MICROECONOMICS

MICROECONOMICS

Michael Parkin

University of Western Ontario

Addison-Wesley Publishing Company

Reading, Massachusetts • Menlo Park, California • New York
Don Mills, Ontario • Wokingham, England • Amsterdam
Bonn • Sydney • Singapore • Tokyo • Madrid • San Juan

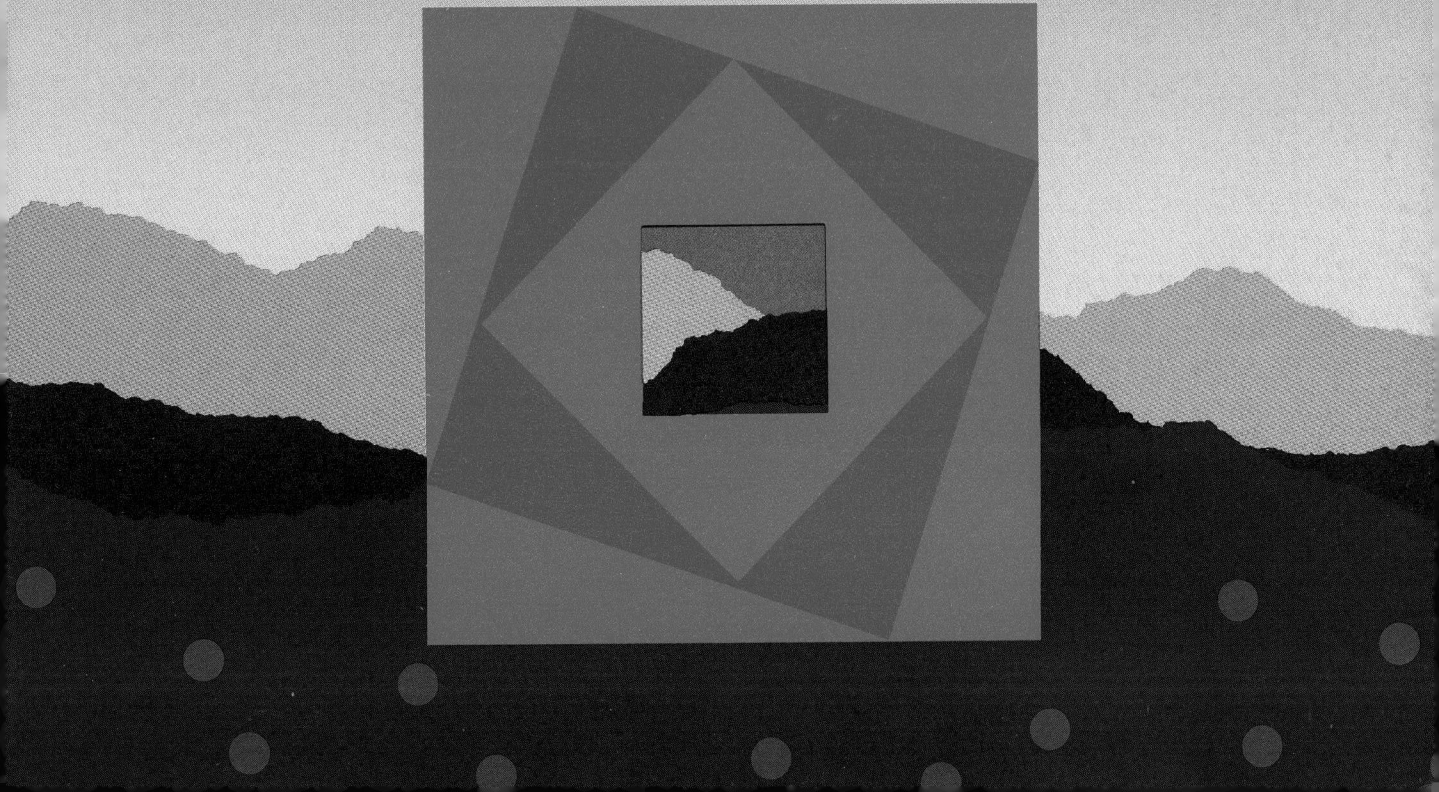

Parkin, Michael, 1939-
Microeconomics / Michael Parkin.
p. cm.
ISBN 0-201-09444-4
1. Microeconomics. I. Title.
HB172.P24 1989

338.5–dc20 89-28034
CIP

Reprinted with corrections April, 1990.

CDEFGHIJ-DO-9543210

Senior Sponsoring Editor: Barbara Rifkind
Development Manager: Sue Gleason
Development Editors: Janice Byer, Robert McGough
Managing Editor: Mary Clare McEwing
Senior Production Supervisor: Kazia Navas
Art and Design Director: Marshall Henrichs
Cover and Interior Designer: Karen Gourley-Lehman
Production Services Manager: Herb Nolan
Art Supervisor: Nancy Blodget
Illustrators: Black Dot Graphics, George Nichols
Photographer for Interviews: Marshall Henrichs
Associate Editor: Christine O'Brien
Copyeditor: Stephanie Magean
Proofreader: Cecilia Thurlow
Layout Artists: Nancy Blodget, Karen Gourley-Lehman
Production Administrator: Loren Stevens
Permissions Editor: Mary Dyer
Indexer: Alexandra Nickerson
Manufacturing Supervisor: Roy Logan
Senior Marketing Manager: Mac Mendelsohn
Promotions Supervisor: Julia Berkley
Compositor: Black Dot Graphics
Color Separator: Black Dot Graphics
Printer: R.R. Donnelley & Sons

Text and photo credits appear on p. I-15, which constitutes a continuation of the copyright page.

To Robin

About Michael Parkin

Michael Parkin received his training as an economist at the Universities of Leicester and Essex in England. Currently in the Department of Economics at the University of Western Ontario, Canada, Professor Parkin has held faculty appointments at Brown University, the University of Manchester, and the University of Essex. He has served on the editorial boards of the *American Economic Review* and the *Journal of Monetary Economics* and as managing editor of the *Canadian Journal of Economics*. He is the author of *Macroeconomics* (Prentice-Hall). Professor Parkin's research on macroeconomics, monetary economics, and international economics has resulted in 160 publications in journals and edited volumes including the *American Economic Review*, the *Journal of Political Economy*, the *Review of Economic Studies*, the *Journal of Monetary Economics*, and the *Journal of Money, Credit and Banking*. It became most visible to the public with his work on inflation that discredited the use of wage and price controls. Michael Parkin also spearheaded the movement toward European monetary union. Professor Parkin is an experienced and dedicated teacher of introductory economics.

Preface

To change the way students see the world: this is my goal in teaching economics and in writing this book.

Economics teaches students to use the economist's lens to view the world more clearly. At every point in the writing, development, and production of this book, I have tried to put myself in the student's place. I have repeatedly recalled my own early struggles to master this discipline, and I have drawn on the learning experiences of the several thousand principles students whom I have been privileged to teach over the past twenty-five years.

Three assumptions (or are they facts?) about students have been my guiding principles in determining the content, organization, features, and visual appearance of this book. First, students are eager to learn, but they are overwhelmed by the seemingly endless claims on their time, interests, and energy. As a result, they want to be told—and in a convincing way—just *why* they are being asked to study a particular body of material. They want to be motivated by a demonstration of its relevance to their everyday experience. Second, once motivated, students want to be presented with a thoughtful, clear, and logical explanation, so that they can understand and begin to apply what they have learned. They do not want to be handed loosely related facts and anecdotes. Third, students are more interested in the present and future than in the past. They want to learn the economics of the 1980s so that, as they enter the 1990s and the twenty-first century, they will be equipped with the most up-to-date tools available to guide them.

Content and Organization

The core of the principles course has been around for more than one hundred years, and other important elements, especially parts of the theory of the firm and Keynesian macroeconomics, have been with us for more than fifty years. But economics has also been developing and changing rapidly during the past few decades. Although all principles texts pay some attention to these more recent developments, they have not succeeded in integrating the new and the traditional. They have created a patchwork quilt rather than a seamless web. I have worked hard to avoid this patchwork approach and to present new ideas in a new way, incorporating them into the body of timeless principles so as to weave a coherent pattern.

Among the many recent developments that you will find in this book are rational expectations, efficient markets, game theory, the principal-agent problem, public choice theory, aggregate demand and aggregate supply, and real business cycle theory. Yet the presence of modern topics does not translate into "high level." Nor does it translate into "bias." The presentation has been crafted to make recent developments in economics thoroughly accessible to the beginning student. Furthermore, where these modern theories are controversial, the more traditional models are also presented and the two (or more) approaches evaluated and compared. Thus, for example, in macroeconomics, all the alternative "schools"—Keynesian, monetarist, rational expectations, and real business cycle—are given an evenhanded treatment.

But this book does have a point of view. It is that economics is a serious, lively, and evolving science—a science that seeks to develop a body of theory powerful enough to explain the economic world around us and that pursues its task by building, testing, and rejecting economic models. In some areas the science has succeeded in its task, but in others it has some way to go and controversy persists. Where matters are settled, I present what we know in the clearest possible light; where controversy persists, I present the alternative viewpoints.

The existence of controversy has implications for the organization of the principles course. As a consequence, I have paid special attention to ensuring that this book can be used in a variety of ways.

Flexibility

Most fundamentally, there is disagreement about the best order in which to present microeconomics and macroeconomics. I have chosen to do microeconomics first, but the book has been written to accommodate courses that are sequenced in either order. The microeconomics and macroeconomics chapters do not depend on each other; concepts and terms are defined and ideas are developed independently in each of the two halves.

I have also tried to accommodate a wide range of teaching approaches by building flexibility and optionality into the book. In addition to the techniques mentioned below, there are several optional chapter sections, which are indicated with an asterisk (*) on the section title and in the table of contents. These may be omitted with no loss of continuity.

Microeconomics In the core areas of consumer and producer theory, there are two optional chapters: one on indifference curves (Chapter 8) and the other on isoquants (Chapter 11). I have provided a full chapter rather than appendixes on these topics because it is my belief that more difficult ideas need a gentle and thoughtful treatment. My own teaching experience has led me to the conclusion that placing more difficult material in short appendixes renders that material almost unteachable. The indifference curve chapter may be treated as a complement of or a substitute for the marginal utility chapter (Chapter 7), and for those instructors using both, there is an appendix showing how they fit together. Because many instructors run out of time when they get to factor markets, the first chapter (Chapter 15) in this part contains the core material, and the remaining chapters may be treated as optional. Finally, I have placed all the material on government choices in a single part (Chapters 19, 20, and 21). However, these chapters may be read before those on factor markets (Chapters 15, 16, 17, and 18), and the chapter on regulation (Chapter 21) may be read immediately after those on competition and monopoly (Chapters 12 and 13).

Special Features

Art Program

One of the most important tools for economists is graphical analysis, yet this is often a real stumbling block for students. The development and art editors at Addison-Wesley and I kept this challenge always in mind as we developed the art program.

We began by observing a distinction between diagrams that represent models and those that display data. Model-based diagrams emphasize analysis and abstraction, whereas empirical graphs emphasize shapes, patterns, and visual correlations. It makes good pedagogical sense to differentiate these two kinds of figures in order to help students work with them better. As a signal to students, we set our model-based diagrams on a white background, and the empirical graphs on a manila background.

Our goal in the model-based art (see the representative figure on the opposite page) is to show clearly "where the economic action is." To achieve this, we observe a consistent protocol in style, nota-

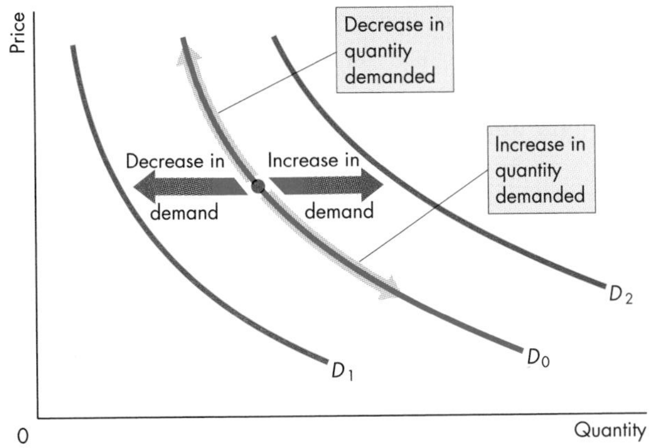

tion, and use of color, including:

- Highlighting shifted curves, points of equilibrium, and the most important features in red.
- Using arrows in conjunction with color to lend directional movement to what are usually static presentations.
- Pairing graphs with data tables from which the curves have been plotted.
- Using color consistently to underscore the content, and referring to such color in the text and captions.
- Labeling key pieces of information in graphs with boxed notes.
- Rendering each piece electronically, so that precision is achieved.

The entire art program has been developed with the study and review needs of the student in mind. We have set up the following features, including:

- Marking the most important figures and tables with a red "key" and listing them at the end of the chapter as "Key Figures and Tables."
- Using complete, informative captions that encapsule major points in the graph so that students can preview or review the chapter by skimming through the art.

We undertook extensive tests of the quality of our art program. For example, we had two art reviewers evaluate every graph. Once a style had been developed, we also conducted informal discussions on the use of color and on the rendering technique. And since accuracy of illustrations and their in-text references is vital, we engaged five economists as accuracy reviewers of the manuscript and three of the galleys and page proofs to check words, numbers, and illustrations. These economists assisted the publisher's in-house development editors and proofreaders, who checked every line, point, label, and cross-reference for clarity and accuracy.

The Interviews

An important goal of the principles course is to develop in students the ability to reason like economists. To aid this process, this book enables students to eavesdrop on a series of conversations that I conducted with twelve eminent economists who have changed the way we think about the world. These interviews open each of the book's parts. It has been a great joy to learn something of how these economists view their area of specialization, of their unique contributions to economics, and also of their general insights which are relevant to beginning students.

Each interview has been carefully edited to be self-contained, and the necessary concepts and terms are defined informally within each one. Since each interview discusses topics that are introduced formally in the following chapters, students can use it as a preview to some of the issues they are about to encounter. A more careful reading afterwards will give students a fuller appreciation of the discussion. Finally, the whole series of interviews can be approached as an informal symposium on the subject matter of economics as it is practiced today.

Reading Between the Lines

Another common goal of the principles course is to develop the student's ability to use economics to analyze current events reported in the media. Recognizing this need, I have developed a feature that may, I hope, be a fruitful model. Each "Reading Between the Lines" spread contains three passes at a story. It begins with a facsimile of an actual (sometimes abbreviated) newspaper or magazine article. It then presents a digest of the article's essential points. Finally, it provides an economic analysis of the news story, based on the economic methods presented in that chapter. It is my intention that students, using this feature, will learn how to do more than just notice the relevance of economics to modern life. I hope that they will also develop the ability to ask good questions, to evaluate the quality of information presented in the media, and to use economic models to deepen their understanding of the economic world.

Our Advancing Knowledge

Another group of special essays reveals the birth and development of economic ideas, not just as abstract models, but as intimately tied to the people and circumstances that formed them.

Learning Aids

We have developed a careful pedagogical plan to ensure that this book complements and reinforces classroom learning. Each chapter contains the following pedagogical elements:

- ***Objectives.*** A list of chapter objectives that enables students to set their goals before embarking on a chapter.
- ***Chapter openers.*** Economic vignettes, questions, puzzles, or metaphors that motivate the analysis and that are resolved in the chapter.
- ***Highlighted in-text reviews.*** Succinct summaries at the end of many main sections.
- ***Key terms.*** Highlighted within the text, these concepts form the first part of a three-tiered review of economic vocabulary. These terms are repeated with page references at chapter ends and compiled in the end-of-book glossary.
- ***Key figures and tables.*** Identified with the "key" logo and listed at chapter ends.
- ***End-of-chapter study material.*** Summaries organized around major headings; lists of key terms with page references; lists of key figures and tables with page references; review questions; and problems. We have worked hard to make the problems meaningful and useful for students.

Design

The design has an important place in the overall pedagogical plan. Our mission with the design of special features was to evoke the colorful feeling of nontextbook print media, notably magazines and annual reports, thus reinforcing the connection of economics to the real world. In the text itself, we strove for a scrupulously clear and honest look that would let the models being presented speak for themselves.

The Teaching and Learning Package

The authors of the supplements, Addison-Wesley, and I have put a tremendous amount of effort into ensuring that each component of the package will help students and instructors derive the maximum benefit from the textbook.

Chapter and Page Numbering System We have given great thought to the best way to enumerate the chapters and paginate the hardcover and split paperback versions of the book so that they work well with all the supplements. Our solution to the problem of confusing numbering systems for chapters in the hardcover and paperback versions was to renumber the pages of each paperback (beginning with page 1) but to keep the chapter numbers the same throughout the three books. This system permits the three books and all of the teaching and learning supplements to work together without confusion.

Study Guide Prepared by David Spencer of Brigham Young University, the Study Guide has been carefully coordinated with the main textbook. Each chapter contains: Chapter in Perspective; Learning Objectives; Helpful Hints; Self-Test (concepts review; true/false, multiple-choice, short-answer questions, and problems) and Answers to Self-Test; and Key Figures and Tables.

Economics in the News This supplement, prepared by Saul Pleeter and Philip Way of the University of Cincinnati, is a unique workbook that extends the "Reading Between the Lines" feature of the textbook. The book includes eighty-five recent news articles organized according to the topical outline of the textbook. An introductory paragraph, objectives, and preview precede a facsimile of the article itself. After the article, two or more pages of analytical questions actively engage students.

Answers to Economics in the News This booklet provides answers to the problems in the supplement above and is available to instructors upon request from the Business and Economics Group at Addison-Wesley.

Test Item File Prepared by Patricia Euzent of the University of Central Florida and David Spencer of Brigham Young University, this file offers over 4000 multiple-choice questions. Each chapter includes a separate section of questions directly from the Study Guide and a section of questions that parallel those in the Study Guide.

Computerized Test Item File This software for qualified adopters is available for IBM-PC and compatible microcomputers and Macintosh microcomputers.

Instructor's Manual Prepared by Patricia Euzent of the University of Central Florida, the Instructor's Manual includes detailed chapter outlines and teaching suggestions, a list of acetates, answers to all review questions and problems in the textbook, and a flexibility guide prepared by Michael Parkin.

Acetates All of the text's key figures are rendered in full color on the acetates. There are 109 acetates for *Microeconomics* and 95 acetates for *Macroeconomics*, and are available to qualified adopters of the textbook by contacting Addison-Wesley.

Graphecon II Software This software for IBM-PC and compatible microcomputers, prepared by Cols. James R. Golden and L. Donne Olvey of the United States Military Academy at West Point, are menu-driven interactive tutorial and quizzing programs that allow students to work with economic graphs.

Student Edition Software Full-function versions of leading software adapted for educational use are available from Addison-Wesley, including Student Edition Software for Lotus® 1-2-3®, Second Edition, MathCAD® 2.0, and MINITAB®.

Acknowledgments

One of the great pleasures of writing an introductory text is the opportunity it affords to learn from so many generous friends and colleagues. Although the extent of my debts cannot be fully acknowledged here, it is nevertheless a joy to record my gratitude to the many people who have helped, some without realizing just how helpful they were.

I want to thank those of my colleagues at the University of Western Ontario who have taught me a great deal that can be found in these pages: Jim Davies, Jeremy Greenwood, Ig Horstmann, Peter Howitt, Greg Huffman, David Laidler, Phil Reny, Chris Robinson, John Whalley, and Ron Wonnacott. I want to extend a special thanks to Glenn MacDonald, who worked well beyond the call of duty discussing this project with me from its outset, helping me develop many of its pedagogical features, and reading and commenting in detail on all the micro chapters.

I also want to acknowledge my debt to those who have had a profound influence on my whole view of and approach to economics and whose influence I can see in these pages. Although I never sat in their classrooms, they are in a very real sense my teachers. I am especially grateful to John Carlson (Purdue University), Carl Christ (Johns Hopkins University), Robert Clower (University of South Carolina), Ed Feige (University of Wisconsin at Madison), Herschel Grossman (Brown University), and Sam Wu (University of Iowa). I also want to place on record my enormous debt to the late Karl Brunner. The energy, drive, and entrepreneurship of this outstanding economist provided me and my generation of economists with incredible opportunities to intereact and learn from each other in a wide variety of conference settings both in the United States and in Europe.

It is also a pleasure to acknowledge my debt to the several thousand students to whom I have been privileged to teach introductory economics. The instant feedback that comes from that look of puzzlement or enlightenment has taught me, more than anything else, how to teach economics.

Producing a text such as this is a team effort, and the members of the Addison-Wesley "Parkin Team" are genuine co-producers of this book. I am especially grateful to and have been truly inspired by my sponsoring editor, Barbara Rifkind. Barbara discovered this book when it was no more than an idea in my mind, while she was working as an Addison-Wesley sales representative in Florida. After two promotions, she came onto the project when Addison-Wesley had already designed the book and when I thought I had finished writing it. Barbara liked what she saw, but saw more in its potential than in its realization. She coaxed me into rewriting the entire book one more time and coaxed Addison-Wesley into another complete overhaul of the design. Because of Barbara, this book is really the second edition of *Economics*! Sue Gleason as development editor has had an enormous influence on both the words and the art program. Sue and I have developed cauliflower ears as a result of working with each other on the telephone over the past two years. Kazia Navas, the production editor, has coordinated the entire production process, keeping us all on track and coping cheerfully with my numerous and sometimes outrageous demands. Great thanks go to Stephanie Magean, Sherry Berg, Nancy Blodget, Janice Byer, Marshall Henrichs, Mary Stuart Lang, Karen Lehman, Mary Clare McEwing, Dick Morton, Christine O'Brien, Loren Stevens, Christine Shuster, and the more than eighty economists (whose names appear separately) who have acted as reviewers or members of focus groups. It is a pleasure to acknowledge my debt to Steven Mautner, the Sponsoring Editor who initiated this project, and to Will Ethridge, who played an important role in the early stages of development. I also wish to express my gratitude to Bob McGough, a superb financial and economic journalist, who provided a thorough and creative edit of my second draft and who also taught me a great deal about how to write more clearly and effectively. David Spencer, Patricia Euzent, Saul Pleeter, and Philip Way were the primary authors of the supplements package and graciously shared their professional insights and teaching expertise with me. I also want to thank the many secretaries who have helped at various stages of this book, typing and retyping its countless drafts and redrafts. They are Yvonne Adams, Lynda Sollazzo, Kendra McKague, and, most recently, Barbara Craig.

I have left until last four people to whom I want to give special thanks. First, my colleague and best friend Robin Bade has been almost a co-author of this work. She has read every word that I have written, commented in detail on every draft of the work, and has helped manage the project from its conception to its conclusion. Without the anticipation of her help and its availability, I could never have contemplated embarking on this project. Finally, I want to acknowledge the help and inspiration of my children, Catherine, Richard, and Ann. Through the years that I have been developing and writing this work, they have been going through various stages of high school and college. They have forced me to craft a book that they can understand and find interesting.

The empirical test of this textbook's value will be made in the classroom. I would appreciate hearing from instructors and students about how I might improve the book in future editions.

Michael Parkin
Department of Economics
University of Western Ontario
London, Ontario N6A 5C2

Reviewers

Manuscript Reviewers

Berhanu Abegaz
College of William and Mary

Lee J. Alston
University of Illinois

Ted Amato
University of North Carolina at Charlotte

Richard K. Anderson
Texas A & M University

Mohsen Bahmani-Oskooee
University of Wisconsin—Milwaukee

Ian R. Bain
Minnegasco, Inc.

Peter S. Barth
University of Connecticut

Brian R. Binger
University of Arizona

Bruce R. Bolnick
Northeastern University

M. Neil Browne
Bowling Green State University

Clive Bull
Paine Webber

Michael R. Butler
Texas Christian University

Steven Caudill
Auburn University

Steven L. Cobb
University of North Texas

John D. Coupe
University of Maine

Paul N. Courant
University of Michigan

Larry DeBrock
University of Illinois

David Denslow
University of Florida

Donald Dutkowsky
Syracuse University

Nathan Edmonson
Georgia State University

Kenneth G. Elzinga
University of Virginia

Patricia J. Euzent
University of Central Florida

Roger E. A. Farmer
University of California at Los Angeles

Kevin F. Forbes
Catholic University of America

Lynn G. Gillette
Texas A & M University

Edward Greenberg
Washington University

John Grobey
Humbolt State University

Timothy J. Gronberg
Texas A & M University

John R. Hanson II
Texas A & M University

Stephen Happel
Arizona State University

Elizabeth Hoffman
University of Arizona

Glenn Hueckel
Purdue University

Dennis W. Jansen
Texas A & M University

Bruce E. Kaufman
Georgia State University

Arjo Klamer
University of Iowa

Levis A. Kochin
University of Washington

Don N. MacDonald
Northeast Louisiana University

Michael Magura
University of Toledo

George J. Mailath
University of Pennsylvania

Steven J. Matusz
Michigan State University

Sam Mirmirani
Bryant College

W. Douglas Morgan
University of California, Santa Barbara

Anthony L. Ostrosky
Illinois State University

Harold Petersen
Boston College

Frank Petrella
Holy Cross College

Thomas J. Pierce
California State University, San Bernadino

Mark W. Plant
U.S. Department of Commerce

Andrew J. Policano
State University of New York at Stony Brook

Robert Puth
University of New Hampshire

Krishnamurthy Ramagopal
University of Vermont

J. David Reed
Bowling Green State University

Robert Rosenman
Washington State University

Mark Rush
University of Florida

Allen R. Sanderson
The University of Chicago

Michael P. Shields
Southern Illinois University at Carbondale

Ronald Soligo
Rice University

David E. Spencer
Brigham Young University

Robert W. Thomas
Iowa State University

Marie Thursby
Purdue University

Arthur L. Welsh
Pennsylvania State University

Walter J. Wessels
North Carolina State University

James N. Wetzel
Virginia Commonwealth University

Jeffrey Wolcowitz
Harvard University

William C. Wood
James Madison University

Gavin Wright
Stanford University

Peter A. Zaleski
Villanova University

Gary Zarkin
Research Triangle Institute

Art Reviewers

Donald Dutkowsky
Syracuse University

Willard W. Radell, Jr.
Indiana University of Pennsylvania

Accuracy Reviewers

Eugene Bland
National Education Center's Tampa Technical Institute

Robert P. Edwards
County College of Morris (NJ)

Edward Monkman
County College of Morris (NJ)

David Spencer
Brigham Young University

Jeffrey Wrase
Arizona State University

Brief Contents

Contents

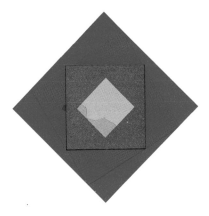

†Summary, Key Concepts, Review Questions, and Problems appear at the end of each chapter.

*Optional section (may be omitted without loss of continuity)

Part 5 *Markets for Goods and Services*

MICROECONOMICS

Part 1 Introduction

Talking with Assar Lindbeck

Assar Lindbeck is a professor of economics and director of the Institute for International Economic Studies at the University of Stockholm. He has been a visiting professor at Columbia University, the University of Michigan, and Yale University. Since 1981, he has been chairman of the committee that annually awards the Nobel Prize for economic science. Michael Parkin talked with Professor Lindbeck about the nature of economics, the economic landscape of the 1990s, and the way economists do their work.

Professor Lindbeck, how did you decide to become an economist?

My father was a politician in northern Sweden, so I was interested myself in studying political science at college. After three semesters, I decided to learn economics as a background. The problem is that I never finished learning economics!

What was it about economics that was so compelling?

I discovered that political science dealt mainly with the forms of political events, the way political decisions are made. But it dealt very little with the consequences of political decisions. Economics, on the other hand, does just that, by looking at how political decisions and economic policy actually affect families, businesses, or nations.

"I wonder if we aren't straining out young people with creativity by forcing them into elaborate analysis."

What makes economics different from political science or the other social sciences?

First, economics asks different questions. Questions about employment; output; the allocation of resources, including labor; the distribution of income. Next, economics has been able to build up a general analytical structure. We don't need a special kind of economics to discuss housing or agriculture or education. We apply the same economic principles to each different field. Other social sciences tend to build specific theories for each issue or field. Family sociology is different from criminal sociology, for example. Finally, economics can use narrower assumptions to produce reasonably good predictions. For instance, if you ask me about factors that influence the demand for butter or margarine, I don't have to go into philosophical issues about the basis for human behavior.

Do microeconomics and macroeconomics, the two traditional branches of economics, use the same principles?

Well, there has been a discontinuity between microeconomics and macroeconomics. Macroeconomics is based on the idea that there are systematic movements of broad aggregates—total output, national economic growth, unemployment, or inflation—and that we can explain one aggregate by another, as a kind of short cut. You don't have to explain all relative prices and the allocation of resources to be able to explain a recession. But it *is* important that what you're saying about these aggregate movements should be consistent with the microeconomic assumptions you would make about the behavior of individual firms or consumers. Milton Friedman, Franco Modigliani, James Tobin, and others started this approach in the 1950s because they were dissatisfied with the absence of microeconomic foundations for the empirical generalizations that characterized macroeconomics at the time.

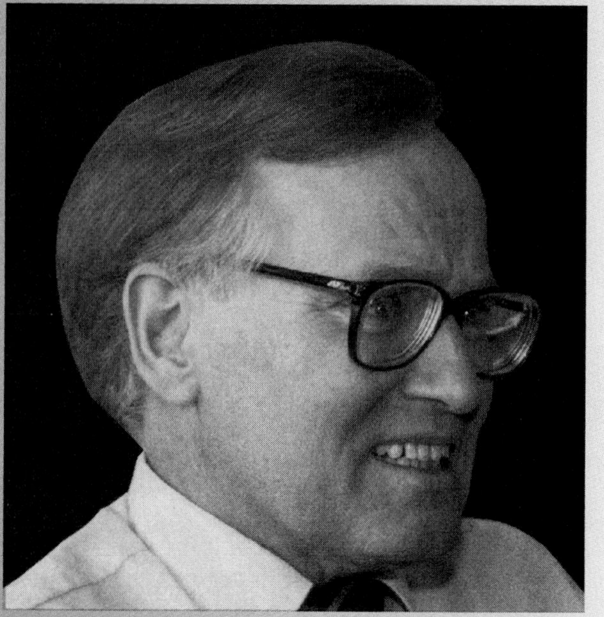

If you want to talk about "the economy," you need to work with aggregate concepts because the human brain is just too small to consider all the variables at one time. For economics to be useful to you as an individual, you have to be able to play with the model in your head. You should be able to read the newspaper or watch the TV news and process it mentally. For economics to be useful to society, an economist must be able to talk with journalists and politicians, or to draw diagrams on the blackboard for students. If you cannot transform your thinking into broad categories, you can never communicate outside a group of specialists.

You've been chairman of the committee that awards the Nobel Prize for economic science. What characterizes the great economists?

The Prize Committee—and economists in general—recognize the value both of people who have influential ideas, even if they haven't formalized them into complete models, and of people who formalize ideas borrowed partly from others. There are very few people with both bright ideas and the ability or opportunity to formalize them. I think that today economists with interesting and realistic visions are scarcer than technical economists. I have always been a strong advocate for rigorous training, but I sometimes wonder if we aren't straining out some young people with common sense and creativity by forcing them into elaborate technical analysis.

What do you see as the most important economic issue facing us in the 1990s?

Let me begin by looking back at some of the events that have led us to where we are today. The 25 years after World War II are regarded now as a golden age—expanding world trade, low unemployment, rapid

growth, and prosperity. Unique historical events contributed to that era—workers were available to move from agriculture to industry; prewar trade protectionism gave way; there were great advances in technology after years of stagnation. In the 1960s and 1970s, politicians started to believe, however, that economic growth and prosperity were manna from heaven. And we began to consume the very source of our economic success—by tampering with the efficiency of our market economies. In the 1970s, the OPEC oil shocks came, and, at least in Europe, great explosions in wages. There were also extraordinary policy efforts to squeeze out inflation, which was a basic reason for the depths of the recessions in the 1970s and 1980s. The late 1980s have been a period of recovery from the turmoil of the previous decade. The growth rate has started to improve, unemployment has fallen in the United States and England. What is happening? There's a distinct possibility that we're finally returning the strength of the market to market economies.

And in the future?

I see the issue of the 1990s as how far deregulation can go without interest groups protesting—many people feel the pinch of deregulation. In global terms, with the European Economic Community, how much control will any

national government give up to international market forces? Will a government be willing to say that they can't do anything about a problem because they've deregulated both the domestic economy and its foreign economic relations? Can a government do that without its domestic population throwing them out of office?

In addressing such difficult issues, can economists really separate scientific analysis from passionate advocacy of policy?

"I see the issue of the 1990s as how far deregulation can go without interest groups protesting."

If someone asks an economist what will be the effects of a tax on imported oil, the answer should be completely independent of his or her

opinion about whether those effects are good or bad. A liberal or a conservative economist should give the same answer if they've each used the same type of economic model. So why don't they always? Perhaps because they have inadvertently been influenced by their political beliefs to choose a model that tends to support a certain political value or world view.

"We cannot make economic forecasts without forecasting policies."

The purpose of science, of economic science, is to discriminate correctly among different models in order to produce an honest assessment. It's never easy to do this, but it's critical to the justification of economics as a positive science.

You've tried in some of your writing to apply positive economics to explain the policy choices made by politicians—what is called "public choice." Why is this an important area of economic research and what progress have we made in understanding political decision making?

This is a vital area of research. We cannot make economic forecasts without forecasting policies. And we cannot forecast policies without having a theory that predicts how politicians will react to new economic events in the future. But so far, I think that there

are few generally solid results—because politicians naturally have a very complex pattern of behavior that we can't yet really explain. For example, there are often conflicts between the policy agenda that politicians believe they should pursue and the policy decisions they may have to make in order to stay in office. The chief result of research in this area, so far, is that economists have become much more aware of how complicated it really is to give good advice on policy.

What have been the guiding principles that have helped you as an economist and as a person concerned with economic policy?

I like to be inspired by real-world problems. I want to look around and see something that puzzles me, something I don't understand, and try to find a plausible explanation. Next, I sit down at my desk and try to write the problem down. I try to make sense of it in both ordinary words and formal terms, with graphs and equations. I often find out that the answer was different from what I had expected.

What advice would you give to a student in the first weeks of a principles of economics course?

Try to understand the principles intuitively and not just mechanically. Try to understand the common sense, if there is any, of the examples your teachers and textbooks provide. If you only memorize the facts, after two years you'll have forgotten it all. But if you learn economics with your intuition backing you up, you'll keep something of great value.

Chapter 1

What Is Economics?

After studying this chapter, you will be able to:

- State the kinds of questions that economics tries to answer
- Explain why all economic questions and economic activity arise from scarcity
- Explain why scarcity forces people to make choices
- Define opportunity cost
- Describe the function and the working parts of an economy
- Distinguish between positive and normative statements
- Explain what is meant by an economic theory and how economic theories are developed by building and testing economic models

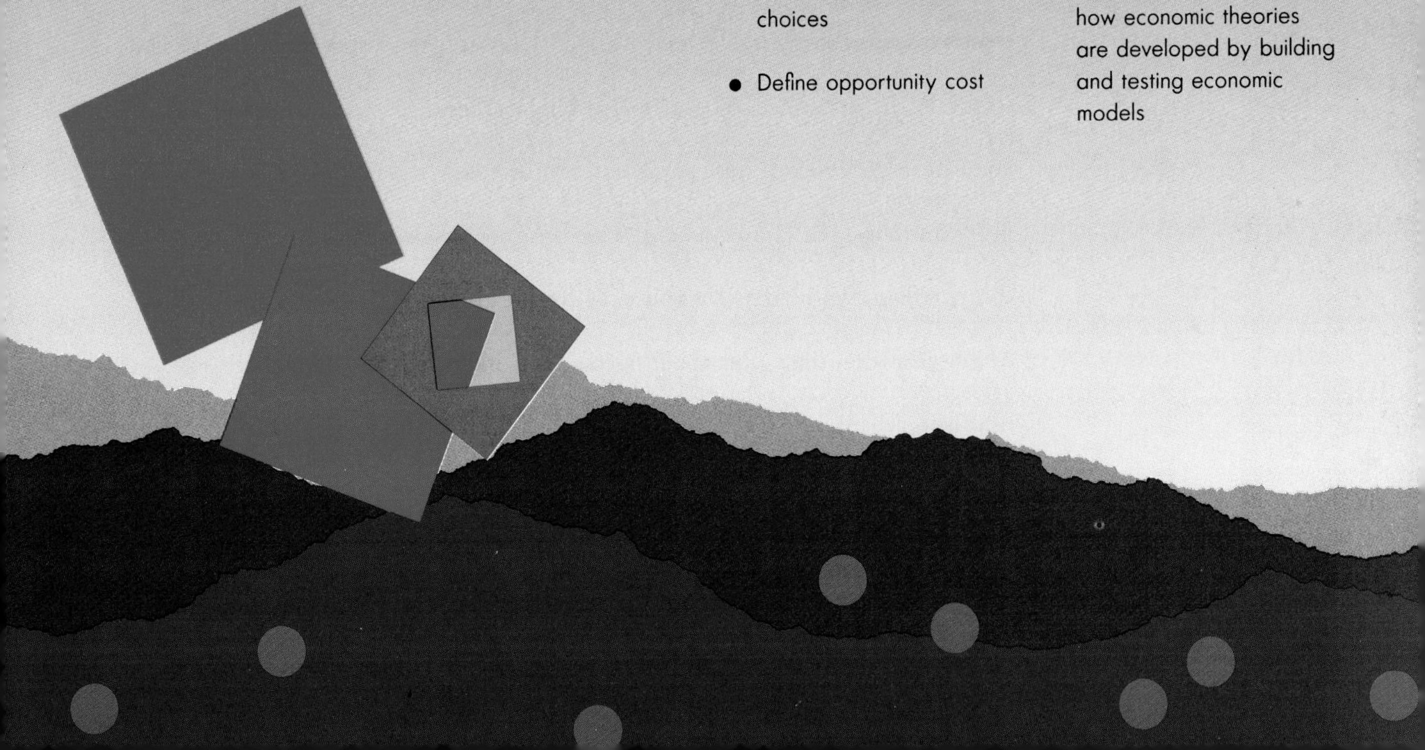

Seven Big Questions

PRODUCTION, CONSUMPTION, AND TECHNOLOGICAL CHANGE

If you wanted to watch a movie in your home in 1975, you had to rent a movie projector and a screen—as well as the movie itself. The cost of such entertainment would have been as high as what a theater would pay to show the movie to several hundred people. Only the rich chose to watch movies in the comfort of their own homes. ■ In 1976, the video cassette recorder (VCR) became available to consumers. Its typical price tag was $2000 (which in today's dollars is $4000). Since that time, the price of VCRs has steadily fallen so that today you can buy a reliable machine for $200. A video can be rented for a dollar a day and can be bought for less than $30. In just a few years, watching a movie at home changed from a luxury available to the richest few to an event enjoyed by millions. ■ Advances in technology affect the way we consume. We now watch far more movies at home than we did a decade ago because new technologies have lowered the cost. ■ New technologies also affect the way we *produce* things. Johnny Wilder, Jr., was a successful popular musician in the 1970s with such hits as "Boogie Nights" and "Always and Forever." A car accident in 1979 left Wilder paralyzed from the neck down. Today, Wilder again produces music but of a new kind. The artist now works with a Macintosh computer and synthesizers controlled by his breath and by beams of light. ■ We hear a great deal these days about lasers. Their most dramatic use may be in futuristic defense systems such as the Strategic Defense Initiative—or "Star Wars" as it is popularly known. But lasers already affect us every day. They scan prices at the supermarket checkout. They create holograms on credit cards, making them harder to forge. Neurosurgeons and eye surgeons use them in our hospitals.

■ It is clear that new technologies affect the way that we produce goods and services. The examples that we have given, whether they affect our consumption or production, give rise to the first big economic question:

How do people choose *what* to consume and *how* to produce, and how are these choices affected by the discovery of new ways of doing things—of new technologies?

Wages and Earnings

On a crisp, bright winter day on the ski slopes at Aspen, a bronzed 23-year-old instructs some beginning skiers in the snowplow turn. For this pleasant and uncomplicated work, the young man, who quit school after eleventh grade, is paid $10 an hour.

In a lawyer's office in the center of a busy city, a 23-year-old secretary handles a large volume of correspondence, filing, scheduling, and meetings. She arrives home most evenings exhausted. She has a bachelor's degree in English and has taken night courses in computer science and word processing. She receives $8 an hour for her work.

On September 10, 1988, Steffi Graf and Gabriela Sabatini played a stunning tennis match in the final of the Women's U.S. Open Championship. At the end of the close and hard-fought match, the winner, Steffi Graf, received $275,000; Ms. Sabatini collected only half that amount. A similar phenomenon can be seen in the headquarters of large corporations. Chief executive officers who work no harder (and in some cases, even less hard) than the people immediately beneath them receive far higher salaries than their subordinates.

Situations like these raise the second big economic question:

What determines people's incomes and why do some people receive much larger rewards than others whose efforts appear to be similar?

Unemployment

During the Great Depression, the four years from 1929 to 1933, unemployment afflicted almost one fifth of the labor force in the industrial world. For months and in some cases years on end, many families had no income other than meager payments from the government or from private charities. In the 1950s and 1960s, unemployment rates stayed below 5 percent in most countries and in some, below 2 percent. During the 1970s and early 1980s, unemployment steadily increased so that by late 1982 and early 1983 almost 11 percent of the U.S. labor force was looking for work. But in 1989, the U.S. unemployment rate had fallen to 5 percent.

Unemployment hurts different groups unequally. When the average unemployment rate in the United States was 5 percent—as it was in 1989—the unemployment rate among young people 16 to 19 years old was 19 percent, but for young blacks, it was 43 percent. These facts raise the third big economic question:

What are the causes of unemployment and why are some groups more severely affected than others?

Inflation

Between August 1945 and July 1946, prices in Hungary rose by an average of 20,000 percent per month. In the worst month, July 1946, they rose 419 quadrillion percent (a quadrillion is the number one followed by 15 zeros).

In 1985, the cost of living in Bolivia rose by 11,750 percent. This meant that in downtown La Paz a McDonald's hamburger that cost 20 bolivianos on January 1, cost 2370 bolivianos by the end of the year. That same year, prices rose only 3.2 percent in the United States. But in the late 1970s, prices in the United States were rising at a rate well in excess of 10 percent a year. These facts raise the fourth big economic question:

Why do prices rise and why do some countries sometimes experience rapid price increases while others have stable prices?

Government

The government touches many aspects of life. It maintains the army, air force, navy, and marines for our national defense. It provides law enforcement, health care, insurance, and education. Its agencies regulate food and drug production, nuclear energy, and agriculture.

The cost of government has increased dramatically over the years. In the early 1900s, the federal government took in taxes and spent about 3¢ out of every dollar earned by the average American, and state and local governments took in and spent about 5¢—for a total of about 8¢ for every dollar earned. Government budgets were balanced. In 1987, the federal government collected 20¢ in taxes out of every dollar earned, but it spent 24¢, thereby generating a 4¢ deficit, or a 4¢ excess of spending over taxes for every dollar earned. If you add state and local government spending to that of the federal government, approximately 35¢ of every dollar earned by Americans is spent by the government.

These facts about government raise the fifth big economic question:

How do government spending and taxes influence economic life and what happens when the government has a deficit, as it does at the present time?

International Trade

In the 1960s, almost all the cars and trucks on the highways of the United States were Fords, Chevrolets, and Chryslers. By the 1980s, Toyotas, Hondas, Volkswagens, and BMWs were a common sight on these same highways. As a matter of fact, by 1985 one third of all new cars sold in the United States were imported; in the mid-1950s, less than 1 percent were.

Cars are not exceptional. The same can be said of television sets, clothing, and computers.

Governments regulate international trade in cars and in most other commodities. They impose taxes on imports, called tariffs, and also establish quotas, which restrict the quantities that may be imported. These facts raise the sixth big economic question:

What determines the pattern and the volume of trade between nations and what are the effects of tariffs and quotas on international trade?

Wealth and Poverty

At the mouth of the Canton River in southeast China is a small rocky peninsula and a group of islands with virtually no natural resources. But this bare land supports more than five million people who, though not excessively rich, live in rapidly growing abundance. They produce much of the world's fashion goods and electronic components. They are the people of Hong Kong.

On the eastern edge of Africa bordering the Red Sea, a tract of land a thousand times larger supports a population of 34 million people—only seven times that of Hong Kong. The region suffers such abject poverty that in 1985 rock singers from Europe and North America organized one of the most spectacular worldwide fund-raising efforts ever seen—Live Aid—to help them. These are the desperate and dying people of Ethiopia.

Hong Kong and Ethiopia, two extremes in income and wealth, are not isolated examples. The poorest two thirds of the world's population consumes less than one fifth of all the things produced. A middle income group accounts for almost one fifth of the world's population and consumes almost one fifth of the world's output. A further one fifth of the world's population—living in rich countries such as the United States, Canada, Western Europe, Japan, Australia, and New Zealand—consumes two thirds of the world's output.

These facts raise the seventh big economic question:

What causes differences in wealth among nations, making the people in some countries rich and in others poor?

Big Questions with No Easy Answers

These seven big questions provide an overview of economics. They are *big* questions for two reasons. First, they affect the quality of human life with great intensity. Second, they are hard questions to answer. They generate passionate argument and debate, and just about everybody has an opinion about them. Self-appointed experts abound. One of the hardest things for students of economics, whether beginners or seasoned practitioners, is to stand clear of the passion and emotion, and to approach their work with the detachment, rigor, and objectivity of a scientist.

Later in this chapter, we will explain how economists try to find answers to economic questions. But before doing that, let's go back to the seven big questions. What do these questions have in common? What distinguishes them from non-economic questions?

Scarcity

All economic questions arise from a single and inescapable fact: You can't always get what you want. We live in a world of scarcity. An economist defines **scarcity** to mean that wants always exceed the resources available to satisfy them. A child wants a 75¢ can of soft drink and a 50¢ pack of gum but has only $1.00 in her pocket. She experiences scarcity. A student wants to go to a party on Saturday night but also wants to spend that same night catching up on late assignments. He also experiences scarcity. The rich and the poor alike face scarcity. The U.S. government with its $1 trillion budget faces scarcity. The total amount that the federal government wants to spend on defense, health, education, welfare, and other services exceeds what it collects in taxes. Even parrots face scarcity—there just aren't enough crackers to go around.

Wants do not simply exceed resources; they are unlimited. In contrast, resources are limited, or finite. People want good health and a long life, material comfort, security, physical and mental recreation, and, finally, an awareness and understanding of themselves and their environment.

None of these wants are satisfied for everyone; and everyone has some unsatisfied wants. While many Americans have all the material comfort they want, many do not. No one is entirely satisfied with his or her state of health and length of life. No one feels entirely secure, especially in this nuclear age, and no one—not even the wealthiest person—has the time to enjoy all the travel, vacations, and art that he or she would like. Not even the wisest and most knowledgeable philosopher or scientist knows as much as he or she would like to know.

We can imagine a world that satisfies people's wants for material comfort and, perhaps, even security. But we cannot imagine a world in which people live as long and in as good a state of health as they would like. Nor can we imagine people having all the time, energy, and resources to enjoy all the sports, travel, vacation, and art that they would like. Natural resources and human resources—in the form of time, muscle-power, and brain-power—as well as all the dams, highways, buildings, machinery, tools, and other equipment that have been built by past human efforts amount to an enormous heritage, but they are limited. Our unlimited wants will always outstrip the resources available to satisfy them.

"Not only do I want a cracker—we all want a cracker!"

Drawing by Modell; © 1985 The New Yorker Magazine, Inc.

Economic Activity

The confrontation of unlimited wants with limited resources results in economic activity. **Economic activity** is what people do to cope with scarcity. **Economics**, then, is the study of how people use their limited resources to try to satisfy unlimited wants. Defined in this way, economic activity and economics deal with a wide range of issues and problems. The seven big questions posed earlier are examples of the more important problems economists study. Let's see how those questions could not arise if resources were infinitely abundant and scarcity did not exist.

With unlimited resources, there would be no need to devise better ways of producing more goods. Studying how we all spend our time and effort would not be interesting because we would simply do what we enjoyed without restriction. There would be no wages. We would do only the things that we enjoyed because there would be enough goods and services to satisfy everyone without effort. Unemployment would not be an issue because no one would work—except for people who wanted to work simply for the pleasure that it gave them. Inflation—rising prices—would not be a problem because no one would care about prices. Questions about government intervention in economic life would not arise because there would be no need for government-provided goods and no taxes. We would simply take whatever we wanted from the infinite resources available. There would be no international trade since, with complete abundance, it would be pointless to transport things from one place to another. Finally, differences in wealth among nations would not arise because we would all have as much as we wanted. There would be no such thing as rich and poor countries—all countries would be infinitely wealthy.

You can see that this science fiction world of complete abundance would have no economic questions. It is the universal fact of scarcity that produces economic questions.

Choice

Faced with scarcity, people must make *choices*. When we cannot have everything that we want, we have to choose among the available alternatives. Because scarcity forces us to choose, economics is sometimes called the science of choice—the science that explains the choices that people make and predicts how changes in circumstances affect their choices.

To make a choice, we balance the benefits of having more of one thing against the costs of having less of something else. Balancing benefits against costs and doing the best within the limits of what is possible is called **optimizing.** There is another word that has a similar meaning—*economizing*. **Economizing** is making the best use of the resources available. Once people have made a choice and have optimized, they cannot have more of *everything*. To get more of one thing means having less of something else. Expressed in another way: In making choices, we face costs. Whatever we choose to do, we could always have chosen to do something else instead.

Opportunity Cost

Economists use the term opportunity cost to emphasize that making choices in the face of scarcity implies a cost. The **opportunity cost** of any action is the best alternative forgone. If you cannot have everything that you want, then you have to choose among the alternatives. The best thing that you choose not to do—the alternative forgone—is the cost of the thing that you choose to do. This is the meaning of opportunity cost. We must be careful to measure opportunity cost accurately. To understand how to do this, let's examine a familiar situation.

You are supposed to attend a lecture at 8:30 on a Monday morning. There are two alternatives to attending this lecture: to stay in bed for an hour or to go jogging for an hour. You cannot, of course, stay in bed *and* go jogging for that one same hour. The opportunity cost of attending the lecture is not the cost of an hour in bed *and* the cost of jogging for an hour. If these are the only two alternatives that you would contemplate, then you have to decide which one you would do if you did not go to the lecture. The opportunity cost of attending a lecture for a jogger is an hour of exercise; the opportunity cost of attending a lecture for a late sleeper is an hour in bed.

Suppose you always have a muffin and a cup of coffee for breakfast. On the day that you go to your lecture, you pick these items up in the college cafeteria as you race to class. If you did not spend $1.50 every day on your breakfast, you would go to the movies more often than you are now able to afford. The movies that you forgo are the opportunity cost of your breakfast. But they are not part of the opportunity cost of going to class—you spend $1.50 on your breakfast every day whether or not you attend your class.

Not all of the opportunity costs that you incur are the result of your own choices. Sometimes others make choices that impose opportunity costs on you. For example, when you cannot get onto a bus at rush hour, you have to bear the cost of the choices made by all the other people who filled the bus.

Everything has an opportunity cost. In choosing one activity, an individual decides that the cost of that activity—the activity forgone—is worth paying. Scarcity not only implies cost, it implies one other fundamental feature of human life—competition.

Competition and Cooperation

Competition If wants exceed resources, wants must compete against each other for what is available. **Competition** is a contest for command over scarce resources. In the case of the child with $1.00 in pocket money who wants a soft drink and gum that add up to $1.25, the soft drink and gum compete for the $1.00 in her pocket. For the student who has allowed assignments to accumulate, the party and the assignments compete with each other for Saturday night. For the government, defense and social services compete with each other for limited tax dollars.

Scarcity also implies competition between people. If it is not possible to have everything that you want, then you must compete with others for what is available. In modern societies, competition has been organized within a framework of almost universally accepted rules that have evolved. This evolution of rules is itself a direct response to the problem of scarcity. Not all societies, even modern societies, employ identical rules to govern competition. For example, the way that economic life is organized in the United States differs greatly from that in the Soviet Union. In Chapter 38, we will examine these differences and compare alternative economic systems. For now, we will restrict our attention to the rules that govern competition in the United States.

A key rule of competition is that people own what they have acquired through voluntary exchange. People can compete with each other by offering more favorable exchanges—for example, selling something for a lower price or buying something for a higher price. But they cannot compete with each other by simply taking something from someone else.

Cooperation Perhaps you are thinking that scarcity does not make competition inevitable and that cooperation would better solve economic problems. **Cooperation** means working with others to achieve a common end. If instead of competing with each other we cooperated, wouldn't that eliminate economic problems? This line of reasoning is appealing because it emphasizes the possibility that we might be able to solve our economic problems by using reason. Unfortunately, cooperation does not eliminate economic problems, because it does not eliminate scarcity. Cooperation may, though, be one way to get the best use of our scarce resources. Indeed, we cooperate when we agree to rules of the game that limit competition to avoid violence.

Other more specific examples of solving economic problems through cooperation abound. Marriage partners cooperate. Most forms of business also entail cooperation. Workers cooperate with each other on the production line; members of a management team cooperate with each other to design, produce, and market their products; management and workers cooperate; business partners cooperate.

Common as it is, cooperative behavior neither solves the economic problem nor eliminates competition. Almost all cooperative behavior implies some prior competition to find the best individuals with whom to cooperate. Marriage provides a good example. Although marriage is a cooperative affair, unmarried people compete intensely to find a marriage partner. Similarly, although workers and management cooperate with each other, firms compete for the best workers and workers compete for the best employers. Professionals such as lawyers and doctors compete with each other for the best business partners.

Competition does not end when a partner has been found. Groups of people who cooperate together compete with other groups. For example, although a group of lawyers may have formed a partnership and may work together, they will be in competition with other lawyers.

R E V I E W

Economics studies the activities arising from scarcity. Scarcity forces people to make choices. Economists try to understand the choices that people make. To make choices, people optimize. To optimize, they evaluate the costs of alternative actions. We call these opportunity costs, to emphasize that doing one thing removes the opportunity to do something else. Scarcity also implies that people must compete with each other. ■

You now know the types of questions that economists try to answer and that all economic questions and economic activity arise from scarcity. In the following chapters, we are going to study economic activity and discover how a modern economy such as that of the United States works. But before we do that, we need to stand back and take an overview of our economy. What exactly do we mean by "the economy"?

The Economy

What is an economy? How does an economy work? Rather than trying to answer these questions directly, let's begin by asking similar questions but on a more familiar subject. What is an airplane? How does an airplane work?

Without delving into the detail that would satisfy an aeronautical engineer, most of us could take a shot at answering these two questions. We would describe an airplane as a flying machine that transports people and cargo. To explain how an airplane works, we would describe its key components—fuselage (or body), wings, and engines, and also perhaps its flaps, rudder, and control and navigation systems. We would also explain that as powerful engines move the machine forward, its wings create an imbalance in air pressure that lifts it into the air.

This example nicely illustrates four things. First, it is hard to explain what something is without saying what it does. To say that an airplane is a machine does not tell us much. We have to go beyond that and say what the machine is for, and how it works.

Second, it is hard to explain how something works without being able to divide it up into components. Once we have described something in terms of its components, we can explain how those components work and how they interact with each other.

Third, it is hard to explain how something works without leaving out some details. Notice that we did not describe an airplane in all its detail. Instead, we isolated the most important parts in order to explain how the whole works. We did not emphasize the inflight movie system, the seat belts, or the color of the paint on the wings. We supposed that these things were largely, or even totally, irrelevant to an explanation of how an airplane works.

Fourth and finally, there are different levels of understanding how something works. We gave a superficial account of how an airplane works. An aeronautical engineer would have given a deeper explanation and experts in the individual components—engines, navigation systems, control system, and so on—would have given an even more detailed and precise explanation than a general engineer.

Now let's return to questions about the economy. What is an economy? How does it work?

What Is an Economy?

An **economy** is a mechanism that allocates scarce resources among competing uses. This mechanism achieves three things:

- What
- How
- For whom

1 *What* goods and services will be produced and in *what* quantities? How many VCRs will be made and how many movie theaters will be built? Will young professionals vacation in Europe or live in large houses? How many high performance cars will be built, and how many trucks and station wagons?

2 *How* will the various goods and services be produced? Will a supermarket operate with three checkout lines and clerks using laser scanners or six checkout lines and clerks keying in prices by hand? Will workers weld station wagons by hand or will robots do the job? Will farmers keep track of their livestock feeding schedules and inventories by using paper and pencil records or personal computers? Will credit card companies use computers to read charge slips in New York or ship paper records to Barbados for hand processing?

3 *For whom* will the various goods and services be produced? The distribution of economic benefits depends on the distribution of income and wealth. Those with a high income and great wealth consume more goods and services than those with low income and little wealth. Who gets to consume what thus depends on income. Will the ski instructor consume more than the lawyer's secretary? Will the people of Hong Kong get to consume more than the people of Ethiopia?

The Economy's Working Parts

To understand how an economy works, we must identify its major working parts and see how they interact with each other. The working parts of an economy and the interrelations between them are illustrated in Fig. 1.1. The working parts of the economy fall into two categories:

- **Decision makers**—any person or organized group of persons that make choices
- **Coordination mechanisms**—arrangements that make the choices of one person or group compatible with the choices of others

Decision Makers Decision makers fall into three groups:

- Households
- Firms
- Governments

A **household** is any group of people living together as a decision-making unit. Every individ-

Figure 1.1 A Picture of the Economy

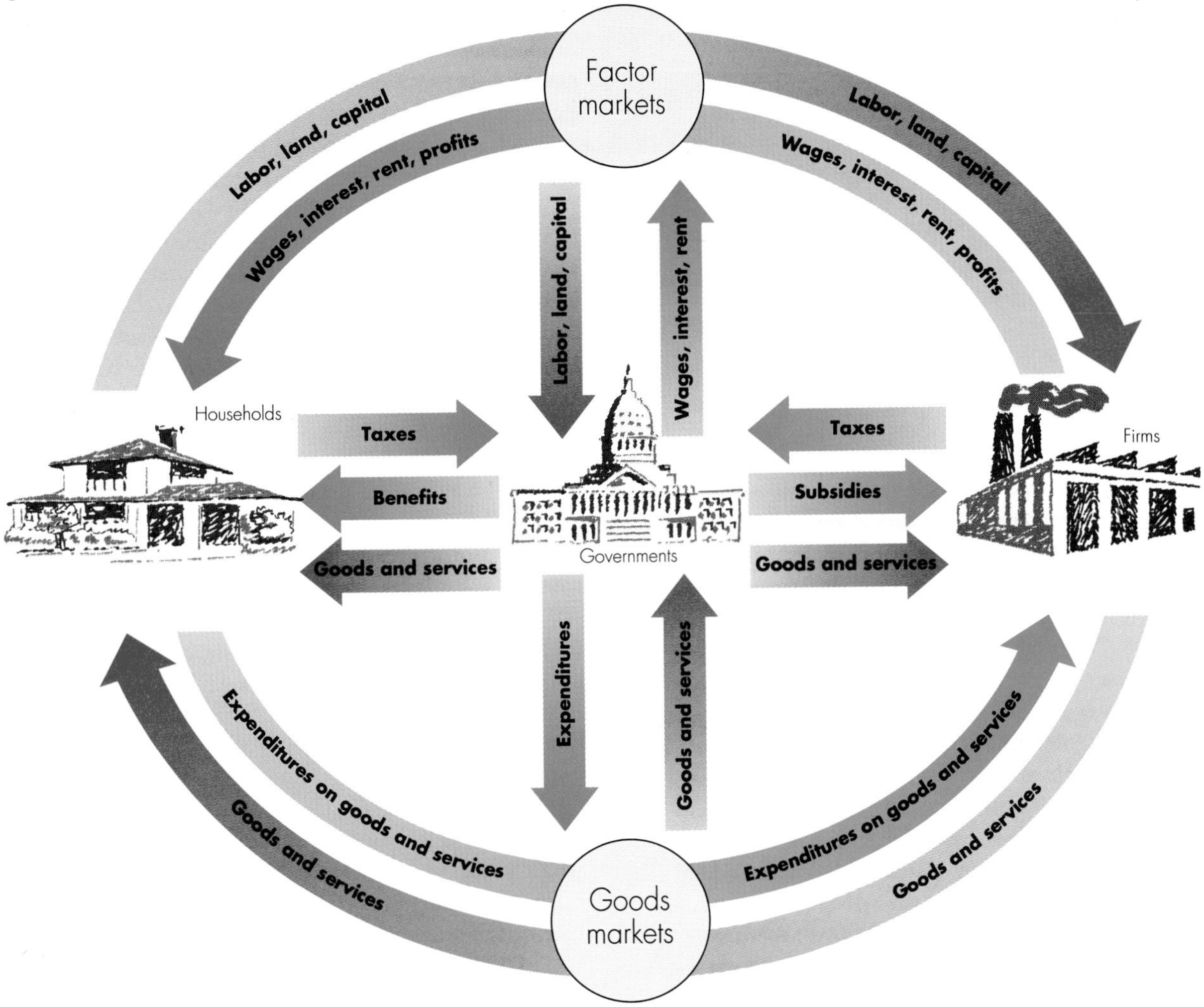

The economy has three groups of decision makers: households, firms, and governments. It also has two groups of markets: factor markets and goods markets. Households provide factors of production to both firms and governments through the factor markets. Firms and governments pay households wages, interest, rent, and profits in exchange. Firms supply goods and services to households and to governments through the goods markets. Households and governments pay firms for these goods and services. In addition, governments provide goods and services directly to households and firms. Households and firms pay taxes to governments, and governments make transfer payments—subsidies and benefits—to firms and households. In this figure, money and other expenditures move along the green arrows; goods, services, land, labor, and capital move along the red arrows.

ual in the economy belongs to a household. Some households consist of a single person while others consist either of families or of groups of unrelated individuals, such as two or three students sharing an apartment.

A **firm** is an organization that produces goods and services. All producers are called firms, no matter how big they are or what they produce. Car makers, farmers, banks, and insurance companies are all firms.

A **government** is an organization that has two functions: the provision of goods and services to households and firms and the redistribution of income and wealth. Examples of the goods and services supplied by government are national defense, law enforcement, public health, transportation, and education.

You can see these three groups of decision makers in Fig. 1.1. You can also see in this figure the decisions that they make. Households supply factors of production to firms and governments. **Factors of production** are the economy's productive resources, usually classified under three headings:

- Labor
- Land
- Capital

Labor is the brain-power and muscle-power of human beings; **land** is natural resources of all kinds; **capital** is all the equipment, buildings, tools, and other manufactured goods that can be used in production. Households sell or rent factors of production to firms and governments and receive an income in payment for their supply. Households also receive benefits from the government and pay taxes to the government. With what is left, households buy goods and services produced by firms.

Firms hire factors of production from households and choose how to use them to produce goods and services. They also decide what goods and services to produce and in what quantities. Expenditures by households and governments on goods and services are received by firms. Firms use these receipts to make payments to households for the factors of production supplied. Firms also receive subsidies from and pay taxes to governments.

Governments decide on the scale of purchases of factors of production from households and of goods and services from firms. They also decide on the scale of provision of goods and services to households and firms, as well as on the rates of benefits and subsidies and taxes.

Coordination Mechanisms

Perhaps the most striking thing about the choices made by households, firms, and governments, as illustrated in Fig. 1.1, is that they surely must come into conflict with each other. For example, households choose how much work to do and what type of work to specialize in, but firms choose the type and quantity of labor to employ in the production of various goods and services. In other words, households choose the types and quantities of labor to sell and firms choose the types and quantities of labor to buy. Similarly, in markets for goods and services, households choose the types and quantities of goods and services to buy, while firms choose the types and quantities to sell. Government choices regarding taxes, benefits, subsidies and the provision of goods and services also enter the picture. Taxes taken by the government affect the amount of income that households and firms have available for spending and saving. Also, decisions by firms and households depend on the types and quantities of goods and services governments make available. For example, if the government provides excellent highways but a dilapidated railroad system, households will allocate more of their income to buying motor vehicles and less to buying train rides.

How is it possible for the millions of individual decisions taken by households, firms, and governments to be consistent with each other? What makes households want to sell the same types and quantities of labor that firms want to buy? What happens if the number of households wanting to work as economics professors exceeds the number that universities want to hire? How do firms know what to produce so that households will buy their output? What happens if firms want to sell more hamburgers than households want to buy?

There are two mechanisms that can achieve a coordination of individual economic choices:

- Command mechanism
- Market mechanism

A **command mechanism** is a method of determining *what*, *how*, and *for whom* goods and services are produced, based on the authority of a ruler or ruling body—such as a king or a ruling political party. The best example of a command mechanism in the modern world is in the USSR and some other Eastern European countries. In those economies, a central planning bureau makes decisions about *what* will be produced, *how* it will be produced, and *for whom* it will be produced. We'll study command economies and compare them with other types of economies in the last chapter of this book.

A **market mechanism** is a method of determining *what*, *how*, and *for whom* goods and services are produced, based on individual choices coordinated through markets. In ordinary speech, the word *market* means a place where people buy and sell goods such as fish, meat, fruits, and vegetables. In economics, the word *market* has a more general meaning. A **market** is any arrangement that facilitates the buying and selling (trading) of a good, service, or factor of production.

As an example of a market, consider that in which oil is bought and sold—the world oil market. The world oil market is not a place. It is all the many different institutions, buyers, sellers, brokers and so on who buy and sell oil. The market is a coordination mechanism because it pools together the separate plans of all the individual decision makers who try to buy and sell any particular good. Decision makers do not have to meet in a physical sense. In the modern world, telecommunications have replaced direct contact as the main link between buyers and sellers.

Markets are classified according to the types of things traded in them. Figure 1.1 shows the two types of market. The markets in which goods and services are traded are called **goods markets.** The markets in which factors of production are traded—markets for labor, land, and capital—are called **factor markets.** These markets enable the plans of individual households and firms and the government to be coordinated and made consistent with each other.

The U.S. economy relies extensively on the market as the mechanism for coordinating the plans of individual households and firms. There is, though, an element of command in the U.S. economy. Markets do not operate in isolation of the legal framework established and enforced by the government sector of the economy. In recognition of the role played both by command and market coordination mechanisms, modern economies are referred to as mixed economies. A **mixed economy** is one that uses both market and command mechanisms to coordinate economic activity.

The U.S. economy is a mixed economy but one that relies much more heavily on the market than on a command mechanism. However, actions taken by the government sector modify the allocation of scarce resources, changing *what*, *how*, and *for whom* the various goods and services are produced.

How Market Coordination Works The market coordinates individual decisions through price adjustments. To see how, think about the market for hamburgers in your local area. Suppose that the quantity of hamburgers being offered for sale is less than the quantity that people would like to buy. Some people who want to buy hamburgers will not be able to do so. To make the choices of buyers and sellers compatible, buyers will have to scale down their appetites and more hamburgers will have to be offered for sale. An increase in the price of hamburgers will produce this outcome. A higher price will encourage producers to offer more hamburgers for sale. It will also curb the appetite for hamburgers and change some lunch plans. Fewer people will buy hamburgers and more will buy hot dogs (or some other alternative to hamburgers). More hamburgers (and more hot dogs) will be offered for sale.

Now imagine the opposite situation. More hamburgers are available than people want to buy. In this case, the price is too high. A lower price will discourage the production and sale of hamburgers, and encourage their purchase and consumption. Decisions to produce and sell, and to buy and consume, are continuously adjusted and kept in balance with each other by adjustments in prices.

In some cases, prices get stuck or fixed. When this happens, some other adjustment has to make the plans and choices of individuals consistent. Customers waiting in lines and stocks of inventories operate as a temporary safety valve when the market price is stuck. If people want to buy more than the quantity that firms have decided to sell, and if the price is temporarily fixed, then one of two things will have to happen. Firms wind up selling more than they would like and their inventories will shrink; or, lines of customers will develop and only those who get to the head of the line before the goods run out will be able to make a purchase. The longer the line or the bigger the decline in inventories, the more prices will have to adjust to keep buying and selling decisions in balance.

We have now seen how the market solves the question of *what* quantity to produce—how many hamburgers to make. The market also solves the question of *how* to produce in similar fashion. For example, hamburger producers can use gas, electric power, or charcoal to cook their hamburgers.

Figure 1.2 International Linkages

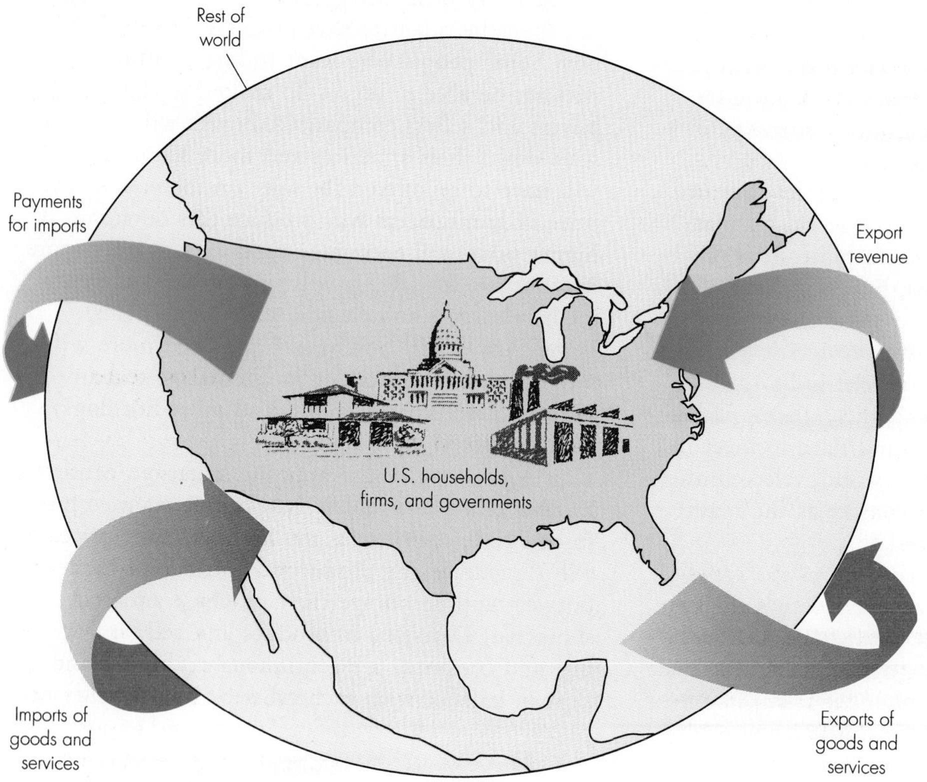

The U.S. economy exports and imports goods and services. It receives a flow of revenue from its exports of goods and services and makes payments for imports. The difference between these two flows is the country's net foreign borrowing or lending. In recent years, the United States has been a net borrower.

Which fuel is used depends in part on the flavor that the producer wants to achieve and on the cost of the different fuels. If a fuel becomes very expensive, as did oil in the 1970s, less of it will be used and more of other fuels will be used in its place. By substituting one fuel for another as the costs of the different fuels change, the market solves the question of how to produce.

Finally, the market helps solve the question of *for whom* to produce. Skills, talents, and resources that are in very short supply will command a higher price than those in greater abundance. The owners of rare resources and skills will obtain a larger share of the output of the economy than the owners of those resources in abundant supply.

Closed and Open Economies

The economy depicted in Fig. 1.1 is a closed one. A **closed economy** is one that has no links with any other economy. The only truly closed economy is that of the entire world. The U.S. economy is an open economy. An **open economy** is one that has economic links with other economies. Firms in an open economy export some of their production to other countries, rather than selling only to households within their own country. Firms, households, and governments in an open economy also buy some of the goods and services that they use from firms in other countries. These imports and exports of goods and services are illustrated in Fig. 1.2.

The total values of exports and imports are not necessarily equal to each other. The difference between those two values is the net amount that a country lends to or borrows from the rest of the world.

In the United States, there has been a deficit on international payments in recent years, with the government borrowing more than $100 billion each year. The consequence of our importing more goods and services than we export is that the United States is a net borrower from—not a net lender to—the rest of the world. We will study the international linkages between the U.S. economy and the rest of the world later in this book.

R E V I E W

An economy is a mechanism that determines what is produced, how it is produced, and for whom it is produced. In the U.S. economy, these choices are made by households, firms, and government, and they are coordinated through markets. Governments influence these choices by taxing, subsidizing, regulating, and lawmaking. The U.S. economy is an open economy, having extensive links with other economies. ■

We have now described an economy in about as much detail as we described an airplane. But we're about to become the economic equivalent of aeronautical engineers! We're going to build economies that fly! To do that, we have to understand the principles of economics as thoroughly as aeronautical engineers understand the principles of flight. To discover these principles, economists approach their work with the rigor and objectivity of natural scientists—they do economic science.

Economic Science

Economic science, like the natural sciences (such as physics and biology) and the other social sciences (such as political science, psychology, and sociology), is an attempt to find a body of laws of nature. All sciences have two components:

- Careful and systematic observation and measurement
- Development of a body of theory to direct and interpret observations

All sciences are careful to distinguish between two types of statements:

- Statements about what *is*
- Statements about what *ought* to be

What Is and What Ought to Be

Statements about what *is* are **positive statements.** Statements about what *ought* to be are **normative statements.** Let's illustrate the distinction between positive and normative statements with two examples.

First, consider the controversy over the Strategic Defense Initiative, or "Star Wars." The question *Is it possible* to build an effective strategic defense system? is positive. The question *Ought* we to try to build a strategic defense system? is normative. Second, consider the economic controversy over tax cuts and cutbacks on social programs. The question *Will* lower taxes and less generous social programs make people work harder? is positive. The question *Should* taxes and social programs be cut? is normative.

Science—whether natural, social, or economic—tries to discover and catalog positive statements that are consistent with what we observe in the world. Science is silent on normative questions. It is not that such questions are unimportant. On the contrary, they are often the most important questions of all. Nor is it that scientists as people do not have opinions on such questions. It is simply that the activity of doing science cannot settle a normative matter and the possession of scientific knowledge does not equip a person with superior moral precepts or norms. A difference of opinion on a positive matter can ultimately be settled by careful observation and measurement. A difference of opinion on a normative matter cannot be settled in that way. In fact, there are no well-defined rules for settling a normative dispute and sometimes reasonable people simply have to agree to disagree.

When they cannot, political and judicial institutions intervene in order for decisions to be made. We settle normative disagreements in the political, not the scientific, arena. The scientific community can, and often does, contribute to the normative debates of political life. But science is a distinct activity. Even though scientists have opinions about what ought to be, those opinions have no part in science itself.

Now let's see how economists attempt to discover and catalog positive statements that are consistent with their observations and that enable them to answer economic questions such as the seven big questions that we reviewed earlier.

Observation and Measurement

Economic phenomena can be observed and measured in great detail. For example, we can catalog the amounts and locations of natural and human resources. We can describe who does what kind of work, for how many hours, and how they are paid. We can catalog the things that people produce, consume, and store, and their prices. We can describe in detail who borrows and who lends and at what interest rates. We can also catalog the things that government taxes and at what rates, the programs it finances and at what cost.

Our list is not exhaustive. It gives a flavor, though, of the array of things that economists can describe through careful observation and measurement of economic activity.

In today's world, computers have given us access to an enormous volume of economic description. Government agencies around the world, national statistical bureaus, private economic consultants, banks, investment advisors, and research economists working in universities generate an astonishing amount of information about economic behavior.

But economists do more than observe and measure economic activity, crucial as that is. Describing something is not the same as understanding it. You can describe your digital watch in great detail, but that does not mean you can explain what makes it work. Understanding what makes things work requires the discovery of laws. That is the main task of economists—the discovery of laws governing economic behavior. How do economists go about this task?

Economic Theory

We can describe in great detail the ups and downs, or cycles, in unemployment, but can we explain *why* unemployment fluctuates? We can describe the fall in the price of a VCR or a pocket calculator and the dramatic increase in its use, but can we explain the low price and popularity of such items? Did the fall in the price lead more people to use pocket calculators, or did their popularity lower the costs of production and make it possible to lower the price? Or did something else cause both the fall in the price and the increase in use?

Questions like these can be answered only by developing a body of economic theory. An **economic theory** is a reliable generalization that enables us to understand and predict the economic choices that people make. We develop economic theories by building and testing economic models. What is an economic model?

Economic Model

You have just seen an economic model. To answer the question What is an economy and how does it work? we built a model of an economy. We did not describe in all its detail all the economic actions that take place in the United States. We concentrated our attention only on those features that seemed important for understanding economic choices, and ignored everything else. You will perhaps better appreciate what we mean by an economic model if you think about more familiar models.

We have all seen model trains, cars, and airplanes. Although we do not usually call dolls and stuffed animals models, we can think of them in this way. Architects make models of buildings, and biologists make models of DNA (the double helix carrier of the genetic code).

A model is usually smaller than the real thing that it represents. But models are not always smaller in scale (e.g., the biologist's model of the components of cells) and, in any case, the scale of a model is not its most important feature. A model also shows less detail than its counterpart in reality. For example, all the models we have mentioned resemble the real thing in *appearance*, but they are not usually made of the same substance nor do they work like the real thing that they represent. The architect's model of a new high-rise shows us what the building will look like and how it will conform with the buildings around it—but it does not contain plumbing, telephone cables, elevator shafts, air conditioning plants, and other interior workings.

All the models that we have discussed (including those that are typically used as toys) represent something that is real, but they lack some key features. The model abstracts from the detail of the real thing. It includes only those features needed for the purpose at hand. It leaves out the inessential or unnecessary. What a model includes and what it leaves out is not arbitrary; it results from a conscious and careful decision.

The models that we have just considered are all "physical" models. We can see the real thing and we can see the model. Indeed, the purpose of those models is to enable us to "visualize" the real thing. Some models, including economic models, are not physical. We cannot look at the real thing and look at the model and simply decide whether the model is a good or bad representation of the real thing. But the idea of a model as an abstraction from reality still applies to an economic model.

An economic model has two components:

- Assumptions
- Implications

Assumptions form the foundation on which a model is built. They are propositions about what is important and what can be ignored; about what can be treated as being constant and, therefore, reliably used to make predictions.

Implications are the outcome of a model. The link between a model's assumptions and its implications is a process of logical deduction.

Let's illustrate these components of a model by building a simple model of your daily journey to school. The model has three assumptions:

1 Class begins at 9:00 A.M.

2 The bus ride takes 30 minutes.

3 The walk from the bus to class takes five minutes.

The implication of this model is that to be in class on time, you have to be on the bus by 8:25 A.M.

The assumptions of a model depend on the model's purpose. The purpose of an economic model is to understand how people make choices in the face of scarcity. Thus in building an economic model, we abstract from the rich detail of human behavior and focus only on behavior that is relevant for coping with scarcity. Everything else is ignored. Economists know that people fall in love and form deep friendships; that they experience great joy and security or great pain and anxiety. But economists assume that in seeking to understand economic behavior, they may build models that ignore many aspects of life. They focus on one and only one feature of the world: People have wants that exceed their resources and so, by their choices, have to make the best of things.

Assumptions of an Economic Model Economic models are based on four key assumptions:

1 *People have preferences.* Economists use the term **preferences** to denote likes and dislikes and the intensity of those likes and dislikes. People can judge whether one situation is better, worse, or just as good as another one. For example, you can judge whether for you, one loaf of bread and no cheese is better, worse, or just as good as a half a loaf of bread and four ounces of cheese.

2 *People are endowed with a fixed amount of resources and a technology that can transform those resources into goods and services.* Economists use the term **endowment** to refer to the resources that people have and the term **technology** to describe the methods of converting those endowments into goods and services.

3 *People economize.* They choose how to use their endowments and technologies in order to make themselves as well-off as possible. Such a choice is called a rational choice. A **rational choice** is the best possible course of action from the point of view of the person making the choice. Each choice, no matter what it is or how foolish it may seem to an observer, is interpreted, in an economic model, as a rational choice.

Choices are made on the basis of the information available. With hindsight, and with more information, people may well feel that some of their past choices were bad ones. This fact does not make such choices irrational. Again, a rational choice is the best possible course of action, from the point of view of the person making the choice, given that person's preferences and *given the information available when the choice is made.*

4 *People's choices are coordinated.* One person's choice to buy something must be matched by another person's choice to sell that same thing. One person's choice to work at a particular job must be matched by another person's choice to hire someone to do that job. The coordination of individual choices is made either by a market mechanism or a command mechanism.

Implications of an Economic Model The implications of an economic model are the equilibrium values of various prices and quantities. An **equilibrium** is a situation in which everyone has economized—that is, all individuals have made the best possible choices in the light of their own preferences and given their endowments, technologies, and information—and in which those choices have been coordinated and made compatible with the choices of everyone else. Equilibrium is the solution or outcome of an economic model.

The term equilibrium conjures up the picture of a balance of opposing forces. For example, a balance scale can be said to be in equilibrium if a pound of butter is placed on one side of the balance and a one-pound weight is placed on the other side. The two weights exactly equal each other and so offset each other, leaving the balance arm horizontal. A soap bubble provides another excellent physical illustration of equilibrium. The delicate spherical film of soap is held in place by a balance of forces of the air inside the sphere and the air outside it.

This second physical analogy illustrates a further important feature of an equilibrium. An equilibrium is not necessarily static but may be dynamic—constantly changing. By squeezing or stretching the bubble, you can change its shape, but its shape is always determined by the balance of the forces acting upon it (including the forces that you exert upon it).

An economic equilibrium has a great deal in common with that of the soap bubble. First, it is in a constant state of motion. At each point in time, each person makes the best possible choice, given the endowments and actions of others. But changing circumstances alter those choices. For example, on a busy day in Manhattan, there are more cars looking for parking spaces than the number of spaces available. In this situation, the equilibrium number of free spaces is zero. But people do get to park. Individual cars are leaving and arriving at a steady pace. As soon as one car vacates a parking space, another instantly fills it. Being in equilibrium does not mean that everyone gets to park instantly. There is an equilibrium amount of time spent finding a vacant space. People hunting for a space are frustrated and experience rising blood pressure and increased anger. But there is still an equilibrium in the hunt for available parking spaces.

"And now a traffic update: A parking space has become available on Sixty-fifth Street between Second and Third. Hold it! A bulletin has just been handed me. That space has been taken."

Drawing by H. Martin; © 1987 The New Yorker Magazine, Inc.

Similarly, an economic equilibrium does not mean that everyone is experiencing economic prosperity. The constraints may be such that some people are very poor. Nevertheless, given their preferences, endowments, the available technologies, and the actions of everyone else, each person has made the best possible choice and sees no advantage in modifying his or her current action.

Microeconomic and Macroeconomic Models

Economic models fall into two categories: microeconomic and macroeconomic. **Microeconomics** is the branch of economics that studies the decisions of individual households and firms. Microeconomics also studies the way that individual markets work and the detailed way that regulation and taxes affect the allocation of labor and of goods and services.

Macroeconomics is the branch of economics that studies the economy as a whole. It seeks to understand the big picture rather than the detailed individual choices. In particular, it studies the determination of the overall level of economic activity—of unemployment, aggregate income, average prices, and inflation.

Of the seven big questions, those dealing with technological change, production and consumption, and wages and earnings are microeconomic. Those dealing with unemployment, inflation, and differences in wealth among nations are macroeconomic.

Model, Theory, and Reality

People who build models often get carried away and start talking as if their model *is* the real world—as if their model is reality. No matter how useful it is, there is no sense in which a model can be said to be reality.

A model is an abstract entity. It lists assumptions and their implications. When economists talk about people who have made themselves as well-off as possible, they are not talking about real people. They are talking about artificial people in an economic model. Do not lose sight of this important but easily misunderstood fact.

Economic theory bridges the gap between an economic model and the real world. Economic theory proposes that the economic behavior of people in actual economies can be predicted by using models in which people who make rational choices interact with each other in an equilibrium. Economics develops models based on this idea to explain all aspects of economic behavior. But economic models have to be tested.

To test an economic model, its implications are matched against actual events in the real world. That is, the model is used to make predictions about the real world. The model's predictions may correspond to or be in conflict with the facts. It is by comparing the model's predictions with the facts that we are able to test a model. The process of developing economic theories by using models is illustrated in Fig. 1.3. We begin by building a model. The model's implications are used to generate predictions about the world. These predictions and their test form the basis of a theory. When predictions are in conflict with the facts, either a theory is discarded in favor of a superior alternative or we return to the model building stage, modifying our assumptions and creating a new model. Economics itself provides guidance on how we might discover a better model. It prompts us to look for some aspect of preferences, endowments, technology, or the coordination mechanism that has been overlooked.

Figure 1.3 How Theories Are Developed

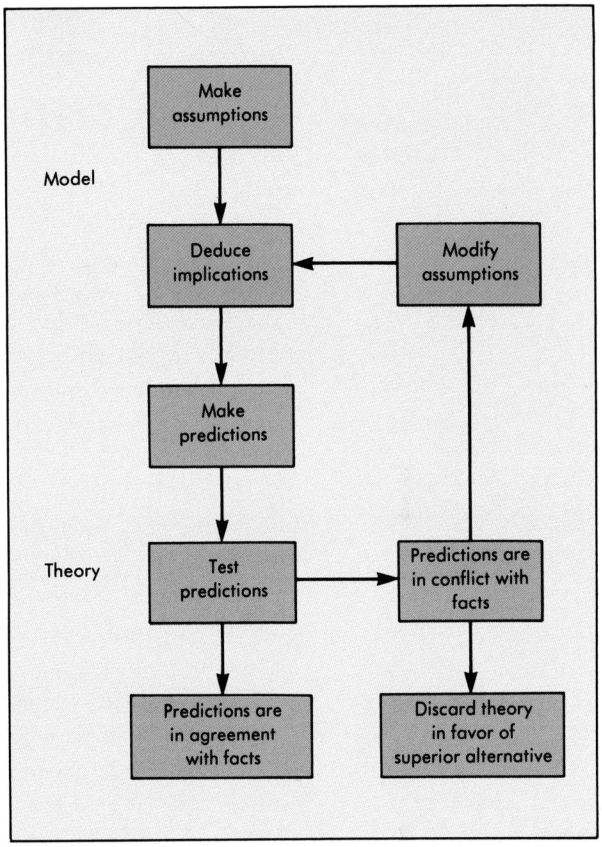

Economic theories are developed by building and testing economic models. An economic model is a set of *assumptions* about what is important and what can be ignored and the *implications* of those assumptions. The implications of a model form the basis of *predictions* about the world. These predictions are tested by being checked against the facts. If the predictions are in conflict with the facts, either the theory is discarded in favor of a superior alternative or the model-building process begins anew with modified assumptions. It is only when predictions are in agreement with the facts that a useful theory has been developed.

Adam Smith and the Birth of Economic Science

In the year that colonists in far-off America revolted against Britain, a Scottish thinker touched off a different kind of revolution. For it was in 1776 that Adam Smith published *An Inquiry into the Nature and Causes of the Wealth of Nations*, the book that began economics as a science. Even today, more than two hundred years after its publication, the book is reprinted, reinterpreted, and reread repeatedly.

Smith led a quiet, scholarly life. He was born in 1723 in Kirkaldy, Scotland, a small community near Edinburgh where he spent his first 14 years. At the remarkably early age of 14, he became a student at the University of Glasgow. He graduated at 17 and then went on to Oxford University where he spent the next six years. His first major academic appointment, at age 28, was as Professor of Logic, and subsequently as Professor of Logic and Moral Philosophy, at Glasgow. After 13 years at Glasgow, Smith became a tutor to a wealthy Scottish duke who lived in France. After Smith spent two years in that position, the Duke gave him a pension—an income for the rest of his life—of £300 a year. (An income of this size would have bought a great deal in the eighteenth century, when the average wage was about £30 a year.)

With the financial security of a pension, Smith devoted the next ten years of his life—from 1766 to 1776—to his great treatise. He was writing his *Wealth of Nations* at a time when the British economy was undergoing what came to be called the Industrial Revolution. New technologies were being invented and applied to the manufacture of cotton and wool, iron, transportation, and agriculture. The prevailing intellectual climate held that Britain needed to be protected from cheap foreign imports so that the nation could build up its stock of gold and finance its continuing process of industrialization.

Adam Smith

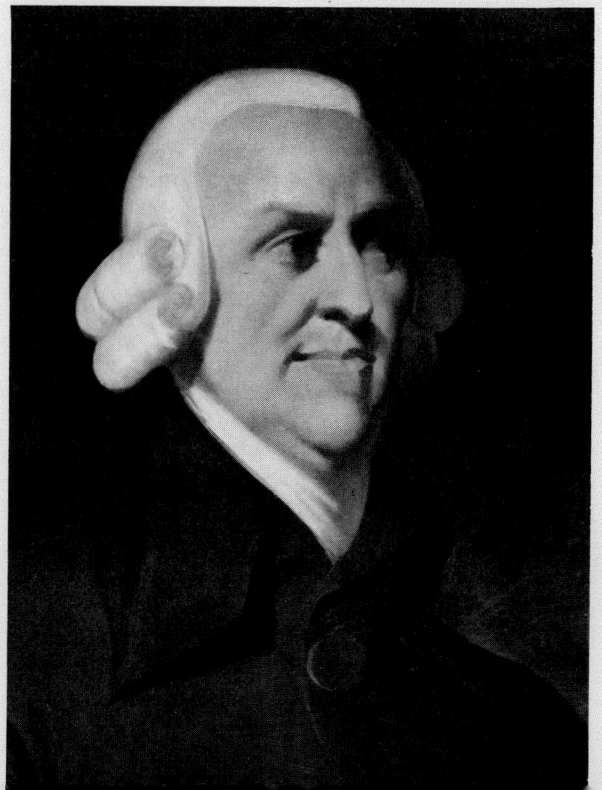

Smith scoffed at this idea and developed a massive case against protection and in favor of "free trade." *The Wealth of Nations* argued that when each person makes the best economic choice possible, that choice leads, as if by "an invisible hand," to the best economic outcome for society as a whole. This best possible social outcome arises not because people pay attention to the needs of others but from self-interest. Said Smith, "It is not from the benevolence of the butcher, the brewer, or the baker, that we can expect our dinner, but from their regard to their own interest."*

The Wealth of Nations proposed that all economic behavior can be understood as the rational pursuit of self-interest. The book begins much like the one that you are now studying, but much more profoundly, for Smith's was the first systematic treatment of these ideas. Smith explained how specialization, exchange, and the development of money lead to massive increases in goods and services. He applied his basic theory to a sweep of human history, starting from the fall of the Roman Empire. He explained the rise and progress of towns and cities, how commerce between towns and farmlands benefits both, and why free international trade leads to improved living standards. He also applied the theory of rational self-interest to explain why the universities of the eighteenth century were organized not for the benefit of the students but, as he put it, "for the ease of the professors." He even used his theory to explain the proliferation of new religions.

Many thinkers had written earlier on economic questions, but Smith was the first to make a science of economics.

> It was Smith who provided so broad and authoritative an account of the known economic doctrine that henceforth it was no longer permissible for any subsequent writer on economics to advance his own ideas while ignoring the state of general knowledge. A science consists of interacting practitioners, and henceforth no one could decently ignore Smith's own work and in due time the work of Malthus, Ricardo, and the galaxy of economists who populated the first half of the nineteenth century.**

This first box on our advancing knowledge in economic science has been devoted to Adam Smith, who stands alone as the founder of this discipline. Subsequent boxes in this series will give you a taste of how various branches of the subject have advanced from this founding father through to the present. The goal is to enable you to see how the science of economics advances and perhaps even to inspire you to become one of that community of scholars seeking to deepen our understanding of economic phenomena.

---

*Adam Smith, *An Inquiry into the Nature and Causes of the Wealth of Nations*, ed. Edwin Cannan, with a new preface by George J. Stigler (Chicago: University of Chicago Press, 1976), p. 18.

**George J. Stigler, "Nobel Lecture: The Process and Progress of Economics," *Journal of Political Economy* 91 (August 1983): 529–45.

Economics is a young science and a long way from having achieved its goal. Its birth can be dated fairly precisely in the eighteenth century with the publication of Adam Smith's *The Wealth of Nations* (see Our Advancing Knowledge, p. 22). In the closing years of the twentieth century, economic science has managed to discover a sizable number of useful generalizations. In many areas, however, we are still going around the circle—changing assumptions, performing new logical deductions, generating new predictions, and getting wrong answers yet again. The gradual accumulation of correct answers gives most practitioners some faith that their methods will, eventually, provide usable answers to the big economic questions.

As we make progress, though, more and more things become clearer and seem to fit together. Theoretical advances lead to deeper understanding. This feature of economics is shared with scientists in all fields. As Albert Einstein, the great physicist, said: "Creating a new theory is not like destroying an old barn and erecting a skyscraper in its place. It is rather like climbing a mountain, gaining new and wider views, discovering new connections between our starting point and its rich environment. But the point from which we started still exists and can be seen, although it appears smaller and forms a tiny part of our broad view gained by the mastery of the obstacles on our adventurous way up."[1]

■ In the next chapter, we will study some of the tools that economists use to build economic models. Then, in Chapter 3, we'll build an economic model and use that model to understand the world around us and to start to answer some of the seven big economic questions.

[1]These words are attributed to Einstein in a letter by Oliver Sacks to *The Listener* 88, no. 2279, 30 Nov. 1972, 756.

S U M M A R Y

Seven Big Questions

Economics tries to answer difficult questions that affect our daily lives. These questions concern the production and consumption of goods and services; wages and earnings; unemployment; inflation; government spending, taxation, and regulation; international trade; and the distribution of wealth and poverty in the United States and throughout the world. There are no easy answers to the big economic questions, which must be approached in a scientific manner. (pp. 6–8)

Scarcity

All economic questions arise from the fundamental fact of scarcity. Scarcity means that wants exceed resources. Human wants are effectively unlimited but the resources available to satisfy them are finite.

Economic activity is what people do to cope with scarcity. Scarcity forces people to make choices. Making the best choice possible from what is available is called optimizing. In order to make the best possible choice, a person weighs the costs and benefits of the alternatives.

Opportunity cost is the cost of one choice in terms of the best forgone alternative. The opportunity cost of any action is the best alternative action that could have been undertaken in its place. Attending class instead of staying in bed has an opportunity cost—the cost of one hour of rest.

Scarcity forces people to compete with each other for scarce resources. People may cooperate in certain areas, but all economic activity ultimately results in competition among individuals acting alone or in groups. (pp. 9–11)

The Economy

The economy is a mechanism that allocates scarce resources among competing uses, determining *what*, *how*, and *for whom* the various goods and services will be produced.

The economy's working parts are divided into two categories: decision makers and coordination mechanisms. Economic decision makers are households, firms, and governments. Households decide how much of their factors of production to sell to firms and government, and what goods and services to buy from firms. Firms decide what factors of production to hire and which goods and services to produce. Governments decide on the scale of purchases of factors of production from households and of goods and services from firms. They also decide on the scale of provision of goods and services to households and firms, as well as on the rates of benefits and subsidies and taxes.

There are two types of coordination mechanisms: the command mechanism and the market mechanism. The U.S. economy relies mainly on the market mechanism, but the actions taken by the government sector do modify the allocation of scarce resources. The U.S. economy is therefore a mixed economy. (pp. 11–17)

Economic Science

Economic science, like the natural sciences and the other social sciences, attempts to find a body of laws of nature. Economic science seeks to understand what *is* and is silent about what *ought* to be. Economists try to find economic laws by developing a body of economic theory, and economic theory, in turn, is developed by building and testing economic models. Economic models are abstract, logical constructions that contain two components: assumptions and implications. An economic model has four key assumptions:

1 People have preferences.
2 People have a given endowment of resources and technology.
3 People economize.
4 Peoples' choices are coordinated through market or command mechanisms.

The implications of an economic model are the equilibrium values of various prices and quantities that result from each individual doing the best that is possible, given the individual's preferences, endowments, information, and technology and given the coordination mechanism. (pp. 17–24)

K E Y C O N C E P T S

Key Figure

REVIEW QUESTIONS

1 Give two examples, different from those in the chapter, that illustrate each of the seven big economic questions.

2 Why does scarcity force us to make choices?

3 What do we mean by "rational choice"? Give examples of rational and irrational choices.

4 Why does scarcity force us to optimize?

5 Why does optimization require us to calculate costs?

6 Why does scarcity imply competition?

7 Why can't we solve economic problems by co-operating with each other?

8 Name the main economic decision makers.

9 List the economic decisions made by households, firms, and governments.

10 What is the difference between a command mechanism and a market mechanism?

11 Distinguish between positive and normative statements by listing three examples of each type of statement.

12 What are the four key assumptions of an economic model?

13 Explain the difference between a model and a theory.

PROBLEMS

1 Which of the following are part of your opportunity cost of attending school? Explain why they are or are not.

a) The money you spend on haircuts

b) The vacation you would have taken if you had been working rather than being in school

c) The tapes and compact discs that you don't have because you've had to spend so much on economics textbooks

d) The amount you pay for your lunch in the college cafeteria each week

e) The $20,000 annual salary you could have made in your Uncle Fred's store

2 List some examples of opportunity costs that you have incurred today.

3 Give some examples of opportunity costs you incurred that are the results of someone else's actions. Give some examples of opportunity costs incurred by someone else that are the result of your actions.

4 Which of the following statements are positive and which are normative?

a) Low rents will restrict the supply of housing.

b) High interest rates lower the demand for mortgages and new homes.

c) No family ought to have to pay more than one quarter of its income to rent decent housing.

d) Owners of apartment buildings ought to be free to charge whatever rent they like.

e) The government ought to restrict the rents that apartment owners are allowed to charge.

5 You have been hired by a company that makes and markets tapes, records, and compact discs. Your employer is going to start selling these products in a new market that has a population of 100 million people. A survey has revealed that 40 percent of this market buys only popular music and 5 percent of it buys only classical music. No one buys both types of music. The average income of the pop music fan is $10,000 a year and that of the classical fan is $50,000 a year. It has also been discovered that people with low incomes spend one quarter of 1 percent of their income on tapes, records, and CDs while those with high incomes spend 2 percent of theirs. You have been asked to predict how much is likely to be spent in this market on pop music and classical music in one year.

Build a model to answer this question. List your assumptions and work out their implications. Draw attention to the potential for unreliablility in your answers. Why might your model give wrong answers?

Chapter 2

Making and Using Graphs

After studying this chapter, you will be able to:

- Make and interpret a time-series graph and a scatter diagram
- Distinguish between linear and nonlinear relationships and relationships that have a maximum and a minimum
- Define and calculate the slope of a line
- Graph relationships among more than two variables

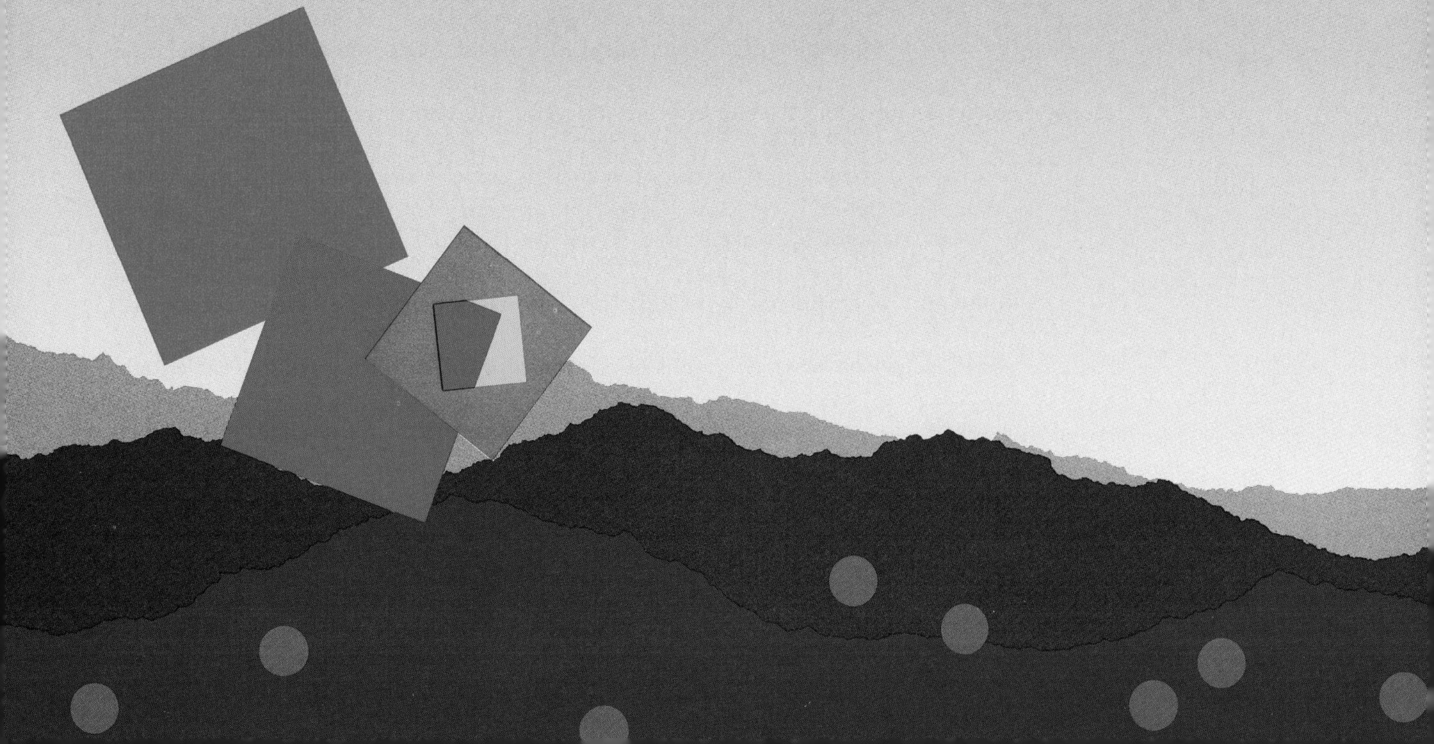

Three Kinds of Lies

Benjamin Disraeli, British prime minister in the late nineteenth century, is reputed to have said that there are three kinds of lies: lies, damned lies, and statistics. One of the most powerful ways of conveying statistical information is in the form of a picture—a graph. Thus graphs, too, like statistics, can tell lies. But the right graph does not lie. Indeed, it reveals data and helps its viewer to see and think about relationships that would otherwise be obscure. ■ Graphs are a surprisingly modern invention. The first graphs appeared in the late eighteenth century, long after the discovery of mathematically sophisticated ideas such as logarithms and calculus. But today, especially in the age of the personal computer and the video display, graphs have become almost more important than words. The ability to make and use graphs is as important as the ability to read and write. ■ How do economists use graphs? What are the different types of graphs that economists use? What do economic graphs reveal and what can they hide? What are the main pitfalls that can result in a graph that lies? ■ It will be clear to you from the seven big questions that you studied in Chapter 1 that the problems that economics seeks to solve are difficult ones. You will also suspect, and rightly so, that hardly anything in economics has a single cause. Variations in the quantity of ice cream consumed are not caused merely by variations in the air temperature or in the price of cream but by at least these two factors and probably several others as well. How can we draw graphs of relationships that involve several variables, all of which vary simultaneously? How can we interpret such relationships? ■ In this chapter, we are going to look at the different kinds of graphs that are used in economics. We are going to learn how to make them and read them.

■ We are going to look at examples of useful graphs as well as misleading graphs. We are also going to study how we can calculate the strength of the effect of one variable on another.

There are no graphs or techniques used in this book that are more complicated than those explained and described in this chapter. If you are already familiar with graphs, you may want to skip or at least only skim this chapter. Whether you study this chapter thoroughly or give it a quick pass, you should regard it as a handy reference chapter to which you can return if you feel that you need additional help understanding the graphs that you encounter in your study of economics.

Graphing Data

Graphs represent a quantity as a distance. Figure 2.1 gives two examples. Part (a) shows temperature, measured in degrees Fahrenheit, as the distance on a scale. Movements from left to right represent increases in temperature. Movements from right to left represent decreases in temperature. The point marked zero represents zero degrees Fahrenheit. To the right of zero, the temperatures are positive. To the left of zero, the temperatures are negative (as indicated by the minus sign in front of the numbers).

Figure 2.1(b) provides another example. This time altitude, or height, is measured in thousands of feet above sea level. The point marked zero represents sea level. Points to the right of zero represent feet above sea level. Points to the left of zero (indicated by a minus sign) represent depths below sea level.

There are no rigid rules about the scale for a graph. The scale is determined by the range of the variable being graphed and the space available for the graph.

The two graphs in Fig. 2.1 show just a single variable. Marking a point on either of the two scales indicates a particular temperature or a particular height. Thus the point marked *a* represents 32°F, the freezing point of water. The point marked *b* represents 20,320 feet, the height of Mount McKinley, the highest mountain in North America.

Graphing a single variable as we have done does not usually reveal much. Graphs become powerful when they show how two variables are related to each other.

Figure 2.1 Graphing a Single Variable

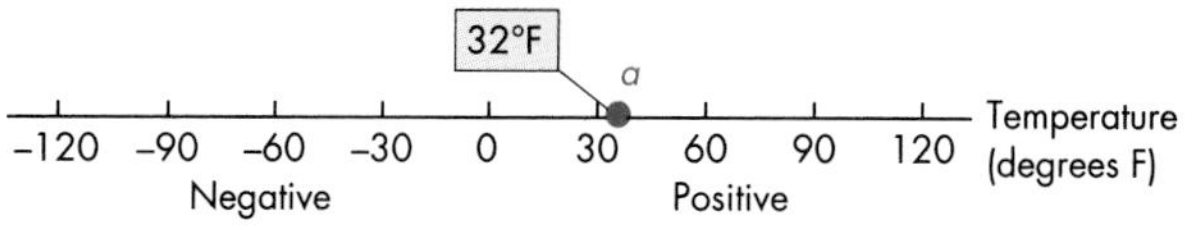

(a) Temperature

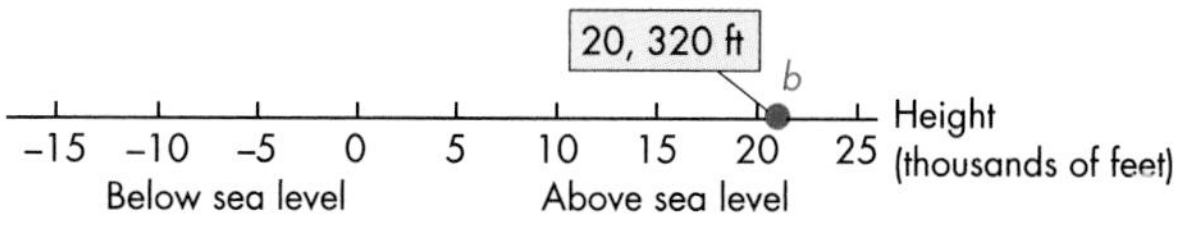

(b) Height

All graphs have a scale that measures a quantity as a distance. The two scales here measure temperature and height. Numbers to the right of zero are positive. Numbers to the left of zero are negative.

Two-Variable Graphs

To construct a two-variable graph, we set two scales perpendicular to each other. Let's continue to use the same two variables as those in Fig. 2.1. We will measure temperature in exactly the same way, but we will turn the height scale to a vertical position. Thus temperature is measured exactly as it was before but height is now represented by movements up and down a vertical scale.

The two scale lines in Fig. 2.2 are called **axes.** The vertical line is called the ***y*-axis** and the horizontal line is called the ***x*-axis.** The letters *x* and *y* appear on the axes of Fig. 2.2. Each axis has a zero point shared by the two axes. The zero point, common to both axes, is called the **origin.**

To represent something in a two-variable graph, we need two pieces of information. For example, Mount McKinley is 20,320 feet high and, on a particular day, the temperature at its peak is 20°F. We can represent this information in Fig. 2.2 by marking the height of the mountain on the *y*-axis at 20,320 feet and the temperature on the *x*-axis at 20°F. We can now identify the values of the two variables that appear on the axes by marking point *c*.

Two lines, called coordinates, can be drawn from point *c*. **Coordinates** are lines running from a point on a graph perpendicularly to its axis. The line

Figure 2.2 Graphing Two Variables

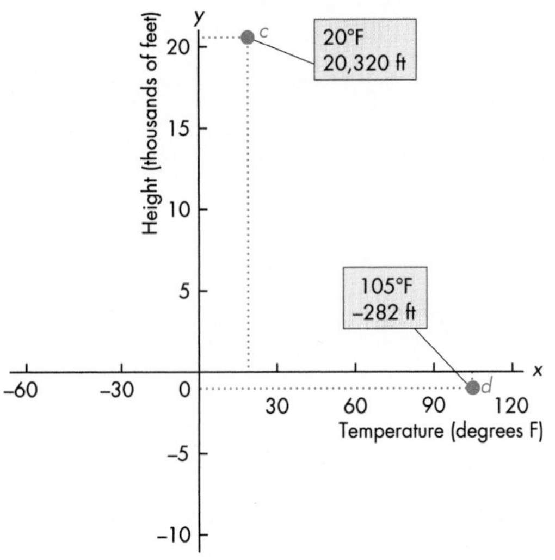

The relationship between two variables is graphed by forming two axes perpendicular to each other. Height is measured here on the y-axis and temperature on the x-axis. Point c represents the top of Mt. McKinley, 20,320 feet above sea level (measured on the y-axis), with a temperature of 20°F (measured on the x-axis). Point d represents Death Valley, 282 feet below sea level, with a temperature of 105°F.

running from *c* to the *x*-axis is the ***y*-coordinate,** because its length is the same as the value marked off on the *y*-axis. Similarly, the line running from *c* to the vertical axis is the ***x*-coordinate,** because its length is the same as the value marked off on the *x*-axis.

Now let's leave the top of Mount McKinley, at 20,320 feet and 20°F, and go to Death Valley in the Mojave Desert, the lowest point in the United States at 282 feet *below* sea level. Death Valley is represented by point *d*, which shows that we are 282 feet below sea level (the *y*-coordinate) and that the temperature is 105°F (the *x*-coordinate).

Economists use graphs similar to this one in a variety of ways. Let's look at two examples.

Time-Series Graphs

One of the most common and powerful graphs used in economics is the time-series graph. A **time-series graph** measures time (for example, in years or months) on the *x*-axis and the variable or variables in which we are interested on the *y*-axis.

Figure 2.3 illustrates a time-series graph. Time is measured in years on the *x*-axis. The variable that we are interested in—the U.S. unemployment rate (the percentage of the labor force unemployed)—is measured on the *y*-axis. The time-series graph conveys an enormous amount of information quickly and easily:

1 It tells us the *level* of the unemployment rate—when it is *high* and *low*. When the line is a long way from the *x*-axis, the unemployment rate is high. When the line is close to the *x*-axis, the unemployment rate is low.

2 It tells us how the unemployment rate *changes*—whether it *rises* or *falls*. When the line slopes upward, as in the early 1930s, the unemployment rate is rising. When the line slopes downward, as in the early 1940s, the unemployment rate is falling.

3 It tells us the *speed* with which the unemployment rate is *changing*—whether it is rising or falling *quickly* or *slowly*. If the line rises or falls very steeply, then unemployment is changing quickly. If the line is not steep, unemployment is rising or falling slowly. For example, unemployment rose sharply between 1930 and 1932. Unemployment went up again in 1933 but more slowly. Similarly, when unemployment was falling in the early 1950s, it fell quickly between 1950 and 1951, but then it began to fall much more gently in 1952 and 1953.

A time-series graph can also be used to depict a trend. A **trend** is a general tendency for a variable to rise or fall. You can see that unemployment had a general tendency to rise from the mid-1940s to the mid-1980s. That is, although there were ups and downs in the unemployment rate, there was an upward trend.

Graphs also allow us to compare different periods quickly. It is apparent, for example, that the 1930s were different from any other period in the twentieth century because of exceptionally high unemployment. You can also see that unemployment fluctuated more violently in the years before 1920 than it did in the years since 1950. The sawtooth pattern is more jagged in the period from 1900 to 1930 than it is in the period after 1950.

Figure 2.3 A Time-Series Graph

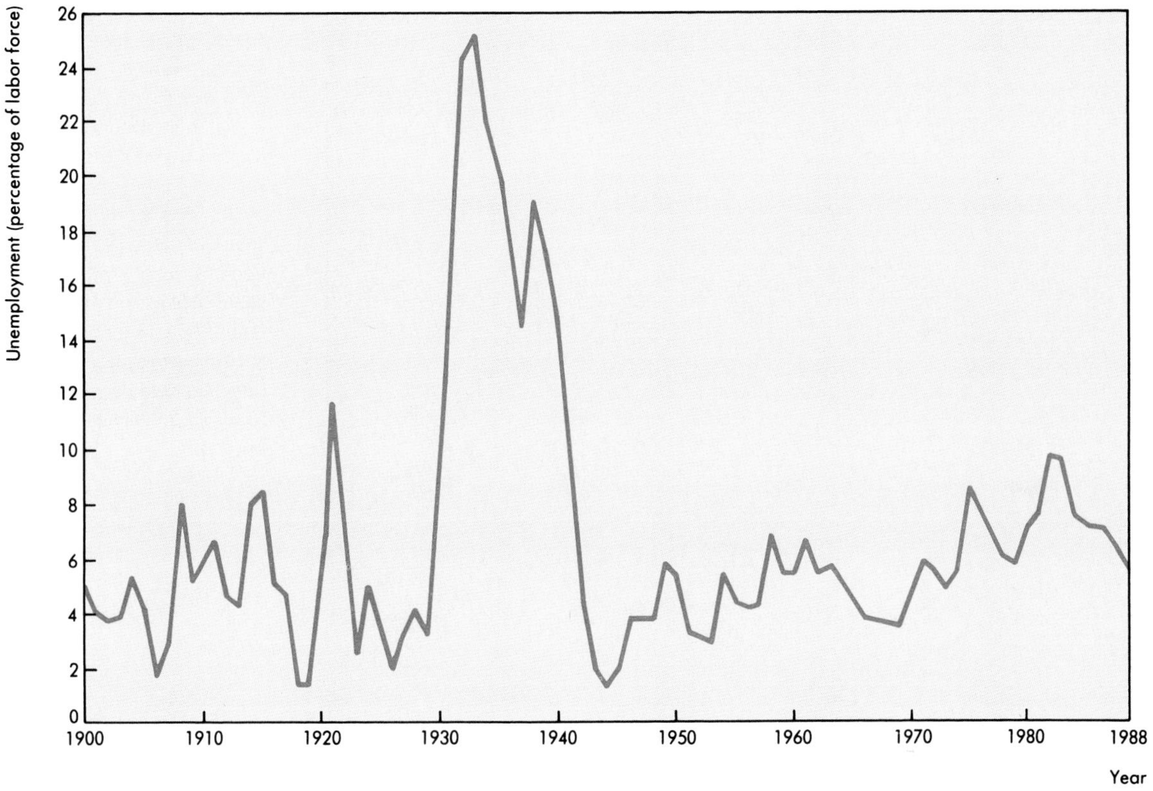

A time-series graph plots the level of a variable on the y-axis against time (day, week, month, or year) on the x-axis. This graph shows the U.S. unemployment rate each year from 1900 to 1988.

We can thus see that not only does Fig. 2.3 convey a wealth of information, it does so in a much shorter space than we have used to describe only some of its features.

Misleading Time-Series Graphs Although time-series graphs are powerful devices for conveying a large amount of information, they can also be used to distort data and to create a misleading picture.

One common way of misleading is to place two graphs that have different scales, side by side. Figure 2.4 provides an illustration. This figure contains exactly the same information as Fig. 2.3, but the information is packaged in a different way. In part (a), the scale on the y-axis has been compressed; in part (b), it has been expanded. When we look at these two parts as a whole, they suggest that unemployment was pretty stable during the first half of this century but that it has trended upward dramatically in the last 40 years or so.

You may think that this graphical way of distorting data is so outrageous that no one would ever attempt to use it. If you scrutinize the graphs that you see in newspapers and magazines, you will be surprised how common this device is.

Omitting the Origin Sometimes a graph is drawn with the origin (0 on the axis) omitted. Sometimes omitting the origin is precisely the correct thing to do, as it enables the graph to reveal its information. But there are also times when omitting the origin is misleading.

Figure 2.4 Misleading Graphs: Squeezing and Stretching Scales

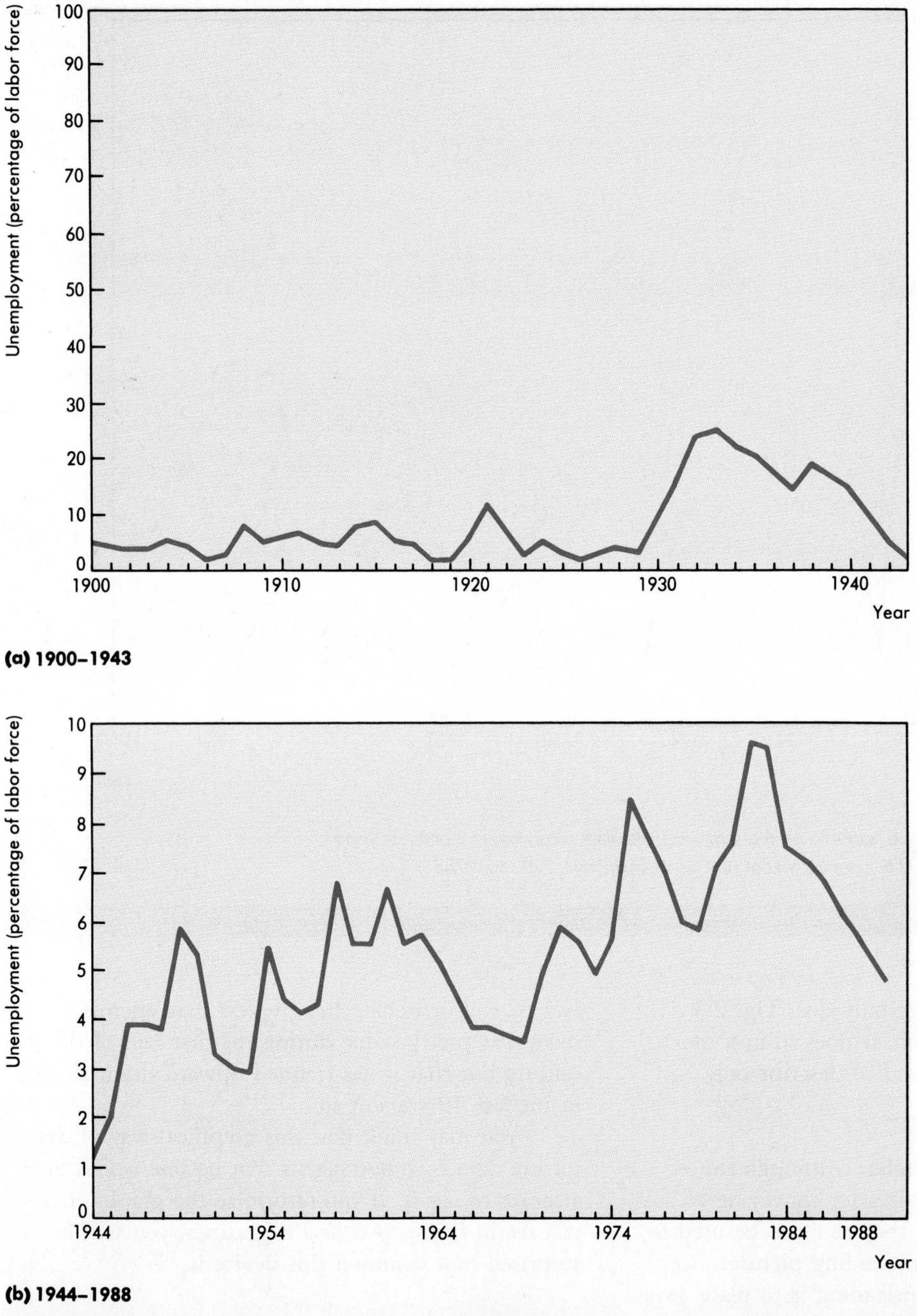

Graphs can mislead by squeezing and stretching the scales. These two graphs show exactly the same thing as Fig. 2.3—U.S. unemployment from 1900 to 1988. Part (a) has squeezed the *y*-axis, while part (b) has stretched that axis. The result appears to be a low and stable unemployment rate before 1943 and a rising, highly volatile unemployment rate after that date. Contrast the lie of Fig. 2.4 with the truth of Fig. 2.3.

Figure 2.5 illustrates the effect of omitting the origin. In parts (a) and (b), you can see a graph of the unemployment rate between 1970 and 1988. Part (a) includes the origin, and part (b) does not. The graph in part (a) provides a clear account of what happened to unemployment over the time period in question. You can use that graph in the same way that we used Fig. 2.3 to describe all the features

Figure 2.5 Omitting the Origin

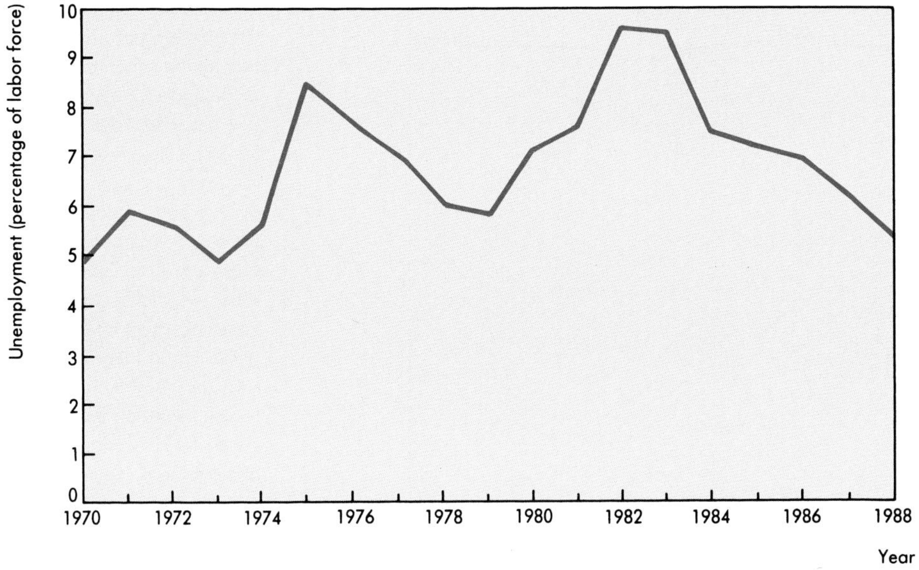

(a) Revealing graph with origin

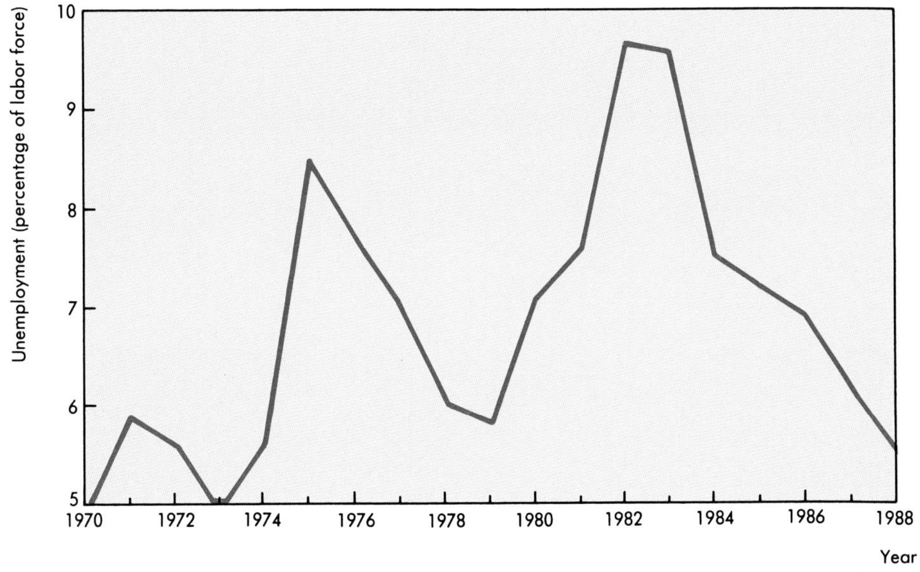

(b) Misleading graph with origin omitted

Sometimes the origin is omitted from a graph. This practice can be either revealing or misleading, depending on how it is used. Parts (a) and (b) graph the U.S. unemployment rate between 1970 and 1988. Part (a) is graphed with the origin and part (b) without it. Part (a) reveals a large amount of information about the level and changes in the unemployment rate over this time period. Part (b) overdramatizes the rises and falls in unemployment and gives no direct visual information about its level.

(Figure 2.5, parts c and d, continued on following page.)

of unemployment during that time period. But the graph in part (b) is less revealing and distorts the picture. It fails to reveal the level of unemployment. It focuses only on, and exaggerates the magnitude of, the increases and decreases in its rate. In particular, the increases in the unemployment rate in 1974–75 and in 1981–82 look enormous when compared with the increases that appear in part (a). By omit-

Figure 2.5 (continued)

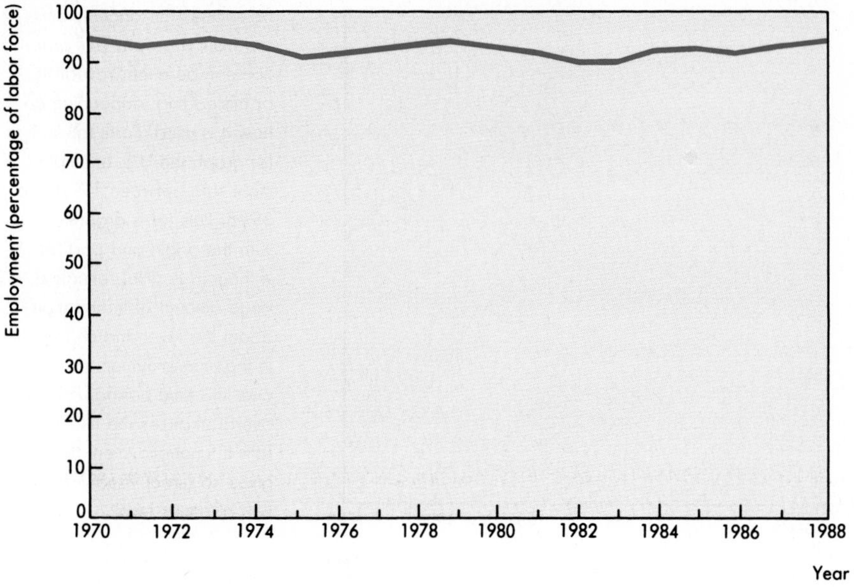

(c) Uninformative graph with origin

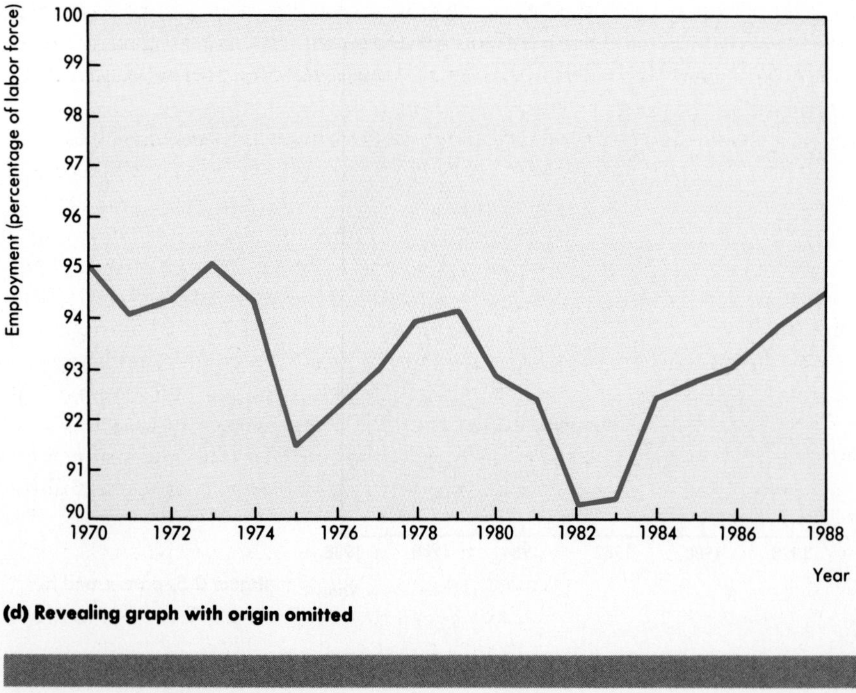

(d) Revealing graph with origin omitted

Sometimes the origin is omitted from a graph. This practice can be either revealing or misleading, depending on how it is used. Parts (c) and (d) graph the employment rate. Part (c) contains an origin and part (d) does not. In this case, the graph with the origin is uninformative and shows virtually no variation in the employment rate. The graph in part (d) gives a clear picture of fluctuations in the employment rate and is more informative than part (c) about those fluctuations.

ting the origin, small percentage changes in unemployment look like many hundredfold changes.

Parts (c) and (d) of Fig. 2.5 graph the employment rate—the percentage of the labor force employed. Part (c) includes the origin, and part (d) omits it. As you can see, the graph in part (c) reveals very little about movements in the employment rate. It seems to suggest that the employment rate was pretty constant and lying between 90 and 95 percent. The main feature of part (c) is an enormous amount of empty space and an inefficient use of the space available. Part (d) shows the same information but with the origin omitted. The scale begins at 90 percent. In this case, we can see very clearly the ups and downs in the employment rate. This graph does not provide a visual impression of the level of employment but it does provide a clear picture of variations in its rate.

The decision about whether to include or exclude the origin of the graph depends on what the graph is designed to reveal. To convey information about the level of employment and unemployment and variations in their rates, the graphs in parts (a) and (d) of Fig. 2.5 are almost equally revealing. By comparison, the graphs in parts (b) and (c) convey almost no information.

Comparing Two Time-Series Sometimes we want to use a time-series graph to compare two different variables. For example, suppose you wanted to know how the balance of the government's budget—its surplus or deficit—fluctuated and how those fluctuations compared with fluctuations in the unemployment rate. You can examine two such series by drawing a graph of each of them in the manner shown in Fig. 2.6(a). The scale for the unemployment rate appears on the left side of the figure and the scale for the government's budget surplus appears on the right. The (black) line shows unemployment and the (red) line shows the government's budget. You will probably agree that it is pretty hard work figuring out from Fig. 2.6(a) just what the relationship is between the unemployment rate and the government's budget. But it does look as if there is a tendency for the government's budget to go into a bigger deficit (red line goes downward) when the unemployment rate increases (black line goes upward). In other words, it seems as if these two variables have a tendency to move in opposite directions to each other.

In a situation such as this, it is often more revealing to flip the scale of one of the variables over, and graph it upside-down. Figure 2.6(b) does this. The unemployment rate in part (b) is graphed in exactly the same way as in part (a). But the government's budget has been flipped over. Now, instead of measuring the deficit (a negative number) in the down direction and the surplus (a positive number) in the up direction, we measure the deficit upward and the surplus downward. You can now "see" very clearly the relationship between these two variables. There is indeed a tendency for the government's deficit to get bigger when the unemployment rate gets higher. But the relationship is by no means an exact one and there are significant periods, clearly revealed in the graph, when the deficit and the unemployment rate move apart. You can "see" these periods as those in which the gap between the two lines widens.

Time-series graphs, whether simple ones with a single variable or more complex ones, such as those in Fig. 2.6 that show two variables, enable us to see how things change over time. But sometimes we are more interested in how variables relate to each other than in how they move over time. To study such relationships, we need to use a different but common kind of graph employed in economics—the scatter diagram.

Scatter Diagrams

A **scatter diagram** plots the value of one economic variable associated with the value of another. It measures one of the variables on the *x*-axis and the other variable on the *y*-axis.

Figure 2.7 illustrates three scatter diagrams. Part (a) shows the relationship between average consumption and average income. The *x*-axis measures average income and the *y*-axis measures average consumption. Each point represents average consumption and average income in the United States from 1970 to 1988. The years are identified by the two-digit numbers "scattered" within the graph. For example, the point marked 83 tells us that in 1983 average consumption was $9200 and average income was $10,000. The pattern formed by the points in part (a) tells us that when income rises, consumption also rises.

In part (b), the *x*-axis shows the percentage of households owning a video cassette recorder and the vertical axis shows its average price. The two-digit numbers each represent a year. Thus the point marked 81 tells us that the average price of a VCR in 1981 was $600 and that VCRs were owned by 20 percent of all households. The pattern formed by the points in part (b) tells us that as the price of a VCR falls, more people own one.

Figure 2.6 Seeing Relationships in Time-Series Graphs

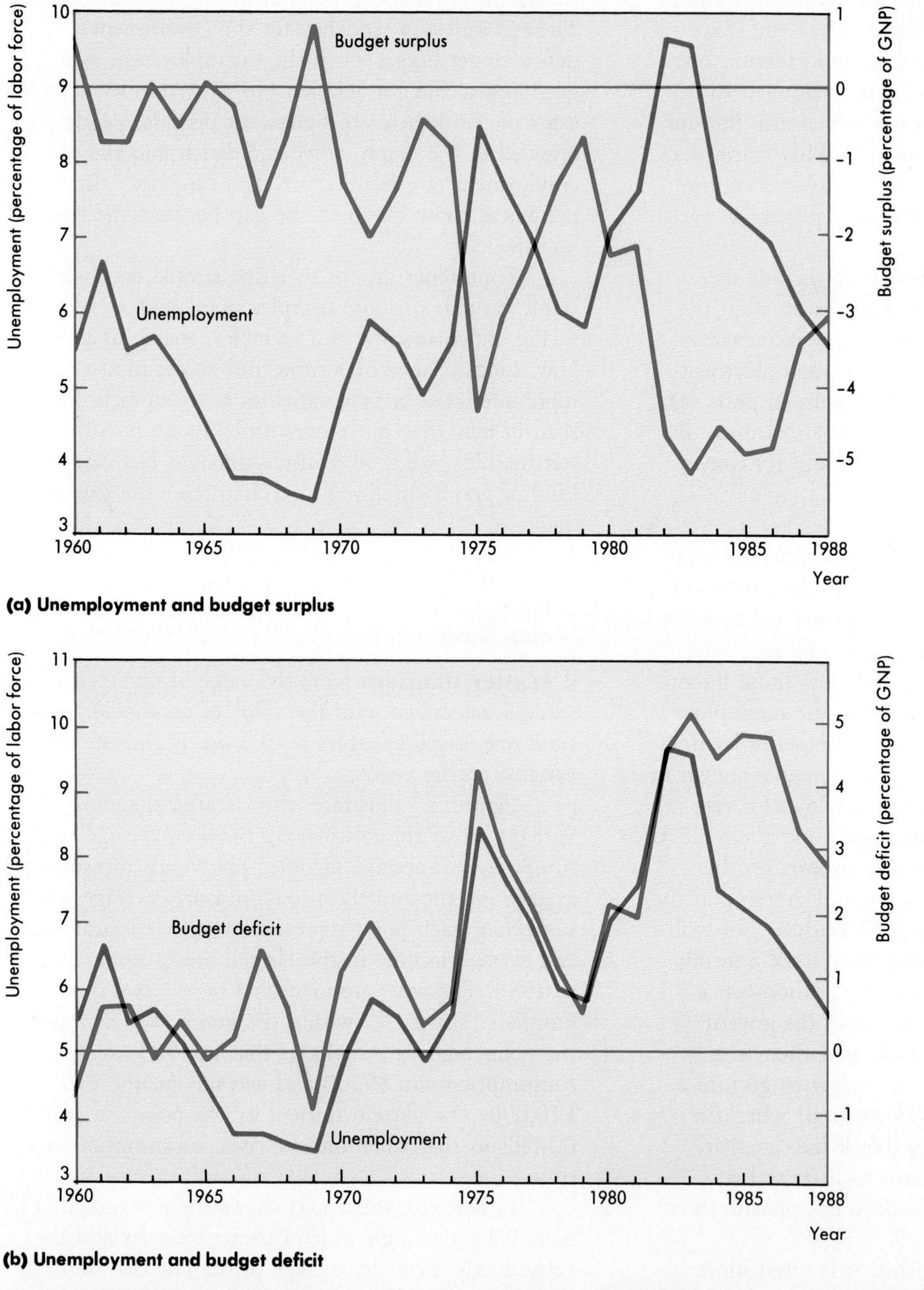

A time-series graph can be used to reveal relationships between two variables. These two graphs show the unemployment rate and the balance of the government's budget between 1960 and 1988. The unemployment line is identical in the two parts. In part (a), the budget balance is shown measuring surpluses upward and deficits downward (as negative numbers) on the right scale. It looks as if the budget goes into a bigger deficit when unemployment rises, but not much else is shown by part (a). Part (b) inverts the scale on which the budget is measured. Now a deficit is measured in the up direction and a surplus in the down direction on the right scale. The relationship between the budget deficit and unemployment is now clearer. There is a tendency for unemployment and the deficit to move together. But there are times, such as 1967–69 and 1984–88, when the variables move apart.

Part (c) is another scatter diagram. Its x-axis measures unemployment in the United States and its y-axis measures inflation. Again, each two-digit number represents a year. The point marked 85 tells us that in 1985 unemployment was 7.2 percent and inflation was 3.3 percent. The pattern formed by the

Figure 2.7 Scatter Diagrams

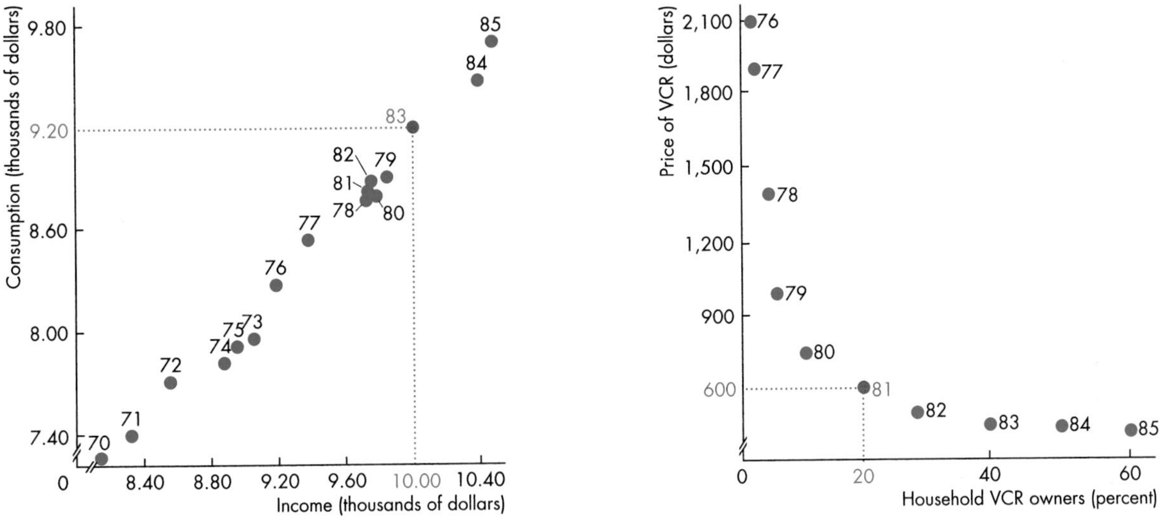

(a) Consumption and income

(b) VCR ownership and price

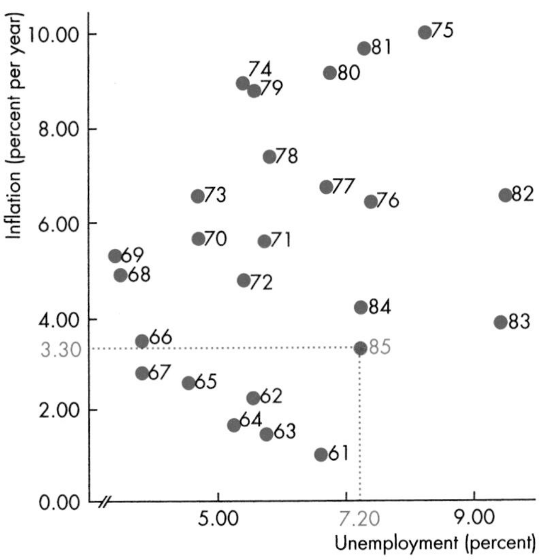

(c) Unemployment and inflation

A scatter diagram shows a relationship between two variables. Each point on these scatter diagrams represents an observation of two variables in a specific year. Part (a) shows that as income increases, so does consumption. Part (b) shows that as the price of a VCR falls, the number of VCRs owned increases. Part (c) shows that there is no relationship between inflation and unemployment.

points in part (c) does not reveal a clear relationship —upward-sloping or downward-sloping—between the two variables. The graph thus informs us, by its lack of a distinct pattern, that there is no relationship between these two variables.

Now that we have seen how we can use graphs in economics to represent economic data and to show the relationship between variables, let us examine how economists use graphs in a more abstract way to construct and analyze economic models.

Graphs Used in Economic Models

Although you will encounter many different kinds of graphs in economics, there are some patterns which, once you have learned to recognize them, will instantly convey to you the meaning of a graph. There are graphs that show each of the following:

- Things that go up and down together
- Things that move in opposite directions
- Things that are not related to each other at all
- Things that have a maximum or a minimum

Let's look at these four cases.

Things That Go Up and Down Together

Graphs that show the relationship between two variables that move up and down together are shown in Fig. 2.8. The relationship between two variables that move in the same direction is called a **positive relationship.** Such a relationship is shown by a line that slopes upward.

Part (a) shows the relationship between the number of miles traveled in 5 hours and speed. For example, the point marked *a* tells us that we will travel 200 miles in 5 hours if our speed is 40 miles an hour. If we double our speed and travel at 80 miles an hour, we will cover a distance of 400 miles. The relationship between the number of miles traveled in 5 hours and speed is represented by an upward-sloping straight line. A relationship depicted by a straight line is called a **linear relationship.** A linear relationship is one that has a constant slope.

Part (b) shows the relationship between distance sprinted and exhaustion (exhaustion being measured by the time it takes the heart rate to return to normal). This relationship is an upward-sloping one depicted by a curved line that starts out with a gentle slope but then becomes steeper.

Part (c) shows the relationship between the number of problems worked by a student and the amount of study time. This relationship is illustrated

Figure 2.8 Positive Relationships

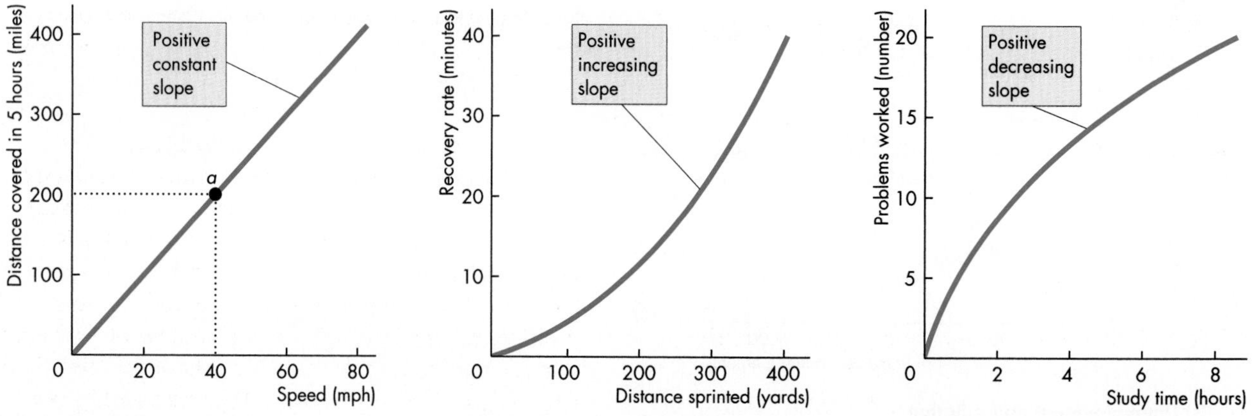

(a) Positive constant slope **(b) Positive increasing slope** **(c) Positive decreasing slope**

Each part of this figure shows a positive relationship between two variables. That is, as the value of the variable measured on the x-axis increases, so does the value of the variable measured on the y-axis. Part (a) illustrates a linear relationship—a relationship whose slope is constant as we move along the curve. Part (b) illustrates a positive relationship whose slope becomes steeper as we move along the curve away from the origin. It is a positive relationship with an increasing slope. Part (c) shows a positive relationship whose slope becomes flatter as we move away from the origin. It is a positive relationship with a decreasing slope.

Figure 2.9 Negative Relationships

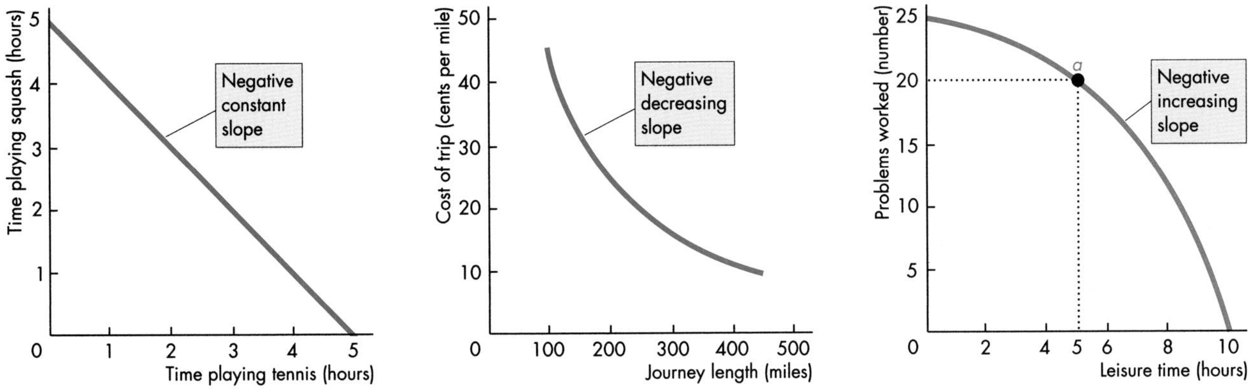

(a) Negative constant slope **(b) Negative decreasing slope** **(c) Negative increasing slope**

Each part of this figure shows a negative relationship between two variables. Part (a) shows a linear relationship—a relationship whose slope is constant as we travel along the curve. Part (b) shows a negative relationship of decreasing slope. That is, the slope of the relationship gets less steep as we travel along the curve from left to right. Part (c) shows a negative relationship of increasing slope. That is, the slope becomes steeper as we travel along the curve from left to right.

by an upward-sloping curved line that starts out with a steep slope but then becomes more gentle.

There are three types of upward-sloping lines in the graphs in Fig. 2.8, one straight and two curved. But they are all called curves. Any line on a graph—no matter whether it is straight or curved—is called a **curve.**

Things That Move in Opposite Directions

Figure 2.9 shows relationships between things that move in opposite directions. A relationship between variables that move in opposite directions is called a **negative relationship.**

Part (a) shows the relationship between the number of hours available for playing squash and the number of hours for playing tennis. One extra hour spent playing tennis means one hour less playing squash and vice versa. This relationship is negative and linear.

Part (b) shows the relationship between the cost per mile traveled and the length of a journey. The longer the journey, the lower is the cost per mile. But as the journey length increases, the cost per mile decreases at a decreasing rate. This feature of the relationship is illustrated by the fact that the curve slopes downward starting out steep at a short journey length and then becoming flatter as the journey length increases.

Part (c) shows the relationship between the amount of leisure time and the number of problems worked by a student. If the student takes no leisure, 25 problems can be worked. If the student takes 4 hours of leisure, only 20 problems can be worked (point *a*). Increasing leisure time beyond 4 hours produces a large reduction in the number of problems worked and, if the student takes 8 hours of leisure a day, no problems get worked. This relationship is a negative one that starts out with a gentle slope at a low number of leisure hours and becomes increasingly steep as leisure hours increase.

Things That Have a Maximum and a Minimum

Economics is about optimizing, or doing the best with limited resources. Making the highest possible profits or achieving the lowest possible costs of production are examples of optimizing. Economists make

Figure 2.10 Maximum and Minimum Points

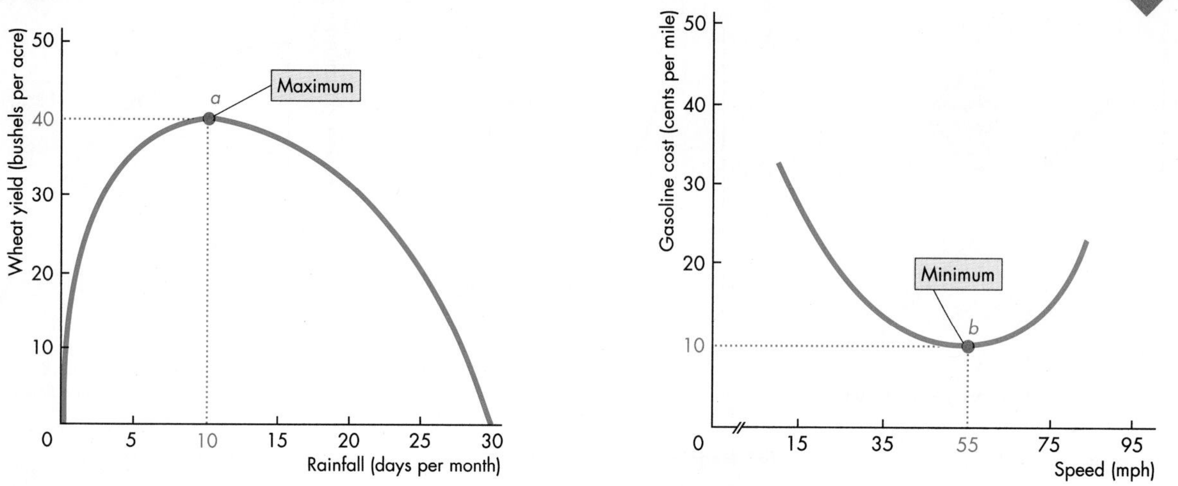

(a) Maximum **(b) Minimum**

Part (a) shows a relationship that has a maximum point, *a*. The curve rises at first, reaches its highest point, and then falls. Part (b) shows a relationship with a minimum point, *b*. The curve falls to its minimum and then rises.

frequent use of graphs depicting relationships that have a maximum or a minimum. Figure 2.10 illustrates such relationships.

Part (a) shows the relationship between rainfall and wheat yield. When there is no rainfall, wheat will not grow, so the yield is zero. As the rainfall increases up to 10 days a month, the wheat yield also increases. With 10 rainy days each month, the wheat yield reaches its maximum at 40 bushels an acre (point *a*). Rain in excess of 10 days a month starts to lower the yield of wheat. If every day is rainy, the wheat suffers from a lack of sunshine and the yield falls back almost to zero. This relationship is one that starts out positive, reaches a maximum, and then becomes negative.

Part (b) shows the reverse case—a relationship that begins with a negative slope, falls to a minimum, and then becomes positive. An example of such a relationship is the gasoline cost per mile as the speed of travel varies. At low speeds, the car is creeping along in a traffic snarl-up. The number of miles per gallon is low so the gasoline cost per mile is high. At very high speeds, the car is operated beyond its most efficient rate and, again, the number of miles per gallon is low and the gasoline cost per mile is high. At a speed of 55 miles an hour, the gasoline cost per mile traveled is at its minimum (point *b*).

Things That Are Independent

There are many situations in which one variable is independent of another. No matter what happens to the value of one variable, the other variable remains constant. Sometimes we want to show the independence between two variables in a graph. Figure 2.11 shows two ways of achieving this. In Fig. 2.11(a), your grade in economics is shown on the vertical axis against the price of bananas on the horizontal axis. Your grade (75 percent in this example) does not depend on the price of bananas. The relationship between these two variables is shown by a horizontal straight line. In part (b), the output of French wine is shown on the horizontal axis and the number of rainy days a month in California is shown on the vertical axis. Again, the output of French wine (3 billion gallons a year in this example) does not change when the number of rainy days in California changes. The relationship between these two variables is shown by a vertical straight line.

Figures 2.8 through 2.11 illustrate ten different shapes of graphs that we will encounter in economic

Figure 2.11 Variables with No Relationship

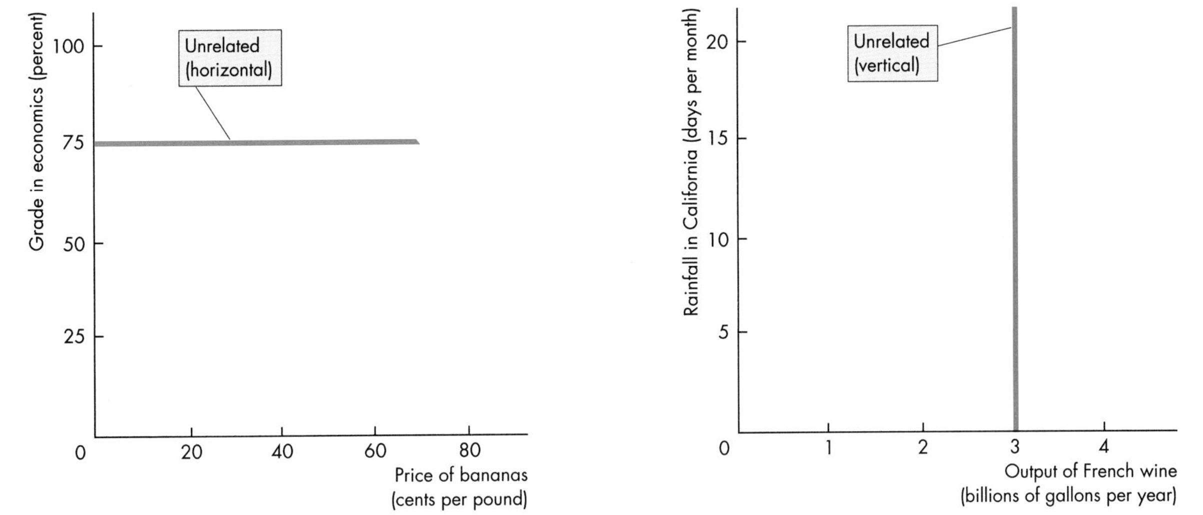

(a) Unrelated: horizontal **(b) Unrelated: vertical**

This figure shows how we can graph two variables that are unrelated to each other. In part (a), a student's grade in economics is plotted at 75 percent regardless of the price of bananas on the x-axis. In part (b), the output of the vineyards of France does not vary with the rainfall in California.

models. In describing these graphs, we have talked about curves that slope upward or slope downward and slopes that are steep or gentle. The concept of slope is an important one. Let's spend a little time discussing exactly what we mean by slope.

The Slope of a Relationship

The Definition of Slope

The **slope** of a relationship is the change in the value of y divided by the change in the value of x. We use the Greek letter Δ to represent "change in." Thus Δy means the change in the value of y, and Δx means the change in the value of x. Therefore, the slope of the relationship between x and y is

$$\frac{\Delta y}{\Delta x}$$

If a large change in y is associated with a small change in x, the slope is large and the curve is steep. If a small change in y is associated with a large change in x, the slope is small and the curve is flat.

We can make the idea of slope sharper by doing some calculations.

Calculating Slope

A Straight Line The slope of a straight line is the same regardless of where on the line you calculate it. Thus the slope of a straight line is constant. Let's calculate the slopes of the lines in Fig. 2.12. In part (a), when x increases from 2 to 6, y increases from 3 to 6. The change in x is $+4$—that is, Δx is 4. The change in y is $+3$—that is, Δy is 3. The slope of that line is

$$\frac{\Delta y}{\Delta x} = \frac{3}{4}$$

In part (b), when x increases from 2 to 6, y decreases from 6 to 3. The change in y is *minus* 3—that is, Δy is -3. The change in x is *plus* 4—that is, Δx is $+4$. The slope of the curve is

$$\frac{\Delta y}{\Delta x} = \frac{-3}{4}$$

Figure 2.12 The Slope of a Straight Line

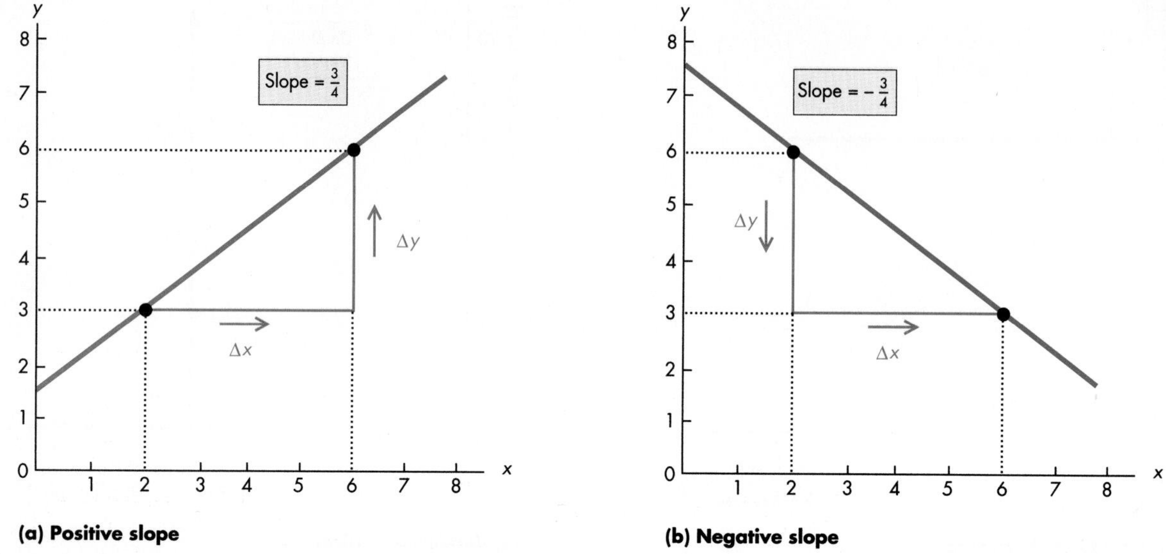

To calculate the slope of a straight line, we divide the change in the value of y by the change in the value of x. Part (a) shows the calculation of a positive slope—where both x and y go up together. When x goes up from 2 to 6, the change in x is 4—that is, Δx equals 4. That change in x brings about an increase in y from 3 to 6, so that Δy equals 3. The slope (Δy/Δx) equals 3/4. Part (b) shows a negative slope (when x goes up, y goes down). When x goes up from 2 to 6, Δx equals 4. That change in x brings about a decrease in y from 6 to 3, so that Δy equals −3. The slope (Δy/Δx) equals −3/4.

Notice that the two slopes have the same magnitude (3/4), but the slope of the line in part (a) is positive ($+3/+4 = 3/4$), while that in part (b) is negative ($-3/+4 = -3/4$). The slope of a positive relationship is positive; the slope of a negative relationship is negative.

A Curved Line Calculating the slope of a curved line is trickier. The slope of a curved line is not constant. Its slope depends on where on the line we calculate it. There are two ways to calculate the slope of a curved line: You can calculate the slope at a point on the line or you can calculate the slope across an arc of the line. Let's look at the two alternatives.

Slope at a point To calculate the slope at a point on a curved line, you need to construct a straight line that has the same slope as the curve at the point in question. Figure 2.13 shows how such a calculation is made. Suppose you want to calculate the slope of the curve at the point marked *a*. Place a ruler on the graph so that it touches point *a* and no other point on the curve, then draw a straight line along the edge of the ruler. The straight red line in part (a) is such a line. If the ruler touches the curve only at point *a*, then the slope of the curve at point *a* must be the same as the slope of the edge of the ruler. If the curve and the ruler do not have the same slope, the line along the edge of the ruler will cut the curve instead of just touching it.

Having now found a straight line with the same slope as the curve at point *a*, you can calculate the slope of the curve at point *a* by calculating the slope of the straight line. We already know how to calculate the slope of a straight line, so the task is straightforward. In this case, as *x* increases from 0 to

Figure 2.13 The Slope of a Curve

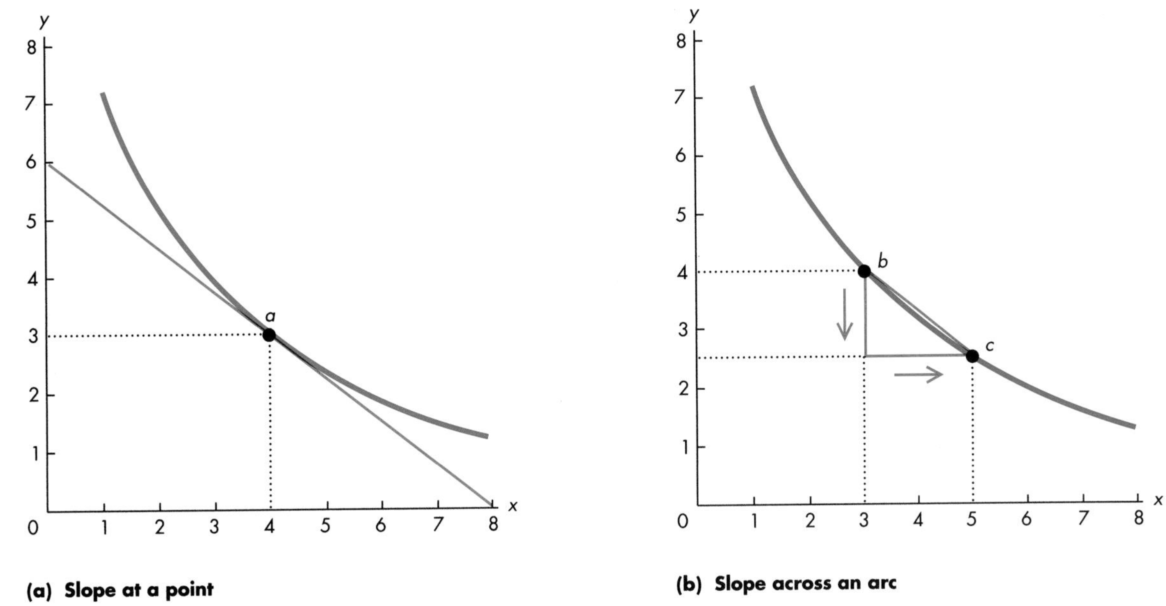

The slope of a curve can be calculated either at a point, as in part (a), or across an arc, as in part (b). The slope at a point is calculated by finding the slope of a straight line that touches the curve only at one point. One such straight line touches the curve at point *a*. The slope of that straight line is calculated by dividing the change in *y* by the change in *x*. When *x* increases from 0 to 8, Δx equals 8. That change in *x* is associated with a fall in *y* from 6 to 0, so Δy equals -6. The slope of the line is $-6/8$ or $-3/4$. To calculate the slope across an arc, we place a straight line across the curve from one point to another and then calculate the slope of that straight line. One such line is that from *b* to *c* in part (b). The slope of the straight line *bc* is calculated by dividing the change in *y* by the change in *x*. In moving from *b* to *c*, *x* goes up by 2, Δx equals 2, and *y* goes down by 1½, Δy equals $-1½$. The slope of the line *bc* is $-1½$ divided by 2, or $-3/4$.

8 ($\Delta x = 8$), y decreases from 6 to 0 ($\Delta y = -6$). Therefore, the slope of the straight line is

$$\frac{\Delta y}{\Delta x} = \frac{-6}{+8} = \frac{-3}{4}$$

Thus the slope of the curve at point a is $-3/4$.

Slope across an arc Calculating a slope across an arc is similar to calculating an average slope. In Fig. 2.13(b), we are looking at the same curve as in part (a), but instead of calculating the slope at point a, we calculate the slope for a change in x from 3 to 5. As x increases from 3 to 5, y decreases from 4 to 2½. The change in y is $-1½$ ($\Delta y = -1½$). The change in x is $+2$ ($\Delta x = 2$). Therefore, the slope of the line is

$$\frac{\Delta y}{\Delta x} = \frac{-1½}{2} = \frac{-3}{4}$$

This calculation gives us the slope of the red line between points b and c. In this particular example, the slope of the arc bc is identical to the slope of the curve at point a in part (a). Calculating the slope across an arc does not always work out so neatly. You might have some fun constructing other examples that do not give such an outcome.

Figure 2.14 Graphing a Relationship Among Three Variables

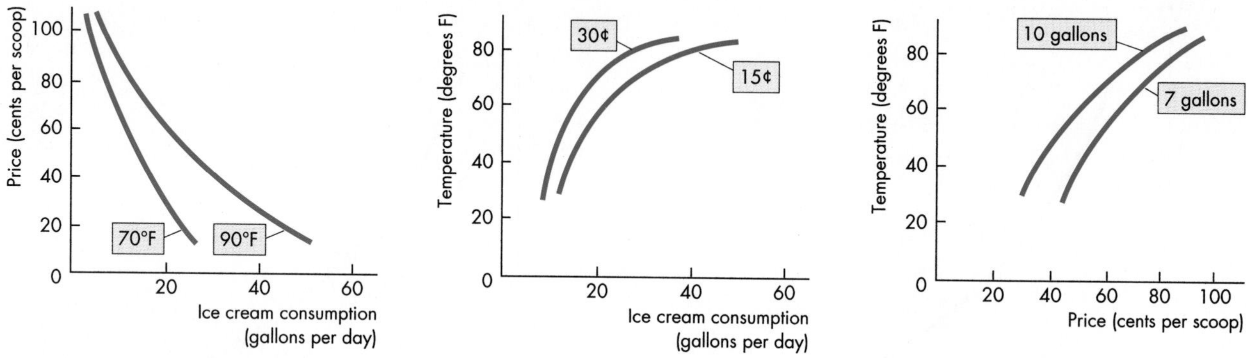

(a) Price and consumption at a given temperature

(b) Temperature and consumption at a given price

(c) Temperature and price at a given consumption

Price (cents per scoop)	**Ice Cream Consumption (gallons per day)**			
	30°F	50°F	70°F	90°F
15	12	18	25	50
30	10	12	18	37
45	7	10	13	27
60	5	7	10	20
75	3	5	7	14
90	2	3	5	10
105	1	2	3	6

The quantity of ice cream consumed (one variable) depends on its price (a second variable) and the air temperature (a third variable). The table provides some hypothetical numbers that tell us how many gallons of ice cream are consumed each day at different prices and different temperatures. For example, if the price is 45¢ per scoop and the temperature is 50°F, 10 gallons of ice cream will be consumed. In order to graph a relationship among three variables, the value of one variable must be held constant. Part (a) shows the relationship between price and consumption, holding temperature constant. One curve holds temperature constant at 90°F and the other at 70°F. Part (b) shows the relationship between temperature and consumption, holding price constant. One curve holds the price at 30¢ and the other at 15¢. Part (c) shows the relationship between temperature and price, holding consumption constant. One curve holds consumption constant at 10 gallons and the other at 7 gallons.

Graphing Relationships Among More Than Two Variables

We have seen that we can graph a single variable as a point on a straight line and we can graph the relationship between two variables as a point formed by the *x*- and *y*-coordinates in a two-dimensional graph. You may be suspecting that although a two-dimensional graph is informative, most of the things in which you are likely to be interested involve relationships among not just two variables but many.

Examples of relationships among more than two variables abound. For example, consider the relationship between the price of ice cream, the air temperature, and the amount of ice cream eaten. If ice cream is expensive and the temperature is low, people eat much less ice cream than when ice cream is inexpensive and the temperature is high. For any given price of ice cream, the quantity consumed varies with the temperature, and for any given temperature, the quantity of ice cream consumed varies with its price.

Other Things Being Equal

Figure 2.14 illustrates such a situation. The table shows the number of gallons of ice cream that will be eaten each day at various temperatures and ice cream prices. How can we graph all these numbers?

To graph a relationship that involves more than two variables, we consider what happens if all but two of the variables are held constant. This device is called ceteris paribus. **Ceteris paribus** is a Latin phrase that means "other things being equal." For example, in Fig. 2.14(a) you can see what happens to the quantity of ice cream consumed when the price of ice cream varies while the temperature is held constant. The line labeled 70°F shows the relationship between ice cream consumption and the price of ice cream when the temperature stays at 70°F. The numbers used to plot that line are those in the third column of the table in Fig. 2.14. The curve labeled 90°F shows the consumption of ice cream when the price varies and the temperature is 90°F.

Alternatively, we can show the relationship between ice cream consumption and temperature while holding the price of ice cream constant, as is shown in Fig. 2.14(b). The curve labeled 30¢ shows how the consumption of ice cream varies with the temperature when ice cream costs 30¢, and a second curve shows the relationship when ice cream costs 15¢. Part (c) shows the combinations of temperature and price that result in a constant consumption of ice cream. One curve shows the combination that results in 10 gallons a day being consumed and the other shows the combination that results in 7 gallons a day being consumed. A high price and a high temperature lead to the same consumption as a lower price and lower temperature. For example, 7 gallons are consumed at 30°F and 45 cents per scoop and at 70°F and 75 cents per scoop.

■ With what you have now learned about graphs, you can move forward with your study of economics. There are no graphs in this book that are more complicated than those that have been explained here.

SUMMARY

Graphing Data

There are two main types of graphs used to represent economic data: time-series graphs and scatter diagrams. A time-series graph plots the value of one or more economic variables on the vertical axis (y-axis) and time on the horizontal axis (x-axis). A well-constructed time-series graph quickly reveals the level, direction of change, and speed of change of a variable. It also reveals trends. Graphs sometimes mislead, especially when scales are stretched or squeezed to exaggerate or understate a variation.

Scatter diagrams plot the value of one economic variable associated with the value of another. These diagrams reveal whether or not there is a relationship between two variables and, if there is a relationship, its nature. (pp. 29–37)

Graphs Used in Economic Models

Graphs are used in economic models to illustrate relationships between variables. There are four cases: positive relationships, negative relationships, relationships that have a maximum or a minimum, and variables that are not related to each other. Examples of these different types of relationships are summarized in Figures 2.8 through 2.11. (pp. 38–41)

The Slope of a Relationship

The slope of a relationship is calculated as the change in the value of y divided by the change in the value of x—$\Delta y/\Delta x$. A straight line has a constant slope, but a curved line has a varying slope. To calculate the slope of a curved line, we either calculate the slope at a point or across an arc. (pp. 41–43)

Graphing Relationships Among More Than Two Variables

To graph a relationship among more than two variables, we hold constant the values of all the variables except two. We then plot the value of one of the variables against the value of another. Holding constant all the variables but two is called the ceteris paribus assumption—other things being equal. (pp. 44–45)

KEY CONCEPTS

Key Figures

REVIEW QUESTIONS

1 Why do we use graphs?

2 What are the two scale lines on a graph called?

3 What is the origin on a graph?

4 What do we mean by the *y*-coordinate and *x*-coordinate?

5 What is a time-series graph?

6 List three things that a time-series graph shows quickly and easily.

7 What do we mean by trend?

8 What is a scatter diagram?

9 Sketch some graphs to illustrate the following:
  a) Two variables that move up and down together
  b) Two variables that move in opposite directions
  c) A relationship between two variables that has a maximum
  d) A relationship between two variables that has a minimum

10 Which of the relationships in question 9 is a positive relationship and which a negative relationship?

11 What is the definition of the slope of a relationship?

12 What are the two ways of calculating the slope of a curved line?

13 How do we graph relationships among more than two variables?

PROBLEMS

1 The rate of inflation in the United States between 1970 and 1987 was as follows:

Year	Inflation Rate	Year	Inflation Rate
1970	5.7	1979	11.3
1971	4.4	1980	13.5
1972	3.2	1981	10.3
1973	6.2	1982	6.2
1974	11.0	1983	3.2
1975	9.1	1984	4.3
1976	5.8	1985	3.6
1977	6.5	1986	1.9
1978	7.6	1987	3.6

Draw a time-series graph of these data; use your graph to answer the following questions:

a) In which year was inflation highest?

b) In which year was inflation lowest?

c) In which years did inflation rise?

d) In which years did inflation fall?

e) In which year did inflation rise/fall the fastest?

f) In which year did inflation rise/fall the slowest?

g) What have been the main trends in inflation?

2 Interest rates on treasury bills in the United States between 1970 and 1987 were as follows:

Year	Interest Rate	Year	Interest Rate
1970	6.5	1979	10.0
1971	4.3	1980	11.5
1972	4.1	1981	14.0
1973	7.0	1982	10.7
1974	7.9	1983	8.6
1975	5.8	1984	9.6
1976	5.0	1985	7.5
1977	5.3	1986	6.0
1978	7.2	1987	5.8

Use these data together with those in problem 1 to draw a scatter diagram showing the relationship between inflation and the interest rate. Use this diagram to determine whether there is a relationship between inflation and the interest rate and whether it is positive or negative.

3 Use the following information to draw a graph showing the relationship between x and y.

x	0	1	2	3	4	5	6	7	8
y	0	1	4	9	16	25	36	49	64

a) Is the relationship between x and y positive or negative?

b) Does the slope of the relationship rise or fall as the value of x rises?

4 Using the data in problem 3,

a) Calculate the slope of the relationship between x and y when x equals 4.

b) Calculate the slope of the arc when x rises from 3 to 4.

c) Calculate the slope of the arc when x rises from 4 to 5.

d) Calculate the slope of the arc when x rises from 3 to 5.

e) What do you notice that is interesting about your answers to (b), (c), and (d), compared with your answer to (a)?

5 Calculate the slopes of the following two relationships between x and y.

a)

x	0	2	4	6	8	10
y	20	16	12	8	4	0

b)

x	0	2	4	6	8	10
y	0	8	16	24	32	40

6 Draw a graph showing the following relationship between x and y:

x	0	1	2	3	4	5	6	7	8	9
y	0	2	4	6	8	10	8	6	4	2

a) Is the slope positive or negative when x is less than 5?

b) Is the slope positive or negative when x is greater than 5?

c) What is the slope of this relationship when x equals 5?

d) Is y at a maximum or at a minimum when x equals 5?

7 Draw a graph showing the following relationship between x and y:

x	0	1	2	3	4	5	6	7	8	9
y	10	8	6	4	2	0	2	4	6	8

a) Is the slope positive or negative when x is less than 5?

b) Is the slope positive or negative when x is greater than 5?

c) What is the slope of this relationship when x equals 5?

d) Is y at a maximum or at a minimum when x equals 5?

Chapter 3

Production, Specialization, and Exchange

After studying this chapter, you will be able to:

- Define the production possibility frontier
- Calculate opportunity cost
- Explain why economic growth and technical change do not provide free gifts
- Explain comparative advantage
- Explain why people specialize and how they gain from trade
- Explain why property rights and money have evolved

Making the Most of It

We live in a style that most of our grandparents could not even have imagined. Medicine has cured diseases that terrified them. Most of us live in better and more spacious homes. We eat more, we grow taller, we are even born larger than they were. Our parents are amazed at the matter-of-fact way we handle computers. We casually use products—microwave ovens, graphite tennis rackets, digital watches—that didn't exist in their youth. Economic growth has made us richer than our parents and grandparents. ■ But economic growth and technical change, and the wealth they bestow, have not liberated us from scarcity. Why not? Why, despite our immense wealth, do we still have to face costs? Why are there no "free lunches"? ■ We see an incredible amount of specialization and trading in the modern world. Each one of us specializes in a particular job—as lawyer, car maker, homemaker. Countries and regions also specialize—Florida in orange juice, Idaho in potatoes, Detroit in cars, and the Silicon Valley in computer-related products. We have become so specialized that one farm worker can feed 100 people. Only one in five of us works in manufacturing. More than half of us work in wholesale and retail trade, banking and finance, other services, and government. ■ Why do we specialize? How do we benefit from specialization and exchange? How do money and the legal institution of private property extend our ability to specialize and increase production? These are the questions that we tackle in this chapter.

■ We will begin by making the idea of scarcity more precise. Then we will go on to see how we can measure opportunity cost. We will also see how, when each individual tries to get the most out of scarce resources, specialization and exchange occur. That is, people will specialize in doing what they do best and exchange their products with other specialists. We are also going to see why such institutions as private property and money exist and how they spring from people's attempts to make the most of their limited resources.

The Production Possibility Frontier

What do we mean by production? **Production** is the conversion of natural, human, and capital resources into goods and services. In defining production, we have used several terms that need to be defined. Let's review them.

Natural resources are all the gifts of nature. They include the air, the water, and the land, and the minerals that lie on top of or beneath the surface of the earth. They are the factor of production called *land.* **Human resources** are all the muscle-power and brain-power of human beings. The voices and artistry of singers and actors, the strength and coordination of athletes, the daring of astronauts, the political skill of diplomats, as well as the physical and mental skills of the many millions of people who make cars and cola, gum and glue, wallpaper and watering cans, are included in this category. They are the factor of production called *labor.*

Capital resources are goods that have been produced and can now be used in the production of other goods and services. Examples include the interstate highway system, the fine buildings of great cities, dams and power projects, airports and jumbo jets, car production lines, shirt factories, and cookie shops. Capital resources also include human capital. **Human capital** is the accumulated skill and knowledge of human beings, which arise from their training and education. These are the factor of production called *capital.*

Goods and services are all the valuable things that people produce. Goods are tangible—cars, spoons, VCRs, and bread. Services are intangible—haircuts, amusement park rides, and telephone calls. There are two types of goods: capital goods and consumption goods. **Capital goods** are goods that are added to our capital resources. **Consumption goods** are goods that are used up as soon as they are produced. **Consumption** is the process of using up goods and services.

The **production possibility frontier** (PPF) marks the boundary between production levels that can and cannot be attained. It is important to understand the production possibility frontier in the real world, but in order to achieve that goal more easily, we will first study an economy—a model economy—that is simpler than the one in which we live.

A Model Economy

Instead of looking at the real world economy with all its complexity and detail, we will build a model of an economy. The model will have features that are essential to understanding the real economy, but we will ignore most of reality's immense detail. Our model economy will be simpler in three important ways:

1. For the time being, we will suppose that everything that is produced is also consumed. This simplification means that, in our model, capital resources neither grow nor shrink. Later we will examine what happens if we consume less than we produce and add to capital resources.
2. In our model economy, there will be just two goods—even though in the real world we use our scarce resources to produce countless goods and services.
3. Although there are approximately five billion people living on this planet, our model economy initially has just one person, Jane, who lives on a deserted island and has no dealings with other people.

Let's suppose that all the resources of Jane's island economy can be used to produce two goods, corn and cloth. Suppose also that Jane can work twelve hours each day. The amount of corn and cloth that Jane can produce will depend on how many hours she devotes to producing them. Table 3.1 sets out Jane's production possibilities for corn and cloth. If she does no work, she produces nothing. Three hours a day devoted to corn farming produces 9 pounds of corn per month. Devoting more hours to corn increases the output of corn, but there is a decline in the extra amount of corn that comes from extra effort. The reason for this decline is that Jane has to use increasingly unsuitable land for growing corn. At first, she plants corn on a lush, flat plain. Eventually, when she has used all the arable land, she has to start planting on the rocky hills and the edge

Table 3.1 Jane's Production Possibilities

Hours worked per day		Corn grown (pounds per month)		Cloth produced (yards per month)
0	either	0	or	0
3	either	9	or	4
6	either	15	or	7
9	either	20	or	9
12	either	25	or	10

If Jane does no work, she produces no corn or cloth. If she works for 3 hours per day and spends the entire amount of time on corn production, she produces 9 pounds of corn per month. If that same time is used for cloth production, 4 yards of cloth are produced but no corn. The last three rows of the table show the amounts of corn or cloth that can be produced per month as more hours are devoted to each activity.

of the beach. The numbers in the second column of the table show how the output of corn rises as the hours devoted to cultivating it rise.

To produce cloth, Jane gathers wool from the sheep that live on the island. Some of the sheep are tame, so the first few hours she works produce a large amount of cloth. As she devotes more hours to collecting wool and making cloth, her output rises but, as in the case of corn, each additional hour produces less wool. Jane has to find and catch less cooperative sheep to make more wool.

If Jane devotes all her time to growing corn, she can produce 25 pounds of corn in a month. In that case, however, she cannot produce any cloth. Conversely, if she devotes all her time to making cloth, she can produce 10 yards a month but will have no time left for growing corn. Jane can devote some of her time to corn and some to cloth but not more than 12 hours a day total. Thus she can spend 3 hours growing corn and 9 hours making cloth or 6 hours on each (or any other combination of hours that add up to 12 hours).

We have defined the production possibility frontier as the boundary between what is attainable and what is not attainable. You can calculate Jane's production possibility frontier by using the information in Table 3.1. These calculations are summarized in the table in Fig. 3.1 and graphed in that figure as *Jane's production possibility frontier.* To see how we calculated that frontier, let's concentrate first on the table in Fig. 3.1.

Possibility *a* shows Jane devoting no time to cloth and her entire 12-hour working day to corn. In this case, she can produce 25 pounds of corn per month and no cloth. For possibility *b*, she spends 3 hours a day making cloth and 9 hours growing corn, to produce a total of 20 pounds of corn and 4 yards of cloth per month. The pattern continues on to possibility *e*, where she devotes 12 hours a day to cloth and no time to corn. These same numbers are plotted in the graph shown in Fig. 3.1. Yards of cloth are measured on the horizontal axis and pounds of corn on the vertical axis. Points *a*, *b*, *c*, *d*, and *e* represent the numbers in the corresponding row of the table.

Of course, Jane does not have to work in blocks of 3 hours, as in our example. She can work 1 hour or 1 hour and 10 minutes growing corn and devote the rest of her time to making cloth. All other feasible allocations of Jane's 12 hours will result in a series of production possibilities represented by the line that joins points *a*, *b*, *c*, *d*, and *e*. This line shows Jane's production possibility frontier. She can produce at any point on the frontier or inside it, within the orange area. These are attainable points. Points outside the frontier are unattainable. To produce at points beyond the frontier, Jane needs more time than she has. By working 12 hours a day producing both corn and cloth, Jane can choose any point she wishes on the frontier. By working less than 12 hours a day, she produces at a point inside the frontier.

On the Frontier Is Best

Jane produces corn and cloth, not for the fun of it, but so that she can eat and keep warm. The larger the quantities of corn and cloth she produces, the more she can consume. Her wants for corn and cloth outstrip her production possibilities, and the best that she can do is to produce—and, therefore, consume—at a point *on* her production possibility frontier. To see why, consider a point such as *z* in the attainable region. At point *z*, Jane can improve her situation by moving to a point such as *b* or *d* or to a point on the frontier between *b* and *d*, such as point *c*. Jane can have more of everything on the frontier

Figure 3.1 Jane's Production Possibility Frontier

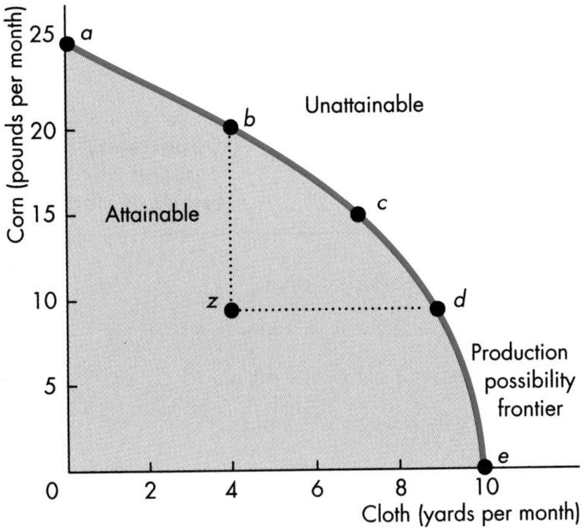

Possibility	Corn (pounds per month)		Cloth (yards per month)
a	25	and	0
b	20	and	4
c	15	and	7
d	9	and	9
e	0	and	10

The table lists five points on Jane's production possibility frontier. Row *d* tells us that if Jane produces 9 pounds of corn, the maximum cloth production that is possible is 9 yards. These same points are graphed as points *a*, *b*, *c*, *d*, and *e* in the figure. The line passing through these points is Jane's production possibility frontier, which separates the attainable from the unattainable. The orange attainable area contains all the possible production points. Jane can produce anywhere inside this area or on the production possibility frontier. Points outside the frontier are unattainable. Jane prefers points on the frontier to any point inside. Points between *b* and *d* on the frontier are better than point *z* inside the frontier because they give Jane more of both goods.

than at points inside it. At point *b*, she can consume more corn and no less cloth than at point *z*. At point *d*, she can consume more cloth and no less corn than at point *z*. At point *c* she can consume more corn and more cloth than at point *z*. Jane will never choose points such as *z* because better choices, such as *c*, will always be available. That is, some point on the frontier is always better than a point inside the frontier.

In comparing points *b*, *c*, and *d* with point *z*, we can see that *z* is an inferior point and one that Jane will not choose. It is easy to see that Jane will want to produce at some point on her production possibility frontier, but she will still be faced with the problem of choosing the best point. In choosing between one point and another, Jane is confronted with opportunity costs. At point *b*, for example, she will have less cloth and more corn than at point *c*. If she chooses point *c*, she will do so because she figures that the extra cloth is worth the corn forgone. Let's go on to explore opportunity cost more closely and see how we can measure it.

Opportunity Cost

We've defined opportunity cost as the best alternative forgone: For a late sleeper, the opportunity cost of attending an early morning class is an hour in bed; for a jogger, it is an hour of exercise. The concept of opportunity cost can be made more precise by using a production possibility frontier such as the one shown in Fig. 3.1. Let's see what that curve tells us.

The Best Alternative Forgone

The production possibility frontier in Fig. 3.1 traces the boundary between attainable and unattainable combinations of corn and cloth. Since there are only two goods, there is no difficulty in working out what is the best alternative forgone. More corn can be grown only by paying the price of having less cloth, and more cloth can be made only by bearing the cost of having less corn. Thus the opportunity cost of cloth is the corn forgone and the opportunity cost of corn is the cloth forgone. Let's put numerical values on the opportunity costs of corn and cloth.

Measuring Opportunity Cost

We are going to measure opportunity cost by using Jane's production possibility frontier. We will calculate how much cloth she has to give up to get more corn and how much corn she has to give up to get more cloth.

If all Jane's time is used to produce cloth, she produces 10 yards of cloth and no corn. If she decides to give up 1 yard of cloth in order to get some corn, how much corn can she produce? You can see the answer in Fig. 3.1. By giving up 1 yard of cloth to produce some corn, Jane moves from *e* to *d* and produces 9 pounds of corn. Thus the opportunity cost of the first 9 pounds of corn is 1 yard of cloth.

Consider next the reverse move, from *d* to *e*. Jane increases her cloth production by 1 yard but she has to give up 9 pounds of corn. Thus the opportunity cost of the tenth yard of cloth is 9 pounds of corn. The opportunity cost of cloth when moving from *d* to *e* is the inverse of the opportunity cost of corn when moving from *e* to *d*. If giving up the last 1 yard of cloth allows Jane to produce 9 pounds of corn, then, conversely, getting the last yard of cloth costs her 9 pounds of corn.

We have just worked out the opportunity cost of corn if we move from *e* to *d* and the opportunity cost of cloth if we move from *d* to *e* in Fig. 3.1. These opportunity costs are recorded in Table 3.2. The first row records the opportunity cost of the first 9 pounds of corn. That opportunity cost is 1 yard of cloth, which means that the opportunity cost of 1 pound of corn is 1/9 of a yard of cloth. The last row of the table records the opportunity cost of the last yard of cloth. That opportunity cost is 9 pounds of corn. Table 3.2 also sets out the opportunity costs of moving between points *a*, *b*, *c*, and *d* on the production possibility frontier. You may want to work out another example on your own to be sure that you understand what is going on. Calculate Jane's opportunity cost of moving from point *b* to *c*, or from *c* back to *b*.

Table 3.2 Jane's Opportunity Costs of Corn and Cloth

(a) Opportunity cost of corn

As Jane increases her cloth production:	**Opportunity cost of 1 pound of corn (yards of cloth)**
First 9 pounds of corn cost 1 yard of cloth	1/9
Next 6 pounds of corn cost 2 yards of cloth	1/3
Next 5 pounds of corn cost 3 yards of cloth	3/5
Last 5 pounds of corn cost 4 yards of cloth	4/5

(b) Opportunity cost of cloth

As Jane increases her cloth production:	**Opportunity cost of 1 yard of cloth (pounds of corn)**
First 4 yards of cloth cost 5 pounds of corn	1 1/4
Next 3 yards of cloth cost 5 pounds of corn	1 2/3
Next 2 yards of cloth cost 6 pounds of corn	3
Last yard of cloth costs 9 pounds of corn	9

Part (a) shows Jane's opportunity cost of corn. The first 9 pounds of corn cost 1 yard of cloth or 1 pound of corn costs 1/9 of a yard of cloth. The next 6 pounds of corn cost 2 yards of cloth. The opportunity cost of corn rises as Jane produces more corn, with the last 5 pounds of corn costing 4 yards of cloth. Part (b) shows Jane's opportunity cost of cloth. The first 4 yards of cloth cost 5 pounds of corn or 1 yard of cloth costs 1 1/4 pounds of corn. The opportunity cost of cloth rises as Jane produces more cloth, with the last yard of cloth costing 9 pounds of corn.

Increasing Opportunity Cost

As you can see, opportunity cost varies with the quantity produced. The first 9 pounds of corn cost only 1 yard of cloth. The next 6 pounds of corn cost 2 yards of cloth. The last 5 pounds of corn cost 4 yards of cloth. Thus the opportunity cost of corn increases as Jane grows more corn.

The same is true for cloth. The first 4 yards of cloth cost 5 pounds of corn. The next 3 yards of cloth also cost 5 pounds of corn. The last yard of cloth costs 9 pounds of corn. Thus the opportunity cost of cloth also increases as Jane makes more cloth.

The Shape of the Frontier

Pay special attention to the shape of the production possibility frontier in Fig. 3.1. When a large amount of corn and not much cloth is produced—between points *a* and *b*—the frontier has a gentle slope. When a large amount of cloth and not much corn is produced—between points *d* and *e*—the frontier is steep. The whole frontier bows outward. These features of the production possibility frontier are a reflection of increasing opportunity cost. Between points *a* and *b*, a large amount of cloth can be obtained by giving up a small amount of corn so that the opportunity cost of cloth is low and the opportunity cost of corn is high. Between points *d* and *e*, a large amount of corn must be given up to produce a small extra amount of cloth. In this region, the opportunity cost of cloth is high and the opportunity cost of corn is low.

Increasing opportunity cost and the outward bow of the production possibility frontier arise from the fact that scarce resources are not equally useful in all activities. For instance, some of the land on Jane's island is extremely fertile and produces a high crop yield, while other land is rocky and barren. The sheep on the island, however, prefer the rocky, barren land.

Jane uses the most fertile land for growing corn and the most barren areas for raising sheep. Only if she wants a larger amount of corn does she try to cultivate relatively barren areas, and only if she wants a larger amount of wool does she start raising sheep on the more fertile corn-growing land. If she uses all her time to grow corn, she has to use some very unsuitable, low-yielding land. Devoting some time to making cloth, and reducing the time spent growing corn by the same amount, produces a small drop in corn production but a large increase in the output of cloth. Conversely, if Jane uses all her time to make cloth, a small reduction in woolgathering yields a large increase of corn production.

Production Possibilities in the Real World

Jane's island is dramatically different from the world that we live in. The fundamental lesson it teaches us, however, applies to the real world. The world has a fixed number of people with a limited time to spend producing things. The world also has a fixed amount of natural and capital resources. Thus there is a limit to the goods and services that can be produced, a boundary between what is attainable and what is not attainable. That boundary is the real-world economy's production possibility frontier. On that frontier, producing more of any one good requires producing less of some other good or goods.

For example, a presidential candidate who promises better welfare and education services must at the same time, to be credible, promise either cuts in defense spending or higher taxes. Higher taxes mean less money left over for vacations and other consumption goods and services. The cost of better welfare and educational services is less of other goods. On a smaller scale but equally important, each time you decide to rent a video you decide not to use your limited money to buy soda, or popcorn, or some other good. The cost of one more video is less of something else.

On Jane's island, we saw that the opportunity cost of a good increased as the output of the good increased. Opportunity costs in the real world increase for the same reasons that Jane's opportunity costs increase. Consider, for example, two goods vital to our well being—food and health care. In allocating our scarce resources, we use the most fertile land and the most skillful farmers to produce food. We use the best doctors and the least fertile land for health care. If we shift fertile land and tractors away from farming and ask farmers to do surgery, the production of food drops drastically and the increase in the production of health care services is small. The opportunity cost of health care services rises. Similarly, if we shift our resources away from health care toward farming, we have to use more doctors and nurses as farmers and more hospitals as hydroponic tomato factories. The drop in health care services is large, but the increase in food production small. The opportunity cost of producing more food rises.

This example is extreme and unlikely, but these same considerations apply to any pair of goods that you can imagine: guns and butter; housing for the needy and diamonds for the rich; wheelchairs and golf carts; television programs and breakfast cereals. We cannot escape from scarcity and opportunity cost. More of one thing always means less of something else, and the more of anything that we have or do, the higher is its opportunity cost.

R E V I E W

The production possibility frontier is the boundary between the attainable and the unattainable. There is always a point on the frontier that is better than any point inside it. Moving from one point on the frontier to another means having less of one good to get more of another. The frontier is bowed outward or, equivalently, the opportunity cost of a good increases as more of it is produced. ■

Changing Production Possibilities

Although the production possibility frontier defines the boundary between what is attainable and what is unattainable, that boundary is not static. It is constantly changing. Sometimes the production possibility frontier shifts *inward,* reducing our production possibilities. For example, droughts or other extreme climatic conditions shift the frontier inward. Sometimes the frontier moves outward. For example, excellent growing and harvest conditions have this effect. Sometimes the frontier shifts outward because we get a new idea. It suddenly occurs to us that there is a better way of doing something that we never before imagined possible—we invent the wheel.

Over the years, our production possibilities have undergone enormous expansion. The persistent expansion of our production possibilities is called **economic growth.** As a consequence of economic growth we can now produce much more than we could 100 years ago and quite a bit more than even ten years ago. By the mid–1990s, if the same pace of growth continues, our production possibilities will be even greater. By pushing out the frontier, can we avoid the constraints imposed on us by our limited resources? That is, can we get our free lunch after all?

The Cost of Shifting the Frontier

We are going to discover that although we can and do shift the production possibility frontier outward over time, we cannot increase the pace at which we do so without incurring costs. The faster the pace of economic growth, the less we can consume at the present time. Let's investigate the costs of growth by examining why economies grow and prosper.

Two key activities generate economic growth: capital accumulation and technological progress. **Capital accumulation** is the growth of capital resources. **Technological progress** is the development of new and better ways of producing goods and services. As a consequence of capital accumulation and technological progress, we have an enormous quantity of cars and airplanes that enable us to produce more transportation than when we only had horses and carriages; satellites that make transcontinental communications possible on a scale much larger than that produced by the earlier cable technology. But accumulating capital and developing new technology is costly. To see why, let's go back to Jane's island economy.

Capital Accumulation and Technological Change

We know that if Jane spends her entire 12 hours of working time each day producing corn and cloth, she will be somewhere on the production possibility frontier illustrated in Fig. 3.1. If Jane produces at a point on the frontier, she cannot devote any time to making tools or equipment that can be used to grow corn or to make cloth. Her production possibilities for next year will be the same as this year. She will have no more capital and no better technology in the future than she has now. To expand her future production, Jane must produce less corn and cloth today and devote resources to making tools or developing better methods of growing corn and making cloth. The cut in her output of corn and cloth today will be the opportunity cost of expanding her production in the future.

Figure 3.2 provides a more concrete example. The table sets out Jane's production possibilities for producing tools as well as corn and cloth. If she devotes all her working hours to corn and cloth production (row *e*), she produces no tools. If she devotes enough time to produce 1 tool per month (row *d*), her corn and cloth production is cut back to 90 percent of its maximum possible level. She can devote still more time to toolmaking and, as she does so, her corn and cloth production falls by successively larger amounts.

The numbers in the table are graphed in the figure. Each point, from *a* through *e*, represents a row of the table. Notice the similarity between Figs. 3.2 and 3.1. Each shows a production possibility frontier. In the case of Fig. 3.2, the frontier is that between producing tools and producing current consumption goods—corn and cloth. If Jane produces at point *e* in Fig. 3.2, she produces no tools and remains stuck on the production possibility frontier for corn and cloth shown in Fig. 3.1. However, if she moves to point *d* in Fig. 3.2, she can produce 1 tool each month. But to do so, Jane must reduce her production of corn and cloth to 90 percent of what she can produce if all her time is devoted to those activities.

By lowering her production of corn and cloth and producing tools, Jane is able to increase her production possibilities. She will have an increasing stock of tools and can use these tools to become more productive at growing corn and making cloth. She can even use tools to make better tools. As a consequence, Jane's production possibility frontier shifts outward as shown by the shift arrow—she experiences economic growth. The amount by which the frontier shifts out depends on how much time she devotes to toolmaking. If she devotes no time to making tools, the frontier remains at *abcde*—the original production possibility frontier. If she cuts back on the production of corn and cloth and produces one tool (at point *d*), her frontier moves out to the position of the red curve shown in the figure. The less time she devotes to corn and cloth production and the more time to toolmaking, the farther out the frontier shifts. But economic growth is not a free gift for Jane. To make it happen she has to devote more time to producing tools and less to producing corn and cloth. Economic growth is no magic formula for abolishing scarcity.

Figure 3.2 Jane's Tool Production Possibilities

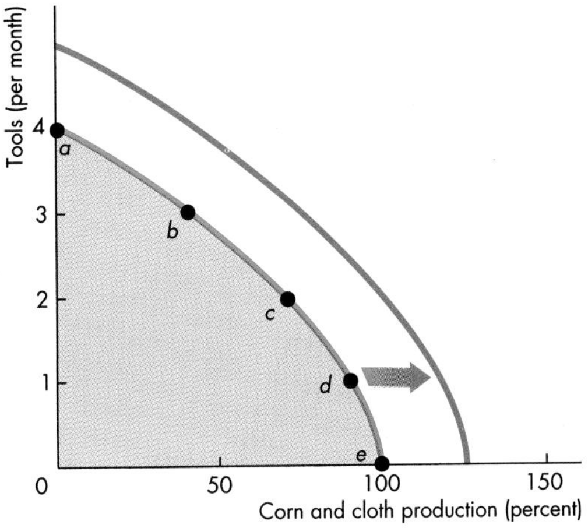

Possibility	Tools (per month)	Corn and cloth production (percent)
a	4	0
b	3	40
c	2	70
d	1	90
e	0	100

If Jane devotes all her time to corn and cloth production, she produces no tools (row e of the table). As she devotes more time to tool production, she can produce successively smaller amounts of corn and cloth. If all her time is devoted to tool production (possibility a), no corn and cloth and 4 tools are produced. In the figure, the curve *abcde* is Jane's production possibility frontier for tools and consumption goods (corn and cloth). If Jane produces at point e (producing no tools), her production possibility frontier remains fixed at *abcde*. If she cuts her production of corn and cloth and makes one tool (producing at point *d*), her future production possibility frontier shifts outward as shown in the figure. The more tools and the less corn and cloth Jane produces, the farther out the frontier shifts. The reduced output of corn and cloth is the opportunity cost of increasing future production possibilities.

The Real World Again

The ideas that we have explored in the setting of Jane's island apply with equal force to our real-world economy. If we devote all our resources to producing food, clothing, housing, vacations, and the many other consumer goods that we enjoy, and none to research, development, and accumulating capital, we will have no more capital and no better technologies in the future than we have at present. Our production possibilities in the future will be exactly the same as those today. If we are to expand our production possibilities in the future, we must produce fewer consumption goods today. The

Figure 3.3 Economic Growth in the United States and Japan

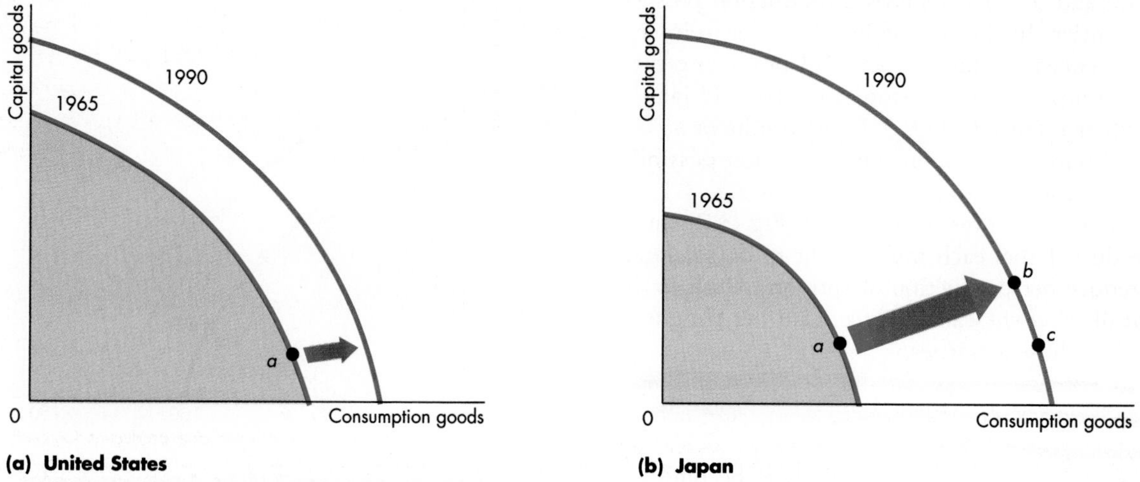

In 1965, the production possibilities per capita in the United States, part (a), were much larger than those in Japan, part (b). But Japan devoted one third of its resources to producing capital goods, while the United States devoted only one fifth. Japan's more rapid increase in capital resources resulted in its production possibility frontier shifting out more quickly than that in the United States. The two production possibilities per capita in 1990 are similar to each other. If Japan produces at point *b* on its 1990 frontier, it will continue to grow more quickly than the United States. If Japan increases consumption and produces at point *c* on its 1990 frontier, its growth rate will slow down to that of the United States.

resources we free up today will enable us to accumulate capital and to develop better technologies for producing consumption goods in the future. The cut in the output of consumption goods today is the opportunity cost of economic growth.

The recent experience of the United States and Japan provides a striking example of the effects of our choices on the rate of economic growth. In 1965, the production possibilities per capita in the United States were much larger than those in Japan (see Fig. 3.3). The United States devoted one fifth of its resources to producing capital goods and the other four fifths to producing consumption goods, as illustrated by point *a* in Fig. 3.3(a). But Japan devoted one third of its resources to producing capital goods and only two thirds to producing consumption goods, as illustrated by point *a* in Fig. 3.3(b). Both countries experienced economic growth, but the growth in Japan was much more rapid than the growth in the United States. Because Japan devoted a bigger fraction of its resources to producing capital goods, its stock of capital equipment grew more quickly than ours, and its production possibilities expanded more quickly. As a result, Japanese production possibilities per capita are now so close to those in the United States that it is hard to say which country has the larger per capita production possibilities. If Japan continues to devote a third of its resources to producing capital goods (at point *b* on its 1990 production possibility frontier), it will continue to grow much more rapidly than the United States and its frontier will move out beyond our own. If Japan increases its production of consumption goods and reduces its production of capital goods (moving to point *c* on its 1990 production possibility frontier), then its rate of economic expansion will slow down to that of our own.

REVIEW

Economic growth results from the accumulation of capital and the development of better technologies. To reap the fruits of economic growth, we must incur the cost of fewer goods and services for current consumption. By cutting the current output of consumption goods, we can devote more resources to accumulating capital and to the research and development that lead to technological change—the engines of economic growth. Thus economic growth does not provide a free lunch. It has an opportunity cost—the fall in the current output of consumption goods. ■

Gains from Trade

No one excels at everything. One person is more athletic than another, another person may have a quicker mind or a better memory. What one person does with ease, someone else may find difficult.

Comparative Advantage: Jane Meets Joe

Differences in individual abilities mean that there are also differences in individual opportunity costs of producing various goods. Such differences give rise to **comparative advantage**—we say that a person has a comparative advantage in producing a particular good if that person can produce the good at a lower opportunity cost than anyone else.

People can produce for themselves all the goods that they want to consume or they can concentrate on producing one good (or perhaps a few goods) and then exchange some of their own products for the output of others. Concentrating on the production of only one good or a few goods is called **specialization.** We are going to discover how people can gain by specializing in that good at which they have a comparative advantage and then trading their output with others.

Let's return again to our island economy. Suppose that Jane has discovered another island very close to her own on which a fellow voyager named Joe is stranded. Joe's island is much like Jane's. Jane and Joe each have access to a simple boat that is adequate for transporting themselves and their goods between the two islands.

Joe's island, too, can produce only corn and cloth, but its terrain differs from that on Jane's island. While Jane's island has a lot of fertile corn-growing land and a small sheep population, Joe's island has little fertile corn-growing land and plenty of sheep. This important difference between the two islands means that Joe's production possibility frontier is different from Jane's—in fact, it is a mirror image of Jane's. The table in Fig. 3.4 presents the production possibility frontiers of Jane and Joe. Note that if Jane devotes all her time to cloth production, she can make 10 yards of cloth, but if Joe devotes all his time to cloth, he can make 25 yards of cloth. Conversely, if Jane devotes all her time to corn farming, she can produce 25 pounds of corn, but Joe can produce only 10 pounds.

The graph in Fig. 3.4 illustrates the same production possibility frontiers. Jane's frontier, labeled "Jane's PPF," looks different here from the way it looked in Fig. 3.1 because we have had to change the scale on the x-axis to make room for Joe's frontier, labeled "Joe's PPF."

Jane and Joe can be self-sufficient in corn and cloth. **Self-sufficiency** is a state that occurs when people produce only for their own consumption. Suppose that Jane and Joe are each self-sufficient and that each chooses to produce 9 yards of cloth and 9 pounds of corn. (They could have chosen any other point on their own production possibility frontier.) Given this choice, each of them is at point x in Fig. 3.4. Total production of corn and cloth is twice the amount shown at x. That is, Jane and Joe individually produce at point x, which means that total production is at point n. Together, Joe and Jane produce 18 pounds of corn and 18 yards of cloth.

Jane's Comparative Advantage In which of the two goods does Jane have a comparative advantage? We have defined comparative advantage as a situation in which one person's opportunity cost of producing a good is lower than another person's opportunity cost of producing that same good. Jane, then, has a comparative advantage in producing whichever good she produces at a lower opportunity cost than Joe. What is that good?

Figure 3.4 The Gains from Specialization and Trade

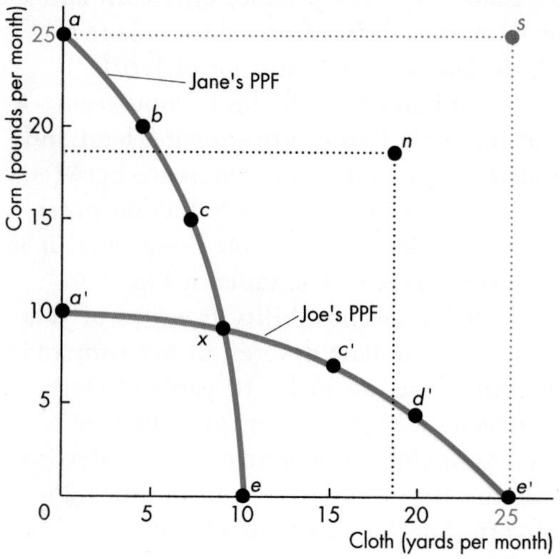

	Jane				Joe		
	Corn (pounds per month)		Cloth (yards per month)		Corn (pounds per month)		Cloth (yards per month)
a	25	and	0	a′	10	and	0
b	20	and	4	b′	9	and	9
c	15	and	7	c′	7	and	15
d	9	and	9	d′	4	and	20
e	0	and	10	e′	0	and	25

Jane's and Joe's production possibility frontiers (PPFs) are shown. Suppose that Joe and Jane each produce at point *x*. Their total production is at point *n*. Joe and Jane can do better by specialization and exchange. Jane has a lower opportunity cost of producing corn than Joe, and Joe has a lower opportunity cost of producing cloth than Jane. Jane has a comparative advantage in corn production. If she specializes in corn production, she produces 25 pounds of corn and no cloth. Joe has a comparative advantage in cloth production. If he specializes in that activity, he produces 25 yards of cloth and no corn. That is, Jane chooses row *a* and Joe chooses row *e′* of the table. Total production is then 25 pounds of corn and 25 yards of cloth (point *s*). If Jane exchanges some of her corn for Joe's cloth and if Joe exchanges some of his cloth for Jane's corn, each can consume more corn and cloth than in a state of self-sufficiency. If each exchanges half of his or her output with the other, they will each consume 12.5 pounds of corn and 12.5 yards of cloth. The increased corn and cloth consumption is the gain from specialization and trade.

You can answer the question by looking at the production possibility frontiers for Jane and Joe in Fig. 3.4. If each of them is producing at point *x*—the point of self-sufficiency—Jane's production possibility frontier is much steeper than Joe's. To produce more corn, Jane gives up much less cloth than Joe. Hence Jane's opportunity cost of a pound of corn is much lower than Joe's. This means that Jane has a comparative advantage in producing corn.

Joe's Comparative Advantage Joe's comparative advantage is in producing cloth. His production possibility frontier at *x*—the point of self-sufficiency—is much flatter than Jane's. This means that Joe has to give up much less corn to produce more cloth than Jane does. Joe's opportunity cost of a yard of cloth is lower than Jane's, so Joe has a comparative advantage in cloth production.

Reaping the Gains from Trade

Can Jane and Joe do better than be self-sufficient? In particular, what would happen if each were to specialize in producing the good at which each has a comparative advantage and then trade with the other?

If Jane, who has a comparative advantage in corn production, puts all her resources into growing corn, she can grow 25 pounds (the amount labeled *a* on the vertical axis of Fig. 3.4). If Joe, who has a comparative advantage in cloth production, puts all his resources into making cloth, he can make 25 yards (the amount labeled *e′* on the horizontal axis). By specializing, Jane and Joe together can produce 25 pounds of corn and 25 yards of cloth (the amount labeled *s* in the figure). Point *s* shows the production of 25 pounds of corn (all produced by Jane) and 25 yards of cloth (all produced by Joe). Clearly, at point *s* Jane and Joe produce more cloth and corn than they were producing at point *n*, when each took care only of his or her own requirements. Point *s* is a better point than *n* because, between them, Jane and Joe have more of both corn and cloth than at point *n*.

To obtain the gains from trade, Jane and Joe must do more than specialize in producing the good at which each has a comparative advantage. They must exchange the fruits of their specialized production. Suppose that Jane and Joe agree to exchange one half of their output. Jane pays Joe 12.5 pounds of corn in exchange for 12.5 yards of cloth. Joe pays Jane 12.5 yards of cloth in exchange for 12.5 pounds of corn. Both Jane and Joe will now have consumption greater than what they had under a self-sufficiency arrangement. Under self-sufficiency, each was consuming 9 pounds of corn and 9 yards of cloth. With specialization and exchange, each is consuming 12.5 pounds of corn and 12.5 yards of cloth. The gain from trade is represented by the increase in consumption of both goods that each person obtains. In this example, the gain from trade is 3.5 pounds of corn and 3.5 yards of cloth for each individual—a gain of almost 39 percent.

Absolute Advantage

Whenever a person can produce more of all goods than anyone else, that person has an **absolute advantage.** In our example, no one has an absolute advantage. Jane and Joe have production possibilities that are mirror images of each other. Jane produces corn as easily as Joe produces cloth, and she is as bad at making cloth as Joe is at growing corn. Suppose that Jane becomes more productive, so that she has an absolute advantage over Joe. In particular, suppose that she becomes twice as productive. Her new production possibilities appear in Table 3.3.

Table 3.3 Jane's New Production Possibilities

Possibility	Corn (pounds per month)		Cloth (yards per month)
a	50	and	0
b	40	and	8
c	30	and	14
d	18	and	18
e	0	and	20

We have already worked out that the gains from trade arise when each person specializes in producing that good with the lower opportunity cost. Joe's opportunity costs remain exactly the same as they were before. What has happened to Jane's opportunity costs now that she has become twice as productive?

You can work out Jane's opportunity costs by using exactly the same calculation that was used in Table 3.2. Start by looking at Jane's opportunity cost of corn. The first 18 pounds of corn that Jane grows cost her 2 yards of cloth. So the opportunity cost of 1 pound of corn is $\frac{1}{9}$ of a yard of cloth—the same as Jane's original opportunity cost of corn. If you calculate the opportunity costs for Jane's production possibilities *a* through *e*, you will discover that each of them has remained the same.

Since the opportunity cost of cloth is the inverse of the opportunity cost of corn, Jane's opportunity costs of cloth also have remained unchanged. Let's work through one example. If Jane moves from *a* to *b* to make 8 yards of cloth, she will have to reduce her corn production by 10 pounds—from 50 to 40 pounds. Thus the first 8 yards of cloth cost 10 pounds of corn. The cost of 1 yard of cloth is, therefore, $1\frac{1}{4}$ pounds of corn—again exactly the same as before.

When Jane becomes twice as productive as before, each hour of her time produces more output, but her opportunity cost remains the same. One more unit of corn costs the same in terms of cloth forgone as it did previously. Since Jane's opportunity costs have not changed and since Joe's have not changed, Joe continues to have a comparative advantage in producing cloth. Both Jane and Joe can have more of both goods if Jane specializes in corn production and Joe in cloth production.

The key point to recognize is that it is ***not*** possible for a person having an absolute advantage to have a comparative advantage in everything.

REVIEW

Gains from trade come from comparative advantage. Unless two individuals have the same opportunity costs, each has a comparative advantage in some activity. Differences in opportunity costs provide the basis for comparative advantage and the gains from specialization and exchange. Even a person with an absolute advantage gains from specialization and exchange. ■

Exchange in the Real World

In the real world, where there are billions of people specializing in millions of different activities, gains from specialization and trade exist, but they are harder to exploit. Trade has to be organized. To organize trade, we have evolved rules of conduct and mechanisms for enforcing those rules. One such mechanism is private property rights. Another is the institution of money. In the island economy of Jane and Joe, direct exchange of one good with another is feasible. In the real-world economy, direct exchange of one good for another would be very cumbersome. To lubricate the wheels of exchange, societies have created money—a medium that enables indirect exchange of goods for money and money for goods. Let's examine these two aspects of exchange arrangements in more detail.

Property rights

Property rights are social arrangements that govern the ownership, use, and disposal of property. **Property** is anything of value: It includes land and buildings—the things we call property in ordinary speech; it also includes stocks and bonds, durable goods, plant and equipment; it also includes intellectual property. **Intellectual property** is the intangible product of creative effort, protected by copyrights and patents. This type of property includes books, music, computer programs, and inventions of all kinds.

What if property rights did not exist? What would such a social science fiction world be like?

A World Without Property Rights Without property rights, people could take possession of whatever they had the strength to obtain for themselves. In such a world, people would have to devote a good deal of their time, energy, and resources to protecting what they had produced or acquired.

In a world without property rights, it would be impossible to reap any gains from specialization and exchange. People would have no incentive to specialize in producing those goods at which they each had a comparative advantage. In fact, the more of a particular good someone produced, the bigger the chance that others would simply help themselves to it. Also, if a person could take the goods of others without giving up something in exchange, then there would be no point in specializing in producing something for exchange. In a world without property rights, no one would enjoy the gains from specialization and exchange, and everyone would specialize only in unproductive acts of piracy. It is to overcome the problems that we have just described that property rights have evolved. Let's examine these property rights as they operate to govern economic life in the United States today.

Property Rights in Private Enterprise Capitalism The U.S. economy operates for the most part on the principles of private enterprise capitalism. **Private enterprise** is an economic system that permits individuals to decide on their own economic activities. **Capitalism** is an economic system that permits private individuals to own the capital resources used in production.

Under the property rights in such an economic system, individuals own what they have made, or what they have acquired in a voluntary exchange with others, or what they have been given. Any attempt to remove the property of someone against that person's will is considered theft, a crime punished by a sufficiently severe penalty to deter most people from becoming thieves.

It is easy to see that property rights based on these ideas can generate gainful trade: People can specialize in producing those goods that, for them, have the least opportunity cost. Some people will specialize in enforcing and maintaining property rights (for example, politicians, judges, and police officers) and all individuals will have the incentive to trade with each other, offering the good in which they have a comparative advantage in exchange for the goods produced by others.

Although the U.S. economic system is based on a system of private property with voluntary exchange, property rights even in this country have limits. Let's look at some of these.

Taxes Limit Private Property Rights The most important and pervasive limit on people's rights to private property comes from taxes. All of us have to pay taxes to federal, state, and local governments. Many people regard the taxes that they pay as a fair price for the services provided by government. Many others, however, regard the taxes that they pay as exorbitant. Taxing part of the property that people have created limits people's efforts to create more property and reduces their gain from specialized production.

Even though taxes constitute a partial intrusion into private property rights, the taxes themselves are not arbitrary. Everyone faces the same rules and can calculate the effects of their own actions on the taxes for which they will be liable.

Regulation Limits Private Property Rights Other restrictions on private property rights prohibit certain kinds of voluntary exchange. For example, food and drug manufacturers cannot place a product on the market without first obtaining approval from a government agency. The government controls or prohibits the sale of many types of drugs, and also restricts trading in human beings and their component parts—that is, it prohibits the selling of slaves, children, and human organs.

These restrictions on the extent of private property and on the legitimacy of voluntary exchange, though important, do not, for the most part, seriously impede specialization and gainful trade. Most people take the view that the benefits of regulation—for example, prohibiting the sale of dangerous drugs—far outweigh the costs imposed on the sellers.

Let's now turn to the other major social institution that permits specialization and exchange—the development of an efficient means of exchange.

Money

We have seen that well-defined property rights based on voluntary exchange allow individuals to specialize and exchange their output with each other. In our island economy, we studied only two people and two goods. Exchange in such a situation was a simple matter. In the real world, however, how can billions of people exchange the millions of goods that are the fruits of their specialized labor?

Barter Goods can be simply exchanged for goods. This system is known as **barter.** However, exchanging goods only through the barter system severely limits the amount of trading that can take place. Imagine that you have roosters, but you want to get roses. First, you must look for someone with roses who wants roosters. Economists call this a **double coincidence of wants**—when person A wants to sell exactly what person B wants to buy, and person B wants to sell exactly what person A wants to buy. As the term implies, such occurrences are coincidences and will not arise frequently. A second way of trading by barter is to undertake a sequence of exchanges. If you have oranges and you want apples, you may have to trade oranges for plums and plums for pomegranates and pomegranates for pineapples and then eventually pineapples for apples.

Cumbersome though it is, quite a large amount of barter trade does take place. For example, when British rock star Rod Stewart played in Budapest, Hungary, in August 1986, he received part of his $30,000 compensation in Hungarian sound equipment, electrical cable, and the use of a forklift truck. Hairdressers in Warsaw, Poland, obtain their barbershop equipment from England in exchange for hair clippings that they supply to London wigmakers.

Although barter exchange does occur, it is an inefficient means of exchanging goods. Fortunately, a better alternative has been invented.

Monetary Exchange An alternative to barter is **monetary exchange**—a system in which some commodity or token serves as the medium of exchange. A **medium of exchange** is anything that is generally acceptable in exchange for goods and services. **Money** can also be defined as a medium of exchange—something that can be passed on to others in exchange for goods and services. In a monetary exchange system, people exchange money for goods and goods for money, but they do not directly exchange goods for goods.

Overcoming Obstacles to the Gains from Trade

In Romania, Smoking A Kent Cigarette Is Like Burning Money

It isn't true that Romania, a hard-core Communist country, doesn't operate on the market principle. It does. Call it the farmers' market principle, and this is how it works:

As dawn breaks, a crowing rooster on sale at the downtown market signals the opening of an intense round of barter trading. Apples will get you peppers. Cauliflower will get you beets. Turnips will get you garlic. And Kent cigarettes will get you everything.

"Psssst. Mister. With the Kents," whispers a young farmer rushing from behind his fruit and vegetable stand to pursue someone who has just flashed a pack of Kents. Never mind the line of customers at the stand. They can wait; they have only *lei*, the official Romanian currency. The other guy has Kents.

"You sell?" asks the farmer, now being joined by four fellow farmers. He presents his left palm and begins writing on it. "Twenty-five," he writes. That is 25 *lei*, or about $2.20, for one pack of Kents. The man with the Kents sells two packs for 50 *lei* and inquires about the apples on sale.

"You want apples?" asks the farmer. He pulls out a bag hidden at the bottom of the pile. These aren't the yellow apples for the regular customers—the ones with *lei*. These are red apples for the man with the Kents.

Under the farmers' market principle, the fruit and vegetable farmer perhaps will trade away his Kents to get his tractor fixed. The mechanic will use the Kents to get a rare and relatively good cut of meat at the butcher shop. The butcher will pass on the Kents to get a table at a packed restaurant. The maitre d' will use the Kents to pay his doctor. The doctor will flash the Kents at the farmers' market to get some attention. And some farmer, writing on his hand, will come running after.

"In Romania, Kents are the ultimate affirmation of the market theory," says a Western diplomat here. "You've heard of the gold standard. Well this is the Kent standard. Everyone in this country wants Kents." And only Kents. Winston, Marlboro, Pall Mall won't do.

Want to be a big shot in Romania? Flash a pack of Kents. Want a taxi? Wave some Kents. (With the distinctive gold box used for the European Kents, they can be spotted at surprising distances.) Want to get past a troublesome passport officer at the airport? A couple of packs of Kents will do. Kents will open most every door in this country, including the door to the outside world.

***The Wall Street Journal*, January 3, 1986**

by Roger Thurow, Staff Reporter

The Essence of the Story

In Romania, people buy and sell goods in three ways:

- By barter—exchanging apples for peppers and cauliflower for beets
- By using their official currency—giving and receiving lei in exchange for goods and services
- By using Kents—giving and receiving packs of Kent cigarettes in exchange for goods and services.

People offering Kents get a better deal than people offering lei. Kents circulate as a medium of exchange:

- The "man with the Kents" buys apples
- The farmer uses Kents to get his tractor fixed
- The mechanic uses Kents to buy meat
- The butcher uses Kents at a restaurant
- The head waiter uses Kents to get medical treatment
- The doctor uses Kents to buy apples—and so on.

Kents thus allow people to undertake a wide variety of trades (or exchanges).

Background and Analysis

Romania is a socialist country in Eastern Europe. Private property rights are restricted and the government controls most aspects of economic life. Some examples of what the government dictates:

- The things that people may produce
- The quantities that may be produced
- The prices at which goods may be sold

Romanians specialize in producing the things at which they have a comparative advantage. If they were to sell their output at the prices fixed by the government, they would receive less than the opportunity cost of production.

For this reason, people try to evade the government's controlled prices by direct barter or by using Kent cigarettes as money. Because people widely accept Kents as a means of payment, these cigarettes have come to serve as a medium of exchange—as money.

Conclusion

The people of Romania have invented the social contract of using Kents as money. By so doing, they have lessened the severity of restricted property rights and removed, at least partly, a major obstacle to achieving the gains from specialization and exchange.

Metals such as gold, silver, and copper have long served as money. Most commonly, they serve as money by being stamped as coins. Primitive societies have traditionally used various commodities, such as sea shells, as money. During the Civil War and for several years after, people used postage stamps as money. Prisoners of war in German camps in World War II used cigarettes as money. Even today in Bucharest, the capital of Romania, people use cigarettes as money (see Reading Between the Lines, pp. 64–65).[1] Using cigarettes as a medium of exchange should not be confused with barter. Under the circumstances described, cigarettes play the role of money, and people buy and sell goods by using cigarettes as a medium of exchange.

In modern societies, governments provide paper money. The banking system also provides money in the form of checking accounts. Checking accounts can be used for settling debts simply by writing an instruction—writing a check—to the bank requesting that funds be transferred to another checking account. Electronic links between bank accounts, now becoming more widespread, enable direct transfers between different accounts without any checks being written.

■ You have now begun to see how economists go about the job of trying to answer some important questions. The simple fact of scarcity and the associated concept of opportunity cost allow us to understand why people specialize, why they trade with each other, why they have social conventions that define and enforce private property rights, and why they use money. One simple idea—scarcity and its direct implication, opportunity cost—explains so much!

[1]This is the first in a series of "Reading Between the Lines" boxes. Each box begins with an extract from a newspaper or news magazine. The news story is then retold in stripped down form and analyzed by using the tools of economics that have been developed in the chapter.

SUMMARY

The Production Possibility Frontier

The production possibility frontier is the boundary between what is attainable and what is not attainable. Production can take place at any point inside or on the production possibility frontier. But it is not possible to produce outside the frontier. There is always a point on the production possibility frontier that is better than a point inside it. (pp. 51–53)

Opportunity Cost

The opportunity cost of any action is the best alternative action forgone. The opportunity cost of acquiring one good is equivalent to the amount of another good that must be given up. The opportunity cost of a good increases as the quantity of it produced increases. (pp. 53–56)

Changing Production Possibilities

Although the production possibility frontier marks the boundary between the attainable and the unattainable, that boundary does not remain fixed. It changes, partly because of natural forces (changes in climate and the accumulation of ideas about better ways of producing) and partly by the choices that we make. If we use some of today's resources to produce capital goods and for research and development we will be able to produce more goods and services in the future. The economy will grow. But growth cannot take place without incurring costs. The opportunity cost of more goods and services in the future is consuming fewer goods and services today. (pp. 56–59)

Gains from Trade

When people have different opportunity costs, they can gain from specialization and exchange. Each person specializes in producing the good for which their opportunity cost is lower than everyone else's—the good in which he or she has a comparative advantage. They then exchange part of their output with each other. (pp. 59–62)

Exchange in the Real World

Property rights and a system of monetary exchange enable people to specialize, exchanging their labor for money and their money for goods, thereby reaping the gains from trade. (pp. 62–66)

KEY CONCEPTS

Absolute advantage, 61
Barter, 63
Capitalism, 62
Capital accumulation, 56
Capital goods, 51
Capital resources, 51
Comparative advantage, 59
Consumption, 51
Consumption goods, 51
Double coincidence of wants, 63
Economic growth, 56
Goods and services, 51
Human capital, 51
Human resources, 51
Intellectual property, 62
Medium of exchange, 63
Monetary exchange, 63
Money, 63
Natural resources, 51
Private enterprise, 62
Production, 51
Production possibility frontier, 51
Property, 62
Property rights, 62
Self-sufficiency, 59
Specialization, 59
Technological progress, 56

Key Figures

REVIEW QUESTIONS

1 How does the production possibility curve illustrate scarcity?
2 How does the production possibility curve illustrate opportunity cost?
3 Explain what shifts the production possibility frontier outward and what shifts it inward.
4 Explain how our choices influence economic growth. What is the cost of economic growth?
5 Why does it pay people to specialize and trade with each other?
6 What are the gains from trade? How do they arise?
7 Why do social contracts such as property rights and money become necessary?
8 Why is monetary exchange more efficient than barter?

PROBLEMS

1 Suppose that there is a change in the weather conditions on Jane's island that makes the corn yields much higher. This enables Jane to produce the following amounts of corn:

Hours worked per day	Corn (pounds per month)
0	0
3	66
6	96
9	110
12	120

Her cloth production possibilities are the same as those that appeared in Table 3.1.

a) What are five points on Jane's new production possibility frontier?

b) What are Jane's opportunity costs of corn and cloth?

c) Comparing Jane's opportunity cost of corn with that in Table 3.2, has her opportunity cost of corn gone up, down, or remained the same? Explain why.

2 Suppose that Joe has the following production possibilities:

Corn (pounds per month)		Cloth (yards per month)
6	and	0.0
5	and	0.5
4	and	1.0
3	and	1.5
2	and	2.0
1	and	2.5
0	and	3.0

Jane has the following production possibilities:

Corn (pounds per month)		Cloth (yards per month)
3.0	and	0
2.5	and	1
2.0	and	2
1.5	and	3
1.0	and	4
0.5	and	5
0.0	and	6

Find the maximum quantity of corn and cloth that they can produce if each specializes in the activity at which he or she has the lower opportunity cost.

3 Suppose that Jane has become twice as productive and that she can now produce the following quantities:

Corn (pounds per month)		Cloth (yards per month)
6	and	0
5	and	2
4	and	4
3	and	6
2	and	8
1	and	10
0	and	12

a) Show the effect of Jane's increased productivity on her production possibility frontier.

b) Will it still pay Jane to specialize and trade with Joe now that she is twice as productive?

c) Will it still pay Joe to trade with Jane?

Chapter 4

Demand and Supply

After studying this chapter, you will be able to:

- Explain how prices are determined
- Explain why some prices rise, some fall, and some fluctuate
- Explain how quantities bought and sold are determined
- Construct a demand schedule and a demand curve
- Construct a supply schedule and a supply curve
- Make predictions about price changes using the demand and supply model

Slide, Rocket, and Roller Coaster

Disneyland rides? No. Commonly used descriptions of the behavior of prices. ■ There are lots of examples of price slides. One particular example is probably very familiar to you. In 1979, Sony began to market a pocket-sized cassette player that delivered its sound through tiny earphones. They named their new product the Walkman and they gave it a price tag of around $300—more than $500 in today's money. Today Sony has been joined by many other producers of Walkman clones, and you can buy a Walkman (or its equivalent) that's even better than the 1979 prototype, for less than one tenth of the original price. During the time that the Walkman has been with us, the quantity bought has increased steadily each year. Why has there been a long and steady slide in the price of the Walkman? Why hasn't the increase in the quantity bought kept its price high? ■ Rocketing prices are also a familiar phenomenon. An important recent example is that of rents paid for apartments and houses, especially in central locations in big cities. Huge increases in rents and house prices have not deterred people from living in the centers of cities—on the contrary, their numbers have increased slightly in recent years. Why do people continue to seek housing in city centers when rents have rocketed so sharply? ■ There are lots of price roller coasters—cases in which prices rise and fall from season to season or year to year. Prices of coffee, strawberries, and many other agricultural commodities fit this pattern. Why does the price of coffee roller-coaster even when people's taste for coffee hardly changes at all? ■ Though amusement park rides provide a vivid description of the behavior of prices, many of the things that we buy have remarkably steady prices. The audiocassette tapes that we play in a Walkman are an example. The price of a tape has barely changed over the past ten years.

Nevertheless, the number of tapes bought has risen steadily year after year. Why do firms sell more and more tapes, even though they're not able to get higher prices for them and why do people willingly buy more tapes even though their price is no lower than it was a decade ago?

■ We will discover the answers to these and similar questions by studying demand and supply. We are first going to discover what determines the demand for different goods and the supply of them. Then we are going to discover how demand and supply together determine price. This powerful theory enables us to analyze many important economic events that affect our lives and even to make predictions about future prices.

Demand

The **quantity demanded** of a good or service is the amount that consumers plan to buy in a given period of time. Demands are different from wants. **Wants** are the unlimited desires or wishes that people have for goods and services. How many times have you thought that you would like something "if only you could afford it" or "if it weren't so expensive"? Scarcity guarantees that many —perhaps most—of our wants will never be satisfied. Demand reflects a decision about which wants to satisfy. If you demand something, then you've made a plan to buy it.

The quantity demanded is not necessarily the same amount as the quantity actually bought. The quantity that people actually buy and sell is called the **quantity traded.** Sometimes the quantity demanded is greater than the amount of goods available, so the quantity traded is less than the quantity demanded.

The quantity demanded is measured as an amount per unit of time. For example, suppose a person consumes one cup of coffee a day. The quantity of coffee demanded by that person can be expressed as one cup per day or seven cups per week or 365 cups per year. Without a time dimension, we cannot tell whether a particular quantity demanded is large or small.

What Determines the Quantity Demanded?

The amount that consumers plan to buy of any particular good or service depends on many factors. Among the more important ones are:

- The price of the good
- The prices of other goods
- Income
- Population
- Tastes

The theory of demand and supply makes predictions about the prices at which goods are traded and the quantities bought and sold. Our first focus, therefore, is on the relationship between the quantity demanded and the price of a good. To study this relationship, we hold constant all other influences on consumers' planned purchases. We can then ask: How does the quantity demanded of the good vary as its price varies?

The Law of Demand

The law of demand states:

Other things being equal, the higher the price of a good, the lower is the quantity demanded.

Why does a higher price reduce the quantity demanded? The answer is that each good, although unique, can usually be replaced by some other good. As the price of a good climbs higher, people buy less of that good and more of some substitute that serves almost as well.

Let's consider an example—blank audiocassette tapes, which we'll refer to as "tapes." Many different goods provide a similar service to a tape; for example, records, compact discs, prerecorded tapes, radio and television broadcasts, and live concerts. Tapes sell for about \$3 each. If the price of a tape doubles to \$6 while the prices of all the other goods remain constant, the quantity of tapes demanded will fall dramatically. People will buy more records and prerecorded tapes and fewer blank tapes. If the price of a tape falls to \$1 while the prices of all the other goods stay constant, the quantity of tapes demanded will rise and the demand for records, albums, and prerecorded tapes will fall dramatically.

Figure 4.1 The Demand Schedule and the Demand Curve

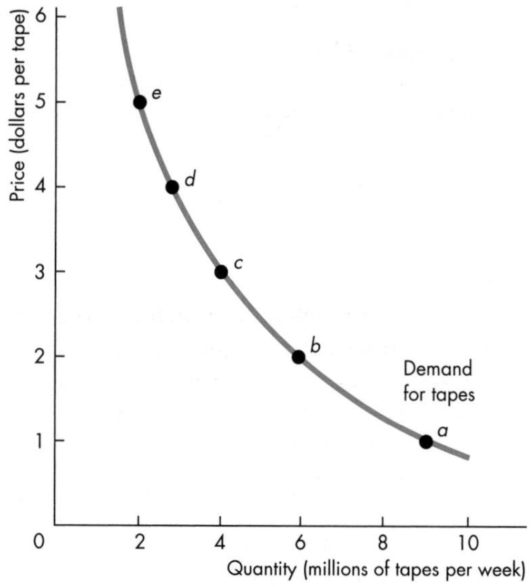

	Price (dollars per tape)	Quantity (millions of tapes per week)
a	1	9
b	2	6
c	3	4
d	4	3
e	5	2

The table shows a demand schedule listing the quantity of tapes demanded at each price if all other influences on buyers' plans are held constant. At a price of \$1 a tape, 9 million tapes a week are demanded; at a price of \$3 a tape, 4 million tapes a week are demanded. The demand curve shows the relationship between quantity demanded and price, holding everything else constant. The demand curve slopes downward: as price decreases, the quantity demanded increases. The demand curve can be read two ways. For a given price it tells us the quantity that people plan to buy. For example, at a price of \$3 a tape, the quantity demanded is 4 million tapes a week. For a given quantity, the demand curve tells us the maximum price that consumers are willing to pay for the last tape bought. For example, the maximum price that consumers will pay for the 6 millionth tape is \$2.

Demand Schedule and Demand Curve

A **demand schedule** lists the quantities demanded at each different price, when all the other influences on consumers' planned purchases—such as the prices of other goods, income, population, and tastes—are held constant.

The table in Fig. 4.1 sets out a demand schedule for tapes. For example, if the price of a tape is \$1, the quantity demanded is 9 million tapes a week. If the price of a tape is \$5, the quantity demanded is 2 million tapes a week. The other rows of the table show us the quantities demanded at prices between \$2 and \$4.

A demand schedule can be illustrated by drawing a demand curve. A **demand curve** graphs the relationship between the quantity demanded of a good and its price, holding constant all other influences on consumers' planned purchases. The graph in Fig. 4.1 illustrates the demand curve for tapes. By convention, the quantity demanded is always measured on the horizontal axis and the price is measured on the vertical axis. The points on the demand curve labeled *a* through *e* represent the rows of the demand schedule. For example, point *a* on the graph represents a quantity demanded of 9 million tapes a week at a price of \$1 a tape.

Willingness to Pay

There is another way of looking at the demand curve: It shows the highest price that people are willing to pay for the last unit bought. If a large quantity is available, that price is low; but if only a small quantity is available, that price is high. For example, if 9 million tapes are available each week, the highest price that consumers are willing to pay for the 9 millionth tape is \$1. But if only 2 million tapes are available each week, consumers are willing to pay \$5 for the last tape available.

This view of the demand curve may become clearer if you think about your own demand for tapes. If I give you a list of possible prices of tapes, you could write down alongside each price your planned weekly purchase of tapes. On the other hand, if I tell you that there is just one tape available each week, you could tell me how much you'd be willing to pay for it. If I then told you that there is one more tape available, you could tell me the maximum price that you will be willing to pay for that second tape. We could continue this process, increasing the number of tapes by one, with you saying the maximum price that you're prepared to pay for each extra tape. The schedule of prices and quantities that we'd arrive at would be your demand schedule.

A Change in Demand

The term **demand** refers to the entire relationship between the quantity demanded and the price of a good. The demand for tapes is described by both the demand schedule and the demand curve in Fig. 4.1. To construct a demand schedule and demand curve, we hold constant all the other influences on consumers' buying plans. But what are the effects of each of those other influences?

1. Prices of Other Goods The quantity of tapes that consumers plan to buy does not depend only on the price of tapes. It also depends in part on the prices of other relevant goods. These other goods fall into two categories: substitutes and complements.

A **substitute** is a good that can be used in place of another good. For example, a bus ride substitutes for a train ride; a hamburger substitutes for a hot dog; a pear substitutes for an apple. As we have seen, tapes have many substitutes—records, prerecorded tapes, compact discs, radio and television broadcasts, and live concerts. If the price of one of these substitutes increases, people economize on its use and buy more tapes. For example, if the price of records doubles, fewer records are bought and the demand for tapes increases—there is much more taping of other people's records. Conversely, if the price of one of these substitutes decreases, people use the now cheaper good in larger quantities, and they buy fewer tapes. For example, if the price of prerecorded tapes decreases, people play more of these tapes and make fewer of their own tapes—the demand for blank tapes falls.

The effects of a change in the price of a substitute occur no matter what the price of a tape. Whether tapes have a high or a low price, a change in the price of a substitute encourages people to make the substitutes that we've just reviewed. As a consequence, a change in the price of a substitute changes the entire demand schedule for tapes and shifts the demand curve.

A **complement** is a good used in conjunction with another good. Some examples of complements are hamburgers and french fries, party snacks and drinks, spaghetti and meat sauce, running shoes and jogging pants. Tapes also have their complements: Walkmans, tape recorders, and stereo tape decks. If the price of one of these complements increases, people buy fewer tapes. For example, if the price of a Walkman doubles, fewer Walkmans are bought and, as a consequence, fewer people are interested in buying tapes—the demand for tapes decreases. Conversely, if the price of one of these complements decreases, people buy more tapes. For example, if the price of the Walkman halves, more Walkmans are bought and a larger number of people buy tapes—the demand for tapes increases.

2. Income Another influence on demand is consumer income. When income increases, consumers demand more of most goods. When income decreases, consumers demand less of most goods. Higher average income means consumers demand more of most goods. Lower average income means consumers demand less of most goods. Rich people consume more food, clothing, housing, art, vacations, and entertainment than do poor people.

Although an increase in income leads to an increase in the demand for most goods, it does not lead to an increase in the demand for all goods. Goods that do increase in demand as income increases are called **normal goods.** Goods that decrease in demand when income increases are called **inferior goods.** Examples of inferior goods are rice and potatoes. These two goods are a major part of the diet of people with very low incomes. As incomes increase, the demand for these goods declines as more expensive meat and dairy products are substituted for them.

3. Population Demand also depends on the size of the population. The larger the population, the greater is the demand for all goods and services. The smaller the population, the lower is the demand for all goods and services.

4. Tastes Finally, demand depends on tastes. **Tastes** are an individual's attitudes or preferences toward goods and services. For example, a rock music fanatic has a much greater taste for tapes than does a tone-deaf workaholic. As a consequence, even if they have the same incomes, their demands for tapes will be very different. There is, however, a fundamental difference between tastes and all the other influences on demand. Tastes cannot be directly observed. We can observe the price of a good and of its substitutes and complements. We can observe income and population size. But we cannot observe people's tastes. Economists assume that tastes do not change or that they change only slowly, and that they are independent of all the other influences on demand.

A summary of influences on demand and the direction of those influences is presented in Table 4.1.

Movement Along Versus a Shift in the Demand Curve

Changes in the influences on buyers' plans cause either a movement along the demand curve or a shift in it. Let's discuss each case in turn.

Movement Along the Demand Curve If the price of a good changes but everything else remains the same, then we say that the quantity demanded of that good has changed. We illustrate the effect as a movement along the demand curve. For example, if the price of a tape changes from $3 to $5, the result is a movement along the demand curve, from point *c* to point *e* in Fig. 4.1.

Table 4.1 The Demand for Tapes

The law of demand	
The quantity of tapes demanded	
Falls if:	*Rises if:*
• The price of a tape rises	• The price of a tape falls
Changes in demand	
The demand for tapes	
Falls if:	*Rises if:*
• The price of a substitute falls	• The price of a substitute rises
• The price of a complement rises	• The price of a complement falls
• Income falls	• Income rises
• The population decreases	• The population increases

A Shift in the Demand Curve If the price of a good remains constant but another influence on buyers' plans changes, we say that there is a change in demand for that good. We illustrate the change in demand as a shift in the demand curve. For example, a dramatic fall in the price of the Walkman—a complement of tapes—increases the demand for tapes. We illustrate this increase in demand for tapes with a new demand schedule and a new demand curve. Consumers demand a larger quantity of tapes at each and every price.

The table in Fig. 4.2 provides some hypothetical numbers that illustrate such a shift. The table sets out the original demand schedule and the new demand schedule resulting from a fall in the price of a Walkman. These numbers record the change in demand. The graph in Fig. 4.2 illustrates the corresponding shift in the demand curve. When the price of the Walkman falls, the demand curve for tapes shifts to the right.

A Change in Demand Versus a Change in Quantity Demanded The quantity demanded at a given price is shown by a point on a demand curve. The entire demand curve shows demand. It follows, then, that a **change in demand** is a shift in the entire demand curve. It also follows that a movement along a demand curve is a **change in the quantity demanded.** Figure 4.3 illustrates these distinctions. If the price of a good falls but nothing else changes, then there is an increase in the quantity demanded of that good (a movement down the demand curve D_0). If the price rises, but nothing else changes, then there is a decrease in the quantity demanded (a movement up the demand curve D_0). When any other influence on buyers' planned purchases changes, the demand curve shifts and there is a *change* (an increase or a decrease) *in demand*. A rise in income, in population, or in the price of a substitute, or a fall in the price of a complement shifts the demand curve to the right (to the red demand curve D_2). This represents an *increase in demand*. A fall in income, in population, or in the price of a substitute, or a rise in the price of a complement shifts the demand curve to the left (to the red demand curve D_1). This represents a *decrease in demand*.

Figure 4.2 A Change in the Demand Schedule and a Shift in the Demand Curve

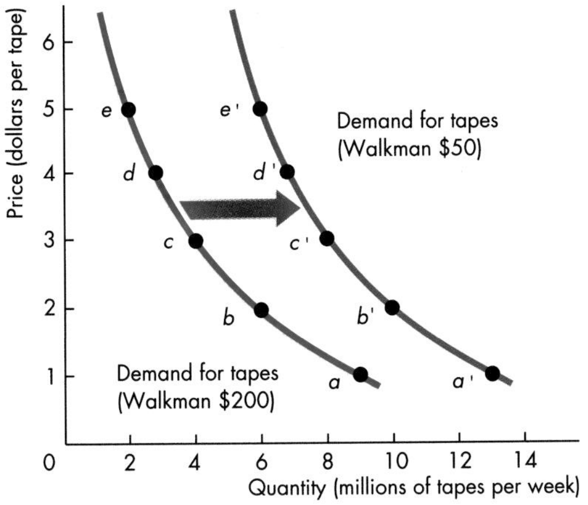

	Original demand schedule (Walkman $200)			New demand schedule (Walkman $50)	
	Price (dollars per tape)	Quantity (millions of tapes per week)		Price (dollars per tape)	Quantity (millions of tapes per week)
a	1	9	a′	1	13
b	2	6	b′	2	10
c	3	4	c′	3	8
d	4	3	d′	4	7
e	5	2	e′	5	6

A change in any influence on buyers other than the price of the good itself results in a new demand schedule and a shift in the demand curve. Here, a fall in the price of a Walkman—a complement of tapes—increases the demand for tapes. At a price of $3 a tape (row c of table), 4 million tapes a week are demanded when the Walkman costs $200 and 8 million tapes a week are demanded when the Walkman costs only $50. The demand curve shifts to the right, as shown by the shift arrow and the resulting red curve.

Figure 4.3 A Change in Demand Versus a Change in the Quantity Demanded

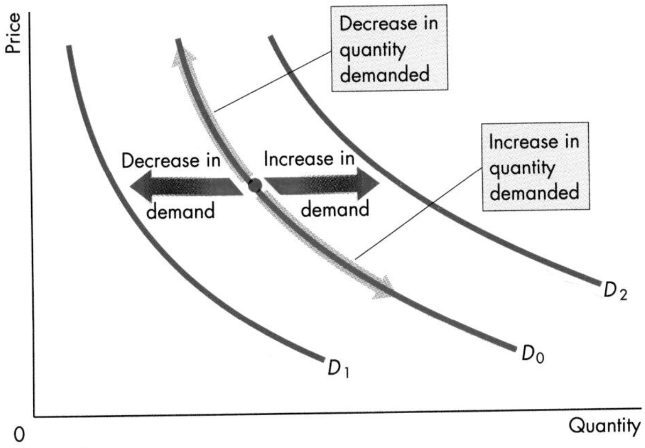

When the price of a good changes, there is a movement along the demand curve and a *change in the quantity of the good demanded*. For example, if the demand curve is D_0, a rise in the price of the good produces a decrease in the quantity demanded and a fall in the price of the good produces an increase in the quantity demanded. The arrows on demand curve D_0 represent these movements along the demand curve. If some other influence on demand changes, which increases the quantity that people plan to buy, there is a shift in the demand curve to the right (from D_0 to red D_2) and an *increase in demand*. If some other influence on demand changes, which reduces the quantity people plan to buy, there is a shift in the demand curve to the left (from D_0 to red D_1) and a *decrease in demand*.

R E V I E W

The quantity demanded is the amount of a good that consumers plan to buy in a given period of time. Other things being equal, the quantity demanded of a good increases if its price falls. Demand can be represented by a schedule or curve that sets out the quantity demanded at each price. Demand describes the quantity that consumers plan to buy at each possible price, or the highest price that consumers are willing to pay for the last unit bought. Demand increases if the price of a substitute rises, if the price of a complement falls, if income rises, or if the population increases; demand decreases if the price of a substitute falls, if the price of a complement rises, if income falls, or if the population decreases.

If the price of a good changes but all other influences on buyers' plans are held constant, there is a change in the quantity demanded and a movement along the demand curve. All other influences on consumers' planned purchases shift the demand curve. ■

Supply

The **quantity supplied** of a good is the amount that producers plan to sell in a given period of time. The quantity supplied is not the amount a firm would like to sell but the amount it definitely plans to sell. However, the quantity supplied is not necessarily the same amount as the quantity actually sold, or traded. If consumers do not want to buy the quantity a firm plans to sell, the firm's sales plans will be frustrated. Like quantity demanded, the quantity supplied is expressed as an amount per unit of time.

What Determines the Quantity Supplied?

The quantity supplied depends on the number of firms supplying a good and the plans of each firm. The amount of any good that each firm plans to supply depends on many factors. Among the more important ones are:

- The price of the good
- The prices of other goods
- The prices of the resources used to produce the good
- The number of suppliers
- Technology

Since the theory of demand and supply makes predictions about prices and quantities traded, we focus first on the relationship between the price of a good and the quantity supplied. In order to study this relationship, we hold constant all the other influences on the quantity supplied. We ask: How does the quantity supplied of a good vary as its price varies?

The Law of Supply

The law of supply states:

Other things being equal, the higher the price of a good, the greater is the quantity supplied.

Why does a higher price lead to a greater quantity supplied of a good? The key to the answer is profitability. If the prices of the resources used to produce a good are held constant, a higher price for the good means a higher profit for the producer. Higher profits encourage existing producers to increase the quantity they supply. Higher profits also attract additional producers.

Supply Schedule and Supply Curve

A **supply schedule** lists the quantities supplied at each different price, when all other influences on the amount firms plan to sell are held constant. Let's construct a supply schedule. To do so, we examine how the quantity supplied of a good varies as its price varies, holding constant the prices of other goods, the prices of resources used to produce it, and the state of technology.

The table in Fig. 4.4 sets out a supply schedule for tapes. It shows the quantity of tapes supplied at each possible price. For example, if the price of a tape is $1, no tapes are supplied. If the price of a tape is $4, 5 million tapes are supplied each week.

A supply schedule can be illustrated by drawing a supply curve. A **supply curve** graphs the relationship between the quantity supplied and the price of a good, holding everything else constant.

Using the same numbers listed in the table, the graph in Fig. 4.4 illustrates the supply curve for tapes. For example, point *d* represents a quantity supplied of 5 million tapes a week at a price of $4 a tape.

Minimum Supply Price

Just as the demand curve has two interpretations, so too does the supply curve. So far we have thought about the supply curve and the supply schedule as showing the quantity that firms will supply at each possible price. But we can also think about the supply curve as showing the minimum price at which the last unit will be supplied. Looking at the supply schedule in this way, we ask what is the minimum price that brings forth a supply of a given quantity. For firms to supply the 3 millionth tape each week, the price has to be at least $2 a tape. For firms to supply the 5 millionth tape each week, they have to get at least $4 a tape.

A Change in Supply

The term **supply** refers to the entire relationship between the quantity supplied of a good and its price. The supply of tapes is described by both the supply schedule and the supply curve in Fig. 4.4. To construct a supply schedule and supply curve, we hold constant all the other influences on suppliers' plans. Let's now consider these other influences.

1. Prices of Other Goods The supply of a good can be influenced by the prices of other goods. For example, if an automobile assembly line can produce either sports cars or sedans, the quantity of sedans produced will depend on the price of sports cars and the quantity of sports cars produced will depend on the price of sedans. These two goods are substitutes in production. An increase in the price of a substitute in production lowers the supply of the good. Goods can also be complements in production. Complements in production arise when two things are, of necessity, produced together. For example, extracting chemicals from coal produces coke, coal tar, and nylon. An increase in the price of any one of these by-products of coal increases the supply of the other by-product.

Tapes have no obvious complements in production, but they do have substitutes: prerecorded tapes. An increase in the price of prerecorded tapes will decrease the supply of blank tapes.

Figure 4.4 The Supply Schedule and the Supply Curve

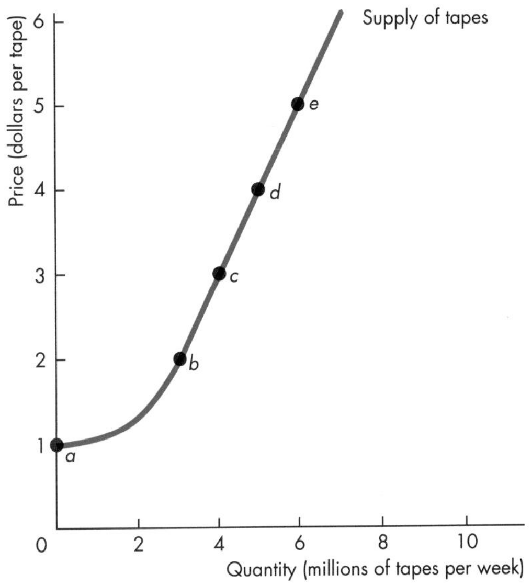

	Price (dollars per tape)	Quantity (millions of tapes per week)
a	1	0
b	2	3
c	3	4
d	4	5
e	5	6

The table shows the supply schedule of tapes. For example, at $2 a tape, 3 million tapes a week are supplied; at $5 a tape, 6 million tapes a week are supplied. The supply curve shows the relationship between the quantity supplied and price, holding everything else constant. The supply curve usually slopes upward: as the price of a good increases, so does the quantity supplied. A supply curve can be read in two ways. For a given price, it tells us the quantity that producers plan to sell. For example, at a price of $3 a tape, producers plan to sell 4 million tapes a week. The supply curve also tells us the minimum acceptable price at which a given quantity will be offered for sale. For example, the minimum acceptable price that will bring forth a supply of 4 million tapes a week is $3 a tape.

2. Prices of Resources The prices of the resources used to produce a good will exert an important influence on its supply. For example, an increase in the prices of the labor and the capital equipment used to produce tapes decreases the supply of tapes.

3. The Number of Suppliers. Other things being equal, the larger the number of firms supplying a good, the larger is the supply of the good.

4. Technology Technology also influences supply. New technologies that enable producers to use fewer resources will lower the cost of production and increase supply. For example, the development of a new technology for tape production by companies such as Sony and Minnesota Mining and Manufacturing (3M) has lowered the cost of producing tapes and increased their supply. A summary of influences on supply and the directions of those influences is presented in Table 4.2.

Table 4.2 The Supply of Tapes

The law of supply

The quantity of tapes supplied

Falls if:	*Rises if:*
• The price of a tape falls	• The price of a tape rises

Changes in supply

The supply of tapes

Falls if:	*Rises if:*
• The price of a substitute in production rises	• The price of a substitute in production falls
• The price of a complement in production falls	• The price of a complement in production rises
• The price of a resource used to produce tapes increases	• The price of a resource used to produce tapes decreases
• The number of firms supplying tapes decreases	• The number of firms supplying tapes increases
	• More efficient technologies for producing tapes are discovered

Movement Along Versus a Shift in the Supply Curve

Changes in the influences on producers cause either a movement along the supply curve or a shift in it.

Movement Along the Supply Curve If the price of a good changes but everything else influencing suppliers' planned sales remains constant, there is a movement along the supply curve. For example, if the price of tapes increases from $3 to $5 a tape, there will be a movement along the supply curve from point *c* (4 million tapes a week) to point *e* (6 million tapes a week).

A Shift in the Supply Curve If the price of a good remains constant but another influence on suppliers' planned sales changes, then there is a change in supply and a shift in the supply curve. For example, as we have already noted, technological advances lower the cost of producing tapes and increase their supply. As a result, the supply schedule changes. The table in Fig. 4.5 provides some hypothetical numbers that illustrate such a change. The table contains two supply schedules: the original, based on "old" technology, and one on "new" technology. With the new technology, more tapes are supplied at each price. The graph in Fig. 4.5 illustrates the resulting shift in the supply curve. When tape-producing technology improves, the supply curve of tapes shifts to the right, as shown by the shift arrow and the red supply curve.

A Change in Supply Versus a Change in Quantity Supplied The quantity supplied at a given price is shown by a point on a supply curve. The entire supply curve shows supply. A **change in supply** occurs whenever there is a shift in the supply curve. A **change in the quantity supplied** occurs when there is a movement along the supply curve.

Figure 4.6 illustrates and summarizes these distinctions. If the price of a good falls but nothing else changes, then there is a decrease in the quantity supplied of that good (a movement down the supply curve S_0). If the price of a good rises but nothing else changes, there is an increase in the quantity supplied (a movement up the supply curve S_0). When any other influence on sellers changes, the supply curve shifts and there is a

Figure 4.5 A Change in the Supply Schedule and a Shift in the Supply Curve

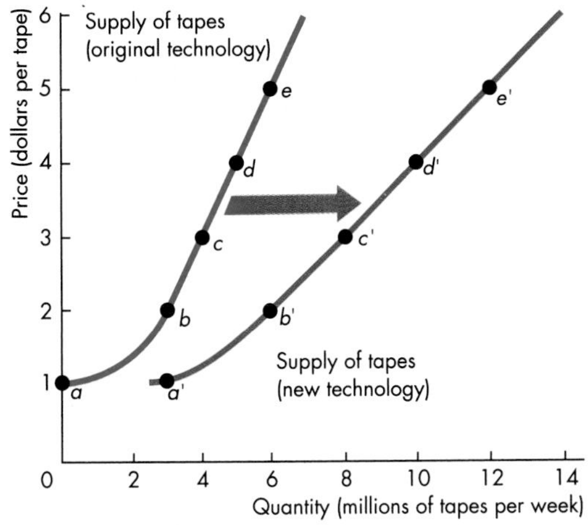

	Original technology			New technology	
	Price (dollars per tape)	Quantity (millions of tapes per week)		Price (dollars per tape)	Quantity (millions of tapes per week)
a	1	0	a'	1	3
b	2	3	b'	2	6
c	3	4	c'	3	8
d	4	5	d'	4	10
e	5	6	e'	5	12

If the price of a good remains constant but another influence on its supply changes, there will be a new supply schedule and the supply curve will shift. For example, if Sony and 3M invent a new, cost-saving technology for producing tapes, the supply schedule changes, as shown in the table. At $3 a tape, producers sell 4 million tapes a week with the old technology and 8 million tapes a week with the new technology. Improved technology increases the supply of tapes and shifts the supply curve of tapes to the right.

Figure 4.6 A Change in Supply Versus a Change in the Quantity Supplied

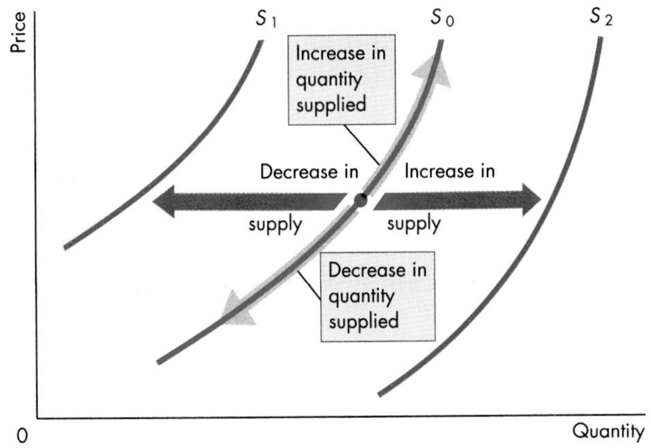

When the price of a good changes, there is a movement along the supply curve and a *change in the quantity of the good supplied*. For example, if the supply curve is S_0, a rise in the price of the good produces an increase in the quantity supplied and a fall in the price produces a decrease in the quantity supplied. The arrows on curve S_0 represent these movements along the supply curve. If some other influence on supply changes, which increases the quantity that producers plan to sell, there is a shift in the supply curve to the right (from S_0 to red S_2) and an *increase in supply*. If some other influence on supply changes, which reduces the quantity that producers plan to sell, there is a shift to the left in the supply curve (from S_0 to red S_1) and a *decrease in supply*.

change in supply. If the supply curve is S_0 and there is, say, a technological change that reduces the amounts of the resources needed to produce the good, then supply increases and the supply curve shifts to S_2. If production costs rise, supply decreases and the supply curve shifts to S_1.

R E V I E W

The quantity supplied is the amount of a good that producers plan to sell in a given period of time. Other things being equal, the quantity supplied of a good increases if its price rises. Supply can be represented by a schedule or a curve that shows the relationship between the quantity supplied of a good and its price. Supply describes the quantity that will be supplied at each possible price or the lowest price at which producers will supply the last unit. Supply increases if the price of a substitute in production falls, if the price of a complement in production rises, if the prices of the resources used to produce the good fall, or when technological advances lower the cost of production. If the price of a good changes but all other influences on producers' plans are held constant, there is a change in the quantity supplied and a movement along the supply curve. A change in any other influence on producers' plans shifts the supply curve. Changes in the prices of substitutes and complements in production, changes in the prices of resources, or improvements in technology shift the supply curve and are said to change supply. ■

Now that we have studied demand and supply, let's bring these two concepts together and see how prices are determined.

Price Determination

We have seen that when the price of a good rises, the quantity demanded decreases and the quantity supplied increases. We are now going to see how adjustments in price achieve an equality between the quantities demanded and supplied.

Price as a Regulator

The price of a good regulates the quantities demanded and supplied. If the price is too high, the quantity supplied exceeds the quantity demanded. If the price is too low, the quantity demanded exceeds the quantity supplied. There is one price, and only one price, at which the quantity demanded equals the quantity supplied. We are going to work out what that price is. We are also going to discover that natural forces operating in a market move the price toward the level that makes the quantity demanded equal the quantity supplied.

The demand schedule shown in the table in Fig. 4.1 and the supply schedule shown in the table in Fig. 4.4 appear together in the table in Fig. 4.7. If the price of a tape is $1, the quantity demanded is 9 million tapes a week but no tapes are supplied. The quantity demanded exceeds the quantity supplied by 9 million tapes a week. In other words, at a price of $1 a tape, there is a shortage of 9 million tapes a week. This shortage is shown in the final column of the table. At a price of $2 a tape, there is still a shortage but only of 3 million tapes a week. If the price of a tape is $5, the quantity supplied exceeds the quantity demanded. The quantity supplied is 6 million tapes a week, but the quantity demanded is only 2 million. There is a surplus of 4 million tapes a week. There is one price and only one price at which there is neither a shortage nor a surplus. That price is $3 a tape. At that price the quantity demanded is equal to the quantity supplied—4 million tapes a week. That quantity is also the quantity traded.

The market for tapes is illustrated in the graph in Fig. 4.7. The graph shows both the demand curve of Fig. 4.1 and the supply curve of Fig. 4.4. The demand curve and the supply curve intersect when the price is $3 a tape, and the quantity traded is 4 million tapes a week. At prices above $3 a tape, the quantity supplied exceeds the quantity demanded and there is a surplus of tapes—shown by the blue area labeled "Surplus" in the figure. At prices below $3 a tape, the quantity demanded exceeds the quantity supplied and there is a shortage of tapes—shown by the red area labeled "Shortage."

Equilibrium

We defined *equilibrium* in Chapter 1 as a situation in which opposing forces exactly balance each other and in which no one is able to make a better choice given the available resources and actions of others. So, in an equilibrium, the price is such that opposing forces exactly balance each other. The **equilibrium price** is the price at which the quantity demanded equals the quantity supplied. To see why this situation is an equilibrium, we

Figure 4.7 Equilibrium

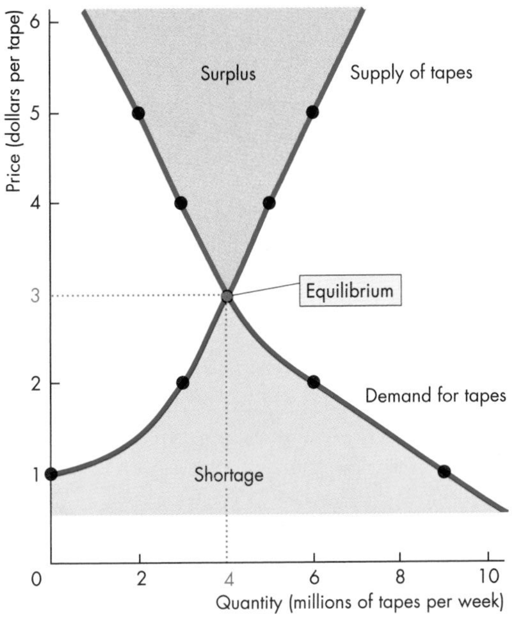

The table lists the quantities demanded and quantities supplied as well as the shortage or surplus of tapes at each price. (Note that the numbers in the final column of the table represent the shortages as negative numbers and the surpluses as positive numbers.) If the price of a tape is $2, 6 million tapes a week are demanded and 3 million are supplied. There is a shortage of 3 million tapes a week and the price rises. If the price of a tape is $4, 3 million tapes a week are demanded but 5 million are supplied. There is a surplus of 2 million tapes a week and the price falls. If the price of a tape is $3, 4 million tapes a week are demanded and 4 million are supplied. There is neither a shortage nor a surplus. Neither buyers nor sellers have any incentive to change the price. The price at which the quantity demanded equals the quantity supplied is the equilibrium price.

Price (dollars per tape)	Quantity demanded (millions of tapes per week)	Quantity supplied (millions of tapes per week)	Shortage (−) or surplus (+) (millions of tapes per week)
1	9	0	−9
2	6	3	−3
3	4	4	0
4	3	5	+2
5	2	6	+4

need to examine the behavior of buyers and sellers a bit more closely. First, let's look at the behavior of buyers.

The Demand Curve and the Willingness to Pay

Suppose the price of a tape is $2. In such a situation, producers plan to sell 3 million tapes a week. Consumers cannot force producers to sell more than they want to sell, so the quantity sold will also be 3 million tapes a week. What is the highest price that buyers are willing to pay for the 3 millionth tape each week? The answer can be found on the demand curve in Fig. 4.7—it is $4 a tape.

If the price remains at $2 a tape, the quantity of tapes demanded is 6 million tapes a week—3 million tapes more than are available. In such a situation, the price of a tape does not remain at $2. Because people want more tapes than are available at that price and because they are willing to pay up to $4 a tape, the price rises. If the quantity supplied stays at 3 million tapes a week, the price rises all the way to $4 a tape.

In fact, the price doesn't have to rise by such a large amount because at higher prices the quantity supplied increases. The price will rise from $2 a tape to $3 a tape. At that price, the quantity supplied is 4 million tapes a week, and $3 a tape is the highest price that consumers are willing to pay. At $3 a tape, buyers are able to make their planned purchases and producers are able to make their planned sales. Therefore no one has an incentive to bid the price higher.

The Supply Curve and the Minimum Supply Price Suppose that the price of a tape is $4. In such a situation, the quantity demanded is 3 million tapes a week. Producers cannot force consumers to buy more than they want, so the quantity bought is 3 million tapes a week. Producers are willing to sell 3 million tapes a week for a price lower than $4 a tape. In fact, you can see on the supply curve in Fig. 4.7 that suppliers are willing to sell the 3 millionth tape each week at a price of $2. At $4 a tape, they would like to sell 5 million tapes each week. Because they want to sell more than 3 million tapes a week at $4 a tape, and because they would be willing to sell the 3 millionth tape for as little as $2, they will continuously undercut each other in order to get a bigger share of the market. They will cut their price all the way to $2 a tape if only 3 million tapes a week can be sold.

In fact, producers don't have to cut their price to $2 a tape because the lower price brings forth an increase in the quantity demanded. When the price falls to $3, the quantity demanded is 4 million tapes a week, which is exactly the quantity that producers want to sell at that price. So, when the price reaches $3 a tape, producers have no incentive to cut the price any further.

The Best Deal Available for Buyers and Sellers Both situations we have just examined result in price changes. In the first case, the price starts out at $2 and is bid upward. In the second case, the price starts out at $4 and producers undercut each other. In both cases, prices change until they hit the price of $3 a tape. At that price, the quantity demanded and the quantity supplied are equal and no one has any incentive to do business at a different price. Consumers are paying the highest acceptable price and producers are selling at the lowest acceptable price.

When people can freely make bids and offers and when they seek to buy at the lowest price and sell at the highest price, the price at which they trade is the equilibrium price—the quantity demanded equals the quantity supplied.

REVIEW

The equilibrium price is the price at which the plans of buyers and sellers match each other—the price at which the quantity demanded equals the quantity supplied. If the price is below equilibrium, the quantity demanded exceeds the quantity supplied, buyers offer higher prices, sellers ask for higher prices, and the price rises. If the price is above equilibrium, the quantity supplied exceeds the quantity demanded, buyers offer lower prices, sellers ask for lower prices, and the price falls. Only when the price is such that the quantity demanded and the quantity supplied are equal are there no forces acting on the price to make it change. Therefore that price is the equilibrium price. At that price, the quantity traded is also equal to the quantity demanded and the quantity supplied. ■

The theory of demand and supply that you have just studied, is now a central part of economics. But that was not always so. Only 100 years ago, the best economists of the day were quite confused about these matters, which today even students in introductory courses find relatively easy to get right (see Our Advancing Knowledge on pp. 84–85).

As you'll discover in the rest of this chapter, the theory of demand and supply enables us to understand and make predictions about changes in prices—including the price slides, rockets, and roller coasters described in the chapter opener.

Predicting Changes in Price and Quantity Traded

The theory we have just studied provides us with a powerful way of analyzing influences on prices and quantities traded. According to the theory, a change in price stems from either a change in demand or a change in supply. Let's look first at the effects of a change in demand.

Figure 4.8 The Effect of a Change in Demand

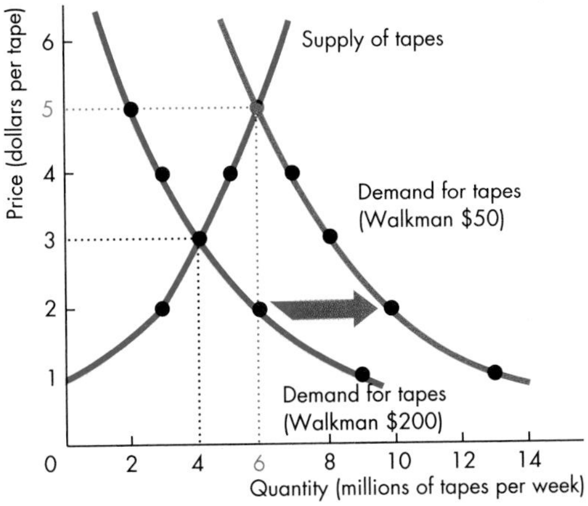

If the price of a Walkman is $200, the quantity of tapes demanded and the quantity traded is 4 million tapes a week at a price of $3 a tape. If the price of a Walkman falls from $200 to $50, the quantity of tapes demanded at a price of $3 is 8 million tapes a week. If the price stays at $3, there is a shortage of 4 million tapes a week. The quantities of tapes demanded and supplied are equal when the price is $5 a tape and the quantity traded is 6 million tapes a week. The increase in demand raises the equilibrium price by $2 and raises the equilibrium quantity traded by 2 million tapes a week.

Price (dollars per tape)	Quantity demanded (millions of tapes per week)		Quantity supplied (millions of tapes per week)
	Walkman $200	Walkman $50	
1	9	13	0
2	6	10	3
3	4	8	4
4	3	7	5
5	2	6	6

A Change in Demand

What happens to the price of tapes and the quantity traded if demand for tapes increases? We can answer this question with a specific example. If the price of a Walkman falls from $200 to $50, the demand for tapes will increase as is shown in the table in Fig. 4.8. The original demand schedule and the new one are set out in the first three columns of the table. The table also shows the supply schedule.

The original equilibrium price was $3 a tape. At that price, 4 million tapes a week were demanded and supplied. When demand increases, the price that makes the quantity demanded equal the quantity supplied is $5 a tape. At this price 6 million tapes are traded each week. When demand increases, the price rises and the quantity traded increases.

We can illustrate these changes in the graph in Fig. 4.8. The graph shows the original demand for and supply of tapes. The original equilibrium price is $3 a tape and the quantity traded is 4 million tapes a week. When demand increases, the demand curve shifts to the right. The equilibrium price rises to $5 a tape and the quantity traded increases to 6 million tapes a week, as is highlighted in the figure.

The exercise that we've just conducted can easily be reversed. If we start at a price of $5 a tape, trading 6 million tapes a week, we can then work out what happens if demand falls back to its original level. You will see that a fall in demand lowers price and decreases the quantity traded.

Discovering the Laws of Demand and Supply

How are the prices of goods and services determined? Why are some vital-to-life resources, such as the air that we breathe and the water that we drink, virtually free while luxurious but inessential commodities such as diamonds are so expensive? For centuries, people have puzzled over these and similar questions. The questions were finally answered when the theories of demand, supply, and equilibrium price, which you have been studying in this chapter, were discovered and refined. But this discovery was not completed until the 1890s.

Let's transport ourselves back in time to the early part of the nineteenth century. We are planning to make a sizable investment in railroads and we are using the prevailing theory of prices to guide our decision. Economists believe that prices are determined by costs of production. So we predict that the price of railroad transportation will stay in line with production costs and that a reasonable rate of return will be made on our investment. As a result, we (and millions of others) invest heavily in this new mode of transportation. Rates of return turn out to be much lower than we predicted. Why? What went wrong? Ignorant of the laws of demand and supply, we failed to realize that a massive increase in the supply of railroad transportation services would drive their prices down and therefore lower the returns on investing in them. Let's look at the main milestones on the road to discovering the theory of demand and supply.

The road begins with the work of Antoine-Augustin Cournot. Cournot (1801–1877) was born near Dijon, France. In 1834, he became professor of mathematics at the University of Lyon. Four years later he published a book entitled *Recherches sur les principes mathématiques de la théorie des richesses* (*The Mathematical Principles of the Theory of Wealth*). In that book Cournot wrote down the law of demand. But he wrote it in abstract mathematical language. Cournot's book was a work of amazing clarity, but, because it used a mathematical language unfamiliar at that time to most students of economics, and because the book was in French, it did not have much influence until many years later.

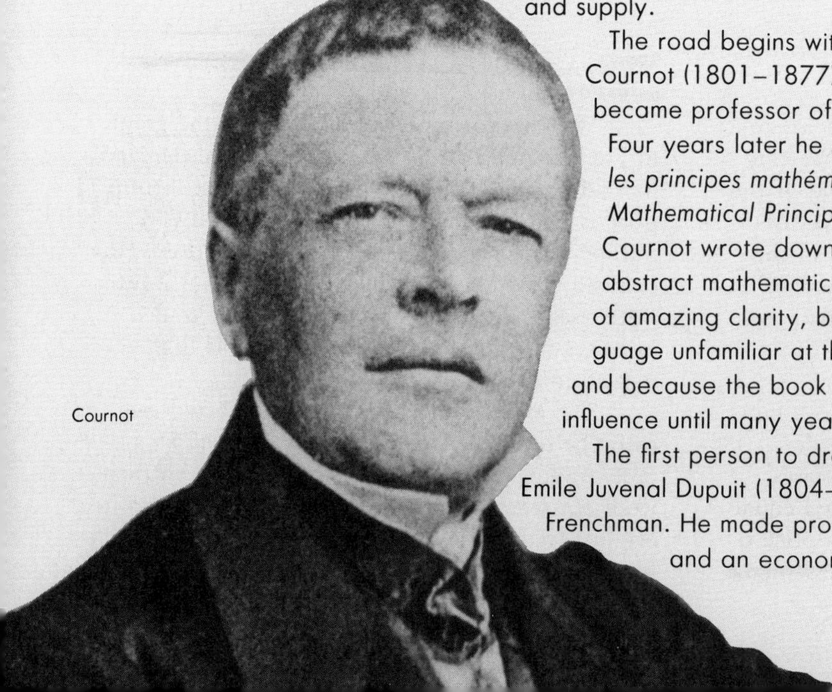

Cournot

The first person to draw a demand curve was Arsène-Jules-Emile Juvenal Dupuit (1804–1866). Like Cournot, Dupuit was a Frenchman. He made profound contributions as both an engineer and an economic theorist. Dupuit's demand curve, which he called "the curve of consumption" (*courbe de consommation*) appeared in 1844.

The law of demand was independently discovered a few years later, and given its first practical application by Dionysius Lardner (1793–1859), an Irishman who was professor of philosophy at the University of London. In his book *Railway Economy*, published in 1850, Lardner drew and used a demand curve for transportation services.

The first person to draw a demand and supply curve together and to use demand and supply theory to determine price was Fleeming Jenkin (1833–1885), an Englishman who was also a professor of philosophy at the University of London. Jenkin's demand and supply curves appeared in a paper entitled "The Graphic Representation of the Laws of Supply and Demand," published in 1870. Jenkin also was the first to use the theories of demand and supply to make predictions about the effects of taxes, in a paper entitled "On the Principles Which Regulate the Incidence of Taxes," published in 1872.

Many others had a hand in the refinement of the theory of demand and supply, but the first thorough and complete statement of the theory, in terms sufficiently modern for it to be recognized as the same theory that you have studied in this chapter, was provided by Alfred Marshall (1842–1924). Marshall was a professor of political economy at the University of Cambridge, and in 1890, he published a monumental treatise—*Principles of Economics*. Marshall's *Principles* was *the* textbook on this subject for almost half a century. In the preface to *Principles*, Marshall acknowledged his own debt to Cournot. He also expressed his view that the theory of demand and supply provides a unifying analysis applicable to all aspects of economics.

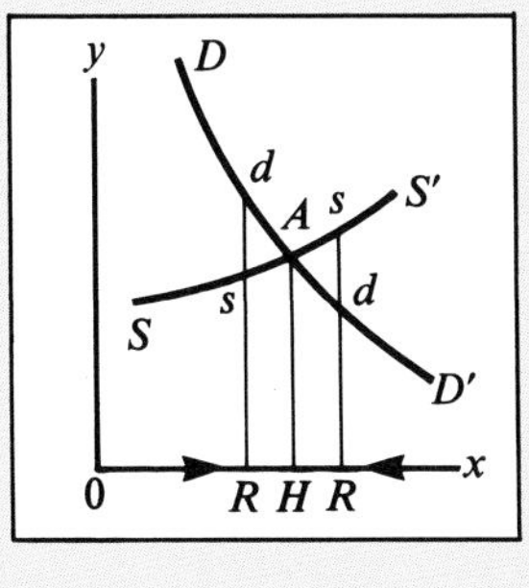

Although Marshall was an outstanding mathematician, he kept mathematics and even diagrams in the background. His own supply and demand diagram and discussion of how the equilibrium price arises appears only in a footnote. It is reproduced here. Although Marshall's diagram is far less striking than those you have been studying, note the strong similarities it has with Fig. 4.7.

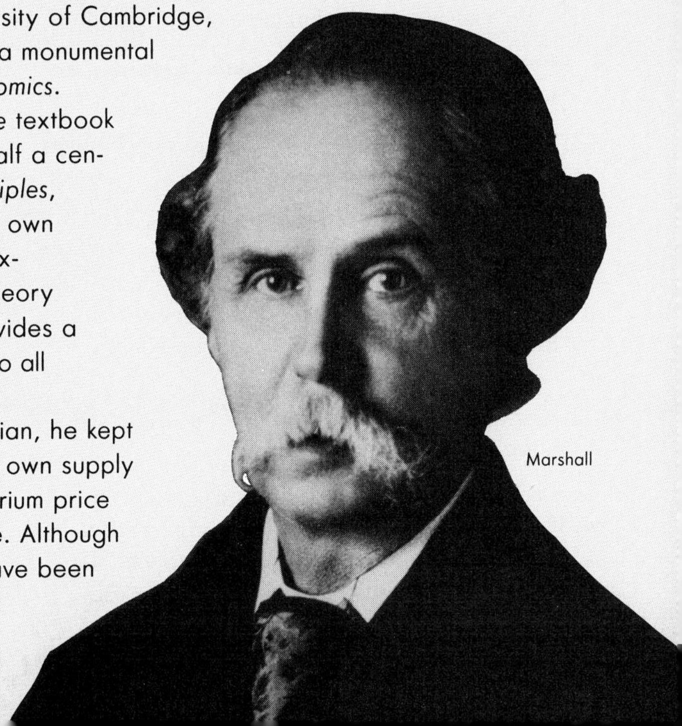

Marshall

Figure 4.9 The Effect of a Change in Supply

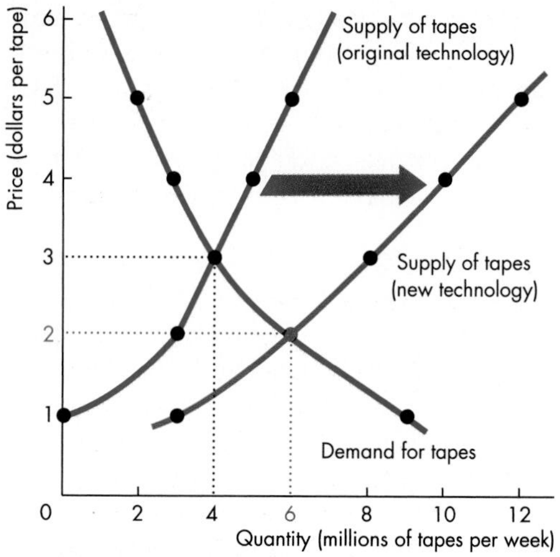

Price (dollars per tape)	Quantity demanded (millions of tapes per week)	Quantity supplied (millions of tapes per week)	
		Original technology	New technology
1	9	0	3
2	6	3	6
3	4	4	8
4	3	5	10
5	2	6	12

When the supply schedule changes as a result of introducing a new technology, the quantity of tapes supplied at $3 a tape exceeds the quantity demanded at that price. The quantity supplied is 8 million tapes at a price of $3. The table shows that the quantity demanded equals the quantity supplied when the price of tapes falls to $2. At this price, 6 million tapes are demanded and supplied each week. The new technology results in a shift in the supply curve to the right. The original technology supply curve intersects the demand curve at a price of $3 and at a quantity traded of 4 million tapes a week. The new technology supply curve intersects the demand curve at a price of $2 and a quantity traded of 6 million tapes a week. The increase in supply lowers the price of tapes by $1 and increases the quantity traded by 2 million tapes a week.

We can now make our first two predictions:

- When demand increases, the price rises and the quantity traded increases.
- When demand decreases, the price falls and the quantity traded decreases.

Reading Between the Lines on pp. 90–91 provides further illustration of demand and supply in action—explaining what happened when a massive but temporary rise in demand for boat rides around Liberty Island occurred on the Fourth of July in 1986.

A Change in Supply

Let's ask what happens if supply changes. Again, we'll start out with a price of $3 a tape and 4 million tapes a week being traded. Suppose that Sony and 3M have just introduced a new cost-saving technology in their tape-production plants. The new technology shifts the supply schedule and the supply curve. The new supply schedule (the same one that was shown in Fig. 4.5) is presented in the table in Fig. 4.9. What is the new equilibrium price and quantity traded? The answer is highlighted in the table: The price falls to $2 a tape and the number of tapes traded rises to 6 million a week. You can see why by looking at the quantities demanded and supplied at the old price of $3 a tape. The quantity supplied at that price is 8 million tapes a week and there is a surplus of tapes. The price falls. Only when the price is $2 a tape is the quantity supplied equal to the quantity demanded.

The graph in Fig. 4.9 illustrates the effect of an increase in supply. The graph shows the demand curve for tapes and the original and new supply curves. The initial equilibrium price is $3 a tape and the original quantity traded is 4 million tapes a week. When the supply increases, the supply curve shifts to the right. The new equilibrium price is $2 a tape and the quantity traded is 6 million tapes a week, highlighted in the figure.

The exercise that we've just conducted can easily be reversed. If we start out at a price of $2 a tape with 6 million tapes a week being traded, we can work out what happens if the supply curve shifts back to its original position. You can see that the fall in supply increases the equilibrium price to $3 a tape and decreases the quantity traded to 4 million tapes a week. Such a fall in supply could arise from an increase in the cost of labor and raw materials. We can now make two more predictions:

- When supply increases, the quantity traded increases and the price falls.
- When supply decreases, the quantity traded decreases and the price rises.

Reading Between the Lines on pp. 92–93 shows the effects of increases in the supply of compact discs and CD players on their prices and quantities traded.

Changes in Both Supply and Demand

In the above exercises, we changed either demand or supply but only one at a time. If we change just one of these, we can predict the direction of change of the price and the quantity traded. If we change both demand and supply, we cannot always say what will happen to both the price and the quantity traded. For example, if both demand and supply increase, we know that the quantity traded increases but we cannot predict whether the price will rise or fall. To make such a prediction, we need to know the relative importance of the increase in demand and supply. If demand increases and supply decreases, we know that the price rises but we cannot predict whether the quantity traded will increase or decrease. Again, to be able to make a prediction about the quantity traded, we need to know the relative magnitudes of the changes in demand and supply.

As an example of a change in both supply and demand, let's take one final look at the market for tapes. We've seen how demand and supply determine the price and quantity of tapes traded; how an increase in demand resulting from a fall in the price of a Walkman both raises the price of tapes and increases the quantity traded; how an increase in the supply of tapes resulting from an improved technology lowers the price of tapes and increases the quantity traded. Let's now examine what happens when both of these changes—a fall in the price of a Walkman (which increases the demand for tapes) and an improved production technology (which increases the supply of tapes)—occur together.

The table in Fig. 4.10 brings together the numbers that describe the original quantities demanded and supplied and the new quantities demanded and supplied after the fall in the price of the Walkman and the improved tape production technology. These same numbers are illustrated in the graph. The original demand and supply curves intersect at a price of $3 a tape and a quantity traded of 4 million tapes a week. The new supply and demand curves also intersect at a price of $3 a tape but at a quantity traded of 8 million tapes a week. In this example, there is an equal increase in both demand and supply. As a result, the rise in price brought about by an increase in demand is offset by the fall in price brought about by an increase in supply—so the price does not change. An increase in either demand or supply increases the quantity traded. Therefore, when both demand and supply increase, so does the quantity traded. Note that if demand had increased slightly more than shown in the figure, the price would have risen. If supply had increased by slightly more than shown in the figure, the price would have fallen. But in both cases the quantity traded would have increased.

Walkmans, Apartments, and Coffee

At the beginning of this chapter, we looked at some facts about prices and quantities traded of Walkmans, apartments, and coffee. Let's use the theory of demand and supply that we have just studied to explain the movements in the prices and the quantities traded of those goods. Figure 4.11 illustrates the analysis.

First, let's consider the Walkman, shown in part (a). In 1980, using the original technology, the supply of Walkmans is described by the supply curve S_0. The 1980 demand curve is D_0. The quantities supplied and demanded in 1980 are equal at

Figure 4.10 The Effect of a Change in Both Demand and Supply

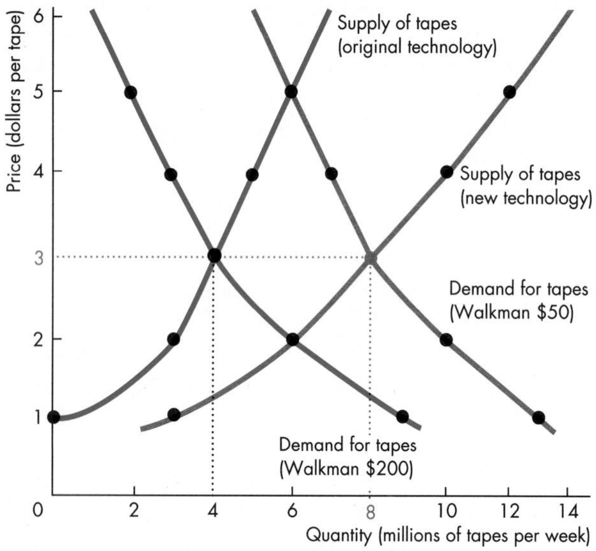

When a Walkman costs $200, the price of a tape is $3 and the quantity traded is 4 million tapes a week. A fall in the price of a Walkman increases the demand for tapes and improved technology increases the supply of tapes. The new technology supply curve intersects the higher demand curve at $3, the same price as before, but at a higher quantity traded of 8 million tapes a week. The simultaneous increase in both demand and supply increases the quantity traded but leaves the price unchanged.

	Original Quantities (millions of tapes per week)		**New Quantities (millions of tapes per week)**	
Price (dollars per tape)	Quantity demanded (Walkman $200)	Quantity supplied (Original technology)	Quantity demanded (Walkman $50)	Quantity supplied (New technology)
1	9	0	13	3
2	6	3	10	6
3	4	4	8	8
4	3	5	7	10
5	2	6	6	12

Q_0 and the price is P_0. Advances in technology and the building of additional production plants increase supply and shift the supply curve from S_0 to S_1. At the same time, increasing incomes increase the demand for Walkmans but not by nearly as much as the increase in supply. The demand curve shifts from D_0 to D_1. With the new demand curve D_1 and supply curve S_1, the equilibrium price is P_1 and the quantity traded is Q_1. The large increase in supply combined with a smaller increase in demand results in an increase in the quantity of Walkmans traded and a dramatic fall in their price.

Next, let's consider apartments in the center of the city, as in part (b). The supply of apartments is described by supply curve S. The supply curve is steep, reflecting the fact that there is a fixed amount of land and a fixed number of apartment buildings. As the number of young urban professionals increases and the number of two-income families increases, the demand for urban apartments increases sharply. The demand curve shifts from D_0 to D_1. As a result, the price increases from P_0 to P_1 and the quantity traded also increases but not as dramatically as price.

Figure 4.11 More Changes in Supply and Demand

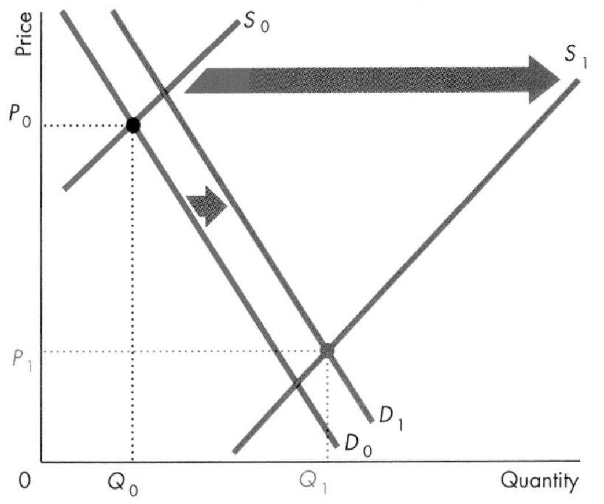

(a) Walkmans

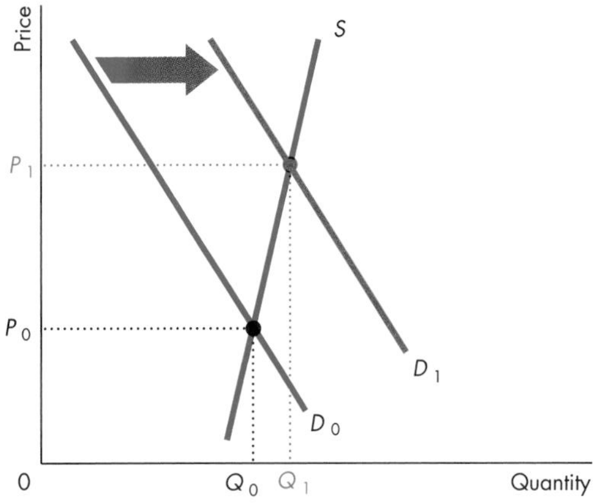

(b) Apartments

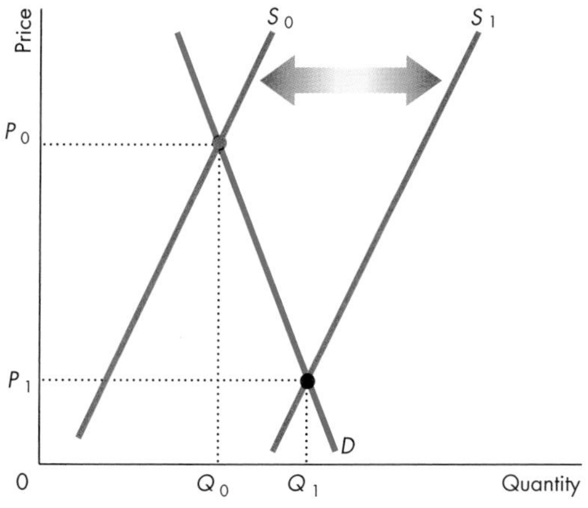

(c) Coffee

A large increase in the supply of Walkmans, from S_0 to S_1, combined with a small increase in demand, from D_0 to D_1, results in a fall in the price of the Walkman, from P_0 to P_1, and an increase in the quantity traded, from Q_0 to Q_1 (part a). An increase in the demand for apartments produces a large increase in the price, from P_0 to P_1, but only a small increase in the quantity traded, from Q_0 to Q_1 (part b). Variations in the weather and in growing conditions lead to fluctuations in the supply of coffee, between S_0 and S_1, which produce fluctuations in the price of coffee, between P_0 and P_1, and in the quantity traded, between Q_0 and Q_1 (part c).

Finally, let's consider the market for coffee, shown in part (c). The demand for coffee is described by curve *D*. The supply of coffee fluctuates between S_0 and S_1. When growing conditions are good, the supply curve is S_1. When there are adverse growing conditions such as frost, the supply decreases and the supply curve is S_0. As a consequence of fluctuations in supply, the price of coffee fluctuates between P_0 (the maximum price) and P_1 (the minimum price). The quantity traded fluctuates between Q_0 and Q_1.

■ By using the theory of demand and supply, you will be able to explain past fluctuations in prices and quantities traded and make predictions about future fluctuations. But you will want to do more than predict whether prices are going to rise or fall. In your study of microeconomics, you will learn to predict *by how much* they will change. In your study of macroeconomics, you will learn to explain fluctuations in the economy as a whole. In fact, the theory of demand and supply can help answer almost every economic question.

Demand and Supply in Action: A Temporary Increase in Demand

Planning Early for the 4th of July

Let others grouse about Christmas coming so early in the year. New Yorkers are frantically making plans for the Fourth of July.

The city's chronic scramble for space—space to walk, space to dine, space to rent—focuses now on finding a spot to view the historic, histrionic relighting of the Statue of Liberty on July 4 and related extravaganzas, Frank Sinatra and an armada of tall ships among them.

Some hotels and restaurants are already booked. Rudy Montgomery has been offered $3,600—three times his monthly rent—to sublet his modest Brooklyn Heights apartment, a short walk from the Promenade and a view of the statue, for the four-day holiday weekend.

Boats that normally charge $25 to $50 per person for trips around the harbor have raised their fees to $1,000 per person or more. Neiman Marcus has made a Fourth of July harbor excursion one of its extravagant Christmas catalogue items. And the scramble for a place at the bar at Windows On The World has begun. . . .

One of the unanswered questions is: Is there enough water in the harbor? The Coast Guard estimates that there will be at least 25,000 private pleasure boats in the harbor to observe the flotilla and fireworks. "You will be able to walk across the hulls," said one boater. "It will be a bumper-boat situation."

"Everything that floats is being rented," said Bill Sills, another boater. "Some of the boats ain't much more than a piece of driftwood."

Marilyn Vogel, commodore of the Sebago Canoe Club of Brooklyn, said that a boat at the 79th Street Marina that doesn't even run was rented for the holiday weekend for $7,000.

She said the canoe club receives requests to rent canoes for that weekend, and that the club is considering becoming part of the festivities. "It would be their last outing . . . gridlock on the waters."

"The only thing they forgot," said Mr. O'Keefe [owner of the River Cafe] is that there is nowhere to embark and disembark. You figure 1,000 yachts minimum and maybe, just maybe, Manhattan's three marinas can service 15 extra boats, so what do the other 985 do?"

"This will be 10 times the colossal jam caused by the boats at the Brooklyn Bridge celebration," he said. "That was a New York party. This is national and international. I get five calls a day from Florida, Texas, the Carribean and everywhere to tie up at our restaurant." "You will see launch services springing up to take people out to the boats," he said.

Captain Parker [of The Ethel] is leasing some dock space for $2,500 for the weekend and plans to rent it out at high rates: about $3,000 for a single 100-foot boat to pick up passengers. He will hire security guards to make sure only customers use the space. "Boats will be landing wherever they can," he said. "This will look like Dunkirk."

The New York Times, November 6, 1985

by William E. Geist

The Essence of the Story

- A unique and massive spectacular was held in the waters surrounding Liberty Island, on the weekend of the Fourth of July in 1986. The refurbished Statue of Liberty was illuminated amidst fireworks, tall ships, and "related extravaganzas."

- The demand for space to view these events was extraordinarily high. Boats, restaurants, and any places with a view of the Liberty celebrations were demanded on a scale much larger than the demand for those same facilities on an ordinary day.

- The prices increased astronomically and the quantities available increased (to the point of total congestion).

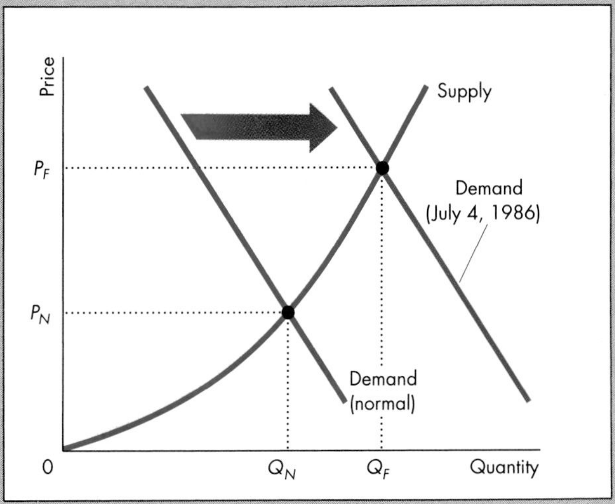

Background and Analysis

The events of this weekend illustrate the effects of a large temporary increase in the demand for boat rides. The figure on the left shows what happened.

- The demand curve for boat rides and places with a view of the Liberty celebrations shifted to the right.

- The quantity of boat rides and viewing places supplied increased but could not do so without limit.

- The increase in demand produced a large price rise (to P_F) but only a small increase in the quantity of boat rides and viewing places traded (to Q_F).

After the Fourth of July weekend, demand returned to its normal level and so did the price and the quantity traded—to P_N and Q_N.

Demand and Supply in Action: An Increase in Supply

A Compact Sonic Boom

Listen to this: *Bam.* Sssh, now wait for this: *Tinkle.* And get a load of what's next: *Twang.* Whether they're playing thundering Tchaikovsky, delicate Debussy or stand-on-your-feet Springsteen, music fans love what they get from their new compact-disc systems—and that enthusiasm is producing a resounding result for the home-electronics industry: *Boom.*

Compact-disc players and recordings only hit the market in early 1983, but the takeoff has been astonishing. . . . This year [1985] retail sales are expected to total a hefty $500 million—2½ times 1984 sales—and they may double in 1986 to $1 billion. Leslie Rosen, executive director of the Compact Disc Group, a trade association, claims compact-disc products are the fastest-selling consumer electronics merchandise ever. "It took VCR's seven years to get to the point where we got in just two years," she says.

The big beneficiaries of the surge are Philips of Holland and Japan's Sony, which copioneered the CD system, and other Japanese companies such as Matsushita and Hitachi that already dominate other areas of the American consumer-electronics market. For the industry, the disc boom came just in time. Sales of recorded music and stereo equipment were stagnating in 1983. The fast growth of prerecorded cassettes eased some of the pain, but other innovations like quadrophonic sound and eight-track tapes had failed to help. At first, manufacturers were nervous about the prospect for CD products. With players typically priced at $1000 and discs selling for more than $20, sales did begin as a trickle. As in the case of VCR's, it took a price break to open the floodgates. Today the average player sells for about $225, discs go for $11 and up, and customers are grabbing everything in sight.

Happily for consumers, they don't have to choose between competing CD technologies as they do with VCR's. That's because the manufacturers banded together in the Compact Disc Group at the outset to settle on a single standard. . . .

One thing the trade group couldn't do was put an end to disc and player shortages. There are only 10 major disc-making plants in the world—only one in the United States—and they typically have back orders of 18 months. Some relief is in sight. The one American plant, in Terre Haute, Ind., has been expanded. CBS, which is selling its interest in the Indiana plant to its partner, Sony, says it may build another facility of its own. And Philips and Du Pont plan a joint plant in North Carolina.

The first buyers of CD players tended to be classical-music buffs, and now almost all new classical recordings come in disc form. Pop music on CDs got off to a slower start—partly because the multitrack recording process favored by pop artists is more complicated. But increasingly, the list of best-selling CDs mimics that of top-selling LPs and tapes. Record companies are also reissuing old favorites in digital versions—but the supply of oldies is limited by the availability of good master recordings. . . .

Given the voracious appetites of CD fans, disc supplies may continue to be tight for some time. A few nervous companies like Motown and Warner Brothers, however, fear that sales growth may taper off to more reasonable levels and some retail inventories may begin to pile up next year. It seems more likely that . . . when off-brand manufacturers from South Korea and elsewhere begin to flood the market, . . . player prices may dip as low as $99, against today's low-ball price of $140.

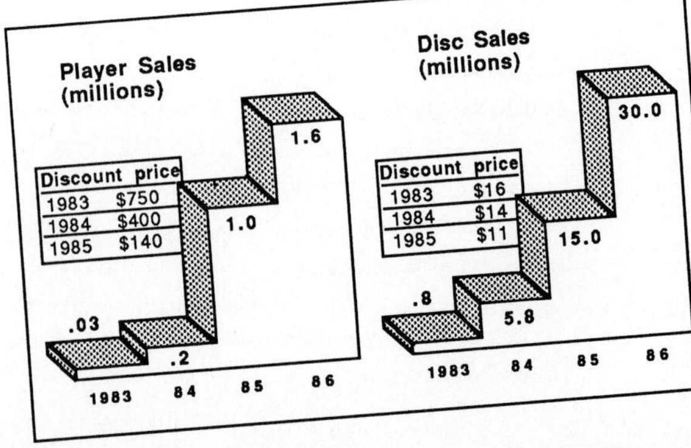

NEWSWEEK, December 16, 1985

David Pauly with Penelope Wang in New York, Patricia King in Chicago, and bureau reports.

The Essence of the Story

- Compact disc players and recordings were first offered for general sale in 1983. Players were priced at more than \$1000 and discs at more than \$20. Sales were low.
- Even in 1983, prices began to fall, and the discount prices were \$750 for CD players and \$16 for discs.
- Prices continued to fall rapidly and by 1985 CD players averaged \$225 and sold at discount for \$140. Disc prices fell to \$11. Sales grew quickly.
- Large increases in the supply of players (especially from Korea) are expected, so prices are expected to fall still further, to less than \$100.

Background and Analysis

- The quantity of CD players demanded depends on the price of CD players. In 1983, the demand for CD players was D_{83} (Fig. a).
- The quantity of discs demanded depends on the price of discs. In 1983, the demand for discs was D_{83} (Fig. b).
- In 1983, the supply of both players and discs was low (S_{83} in Figs. a and b).
- In 1983 the demand and supply curves for players intersected at a price of \$750 and at a quantity traded of 30,000 players (Fig. a). The demand and supply curves for discs intersected at a price of \$16 and at a quantity traded of 800,000 discs (Fig. b).
- After 1983, the supply of both players and discs increased. The supply curves for 1986 (consistent with the predictions in the story) are those marked S_{86}.
- Compact disc players and discs are complements. The lower the price of a player, the greater is the demand for discs; the lower the price of discs, the greater is the demand for players. All CD players use a single technology standard (unlike VCRs, which use two technologies —VHS and Beta). This single standard reinforces the complementarity between players and discs.
- In Fig. a, the lower prices of discs shifted the demand for players from D_{83} to D_{86} for 1986. In Fig. b, lower prices of players shifted the demand for discs from D_{83} to D_{86} for 1986.
- In Fig. a, the price of players in 1986 is predicted to be \$100 and the quantity traded 1.6 million players.
- In Fig. b, the price of a disc in 1986 is predicted to be \$11 and the quantity traded 30 million discs. (The story does not predict the price of discs in 1986, but if the supply of discs increases more than the increase in demand, the price will fall.)

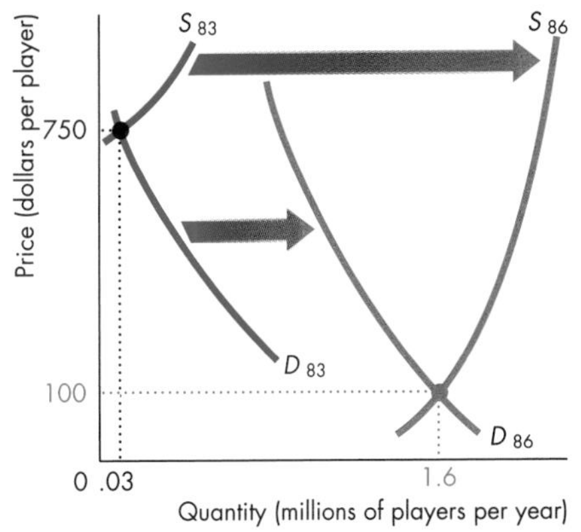

(a) Players

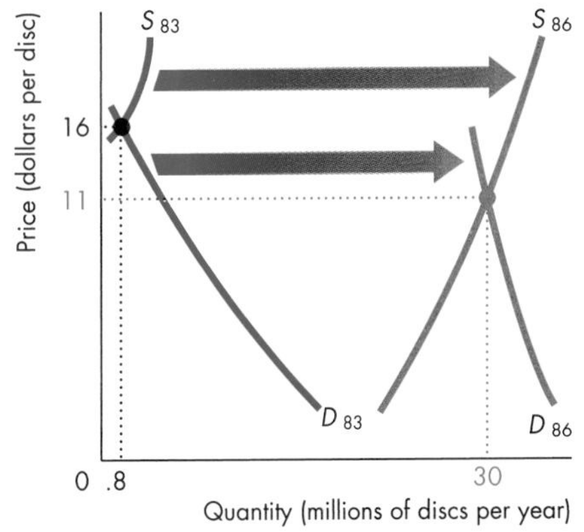

(b) Discs

SUMMARY

Demand

The quantity demanded of a good or service is the amount that consumers plan to buy in a given period of time. Demands are different from wants. Wants are unlimited, whereas demands reflect decisions to satisfy specific wants. The quantity that consumers plan to buy of any good depends on:

- The price of the good
- The prices of other goods—substitutes and complements
- Income
- Population
- Tastes

The demand schedule lists the quantities that will be demanded at each price, holding constant all other influences on consumers' planned purchases.

A demand curve graphs the quantity demanded at each price, holding everything else constant. A change in the price of a good produces a movement along the demand curve for that good. Such a movement is called a change in the quantity demanded. Changes in things other than the price of a good shift the demand curve. Such changes are said to change demand. (pp. 71–76)

Supply

The quantity supplied of a good or service is the amount that producers plan to sell in a given period of time. The quantity that producers plan to sell of any good or service depends on:

- The price of the good
- The prices of other goods
- The prices of the resources used to produce the good
- The number of suppliers
- Technology

The supply schedule lists the quantities that will be supplied at each price, holding constant all other influences on producers' planned sales. The supply curve graphs that relationship. Changes in the price of the good produce movements along the supply curve of that good. Such movements are called changes in the quantity supplied. Changes in variables other than the price shift the supply curve. Such shifts are called changes in supply. (pp. 76–80)

Price Determination

Price regulates the quantities supplied and demanded. The higher the price, the greater is the quantity supplied and the smaller is the quantity demanded. At high prices, there is a surplus—an excess of the quantity supplied over the quantity demanded. At low prices, there is a shortage—an excess of the quantity demanded over the quantity supplied. There is one price and only one price at which the quantity demanded equals the quantity supplied. That price is the equilibrium price. At that price, buyers have no incentive to offer a higher price and suppliers have no incentive to sell at a lower price. (pp. 80–82)

Predicting Changes in Price and Quantity Traded

Changes in demand and supply lead to changes in price and in the quantity traded. An increase in demand leads to a rise in the price and to an increase in the quantity traded. A decrease in demand leads to a fall in price and to a decrease in the quantity traded. An increase in supply leads to an increase in the quantity traded and to a fall in price. A decrease in supply leads to a decrease in the quantity traded and a rise in price. (pp. 82–89)

KEY CONCEPTS

Key Figures and Tables

REVIEW QUESTIONS

1 Define the quantity demanded of a good or service.

2 Define the quantity supplied of a good or service.

3 Define the quantity traded and distinguish between the quantities demanded, supplied, and traded.

4 What determines the quantity demanded of a good? List the more important factors and say whether an increase in the factor increases or decreases the amount that consumers plan to buy.

5 What determines the quantity supplied? List the more important factors and say whether an increase in that factor increases or decreases the quantity that firms plan to sell.

6 State the law of demand and the law of supply.

7 The demand curve shows the quantity of a good demanded at each price. If a fixed amount of the good is available, what does the demand curve tell us about the price that consumers are willing to pay for that fixed quantity?

8 The supply curve shows the quantity supplied at each price. If consumers are only willing to buy a certain fixed quantity, what does the supply curve tell us about the price at which firms will supply that quantity?

9 Distinguish between:

a) A change in demand and a change in the quantity demanded

b) A change in supply and a change in the quantity supplied

10 Why is the price at which the quantity demanded equals the quantity supplied the equilibrium price?

11 What happens to the price and the quantity traded of a good if:

a) Demand increases

b) Supply increases

c) Both demand and supply increase

d) Demand decreases

e) Supply decreases

f) Both demand and supply decrease

PROBLEMS

Suppose that one of the following events occur:

a) The price of gasoline rises.
b) The price of gasoline falls.
c) All speed limits on highways are abolished.
d) A new fuel-effective engine that runs on cheap alcohol is invented.
e) The population doubles.
f) Robotic production plants lower the cost of producing cars.
g) A law banning car imports from Japan is passed.
h) The rates for auto insurance double.
i) The interstate highway system is greatly improved.
j) The minimum age for drivers is increased to 19 years.
k) A massive and high-grade oil supply is discovered in Mexico.
l) The environmental lobby succeeds in closing down all nuclear power stations.
m) The price of cars rises.
n) The price of cars falls.
o) The summer temperature is ten degrees higher than normal and the winter temperature is ten degrees lower than normal.
p) GM stops making cars.

State which of the preceding events will:

1 Increase the quantity of gasoline demanded.
2 Decrease the quantity of gasoline demanded.
3 Increase the quantity of cars demanded.
4 Decrease the quantity of cars demanded.
5 Increase the quantity of gasoline supplied.
6 Decrease the quantity of gasoline supplied.
7 Increase the quantity of cars supplied.
8 Decrease the quantity of cars supplied.
9 Increase the demand for gasoline.
10 Decrease the demand for gasoline.
11 Increase the demand for cars.
12 Decrease the demand for cars.
13 Increase the supply of gasoline.
14 Decrease the supply of gasoline.
15 Increase the supply of cars.
16 Decrease the supply of cars.
17 Increase the price of gasoline.
18 Decrease the price of gasoline.
19 Increase the price of cars.
20 Decrease the price of cars.
21 Increase the quantity of gasoline purchased.
22 Decrease the quantity of gasoline purchased.
23 Increase the quantity of cars purchased.
24 Decrease the quantity of cars purchased.

Part 2 How Markets Work

Talking with Milton Friedman

Milton Friedman spent most of his career at the University of Chicago, where he was one of the most forceful exponents of the Chicago view of economics. Currently a senior fellow at the Hoover Institution at Stanford University, he has made contributions to the theories of consumption, money, the functioning of markets, and comparative economic systems, and to the methods of scientific inquiry in economics. In 1977, Dr. Friedman was awarded the Nobel Prize in economic science.

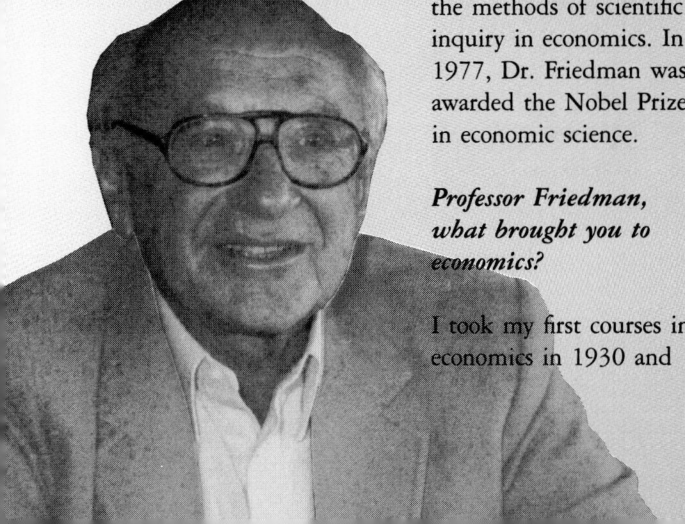

Professor Friedman, what brought you to economics?

I took my first courses in economics in 1930 and 1931, during the depths of the Depression. The choice for me was very easy, since the Depression was clearly the single most important issue facing the world.

What was your college experience in economics like?

I was lucky enough to study with two people who had a great influence on me: Homer Jones, a student of Frank Knight's, and Arthur Burns, later chairman of the Fed. I took a seminar with Burns that was devoted entirely to poring over his Ph.D. thesis on U.S. production trends, sentence by sentence. It was probably the best research training I ever got!

"It always comes down to trying to understand the forces of demand and supply."

Your lifetime contributions have spanned an enormous breadth. What is the unifying theme in all your work?

Most important is taking economics seriously. There are two ways to look at economics, I believe. One is to regard it as a game, a mathematical recreation judged by its elegance. Some of that is very impressive intellectually and contributes to our understanding of the world. The other approach descends from Alfred Marshall and his idea that economics is an engine for analyzing concrete problems. That's how I

approach economics. In practice, it always comes down to trying to understand the forces of demand and supply, based on the idea of using scarce resources to achieve alternative goals. There is no major economic problem that ultimately does not reduce to this.

Can you give some examples that illustrate how economic problems of all sorts reduce to demand and supply?

When people decide what fraction of their income to consume, it's clear that they have scarce resources that they'd like to apply to alternative ends. In the realm of macroeconomics, when you're deciding how to conduct monetary policy, the paper on which currency is printed may be, in effect, unlimited, but the resources that they command are scarce. You have to decide how they should be applied. It's the same

approach that Gary Becker originally used, in his dissertation, to study racial discrimination. People have scarce resources and can use them to discriminate against people. That's one goal—you may not like it, but that's a different question. So finally, my approach includes the belief that economics is capable in principle of being value-free. It's a technique of analysis, not a begging of the question of what's good or bad.

Your approach includes a methodology that some people have criticized—that you say that assumptions don't matter. Is this fair?

What I've said is that the crucial test of any hypothesis is found in its predictions, not in its assumptions. I'll give you an analogy from outside economics. I hypothesize, for example, that if I drop a ball from a building, it will hit the ground in an amount of time given by a certain formula. The formula only gives an accurate answer in a perfect vacuum. So am I actually assuming that there's a vacuum all around me as I drop the ball from the rooftop? No, of course not. I know there isn't a vacuum. But it doesn't make any difference. How do I know? There's only one way to tell. I predict that the ball will hit the ground in so much time. You tell me what range of error you'll permit. Then we drop the ball. If it

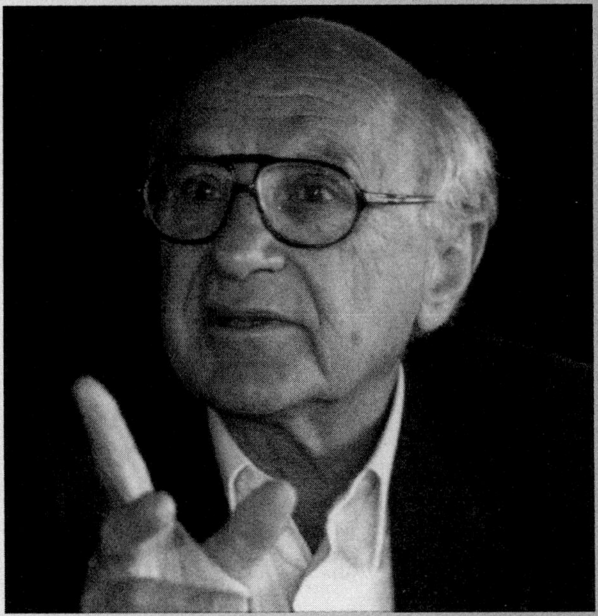

hits the ground within the range you set, then I'm getting correct results by *assuming* that there is a vacuum.

Another use of assumptions is to let them stand in for a body of complex propositions.

For example, I can predict the density of distribution of leaves on a tree by supposing that the leaves deliberately position themselves to get maximum sunlight. Now that gives me good predictions, but I obviously don't really believe that the leaves do this. In economics, we say that people in business behave as if they know what their production functions are. It's just a shorthand—a good one if it works.

By the way, the article in which I made these comments about assumptions has given rise to more comments and attacks than any other I've written. I never replied to any of them, because I decided that I'd rather spend my time doing economics than

talking about how economics should be done.

"The crucial test of any hypothesis is in its predictions, not its assumptions."

You've studied the effectiveness of markets. What do we know about how markets work?

I always say that economists may not know much, but we know one thing very well, and that's how to create shortages and surpluses. Just tell us which you want! If you want a shortage, all we have to do is to set a price that's below the market price and I'll guarantee you a shortage. If you want a surplus, set a price too high and you'll have your surplus.

The contrast between the taxicab markets in New York and Washington, D.C., is a good example with many implications. In Washington, because government officials, who control the city, want cheap taxicab rides, entry into the taxicab industry is virtually free. Prices are fixed, but also elastic and responsive to change. In New York, however, there is essentially a taxicab cartel, a limit on the number of taxicab medallions. A breakdown of the market. Therefore, these licenses have a very high value—somewhere over a hundred thousand dollars. One consequence is that it's often difficult to find a cab in New York, while there are almost always cabs available in Washington. But the most important effect, in my mind, is that the fraction of black and Latin cab drivers and owners is high in Washington but very low in New York. That's because many members of minority groups can't afford to break into the business. And that's a tragedy.

"What's true for the individual is the opposite of what's true for the society."

What have been the most important developments in economics of the past 20 years?

Let's divide that question into developments in the theoretical discipline and in the world of economics. In the discipline, I'd say the rational expectations revolution, the public choice approach, and the revival of money as an important factor in macroeconomics. In the world of economics, there's no doubt that the most important change is the complete loss of faith in socialism. The triumph of capitalism over socialism as an ideology, though not as an actual practice. In fact, there's been very little change in practice, but there's been the enormous change that practically nobody believes that a centrally planned economy is the right way to get prosperity. Twenty years ago that wasn't true.

What advice would you share with a student studying economics for the first time?

Try to get a feel for the central principles of demand and supply, for how these two forces are reconciled with each other. Work to understand the function of prices and the price system. Don't worry about all the intricate details of the banking system or the institutions you're familiar with now. I'd also propose the statement that it's generally correct that what's true for the individual is the opposite of what's true for the society. Find out why that's so.

Chapter 5

Elasticity

After studying this chapter, you will be able to:

- Define and calculate the price elasticity of demand
- Explain what determines the elasticity of demand
- Distinguish between short-run demand and long-run demand
- Use elasticity to determine whether a price change will increase or decrease revenue
- Define and calculate other elasticities of demand and supply
- Distinguish between momentary supply, long-run supply, and short-run supply

OPEC's Dilemma

If the supply of a good falls, its price rises. But by how much? To answer this question, you will have to don a flowing caftan: You have just been named chief economic strategist for OPEC—the Organization of Petroleum Exporting Countries. You want to bring more money into OPEC. Would you restrict the supply of oil to raise prices? Or would you produce more oil? ■ You know that a higher price will bring in more dollars per barrel, but lower production means that fewer barrels will be sold. Will the price rise high enough to offset the smaller quantity that OPEC will sell? ■ As OPEC's economic strategist, you need to know about the demand for oil in great detail. For example, as the world economy grows, how will that growth translate into an increasing demand for oil? What about substitutes for oil? Will we discover inexpensive methods to convert coal and tar sands into usable fuel? Will nuclear energy become safe and cheap enough to compete with oil?

■ In this chapter, you will learn how to tackle questions such as the ones just posed. You will learn how we can measure in a precise way the responsiveness of the quantities bought and sold to changes in prices and other influences on buyers or sellers.

Price Elasticity of Demand

Let's begin by looking a bit more closely at your task as OPEC's economic strategist. You are trying to decide whether to advise a cut in output to shift the supply curve and raise the price of oil. To make this decision, you need to know how the quantity of oil demanded responds to a change in price. You also need some way to measure that response.

Two Possible Scenarios

To understand the importance of the responsiveness of the quantity of oil demanded to a change in its price, let's compare two possible (hypothetical) scenarios in the oil industry, shown in Fig. 5.1. In the two parts of the figure, the supply curves are identical, but the demand curves differ.

Focus first on the supply curve labeled S_0 in each part of the figure. This curve represents the initial supply. Notice that S_0 cuts the demand curve, in both cases, at a price of \$10 a barrel and a quantity traded of 40 million barrels a day.

Now suppose that you contemplate a cut in supply that shifts the supply curve from S_0 to S_1. In part (a), the new supply curve S_1 cuts the demand curve D_a at a price of \$30 a barrel and a quantity traded of 23 million barrels a day. In part (b), the same shift in the supply curve results in the new supply curve cutting the demand curve D_b at a price of \$15 a barrel and a quantity traded of 15 million barrels a day.

Figure 5.1 Demand, Supply, and Revenue

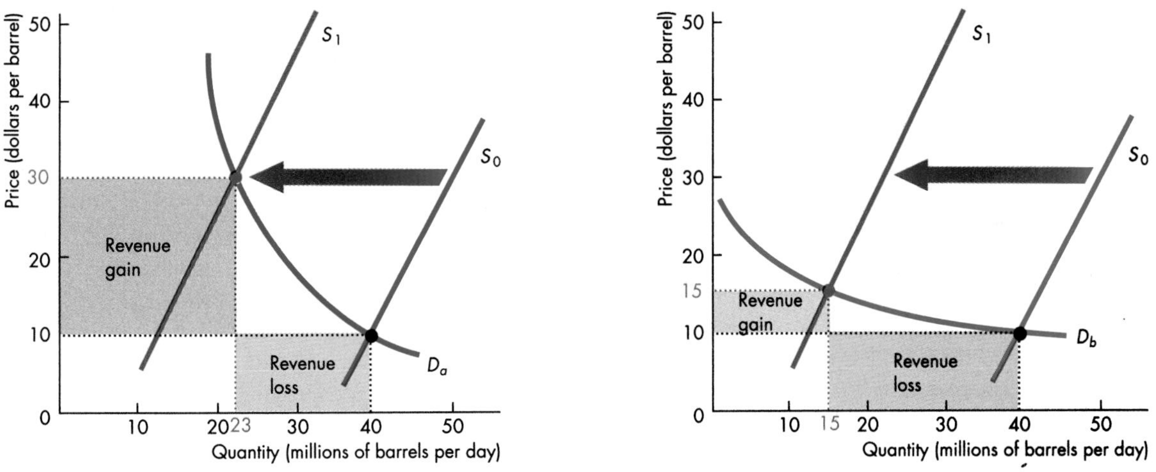

(a) More revenue **(b) Less revenue**

If supply is cut from S_0 to S_1, the price rises and the quantity traded falls. In part (a), revenue—quantity multiplied by price—rises from \$400 million to \$690 million a day (the increase in revenue from a higher price—blue area—exceeds the decrease in revenue from lower sales—red area). In part (b), revenue falls from \$400 million to \$225 million a day (the increase in revenue from a higher price—blue area—is smaller than the decrease in revenue from lower sales—red area). These two different responses in revenue arise from different responses of the quantity demanded to a change in price. In the figure, revenue increases when the demand curve is steep; it falls when the demand curve is flat. To compare the responsiveness of two demand curves, we must draw them on the same scale. Changing the scale or the units of measurement will change the slope of the demand curve, thus creating the illusion of a different degree of responsiveness.

You can see that in part (a) the price rises by more and the quantity traded falls by less than it does in part (b). What happens to the revenue of the oil producers in these two cases? The **revenue** from the sale of a good equals the price of the good multiplied by the quantity sold.

An increase in price has two opposing effects on revenue. The higher price brings in more revenue on each unit sold (blue area) and the higher price leads to a decrease in the quantity sold, which in turn results in less revenue (red area). In case (a) the first effect is larger (blue area exceeds red area), so revenue rises. In case (b) the second effect is larger (red area exceeds blue area), so revenue falls.

You can confirm these results by doing some multiplication. In both cases, the original revenue was $400 million a day ($10 a barrel multiplied by 40 million barrels a day). What happens to the revenue after the supply is reduced? In part (a), revenue goes up to $690 million a day ($30 a barrel multiplied by 23 million barrels a day). In part (b), revenue falls to $225 million a day ($15 a barrel multiplied by 15 million barrels a day).

Slope Depends on Units of Measurement

What differs in these two cases is how the quantity demanded responds to a change in the price of oil. Demand curve D_a is much steeper than demand curve D_b. For the same cut in supply, the steeper demand curve causes a higher price rise and a smaller drop in the quantity traded. The steepness of the demand curve is one way of measuring how the quantity demanded of a good is affected by its price. A steep demand curve means that the quantity demanded does not respond much to price changes. A relatively flat demand curve means that the quantity demanded will change greatly with price changes.

But the slope of a demand curve depends on the units that we put on the axes of the diagram. In Fig. 5.1, we use the same units in both parts so that we can compare the demand curves D_a and D_b. However, we could easily make the demand curve D_b look as steep as D_a by changing the units on the axes of the figure. If, in part (b), we measured quantity in hundreds of millions of barrels a day, the demand curve D_b would be almost vertical. It would "look" much steeper than demand curve D_a, but the appearance would be an illusion. If, again in part (b), we measured the price in cents per barrel, the demand curve D_b would appear as a much steeper curve than D_a. Again, the appearance would be an illusion.

Since we can influence the slope of a demand curve purely by our choice of the units in which we measure prices and quantities, we cannot hope to find a rule that tells us how revenue responds to a price change that is based on the slope of the demand curve. What we need is a measure of response that is independent of our units of measurement of prices and quantities. Elasticity is such a measure.

A Units-Free Measure of Response

Price elasticity of demand measures the responsiveness of the quantity demanded of a good to a change in its price. It measures responsiveness by calculating the percentage change in the quantity demanded divided by the percentage change in its price.

Price elasticity of demand is represented by the Greek letter *eta* (η). We use the following formula to calculate the price elasticity of demand:

$$\eta = \frac{\text{Percentage change in quantity demanded}}{\text{Percentage change in price}}$$

When the price of a good rises, the quantity demanded falls. If the percentage change in price is positive, the percentage change in quantity demanded will be negative. As a consequence, the price elasticity of demand will be a negative number. Because the price elasticity of demand is always negative, we adopt the convention of dropping the minus sign and speaking only of the magnitude of the elasticity. Also, for simplicity (provided no ambiguity will result), we often drop the word *price* and simply refer to the elasticity of demand. Whenever we use the term **elasticity of demand,** we mean *price* elasticity of demand. Let's practice using the formula for the elasticity of demand.

Calculating Elasticity

In order to calculate an elasticity, we need to know the quantities demanded at different prices. We also need some reasonable assurance that when the price changes, nothing else that influences consumers' buying plans changes. As an example, let's assume we have the relevant data on prices and quantities de-

Table 5.1 Calculating the Price Elasticity of Demand

	Numbers	Symbols and Formulas*
Prices (dollars per barrel)		
Original price	\$ 9.50	P_0
New price	\$10.50	P_1
Change in price	\$ 1.00	$\Delta P = P_1 - P_0$
Average price	\$10.00	$P = (P_0 + P_1)/2$
Percentage change in price	10%	$(\Delta P/P) \times 100$
Quantities (millions of barrels per day)		
Original quantity demanded	41	Q_0
New quantity demanded	39	Q_1
Change in quantity demanded	2	$\Delta Q = Q_0 - Q_1$
Average quantity demanded	40	$Q = (Q_0 + Q_1)/2$
Percentage change in quantity demanded	5%	$(\Delta Q/Q) \times 100$
Price elasticity of demand	0.5	$\eta = (\Delta Q/Q)/(\Delta P/P)$

*The Greek letter *delta*, (Δ), stands for "change in."

manded for the oil industry. The calculations that we will perform are summarized in Table 5.1. You can use the symbols and the formulas shown in the final column of the table to perform the same calculations on any set of numbers.

At \$9.50 a barrel, 41 million barrels a day are sold. As the price increases to \$10.50 a barrel, the quantity demanded falls to 39 million barrels a day. When the price rises by \$1 a barrel, the quantity demanded falls by 2 million barrels a day. To calculate the elasticity of demand, we have to express changes in price and quantity demanded as percentage changes. But there are two prices and two quantities—the original and the new. Which price and which quantity do we use for calculating the percentage change? By convention, we use the *average* price and the *average* quantity. The formula for calculating a percentage change (in either the price or the quantity) is:

$$\text{Percentage change} = \frac{\text{Change in value}}{\text{Average value}} \times 100$$

Let's use this formula to calculate the percentage changes in price and quantity. The original price was \$9.50 and the new price is \$10.50, so the average price is \$10. When the price rises by \$1, it changes one tenth, or 10 percent, of the average price. The original quantity was 41 million barrels and the new quantity is 39 million barrels, so the average quantity demanded is 40 million barrels. When the quantity falls by 2 million barrels a day, it changes by one twentieth, or 5 percent, of the average quantity.

Remember, price elasticity of demand (η) is the ratio of the percentage change in the quantity demanded to the percentage change in the price. That is,

$$\eta = \frac{\Delta Q/Q}{\Delta P/P} = \frac{5\%}{10\%} = 0.5$$

Notice three things about the calculation of the price elasticity of demand:

1 The change in price and the change in the quantity demanded are both recorded as positive numbers. It is true that as the price increases, the quantity demanded decreases. Usually, a rise in something is called a positive change and a fall in something is a negative change. Since the quantity demanded *always* falls when the price rises (other things being equal), there is no need to attach a negative sign. The elasticity, a positive number, tells us the responsiveness of a quantity *fall* to a price *rise* or of a quantity *rise* to a price *fall.*

2 The changes in prices and quantities demanded are expressed as percentages of the *average* price and *average* quantity demanded. We do this to avoid the awkwardness of having two values for the elasticity, depending on whether we move from the original price to the new price or from the new price back to the original price. The price and quantity demanded change by the same amount in each case—in our example, \$1 a barrel and 2 million barrels a day. But whereas \$1 is 10.5 percent of \$9.50, it is only 9.5 percent of \$10.50. Furthermore, 2 million barrels a day is 4.9 percent of 41 million barrels but 5.1 percent of 39 million barrels. If we use these numbers to calculate the elasticity, we get a value of 0.54 for a price rise from \$9.50 to \$10.50 and 0.47 for a price cut from \$10.50 to \$9.50. By using the average price and quantity demanded, we calculate an elasticity that is the same, 0.5, regardless of whether the price rises or falls.

3 Although it is convenient to think of elasticity as the ratio of the *percentage* change in the quantity demanded to the *percentage* change in the price, it is also, equivalently, the *proportionate* change in the quantity demanded divided by the *proportionate* change in the price. In Table 5.1, notice that although the formula multiplies both the change in price and the change in quantity demanded by 100, to create a percentage, those hundreds cancel when we divide.

R E V I E W

Elasticity is a units-free measure of response. The price elasticity of demand—or simply, the elasticity of demand—is calculated as the percentage change in the quantity demanded divided by the percentage change in price. ■

Elastic and Inelastic Demand

The elasticity that we have just calculated in our example is 0.5. Is that a large or a small value for an elasticity? The size of the elasticity of demand can range between zero and infinity. The elasticity of demand would be zero if the quantity demanded did not change when the price changed. You can see that by assuming that the percentage change in the quantity demanded is zero and then doing a little calculation. It doesn't matter what the percentage change in the price is because if we divide zero by any positive number, we get zero. An example of a good that has a very low elasticity of demand (perhaps zero) is insulin. This commodity is of such importance to many diabetics that they would buy the quantity they need for their health at almost any price.

If a price rise causes a fall in the quantity demanded, the elasticity is greater than zero. When the percentage change in the quantity demanded is less than the percentage change in price, the elasticity is a fraction (the example that we calculated in Table 5.1 is such a case).

If the percentage change in the quantity demanded exactly equals the percentage change in price, then the elasticity of demand is 1. If the percentage change in the quantity demanded exceeds the percentage change in price, then the elasticity is greater than 1.

In an extreme case, the quantity demanded may be infinitely sensitive to price changes. At a particular price, people demand any quantity of a good, but if the price rises by one cent, then the quantity demanded will drop to zero. In this case, an almost zero percentage change in the price produces an infinite percentage change in the quantity demanded, so the elasticity of demand is infinity. An example of a good whose elasticity is infinite is Schweppes soda. If the price of Schweppes soda increased, while all other prices, including the pric-

Table 5.2 Elastic and Inelastic Demand (effects of a 10% price change)

	Original quantity demanded	New quantity demanded	Change in quantity demanded	Average quantity demanded	Percentage change in quantity demanded	Elasticity of demand
Inelastic	41	39	2	40	5	0.5
Unit elastic	42	38	4	40	10	1.0
Elastic	50	30	20	40	50	5.0

es of competing sodas, remained constant, there would be an indefinitely large decrease in the quantity of Schweppes soda consumed. Other sodas are almost perfect substitutes for Schweppes soda.

For elasticities between zero and 1, demand is called **inelastic.** When the elasticity is greater than 1, demand is said to be **elastic.** The dividing line between inelastic and elastic demand is called **unit elastic demand.** When elasticity is equal to infinity, demand is sometimes called **perfectly elastic;** when elasticity is equal to zero, demand is called **perfectly inelastic.**

Table 5.2 shows examples of inelastic, elastic, and unit elastic demands. We can see in this table the changes in quantities demanded for a 10 percent change in price. The first row simply reproduces the calculations that you worked through in Table 5.1. The second row shows the case of a unit elastic demand. The initial quantity demanded was 42 million barrels a day and the new quantity demanded is 38. Thus the average quantity demanded is 40 and the change in the quantity demanded is 4. The percentage change in the quantity demanded is 10 percent—the same as the percentage change in price. Therefore the elasticity is 1. The final case is one where the original quantity demanded was 50 but the new quantity demanded is 30. The average quantity demanded is still 40 but the change in quantity demanded is now 20, which is 50 percent. In this case, the elasticity is 50 percent divided by 10 percent, which is 5.

Elasticity is not just a number calculated by economists. Whether demand is elastic or inelastic is of enormous importance to each of us on an individual level. In the 1970s, when OPEC did in fact cut back on the supply of oil, Americans discovered that their demand for oil was inelastic. Despite the lower supplies, we still demanded a lot of oil and gasoline, which led to cuts in spending on other things—people took fewer vacations; vast companies were thrown into a panic as they tried to adjust; schools had to cut the salaries of teachers so that they could pay for heating oil; speed restrictions were imposed and angry car owners had to face the premature obsolescence of their gas guzzlers.

Elasticity and the Slope of the Demand Curve

Elasticity is not the same as slope, but the two are related. However, that connection is not entirely straightforward. To understand the relation better, we'll consider the elasticity along a demand curve that has a constant slope. Such a demand curve is a straight line.

Let's calculate the elasticity of the straight-line demand curve shown in Fig. 5.2. To do so, we first pick an initial price and quantity demanded. Next, we change the price and observe the change in the quantity demanded. Finally, we combine the information on prices and quantities to calculate elasticity by using the formula (summarized in Table 5.1, page 105):

$$\eta = (\Delta Q/Q)/(\Delta P/P)$$

Let's start with a price of $50 a barrel. What is the elasticity if we lower the price from $50 to $40? The change in the price is $10 and the

Figure 5.2 Elasticity Along a Straight-Line Demand Curve

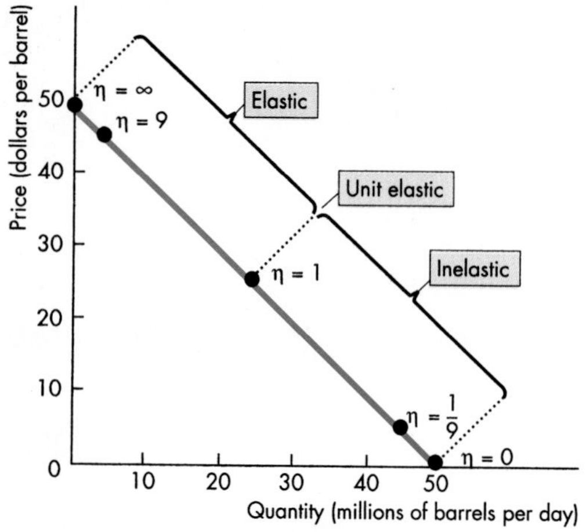

On a straight-line demand curve, elasticity falls as the price falls and the quantity demanded rises. Demand is unit elastic at the midpoint of the demand curve (elasticity is 1). Above the midpoint, demand is elastic (elasticity is greater than 1); below the midpoint, demand is inelastic (elasticity is less than 1).

average price is $45 (average of $50 and $40), which means that the proportionate change in price is:

$$\Delta P/P = 10/45$$

The original quantity demanded was zero and the new quantity demanded is 10 million barrels a day, so the change in the quantity demanded is 10 million barrels a day and the average quantity is 5 million barrels a day (the average of 10 million and zero). We can use these numbers to calculate the proportionate change in the quantity demanded as:

$$\Delta Q/Q = 10/5$$

To calculate the elasticity of demand, we divide the proportionate change in the quantity demanded by the proportionate change in the price. That is:

$$\eta = (\Delta Q/Q)/(\Delta P/P) = (10/5)/(10/45) = 9$$

Using this same formula, we can calculate the elasticity of demand when the price of a barrel is cut repeatedly by $10—from $45 to $35, from $40 to $30, from $35 to $25, and so on. You can verify the elasticity of demand at each point on the demand curve in Fig. 5.2. Notice that on a straight-line demand curve, the elasticity falls as the price falls.

Figure 5.3 Demand Curves with Constant Elasticity

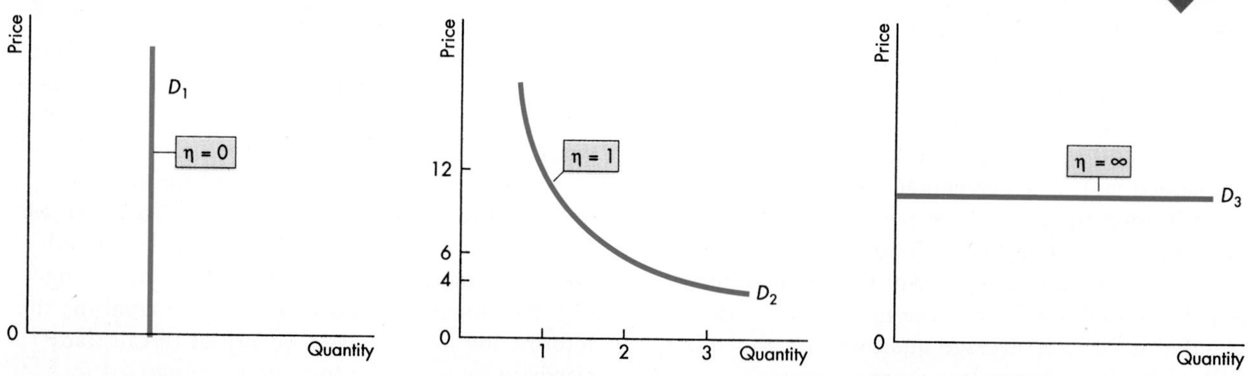

(a) Zero elasticity **(b) Unit elasticity** **(c) Infinite elasticity**

Each demand curve shown here has a constant elasticity. The demand curve in part (a) has zero elasticity. The demand curve in part (b) has unit elasticity. The demand curve in part (c) has infinite elasticity.

At the midpoint of the demand curve, where the price is $25 a barrel and the quantity demanded is 25 million barrels a day, elasticity is exactly 1. Above the midpoint, the elasticity is bigger than 1 and it rises as the price rises. Below the midpoint, the elasticity is less than 1 and it falls as the price falls.

Elasticity is infinity when the price is $50 a barrel and the quantity demanded is zero, and elasticity is zero when the quantity demanded is 50 million barrels a day and the price is zero. By using the formula for elasticity, you will be able to verify these calculations.

A demand curve can have a constant elasticity. A perfectly inelastic demand curve has a constant elasticity of zero ($\eta = 0$) and is vertical. A perfectly elastic demand curve has a constant elasticity of infinity ($\eta = \infty$) and is horizontal. Other constant elasticity demand curves are *curved*. Figure 5.3 illustrates three constant elasticity demand curves—the cases of zero, unity, and infinity.

The example we gave earlier, of a good with very low elasticity of demand (shown as zero in part a of the figure) is insulin. Regardless of the price, the quantity demanded remains constant in part (a). An example of a good whose elasticity is close to 1 (part b) is electricity. As its price increases, the quantity demanded decreases by the same percentage amount. The example we gave of a good whose elasticity is infinite (part c) is Schweppes soda. Schweppes is bought only if its price equals that of identical competing sodas. If the price of Schweppes exceeds the price of competing sodas, the quantity of Schweppes demanded is zero. If the price of competing soda exceeds that of Schweppes, Schweppes is the only soda bought. When the prices are equal, there is no unique quantity demanded.

Actual Elasticities Actual values of elasticities of demand have been estimated from the average spending patterns of consumers and some examples are set out in Table 5.3.

Table 5.3 Some Price Elasticities in the U.S. Economy

Industry	Elasticity
Elastic demands	
Metals	1.52
Electrical engineering products	1.39
Mechanical engineering products	1.30
Furniture	1.26
Motor vehicles	1.14
Instrument engineering products	1.10
Professional services	1.09
Transportation services	1.03
Inelastic demands	
Gas, electricity, and water	0.92
Oil	0.91
Chemicals	0.89
Beverages (all types)	0.78
Tobacco	0.61
Food	0.58
Banking and insurance services	0.56
Housing services	0.55
Clothing	0.49
Agricultural and fish products	0.42
Books, magazines, and newspapers	0.34
Coal	0.32

Source: Ahsan Mansur and John Whalley, "Numerical Specification of Applied General Equilibrium Models: Estimation, Calibration, and Data," in *Applied General Equilibrium Analysis*, eds. H.E. Scarf and J.B. Shoven (New York: Cambridge University Press, 1984), 109.

The Size of the Elasticity of Demand

What makes the demand for some goods elastic and the demand for others inelastic? Elasticity depends on:

- The ease with which one good can be substituted for another
- The proportion of income spent on the good
- The amount of time elapsed since the price change

Substitutability Substitutability depends on the nature of the good itself. For example, oil, a good with an inelastic demand, certainly has substitutes but none that are very close (imagine a steam-driven, coal-fueled car or a nuclear-powered jetliner). On the other hand, metals, a group of goods with elastic demands, have very good substitutes in the form of plastics.

The degree of substitutability between two goods depends on how narrowly (or broadly) we define them. For example, even though oil does not have a close substitute, different types of oil substitute for each other without much difficulty. Oils from different parts of the world differ in weight and chemical composition. Let's consider a particular kind of oil—called Saudi Arabian Light. Its elasticity will be relevant if you happen to be the economic advisor to Saudi Arabia (as well as the OPEC economic strategist!). Suppose Saudi Arabia is contemplating a unilateral price rise, which means that prices of other types of oil will stay the same. Although Saudi Arabian Light has some unique characteristics, other oils can easily substitute for it, and most buyers will be very sensitive to its price relative to the prices of other types of oil. Demand in this case is highly elastic.

This example, which distinguishes between oil in general and different types of oil, has broad applications. For example, the elasticity of demand for meat in general is low while the elasticity of demand for beef, lamb, or pork is high. The elasticity of demand for personal computers is low, but the elasticity of demand for an IBM, Zenith, or Apple is high.

Proportion of Income Spent on a Good Other things being equal, the higher the elasticity, the higher is the proportion of income spent on a good. If only a small fraction of income is spent on a good, then a change in its price will have little impact on the consumer's overall budget. In contrast, even a small rise in the price of a good that commands a large part of a consumer's budget will induce the consumer to undertake a radical reappraisal of expenditures.

To appreciate the importance of the proportion of income spent on a good, consider your own elasticity of demand for textbooks and chewing gum. If the price of textbooks doubled (increased 100 percent) there would be an enormous fall in the quantity of textbooks bought. There would be an increase in sharing and in illegal photocopying. If the price of chewing gum doubled, also a 100 percent increase, there would be almost no change in the quantity of gum demanded. Why the difference? Textbooks take a large proportion of your budget while gum takes only a tiny portion. You don't like either price increase, but you hardly notice the effects of the increased price of gum, while the increased price of textbooks blows you away!

Time Elasticity also depends on the amount of time elapsed since a price change. In general, the greater the lapse of time, the higher the elasticity of demand. The reason is related to substitutability. The greater the passage of time, the more it becomes possible to develop substitutes for a good whose price has increased. Thus at the moment of a price increase, the consumer often has little choice but to continue consuming similar quantities of a good. However, given enough time, the consumer finds alternatives or cheaper substitutes and gradually lowers the rate of purchase of items that have become more expensive.

R E V I E W

The elasticity of demand ranges between zero and infinity. Goods that have a high elasticity of demand are those that have close substitutes and on which a large proportion of income is spent. Goods that have a low elasticity of demand are those that do not have good substitutes and on which a small portion of income is spent. Elasticity also is higher, the longer the time lapse since a price change. ■

Two Time-Frames for Demand

To take account of the importance of time on the elasticity of demand, we distinguish between two time-frames for demand—the short run and the long run. Let's examine them now.

Short-run Demand

The **short-run demand curve** describes the initial response of buyers to a change in the price of a good. The short-run response depends on whether the price change is seen as permanent (or, at least, long-lasting) or temporary. A price change that is believed to be temporary produces a highly elastic buyer response. Why would you pay a higher price now if you can get the same thing for a lower price a few days from now? And if the price is temporarily low, why wouldn't you take advantage of it and buy a lot before the price goes up again?

Examples of temporary price changes abound. For example, you can make telephone calls at much lower rates on weekends than during the week. The drop in price on Saturday and the rise in price on Monday produces a large change in the quantity demanded—demand is highly elastic. Of course, many calls are made during normal business hours, but the lower price on the weekend induces a large switch from business day calling to weekend calling. Other examples are seasonal variations in the price of travel and of certain fresh fruits and vegetables.

When a price change seems permanent, the quantity bought does not change much in the short run. That is, short-run demand is inelastic. The reason is that people find it hard to change their buying habits. More importantly, they often have to adjust their consumption of other complementary goods, an expensive and time-consuming undertaking.

An example of a permanent, or at least a long-lasting, price change occurred in the market for oil in the early 1970s. At the end of 1973 and the beginning of 1974, the price of oil increased fourfold, leading in turn to a sharp rise in the costs of home heating and of gasoline. Initially, consumers had little choice but to accept the price increases and maintain consumption at more or less their original levels. Home heating equipment and cars may not have been the most energy-efficient, but there was nothing else available. Drivers could lower their average speed and economize on gasoline. Thermostats could be turned down but that too imposed costs—costs of discomfort. As a consequence, there were severe limits in the extent to which people felt it worthwhile cutting back on their consumption of the now much more costly fuel, oil, and gasoline. The short-run buyer response in the face of this sharp price increase was inelastic.

Long-run Demand

The **long-run demand curve** describes the response of buyers to a change in price after all possible adjustments have been made. Long-run demand is more elastic than short-run demand. The 1974 rise in the price of oil and gasoline produced a clear demonstration of the distinction between long-run and short-run demand. Initially, buyers responded to higher gasoline and oil prices by using their existing capital equipment—furnaces and gas guzzlers—in a way that economized on the more expensive fuel. With a longer time to respond, people bought more energy-efficient capital equipment. Cars became smaller and more fuel-efficient, car engines also became more efficient.

Figure 5.4 Short-run and Long-run Demand

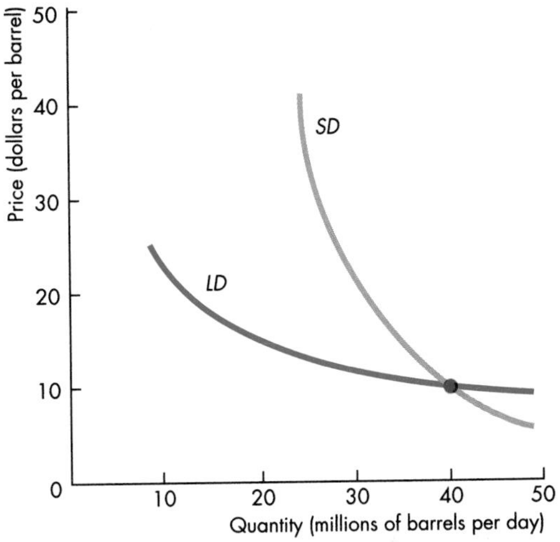

The light blue short-run demand curve (*SD*) shows the initial response of the quantity demanded to a change in the price of a good, before buyers have had sufficient time to make all possible adjustments. The dark blue long-run demand curve (*LD*) shows how the quantity demanded varies with the price of a good when buyers have made all possible adjustments to their buying plans.

Two Demand Curves

The short-run and long-run demand curves for oil in 1974 appear in Fig. 5.4. The light blue short-run demand curve (*SD*) shows the initial response of the quantity demanded to a permanent change in price. The dark blue long-run demand curve (*LD*) shows the change in the quantity demanded after buyers have made all possible adjustments.

The price of a barrel of oil in 1974 was $10 and the quantity of oil traded in that year was 40 million barrels a day. The two demand curves have been drawn to intersect at that price and quantity. At that point of intersection, the long-run demand curve is more elastic than the short-run demand curve.

In Chapter 6, we'll use the short-run and long-run demand curves to work out what happens in a market when supply changes.

Elasticity, Revenue, and Expenditure

We've defined *revenue* as the price of a good multiplied by the quantity sold. **Expenditure** is the price of a good multiplied by the quantity *bought*. Thus revenue and expenditure are two sides of the same coin—revenue is the receipts of the sellers while expenditure is the outlays of the buyers. When the price of a good rises, the quantity sold falls. What happens to revenue (and expenditure) depends on the extent to which the quantity sold falls as the price rises. If a 1 percent rise in the price reduces the quantity sold by less than 1 percent, revenue increases. If a 1 percent rise in price lowers the quantity sold by more than 1 percent, revenue falls. If a 1 percent rise in price lowers the quantity sold by 1 percent, the price rise and the quantity fall just offset each other and revenue stays constant. But we now have a precise way of linking the percent change of the quantity sold to the percent change in price—the elasticity of demand. When the price of a good rises, the size of the elasticity of demand determines whether revenue rises or falls. Table 5.4 provides some examples based on the three cases in Table 5.2.

In case *a,* the elasticity of demand is 0.5. When the price goes up from $9.50 to $10.50, the quantity sold falls from 41 million to 39 million barrels a day. Revenue, which is equal to price multiplied by quantity sold, was originally $9.50 multiplied by 41 million, which is $389.50 million a day. After the price rises, revenue rises to $409.50 million a day. Thus a rise in the price leads to a *rise* in revenue of $20 million a day.

In case *b,* the elasticity of demand is 1. The quantity sold falls from 42 million to 38 million barrels a day as the price rises from $9.50 to $10.50. Revenue in this case is the same at each price, $399 million a day. Thus when the price changes and the elasticity of demand is 1, revenue *does not change.*

In case *c,* the elasticity of demand is 5. When the price rises by $1, the quantity sold falls by 20 million barrels a day. The original revenue was $475 million a day but the new revenue is $315 million a day. Thus in this case, a rise in the price leads to a *fall* in revenue of $160 million a day.

Elasticity and revenue are closely connected. When the elasticity of demand is greater than 1, the percentage fall in the quantity demanded exceeds the percentage rise in price and therefore revenue falls. When the elasticity of demand is less

Table 5.4 Elasticity of Demand, Revenue, and Expenditure

	Elasticity	Price (dollars per barrel)		Quantity demanded (millions of barrels per day)		Revenue/Expenditure (millions of dollars per day)		
		Original	New	Original	New	Original	New	Change
a	0.5	9.50	10.50	41	39	389.50	409.50	+ 20.00
b	1.0	9.50	10.50	42	38	399.00	399.00	0
c	5.0	9.50	10.50	50	30	475.00	315.00	−160.00

Figure 5.5 Income Elasticity of Demand

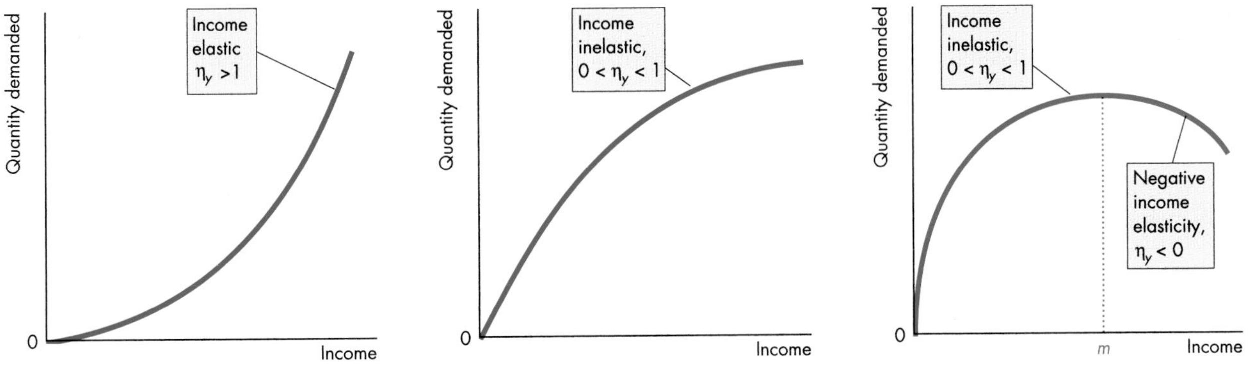

(a) Elasticity greater than 1

(b) Elasticity between zero and 1

(c) Elasticity less than 1 and becomes negative

There are three ranges of values for income elasticity of demand. In part (a), income elasticity of demand is greater than 1. In this case, as income increases, the quantity demanded increases but by a bigger percentage than the increase in income. In part (b), income elasticity of demand is between zero and 1. In this case, as income increases, the quantity demanded increases but by a smaller percentage than the increase in income. In part (c), the income elasticity of demand is positive at low incomes but becomes negative as income rises above the level *m*. Maximum consumption occurs at the income *m*.

than 1, the percentage fall in the quantity demanded is less than the percentage rise in price and therefore revenue rises. When the elasticity of demand is 1, the percentage fall in the quantity demanded equals the percentage rise in price and revenue remains constant. Extra revenue from a higher price is exactly offset by the loss in revenue from the smaller quantities sold.

As we have seen, long-run demand curves are more elastic than short-run demand curves. It is possible, therefore, that an increase in price will result in an increase in revenue in the short run but not in the long run. If the short-run elasticity is less than 1 but the long-run elasticity is greater than 1, this outcome will occur.

The price elasticity of demand that you have just learned to calculate and interpret is the most important of all the elasticities. Whenever economists refer to the elasticity of demand without qualification, they mean the price elasticity of demand. There are, however, some other elasticities of demand. Let's now turn our attention to them.

More Demand Elasticities

The quantity demanded of any good (or service or factor of production) is influenced by many things other than its price. It depends on, among other things, incomes and the prices of other goods. We can calculate elasticities of demand with respect to these other variables as well. Let's now examine some of these additional elasticities.

Income Elasticity of Demand

As income grows, how will the demand for a particular good change? The answer depends on the income elasticity of demand for the good. The **income elasticity of demand** is the percentage change in the quantity demanded divided by the percentage change in income. It is represented by η_y.

Table 5.5 Some Income Elasticities of Demand

Elastic	
Airline travel	5.82
Movies	3.41
Foreign travel	3.08
Drugs and medicines	3.04
Housing services	2.45
Toys	2.01
Electricity	1.94
Intercity buses	1.89
Stationery	1.83
Restaurant meals	1.61
Books and maps	1.42
Local buses and trains	1.38
Gasoline and oil	1.36
Haircutting	1.36
Car insurance	1.26
Household appliances	1.18
Taxicabs	1.15
Physicians' services	1.15
Cars	1.07
Unit Elasticity	
Dentists' services	1.00
Inelastic	
Shoes and other footwear	0.94
Car repairs	0.90
Tobacco	0.86
China, glassware, and utensils	0.77
Shoe repairs	0.72
Alcoholic beverages	0.62
Water	0.59
Furniture	0.53
Clothing	0.51
Newspapers and magazines	0.38
Telephone	0.32

Source: H.S. Houthakker and Lester D. Taylor, *Consumer Demand in the United States* (Cambridge, Mass.: Harvard University Press, 1970).

That is:

$$\eta_y = \frac{\text{Percentage change in quantity demanded}}{\text{Percentage change in income}}$$

Income elasticities of demand can be positive or negative; however, there are three interesting ranges for the income elasticity of demand:

- Greater than 1 (income elastic)
- Between zero and 1 (income inelastic)
- Less than zero (negative income elasticity)

These three cases are illustrated in Figure 5.5. Part (a) shows an income elasticity of demand that is greater than 1. As income rises, the quantity demanded rises, but the quantity demanded rises faster than income. The curve slopes upward and has an increasing slope. Goods that fall into this category include ocean cruises, custom clothing, international travel, jewelry, and works of art.

Part (b) shows an income elasticity of demand that is between zero and 1. In this case, the quantity demanded rises as income rises, but income rises faster than the quantity demanded. The curve slopes upward but the slope declines as income rises. Goods that fall into this category include basic food, clothing, housing, and local bus transportation.

Part (c) illustrates a third category of goods that is a bit more complicated. For these goods, as income rises, the quantity demanded increases until it reaches a maximum at income *m*. Beyond that point, as income continues to rise, the quantity demanded declines. The elasticity of demand is positive but less than 1 up to point *m*. Beyond *m*, the income elasticity of demand is negative. Examples of goods in this category include one-speed bicycles, small motorbikes, potatoes, and rice. Low income consumers buy most of these goods. At low income levels, the demand for such goods rises as income rises. Eventually, income reaches a level (at point *m*) where consumers replace these goods with superior alternatives. For example, a small car replaces the motorbike; fruit, vegetables, and meat begin to appear in a diet that was heavy in rice or potatoes.

Goods whose income elasticities of demand are positive are called *normal goods*. Goods whose income elasticities of demand are negative are called *inferior goods*. These goods are "inferior" in the sense that as income increases they are replaced with "superior," but more expensive substitutes.

Let's now look at some estimates of actual income elasticities of demand in the United States. Table 5.5 provides a summary. The various goods and services are listed in three groups. The first group lists goods and services whose income elasticity is greater than 1. The second group, in which there is just one example, has a unit elasticity. The third group lists goods whose income elasticity is less than 1 and whose demands are said to be income inelastic.

By using estimates of income elasticity of demand, we can translate projections of average income growth rates into growth rates of demand for particular goods and services. For example, if average incomes grow by 3 percent a year, the demand for gasoline and oil will grow by 4 percent a year (3 percent multiplied by the income elasticity of demand for gasoline and oil which, as shown in Table 5.5, is 1.36).

Cross Elasticity of Demand

The quantity of any good demanded depends on the prices of its substitutes and complements. The responsiveness of the quantity demanded of a particular good to the prices of its substitutes and complements is measured by **cross elasticity of demand**, which is represented by η_x. The cross elasticity of demand is calculated as the percentage change in the quantity demanded of one good divided by the percentage change in the price of another good (a substitute or a complement).

That is:

$$\eta_x = \frac{\text{Percentage change in quantity demanded of one good}}{\text{Percentage change in the price of another good}}$$

Figure 5.6 Cross Elasticities: Substitutes and Complements

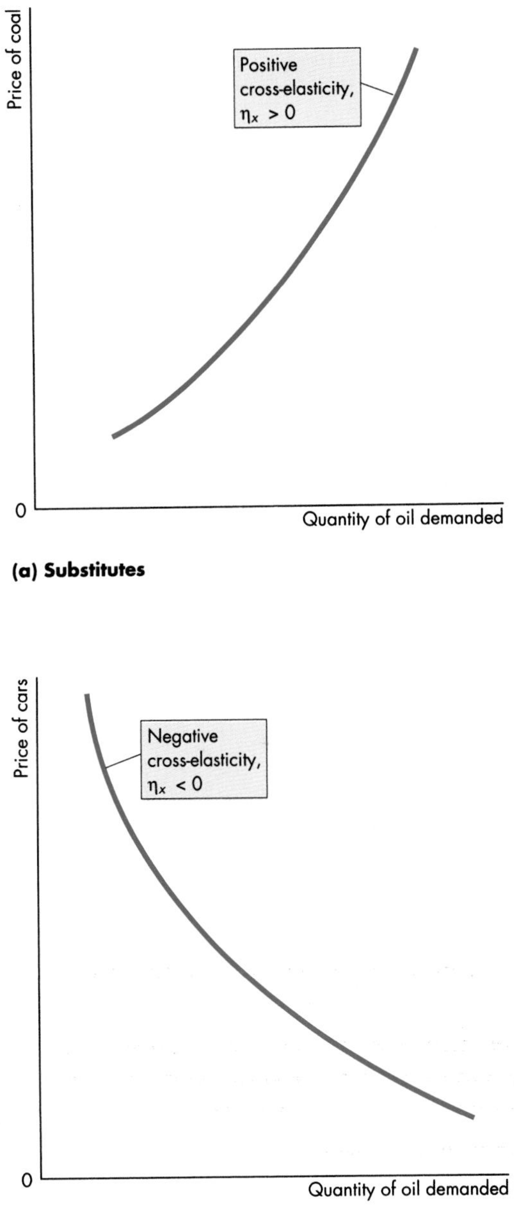

(a) Substitutes

(b) Complements

Part (a) shows the cross elasticity of demand with respect to the price of a substitute. When the price of coal increases, the quantity of oil demanded also increases. Part (b) shows the cross elasticity of demand with respect to the price of a complement. When the price of cars increases, the quantity of oil demanded decreases.

Table 5.6 A Compact Glossary of Elasticities of Demand

Price elasticities (η)

When η is:	The relationship is described as:	Which means that:
Infinity	Perfectly elastic or infinitely elastic	The smallest possible price rise (fall) causes an infinitely large fall (rise) in the quantity demanded.
Less than infinity but greater than 1	Elastic	The percentage rise (fall) in the quantity demanded exceeds the percentage fall (rise) in price.
1	Unit elasticity	The percentage rise (fall) in the quantity demanded equals the percentage fall (rise) in price.
Greater than zero but less than 1	Inelastic	The percentage rise (fall) in the quantity demanded is less than the percentage fall (rise) in price.
Zero	Perfectly inelastic or completely inelastic	The quantity demanded is the same at all prices.

Income Elasticities (η_y)

When η_y is:	The relationship is described as:	Which means that:
Greater than 1	Income-elastic (normal good)	The percentage rise (fall) in the quantity demanded is greater than the percentage rise (fall) in income.
Less than 1 but greater than zero	Income-inelastic (normal good)	The percentage rise (fall) in the quantity demanded is less than the percentage rise (fall) in income.
Less than zero	Negative income elasticity (inferior good)	When income rises, quantity demanded falls.

Cross Elasticities (η_x)

When η_x is:	The relationship is described as:	Which means that:
Infinity	Perfect substitutes	The smallest possible rise (fall) in the price of one good causes an infinitely large rise (fall) in the quantity demanded of the other good.
Less than infinity but greater than zero	Substitutes	If the price of one good rises (falls), the quantity demanded of the other good also rises (falls).
Zero	Independent	The quantity demanded of one good remains constant regardless of the price of the other good.
Less than zero (negative)	Complements	The quantity demanded of one good falls (rises) when the price of the other good rises (falls).

The cross elasticity of demand with respect to the price of a substitute is positive. The cross elasticity of demand with respect to the price of a complement is negative. Figure 5.6 makes it clear why. When the price of coal (a substitute for oil) rises, the demand for oil rises. When the price of cars (a complement with oil) rises, the demand for oil declines. The degree to which demand changes depends on how close the substitute or complement is. That is, the more easily coal and oil substitute for each other, the bigger the cross elasticity of demand between them. The more complementary are cars and oil, the more negative the cross elasticity of demand for oil with respect to the price of a car.

Table 5.6 provides a compact summary of all the different kinds of demand elasticities you've just studied, and Reading Between the Lines (pp. 118–119) gives an example of how these elasticities may be used in practical calculations.

Let's now turn our attention to the supply curve and study the concept of the elasticity of supply.

Elasticity of Supply

We have seen that the concept of elasticity of demand may be used to determine the extent to which price and the quantity traded change when there is a change in supply. But suppose we want to predict the effects on price and the quantity traded of a change in demand. To make such a prediction, we need to know how responsive the quantity supplied is to the price of a good. That is, we need the concept of the elasticity of supply.

The **elasticity of supply** is the percentage change in the quantity supplied of a good divided by the percentage change in its price. It is represented by η_s. That is:

$$\eta_s = \frac{\text{Percentage change in quantity supplied}}{\text{Percentage change in price}}$$

The supply curves that we have considered in this chapter (and those in Chapter 4) all slope upward. When the price increases, the quantity supplied increases. Upward-sloping supply curves have a positive elasticity.

There are two interesting cases of the elasticity of supply. If the quantity supplied is fixed regardless of the price, the supply curve is vertical. In this case, the elasticity of supply is zero. An increase in price leads to no change in the quantity supplied. If there is a price below which nothing will be supplied and at which suppliers are willing to sell any quantity demanded, the supply curve is horizontal. In this case, the elasticity of supply is infinite. The small fall in price would reduce the quantity supplied from an indefinitely large amount to zero.

The magnitude of the elasticity of supply depends on:

- The technological conditions governing production
- The amount of time elapsed since the price change

The importance of technological conditions is best illustrated by considering two extreme examples. Some goods, such as a painting by Georgia O'Keeffe, are unique. There is just one of each of her paintings. Its supply curve is vertical and its elasticity of supply is zero. At the other extreme, the supply of sand for making silicon chips is available in indefinitely large quantities at a virtually constant cost of production. Its supply curve is horizontal and its elasticity of supply is infinitely large.

To study the influence of the length of time elapsed since a price change, we distinguish three time-frames of supply: momentary, short-run, and long-run.

Momentary Supply

When the price of a good rises or falls in a sudden, unforeseen way, we use the momentary supply curve to describe the initial change in the quantity supplied. The **momentary supply curve** shows the response of the quantity supplied immediately following a price change.

For many goods, the momentary supply curve is perfectly inelastic—which means that the supply curve is vertical. Consider perishable fruits and vegetables. The amounts that can be supplied depend on crop planting decisions made several months earlier. In the case of fruit such as oranges, for example, the planting decisions have to be made many years in advance. All crops and all animal products take *some* time to grow, and so the

Warning: Travel with Care

Terrorism Spurs U.S. Tourists to Change Their Vacation Plans in Droves

It is Eastertide in Rome, April in Paris and the eve of Passover in Jerusalem. But suddenly, for millions of American tourists, this is chiefly the season for caution in making travel plans. In 1986, in sharp contrast to the overseas-travel surge of a year ago, Americans and their sought-after dollars are making themselves scarce in many parts of Western Europe and the Mediterranean. The phones of travel agents are as busy as ever, but many of the callers now want to change their vacation plans. Some are canceling their trips abroad entirely. Others are choosing more circuitous means and routes to reach their destinations, rather than having to pass through airports in Rome, Athens and other cities along the Mediterranean littoral. The fear of terrorism has suddenly become an important factor in the $250 billion U.S. travel industry.

Many U.S. holidaymakers are hurriedly lining up presumably safer summer excursions, including Caribbean cruises and even charter tours to Moscow. But above all, Americans this year are deciding that they would rather take in the splendors of their own land, on motor-home jaunts to Disney World, camping trips to U.S. national parks, and surfing safaris to Hawaii. The travel industry expects a jump of 10% or more in domestic bookings this year. Says Harold Van Sumeren, president of the Chamber of Commerce in Traverse City, Mich., a boating and camping mecca: "We're really anticipating one of the biggest and finest summer seasons we've ever had."

The apprehension over travel to Europe and the Mediterranean is a direct result of the recent rash of bloody attacks directed against U.S. citizens in Italy and West Germany, of rioting in Egypt and of random bombings in France. Last week travelers had further cause to be spooked by the harsh words and bellicose gestures flying between the U.S. and Libya. Reasons other than the terrorism scare, such as a sharp decline in the value of the U.S. dollar abroad and an abundance of cheap gasoline at home, are also involved in the shuffle of itineraries. Even so, says Sam Massell, an Atlanta travel agent, "if you're going on vacation, you want to start off happy. You're not supposed to go where you have to think about stress management."

The change in U.S. traveling patterns is already starting to have substantial effects. Until late last year, U.S. travel to Europe and the Mediterranean was setting records, thanks partly to the buying power of the strong dollar. Some 6.4 million Americans visited European countries in 1985, up from 5.8 million the previous year. Now the trade magazine *Travel Industry Monthly* expects European tourism by Americans to fall by about 25% in 1986.

***Time*, April 21, 1986**

By Stephen Koepp, reported by Thomas McCarroll/New York, with other bureaus

The Essence of the Story

Facts

- In 1984, 5.8 million Americans visited Europe.
- In 1985, 6.4 million Americans visited Europe, a 10 percent increase.
- In April 1986, it was predicted that European tourism by Americans would fall by 25 percent of its 1985 level.
- In April 1986, the U.S. travel industry expected a rise of 10 percent in domestic business.
- In 1986, the U.S. dollar fell in value—i.e., it bought fewer goods abroad than in 1985.
- In 1986, the price of gasoline fell.
- In the winter of 1985 and the spring of 1986, there was a wave of terrorism directed at U.S. citizens in several European and Mediterranean countries.

Alleged explanation

- People switched from European to domestic vacations mainly because of the rise in anti-American terrorism and partly because of the drop in the value of the dollar and in the price of gasoline.

Background and Analysis

Prices

- A fall in the price of a good leads to an increase in the quantity demanded.
- An increase in the price of a substitute leads to an increase in demand.
- In 1985, the price of a European vacation fell by 1.8 percent. (The dollar cost of a European vacation rose by 1.7 percent but prices in the United States rose by 3.5 percent so that the relative price (opportunity cost) of a European vacation fell by the difference—1.8 percent).
- In 1986 the price of a European vacation increased by 18.2 percent. (In that year the dollar fell in value resulting in an increased dollar cost of a European vacation of 21.3 percent. Prices rose in the United States by 3.1 percent so the relative price (opportunity cost) of a European vacation rose by the difference—18.2 percent).

Incomes

- In 1985 disposable income per head rose by 1 percent.
- In 1986 disposable income per head rose by 2 percent.

Elasticities

- The income elasticity of demand for foreign travel is estimated to be 3 (see Table 5.5, p. 114).
- The price elasticity of demand for European vacations is not known but is likely to be much bigger than 1 because vacations in Europe, Asia, Latin America, Canada, and the United States are close substitutes for each other.
- The formula used for predicting the percentage change in the quantity demanded of a good is:

  Percent rise in quantity demanded =

  Price elasticity × percent fall in price +

  Income elasticity × percent rise in income

- The table gives predicted percentage changes in the quantity of European vacations demanded for three different values of the price elasticity of demand and for an income elasticity of demand of 3.
- If the price elasticity of demand is about 2, then the price and income changes in 1985 and 1986 come close to predicting the actual changes in travel.
- The rise in the quantity demanded in 1985 is slightly bigger than would have been predicted, but the fall in the quantity demanded in 1986 is smaller than predicted.
- The puzzle raised by the numbers in the table is not that European travel by Americans fell in 1986. Rather, it is that European travel fell by so little! It is thus plausible that terrorism had no effect.
- But why would European travel fall by only 25 percent when the relative price had risen by 18 percent? Perhaps something else changed.
- Since vacations in Japan and the Far East are substitutes for vacations in Europe, a rise in the price of an Asian vacation would lead to a rise (or a smaller fall) in the demand for European vacations.
- Prices in Japan rose by 1.6 percent, but the dollar *fell* in value against the Japanese yen by 26.3 percent, so the dollar cost of a Japanese vacation rose by 27.9 percent.
- Since European travel costs, in dollars, rose by only 18.2 percent, the price of a European vacation relative to that of a Japanese vacation *fell* by almost 10 percent.
- The rise in the cost of a Japanese vacation relative to that of a European vacation would moderate the fall in the quantity demanded of European vacations.

	1985	1986
Elasticity		
1	+ 4.8%	−12.2%
2	+ 6.6%	−30.4%
3	+ 8.4%	−48.6%
Actual	+10%	−25%

Conclusion

- The journalists reporting this story probably overemphasized the importance of terrorism and underemphasized the importance of price and income changes in explaining the changes in the vacation plans of Americans.

momentary supply curve for these goods is always perfectly inelastic.

Other goods have elastic momentary supply curves. One such good is electricity. If we all turned on our TV sets and air conditioners simultaneously, there would be a big surge in the demand for electricity. If the supply of electricity were inelastic, this surge in demand would cause a sharp rise in price and no change in the quantity of electricity actually bought. Surges in demand are common, but when they occur, the quantity bought increases and the price remains constant. Electricity producers can usually anticipate fluctuations in demand and bring more generators into operation to ensure that the quantity supplied equals the quantity demanded without raising the price. (There is, of course, an upper limit to what can be produced, but normally increased output can meet the extra demand.) In this example, the momentary supply is perfectly elastic. But the momentary supply curve for most goods is inelastic, perhaps perfectly inelastic.

Let's now look at the other extreme—the long run.

Long-run Supply

The **long-run supply curve** shows the response of the quantity supplied to a change in price after all the technologically possible ways of adjusting supply have been exploited. In the case of oranges, the long run is the time it takes new plantings to grow to full maturity—about 15 years. In some cases, the long-run adjustment occurs only after a completely new production plant has been built and workers have been trained to operate it—typically a process that may take several years.

Between the momentary and the long-run time-frames, there are many intermediate time-frames. We call these the short run.

Short-run Supply

The **short-run supply curve** shows how the quantity supplied responds to a price change when only *some* of the technologically possible adjustments to production have been made. The first adjustment that is usually made is in the amount of labor employed. To increase output in the short-run, firms work their labor force overtime and perhaps hire additional workers. To decrease their output in the short-run, firms lay off workers or reduce their hours of work. With the passage of more time, firms can make additional adjustments, perhaps training additional workers or buying additional tools and other equipment. The short-run response to a price change, unlike the momentary and long-run responses, is not a unique response but a sequence of adjustments.

Figure 5.7 Supply: Momentary, Short-run, and Long-run

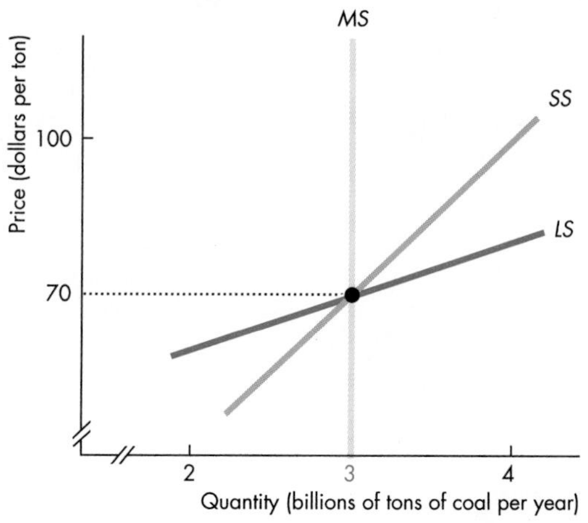

The momentary supply curve (*MS*) shows how quantity supplied responds to a price change the moment that it occurs. The light blue momentary supply curve shown here is perfectly inelastic. The medium blue short-run supply curve (*SS*) shows how the quantity supplied responds to a price change after some adjustments to production have been made. The dark blue long-run supply curve (*LS*) shows how the quantity supplied responds to a price change when all the technologically possible adjustments to the production process have been made.

Three Supply Curves

Three supply curves corresponding to the three time-frames are illustrated in Fig. 5.7. They are the supply curves in the world market for coal in a year in which the price is \$70 a ton and the quantity of coal produced is 3 billion tons. The three supply curves all pass through that point. The light blue momentary supply curve (*MS*) is perfectly inelastic at 3 billion tons. The dark blue long-run supply curve (*LS*) is the most elastic of the three curves.

The medium blue short-run supply curve (*SS*) lies between the other two curves. In fact, there is a series of successively more elastic short-run supply curves between the momentary and the long-run curves. As more time elapses following a price change, more changes can be made in the method of production to increase output. The short-run supply curve (*SS*) shown in Fig. 5.7 is an example of one of these short-run supply curves.

The momentary supply curve (*MS*) is vertical because, at a given moment in time, no matter what the price of coal, producers cannot change their output. They have a certain labor force and a certain amount of coal mining equipment in place and there is a given amount of output that can be produced. But as time elapses, coal producing companies can increase their capacity. They can hire and train more miners and buy more equipment. In the long run, they can sink new mines, discover more accessible coal deposits, and increase the quantity supplied even more in response to a given price rise.

■ You have now studied the theory of demand and supply, and you have learned how to measure the responsiveness of the quantities demanded and supplied to changes in price and income. In the next chapters we are going to use what we have learned, to study some real world markets—markets in action.

SUMMARY

Price Elasticity of Demand

Price elasticity of demand is a precise measure of the responsiveness of the quantity demanded of a good to a change in its price. It enables us to calculate the effect of a change in supply on price, quantity traded, and revenue. Price elasticity of demand (η) is calculated using the formula:

$$\eta = \frac{\text{Percentage change in quantity demanded}}{\text{Percentage change in price}}$$

When elasticity is between zero and 1, demand is inelastic. When elasticity is 1, demand is unit elastic. When elasticity is greater than 1, demand is elastic.

Elasticity varies along a straight-line demand curve. The elasticity falls as the price falls and the quantity demanded rises.

The size of the elasticity depends on how easily one good may serve as a substitute for another, on the proportion of income spent on the good, and on the time that has elapsed since the price change. (pp. 103–110)

Two Time-Frames for Demand

We use two time-frames to analyze demand: short-run and long-run. Short-run demand describes the initial response of buyers to a price change. Long-run demand describes the response of buyers to a price change after all possible adjustments have been made. Short-run demand is usually less elastic than long-run demand. (pp. 110–112)

Elasticity, Revenue, and Expenditure

If the elasticity of demand is less than 1, a decrease in supply leads to an increase in revenue—the percentage increase in price is greater than the percentage decrease in the quantity traded. If the elasticity of demand is greater than 1, a decrease in supply leads to a decrease in revenue—the percentage increase in price is less than the percentage decrease in the quantity traded. (pp. 112–113)

More Demand Elasticities

Income elasticity of demand measures the responsiveness of demand to a change in income. Income elasticity of demand is calculated as the percentage change in the quantity demanded divided by the percentage change in income. Income elasticities may be greater than 1 (income elastic), between zero and 1 (income inelastic), or less than zero (negative income elasticity). Income elasticities are greater than 1 for items typically consumed by the rich; they are positive but less than 1 for more basic consumption items. Income elasticities are less than zero for inferior goods—goods that are consumed only at low incomes and that disappear as budgets increase.

Cross elasticity of demand measures the responsiveness of demand for one good to a change in the price of another good. Cross elasticity of demand is calculated as the percentage change in the quantity demanded of one good divided by the percentage change in the price of another good (a substitute or a complement). The cross elasticity of demand with respect to the price of a substitute is positive. The cross elasticity of demand with respect to the price of a complement is negative. (pp. 113–117)

Elasticity of Supply

The elasticity of supply measures the responsiveness of the quantity supplied to a change in price. Elasticity of supply is calculated as the percentage change in the quantity supplied of a good divided by the percentage change in its price. Supply elasticities are usually positive but range between zero (vertical supply curve) and infinity (horizontal supply curve).

We classify supply according to three different time-frames: momentary, long-run, and short-run. Momentary supply refers to the response of suppliers to a price change at the instant that it happens. Long-run supply refers to the response of suppliers to a price change when all the technologically feasible adjustments in production have been made. Short-run supply refers to the response of suppliers to a price change after some adjustments in production have been made. For many goods, the momentary supply curve is perfectly inelastic. Supply becomes more elastic as suppliers have more time to respond to price changes. (pp. 117–121)

KEY CONCEPTS

Key Figures and Tables

REVIEW QUESTIONS

1 Define the price elasticity of demand.

2 Why is elasticity a more useful measure of responsiveness than slope?

3 Draw a graph of, or describe the shape of, a demand curve that along its whole length has an elasticity of:

a) Infinity

b) Zero

c) Unity

4 What three factors determine the size of the elasticity of demand?

5 What do we mean by short-run demand and long-run demand?

6 Explain why the short-run demand curve is usually less elastic than the long-run demand curve.

7 What is the connection between elasticity and revenue? If the elasticity of demand is 1, by how much does a 10 percent price increase change revenue?

8 Define the income elasticity of demand.

9 Give an example of a good whose income elasticity is:

a) greater than 1

b) positive but less than 1

c) less than zero

10 Define the cross elasticity of demand. Is the cross elasticity of demand positive or negative?

11 Define the elasticity of supply. Is the elasticity of supply positive or negative?

12 Give an example of a good whose elasticity of supply is

a) Zero

b) Greater than zero but less than infinity

c) Infinity

13 What do we mean by momentary, short-run, and long-run supply?

14 Why is the momentary supply curve perfectly inelastic for many goods?

15 Why is the long-run supply curve more elastic than the short-run supply curve?

PROBLEMS

1 The demand schedule for videotape rentals is:

Price (dollars)	Quantity demanded per day
0	120
1	100
2	80
3	60
4	40
5	20
6	0

a) At what price is the elasticity of demand equal to

(i) 1

(ii) infinity

(iii) zero

b) What price brings in the most revenue per day?

c) Calculate the elasticity of demand for a rise in price from \$3 to \$4.

2 Assume that the quantity of videotape rentals demanded in problem 1 increases by 10 percent at each price.

a) Draw the old and new demand curves.

b) Calculate the elasticity of demand for a rise in the rental price from \$3 to \$4. Compare your answer with that of problem 1(c).

3 Which item in each of the following pairs has the larger elasticity of demand:

a) Daily newspapers or *The New York Times*

b) Exercise equipment or rowing machines

c) Soda or Diet Pepsi

4 You have been hired as an economic consultant by OPEC and given the following schedule showing the world demand for oil:

Price (dollars per barrel)	Quantity demanded (millions of barrels per day)
10	60,000
20	55,000
30	45,000
40	20,000
50	5,000

Your advice is needed on the following questions:

a) If the supply of oil is cut back so that the price rises from \$10 to \$20 a barrel, will the revenue from oil sales rise or fall?

b) What will happen to revenue if the supply of oil is cut back further and the price rises to \$30 a barrel?

c) What will happen to revenue if the supply of oil is cut back further still so that the price rises to $40 a barrel?

d) What is the price that will achieve the highest revenue?

e) What quantity of oil will be sold at the price that answers problem 4(d)?

f) What are the values of the price elasticity of demand for price changes of $10 a barrel at average prices of $15, $25, $35, and $45 a barrel?

g) What is the elasticity of demand at the price that maximizes revenue?

5 State the sign (positive or negative) and, where possible, the range (less than 1, 1, greater than 1) of the following elasticities:

a) The price elasticity of demand for coal at the point of maximum revenue

b) The cross elasticity of demand for coal with respect to the price of oil

c) The income elasticity of demand for diamonds

d) The income elasticity of demand for toothpaste

e) The elasticity of supply of Maine lobsters

f) The cross elasticity of demand for floppy discs with respect to the price of personal computers

6 The following table gives some data on the quantities of chocolate chip cookies demanded:

Price (cents per cookie)	**Quantity demanded (thousands per day)**	
	Short-run	Long-run
10	700	1,000
20	500	500
30	200	0

Using 20¢ as the average price of a cookie and 500,000 cookies a day as the average quantity, calculate:

a) The short-run elasticity of demand

b) The long-run elasticity of demand

7 The following table gives some data on the quantities of chocolate chip cookies supplied:

Price (cents per cookie)	**Quantity supplied (thousands per day)**		
	Momentary	Short-run	Long-run
10	500	200	0
20	500	500	500
30	500	700	10,000

Using 20¢ as the average price of a cookie and 500,000 cookies a day as the average quantity, calculate:

a) The momentary elasticity of supply

b) The short-run elasticity of supply

c) The long-run elasticity of supply

Chapter 6

Markets in Action

After studying this chapter, you will be able to:

- Explain the short-run and long-run effects of a change in supply on price and the quantity traded
- Explain the short-run and long-run effects of a change in demand on price and the quantity traded
- Explain the effects of price controls
- Explain why price controls can lead to black markets
- Explain how people cope with uncertainty and make decisions in the face of unpredictable fluctuations in demand and supply
- Explain how inventories and speculation limit price fluctuations

Turbulent Times

On April 18, 1906, San Francisco suffered a devastating earthquake. From April 18 to April 20, massive fires destroyed countless buildings on 3400 acres in the heart of the city. Despite the extreme destruction of property, fewer than 1000 people died. The remaining population somehow had to fit into a vastly smaller number of houses and apartments. How did the San Francisco housing market cope with this enormous shock? What happened to rents and to the quantity of housing services available? ■ Almost every day, new machines and techniques are being invented that save labor and increase productivity. But the invention and adoption of new technologies doesn't reduce the demand for labor—it changes its composition. The simplest tasks performed by the least skilled workers are the ones most easily mechanized. So the march of technological change brings a persistent decrease in the demand for the least skilled types of labor. But ever more sophisticated equipment needs ever more sophisticated management and maintenance. As a consequence, it brings a steady increase in the demand for more highly skilled types of labor. How do labor markets cope with the changing patterns in demand for labor and what happens to the wages of the unskilled in the process? Does falling demand make those wages fall lower and lower? ■ Wages and housing costs are the two most important items in the budget of every household. Because of this fact, politicians take a great interest in the markets for housing and labor. If rents get too high, rent controls are introduced. If wages get too low, minimum wage laws are introduced. What are the effects of rent controls and minimum wage laws? How do rent controls affect the rents that people pay and the housing services that are available? How do minimum wages affect wages and employment prospects? ■ When the winter is severe and the summer is hot and humid, there is an increase in the number of days on which people run furnaces and air conditioners. The number of such days in the year has an important effect on the total demand for electricity and, in turn, for fuels used to generate electricity. As we all know from experience, fluctuations in the weather cannot be forecast with any real accuracy—at least not a whole season ahead. We know the range of possibilities, but there is no way of predicting whether the coming winter will turn out to be mild or severe. Producers of electricity and of the fuels they use must devise ways of coping with the inherent unpredictability in the demand for their products. How do these producers cope with uncertainty about demand? What are the effects of unpredictable fluctuations in demand on prices and the quantities traded?

The weather also creates unpredictable fluctuations in supply. The output of virtually every agricultural product is subject to unpredictable fluctuations of weather—hours of sunshine, rainfall, and temperature—and their effect on growing conditions. For example, the grain yield in 1982 was very high, but in 1988 it was extremely low as crops were devastated by the drought.

Fluctuations in demand and supply cause fluctuations in the price of a good and the quantity traded. In some cases, the price fluctuates a great deal and the quantity traded hardly changes. In other cases, the quantity traded fluctuates dramatically and price changes very little. What determines the amount by which price and quantity traded fluctuate?

Every day, the pages of any newspaper—from your local daily to the *Wall Street Journal*—report the latest fortunes of the stock market. Attention focuses on various indexes, such as the Dow-Jones industrial average. On one particular day—October 19, 1987—a page in history was written. The Dow-Jones average fell by more than 36 percent from its peak value. A movement of this magnitude is, of course, unusual. Nevertheless, stock prices do go up and down—and they do so much more than the prices of most of the ordinary goods and services we buy. Why are stock prices so volatile? Is it speculation that makes the stock market fluctuate so much?

■ In this chapter, we use the theory of demand and supply (of Chapter 4) and the concept of elasticity (of Chapter 5) to answer questions such as those we have just asked. We'll study how unregulated markets work, and we'll study government intervention to regulate prices. We'll see how such regulation can produce black markets and unemployment. We'll extend the demand and supply model to take account of the fact that production decisions made today often do not affect output until a later date. For example, if a producer decides today to grow more oranges, the actual supply of oranges will not increase until the new orange trees mature—in about 15 years. In a situation such as this, suppliers have to make today's production decisions on the basis of forecasts of future prices. We'll see how they go about making such forecasts. A final extension of the demand and supply model that we'll make takes account of the fact that many goods can be stored. We'll study the way in which inventories of goods, and changes in those inventories, affect the prices of goods and the quantities traded. We'll emerge from this chapter with a richer model of demand and supply that explains many features of the real world.

Let's begin by studying how a market responds to a severe supply shock in both the short run and the long run. We'll see how an unregulated market responds and also we'll see what happens when the government intervenes in the market to limit price changes.

Housing Markets and Rent Ceilings

To see how an unregulated market copes with a massive supply shock, let's transport ourselves to the city of San Francisco in April 1906 as the city is facing the effects of its massive earthquake and fire. You can sense the enormity of San Francisco's problems by reading some headlines from *The New York Times* on the first days of the crisis.

On April 19, 1906:

> *Over 500 Dead, $200,000,000 Lost in San Francisco Earthquake.*
>
> *Nearly Half the City Is in Ruins and 50,000 Are Homeless.*

On April 20, 1906:

> *Army of Homeless Fleeing from Devastated City.*
>
> *200,000 Without Shelter and Facing Famine.*

And again on April 21, 1906:

> *San Francisco's New Peril; Gale Drives Fire Ferryward.*
>
> *Fighting Famine and Disease Among the 200,000 Refugees.*
>
> *San Francisco Multitudes Camped Out Shelterless and in Want.*

The commander of the federal troops in charge of the resulting emergency described the magnitude of the problem:

> Not a hotel of note or importance was left standing. The great apartment houses had vanished . . . two-hundred-and-twenty-five thousand people were . . . homeless.[1]

Almost overnight, more than half the people in a city of 400,000 had lost their homes. Temporary shelters and camps alleviated some of the problem, but it was also necessary to utilize the apartment buildings and houses left standing. As a consequence, they had to accommodate 40 percent more people than they had prior to the earthquake.

The *San Francisco Chronicle* was not published for more than a month after the earthquake. When the newspaper reappeared on May 24, 1906, the city's housing shortage—what would seem like a major news item that would still be of grave importance—was not mentioned. Milton Friedman and George Stigler describe the situation:

> *There is not a single mention of a housing shortage!* The classified advertisements listed sixty-four offers of flats and houses for rent, and nineteen of houses for sale, against five advertisements of flats or houses wanted. Then and thereafter a considerable number of all types of accommodation except hotel rooms were offered for rent.[2]

[1]Reported in Milton Friedman and George J. Stigler, "Roofs or Ceilings? The Current Housing Problem," in *Popular Essays on Current Problems,* vol. 1, no. 2 (New York: Foundation for Economic Education, 1946), 3–15, 3.

[2]*Ibid., 3.*

How did San Francisco cope with such a devastating reduction in the supply of housing?

The Market Response to an Earthquake

We can work out how the unregulated San Francisco housing market responded to the earthquake of 1906 by using the theory of demand and supply that we studied in Chapters 4 and 5. Figure 6.1 analyzes this market. Part (a) shows the situation before the earthquake and parts (b) and (c), after the earthquake. The horizontal axis of each part measures the quantity of housing units and the vertical axis measures the monthly rent of a unit of housing.

Look first at the situation before the earthquake (part a). The demand curve for housing is *D.* There are two supply curves: the short-run supply curve, which is labeled *SS* and the long-run supply curve, which is labeled *LS.* The short-run supply curve shows how the quantity of housing supplied varies as the price (rent) varies, while the number of houses and apartment buildings remains constant. This supply response arises from a variation in the intensity with which existing buildings are used. The quantity of housing supplied increases as families rent out rooms or parts of their houses and apartments to others, and the quantity supplied decreases as families occupy a larger number of the rooms under their control.

The long-run supply curve shows how the quantity supplied varies after enough time has elapsed for new apartment buildings and houses to be erected or existing buildings to be destroyed. The long-run supply curve is shown as being perfectly elastic. We do not actually know that the long-run supply curve is perfectly elastic, but it is a reasonable assumption. It implies that the cost of building an apartment is pretty much the same regardless of whether there are 50,000, 100,000, or 150,000 apartments in existence.

The equilibrium price and quantity traded are determined at the point of intersection of the short-run supply curve and the demand curve. Before the earthquake, that equilibrium rent is $110 a month and the quantity of housing units traded is 100,000. In addition (but only because we are assuming it to be so), the housing market is on its long-run supply curve, *LS.* Let's now look at the situation immediately after the earthquake.

Figure 6.1 The San Francisco Housing Market in 1906

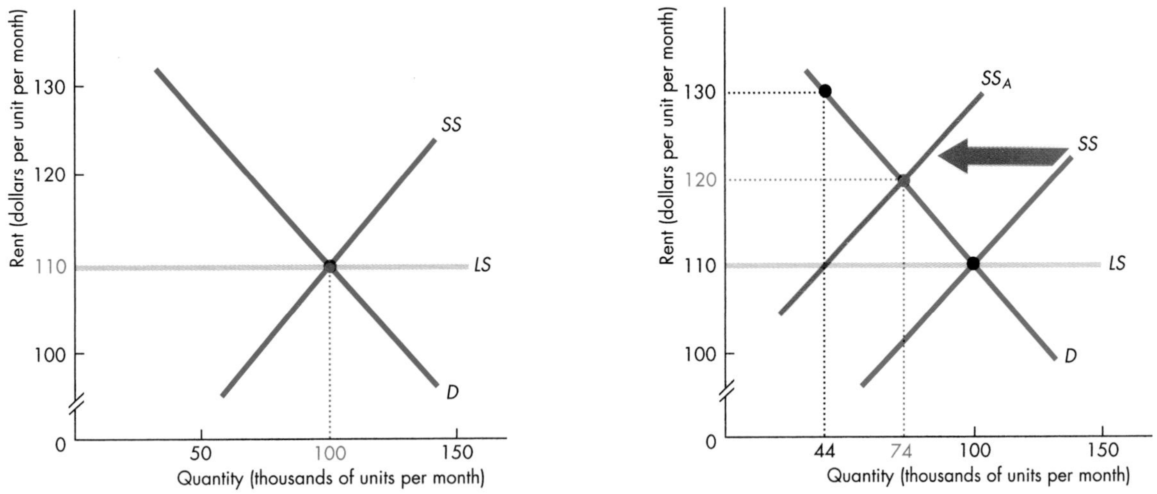

(a) Before earthquake

(b) After earthquake

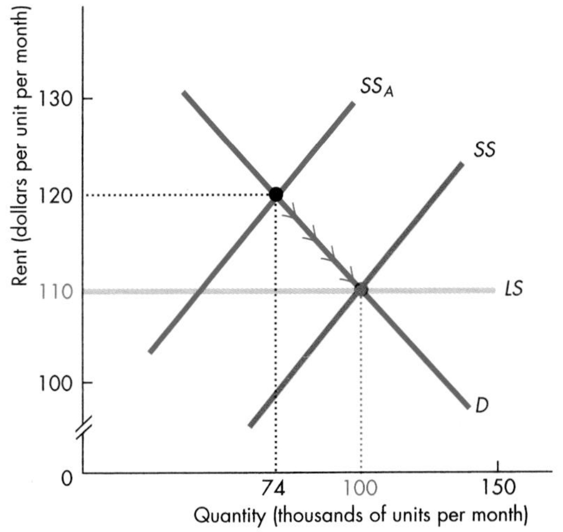

(c) Long-run adjustment

Before the earthquake, the San Francisco housing market is in equilibrium with 100,000 housing units being traded each month at an average rent of $110 a month. This equilibrium is at the intersection of demand curve *D*, short-run supply curve *SS*, and long-run supply curve *LS*. After the earthquake, the short-run supply curve shifts from *SS* to SS_A (part b). The equilibrium rent rises to $120 a month and the number of housing units available falls to 74,000 a month. The rent rises because only 44,000 units of housing will be supplied at the old rent of $110 a month, and the price that demanders will willingly pay for the forty-four thousandth unit is $130 a month. With rents at $120 a month, there is profit in building new apartments and houses. As the building program proceeds, the short-run supply curve shifts to the right. As it does so (part c), rents gradually fall back to $110 a month and the number of housing units available increases gradually to 100,000. Note that we use a special arrowed line to indicate such gradual movements along a curve.

After the Earthquake

After the earthquake and the subsequent fires, housing for 56 percent of the population is destroyed. Figure 6.1(b) reflects the new situation by shifting the short-run supply curve *SS* to the left by 56,000 units, to become the short-run supply curve SS_A (*A* for after the earthquake). If people use the remaining housing units with the same intensity as before the earthquake and if the rent remains at $110 a month, only 44,000 units of housing are available.

But rents do not remain at $110. With only 44,000 units of housing available, the maximum rent that will willingly be paid for the last available apartment is $130 a month. Since people value the available housing more highly than the long-run price of $110 a month, they offer to pay higher rents. At higher rents, people with accommodations economize on their use of space and make their spare rooms, attics, and basements available to others. Thus the quantity of housing units offered increases. The market achieves a new, short-run equilibrium at a rent of $120 a month, where 74,000 units of housing are available. In this new short-run equilibrium, approximately 20 percent of the population has left the city and a further 6 percent has been housed in temporary camps.[3]

You've now seen how the housing market reacts, almost overnight, to a devastating shock. When supply decreases, the intersection point of the new short-run supply curve and the demand curve determines the price and the quantity traded. The price rises; those willing to pay the higher price find housing, and those with housing are willing to economize on its use. People who are unwilling or unable to pay the higher rents either leave the city or are housed in temporary shelters.

Long-run Adjustments The new equilibrium depicted in Fig. 6.1(b) is not the end of the story. The long-run supply curve tells us that with sufficient time for new apartment buildings and houses to be constructed, housing will be supplied at a rent of $110 a month. Since the current rent of $120 a month is higher than the long-run supply price of housing, there will be a rush to build and supply new apartments and houses. As time passes, more apartments and houses are built, and the short-run supply curve starts moving back gradually to the right.

Figure 6.1(c) illustrates the long-run adjustment. As the short-run supply curve shifts back to the right, it intersects the demand curve at lower rents and higher quantities. The market follows the arrows down the demand curve. The process ends when there is no further profit in building new housing units. Such a situation occurs at the original rent of $110 a month and the original quantity of 100,000 units of housing.

[3]*Ibid.*, 3.

R E V I E W

An earthquake reduces the short-run supply, raising rents and lowering the quantity traded. Higher rents immediately bring forth an increase in the quantity of housing supplied as people economize on their own use of space and make rooms available for rent to others. High rents also lead to increased building activity, which causes the short-run supply curve to shift gradually back to the right. As this process continues, the price of housing falls and the quantity rises. The original (pre-earthquake) equilibrium eventually is restored (because nothing has happened in the meantime to shift the long-run supply curve or the demand curve). ■

A Regulated Housing Market

We've just seen how the housing market of San Francisco coped with a massive supply shock. One of the things that happened was that rents increased sharply. Let's now suppose that the San Francisco city government imposed a **rent ceiling.** A rent ceiling is a regulation making it illegal to charge a rent higher than a specified level. What would have happened if a rent ceiling of $110 a month—the rent before the earthquake—had been imposed? This question is answered in Fig. 6.2.

First let's work out what will happen to the quantities supplied and demanded. The quantity supplied at the controlled rent of $110 a month is 44,000 units. The quantity demanded at that rent is 100,000 units. When the quantity demanded exceeds the quantity supplied, what determines the quantity actually bought and sold? The answer is the smaller of the quantities demanded and supplied. At a monthly rent of $110, the suppliers of housing only want to supply 44,000 units. They cannot be forced to supply more. The demanders would like to rent 100,000 units at that price, but they cannot do so. The difference between the quantity demanded and the quantity supplied is called the excess quantity demanded.

When a rent ceiling of $110 a month is imposed, the quantity of housing available falls to 44,000 units, but the quantity demanded remains constant at 100,000 units. There is an excess demand of 56,000 units. Is that the end of the story? Is this situation an equilibrium? To answer this question, we need to explore a bit more closely what the demanders are doing.

If the rent really is $110 a month, a lot of people who would like to rent more housing will not be able to do so. Moreover, some people would be willing to pay much more than $110 a month to get an apartment. To understand why, recall that there are two ways of interpreting a demand curve. One interpretation is that the curve tells us the quantities demanded at each price. But the demand curve also tells us the highest price that demanders will pay for the last unit available. What is the highest price that people will pay for the last apartment available? The answer, which can be read from the demand curve, is $130 a month. Since the people who are not able to find housing are willing to pay more than the rent ceiling, the situation that we have just described is not an equilibrium. Two mechanisms come into play in an unbalanced situation such as this one to achieve equilibrium. They are search activity and black markets.

Figure 6.2 A Rent Ceiling

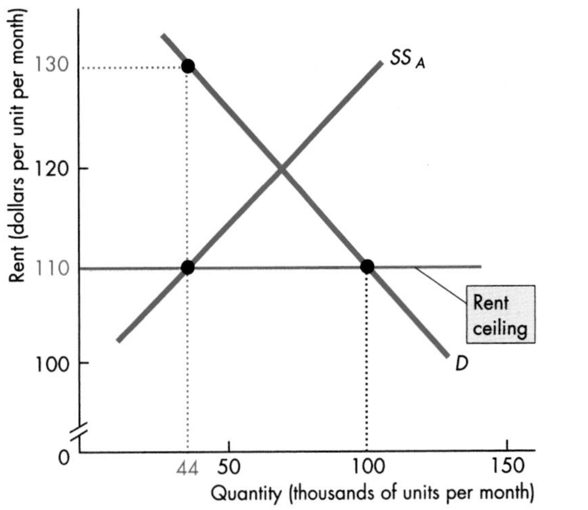

If there had been a rent ceiling of $110 a month following the earthquake, the quantity of housing supplied would have been stuck at 44,000 units. People would willingly pay $130 a month for the forty-four thousandth unit. The difference between the rent ceiling and the maximum price that will willingly be paid is the value of the time used up in searching for an available apartment. The individuals doing the searching are those with the lowest opportunity cost of time. Those whose value of time is high avoid search costs by buying on an illegal black market.

Search Activity

Even when the quantity demanded exceeds the quantity supplied, some suppliers have goods available. But many are sold out. In these circumstances, buyers spend time looking for a supplier with whom they can do business. The time and effort spent in searching for someone with whom to do business is called **search activity.** Even in markets where prices are permitted to fluctuate to bring equality between the quantities demanded and supplied, search activity takes place. But when price is regulated, search activity increases.

The time spent searching for available supplies imposes costs on buyers. Adjustments in the time spent searching bring about an equilibrium. You can see why by thinking about the total amount that the demanders are willing to pay for the last unit of housing available. With only 44,000 housing units available, demanders are willing to pay $130 a month. But the rent is restricted to $110. How does the buyer spend another $20? The answer is by using $20 worth of time in the business of searching for an available apartment. That is, the total cost of housing—the price actually paid for housing obtained—is equal to the rent paid to the owner plus the opportunity cost of time spent searching for the available supply.

Black Markets

Opportunity cost (the value of the best opportunity forgone) enables us to predict *who* will search for available housing. Some people earn high wages and others earn low wages. If it takes one hour to find an apartment, the total price paid is higher for a high-wage earner than a low-wage earner. Therefore the lowest paid people will be those who devote the most time to searching out available supplies. High-wage earners will devote time to search activity only if they place a much higher value on the good than does a low-wage earner.

A person with a high opportunity cost of time has another way of obtaining a good—buying it from someone whose opportunity cost of time is lower. The person with a low wage can devote time to searching out the available supplies and then resell to someone whose opportunity cost of searching is higher. Buying goods in this way is illegal and creates what is known as a black market. A **black market** is an illegal trading arrangement in which buyers and sellers do business at a price higher than the legally imposed price ceiling. The functioning of a black market depends on how tightly the government polices its price regulations, on the chances of being caught violating them, and on the scale of the penalties imposed for violations.

At one extreme, the chance of being caught violating a rent ceiling is small. In this case, the black market will function similarly to an unregulated market, and the black market rent and quantity traded will be close to the unregulated equilibrium. At the other extreme, where policing is highly effective and where large penalties are imposed on violators, the rent ceiling will restrict the quantity traded to 44,000 units. The small number of black marketeers operating in the market will buy at the controlled rent of $110 a month and sell at $130 a month. The government will constantly try to detect and punish such people. The equilibrium in the black market will be such that anyone can obtain an apartment for $130 a month and the profit for the black marketeer is just sufficient compensation for the risk of being caught and punished.

There are many examples of markets, other than housing markets, that are regulated in some way and in which economic forces result in black market trading. One example is the market for personal computers in Poland and other Eastern European countries. (See Reading Between the Lines, pages 134–135.)

We've just looked at what would have happened in a hypothetical situation if there had been rent ceilings following the San Francisco earthquake. But San Francisco actually did have rent ceilings 45 years later—following World War II—so we can see how rent ceilings operated in practice. Let's take a look at that episode in the history of the San Francisco housing market.

Rent Ceilings in Practice

By 1940, the population of San Francisco had increased to 635,000. At that time, only 93 percent of the city's houses and apartments were occupied. The situation stayed much the same throughout World War II. Then, after the war, the population increased by 30 percent, but the number of houses and apartments increased by only 20 percent. As a result, each dwelling unit had to house 10 percent more people in 1946 than one year earlier. The housing problems that San Francisco suffered in 1946 were only a quarter of the magnitude of the problems that followed the earthquake in 1906. Yet the 1946 housing shortage was a major political problem.

> On January 8 [1946] the California State Legislature was convened, and the Governor listed the housing shortage as "the most critical problem facing California." During the first five days of the year there were altogether only four advertisements offering houses or apartments for rent . . . [and] . . . there were thirty advertisements per day by persons wanting to rent houses or apartments. . . .[4]

The key difference between San Francisco in 1906 and in 1946 was the way in which scarce housing was rationed. In 1906, the scarce housing was allocated by an unregulated market. Rent increases achieved an equilibrium between the quantity of housing supplied and the quantity demanded and resulted in a steady increase in the quantity of housing available. In 1946, rent ceilings were in place. Scarce housing was allocated by people devoting time and effort to searching out and advertising for available houses and apartments. The actual cost of housing, taking account of the frustration and effort involved in finding accommodation, exceeded the controlled rent level and even exceeded the rents that would have prevailed in an unregulated market.

We've now studied the way in which a market responds, in both the short run and the long run, to a change in supply and how a regulated market would work in the face of such a supply shock. Let's now study how a market responds, both in the short run and the long run, to a change in demand. We'll study how an unregulated market handles such a shock and the effects of government intervention to limit price movements.

---

[4] *Ibid., 4.*

The Labor Market and Minimum Wage Regulation

Labor-saving technology is constantly being invented and, as a result, the demand for certain types of labor, usually the least skilled types, is constantly decreasing. How does the labor market cope with this continuous decrease in the demand for unskilled labor? Doesn't it mean that the wages of the unskilled will constantly be falling? To study this question, let's examine the market for unskilled labor.

Figure 6.3(a) shows this market. The quantity of labor (millions of hours per year) is measured on the horizontal axis and the wage rate (dollars per hour) on the vertical axis. The demand curve is *D*. There are two supply curves: the upward-sloping short-run supply curve *SS* and the horizontal long-run supply curve *LS*.

Figure 6.3 A Market for Unskilled Labor

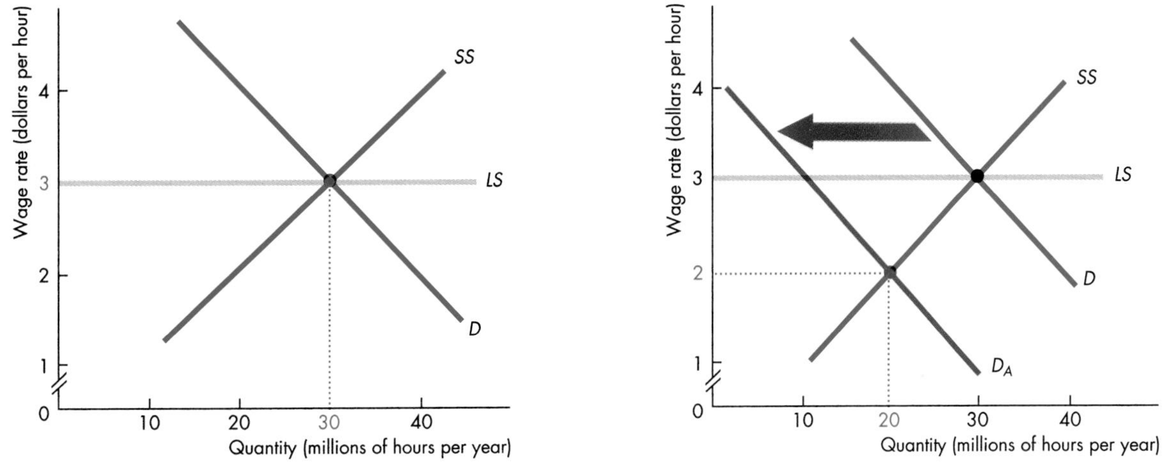

(a) Before invention

(b) After invention

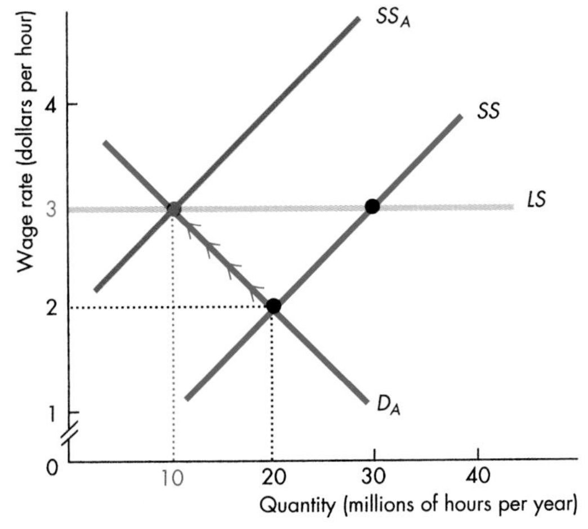

(c) Long-run adjustment

A market for unskilled labor is in equilibrium (part a) at a wage rate of $3 an hour with 30 million hours of labor a year being traded. The short-run supply curve (*SS*) slopes upward because employers have to pay a higher wage to get more hours out of a given number of workers. The long-run supply curve (*LS*) is perfectly elastic because workers will eventually enter this labor market if the wage rate is above $3 an hour or leave it if the wage rate is below $3 an hour. The invention of a labor-saving machine shifts the demand curve from *D* to D_A (part b). The wage rate falls to $2 an hour and employment falls to 20 million hours a year. With the lower wage, workers begin to leave this market to undertake training for other types of work. As they do so, the short-run supply curve shifts to SS_A (part c). As the supply curve shifts, the wage rate gradually increases and the employment level decreases. Ultimately, wages return to $3 an hour and employment falls to 10 million hours a year.

A Black Market for Personal Computers

High Tech Leak: Astute Poles Purchase Capitalist Computers, Sell Them to the State

What would a Polish bus conductor do if he had a couple of IBM-compatible mother boards, each with a 16-MHz 386 processor, 2MB of RAM, an FDD/HDD controller and a TEAC 360KB floppy disk drive?

Sell them to buy a taxi.

What would a Polish taxi driver do with the above, fitted out with EGA cards, enhanced keyboards and 40MB SEAGATE hard disks?

Sell them to build a house.

Capitalist computers have become hot items for nimble Polish entrepreneurs seeking quick profits in the complicated world of embargoes, export licenses, and black-market currencies. A quick computer killing takes just a few fancy steps, a bribe or two and a buyer willing to pay in Polish zlotys at triple the dollar's black market rate.

Thus, a $2,000 computer will cost two million zlotys (the price of those dollars in the black market) and sell here for six million. The seller pays a tax of one million zlotys and comes away three million zlotys richer. It takes most Poles 10 years to make that much.

Desperate Desire

But who in Poland would be fool enough to pay three times the black-market rate for a personal computer? It would have to be a customer with a desperate desire to enter the high-tech age, plenty of zlotys, and not a dollar to spare. A customer, in short, like the Polish state.

"The government gets the computers free," says Marek Kaluzny, a software writer who hands out the perfumed business cards of a Taiwanese clone maker. "It just prints zlotys." Its shrewder citizens then parlay that paper into more computers. Says a man who buys PCs for the state: "It's big money. Everybody benefits."

This isn't quite what the industrial democracies had in mind when they embargoed high-technology exports to the Soviet bloc. Nor is it what the Soviet bloc has in mind now that it is setting out to build PCs of its own.

Relatives' Dollars

Always on the lookout for loopholes, the Poles have become the East bloc's biggest PC traders, thanks largely to the greenbacks provided by their Polish-American relatives. One Taiwan company shipped 1,500 machines to Poland in 1986. Amstrad computers from Britain account for 70% of the air freight between London and Warsaw. On Warsaw airport's import dock, close to 100 PCs pile up daily.

A Polish dealer figures that tens of thousands arrive in a year. "We are talking," he says, "about tens of millions of dollars." Since the boom began in 1985, PC prices have actually fallen in Poland. The cause isn't a drop in demand but a surge of supply.

All of which has made life easier in the Warsaw University physics department. Private middlemen have delivered 50 powerful PCs from Taiwan to Roman Szwed (a young physicist), who is in the market for 50 more.

"I'd prefer to buy direct from the U.S.," he says, standing in the doorway of the department's basement computer center, "but it's my duty to keep things going in our little environment."

Work stations fill the room before him, each with a PC and a number-crunching researcher. Beyond them, in a room behind a glass wall, stands a big mainframe from Czechoslovakia. The room is dark. Nobody goes in there anymore.

***The Wall Street Journal*, January 7, 1988**

By Barry Newman, staff reporter

The Essence of the Story

- The industrial countries that produce PCs have placed an embargo on the shipment of computers to the Soviet Union and Eastern European countries such as Poland.
- There is a large demand for PCs in Poland, much of it by the state and the universities.
- Computers are illegally shipped into Poland on a very large scale and sold on a black market.
- A PC that costs $2000 in the United States sells for $6000 on the Polish black market, but since 1985 the price has fallen.
- Scientists and others make heavy use of their PCs and have stopped using inferior mainframe computers made in Czechoslovakia.

Background and Analysis

- The black market for computers in Poland is illustrated in the figure. The demand curve for PCs is labeled *D*. The light blue horizontal supply curve labeled S_N is the (assumed) supply curve of PCs in Poland without restrictions.
- If no PCs get into Poland, there will be a large unsatisfied demand. People will be willing to pay a much higher price than the $2000 that PCs cost in the United States.
- Finding ways around embargoes takes time and effort and is also risky. But it is profitable. Black-market traders, evading the embargo, had a supply curve in 1985 labeled S_{1985}.
- In 1985, the equilibrium price in Poland for PCs was $8000 and the equilibrium quantity traded was 10,000.*
- As more people sought to profit from the illegal trade in PCs, the supply curve shifted to the right so that, by 1988, it was S_{1988}. The price fell and the quantity traded increased.

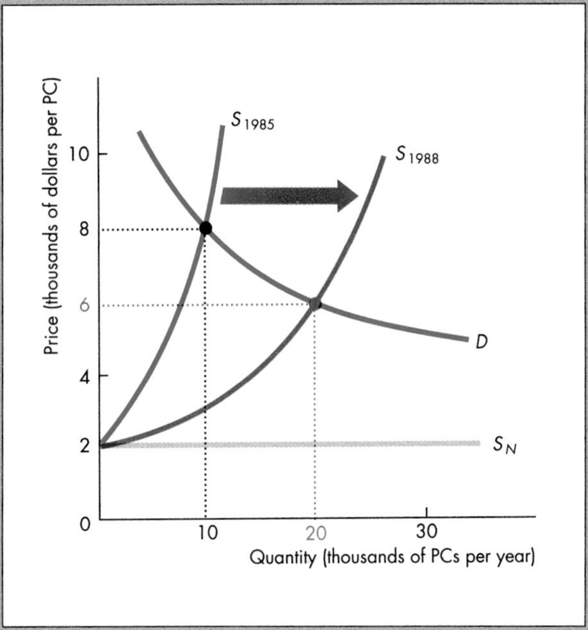

- In 1988, the equilibrium price of PCs was $6000 and the quantity traded was 20,000. (The price of $6000 is the actual price reported in the article. The quantity traded is not specified exactly in the article, but we are told that "tens of thousands arrive in a year.")
- As the world supply of PCs increases, and as the number of supply sources increases, we may predict that the supply curve for PCs in Poland will continue to shift to the right. As a consequence, the price will continue to fall and the quantity traded will continue to increase.

---

*The prices used in this analysis come from the article but the quantities are hypothetical. The article does not contain enough information to locate the positions of the supply curve and the demand curve.

The short-run supply curve shows how the hours of labor supplied by a given number of workers varies as the wage rate varies. To get workers to work longer hours, firms have to offer higher wages. The long-run supply curve shows the relationship between the quantity of labor supplied and the wage rate when the number of workers in the market varies. The number of people in this unskilled labor market depends on the wage in this market compared with other opportunities. If the wage is high enough, people will enter this market. If the wage is too low, people will leave this unskilled labor market and seek training to enter a different, more skilled market. The long-run supply curve tells us the conditions under which workers supply labor in this unskilled market after enough time has passed for people to have acquired new skills and moved to new types of jobs.

The labor market is initially in equilibrium at a wage rate of \$3 an hour and with 30 million hours of labor being supplied. We're now going to analyze what happens in the labor market if the demand for this particular type of labor falls as a result of the invention of some labor-saving technology. Figure 6.3(b) shows the short-run effects of such a change. The demand curve before the new technology is introduced is D. After the introduction of the new technology, the demand curve shifts to the left, to D_A. The wage rate falls to \$2 an hour and the quantity of labor employed falls to 20 million hours. This short-run effect on wages and employment is not the end of the story.

People who are now earning only \$2 an hour look around for other opportunities. They see, for example, that the new labor-saving equipment doesn't always work properly and, when it breaks down, it is maintained by more highly paid, highly skilled workers. There are many other jobs (in markets for other types of skills) paying higher wages than \$2 an hour. One by one, workers decide to quit this particular market for unskilled labor. They go back to school or they take jobs that pay less but offer on-the-job training. As a result of these decisions, the short-run supply curve begins to shift to the left.

Figure 6.3(c) shows the long-run adjustment. As the short-run supply curve shifts to the left, it intersects the demand curve D_A at higher wage rates and lower levels of employment. In the long run, the short-run supply curve will have shifted all the way to SS_A. At this point, the wage has returned to \$3 an hour, and the level of employment has fallen to 10 million hours.

Sometimes, the adjustment process that we have just described will take place quickly. At other times, it will be a long drawn-out affair. If the adjustment process is long and drawn out and wages remain low for a prolonged period, there will be a temptation on the part of government to intervene in the market, setting a minimum wage to protect the incomes of the lowest-paid workers. What are the effects of imposing a minimum wage?

The Minimum Wage

Suppose that when the demand for labor decreases from D to D_A, as illustrated in Fig. 6.3(b), and the wage falls to \$2 an hour, the government passes a minimum wage law. A **minimum wage law** is a regulation that makes trading labor below a specified wage illegal. In particular, suppose that the government declares that the minimum wage is \$3 an hour. What are the effects of this law?

The answer can be found by studying Fig. 6.4. In that figure, the minimum wage is shown as the horizontal red line labeled "Minimum wage." At the minimum wage, only 10 million hours of labor are demanded (point *a*). But there are 30 million hours of labor available at that wage (point *b*). Because the number of hours demanded is less than the number of hours supplied, 20 million hours of available labor go unemployed.

What are the workers doing with their unemployed hours? They are looking for work. It pays to spend a lot of time searching for work. With only 10 million hours of labor being employed, there are many people willing to supply their labor for wages much lower than the minimum wage. In fact, the ten-millionth hour of labor will be supplied for as little as \$1. How do we know that there are people willing to work for as little as \$1 an hour?

Look again at Fig. 6.4. As you can see, when there are only 10 million hours of work available, the lowest wage at which workers will supply that ten-millionth hour—read off from the supply curve—is \$1. Someone who manages to find a job will earn \$3 an hour—\$2 an hour more than the lowest wage at which someone is willing to work.

Figure 6.4 The Minimum Wage and Unemployment

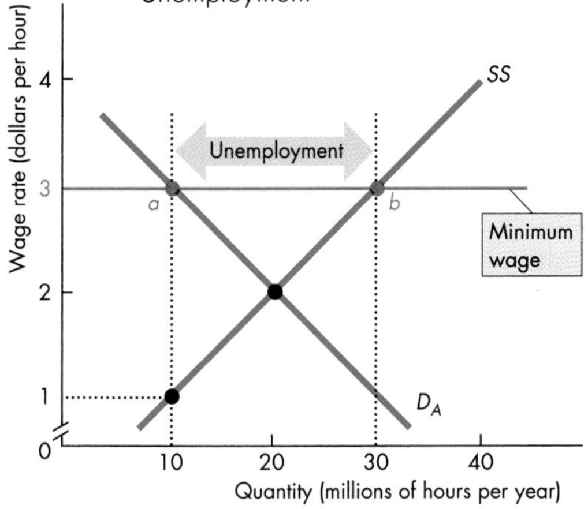

The demand curve for labor is D_A and the supply curve is *SS*. In an unregulated market, the wage rate is $2 an hour and 20 million hours of labor a year are employed. If a minimum wage of $3 an hour is imposed, only 10 million hours of labor are hired but 30 million hours are available. This results in unemployment—*ab*—of 20 million hours of labor a year. With only 10 million hours of labor being demanded, workers will willingly supply that ten millionth hour for $1. It will pay such suppliers to spend the difference between the minimum wage and the wage for which they are willing to work—$2 an hour—in time and effort looking for a job.

It pays the unemployed, therefore, to spend a considerable amount of time and effort looking for work. Even though only 10 million hours of labor actually find employment, each person will spend time and effort searching for one of the scarce jobs.

The severity of the unemployment generated by a minimum wage depends on the demand and supply for labor. You can see that if the supply curve were farther to the left, unemployment would be less. In fact, if the supply curve cut the demand curve at point *a,* the minimum wage would be the same as the unregulated wage. In such a situation, there would be no unemployment. Also, the farther to the right is the demand for labor, the smaller is the amount of unemployment. If the demand curve cut the supply curve at point *b*, then, again, the minimum wage would be the same as the unregulated wage, and there would be no unemployment.

The Minimum Wage in Reality

The **Fair Labor Standards Act** makes it illegal to hire an adult worker for less than $3.35 an hour. Economists are not in agreement on the effects of the minimum wage or on how much unemployment it causes. However, they do agree that minimum wages bite hardest on the unskilled. Since there is a preponderance of unskilled workers among the young—the young have had less opportunity to obtain work experience and acquire skills—we would expect the minimum wage to cause more unemployment among young workers than among older workers. And that is exactly what happens. The unemployment for teenagers is more than twice the average rate. Although there are many factors other than the minimum wage influencing unemployment among young people, it is almost certainly the case that part of the higher unemployment among the young arises from the impact of minimum wage laws.

REVIEW

Governments intend minimum wages to protect the incomes of the lowest paid. But a minimum wage lowers the quantity of labor demanded and hired. Some people will want to work, but they will be unemployed and will spend time searching for work. The young and the unskilled are hit hardest by the minimum wage. ■

We have now studied how changes in either supply or demand bring about changes—in the short run and the long run—in price and in the quantity traded. But the examples that we've studied are of shocks that come like bolts from the blue—an earthquake lowers the supply of housing or a technological change lowers the demand for unskilled labor. But many changes in demand and supply are predictable. How do predictable changes in demand and supply affect prices and quantities traded? And how do people go about making predictions? Let's now study these questions.

Anticipating the Future

Producers are especially concerned about two uncertainties: the price at which they will be able to sell their product and the conditions affecting how much of their product will be produced. Farmers provide a clear illustration of the importance of these two uncertainties. First, when farmers decide how many acres of corn to plant, they do not know the price at which the corn will be sold. Knowing the price of corn today does not help them make decisions about how much seed to sow today. Today's planting becomes tomorrow's crop, and so tomorrow's price determines how much revenue farmers get from today's sowing decisions. Second, when farmers plant corn, they do not know what the growing conditions will turn out to be. Conditions may be excellent, producing a high yield and a bumper crop, or conditions such as drought and inadequate sunshine may lead to a low crop yield and disaster.

Uncertainty about the future price of a good can arise from uncertainty about its future demand or its future supply. We have just considered some uncertainties about supply. There are also many uncertainties about demand. We know that demand for a good depends on the prices of its substitutes and complements, income, population, and tastes. Demand varies as a result of fluctuations in all these influences on buyers' plans. Since these influences *do* fluctuate and are impossible to predict exactly, the level of future demand is always uncertain.

Uncertainties about future supply and demand also make future prices uncertain. But producers must make decisions today even though they do not know the price at which their output will be sold. In making such decisions, they have no choice but to rely on a forecast of the future price.

The higher the expected price, the greater is the amount that each producer will supply. The total market supply combines the supplies of all producers and it too depends on the expected future price. In Fig. 6.5, the market supply curve (*ES*) shows how the quantity supplied one year in the future responds to producers' current expectations or forecasts of the price of a good—not to next year's price of that good. To determine what actions to take today to influence the quantity supplied next year, producers must first form expectations of next year's price. How do they do that?

Figure 6.5 Supply and Expected Prices

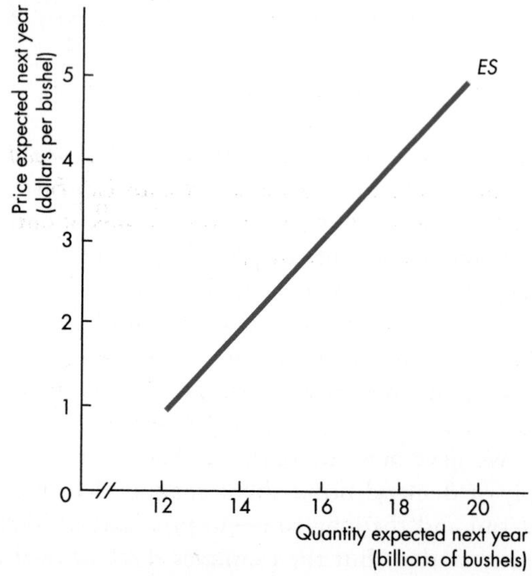

When the quantity supplied depends on past production decisions, quantity supplied depends on the price expected at the time the production decision is made rather than on the actual price. Expected supply is represented by the supply curve *ES*. The expected future quantity supplied rises as the expected future price rises.

Making Forecasts

The time and effort devoted to making forecasts varies considerably from one individual to another. Most people devote hardly any time to this activity at all. Instead, they follow rules of thumb that, most of the time, seem to work well. But in important matters that directly affect their incomes, people will try to do better than that. One way of doing better is to simply imitate the actions of others who have a track record of success. Another way of doing better is to buy forecasts from specialists. A large number of forecasting agencies exist—from investment advisors and stock and commodity brokers to professional economic forecasting agencies. Such agencies have a strong incentive to make their forecasts correct, at least on the average.

The particular methods used to make forecasts are, of course, highly diverse, but our task is not to describe all of the actual methods used to make forecasts. Instead, our task is to build a model of forecasting. To build such a model, we use the fundamental assumption of economics—the assumption that people are seeking to get the most they can out of their scarce resources. In pursuit of that goal, forecasts will be correct on the average and forecasting errors will be as small as possible. If any information is available that can improve a forecast, that information will be used. The forecast that uses all of the relevant information available about past and present events and that has the least possible error is called a **rational expectation.**

How does an economist go about calculating a rational expectation? The answer is by using an economic model. The economic model that explains prices is the model of demand and supply. Therefore, we use the demand and supply model to forecast prices—to calculate a rational expectation of a future price. We know that the point at which next year's demand curve intersects next year's supply curve determines next year's price. But until next year arrives, we don't know where those demand and supply curves will be located. However, we do know the factors that determine their position and by forecasting those factors we can forecast next year's demand and supply curves and forecast their point of intersection—next year's price. Let's work out a rational expectation of the future price of corn.

Expected Demand and Expected Supply Our goal is to make the best forecast we can of the future price of corn. To make that forecast, we must forecast the positions of next year's demand and supply curves for corn. We learned earlier that the position of the demand curve for a good depends on the prices of its substitutes and complements, income, population, and tastes. The expected position of a demand curve, therefore, depends on the expected values of all these variables. In order to form an expectation about the future position of the demand curve of corn, it is necessary to forecast the future prices of corn's substitutes and complements, of income, of population, and of current trends that might influence tastes. By taking into account every conceivable piece of available information that helps forecast such variables, farmers—or the specialists from whom farmers buy forecasts—can form a rational expectation of next year's demand for corn.

We also learned earlier that the position of the supply curve of a good depends on the prices of its substitutes and complements in production, the prices of the resources used to produce the good, and technology. An important part of the technology of farming is the biological process that converts seed to crop. That process, of course, depends in an important way on the temperature, the amount of sunshine, and the amount of rain. Expected supply depends on the expected values of all these variables. In order to form an expectation about the future supply of corn it is necessary to forecast the future prices of corn's substitutes and complements in production, the prices of the resources used to produce the corn (the wages of farm workers and the prices of seed and fertilizers) as well as any current trends in weather patterns that might influence growing conditions. By taking into account every available piece of information that helps forecast such variables, people can form a rational expectation of the next year's corn supply.

Calculating a Rational Expectation A rational expectation of next year's price of corn can be formed by bringing together expectations about next year's demand and supply. Figure 6.6 illustrates how to accomplish this. The quantities measured on the two axes are expectations of next year's price and quantity. The curve labeled *ED* is the best forecast available of next year's demand for corn. The curve labeled *ES* is the best forecast available of next year's supply of corn.

What do people expect the price of corn to be next year? They expect it to be $3 a bushel. That is the price at which expected quantity demanded equals the expected quantity supplied. People also can forecast next year's quantity traded. That forecast is 16 billion bushels. The price of $3 a bushel is the rational expectation of next year's price of corn. It is the forecasted price based on all the available relevant information. Producers use that forecast of the price to decide how many acres of corn to plant.

Figure 6.6 A Rational Expectation of Price

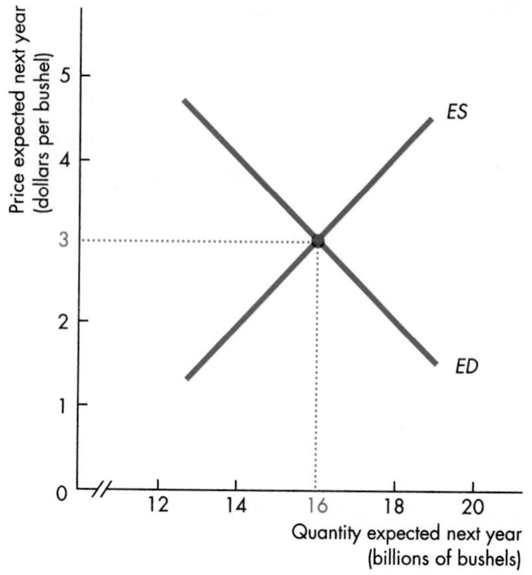

Since actual price is determined by actual supply and demand, expected price is determined by expected supply and expected demand. The point where expected demand (*ED*) cuts expected supply (*ES*) determines the rational expectation of the price ($3 a bushel) and quantity traded (16 billion bushels).

REVIEW

The rational expectation of a future price is the best forecast that can be made using all the available information. It is the price at which the expected quantity demanded equals the expected quantity supplied. Expected demand and expected supply are themselves the best forecasts available of the positions of the supply and demand curves. ■

We have seen how people form a rational expectation of a future price. What determines the actual future price?

Demand Fluctuations

Producers make the best forecast they can of future demand and future price—but almost certainly they will turn out to be wrong. The future hardly ever turns out to be exactly as expected. Let's suppose that the demand for corn fluctuates between a high level (D_1) and a low level (D_0) but that on the average it is *ED* (expected demand). These demand curves are shown in Fig. 6.7(a). Let's also suppose that it is impossible to forecast the fluctuations in demand. The best that people can do in forecasting demand is to suppose that demand will be at its average level. The rational expectation of this year's demand for corn is the demand curve *ED*. But this expectation was made last year. The curves D_0 and D_1 are possible actual demand curves for the current year.

We will be able to understand the effects of fluctuations in demand if we focus exclusively on that source of future uncertainty. To do that, let's suppose just for the moment that there is no uncertainty about supply. Expecting the price next year to be $3 a bushel, farmers plant enough acres of corn for the actual output to equal the actual output they expected—16 billion bushels. Growing conditions turn out to be exactly the same as they forecasted, so not only did they plan to produce 16 billion bushels, they actually achieve that plan. Since the quantity of corn actually produced is 16 billion bushels, the momentary supply curve of corn (*MS*) is completely inelastic.

Price Determination If demand turns out to be exactly as expected, the price of corn this year will be exactly the same as was forecasted a year ago. That is, with this year's demand turning out to be *ED* and with this year's momentary supply curve *MS*, the quantity demanded equals the quantity supplied at a price of $3 a bushel—exactly the same price that was forecasted a year ago and shown in Fig. 6.6.

Let's now look at the two other cases where demand is either higher or lower than expected, both shown in Fig. 6.7(a). First, suppose that demand is D_1. In this case, demand and momentary supply intersect at a price of $5 a bushel. When demand is higher than expected, the price turns out to be higher than it was forecasted to be. If demand is D_0, then the demand and momentary supply curves intersect at a price of $1 a bushel. When demand is lower than expected, the price turns out to be lower than it was forecasted to be.

It is interesting to note that suppliers are disappointed with the outcome whenever demand turns out to be different from its expected level. If

Figure 6.7 The Effects of Temporary Fluctuations in Demand

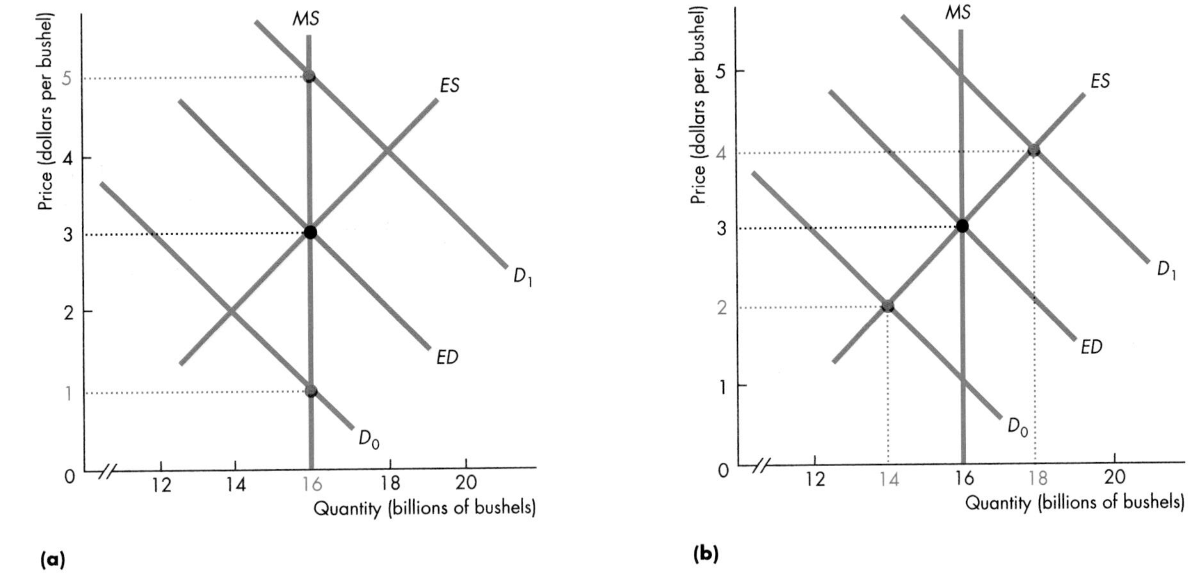

Demand fluctuates between D_0 and D_1, but on the average, demand is as expected, *ED*. Expected supply is *ES*. The rational expectation of the price is \$3 a bushel. Producers plan to produce 16 billion bushels. Actual supply equals planned supply and the momentary supply curve is *MS*. As demand fluctuates, the price fluctuates. In part (a), when demand is D_0, the price falls to \$1 a bushel. When demand is D_1, the price rises to \$5 a bushel. In part (b), if suppliers could anticipate the demand fluctuations correctly, the quantity supplied would fluctuate along curve *ES* and price fluctuations would be less severe than those that actually occur. But because the future is uncertain, suppliers can do no better than produce 16 billion bushels and put up with the price fluctuations that result.

demand is D_1, then suppliers will regret that they did not plant a bigger acreage to produce a bigger quantity. They would have liked, in this case, to have produced 18 billion bushels and sold them for \$4 a bushel, as shown in Fig. 6.7(b). This point is where the demand curve D_1 intersects the expected supply curve *ES*. That is, if they could have correctly forecasted demand at D_1, they would have forecasted a price of \$4 a bushel and produced 18 billion bushels. At a price of \$5 a bushel, farmers have produced less than they would have liked to produce. But bygones are bygones. They couldn't do any better than forecast demand at *ED* and so, at the time they made their planting decision, they made the correct decision.

If demand turns out to be D_0, then suppliers will regret that they did not plant a smaller acreage which would have produced 14 billion bushels of corn and sold at \$2 a bushel, in Fig. 6.7(b). This quantity and price are at the point where the demand curve D_0 intersects the expected supply curve *ES*. That is, if farmers could have correctly forecasted demand at D_0, they would have forecasted a price of \$2 a bushel and planted sufficient acres to grow 14 billion bushels. At a price of \$1 a bushel, farmers would have liked to produce less than they did. Again, bygones are bygones. They did the best they could at the time they had to make their decisions.

Supply Fluctuations

Let's now study the effects of supply fluctuations on price and the quantity traded. We'll understand these effects more clearly if we isolate supply as the only source of uncertainty. To do this, let's suppose

Figure 6.8 The Effects of Temporary Fluctuations in Supply

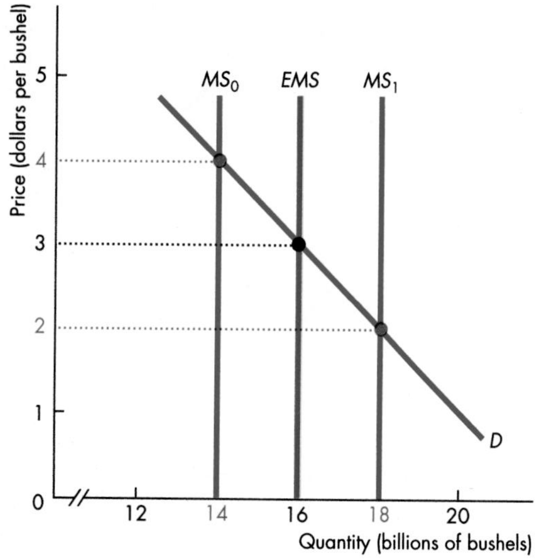

Growing conditions fluctuate and momentary supply fluctuates between MS_0 and MS_1. Expected momentary supply is *EMS*. Demand is expected to be and actually turns out to be *D*. The rational expectation of the price is $3 a bushel. When supply is low (MS_0), the quantity produced falls to 14 billion bushels and the price rises to $4 a bushel. When supply is high, (MS_1), the quantity produced increases to 18 billion bushels and the price falls to $2 a bushel.

that demand is forecasted correctly. The actual demand curve turns out to be the same one that was expected. What is uncertain now is the size of the crop.

There are three possibilities regarding growing conditions: First, they may turn out to be excellent, resulting in a bumper crop. Although ideal growing conditions do sometimes occur, farmers cannot forecast them. When they do happen, farmers grow more corn than they originally planned or expected. Second, growing conditions may turn out to be unusually poor, resulting in a crop yield much lower than expected. Third, growing conditions may turn out to be average, resulting in a crop yield equal to what was expected.

Figure 6.8 illustrates how each of these situations affects price. The demand curve *D* is the same as the demand curve that was forecasted a year ago. The figure contains three momentary supply curves: the curve *EMS* arises if growing conditions are average; the curve MS_0 arises if there is a drought and a low crop yield results; the curve MS_1 describes the situation when excellent growing conditions occur and a bumper crop results.

Price Determination The price is determined at the point of intersection of the momentary supply curve and the demand curve. In a drought, that price will be $4 a bushel, with a bumper crop it will be $2 a bushel, and, on the average, when expectations are correct, it will be $3 a bushel.

Notice that when supply is correctly forecasted, the actual price equals the forecasted price. If supply turns out to be lower than its forecasted level, the price is higher than it was forecasted to be; if supply turns out to be higher than its forecasted level, the price is lower than forecasted.

In the examples that we've just worked through, momentary supply is perfectly inelastic, so price fluctuations have to do all of the work to achieve an equilibrium. What happens to these price fluctuations if corn is stored in inventories? We will now spend a bit of time examining this common situation.

*Inventories

Many goods, including a wide variety of agricultural products, can be stored. These inventories provide a cushion between production and consumption. If demand increases or if production decreases, goods can be sold from inventory; if demand decreases or if production increases, goods can be put into inventory.

Inventory holders speculate. They try to buy at a low price and sell at a high price. That is, they try to buy goods and put them into inventory when the price is low, and sell them from inventory when the price is high. Their aim is to make a profit equal to the difference between their buying price and selling price, minus the cost of storage.[5]

*This section is more demanding and may be omitted.

[5]We will suppose that the cost of storage is so small that we can ignore it. This assumption, though not essential, enables us to see more sharply the effects of inventory holders' decisions on prices.

But how do inventory holders know when to buy and when to sell? How do they know whether the price is high or low? To decide whether a price is high or low, and to make their buying and selling decisions, inventory holders have to forecast future prices. To do this, they form a rational expectation of the future price. If the price is above its expected future level, they sell goods from inventory. If the price is below its expected future level, they buy goods to put into inventory.

Selling goods from inventory is equivalent to increasing supply. Buying goods to put into inventory is equivalent to decreasing supply. If the price is one penny above the inventory holder's rational expectation, goods will be supplied from inventory. If the price is one penny below the inventory holder's rational expectation, the supply available to the market will be reduced as the inventory holder puts goods into inventory. This behavior by the inventory holder makes the supply curve perfectly elastic at the inventory holder's rational expectation of the price.

In a market that has inventories, we need to distinguish the producer's supply, the inventory holder's supply, and the market supply. Let's now work out what happens to the price and quantity traded when there are unexpected fluctuations in demand and in producers' supply in a market in which inventories are held. We'll study demand fluctuations first.

Demand Fluctuations

To make things concrete, we'll continue to study the market for corn. Figure 6.9(a) illustrates the analysis of demand fluctuations. We'll suppose, for the moment, that the producer's supply of corn is perfectly inelastic and determined by the momentary supply curve *MS* at 16 billion bushels. The rational expectation of the price level is $3 a bushel. Therefore, the inventory holders' supply curve *SI*, highlighted in red, is perfectly elastic at that price. Demand fluctuates between D_1 and D_0.

In the absence of inventories, the quantity traded stays fixed at 16 billion bushels and the price fluctuates to maintain equality between the quantity demanded and the fixed quantity supplied. But things turn out very differently when there are inventory holders. If demand is D_0 (a low level of demand), the quantity bought by consumers falls to 14 billion bushels. Producers still supply 16 billion bushels. The difference between the quantity supplied by producers and the quantity demanded by consumers is taken off the market and put into inventory. Thus inventories increase, in this example by 2 billion bushels. If the demand is high (D_1), consumers buy 18 billion bushels. Farmers produce 16 billion bushels and the additional 2 billion bushels come from inventory. Demand fluctuations lead to fluctuations in the quantity bought and to fluctuations in the size of inventory holdings, but the price stays constant at the inventory holder's rational expectation of its future level. The expectation of the future price becomes the actual price.

Now let's consider fluctuations in supply.

Supply Fluctuations

Supply fluctuations are analyzed in Fig. 6.9(b). Here the demand curve is expected to be and actually turns out to be *D*. The rational expectation of the price level is $3 again, so inventory holders' supply curve (*SI*) is perfectly elastic at that price. The producers' momentary supply now fluctuates between MS_0 and MS_1. Recall that without inventories, when supply fluctuates, the price and the quantity traded fluctuate, the price falling when supply increases and rising when supply decreases.

With inventories, there are no price fluctuations. When supply is low (at MS_0), the quantity supplied by producers falls to 14 billion bushels. The quantity bought remains 16 billion bushels and inventory holders supply the 2 billion bushels that make up the difference. When producers' supply is high (at MS_1), producers sell 18 billion bushels. Consumers continue to buy 16 billion bushels and 2 billion bushels are taken into inventory. Again, the actual price is equal to the inventory holders' expectations of the future price.

The model of a market with inventories that we have reviewed is the simplest possible. It serves to show how inventories and inventory holders' expectations about future prices reduce price fluctuations. In the above example, the price fluctuations are entirely eliminated. When there are costs of carrying inventories and when inventories become almost depleted, some price fluctuations do occur, but these fluctuations are much smaller then those occurring in a market without inventories.

People's holdings of stock are similiar to holdings of inventories. They are also a good example of an inventory that in fact does have a zero (or almost zero) cost of storage—you can store shares

Figure 6.9 How Inventories Limit Price Changes: When Demand Fluctuates

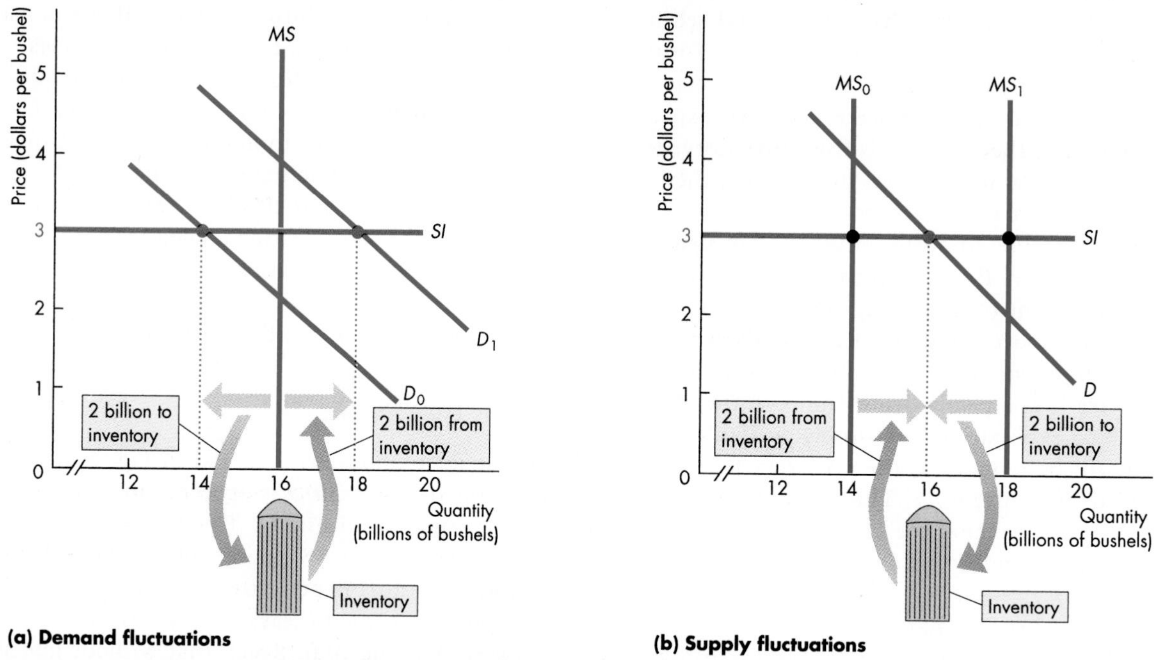

The rational expectation of the price is $3 a bushel. Inventory holders supply from inventory if the price rises above $3 and take goods into inventory if the price falls below $3. The inventory holders' supply curve is the perfectly elastic curve *SI* at the rationally expected price of $3 a bushel. When demand fluctuates between D_0 and D_1, the price stays constant at $3 a bushel, as shown in part (a). When demand is low (at D_0), production exceeds consumers' purchases by 2 billion bushels and that amount is taken into inventory. When demand is high (at D_1), consumers buy more than producers are supplying and the difference is made up from inventories. Fluctuations in supply lead to fluctuations in the producers' momentary supply curve between MS_0 and MS_1, as shown in part (b). The price stays constant at $3 a bushel and consumers buy a constant 16 billion bushels. When supply falls to 14 billion bushels, 2 billion bushels are supplied from inventory. When supply increases to 18 billion bushels, 2 billion bushels are taken into inventory.

of IBM or AT&T at virtually zero cost. Do inventories of stocks work like inventories of corn to reduce the range of price fluctuations? And if they do, why do the prices on the stock market fluctuate so dramatically?

The Stock Market

The stock market is the market on which the stocks of corporations are traded. Fig. 6.10 illustrates how a stock price is determined. The horizontal axis measures the quantity expected next period. The vertical axis measures the price expected next period and the actual price this period. This period's expectations of next period's demand and supply curves are shown as *ED* and *ES*. The intersection point of those curves determines the rational expectation of next period's price, *EP*. If the actual price rose by a penny above that expected price, people would supply stocks from their inventories. If the price fell to a penny below that price, people would put stocks into their inventory. Thus the supply of stocks, taking into account inventory behavior, is the perfectly elastic supply curve *SI* at the price level that is rationally expected for next period. The actual price (*P*) is equal to the expected price (*EP*). No matter how the demand and supply curves actually fluctuate, as long as the expected demand and expected supply curves are those shown in the figure, inventory holders supply from inventory or take stock into inventory and, by so doing, keep the price at its expected level.

We have seen that a rational expectation is an expectation that uses all the available information that is relevant for forecasting a future price. Since the actual stock price is equal to the rational expectation of the future stock price, that stock price also embodies all the relevant information that is available. A market in which the actual price embodies all currently available relevant information is called an **efficient market.** In an efficient market, it is impossible to forecast changes in price. Why? If your forecast is that the price is going to rise next period, you will buy now (since the price is low today compared with what you predicted it is going to be in the future). Your action of buying today acts like an increase in demand today and increases today's price. It's true that your action—the action of a single trader—is not going to make much difference to a huge market like the New York Stock Exchange. But if traders in general expect a higher price next period and they all act today on the basis of that expectation, then today's price will rise. It will keep on rising until it reaches the expected future price. For only at that price do traders see no profit in buying more stock today.

There is an apparent paradox about efficient markets. Markets are efficient because people try to make a profit. They seek a profit by buying at a low price and selling at a high price. But the very act of buying and selling to make a profit means that the market price moves to its expected future value. Having done that, no one, not even those who are seeking to profit, can *predictably* make a profit. Every profit opportunity seen by a trader leads to an action that produces a price change that removes the profit opportunity for others.

Thus an efficient market has two features:

- Its price equals the expected future price and embodies all the available information
- There are no forecastable profit opportunities available

The key thing to understand about an efficient market such as the stock market is that if something can be anticipated, it will be and the anticipation will be acted upon.

Figure 6.10 The Stock Market

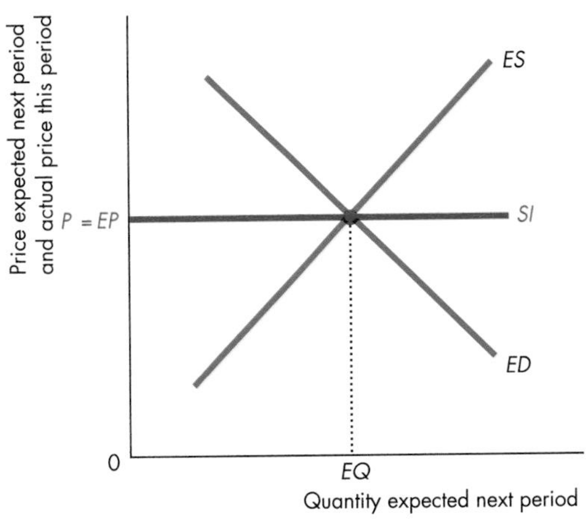

Holders of stocks behave like inventory holders. They form a rational expectation of the future price of a stock (*EP*) at the point of intersection of the expected demand curve (*ED*) and the expected supply curve (*ES*). If the price is a penny above their expectation of the future price, stockholders sell. If the price is a penny below their expectation of the future price, they buy. These transactions keep the actual price (*P*) equal to the expected future price. Such a market is called an efficient market. In an efficient market, it is not possible to forecast a future price change and profit from that forecast. A foreseen price change is acted on immediately, and the actual price adjusts to eliminate the profit opportunity.

Volatility in Stock Prices

If the price of a stock is always equal to its expected future price, why is the stock market so volatile? The answer must be that expectations themselves are subject to fluctuation. Expectations depend on the information available. As new information becomes available, stock traders form new expectations about the future state of the economy and in turn new expectations of future stock prices. Expectations about the economy are of crucial importance: Is the economy going to enjoy sustained rapid expansion? Or is it going to suffer a recession? The macroeconomic events, such as expansion and recession, influence stock prices. Individual stock prices are influenced by technological change, which in turn influences the supply of and demand for particular goods and services. Since new information is being accumulated daily about all these

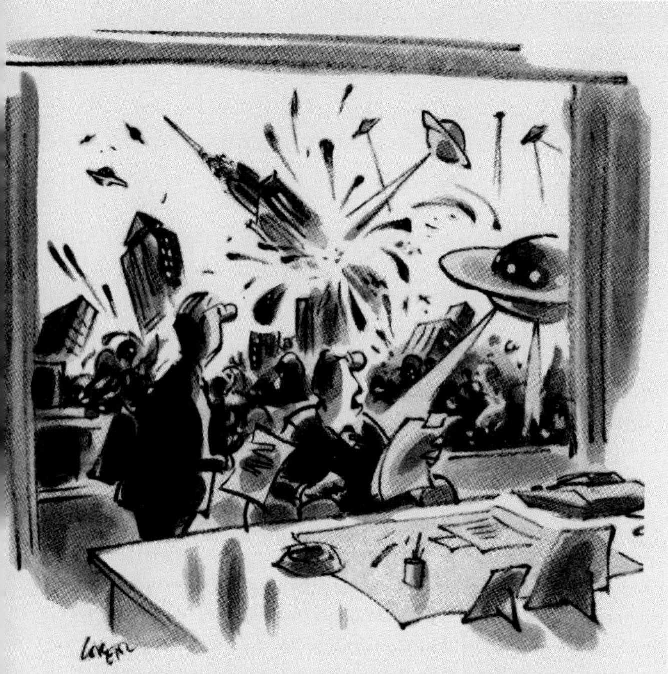

"Drat! I suppose the market has already discounted this, too."

all these matters, expectations about the future price of a stock are constantly being re-evaluated. It is this process of re-evaluation that leads to high volatility in the stock market. As expectations change from being optimistic to pessimistic, the stock market can plunge many percentage points—as it did dramatically on October 19, 1987. On the other hand, a sustained period of increasing optimism can produce a long upswing in stock prices. The five-year run from mid-1982 to mid-1987 is an example of such stock market behavior.[6]

■ We've now completed our study of demand and supply and its applications. You've seen how this powerful model enables us to make predictions about prices and quantities traded and also how it enables us to understand a wide variety of markets and situations.

We're now going to start digging a bit more deeply into people's economic choices, and, in the next section, we'll study the economic choices of households.

[6]We will study the stock market in more detail in Chapter 17.

SUMMARY

Housing Markets and Rent Ceilings

A sudden decrease in the supply of housing shifts the short-run supply curve to the left. Rents increase. In the short run, higher rents bring forth an increase in the quantity of housing supplied as people economize on the available space. In the long run, the higher rents stimulate building activity, resulting in a shift to the right in the short-run supply curve. Through this process, rents gradually decrease, and the quantity of housing available gradually increases.

If a rent ceiling prevents rents from increasing, the quantity of housing supplied is lower, in both the short run and the long run, than it would be in an unregulated market. There is no inducement to economize on space in the short run and no incentive to build new houses and apartments in the long run. Equilibrium is achieved by people spending time searching for housing. The total cost of housing, including the value of the time spent searching, exceeds the cost in an unregulated market. (pp. 127–132)

The Labor Market and Minimum Wage Regulation

A decrease in the demand for unskilled labor lowers wages and reduces employment in the short run. Low wages encourage people to quit a particular market and to acquire skills and seek different, more highly paid work. As they do so, the short run supply curve for unskilled labor shifts to the left. As it does so, it intersects the demand curve at higher wages and lower levels of employment. Eventually, the wage will return to its previous level but at a much lower employment level.

If the government imposes a minimum wage, a decrease in the demand for labor will result in an increase in unemployment and an increase in the amount of time spent searching for a job. Minimum wages bite hardest on people having the fewest skills and such workers tend to be young persons. The unemployment rate among young people is more than twice the average rate. (pp. 133–137)

Anticipating the Future

Producers have to make decisions about how much of a good to supply before they know the price at which they can sell it. In order to make supply decisions, producers form expectations about future prices. There is uncertainty about both demand and supply.

Producers form rational expectations about future prices based on their forecasts of future demand and supply. The actual price fluctuates around its expected level. Higher-than-expected demand produces a higher-than-expected price. Higher-than-expected supply produces a lower-than-expected price. (pp. 138–142)

Inventories

Goods that can be stored in inventory have smaller price flucutations than those that cannot be stored. If demand or supply fluctuate, such goods can be put into or taken out of inventory. When goods are put into inventory, the supply to the market is reduced; when goods are taken out of inventory, the supply to the market is increased. Inventory holders try to buy at a low price and sell at a high price. To do so, they forecast the future price—they make a rational expectation—and sell when the price is above that expectation and buy when it is below it. Inventory holders' supply curves are perfectly elastic at their expected price (if we ignore the costs of holding inventories).

Actual prices are determined by inventory holders' rational expectations. Inventories fluctuate in response to fluctuations in demand and in producers' supply.

A rational expectation embodies all relevant information that is available. In a market in which the price equals its rational expectation, that price embodies all relevant information. Such a market is called an efficient market. Since the actual price equals the expected price, no systematic profit can be made in such a market. The actual price fluctuates in an efficient market because new information leads to a revision of the rational expectation of the price. (pp. 142–146)

KEY CONCEPTS

Black market, 132
Efficient market, 145
Fair Labor Standards Act, 137
Minimum wage law, 137
Rational expectation, 139
Rent ceiling, 130
Search activity, 131

Key Figures

Figure 6.1	The San Francisco Housing Market in 1906, 129
Figure 6.2	A Rent Ceiling, 131
Figure 6.3	A Market for Unskilled Labor, 133
Figure 6.4	The Minimum Wage and Unemployment, 136
Figure 6.6	A Rational Expectation of Price, 140

REVIEW QUESTIONS

1 Describe what happens to rent and to the quantity of housing available if an earthquake suddenly and unexpectedly reduces the supply of housing. Trace the evolution of the rent and the quantity traded over time.

2 In the situation described in question 1, how

will things be different if a rent ceiling is imposed?

3 Describe what happens to the price and quantity traded in a market in which there is a sudden and unforeseen increase in supply. Trace the evolution of the price and quantity traded in the market over time.

4 Describe what happens to the price and quantity traded in a market in which there is a sudden and unforeseen increase in demand. Trace the evolution of the price and quantity traded in the market over time.

5 Describe what happens to the wage rate and quantity of labor employed when there is a sudden and unforeseen increase in demand for labor. Trace the evolution of the wage rate and employment over time.

6 In the situation described in question 5, how are things different if a minimum wage is introduced?

7 When a government regulation prevents a price from changing, what forces come into operation to achieve an equilibrium?

8 What are the main uncertainties that producers face?

9 What is a rational expectation?

10 How are the price and quantity traded of a good determined in a market in which expectations are rational but the good cannot be stored in inventory?

11 How are the price and quantity traded of a good determined in a market in which expectations are rational but the good can be stored in inventory?

12 What determines the price per share of a corporation's stock? Why will the actual price always equal the expected price?

13 Why is the stock market so volatile?

PROBLEMS

You may find it easier to answer some of these problems by drawing the supply and demand curves on graph paper.

1 You have been given the following information about the market for rental housing in your town:

Rent (dollars per month)	Quantity demanded	Quantity supplied
50	20,000	0
100	15,000	5,000
150	10,000	10,000
200	5,000	15,000
250	2,500	20,000
300	1,500	25,000

a) What is the equilibrium rent?

b) What is the equilibrium quantity of housing traded?

2 Now suppose that a rent ceiling of $100 a month is imposed in the housing market described in problem 1:

a) What is the quantity of housing demanded?

b) What is the quantity of housing supplied?

c) What is the excess quantity of housing demanded?

d) What is the maximum price that demanders are be willing to pay for the last unit available?

e) Suppose that the average wage rate is $5 per hour. How many hours a month will a person spend looking for housing?

3 The demand for and supply of teenage labor are as follows:

Wage rate (dollars per hour)	Hours demanded	Hours supplied
1	3000	1000
2	2500	1500
3	2000	2000
4	1500	2500
5	1000	3000

(continued)

a) What is the equilibrium wage rate?
b) What is the level of employment?
c) What is the level of unemployment?
d) If the government imposes a minimum wage of $2.50 an hour for teenagers, how many hours do teenagers work?
e) If the government imposes a minimum wage of $3.50 an hour for teenagers, what are the employment and unemployment levels?
f) If there is a minimum wage of $3.50 an hour and demand increases by 500 hours, what is the level of unemployment?

4 Why does a minimum wage create unemployment?

5 The following table illustrates three supply curves for train travel:

Price (cents per passenger mile)	**Quantity supplied (billions of passenger miles)** *Momentary*	*Short run*	*Long run*
10	500	300	100
20	500	350	200
30	500	400	300
40	500	450	400
50	500	500	500
60	500	550	600
70	500	600	700
80	500	650	800
90	500	700	900
100	500	750	1000

a) If the price is 50 cents per passenger mile, what is the quantity supplied
   (i) In the long run
   (ii) In the short run
b) Suppose that the price is initially 50 cents but that it then rises to 70 cents. What will be the quantity supplied
   (i) Immediately following the price rise
   (ii) In the short run
   (iii) In the long run

6 Suppose that the supply of train travel is the same as in problem 5. The following table gives two demand schedules—original and new:

Price (cents per passenger mile)	**Quantity demanded (billions of passenger miles)** *Original*	*New*
10	10,000	10,300
20	5,000	5,300
30	2,000	2,300
40	1,000	1,300
50	500	800
60	400	700
70	300	600
80	200	500
90	100	400
100	0	300

a) What is the original equilibrium price and quantity?
b) After the increase in demand has occurred, what is
   (i) The momentary equilibrium price and quantity
   (ii) The short-run equilibrium price and quantity
   (iii) The long-run equilibrium price and quantity

7 The short-run and long-run demand for travel is as follows:

Price (cents per passenger mile)	**Quantity demanded (billions of passenger miles)** *Short run*	*Long run*
10	700	10,000
20	650	5,000
30	600	2,000
40	550	1,000
50	500	500
60	450	400
70	400	300
80	350	200
90	300	100
100	250	0

The supply of train travel is the same as in problem 5.

a) What is the long-run equilibrium price and quantity of train travel?
b) Serious floods destroy one fifth of the train tracks and rolling stock, and supply falls by 100 billion passenger miles. What happens

to the price and the quantity of train travel

(i) In the short run

(ii) In the long run

8 Assume that corn is not stored. The demand for corn and the supply of corn are expected to be as follows:

Price (dollars)	Expected quantity demanded	Expected quantity supplied
1	700	100
2	600	200
3	500	300
4	400	400
5	300	500
6	200	600
7	100	700

a) The average levels of demand and supply are expected to remain constant, and farmers expect no unusual events. What is their rational expectation of the price of corn?

b) A drought occurs and corn production is 100 units less than expected.

(i) What is the actual quantity of corn traded?

(ii) What is the actual price of corn at that quantity?

(iii) How much corn will producers like to have supplied if they had been able to forecast the drought accurately?

c) Growing conditions turn out to be exactly as expected, and actual supply equals average supply. At the same time, a drought in the Soviet Union increases Soviet demand for U.S. corn by 100 units.

(i) What is the actual price of corn?

(ii) What is the actual quantity of corn traded?

(iii) How much corn will U.S. growers like to have produced if they had been able to predict the rise in Soviet demand?

9 Assume that corn *is* stored and that the average demand and supply described in problem 8 still apply.

a) If farmers expect the average levels of demand and supply, and they forecast no unusual events, what is their rational expectation of

(i) The price of corn

(ii) The quantity of corn

b) A drought occurs and corn production is 100 units less than expected.

(i) What is the actual price of corn?

(ii) What is the actual quantity of corn traded?

(iii) How much corn will producers like to have supplied if they had been able to forecast the drought accurately?

(iv) Is corn added to inventories or taken out of inventories? By how much do inventories change?

c) Growing conditions turn out to be exactly as expected, and actual supply equals average supply. At the same time, a drought in the Soviet Union increases Soviet demand for U.S. corn by 100 units.

(i) What is the actual price of corn?

(ii) What is the actual quantity of corn traded?

(iii) How much corn will U.S. growers like to have produced if they had been able to predict the rise in Soviet demand?

(iv) Is corn added to inventories or taken out of inventories? By how much does the inventory level change?

Part 3

Households' Choices

Talking with Gary Becker

Gary Becker has devoted much of his lifetime research to applying the economic way of thinking to problems traditionally studied by sociologists. Professor Becker holds professorships in the departments of economics and sociology at the University of Chicago. Michael Parkin spoke with him about how the economics of human behavior sheds light on social issues.

Professor Becker, can we really hope to explain all human choices by using models that were invented to explain and predict choices about the allocation of income among ... consumer

... decisions in- ... Should I watch television or read a book? Should I go out on a date or drink beer with my friends? Should I get married now or remain single? In all these problems, I'm deciding how to allocate my money, my time, my effort, and my love among various uses. We live in a rich society, but we're not rich in time or energy. We're limited even in money. It's natural to ask, how do people make their choices? Do they make different types of choices when they decide what to watch on television than when they plan how to spend their money in a grocery store? Do they make different types of choices in deciding whether to get divorced or what job they should take? When I try to understand what people are doing, I do not believe that they make rational choices

sometimes and at other times they make irrational choices. It's far more natural to suspect that they use the same criteria in making all their decisions. That's really the economic approach to choice, or what's called the rationality assumption.

"I don't believe that people make rational choices sometimes and irrational choices other times."

Other social sciences consider social issues and problems. How do they differ from economics?

Economics is, uniquely I believe, a way of thinking about social issues. I think it's fair to say that economics is the most powerful of all the social sciences in providing a general organizing theory. In other respects, it's inferior to the other social sciences. Sociologists are more ingenious at conducting surveys. Anthropologists are wonderful observers and recorders of information. Psychologists are good experimenters. So all the social sciences contribute, but economics' main contribution is its analytical framework.

In this economic framework, which principles have been most fruitful for your own work?

I like to stress four principles. First, that people maximize—that's what economists sometimes associate with rational behavior. People try to do the best they can given limited income or time. They want to use their time and resources effectively. Next, people's goals are stable over time and don't shift around. If people's goals changed readily, it would be very hard for us to talk about their behavior. And third, people try to anticipate the adverse consequences of their behavior. If I'm going to smoke, what's going to happen to me? I may still do it, but I try to anticipate the consequences. Finally, at the group level, these different individuals, interact and end up with some aggregate solution, or what we call equilibrium. These are the basic principles. They sound simple, but it's a little more complicated to see all their implications.

What are the achievements of the economics of human behavior? To what questions do we have convincing answers?

We have answers to many questions! For example, if we raise the tax on cigarettes, we can predict with confidence not only that the consumption of cigarettes will decline but by how

much. If the price goes up, people consume less. Even those addicted to cigarettes will consume less. We can predict outcomes in labor markets, and say, for example, that when firms have to provide paid child care, the wages of women will fall. Or perhaps firms will try not to hire women.

I'm willing to say we also know a good deal about less conventional areas. We know that if you increase the likelihood that you'll catch criminals and stiffen their punishment, you get less crime. Lots of recent studies demonstrate that. We know that if you have unemployment you'll increase the amount of crime.

When you first suggested that children could be treated as durable consumer goods, the suggestion was treated with derision. Thirty years later, what are the concrete payoffs gained from making that assumption?

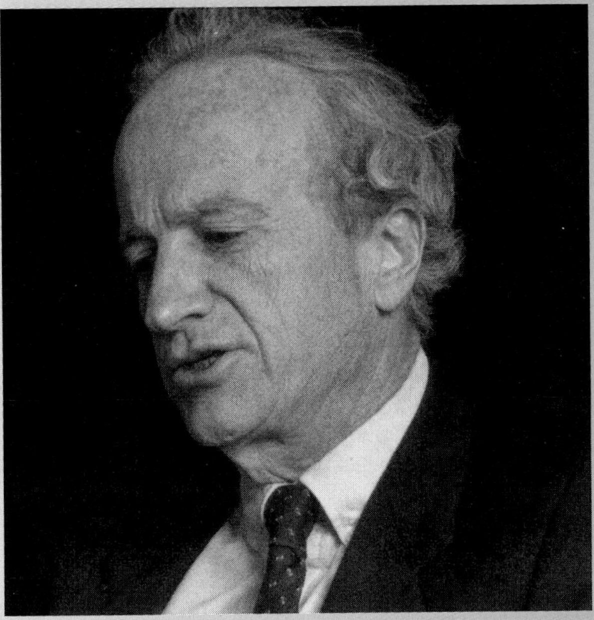

Thirty years later many more economists are taking this approach. And it's accepted not only by economists but by groups who didn't accept it then, by sociologists, demographers, and the like. Let me give you an example of its success. What would the economic approach emphasize in looking at the demand for children? It would naturally look at the benefits and costs of having children, including the value of the mother's time. You would predict with this approach that if the value of the mother's time went up, it would raise the cost of having children and mothers would have fewer children. Now some people would say, that's such a materialistic view. People have children because they love them. Well, of course people have children because of love. We wouldn't have any children with all the difficulties of raising kids if we didn't love them, but love has its price.

Now, if you're a skeptic, you'll want to see the evidence. And the evidence shows that as the value of the time of women has gone up, they have fewer children, in every country that I know of. The theory also says that you might substitute. When people have fewer children, they give them more education, they may spend more time with each child. For example, China has had an official "one child policy" of family planning. There's much discussion now in Chinese newspapers about the so-called Emperor Child. The child who gets lots of toys, whose parents are pushing him to get him into the best nursery school. That's just what the theory predicts. This substitution between quantity and quality.

"As the value of the time of women has gone up, they have fewer children."

Some people think it's immoral to reduce choices of a deeply personal nature to mere economic calculations. How do you respond to this objection?

First of all, when we use an economic approach, we don't concentrate on money alone. I never claim that people marry only according to how much money they're going to get out of it, or that when they have children, they reckon up each child as a profit or loss. That's ridiculous. Money is just a part of it. There have certainly been lots of family fights over money, but it's not the whole of life or any human behavior. The economic approach doesn't say it's the whole of life. It just says that people maximize. What they're maximizing may include love toward children or a spouse. I think it's a great virtue to say, life is short and full of hardships, so let's try to get as much out of life as we can. Not the least, but the most.

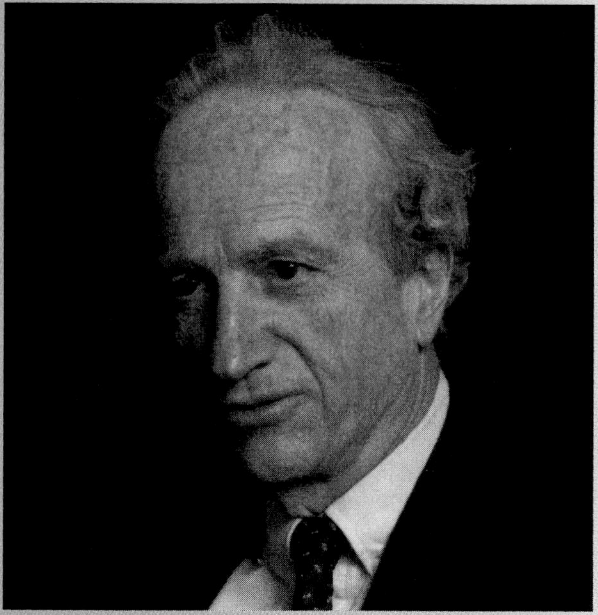

"When people solve problems rationally, they don't look at their marginal utility any more than Orel Hershiser is Einstein."

Many people who are not economists don't believe that the "rationality assumption" should be taken seriously. They look inside themselves, examine their own behavior, and don't find it rational. So how can you fairly assume that other people behave rationally?

I disagree with the premise of that question. I believe that, on reflection, people will say that a lot of the things they do are in fact rational. Let me pose some simple questions. You're a college student and you're thinking of going to the movies and a happy hour. You're worried about how much the evening will cost. You say, of course I'm going to think about the cost. Suppose there's no student discount and the movie will cost $6. Will you change your behavior? Well if you don't think you can afford $6, you'll maybe go and watch television. Are you behaving rationally? Are you thinking about the consequences? Yes. That's rationality.

I'd ask more questions of this 19-year-old: How many beers are you going to have at the happy hour? Well, the legal drinking age is 21, but maybe you have a fake ID, so you get in under age. But suppose you're caught by campus security. You've got to spend the night in jail and get thrown out of school. Do you think you'd be willing to try to get in under age? Well, you might very well answer, what's my chance of being caught? And that's exactly a rational choice. Worrying about your chances of being caught and about the likely punishment.

But even if you don't actually analyze your actions in these terms doesn't mean you're acting irrationally. Let me give you another example. Orel Hershiser is a top baseball player. He effectively knows all the laws of motion, of eye and hand coordination, about the speed of the bat and the ball, and so on. He's in fact solving a complicated physics problem when he steps up to pitch, but obviously he doesn't have to know physics to do that. Likewise, I'm saying that when people solve problems rationally, they're really not thinking that, well, I have this budget and I read this textbook, and I look at my marginal utility or my indifference curve. They don't do that, but it doesn't mean they're not being rational any more than Orel Hershiser is Einstein.

Chapter 7

Utility and Demand

After studying this chapter, you will be able to:

- Explain the connection between individual demand and market demand
- Define utility and marginal utility
- Explain the marginal utility theory of consumer choice
- Use the marginal utility theory to predict the effects of changing prices
- Use the marginal utility theory to predict the effects of changing income
- Define and calculate consumer surplus
- Explain the paradox of value

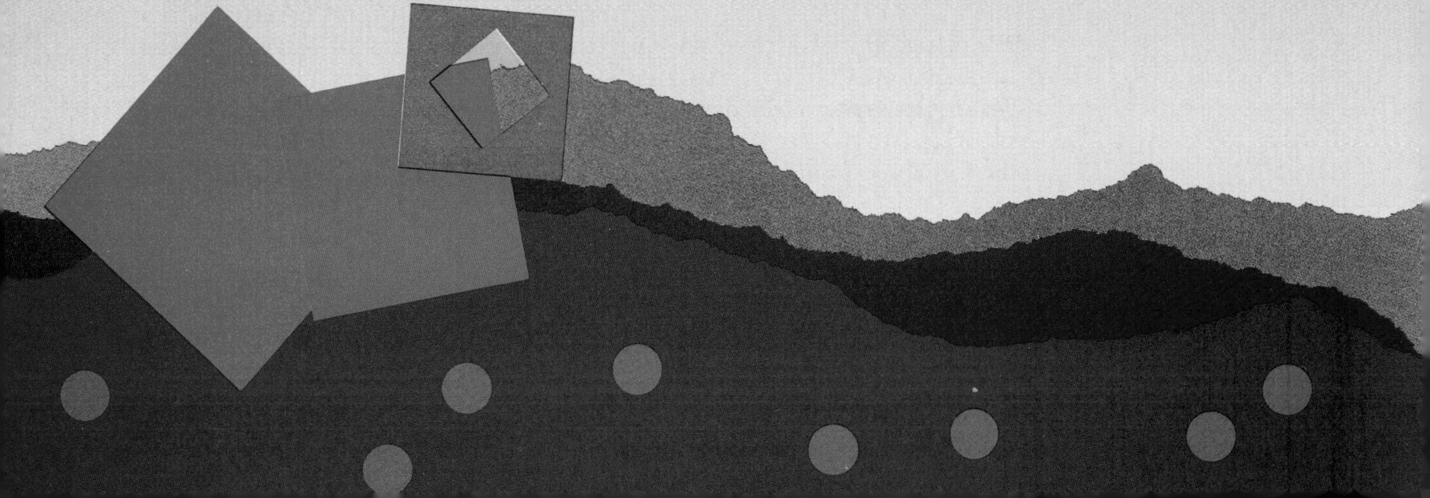

Water, Water, Everywhere

We need water to live. We don't need diamonds for much besides decoration. If the benefits of water far outweigh the benefits of diamonds, why, then, does water cost practically nothing while diamonds are terribly expensive? ■ When OPEC restricted its sale of oil in 1973, it created a dramatic rise in price, but people continued to use almost as much oil as they had before. Our demand for oil was inelastic. But why? ■ When Sony introduced the Walkman in 1979, it cost about $300, and consumers didn't buy very many of them. Since then, the price has decreased dramatically, and people are buying them in enormous quantities. Our demand for portable audio headsets is elastic. But why? What makes the demand for some things elastic while the demand for others is inelastic? ■ Over the past 15 years, incomes have increased by 40 percent. Over that same period, expenditure on electricity has increased by 66 percent, while expenditure on transportation has increased by only 18 percent. Thus the proportion of income spent on electricity has increased while the proportion spent on transportation has decreased. Why, as incomes rise, does the proportion of income spent on some goods rise and on others fall?

■ In the last three chapters, we've seen that demand has an important effect on the price of a good. But we have not analyzed what exactly shapes a person's demand. This chapter explains why demand is elastic for some goods and inelastic for others. It also explains why the prices of some things, such as diamonds and water, are so out of proportion with their benefits.

Individual Demand and Market Demand

When we studied how demand and supply determine price and the quantity bought and sold, we used the concept of **market demand**—the relationship between the total quantity of a good demanded and its price. Goods and services are demanded, though, by individuals. The relationship between the quantity demanded by a single individual and the price of a good is called **individual demand.**

Obviously, there is a relationship between market demand and individual demand. In fact, market demand is the sum of all individual demands. The table in Fig. 7.1 illustrates the relationship between individual demand and market demand. In this example Lisa and Chuck are the only people. The market demand is the total demand of Lisa and Chuck. At $3 a movie, Lisa demands 5 movies and Chuck 2, so that the total quantity demanded by the market is 7 movies.

We can represent the relationship between individual and market demands in a diagram such as that in Fig. 7.1. Here Lisa's demand curve for movies appears in part (a) and Chuck's appears in part (b). The market demand curve, shown in part (c), adds Chuck's quantity demanded to Lisa's quantity demanded at each price.

The market demand curve is the sum of the quantities demanded by each individual at each price.

Figure 7.1 Individual and Market Demand Curves

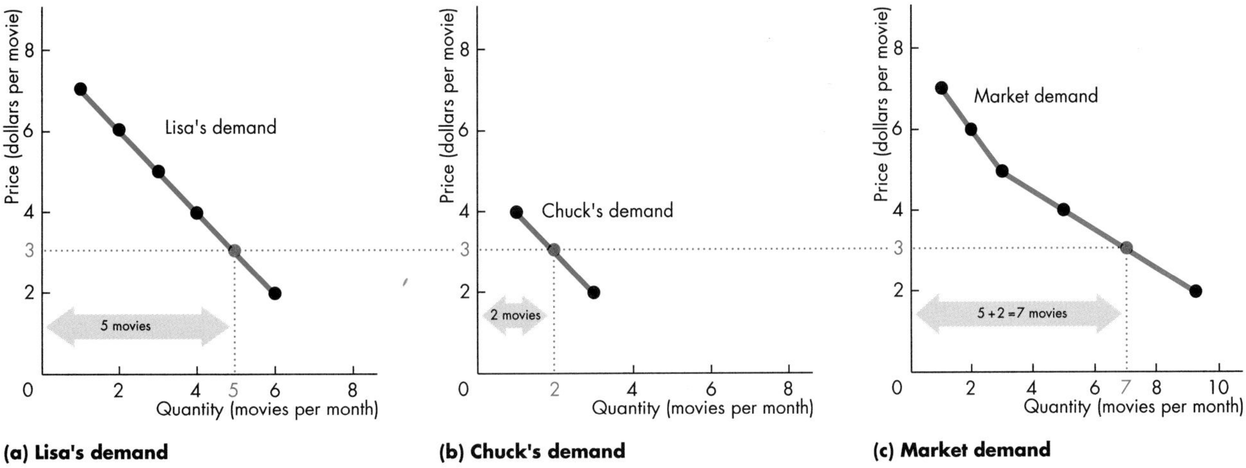

Price (dollars per movie)	Quantity (movies per month) Lisa	Chuck	Market
7	1	0	1
6	2	0	2
5	3	0	3
4	4	1	5
3	5	2	7
2	6	3	9

The table and diagram illustrate how the quantity of movies demanded varies as the price of a movie varies. The market demand is the sum of the individual demands. For example, at a price of $3, Lisa demands 5 movies and Chuck demands 2 movies, so the total quantity demanded in the market is 7 movies.

Let's now investigate an individual demand curve by studying how an individual household makes its consumption choices.

Household Consumption Choices

Suppose that a household has a certain amount of money to spend and that it cannot influence the prices of the goods and services that it buys. How does the household choose the consumption goods on which to spend its income? The answer to this question that you're about to study is called the marginal utility theory. It was invented almost 100 years ago by Alfred Marshall (see Our Advancing Knowledge on pp. 84–85)

To study the marginal utility theory, we'll examine Lisa's consumption choices. Lisa has a monthly income of $30, and spends all of it on only two goods—movies and soda. Movies cost $6 each and soda costs 50 cents a can or $3 for a six-pack. How does Lisa divide her $30 between these two goods? The answer depends on her likes and dislikes—on what economists call *preferences.* The marginal utility theory of consumption choice has a particular way of describing preferences—it uses the concept of utility.

Utility

The benefit or satisfaction that a person gets from the consumption of a good or service is called **utility.** But what exactly is utility and in what units can we measure it? Utility is an abstract theoretical concept and units of utility are chosen arbitrarily, just like the units in which we measure temperature.

Temperature—an Analogy Temperature is a concept with which you are familiar. You know when you feel hot and when you feel cold. But you can't *observe* temperature. You can observe water turning to steam if it is hot enough or turning to ice if it is cold enough. You can construct an instrument, called a thermometer, that will predict when such changes of state will occur. The scale on the thermometer is what we call temperature. But the units in which we measure temperature are arbitrary. For example, we can accurately predict that when a Fahrenheit thermometer shows a temperature of 32°, water will turn to ice. But the units of measurement do not matter, because this same event will also occur when a centigrade thermometer shows a temperature of zero.

The concept of utility helps us make predictions about consumption choices in much the same way that the concept of temperature helps us make predictions about physical phenomena. It has to be admitted, though, that the marginal utility theory is not as precise as the theory that enables us to predict when water will turn to ice or steam.

Let's now see how we can use the concept of utility to describe preferences.

Utility and Consumption

The amount of utility that a person gets depends on the person's level of consumption—more consumption gives more utility. Table 7.1 gives an example of Lisa's utility derived from consuming different quantities of movies and soda. If she sees no movies, she gets no utility from movies. If she sees 1 movie in a month, she gets 50 units of utility. As the number of movies she sees in a month increases, her utility increases so that if she sees 10 movies a month, she gets 250 units of utility. The other part of the table shows Lisa's utility from soda. If she drinks no soda, she gets no utility. As the amount of soda she drinks rises, her utility increases.

Table 7.1 Lisa's Utility from Movies and Soda

Movies		Soda	
Quantity per month	Utility	Six-packs per month	Utility
0	0	0	0
1	50	1	30
2	88	2	57
3	121	3	81
4	150	4	102
5	175	5	122
6	196	6	141
7	214	7	159
8	229	8	176
9	241	9	192
10	250	10	207

Figure 7.2 Utility and Marginal Utility

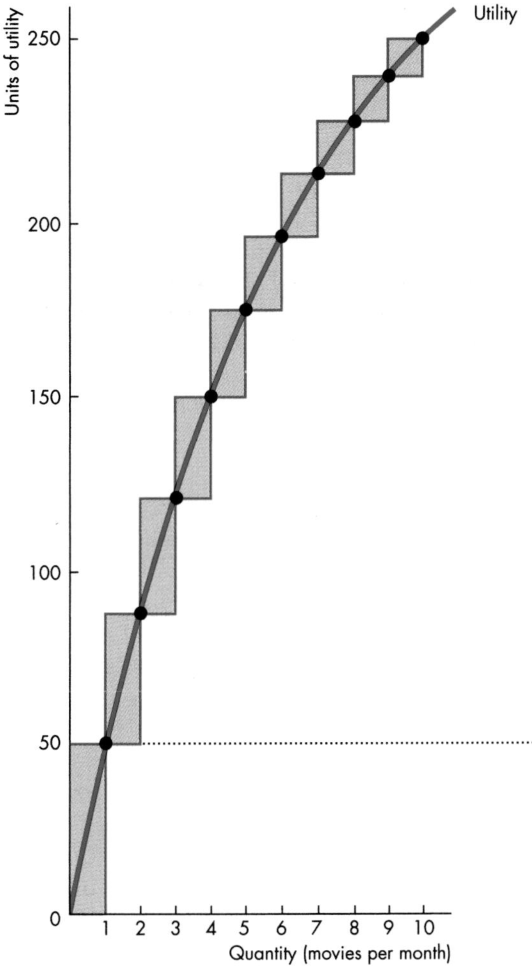

(a) Utility

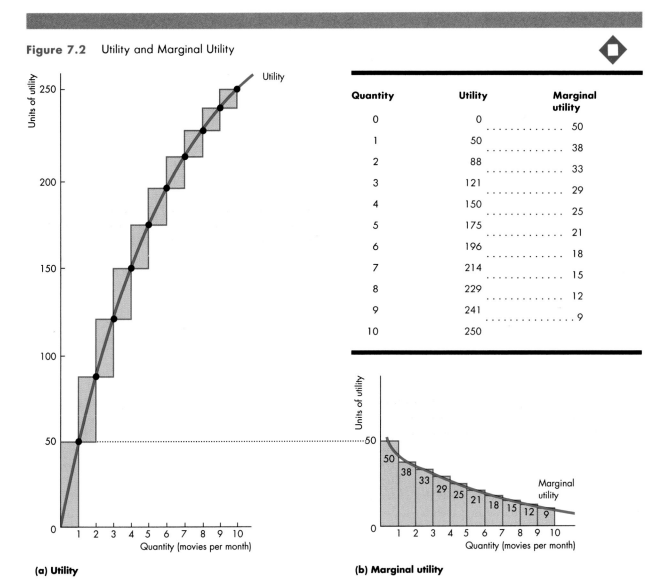

Quantity	Utility	Marginal utility
0	0	
		50
1	50	
		38
2	88	
		33
3	121	
		29
4	150	
		25
5	175	
		21
6	196	
		18
7	214	
		15
8	229	
		12
9	241	
		9
10	250	

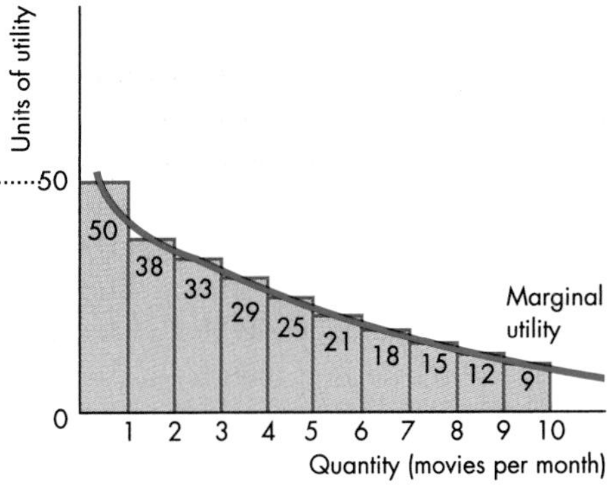

(b) Marginal utility

The table shows that as Lisa's consumption of movies increases, so does the utility she derives from movies. For example, 4 movies gives 150 units of utility while 5 movies give 175 units. The table also shows her marginal utility—the change in utility resulting from the last movie seen. Marginal utility declines as consumption increases. For example, the marginal utility from the fourth movie is 29 units while that from the fifth movie is 25 units. Lisa's utility and marginal utility from movies are graphed in the figure. Part (a) shows the extra utility gained from each additional movie as an orange bar. Part (b) shows the marginal utility of each new movie as a declining series of steps.

Marginal Utility

Marginal utility is the additional utility derived from the last unit of a good consumed. We calculate marginal utility as the change in utility that occurs when one more unit of a good is consumed. Such a calculation is shown in the table in Fig. 7.2. When Lisa's consumption of movies increases from 4 to 5 movies a month, her utility from movies increases from 150 units to 175 units. Thus the marginal utility of Lisa's fifth movie each month is 25 units. The table displays calculations of marginal utility for each level of movie consumption. Notice that the units of marginal utility appear midway between the quantities of consumption. It is the *change* in consumption from 4 to 5 movies that produces the *marginal* utility of 25 units.

Lisa's utility and marginal utility can be illustrated in a graph. Figure 7.2(a) illustrates the utility that Lisa gets from movies. As you can see, the more movies Lisa sees in a month, the more utility she gets. Part (b) illustrates her marginal utility. This graph tells us that as Lisa sees more movies, the marginal utility that Lisa gets from watching movies falls. For example, her marginal utility from the first movie is 50 units, from the second, 38 units, and from the third, 33 units. We call this decline in marginal utility as the consumption of a good increases the principle of **diminishing marginal utility.**

Marginal utility is positive but diminishes as the consumption of a good increases. Why does marginal utility have these two features? In Lisa's case, she likes movies, and the more she sees the better. That's why marginal utility is positive. The benefit that Lisa gets from the last movie seen is its marginal utility. To see why marginal utility diminishes, think about how you'd feel in the following two situations: In one, you've just been studying for 29 evenings in a row. An opportunity arises to see a movie. The utility that you get from that movie is the marginal utility from seeing one movie in a month. In the second situation, you've been on a movie binge. For the past 29 nights, you have not even seen an assignment or test. You are up to your eyeballs in movies. You are happy enough to go to a movie on yet one more night. But the kick that you get out of that thirtieth movie in 30 days is not very large. It is the marginal utility of the thirtieth movie in a month.

R E V I E W

Lisa divides her income of $30 a month between movies that cost $6 each and soda that costs $3 a six-pack. Lisa's preferences are described by using the concept of utility: The more movies Lisa sees in a given month, the more utility she gets; the more cans of soda she drinks in a month, the more utility she gets. The increase in utility that results from the last unit of a good consumed is called marginal utility. As the quantity of a good consumed increases, marginal utility decreases. ■

Utility Maximization

Utility maximization is the attainment of the greatest possible utility. But a household's income and the prices that it faces limit the utility that it can obtain. We assume that a household consumes in a way that maximizes its utility, taking into consideration its income and the prices that it faces. In Lisa's case, we examine how she allocates her spending between movies and soda to maximize her utility, assuming that movies cost $6 each, soda costs $3 a six-pack, and Lisa only has $30 a month to spend.

The Utility-Maximizing Choice Let's calculate how Lisa spends her money to maximize her utility by constructing a table. Table 7.2 has two parts. Part (a) records Lisa's expenditure and part (b), her utility. Part (a) shows six ways in which Lisa can allocate her $30 of income between movies and soda. For example, she can buy 2 movies at a cost of $12, in which case she will be able to buy 6 six-packs for a cost of $18. Each row in part (a) shows the combinations of movies and soda that exhaust her income.

Part (b) considers the same affordable combinations of movies and soda that are set out in part (a). Part (b) records three things: first, the number of movies consumed and the utility derived from them (the left side of the table); second, the number of six-packs of soda consumed and the utility derived from them (the right side of the table); and third, the total utility derived from both movies and soda (the middle column of the table).

Consider, for example, the first row. It shows Lisa watching no movies, getting no utility from them but getting 207 units of utility from drinking 10 six-packs of soda. Her total utility, in this case, is 207 units.

Now consider the second row. Lisa watches 1 movie, getting 50 units of utility from it, and drinks 8 six-packs of soda, getting another 176 units of utility. In this case, her total utility is the sum of 50 units from movies and 176 units from soda, or 226 units. The rest of part (b) is constructed in exactly the same way.

Table 7.2 Lisa's Utility Maximizing Combinations of Movies and Soda

(a) Expenditure

Movies			Soda	
Quantity	Expenditure (dollars)	Total expenditure (dollars)	Expenditure (dollars)	Six-packs
0	0	30	30	10
1	6	30	24	8
2	12	30	18	6
3	18	30	12	4
4	24	30	6	2
5	30	30	0	0

(b) Utility

Movies			Soda	
Quantity	Utility	Total utility	Utility	Six-packs
0	0	207	207	10
1	50	226	176	8
2	88	229	141	6
3	121	223	102	4
4	150	207	57	2
5	175	175	0	0

Notice also that Table 7.2 does not consider allocations in which Lisa consumes odd numbers of six-packs of soda (1, 3, 5, 7, or 9). The reason is that she cannot buy half a movie. She has to buy movies in whole numbers and, since movies cost $6, twice as much as a six-pack of soda, she can only consume 0, 2, 4, 6, 8, or 10 six-packs of soda if she spends all her income on these two goods.

The consumption of movies and soda that maximizes Lisa's utility is highlighted in part (b) of the table. When Lisa consumes 2 movies and 6 six-packs of soda, she gets 229 units of utility. This is the best Lisa can do given that she has only $30 to spend and given the prices of movies and six-packs. If she buys 8 six-packs of soda, she can see only 1 movie and gets 226 units of utility, 3 less than the maximum attainable. If she sees 3 movies and drinks only 4 six-packs, she gets 223 units of utility, 6 less than the maximum attainable. Thus Lisa can do no better than consume 2 movies and 6 six-packs—the allocation of her $30 that maximizes her utility.

The situation that we've just described is a consumer equilibrium. A **consumer equilibrium** is a situation in which a consumer has allocated his or her income in a manner that maximizes utility. In calculating Lisa's consumer equilibrium, we have measured her total utility from the consumption of movies and soda. There is another, better way of determining a consumer equilibrium that does not involve measuring total utility at all. Let's look at this alternative.

Equalizing Marginal Utility per Dollar Spent

Another way to find out the allocation that maximizes a consumer's utility is to make the marginal utility per dollar spent equal for all goods. The **marginal utility per dollar spent** on a good is the marginal utility obtained from the last good consumed divided by the price of the good. For example, Lisa's marginal utility from consuming the first movie is 50 units of utility. The price of a movie is $6, which means that the marginal utility per dollar spent on movies is 50 units divided by $6, or 8.33 units of utility per dollar.

Table 7.3 sets out Lisa's marginal utilities per dollar spent for both movies and soda. Again, the table has been arranged so that each row represents an allocation of Lisa's income that uses up her $30. You can see that Lisa's marginal utility per dollar spent on either good, like marginal utility itself, declines as consumption of the good rises. The marginal utility per dollar spent on movies falls from 8.33 for the first movie to 6.33 for the second to 4.16 for the fifth. The marginal utility per dollar spent on soda is 9.00 for 2 six-packs, 7.00 for 4 six-packs, 6.33 for 6 six-packs, and 5.00 for 10 six-packs.

Notice that when Lisa consumes 2 movies and 6 six-packs of soda, she gets the same marginal utility per dollar spent from movies as she does from soda. This allocation of her income maximizes her utility. It is the same allocation that we calculated in Table 7.2.

Utility is maximized when the marginal utility per dollar spent is equal for all goods.

In calculating the utility-maximizing allocation of income in Table 7.3, we have not used the concept of total utility at all. All the calculations have been performed using marginal utility and price. By making the marginal utility per dollar spent equal for both goods, we know that we have maximized utility but we have not calculated what the maximum level of utility is. As a matter of fact, we do not need to know what the level of utility is. We need only to know that the maximum utility has been attained. This way of viewing maximum utility is important; it means that the units in which utility is measured do not matter. We could double or halve all the numbers measuring utility, or multiply them by any other positive number, or square them, or take their square roots. None of these transformations of the units used to measure utility will make any difference to the outcome. Utility is maximized when the marginal utility per dollar spent is equal for all goods. It is in this respect that utility is analogous to temperature. Our prediction about the freezing of water does not depend on the temperature scale; our prediction about maximizing utility does not depend on the units of utility.

Table 7.3 Maximizing Utility by Equalizing Marginal Utilities per Dollar Spent

Movies ($6 each)			Soda ($3 per six-pack)		
Quantity	Marginal utility	Marginal utility per dollar spent	Six-packs	Marginal utility	Marginal utility per dollar spent
0	0		10	15	5.00
1	50	8.33	8	17	5.66
2	38	6.33	6	19	6.33
3	33	5.50	4	21	7.00
4	29	4.83	2	27	9.00
5	25	4.16	0	0	

You can see why the rule "equalize marginal utility per dollar spent on all goods" works by considering what happens if Lisa spends differently. Suppose that instead of consuming 2 movies and 6 six-packs of soda, Lisa consumes 1 movie and 8 six-packs of soda (the second row of Table 7.3). She will then get 8.33 units of utility from the last dollar spent on movies and 5.66 units of utility from the last dollar spent on soda. It will pay Lisa to spend less on soda and more on movies. Spending a dollar less on soda lowers her utility by 5.66 units, while spending the extra dollar on movies gives her an additional 6.33 units. Lisa's utility rises if she spends less on soda and more on movies.

Or, suppose that Lisa consumes 3 movies and only 4 six-packs of soda (the fourth row of the table). In this situation, she will get 5.50 units of utility from the last dollar spent on movies and 7.00 units of utility from the last dollar spent on soda. It will now pay Lisa to cut her spending on movies, at a cost of 5.50 units of utility per dollar, and raise her spending on soda, where she gets 7.00 units of utility per dollar. When Lisa's marginal utility per dollar spent on both goods is equal, she cannot get more utility by spending differently. Her utility is maximized.

R E V I E W

Consumers maximize utility. A consumer spends his or her income in order to make the marginal utility per dollar spent on each good equal. In such a situation, the consumer cannot reallocate spending to get more utility. The absolute level of utility is irrelevant—all that matters is its maximization. The units in which utility is measured are irrelevant—all that matters is that the marginal utility per dollar is equal for all goods. ■

Predictions of Marginal Utility Theory

Now let's go on to use marginal utility theory to make some predictions. In particular, let's see what happens to Lisa's consumption of movies and soda when their prices change and also when her income changes.

First, we'll work out what happens to Lisa's consumption if the price of a movie drops by half, to $3. Next, we'll work out what happens if the price of a movie stays at $3 and the cost of soda doubles to $6 per six-pack.

The Effects of Changes in Prices

To determine the effects of changes in prices on consumption requires three steps. First, we need to determine the combinations of movies and soda that can be bought at the new prices. Second, we need to calculate the new marginal utilities per dollar spent. Third, we need to determine the consumption of each good that makes the marginal utility per dollar spent on each good equal and that just exhausts the money available for spending. Table 7.4 works out the answers for two price changes: first halving the price of a movie (from $6 to $3) and then doubling the price of soda (from $3 to $6) while the price of a movie remains at $3.

A Fall in the Price of Movies Case 1 in Table 7.4 shows ways of consuming movies at $3 each and soda at $3 a six-pack. Once again, each row of the table shows quantities consumed that exactly use up the $30 of income available. The marginal utility per dollar spent is marginal utility of the good divided by its price. Marginal utility, which was shown in the table in Fig. 7.2, describes Lisa's preferences. Her preferences do not change when prices change, so her marginal utility schedule remains the same as that in Fig. 7.2. But now we divide her marginal utility from movies by $3, the new price of a movie, to get the marginal utility per dollar spent on movies. You can see that Lisa's marginal utility per dollar spent on movies declines from 16.67 at 1 movie all the way down to 3.00 at 10 movies.

Lisa's marginal utility per dollar spent on soda declines from 10.00 at 1 six-pack to 5.00 at 10 six-packs. The marginal utilities per dollar spent on movies and on soda are each equal to 7.00 when Lisa watches 6 movies and drinks 4 six-packs.

What has been the effect of the fall in the price of a movie on Lisa's consumption? You can find the answer by comparing Lisa's utility-maxi-

Table 7.4 How a Change in Price Affects Lisa's Choices

Case I: Movies $3.00 each
Soda $3.00 per six-pack

Movies		Soda	
Quantity	Marginal utility per dollar spent	Six-packs	Marginal utility per dollar spent
0		10	5.00
1	16.67	9	5.33
2	12.67	8	5.67
3	11.00	7	6.00
4	9.67	6	6.33
5	8.33	5	6.67
6	7.00	4	7.00
7	6.00	3	8.00
8	5.00	2	9.00
9	4.00	1	10.00
10	3.00	0	

Case 2: Movies $3.00 each
Soda $6.00 per six-pack

Movies		Soda	
Quantity	Marginal utility per dollar spent	Six-packs	Marginal utility per dollar spent
0		5	3.33
2	12.67	4	3.50
4	9.67	3	4.00
6	7.00	2	4.50
8	5.00	1	5.00
10	3.00	0	

mizing allocation shown in Case 1 in Table 7.4 with her allocation in Table 7.3. You can see that as a result of the fall in the price of a movie, Lisa watches more movies (up from 2 to 6 a month) and she drinks less soda (down from 6 six-packs to 4 six-packs a month).

A Rise in the Price of Soda Let us now look at Case 2 in Table 7.4. The price of a movie stays at $3, but the price of soda doubles to $6 a six-pack. The rows of the table show the possible ways of consuming soda and movies at these new prices. Because soda now costs $6, Lisa cannot consume more than 5 six-packs. Five six-packs of soda cost $30, exactly the amount that Lisa has available. Since we are assuming that a six-pack cannot be split into single cans, Lisa can consume only 0, 2, 4, 6, 8, or 10 movies. Because movies cost the same in Case 1 and Case 2, the marginal utility per dollar spent on movies remains the same. You can see that if Lisa sees 2 movies, her marginal utility per dollar spent on movies is 12.67 in both cases. If Lisa sees 10 movies, her marginal utility per dollar spent on movies is 3.

Lisa's marginal utility per dollar spent on soda is the marginal utility of soda divided by the new price of soda ($6). These marginal utilities per dollar spent are set out in the extreme right-hand column of Table 7.4. As you can see in Case 2, the marginal utility per dollar spent on movies and on soda are equal when Lisa watches 8 movies and drinks 1 six-pack a month. You can calculate the effects of the rise in the price of soda on Lisa's consumption by comparing Case 2 with Case 1. Lisa's consumption of soda has fallen from 4 six-packs to 1 six-pack and her consumption of movies has increased from 6 to 8 a month. For Lisa, soda and movies are substitutes. When there is a rise in the price of soda, Lisa substitutes movies for soda. She sees more movies and drinks less soda.

REVIEW

Let's review how Lisa changes her consumption when prices change. When the price of a movie falls but the price of soda stays constant, Lisa increases her consumption of movies and cuts her consumption of soda. When the price of a movie stays constant but the price of soda increases, Lisa cuts her consumption of soda and increases her consumption of movies. When the price of a movie falls or the price of soda rises, with unchanged consumption, the marginal utility per dollar spent on movies exceeds that on soda. To restore the equality of the marginal utility per dollar spent on each good, the consumption of movies must rise and the consumption of soda must fall. ■

Marginal utility theory predicts these two results: When the price of a good rises, the quantity demanded falls. When the price of one good rises, the demand for another good that can serve as a substitute increases. Does this sound familiar? It should. These predictions of marginal utility theory correspond to the assumptions that we made about consumer demand in Chapter 4. There we *assumed* that the demand curve for a good sloped downward, and we *assumed* that a rise in the price of a substitute increased demand. Marginal utility theory predicts these responses to price changes. It makes these predictions by assuming three things: First, that consumers maximize utility. Second, that they get more utility as they consume more of a good. Third, as consumption increases, marginal utility declines.

Thus the assumption of diminishing marginal utility implies the law of demand. But this is not the only implication of diminishing marginal utility. It also has implications for the response of consumption to a change in income. Let's see how by studying the effects of a change in Lisa's income on her consumption.

The Effects of a Rise in Income

Let's suppose that Lisa gets a raise of $12 a month, which means that she now has $42 a month to spend on movies and soda. Let's also suppose that movies cost $3 each and a six-pack costs $3 (as in Case 1 in Table 7.4). We now want to compare Lisa's consumption of movies and soda at her original income of $30 with her consumption at her new income of $42. The calculations for such a comparison are presented in Table 7.5. Case 1 (which is identical to Case 1 in Table 7.4) shows Lisa's utility-maximizing consumption of movies and soda when she earns $30. Case 2 shows what happens when Lisa's income goes up to $42. With $42, Lisa can buy 14 movies a month and no soda or 14 six-packs a month and no movies or any combination of the two goods shown in the rows of Table 7.5.

We can calculate the marginal utility per dollar spent on movies and soda in exactly the same way as we did before. Only now, because Lisa has more income, she can consume more soda for any given consumption of movies or, equivalently, more movies for any given consumption of soda. For example, Lisa can watch 1 movie and drink 13 six-packs of soda when she earns $42. When her income is $30, however, she can buy only 9 six-packs of soda if she sees 1 movie. Lisa maximizes her utility when the marginal utilities per dollar spent on movies and on soda are equal. At an income of $42, such a situation occurs when the marginal utility per dollar spent on each good is 6 units. Lisa watches 7 movies a month and drinks 7 six-packs of soda.

By comparing Case 2 with Case 1, we can see another important prediction of the marginal utility theory of consumption. When Lisa earns more income, she increases her consumption of both goods—but she does not increase her consumption of both goods by the same amount. She consumes 3 more six-packs of soda but sees only 1 more movie each month. Lisa's response arises from her preferences, as described by her marginal utilities of movies and soda.

For Lisa, soda and movies are normal goods. When her income rises, Lisa buys more of both goods. This prediction of the marginal utility theory corresponds to another assumption that we made when studying the theory of demand in Chapter 4. There we *assumed* that demand rises when income rises. Here we have obtained that result as a prediction of marginal utility theory.

The marginal utility theory of consumption is summarized in Table 7.6. We can use the marginal utility theory of consumer behavior to make sense

Table 7.5 How a Change in Income Affects Lisa's Choices

Case 1: Income $30

Movies ($3 each) Quantity	Marginal utility per dollar spent	Soda ($3 per six-pack) Six-packs	Marginal utility per dollar spent
0		10	5.00
1	16.67	9	5.33
2	12.67	8	5.67
3	11.00	7	6.00
4	9.67	6	6.33
5	8.33	5	6.67
6	7.00	4	7.00
7	6.00	3	8.00
8	5.00	2	9.00
9	4.00	1	10.00
10	3.00	0	

Case 2: Income $42

Movies ($3 each) Quantity	Marginal utility per dollar spent	Soda ($3 per six-pack) Six-packs	Marginal utility per dollar spent
0		14	
1	16.67	13	
2	12.67	12	
3	11.00	11	
4	9.67	10	5.00
5	8.33	9	5.33
6	7.00	8	5.67
7	6.00	7	6.00
8	5.00	6	6.33
9	4.00	5	6.67
10	3.00	4	7.00
11		3	8.00
12		2	9.00
13		1	10.00
14		0	

of some of the features of the world described at the beginning of this chapter. For example, it explains why the demand for some goods, such as audio headsets, are elastic and others, such as oil, are inelastic. It also explains why, as income increases, the proportion of income spent on some goods, such as electricity, increases, while the proportion spent on other goods, such as transportation, decreases. These effects occur because of our preferences. The speed with which our marginal utility for each good diminishes as we increase our consumption of the good affects the way in which we reallocate our income in response to price changes and the way in which our spending responds to a change in income. The calculations that we've performed for Lisa illustrate these effects.

Criticisms of Marginal Utility Theory

Marginal utility theory helps us to understand the choices people make, but there are some criticisms of this theory. Let's look at them.

Utility Can't Be Observed or Measured

Agreed—we can't observe utility. But we do not need to observe it to use it. We can and do observe the quantities of goods and services that people consume, the prices of those goods and services, and people's incomes. Our goal is to understand the consumption choices that people make and to predict the effects of changes in prices and incomes on these choices. To make such predictions, we *assume* that people derive utility from their consumption, that more consumption yields more utility, and that marginal utility diminishes. From these assumptions, we make predictions about the directions of change in consumption when prices and incomes change. As we've already seen, the actual numbers we use to express utility do not matter. Consumers maximize utility by making the marginal utility per dollar spent on each good equal. As long as we use the same scale to express utility for all goods, we'll get the same answer regardless of the units on our scale. In this regard, utility is similar to temperature—water freezes when it's cold enough, and that occurs independently of the temperature scale used.

"People Aren't That Smart"

Some critics maintain that marginal utility theory assumes that people are super-computers. It requires people to look at the marginal utility of every good at every different quantity they might consume, divide those numbers by the prices of the goods, and then calculate the quantities at which the marginal utility of each good divided by its price is equal.

But such criticism of marginal utility theory confuses the actions of people in the real world with those of people in a model economy. A model economy is no more an actual economy than a model railway is an actual railway. The people in the model economy perform the calculations that we have just described. People in the real world just consume. We observe their consumption choices, not their mental gymnastics. The marginal utility theory proposes that the consumption patterns that we observe in the real world are similar to those implied by the model economy in which people do compute the quantities of goods that maximize utility. We test how closely the marginal utility model resembles reality by checking the predictions of the theory against observed consumption choices.

Marginal utility theory also has some broader implications that provide an interesting way of testing its usefulness. Let's examine two of these.

Table 7.6 Marginal Utility Theory

Assumptions

(a) A consumer derives utility from the goods consumed.

(b) Each additional unit of consumption yields additional utility; marginal utility is positive.

(c) As the quantity of a good consumed increases, marginal utility decreases.

Implication

Utility is maximized when the marginal utility per dollar spent is equal for all goods.

Predictions

(a) Other things being equal, the higher the price of a good, the lower is the quantity bought (the law of demand).

(b) The higher the price of a good, the higher is the consumption of substitutes for that good.

(c) The higher the consumer's income, the greater is the quantity demanded of normal goods.

Some Implications of Marginal Utility Theory

We all love bargains—paying less for something than its usual price. One implication of the marginal utility theory is that we almost *always* get a bargain when we buy something. That is, we place a higher total value on the things we buy than the amount that it costs us. Let's see why.

Consumer Surplus and the Gains from Trade

In Chapter 3, we saw how people can gain by specializing in the things at which they have a comparative advantage and then trading with each other. Marginal utility theory provides a precise way of measuring the gains from trade.

When Lisa buys movies and soda, she exchanges her income for them. Does Lisa profit from

Figure 7.3 Consumer Surplus

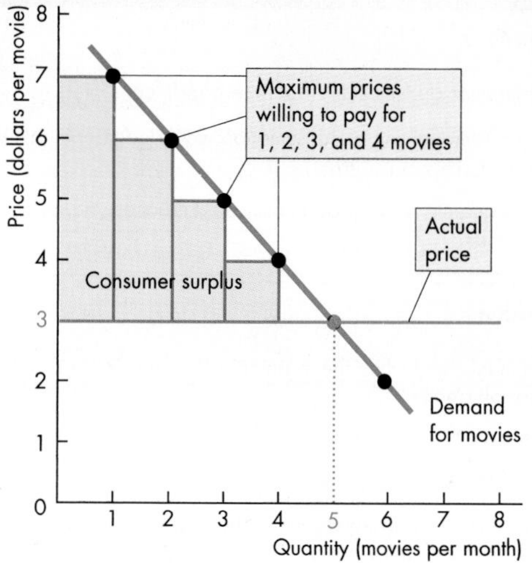

Lisa is willing to pay $7 to watch her first movie, $6 to watch her second, $5 to watch her third, and $4 to watch her fourth. She actually has to pay only $3 for each movie. At that price, she sees 5 movies. She has a consumer surplus on the first four movies equal to $10—the difference between the highest price she is willing to pay and the price actually paid ($4 + $3 + $2 + $1).

this exchange? Are the dollars she has to give up worth more or less than the movies and soda are worth to her? As we are about to discover, the principle of diminishing marginal utility guarantees that Lisa, and everyone else, gets more value from the things they buy than the amount of money they give up in exchange.

Calculating Consumer Surplus

The **value** of a good is the maximum amount that a person would be willing to pay for it. The amount that a person has actually paid for a good is its price. **Consumer surplus** is the difference between the value of a good and its price. The principle of diminishing marginal utility guarantees that a consumer always makes some consumer surplus. To understand why, let's look again at Lisa's consumption choices.

As before, let's assume that Lisa has $30 a month to spend, that movies cost $3 each, and that she watches 6 movies each month. Now let's look at Lisa's demand curve for movies, shown in Fig. 7.3. We can see from Lisa's demand curve that if she were able to watch only 1 movie a month she would be willing to pay $7 to see it. She would be willing to pay $6 to see a second movie, $5 to see a third, and so on.

Luckily for Lisa, she has to pay only $3 for each movie she sees. Although she values the first movie she sees in a month at $7, she pays only $3—$4 less than she would be willing to pay. The second movie she sees in a month is worth $6 to her. The difference between the value she places on the movie and what she has to pay is $3 in this case. The third movie she sees in a month is worth $5 to her—$2 more than she has to pay for it, and the fourth movie is worth $4—$1 more than she has to pay for it. You can see this progression in Fig. 7.3, which highlights the difference between the price she pays ($3) and the higher value she places on the first, second, third, and fourth movies. These differences are a gain to Lisa. Let's calculate her total gain.

The total amount that Lisa is willing to pay for the 5 movies that she sees is $25 (the sum of $7, $6, $5, $4, and $3). She actually pays $15 (5 movies multiplied by $3). The extra value she receives from the movies is therefore $10. This amount is the value of Lisa's consumer surplus. From watching 5 movies a month, she gets $10 worth of value in excess of what she has to spend to see them.

Let's now look at another implication of the marginal utility theory.

The Paradox of Value

More than 200 years ago, Adam Smith posed a paradox that we also raised at the start of this chapter. Water, which is essential to life itself, costs little, but diamonds, which are useless compared to water, are expensive. Why? Adam Smith could not solve the paradox. Not until the theory of marginal utility had been invented could anyone give a satisfactory answer.

You can solve Adam Smith's puzzle by distinguishing between total utility and marginal utility. The total utility that we get from water is enormous. But remember, the more we consume of something, the smaller is its marginal utility. We use so much water that the marginal utility—the benefit we get from one more glass of water—diminishes to a tiny value. Diamonds, on the other hand, have a small total utility relative to water, but because we buy few diamonds, they have a high marginal utility.

Our theory also tells us that consumers spend in a way that makes the marginal utility from each good divided by its price equal for all goods. This also holds true for their spending on diamonds and water: Diamonds have a high marginal utility divided by a high price, while water has a low marginal utility divided by a low price. In each case, the marginal utility per dollar spent is the same.

■ We've now completed our study of the marginal utility theory of consumption. We've used that theory to examine how Lisa allocates her income between the two goods that she consumes—movies and soda. We've also seen how the theory can be used to resolve the paradox of value. Furthermore, we've seen how the theory can be used to explain our real-world consumption choices.

In the next chapter, we're going to study an alternative theory of household behavior. To help you see the connection between the marginal utility theory of this chapter and the more modern theory of consumer behavior of the next chapter, we'll continue with the same example. We'll meet Lisa again and discover another way of understanding how she gets the most out of her $30 a month.

S U M M A R Y

Individual Demand and Market Demand

Individual demand represents the relationship between the price of a good and the quantity demanded by a single individual. Market demand is the sum of all individual demands. (pp. 157–158)

Household Consumption Choices

The marginal utility theory explains how people divide their spending between goods and services. The theory is based on a model that assumes certain characteristics about the consumer: The consumer derives utility from the goods consumed. This utility rises as consumption of the good increases. The change in utility resulting from a one-unit increase in the consumption of a good is called marginal utility. Marginal utility declines as consumption rises. The consumer's goal is to maximize total utility, which occurs when the marginal utility per dollar spent on each good is equal. (pp. 158–163)

Predictions of Marginal Utility Theory

Marginal utility theory predicts how prices and income affect the amounts of each good consumed. First, it predicts the law of demand. That is, other things being equal, the higher the price of a good, the lower is the quantity demanded of that good. Second, it predicts that, other things being equal, the higher the consumer's income, the greater is the consumption of all normal goods. (pp. 163–166)

Criticisms of Marginal Utility Theory

Some people criticize marginal utility theory because utility cannot be observed or measured. However, the size of the units of measurement of utility do not matter. All that matters is that the ratio of the marginal utility from each good to its price is equal for all goods. Any units of measure consistently applied will do. The concept of utility is analogous to the concept of temperature—it cannot be directly observed but it can be used to make predictions about events that are observable.

Another criticism of marginal utility theory is that consumers can't be as smart as the theory implies. In actuality, the theory makes no predictions about the thought processes of consumers. It only makes predictions about their actions and assumes that people spend their income in what seems to them to be the best possible way. (pp. 166–167)

Some Implications of Marginal Utility Theory

Marginal utility theory implies that every time we buy goods and services we get more value for our expenditure than the money we spend. We benefit from consumer surplus, which is equal to the difference between the maximum amount that we are willing to pay for a good and the price that we actually pay.

Marginal utility theory resolves the paradox of value: Water is extremely valuable but cheap, while diamonds are less valuable though expensive. When we talk loosely about value, we are thinking of total utility. The total utility of water is higher than the total utility of diamonds. The marginal utility of water, though, is lower than the marginal utility of diamonds. People choose the amount of water and diamonds to consume so as to maximize utility. In maximizing utility, they make the marginal utility per dollar spent the same for water as for diamonds. (pp. 167–169)

KEY CONCEPTS

Key Figures and Tables

REVIEW QUESTIONS

1 What is the relationship between individual demand and market demand?

2 How do we construct a market demand curve from individual demand curves?

3 What do we mean by utility?

4 What is marginal utility?

5 How does marginal utility change as the level of consumption of a good changes?

6 Susan is a consumer living in Chicago. When is Susan's utility maximized? Explain your answer.

a) When she has spent all her income

b) When she has spent all her income and marginal utility is equal for all goods

c) When she has spent all her income and the marginal utility per dollar spent is equal for all goods

7 What does the marginal utility theory predict about the effect of a change in price on the quantity of a good consumed?

8 What does the marginal utility theory predict about the effect of a change in the price of one good on the consumption of another good?

9 What does the marginal utility theory predict about the effect of a change in income on consumption?

10 How would you answer someone who says that the marginal utility theory is useless because utility cannot be observed?

11 How would you respond to someone who tells you that the marginal utility theory is useless because people are not smart enough to compute a consumer equilibrium in which the marginal utility per dollar spent is equal for all goods?

12 What is consumer surplus? How is consumer surplus calculated?

13 What is the paradox of value? How does the marginal utility theory resolve it?

14 Calculate Lisa's marginal utility from soda from the numbers given in Table 7.1. Draw two graphs, one of her utility and the other of her marginal utility from soda. Your graphs should look similar to those for movies in Fig. 7.2.

PROBLEMS

1 Shirley's demand for yogurt is given by the following:

Price (dollars per pound)	Quantity (cartons per week)
1	9
2	7
3	5
4	3
5	2

a) Draw a graph for Shirley's demand for yogurt.

Dan also likes yogurt. His demand for yogurt is given by the following:

Price (dollars per pound)	Quantity (cartons per week)
1	5
2	4
3	3
4	2
5	1

b) Draw a graph of Dan's demand curve.

c) If Shirley and Dan are the only two individuals, construct the market demand schedule for yogurt.

d) Draw a graph of the market demand for yogurt.

e) Draw a graph to show that the market demand curve is the horizontal sum of Shirley's demand curve and Dan's demand curve.

2 Max enjoys windsurfing and snorkeling. He obtains the following utility from each of these sports:

Half-hours per month	Utility from windsurfing	Utility from snorkeling
1	60	20
2	110	38
3	150	53
4	180	64
5	200	70
6	210	70

a) Draw graphs showing Max's utility from windsurfing and from snorkeling.

b) Compare the two utility graphs. Can you say anything about Max's preferences?

c) Draw graphs showing Max's marginal utility from windsurfing and from snorkeling.

d) Compare the two marginal utility graphs. Can you say anything about Max's preferences?

3 Max has $35 to spend. Equipment for windsurfing rents for $10 a half-hour while snorkeling equipment rents for $5 a half-hour. Use this information together with that given in problem 1 to answer the following questions:

a) What is the marginal utility per dollar spent on snorkeling if Max snorkels for
   (i) Half an hour
   (ii) One and a half hours

b) What is the marginal utility per dollar spent on windsurfing if Max windsurfs for
   (i) Half an hour
   (ii) One hour

c) How long can Max afford to snorkel if he windsurfs for
   (i) Half an hour
   (ii) One hour
   (iii) One and a half hours

d) Will Max choose to snorkel for one hour and windsurf for one and a half hours?

e) Will he windsurf for more or less than one and a half hours?

f) How long will Max choose to windsurf and to snorkel?

4 Max's sister gives him $20 to spend on his leisure pursuits, so he now has $55 to spend. How long will Max windsurf and snorkel?

5 If Max has only $35 to spend and the rent on windsurfing equipment doubles to $20 a half-hour, how will Max now spend his time windsurfing and snorkeling?

6 Does Max's demand curve for windsurfing slope downward or upward?

7 Max takes a Club Med holiday, the cost of which includes unlimited sports activities—including windsurfing, snorkeling, and tennis. There is no extra charge for any equipment. Max decides to spend two hours each day on both windsurfing and snorkeling. How long does he windsurf? How long does he snorkel?

8 Sara also enjoys windsurfing. Her demand for windsurfing is given by the following:

Price (dollars per half-hour)	Time windsurfing (half-hours per month)
2.50	8
5.00	7
7.50	6
10.00	5
12.50	4
15.00	3
17.50	2
20.00	1

a) Windsurfing costs $10.00 a half-hour. If Sara windsurfs for a half an hour, what is her consumer surplus?

b) If Sara windsurfs for two and a half hours, what is her consumer surplus?

Chapter 8

(Alternative to Chapter 7)

Possibilities, Preferences, and Choices

After studying this chapter, you will be able to:

- Calculate and graph a household's budget line
- Work out how the budget line changes when prices and income change
- Make a map of preferences by using indifference curves
- Calculate a household's optimal consumption plan
- Predict the effects of price and income changes on the pattern of consumption
- Explain why the workweek gets shorter as wages rise
- Explain how budget lines and indifference curves can be used to understand all household choices

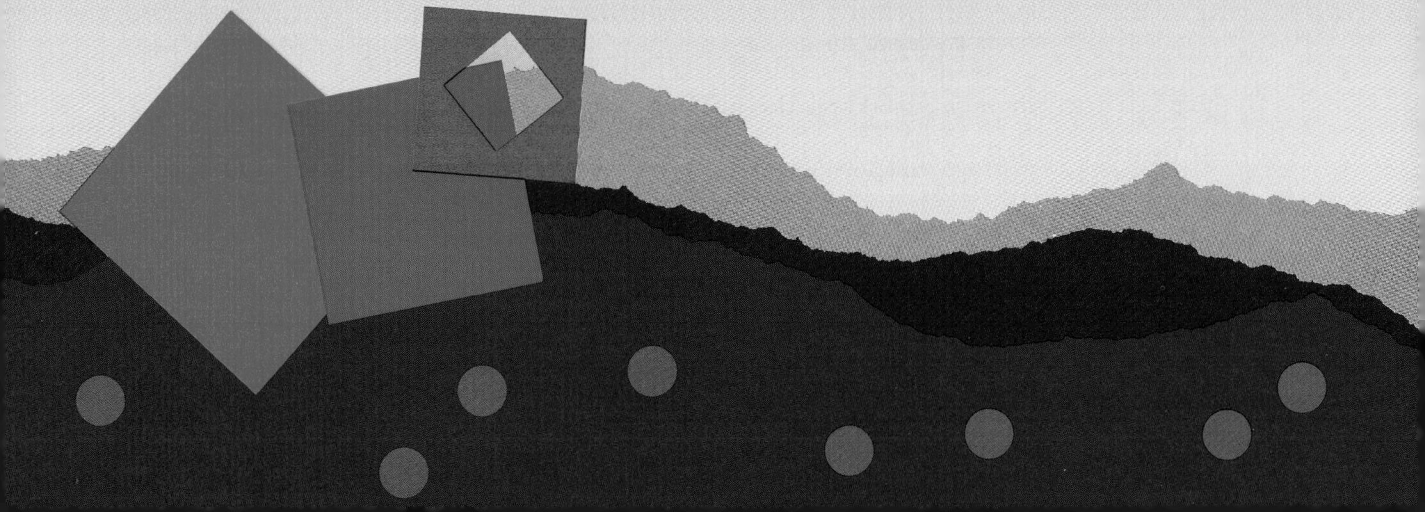

Subterranean Movements

The past 30 years have seen great changes in how we spend our incomes. Some goods—from home videos to microwave popcorn—that now regularly appear on our shopping lists didn't exist before. Other goods, such as Davy Crockett coonskin caps and horse-drawn carriages, have virtually disappeared. Yet other goods, such as miniskirts, appear, disappear, and reappear in cycles of fashion. ■ But the glittering surface of our consumption obscures deeper and slower changes in how we spend. In the last few years, we've seen a proliferation of gourmet food shops and designer clothing boutiques. Yet we spend a smaller percentage of our income today on food and clothing than we did in 1950. Despite the proliferation of jet travel and interstate highways, we spend about the same percentage of our income on transportation today as we did 40 years ago. At the same time, the percentage of our income spent on fuel, housing, and medical care has grown steadily. Like the continents floating on the earth's mantle, our spending patterns change steadily over time. On such subterranean movements, business empires rise and fall. Why does consumer spending change over the years? How do people react to changes in income and changes in the prices of the things they buy? ■ There are similar subterranean movements governing most aspects of household behavior. For example, the average workweek has fallen steadily from 70 hours a week in the nineteenth century down to 35 hours a week today. Why has the average workweek declined? Similarly, there have been steady trends in fertility, marriage, education, crime, and social interactions. Why do the habits and social mores of one generation become the old-fashioned ideas of another?

■ We're going to study a model of household behavior that has predictive power over an enormous range of choices. We'll first use the model to study consumption choice. We'll learn how to predict the way in which people spend their income and how spending changes when income and prices change. Then we'll see how this same model helps us to understand people's choices of hours of work and leisure, borrowing and lending, and even such sociological issues as fertility and the incidence of crime.

Consumption Possibilities

How does a household divide its income among the goods and services available? We are going to study a model of household behavior that can answer this question and that predicts how consumption patterns change when income and prices change. Our first step is to examine the constraint on the household's possible choices.

Constraint

A household's consumption choices are constrained by the household's income and by the prices of the goods and services available. We're going to study a household that has a given amount of income to spend and that cannot influence the prices of the goods and services that it buys. It has to take those prices as given.

The limits to a household's consumption choices are described by its **budget line.** In order to make the concept of the household's budget line as clear as possible, we'll consider the example of Lisa, who has an income of $30 a month to spend.[1] She buys two goods—movies and soda. Movies cost $6 each; soda costs $3 for a six-pack. If Lisa spends all of her income, she will reach the limits to her consumption of movies and soda.

[1]If you have read the preceding chapter on marginal utility theory, you have already met Lisa. This tale of her thirst for soda and zeal for movies will sound familiar to you—up to a point. But in this chapter, we're going to use a different method for representing preferences—one that does not require us to resort to the idea of utility. The appendix to this chapter explains the differences and the connections between the marginal utility approach and the approach of this chapter.

Figure 8.1 The Budget Line

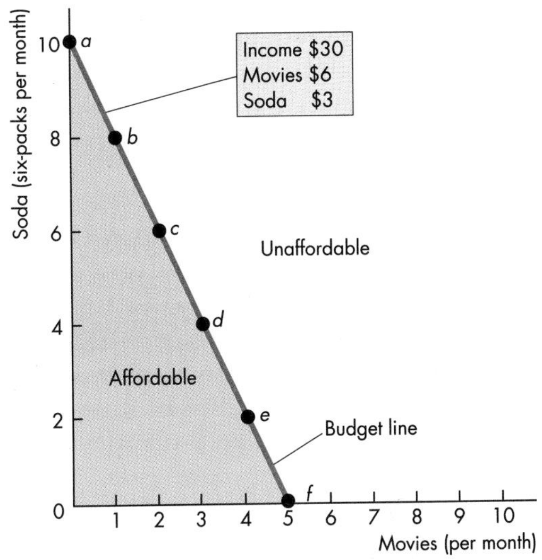

Consumption possibility	Movies (per month)	Soda (six-packs per month)
a	0	10
b	1	8
c	2	6
d	3	4
e	4	2
f	5	0

Lisa's budget line shows the boundary between what Lisa can and cannot afford. The table lists Lisa's affordable combinations of movies and soda when she has an income of $30 and when soda costs $3 a six-pack and movies cost $6 each. For example, row *a* tells us that Lisa can buy 10 six-packs and see no movies—a combination that exhausts her $30 income. The figure graphs Lisa's budget line. Points *a* through *f* on the graph represent rows of the table. For divisible goods, the budget line is the continuous line *af*.

In Fig. 8.1, each row of the table shows an affordable way for Lisa to consume movies and soda. Row *a* indicates that she can buy 10 six-packs of soda and see no movies. You can see that this combination of movies and soda exhausts her monthly income of \$30. Now look at row *f*. It says that Lisa can watch 5 movies and drink no soda—another combination that exhausts the \$30 available. Each of the other rows in the table also exhausts Lisa's income. (Check that each of the other rows costs exactly \$30.) The numbers in the table define Lisa's consumption possibilities. We can graph Lisa's consumption possibilities as points *a* through *f*.

Divisible and Indivisible Goods Some goods can be bought in any quantity desired. Such goods are called divisible. Examples of divisible goods are gasoline and electricity, both of which can be bought in almost any quantity at all. Other goods—called indivisible goods—can be bought only in whole units. Movies are an example of an indivisible good. Although you can watch a fraction of a movie (as presumably you've done when you've picked a loser), you can buy movies only in whole units.

We can best understand the model of consumer behavior that we are about to study if we suppose that all goods and services are divisible. In this case, the consumption possibilities are not just the points *a* through *f* shown in Fig. 8.1, but those points plus all the intermediate points that form a continuous straight line running from *a* to *f*. Such a line is a budget line. Thus, for example, if instead of movies and soda we measure gallons of gasoline on the vertical axis and yards of cloth on the horizontal axis, Lisa can buy at any point along the line, consuming any fraction of a gallon or a yard.

Though Lisa can consume at only one of the six points represented by each row of the table in our example, we'll develop the model so that it can deal with the more general case in which goods are divisible into any desired units.

Lisa's budget line is a constraint on her choices. It marks the boundary between what is affordable and what is unaffordable. She can afford all the points on the line and inside it. She cannot afford points outside the line. The constraint on her consumption depends on prices and on her income, and the constraint changes when prices and her income change.

The Budget Equation

To discover how the constraint on consumption changes when prices and income change, we need to describe the budget line in the form of an equation. Such an equation is called the budget equation. The **budget equation** states the limits to consumption for a given income and for given prices. We're going to work out such an equation and, to keep things tidy, we'll summarize our calculations in Table 8.1.

The left side of the table works out the budget equation by using symbols that apply to any consumer; the right side of the table works out the equation by using numbers that describe Lisa's situation. The first section of the table lists the variables that affect a household's budget. Those variables are income, the prices of the goods consumed, and the quantities consumed. To make our calculations clear, we have assigned symbols to each of these variables. In Lisa's case, her income is \$30, the prices are \$6 for movies and \$3 for soda, and Lisa will choose the quantities of movies and soda to consume.

The consumer's budget is set out in the second section of the table. It states that expenditure (on the left side of the equation) equals income (on the right side of the equation). Look at the elements of expenditure. Expenditure is equal to the sum of the expenditures on each of the goods. Expenditure on any one good equals its price multiplied by the quantity consumed. In Lisa's case, income (on the right side) is \$30, and the most that she can spend (on the left side of the equation) is the amount of soda consumed (Q_s) multiplied by the price of a soda (\$3) plus the number of movies consumed (Q_m) multiplied by their price (\$6).

The third section of the table shows you how to derive the budget equation from the consumer's budget. There are just two steps. First, divide both sides by the price of soda. Second, subtract $(P_m/P_s)Q_m$ from both sides of the resulting equation. The result is the budget equation shown in the last line of the table. This equation tells us how the consumption of one good varies as consumption of the other good varies. To interpret the equation, let's go back to the budget line of Fig. 8.1.

Let's first check that the budget equation that we have derived in Table 8.1 delivers the graph of the budget line in Fig. 8.1. Begin by setting Q_m equal to zero. In this case, the budget equation tells us that Q_s will be 10. This combination of Q_s and Q_m is the same as that shown in row *a* of the table in Fig. 8.1. Setting Q_m equal to 5 makes Q_s equal to zero (row *f* of the table in Fig. 8.1). Check that you can derive the other rows of the table in Fig. 8.1.

The budget equation contains two variables under the control of the individual (Q_m and Q_s) and two numbers outside the individual's control. Let's look more closely at the two numbers outside the individual's control (y/P_s and P_m/P_s).

Table 8.1 Calculating the Budget Equation

In General		In Lisa's Case	
1. The variables			
Income	$= y$	y	$= \$30$
Price of movies	$= P_m$	P_m	$= \$6$
Price of soda	$= P_s$	P_s	$= \$3$
Quantity of movies	$= Q_m$	Q_m	= Lisa's choice
Quantity of soda	$= Q_s$	Q_s	= Lisa's choice
2. The budget			
$P_sQ_s + P_mQ_m = y$		$\$3Q_s + \$6Q_m = \$30$	
3. Calculating the budget equation			
• Divide by P_s to obtain:		• Divide by \$3 to obtain:	
$Q_s + \frac{P_m}{P_s} Q_m = \frac{y}{P_s}$		$Q_s + 2\ Q_m = 10$	
• Subtract $(P_m/P_s)Q_m$ from both sides to obtain:		• Subtract $2\ Q_m$ from both sides to obtain:	
$Q_s = \frac{y}{P_s} - \frac{P_m}{P_s} Q_m$		$Q_s = 10 - 2\ Q_m$	

The first number y/P_s, or 10 in Lisa's case, is the maximum number of six-packs that can be bought. It is called real income in terms of soda. **Real income** is income expressed in units of goods. Real income in terms of a particular good is income divided by the price of that good. In Lisa's case, her real income is 10 six-packs. In Fig. 8.1, the budget line intersects the vertical axis at Lisa's real income in terms of soda. That is, if Lisa spends all her income on soda, she can buy 10 six-packs.

Let's now look at the second number in the budget equation that is outside the consumer's control (P_m/P_s), or 2 in Lisa's case. This number shows the relative price of the two goods. A **relative price** is the price of one good divided by the price of another good. In the equation, P_m/P_s is the relative price of movies in terms of soda. For Lisa, that relative price is 2. That is, in order to see one more movie, she has to give up 2 six-packs.

You can see the relative price of movies to soda in Fig. 8.1 (p. 175) as the magnitude of the slope of the budget line. To calculate the slope of the budget line, recall the formula for slope that was introduced in Chapter 2: Slope equals the change in soda divided by the change in movies. In Lisa's case, the change in movies is 5 and the change in soda is -10. (As movies increase from 0 to 5, soda falls from 10 to 0.) Therefore the slope of the budget line is $-10/5$, or -2. The flatter the slope of the budget line, the less expensive is the good measured on the horizontal axis relative to the good measured on the vertical axis. The steeper the line, the more expensive is the good measured on the horizontal axis relative to the one on the vertical axis. In other words, the slope of the budget line is the relative price of the good whose quantity appears on the horizontal axis.

The relative price of one good in terms of another is the opportunity cost of the first good in terms of the second. In Lisa's case, the opportunity cost of one movie is 2 six-packs of soda. Equivalently, the opportunity cost of 2 six-packs of soda is one movie.

Changes in Prices and Income

Let's now work out what happens to the budget line when prices and income change. We'll begin with a change in the price of one good.

A change in the price of movies Suppose that the price of movies rises. What happens to Lisa's budget line? To make things vivid, let's suppose that the price of movies halves to \$3 a movie. By working through the calculations in Table 8.1, you can work out Lisa's budget line with the new price of movies. Recall that the budget equation is

$$Q_s = \frac{y}{P_s} - \frac{P_m}{P_s} Q_m.$$

Nothing has happened to income (y) or the price of soda (P_s). Lisa's real income in terms of soda remains 10. But the price of movies has fallen and is now equal to the price of soda. Therefore the relative price of movies P_m/P_s has decreased to 1. Lisa's new budget equation is

$$Q_s = 10 - Q_m.$$

Let's check that this new budget equation works. With movies costing \$3 each, Lisa can see as many

Figure 8.2 Prices, Income, and the Budget Line

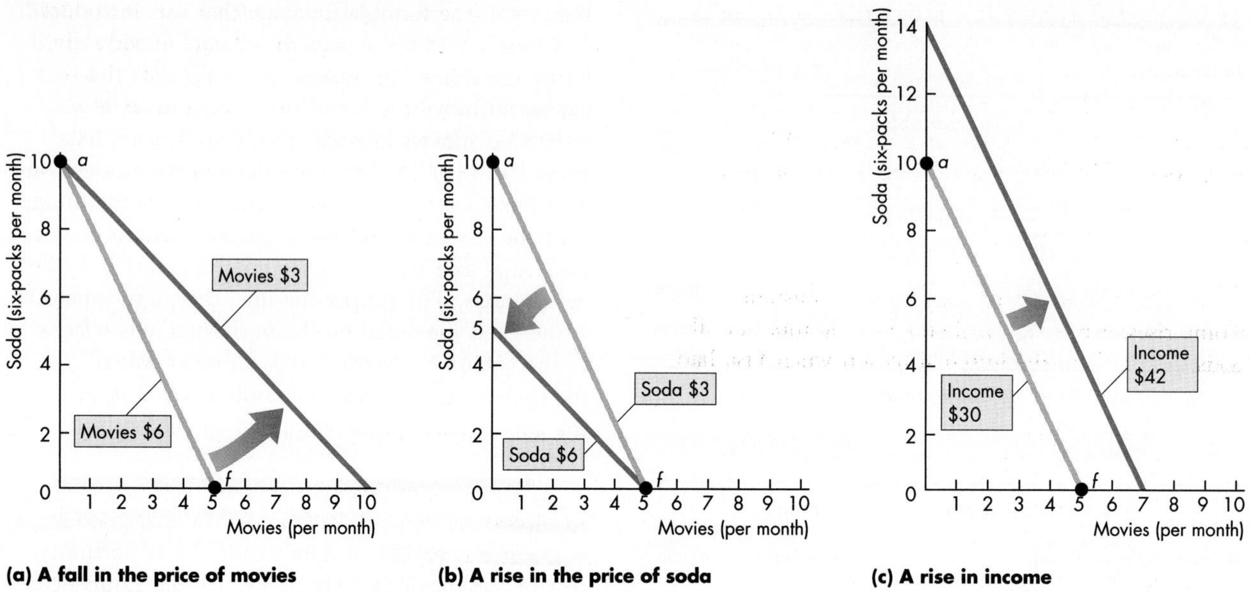

In part (a), the price of a movie falls from \$6 to \$3. In part (b), the price of a six-pack of soda increases from \$3 to \$6. In part (c), income increases from \$30 to \$42, but prices remain constant. The arrow in each part indicates the shift in the budget line.

as 10 movies with her income. Using Lisa's new budget equation, you will see that substituting 10 for Q_m results in zero for Q_s. We know that this answer is correct because if Lisa sees 10 movies, she spends all her income on movies and has nothing left for soda.

Figure 8.2(a) shows how the fall in the price of movies affects the budget line. Because the price of movies has gone down, the new budget line is flatter than budget line *af*. But notice that point *a* has not changed. If Lisa spends all her income on soda, she can still buy 10 six-packs. In other words, Lisa's real income in terms of soda has not changed. Only the price of movies has changed. Movies have become cheaper in terms of soda. Previously, 1 movie was worth 2 six-packs. In the new situation, the relative price or opportunity cost of 1 movie is 1 six-pack.

Let's see what happens to the budget line when the price of soda changes.

A Change in the Price of Soda Let's go back to the original situation in which movies cost \$6 each and soda \$3 a six-pack. What happens to Lisa's budget line if the price of a six-pack rises? Let's suppose that the price goes up from \$3 to \$6. If Lisa spends all her income on soda, she can buy 5 six-packs. Her real income in terms of soda has gone down. Since movies cost \$6 each and soda costs \$6 a six-pack, the relative price of movies is 1, the same as in the previous example. The opportunity cost of 1 movie is 1 six-pack of soda. We can work out the new budget line by using the budget equation:

$$Q_s = \frac{y}{P_s} - \frac{P_m}{P_s} Q_m.$$

The price of soda P_s is now \$6. Lisa's income is still \$30 and the price of a movie is still \$6. So Lisa's budget equation is

$$Q_s = \frac{30}{6} - \frac{6}{6} Q_m,$$

$$\text{or } Q_s = 5 - Q_m.$$

Figure 8.2(b) shows the new budget line. Notice this time point *f* has not moved. If Lisa spends all her income on movies, she can still see only 5 movies. Her real income in terms of movies has not changed.

Look at the new budget lines in parts (a) and (b). In part (a), both movies and soda cost $3; in part (b), they both cost $6. Lisa earns $30 in both cases. Therefore in part (b), she can consume less of everything than in part (a), but movies have the same opportunity cost in the two cases—to see 1 more movie she must give up 1 six-pack of soda. Notice that the new budget line in part (b) has the same slope as the new budget line in part (a).

Let's now see what happens to the budget line when income changes.

A Change in Income If prices remain constant and income rises, a person can then consume more of all goods. Go back to the initial situation when Lisa had an income of $30, a movie cost $6, and a six-pack cost $3. Keeping the prices of the two goods constant, let's work out what happens if Lisa's income goes up from $30 to $42. Again, recall the budget equation:

$$Q_s = \frac{y}{P_s} - \frac{P_m}{P_s} Q_m.$$

Let's put into this equation the numbers for prices and for the new income. The price of soda (P_s) is $3 and the price of movies (P_m) is $6. Income ($y$) is $42. Putting these numbers into the equation gives

$$Q_s = \frac{42}{3} - \frac{6}{3} Q_m,$$

$$\text{or } Q_s = 14 - 2\,Q_m.$$

Lisa's real income has gone up because her money income has gone up, while the prices of movies and soda have stayed the same. Her real income in terms of soda has gone up from 10 to 14. That is, if she spends all her income on soda, she can now buy 14 six-packs. Her real income in terms of movies has also gone up. If she spends all her income on movies, she can see 7 movies.

The shift in Lisa's budget line is shown in Fig. 8.2(c). The initial budget line is the same one that we began with in parts (a) and (b) when Lisa's income was $30. The new budget line shows Lisa able to consume more of each good. The new line is parallel to the old one but farther out. The two budget lines are parallel, or have the same slope, because the relative price is the same in both cases. With movies costing $6 each and a six-pack $3 each, Lisa must give up 2 six-packs to see 1 movie. The new budget line is farther out than the initial one because her real income has risen.

R E V I E W

The budget line describes the maximum amounts of consumption that a household can undertake given its income and the prices of the goods that it buys. A change in the price of one good changes the slope of the budget line. If the price of the good measured on the horizontal axis rises, the budget line gets steeper. A change in income makes the budget line shift, but its slope does not change. ■

Let's now leave the budget line and look at the second ingredient in the model of consumer choice: preferences.

Preferences

Preferences are a person's likes and dislikes. There are three fundamental assumptions about preferences:

- Preferences do not depend on the prices of goods.
- Preferences do not depend on income.
- More of any good is preferred to less of that good.

The first two assumptions amount to the proposition that people's likes and dislikes do not depend on what they can afford to buy. This assumption does *not* mean that people's preferences do not change over time. Nor does it mean that their preferences are not influenced by the things that they have consumed and experienced. It *does* mean that just because income increases or the price of a good decreases, people do not, *for one of those reasons,* suddenly decide that they like a particular good more than they did before.

The third assumption—more of any good is preferred to less of that good—is just a different way of saying that wants are unlimited. Of course, in reality, you can imagine having enough of any one good to want no more of it, but there will always be something that you will prefer to have more of—that you will not prefer to have less of.

We are going to discover in this section a very neat idea—that of drawing a map of a person's preferences.

Figure 8.3 Mapping Preferences

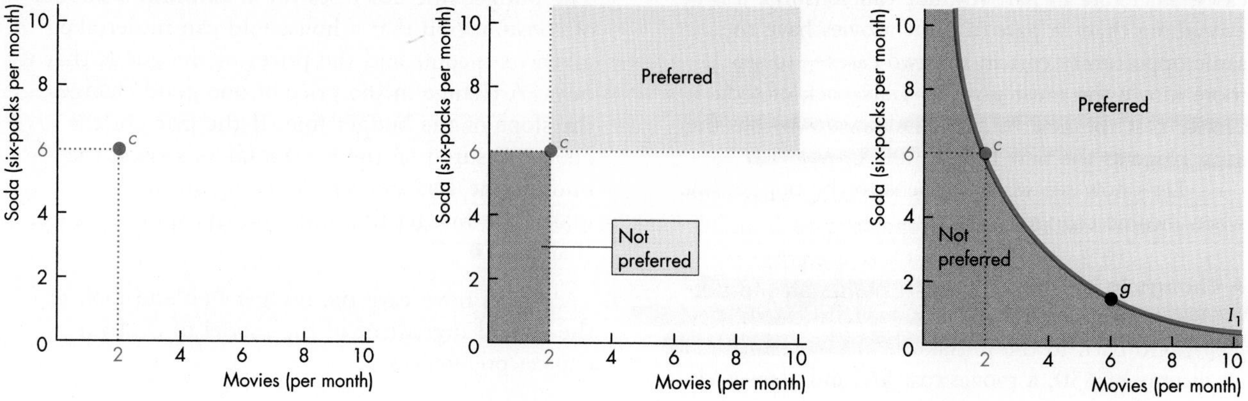

(a) A consumption point **(b) Preference relations** **(c) Indifference curve**

If Lisa consumes 6 six-packs of soda and 2 movies, she consumes at point c in part (a). Lisa prefers more goods to fewer goods. This fact is illustrated in part (b). She prefers any point at which she consumes more of both soda and movies to point c (all the points in the yellow area). She prefers point c to any point at which fewer movies and six-packs are consumed (all the points in the gray area). If she sees more movies but has less soda than at point c, whether she prefers c or not depends on how many more movies and how much less soda she has. Similarly, if she consumes more soda and sees fewer movies than at point c, whether she prefers that situation to c depends on how much more soda and how many fewer movies she has. The boundary between points that she prefers to points c and those to which c is preferred is shown in part (c). That boundary is called an indifference curve. Lisa is indifferent between points such as g and c on the indifference curve. She prefers any point above the indifference curve (yellow area) to any point on it, and she prefers any point on the indifference curve to any point below it (gray area).

A Preference Map

Let's see how we can draw a map of a person's preferences by constructing a map of Lisa's preferences for movies and soda. This map, which appears in Fig. 8.3, measures the number of movies seen on the horizontal axis and the number of six-packs consumed on the vertical axis. Let's start with Fig. 8.3(a) and focus on point *c*, where Lisa sees 2 movies and consumes 6 six-packs of soda. We will use this point as a reference and ask how Lisa likes all the other points in relation to point *c*.

Figure 8.3(b) takes us to the next step. It is divided into four areas. The area shaded orange has, at each point, more movies and more soda than at point *c*. Lisa prefers all the points in this area to point *c*. The area shaded gray has, at each point, fewer movies and less soda than at point *c*. She prefers point *c* to all the points in this area.

Points in the two white areas have either more movies and less soda than point *c* or more soda and fewer movies than point *c*. How does Lisa rank points in these areas against point *c*? To answer this question, we need to take the final step in constructing a map of Lisa's preferences.

Figure 8.3(c) takes the final step. It contains a line—I_1—passing through point *c* and through what were the two white areas. That line defines the boundary between points that Lisa prefers to point *c* and points she regards as inferior to point *c*. Lisa is indifferent between point *c* and the other points on line I_1 such as point *g*. The line itself is called an indifference curve. An **indifference curve** is a line that shows all combinations of two goods among which the consumer is indifferent. The indifference curve shown in Fig. 8.3(c) shows all the combinations of movies and soda among which Lisa is indifferent.

The indifference curve shown in Fig. 8.3(c) is just one of a whole family of such curves. This indifference curve appears again in Fig. 8.4. It is labeled I_1, and passes through points c and g. Two other indifference curves are I_0 and I_2. Lisa prefers any point on indifference curve I_2 to those on indifference curve I_1 and she prefers any point on I_1 to those on I_0. We refer to I_2 as being a higher indifference curve to I_1 and I_1 as higher than I_0.

Indifference curves never intersect each other. To see why, consider indifference curves I_1 and I_2 in Fig. 8.4. We know that point j is preferred to point c. We also know that all points on indifference curve I_2 are preferred to all points on indifference curve I_1. If these indifference curves did intersect, the consumer would be indifferent between the combination of goods at the intersection point and combinations c and j. But we know that point j is preferred to point c, so such a point cannot exist. Hence the indifference curves never intersect.

A preference map consists of a series of indifference curves. The indifference curves shown in Fig. 8.4 are only a part of Lisa's preference map. Her entire map consists of an infinite number of indifference curves, all of them sloping downward and none of them intersecting. They resemble the contour lines on a map measuring the height of mountains. An indifference curve joins points representing combinations of goods among which a consumer is indifferent in much the same way that contour lines on a map join points of equal height above sea level. By looking at the shape of the contour lines on a map, we can draw conclusions about the terrain. In the same way, by looking at the shape of a person's indifference curves we can draw conclusions about preferences. But interpreting a preference map requires a bit of work. It also requires some way of describing the shape of the indifference curves. In the next two sections, we'll learn how to "read" a preference map.

Figure 8.4 A Preference Map

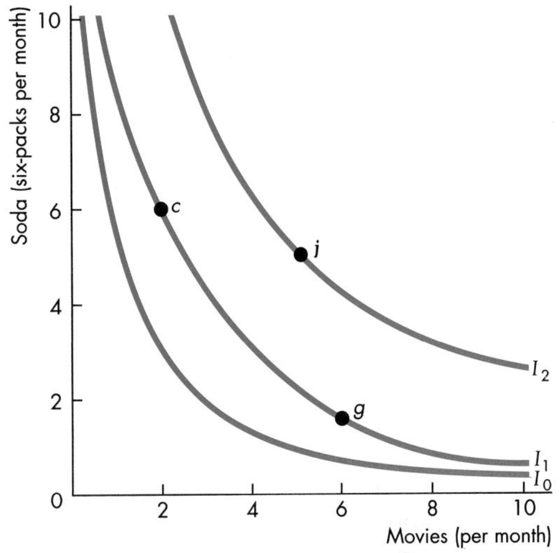

A preference map consists of an infinite number of indifference curves. Here, we show just three—I_0, I_1, and I_2—that are part of Lisa's preference map. Each indifference curve shows points among which Lisa is indifferent. For example, she is indifferent between point c and point g on indifference curve I_1. But Lisa prefers point j to points c or g; she prefers all the points on indifference curve I_2 to all the points on indifference curve I_1. Points on a higher indifference curve are preferred to points on a lower curve.

Indifference Curves and Preferences

We use the concept of the marginal rate of substitution to describe the shape of an indifference curve. The **marginal rate of substitution** (or **MRS**) is the rate at which a person will give up good y in order to get more of good x and at the same time remain indifferent. The marginal rate of substitution is measured from the slope of an indifference curve. If the indifference curve is steep, the marginal rate of substitution is high. The person is willing to give up a large quantity of good y (measured on the vertical axis) in exchange for a small quantity of good x (measured on the horizontal axis) while remaining indifferent. If the indifference curve is flat, the marginal rate of substitution is low. The person is willing to give up only a small amount of good y and must be compensated with a large amount of good x to remain indifferent.

Let's work out the marginal rate of substitution in two cases, both illustrated in Fig. 8.5. The curve labeled I_1 is one of Lisa's indifference curves. Suppose that Lisa drinks 6 six-packs of soda and watches 2 movies (point c in the figure). What is her marginal rate of substitution at this point? It is calculated by measuring the magnitude of the slope of the indifference curve at that point. To measure the slope, place a straight line against, or tangential

Figure 8.5 The Marginal Rate of Substitution

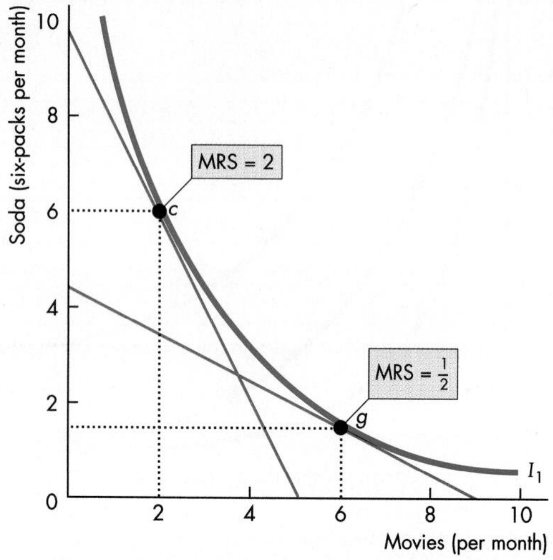

The slope of an indifference curve is called the marginal rate of substitution, or MRS. The marginal rate of substitution measures how much of one good a person is willing to give up to gain more of another good, while remaining indifferent. The marginal rate of substitution at point *c* is 2; at point *g* it is ½.

to, the indifference curve at that point. The slope of that line is the change in soda divided by the change in movies. As movies increase by 5, soda falls by 10. The slope of that line is -2. Thus when Lisa is consuming 2 movies and 6 six-packs of soda, her marginal rate of substitution is 2.

Now, suppose that Lisa is consuming 6 movies and 1.5 six-packs (point *g* in Fig. 8.5). What is her marginal rate of substitution at this point? The answer is found by calculating the slope of the indifference curve at that point. That slope is the same as the slope of the straight line that is drawn tangential to the point. Again, the slope equals the change in soda divided by the change in movies. As movies increase by 9, soda falls by 4.5. The slope of the line is $-1/2$. Thus when Lisa sees 6 movies and consumes 1.5 six-packs of soda, she is willing to substitute movies for soda at the rate of half a six-pack per movie while remaining indifferent. Her marginal rate of substitution is $1/2$.

Notice that if Lisa drinks a lot of soda and does not see many movies, her marginal rate of substitution is high. If she watches a lot of movies and does not drink much soda, her marginal rate of substitution is low. This feature of the marginal rate of substitution is the central assumption of the theory of consumer behavior and is referred to as diminishing marginal rate of substitution. The assumption of **diminishing marginal rate of substitution** is the general tendency for the marginal rate of substitution to diminish as the consumer moves along an indifference curve, increasing consumption of good *x* and decreasing consumption of good *y*.

You may be able to appreciate why we assume that the marginal rate of substitution diminishes by thinking about your own preferences. Imagine two situations: In one, you are watching 3 movies a night but have no soda. In the other, you have 6 six-packs of soda and no movies. In the first situation, you will probably willingly give up seeing 1 movie if you can get just a small amount of soda in exchange. In the second situation, you will probably be willing to give up quite a lot of soda to watch just 1 movie. Your preferences satisfy the assumption of diminishing marginal rate of substitution.

The shape of the indifference curves incorporates the assumption of diminishing marginal rate of substitution because these curves are bowed toward the origin. The tightness of the bend of an indifference curve tells us how willing a person is to substitute one good for another while remaining indifferent. Let's look at some examples that will clarify this point.

Degree of Substitutability

Most of us would not regard movies and soda as being close substitutes for each other. We probably have some fairly clear ideas about how many movies we want to see each month and how many cans of soda we want to drink. Nevertheless, to some degree, we are willing to substitute between these two goods. No matter how big a soda freak you are, there is surely some increase in the number of movies you can see that will compensate you for being deprived of a can of soda. Similarly, no matter how addicted you are to the movies, surely some number of cans of soda will compensate you

Figure 8.6 The Degree of Substitutability

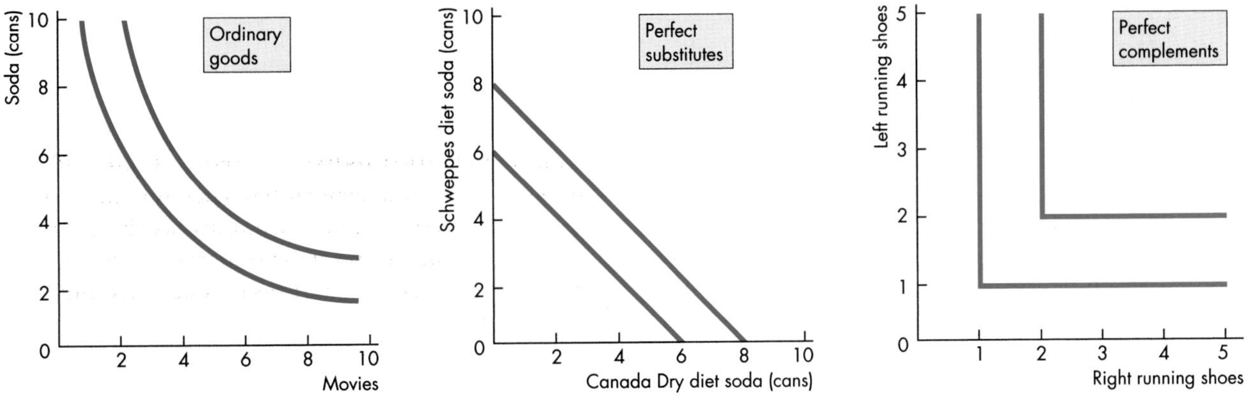

(a) Ordinary goods **(b) Perfect substitutes** **(c) Perfect complements**

The shape of the indifference curves reveals the degree of substitutability between two goods. Part (a) shows the indifference curves for two ordinary goods: movies and soda. To remain indifferent as less soda is consumed, one must see more movies. The number of movies that compensates for a reduction in soda increases as less soda is consumed. Part (b) shows the indifference curves for two perfect substitutes. For the consumer to remain indifferent, one fewer can of Schweppes diet soda must be replaced by one extra can of Canada Dry diet soda. Part (c) shows two perfect complements—goods that cannot be substituted for each other at all. Two left running shoes with one right running shoe is no better than one of each. But two of each is preferred to one of each.

for being deprived of seeing one movie. A person's indifference curves for movies and soda might look something like those shown in Fig. 8.6(a).

Close Substitutes Some goods substitute so easily for each other that most of us do not even notice which we are consuming. A good example concerns different brands of personal computers. Zenith, Leading Edge, and Tandy are all clones of the IBM PC—but most of us can't tell the difference between the three clones and indeed the IBM machine itself. The same holds true for soda. Except for a few connoisseurs, most of us don't care whether we are drinking Canada Dry or Schweppes diet soda. When two goods are perfect substitutes for each other, their indifference curves are straight lines that slope downward, as illustrated in Fig. 8.6(b). The marginal rate of substitution between perfect substitutes is constant.

Complements Some goods cannot substitute for each other at all. Instead they are complements. The complements in Fig. 8.6(c) are left and right running shoes. Indifference curves of perfect complements are L-shaped. One left running shoe and one right running shoe are as good as one left shoe and two right ones. Two of each is preferred to one of each, but two of one and one of the other is no better than one of each.

The extreme cases of perfect substitutes and perfect complements shown here don't often happen in reality. They do, however, illustrate that the shape of the indifference curve shows the degree of substitutability between two goods. The more perfectly substitutable the two goods, the more nearly are their indifference curves straight lines and the less quickly does the marginal rate of substitution fall. Poor substitutes for each other have tightly curved indifference curves, approaching the shape of those shown in Fig. 8.6(c).

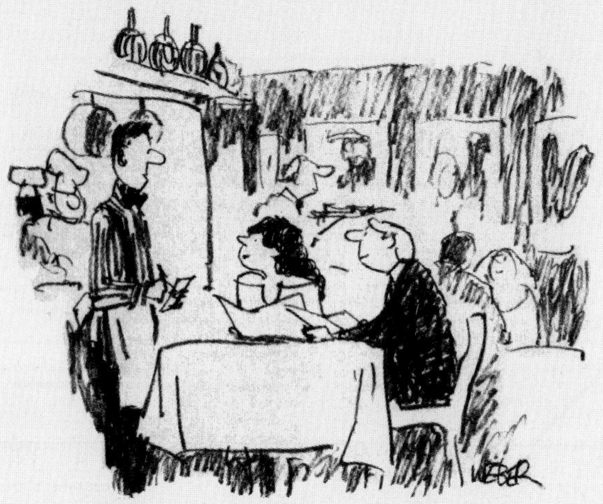

"With the pork I'd recommend an Alsatian white or a Coke."

As you can see in the cartoon, according to the waiter's preferences, Coke and Alsatian white wine are perfect substitutes for each other and are each complements with pork. We hope the customers agree with him.

REVIEW

A person's preferences can be represented by a preference map. A preference map consists of a series of indifference curves. Indifference curves slope downward, bow toward the origin, and do not intersect each other. The slope of an indifference curve is called the marginal rate of substitution. The marginal rate of substitution falls as a person consumes less of good *y* and more of good *x*. The tightness of an indifference curve tells us how well two goods substitute for each other. Indifference curves that are almost straight lines indicate that the goods are close substitutes. Indifference curves that are tightly curved and that approach an L-shape indicate that the two goods complement each other. ■

The two components of the model of consumer behavior are now in place: the budget line and the preference map. We will now use these two components to work out the consumer's choice.

Choice

Recall that Lisa has $30 to spend and she buys only two goods: movies (at $6 each) and soda (at $3 a six-pack). We've learned how to construct Lisa's budget line, which summarizes what she can buy, given her income and the prices of movies and soda (Fig. 8.1). We've also learned how to characterize Lisa's preferences in terms of her indifference curves (Fig. 8.4). We are now going to bring Lisa's budget line and indifference curves together and discover her best affordable way of consuming movies and soda.

The analysis is summarized in Fig. 8.7. You can see in that figure the budget line from Fig. 8.1 and the indifference curves from Fig. 8.4. Let's first focus on point *h* on indifference curve I_0. That point is on Lisa's budget line, so we know that she can afford it. But does she prefer this combination of movies and soda over all the other affordable combinations? The answer is no, she does not. To see why not, consider point *c* where she consumes 2 movies and 6 six-packs. Point *c* is also on Lisa's budget line, so we know she can afford to consume at this point. But point *c* is on indifference curve I_1, a higher indifference curve than I_0. Therefore we know that Lisa prefers point *c* to point *h*.

Are there any affordable points that Lisa prefers to point *c*? The answer is that there are not. All Lisa's other affordable consumption points—all the other points on or below her budget line—lie on indifference curves that are below I_1. Indifference curve I_1 is the highest indifference curve on which Lisa can afford to consume.

Let's look more closely at Lisa's best affordable choice.

Properties of the Best Affordable Point

Two properties of point *c* need to be highlighted. First, the best affordable point is *on* the budget line. If Lisa chooses a point inside the budget line, she will have an affordable point on the budget line where she can consume more of both goods. Lisa prefers that point to the one inside the budget line. The best affordable point cannot be outside the budget line because Lisa cannot afford such a point.

Second, the chosen point is where the highest attainable indifference curve has the same slope as the budget line. Stated another way, the marginal

Figure 8.7 The Best Affordable Point

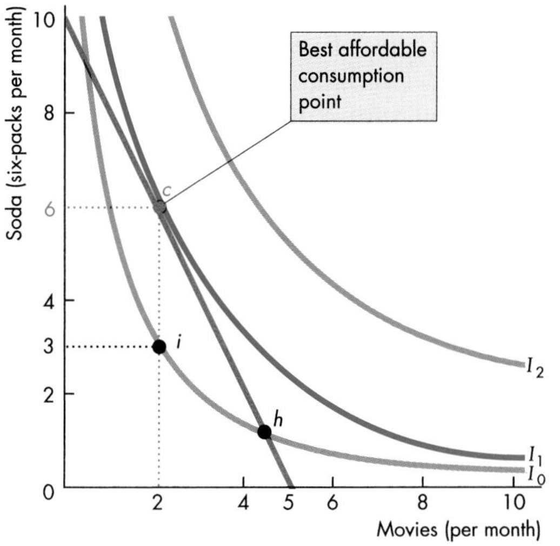

Lisa's best affordable point is c. At that point, she is on her budget line and so spends her entire income on the two goods. She is also on the highest attainable indifference curve. Indifference curves above I_1 (such as I_2) do not touch her budget line and so she cannot afford any point on them. At point c, the marginal rate of substitution (the slope of the indifference curve) equals the relative price of movies (the slope of the budget line). A point such as h on the budget line is not Lisa's best affordable point because at that point she is willing to give up more movies in exchange for soda than she has to. She can move to a point such as i, which she regards as being just as good as point h and which allows her to still have some income left over. She can spend that income and move to c, a point that she prefers to point i.

rate of substitution between the two goods (the slope of the indifference curve) equals their relative price (the slope of the budget line).

To see why this condition describes the best affordable point, consider point *h*, which Lisa regards as inferior to point *c*. At point *h*, Lisa's marginal rate of substitution is less than the relative price—indifference curve I_0 has a flatter slope than Lisa's budget line. As Lisa gives up movies for soda and moves up indifference curve I_0, she moves inside her budget line and has some money left over. She can move to point *i*, for example, where she consumes 2 movies and 3 six-packs and has $9 to spare. She is indifferent between the combination of goods at point *i* and at point *h*. But she prefers point *c* to point *i*, since at *c* she has more soda than at *i* and sees the same number of movies.

By moving along her budget line from point *h* toward point *c*, Lisa passes through a whole array of indifference curves (not shown in the figure) located between indifference curves I_0 and I_1. All of these indifference curves are higher than I_0 and therefore any point on them is preferred to point *h*. Once she gets to point *c*, Lisa has reached the highest attainable indifference curve. If she keeps moving along the budget line, she will now start to encounter indifference curves that lie below I_1.

REVIEW

The consumer has a given income and faces fixed prices. The consumer's problem is to allocate that fixed income in the best possible way. Affordable combinations of goods are described by the consumer's budget line. The consumer's preferences are represented by indifference curves. The consumer's best allocation of income occurs when all income is spent (on the budget line) and when the marginal rate of substitution (the slope of the indifference curve) equals the relative price (the slope of the budget line). ■

We will now use this model of consumer choice to make some predictions about the effects of changes in prices and income on consumption patterns.

Predicting Consumer Behavior

Let's examine how consumers respond to changes in prices and income. We'll start by looking at the effect of a change in price. By studying the effect of a change in price on a consumer's choice, holding all other effects constant, we are able to derive a consumer's demand curve.

Figure 8.8 The Price Effect and the Demand Curve

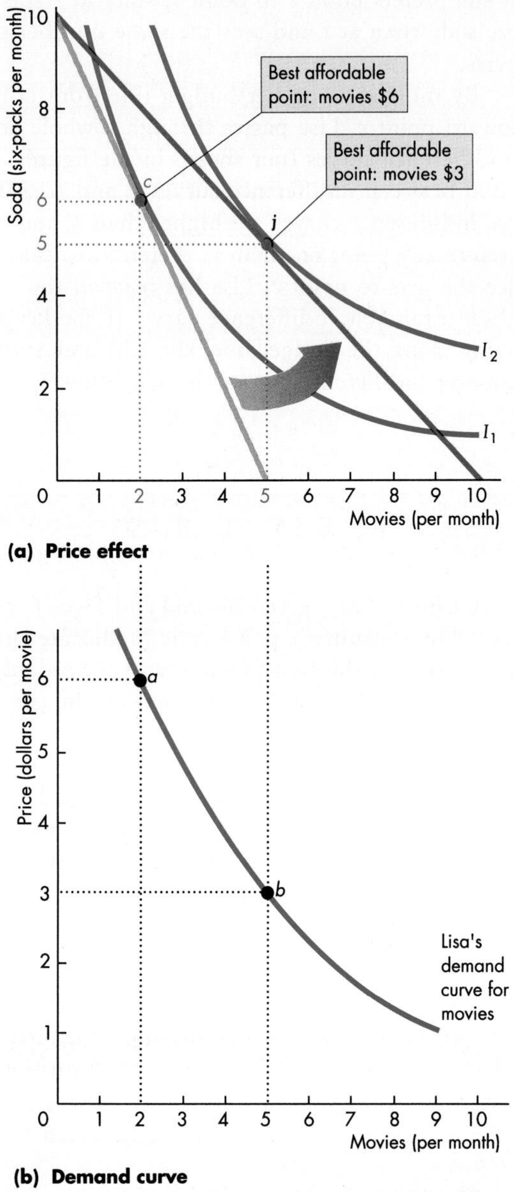

Initially, Lisa consumes at point c (part a). If the price of a movie falls from \$6 to \$3, she consumes at point j. The increase in the consumption of movies from 2 to 5 per month is the price effect. When the price of a movie falls, Lisa consumes more movies. She also consumes less soda. Lisa's demand curve for movies is shown in part (b). When the price of movies is \$6, she consumes 2 a month, at point a. When the price of movies falls to \$3, she consumes 5 a month, at point b. The demand curve is traced by varying the price of movies and calculating Lisa's best affordable consumption of movies for each different price.

A Change in Price: The Demand Curve

The effect of a change in price on the quantity of a good consumed is called the **price effect.** Let's work out the price effect of a fall in the price of movies and derive Lisa's demand curve for movies. We'll start out with movies costing \$6 each, soda costing \$3 a six-pack, and with Lisa's income being \$30 a month. In this situation, she consumes at point *c* (Fig. 8.8a) where her budget line is tangential to her highest attainable indifference curve, I_1. She consumes 6 six-packs and 2 movies a month.

Now suppose that the price of a movie falls to \$3. We've already seen how a change in price (in Fig. 8.2a) affects the budget line. With a lower price of movies, the budget line moves outward and becomes less steep. You can see the new budget line (dark red) in Fig. 8.8(a).

Lisa's new best affordable point is *j*, where she consumes 5 movies and 5 six-packs of soda. As you can see, Lisa drinks less soda and watches more movies now that movies cost less. Her soda consumption has been cut from 6 to 5 six-packs, and her movie consumption has gone up from 2 to 5.

This analysis of the effect of a change in the price of movies enables us to derive Lisa's demand curve for movies. Lisa's demand curve is derived by gradually lowering the price and calculating the best affordable point at each different price. Figure 8.8(b) highlights just two prices and two points that lie on Lisa's demand curve for movies. When the price of movies is \$6, Lisa consumes two movies a month at point *a*. When the price falls to \$3, she increases her consumption to 5 movies a month at point *b*. The entire demand curve is made up of the two points that we've derived plus all the other points that tell us Lisa's best affordable consumption of movies at each price—above \$6, between \$6 and \$3, and below \$3. As you can see, Lisa's demand curve for movies slopes downward—the lower the price of a movie, the more movies she watches each month.

Next, let's examine what happens when Lisa's income changes.

A Change in Income

We've already seen, earlier in this chapter, how a change in income shifts the budget line. We worked out and illustrated (in Fig. 8.2c) that a rise in income shifts the budget line outward, with its slope unchanged.

Figure 8.9 The Income Effect

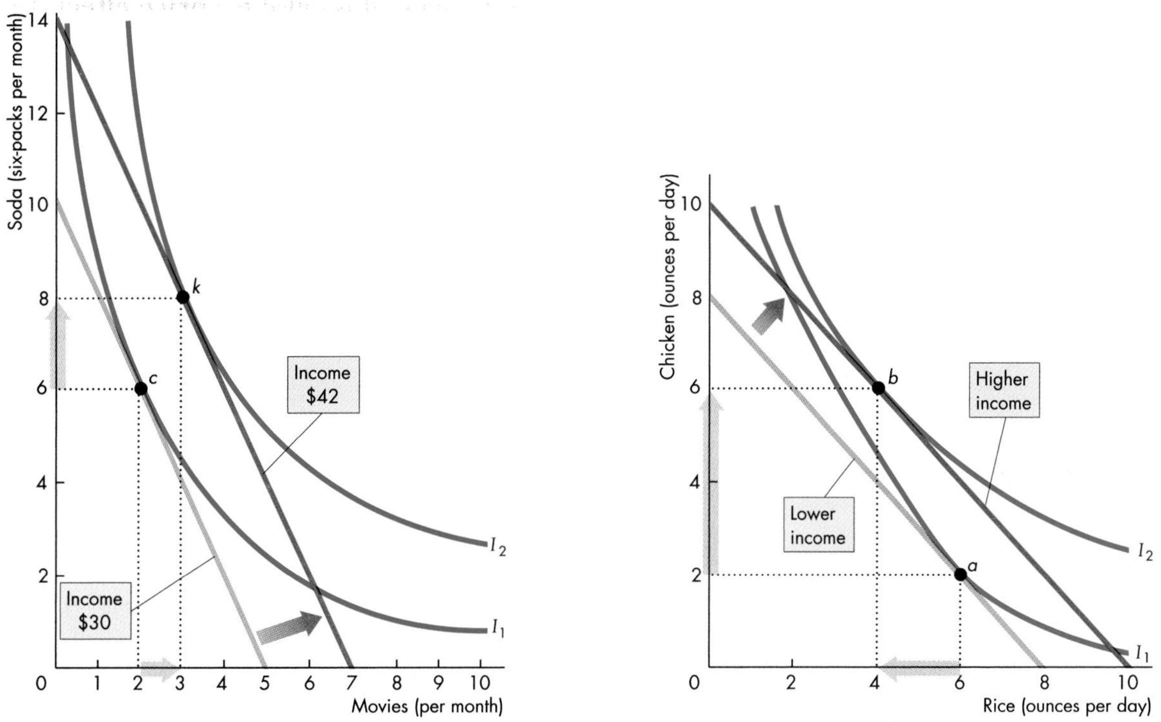

(a) Normal goods **(b) Inferior good**

An increase in income increases the consumption of most goods. These goods are normal goods. In part (a), Lisa consumes more of both soda and movies (as shown by the orange arrows) as her income increases.

Soda and movies are normal goods, but some goods are inferior goods. The consumption of inferior goods decreases as income increases. In part (b), as income increases, the consumption of rice decreases (and more chicken is consumed), again shown by the orange arrows. For this consumer, rice is an inferior good.

It will be clear to you that, as income rises, a person can consume more of all goods. But being able to consume more of all goods does not mean that a person will consume more of all goods. Goods are classified into two groups: normal goods and inferior goods. *Normal goods* are goods whose consumption increases as income increases. *Inferior goods* are goods whose consumption decreases as income increases. As the name implies, most goods are normal goods. A few examples of inferior goods, however, do exist. Rice and potatoes are perhaps the most obvious. People with low incomes have a heavy rice or potato component to their diet. As incomes rise, people substitute chicken or beef—normal goods—for rice and potatoes. Thus as income increases, the consumption of chicken and beef increases but that of rice and potatoes decreases.

The effect of a change in income on consumption is called the **income effect.** The income effect for a normal good is positive. That is, a rise in income produces a rise in consumption of a normal good. If all goods are normal, then the consumption of each good rises as income rises. In Lisa's case, both movies and soda are normal goods. Therefore as Lisa's income rises, she consumes more movies and more soda.

Parts (a) and (b) of Fig. 8.9 illustrate the two types of income effect. Part (a) shows the income effect for normal goods, using Lisa's consumption

Figure 8.10 Price Effect, Substitution Effect, and Income Effect

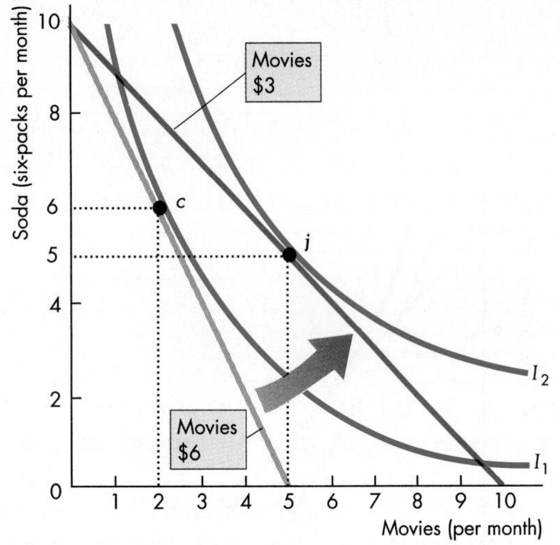

(a) Price effect

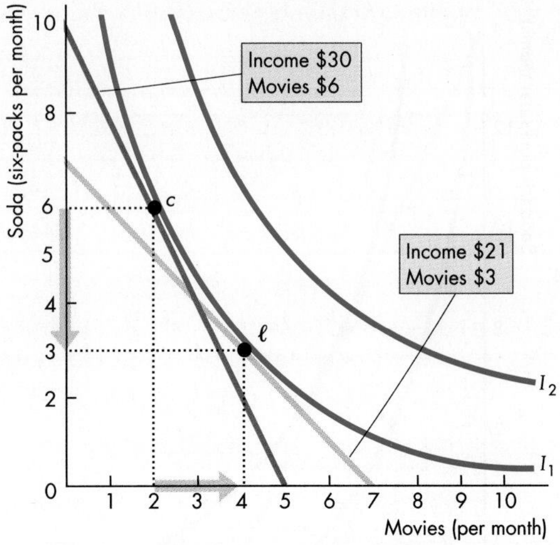

(b) Substitution effect

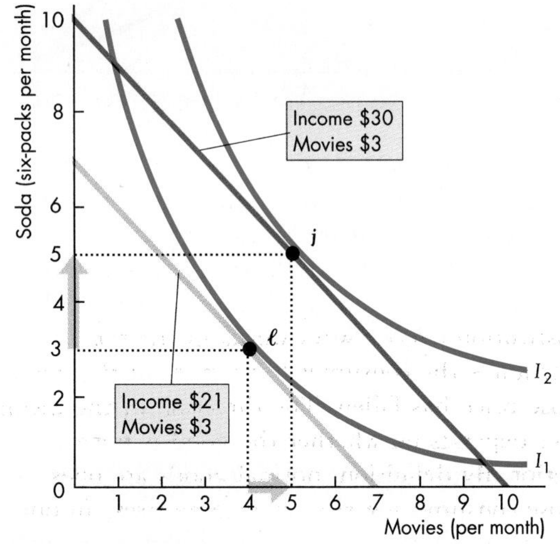

(c) Income effect

The price effect can be separated into a substitution effect and an income effect. The price effect is shown in part (a) and is the same as that in Fig. 8.8(a).

The substitution effect in part (b) is calculated by imagining that Lisa's income falls at the same time as the fall in the price of a movie, so that when she chooses her best affordable point ℓ, she is indifferent between that and the original situation. The move from c to ℓ is the substitution effect. The substitution effect of a price change always results in more consumption of the good whose price has fallen. The orange arrows show the changes in consumption.

The income effect (part c) is calculated by reversing the imaginary pay cut. Income is increased while holding prices constant at their new level. The budget line moves outward and more of both goods is consumed, as shown by the orange arrows. The move from ℓ to *j* is the income effect.

as an example. With an income of $30 and with movies costing $6 each and soda $3 for a six-pack, she consumes at point *c*—2 movies and 6 six-packs. If her income goes up to $42, she consumes at point *k*—consuming 3 movies and 8 six-packs. Thus with a higher income, Lisa consumes more of both goods. Part (b) of Fig. 8.9 shows the income effect for an inferior good—rice. At the initial income level, the household consumes at point *a*, by consuming 2 ounces of chicken and 6 ounces of rice a day. When income increases, chicken consumption increases to 6 ounces a day, but rice consumption decreases to 4 ounces a day, at point *b*.

A Change in Price: Income and Substitution Effects

We've now worked out the effects of a change in the price of movies and the effects of a change in Lisa's income on the consumption of movies and soda. We've discovered that when her income increases, she increases her consumption of both goods. When the price of movies falls, she increases her consumption of movies and decreases her consumption of soda. Movies and soda are *normal goods*. For a normal good, a fall in its price leads to an increase in consumption of that good, as well as to a decrease in the consumption of the substitutes for that good. In this example, a fall in the price of movies leads to an increase in the consumption of movies and to a decrease in the consumption of soda, a substitute for movies. To see why these changes in spending patterns occur when there is a change in price, we separate the effect of the change into two parts. One part is called the substitution effect; the other part is called the income effect. You will discover that the income effect of a price change is exactly the same as the effect of a change in income such as the one that we have already studied. But first let's study the substitution effect.

The Substitution Effect The **substitution effect** is the effect of a change in price on the quantities consumed when the consumer (hypothetically) remains indifferent between the original and the new combinations of goods consumed. To work out Lisa's substitution effect, we have to imagine that when the price of movies falls, Lisa's income also falls by an amount that is just enough to leave her on the same indifference curve as before.

The substitution effect is illustrated in Fig. 8.10(b). When the price of movies falls from \$6 to \$3, let's suppose (hypothetically) that Lisa's income falls to \$21. What's special about \$21? It is the income that is just enough, at the new price of movies, to enable Lisa to buy 4 movies and 3 six-packs, a combination at ℓ, which is on the same indifference curve as her initial consumption point c. Lisa's budget line in this situation is the light red line shown in Fig. 8.10(b). With the new price of movies and the new lower income, Lisa's best affordable point is ℓ on indifference curve I_1. The move from c to ℓ isolates the substitution effect of a price change. The substitution effect of the fall in the price of movies is an increase in the consumption of movies from 2 to 4 and a decrease in the consumption of soda. The direction of the substitution effect never varies: when the relative price of a good falls, the consumer substitutes more of that good for the other good.

Income Effect To calculate the substitution effect, we gave Lisa a \$9 pay cut. Now let's give Lisa her money back. This means shifting Lisa's budget line, as shown in Fig. 8.10(c). That move does not involve any change in prices. The budget line moves outward but its slope does not change. This change in the budget line is similar to the one that occurs in Fig. 8.9 where we study the effect of income on consumption. As Lisa's budget line shifts outward, her consumption possibilities expand and her best affordable point becomes j on indifference curve I_2. The move from ℓ to j isolates the income effect of a price change. In this example, the increase in income increases the consumption of both movies and soda; they are normal goods.

Price Effect We have separated the effect of a change in price, as Fig. 8.10(a) illustrates, into two parts—part (b) keeps the consumer indifferent between the two situations (by making a hypothetical income change at the same time) and looks at the substitution effect of the price change; part (c) keeps prices constant and looks at the effect of undoing the hypothetical change in income. The substitution effect always works in the same direction—the consumer buys more of the good whose price has fallen. The direction of the income effect depends on whether the good is normal or inferior. By definition, normal goods are ones whose consumption rises as income rises. In our example, movies and soda are normal goods because the income effect raises their consumption. Both the income effect and the substitution effect raise Lisa's consumption of movies.[2]

[2]The example that we have just studied is that of a normal good. The effect of the change in price of an inferior good is different. Recall that an inferior good is one whose consumption falls as income increases. For an inferior good, the income effect is negative. It is not always the case that a lower price leads to an increase in the quantity demanded of an inferior

(continued)

The substitution and income effects of a price change are marked off on the axes in parts (b) and (c) of Fig. 8.10. The move from point c to ℓ is the substitution effect, and the move from point ℓ to point j is the income effect.

Reading Between the Lines (pp. 192–193) takes a look at some recent real-world examples of income and price changes and their effects on consumption patterns.

Model, Theory, and Reality

We have built a model of household behavior that makes predictions about consumption choices and how those choices are affected by changes in income and prices. This model leads to a theory of consumer behavior that helps us to understand past spending patterns and to predict future ones. Let's summarize this model.

The Model

All models begin with assumptions. By using logic, we work out the implications of those assumptions. Let's look at the assumptions and implications in the model of consumer choice.

Assumptions

- A household has a fixed income to allocate among various goods.
- The prices of goods cannot be influenced by the household.
- The household has preferences and can compare alternative combinations of goods as preferred, not preferred, or indifferent.
- Preferences can be represented by indifference curves.
- Indifference curves bow toward the origin—the marginal rate of substitution falls as consumption of good x rises and consumption of good y falls.
- The household chooses its best affordable combination of goods.
- Preferences do not change when prices and incomes change. *Choices* change but the new choices result from given preferences and changed constraints.

Implications

- The chosen consumption point is affordable and is *on* the budget line.
- The chosen consumption point is on the highest attainable indifference curve.
- At the chosen consumption point, the slope of the indifference curve equals the slope of the budget line. Expressed in another way, the marginal rate of substitution equals the relative price of the two goods.
- For normal goods, a rise in income raises demand.
- For inferior goods, a rise in income lowers demand.
- For any good, a rise in its price has a substitution effect that lowers the quantity demanded of it.
- For a normal good, a rise in its price lowers the quantity demanded of it—the income effect and the substitution effect reinforce each other. This is the law of demand.
- For an inferior good, a rise in its price can lead to a rise in the quantity demanded of it if the income effect is bigger than the substitution effect.

---

good. A lower price has a substitution effect that tends to increase the quantity demanded. But the lower price raises real income and the higher real income lowers the demand for an inferior good. Thus the income effect offsets the substitution effect to some degree.

It has been suggested that the negative income effect is so large for some goods that it dominates the substitution effect. As a result, a lower price leads to a decrease in the quantity demanded for such a good. Goods of this type are called "Giffen" goods, named after Sir Robert Giffen, an Irish economist. During a potato famine in Ireland in the nineteenth century, Giffen noticed that when the price of potatoes increased, the quantity of potatoes consumed also increased. Potatoes made up such a large part of the diets of these impoverished people that when the price of potatoes rose, consumers couldn't afford to buy meat or other more expensive foods. Though it is likely that there are many inferior goods, Giffen goods are very uncommon. Thus even though some goods do have a negative income effect, that negative income effect is usually not large enough to offset the substitution effect. So the law of demand still operates—when the price of a good falls, the quantity of that good consumed rises.

The above, in a nutshell, is the model of consumer choice that we have studied in this chapter. That model provides a basis for developing a theory that explains the patterns of consumption.

The Theory

The theory of consumer choice can be summarized as follows:

- The choices made by real people resemble the choices made by the artificial people in the model economy.
- Spending patterns in the model look like the actual spending patterns in the real world.

What the Theory Is Not

- The theory of consumer choice does *not* say that people compute marginal rates of substitution and then set them equal to relative prices to decide how much of each good to buy.
- Economists do not have a theory about the mental processes people use to arrive at their choices.

Back to the Facts

We started this chapter by observing how consumer spending has changed over the years. The theory of consumption choice studied in this chapter can be used to explain those changes. Spending patterns are interpreted as being the best choices households can make, given their preferences and incomes and given the prices of the goods they consume. Changes in prices and in income lead to changes in the best possible choice—changes in consumption patterns.

Models based on the same ideas that you've studied here are used to explain the actual changes that occur and to measure the response of consumption to changes in prices and in income—the price and income elasticities of demand. You met some measures of these elasticities in Chapter 5. Most of those elasticities were measured by using models of exactly the same type that we've studied here (but models that have more than two goods).

But the model of household choice can do much more than explain consumption choices. It can be used to explain a wide range of other aspects of household behavior. Let's look at some of these.

Other Household Choices

Households make many choices other than those about how to spend their income on the various goods and services available. There are two key choices that households must make:

- The type and amount of work to do
- How much to consume and how much to save

Time Allocation and Labor Supply

Every day, we have to allocate our 24 hours between leisure, working for ourselves, and working for someone else. When we work for someone else, we are supplying labor.

We can understand our labor supply decisions by using the theory of household choice. Supplying more labor is exactly the same thing as consuming less leisure. Leisure is a good, just like movies and soda. Other things being equal, a situation that has more leisure is preferred to one that has less leisure. We have indifference curves for leisure and consumption goods similar to those we've already studied. For example, we can relabel the axes of Fig. 8.4 so that instead of soda, we measure all consumption goods on the vertical axis and instead of movies, we measure leisure on the horizontal axis.

We can't have as much leisure and consumption as we'd like. Our choices are constrained by the wages that we can earn. For a given hourly wage rate, increasing our consumption of goods and services is only possible if we decrease our leisure time and increase our supply of labor. The wage rate that we can earn determines how much extra consumption we can undertake by giving up an extra hour of leisure. The slope of our indifference curve tells us the marginal rate of substitution—the rate at which we will be willing to give up consumption of goods and services to get one more hour of leisure while remaining indifferent. Our best choice of consumption and leisure has exactly the same properties as our best choice of movies and soda. We get onto the highest possible indifference curve by making the marginal rate of substitution between consumption and leisure equal to the wage rate relative to the price of consumption goods.

Growing Pains at 40

As They Approach Mid-Life, Baby Boomers Struggle to Have It All

The generation that wanted to stay forever young is entering middle age. This year the leading edge of the Baby Boom, the 76 million Americans born in the fecund years between 1946 and 1964, reaches mid-life. Former White House Wunderkind David Stockman and Actor Sylvester Stallone (Rocky, Rambo) turn 40 in 1986. So do ex-Mouseketeer Carl ("Cubby") O'Brien, Arms Control and Disarmament Agency Director Kenneth Adelman, and Real Estate Mogul Donald Trump.

The generation idealized by Madison Avenue for its superior muscle tone and free-spending habits is ruefully discovering that, contrary to the promise of the ads, it cannot have it all. . . . Says Mern Wildcat, 30, . . . in Olathe, Kans., "People want a home, two cars and all the new technologies, like VCRs, but it's hard to afford it all."

The Baby Boom, says Richard C. Michel of the Urban Institute, was hit by a quadruple whammy: inflation, fierce competition for jobs, exorbitant housing costs and the recessions of the '70s and early '80s. "They grew up with the expectation that they would live better than their parents no matter what they did," says Michel. "The 1970s ended that. It was a time of tremendous economic disillusionment for many people." Between 1973 and 1983 the median real income of a typical young family headed by a person aged 25 to 34 fell by 11.5% . . . "If you can't afford a home, you want the best espresso machine you can buy," observes Los Angeles Psychologist Shelley Taylor, 39. Manhattan Ad Executive Julianne Hastings, 39, wears designer clothes and jets off to the Caribbean for vacations. But she lives in an apartment "the same size as the bedroom I grew up in."

***Time*, May 19, 1986**

By Evan Thomas, reported by Ann Blackman/Washington, Cathy Booth/New York, and Jon D. Hull/Los Angeles

The Essence of the Story

- No matter what our aspirations, there are limits to what we can consume: Scarcity is a fact of life for everyone.
- The following four negative factors have lowered consumption possibilities: inflation, a competitive job market, high housing prices, and recession.
- The net result of the four negative factors is a cut in real income of 11.5% for a typical family headed by a person aged 25 to 34.
- People would prefer to have avoided a fall in real income.
- Even for people whose real income has risen, their demand for housing has remained fairly constant while their demand for other goods—such as designer clothes, Caribbean vacations, VCRs and espresso machines—has increased.

Background and Analysis

- We can use the theory of consumer choice to analyze this article. The household's budget line defines the limit of the household's consumption possibilities. Points beyond that line are not attainable.

- Between 1973 and 1983, two things happened to the budget line of the median family: It shifted inward and the relative price of housing increased.

- The top figure illustrates these changes. The horizontal axis measures the consumption of housing and the vertical axis measures the consumption of other goods such as VCRs, Caribbean vacations, designer clothes, and espresso machines.

- People prefer to be on the 1973 budget line rather than on the 1983 one.

- Income for some people increased between 1973 and 1983, but housing costs also increased. The bottom figure illustrates the situation facing such individuals. (For example, Julianne Hastings in the story.)

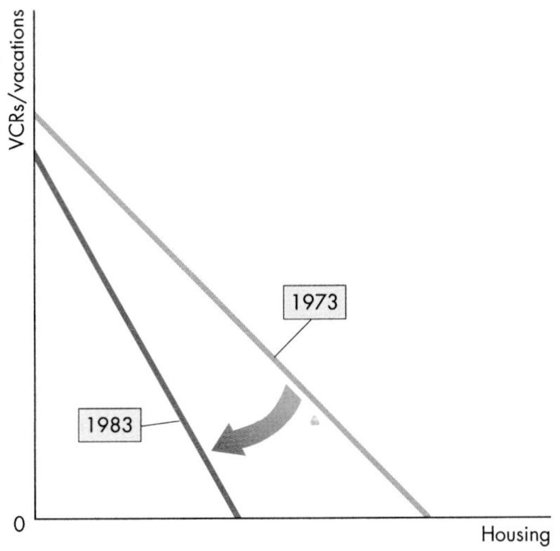

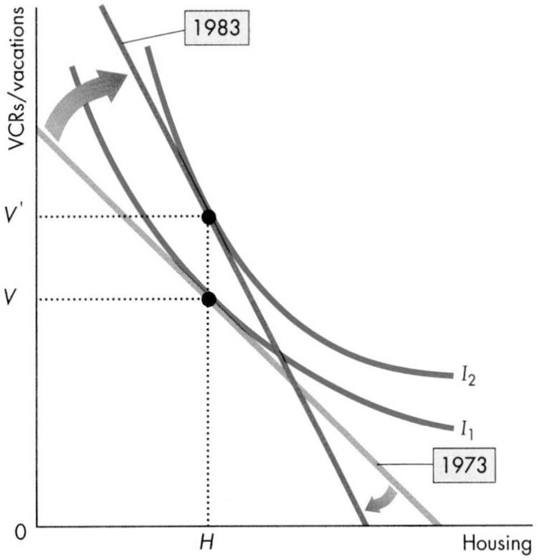

- In 1973, the budget line was the light red line; in 1983, it was the dark red line.

- In 1973, consumption of housing was H and of other goods V.

- A rise in income produces a rise in the demand for all goods.

- A rise in the price of housing produces a substitution effect away from housing toward other goods.

- For some people, the combination of a rise in the price of housing and a rise in income results in a larger quantity demanded of designer clothes and Caribbean vacations (V'), but no change in the quantity of housing demanded (H).

Conclusion

- "Growing Pains at 40" is an interesting and clear example of scarcity and how the behavior of mid-life baby boomers can be entirely predicted by an economic model of consumer choice.

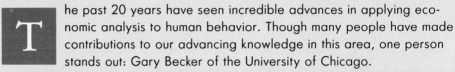

Understanding Human Behavior

Jeremy Bentham

The past 20 years have seen incredible advances in applying economic analysis to human behavior. Though many people have made contributions to our advancing knowledge in this area, one person stands out: Gary Becker of the University of Chicago.

But the economic approach to human behavior did not begin with his work. Adam Smith (see "Our Advancing Knowledge" in Chapter 1) used the approach to understand political choices. The approach was also taken by one of Smith's contemporaries, Jeremy Bentham. Bentham lived in London, England, throughout his life—from 1748 to 1832. He believed that what he called the pleasure-pain calculus was applicable to all human behavior: "Nature has placed mankind under the governance of two sovereign masters, *pain and pleasure*. It is for them alone to point out what we ought to do, as well as to determine what we shall do. . . . They govern us in all we do, in all we say, in all we think."*

Many years passed between the writings of Bentham and Becker with little development in the economics of human behavior. In the last 20 years, many scholars have worked to extend the economic approach to a variety of nontraditional problems. The economics of the family and the economics of crime are just two such areas.

The economics of the family have attracted a lot of attention and a good deal of controversy. The Chicago view, led by Gary Becker (see "Talking with Gary Becker" on pages 151–154), is that we must seek explanations of family behavior as the outcome of given preferences and changing constraints. Chicago students of the economics of the family, such as Robert Michael and Robert J. Willis (both at the University of Chicago's National Opinion Research Center), have used this approach to conduct extensive studies of fertility designed to understand the postwar baby boom (and its subsequent bust).

A competing view, sometimes called the "Pennsylvania school," inspired primarily by Richard Easterlin of the University of Pennsylvania, assumes that preferences have changed in a systematic way to affect postwar fertility.

Among the more active investigators of the economics of crime are Isaac Ehrlich (State University of New York at Buffalo), Stephen Layson (University of North Carolina at Greensboro), Mitchell A. Polinsky (Stanford Law School), and Steven Shavell (Harvard Law School). These scholars are attempting to discover what might be called "supply of offenses" and "demand for enforcement or protection" curves that can be used to provide guidance on how best to design a system of law and enforcement that balances the gains from low crime rates against the costs of achieving them.

*The Bentham quotation is from Gary Becker, *The Economic Approach to Human Behavior* (Chicago: University of Chicago Press, 1976), p. 8.

Changes in wages affect our choice of consumption and leisure in a similar way to that in which a change in the price of movies affects our consumption of movies and soda. A higher wage rate makes leisure more expensive. There is a substitution effect encouraging us to take less leisure and work longer hours, thereby consuming more goods and services. But a higher wage rate also has an income effect. A higher wage leads to a higher income, and with a higher income we consume more of all normal goods. Leisure is a normal good. Other things being equal, the higher the income, the more leisure we take.

People who can earn only a very low hourly wage rate tend to work fewer hours, or perhaps not at all. As the wage rate increases, the substitution effect encourages less leisure and more work to be undertaken. But as the wage rate keeps on increasing, eventually, the income effect comes to dominate the substitution effect. The higher wage leads to higher consumption of goods and services and to additional leisure. It is the ultimately dominant role of the income effect that has resulted in the workweek getting steadily shorter despite the fact that wages have increased.

Consumption and Saving

We don't have to spend all our income here and now. Nor are we constrained to consuming only our current income. We can consume less than our current income, saving the difference for future consumption. Or we can consume more than our current income, borrowing the difference but putting ourselves in a position where we must consume less later in order to repay our loan. Choosing when to consume, how much to save, and how much to borrow can also be understood by using the same theory of household choice that explained Lisa's allocation of her income to movies and soda.

Other things being equal, more consumption today is preferred to less. Also, other things being equal, more consumption in the future is preferred to less. As a consequence, we have indifference curves for consumption now and in the future that are similar to our indifference curves for any pair of goods. Of course, we cannot consume as much as we'd like to today or in the future. Our choices are constrained. The constraint on our choices is our income, and the interest rate that we can earn on our savings or that we have to pay on our borrowings. The interest rate is a relative price—the relative price of consumption today versus consumption in the future. We make our choice of the timing of consumption (and the amount of saving or borrowing to undertake) by making the marginal rate of substitution between current and future consumption equal to the interest rate. Thus high interest rates will discourage borrowing and lead to lower current consumption and higher future consumption.

Other Choices

Many other choices can be understood by using this same theory of household behavior. Some of these choices are discussed in Our Advancing Knowledge (p. 194).

■ We've now completed our study of household choices. We've seen how we can derive, from a model of household choice, the law of demand. We've also seen how that same model can be applied to a wide range of other choices, including the demand for leisure and the supply of labor.

In Part 4, we're going to study the choices made by firms. We'll see how, in the pursuit of profit, firms make choices governing the supply of goods and services and the demand for factors of production (inputs).

After completing these chapters, we'll then bring the analysis of households and firms back together again, studying their interactions in markets for goods and services and factors of production.

S U M M A R Y

Consumption Possibilities

A household's budget line shows the limits to consumption given the household's income and the prices of goods. The budget line is the boundary between what the consumer can and cannot afford.

Changes in prices and changes in income produce changes in the budget line. The slope of the budget line equals the relative price. The point at which the budget line intersects each axis marks the consumer's real income in terms of the good measured on that axis. (pp. 175–179)

Preferences

A consumer's preferences can be represented by indifference curves. An indifference curve joins all the combinations of goods among which the consumer is indifferent. A consumer prefers points above an indifference curve to the points on it and points on an indifference curve to all points below it. Indifference curves bow toward the origin.

The slope of an indifference curve is called the marginal rate of substitution. A key assumption is the diminishing marginal rate of substitution. In other words, the marginal rate of substitution falls as the consumption of good y falls and the consumption of good x increases. The more perfectly two goods substitute for each other, the straighter are the indifference curves. The less easily they substitute, the more tightly curved are the indifference curves. Goods that are always consumed together are complements and have L-shaped indifference curves. (pp. 179–184)

Choice

A household consumes at the best affordable point. Such a point is on the budget line and on the highest attainable indifference curve. At that point the indifference curve and the budget line have the same slope—the marginal rate of substitution equals the relative price. (pp. 184–185)

Predicting Consumer Behavior

Goods are classified into two groups: normal goods and inferior goods. Most goods are normal. When income increases, a consumer buys more normal goods and fewer inferior goods. If prices are held constant, the change in consumption resulting from a change in income is called the income effect.

The change in consumption resulting from a change in the price of a good is called the price effect. The price effect can be divided into a substitution effect and an income effect. The substitution effect is calculated as the change in consumption resulting from the change in price accompanied by a (hypothetical) change in income that leaves the consumer indifferent between the initial situation and the new situation. The substitution effect of a price change always results in an increase in consumption of the good whose prices have decreased. The income effect of a price change is the effect of (hypothetically) restoring the consumer's original income but keeping the price of the good constant at its new level. For a normal good, the income effect reinforces the substitution effect. For an inferior good, the income effect offsets the substitution effect. (pp. 185–190)

Model, Theory, and Reality

A model of household behavior based on the assumption that households' preferences can be represented by indifference curves that bow toward the origin (that have a diminishing marginal rate of substitution) has the implication that the household will choose to consume on its budget line at a point at which the marginal rate of substitution and relative price are equal. A change in price or a change in income leads to a new choice that corresponds to the law of demand: When the price of a good falls, the quantity consumed increases; when income increases, the demand for (normal) goods increases.

The theory of consumer behavior based on this model is that the choices made in the real world correspond to choices made in the model economy. Such a model is used to measure the response of consumption to changes in price and income—the price and income elasticities of demand that appeared in Chapter 5. (pp. 190–191)

Other Household Choices

The model of household behavior also enables us to understand other household choices such as the allocation of time between leisure and work, the allocation of consumption over time, and decisions regarding borrowing and saving. (pp. 191–195)

KEY CONCEPTS

Key Figures and Tables

REVIEW QUESTIONS

1 What determines the limits to a household's consumption choices?

2 What is the budget line?

3 What determines the intercept of the budget line on the vertical axis?

4 What determines the slope of the budget line?

5 What do all the points on an indifference curve have in common?

6 What is the marginal rate of substitution?

7 How can you tell by looking at the consumer's indifference curves how closely two goods substitute for each other?

8 What two conditions are satisfied at the best affordable consumption point?

9 What is the effect of a change in income on consumption?

10 What is the effect of a change in price on consumption?

11 Distinguish between the income effect and the substitution effect of a price change.

PROBLEMS

1 Marc has a monthly income of $20. Beer costs $1 a can and chips cost 50 cents a bag. He consumes 10 cans of beer and 20 bags of chips.

a) What is the relative price of beer in terms of chips?

b) What is the opportunity cost of a can of beer?

c) What is Marc's budget equation?

d) Is Marc on his budget line?

e) What is his marginal rate of substitution of beer for chips?

2 Now suppose that the price of beer rises to $1.50 a can and the price of chips falls to 25 cents a bag.

a) Can Marc still buy the same quantities of beer and chips as before if he wants to?

b) Will he want to?

c) If he changes his consumption, which good does he buy more of and which less?

d) Which situation does Marc prefer: beer at $1 a can and chips at 50 cents a bag or beer at $1.50 and chips at 25 cents?

Appendix to Chapter 8

Utility and Preferences

If you have studied both Chapters 7 and 8, you know that they both explain people's consumption choices. Each chapter presents a different model of consumer choice but they both do the same job. They even use the same example—Lisa and her consumption of movies and soda. This appendix deals with the connection between the two models. When you have read this appendix, you will be able to reinterpret each model in terms of the other.

Utility and Indifference Curves

A key element in each theory of choice is its way of describing the consumer's preferences. The marginal utility theory of Chapter 7 describes preferences in terms of the utility derived from consumption. In the indifference curve theory of Chapter 8, indifference curves represent preferences. You can understand how the two models relate to each other by thinking of an indifference curve as connecting points of equal utility. Let's say that Lisa is indifferent between watching 3 movies and drinking 4 six-packs of soda and watching 2 movies and drinking 6 six-packs of soda. Another way of saying that she is indifferent is that she gets equal utility from the two.

You can literally see the connection between utility and indifference curves by looking at the two parts of Fig. A8.1. Part (a) of this figure has three dimensions: the quantity of soda consumed, the quantity of movies watched, and the level of utility. Part (b) has just two dimensions—the quantities of soda and movies consumed.

The utility that Lisa gets from soda alone (with no movies) appears here as the left-hand yellow line. It shows that as Lisa's consumption of soda rises, so does the utility she gets from soda. Lisa's utility from movies, which appeared in Fig. 7.2, appears as the right-hand yellow line. It shows that as Lisa's consumption of movies rises, so does the utility she gets from movies. Lisa's indifference curve for movies and soda is also visible in both parts of the figure. It appears as the blue line in part (b). It can also be seen in part (a). There it appears as a contour line on a map that shows the height of the terrain. Viewed in this way, an indifference curve is a contour line that measures equal levels of utility.

We can work either with utility curves, as we did in Chapter 7, or with indifference curves, as we did in Chapter 8. They each give the same answers. There are, though, some interesting differences between the two theories.

Figure A8.1 Utility and Indifference Curves

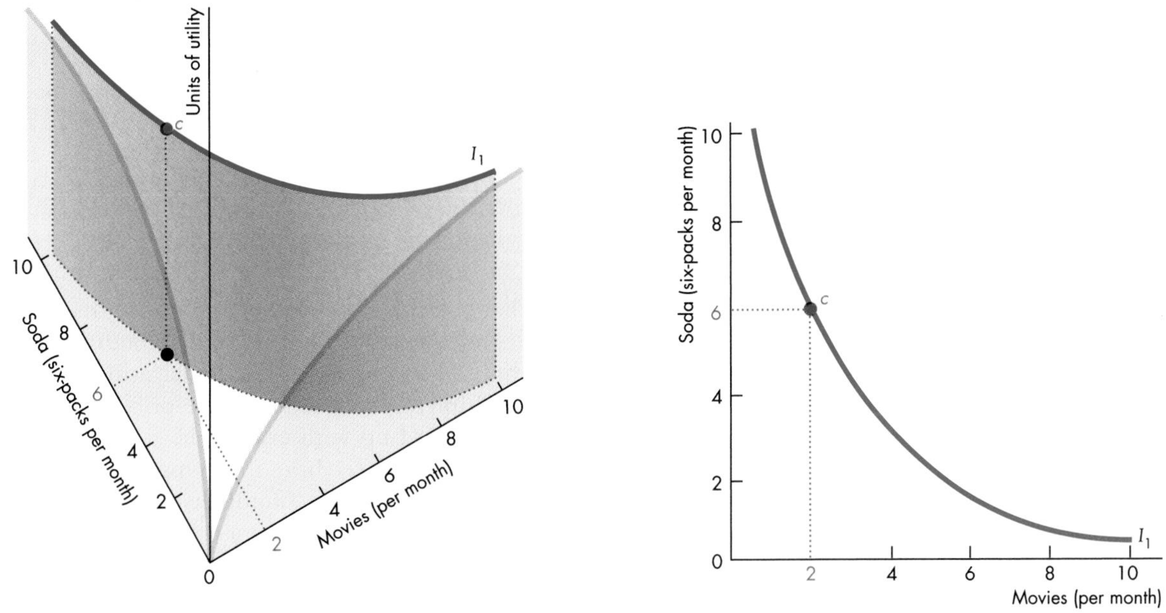

(a) Utility from soda and movies **(b) Indifference curve for soda and movies**

We can represent preferences in two ways: by using utility curves or indifference curves. These two methods are different ways of looking at the same thing. Part (a) shows the utility received from soda when no movies are consumed (the left-hand yellow curve) and the utility received from movies when no soda is consumed (the right-hand yellow curve). It also shows an indifference curve that tells us the combinations of soda and movies that give equal (constant) utility (the blue curve).

Part (b) shows an indifference curve for movies and soda. You can see that it is the same as the indifference curve in part (a). Point c in part (a) is exactly the same as point c in part (b). The indifference curve in part (b) is what you would see if you looked straight down on top of the three-dimensional diagram shown in part (a).

Maximizing Utility and Choosing the Best Affordable Point

According to marginal utility theory, the consumer maximizes utility by dividing the available income among different goods and services so that the marginal utility per dollar spent on each is equal. In Lisa's case, she maximizes utility by making the marginal utility of a dollar spent on movies equal to the marginal utility of a dollar spent on soda. Her choice of movies and soda satisfies the following equation:

$$\frac{\text{Marginal utility of movies}}{\text{Price of movies}} = \frac{\text{Marginal utility of soda}}{\text{Price of soda}}.$$

According to the indifference curve theory, the best consumption point is chosen by making the marginal rate of substitution between the two goods equal to their relative price. In terms of our example, Lisa makes her marginal rate of substitution of movies for soda equal to the relative price of movies in terms of soda. That is, her choice of movies and soda satisfies the following equation:

$$\text{Marginal rate of substitution} = \frac{\text{Price of movies}}{\text{Price of soda}}.$$

In Chapter 8, we learned how to calculate the marginal rate of substitution as the slope of the indifference curve. The marginal rate of substitution is, therefore, the change in the quantity of movies divided by the change in the quantity of soda, such that Lisa remains indifferent.

Indifference in the indifference curve theory means the same thing as constant utility in the marginal utility theory. The two situations that derive the same utility are two situations between which Lisa is indifferent. The marginal rate of substitution, therefore, is the change in the consumption of movies divided by the change in the consumption of soda, holding utility constant. But, according to the utility theory, when consumption levels change utility changes. Total utility, in fact, changes in accordance with the following equation:

$$\text{Change in utility} = \text{Marginal utility of movies} \cdot \Delta Q_m + \text{Marginal utility of soda} \cdot \Delta Q_s.$$

where Δ stands for "change in." If Lisa is indifferent, the change in utility must be zero, which means that

$$\text{Marginal utility of soda} \cdot \Delta Q_s = -\text{Marginal utility of movies} \cdot \Delta Q_m.$$

If we divide both sides of the above equation by the ΔQ_m, and both sides by the marginal utility of soda, we get

$$\frac{\Delta Q_s}{\Delta Q_m} = \frac{-\text{Marginal utility of movies}}{\text{Marginal utility of soda}}.$$

We've just calculated the change in soda divided by the change in movies, while holding utility constant or, equivalently, while staying on an indifference curve. Therefore what we've calculated is nothing other than the marginal rate of substitution. That is,

$$\text{Marginal rate of substitution} = \frac{\text{Marginal utility of movies}}{\text{Marginal utility of soda}}.$$

(Recall that we ignore the minus sign when talking about the magnitude of the marginal rate of substitution.)

You are now ready to see directly the connection between the two theories. The utility theory says that Lisa chooses her consumption of movies and soda to ensure that

$$\frac{\text{Marginal utility of movies}}{\text{Price of movies}} = \frac{\text{Marginal utility of soda}}{\text{Price of soda}}$$

The indifference curve theory says that Lisa chooses her consumption of movies and soda to ensure that

$$\text{Marginal rate of substitution} = \frac{\text{Marginal utility of movies}}{\text{Marginal utility of soda}} = \frac{\text{Price of movies}}{\text{Price of soda}}.$$

All that you now have to do is to notice that you can manipulate the marginal utility condition by dividing both sides by the marginal utility of soda and multiplying both sides by the price of movies. Thus you wind up with exactly the same equation that the indifference curve theory uses to characterize the consumer's best affordable choice.

Equivalently, you can go the other way and start with the indifference curve equation. Multiply both sides by the marginal utility of soda and divide both sides by the price of movies and you arrive at the condition for maximizing utility. Thus the condition for maximizing utility, according to the marginal utility theory, and the condition for choosing the best affordable consumption point, according to the indifference curve theory, are equivalent to each other.

Differences Between the Theories

The key difference between the two models of consumer choice is that the indifference curve approach does not require us to use the concept of utility. We merely have to talk about preferences between different pairs of goods. We have to say whether the consumer prefers one combination to another or is indifferent between the two combinations. We don't have to say anything about *how* the consumer makes such evaluations. Though the indifference curve theory does not require the concept of utility, as we've seen, it is not inconsistent with marginal utility theory.

Part 4

Firms' Choices

Talking with Oliver Williamson

Oliver Williamson, the author of *Markets and Hierarchies* and *The Economic Institutions of Capitalism,* is one of the architects of what is called the "new institutional economics." Now a professor of economics at the University of California, Berkeley, he has worked in the antitrust division of the U.S. Department of Justice. Michael Parkin spoke with Professor Williamson about the nature of markets and firms, and how the internal structure and organization of firms affects their behavior.

What are some of the basic issues that you consider when you look at economic organizations?

One issue is when people engage in an economic activity within a firm rather than contract for the same thing in the market. When the job is done, you have the same product but how you get it may make a real difference. Even within the firm there are different internal structures, some more advantageous and some less. The science of organizations looks at a firm's composition and limitations, its formal and informal structure.

What was the course of events that brought you to the study of economic organizations?

I was an undergraduate at M.I.T. studying chemical engineering and business administration.

"When the job is done, you have the same product, but how you get it may make a real difference."

I then went to work for the government as a project engineer and got exposed to the way engineering projects get shaped, the way contracts are made. Dealing with private firms—large and small—that were doing R&D, and with the government gave me an incredible appreciation for bureaucracy. Later when I took courses in organizational theory, the courses meant a great deal more to me because I had seen bureaucracy in motion. After an M.B.A. and graduate school in economics, when I was teaching at Berkeley, I inherited a course of Julie [Julius] Margolis's on the pricing of public services. This course got me deeply into the market failure literature. Trying to puzzle out what's behind market failure and why it's important. I worked with Julie Margolis again at the University of Pennsylvania when I was asked to teach organization theory. The field was new to me, so I decided to teach it by reexamining market failure. That got me thinking in more microanalytic terms—were organizational and contractual issues behind some of these market failures?

In your work, you've distinguished between two concepts of the firm—what you call a "governance structure" and a "production function." Why do you think that viewing the firm as a governance structure is more revealing than thinking of it as a production function?

The production function describes the firm as a transformation of inputs into outputs. It looks at things like the choice of labor and capital, the effect of taxes, and how firms set prices. This approach assumes that the firm's business activities can be taken as givens. We are producing shoes and we have certain kinds of relationships with suppliers and contractors.

The concept of a governance structure says that there are a variety of ways to produce any particular good or service. The firm can produce it internally, can buy it from another firm, can engage in a joint venture, or can have a long-term or a short-term contract. The notion here is that organization matters, that some kinds of contracting relations work well for some purposes and poorly for others. Some contracts are subject to hazards. If we take these transactions out of markets and organize them internally, we may be able to introduce additional protections against breakdown of the contract. There are two extremes. One is spot contracting and using court-enforced contracts. The other is internal organization and using administration to control contracts. These are alternative ways of governing a contractual relation, or two different governance structures.

How do we observe governance structures in real business practice?

A classic case was the contract between Fisher Body and General Motors in the 1920s. GM originally produced cars with wooden bodies that were supplied by Fisher. But then wooden body technology was replaced by metal body technology, which required new and expensive specialized plant investments. The two companies had contracting problems in conjunction with this move from wooden body construction to metal. GM wanted Fisher to do some things that Fisher didn't want to do. When the two firms were unable to work these things out, what had been a good contracting relationship was eventually replaced by an ownership relation. Fisher Body became a division of the General Motors Corporation.

The notion here is that there is a logic to making and buying and selling. This logic is determined less by technological considerations than it is by contracting considerations.

You never encountered him in the classroom, but you've said that you always thought of Ronald Coase as one of your teachers. Coase suggested that transactions costs were the key factor that determined whether an activity would be carried out within a firm or by individuals coordinated through markets. What are transactions costs and why are they important?

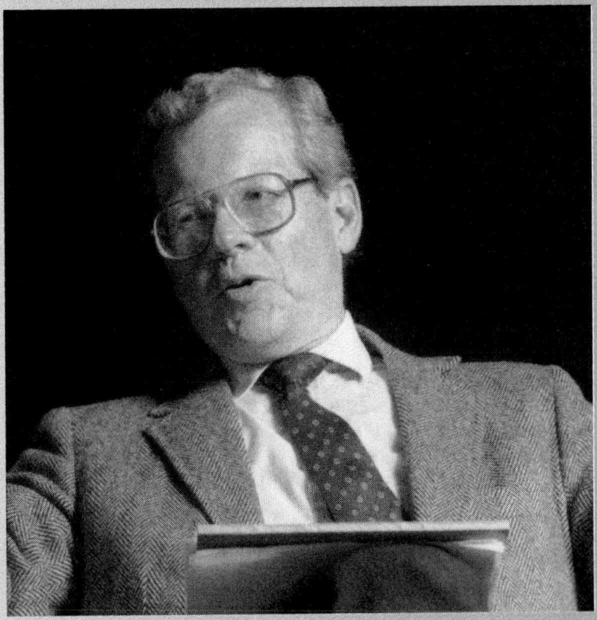

Kenneth Arrow calls them the costs of running the economic system. I like to think about transactions costs mainly from a contractual point of view. Things don't get done simply because we agree to them. That is, it's costly to write and negotiate a contract. Next, there are all kinds of surprises and adjustments in life. Sometimes people renege on agreements. So, it's costly to enforce a contract. The really critical transactions costs are those that make a difference as to whether you organize in one way or another. Of special importance are the costs of adaptation. These costs principally come up when the parties to the contract want to change the terms of the contract because of unanticipated events.

"Bureaucratic organizations can't pay commensurate rewards to those who make huge contributions."

What effect do the costs of adaptation have on the relative effectiveness of firms and markets?

The principle is that there is an underlying tradeoff between incentive intensity and adaptability. Markets provide stronger incentives—for cost control, for many forms of innovation—than do large firms. The problem with firms in terms of incentives is that bureaucratic forms of organization simply can't deliver on promises to pay commensurate rewards to those who make huge contributions. Markets are therefore superior to firms in this respect.

But firms are superior to markets in terms of adaptability when the parties have no choice but to work things out between themselves. Where a dependency builds up between parties, as in the case of Fisher Body and General Motors, markets have limitations. Markets therefore give way to firms when specialized investments in human and physical capital are called for.

Let's turn from questions about how ***a firm functions to*** why ***it functions. You, among other economists, have questioned the notion that firms actually seek to maximize profits by suggesting that the objectives of owners or stockholders and the objectives of managers are different and sometimes***

in conflict. What does this suggest about a firm's ability to maximize profits?

I would say that managers are like everyone else. They're neither better nor worse. They behave in a principled way, but they also have their own interests in mind. Put differently, they're not given to faultless behavior. If you tell a manager to maximize profits, he may not really know what that means. Even if he does, if it runs counter to his own purposes he'll provide you with a mixture of his preferences and yours. As a profession, we've almost abandoned the notion of profit maximization as far as managers go.

Managers, as I said, are like everyone else. Maybe they have a bit more energy. Maybe a bit more ambition, but basically they're interested in income, security, prestige, power, an easy life. Shareholders, in contrast, have a simple relation to the firm. They derive satisfaction from dividends and stock prices and they favor activities that enhance them. That's it. Not everything a manager does contributes equally to improve the firm's earnings and stock prices. That's when there's a problem.

What are some of the professional applications of studies in the economics of organizations? Where do people trained in these studies work in the business world?

Corporations need people that understand how economic organizations work. People that can shed light on important organization questions. In marketing, questions like how do you organize your distribution systems? How do you pay your salespeople? Financial questions such as what are the tradeoffs between debt and equity, in terms of transactions costs. Management issues that involve strategic behavior. Obviously, legal questions, antitrust work, about whether there are underlying economic rationales for mergers and acquisitions.

"Not everything a manager does contributes equally to improve the firm's earnings and stock prices."

Chapter 9

Organizing Production

After studying this chapter, you will be able to:

- Explain what a firm is, and describe the economic problems that *all* firms face
- Describe and distinguish between different forms of business organization
- Explain how firms raise the money to finance their operations
- Calculate and distinguish between a firm's historical costs and opportunity costs
- Define technological efficiency and economic efficiency and distinguish between them
- Explain why firms solve some economic problems and markets solve others

Trees, Forests, and Apples

Every day tens of thousands of trees are harvested and a similar number of new seedlings are planted. Billions of individual trees become one day older. The forest looks much the same from one day to the next, but the evolution of the birth and death of trees means that the individual trees that make up the forest are continuously changing. It is much the same with businesses. Every day thousands of new businesses are born and a similar number die. From one day to the next, the industries that produce the goods and services we consume look much the same, but the individual firms that make up those industries are constantly changing. ■ On a July day in 1977, a tiny new firm was born that grew into and remains a giant—Apple Computer. Apple began its life when Steven Jobs and Stephen Wozniak—two Stanford University students working out of a garage—bought a few components and produced the world's first commercially successful personal computer, the Apple. From that modest start, Apple Computer has grown into a giant, with revenue in 1987 of $2.7 billion. But neither founder now works at Apple: both have gone off and founded new companies. ■ As Apple grew, it passed through several stages of organization, much as a growing tree passes from seed to sapling to maturity. Just as a tree needs nourishment to grow, so does a business. The main form of nourishment that encourages business growth is financial, and it is obtained from investors. Why do companies take different forms? How does a company get the money it needs to build plants and to do research? What do investors expect in return when they put money into a company? ■ At the same time that Apple was growing, other computer companies were dying. You may have heard of Entre Computer Center, ECS Computers, Abacus Computer Centers, and ComputerWorks, but don't try applying for jobs there. They are all firms that fizzled! Sometimes disaster can follow hard on the heels of success. Worlds of Wonder, Inc., a toymaker that created a talking bear, was one of the fastest growing companies in history in 1986. In 1987, it filed for bankruptcy. How does an economist measure a firm's health? What happens to owners and investors of business organizations that die? ■ Economists call business organizations firms. Some 16.5 million firms operate in the United States today in a startling diversity of forms. They range from multinational giants such as IBM, Exxon, and Sony to small family businesses such as painters, gardeners, and restaurants. Some types of business can be done in several forms: Some bookstores have single owners, others belong to corporations. Three quarters of all firms are operated by their owners, as Apple once was. But corporations (like Apple today) account for 90 percent of all business sales. Why are owner-operated firms so predominate in number, but corporations predominate in sales? ■ We have learned that the market is an amazing instrument for coordinating the economic actions of millions of individuals. Firms are another type of instrument for coordinating individual activity. Why do we need firms to organize and coordinate activity? Why don't people simply buy everything they need from other individuals in markets?

■ In this chapter, we are going to address the questions that have just been posed. Although we are going to learn about the many different types of firms, we will understand better the behavior of all firms if we focus on the things they have in common.

The Firm's Economic Problem

The 16.5 million firms in the United States differ enormously in size, in what they do, and in their survival power. What do they have in common? What is the distinguishing characteristic of a firm? What are the different ways in which firms are organized? Why are there different forms of organization? These are the questions that we will tackle first.

What Is a Firm?

A **firm** is an institution that buys or hires factors of production and *organizes* these resources to produce and sell goods and services. The important word in the definition of a firm is "organizes." Someone, or some hierarchy of managers, runs the firm.

What Firms Have in Common

Firms exist because of scarcity. We use firms to get as much as we can out of our scarce resources. Each firm has to solve its own economic problem. That is, each firm has to get the most it can out of the scarce resources under its control. To do so, a firm has to decide on the following:

- What to produce and in what quantities
- Which techniques of production to use
- The quantities of each factor of production to employ
- Its organization and management structure
- The arrangements for compensating factors of production

A firm's receipts from the sale of goods and services are called *revenue*. The total payment made by a firm for the services of factors of production is called **cost.** The difference between a firm's revenue and cost is its **profit** (if revenue exceeds cost) or its **loss** (if cost exceeds revenue). A firm's revenue, cost, and profits (or losses) are obviously affected by the choices that a firm makes to solve its economic problem. Though all firms face common problems, they do not solve those problems in the same way. In particular, the management arrangements and the arrangements for compensating factors of production vary and lead to different forms of business organization. Let's look at these different forms.

Forms of Business Organization

There are three main forms of business organization:

- Proprietorship
- Partnership
- Corporation

Which form a firm takes influences both its management structure and how it compensates factors of production. It also affects how much tax the firm and its owners have to pay. Finally, it affects who receives the firm's profits and who is liable for its debts in the event that it has to go out of business.

Proprietorship Most firms are proprietorships. Corner stores, computer programmers, and freelance editors and artists are all examples of proprietorships. A **proprietorship** is a firm with a single owner—a proprietor—who has unlimited liability. **Unlimited liability** is the legal responsibility for all the debts of a firm up to an amount equal to the entire wealth of the owner. If a proprietorship cannot pay its debts, the personal property of the owner can be claimed by those to whom the firm owes money.

The management structure of a proprietorship is very simple. The sole owner makes all the management decisions—what to produce, in what quantities, and with what techniques; what capital equipment to buy and how much labor to hire; how much money to put into the firm and how much to borrow from others. The proprietor is also the firm's sole residual claimant. A firm's **residual claimant** is the agent or agents who receive the firm's profits and are responsible for its losses.

The profits of a proprietorship are treated as the income of the proprietor. They are simply added to any other income that the proprietor has and taxed as personal income. The proprietorship does not pay taxes in its own right. Profits are taxed just once, when the owner receives them.

Partnership Partnerships are the second most common type of business organization. Most law firms and accounting firms are partnerships. A **partnership** is a firm with two or more owners who have unlimited liability. A partnership has a more complicated management structure than a proprietorship. The partners must agree on an appropriate management structure and how to run the firm. They also must agree on how to divide the firm's

Table 9.1 The Pros and Cons of Different Types of Firms

Type of firm	Pros	Cons
Proprietorship	• Easy to set up • Simple decision making • Profits taxed only once as owner's income	• Bad decisions not checked by need for consensus • Owner's entire wealth at risk • Firm dies with owner • Capital is expensive • Labor is expensive
Partnership	• Easy to set up • Diversified decision making • Can survive withdrawal of partner • Profits taxed only once as owners' incomes	• Achieving consensus may be slow and expensive • Owners' entire wealth at risk • Withdrawal of partner may create capital shortage • Capital is expensive
Corporation	• Owners have limited liability • Large scale, low-cost capital available • Professional management not restricted by ability of owners • Perpetual life • Long-term labor contracts cut labor costs	• Complex management structure can make decisions slow and expensive • Profits bear corporation tax and dividends are taxed as income of stockholders

profits among themselves. As in a proprietorship, the profits of a partnership are taxed as the personal income of the owners. But each partner is legally liable for all the debts of the partnership (only limited by the wealth of an individual partner). Liability for the full debts of the partnership is called **joint unlimited liability.**

Corporation Corporations are the best known types of business organizations, though they are not the most common. IBM, Exxon, and Sony are all examples of corporations. Many corporations, including these three, are multinational giants. A **corporation** is a firm owned by one or more limited liability stockholders. **Limited liability** means the owners have legal liability only for the value of their initial investment. Furthermore, the stock of a corporation is divided into shares. A **share** is a fraction of the stock of a corporation. Shares in some corporations are held privately and can be bought and sold only by mutual agreement between two people. Shares in other corporations can be bought and sold on stock markets like the New York Stock Exchange. Only larger corporations, however, have shares traded on major stock exchanges. The shares of smaller corporations are bought and offered for sale by individual stockbrokers.

The management structures of corporations vary enormously. Some corporations, no bigger than a proprietorship, have just one effective owner. Such corporations are managed in exactly the same way as a proprietorship. Large corporations have elaborate management arrangements. Typically, they have an organization structure headed by a chief executive officer. Below that officer, there are usually senior vice-presidents responsible for such areas as production, finance, marketing, and perhaps research. These senior executives are in turn served by a series of specialists and subspecialists. Each layer in the management structure knows enough about what happens in the layer below to exercise control, but the entire management consists of specialists who concentrate on a narrow aspect of the corporation's activities.

The corporation receives much of its money from its owners—the stockholders. The stockholders' compensation comes in part from dividends and in part from changes in the market price of their shares. Corporations also raise money by issuing bonds (see pages 211–215). Bondholders are compensated by an agreed fixed interest payment.

For as long as a corporation makes profits, the residual claimants to those profits are the stockholders. If a corporation incurs losses on such a scale that it becomes bankrupt, the residual loss is absorbed by the banks and other corporations to whom the troubled corporation is in debt. The stockholders themselves, by virtue of their limited liability, are responsible for the debt of the corporation only up to the value of their initial investment.

Government taxes the profits of a corporation independently of the incomes of the stockholders. The rate of tax on corporations is 34 percent. Corporate profits are, in effect, taxed twice. After the corporation has paid tax on its profits, the stockholders themselves pay taxes on their dividend income. The rate of tax paid by the stockholder depends on that individual stockholder's total income.

Other Types of Firms Although most firms are proprietorships, partnerships, or corporations, there are two other less common types of firms—not-for-profit firms and government firms.

A **not-for-profit** firm is an organization that either chooses or is required to have equal costs and revenue. Examples are universities and colleges, churches, and some insurance companies called mutual insurance companies. A **government firm** is a firm that is owned and operated by a government. Common examples of government firms are those in industries such as water supply, garbage collection, and in some countries airlines, railroads, and utilities.

What are the pros and cons of the various different forms of business organization?

The Pros and Cons of the Different Forms

Since each of the three main types of firms exists in large numbers, each type obviously has advantages in particular situations. Each type also has its disadvantages, which explains why it has not driven out the other two. Table 9.1 summarizes the pros and cons of each type of firm. Let's see how the advantages and disadvantages balance out for each type of business, beginning with a proprietorship.

Proprietorship The pros and cons of a proprietorship balance out in favor of this form of business organization mainly for small operations in which the proprietor is an expert. Though the risk of a bad

Table 9.2 The Relative Importance of the Three Main Types of Firms in Various Industries in 1982

Industry	Percentage of firms in industry			Percentage of industry revenues		
	Proprietorship	Partnership	Corporation	Proprietorship	Partnership	Corporation
Agriculture, forestry, and fishing	91	5	4	59	4	37
Mining	61	24	15	8	11	81
Construction	79	4	17	15	6	79
Manufacturing	54	4	42	1	1	98
Transportation and public utilities	77	3	20	4	1	95
Wholesale trades	40	5	55	2	2	96
Retail trades	74	6	20	14	3	83
Finance, insurance, and real estate	44	34	22	6	16	78
Services	80	5	15	21	13	66
All industries	73	9	18	7	4	89

Almost three quarters of all firms are proprietorships. The least common type of firm is a partnership (accounting for less than 10 percent of all firms). Corporations account for 18 percent of all firms. In contrast to the percentage of firms, the percentage of industry revenues is by far the largest for corporations (except in agriculture, forestry, and fishing).

Source: U.S. Bureau of the Census, *Statistical Abstract of the United States: 1987*, 107th ed. (Washington, D.C.: 1986): 504 and 623.

decision always exists, the expertise of the proprietor keeps mistakes to a minimum. For example, experienced computer programmers with a good grasp of their field often work as proprietorships. The proprietorship also works well in businesses that require relatively low-skilled labor and where a high rate of labor turnover does not hurt efficiency. Most farms, which require the expertise of the owners but which also use unskilled labor, are proprietorships.

Table 9.2 shows the relative importance of the three main types of firms in various industries. As illustrated in the table, proprietorships are particularly important in agriculture, forestry, and fishing and in the service sector.

Proprietorships are often a step on the way to becoming a corporation—the first step in the evolution of a firm. Proprietorships are risky. Those with profitable ideas and expert abilities can earn a large income. Those whose ideas don't fly die quickly. The survivors, with the wealth coming from their success, may go on to create and manage corporations.

For example, the largest greeting card company in the United States—Hallmark Cards—started out as a proprietorship. Its founder, Joyce Hall, kept his first greeting cards under a bed in his room at the YMCA in Kansas City. Today Hallmark is a corporation with annual sales of more than a billion dollars.

Partnership The partnership suits skilled professionals who share a body of knowledge and discipline such as accounting, architecture, law, and medicine. The common viewpoint and background of a group of lawyers, for example, usually means that they can reach a consensus easily. Partnerships have thrived in professions. Table 9.2 shows that partnerships are important in finance, insurance, and real estate, as well as in the services sector. Somewhat surprisingly, a significant percentage of mining firms are partnerships—mainly small prospecting firms.

Corporation The corporation has become the dominant form of business organization in the modern economy because of its advantages in financing, in hiring professional managers, and in hiring and training labor. Although there are far more proprietorships, as you can see in Table 9.2, corporations account for more than 50 percent, and in many cases more than 90 percent, of industry revenue except in agriculture, forestry, and fishing.

R E V I E W

A firm is an organization that organizes factors of production to produce goods and services. There are three main types of firm: proprietorships, partnerships, and corporations. Each has its advantages and each plays a role in every sector of the economy. The pros and cons of the different types of firm are summarized in Table 9.1 and the importance of each type of firm in the various sectors of the economy are summarized in Table 9.2. ■

Business Finance

Now let's look at some financial aspects of firms. First we will examine the ways in which firms raise money. Then we will see how we can measure their costs. And finally, we will look at the ways in which accountants measure costs and compare them with the economist's concept of cost—opportunity cost.

How Firms Raise Money

All firms get some of their money from their owner. The owner's stake in a business is called **equity** or **equity capital.** Proprietorships and partnerships raise additional money by borrowing from the bank or from friends. This limits the amount of money that they can raise. Corporations raise much more money than partnerships and proprietorships. An airline, for example, may raise hundreds of millions of dollars to buy a bigger fleet of jets. A steel manufacturer may raise hundreds of millions of dollars to build a new plant. The more permanent structure of corporations gives them two important ways of raising large sums of money that are not generally available to households and unincorporated businesses.

- Selling bonds
- Issuing stock

Let's look at these two ways in which corporations raise billions of dollars each year.

Selling Bonds A **bond** is a legally enforceable obligation to pay specified sums of money at specified future dates. Usually a corporate bond specifies that a certain sum of money called the **redemption value** of the bond will be paid at a certain future date called the **redemption date.** In addition, another sum will be paid each year between the date of issue of the bond and the redemption date. The sum of money paid each year is called the **coupon payment.**

Let's look at the example shown in Fig. 9.1. On June 25, 1987, the General Cinema Corporation raised more than $100 million by selling bonds. On that day, General Cinema obligated itself to make a payment on the redemption date, July 1, 1997, of $125 million plus any interest then owing. It also committed itself to making a coupon payment of 9⅜ percent on July 1 each year. General Cinema did not expect to get $125 million on July 1, 1987. The bonds were sold for 99¼ percent. That is, General Cinema was to receive $99.25 in 1987 for every $100 that it promised to pay back in 1997.

Let's suppose that the bonds issued by General Cinema are divided into lots that have a redemption value of $100. An investor buys one of these $100 bonds from General Cinema, and each year until 1997 General Cinema makes a coupon payment to the investor. The flow of cash between bond issuer and bond holder is set out in Table 9.3. As you can see, General Cinema receives $99.25 on July 1, 1987, and then makes coupon payments of $9.37 (9⅜ percent of $100) each year through 1996. Finally, in 1997 it redeems the bond for $100 and makes the coupon payment for the last year. At that time, General Cinema will

Figure 9.1 Selling Bonds

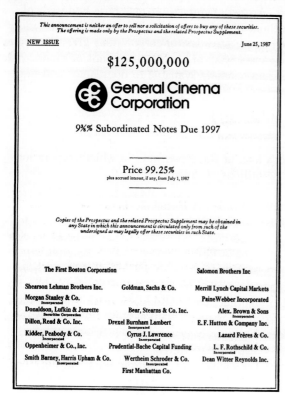

This announcement is neither an offer to sell nor a solicitation of offers to buy any of these securities. The offering is made only by the Prospectus and the related Prospectus Supplement.

NEW ISSUE — June 25, 1987

$125,000,000

General Cinema Corporation

9⅜% Subordinated Notes Due 1997

Price 99.25%

plus accrued interest, if any, from July 1, 1987

Copies of the Prospectus and the related Prospectus Supplement may be obtained in any State in which this announcement is circulated only from such of the undersigned as may legally offer these securities in such State.

The First Boston Corporation		Salomon Brothers Inc
Shearson Lehman Brothers Inc.	Goldman, Sachs & Co.	Merrill Lynch Capital Markets
Morgan Stanley & Co. Incorporated		PaineWebber Incorporated
Donaldson, Lufkin & Jenrette Securities Corporation	Bear, Stearns & Co. Inc.	Alex. Brown & Sons Incorporated
Dillon, Read & Co. Inc.	Drexel Burnham Lambert Incorporated	E. F. Hutton & Company Inc.
Kidder, Peabody & Co. Incorporated	Cyrus J. Lawrence Incorporated	Lazard Frères & Co.
Oppenheimer & Co., Inc.	Prudential-Bache Capital Funding	L. F. Rothschild & Co. Incorporated
Smith Barney, Harris Upham & Co. Incorporated	Wertheim Schroder & Co. Incorporated	Dean Witter Reynolds Inc.
	First Manhattan Co.	

A bond is an obligation to make coupon payments and a redemption payment. General Cinema issued bonds in 1987 promising to pay 9⅜ percent each year as a coupon payment. For each $100 of redemption value, General Cinema received $99.25.

have paid out $94.50 per bond more than it received from the bondholder. For all bondholders, the net outflow will come to slightly more than $118 million. In other words, General Cinema receives about $124 million in 1987 (99¼ percent of the $125 million bond issue) and it contracts, over the next 10 years, to pay back that $124 million plus another $118 million.

On the face of it, this appears to be a terrible way of doing business. Why would General Cinema find that a worthwhile deal? To answer this question, we need to understand a fundamental principle of business (and indeed personal) finance.

Discounting and Present Value We have seen that a bond is an obligation to make a series of *future* payments. Also, a bond is sold for a *current* receipt. Money flows into General Cinema in 1987 and out in 1988 through 1997.

If you were given the choice between a dollar today and a dollar a year from today, you would choose a dollar today. The same is true for General Cinema. A dollar in 1987 is worth more to General Cinema than that same dollar in 1988 and even more still than that same dollar in 1997. A dollar today is worth more than a dollar in the future because today's dollar can be invested to earn interest.

The next two paragraphs contain a hefty load of calculations, but they are well worth sticking with. There are many situations in your own life where an understanding of this material will help you to make the right decisions—decisions about whether to rent or to buy a videotape or a VCR, whether to buy for cash or buy on credit, whether to buy in bulk or buy more frequently in smaller quantities. Any calculation that involves comparing a sum of money today with a different sum of money at a later date involves calculating a present value. Let's learn how to do such a calculation.

Suppose that the interest rate is 10 percent a year. One hundred dollars invested this year at 10 percent produces $110 one year from now. We can turn the tables and say that $110 a year from now is worth $100 today. The **present value** of a future sum of money is the amount which, if invested today, will grow as large as that future sum, taking into account the interest that it will earn. Let's express this idea with an equation:

$$\text{Future sum} = \text{Present value} \times (1 + r).$$

If you have $100 today and the interest rate (r) is 10 percent a year ($r = 0.1$), one year from today you will have $110. Check that the above formula delivers that answer. One hundred dollars multiplied by 1.1 equals $110.

The formula that we have just used calculates a future sum from the present value and an interest rate. To calculate the present value, we just have to work backward. Instead of multiplying the present value by $(1 + r)$, we divide the future sum by $(1 + r)$. That is,

$$\text{Present value} = \frac{\text{Future sum}}{(1 + r)}.$$

You can use this formula to calculate present value. Calculating present value is called discounting. **Discounting** is the conversion of a future sum of money to its present value. Let's check that we can use the present value formula by calculating the present value of \$110 one year from now when the interest rate is 10 percent a year. You'll be able to guess that the answer is \$100 because we just calculated that \$100 invested today at 10 percent a year becomes \$110 in one year. Thus it follows immediately that the present value of \$110 in one year's time is \$100. But let's use the formula. Putting the numbers into the above formula we have

$$\text{Present value} = \frac{\$110}{(1 + 0.1)} = \frac{\$110}{1.1} = \$100.$$

Calculating the present value of a sum of money one year from now is the easiest case. But we can also calculate the present value of a sum any number of years in the future. As an example, let's see how we calculate the present value of a sum of money available two years from now.

Suppose that you invest \$100 today for two years at an interest rate of 10 percent a year. The money will earn \$10 in the first year, which means that by the end of the first year you will have \$110. If the interest of \$10 is invested, then the interest earned in the second year will be a further \$10 on the original \$100 plus \$1 on the \$10 interest. Thus the total interest earned in the second year will be \$11. The total interest earned overall will be \$21 (\$10 in the first year and \$11 in the second year). After two years, you will have \$121. From the definition of present value, you can see that the present value of \$121 two years hence is \$100. That is, \$100 is the present sum which, if invested at 10 percent interest, will grow to \$121 two years from now.

To calculate the present value of a sum of money two years in the future we use the formula

$$\text{Present value} = \frac{\text{Sum of money two years in future}}{(1 + r)^2}.$$

Let's see if the formula works by calculating the present value of \$121 two years in the future when the rate of interest is 10 percent a year. Putting these numbers into the above formula gives:

$$\text{Present value} = \frac{\$121}{(1 + 0.1)^2} = \frac{\$121}{(1.1)^2} = \frac{\$121}{1.21} = \$100.$$

We can calculate the present value of a sum of money any number of years in the future by using a formula based on the two that we've already used. The general formula is

$$\text{Present value} = \frac{\text{Money available } n \text{ years in future}}{(1 + r)^n}$$

For example, if the rate of interest is 10 percent a year, \$100 received 10 years from now will have a present value of \$38.55. That is, if \$38.55 is invested today at an interest rate of 10 percent, it will accumulate to \$100 in 10 years. (You may want to check that calculation on your pocket calculator.)

Now that you understand and can calculate a present value, we can return to the main question: Why does it pay General Cinema to borrow \$124 million in 1987 and pay out \$242 million over the next 10 years?

The Present Value of a Bond First, General Cinema isn't planning to pay out \$242 million on a \$124 million loan just for fun. It plans to use the money for its business. Let's suppose that General Cinema plans to build \$124 million worth of movie theaters in college towns across the country. It doesn't have \$124 million in its pocket to spare. It can borrow the money from the bank for 9.5 percent interest. Alternatively, it can sell the bonds that we have just been describing. Let's suppose it sells the bonds.

You know from what you have learned about discounting that a sum of money paid two or five or 10 years in the future is worth a smaller sum today. Discounting tells you that the money General Cinema pays in future years to its bondholders is worth less today. How much less? To find out, let's calculate the present value of the bond payments.

We will use the formulas that we have just learned. To begin, we need to list the sums of

Table 9.3 General Cinema Corporation Bonds (per $100 of redemption value)

Year	Cash flow (dollars)	Present value at 9½% (dollars)
1987	+99.250	+99.250
1988	−9.375	−8.562
1989	−9.375	−7.819
1990	−9.375	−7.141
1991	−9.375	−6.521
1992	−9.375	−5.955
1993	−9.375	−5.439
1994	−9.375	−4.967
1995	−9.375	−4.536
1996	−9.375	−4.141
1997	−109.375	−44.134
Net	−94.500	0.035

money that General Cinema is going to receive and to pay out. Such a list appears in Table 9.3, in the column headed "Cash Flow." A plus sign (+) means that money flows into General Cinema and a minus sign (−) means that money flows out from General Cinema. In 1987, General Cinema receives $99.25 on each $100 worth of bonds. Between 1988 and 1996, the company makes coupon payments of $9.375. In 1997, the company makes a final coupon payment of $9.375 and redeems each bond for $100; so it makes a total payment of $109.375. To calculate the present value of this stream of receipts and payments, we divide each item by $(1 + r)^n$. The variable n is the number of years in the future that the money is paid and r is the interest rate. Since General Cinema could have borrowed the money that it needs from the bank for 9.5 percent, that is the interest rate that we will use for calculating the present value of a bond. The interest rate (r) is 0.095.

The results of our calculations are set out in Table 9.3, in the column headed "Present Value." The present value of a sum of money today is the sum itself. So for 1987, the present value of the cash flow is $99.25. The present value of $9.375 one year hence is $8.562. How did we arrive at that figure? We used our formula

$$\text{Present value} = \frac{\$9.375}{1 + 0.095} = \frac{\$9.375}{1.095} = \$8.562.$$

You can use your pocket calculator to verify this calculation. The further out we go into the future, the smaller are the present values. In the final year when General Cinema makes a $100 payment to redeem the bond plus the coupon payment of $9.375 for the last year, the present value of that payment is $44.134.

The sum of the present values is called the net present value. The **net present value** of a stream of future payments is the sum of the present values of the payments in each year. As you can see, the net present value per $100 worth of bonds is 3.5 cents when the rate of interest is 9.5 percent. Expressed another way, the present value of the future payments General Cinema will make is almost equal to the $124 million it borrowed. To be precise, since the net present value of each $100 worth of bonds is 3.5 cents, the net present value of the bond issue of $124,000,000 equals approximately $44,000. That is, the present value of the payments is $44,000 less than the amount received in the first place.

Now you can see that General Cinema was not so crazy to take in $124 million in 1987 and pay out $242 million over the next 10 years. The present value of its future payments is far smaller than $242 million. In our example, we used an interest rate of 9.5 percent to calculate the present value. Using other interest rates will yield different results. But if a bank loan at an interest rate of 9.5 percent is the alternative, issuing the bond is better than borrowing from the bank. The wisdom of borrowing at all will finally depend on the profits of the new college town movie theaters. General Cinema will want the theaters to earn enough profits to meet the payments on the bonds.

The Attractions of Bonds Bonds provide a corporation with predictable long-term financing at guaranteed cost. Large corporations typically sell some bonds every year or two and redeem others in sequence so that the firm has a fairly constant maturity structure of bonds outstanding. The **maturity structure** of bonds is the distribution of future dates on which bonds are to be redeemed.

Bonds are attractive to purchasers because of the security they provide. Just as they give the corporation predictable interest costs, so do they provide the investor with predictable interest income. Bonds are risky in the sense that if a corporation goes bankrupt it may not be able to pay the bondholders. Nevertheless, the bondholders get paid with any residual value of the corporation before stockholders get any payments. Though bondholders have a prior claim on the residual value of the company in the event of bankruptcy, they have less control over the company than stockholders do. They have no rights to select the directors who oversee management or to select the management that runs the corporation.

Figure 9.2 Issuing Stock

This is not an offer to sell nor a solicitation of offers to buy any of these securities.
This offer is made only by the Prospectus.

June 26, 1987

1,400,000 Shares

WISCONSIN TOY

Wisconsin Toy Company, Inc.

Common Stock

Price $9 Per Share

Copies of the Prospectus may be obtained within any State from any Underwriter who may lawfully offer these securities within such State.

William Blair & Company
Robert W. Baird & Co. Incorporated
Alex. Brown & Sons Incorporated
Dillon, Read & Co. Inc.
Donaldson, Lufkin & Jenrette Securities Corporation
Drexel Burnham Lambert Incorporated
Hambrecht & Quist Incorporated
Kidder, Peabody & Co. Incorporated
Lazard Frères & Co.
Montgomery Securities
PaineWebber Incorporated
Prudential-Bache Capital Funding
Robertson, Colman & Stephens
L. F. Rothschild & Co. Incorporated
J. C. Bradford & Co. Incorporated
Dain Bosworth Incorporated
McDonald & Company Securities, Inc.
Piper, Jaffray & Hopwood Incorporated
Prescott, Ball & Turben, Inc.
Blunt Ellis & Loewi Incorporated
The Chicago Corporation
The Milwaukee Company
Stifel, Nicolaus & Company Incorporated
George K. Baum & Company
R. G. Dickinson & Co.
First Analysis Securities Corporation
Frederick & Company, Inc.
Oberweis Securities, Inc.
Rodman & Renshaw, Inc.
Roney & Co.
Steiner Diamond & Co. Incorporated

Wisconsin Toy issued stock in 1987 at $9 a share. The price of a share is the present value of the expected future dividends, based on the company's profits.

Issuing Stock The second major way in which corporations raise money is by issuing stock. Money raised in this way is the corporation's *equity capital* because the stockholders of a corporation are its owners. They have bought shares of the corporation's stock.

There are three types of corporate stock:

- Common stock
- Preferred stock
- Convertible stock

Common stock gives voting rights at stockholders' meetings but gives a claim to a dividend only if the directors vote to pay one and at a variable rate, determined by the directors and varying according to the firm's profits.

Preferred stock gives no voting rights but gives a prior claim on dividends at a fixed rate, regardless of the profit level. Preferred stockholders stand before common stockholders but after bondholders if the corporation cannot meet all its obligations.

Convertible stock is not quite a bond and not quite a stock. Its owner receives a fixed coupon payment, as a bondholder does, but has the privilege of being able to convert the bond into a fixed number of shares of common stock.

Corporations issue billions of shares of their stock and these shares regularly trade on stock exchanges. A **stock exchange** is an organized market for trading in stock. The most important stock exchanges in the United States are the New York Stock Exchange (NYSE) and the American Stock Exchange (ASE) in New York City. Although only the NYSE is physically located on Wall Street, in the parlance of finance they are both "on Wall Street." Other major stock exchanges are in Boston, Philadelphia, Chicago, and San Francisco.

The Price of a Share of Stock In June 1987, Wisconsin Toy Company, Inc., sold 1.4 million shares of common stock for $9 a share (see Fig. 9.2). What determined the price for the shares of Wisconsin Toy's common stock? Why couldn't it get $10 a share? Why were people willing to pay more than $8 a share?

To answer these questions, we need to examine common stock as an investment. The holder of a share receives a dividend each year. That dividend may be zero. If the dividend is zero and is expected to be zero forever, the value of the stock will be exactly zero! Suppose that a corporation is expected to pay a dividend of $110 a share one year from now and nothing thereafter. What will such a share be worth? You probably guessed it: The share will be worth the present value of $110 one year from now. If the interest rate is 10 percent a year, the present value of $110 one year from now is $100. People will be willing to pay $100 for the share today. If the share sells for less than $100, there will be a strong demand for it since the expected return on the share will exceed 10 percent, the prevailing rate of interest. For example, if you can buy the stock for $90, and you receive $110 next year, you will have earned $20, or 22 percent, on your initial $90 investment. If someone tries to sell the share for more than $100, no one will buy it. No one will pay more than $100 for a claim to $110 one year from now if the interest rate is 10 percent. You will do better by simply putting $100 in the bank and collecting $110 in one year's time.

In general, the price of a share is the present value of its expected future dividends. To drive this fact home, let's consider another example. Suppose that investors expect a corporation to pay a dividend of $10 a share each and every year into the indefinite future. Suppose also that the interest rate is 10 percent a year. What will that corporate share be worth? The answer is $100. An investment of $100 in the share will produce $10 a year, or a return of 10 percent a year. That is the same as the interest rate available on other things. The net present value of $10 a year forever, discounted at a 10 percent interest rate, is $100.[1]

Investors can estimate future dividends, but they cannot know them for sure, and their estimates can change. These changing expectations cause share prices to fluctuate dramatically. Because corporations pay dividends out of their profits, news about a corporation's profitability can change investors expectations of future dividends.

One number that investors pay attention to is called the price-earnings ratio. The **price-earnings ratio** is the current price of a stock divided by the current profit per share. A high price-earnings ratio means that investors are willing to pay a high price for a share compared to the profits that the share is currently earning. Such a situation arises when the firm's future profits are expected to be high relative to its current profits. A low price-earnings ratio means that investors are willing to pay only a low price for a share relative to its current earnings. This situation arises when future profits are expected to be low compared with current profits.

In this example, we have worked out how the price of a share of common stock is determined. The prices of preferred stock and convertible stock are determined in a similar manner and depend on the expected future stream of payments that will be made to the holders of those stocks.

Cost: Accountant's and Economist's Measures

What is cost? Cost is the total payment made by a firm for the services of factors of production. There are two ways of measuring cost—the accountant's way and the economist's way.

Accountants measure historical cost. **Historical cost** values resources at the prices actually

[1]If you are comfortable with algebra you may find the following demonstration of this result helpful. First, write out the formula for the present value of $10 forever, at an interest rate of 10 percent (0.1):

$$PV = \frac{\$10}{1.1} + \frac{\$10}{(1.1)^2} + \cdots\cdots + \frac{\$10}{(1.1)^n} + \cdots\cdots.$$

The dots stand for the years between year 2 and year n and the years beyond year n. Next, divide this equation by (1.1) to give

$$\frac{PV}{1.1} = \frac{\$10}{(1.1)^2} + \cdots\cdots + \frac{\$10}{(1.1)^n} + \cdots\cdots.$$

Now subtract the second equation from the first to give

$$PV - \frac{PV}{1.1} = \frac{\$10}{1.1}.$$

Multiply both sides of the equation by 1.1 to give

$$(1.1)PV - PV = \$10 \quad \text{or} \quad (0.1)PV = \$10.$$

Finally divide both sides of the previous equation by 0.1 to give

$$PV = \frac{\$10}{(0.1)} = \$100.$$

So, the present value of $10 forever at an interest rate of 10 percent is $100.

paid for them. Economists measure opportunity cost. Opportunity cost is the best forgone alternative. For example, the opportunity cost of an hour in the classroom is an hour of swimming, if that is the best alternative forgone. Although opportunity cost is something real, it is convenient, when analyzing the costs of firms, to talk about the dollar equivalent of opportunity cost. Thus we can ask how many dollars would we have had available to spend on a good if we had not produced some quantity of another good. Here we'll value opportunity cost in terms of dollars. But don't lose sight of the fact that such a measure is just a convenience. When we calculate the opportunity cost of producing something, we're really asking another question: What did we give up to produce this good? We're using dollars as a convenient unit of accounting.

In some cases, historical cost and opportunity cost measures are the same. In others, important differences arise. Let's look first at the cases where they are the same.

When Historical Cost Equals Opportunity Cost

Historical cost equals opportunity cost when a company uses up resources soon after buying them. The historical cost is the money paid for those resources. The opportunity cost (expressed in dollars) is the same as the historical cost because the money could have bought other resources to produce something else or could have bought the goods directly from someone else. Examples of such resources are labor, raw materials, and services such as gas, electricity, and water consumed in production.

When Historical Cost and Opportunity Cost Differ

There are two main sources of difference between historical cost and opportunity cost:

- Durable input costs
- Costs of inputs not directly purchased

Durable inputs are factors of production that are not entirely used up in a single production period. They are bought in a lump and then used gradually over a prolonged period of time. A firm may spend a large sum of money on buildings, plant, and equipment in a single year and then spend nothing on them for another five years. Similarly, a firm may carry large inventories of raw materials and semifinished products that it does not use up completely in a single year. It may use items that it bought a year or two earlier. What is the opportunity cost of using capital equipment bought several years earlier? What is the opportunity cost of taking inputs from inventory? We'll answer these questions below.

A second difference between historical cost and opportunity cost occurs when a firm uses inputs that it does not directly pay for. Examples are the time of the owner and the owner's reputation for reliable service.

Let's examine the differences by looking first at plant and machinery costs, then inventory costs, and finally at the costs of inputs not directly purchased.

Plant and Machinery

Historical Cost Measures The historical cost of buildings, plant, and equipment is calculated by applying a conventional depreciation rate to the original purchase price. **Depreciation** is the fall in the value of a durable input over a given period of time. For buildings, a conventional depreciation allowance is 5 percent a year. Thus if a firm builds a factory for \$100,000, the accountant will regard 5 percent of that amount, \$5000, as a cost of production in the first year. At the end of the first year, the accountant will record the value of the building as \$95,000 (the original cost minus the 5 percent depreciation). In the next year, the accountant will regard \$4750 as a cost of production (5 percent of the remaining \$95,000 value of the building), and so on. The accountant uses different depreciation rates for different types of inputs. Fifteen percent is a common rate for plant and equipment.

If a firm borrows money to buy a building, plant, or equipment the accountant will also count the interest on the borrowing as a cost of production. So, in this case, if the firm borrows the entire \$100,000 and if the interest rate is 10 percent a year, the accountant will treat the \$10,000 interest payment as a cost of production. If the firm has not borrowed anything to build the factory but instead has used its own previously earned profits, the accountant will regard the interest cost incurred in production as zero.

Opportunity Cost Measures To measure opportunity cost, we calculate the implicit rental rate of the inputs. The **implicit rental rate** is defined as the rent that the firm implicitly pays to itself for the use of the durable inputs that it owns. You are familiar with the idea of renting equipment. People commonly rent houses, apartments, cars, televisions, VCRs, videotapes; firms commonly rent earthmoving equipment, satellite launching services, etc. When someone rents a piece of equipment, that person pays an *explicit* rent. When an owner uses a piece of equipment rather than renting it out, the economist notes that the owner could have rented the equipment out instead. By not doing so, owners *implicitly* rent from themselves.

Another term that is sometimes used to describe an implicit cost or rent is an imputed cost. An **imputed cost** is an opportunity cost that does not require an actual expenditure of cash. How does the economist work out the implicit (or imputed) cost of a firm using such durable inputs as its own buildings, plant, and equipment?

Economic Depreciation **Economic depreciation** is the change in the market price of a durable input over a given period. For example, economic depreciation over a year is calculated as the market price of the input at the beginning of the year minus its market price at the end of the year. That amount is part of the implicit cost of using the input. The original cost of the equipment is not directly relevant to this calculation. The equipment could have been sold at the beginning of the year for the market price then prevailing. The opportunity cost of hanging on to the equipment, therefore, is the value lost by not selling it. If a firm has kept the equipment for a year and used it, the difference between its market prices at the beginning of the year and at the end of the year tells us how much of its value has been used up in production.

Interest Costs The other cost of using durable inputs is interest. Whether a firm borrows to buy its buildings, plant, and equipment or uses previously earned profits to pay for them, it makes no difference to the opportunity cost of the funds tied up in the productive assets. If a firm borrows the money, then it makes an interest payment. That's the payment the accountant picks up using the historical cost method. If a firm uses its own funds, then the opportunity cost is the amount that could have been earned by using those funds for something else. The firm could have sold the equipment at the beginning of the year and used the funds from the sale for some other purpose. At the very least, the firm could have put the money in the bank and earned interest. The interest passed up is the opportunity cost of the funds tied up in equipment, regardless of whether that money is borrowed or not. So, the implicit interest cost of a durable resource is the value of the input at the beginning of the year multiplied by the current year's rate of interest.

The implicit cost of the firm using its own buildings, plant, and equipment is the sum of their depreciation and interest costs—that is, the change in their market value over the year, plus their market value at the beginning of the year multiplied by the interest rate prevailing during the year.

Inflation Inflation complicates the calculation of opportunity cost. A change in prices that results purely from inflation—a rise in all prices—does not affect opportunity cost. To avoid being misled by inflation, we measure opportunity cost in terms of the prices prevailing in a single year. As a result of the high inflation rates experienced in the 1970s and early 1980s, accountants also have begun to pay attention to the distortions that inflation can cause in measuring historical cost and comparing costs between one year and another.

Sunk Costs A situation sometimes arises in which a firm has bought some capital equipment and the equipment is in place, functioning well, but has no resale value. The historical cost of buying that equipment is called a sunk cost. A **sunk cost** is the historical cost of buying plant and machinery that have no current resale value. The opportunity cost of using such equipment is zero.

Inventory Costs **Inventories** are stocks of raw materials, semifinished goods, and finished goods held by firms. Some firms have small inventories or inventories that turn over very quickly. In such cases, the accountant's historical cost and the economist's opportunity cost are the same. When a production process requires inventories to be held for a long time, the two measurements differ and possibly in important ways.

Historical Cost Measures To measure the cost of using inventories, accountants use a historical cost method called FIFO, which stands for "First In,

First Out." This method of pricing the use of inventories assumes, as a convenient fiction, that the first item placed into the inventory is literally the first one out. An alternative accountant's measure that is used in some cases is called LIFO, which stands for "Last In, First Out." This measure, though not quite opportunity cost, is sometimes close to it.

Opportunity Cost Measures The opportunity cost of using inventories is their current replacement cost. If an item is taken out of inventory, it will have to be replaced by a new item. The cost of that new item is the opportunity cost of using the inventory. Again, we have to be careful to avoid contaminating our measure with the effects of inflation. If the cost of some inventory item has risen purely because the prices of all things have risen, then the higher dollar cost does not reflect a higher opportunity cost.

Other Costs

Owners' Wages The owner of a firm often puts a great deal of time and effort into working for the firm but rarely takes an explicit wage payment for this work. Instead, the owner withdraws cash from the business to meet living expenses. Accountants regard such withdrawals of cash as the owner taking "profits" from the business and they do not take into account the cost of the owner's time. But the owner could have worked at some other activity and earned a wage. The opportunity cost of the owner's time is the income forgone by the owner by not working in the best alternative job.

Patents, Trademarks, and Names Many firms have patents, trademarks, or a name that has come to be associated with reliability, service, or some other desirable characteristic. Sometimes firms have acquired these things by their own past efforts. In other cases, they have bought them. A firm always has the option of selling its patents, trademarks, or name to other firms.

In calculating historical cost, these items are ignored unless the firm actually bought them. But they have an opportunity cost regardless of whether or not they were bought. The opportunity cost of a firm's patents, trademarks, or name used in this year's production is the change in their market value—the change in the best price for which they could be sold. If their value falls over the year, there is an additional opportunity cost of production. If their value rises, there is a negative opportunity cost, or a reduction in the opportunity cost of production.

The Bottom Line What does all this add up to? Is the historical measure of cost higher or lower than the opportunity cost measure? And what about the bottom line—the profit or loss of the firm. Does the accountant come up with the same answer as the economist or is there a difference in the measurement of profit as well?

In general, opportunity cost includes more things than historical cost, so the historical measure of cost understates the opportunity cost of production. There is no difference in the accountant's measure and the economist's measure of a firm's receipts or revenue. Profit is the difference between revenue and cost. Since opportunity cost is bigger than historical cost, economic profit is thus lower than profit calculated on the basis of historical cost.

To see how this works out, let's look at an example. Rocky owns a shop that sells bikes. His revenue, cost, and profit for last year appear in Table 9.4. The historical view of Rocky's cost and profit is on the left-hand side and the economic view is on the right-hand side.

Rocky sold $300,000 worth of bikes during the year. This amount appears as his sales revenue. The wholesale cost of bikes was $150,000, he bought $20,000 worth of utilities and other services, and paid out $50,000 in wages to his mechanic and sales clerk. Rocky also paid $12,000 in interest to the bank. All of the items just mentioned appear in both the accountant's and the economist's statement. The remaining items differ between the two statements and some notes at the foot of the table explain the differences. The only additional cost taken into account by the accountant is depreciation, which the accountant calculates as a fixed percentage of Rocky's assets. The economist imputes a cost to Rocky's time and money invested in the firm and also calculates depreciation based on the change in the market value of Rocky's assets. The historical cost method puts Rocky's cost at $254,000 and his profit at $46,000. In contrast, the opportunity cost of Rocky's year in business was $293,500 and his "economic" profit was $6.500.

Table 9.4 Rocky's Mountain Bikes Revenue, Cost, and Profit Statement

The accountant Item	Amount	**The economist** Item	Amount
Sales revenue	$300,000	Sales revenue	$300,000
Costs:		Costs:	
Wholesale cost of bikes	150,000	Wholesale cost of bikes	150,000
Utilities and other services	20,000	Utilities and other services	20,000
Wages	50,000	Wages	50,000
		Rocky's wages (imputed)[(a)]	40,000
Depreciation	22,000	Fall in market value of assets[(b)]	10,000
Bank interest	12,000	Bank interest	12,000
		Interest on Rocky's money[(c)] invested in firm (imputed)	11,500
Total costs	$254,000	Total costs	$293,500
Profit	$46,000	Profit	$6,500

Notes:

(a) Rocky could have worked elsewhere for $40 an hour, but he worked 1000 hours on the firm's business, which means that the opportunity cost of his time is $40,000.

(b) The fall in the market value of the assets of the firm gives the opportunity cost of not selling them one year ago. That is part of the opportunity cost of using them for the year.

(c) Rocky has invested $115,000 in the firm. If the current rate of interest is 10% a year, the opportunity cost of those funds is $11,500.

REVIEW

Firms raise money by selling bonds and issuing stock. Bondholders receive a fixed income stream. Stockholders receive a future dividend based on the firm's profitability.

A firm's "economic" profit is the difference between its revenue and the opportunity cost of production. Opportunity cost differs from historical cost. Historical cost measures cost as the dollars spent to buy inputs. Opportunity cost measures cost as the value of the best forgone alternative. The most important differences between the two measures arise when assessing the cost of durable inputs and of inputs that the firm does not directly buy, such as the labor of the owner. ■

We are interested in measuring the opportunity cost of production, not for its own sake, but so that we can compare the efficiency of alternative methods of production. What do we mean by efficiency?

Economic Efficiency

Firms make decisions about *how* to produce their output. There is almost always more than one way of making a product. For example, cars can be made on assembly lines that make extensive use of robots but hardly use any people. Cars can also be made without any robots but with a larger number of workers. The first case uses more capital than the second but less labor.

How does a firm choose among alternative methods of production? What is the most efficient way of producing? There are two concepts of efficiency: technological efficiency and economic efficiency. **Technological efficiency** occurs when it is not possible to increase output without increasing inputs. **Economic efficiency** occurs when the cost of producing a given output is as low as possible.

Technological efficiency is an engineering matter. Given what is technologically feasible, something can or cannot be done. Economic efficiency goes further than technological efficiency. It depends on the prices of inputs. Something that is technologically efficient may not be economically efficient. But something that is economically efficient is always technologically efficient.

Let's examine the differences and the connection between technological efficiency and economic efficiency by looking at an example.

Suppose that there are four ways of making TV sets:

- *Method a:* Robot assembly line
- *Method b:* Human assembly line, with each person specializing in a small part of the job as the emerging TV set passes by
- *Method c:* Human assembly line, with each person following the TV set along the assembly line and performing each and every task and using the appropriate piece of machinery as it is needed
- *Method d:* Hand-tooled assembly, with each TV set fashioned by hand tools and assembled completely by each worker who uses just a few hand tools on a bench to build an entire TV set without the help of any machinery

Table 9.5 sets out the amount of labor and capital required to make 10 TV sets a day by each of these four methods. Are all of these alternative methods technologically efficient? By inspecting the numbers in the table you will be able to see that method *c* is not technologically efficient. It requires 100 workers and 10 units of capital to produce 10 TV sets. Those same 10 TV sets can be produced by method *b* with 10 workers and the same 10 units of capital. Therefore method *c* is not technologically efficient.

Are any of the other methods not technologically efficient? The answer is no: Each of the other three methods is technologically efficient. Method *a* uses less labor and more capital than method *b*, and method *d* uses more labor and less capital than method *b*.

Table 9.5 Four Ways of Making 10 TV Sets a Day

		Quantities of inputs	
	Method	Labor	Capital
a	Robot assembly line	1	1000
b	Human assembly line	10	10
c	Human assembly line	100	10
d	Hand-tooled assembly	1000	1

What about economic efficiency? Are all three methods economically efficient? To answer that question, we need to know what the labor and capital costs are. Let's suppose that labor costs $75 per person-day and that capital costs $250 per machine-day. Recall that economic efficiency occurs with the least expensive production process. Table 9.6 calculates the costs of using the four different methods of production. As you can see, the least expensive method of producing a TV set is *b*. Method *a* uses less labor but more capital. The combination of labor and capital needed by method *a* winds up costing much more than method *b*. Method *d*, the other technologically efficient method, uses much more labor and hardly any capital. Like method *a*, it winds up costing far more to make a TV set than method *b*.

Method *c* is technologically inefficient. It uses the same amount of capital as method *b* but 10 times as much labor. It is interesting to notice that although method *c* is technologically inefficient, it costs less to produce a TV set using method *c* than it does using methods *a* and *d*. But method *b* dominates method *c*. Because method *c* is not technologically efficient, there is always a lower cost method available. That is, a technologically inefficient method is never economically efficient.

Although *b* is the economically efficient method in this example, in other circumstances methods *a* or *d* could be economically efficient. Let's see when.

First, suppose that labor costs $150 a person-day and capital only $1 a machine-day. Table 9.7 now shows the costs of making a TV set. In this

Table 9.6 The Costs of Four Ways of Making 10 TV Sets a Day

Method	Labor cost ($75 per day)		Capital cost ($250 per day)		Total cost	Cost per TV set
a	$75	+	$250,000	=	$250,075	$25,007.50
b	750	+	2,500	=	3,250	325.00
c	7,500	+	2,500	=	10,000	1,000.00
d	75,000	+	250	=	75,250	7,525.00

case, Method *a* is economically efficient. Capital is now sufficiently cheap relative to labor that the method using the most capital is the winner.

Now, suppose that labor costs only $1 a day while capital costs $1000 a day. Table 9.8 shows the costs in this case. As you can see, method *d*, which uses a lot of labor and little capital, is now the economically efficient method.

A firm that does not use the economically efficient method of production makes a smaller profit and may attempt to sell its output for higher prices than firms that do use the economically efficient method. Natural selection favors firms that choose the economically efficient method of production and goes against firms that do not. In extreme cases, an inefficient firm may go bankrupt or be taken over by another firm that can see the possibilities for lower cost and greater profit. Efficient firms will be stronger and better able to survive temporary adversity than inefficient ones.

Firms and Markets

At the beginning of this chapter, we defined a firm as an institution that buys or hires factors of production and organizes these resources to produce and sell goods and services. In organizing production, firms coordinate the economic activities of many individuals. But a firm is not the only institution that coordinates economic activity. Coordination can also be achieved by using the market. In Chapter 1, we defined the market as a mechanism for coordinating people's buying and selling plans. By buying inputs and services in many individual markets, each one of us can organize the production of the goods and services that we consume. Consider, for example, two ways in which you might get your creaking car fixed.

- *Firm coordination:* You take the car to the garage. Parts and tools as well as automechanic time are

Table 9.7 The Costs of Three Ways of Making 10 TV Sets a Day: High Labor Costs

Method	Labor cost ($150 per day)		Capital cost ($1 per day)		Total cost	Cost per TV set
a	$150	+	$1000	=	$1,150	$115
b	1,500	+	10	=	1,510	151
d	150,000	+	1	=	150,001	15,000

Table 9.8 The Costs of Three Ways of Making 10 TV Sets a Day: High Capital Costs

Method	Labor cost ($1 per day)		Capital cost ($1000 per day)		Total cost	Cost per TV set
a	$1	+	$1,000,000	=	$1,000,001	$100,000
b	10	+	10,000	=	10,010	1,001
d	1,000	+	1,000	=	2,000	200

coordinated and organized by the garage owner and your car gets fixed. You pay one bill for the entire job.

- *Market coordination:* You hire an automechanic who diagnoses the problems and makes a list of the parts and tools needed to fix them. You buy the parts from the local wrecker's yard and rent the tools from ABC Rentals. You hire the automechanic again to fix the problems. You return the tools and pay your bills—wages to the automechanic, rental to ABC, and the wrecker for the parts used.

What determines the method that you use? The answer is cost. Taking account of the opportunity cost of your own time as well as the costs of the other inputs that you'd have to buy, you will use the method that costs least. In other words, you will use the economically efficient method.

Firms coordinate economic activity when they can perform a task more efficiently than markets. In such a situation, it will pay someone to set up a firm. If markets can perform a task more efficiently than a firm, people will use markets and any attempt to set up a firm to replace such market coordination will be doomed to failure.

Why Firms?

There are three key reasons why, in many instances, firms are more efficient than markets as coordinators of economic activity. Firms achieve:

- Lower transactions costs
- Economies of scale
- Economies of team production

Transactions Costs The idea that firms exist because there are activities in which they are more efficient than markets was first suggested by University of Chicago economist Ronald Coase.[2] Coase focused on the firm's ability to reduce or eliminate transactions costs. **Transactions costs** are the costs arising from finding someone with whom to do business, of reaching an agreement about the price and other aspects of the exchange, and of ensuring that the terms of the agreement are fulfilled. *Market* transactions require buyers and sellers to get together and negotiate the terms and conditions of their trading. Sometimes lawyers have to be hired to draw up contracts. A broken contract leads to still more expenses. A *firm* can lower such transactions costs by reducing the number of individual transactions undertaken.

For example, consider the two ways of getting your car fixed that we've just described. The first method requires that you undertake only one transaction with one firm. It's true that the firm has to undertake several transactions—hiring labor and buying the parts and tools required to do the job. But the firm doesn't have to undertake those transactions simply to fix your car. One set of such transactions enables the firm to fix hundreds of cars. Thus, there is an enormous reduction in the number of individual transactions that take place if people get their cars fixed at the garage rather than going through the elaborate sequence of market transactions that we described above.

[2]Ronald H. Coase, "The Nature of the Firm," *Economica* (November 1977): 386–405.

Economies of scale **Economies of scale** exist when the cost of producing a unit of a good falls as its output rate increases. Many industries experience economies of scale, and automobile and television manufacturing are two examples. Economies of scale can only be reaped by a large organization; thus, they give rise to firm coordination rather than market coordination.

Team Production **Team production** is a production process in which a group of individuals each specializes in mutually supportive tasks. Sport provides the best example of team activity. Some specialize in pitching and some in batting, some in defense and some in offense. But there are many examples of team activity in the production of goods and services. For example, production lines in automobile and TV manufacturing plants work most efficiently when individual activity is organized in teams, each worker specializing in a small task. You can also think of an entire firm as being a team. The team has buyers of raw material and other inputs, production workers, and salespersons. There are even subspecialists within these various groups. Each individual member of the team specializes, but the value of the output of the team and the profit that it earns depend on the coordinated activities of all the team's members.

The idea that firms arise as a consequence of the economies of team production was first suggested by Armen Alchian and Harold Demsetz, of the University of California at Los Angeles.[3]

Because firms can economize on transactions costs, reap economies of scale, and organize efficient team production, it is firms rather than markets that coordinate most of our economic activity. There are, however, limits to the economic efficiency of firms. If firms become too big or too diversified in the things that they seek to do, the cost of management and monitoring per unit of output begins to rise and, at some point, the market becomes more efficient at coordinating the use of resources.

■ In the next two chapters, we are going to study the choices of firms. We will study their production decisions, how they minimize costs, and how they choose the amounts of the various inputs to employ.

[3]Armen Alchian and Harold Demsetz, "Production, Information Costs, and Economic Organization," *American Economic Review* 57, 5 (December 1972): 777–795.

S U M M A R Y

The Firm's Economic Problem

A firm is an institution that organizes the production of goods and services. Firms and markets are alternative mechanisms for coordinating economic activity. All firms have to make certain decisions: what to produce and in what quantities; the techniques of production to use; the quantities of each factor of production to employ; their organization and management structure; and the arrangements for compensating the factors of production.

There are three main forms of business organization: proprietorship, partnership, and corporation. Each has its advantages and disadvantages. Proprietorships are easy to set up and they face lower taxes than corporations, but they are risky and they face higher costs of capital and of labor. Partnerships can draw on diversified expertise but they can also involve decision conflicts. Corporations have limited liability so they can obtain large scale capital at relatively low cost. They hire professional management, but complex management structures can slow down decisions. Corporations pay taxes on profits and their stockholders pay taxes on dividends. Proprietorships are the most common form of business organization, but corporations account for most of the economy's production.
(pp. 207–211)

Business Finance

Firms raise money by selling bonds and issuing stock. Bondholders receive a guaranteed annual interest income and face less risk from bankruptcy than do stockholders. Stockholders are the owners of a corporation. The holders of common stock vote at meetings and elect directors. Their liability is limited, but they do not receive dividends unless voted by the directors.

Business profit is calculated as the difference between revenue and cost. Accountants and economists measure cost in different ways. Accountants measure historical cost, economists measure opportunity cost. Opportunity cost usually exceeds historical cost because it includes imputed costs not counted as part of historical cost. The different measures of cost lead to different measures of profit. Economic profit equals revenue minus opportunity cost. (pp. 210–220)

Economic Efficiency

There are two concepts of efficiency: technological efficiency and economic efficiency. A method of production is economically efficient when the cost of producing a given output is as low as possible. Economic efficiency requires technological efficiency. Economic efficiency also takes into account the relative prices of inputs. Economically efficient firms have a better chance of surviving than do inefficient ones. (pp. 220–222)

Firms and Markets

Firms coordinate economic activities when they are able to achieve lower costs than coordination through markets. Firms are able to economize on transactions costs and to achieve the benefits of economies of scale and of team production. (pp. 222–224)

KEY CONCEPTS

Key Tables

REVIEW QUESTIONS

1 What is a firm?
2 What are the economic problems that all firms face? List the main forms of business organization and their advantages and disadvantages.
3 List the main ways firms can raise money.
4 What is a bond?
5 What is a share?
6 What do we mean by net present value?
7 What determines the value of a bond?
8 What determines the value of a share?
9 Distinguish between historical cost and opportunity cost. What are the main items of opportunity cost that don't get counted as part of historical cost?
10 Define economic efficiency.
11 Distinguish between economic efficiency and technological efficiency.
12 Why do firms, rather than markets, coordinate such a large amount of economic activity?

PROBLEMS

1 Soap Bubbles, Inc., has a bank loan of $1 million on which it is paying an interest rate of 10 percent a year. The firm's financial advisor suggests paying off the loan by selling bonds. Soap Bubbles, Inc., has to offer bonds with a redemption value two years in the future of $1,050,000 and a coupon payment of 9 percent to raise $1 million.

a) Does it pay Soap Bubbles to sell the bonds to repay the bank loan?

b) What is the present value of the profit or loss that would result from repaying the bank loan and selling the bonds?

2 One year ago, Jack and Jill set up a vinegar bottling firm (called JJVB).

- Jack and Jill put $50,000 of their own money into the firm.
- They bought equipment for $30,000 and an inventory of bottles and vinegar for $15,000.
- They hired one employee for an annual wage of $20,000.
- JJVB's sales for the year were $100,000.
- Jack gave up his previous job, at which he earned $30,000, and spent all his time working for JJVB.
- Jill kept her old job, which paid $30 an hour, but gave up 10 hours of leisure each week (for 50 weeks) to work for JJVB.
- The cash expenses of JJVB were $10,000 for the year.
- The inventory at the end of the year was worth $20,000.
- The market value of the equipment at the end of the year was $28,000.
- JJVB's accountant depreciated the equipment by 20 percent a year.

a) Construct JJVB's profit and loss account as recorded by their accountant.

b) Construct JJVB's profit and loss account based on opportunity cost rather than historical cost concepts.

3 There are three methods that you can use for doing your tax return: a personal computer, a pocket calculator, or a pencil and paper. With a PC, you complete the job in an hour; with a pocket calculator, it takes 12 hours; and with a pencil and paper, it takes two days. The PC and its software cost $1000; the pocket calculator costs $10; and the pencil and paper cost $1.

a) Which, if any, of the above methods are technologically efficient?

b) Which of the above methods is economically efficient: (1) if your wage rate is $5 an hour? (2) if your wage rate is $50 an hour? (3) if your wage rate is $500 an hour?

Chapter 10

Output and Costs

After studying this chapter, you will be able to:

- Explain the objective of a firm
- Explain what limits a firm's profitability
- Explain the relationship between a firm's output and its costs
- Define short-run cost and derive a firm's short-run cost curves
- Explain how cost changes when a firm's plant size changes
- Define long-run cost and derive a firm's long-run average cost curve
- Explain why some firms operate with excess capacity and others overutilize their plants.

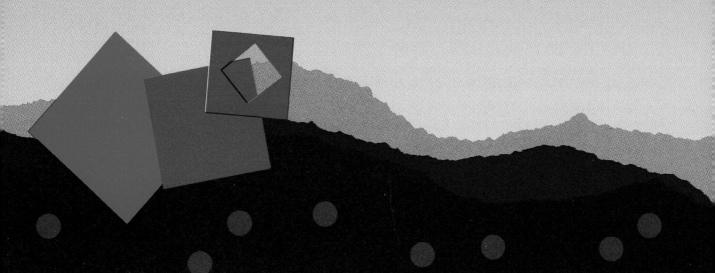

Survival of the Fittest

Size does not guarantee success in business. Of the 100 largest companies in the United States in 1917, according to Forbes magazine, only 22 still remained in that league in 1987. Of the other 78, some had been surpassed in size or swallowed up in takeovers by other companies and some, such as Colorado Fuel & Iron, Studebaker, Willys-Overland—all giants in their day—had gone into bankruptcy. ■ What were all these businesses striving for? If it was for size alone, it didn't ensure their survival. What goals do their successors set for themselves today? How do they decide how to produce and what resources to use? Does a pharmaceutical firm arrive at these decisions the way that a chain of discount stores does or the corner pizza parlor? Or do such businesses have nothing in common except the earning of profits? ■ Every firm tries to keep its costs under control. You would think that to keep costs under control firms would want to have production plants that were fully utilized almost all the time. But most car makers in the United States can produce far more cars than they can sell. Why do car makers have expensive equipment lying around that isn't fully used? In other industries, such as electric power production, there isn't always enough production equipment on hand to meet demand. Firms often have to buy power from other producers. Why don't such firms have a bigger production plant so that they can supply the market themselves?

■ We are going to answer these and similar questions in this chapter. To do so, we are going to study the economic decisions that all firms make about how much to produce and how to keep their costs as low as possible. Although many firms are giants—for example, Exxon and Coca-Cola, or even Willys-Overland—we will make better progress if we concentrate our attention on a small, imaginary firm—Swanky, Inc., a producer of knitted sweaters. The firm is owned and operated by Sidney. By studying Swanky's economic problems and the way Sidney solves them, we will be able to get a clear view of the key problems that face all firms—small ones like Swanky as well as the giants.

Firms' Objectives and Constraints

To understand and predict the behavior of firms, we will start by describing a firm's objectives—what it is trying to achieve.

The Objective: Profit Maximization

The firm that we will study has a single objective: profit maximization. **Profit maximization** can be defined as striving for the highest possible profit. As you know, the fundamental problem from which all economic activity springs is scarcity. Profit maximization is a direct consequence of scarcity. Seeking to make the best possible use of scarce resources is the same thing as trying to make the highest possible profit. A firm that does not try to maximize profit will not survive in a competitive environment. Firms have high birth and death rates. They also frequently get taken over. A firm that does not seek to maximize profit will either lose the competitive race to firms that do or it will be taken over by such a firm.

In studying Swanky, we will suppose that Sidney is constantly striving to make the highest possible profits. However, there are limits to, or constraints on, the profits that a firm can make. What are they?

Constraints

There are two types of constraints that limit the profits a firm can make: market constraints and a technology constraint.

Market Constraints A firm's **market constraints** are the conditions under which it can buy its inputs and sell its output. On the output side, people have a limited demand for each good or service and will buy additional quantities only at lower prices. Firms have to recognize this constraint on how much they can sell. A small firm competing with many other firms in a large market has no choice but to sell its output at the same price as everyone else. It cannot, through its own actions, influence the market price. A large firm that dominates the market for a particular good can manipulate the price to its own advantage. But in so doing, it has to accept the fact that it will sell lower quantities at higher prices.

On the input side, people have a limited supply of the factors of production that they own and will supply additional quantities only at higher prices. Most firms, even large ones, compete with many other firms in the markets for factors of production and have no choice but to buy their inputs at the same prices as everyone else. Except in rare circumstances, firms cannot manipulate the market prices of their factors of production through their own actions.

We will study the output market constraints on firms more thoroughly in Chapters 12 through 14 and the input market constraints in Chapters 15 through 17. Swanky, the firm that we will study in this chapter, is small and cannot influence the prices at which it sells its sweaters or at which it buys the inputs used to make them.

Technology Constraint Firms use inputs to produce outputs. Any feasible way that inputs can be converted into output is called a **technique**. For example, one technique that Swanky can adopt to produce sweaters uses workers equipped with knitting needles. A second technique uses labor and hand-operated knitting machines. A third technique uses automated knitting machines that require a small amount of labor to set them going and to reset them for different sizes and styles of sweaters. A fourth technique uses robotic knitting machines controlled by computers that automatically adjust the size, type, and color of the sweaters with human intervention only at the point of programming the computer. These different techniques use different amounts of labor and capital. But they are all capable of producing the same total output.

Some techniques are capital intensive and some are labor intensive. A **capital-intensive technique** uses a relatively large amount of capital and a relatively small amount of labor. A computer-controlled automated knitting machine is an example of a capital-intensive technique. A **labor-intensive technique** uses a relatively large amount of labor and a relatively small amount of capital. Knitting sweaters by hand—where the only capital equipment used is knitting needles—is an example of a labor-intensive technique.

To maximize profit, a firm will choose a *technologically efficient* production method. Recall the definition of technological efficiency that you encountered in Chapter 9—a state in which no more output can be produced without using more inputs. Technological efficiency does not necessarily require the use of up-to-date or sophisticated equipment. When knitters are working flat out, even if they are using only needles, sweaters are being produced in a technologically efficient way. To produce more sweaters will require more knitters. No resources are being wasted. Similarly, when a computerized automated knitting plant is operating flat out, sweaters are also being produced in a technologically efficient way.

A firm can do no better than use an efficient technique. But it must determine which efficient technique to employ, for not all technologically efficient methods of production are economically efficient. Furthermore, the possibilities open to the firm will depend on the length of the planning period over which the firm is making its decisions. A firm that wants to change its output rate overnight has far fewer options than one that can plan ahead and change its output rate several months in the future. In studying the way a firm's technology constrains its actions, we distinguish between two planning horizons—the short run and the long run.

The Short Run and the Long Run

The **short run** is a period of time in which the quantities of some inputs are fixed and others can be varied. The **long run** is a period of time in which the quantities of all inputs can be varied. Inputs whose quantity can be varied in the short run are called **variable inputs.** Inputs whose quantity cannot be varied in the short run are called **fixed inputs.**

There is no fixed time that can be marked on the calendar to separate the short run from the long run. The short-run and long-run distinction varies from one industry to another. For example, if an electric power company decides that it needs a bigger production plant, it will take several years to implement its decision. If United Airlines decides that it needs 100 additional Boeing 737s, it will take a few years for Boeing to turn out the new planes needed to accommodate United's demand. The short-run for these firms is several years in length. At the other extreme, a laundromat or a copying service has a short run of just a month or two. New premises can be acquired and new machines installed and made operational quickly.

Swanky has a fixed amount of capital equipment in the form of knitting machines and to vary its output in the short run it has to vary the quantity of labor that it uses. For Swanky, labor is the variable input. The quantity of knitting machinery is fixed in the short run and this equipment is Swanky's fixed input. In the long run, Swanky can vary the quantity of both knitting machines and labor employed.

Let's look a bit more closely at how Sidney makes his output decisions in the short run.

*The Short-run Production Function

A firm's **short-run production function** describes how the maximum attainable output varies as the quantity of labor employed in a given production plant varies. In our example, Swanky can produce more sweaters if it employs more workers. The short-run production function for sweaters shows how the output rate of a fixed number of knitting machines varies as the number of workers varies. There are three ways of describing the short-run production function:

- Total product curve
- Marginal product curve
- Average product curve

Total, Marginal, and Average Product Curves

Swanky's short-run production function appears first in Fig. 10.1. The table shows us how the firm's total quantity produced (output)—the number of sweaters that can be knitted in a day—varies as the quantity of labor employed varies. As you can see, when employment is zero, no sweaters are knitted. As employment rises, so does the number of sweaters knitted. The total quantity produced is called **total product.**

*The reader who is anxious to move more quickly to a study of costs may omit this section and jump immediately to the section entitled "Short-run Cost."

Figure 10.1 Total Product

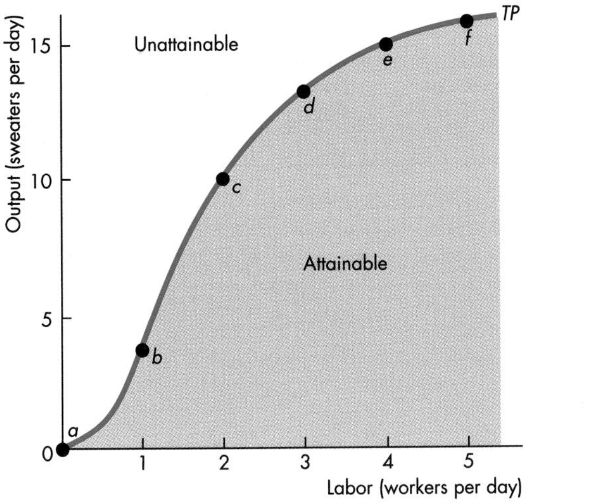

	Labor (workers per day)	Output (sweaters per day)
a	0	0
b	1	4
c	2	10
d	3	13
e	4	15
f	5	16

The numbers in the table show how, with one knitting machine, Swanky can vary the total output of sweaters by varying the amount of labor it employs. For example, 1 worker (row *b*) produces 4 sweaters a day; 2 workers (row *c*) produce 10 sweaters a day. The short-run production function is graphed here as the total product curve (*TP*). Points *a* through *f* on the curve correspond to the rows of the table. The total product curve separates the attainable output from the unattainable.

Total product can be illustrated as a total product curve. The **total product curve** shows the maximum output attainable with a given amount of capital as the amount of labor employed is varied. The total product curve for Swanky is graphed in Fig. 10.1 and labeled *TP*. Points *a* through *f* on the curve correspond to the same rows in the table. The total product curve separates the attainable output levels from those that are unattainable. All the points above the curve are unattainable. The points below the curve, in the orange area, are attainable, but they are inefficient.

The **marginal product** of any input is the increase in total product resulting from an increase of one unit of that input. The **marginal product of labor** is the change in total product resulting from a one-unit increase in the quantity of labor employed, holding the quantity of capital constant. In Swanky's case, the marginal product of labor is the additional number of sweaters knitted each day that results from hiring one additional worker. The magnitude of that marginal product depends on how many workers Swanky is employing. Swanky's marginal product of labor is calculated in the table in Fig. 10.2. The first two columns of the table are the same as the table in Fig. 10.1. The last column shows the calculation of marginal product. For example, when the quantity of labor rises from 1 to 2 workers, total product rises from 4 to 10 sweaters. The change in total product—6 sweaters—is the marginal product of the second worker.

Swanky's marginal product of labor is illustrated in the two parts of Fig. 10.2. Part (a) reproduces the total product curve that you met in Fig. 10.1. Part (b) shows the marginal product curve (labeled *MP*). In part (a), the marginal product of labor is illustrated by the orange bars. The height of each bar measures marginal product. Marginal product is also measured as the slope of the total product curve. Recall that the slope of a curve is measured as the change in y—output—divided by the change in x—labor input. A 1-unit increase in labor input, from 1 to 2 workers, increases output from 4 to 10 sweaters, so the slope from point *b* to point *c* is 6, exactly the same as the marginal product that we've just calculated.

Notice the relationship between the total and marginal product curves. The steeper the *slope* of the total product curve, the higher is the *level* of the marginal product curve. The total product curve in part (a) shows that a rise in employment from 1 to 2 workers raises output from 4 to 10 sweaters (an increase of 6). The increase in output of 6 sweaters appears on the vertical axis of part (b) as the marginal product of the second worker. We plot that marginal product at the midpoint between 1 and 2 workers per day. Notice that marginal product shown in Fig. 10.2(b) reaches a peak at 1 unit of labor and at that point marginal product is more than 6. The

Figure 10.2 Total Product and Marginal Product

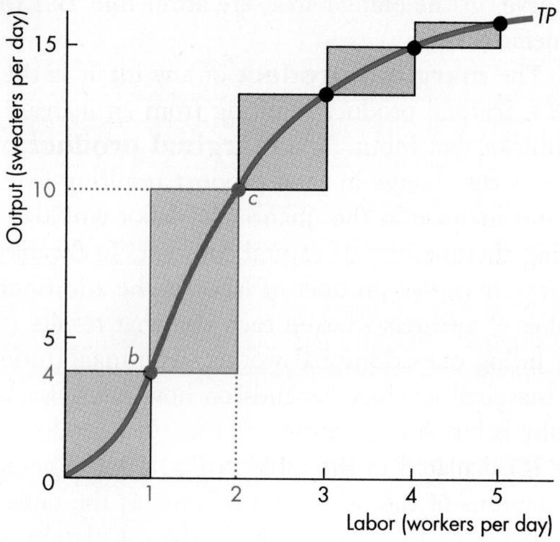

(a) Total product

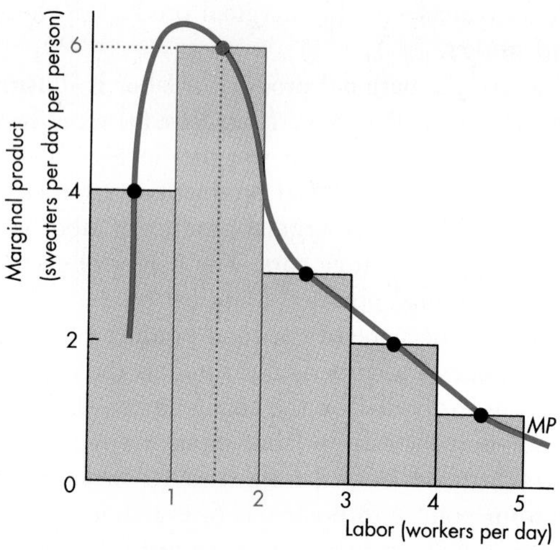

(b) Marginal product

	Labor (workers per day)	Output (sweaters per day)	Marginal product (sweaters per day per person)
a	0	0	
			4
b	1	4	
			6
c	2	10	
			3
d	3	13	
			2
e	4	15	
			1
f	5	16	

The table calculates marginal product as the change in total product resulting from a one-unit increase in labor input. For example, when labor increases from 1 to 2 workers (row *b* to row *c*), total product increases from 4 to 10 sweaters a day. Marginal product is 6 sweaters. (Marginal product is shown midway between the rows to emphasize that it is the result of *changing* inputs—moving from one row to the next.)

Marginal product is illustrated in both parts of the figure by the orange bars. The height of the bars indicates the size of the marginal product. For example, when labor increases from 1 to 2, marginal product is the highlighted orange bar whose height is 6 sweaters (visible in each part of the figure). The steeper the slope of the total product curve (*TP*), in part (a), the higher the marginal product (*MP*) in part (b). Marginal product rises to a maximum (when 1 worker is employed in this example) and then declines—diminishing marginal product.

peak occurs at 1 unit of labor because the total product curve is steepest at 1 unit of labor.

Average product is total product per unit of variable input. In Swanky's case, average product is the total number of sweaters produced each day, divided by the number of workers employed. Swanky's average product is calculated in the table in Fig. 10.3. For example, 3 workers can knit 13 sweaters a day, so the average product is 13 divided by 3, which is 4.33 sweaters per day.

Average product is illustrated in the two parts of Fig. 10.3. First, average product can be measured in part (a) as the slope of a line from the origin to a point on the total product curve. For example, at point *d*, 3 workers knit 13 sweaters. The slope of the red line from the origin to point *d* is equal to the level of output—13 sweaters—divided by the quantity of labor used—3 workers. The result is an average product for 3 workers of 4.33 sweaters a day. You can use this method of calculating average prod-

Figure 10.3 Total, Marginal, and Average Product

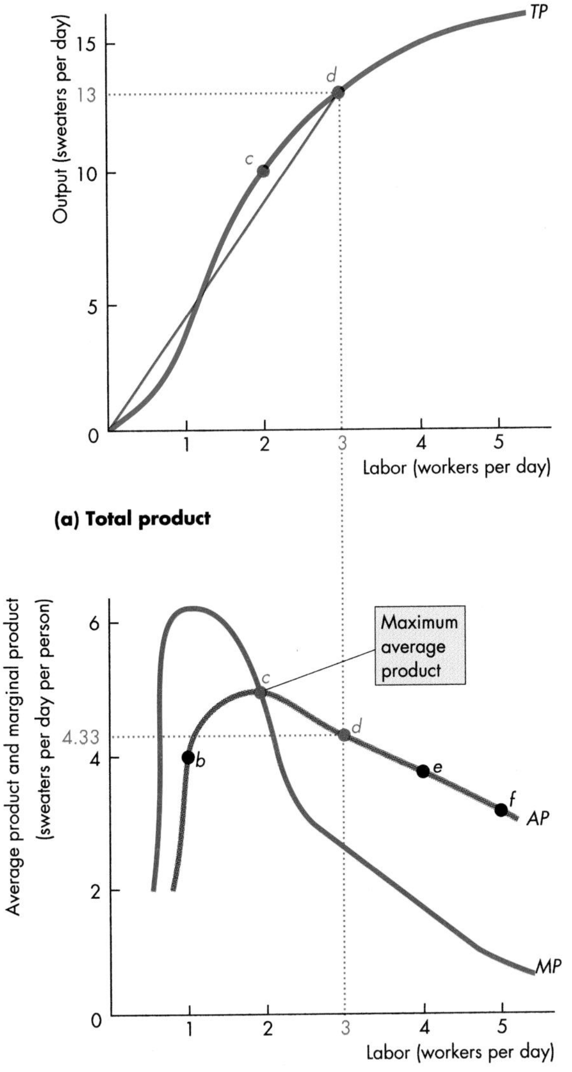

(a) Total product

(b) Marginal and average product

	Labor (workers per day)	Output (sweaters per day	Average product (sweaters per day per person)
b	1	4	4.00
c	2	10	5.00
d	3	13	4.33
e	4	15	3.75
f	5	16	3.20

Average product—total product per unit of labor—is calculated in the table by dividing total product by the quantity of labor employed. For example, 3 workers produce 13 sweaters a day, so the average product of 3 workers is 4.33 sweaters a day. The two parts of the figure show two ways of representing average product on a graph. In part (a), average product is measured as the slope of a straight line from the origin to a point on the total product curve. The straight line to point *d* is such a line. The slope of that line is 4.33 (13 sweaters a day divided by of 3 workers). Part (b) graphs average product. Points *b* through *f* on the average product curve, *AP*, correspond to the rows of the table. Part (b) also shows the connection between the average product and marginal product curves. Marginal product is above average product when average product is rising and below it when average product is falling. Average product and marginal product are equal at the maximum average product. Part (b) also shows that marginal product increases from 0 to 1 worker and decreases thereafter and that average product increases from 0 to 2 workers and decreases thereafter.

uct to check that point *c* is the point of maximum average product. The steepest line from the origin that touches the total product curve touches only at point *c*. Place a ruler on the curve and check that. Since the slope of such a line measures average product and this line is steepest when 2 workers are employed, average product is at a maximum at that point.

Part (b) graphs the average product curve, *AP*, and also shows the relationship between average product and marginal product. Points *b* through *f* on the average product curve correspond to those same rows in the table. Average product rises from 1 to 2 workers (its maximum value at point *c*), but then falls as yet more workers are employed. Notice also that the highest average product occurs where average and marginal product are equal to each other. That is, the marginal product curve cuts the average product curve at the point of maximum average product. When the average product curve is rising, marginal product is higher than average product. When the

Table 10.1 Average and Marginal Test Scores

Test	Test score	Aggregate score	Average score	Marginal score
Sidney				
1	55	55	55	
2	65	120	60	65
3	75	195	65	75
4	85	280	70	85
Steve				
1	85	85	85	
2	75	160	80	75
3	65	225	75	65
4	55	280	70	55
Sam				
1	70	70	70	
2	70	140	70	70
3	70	210	70	70
4	70	280	70	70

On the second test, Sidney scores 65 percent. After the first two tests, Sidney has an average score of 60 percent. On the third test, Sidney scores 75 percent. Sidney's marginal score is the change in his aggregate score as the result of doing one more test. The marginal score after three tests is 75 percent. This score is located midway between the scores for the second and third tests to emphasize that it is associated with doing one more test. His marginal score now exceeds his previous average (60 percent), which means that his average after three tests is higher (65 percent). Steve's marginal score is below his average score, so his average falls. Sam's marginal score equals his average score, so his average remains constant.

average product curve is falling, marginal product is below average product.

Why does Swanky care about diminishing marginal and average product? Because they have an important influence on the costs of producing sweaters and the way those costs vary as the production rate varies. We will examine these matters soon, but first we will take one more look at how marginal product and average product are related, for you will meet this type of relationship many times in your study of economics. You can also see it in your everyday life.

Relationship Between Marginal and Average Values We have seen, in Fig. 10.3, that when marginal product exceeds average product, average product is rising and when marginal product is below average product, average product is falling. We have also seen that when marginal product equals average product, average product is neither rising nor falling—it is at its peak and it is constant. These relationships between the average and marginal product curves are a general feature of the relationship between the average and marginal values of any variable. Let's look at a familiar example.

Sidney (the owner of Swanky) attends an introductory economics class with his friends Steve and Sam. They each receive a grade of 70 percent in the course the first semester, but they achieved this in different ways. Table 10.1 illustrates how. They took four tests, each worth a quarter of the final mark. Sidney, preoccupied with managing Swanky, started out disastrously with 55 percent but then steadily improved. Steve started out brilliantly but then nosedived, while Sam scored 70 percent on every test.

We can calculate the average and the marginal scores of these three students. The average score is simply the total marks obtained divided by the number of tests written. After two tests, Sidney has an aggregate score of 55 percent plus 65 percent, which is 120 percent, so his average score is 60 percent. A student's marginal score is the score on the last test written. After two tests, Sidney's marginal score is 65 percent.

Over the four tests, Sidney's marginal score rises, Steve's falls and Sam's is constant. But notice what the average scores are doing. For Sidney, the average is rising. His marginal score is higher than his average score and his average rises. For Steve, the marginal score falls. So, too, does his average. Steve's marginal score is always below his average score and pulls his average down. Sam's marginal score equals his average score, so his average stays constant.

These examples of an everyday relationship between marginal and average values agree with the relationship between marginal and average product that we have just discovered. Average product rises when marginal product exceeds average product (Sidney). Average product falls when marginal product is below average product (Steve). Average product is at a maximum and constant (it neither rises nor falls) when marginal product equals average product (Sam).

The Shape of the Short-run Production Function

Now let's get back to studying production. Pretty obviously, the short-run production function, as described by the total, marginal, and average product curves, will be different for different firms and different types of goods. Ford Motor Company's production function will be different from that of Jim's Burger Stand, which in turn will be different from that of Sidney's sweater factory. But the shape of the product curves will be similar, because almost every production process incorporates two features:

- Increasing marginal returns initially
- Diminishing marginal returns eventually

Increasing Marginal Returns **Increasing marginal returns** occur when the marginal product of an additional worker exceeds the marginal product of the previous worker. If Sidney employs just one worker at Swanky, that person has to learn all the different aspects of sweater production: running the knitting machines, fixing breakdowns, packaging and mailing sweaters, buying and checking the type and color of the wool. All of these tasks must be done by that one person. If Sidney hires a second person, the two workers can specialize in different parts of the production process. As a result, two workers produce more than twice as much as one. This is the range over which marginal returns are increasing.

Diminishing Marginal Returns **Diminishing marginal returns** occur when the marginal product of an additional worker falls short of the marginal product of the previous worker. If Sidney hires a third worker, output increases but not by as much as it did when he added the second worker. With a third worker, the factory produces more sweaters, but the equipment is being operated closer to its limits. Furthermore, there are times when the third worker has nothing to do because the plant is running without the need for further attention. Adding yet more and more workers continues to increase output but by successively smaller amounts. This is the range over which marginal returns are diminishing. This phenomenon is such a pervasive one that it is called "the law of diminishing returns." The **law of diminishing returns** states that:

As a firm uses more of a variable input, with the quantity of fixed inputs constant, its marginal product eventually diminishes.

Because marginal product eventually diminishes, so does average product. Recall that average product falls when marginal product is below average product. If marginal product is falling, it must eventually fall below average product and, when it does so, average product begins to decline.

R E V I E W

The short-run production function shows how the output rate of a given plant varies as the input of labor is varied. Three curves—total product, marginal product, and average product—describe the short-run production function. As the amount of labor rises but the total labor input is small, average and marginal product rise. With larger amounts of labor, average and marginal product fall. Average product rises when marginal product exceeds average product. Average product falls when marginal product is below average product. Marginal product and average product are equal at the point at which average product begins to decline. ■

Short-run Cost

We have seen how a firm's *output* can be varied in the short run by varying its labor inputs. We now examine how a firm's *costs* vary as it varies its output. Swanky cannot influence the prices of its inputs and has to pay the market price for them. Given the prices of its inputs, Swanky's lowest attainable cost of production for each output level is determined by its short-run production function. Let's see how.

Figure 10.4 Short-run Costs

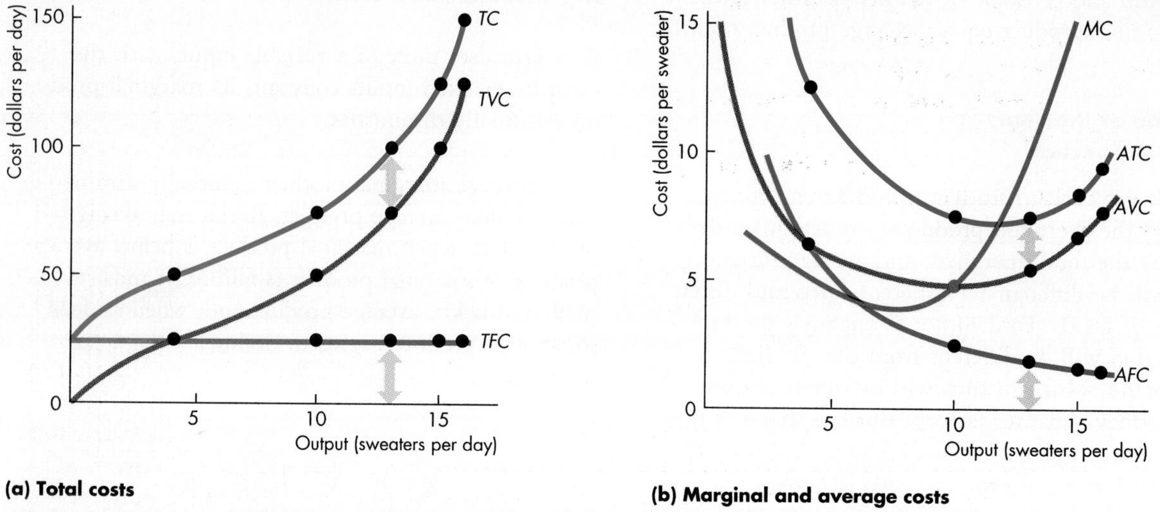

Labor (workers per day)	Output (sweaters per day)	Total fixed cost (TFC)	Total variable cost (TVC)	Total cost (TC)	Marginal cost (change in dollars per change in output) (MC)	Average fixed cost (AFC)	Average variable cost (AVC)	Average total cost (ATC)
		(dollars per day)				(dollars per sweater)		
0	0	25	0	25		..	..	..
					.... 6.25			
1	4	25	25	50		6.25	6.25	12.50
					.... 4.17			
2	10	25	50	75		2.50	5.00	7.50
					.... 8.33			
3	13	25	75	100		1.92	5.77	7.69
					.......12.50			
4	15	25	100	125		1.67	6.67	8.33
					.......25.00			
5	16	25	125	150		1.56	7.81	9.38

Short-run costs are calculated in the table and illustrated in the graphs. At each level of employment and output in the table, total variable cost (*TVC*) is added to total fixed cost (*TFC*) to give total cost (*TC*). The change in total cost per unit change in output gives marginal cost (*MC*). Average costs are calculated by dividing total costs by output.

The firm's total cost curves are shown in part (a). Total cost (*TC*) increases as output increases. Total fixed cost (*TFC*) is constant—it graphs as a horizontal line—and total variable cost (*TVC*) increases in a similar way to total cost. The vertical distance between the *TC* and *TVC* curves equals total fixed cost (*TFC*) as illustrated by the green arrows.

The average and marginal cost curves are shown in part (b). Average fixed cost (*AFC*) falls as the constant total fixed cost is divided by ever higher output levels. The curves showing average total cost (*ATC*) and average variable cost *AVC* are U-shaped. The vertical distance between them is equal to average fixed cost, which gets smaller as output increases. The marginal cost curve (*MC*) is also U-shaped. It cuts the average variable cost curve and the average total cost curve at their minimum points.

Total, Marginal, and Average Cost

Total cost *(TC)* is the sum of the costs of all the inputs used in production. Total cost is divided into two categories: fixed cost and variable cost. A **fixed cost** is a cost that is independent of the output level. A **variable cost** is a cost that varies with the output level. A fixed cost cannot be avoided, whereas a variable cost can. **Total fixed cost** *(TFC)* is the cost of all the fixed inputs. **Total variable cost** *(TVC)* is the cost of all the variable inputs.

Swanky's total cost and its division into total fixed cost and total variable cost appears in the table in Fig. 10.4. The first two columns show the short-run production function from Fig. 10.1. Swanky has fixed inputs in the form of knitting machines and factory space. Let's suppose that the cost of these fixed inputs—total fixed cost—is $25 a day. Furthermore, let's suppose that a worker costs $25 a day (the wage rate). Total variable cost rises as the quantity of labor rises. For example, when Swanky employs 3 workers, total variable cost is $75 (3 multiplied by $25). Total cost is the sum of total fixed cost and total variable cost. For example, when Swanky employs 3 workers, total variable cost is $75, total fixed cost is $25, and total cost is $100.

Marginal cost is the increase in total cost resulting from a unit increase in output. To calculate marginal cost, we find the change in total cost and divide it by the change in output. For example, when output (total product) goes up from 4 to 10 sweaters, total cost rises from $50 to $75. The change in output is 6 sweaters and the change in total cost is $25. The marginal cost of one of those 6 sweaters is $4.17 ($25 divided by 6).

Average cost is the cost per unit of output. There are three average costs:

- Average fixed cost *(AFC)*,
- Average variable cost *(AVC)*, and
- Average total cost *(ATC)*.

Average fixed cost is total fixed cost per unit of output. **Average variable cost** is total variable cost per unit of output. **Average total cost** is total cost per unit output. Average fixed cost plus average variable cost equals average total cost. For example, in the table in Fig. 10.4 when output is 10 sweaters, average fixed cost is $2.50 ($25 divided by 10), average variable cost is $5.00 ($50 divided by 10), and average total cost is $7.50 ($75 divided by 10 or, equivalently, $2.50 average fixed cost plus $5.00 average variable cost).

Short-run Cost Curves

We can illustrate Swanky's short-run costs as short-run cost curves (Fig. 10.4a). Total fixed cost is a constant $25. It appears in the figure as the horizontal green curve labeled *TFC*. Total variable cost and total cost both increase with output. They are graphed as the purple total variable cost curve (*TVC*) and the blue total cost curve (*TC*) in the figure. The vertical distance between those two curves is equal to total fixed cost—as indicated by the arrows.

There is a close relationship between the total variable cost curve in Fig. 10.4(a) and the total product curve of Fig. 10.1. They both slope upward. But the more gently sloped the product curve, the more steeply sloped is the variable cost curve. The more gently sloped the total product curve, the slower output rises with a given increase in labor. But cost and labor input changes are proportional, so, turning it around, the faster variable cost rises for a given rise in output, the more steeply sloped is the total variable cost curve.

The average cost curves appear in Fig. 10.4(b). The green average fixed cost curve (*AFC*) slopes downward. As output rises, the same constant fixed cost is spread over a larger output: When Swanky produces only 4 sweaters, average fixed cost is $6.25; when it produces 16 sweaters, average fixed cost is $1.56.

The blue average total cost curve (*ATC*) and the purple average variable cost curve (*AVC*) are U-shaped curves. The vertical distance between the average total cost and average variable cost curves is equal to average fixed cost—as indicated by the arrows. That distance shrinks as output rises, since average fixed cost falls with rising output.

Figure 10.4(b) also illustrates the red marginal cost curve. It is the red curve labeled *MC*. That curve is also U-shaped. It cuts the average variable cost curve and the average total cost curve at their minimum points. That is, when marginal cost is above average cost, average cost is rising and when marginal cost is below average cost, average cost is falling. This relationship holds for both the *ATC* curve and the *AVC* curve. You may wonder

Table 10.2 A Compact Glossary on Product and Cost

Term	Symbol	Equation	Definition
Fixed input			An input whose quantity used cannot be varied in the short run
Variable input	*L*		An input (labor in our examples) whose quantity used can be varied in the short run
Total product	*TP*		Output produced
Marginal product	*MP*	$MP = \Delta TP \div \Delta L$	Change in total product resulting from a unit rise in variable input (equals change in total product divided by change in variable factor)
Average product	*AP*	$AP = TP \div L$	Total product per unit of variable input (equals total product divided by number of units of variable factor)
Point of maximum average product			Output rate above which average product diminishes
Point of maximum marginal product			Output rate above which marginal product diminishes
Fixed cost			Cost that is independent of the output level
Variable cost			Cost that varies with the output level
Total fixed cost	*TFC*		Cost of the fixed inputs (equals their number times their unit price)
Total variable cost	*TVC*		Cost of the variable inputs (equals their number times their unit price)
Total cost	*TC*	$TC = TFC + TVC$	Cost of all inputs (equals fixed costs plus variable costs)
Marginal cost	*MC*	$MC = \Delta TC \div \Delta TP$	Change in total cost resulting from a unit rise in total product (equals the change in total cost divided by the change in total product)
Average fixed cost	*AFC*	$AFC = TFC \div TP$	Total fixed cost per unit of output (equals total fixed cost divided by total product)
Average variable cost	*AVC*	$AVC = TVC \div TP$	Total variable cost per unit of output (equals total variable cost divided by total product)
Average total cost	*ATC*	$ATC = AFC + AVC$	Total cost per unit of output (equals average fixed cost plus average variable cost)

why the marginal cost curve cuts both the average total cost curve and the average variable cost curve at their minimum points. It does so because the source of the change in total cost, from which we calculate marginal cost, is variable cost. For average variable cost to fall, marginal cost must be less than average variable cost and for average variable cost to rise, marginal cost must be higher than average variable cost. Similarly, for average total cost to fall, marginal cost must be below average total cost, and for average total cost to rise, marginal cost must be above average total cost. This is exactly the same relationship that we found when studying students' grades in Table 10.1.

There is an interesting and important relationship between the average and marginal product curves, shown in Fig. 10.3(b), and the average and marginal cost curves, shown in Fig. 10.4(b). The average and marginal cost curves are like the flip side of the relationship between the average and marginal product curves. Average variable cost is at a minimum at the same output at which average product is at a maximum (10 sweaters). The output range over which average variable cost is decreasing is the same as that over which average product is increasing. Similarly, the output range over which average variable cost is increasing is the same as that over which average product is decreasing.

The product and cost concepts that we have just studied are summarized in Table 10.2.

Real World Short-run Costs

Swanky's costs are a lot like the costs of a real world firm. Let's confirm this fact by looking at the costs of a group of real firms, the New England Power Pool (NEPOOL). NEPOOL is an association of 92 electric power companies serving more than 5 million customers in the six New England states. If the NEPOOL producers work their production plants to their physical limits, they can generate about 18,500 megawatt-hours of electric power.

NEPOOL's actual production is never that high. It fluctuates between 11,500 and 17,000 megawatt-hours, depending partly on the time of day, partly on the day of the week, and partly on the temperature. To vary their output in the short run, the power producers vary the amount of fuel that they use. Fuel is the variable input of a power producer. The power source with the lowest fuel cost in the New England system is nuclear. Large coal-burning and oil-burning generators come next. The power sources with the highest fuel cost are small gas-turbine generators that use the same kind of fuel as jet aircraft.

NEPOOL operates the New England Power Exchange (NEPEX), whose master control center is in West Springfield, Massachusetts. Engineers equipped with powerful computers make minute by minute decisions to turn power generators on and off in order to minimize the total cost of production. The engineers bring generators into operation to meet demand by choosing the remaining power source with the lowest fuel cost. That is, to increase the amount of electricity, the engineers tap into the power source with the lowest marginal cost. Only at the peak of demand do they use the generators with the highest marginal cost.

On January 28, 1987, a fairly cold winter day, the hour by hour output of the NEPOOL producers and the marginal cost per 1000 megawatt-hours fluctuated in the manner shown in Fig. 10.5. As you can see, there are two cycles over a 24-hour period in electric power production. From 1:00 A.M. to 6:00 A.M., output (shown by the blue curve) is between 11,500 and 12,000 megawatt-hours. Then between 6:00 A.M. and 7:00 A.M., output rises as we all turn on morning TV shows, toasters, and coffeemakers. Output reaches a peak at 9:00 A.M. and then falls off slightly during the day to a low point at 4:00 P.M. In the early evening, there is another TV viewing and meal-preparation peak, and then a gradual fall through to midnight as people go to bed. The marginal cost of production follows a similar cycle and fluctuates between \$29 a megawatt-hour at the trough and \$44 a megawatt-hour at the peak.

The relationship between output and marginal cost is not perfect. Mechanical failure or maintenance shutdowns often make it impossible to use the idle generator with the lowest marginal cost. Nevertheless, the relationship between output and marginal cost is pretty close. To see how close, let's plot NEPOOL's marginal cost curve—shown in Fig. 10.6. Each point in that figure represents the marginal cost and output at a particular hour. For example, you can see in Fig. 10.5 that, between 10.00 P.M. and 11.00 P.M., 14,000 megawatt-hours were produced at a marginal cost of \$32 a megawatt-hour. That output and marginal cost generate point *a* in Fig. 10.6. The continuous red curve labeled *MC* is the marginal cost curve for NEPOOL.

Notice the similarity between the marginal cost curves for NEPOOL and Swanky. All production processes have marginal cost curves that have the features of those that we have just studied.

Swanky adjusts its rate of sweater production by varying the amount of labor it employs and varying the extent to which it utilizes its fixed

Figure 10.5 New England Power Pool Output and Cost

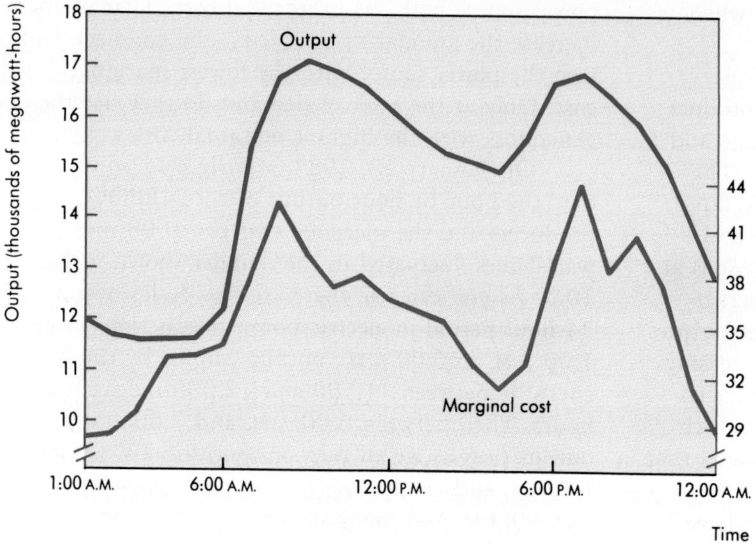

During a 24-hour period, electric power production fluctuated between 11,500 and 17,000 megawatt-hours. Over the same period, marginal cost fluctuated between $29 and $44 per megawatt-hour. The empirical relationship between output and marginal cost is not exact because of maintenance scheduling and uncontrollable factors such as plant breakdowns.

amount of knitting machinery—its physical plant. NEPOOL meets fluctuations in the production of electric power by varying the fuel input and varying the output of a fixed physical generating plant. Over the long run, as the demand for sweaters grows, Swanky might increase output by installing additional knitting machines. Similarly, as the demand for electric power grows, NEPOOL might produce additional output by installing new generators. When does it pay Swanky to install new knitting machines and the New England power producers to install new and larger generators? It is this type of question to which we now turn.

Plant Size, Cost, and Capacity

We have studied how the cost of production varies for a given sweater plant when different quantities of labor are used. The output rate at which a plant's average total cost is at a minimum is called the **capacity** of the plant. If a plant's output is below the point of minimum average total cost—that is, if it produces a lower amount than its capacity—it is said to have **excess capacity.** If a plant's output is above the point of minimum average total cost—that is, if it produces a higher amount than its capacity—it is said to have **overutilized capacity.**

The economist's use of the word capacity differs from the everyday use. It seems more natural to talk about a plant operating at capacity when it cannot produce anymore. However, when we want to refer to the maximum output that a plant can produce, we call that output the **physical limits** of the plant.

The cost curves that were shown in Fig. 10.4 apply to a plant size of one knitting machine that has a fixed cost of $25. There is a set of short-run cost curves, like those shown in Fig. 10.4, for each

Figure 10.6 New England Power Pool Marginal Cost Curve

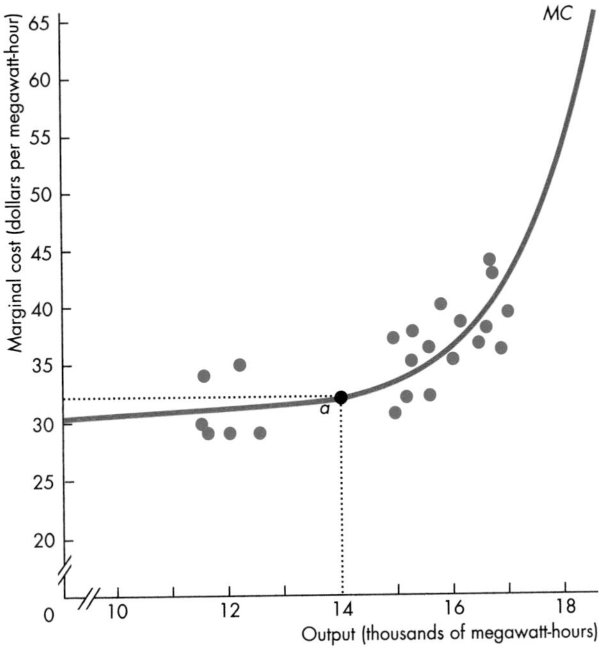

Each point in the figure represents marginal cost at a particular hour on January 28, 1987. For example, point *a* represents a marginal cost of $32 per megawatt-hour and an output rate of 14,000 megawatt-hours. The marginal cost curve for electric power in New England rises steeply as output approaches the physical limits of the generating plant.

different plant size. In the short run, a firm will be economically efficient if it produces at a point on the short-run cost curve for its given plant. In the long run, though, the firm can do better. It can choose its plant size and therefore can create a different short-run cost curve on which it will operate.

The Capacity Utilization Puzzle

The producers of electric power in the New England Power Pool sometimes operate their plant at outputs above capacity and close to their physical limits. Their situation is not uncommon. High-quality gardeners, plumbers, electricians, painters, and other suppliers of services often work so hard that they produce at an average total cost that is higher than their minimum average cost. To get the work done, they have to hire extra help at overtime wage rates and work evenings and weekends, thereby incurring high marginal costs of production.

Operating with increasing average total cost looks uneconomic. Why don't such firms buy more capital equipment and increase the scale of their business to meet the obvious high demand for their output? Is there an economic reason why they don't?

In contrast, it is not uncommon in many industries to have an almost permanent excess capacity. Steel production is an example. Excess capacity also occurs in the auto industry, in many mining operations, and in a host of other industries. These producers claim that they could increase their output if the demand for their product was higher and, as a result, could produce at a lower average total cost.

It sounds as if these firms have invested in too big a production plant. It seems as if the steel producers and automakers would be better off if they had smaller plants so that they could produce closer to the point of minimum average total cost. Is this in fact the case? Or is there some economic explanation for why firms in such industries persistently have excess capacity? This section, provides a large part of the answers to these questions.

You have already studied how a firm's costs change when it varies its use of labor, while holding constant the size of its production plant. This cost behavior is described by the firm's short-run cost curves. Now we are going to study how a firm's costs vary when *all* its inputs vary—both labor and the scale of the production plant. These variations in costs are described by the firm's long-run cost curves.

Although we want to understand the behavior of real firms, we will, as before, spend most of our time studying the long-run costs of our imaginary firm—Swanky, Inc. We will then use the insights that we get from Sidney's sweater factory to make sense of the behavior of real firms.

Short-run Cost and Long-run Cost

Short-run cost is made up of the fixed cost of a fixed plant and the variable cost of labor. The

Figure 10.7 The Production Function

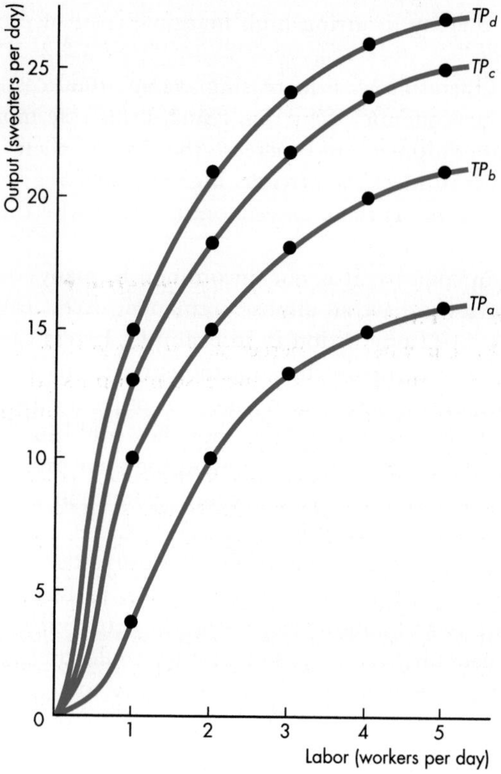

Labor (workers per day)	Plant size (number of knitting machines)			
	1	2	3	4
1	4	10	13	15
2	10	15	18	21
3	13	18	22	24
4	15	20	24	26
5	16	21	25	27

The table shows four different short-run production functions for four different plant sizes. These production functions are plotted in the graph and are labeled TP_a (1 knitting machine), TP_b (2 knitting machines), TP_c (3 knitting machines), and TP_d (4 knitting machines). Each total product curve displays diminishing marginal product. The bigger the plant, the higher is the total product for any given amount of labor employed. The highlighted numbers in the table show what happens as the firm changes its scale of production. Doubling the scale from 1 machine and 1 worker to 2 machines and 2 workers more than doubles the output—increasing returns to scale. Increasing the scale again from 2 workers and 2 machines to 3 workers and 3 machines and to 4 workers and 4 machines increases output by a smaller percentage than the increase in inputs—decreasing returns to scale.

behavior of short-run cost depends on the short-run production function. **Long-run cost** is the cost of production when a firm uses the economically efficient plant size. The behavior of long-run cost depends on the firm's production function. A **production function** is the relationship between the maximum output attainable and the quantities of inputs used.

The Production Function

Swanky's production function is shown in Fig. 10.7. In the table, we look at four different plant sizes and five different quantities of labor input. Perhaps you will recognize the numbers in the column for a plant size of one knitting machine. This is the sweater factory whose short-run product and cost curves we have just studied. With one knitting machine, output varies as the labor input is varied, as described by the numbers in that column. The table also shows three other plant sizes—two, three, and four times the size of the original one. If Sidney doubles the plant size (to two knitting machines), the various amounts of labor can produce the outputs shown in the second column of the table. The other two columns show the outputs of yet larger plants. Each of the columns of the table is a short-run production function. The production function itself is just the collection of all the short-run production functions.

The total product curves for these four different plant sizes appear in Fig. 10.7. As you can see, each total product curve has the same basic shape, but the bigger the sweater plant, the larger is the number of sweaters knitted each day by a given number of workers. One of the fundamental technological facts reflected in the shape of a total product curve is the law of diminishing returns.

Diminishing Returns

Diminishing returns occur in all four plants as the labor input increases. You can check that fact by doing calculations for the larger plants similar to those done in Fig. 10.2. Regardless of the size of the plant, the larger the labor input, the lower (eventually) its marginal product.

Just as we can calculate the marginal product of labor for each plant size, we can also calculate the marginal product of capital for each quantity of labor. The **marginal product of capital** is the change in total product resulting from a one-unit increase in the quantity of capital employed, holding the quantity of labor constant. It is calculated in a similar way to the marginal product of labor. Also, it behaves in a similar way to the marginal product of labor. That is, if the labor input is held constant as the capital input is increased, the marginal product of capital diminishes.

The law of diminishing returns tells us what happens to output when a firm changes one input, either labor or capital, and holds the other input constant. What happens to output if a firm changes both labor and equipment?

Returns to Scale

A change in scale occurs when there is an equal percentage change in the use of all the firm's inputs. For example, if Swanky has been employing one worker and has one knitting machine and then doubles its use of both inputs (to use two workers and two knitting machines), the scale of the firm doubles. **Returns to scale** are the increases in output that result from increasing all inputs by the same percentage. There are three possible cases.

- Constant returns to scale
- Increasing returns to scale
- Decreasing returns to scale

Constant Returns to Scale **Constant returns to scale** occur when the percentage increase in a firm's output is equal to the percentage increase in its inputs. If constant returns to scale are present, when a firm doubles all its inputs, its output exactly doubles. Constant returns to scale occur if a rise in output is achieved by replicating the original production process. For example, General Motors can double its production of Cavaliers by doubling its production facility for those cars. It can build an identical production line and hire an identical number of workers. With the two identical production lines, GM will produce exactly twice as many cars.

Increasing Returns to Scale **Increasing returns to scale** (also called **economies of scale**) occur when the percentage increase in output exceeds the percentage increase in inputs. If economies of scale are present when a firm doubles all its inputs, its output more than doubles. Economies of scale occur in production processes where increased output enables a firm to use a more productive technology. For example, if GM produces only 100 cars a week, it will not pay to install an automated assembly line. The cost per car will be lower if instead GM uses skilled, but expensive, workers equipped only with inexpensive hand tools. But at an output rate of a few thousand cars a week, it will pay GM to install an automated assembly line. Workers will each specialize in a few tasks at which they will become highly proficient. General Motors may use 100 times more capital and labor, but the number of cars it can make will increase much more than a hundredfold. It will experience increasing returns to scale.

Decreasing Returns to Scale **Decreasing returns to scale** (also called **diseconomies of scale**) occur when the percentage increase in output is less than the percentage increase in inputs. For example, if inputs double and output increases by 50 percent, diseconomies of scale are present. Diseconomies of scale occur in all production processes at some output rate, but perhaps at a very high one. The most common source of diseconomies of scale is the increasingly complex manage ment and organizational structure required to control a large firm. The larger the organization, the larger the number of layers in the management pyramid and the greater the costs of monitoring and maintaining control of all the various stages in the production and marketing process.

Scale Economies at Swanky Swanky's production possibilities, which were presented in Fig. 10.7, display both economies of scale and diseconomies of scale. If Sidney has 1 knitting machine and employs 1 worker, his factory will produce 4 sweaters a day. If he doubles the firm's inputs to 2 knitting machines and 2 workers, the factory's output will rise almost fourfold to 15 sweaters a day. If he increases his inputs another 50 percent to 3 knitting machines and 3 workers, output will rise to 22 sweaters a day—an increase of less than 50 percent. Doubling the scale of Swanky from 1 to 2 units of each input gives rise to economies of scale, but the further increase from 2 to 3 units of each input gives rise to diseconomies of scale.

Whether a firm experiences increasing, constant, or decreasing returns to scale has an important effect on its long-run costs. Let's see how.

Plant Size and Cost

Earlier in this chapter, we worked out Swanky's short-run costs when the firm has a fixed amount of capital—one knitting machine—and a variable number of workers. We can also work out the short-run costs of different plant sizes. It takes longer to change the size of the production plant than to change the size of the plant's work force. That is why we speak of a short run for each different plant size. But Sidney can buy another knitting machine and put it into his existing factory. He will then have a different size of plant. He can vary the amount of labor employed in that plant and, as he does so, we can trace the short-run cost curves associated with those different levels of the variable input.

Let's look at the short-run costs for different plants and see how plant size itself affects the short-run cost curves.

Four Different Plants

We've already studied the costs of a plant with 1 knitting machine. We'll call that plant *a*. The table in Fig. 10.8 sets out the costs for plant *a* and for 3 other plants—what we will call plants *b, c,* and *d.* Plant *b* has 2 knitting machines; plant *c* has 3 knitting machines; and plant *d* has 4 knitting machines.

The average total cost curves associated with the original plant and these 3 larger plants appear in Fig. 10.8(a). The average total cost curve for each of the 4 plant sizes has the same basic U-shape. Which of these cost curves Swanky operates on depends on its plant size. For example, if Swanky has plant *a,* then its average total cost curve will be ATC_a and it will cost $7.69 per sweater to knit 13 sweaters a day. But Swanky can produce 13 sweaters a day with any of these 4 different plant sizes. If it uses plant *b,* the average total cost curve is ATC_b and the average total cost of a sweater is $6.80. If it uses plant *c,* the average cost curve is ATC_c and the average total cost is the same as plant *a*—$7.69. And if it uses plant *d,* the average total cost curve is ATC_d and the average total cost of a sweater is $9.50. If Swanky wants to produce 13 sweaters a day, the economically efficient plant is plant *b*—the one with the lowest average total cost at that level of output.

Long-run Average Cost Curve

The **long-run average cost curve** traces the relationship between the lowest attainable average total cost and output when both capital and labor inputs can be varied. This curve is illustrated in Fig. 10.8(b) as *LRAC.* The curve is derived from the 4 short-run average total cost curves that we have just reviewed in Fig. 10.8(a). As you can see, from either part (a) or (b), and highlighted in red in the table, plant *a* has the lowest average total cost for all output rates up to 10 sweaters a day. Plant *b* has the lowest average total cost for output rates between 10 and 18 sweaters a day. Between output rates of 18 and 24 sweaters a day, plant *c* has the lowest average total cost. Finally, for output rates above 24 sweaters a day, plant *d* has the lowest average total cost. The segments of the four average total cost curves for which each plant has the lowest average total cost are highlighted in Fig. 10.8(b). The scalloped curve made up of these four segments is the long-run average cost curve.

Swanky will be on its long-run average cost curve if it does the following: to produce up to 10 sweaters a day, it uses 1 knitting machine; to produce between 11 and 18 sweaters a day, it uses 2 knitting machines; to produce between 19 and 24 sweaters a day, it uses 3 knitting machines; and, finally, to produce more than 24 sweaters a day, it uses 4 knitting machines. Within these ranges, it varies its output by varying the number of workers employed.

Long-run Cost and Returns to Scale There is a connection between the long-run average cost curve and returns to scale. Figure 10.9 shows this connection. When long-run average cost falls, there are increasing returns to scale (or economies of scale). When long-run average cost rises, there are decreasing returns to scale (or diseconomies of scale). At outputs up to 15 sweaters a day, Swanky experiences economies of scale; at 15 sweaters a day, long-run average cost is at a minimum. When output rises above 15 sweaters a day, Swanky experiences diseconomies of scale.

The long-run average cost curve derived for Swanky has two special features that will not always be found in a firm's long-run cost curve. First, Swanky is able to adjust its plant size only in big jumps. We can imagine varying the plant in tiny increments so that there is an infinite number of plant sizes. In such a situation, there will be an infinite number of short-run average total cost curves, one for each plant. Second, Swanky's long-run average cost curve is either falling (economies of scale) or rising (diseconomies of scale). Some production processes will have constant returns to scale over some intermediate range of output.

Figure 10.10 illustrates this alternative situation in which there is an infinite number of plant sizes and output ranges over which returns to scale are increasing (up to Q_1), constant (between Q_1 and Q_2), and decreasing (above Q_2). To keep the figure clear, only one of the infinite number of short-run average total cost curves, labeled *SRAC,* is shown. Each short-run average total cost curve touches the long-run average cost curve (*LRAC*) at a single point (one output). Thus for each output, there is a unique, economically efficient plant size. The short-run average total cost curve shown in Fig. 10.10 is for the plant that can produce output rate Q_0 at minimum average total cost, ATC_0.

The first time the long-run average cost curve appeared in print, it was drawn incorrectly. Take a look at Our Advancing Knowledge (p. 250) to see why. You will understand the connection between short-run and long-run average cost curves more thoroughly after you have studied the material in that box.

Long-run Costs Are Total Costs When we examine short-run costs, we distinguish between fixed, variable, and total cost. We make no such distinctions for long-run costs. All inputs vary in the long run, so there are no long-run fixed costs. Since there are no long-run fixed costs, long-run total cost and long-run variable cost are the same thing. The long-run average variable cost is the long-run average cost.

There is a long-run marginal cost curve that goes with the long-run average cost curve. The relationship between the long-run average cost curve and the long-run marginal cost curve is similar to that between the short-run average total cost curve and the short-run marginal cost curve. When long-run average cost is falling, long-run marginal cost is below long-run average cost. When long-run average cost is rising, long-run marginal cost is higher than long-run average cost, and when long-run average cost is constant, long-run marginal cost is equal to long-run average cost.

Shifts in Cost Curves

Both short-run and long-run cost curves depend on two things: the production function and input prices. A change in technology shifts the production function and thus shifts the cost curves. Technological advances increase the output that can be produced from given inputs. They also shift the total product curve as well as the average and the marginal product curves upward, and they shift the cost curves downward. For example, advances in genetic engineering are making it possible to increase the milk production of a cow without increasing the amount of food that it eats—a technological advance that lowers the cost of milk production.

Resource or input prices also affect the cost curves. If the price of an input increases, it directly increases cost and shifts the cost curves upward.

Returns to Scale in Reality

Let's close this chapter by looking at some real world examples and see why there is a great deal of excess capacity in some industries while in others firms are operating "flat-out."

Excess Capacity

It has been estimated that one vacuum cleaner factory could produce a quarter of all the vacuum

Figure 10.8 Short-run and Long-run Costs

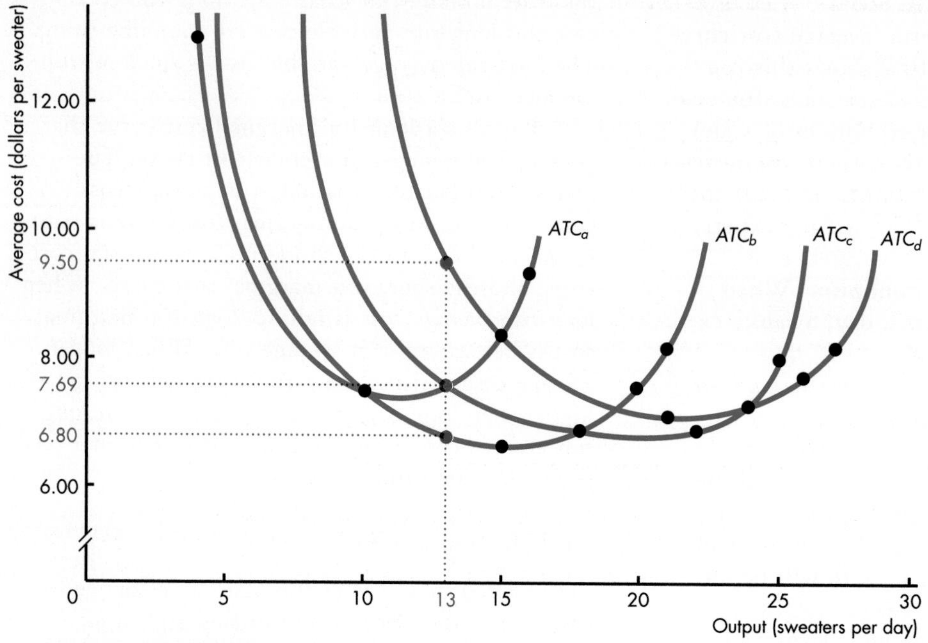

(a) Short-run average cost

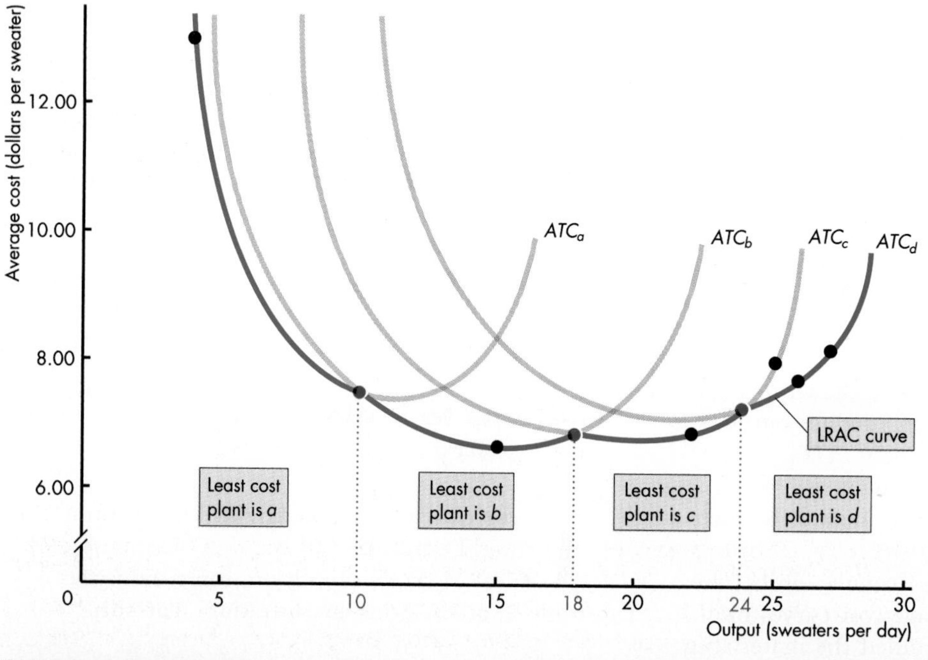

(b) Long-run average cost

The table (opposite page) shows the short-run costs of four different plants. Each plant has a different fixed cost. Plant *a* has 1 knitting machine and a fixed cost of \$25; plant *b* has 2 knitting machines and a fixed cost of \$50; plant *c* has 3 knitting machines and a fixed cost of \$75; and plant *d* has 4 knitting machines and a fixed cost of \$100. The short-run average total cost curve for each plant is graphed in part (a). Part (b) illustrates the construction of the long-run average cost curve. This curve traces the lowest attainable costs of production at each output when both capital and labor inputs are varied. On the long-run average cost curve, and highlighted in the table, Swanky uses plant *a* to produce up to 10 sweaters a day; plant *b* to produce between 11 and 18 sweaters a day; plant *c* to produce between 19 and 24 sweaters a day; and plant *d* to produce more than 24 sweaters a day.

Figure 10.8 (Continued)

Labor (workers per day)	Output (sweaters per day)	Total fixed cost	Total variable cost	Total cost	Average total cost (dollars per sweater)
		(dollars per day)			
***Plant a:* 1 unit of capital—total cost of capital = $25**					
1	4	25	25	50	12.50
2	10	25	50	75	7.50
3	13	25	75	100	7.69
4	15	25	100	125	8.33
5	16	25	125	150	9.38
***Plant b:* 2 units of capital—total cost of capital = $50**					
1	10	50	25	75	7.50
2	15	50	50	100	6.67
3	18	50	75	125	6.94
4	20	50	100	150	7.50
5	21	50	125	175	8.33
***Plant c:* 3 units of capital—total cost of capital = $75**					
1	13	75	25	100	7.69
2	18	75	50	125	6.94
3	22	75	75	150	6.82
4	24	75	100	175	7.29
5	25	75	125	200	8.00
***Plant d:* 4 units of capital—total cost of capital = $100**					
1	15	100	25	125	8.33
2	21	100	50	150	7.14
3	24	100	75	175	7.29
4	26	100	100	200	7.69
5	27	100	125	225	8.33

cleaners produced in the United States before its long-run average cost would fall to a minimum.[1] But there are more than four vacuum cleaner factories in the United States, so each factory is operating at an output rate below that at which long-run average cost is at a minimum. The situation also holds for TV picture tubes and for steel, cars, and

[1]James V. Koch, *Industrial Organization and Prices,* 2nd ed. (Englewood Cliffs, N.J.: Prentice-Hall, 1980), 123–134.

Figure 10.9 Returns to Scale

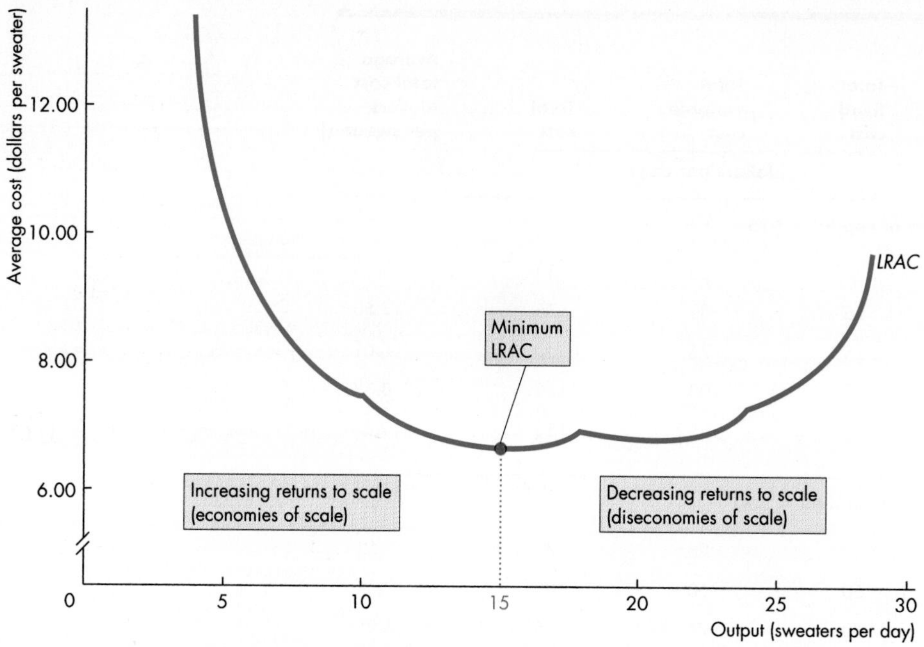

When the long-run average cost curve (*LRAC*) slopes downward, there are increasing returns to scale (or economies of scale). When the long-run average cost curve slopes upward, there are decreasing returns to scale (or diseconomies of scale).

Figure 10.10 Short-run and Long-run Average Costs

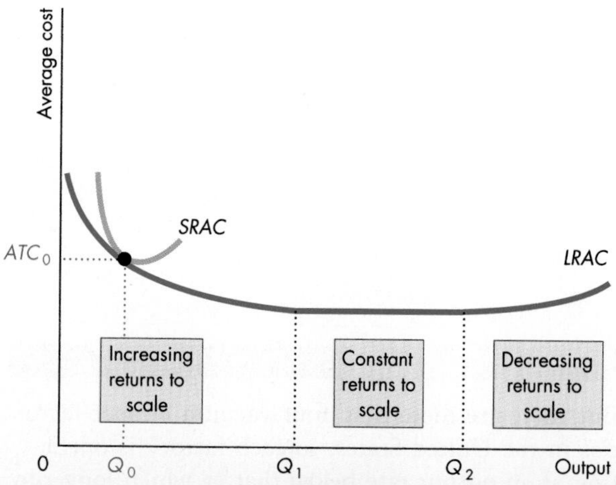

If the capital input can be varied in small units, there are not just four different plant sizes, as in Figure 10.8, but an infinitely large number of them. There are also an infinitely large number of short-run average total cost curves. Each short-run average total cost curve touches the long-run average cost curve at a single point. For example, the short-run average total cost curve (*SRAC*) touches the long-run average cost curve (*LRAC*) at the output rate Q_0 and average total cost ATC_0. The short-run average total cost curve shown is representative of the infinite number of others, each with only one point touching the long-run average cost curve. The long-run average cost curve also illustrates the possibility of constant returns to scale: For outputs up to Q_1, there are increasing returns to scale; between Q_1 and Q_2, there are constant returns to scale; above Q_2, there are decreasing returns to scale.

Figure 10.11 Excess Capacity

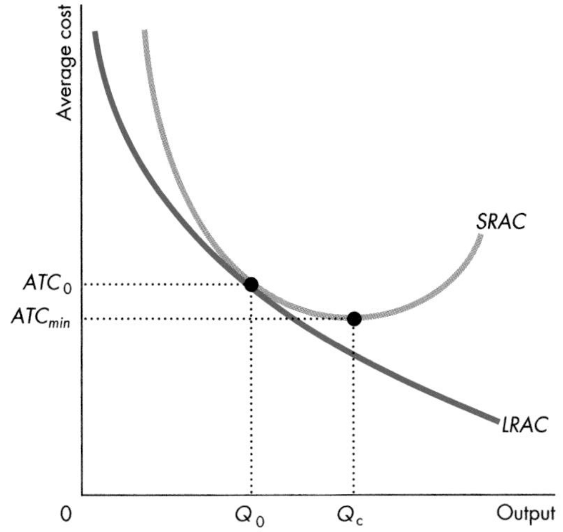

The size of the market limits a firm's output to Q_0. At output Q_0, the long-run average cost curve is downward sloping—there are economies of scale. To produce Q_0 at least cost, the firm installs a plant with a capacity of Q_c and operates the plant below capacity. This situation prevails in many industries, including those manufacturing vacuum cleaners, TV picture tubes, steel, cars, petroleum refining, typewriters, cigarettes, semiconductors and matches.

petroleum refining. Economies of scale also exist for typewriters, cigarettes, semiconductors, and matches.

Figure 10.11 illustrates the situation that prevails in those industries that can lower their average production costs if the market is big enough to permit them to expand to their most efficient scale. Output, limited by the extent of the market, is Q_0. The firm is producing efficiently at an average total cost of ATC_0. But the firm has excess capacity. It can lower its costs to ATC_{min} even with its existing plant if output can be increased to Q_c, and it can lower its costs even more by switching to a bigger plant. But the firm can't sell more than Q_0. So, even when it is operating as efficiently as possible, the firm has excess capacity. The production of vacuum cleaners, TV picture tubes, steel cars, and the other products mentioned above are examples of industries in which the situation shown in Fig. 10.11 prevails.

Operating "Flat-Out"

When we examined the short-run marginal cost of NEPOOL, we discovered that its marginal cost increases as it produces more power. As we saw in Figure 10.6, NEPOOL's marginal cost curve slopes upward and becomes extremely steep at output rates in excess of 17,000 megawatt hours. Why don't the companies in NEPOOL build additional plants? We can answer this question by applying the lessons that you've just learned about the relationship between short-run and long-run costs.

Figure 10.12 shows NEPOOL's short-run marginal cost curve (*MC*) as well as its short-run average total cost curve (*ATC*). Two points are

Figure 10.12 Overutilizing Capacity

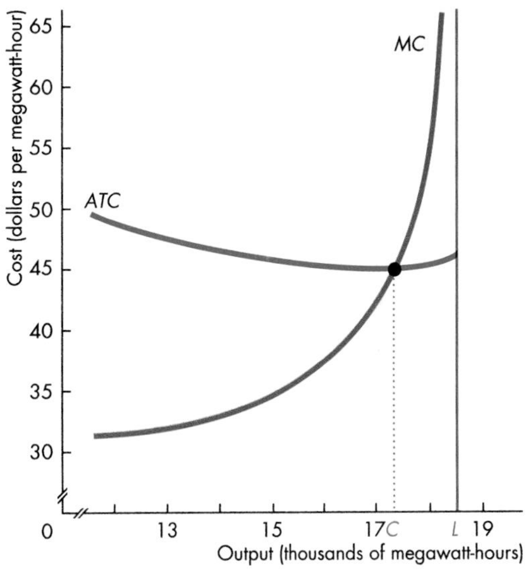

Although NEPOOL producers face steeply increasing marginal costs, their average total cost declines up to output C. The capacity (minimum cost) of NEPOOL'S plant is output C. Output *L* is the physical limit of their plant. Between C and *L*, average total cost rises. When demand increases so that NEPOOL is producing in the range between C and *L* for a significant amount of the time, it will be efficient to increase its plant size to meet the additional demand. It will not be efficient to build a bigger plant to meet current demand even though, at peak demand, NEPOOL is operating "flat-out." Although marginal cost can be lowered with a larger plant, average total cost cannot.

Cost Curves

Jacob Viner

The cost curves that you have studied in this chapter were first expressed in their current form in 1931 by Jacob Viner in an article entitled "Cost Curves and Supply Curves."* Viner, the son of poor immigrant parents from Eastern Europe, was born in Montreal, Canada, in 1892. He did his undergraduate studies at McGill University in Montreal, where he was taught economics by Steven Leacock, the famous humorist. From McGill, Viner went to Harvard where he earned a Ph.D. in 1922. He became a full professor at the University of Chicago at the age of 32. In 1946, he left Chicago for Princeton, where he stayed until his death in 1970.

Viner wrote many important books and articles, mostly on international economic issues. It was his article on cost curves, though, that became his most widely known work. His analysis of cost and cost curves is now studied by every beginning student of economics.

Short-run Cost Curves

Viner's account of the behavior of short-run cost is so clear that it provides a beautifully compact review of what you have studied in this chapter. The following is the essence of Viner's own presentation:

- The short run is a period long enough to permit any desired change of output that is technologically possible without altering the scale of plant but not long enough to permit any adjustment of scale of plant.
- Inputs are classified in two groups—those necessarily fixed in amount in the short run and those freely variable.
- Scale of plant means the amount of the inputs that are fixed in the short run.
- Scale of plant is measured by the output that it produces when average total cost is at a minimum.
- Costs associated with fixed factors are called fixed costs.
- Costs associated with variable factors are called variable costs.**

Viner's diagram of short-run cost curves is reproduced below.†

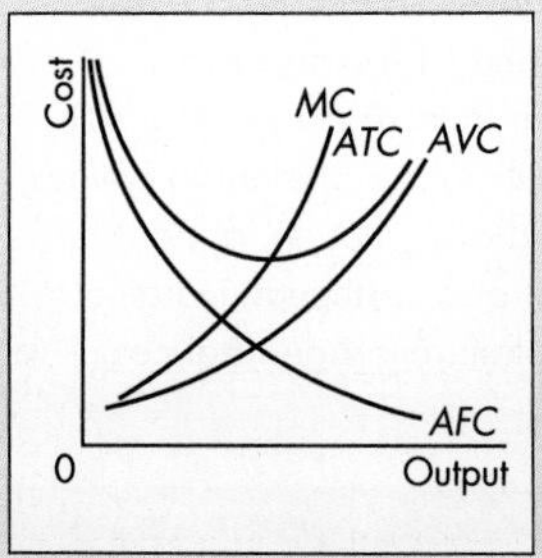

Viner pointed out the following features of the cost curves:

- Average fixed cost (*AFC*) declines as output rises.
- Average variable cost (*AVC*) rises as output rises.
- Marginal cost (*MC*) rises and equals average cost (*ATC*) at the lowest point of average total cost.
- Average cost is the vertical sum of average fixed cost and average variable cost and is necessarily U-shaped "for all industries having any substantial fixed costs."

Long-run Cost Curves

Viner also showed how the short-run cost curves and long-run cost curves are related to each other. In this exercise, he made what has become a famous mistake and one which can reinforce your understanding of the long-run average cost curve. The figure below shows the relation between the long-run average cost curve *(LRAC)* and short-run average total cost curve *(SRAC)* in part (a) and Viner's version in part (b).

When instructing his draftsman, a brilliant Chinese mathematician at the University of Chicago, Viner asked that the long-run average cost curve do two things:

- Pass through the minimum point of each *SRAC* curve.
- Not rise above any *SRAC* curve at any point

Notice that in part (a) the *SRAC* curve is never below the *LRAC* curve. Part (a) thus satisfies Viner's second instruction—that the *LRAC* curve not rise above any *SRAC* curve at any point. But it does not satisfy Viner's first instruction—that the long-run average cost curve pass through the minimum point of each *SRAC* curve.

In part (b), you can see what purports to be a long-run average cost curve and that curve does pass through the minimum points of the *SRAC* curves. This curve satisfies Viner's first condition but not the second.

Viner had given his draftsman what he subsequently called a "technically impossible and economically inappropriate assignment." It is possible to draw a curve that never rises above a *SRAC* curve and that *does not* pass through the points of minimum short-run average total cost [part a] *or* it is possible to draw a curve that passes through the points of minimum short-run average total cost and that *does* rise above the *SRAC* curve (part b), but it is not possible to draw a curve that does both of these things. The curve in part (a) is a long-run average cost curve and the curve in part (b) is not.

Such is the stuff of advancing knowledge. A great economist like Jacob Viner, struggling with a new idea, makes a mistake. Today, a student in an introductory economics course would feel embarrassed to make such an error.

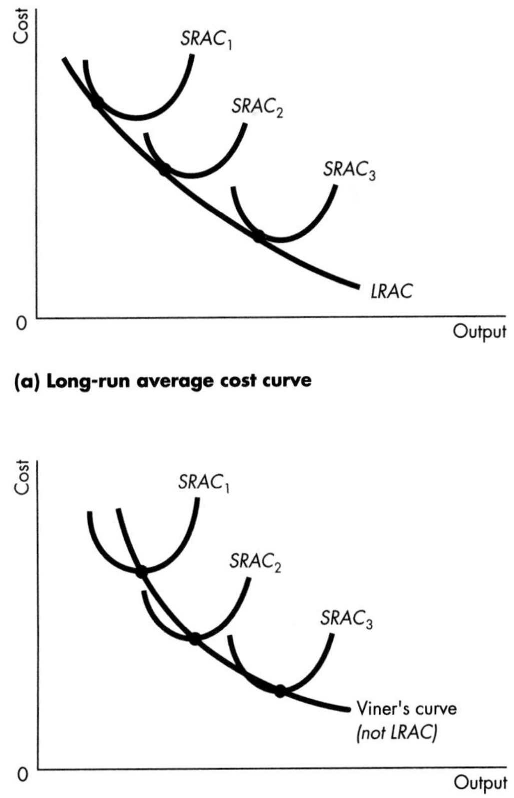

(a) Long-run average cost curve

(b) Viner's error

---

*One of most accessible sources for Viner's article is George J. Stigler and Kenneth E. Boulding (eds.), *Readings in Price Theory* (Chicago: Richard D. Irwin, 1952), 198–232. The brief Viner quotations that appear in this box are taken from this source. The article was first published in *Zeitschrift für Nationalökonomie*, vol. III (1931) pp. 23–46.

**Viner called variable costs "direct costs."

†The figure shown here is a simplified version of the one that appeared in the original article.

marked on the Output axis. Point C is NEPOOL's capacity. (The word *capacity* is being used here in its economic sense as the output rate that minimizes average total cost.) The other point marked is L, the physical limits of the output of the existing plant.

NEPOOL's marginal cost curve slopes upward very steeply because as its output approaches its physical limits, generators are brought into operation that use very expensive fuel (similar to that used by jet aircraft). But the average total cost curve has a much more gentle slope. Why? Because the bulk of NEPOOL's costs are not variable fuel costs at all but fixed costs. NEPOOL's fixed resources—capital equipment and skilled labor—cannot be varied to meet hourly shifts in demand for power. The great proportion of total costs coming from these fixed resources smoothes out NEPOOL's average total cost. NEPOOL's output fluctuates between 11,500 and 17,000 megawatt-hours (see Fig. 10.6). NEPOOL producers operate on the rising part of the marginal cost curve, but they also operate on a falling part of their average total cost curve. Occasionally, output rises above capacity and therefore moves into the range in which average total cost rises. But such cases are rare—occurring only at the peak of demand for the year.

As the demand for electric power gradually rises, the NEPOOL producers will be able to achieve greater economic efficiency by increasing their plant size. Currently, output fluctuates between 11,500 megawatt-hours and 17,000 megawatt-hours. If demand fluctuates between 17,000 and 19,000 megawatt-hours, production will be taking place on the rising part of the short-run average total cost curve and, on some occasions, it will be necessary for NEPOOL to operate "flat-out"—at its physical limits—and to import power from neighboring power pools to meet the demand. It will pay NEPOOL producers to increase their production capacity to meet the additional demand.

It does not pay to increase capacity to meet demand fluctuations in the range shown in the figure. An increased plant will increase the fixed costs and shift the average total cost curve upward. The new average total cost curve will only fall below the current one at higher outputs than can be sold. Thus, it pays the NEPOOL power companies to stick with their existing plants and operate them "flat-out" to meet the peak demand.

■ We have now studied the way in which a firm's costs vary as it varies its inputs and output rate. We've seen how the fact that marginal product eventually diminishes gives rise to eventually increasing average and marginal cost. We've also seen how long-run cost curves take their shape from economies and diseconomies of scale—long-run average cost decreasing as output increases with economies of scale and long-run average cost increasing as output increases with diseconomies of scale.

In the next chapter, we're going to probe a firm's costs and input decisions more closely, studying the way in which its demands for inputs at a given output are affected by input prices. With this model, we'll be able to understand why we see variations in techniques employed and why some industries are much more capital-intensive than others.

SUMMARY

Firms' Objectives and Constraints

Firms aim to maximize profit. Profit maximization stems directly from scarcity. Only firms that maximize profits can survive in a competitive environment.

Constraints are imposed on profit maximization by the market and by technology. Some firms operate in such competitive markets that they have no choice but to sell their output at the going price. Other firms can choose the price of their output. However, at higher prices, they will sell less. Most firms are unable to influence the markets for their inputs and have to buy them at the going prices. Technology limits the production process of firms. If firms are technologically efficient, then they can increase their output only by using more inputs.

In the short run, some inputs cannot be changed. In most cases, the capital input is fixed in the short run while labor can be varied. (pp. 229–230)

The Short-run Production Function

The short-run production function describes the limits to output as a firm changes the quantity of a variable input such as labor. The short-run production function is described by the total, average, and marginal product curves. Total product is the output produced in a given period. Average product is total product per unit of variable input. Marginal product is the change in total product resulting from a one-unit increase in the variable input. As the variable input is increased, average and marginal product rise at first until they reach a peak, and thereafter they fall—diminishing returns begin. When average product rises, marginal product exceeds average product. When average product falls, marginal product is less than average product. When average product is at its maximum, marginal product equals average product. (pp. 230–235)

Short-run Cost

Total cost is divided into total fixed cost and total variable cost. As output rises, total cost rises because total variable cost rises. Marginal cost is the additional cost of producing one more unit of output. Average total cost is total cost per unit of output.

Costs depend on how much a firm produces. Average fixed cost falls as output rises. Average variable cost and average total cost are U-shaped. Marginal cost is also U-shaped. When average cost is falling, marginal cost is below average cost, and when average cost is rising, marginal cost exceeds average cost. When average product is at a maximum, average variable cost is at a minimum. When average product is rising, average variable cost is falling and when average product is falling, average variable cost is rising. (pp. 235–240)

Plant Size, Cost, and Capacity

Plant capacity is the output rate with the lowest average total cost. Firms that produce a smaller amount than their capacity are said to have excess capacity; those that produce a larger amount than their capacity are said to have overutilized their capacity.

Long-run cost is the cost of production when all inputs—labor as well as plant and equipment—have been adjusted to their economically efficient levels. The behavior of long-run cost depends on the firm's production function. As a firm uses more labor while holding capital constant, it eventually experiences diminishing returns. When it uses more capital while holding labor constant, it also experiences diminishing returns. When it varies all its inputs in equal proportions, it experiences returns to scale. Returns to scale can be constant, increasing, or decreasing. (pp. 240–244)

Plant Size and Cost

There is a set of short-run cost curves for each different plant size. There is one least-cost plant for each output. The higher the output, the larger is the plant that will minimize average total cost.

The long-run average cost curve traces the relationship between the lowest attainable average total cost and output when both capital and labor inputs can be varied. With constant returns to scale, the long-run average cost curve is horizontal. With increasing returns to scale, the long-run average cost curve slopes downward. With decreasing returns to scale, the long-run average cost curve slopes upward.

There is no distinction between fixed cost and variable cost in the long run. Since all inputs are variable, all costs are also variable.

Cost curves shift when either input prices or technology change. An improvement in technology raises the output from a given set of inputs and shifts the cost curves downward. A rise in input prices shifts the cost curves upward. (pp. 244–245)

Returns to Scale in Reality

Some firms, including those that make vacuum cleaners, TV picture tubes, and cars, have increasing returns to scale (economies of scale). Usually economies of scale exist when the total market is too small to allow the efficient scale of production. In such industries, firms operate efficiently with excess capacity.

Some firms overutilize their plants, operating

them at an output rate that exceeds capacity. The NEPOOL power producers are an example. Though the marginal cost of electric power rises as output rises, only rarely does NEPOOL produce so much power that producers are operating on the upward-sloping section of their short-run average total cost curves. Only if a firm persistently operates on the upward-sloping part of its short-run average total cost curve is it efficient to increase its plant size. (pp. 245–252)

KEY CONCEPTS

Key Figures and Tables

REVIEW QUESTIONS

1 Why do we assume that firms maximize profit?

2 What are the main constraints on a firm's ability to maximize profit?

3 Distinguish between the short run and the long run.

4 Define total product, average product, and marginal product. Explain the relationships between a total product curve, average product curve, and marginal product curve.

5 State the law of diminishing returns. What does this law imply about the shapes of the total, marginal, and average product curves?

6 Define total cost, total fixed cost, total variable cost, average total cost, average fixed cost, average variable cost, and marginal cost.

7 What is the relationship between the average total cost curve, the average variable cost curve, and the marginal cost curve?

8 Define the long-run average cost curve. What is the relationship between the long-run average cost curve and the short-run average total cost curves?

9 What does the long-run average cost curve tell us?

10 Define economies of scale. What effects do economies of scale have on the shape of the long-run average cost curve?

11 When does the long-run average cost curve touch the minimum point of a short-run average total cost curve?

12 When does the long-run average cost curve touch a point on the short-run average total cost curve to the left of its minimum point?

13 When does the long-run average cost curve touch a point on the short-run average total cost curve to the right of its minimum point?

14 Why might long-run average cost decline? Why might long-run average cost rise?

15 What makes the short-run cost curves shift (a) upward or (b) downward?

PROBLEMS

1 The short-run production function of Rubber Duckies, Inc., a firm making rubber boats, is described by the following:

Labor (number of persons employed per week)	Output (rubber boats per week)
1	1
2	2
3	4
4	7
5	11
6	14
7	16
8	17
9	18
10	18

a) Draw the total product curve.

b) Calculate average product and draw the average product curve.

c) Calculate marginal product and draw the marginal product curve.

d) What is the relationship between average product and marginal product at output rates below 16 boats per week? Why?

e) What is the relationship between average and marginal product at outputs above 16 boats per week? Why?

2 Suppose that the price of labor is $400 per week, total fixed costs are $10,000 a week, and the production possibilities are those presented in question 1.

a) Calculate the firm's total cost, total variable cost, and total fixed costs for each of the outputs given.

b) Draw the total cost, total variable cost, and total fixed cost curves.

c) Calculate the firm's average total cost, average fixed cost, average variable cost, and marginal cost at each of the outputs given.

d) Draw the following cost curves: average total cost, average variable cost, average fixed cost, and marginal cost.

3 Suppose that total fixed costs rise to $11,000 a week. How will this affect the firm's average total cost, average fixed cost, average variable cost, and marginal cost curves in question 2.

4 Suppose that total fixed costs remain at $10,000 a week, but that the price of labor rises to $450 a week. Using these new costs, rework questions 2(a) and (b) and draw the new cost curves.

Chapter 11

(Optional)

Producing at Least Cost

After studying this chapter, you will be able to:

- Define and calculate the marginal rate of substitution between two inputs
- Explain what an isoquant measures
- Explain what an isocost line measures
- Calculate the least-cost technique of production
- Predict the effect of a change in input prices on the least-cost technique
- Explain variations in capital intensity across industries and countries

A Dollar a Day in Amazonia

If you journey to the right part of Amazonia, deep in the interior of Brazil, you will encounter a scene straight from medieval times. As you approach by helicopter, you can see through the mist an enormous pit, several hundred feet wide, dug into the earth. As you draw closer, you can see crude wooden ladders scaling the pit's terraces. Finally, you distinguish the muddy, exhausted shapes of thousands of men scaling the ladders with sacks of dirt on their backs. The scene you are watching is an enormous gold mine, being dug largely by hand by laborers paid little more than a dollar a day. ■ The scene is different at a strip mine in North America. There, far fewer workers, who receive far higher pay, operate earthmovers so large that they make ordinary cars and trucks look like toys. ■ Why do such differences exist? Why do gold mines in Amazonia employ such large numbers of people, risking their lives daily on rickety ladders? Why don't Brazilian mines use the efficient, labor-saving equipment of North American mines? ■ The capital equipment used by all the firms operating in the United States is worth close to three trillion dollars—or $26,000 per person employed. The processed food industry—producing packaged meat and frozen fruits and vegetables—uses about the average amount of capital per worker. Manufacturers of chemicals, especially of plastic materials and industrial gases, use eight times the average amount of capital per person; manufacturers of shirts and other clothing use around one tenth the average capital per person. Why don't shirtmakers use more machinery? Why do plastics makers use so much capital equipment?

■ Capital per person employed varies because different industries, and even different countries, use different techniques of production. The choice of a technique of

Figure 11.1 Swanky's Production Function

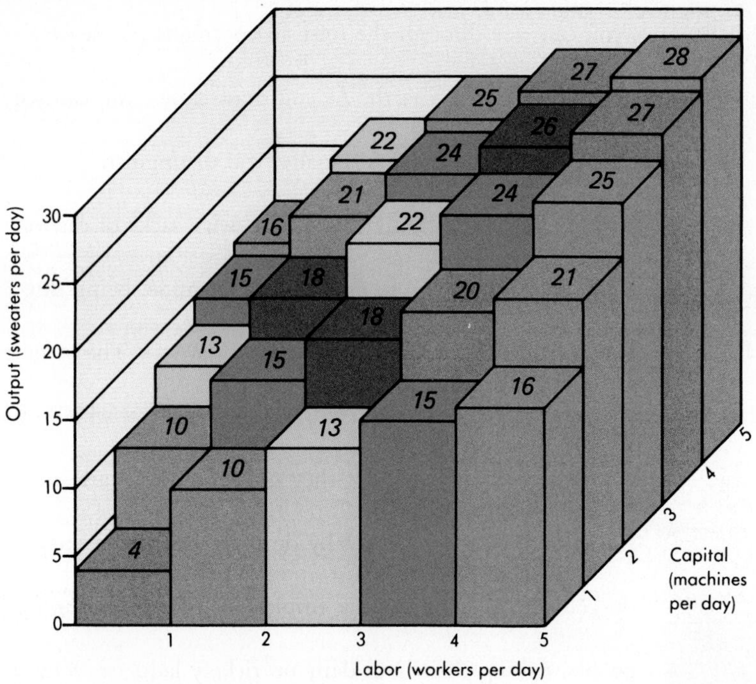

The figure shows how many sweaters can be produced a day by various combinations of labor and capital input. For example, by using 4 workers and 2 knitting machines, Swanky can produce 20 sweaters.

production is a crucial decision to be made by a firm. This chapter examines the way in which firms make such decisions. It also introduces you to some powerful tools of analysis that are well worth the effort required to master them.

Input Substitution

You would be hard-pressed to think of many goods that can be produced in only one way. Just about every good and service can be produced by using a large amount of labor and a small amount of capital or a large amount of capital and a small amount of labor. For example, cars can be made with computer-controlled robotic assembly lines that use enormous amounts of capital and hardly any labor, or they can be built by skilled labor using only hand tools; highways and dams can be built using giant earth-moving machines operated by a small amount of labor or by hoards of workers using picks, shovels, and wheelbarrows.

A production technique that uses a lot of capital per worker is called a *capital-intensive technique.* One that uses a lot of labor and a little capital per worker is called a *labor-intensive technique.* Capital intensity is the ratio of capital to labor employed in a production process. Labor intensity is the ratio of labor to capital.

The technically feasible range of production possibilities is described by the production function. An example of a production function is shown in Fig. 11.1. This production function is that of Swanky, Inc. (the sweater factory owned by Sidney that was introduced in Chapter 10). The figure records the maximum daily output of sweaters that can be produced by using different combinations of labor and capital. For example, if Swanky has 3 knitting machines and employs 1 worker, it can produce 13 sweaters a day. With 3 knitting machines and 5 workers, it can produce 25 sweaters a day.

If you study the numbers in Fig. 11.1, you will see that it shows three ways of producing 15 sweaters a day. It also shows two ways of producing 10, 13, 16, 18, 21, 22, 24, 25, and 27 sweaters a day.

Table 11.1 Substituting Between Capital and Labor to Produce 15 Sweaters a Day

Method	Capital (K)	Labor (L)	Fall in capital ($-\Delta K$)	Rise in labor (ΔL)	Marginal rate of substitution of capital for labor ($-\Delta K/\Delta L$)
a	4	1			
			2	1	2
b	2	2			
			1	2	1/2
c	1	4			

Switching from method *a* to method *b* involves cutting capital ($-\Delta K$) by 2 machines and raising the labor (ΔL) by 1 worker. The marginal rate of substitution of capital for labor—which is the ratio of the fall in capital ($-\Delta K$) to the rise in labor (ΔL)—is 2. Switching from method *b* to method *c* involves cutting capital by 1 machine and raising labor by 2 workers, which means that the marginal rate of substitution of capital for labor is 1/2.

The production function in Fig. 11.1 can be used to calculate the marginal product of labor and the marginal product of capital. As we learned in Chapter 10, *marginal product of labor* is the change in total product per unit change of labor, holding the amount of capital constant. We've already learned how to calculate the marginal product of labor in Chapter 10 and so we will not repeat the calculations here. The *marginal product of capital* is the change in total product per unit change in capital, holding the amount of labor constant. Although we have not calculated examples of marginal products of capital, there is no new principle involved in such calculations. They are performed in exactly the same way as the calculation of the marginal product of labor that you studied in the previous chapter. Furthermore, the law of diminishing returns applies to capital just as it does to labor. That is, holding labor input constant, the marginal product of capital diminishes as the capital input increases.

It's easy to see why the law of diminishing returns applies to capital by imagining this scene in Swanky's knitting factory. Suppose that there is 1 worker with 1 machine. Output (as shown in Fig. 11.1) is 4 sweaters a day. If an extra machine is installed, the one worker can still easily handle the 2 machines. One machine can be set to knit blue sweaters and the other, red sweaters. There's no need to stop the machines to change the wool color. Output more than doubles to 10 sweaters a day. But if a third machine is added, a single worker finds it hard to cope with the increasingly complex factory. For example, there are now three times as many breakdowns as there were with just 1 machine. The worker has to spend an increasing amount of time fixing problems. Output only increases to 13 sweaters a day.

Although all goods and services can be produced by using a variety of alternative methods of production, the ease with which capital and labor can be substituted for each other varies from industry to industry. The production function reflects the ease with which inputs can be substituted for each other. Also, the production function can be used to calculate the degree of substitutability between inputs. Such a calculation involves a new concept—that of the marginal rate of substitution of capital for labor.

The Substitutability of Capital and Labor

The **marginal rate of substitution of capital for labor** is the decrease in capital needed per unit increase in labor that keeps output constant. Table 11.1 illustrates how to calculate the marginal rate of substitution of capital for labor. As we saw in Fig. 11.1, there are three ways of producing 15 sweaters a day. Let's call those methods *a*, *b*, and *c*. They appear again in Table 11.1. A daily output of 15 sweaters can be produced with 4 knitting machines and 1 worker, 2 units of each input, or 1 knitting machine and 4 workers.

Changing the method of production from *a* to *b* reduces the capital input by 2 machines and raises the labor input by 1 worker. The marginal rate of substitution is the ratio of the fall in capital to the rise in labor and, for the switch from technique *a* to *b* equals 2. Switching from method *b* to *c* reduces capital by 1 machine and raises labor by 2 workers. Again, the marginal rate of substitution is the ratio of the fall in capital to the rise in labor, so, for the move from method *b* to *c* the marginal rate of substitution is ½.

The marginal rates of substitution that we have just calculated obey the **law of diminishing marginal rate of substitution** which states that:

> The marginal rate of substitution of capital for labor falls as the amount of capital decreases and the amount of labor increases.

You can see that the law of diminishing marginal rate of substitution makes sense by considering Swanky's sweater factory. With 1 worker racing between 4 knitting machines, desperately trying to keep them all operating, coping with breakdowns, and keeping the wool from tangling, output can be held constant by getting rid 1 machine and hiring only a small additional amount of labor. The marginal rate of substitution is high. At the other extreme, 4 workers are falling over each other to operate 1 machine. In this situation, output can be kept constant by laying off 2 workers and installing 1 additional machine. The marginal rate of substitution is low. This principle of the diminishing marginal rate of substitution applies to (almost) all production processes.

Figure 11.2 An Isoquant

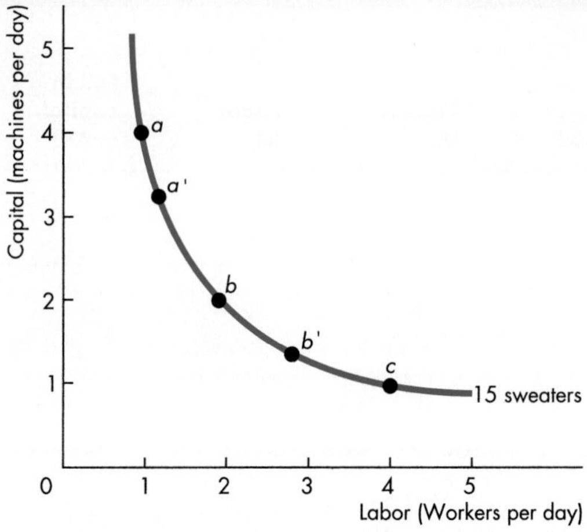

This isoquant shows the different techniques of production, or combinations of capital and labor, that can produce 15 sweaters a day. For example, point a tells us that 4 machines and 1 worker can produce 15 sweaters a day. The same output level can be produced by 2 machines and 2 workers (point b) or 1 machine and 4 workers (point c). Each of these points can be found in Fig. 11.1. The isoquant also shows combinations not found in Fig. 11.1, such as a′ and b′.

Isoquants

Suppose that we want to graph the different combinations of labor and capital that produce 15 sweaters a day. Such a graph would be an isoquant. An **isoquant** is a curve that shows the different combinations of labor and capital required to produce a given quantity of output. The word *isoquant* means "equal quantity"—*iso* meaning equal and *quant* meaning quantity. Fig. 11.2 illustrates an isoquant. Each point (*a, b,* and *c*) represents a technique of production—a combination of workers and knitting machines—that can produce 15 sweaters a day. These three techniques are the same as those that appear in Table 11.1 (and are extracted from Fig. 11.1).

The isoquant in Fig. 11.2 shows more than the three techniques of production set out in the table. It shows *all* the combinations of capital and labor capable of producing 15 sweaters a day. For example, between *a* and *b* there is *a*′. The technique *a*′ combines 3.2 knitting machines with 1.2 workers to produce 15 sweaters a day. Between *b* and *c* is *b*′. Technique *b*′ combines 1.4 units of capital and 2.8 units of labor to produce 15 units of output. (You might think it's strange to talk about fractions of knitting machines and workers. If so, think of Swanky as using three machines full time and another one for one fifth of its time—0.2—so that 3.2 machines are used in total. Similarly, think of Swanky hiring one full-time worker and one part-time worker.)

Marginal Rate of Substitution and Isoquant

The marginal rate of substitution equals the magnitude of the slope of the isoquant. Fig. 11.3 illustrates this relationship. The figure shows the isoquant for 13 sweaters a day. Pick any point on this isoquant and imagine increasing labor by the smallest conceivable amount and decreasing capital in order to keep output constant at 13 sweaters. As we lower the capital input and raise the labor input, we travel along the isoquant. If the isoquant is steep (as at point *a*), the capital input falls by a large amount relative to the rise in the labor input. The marginal rate of substitution is high. But if the isoquant has a gentle slope (as at point *b*), the fall in capital is small relative to the rise in labor and the marginal rate of substitution is small.

The marginal rate of substitution at point *a* is the slope of the straight red line that is tangent to the isoquant at point *a*. The slope of the isoquant at point *a* is the same as the slope of the line. To calculate that slope, use the formula Δy divided by Δx. Along the red line, if capital (y) falls by 5 knitting machines, labor (x) rises by 2.5 workers. The magnitude of the slope is 5 divided by 2.5, which equals 2. Thus when using technique *a* to produce 13 sweaters a day, the marginal rate of substitution of capital for labor is 2.

The marginal rate of substitution at point *b* is the slope of the straight red line that is tangent to the isoquant at point *b*. This line has the same slope as the isoquant at point *b*. That slope is 2.5 knitting machines (Δy) divided by 5 workers (Δx), which equals ½. Thus when using technique *b* to produce 13 sweaters a day, the marginal rate of substitution of capital for labor is ½.

You can now see that the law of diminishing marginal rate of substitution is embedded in the shape of the isoquant. When the capital input is large and the labor input is small, the isoquant is steep. As the capital input decreases and the labor input increases the slope of the isoquant diminishes. Only curves that are bowed toward the origin have this feature; hence, isoquants are always bowed toward the origin.

Figure 11.3 The Marginal Rate of Substitution

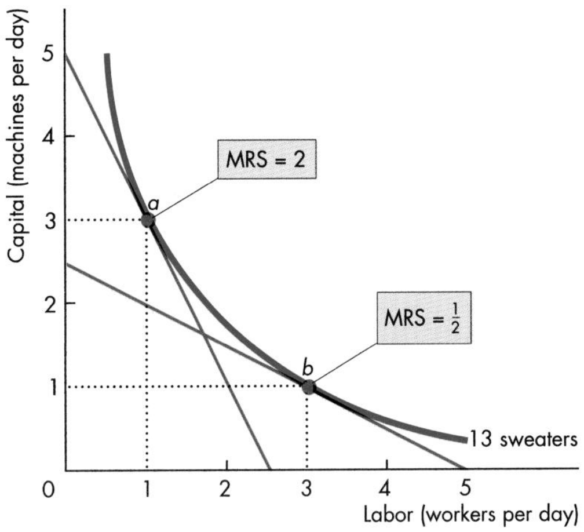

The marginal rate of substitution is measured by the magnitude of the slope of the isoquant. To calculate the marginal rate of substitution at point *a*, use the red line that is tangential to the isoquant at point *a*. Calculate the slope of that line to find the slope of the isoquant at point *a*. The magnitude of the slope at point *a* is 2. Thus at point *a*, the marginal rate of substitution of capital for labor is 2. The marginal rate of substitution at point *b* is found from the slope of the line tangential to the isoquant at that point. That slope is ½. Thus, the marginal rate of substitution of capital for labor at point *b* is ½.

The Isoquant Map

An **isoquant map** shows a series of isoquants, each for a different output. You have already seen two different isoquants in Figs. 11.2 and 11.3 (for 15 and 13 sweaters a day respectively). Figure 11.4(a) shows an isoquant map. It has three isoquants: one for 10 sweaters, the one for 15 sweaters that appears in Fig. 11.2, and one for 21 sweaters. Isoquants for higher outputs are farther from the origin. That is because for any given capital input, to produce more output you need more labor, and for any given labor input, to produce more output you need more capital. Thus starting on any given isoquant if you move to the right (more labor) or upward (more capital) or to the right and upward (more of both capital and labor), you get more output. Each of the isoquants shown in Fig. 11.4(a) is based on the production function presented in Fig. 11.1. But Fig. 11.4(a) does not show all the isoquants.

Figure 11.4 An Isoquant Map

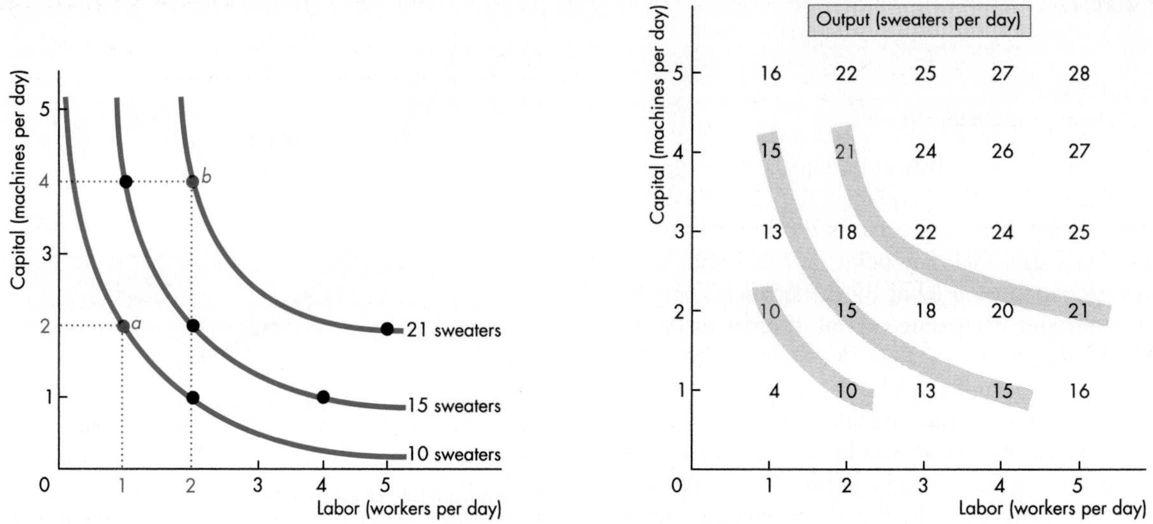

(a) Isoquants **(b) Production function table**

Part (a) is an isoquant map but one that shows only 3 isoquants—those for 10, 15, and 21 sweaters a day. Part (b) highlights from Fig. 11.1 the different ways of producing these output levels. The different ways of producing a given output are connected in part (b) with the light blue curves. These curves correspond to the isoquants in part (a). Each of the points on the isoquants can be found in part (b). For example, point *a* uses 2 machines and 1 worker to produce 10 sweaters, and point *b* uses 4 machines and 2 workers to produce 21 sweaters.

Now, let's make sure that we can see the relationship between the isoquant map in Fig. 11.4(a) and the numbers describing the production function in Fig. 11.1. Figure 11.4(b) is designed to help us do so. It extracts from Fig. 11.1 the three output levels shown by the isoquants in Fig. 11.4(a). Each output level, represented by a number in Fig. 11.4(b), corresponds to a point on an isoquant, and equal outputs are traced by light blue curves that correspond to the isoquants. Let's identify two points on the isoquant map in Fig. 11.4(a) and find them in Fig. 11.4(b). First, consider point *a* on the isoquant for 10 sweaters a day. At point *a,* 2 knitting machines and 1 worker produce the 10 sweaters. We can see that this same information appears in Fig. 11.4(b). Second, consider point *b* on the isoquant for 21 sweaters a day. At point *b,* 4 machines and 2 workers produce 21 sweaters a day. We can also see that this same information appears in Fig. 11.4(b).

R E V I E W

A firm's production function can be shown as an isoquant map. An isoquant shows all the alternative combinations of capital and labor that can produce a given level of output. The slope of an isoquant measures the marginal rate of substitution. The marginal rate of substitution of capital for labor diminishes as the capital input is decreased and the labor input is increased. There is a separate isoquant for each distinct level of output. Thus isoquants are bowed toward the origin. ■

Isoquants are very nice, you might be saying to yourself, but what do we do with them? The answer is that we use them to work out a firm's least-cost technique of production. But to do so, we need a way of illustrating the firm's costs in the same sort of diagram as that containing the isoquants.

Isocost Lines

An **isocost line** shows all the combinations of capital and labor that can be bought for a given total cost. To make the concept of the isocost line as clear as possible, we'll consider the following example. Swanky is going to spend a total of \$100 a day producing sweaters. Knitting-machine operators can be hired for \$25 a day. Knitting machines can be rented for \$25 a day. (We'll consider what happens, below, when these input prices vary.) The table in Fig. 11.5 lists five possible combinations of labor and capital that Swanky can employ for a total cost of \$100. For example, row *b* shows that Swanky can use 3 machines (costing \$75) and 1 worker (costing \$25). The numbers in the table are graphed in the figure and each point, *a* through *e*, represents the corresponding row in the table. If Swanky can employ workers and machines for fractions of a day, then any of the combinations along the line *ae* can be employed for a total cost of \$100. This line is Swanky's isocost line for a total cost of \$100.

Figure 11.5 Swanky's Input Possibilities

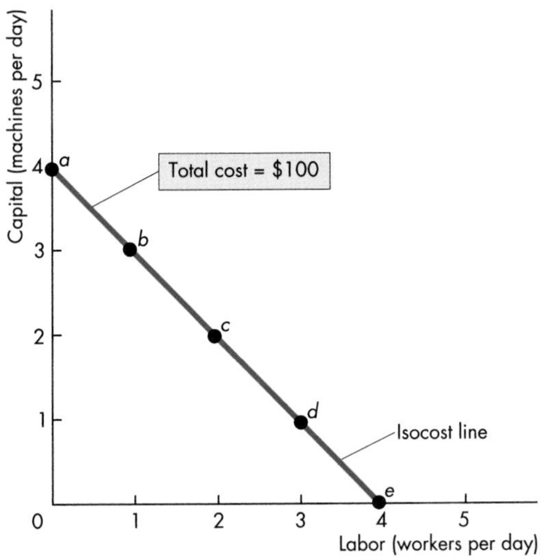

	Capital (machines per day)	Labor (workers per day)
a	4	0
b	3	1
c	2	2
d	1	3
e	0	4

For a given total cost, Swanky's input possibilities depend on input prices. If labor and capital each cost \$25 a day, for a total cost of \$100 Swanky can employ the combinations of capital and labor presented in the table. These combinations are also graphed in the figure. The line passing through points a through e is an isocost line for a total cost of \$100.

Table 11.2 Calculating the Isocost Equation

In general			In Swanky's case
1. The variables			
Total cost	=	TC	$TC = \$100$
Price of labor (daily wage rate)	=	P_L	$P_L = \$25$
Price of capital (daily rental rate of machine)	=	P_K	$P_K = \$25$
Quantity of labor (number of knitting machine operators)	=	L	L = Swanky's choice
Quantity of capital (number of knitting machines)	=	K	K = Swanky's choice
2. Firm's total cost			
$P_L L + P_K K = TC$			$\$25L + \$25K = \$100$
3. Calculating the isocost equation			
■ Divide by P_K to give: $(P_L/P_K)L + K = TC/P_K$			■ Divide by P_K to give: $L + K = 4$
■ Subtract $(P_L/P_K)L$ from both sides to give: $K = TC/P_K - (P_L/P_K)L$			■ Subtract L from both sides to give: $K = 4 - L$

The Isocost Equation

The isocost line can be described by an isocost equation. An **isocost equation** states the relationship between the quantities of inputs that can be hired for a given total cost. Table 11.2 works out the isocost equation by using symbols that apply to any firm and numbers that describe Swanky's situation. The first section of the table lists the variables that affect the firm's total cost. The variables are total cost itself, the prices of the inputs, and the quantities of the inputs employed. We have assigned symbols to each of these variables. In Swanky's case, we're going to look at the amount of labor and capital that can be employed when these two inputs each cost $25 a day and when total cost is $100.

The firm's total cost is set out in the second section of the table. It defines the isocost equation for a given level of total cost. That is, total cost (TC) equals the price of labor (P_L) multiplied by the quantity of labor employed (L) plus the price of capital (P_K) multiplied by the quantity of capital employed (K). In Swanky's case, TC is $100 and the two input prices are $25 each.

The third section of the table shows you how to calculate the isocost equation. There are two steps. First, divide the firm's total cost by the price of capital. Second, subtract $(P_L/P_K)L$ from both sides of the resulting equation. The result is the isocost equation. This equation tells us how the capital input varies as the labor input varies, holding total cost constant. You can check that Swanky's isocost equation corresponds to the isocost line that is graphed in Fig. 11.5. If L is 0, K is 4, which is point *a* in the figure. If L is 1, K is 3, which is point *b* in the figure, and so on.

Figure 11.6 Input Prices and the Isocost Line

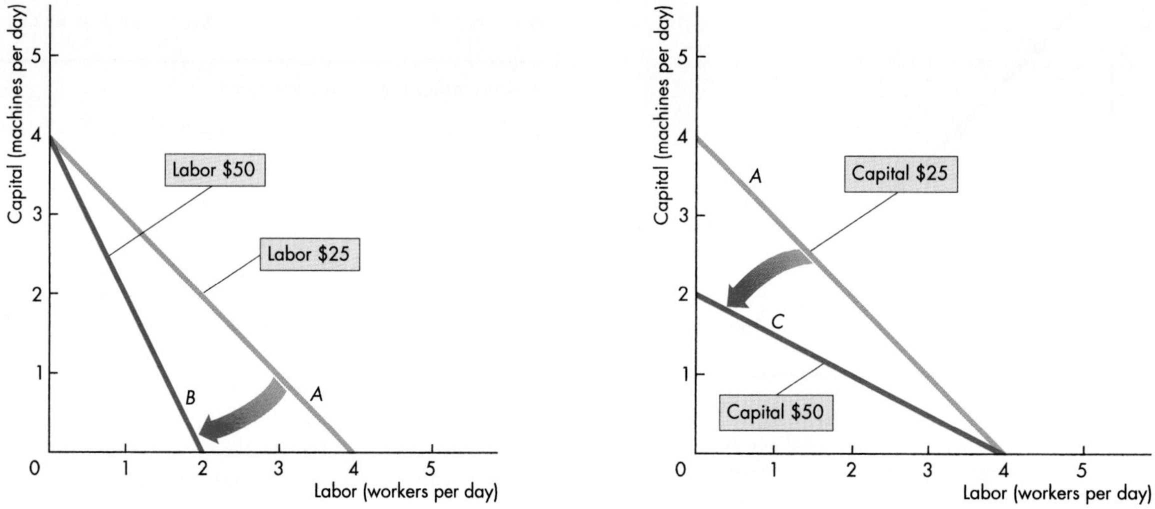

(a) An increase in the price of labor

(b) An increase in the price of capital

Isocost line	Price of capital (rental rate per day)	Price of labor (wage per day)	Isocost equation
A	$25	$25	$K = 4 - L$
B	25	50	$K = 4 - 2L$
C	50	25	$K = 2 - (1/2)L$

The slope of the isocost line depends on the relative input prices. When all the inputs have the same price, the isocost line has a slope of 1. The line labeled *A* shows the isocost line for a total cost of $100 when capital and labor each cost $25 a day. If the price of labor doubles to $50 but the price of capital remains constant at $25, the isocost line for a total cost of $100 will be *B* in part (a). Its slope is twice that of isocost line *A*. If the price of capital doubles to $50 but the price of labor stays at $25, the isocost line for a total cost of $100 will be *C* in part (b). The slope of line *C* is half that of *A*.

The Effect of Input Prices

Along the isocost line that we have just calculated, capital and labor each cost $25 a day. Because these input prices are the same, in order to increase labor by 1 unit, capital must be lowered by 1 unit. The isocost line shown in Fig. 11.5 has a slope of −1. That slope tells us that adding 1 unit of labor costs 1 unit of capital. Isocost lines always slope downward—their slope is always negative. Again, because we know the slope is always negative, we drop the negative sign and talk about the magnitude of the slope. The magnitude of the slope of the isocost line in Fig. 11.5 is 1.

Next, let's consider some different prices, as shown in the table for Fig. 11.6. If the daily wage rate is $50 and the daily rental rate for knitting machines remains at $25, then 1 worker costs the same as 2 machines. Holding total cost constant at $100, to use 1 more worker now requires using 2 fewer machines. With the wage rate double that of the machine rental rate, the isocost line is line *B* in Fig. 11.6(a), and its slope is 2. That is, in order to hire 1 more worker and keep total cost constant, Swanky must give up 2 knitting machines.

If the daily wage rate remains at $25 and the daily rental rate of a knitting machine rises to $50, then 2 workers cost the same as 1 machine. In this case, in order to hire 1 more worker and keep total cost constant, Swanky must give up only half a knitting machine. The slope of the isocost line is now ½—as for line *C* in Fig. 11.6(b).

The higher the relative price of labor, the steeper is the slope of the isocost line. The magnitude of the slope of the isocost line measures the relative price of labor in terms of capital—that is, the price of labor divided by the price of capital.

The Isocost Map

An **isocost map** shows a series of isocost lines, each for a different level of total cost. Obviously, the higher the total cost, the larger the quantities of all inputs that can be employed. Figure 11.7 illustrates an isocost map. In that figure, the middle isocost line is the original one that appears in Fig. 11.5. It is the isocost line for a total cost of $100 when both capital and labor cost $25 a day each. The other two isocost lines in Fig. 11.7 are for a total cost of $125 and $75, holding the prices of the inputs constant at $25 each.

Figure 11.7 An Isocost Map

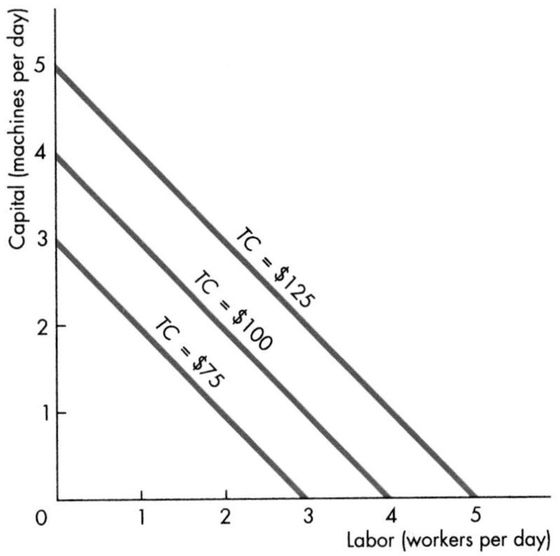

There is an isocost line for each level of cost, and the lines shown here are just a sample. This isocost map shows three isocost lines, one for a total cost of $75, one for $100, and one for $125. For each isocost line, the prices of capital and labor are $25 each. The slope of the lines in an isocost map is determined by the relative price of the two inputs—the price of labor divided by the price of capital. The higher the total cost, the further is the isocost line from the origin.

REVIEW

An isocost line shows all the combinations of capital and labor that can be bought for a given total cost. The slope of an isocost line is the relative price of the two inputs—the price of labor divided by the price of capital. An isocost map shows a series of isocost lines, one for each level of total cost. ■

We now have all the tools that we need to calculate the firm's least-cost technique of production.

The Least-Cost Technique

The **least-cost technique** is the combination of inputs that minimizes total cost of producing a given output. Let's suppose that Swanky wants to produce 15 sweaters a day. What is the least-cost way of doing this? The answer can be seen in Fig. 11.8. The isoquant for 15 sweaters is shown and three points on that isoquant (marked *a*, *b*, and *c*) illustrate the three techniques of producing 15 sweaters that were shown earlier in Fig. 11.1. The figure also contains two isocost lines—each drawn for a price of capital and a price of labor of $25. One isocost line is for a total cost of $125 and the other is for a total cost of $100.

Figure 11.8 The Least-Cost Technique of Production

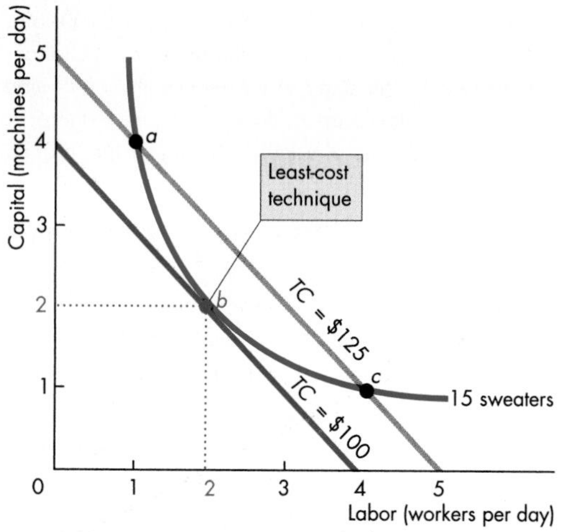

The least-cost technique of producing 15 sweaters occurs when 2 machines and 2 workers are employed at point *b*. An output of 15 sweaters can be produced with the technique illustrated by point *a* (4 machines and 1 worker) or with the technique illustrated by point *c* (1 machine and 4 workers). With either of these techniques, the total cost is $125 and exceeds the total cost at *b* of $100. At *b*, the isoquant for 15 sweaters is tangential to the isocost line for $100. The isocost line and the isoquant have the same slope. If the isoquant intersects the isocost line—for example at *a* and *c*—the least-cost technique has not been found. With the least-cost technique, the marginal rate of substitution (slope of isoquant) equals the relative price of the inputs (slope of isocost line).

First, consider point *a*, which is on the isoquant for 15 sweaters and also on the isocost line with a total cost of $125. Swanky can produce 15 sweaters at point *a* by using 1 worker and 4 machines. The total cost, using this technique of production, is $125. Point *c*, which uses 4 workers and 1 machine, is similar to point *a*, except that it shows another technique by which the firm can produce 15 sweaters for a cost of $125.

Next look at point *b*. At this point, Swanky uses 2 machines and 2 workers to produce 15 sweaters at a total cost of $100. Point *b* is the *least-cost technique* or *the economically efficient technique* for producing 15 sweaters, when knitting machines and workers each cost $25 a day. At those input prices, there is no way that Swanky can produce 15 sweaters for less than $100.

There is an important feature of point *b*, the least-cost technique. At that point, the isoquant on which Swanky is producing (the isoquant for 15 sweaters) has a slope equal to that of the isocost line. The isocost line (for a total cost of $100) is tangential to the isoquant (for 15 sweaters).

Notice that although there is only one way that Swanky can produce 15 sweaters for $100, there are several ways of producing 15 sweaters for more than $100. Techniques shown by point *a* and point *c* are two examples. All the points between *a* and *b* and all the points between *b* and *c* are also ways of producing 15 sweaters for a cost that exceeds $100 but is less than $125. That is, there are isocost lines between those shown, for total costs falling between $100 and $125. Those isocost lines cut the isoquant for 15 sweaters at the points between *a* and *b* and between *b* and *c*. Swanky can also produce 15 sweaters for a cost that even exceeds $125. That is, the firm can change its technique of production by moving to a point on the isoquant higher than point *a* and use a more capital-intensive technique than at point *a* or by moving to a point on the isoquant lower than point *c* and use a more labor-intensive technique than at point *c*. All of these ways of producing 15 sweaters are economically inefficient.

You can see that Swanky cannot produce 15 sweaters for less than $100 by imagining the isocost line for $99. That isocost line will not touch the isoquant for 15 sweaters. That is, the firm cannot produce 15 sweaters for $99. At $25 for a unit of each input, $99 will not buy the inputs required to produce 15 sweaters.

Marginal Rate of Substitution Equals Relative Input Price

When a firm is using the least-cost technique of production, the marginal rate of substitution between the inputs equals their relative price. Recall that the marginal rate of substitution is the slope of an isoquant. Relative input prices are measured by the slope of the isocost line. We've just seen that producing at least cost means producing at a point where the isocost line is tangential to the isoquant. Since the two curves are tangential, their slopes are equal. Hence the marginal rate of substitution (the slope of isoquant) equals the relative input price (the slope of isocost line).

You will perhaps better appreciate the importance of relative input prices if we examine what happens to the least-cost technique when those prices change.

Changes in Input Prices

The least-cost technique of production depends in an important way on the relative prices of the inputs. The case that we've just studied is one in which capital and labor each cost $25 a day. Let's look at two other cases: one where capital costs twice as much as labor and the other where labor costs twice as much as capital.

If knitting machines cost $25 a day and a worker is paid $50 a day, the isocost line becomes twice as steep as the one in Fig. 11.8. That is, to hire one more worker, while holding total cost constant, Swanky has to operate two fewer knitting machines. Let's see how this change in input prices changes the least-cost production technique. Figure 11.9(a) illustrates this. You can see in that figure the isoquant for 15 sweaters a day and the initial inputs of 2 knitting machines and 2 workers. When wages are $50 a day and knitting machines $25 a day, the isocost line becomes steeper. Also, to continue producing 15 sweaters a day, total cost has to rise. That is, the minimum total cost for producing 15 sweaters is higher than originally. The new, steeper isocost line in the figure is that for the minimum cost at which 15 sweaters can be produced at the new input prices. Along that isocost line, Swanky is spending $140. This is the least-cost method of producing 15 sweaters a day; it is achieved by using 3 machines and 1.3 workers

Figure 11.9 Changes in Input Prices

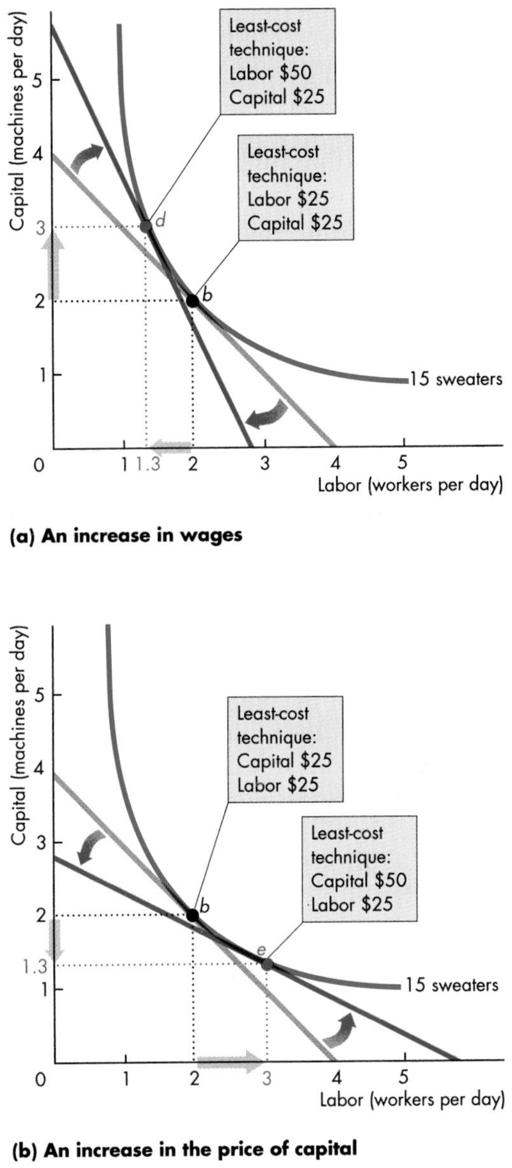

If the price of labor doubles while the price of capital is held constant, the isocost line becomes twice as steep (part a). The least-cost method of producing 15 sweaters a day changes from point *b* to point *d* (using one more machine and 0.7 fewer workers per day). If the price of capital doubles, while the price of labor is held constant, the isocost line becomes half as steep (part b). The least-cost method of producing 15 sweaters a day now changes from point *b* to point *e*. One additional worker is hired and 0.7 fewer machines are used.

a day. (These inputs cost $140: 3 machines × $25 = $75 and 1.3 workers × $50 = $65).

Next, let's see what happens if wages stay constant but the cost of a machine increases. In particular, suppose that knitting machines cost $50 a day while wages stay at $25 a day. In this case, the isocost line becomes less steep. Swanky now has to give up only half a worker-day to get one more machine. The effect of this change on the least-cost technique is illustrated in Fig. 11.9(b). Again, the initial isocost line and least-cost technique are shown in the figure. When the cost of capital increases, the isocost line flattens. The least-cost method of producing 15 sweaters a day now uses 1.3 machines and 3 workers a day. This combination again costs Swanky $140 a day, but it is the least-cost method of producing 15 sweaters a day when machines cost $50 and labor $25 a day.

A change in input prices leads to input substitution. Less of the input whose price has increased and more of the other input are used to produce a given output level. The size of this substitution depends on the technology itself. If the inputs are very close substitutes for each other, the isoquants will be almost straight lines and substitution will be large. If the inputs are not close substitutes for each other, the isoquants will be curved very tightly and quite large changes in input prices would lead to only small substitution effects.

R E V I E W

The least-cost technique of producing a given output is the combination of inputs that minimizes total cost. With the least const technique:

- The slope of the isoquant equals the slope of the isocost line.
- The marginal rate of substitution of capital for labor equals the ratio of the price of labor to the price of capital.
- The higher the price of an input, the less of that input is used to produce a given output. ■

Let's now return to some of the questions with which this chapter opened and see how we can ust the ideas that you've studied here to explain variations in capital intensity, both across different industries and from country to country.

Real World Choice of Technique

We began this chapter by noting that the amount of capital used per unit of labor —capital intensity—varies enormously from one industry to another. We also observed that capital intensity varies across countries. With the tools that you have just discovered, you can interpret these facts.

Industry Variations in Capital Intensity

Variations in capital intensity across industries in a given country arise because of differences in production functions. All firms buy their inputs in common markets, so they have to pay similar input prices. As a result, firms face similar isocost lines. But the isoquants that describe their technologies differ. Figure 11.10 shows possible shapes of isoquants for three industries: plastics, frozen foods, and shirts. With each industry facing a similar isocost line, the least-cost technique chosen varies considerably from one industry to another. In plastics, the chosen point is *a,* a technique using a high capital-labor ratio. Faced with the same input prices, firms producing frozen foods choose point *b,* with an average ratio. Faced with those same input prices, shirt producers choose point *c,* a technique with a low capital-labor ratio.

As input prices change, the least-cost technique changes. The most important such change, over our industrial economic history, has been a steady increase in the relative price of labor. As wages have increased, the isocost line has become steeper over time. As a consequence, firms have substituted capital for labor—they have chosen a more capital-intensive technique. This tendency to increased capital intensity does not only occur in industries such as plastics. It affects all industries.

Differences Across Countries

The differences in capital intensity across countries is explained mainly by differences in wages. In a high-wage country, the isocost lines are steep; in a low-wage country, they are gently sloped. Figure 11.11 shows two isocost lines—one in part (a) for a country in which wages are high and the other in part (b) for a country in which wages are low.

Figure 11.10 Variations in Capital and Labor Inputs Across Industries

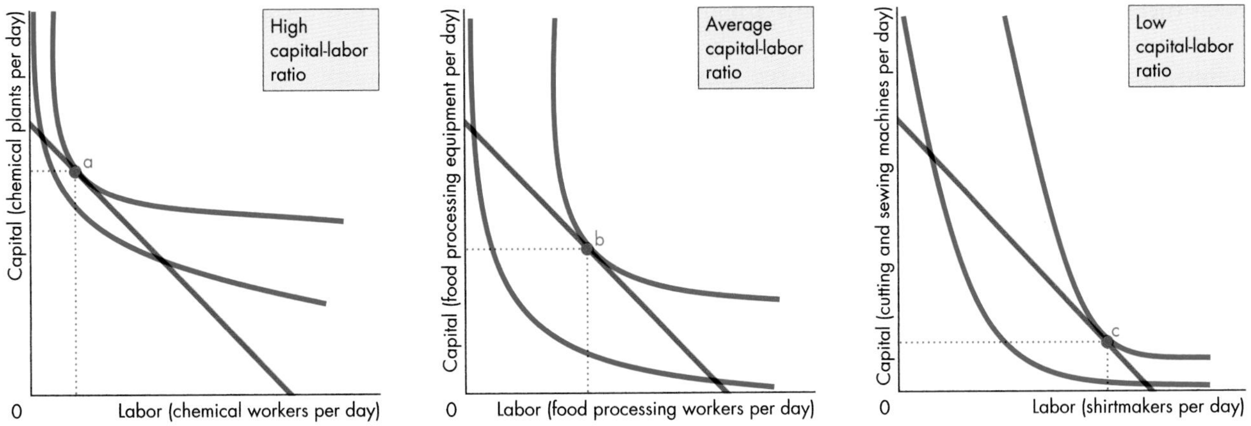

(a) Plastics **(b) Frozen foods** **(c) Shirts**

Variations in the relative amounts of capital and labor employed in different industries arise from differences in technologies. Industries face the same relative input prices (the isocost line) but have different isoquants. Isoquants for plastics (part a), frozen foods (part b), and shirts (part c) are shown in the figure. The least-cost technique for plastics (point *a*) uses a high capital-labor ratio; that for frozen food (point *b*) uses an average capital-labor ratio; and that for shirts (point *c*) uses a low capital-labor ratio.

In contrast with the wages, the isoquants for the two countries are similar. Their similarity arises from the fact that all firms, no matter where they are located, have access to the same technology. (This is true in most cases, but it might not be so if some techniques are protected by patents.) In general, the isoquants in a particular industry are therefore the same for both high-wage and

Figure 11.11 Capital and Labor Inputs in High-Wage and Low-Wage Countries

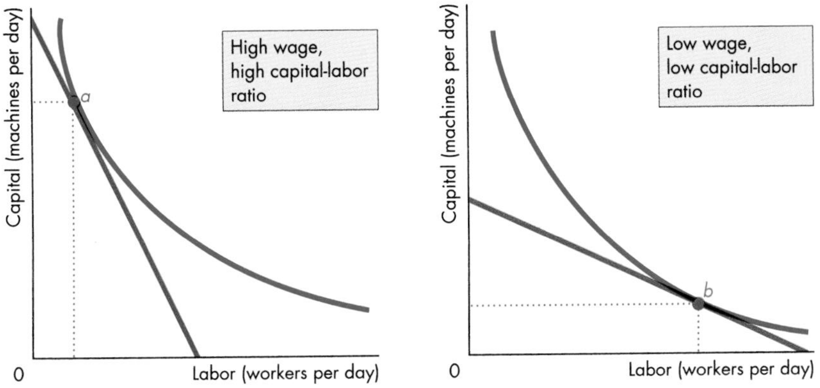

(a) High-wage country **(b) Low-wage country**

In high-wage countries, the isocost line is steep (part *a*), and in low-wage countries, its slope is gentle (part *b*). The same technologies are available in all countries, so the isoquants are the same for both countries. The least-cost technique in a high-wage country (point *a*) uses a high capital-labor ratio. The least-cost technique in a low-wage country (point *b*) uses a low capital-labor ratio.

low-wage countries. One such isoquant is shown in Fig. 11.11. For the high-wage country, the least-cost technique of production is at point *a;* for the low-wage country, it is at point *b.* In low-wage countries, firms use a more labor-intensive technique than in high-wage countries, where a more capital-intensive technique is adopted. As wages rise in poorer countries, firms gradually slide along their isoquants and use a more capital-intensive technique of production. If in high-wage countries wages rise further, relative to the cost of capital, then firms in these countries, too, will use an even more capital-intensive technique of production.

You can now see why gold mines in Amazonia look very different from strip mines in North America. With low wages and a high cost of capital, it pays Brazilian gold mine operators to use a very labor-intensive production technique. With a high wage rate and a low cost of capital, it pays the mining companies of the United States to use a highly capital-intensive technique of production. As wages gradually rise in Brazil, more and more capital will be substituted for labor and those Amazonian gold mines will look like strip mines in the United States.

Marginal Product and Marginal Cost

When we studied short-run and long-run cost in Chapter 10, we learned about the connection between the marginal product curve of a variable input and the marginal cost curve. In the output range over which marginal product increases, marginal cost decreases; in the output range over which marginal product decreases, marginal cost increases. We also learned, in Chapter 10, that it will pay a firm to change its plant size if a different plant can produce the firm's desired output at a lower short-run cost than the existing plant. In this chapter, we learned how to calculate the firm's cost-minimizing combination of capital (plant) and labor. Thus our discussion of product curves and cost curves in Chapter 10 and of isocost lines, isoquants, and least-cost techniques of production in this chapter are both dealing with the same problem. But they're looking at the problem from different viewpoints. Let's examine the connection between these two approaches to the firm's cost minimization problem.

First, we're going to learn about the relationship between the marginal rate of substitution and marginal product.

Marginal Rate of Substitution and Marginal Products

The marginal rate of substitution and the marginal products are linked together in a simple formula:

The marginal rate of substitution of capital for labor equals the marginal product of labor divided by the marginal product of capital.

A few steps of reasoning are needed to establish this fact. First, we know that output changes when a firm changes the amount of labor and capital employed. Furthermore, we know that the effect on output of a change in one of the inputs is determined by the marginal product of the input. That is:

$$\text{Change in output} = \text{Marginal product of labor} \cdot \Delta L + \text{Marginal product of capital} \cdot \Delta K$$

That is, the change in output is equal to the change in the labor input multiplied by its marginal product plus the change in the capital input multiplied by its marginal product.

Suppose now that the firm wants to remain on an isoquant—that is, Swanky wants to produce the same number of sweaters when it changes its labor and capital inputs. To remain on an isoquant, the change in output must be zero. We can make the change of output zero in the above equation, and doing so yields the equation

$$\text{Marginal product of labor} \cdot \Delta L = -\ \text{Marginal product of capital} \cdot \Delta K.$$

This equation tells us what must happen to the capital and labor inputs for Swanky to stay on an isoquant. If the labor input rises, the capital input must fall or, equivalently, if the labor input falls, the capital input must rise. Thus we can write this equation in a slightly different way to state that

$$\text{Marginal product of labor} \cdot \text{Rise in labor input} = \text{Marginal product of capital} \cdot \text{Fall in capital input}$$

If we divide both sides of the above equation by the rise in the labor input and also divide both sides by the marginal product of capital, we get

$$\frac{\text{Fall in capital}}{\text{Rise in labor}} = \frac{\text{Marginal product of labor}}{\text{Marginal product of capital}}.$$

This equation tells us that, when Swanky remains on an isoquant, the fall in its capital input divided by the rise in its labor input is equal to the marginal product of labor divided by the marginal product of capital. But we have defined the marginal rate of substitution of capital for labor as the fall in capital divided by the rise in labor when we remain on a given isoquant. What we have discovered, then, is that the marginal rate of substitution of capital for labor is the ratio of the marginal product of labor to the marginal product of capital.

Marginal Cost

We can use the fact that we have just discovered—that the marginal rate of substitution of capital for labor equals the ratio of the marginal product of labor to the marginal product of capital—to work out an important implication of cost minimization. A few steps are needed and Table 11.3 provides a guide to those steps.

Part (a) defines some symbols. Part (b) reminds us that the marginal rate of substitution of capital for labor is the slope of the isoquant, which in turn equals the ratio of the marginal product of labor (MP_L) to the marginal product of capital (MP_K). Part (b) also reminds us that the slope of the isocost line equals the ratio of the price of labor (P_L) to the price of capital (P_K). Part (c) of the table summarizes some propositions about a firm that is using the least-cost technique of production.

The first of these propositions is that when the least-cost technique is employed, the slope of the isoquant and the slope of the isocost line are the same. That is,

$$MP_L/MP_K = P_L/P_K$$

The second proposition is that total cost is minimized when the marginal product per dollar spent on labor equals the marginal product per dollar spent on capital. To see why, just rearrange the above equation in the following way. First, multiply both sides by the marginal product of capital and then divide both sides by the price of labor.

Table 11.3 The Least-Cost Technique

(a) Symbols

Marginal rate of substitution of capital for labor	*MRS*
Marginal product of labor	MP_L
Marginal product of capital	MP_K
Price of labor	P_L
Price of capital	P_K

(b)Definitions

Slope of the isoquant (*MRS*)	MP_L/MP_K
Slope of the isocost line	P_L/P_K

(c) The least-cost technique

Slope of the isoquant = Slope of the isocost line

Therefore:

$$MP_L/MP_K = P_L/P_K$$

Equivalently:

$$MP_L/P_L = MP_K/P_K$$

That is,

Total cost is minimized when the marginal product per dollar spent on labor equals the marginal product per dollar spent on capital.

Equivalently, flipping the last equation over:

For least-cost technique

$$P_L/MP_L = P_K/MP_K$$

That is,

Marginal cost with fixed capital and a change in labor input equals marginal cost with fixed labor and a change in capital input.

We then get:

$$MP_L/P_L = MP_K/P_K$$

This equation says that the marginal product of labor per dollar spent on labor is equal to the marginal product of capital per dollar spent on capital. In other words, the extra output from the last dollar spent on labor equals the extra output from the last dollar spent on capital. This makes sense. If the extra output from the last dollar spent on labor exceeds the extra output from the last dollar spent on capital, it will pay the firm to use less capital and use more labor. By doing so, it could produce the same output at a lower total cost. Conversely, if the extra output from the last dollar spent on capital exceeds the extra output from the last dollar spent on labor, it will pay the firm to use less labor and use more capital. Again, by so doing, it lowers the cost of producing a given output. A firm achieves the least-cost technique of production only when the extra output from the last dollar spent on all the inputs is the same.

The third proposition is that marginal cost with fixed capital and variable labor equals marginal cost with fixed labor and variable capital. To see this proposition, simply flip the last equation over and write it as

$$P_L/MP_L = P_K/MP_K.$$

Expressed in words, this equation says that the price of labor divided by its marginal product must equal the price of capital divided by its marginal product. But what is the price of an input divided by its marginal product? The price of labor divided by the marginal product of labor is marginal cost when the capital input is held constant. To see why this is so, first recall the definition of marginal cost: *Marginal cost* is the change in total cost resulting from a unit increase in output. If output rises because one more unit of labor is employed, total cost rises by the cost of the extra labor, and output rises by the marginal product of the labor. So marginal cost is the price of labor divided by the marginal product of labor. For example, if labor costs $25 a day and if the marginal product of labor is 2 sweaters, then the marginal cost of a sweater is $12.50 ($25 divided by 2).

The price of capital divided by the marginal product of capital has a similar interpretation. The price of capital divided by the marginal product of capital is marginal cost when the labor input is constant. As you can see from the above equation, with the least-cost technique of production, marginal cost is the same regardless of whether the capital input is constant and more labor is used, or the labor input is constant and more capital is used.

R E V I E W

If a firm wants to increase output, it looks at the various methods available for achieving that end. If one of the methods of increasing output adds less to cost than some other method does, then that method is used. Even if the firm doesn't want to increase output, if the marginal cost of production using one input exceeds that of using another, it will pay the firm to decrease its use of the input whose contribution to marginal cost is highest and increase the use of the input whose contribution to marginal cost is lowest. Only when all inputs have the same impact on marginal cost has the firm achieved the minimum cost method of production. ■

■ We have now seen how firms choose their capital and labor inputs to minimize the cost of producing a given level of output. We've also seen how that choice is influenced by the relative prices of capital and labor. Our next task is to study the interactions of firms and households in markets for goods and services and see how prices, output levels, and profits are determined.

S U M M A R Y

Input Substitution

A given amount of output can be produced by using a small amount of capital and a large amount of labor (a labor-intensive technique) or a small amount of labor and a large amount of capital (a capital-intensive technique). The production function describes the maximum output that can be produced by different combinations of capital and labor. The marginal rate of substitution of capital for labor measures the decrease in capital per unit increase in labor that keeps output constant. (pp. 258–260)

Isoquants

An isoquant is a curve that shows the different combinations of inputs that can produce a fixed amount of output. The magnitude of the slope of the isoquant equals the marginal rate of substitution. An isoquant map shows a series of isoquants, each for a different level of output. Isoquants for larger outputs are farther from the origin. (pp. 260–262)

Isocost Lines

An isocost line shows the combinations of capital and labor that can be bought for a given total cost. An isocost map shows a series of isocost lines, each for a different level of total cost. The slope of an isocost line is the ratio of the price of labor to the price of capital—the relative price of labor. (pp. 263–265)

The Least-Cost Technique

The least-cost technique of production is the least expensive combination of inputs that produces a given output. The least-cost technique of producing a given output occurs where an isocost line is tangential to the isoquant. With the least-cost technique, the marginal rate of substitution of capital for labor equals the ratio of the price of labor to the price of capital.

A change in input prices changes the least-cost production technique. The higher the price of an input, the smaller is the quantity of that input used in the least-cost technique. (pp. 266–268)

Real World Choice of Technique

Variations in capital intensity across industries occur because of differences in production functions. Some industries have isoquants that lead them to choose a capital-intensive technique as the least-cost technique of production. Others have isoquants that lead to a labor-intensive technique of production.

Capital intensity varies in different countries mainly because of differences in wages. In a high-wage country, the isocost lines are steeper; in a low-wage country, they are more gently sloped. Thus firms in high-wage countries use capital-intensive techniques while those in low-wage countries adopt labor-intensive techniques. (pp. 268–270)

Marginal Product and Marginal Cost

The marginal rate of substitution of capital for labor also equals the ratio of the marginal product of labor to the marginal product of capital. When total cost is minimized, the ratio of the marginal product of labor to the marginal product of capital equals the ratio of the price of labor to the price of capital. This fact implies that when the least-cost technique of production is used, the marginal product of labor per dollar spent on labor is equal to the marginal product of capital per dollar spent on capital. (p. 270–272)

KEY CONCEPTS

Key Figures and Tables

REVIEW QUESTIONS

1 What is a production function?

2 Define the marginal rate of substitution.

3 How is the marginal rate of substitution calculated?

4 What is an isoquant?

5 What does the slope of an isoquant measure?

6 What is an isocost line?

7 What does the slope of an isocost line measure?

8 Describe the conditions that are satisfied when a firm has chosen the least-cost technique for producing a given output.

9 How does the least-cost technique change when input prices change?

10 Why do we observe variations in capital intensity across industries in a given country?

11 Why do we observe variations in capital intensity between countries?

12 What is the relationship between the marginal rate of substitution and the marginal product of labor and capital?

13 When costs are minimized, what is the relationship between the marginal cost of increasing output by using more capital and that from using more labor?

PROBLEMS

1 The following table shows the output per hour of a doughnut producer, using alternative combinations of capital and labor.

Units of capital	Units of Labor 1	2	3
3	280	430	490
2	190	280	320
1	100	160	190

Sketch the isoquants for 190 and 280 doughnuts an hour and identify two points on each isoquant.

2 Calculate the marginal rate of substitution of capital for labor in problem 1 if the firm switches the method of production from:

a) 1 unit of labor and 3 units of capital to 2 units of each.

b) 2 units of capital and 1 unit of labor to 1 unit of capital and 3 units of labor.

3 Suppose that labor costs $10 an hour and capital rents for $15 an hour. Calculate the isocost equation.

4 Given the information in problems 1 and 3, what is the least-cost technique of producing:

a) 190 doughnuts an hour

b) 280 doughnuts an hour

(Use only whole units, not fractions of units, of labor and capital.)

5 When the least-cost technique is being used in problem 4, what is the marginal cost of labor and of capital?

6 Suppose that labor costs rise to $15 an hour and the cost of capital equipment falls to $10 an hour. Calculate the isocost equation.

7 Given the information in problem 6, what is the doughnut producer's least-cost technique of producing:

a) 190 doughnuts an hour

b) 280 doughnuts an hour

(Use only whole units, not fractions of units, of labor and capital.)

8 When the least-cost technique is being used in problem 7, what is the marginal cost of labor and of capital?

9 Compare your answers to problems 3 and 6. What do they tell us about the effect of relative input prices on the slope of the isocost line?

10 Compare your answers to problems 4 and 7. What do they tell us about the effects of relative input prices on the least-cost technique of production?

Part 5

Markets for Goods and Services

Talking with Hugo Sonnenschein

Hugo Sonnenschein is a microeconomic theorist whose research has focused on general equilibrium and game theory. For many years a professor of economics at Princeton University, he is now the Dean of Arts and Sciences at the University of Pennsylvania. Michael Parkin spoke with Dean Sonnenschein about how he became interested in economics and his view of the importance of economic theory.

Dean Sonnenschein, what brought you to the study of economics?

My first course in economics, if the truth be told, was not entirely satisfactory. It was definitely not a case of love at first sight. As a senior I enrolled in a statistics course for social scientists to satisfy a distribution requirement, though as a mathematics major, I had actually taken advanced statistics by then. When my professor discovered that I was substantially overprepared, he suggested that I go to the university library, find the journal *Econometrica,* and write some critical reviews of papers that used interesting mathematical methods to do economics. I quickly found an article about Kenneth Arrow's general possibility theorem. It so fascinated me that I tore up my acceptances to mathematics graduate school and set off for graduate school in economics instead. I have never regretted this decision.

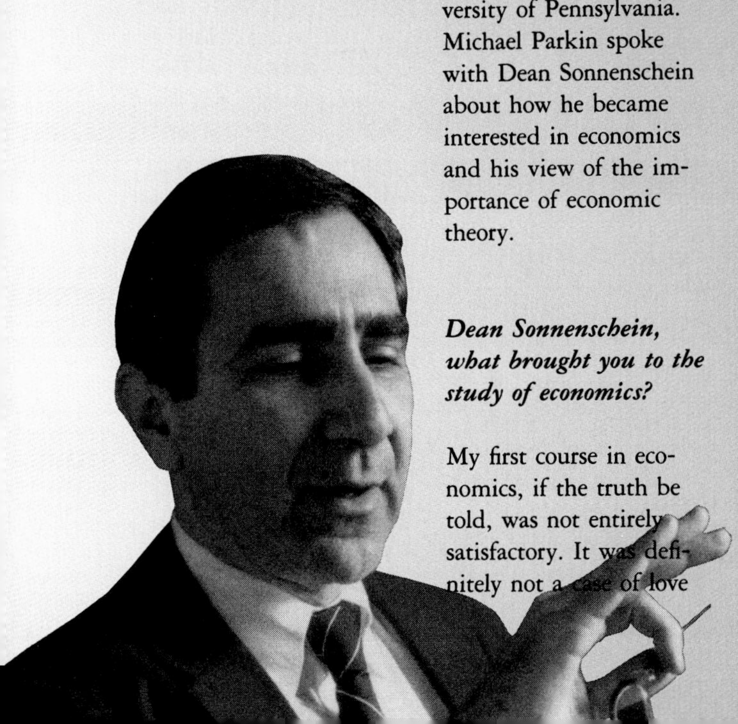

"Economics involves mathematics but within the context of real people in social relationships."

What was it about this work that so appealed to you?

It involves mathematics but within the context of real people in social relationships. I hadn't seen that in my introductory economics courses. Perhaps I should have, but I didn't. Instead, I saw a lot of demand and supply curves. The big picture of "what is to be

produced, the method of production, and the distribution of output" was not at first apparent to me. Economics is concerned with social equilibrium, how people interact, sometimes working together, and sometimes opposing each other. When I finally understood this I started really to love economics.

How do you like to think about social relationships, about how people interact in markets?

My attraction was first to ideas that are similar to game theory, although I didn't recognize that at

the time. I am drawn to problems that have two or three people coming together with different goals, controlling different possible actions, but who will share some kind of outcome as a result of their interaction. When the problem is put this way, it is as much sociology or political science as it is economics. Approaching this setting in formal terms is where economists and game theorists have made particular contributions.

Can you define game theory for us in your own terms?

Game theory tries to explain how individuals behave in situations with elements of both cooperation and conflict. It explains how they *might* behave and also suggests how they *should* behave. It suggests what the outcome of cooperation and conflict will be.

For a long time before game theory, there were well-developed aspects of decision theory that considered how individuals operating independently should act in a situation that had more than one

option, with consequences associated with each option. Everything changes when you speak about how agents will or should behave when there is more than one agent making choices. With many agents, what each individual should do depends on what he believes others will do. In economics, this feature is central to our simplest descriptions of what happens in markets when there are a small number of buyers or sellers.

You've also been known for your work in general equilibrium theory. What does this approach tell us about markets and competition?

General equilibrium is based on the explicit realization that the price of any good is determined not only by traits that are specific to it, such as how much of some other commodity an agent will be willing to surrender for one unit of it, or how much of other commodities are needed to produce it. Instead the price of each commodity is determined by the total menu of trade-offs of every commodity versus every other one by all consumers, the total menu of trade-offs in production, and the distribution of wealth among individuals. As a result, changes in taste or technology, which may to the untrained eye appear to influence only a single market, will have ripple effects throughout the economy. Prices will not settle down until all of these ripples dissipate.

Can you give an example of how general equilibrium theory looks at the world?

Let's say that it has been discovered that grapes in a certain region are being sprayed with a chemical that's harmful to humans if eaten. When the news is reported on television, some consumers become worried and stop buying grapes. They may, for example, prefer cherries at the existing prices. A decrease in the demand for grapes and an increase in the demand for cherries will

decrease the price of grapes and increase the price of cherries. Cherries are harvested with specialized machinery and the demand for the machinery will rise. This will lead to an increase in the production of cherry-picking machines. At the same time you'd expect to see research on safer ways to spray grapes. The demand for biochemists and entomologists will be affected. This may even have some small effect on the demand for Deans of Arts and Sciences. All of these changes and many more from a single economic event, and their impact will depend on a lengthy menu of tradeoffs.

Are game theory and general equilibrium theory compatible approaches?

Yes. I view general equilibrium theory and game theory as complementary. Also, in many ways they are similar in spirit. A major lesson of both approaches is that in economics everything depends on everything else. In general equilibrium the lesson is that what I pay for a commodity depends on other people's tastes, the distribution of income, and the production processes for many different commodities. In game theory the lesson is that what I should choose depends on what others choose, because their actions influence the consequences of my own actions.

One of the most important uses of general

"In economics everything depends on everything else."

equilibrium theory has been to explore Adam Smith's idea that individuals serving their own interests, and not intending to help others, will somehow promote the social good. This problem has been studied for many decades. Currently the best statement of conditions under which self-interested behavior serves to promote the social good is based on the 1950s work of Kenneth Arrow and Gerard Debreu. Game theory has enabled us to appreciate more fully the restrictive nature of their results. It has at the same time led to models that support the general equilibrium theory. One could argue that the most important developments in general equilibrium theory over the past 30 years are a collection of results that provide game theory underpinnings for the general equilibrium theory of competitive markets.

"There are not many areas in which economists can predict what lies more than a few feet down the road."

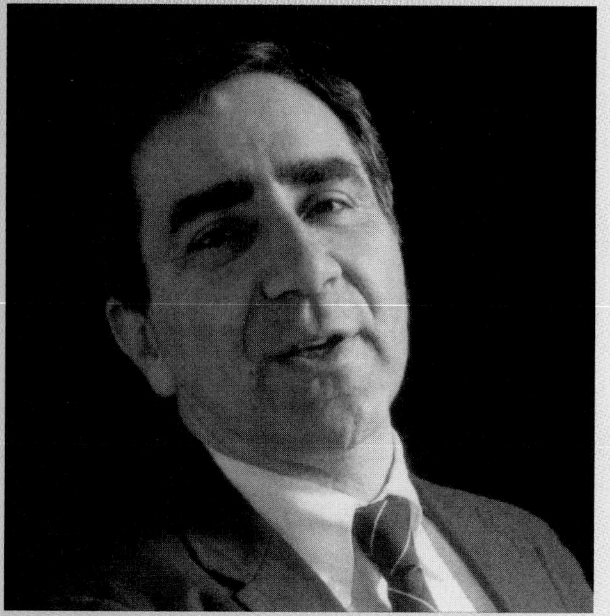

Our discussion has been largely about insights and principles, not about things that have empirical results. Do you have to be interested only in theory to do your kind of economics? Is there any practical value to it?

Insights and principles are not to be disparaged. They are what enable us to put rockets into the air and grow crops more efficiently. They can help a manager to run a firm with success and a legislator to understand more fully the likely impact of proposed quotas and taxes. Theory can be useful and provide powerful insights or it can be vacuous and uninformative. Similarly, some empirical work is meaningless, since it concerns the measurement of quantities which are ill-defined or can only be measured by imposing implausible structural hypotheses.

Empirical work is *per se* no more or less relevant than theory. Even with the best of our theories and the best of our empirical work, there are not many areas in which economists can predict very well what lies more than a few feet down the road. Economics is not for those who are attracted to real-world problems which have simple and clear solutions. For these individuals I recommend astrology. In economics we are fortunate when one or two important aspects of a problem under study have reasonably tractable solutions.

I look at it this way. For economics to be applied well, one must pick carefully the aspects that will be exposed to formal analysis. Theoretical and empirical methods, used with judgment and skill, can often shed important light. Economic theory is especially exciting today, because we are making great strides in our ability to organize ideas that are quite clearly relevant to everyday affairs.

Chapter 12

Competition

After studying this chapter, you will be able to:

- Define perfect competition
- Explain why a perfectly competitive firm cannot influence the market price
- Explain how a competitive industry's output changes when price changes
- Explain why firms sometimes shut down temporarily and lay off workers
- Explain why firms enter and leave an industry
- Predict the effects on an industry and on a typical firm of a change in demand and of a technological advance
- Explain why farmers have had such a bad time in recent years
- Explain why perfect competition is efficient

Hot Rivalry in Ice Cream

Ice cream is big business. In 1988, close to one billion gallons were bought—an average of four gallons per person—at a cost of more than $7 billion. Of the two basic kinds of ice cream—"economy" and "super premium"—the market for economy is the largest but that for super premium is growing fastest. ■ Competition in the ice cream industry is fierce. Great Midwestern Ice Cream, named the best in America by *People* and *Playboy* magazines, nevertheless had to cut back ambitious expansion plans when it discovered that supermarkets were not willing to carry its product. Competition is especially fierce in the super premium category. National names, such as Häagen-Dazs and Frusen Glädjé, are competing with other national, regional, and local brands. Ben and Jerry's, Steve's, Larry's, Emack & Bolio's, Hilary's, Dave's, Damian's, Bart's, and Annabel's are all battling for a place in a crowded market. ■ In this fiercely competitive environment, new firms are entering and trying their luck while other firms are being squeezed out of the business. Some are growing and disappearing in a matter of months. One example is Steve's Homemade Ice Cream, Inc., of Bloomfield, New Jersey. After growing 56 percent in 1987, sales became stagnant in 1988. Although the firm still exists, ice cream is no longer its major product. Steve's is now moving into microwave sundaes and other products. Many other ice cream producers are moving into frozen yogurt. Baskin Robbins has even changed its name to Baskin Robbins Ice Cream and Yogurt.[1] ■ How does competition affect prices and profits? What causes some firms to leave an industry and others to enter it? What are the effects on profits and prices of new firms entering and old firms leaving an industry?

---

[1]This account of the ice cream industry is based on "Ice Cream Makers' Rivalry Heating Up" by Lawrence Ingrassia, *Wall Street Journal,* (December 21, 1988): p. B1.

■ In 1982 and 1983, more than ten million people were unemployed. Of these, six million were unemployed because they had lost their jobs. Many of these job losers had worked for firms that had gone out of business. But most of them were laid off by firms seeking to trim their costs and avoid bankruptcy. Ice cream producers, car producers, computer manufacturers, and firms in almost every sector of the economy were laying off their workers on a massive scale. Those years were unusually harsh ones, but even in a typical year, more than three million people are unemployed as a result of firms trimming back the scale of their labor force. Why do firms lay off workers? When will a firm temporarily shut down, laying off all its workers? ■ Over the past few years, there has been a dramatic fall in the prices of all kinds of consumer goods, such as VCRs, Walkmans, pocket calculators, and personal computers. What exactly goes on in an industry when the price of its output falls dramatically? What causes the price to fall and what happens to the profits of the firms that produce such goods? ■ American farms have been in the news a great deal in recent years. Most farmers have fallen on very hard times. Many of them have gone out of business. What is happening in the farm sector that is creating such serious problems?

■ With what you learn in this chapter you will be able to make sense of the phenomena that we have just described and the questions that we have posed. To tackle these issues, we have to look beyond the individual firm standing in isolation and think about how firms interact with each other. Most goods are produced by more than one firm, so the firms themselves compete with each other. Each firm tries to outdo its rivals by producing at a lower cost and by selling a larger output, thereby making the biggest possible profit. We will study markets in which firms are locked together in such stiff competition with each other that the best a firm can do is to match its rivals in terms of quality and price. We will study other types of markets in the following two chapters. But what we learn in this chapter will help us to understand a wide variety of business situations including the facts and puzzles we have just reviewed.

Perfect Competition

In order to study competitive markets, we are going to build a model of a market in which competition is as fierce and extreme as possible. Economists call the most extreme form of competition perfect competition. **Perfect competition** occurs in a market where:

- There are many firms, each selling an identical product.
- There are many buyers.
- There are no restrictions on entry into the industry.
- Firms in the industry have no advantage over potential new entrants.
- Firms and buyers are completely informed about the prices of the products of each firm in the industry.

Therefore, in perfect competition no single firm can exert a significant influence on the market price of a good. Firms in such markets are said to be price takers. A **price taker** is a firm that cannot influence the price of its product.

Perfect competition does not occur frequently in the real world, but in many industries competition is so fierce that the model of perfect competition that we are about to study is of enormous help in predicting the behavior of the firms in these industries. Ice cream making and retailing, farming, fishing, wood pulping and paper milling, the manufacture of paper cups and plastic shopping bags, grocery retailing, photo-finishing, lawn service, plumbing, painting, and dry cleaning and the provision of laundry services are all examples of industries that are highly competitive.

When a Firm Can't Influence Price

Perfectly competitive or, equivalently, price-taking behavior occurs in markets in which a single firm produces a small fraction of the total output of a particular good. Imagine for a moment that you are a wheat farmer in Kansas. You have a thousand acres under cultivation—which sounds like a lot. But then you go on a drive, first heading west. The flat lands turn into rolling hills as you head toward the Rocky Mountains, but everywhere you look you see thousands and thousands of acres of wheat. The sun goes down in the west behind millions of acres of golden plants. The next morning, it rises in the east above the same scene. Driving to Colorado, Oklahoma, Texas, back up to Nebraska and the Dakotas, reveals similar vistas. You also find unbroken stretches of wheat in Canada, Argentina, Australia, and the Soviet Union. Your thousand acres is a drop in the bucket. To be accurate, it's a molecule in a bucket.

Table 12.1 A Fishery's Elasticity of Demand

(a) Data[1]

- World output of fish is 169 billion pounds a year.[2]
- The average U.S. fishery produces 1.8 million pounds a year.[3]
- The average price of fish is 37.5 cents a pound.[4]
- The elasticity of demand for fish and fish products η_m is 0.42.

(b) Effect on world price

- If an average U.S. fishery raises output by 100 percent, world output rises by 1.8 million pounds—0.00107 percent.
- To calculate change in world price, use the formula

$$\eta_m = \frac{\text{Percentage change in quantity}}{\text{Percentage change in price,}}$$

which means that

$$\text{Percentage change in price} = \frac{\text{Percent change in quantity}}{\eta_m}$$

- To find the fall in price, use the formula

$$\begin{aligned}\text{Percentage change in price} &= 0.00107/0.42 \\ &= 0.00254 \text{ percent}\end{aligned}$$

So, a price fall of 0.00254 percent is a fall of 0.00095 cents.

- When a firm doubles its output, the price falls by 0.00095 cents.

(c) Fishery's elasticity of demand

- The firm's elasticity of demand (η_f) is given by

$$\begin{aligned}\eta_f &= \frac{\text{Percentage change in firm's output sold}}{\text{Percentage change in price}} \\ &= 100/0.00254 \\ &= 39{,}370\end{aligned}$$

Part (a) provides some data about the market for fish. Most fish is sold frozen and the market for fish is a world-wide market. Part (b) calculates the effects on the world market price of fish if one U.S. fishery doubles its output. If one fishery doubles its output, world output will rise by 1.8 million pounds or change by approximately 0.001 percent. As a result of this increase in output, the world price of fish falls by 0.00254 percent or 0.00095¢ a pound. Part (c) calculates the individual producer's elasticity of demand, η_f. That elasticity is almost 40,000!

[1]The quantity and price data refer to 1982 and are from U.S. Bureau of the Census, *Statistical Abstract of the United States: 1986*, 106th ed. (Washington, D.C.: 1985): 681–9. The estimate of the elasticity of demand for fish products is that in Table 5.3.

[2]*Statistical Abstract*, 683.

[3]In 1982, 3600 fishery shore establishments caught 6367 million pounds (6367 million/3600 = 1.77 million). *Statistical Abstract*, 682–3.

[4]*Statistical Abstract*, 682.

You are a price taker. Nothing makes your wheat any better than any other farmer's. If everybody else sells their wheat for $3 a bushel, and you want $3.10, why would people buy from you? They can simply go to the next farmer, and the one after that, and the next, and buy all they need for $3.

Industry and Firm Elasticity of Demand

A price-taking firm faces a demand curve that is perfectly elastic. To see why this is so, let's consider an example. Suppose that there are 1000 firms of equal size producing a good. Even if one firm doubles its output (a big change for an individual firm), industry output will rise by only 0.01 percent (one thousandth is 0.01 percent). Suppose that the industry elasticity of demand for the good is 0.5, then this increase in industry output results in a 0.02 percent fall in price. To put things in perspective, a price change of this magnitude is $1 on a $500 television set, 10¢ on a $50 dress, or a penny on a $5 movie ticket. But these price changes, although small, are much larger than the ones that result from changes in output of a magnitude that a firm might actually make. Therefore, when a firm changes its output rate, the effect of that change on price is tiny and the firm ignores it. The firm behaves as if its own actions have no effect on the market price.

Table 12.1 works through a real world example —the market for fish—and shows the relationship between the elasticity of demand facing an individual competitive fishery and the fish market as a whole. The market elasticity of demand for fish is 0.42 but the elasticity of demand facing an individual producer is almost 40,000.

When we studied the concept of elasticity in Chapter 5, we discovered that a horizontal demand curve has an elasticity of infinity. An elasticity of 40,000 is not quite infinity, but it is very large. A firm whose demand has such an elasticity has, for all practical purposes, an infinitely elastic demand. Such a firm's demand curve is horizontal. The firm is a price taker.

Competition in Everyday Life

We have defined perfect competition as a market where a firm has no choice but to be a price taker. Even massive percentage changes in a firm's own output have only a negligible effect on the market price. In such a situation, there is little point in a firm attempting to set its own price at a level different from the market. If a firm tries to charge a higher price, no one will buy its output; if it offers its goods for a lower price, it will sell them, but it can sell them for the market price so there is no point in price cutting.

The inability of a perfectly competitive firm to compete by price cutting makes it seem as if a perfectly competitive market is not, in fact, very competitive at all. If firms don't compete on price, in what sense are they competing with each other?

Firms compete with each other in much the same way as athletes or football teams do. Firms try to find new tricks that will give them the edge over their competitors and enable them to win. Sometimes, though, the competition that they face is so stiff that they are left with little room to maneuver. This happens in sporting events, too. For example, when two wrestlers are closely matched, they compete with each other, but neither of them has much room to maneuver. They are locked in such fierce competition that the best they can do is to match each other's moves, try not to make a mistake, and accept the inevitable—that the outcome will be close and may even be a tie.

Like evenly matched athletes, firms in perfect competition are locked in such a fierce competitive struggle with each other that they have no choice other than to mimic each other's actions—producing a comparable quality good at a comparable price—and to put up with an outcome analogous to a tie.

Let's now study the behavior of a perfectly competitive industry, beginning with an examination of the choices made by a typical firm in such an industry.

Firms' Choices in Perfect Competition

A perfectly competitive firm has to make three key decisions:

- Whether to stay in the industry or to leave it
- If the decision is to stay in the industry, whether to produce or to temporarily shut down
- If the decision is to produce, how much to produce

In studying the competitive firm's choices, we will continue to look at a model firm whose single objective is to maximize its profit. We'll first consider a situation in which a firm decides to produce. We will then look at the other cases—firms that decide to shut down production temporarily or to leave the industry altogether.

Profit and Revenue

Profit is the difference between a firm's total revenue and total cost. We defined and studied the behavior of total cost in the last two chapters. But what is total revenue? Let's begin by looking at the concepts of revenue.

Total revenue is the value of a firm's sales. It equals the price of the firm's output multiplied by the number of units of output sold (price times quantity). **Average revenue** is total revenue divided by the total quantity sold—revenue per unit sold. Since total revenue is price times quantity sold, average revenue (total revenue divided by quantity sold) equals price. **Marginal revenue** is the change in total revenue resulting from a one-unit increase in the quantity sold. Since, in the case of perfect competition, the price remains constant when the quantity sold changes, the change in total revenue is equal to price multiplied by the change in quantity. Therefore, in perfect competition, marginal revenue equals price.

An example of these revenue concepts is set out for Swanky, Inc., in Fig. 12.1. The table shows three different quantities of sweaters sold. For a price taker, as the quantity sold varies, the price stays constant—in this example at $25. Total revenue is equal to price multiplied by quantity. For example, if Swanky sells 8 sweaters, total revenue is 8 times $25, which equals $200. Average revenue is total revenue divided by quantity. Again, if Swanky sells 8 sweaters, average revenue is total revenue ($200) divided by

Figure 12.1 Demand, Price, and Revenue in Perfect Competition

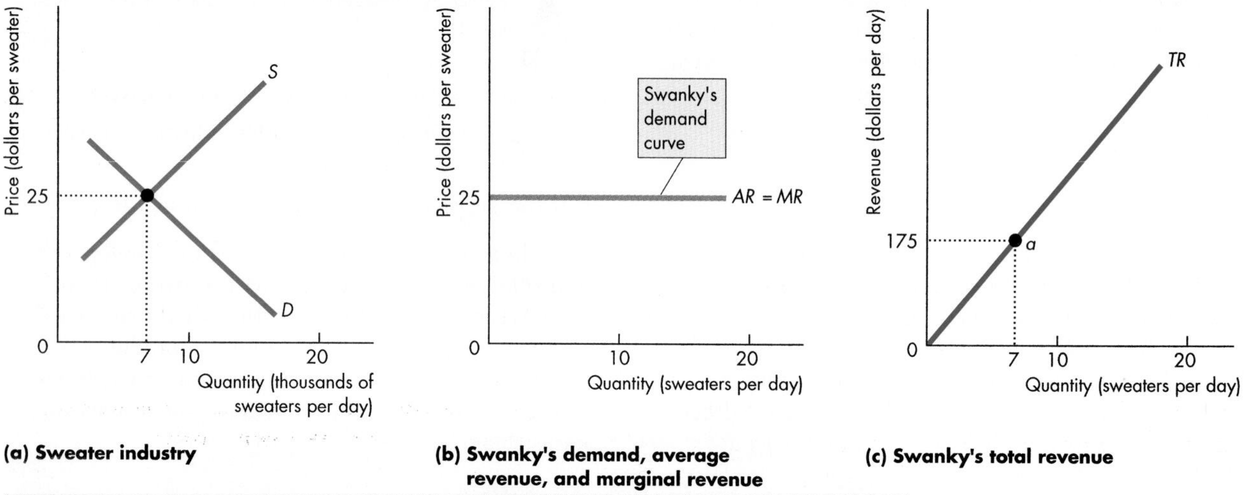

Quantity (Q) (sweaters per day)	Price (P) (dollars per sweater)	Total revenue ($TR = P \times Q$) (dollars)	Average revenue ($AR = TR/Q$) (dollars per sweater)	Marginal revenue ($MR = \Delta TR/\Delta Q$) (dollars per sweater)
7	25	175	25	
				25
8	25	200	25	
				25
9	25	225	25	

In perfect competition, price is determined where the industry demand and supply curves intersect. Such an equilibrium is illustrated in part (a) where the price is $25 and 7000 sweaters are bought and sold. Swanky, a perfectly competitive firm, faces a fixed price, $25 in this example, regardless of the quantity it produces. The table calculates Swanky's total, average, and marginal revenue. For example, when 7 sweaters are sold, total revenue is $175, and average revenue is $25. When sales increase from 7 sweaters to 8 sweaters, marginal revenue equals $25. The demand curve faced by Swanky is perfectly elastic at the market price and is shown in part (b) of the figure. Swanky's demand curve is also its average revenue curve and marginal revenue curve ($AR = MR$). Swanky's total revenue curve (TR) is shown in part (c). Point *a* on the total revenue curve corresponds to the first row of the table.

quantity (8), which equals $25. Marginal revenue is the change in total revenue resulting from a one-unit change in quantity. For example, when the quantity sold rises from 7 to 8, total revenue rises from $175 to $200, so marginal revenue is $25. (Notice that in the table, marginal revenue appears *between* the lines for the quantities sold. This arrangement presents a visual reminder that marginal revenue results from the *change* in the quantity sold.)

Suppose that Swanky is one of a thousand similar small producers of sweaters. The demand and supply curves for the entire sweater industry are shown in Fig. 12.1(a). Demand curve *D* intersects supply curve *S* at a price of $25 and a quantity of 7000 sweaters. Figure 12.1(b) shows Swanky's demand curve. Since the firm is a price taker, its demand curve is perfectly elastic—the horizontal line at $25. The figure also illustrates Swanky's total, average, and marginal revenues, calculated in the table. The average revenue curve and marginal revenue curve are the same as the firm's demand curve. That is, the firm's demand curve tells us the revenue per sweater sold and the change in total revenue that results from selling one more sweater. Swanky's total revenue curve (part c) shows the total revenue for each quantity sold. For example, when Swanky sells 7 sweaters, total revenue is $175 (point *a*). Since each additional sweater sold brings in a constant amount —in this case $25—the total revenue curve is an upward-sloping straight line.

R E V I E W

A firm in a perfectly competitive market is a price taker. The firm's demand curve is perfectly elastic at the market price. The firm's average revenue and marginal revenue are each equal to price so that the marginal revenue and average revenue curves are the same as the firm's demand curve. Total revenue rises as the quantity sold rises. ■

Profit-maximizing Output

Profit is the difference between a firm's total revenue and total cost. Maximizing profit is the same thing as maximizing the difference between total revenue and total cost. Even though a perfectly competitive firm cannot influence its price, it can influence its profit by choosing its level of output. As we have just seen, a perfectly competitive firm's total revenue changes when its output changes. Also, as we discovered in Chapter 10, a firm's total cost varies as its output varies. By changing its inputs and its output, a firm can change its cost. In the *short run,* a firm can change its output by changing its variable inputs and by changing the intensity with which it operates its fixed inputs. In the *long run,* a firm can vary all its inputs. Let's work out how a firm maximizes profit in the short run.

Total Revenue, Total Cost, and Profit Figure 12.2 shows Swanky's total revenue, total cost, and profit both as numbers (in the table) and as curves (in the graphs). Part (a) of the figure shows Swanky's total revenue and total cost curves. These curves are graphs of the numbers shown in the first three columns of the table. The total revenue curve *(TR)* is the same as that in Figure 12.1(c). The total cost curve *(TC)* is similar to the one that you met in Chapter 10. Notice that Swanky's total cost is $25 when output is zero. This amount is Swanky's fixed cost—the cost that is incurred even if nothing is produced and sold. As output increases, so does total cost.

The difference between total revenue and total cost is profit. As you can see in Fig. 12.2(b), Swanky will make a profit at any output above 4 and below 12 sweaters a day. At outputs below 4 sweaters, Swanky makes a loss. A loss is also made if output exceeds 12 sweaters a day. At outputs of 4 sweaters and 12 sweaters, total cost equals total revenue. An output at which total cost equals total revenue is called a **break-even point.**

Swanky's profit, calculated in the final column of the table, is graphed in part (b) of the figure. Notice the relationship between the total revenue, total cost, and profit curves. Profit is measured by the vertical distance between the total revenue and total cost curves. When the total revenue curve in part (a) is above the total cost curve, between 4 and 12 sweaters, the firm is making a profit and the profit curve in part (b) is above the horizontal axis. At the break-even point, where the total cost and total revenue curves intersect, the profit curve cuts the horizontal axis.

When the profit curve is at its highest, the distance between *TR* and *TC* is greatest. In this example, profit maximization occurs at an output of 9 sweaters a day. At this output, profit is $40 a day.

Marginal Calculations

In working out Swanky's profit-maximizing output, we examined its cost and revenue schedules and from all the possibilities picked out the point at which profit is at a maximum. There is a quicker, neater, and more powerful way of figuring out the profit-maximizing output. All Swanky has to do is to calculate its marginal cost and marginal revenue and compare the two. If marginal revenue exceeds marginal cost, it pays to produce more. If marginal revenue is less than marginal cost, it pays to produce less. When marginal revenue and marginal cost are equal, profit is maximized. Let's convince ourselves that this rule works.

Figure 12.2 Total Revenue, Total Cost, and Profit

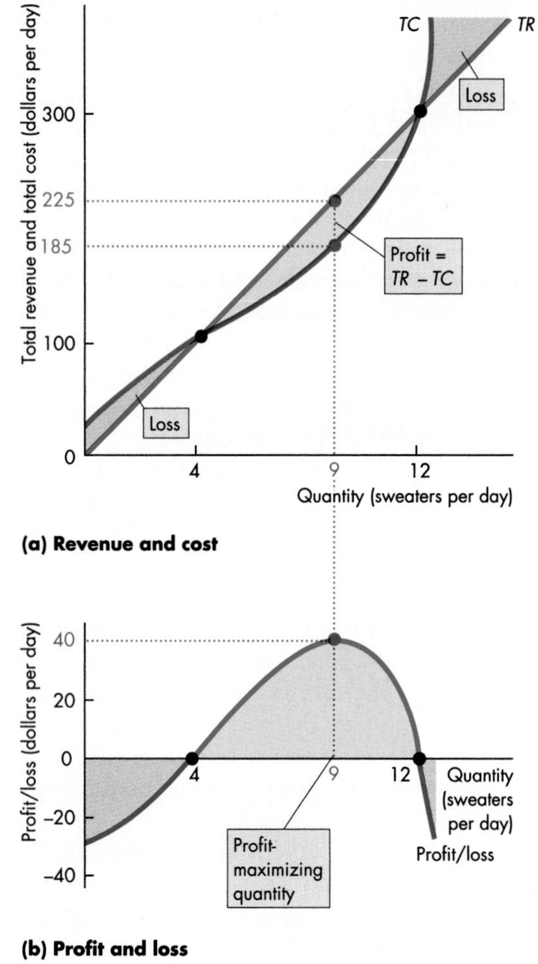

Quantity (Q) (sweaters per day)	Total revenue (TR) (dollars)	Total cost (TC) (dollars)	Profit (TR − TC) (dollars)
0	0	25	−25
1	25	49	−24
2	50	69	−19
3	75	86	−11
4	100	100	0
5	125	114	11
6	150	128	22
7	175	144	31
8	200	163	37
9	225	185	40
10	250	212	38
11	275	246	29
12	300	300	0
13	325	360	−35

The table lists Swanky's total revenue, total cost, and profit. Part (a) graphs the total revenue and total cost curves. Profit is seen in part (a) as the blue area between the total cost and total revenue curves. The maximum profit, $40 a day, occurs when 9 sweaters are produced—where the vertical distance between the total revenue and total cost curves is at its largest. At outputs of 4 sweaters a day and 12 sweaters a day, Swanky makes zero profit—these are break-even points. At outputs below 4 and above 12 sweaters a day, Swanky makes a loss. Part (b) of the figure shows Swanky's profit curve. The profit curve is at its highest when profit is at a maximum and it cuts the horizontal axis at the break-even points.

Look at the table in Fig. 12.3. It records Swanky's marginal cost and marginal revenue. Recall that marginal cost is the change in total cost per unit change in output. For example, when output rises from 8 to 9 sweaters, total cost rises from $163 to $185, a rise of $22, which is the marginal cost of changing the output rate from 8 to 9 sweaters a day. Marginal revenue is the change

Figure 12.3 Marginal Revenue, Marginal Cost, and Profit-Maximizing Output

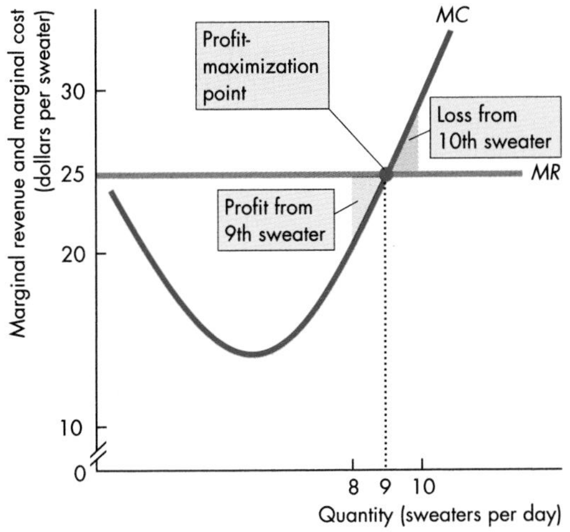

Another way of finding the profit-maximizing output is to determine where marginal revenue equals marginal cost. The table shows that if output rises from 8 to 9 sweaters, marginal cost is $22, which is less than the marginal revenue of $25. If output rises from 9 to 10 sweaters, marginal cost is $27, which exceeds the marginal revenue of $25. The figure shows that marginal cost and marginal revenue are equal when Swanky produces 9 sweaters a day. If marginal revenue exceeds marginal cost, an increase in output increases profit. If marginal revenue is less than marginal cost, an increase in output lowers profit. If marginal revenue equals marginal cost, profit is maximized.

Quantity (*Q*) (sweaters per day)	Total revenue (*TR*) (dollars)	Marginal revenue (*MR*) (dollars per sweater)	Total cost (*TC*) (dollars)	Marginal cost (*MC*) (dollars per sweater)	Profit (*TR* − *TC*) (dollars)
0	0		25		−25
		25		24	
1	25		49		−24
		25		20	
2	50		69		−19
		25		17	
3	75		86		−11
		25		14	
4	100		100		0
		25		14	
5	125		114		11
		25		14	
6	150		128		22
		25		18	
7	175		144		31
		25		19	
8	200		163		37
		25		22	
9	225		185		40
		25		27	
10	250		212		38
		25		34	
11	275		246		29
		25		54	
12	300		300		0
		25		60	
13	325		360		−35

in revenue per unit change in the quantity sold and is, for a perfectly competitive firm, the same as its price. In this case, marginal revenue is $25. The marginal cost and marginal revenue curves corresponding to the table appear in Fig. 12.3.

Now focus on the highlighted row of the table. When output rises from 8 to 9 sweaters, marginal cost is $22. Since marginal revenue is $25, the rise in total revenue exceeds the rise in total cost. Profit goes up by the difference—$3. By looking at the last column of the table, you can see that profit does indeed rise by $3. Because marginal revenue exceeds marginal cost, it pays to expand output from 8 to 9 sweaters. At 8 sweaters a day, profit is $37 and at 9 sweaters a day it is $40—$3 more.

Suppose that output is expanded yet further to 10 sweaters a day. Marginal revenue is still $25, but marginal cost is now $27. Marginal cost exceeds marginal revenue by $2, so expanding output to 10 sweaters increases total cost by $2 more than total revenue and profit falls by $2. So, to maximize profit, all Swanky has to do is to compare marginal cost and marginal revenue. As long as marginal revenue exceeds marginal cost, it pays to increase output. Swanky keeps increasing output until the cost of producing one more sweater equals the price at which the sweater can be sold. At that point, it is making maximum profit. If Swanky makes one more sweater, that sweater will cost more to produce than the revenue it will bring back in, so Swanky will not produce it.

Profits in the Short Run

We've just seen that we can calculate a firm's profit-maximizing output by comparing marginal revenue with marginal cost. But maximizing profit is not the same thing as *making* a profit. Maximizing profit can mean minimizing loss. We cannot tell whether a firm is actually making a profit only by comparing the marginal revenue and marginal cost curves. To check whether a firm is making a profit, we need to look at total revenue and total cost, as we did before, or we need to compare average total cost with price. When a firm makes a profit, average total cost is lower than price. If average total cost exceeds price, the firm makes a loss. When average total cost equals price, the firm breaks even.

Three Possible Profit Outcomes The three possible profit outcomes in the short-run are illustrated in Fig. 12.4. In part (a), Swanky is making an economic profit. At a price of $25, marginal revenue equals marginal cost at an output of 9 sweaters a day. That is, the profit-maximizing output is 9 sweaters a day. Average total cost is lower than the market price and economic profit is represented by the blue rectangle. The height of that rectangle is the gap between price and average total cost, or economic profit per sweater. Its length shows the quantity of sweaters produced. So the rectangle's area measures Swanky's economic profit: profit per sweater (its height—$4.44 a sweater) multiplied by the number of sweaters produced (its length—9 sweaters) equals total profit (its area—$40).

In part (b), Swanky breaks even. At a price of $20, Swanky's profit-maximizing output is 8 sweaters. The average total cost of producing this output level is $20, the same as its price. It is also the minimum average total cost. The maximum profit that Swanky can make in this case is zero.

In part (c), Swanky incurs an economic loss. At a price, of $17, the profit-maximizing output is 7 sweaters. At that output, average total cost is $20.57, so the firm is losing $3.57 a sweater and incurring a total loss of $25.

Temporary Plant Shutdown

There are some situations in which a firm's profit-maximizing decision will be to shut down temporarily, lay off its workers, and produce nothing. Such a situation arises when the price is so low that total revenue is not even enough to cover the variable costs of production. A firm cannot escape its fixed costs. These costs are incurred even at a zero output. A firm that shuts down and produces no output makes a loss equal to its total fixed cost. But this loss is the maximum loss that a firm will make. If the price just equals the average variable cost of production, total revenue equals total variable cost and the loss equals total fixed cost. But if price is below minimum average variable cost, total revenue does not even cover total variable cost and the loss exceeds total fixed cost if the firm produces anything at all. It is in such a situation that the firm minimizes its losses by shutting down, incurring a loss equal to its total fixed cost.

The **shutdown point** is the point at which a firm's maximum profit is the same regardless of whether the firm produces a positive amount of output or produces nothing—temporarily shuts down. The shutdown point is reached when the market price falls to a level equal to the minimum of average variable cost. Table 12.2 illustrates what happens at the shutdown point. The table has two parts: Part (a) shows a case in which it just pays the firm to keep producing, and part (b) shows a case in which it just pays the firm to shut down.

Figure 12.4 Three Possible Profit Outcomes in the Short Run

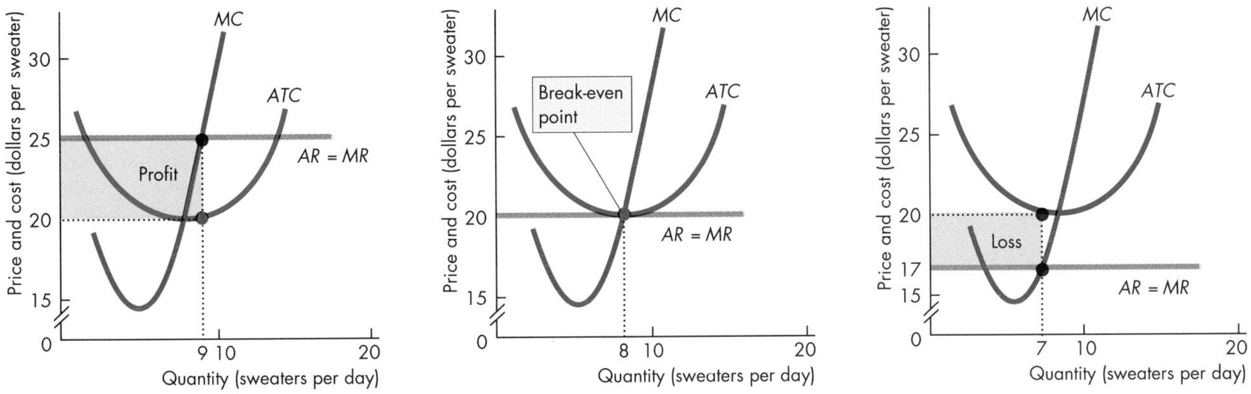

(a) Economic profit **(b) Zero economic profit** **(c) Economic loss**

In the short run, a firm's economic profit may be positive, zero (a breakeven), or negative (a loss). If the market price is greater than the average total cost of producing the profit-maximizing output, the firm makes a profit (part a). If price equals minimum average total cost, the firm breaks even (part b). If the price is below minimum average total cost, the firm makes a loss (part c). The firm's profit is shown as the blue rectangle and the firm's loss is the red rectangle.

The table shows Swanky's total fixed cost, total variable cost, and total cost of producing 6, 7, and 8 sweaters. It also shows the average variable cost and marginal cost. The cost data are the same in both parts (a) and (b) of the table.

Next let's look at the revenue. In part (a), the price of a sweater is $17. To find Swanky's total revenue, multiply the price by the quantity sold. We calculate the profit or loss (and they are all losses in this case) by subtracting total cost from total revenue. For example, if Swanky sells 7 sweaters at $17 each, then total revenue is $119. Total cost is $144, so the loss equals $144 minus $119, which is $25. We calculate the loss from producing 6 sweaters or 8 sweaters in a similar way.

The minimum loss occurs when 7 sweaters are produced. You can see that fact directly by looking at the profit or loss column. You can also check that the loss is minimized by looking at marginal cost and marginal revenue. Increasing output from 6 to 7 sweaters has a marginal cost of $16 but a marginal revenue of $17, so total revenue rises by more than total cost. Increasing output still further, from 7 to 8 sweaters, has a marginal cost of $19, which exceeds marginal revenue, so profit falls (loss rises).

Swanky's loss when producing 7 sweaters exactly equals its total fixed cost—$25. Alternatively, if Swanky produces nothing, it will also lose its $25 of total fixed cost. So, at a price of $17 Swanky is indifferent between producing and shutting down—it makes a loss equal to its fixed cost.

In part (b) the price is $16.99—a lower price but by just a penny. Costs are unchanged. We calculate total revenue and profit in the same way as before. The output that maximizes profit (minimizes loss) is still 7 sweaters but, in this case, the minimum possible loss is $25.07. Swanky loses 7 cents more than it would if it produced nothing at all. The firm will shut down. Its minimum average variable cost is $17. At $17, it just pays to produce and at $16.99 it just pays to shut down. The minimum output that it pays Swanky to produce is 7 sweaters.

Real World Shutdowns Shutdowns occur in the real world either because of a fall in price or be-

Table 12.2 The Shutdown Point

(a) Swanky keeps producing

Output (sweaters per day)	Total fixed cost (dollars)	Total variable cost (dollars)	Total cost (dollars)	Average variable cost (dollars per sweater)	Marginal cost (dollars per sweater)	Price (dollars per sweater)	Total revenue (dollars)	Marginal revenue (dollars per sweater)	Profit(+) loss(−) (dollars)
6	25	103	128	17.17		17	102		−26
					16			17	
7	25	119	144	17.00		17	119		−25
					19			17	
8	25	138	163	17.25		17	136		−27

(b) Swanky shuts down

Output (sweaters per day)	Total fixed cost (dollars)	Total variable cost (dollars)	Total cost (dollars)	Average variable cost (dollars per sweater)	Marginal cost (dollars per sweater)	Price (dollars)	Total revenue (dollars)	Marginal revenue (dollars per sweater)	Profit(+) loss(−) (dollars)
6	25	103	128	17.17		16.99	101.94		−26.06
					16			16.99	
7	25	119	144	17.00		16.99	118.93		−25.07
					19			16.99	
8	25	138	163	17.25		16.99	135.92		−27.08

The shutdown point occurs at the point of minimum average variable cost. If price equals minimum average variable cost, Swanky is indifferent between producing at the shutdown point and producing nothing. If price falls below minimum average variable cost, it pays Swanky to produce nothing. Minimum average variable cost is $17 and occurs at 7 units of output. If the price is $17 and Swanky produces 7 sweaters, its loss equals its total fixed cost of $25 (part a). If the price falls to $16.99, even when it produces at the point of minimum average variable cost, the firm makes a loss that is bigger than its total fixed cost, and so it pays to shut down (part b).

cause of a rise in costs. Shutdowns occur most frequently in raw material producing sectors as a result of fluctuating prices. For example, if the price of gold falls, gold mines temporarily stop producing. If the price of nickel falls, nickel mines shut down. Shutdowns also occur in many industries—such as those producing ice cream, cars, and air transportation services.

A famous example of an airline shutdown occurred in 1982. Braniff, a Dallas-based airline, had grown rapidly following the deregulation of the airline business in 1982. When 1000 new domestic routes became available, Braniff's aggressive chairman, Harding Lawrence, applied for 624 of them, spreading over the Southwest and Southeast. The company also added routes to Asia, Europe, and the Middle East. If airfares had remained stable, the company's expansion plans would have been highly profitable. But the airlines became embroiled in a fare-cutting orgy, and at a time when fuel prices were rising sharply. Braniff, vastly overextended, lost more than $40 million in 1979 and by 1981 it was losing $160 million. In May 1982, after 54 years in the airline business, Braniff laid off all its workers and stopped flying. Because the firm was losing more than its total fixed cost and with no prospect of the situation improving, it shut down.

R E V I E W

In perfect competition, a firm's marginal revenue equals its price. A firm maximizes profit by producing the output at which marginal cost equals marginal revenue (equals price). The lowest output a firm will produce is that at which average variable cost is at a minimum. If price falls below the minimum of average variable cost, the best a firm can do is to stop producing and make a loss equal to its total fixed cost. Maximizing profit is not the same thing as making a profit. In the short run, a firm can make a profit, break even, or make a loss. The maximum loss that a firm will make is equal to its total fixed cost. ■

The Firm's Supply Curve

A **perfectly competitive firm's supply curve** shows how a firm's profit-maximizing output varies as the market price varies. We are now going to derive Swanky's supply curve. Actually, we have already calculated three points on Swanky's supply curve. We discovered that when the price is \$25, Swanky produces 9 sweaters a day; when the price is \$20, Swanky produces 8 sweaters a day; and when the price is \$17, Swanky is indifferent between producing 7 sweaters a day and shutting down. We are now going to derive Swanky's entire supply curve. Figure 12.5 illustrates the analysis.

Figure 12.5(a) shows Swanky's marginal cost and average variable cost curves and Fig. 12.5(b) shows its supply curve. There is a direct connection between the marginal cost and average variable cost curves and the supply curve. Let's see what that connection is.

The smallest quantity that Swanky will supply is at the shutdown point. When the price is equal to the minimum average variable cost, the marginal revenue curve is MR_0 and the firm produces the output at its shutdown point—point s in the figure. If the price falls below minimum average variable cost, Swanky produces nothing. As the price rises above its minimum average variable cost, Swanky's output rises. Since Swanky maximizes profit by producing the output at which marginal cost equals price, we can determine from its marginal cost curve how much the firm produces at each price. At a price of \$25, the marginal revenue curve is MR_1. Swanky maximizes profit by produc-

Figure 12.5 Swanky's Supply Curve

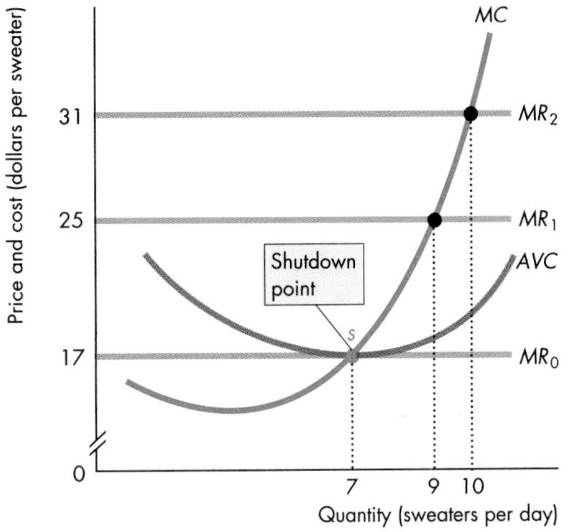

(a) Marginal cost and average variable cost

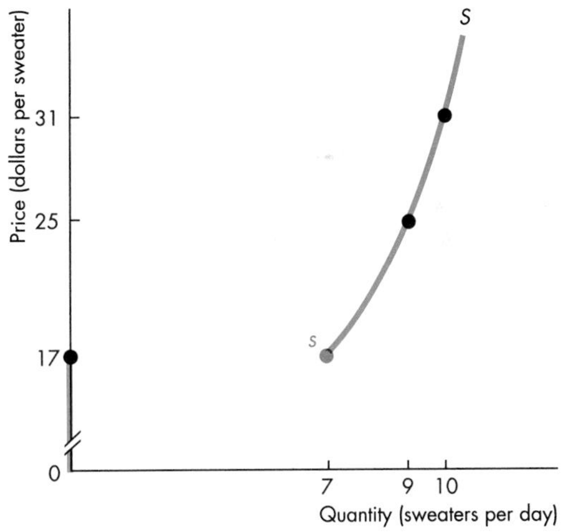

(b) Firm's supply curve

Part (a) shows Swanky's profit-maximizing output at each market price. At \$25 a sweater, Swanky produces 9 sweaters. At \$17 a sweater, Swanky produces 7 sweaters. At any price below \$17 a sweater, Swanky produces nothing. Swanky's shutdown point is at s. Part (b) shows Swanky's supply curve—the number of sweaters Swanky will produce at each price. Swanky's supply curve is made up of its marginal cost curve (part a) at all points above the average variable cost curve and the vertical axis at all prices below minimum average variable cost.

Figure 12.6 Firm and Industry Supply Curves

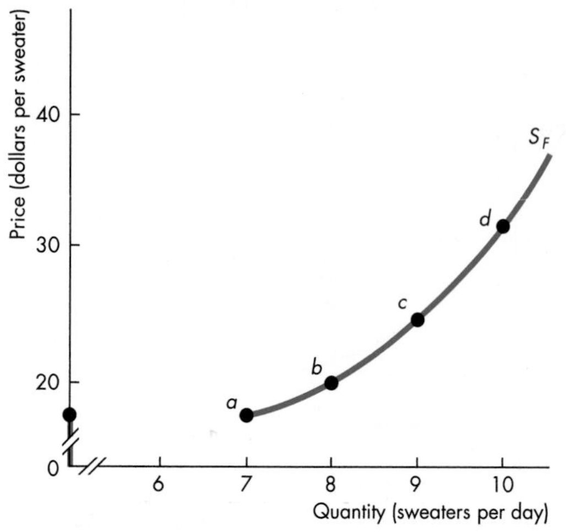

(a) Swanky, Inc.

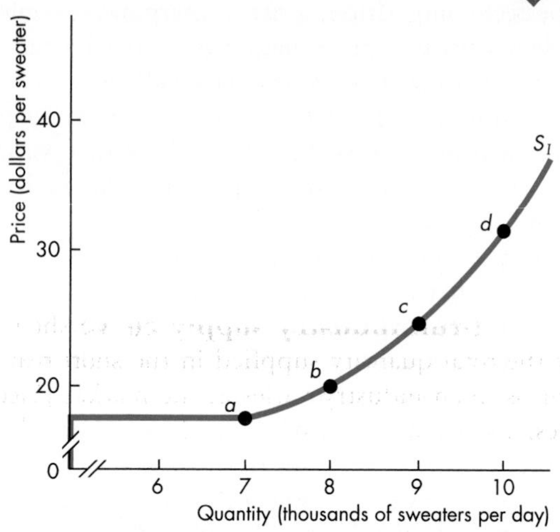

(b) Sweater industry

The industry supply schedule is the sum of the supply schedules of all individual firms. An industry that consists of 1000 identical firms has a supply schedule similar to that of the individual firm. But the quantity supplied by the industry is 1000 times as large as that of the individual firm (see table). At the shutdown price, the firm produces either 0 or 7 sweaters per day. The industry supply curve is perfectly elastic at the shutdown point. Part (a) shows Swanky's supply curve, S_F, and part (b), the sweater industry supply curve, S_I. Points *a*, *b*, *c*, and *d* correspond to the rows of the table. Note that the unit of measurement on the horizontal axis for the industry supply curve is 1000 times the unit for Swanky.

	Price (dollars per sweater)	Quantity supplied by Swanky, Inc. (sweaters per day)	Quantity supplied by industry (sweaters per day)
a	17	0 or 7	0 to 7,000
b	20	8	8,000
c	25	9	9,000
d	31	10	10,000

ing 9 sweaters. At a price of $31, the marginal revenue curve is MR_2 and Swanky produces 10 sweaters. The supply curve, shown in Fig. 12.5(b), has two separate parts. First, in the range of prices that exceed the minimum of average variable cost, the supply curve is the same as the marginal cost curve—above the shutdown point (*s*). Second, at prices below minimum average variable cost, Swanky shuts down and produces nothing and its supply curve runs along the vertical axis.

So far, we have studied a single firm in isolation. We have seen that the firm's profit-maximizing actions depend on the market price—which the firm takes as given. The higher the price, the larger is the quantity that the firm will choose to produce—the firm's supply curve is upward sloping. But how is the market price determined? To answer this question, we need to study not one firm in isolation but the market as a whole.

Short-run Equilibrium

Market price is determined by industry demand and industry supply. It is the price that makes the quantity demanded equal the quantity supplied. But the quantity supplied depends on the supply decisions of all the individual firms in the industry. Those supply decisions, in turn, depend on the market price.

A short-run equilibrium prevails in a competitive market when each firm operates its plant to produce the profit-maximizing output level and when the total quantity produced by all the firms in the market equals the quantity demanded at that price. To find the short-run equilibrium, we first need to construct the short-run industry supply curve.

Short-run Industry Supply Curve

The **short-run industry supply curve** shows how the total quantity supplied in the short run by all firms in an industry varies as the market price varies. The quantity supplied in the short run by the industry at a given price is the sum of the quantities supplied in the short run by all firms in the industry at that price. To construct the industry supply curve, we sum horizontally the supply curves of the individual firms. Let's see how we do that.

Suppose that the competitive sweater industry consists of 1000 firms exactly like Swanky. The relationship between a firm's supply curve and the industry supply curve, for this case, is illustrated in Fig. 12.6. Each of the 1000 firms in the industry has a supply schedule like Swanky's, set out in the table. At a price below $17, every firm in the industry will shut down production so that the industry will supply nothing. At $17, each firm is indifferent between shutting down and producing 7 sweaters. Since each firm is indifferent, some firms will produce and others will shut down. Industry supply will be anything between 0 (all firms shut down) and 7000 (all firms producing 7 sweaters a day each). Thus at $17, the industry supply curve is horizontal—it is perfectly elastic. As the price rises above $17, each firm increases its quantity supplied and the industry quantity supplied also increases, but by 1000 times that of each individual firm.

The supply schedules set out in the table form the basis of the supply curves that are graphed in Fig. 12.6. Swanky and every other firm has the supply curve S_F shown in Fig. 12.6(a); the industry supply curve S_I is shown in Fig. 12.6(b). Look carefully at the units on the horizontal axes of parts (a) and (b) and note that in part (a) the units are individual sweaters while in part (b) they are thousands of sweaters. But there are two important differences. First, at each price, the quantity supplied by the industry is 1000 times the quantity supplied by a single firm. Second, at a price of $17, the firm supplies either nothing or 7 sweaters a day. There is no individual firm supply curve between those two numbers. But for the industry, any quantity between zero and 7000 will be produced, so the industry supply curve is perfectly elastic over that range.

Figure 12.7 Three Short-run Equilibrium Positions for a Competitive Industry

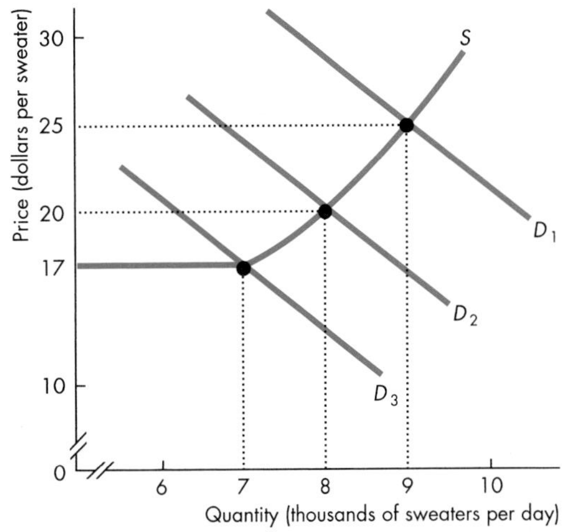

The competitive sweater industry's supply curve is S. If demand is D_1, the price is $25 and the industry produces 9000 sweaters. If demand is D_2, the price is $20, and industry output is 8000 sweaters. If demand is D_3, the price is $17, and industry output is 7000 sweaters. To see what is happening to the individual firms, look back at Fig. 12.4. When the price is $25, the firms are making a profit; when the price is $20, they are breaking even (making zero profit) and when the price is $17, they are incurring a loss. Even when they make a loss, the firms are maximizing profit (minimizing loss).

Short-run Competitive Equilibrium

Price and industry output are determined by industry demand and supply. Three different possible short-run competitive equilibrium positions are shown in Fig. 12.7. The supply curve (S) is the same as S_I, which we derived in Fig 12.6. If the demand curve is D_1, the equilibrium price is \$25 and industry output is 9000 sweaters a day. If the demand curve is D_2, the price is \$20 and industry output is 8000 sweaters a day. If the demand curve is D_3, the price is \$17 and industry output is 7000 sweaters a day.

To see what is happening to each individual firm and its profit in these three situations, you need to check back to Fig. 12.4. With the demand curve D_1, the price is \$25 a sweater, each firm produces 9 sweaters a day and makes a profit as shown in Fig. 12.4(a); if the demand curve is D_2, the price is \$20 a sweater, each firm produces 8 sweaters a day and makes a zero profit, as shown in Fig. 12.4(b); and if the demand curve is D_3, the price is \$17 a sweater, each firm is indifferent between producing 7 sweaters a day and shutting down and, in either event, is making a loss equal to total fixed cost, as shown in Fig. 12.4(c). If the demand curve shifts farther to the left than D_3, the price will remain constant at \$17 since the industry supply curve is horizontal at that price. Some firms will continue to produce 7 sweaters a day and others will shut down. Firms will be indifferent between these two activities and, whichever they choose, will make a loss equal to their total fixed cost. The number of firms continuing to produce will just be enough to satisfy the market demand at a price of \$17.

R E V I E W

In a competitive industry, the price and quantity traded are determined by industry supply and industry demand. Industry supply is the sum of the supplies of all the individual firms. The price determined by industry demand and supply cannot be influenced by the actions of any one individual firm. Each firm takes the market price and, given that price, maximizes profit. The firm maximizes its profit by producing the output at which marginal cost equals marginal revenue (equals price), as long as price is not lower than minimum average variable cost. If the price falls below minimum average variable cost, the firm shuts down and incurs a loss equal to its total fixed cost. ■

Long-run Equilibrium

We have seen that in short-run equilibrium a firm might make a profit, a loss, or break even. Though each of these three situations is a short-run equilibrium, only one of them is a long-run equilibrium. To see why, we need to examine the dynamic forces at work in a competitive industry. An industry adjusts over time in two ways. First, the number of firms in the industry changes; second, the existing firms change the scale of their plants, thereby shifting their short-run cost curves. Let's study the effects of these two dynamic forces in a competitive industry.

Entry and Exit

Entry is the act of setting up a new firm in an industry. **Exit** is the act of closing down a firm and leaving an industry. When will a new firm enter an industry or an existing one leave? How do entry and exit affect the market price, profit, and output in an industry? Let's first look at the causes of entry and exit.

Profits and Losses as Signals What triggers entry and exit? The prospect of profit triggers entry and the prospect of continuing losses triggers exit. Temporary profits and temporary losses that are purely random, like the winnings and losings at a casino, do not trigger entry or exit, but the prospect of profits or losses for some foreseeable future period does. An industry making economic profits attracts new entrants; one making economic losses induces exits; and an industry in which neither economic losses nor economic profits are being made stimulates neither entry nor exit. Thus profits and losses are the signals to which firms respond in making entry and exit decisions.

What are the effects of entry and exit on price and profits?

Effects of Entry and Exit on Price and Profits The immediate effect of entry and exit is to shift the industry supply curve. If more firms enter an industry, the industry supply curve shifts to the right: supply increases. If firms exit an industry, the industry supply curve shifts to the left: supply falls. The effects of entry and exit on price and on

Figure 12.8 Entry and Exit

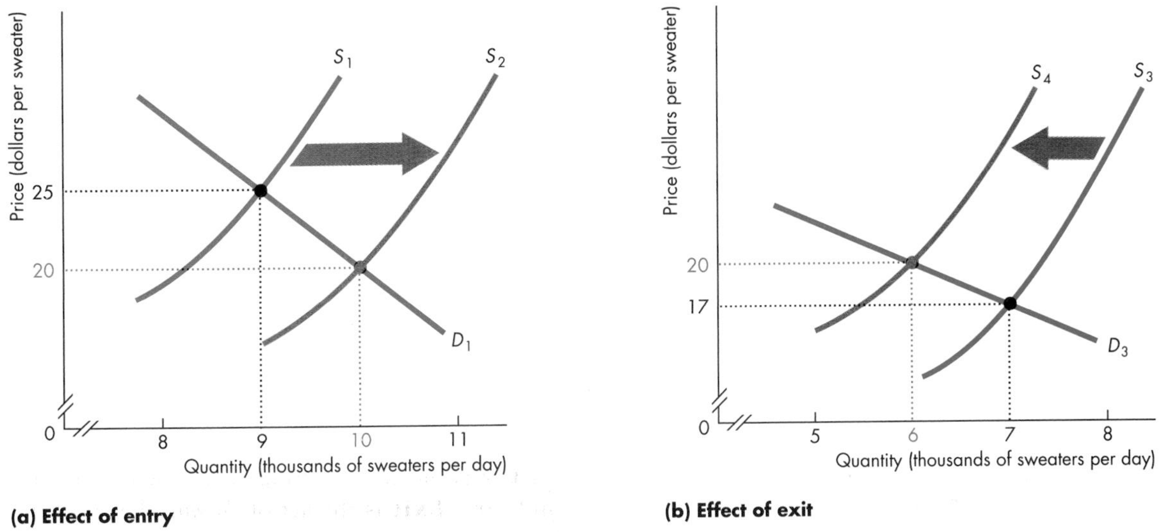

When new firms enter the sweater industry, the industry supply curve shifts to the right, from S_1 to S_2 (part a). The equilibrium price falls from $25 to $20, and the quantity traded rises from 9000 to 10,000 sweaters. When firms exit the sweater industry, the industry supply curve shifts to the left, from S_3 to S_4 (part b). The equilibrium price rises from $17 to $20, and the quantity traded falls from 7000 to 6000 sweaters.

the total quantity traded in the sweater industry are shown in Fig. 12.8.

Entry First, let's look at what happens when new firms enter an industry. Suppose that the demand curve for sweaters is D_1 and the industry supply curve is S_1, so sweaters sell for $25 and 9000 sweaters are being bought and sold. Now suppose that some new firms enter the industry. As they do so, the industry supply curve shifts to the right to become S_2. With the higher supply and unchanged demand, there is a fall in price from $25 to $20 a sweater and a rise in the quantity of sweaters traded from 9000 to 10,000.

As the price falls, Swanky and the other firms in the industry will react by lowering their output. That is, for each existing firm in the industry, its profit-maximizing output falls. Since the price falls, and since each firm sells less, profit falls for each firm. You can see this reduction of profit by glancing back at Fig. 12.4. Initially, when the price is $25, each firm makes a profit and is in the situation shown in Fig. 12.4(a). When the price falls to $20, the firm's profit disappears and it is in the situation shown in Fig. 12.4(b).

You have just discovered an important result:

As new firms enter an industry, the price falls and the profit of each existing firm falls.

A good example of this process has occurred in the last few years in the personal computer industry. When IBM introduced its first personal computer in the early 1980s, the price of PCs gave IBM a big profit. Very quickly thereafter new firms such as Compaq, Zenith, Leading Edge, and a host of others entered the industry with machines technologically identical to the IBM. In fact, they were so similar that they came to be called "clones." The massive wave of entry into the personal computer industry shifted the supply curve to the right and lowered the price and the profits for all firms.

Exit Let's see what happens when firms leave an industry. Again, the impact of a firm leaving is to shift the industry supply curve, but this time to the left. Figure 12.8(b) illustrates. Suppose that initially the demand curve is D_3 with an industry supply curve S_3, so the market price is $17 and 7000 sweaters are being sold. As firms leave the industry, the supply curve shifts to the left and becomes S_4. With the fall in supply, industry output falls from 7000 to 6000 sweaters and the price rises from $17 to $20.

To see what is happening to Swanky, go back again to Fig. 12.4. With the demand curve D_3 and a price of $17, Swanky is in a situation like that illustrated in Fig. 12.4(c). Price is lower than average total cost and Swanky is making a loss. Some firms exit and Swanky (and some others) hang in. As firms exit, the price rises from $17 to $20, so the firms that remain increase their output and their losses vanish. They are then back in a situation like that illustrated in Fig. 12.4(b).

Figure 12.9 Changes in Plant Size

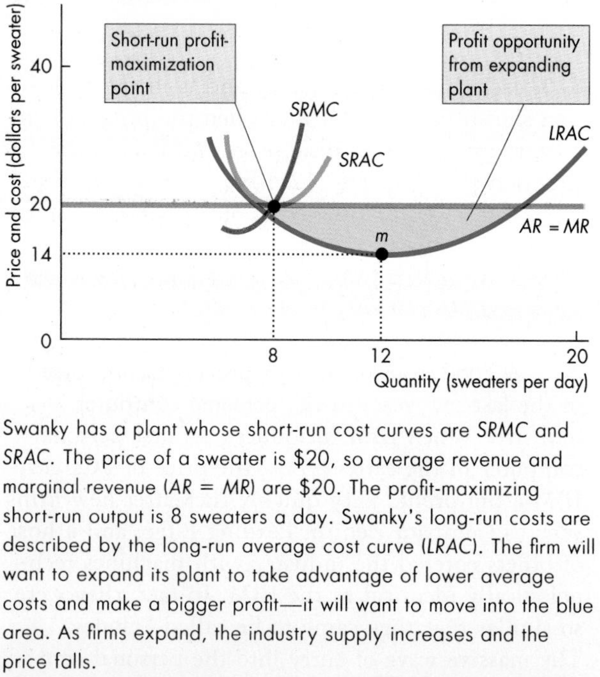

Swanky has a plant whose short-run cost curves are *SRMC* and *SRAC*. The price of a sweater is $20, so average revenue and marginal revenue (*AR* = *MR*) are $20. The profit-maximizing short-run output is 8 sweaters a day. Swanky's long-run costs are described by the long-run average cost curve (*LRAC*). The firm will want to expand its plant to take advantage of lower average costs and make a bigger profit—it will want to move into the blue area. As firms expand, the industry supply increases and the price falls.

You have just worked out the second important result:

As firms leave an industry the price rises and so do the profits of the remaining firms.

An example of a firm leaving an industry is International Harvester, a manufacturer of farm equipment. For decades, people associated the name "International Harvester" with tractors, combines, and other farm machines. But International Harvester wasn't the only maker of farm equipment. The industry became intensely competitive and the firm began losing money. Now the company has a new name, Navistar International, and it doesn't make tractors anymore. After years of losses and shrinking revenues, it got out of the farm business in 1985. Now it makes trucks. Another example is Singer sewing machines. The name "Singer" still means sewing machines to millions of people but Singer no longer makes these machines. It makes electronic equipment for jet aircraft and the like.

Both Singer and International Harvester exited because they were losing money on their operations. Their exits lowered supply and made it possible for the remaining firms in those two industries to break even.

Equilibrium We've seen that the prospect of profit triggers entry and the prospect of continuing loss triggers exit. We have also seen that entry into an industry lowers the profits of the existing firms and that exit from an industry increases the profits of the remaining firms. Long-run equilibrium results from the interaction of profits and losses as signals to entry and exit and the effects of entry and exit on profits and losses.

Long-run equilibrium occurs in a competitive industry when economic profits are zero. If an industry makes economic profits, firms enter the industry and the supply curve shifts to the right. As a result, the market price falls and so do profits. Firms continue to enter and profits continue to fall as long as the industry is earning positive economic profits.

In an industry with economic losses, some firms will exit. As those firms leave the industry, the supply curve shifts to the left and the market price rises. As the price rises, the industry's losses shrink. As long as losses continue, some firms will leave the industry. Only when losses have been eliminated and zero economic profits are being made will firms stop exiting.

Let's now examine the second way in which the competitive industry adjusts in the long run—by existing firms changing their plant size.

Changes in Plant Size

A firm will change its plant size whenever it can increase its profit by doing so. A situation in which a firm can profitably expand its output by increasing its plant is illustrated in Fig. 12.9. In that figure the price (and marginal revenue) is $20. With its current plant, Swanky's marginal and average total cost—its short-run costs—are shown by the curves *SRMC* and *SRAC*. Swanky maximizes profit by producing 8 sweaters a day but with its existing plant, Swanky makes zero economic profit.

Swanky's long-run average cost curve is *LRAC*. By installing more knitting machines—increasing its plant size—Swanky can lower its costs and operate at a positive economic profit. For example, if Swanky increases its plant size so that it operates at point *m*, the minimum of its long-run average cost, it lowers its average cost from $20 to $14 and makes a profit of $6 a sweater. Since Swanky is a price taker, expanding output from 8 to 12 sweaters does not lower the market price and so would be a profitable thing for Swanky to do. Because it takes time to change the production plant, the short-run equilibrium prevails. Nevertheless, over time, the firm will gradually expand its plant.

As firms expand their plants, the short-run industry supply curve starts to shift to the right. (Recall that the industry supply curve is the sum of the supply curves of all the individual firms.) With increases in supply and a given demand, the price gradually falls. As the price falls, so do profits. It will pay firms to expand as long as expansion increases profits. Only when no economic profits are being made will firms stick with their existing plant size. There is only one possible plant size that is consistent with long-run equilibrium in a competitive industry and that is the one associated with the minimum long-run average cost (point *m*) in Fig. 12.9.

Figure 12.10 The Long-run Equilibrium of a Firm

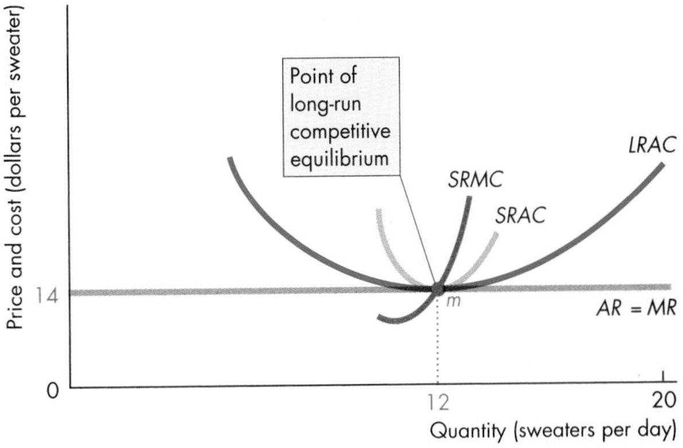

As firms expand their plant, industry supply increases and the price falls. Long-run equilibrium occurs when the price equals $14 and each firm is producing at point *m*, its point of minimum long-run average cost.

Figure 12.10 illustrates the long-run competitive equilibrium. It occurs at a price of $14 with each firm producing 12 sweaters a day. Each firm in the industry has the plant size such that its marginal cost and average total cost curves are *SRMC* and *SRAC*. Each firm produces the output at which its short-run marginal cost equals price. No firm can change its output in the short run and make more profit. As each firm is producing at minimum long-run average cost (point *m* on *LRAC*), no firm has an incentive to expand or contract its production plant—a bigger plant or a smaller plant will lead to a higher long-run average cost and an economic loss. Finally, no firm has an incentive to leave the industry or to enter it.

R E V I E W

Long-run competitive equilibrium is described by three conditions:

- Firms maximize short-run profit so that marginal cost equals marginal revenue (equals price).

- Economic profits are zero so that no firm has an incentive to enter or to leave the industry
- Long-run average cost is at a minimum so that no firm has an incentive to expand or to contract its plant ■

Predictions

Let's now use the theory of perfect competition to make some predictions.

A Permanent Decrease in Demand

There are many examples in the real world of a permanent decrease in demand. Increased awareness of the health hazard of smoking has caused a decrease in the demand for tobacco and cigarettes. The development of inexpensive car and air transportation has caused a huge decrease in the demand for long-distance trains and buses. Solid-state electronics have caused a large decrease in the demand for TV and radio repair. There has been a decrease in the demand for American-made cars as a result of high-quality alternatives from Japan. What happens in a competitive industry when there is a permanent decrease in demand?

Let's suppose that an industry starts out in long-run competitive equilibrium, shown in Fig. 12.11(a). The demand curve labeled D_0 and the supply curve labeled S_0 represent the initial demand and supply in the market. The price initially is P_0 and the total industry output is Q_0. A single firm is shown in Fig. 12.11(b). Initially, it produces the quantity q_0 and makes zero economic profit.

Now suppose that demand decreases to D_1, as shown in part (a). This decrease in demand causes the price to drop to P_1. At this lower price, each firm produces a smaller output (q_1) and the quantity supplied by the industry decreases from Q_0 to Q_1 as the industry slides down its short-run supply curve (S_0). The industry is now in short-run equilibrium but not long-run equilibrium. It is in short-run equilibrium because each firm is maximizing profit. But it is not in long-run equilibrium because each firm is making an economic loss—its average total cost exceeds the price.

In this situation, firms will leave the industry. As they do so, the industry supply curve starts shifting to the left, the quantity supplied shrinks, and the price gradually rises. At each higher price, the profit-maximizing output is higher, so the firms remaining in the industry raise their output as the price rises. Each slides up its marginal cost or supply curve (part b). Eventually, enough firms will have left the industry for the supply curve to have shifted to S_1 (part a). When that has happened, the price will have returned to its original level (P_0). At that price, the firms remaining in the industry will produce the same amount as they did before the fall in demand (q_0). No firms will want to leave the industry because of losses and none will want to enter. The industry supply curve settles down at S_1 and total industry output is Q_2. The industry is again in long-run equilibrium.

The difference between the initial long-run equilibrium and the final long-run equilibrium is the number of firms in the industry. Fewer firms remain after the adjustment. Each remaining firm produces the same output in the new long-run equilibrium as it did initially. While moving from the original equilibrium to the new one, firms that remain in the industry suffer losses. But they keep their losses to a minimum because they adjust their output to keep price equal to marginal cost.

A Permanent Increase in Demand

There are many examples of industries that have experienced a permanent increase in demand. The most spectacular examples stem from technological change. For example, the development of the microwave oven has produced an enormous increase in demand for paper, glass, and plastic cooking utensils, and for plastic wrap. The demand for almost all products is steadily increasing as a result of increasing population and increasing incomes. What happens in a competitive industry when the demand for its product increases? Let's begin the story again in long-run equilibrium, as shown in Fig. 12.12(a). With demand curve D_0 and supply curve S_0, the market price is P_0 and quantity Q_0 is sold by the industry. Figure 12.12(b) shows a single firm. At price P_0, the firm is making zero economic profit and producing an output of q_0. Now suppose that the demand for the industry's output increases from D_0 to D_1. The increased demand raises the price to P_1. The quantity supplied by the industry rises from Q_0 to Q_1 as each

Figure 12.11 A Decrease in Demand

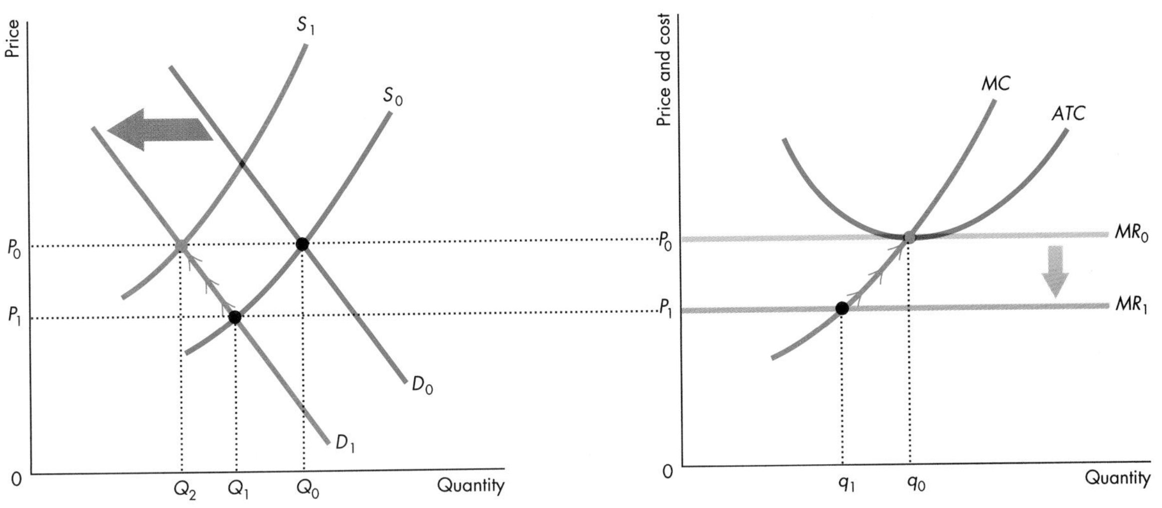

(a) Industry **(b) Firm**

An industry starts out in long-run competitive equilibrium. Part (a) shows the industry demand curve D_0, the industry supply curve S_0, the equilibrium quantity Q_0 and the market price P_0. Each firm sells at price P_0, so its marginal revenue curve is MR_0 in part (b). Each firm produces q_0 and makes a zero profit. Demand decreases from D_0 to D_1 (part a). The equilibrium price falls to P_1, each firm lowers its output to q_1 (part b) and industry output falls to Q_1. In this new situation, firms are making losses and some firms will leave the industry. As they do so, the industry supply curve gradually shifts to the left, from S_0 to S_1. This shift gradually raises the industry price from P_1 back to P_0. While the price is below P_0, firms are making losses and some are leaving the industry. Once the price has returned to P_0, the smaller number of firms whose supply curves add up to the industry supply curve (S_1) will each be making a zero profit. There will be no further incentive for any firm to leave the industry. Each firm produces q_0 and industry output is Q_2.

firm increases its output from q_0 to q_1 (part b). At price P_1 and quantity Q_1, the industry is in short-run equilibrium but not in long-run equilibrium. Firms in the industry are making economic profits. These economic profits will attract new firms into the industry.

As new firms enter, the industry supply curve starts shifting to the right, and as it does so it intersects the demand curve at lower and lower prices and higher and higher quantities. Firms in the industry react to the falling price by cutting their output. That is, in Fig. 12.12(b) each firm slides back down its marginal cost curve in order to maximize profit at each successively lower price. Eventually, enough new firms enter the industry to shift the industry supply curve all the way to S_1. By that time, the market price falls to P_0, the original price, and each firm cuts its output back to its original level, q_0. Each firm is again making zero economic profit and no firms enter or exit the industry. This new situation is a long-run equilibrium. During the adjustment process from the initial long-run equilibrium to the new one, all firms—both those firms that were in the industry originally and those that entered—make economic profits.

External Economies and Diseconomies One feature of the predictions that we have just generated seems odd: In the long-run, regardless of whether demand increases or decreases, the price returns to its original level. Is that outcome inevitable? In

Figure 12.12 An Increase in Demand

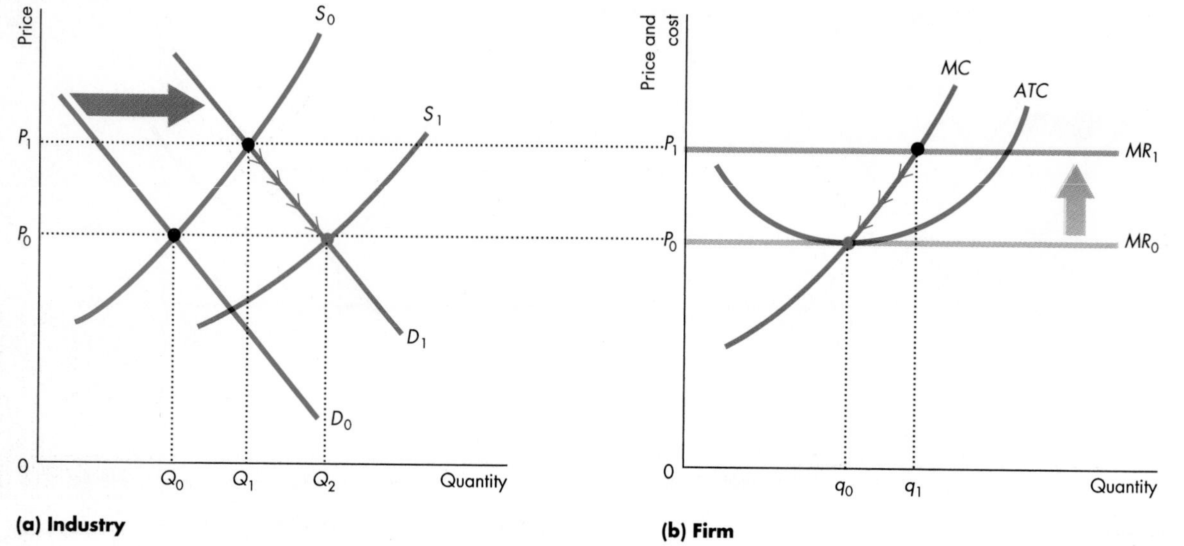

A competitive industry is in long-run equilibrium. The demand curve is D_0 and the supply curve S_0 (part a). The quantity traded is Q_0 and the market price is P_0. Each firm faces the marginal revenue curve MR_0 and maximizes profit by producing q_0 (part b). Demand increases from D_0 to D_1. The price rises to P_1 and industry output rises to Q_1. Each firm increases its output to q_1. In this situation, firms are making a profit (price is greater than average total cost). New firms will enter the industry and as they do so, the industry supply curve shifts to the right. As the supply curve shifts to the right, the price gradually falls and each individual firm gradually cuts its output from q_1 back to q_0. Since firms are entering the industry, total industry output rises even though each firm's output is cut back. The new equilibrium occurs when enough firms have entered the industry for the supply curve to have moved to S_1 with the price restored to its original level, P_0, and with each firm making zero profit. At this point, industry output is at Q_2. Since each firm is making a zero profit, there is no further tendency for new firms to enter the industry, so the supply curve remains stationary at S_1.

fact, it is not. It is possible for the long-run equilibrium price to either rise, fall, or stay the same. Figure 12.13 illustrates these three cases. In part (a), the long-run supply curve (LS_A) is perfectly elastic. In this case, an increase in demand from D_0 to D_1 (or a decrease in demand from D_1 to D_0) results in a change in the quantity traded but an unchanged price. This is the case that we have just analyzed. In part (b), the long-run supply curve (LS_B) slopes upward. In this case, when demand increases from D_0 to D_1, the price increases, and when demand decreases from D_1 to D_0, the price decreases. Finally, part (c) shows a case in which the long-run supply curve (LS_C) slopes downward. In this case, an increase in demand from D_0 to D_1 results in a fall in the price in the long run. A decrease in demand from D_1 to D_0 results in a higher price in the long run.

Whichever outcome occurs depends on external economies and external diseconomies. **External economies** are factors beyond the control of an individual firm that lower its costs as industry output rises. **External diseconomies** are factors outside the control of a firm that raise its costs as industry output rises.

There are many examples of external economies and diseconomies. They are both well illustrated in the agricultural sector. As farm output increased in the nineteenth and early twentieth centuries, the services available to farmers expanded

Figure 12.13 Long-run Price and Quantity Changes

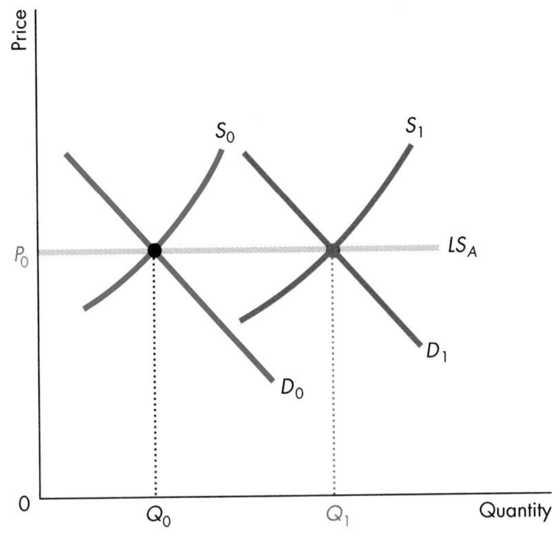

(a) Constant cost industry

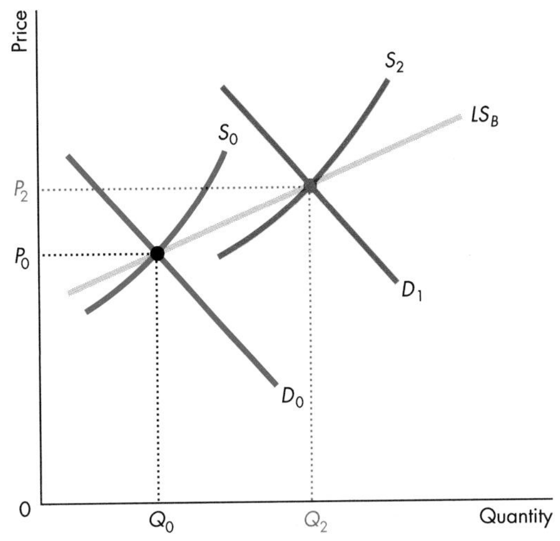

(b) Increasing cost industry

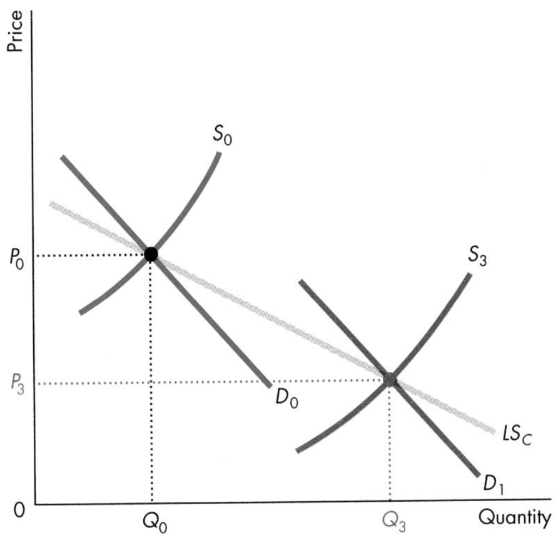

(c) Decreasing cost industry

Three possible long-run changes in price and quantity are illustrated. When demand increases from D_0 to D_1, entry occurs and the industry supply curve shifts from S_0 to S_1. In part (a), the long-run supply curve LS_A is horizontal. The quantity increases from Q_0 to Q_1 and the price remains constant at P_0. In part (b), the long-run supply curve is LS_B; the price increases to P_2 and the quantity traded increases to Q_2. This case occurs in industries with external diseconomies. In part (c), the long-run supply curve is LS_C; the price decreases to P_3 and the quantity traded increases to Q_3. This case occurs in an industry with external economies.

and their costs fell. Farm machinery, fertilizers, transportation networks, storage, and marketing facilities all improved, lowering farm costs. As a consequence, as the demand for farm products has increased, the quantity produced has increased but the price has fallen (as in Fig. 12.13c).

One of the best examples of external diseconomies is congestion. The airline industry provides a good illustration. With bigger airline industry output, there is greater congestion of both airports and airspace, which results in longer delays and extra waiting time for passengers and airplanes. These external diseconomies mean that as the demand for air transportation continues to increase, eventually (in the absence of further technological change), prices will rise.

Technological Change

Industries are constantly discovering lower-cost techniques of production. Most cost-saving production techniques cannot be implemented, however, without investing in new plant and equipment. As a consequence, it takes time for a technological advance to spread through an industry. Some firms whose plants are on the verge of being replaced will be quick to adopt the new technology, while other firms whose plants have recently been replaced will continue to operate with older technology until they can no longer cover their average variable cost. Once average variable cost cannot be covered, it pays a firm to scrap even a relatively new plant (embodying the original technology) in favor of a plant with the new technology.

Let's work out exactly what happens to the output and profit of each firm in an industry reshaped by a new technology. Figure 12.14(a) shows the demand curve for an industry (D) and an initial supply curve (S_0). The price is P_0 and the quantity Q_0. Initially there are only original technology firms in existence (Fig. 12.14b). Each firm has a marginal cost curve MC_O and an average total cost curve ATC_O. At the market price, P_0, each firm faces a marginal revenue curve MR_0, produces an output q_0^O, and makes zero economic profit. The industry is in long-run competitive equilibrium.

New technology allows firms to produce at substantially lower cost than the existing technology. The cost curves of firms with the new technology are shown in part (c). Suppose that one firm with the new technology enters the industry. Since the industry is competitive, this one firm will be a negligible part of the total industry and will hardly affect the industry supply, so that the supply curve remains at S_0. The price remains at P_0 and the new technology firm produces a profit-maximizing output of q_0^N and makes a positive economic profit.

Gradually, more new technology firms enter the industry and, after a period, enough have entered to shift the industry supply curve to become S_1 in part (a). By this time, the market price has fallen to P_1 and the industry output has risen to Q_1. Each firm takes the price P_1 and maximizes its profit. Each new technology firm, in part (c), maximizes profit by producing the output q_1^N and continues to make a positive economic profit. Each original technology firm, in part (b), minimizes its loss by producing the output q_1^O.

More new technology firms will continue to enter since the new technology is profitable. Original technology firms will begin to leave the industry or switch to the new technology because the original technology is unprofitable. Eventually all the firms in the industry will be new technology firms and, by this time, the industry supply curve will have moved to S_2. The supply curve S_2 is based on the marginal cost curves of the new technology firms. The supply curve S_0 is based on the marginal cost curves of the original technology firms. The supply curve S_1 is based on the marginal cost curves for both original technology and new technology firms. With supply curve S_2, the market price is P_2 and the industry output Q_2. At price P_2, the new technology firms produce a profit-maximizing output of q_2, making zero profits. The industry long-run equilibrium price is P_2.

The process that we have just analyzed is one in which some firms experience economic profits and others economic losses. It is a period of dynamic change for an industry. Some firms do well and others do badly. Often a change of the kind that we have just examined will have a geographical dimension to it. For example, the new technology firms may be located in a new industrial region of a country, while the original technology firms may be located in a traditional industrial region. Alternatively, the new technology firms might be in a foreign country, while the original technology firms are in the domestic economy. The struggles of the American textile industry to keep up with the fierce competition from Hong Kong and Taiwan is a good example of this phenomenon. Another example is the dairy industry, which is undergoing a major technological change arising from the use of hormones (see Reading Between the Lines, p. 304).

Farms in Distress

In 1981, there were 2.4 million farms in the United States. The average farm had 425 acres. The population of farms has been steadily declining over the years. In the five years between 1976 and 1981, that decline was close to 1 percent a year. But in the five years between 1981 and 1986, 220,000 farms (9 percent of the total) disappeared —more than three times the number that went out of business in the preceding five years. At the same time, the average size of farms increased by 7 percent to 455 acres. Through the early to mid-

Figure 12.14 Technological Change in a Competitive Industry

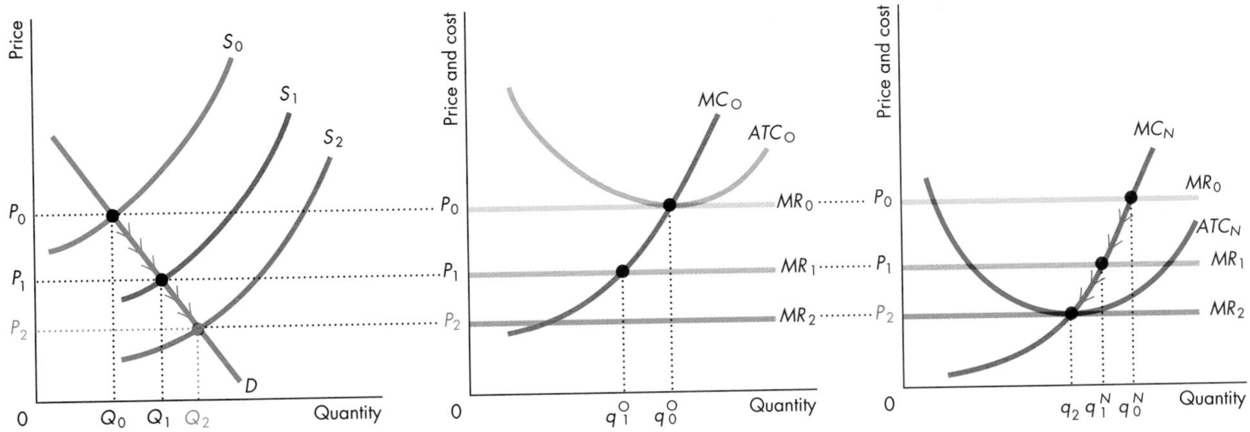

(a) Industry **(b) Original technology firms** **(c) New technology firms**

Initially the industry supply curve is S_0 and the demand curve is D, so the equilibrium price is P_0 and quantity traded is Q_0 (part a). Each individual firm, shown in part (b), produces q_0^O and makes a zero profit. A new technology is developed. The costs associated with the new technology (ATC_N and MC_N) are shown in part (c) and are lower than those for the original technology. A new technology firm, faced with the price P_0, produces a profit-maximizing output of q_0^N and makes a profit. Since the new technology is profitable, more and more firms will use it. As they do so, the industry supply curve begins to shift to the right, from S_0 to S_1. With an increase in industry supply, industry output rises to Q_1, but the price falls to P_1. As a result, new technology firms will cut their output from q_0^N to q_1^N, but they will still be making a profit. Original technology firms will cut their output from q_0^O to q_1^O. They will be making losses. As firms with the original technology begin to close down and more new technology firms enter the industry, the industry supply curve continues to shift to the right, from S_1 to S_2. At S_2, the price is P_2 and industry output is Q_2. Each new technology firm is now producing q_2 and making a zero profit and there are no firms using the original technology.

The effect of the introduction of the new technology has been to raise output and lower price. In the process, firms that adopted the new technology early made profits while firms that stuck with the original technology for too long incurred losses.

1980s, there were many indications of financial distress in the farm sector. By 1985, more than 5 percent of farms were unable to meet their bank loan repayment schedules; almost 40 percent had borrowed up to their loan limits; close to 5 percent a year were going out of business and close to 4 percent were in bankruptcy. Why have American farms gone through a period of such tremendous financial distress? Why have so many farms gone out of business? Why, after such a shakeout, is the remaining farm larger, on the average?

The farm problem is a complex one. In fact, there is no single "farm problem" but many individual problems varying from region to region, crop to crop, and a host of other factors. But there is a single, common problem that affected all farmers to some degree during the early 1980s. It's on this problem that we'll focus.

Although some farmers are wealthy, many are not. They have to buy their land and farm buildings and equipment by borrowing from the bank. In the early 1980s, the cost of bank borrowing increased on an unprecedented scale. Bank loans that in the 1970s had cost an average of 7 or 8 percent a year, suddenly were costing an average of 13 percent and climbed briefly to 20 percent in 1981. The cost remained high at 15 percent a year through 1982. This massive increase in the cost of

Biotechnology in the Milk Industry

After Years of Hype, High Tech Starts to Transform the Business of Farming

After years of hype, the first commercial fruits of biotechnology are nearing the market; the computer is already having an impact in the fields. Over the next two decades, economists and scientists say, these twin technologies will transform agriculture just as mechanization and applied chemistry changed it earlier in this century. . . .

Although elephantine cows and drought-resistant corn remain years away, several companies have used biotechnology to create diagnostic kits, curatives and vaccines for a number of livestock diseases. A hormone that can boost a cow's milk production as much as 40% is expected to hit the market within two years. And a recent General Accounting Office survey showed that nearly five dozen genetically altered plants and organisms will be ready for field tests by 1990. . . .

Produced in animals' pituitary glands, growth hormones play a central role in regulating growth and milk production. Although scientists have known about the powerful effect of these hormones since the 1930s, only genetic engineering allowed them to produce the chemicals in quantities large enough to be commercially applicable. Now, such agribusiness giants as Monsanto Co., American Cyanamid Co., and International Minerals & Chemical Corp. are racing to bring the hormones to the market. Bovine somatotropine, used in dairy cows, is expected to be commercially available by 1988, followed shortly by hormones for hogs, and ultimately byproducts for sheep and beef cattle.

The new hormones will lead to dramatic production spurts, reshaping their respective industries. Bovine somatotropine could boost U.S. milk production by 20% within three years, dropping milk prices by 10% to 15% and eventually forcing 1/4 of the nation's dairy farmers out of business says Cornell University agricultural economist, Robert Kalter. . . .

***Wall Street Journal*, November 10, 1986**

by Wendy L. Wall

The Essence of the Story

- Biotechnology enables the production of growth hormones that can increase a cow's milk production by up to 40 percent.
- It is predicted that within three years (of the date of the article) the use of such hormones will increase U.S. milk production by 20 percent, resulting in milk prices falling by between 10 and 15 percent.
- It is predicted that 25 percent of the nation's dairy farmers will eventually go out of business.

Background and Analysis

- The model of a perfectly competitive industry predicts what will happen to dairy farmers as the new hormone technology is adopted.
- A dairy farmer using the current technology has an average total cost curve ATC_0 and a marginal cost curve MC_0, as shown in part (a) of the figure.
- The market demand curve D and the market supply curve S_0 intersect to determine the equilibrium price, P_0 (part b).
- At the price P_0, the farmer maximizes profit by producing q_0 gallons of milk a day.
- The average total cost curve with the new hormone technology is ATC_N. The marginal cost curve with the new technology is MC_N.
- The hormone can boost production by 40 percent, so the output that minimizes average total cost with the new technology (q_N) is 40 percent larger than q_0.
- Some farmers immediately adopt the new technology and have cost curves ATC_N and MC_N.
- Some stick to original technology and have cost curves ATC_0 and MC_0.
- As farmers adopt new technology, the short-run industry supply curve gradually shifts from S_0 to S_N (part b).
- The market price gradually falls.
- When the price has fallen to P_N, farmers using the new technology break even and those using the original technology make an economic loss.
- Those with the original technology gradually go out of business.
- When all dairy farmers have the new technology, the industry short-run supply curve is S_N, the price is P_N, and farmers make zero economic profit.
- In the new long-run equilibrium, the industry produces Q_N millions of gallons of milk and each farmer remaining in business produces q_N gallons.
- The number of dairy farmers will have fallen by approximately 25 percent.

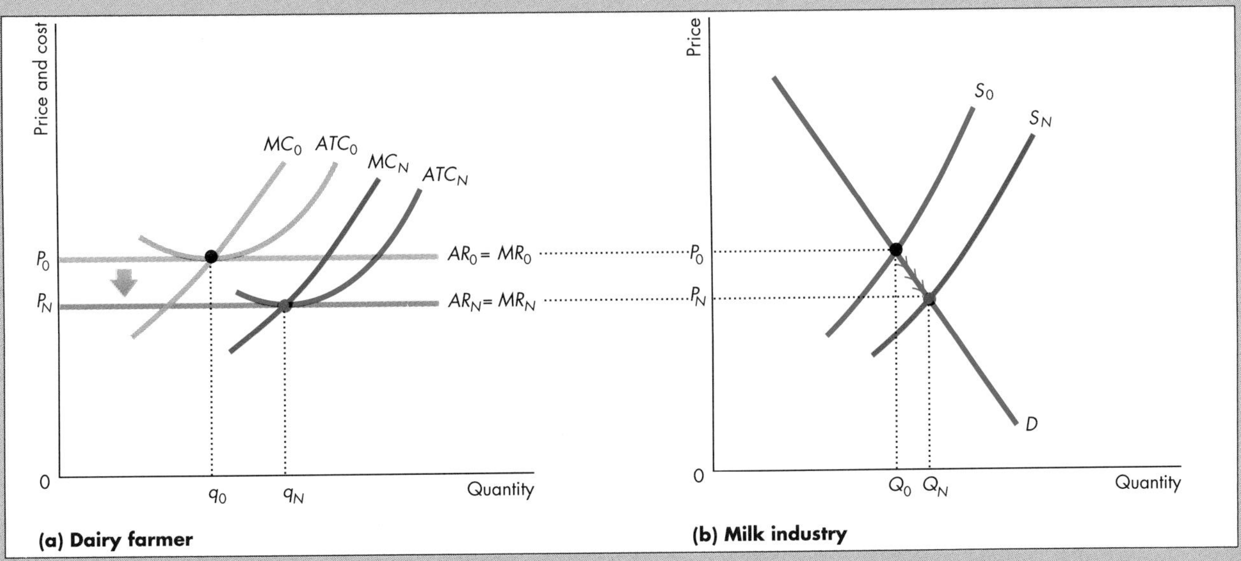

Figure 12.15 The Effects of High Interest Rates on Farm Profits and Prices

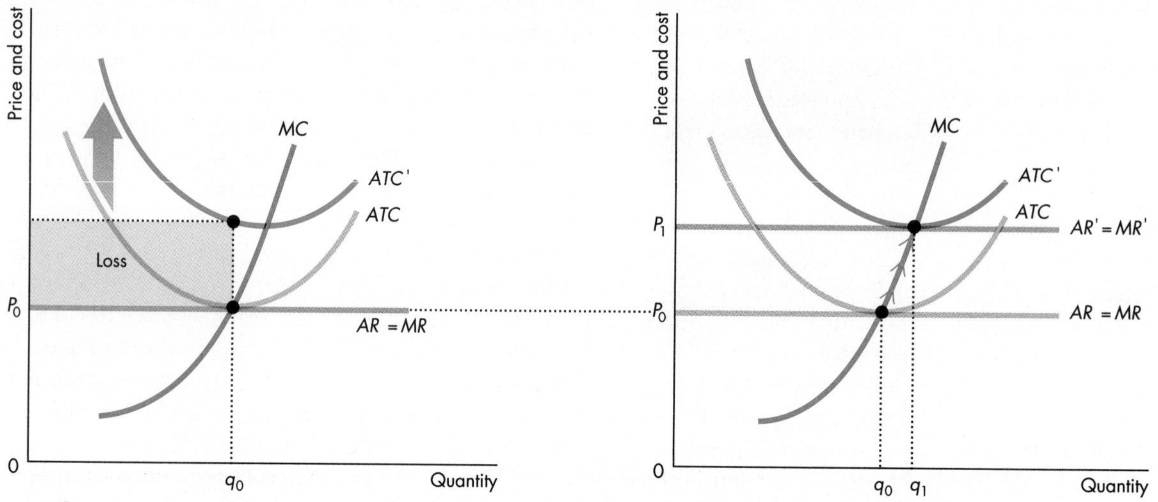

(a) High interest rates cause losses

(b) Exit raises prices—eventually

Initially, an individual farm has an average total cost curve *ATC*, and at a price of P_0 its profit-maximizing output is q_0 (part a). Fixed costs increase, shifting the average total cost curve upward to *ATC'*. Marginal cost and price remain constant and so does the profit-maximizing output. Farms now make a loss shown by the red rectangle. As some farms exit, the industry supply curve shifts to the left and the price begins to rise from P_0 to P_1. The profit-maximizing output increases from q_0 to q_1 (part b). The process of adjustment is not instantaneous and farms make losses for a prolonged period.

borrowing represented an increase in the fixed costs of a farm. Recall that fixed costs are those incurred independently of the volume of output. Even if a farm produces nothing, it has to pay the bank the interest on its loans.

We can analyze the effects of an increase in fixed costs in the farm sector by using the model of a perfectly competitive industry that we've just been studying. Figure 12.15 shows you what happens. In part (a), a farm's average total cost curve is *ATC* and its marginal cost curve is *MC*. The market price is P_0 and the farm's marginal revenue curve is *MR*. The farm's profit-maximizing output is q_0. The initial situation shown in part (a) is a long-run equilibrium with the farm making zero economic profit.

An increase in total fixed cost shifts the average total cost curve upward but does not change the marginal cost curve. (Recall that marginal cost is the cost of producing one additional unit of output. Since the increase in interest charges increases fixed cost but not variable cost, marginal cost is unchanged.) Suppose that the increased fixed cost shifts the average total cost curve to *ATC'*. If the price remains P_0, the farm's profit-maximizing output remains at q_0. But the farm is now losing money. In part (a) of Fig. 12.15, the loss is equal to the red rectangle.

The size of a farm's loss depends on its financial situation. Farms with large debts make the largest losses. Nine percent of farms have loans that exceed 70 percent of the value of their land and buildings. It is these farms that incur the largest losses. These are the farms that will begin to leave the industry. As farms go out of business, the supply curve for farm products starts to shift to the left and the price of farm products begins to increase. Figure 12.15 (b) shows what happens in the long run. When enough farms have left the industry, the price will have increased from P_0 to P_1. At the higher price, farm output increases from q_0 to q_1 and farms are no longer losing money. Individual farm outputs are now bigger than before, which means that the average farm uses more inputs—more labor, machines, and land.

But the situation shown in part (b) takes a long time to come about. The price does not rise quickly from P_0 to P_1. The main factor slowing the rise in price is the fact that even with a large exit of U.S. farms, they represent but a small fraction of the world market for most agricultural products. As a consequence, farms make losses for a prolonged period of time, during which the adjustment process takes place.

You've now studied how a competitive market works and have used the model of perfect competition to interpret and explain a variety of aspects of real world economic behavior. The last topic that we'll study in this chapter is the efficiency of perfect competition.

Competition and Efficiency

In perfect competition, freedom of entry ensures that firms produce at the least possible cost. Also, the fact that each firm is a price taker, facing a perfectly elastic demand curve, results in firms producing a quantity such that marginal cost equals price. These features of a perfectly competitive market have important implications for the efficiency of such a market.

Allocative Efficiency

Allocative efficiency occurs when no resources are wasted—when no one can be made better off without someone else being made worse off. If someone can be made better off without making someone else worse off, a more efficient allocation of resources can be achieved. Three conditions must be satisfied to achieve allocative efficiency:

- Economic efficiency
- Consumer efficiency
- Equality of marginal social cost and marginal social benefit

We defined economic efficiency in Chapter 9 as a situation in which the cost of producing a given output is minimized. Economic efficiency involves technological efficiency—producing the maximum possible output from given inputs—as well as using inputs in their cost-minimizing proportions. Economic efficiency occurs whenever firms maximize profit. Since firms in perfect competition maximize profit, perfect competition is economically efficient.

Consumer efficiency occurs when consumers cannot make themselves better off by reallocating their budget. A consumer's best possible budget allocation is summarized in the consumer's demand curves. That is, a demand curve tells us the quantity demanded at a given price when the consumer has made the best possible use of a given budget. Thus when the quantity bought at a given price is a point on the demand curve, the allocation satisfies consumer efficiency.

The third condition occurs in perfect competition if there are no external costs and benefits. **External costs** are those costs not borne by the producer but borne by other members of society. Examples of such costs are the costs of pollution and congestion. **External benefits** are those benefits accruing to people other than the buyer of a good. Examples of such benefits are the pleasure we get from well-designed buildings and beautiful works of art. As long as *someone* buys these things, *everyone* can enjoy them.

Marginal social cost is the cost of producing one additional unit of output, including external costs. **Marginal social benefit** is the dollar value of the benefit from one additional unit of consumption, including any external benefits. Allocative efficiency occurs when marginal social cost equals marginal social benefit. Figure 12.16 illustrates such a situation. The marginal social benefit curve is *MSB* and the marginal social cost curve is *MSC*. Allocative efficiency occurs at a quantity Q^* and price P^*. In this situation, there is no waste. No one can be made better off without someone else being made worse off. If output is above Q^*, marginal social cost will exceed marginal social benefit. The cost of producing the last unit will exceed its benefit. If output is below Q^*, marginal social benefit will exceed marginal social cost. Producing one more unit will bring more benefit than it costs.

There are some circumstances in which perfect competition delivers allocative efficiency, as shown in Fig. 12.16. Those circumstances are ones in

Figure 12.16 Allocative Efficiency

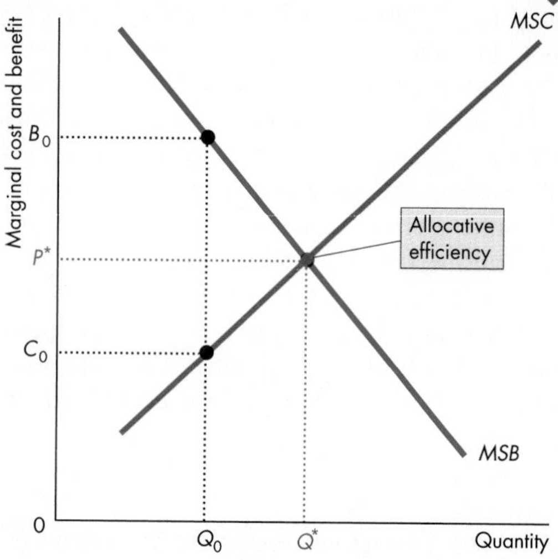

Allocative efficiency, which occurs when no resources are wasted, requires that marginal social cost (*MSC*) be equal to marginal social benefit (*MSB*). Allocative efficiency occurs at output Q^*. If output is Q_0, marginal social cost (C_0) will be less than marginal social benefit (B_0). The benefit from one additional unit of output exceeds its cost. A perfectly competitive market delivers allocative efficiency when there are no external costs and benefits. In such a situation, the marginal social cost curve is the industry supply curve and the marginal social benefit curve is the industry demand curve. The price is P^* and the quantity traded Q^*.

which there are no external costs and benefits. In such a case, all the benefits accrue to the buyers of a good and the costs are borne by its producer. In that case, the marginal social benefit curve is the same as the market demand curve. Also, the marginal social cost curve is the market supply curve. With perfect competition, price and quantity are determined at the point of intersection of the demand and supply curves. Hence, a perfectly competitive market produces an output Q^* at a price P^*. Perfect competition delivers allocative efficiency.

To check that in this situation no resources are being wasted—no one can be made better off without someone being made worse off—consider what will happen if output is restricted to Q_0. At that output, marginal social cost is C_0 but marginal social benefit is B_0. Everyone can be made better off by increasing output. Producers will willingly supply more of the good for a price higher than C_0. Consumers will willingly buy more of the good for a price lower than B_0. Everyone would like to trade more. But once output has increased to Q^*, there are no further available gains from increasing the output of this good. The benefit to the consumer of the last unit produced exactly equals the cost to the producer of the last unit.

The Invisible Hand

The founder of economic science, Adam Smith, suggested that a competitive market acts like an invisible hand to guide buyers and sellers to achieve the best possible social outcome. Each participant in a competitive market is, according to Smith, "led by an invisible hand to promote an end which was no part of his intention." You can see the invisible hand at work in the cartoon on page 309. Adam Smith was not able to work out his conclusion with the clarity and precision with which we are able to do so today. It is the work of Léon Walras and Vilfredo Pareto, and more recently, Nobel Prize-winning American economists Kenneth Arrow and Gérard Debreu that demonstrated the precise conditions under which perfect competition and maximum social welfare coincide.

Obstacles to Efficiency

There are two main obstacles to allocative efficiency:

- External costs and external benefits
- Monopoly

External costs and external benefits mean that many goods cannot be efficiently produced even in perfectly competitive markets. Such goods as national defense, the enforcement of law and order, the provision of clean drinking water and the disposal of sewage and garbage are all examples of goods in which there are enormous external benefits. Left to competitive markets, we would have too small a production of such goods. There are also many examples of goods that impose high external costs. The production of steel and chemicals generate air and water pollution. Perfect competition will result in an overproduction of such goods. One of the key functions of government is to modify the outcome of competitive markets in cases such as these. Government institutions (which we study in Chapters 19 to 21) arise, in part, because of external costs and benefits.

Another obstacle to allocative efficiency is the existence of monopoly. Monopoly, which we study in the next chapter, results in the restriction of output below its competitive level in order to increase price and make a larger profit. Precisely how monopoly achieves this outcome is the subject of the next chapter.

■ We have now completed our study of perfect competition. We have seen how a firm in a perfectly competitive market chooses its profit-maximizing output. We have seen how the actions of all the firms in a market combine to determine the market supply curve and how the market supply and demand curves determine the price and quantity. We have seen how a competitive industry operates in the short run, and we have studied the dynamic forces that move such a market to a long-run equilibrium. We have used the model of perfect competition to understand several important features of real world markets. Finally, we have seen that under some specific circumstances, perfect competition delivers an economically efficient allocation of resources.

Although many markets approximate the model of perfect competition, many do not. Our next task, in Chapters 13 and 14, is to study markets that depart from perfect competition. When we have completed this study, we'll have a toolkit of alternative models of markets that will enable us to study all the possible situations that arise in the real world. We begin, in the next chapter, by going to the opposite extreme of perfect competition—pure monopoly. Then, in Chapter 14, we'll study the markets between perfect competition and pure monopoly—monopolistic competition and oligopoly (competition among a few producers).

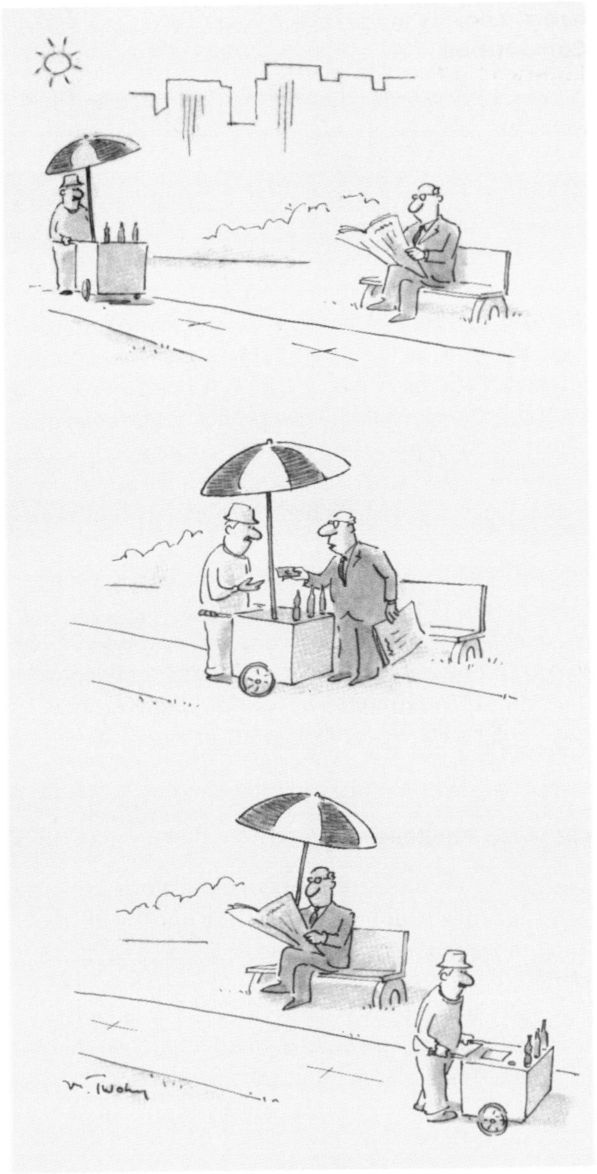

Drawing by M. Twohy; ©1985 The New Yorker Magazine, Inc.

SUMMARY

Perfect Competition

Perfect competition occurs in a market in which a large number of firms produce an identical good; there are many buyers; firms face competition from potential new entrants; and all firms and buyers are fully informed about the prices charged by each firm. In perfect competition, each firm sells its good for the same price and no single firm can influence the market price. Even if one firm doubles its output, the industry output will change by a tiny percentage and the market price will hardly be affected at all. (pp. 281–283)

Firms' Choices in Perfect Competition

A competitive firm takes the market price and has to choose how much to produce, when to temporarily shut down, and when to permanently leave an industry. The firm's choices are motivated by its desire to maximize profit.

A firm's maximum profit is not necessarily a positive profit. If price is above average total cost, the firm makes a profit. If price equals total average cost, the firm breaks even. If price is below average total cost, the firm makes a loss. If price is low enough, the firm maximizes profit by temporarily shutting down and laying off its workers. It pays to shut down production if price is below minimum average variable cost. When price equals minimum average variable cost, the firm makes a loss equal to its total fixed costs whether it produces the profit maximizing output or shuts down.

The firm's supply curve is the upward-sloping part of its marginal cost curve, at all points above the point of minimum average variable cost and runs along the vertical axis at all prices below minimum average variable cost. (pp. 283–292)

Short-run Equilibrium

The short-run industry supply curve shows how the total quantity supplied in the short run by all the firms in an industry varies as the market price varies.

The market price occurs where the quantity supplied and the quantity demanded are equal. Each firm takes the market price as given and chooses the output that maximizes profit. In short-run equilibrium, each firm can make an economic profit or an economic loss, or it can break even. (pp. 292–294)

Long-run Equilibrium

If the firms in an industry make positive economic profits, existing firms will expand and new firms will enter the industry. If the firms in an industry make economic losses, some firms will leave the industry and the remaining firms will produce less. Entry and exit shift the industry supply curve. As firms enter, the industry supply curve shifts to the right. As firms leave, the industry supply curve shifts to the left. Entry causes profits of existing firms to fall and exit causes profits of existing firms to rise (or losses to fall). In long-run equilibrium, firms make zero economic profit. No firm wants to enter or leave the industry and no firm wants to expand or contract its production plant. Long-run competitive equilibrium occurs when each firm maximizes its short-run profit (marginal cost equals marginal revenue equals price); economic profit is zero, so that there is no entry or exit; and each firm produces at the point of minimum long-run average cost; so it has no incentive to change its plant size. (pp. 294–298)

Predictions

In a perfectly competitive market, a permanent decrease in demand leads to a lower industry output and a smaller number of firms in the industry. A permanent increase in demand leads to a rise in industry output and an increase in the number of firms in the industry. If there are no external economies or diseconomies, the market price remains constant in the long-run, as demand changes. If there are external economies, price falls in the long-run as demand rises. If there are external diseconomies, price rises in the long-run as demand rises.

New technology increases the industry supply, and in the long run the market price falls and the quantity traded rises. The number of firms in the industry falls. Firms that are slow to change to the new technology will make losses and eventually will go out of business. Firms that are quick to adopt the new technology will make economic profits initially, but in the long run they will make zero economic profit.

The farm problem of the 1980s, although a complex one, has one central feature that can be understood using the model of perfect competition. A large increase in interest rates increased farms' fixed costs. As a result, their average total cost curves shifted upward. Increased average total cost brought losses. These losses, in turn, forced many farms out of business. As the number of farms declines, the supply curve of farm products shifts to the left and prices increase. But this process takes time—time during which persistent losses occur in the farm sector. Eventually, after the adjustment process is complete, a smaller number of farms will break even. (pp. 298–307)

Competition and Efficiency

Allocative efficiency occurs when no one can be made better off without making someone else worse off. Three conditions for allocative efficiency—economic efficiency, consumer efficiency, and equality of marginal social cost and marginal social benefit—occur in perfect competition when there are no external costs and benefits. It is this situation that Adam Smith was describing when he talked of the economy being led by an "invisible hand."

There are two main obstacles to the achievement of allocative efficiency—the existence of external costs and external benefits and of monopoly. (pp. 307–309)

KEY CONCEPTS

Allocative efficiency, 307
Average revenue, 283
Break-even point, 285
Entry, 294
Exit, 294
External benefits, 307
External costs, 307
External diseconomies, 300
External economies, 300
Marginal revenue, 283
Marginal social benefit, 307
Marginal social cost, 307
Perfect competition, 281
Perfectly competitive firm's supply curve, 291
Price taker, 281
Short-run industry supply curve, 293
Shutdown point, 288

Key Figures

Figure 12.2 Total Revenue, Total Cost, and Profit, 286
Figure 12.3 Marginal Revenue, Marginal Cost, and Profit-Maximizing Output, 287
Figure 12.5 Swanky's Supply Curve, 291
Figure 12.6 Firm and Industry Supply Curves, 292
Figure 12.13 Long-run Price and Quantity Changes, 301
Figure 12.16 Allocative Efficiency, 308

REVIEW QUESTIONS

1 What are the main features of a perfectly competitive industry?

2 Why can't a perfectly competitive firm influence the industry price?

3 List the three key decisions that a firm in a perfectly competitive industry has to make in order to maximize profit.

4 Why is marginal revenue equal to price in a perfectly competitive industry?

5 When will a perfectly competitive firm temporarily stop producing?

6 What is the connection between the supply curve and marginal cost curve of a perfectly competitive firm?

7 What is the relationship between a firm's supply curve and the short-run industry supply curve in a perfectly competitive industry?

8 When will firms enter an industry and when will they leave it?

9 What happens to the short-run industry supply curve when firms enter a competitive industry?

10 What is the effect of entry on the price and quantity produced?

11 What is the effect of entry on profit?

12 Trace the effects of a permanent increase in demand on price, quantity traded, number of firms, and profit.

13 Trace the effects of a permanent decrease in demand on price, quantity traded, number of firms, and profit.

14 Under what circumstances will a perfectly competitive industry have:

a) A perfectly elastic long-run supply curve

b) An upward-sloping long-run supply curve

c) A downward-sloping long-run supply curve

15 Use the model of a perfectly competitive industry to explain why such a large number of farms went out of business in the 1980s.

16 What is allocative efficiency and under what circumstances does it arise?

PROBLEMS

1 Suppose that a firm produces one thousandth of an industry's output. The industry's elasticity of demand is 3. What is the firm's elasticity of demand?

2 Pat's Pizza Kitchen has the following hourly costs:

Output (pizzas per hour)	Total cost (dollars per hour)
0	10
1	12
2	16
3	22
4	30
5	40

a) If pizzas sell for \$9 (and Pat is a price taker), what is his profit-maximizing output per hour?

b) What is Pat's shutdown point?

c) Derive Pat's supply curve.

d) What price will cause Pat to leave the pizza industry?

e) What price would cause other firms with costs identical to Pat's to enter the industry?

f) What is the long-run equilibrium price of pizzas?

3 Why have the prices of pocket calculators and VCRs fallen?

4 What has been the effect of a rise in world population on the wheat market and the individual wheat farmer?

5 How has the diaper service industry been affected by the fall in the U.S. birth rate and the development of disposable diapers?

6 The market demand schedule for record albums is as follows:

Price (dollars per album)	Quantity demanded (albums per week)
0.75	440,000
1.75	430,000
2.75	420,000
3.75	410,000
4.75	400,000
5.75	390,000
6.75	380,000
7.75	370,000
8.75	360,000
9.75	350,000
10.75	340,000
11.75	330,000
12.75	320,000

The market is perfectly competitive and each firm has the same cost structure described by the following table:

Output (albums per week)	Marginal cost (dollars)	Average variable cost (dollars)	Average total cost (dollars)
150	4.82	8.80	15.47
200	4.09	7.69	12.69
250	4.63	7.00	11.00
300	6.75	6.75	10.07
350	9.75	6.91	9.75
400	13.95	7.50	10.00
450	19.62	8.52	10.74
500	26.57	9.97	11.97

There are 1000 firms in the industry.

a) What is the industry price?

b) What is the industry quantity traded?

c) What is the output of each firm?

d) What is the economic profit of each firm?

e) What is the shutdown point?

7 The same demand conditions as those in problem 6 prevail, but total fixed cost increases by $500.

a) What is the short-run profit-maximizing output for each firm?

b) Do firms enter or exit the industry?

c) What is the new long-run equilibrium price?

d) What is the new long-run equilibrium number of firms in the industry?

8 The same cost conditions as those in problem 6 prevail, but the falling price of compact discs decreases the demand for record albums and the demand schedule becomes as follows:

Price (dollars per album)	Quantity demanded (albums per week)
0.75	360,000
1.75	350,000
2.75	340,000
3.75	330,000
4.75	320,000
5.75	310,000
6.75	300,000
7.75	290,000
8.75	280,000
9.75	270,000
10.75	260,000
11.75	250,000
12.75	240,000

a) What is the short-run profit-maximizing output for each firm?

b) Do firms enter or exit the industry?

c) What is the new long-run equilibrium price?

d) What is the new long-run equilibrium number of firms in the industry?

Chapter 13

Monopoly

After studying this chapter, you will be able to:

- Define monopoly
- Explain the conditions under which monopoly arises
- Distinguish between legal monopoly and natural monopoly
- Explain how a monopoly determines its price and output
- Define price discrimination
- Explain why price discrimination leads to a bigger profit
- Compare the performance of a competitive and a monopolistic industry
- Define rent seeking and explain why it arises
- Explain the conditions under which monopoly is more efficient than competition

The Profits of Generosity

You have been hearing a lot in this book about firms that want to maximize profit. But perhaps you've been looking around at some of the places where you do business and wondering if they are really so intent on profit. After all, don't you get a student's discount when you get a haircut? Don't museums and movie theaters give discounts to students, too? And what about the airline that gives a discount for buying a ticket in advance? Are your barber and movie theater owner, as well as the museum and airline operators, simply generous folks to whom the model of profit-maximizing firms does not apply? Aren't they simply throwing profit away by cutting ticket prices and offering discounts? ■ When you want a phone line installed, you really have only one choice—you have to call the local phone company. If you live in New York City and want to buy cable TV service, you only have one option: Buy from Manhattan Cable. Regardless of where you live, you have no choice about the supplier of your local phone service, gas, electricity, or water. If you want to mail a letter, there is only one producer of letter-carrying services (aside from expensive couriers), the U.S. postal service. These are all examples of a single producer of a good or service controlling its supply. Such firms are obviously not like firms in perfectly competitive industries. They don't face a market determined price. They can choose their own price. How do such firms behave? How do they choose the quantity to produce and the price at which to sell it? How does their behavior compare with firms in perfectly competitive industries? Do such firms charge prices that are too high and that damage the interests of consumers? And do such firms bring any benefits?

■ This chapter studies markets in which individual firms can influence the quantity of goods supplied and, as a consequence, exert some influence on price. Whether a firm is a single producer such as the U.S. postal service, or a single producer in a particular location such as a public utility, the firm does not take the market price for its output as given but chooses its price. We begin by studying the conditions under which a single producer controls a market. Then we analyze the price and quantity decisions of such a firm when it sells its output for a single price to all its customers. After that, we study markets in which a firm can charge a higher price to some customers than others. Finally, we ask whether a market controlled by a single firm achieves the same allocative efficiency that arises when a market is perfectly competitive.

How Monopoly Arises

A **monopoly** is an industry in which there is one supplier of a good, service, or resource that has no close substitutes, and in which there is a barrier preventing the entry of new firms. The supply of local phone services, gas, electricity, and water are examples of local monopolies—monopolies restricted to a given location. The U.S. postal service is an example of a national monopoly—a sole supplier of letter-carrying service.

Barriers to Entry

The key feature of a monopoly is the existence of barriers preventing the entry of new firms. **Barriers to entry** are legal or natural impediments protecting a firm from competition from potential new entrants.

Legal Barriers to Entry Legal barriers to entry give rise to legal monopoly. **Legal monopoly** occurs when a law, license, or patent restricts competition by preventing entry. The first legal barrier to entry is a public franchise. A **public franchise** is an exclusive right granted to a firm to supply a good or service. An example of a public franchise is the U.S. postal service, which has the exclusive right to carry first class mail. Another common form of public franchise occurs on freeways and turnpikes where particular firms are given exclusive rights to sell gasoline and food services.

The second legal barrier is a government license. A **government license** controls entry into particular occupations, professions, and industries. Government licensing in the professions is the most important example of this type of barrier to entry. For example, a license is required to practice medicine, law, dentistry, schoolteaching, architecture, and a variety of other professional services and industries. Licensing does not create monopoly, but it does restrict competition.

A third legal restriction on entry is a patent. A **patent** is an exclusive right granted by the government to the inventor of a product or service. A patent is valid for a limited time period that varies from country to country, in the United States it is 17 years. Patents are designed to protect inventors and thereby encourage invention (by preventing others from copying an invention until sufficient time has elapsed for the inventor to have reaped some benefits).

Natural Barriers to Entry Natural barriers to entry give rise to natural monopoly. **Natural monopoly** occurs when there is a unique source of supply of a raw material or when one firm can supply the entire market at a lower price than two or more firms can. As the definition of natural monopoly implies, natural barriers to entry take two forms. First, a single firm may own and control the entire supply of a mineral or natural resource. This type of monopoly occurs in the production of particular types of mineral water, for which there is just a single, unique source, and for some raw materials such as diamonds and chromium. De Beers, a South African company, for example, owns and controls four fifths of the world's diamond mines. Also, all the sources of chromium, again concentrated in southern Africa, are controlled by a small number of producers.

Natural monopoly can also arise because of economies of scale. When a single producer can supply the entire market at a lower average total cost of production than can two or more firms, then only a single firm can survive in the industry. Examples of natural monopoly arising from economies of scale are public utilities, such as the distribution of electricity, natural gas, and water.

Most monopolies in the real world, whether legal or natural, are regulated in some way by government or by government agencies. We will study such regulation in Chapter 21. Here we will consider an unregulated monopoly for two important reasons.

First, we can better understand why governments regulate monopolies and the effects of regulation if we also know how an unregulated monopoly would behave. Second, even in industries with more than one producer, firms often have an element of monopoly power, arising from locational advantages or from important differences in product quality protected by patents. The theory of monopoly sheds important light on the behavior of such firms and industries.

We will begin by studying the behavior of a single-price monopoly. A **single-price monopoly** is a monopoly that charges the same price for each and every unit of its output. How does a single-price monopoly determine the quantity to produce and the price to charge for its output?

Single-Price Monopoly

The starting point for understanding how a single-price monopoly chooses its price and output is to work out the relationship between the demand for the good produced by the monopoly and the monopoly's revenue.

Demand and Revenue

Since in a monopoly there is only one firm, the demand curve facing that firm is the industry demand curve. Let's look at an example: Bobbie's Barbershop, the sole supplier of haircuts in Cairo, Nebraska. The demand schedule that Bobbie faces is set out in Table 13.1. At a price of $20, Bobbie sells no haircuts. The lower the price, the more haircuts per hour Bobbie is able to sell. For example, at a price of $12, consumers demand 4 haircuts per hour (row *e*) and at a price of $4, they demand 8 haircuts per hour (row *i*).

Total revenue (TR) is the price *(P)* multiplied by the quantity sold *(Q)*. For example, in row *d*, Bobbie sells 3 haircuts at $14 each, so total revenue is $42. *Marginal revenue (MR)* is the change in total revenue (ΔTR) resulting from a one-unit rise in the quantity sold. For example, if the price falls from $18 (row *b*) to $16 (row *c*), the quantity sold rises from 1 to 2 haircuts. Total revenue rises from $18 to $32, so the change in total revenue is $14. Since the quantity sold rises by 1 haircut, marginal revenue equals the change in total revenue and is $14. When recording

Table 13.1 Single-Price Monopoly's Revenue

	Price P (dollars per haircut)	Quantity demanded Q (haircuts per hour)	Total revenue $TR = P \times Q$ (dollars)	Marginal revenue $MR = \Delta TR/\Delta Q$ (dollars per haircut)
a	20	0	0	
				18
b	18	1	18	
				14
c	16	2	32	
				10
d	14	3	42	
				6
e	12	4	48	
				2
f	10	5	50	
				−2
g	8	6	48	
				−6
h	6	7	42	
				−10
i	4	8	32	
				−14
j	2	9	18	
				−18
k	0	10	0	

The table shows Bobbie's demand schedule—the number of haircuts demanded per hour at each price. Total revenue *(TR)* is price multiplied by quantity sold. For example, row c shows that when the price is $16 a haircut, two haircuts are sold for a total revenue of $32. Marginal revenue *(MR)* is the change in total revenue resulting from a one-unit rise in the quantity sold. For example, when the price falls from $16 to $14 a haircut, the quantity sold increases from 2 to 3 haircuts and total revenue increases by $10. The marginal revenue of the third haircut is $10. Total revenue rises through row *f*, where 5 haircuts are sold for $10, and it falls thereafter. In the output range over which total revenue is increasing, marginal revenue is positive; in the output range over which total revenue is decreasing, marginal revenue is negative.

marginal revenue, it is written between the two rows to emphasize that marginal revenue relates to the *change* in the quantity sold.

Figure 13.1 shows Bobbie's demand curve (*D*). Each row of Table 13.1 corresponds to a point on the demand curve. For example, row *d* in the table and point *d* on the demand curve tell us that at a price of $14, Bobbie sells 3 haircuts. The figure also shows Bobbie's marginal revenue curve (*MR*). Notice that the marginal revenue curve is below the demand

Figure 13.1 Demand and Marginal Revenue for a Single-Price Monopoly

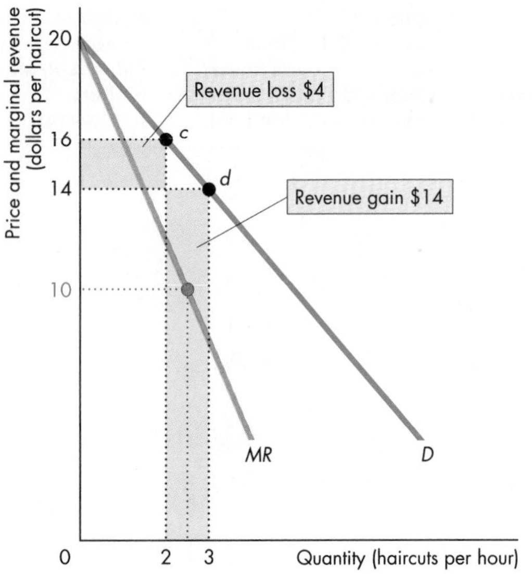

The monopoly demand curve *(D)* is based on the numbers in Table 13.1. At a price of $16 a haircut, Bobbie sells 2 haircuts an hour. If she lowers the price to $14, she sells 3 haircuts an hour. The sale of the third haircut brings a revenue gain of $14 (the price charged for the third haircut). But there is a revenue loss of $4 ($2 per haircut) on the 2 haircuts that she could have sold for $16 each. The marginal revenue (extra total revenue) from the third haircut is the difference between the revenue gain and the revenue loss—$10. The marginal revenue curve *(MR)* shows the marginal revenue at each level of sales. Marginal revenue is lower than price.

curve. That is, at each level of output marginal revenue is less than price. Why is marginal revenue less than price? It is because when the price is lowered to sell one more unit, there are two opposing effects on total revenue. The lower price results in a revenue loss and the increased quantity sold results in a revenue gain. For example, at a price of $16 Bobbie sells 2 haircuts (point *c*). If she reduces the price to $14, she sells 3 haircuts and has a revenue gain of $14 on the third haircut. But she receives only $14 on the first two as well—$2 less than before—so her revenue loss on the first 2 haircuts is $4. She has to deduct this amount from the revenue gain of $14. Marginal revenue—the difference between the revenue gain and the revenue loss—is $10.

Figure 13.2 shows Bobbie's demand curve, marginal revenue curve *(MR),* and total revenue curve *(TR)* and illustrates the connections between them. Again, each row in Table 13.1 corresponds to a point on the curves. For example, row *d* in the table and point *d* on the graphs tell us that when 3 haircuts are sold for $14 each (part a) total revenue is $42 (part b). Notice that as the quantity sold rises, total revenue rises to a peak of $50 (point *f*) and then declines. To understand the behavior of total revenue, notice what happens to marginal revenue as the quantity sold increases. Over the range 0 to 5 haircuts, marginal revenue is positive. When more than 5 haircuts are sold, marginal revenue becomes negative. The output range over which marginal revenue is positive is the same as that over which total revenue is rising. The output range over which marginal revenue is negative is the same as that over which total revenue declines. When marginal revenue is 0, total revenue is at a maximum.

Revenue and Elasticity When we studied elasticity in Chapter 5, we discovered a connection between the elasticity of demand and the effect of a change in price on total expenditure or total revenue. Let's refresh our memories of that connection.

Recall that the elasticity of demand is the percentage change in the quantity demanded divided by the percentage change in price. If the elasticity of demand is greater than 1, a 1 percent decrease in price results in a greater than 1 percent increase in the quantity demanded. If the elasticity of demand is less than 1, a 1 percent decrease in price results in a less than 1 percent increase in the quantity demanded.

But the responsiveness of the quantity demanded to a change in price also influences the change in total revenue. If a 1 percent decrease in price results in an increase in the quantity demanded of more than 1 percent, total revenue increases. We've seen that the output range over which total revenue increases when the price decreases is the same as that over which marginal revenue is positive. Thus the output range over which marginal revenue is positive is also the output range over which the elasticity of demand is greater than 1. The output range over which total revenue decreases when price decreases is the same as that over which marginal revenue is negative. Thus the output range over which marginal revenue is negative is also the output range over which the elasticity of demand is less than 1.

Figure 13.2 A Single-Price Monopoly's Revenue Curves

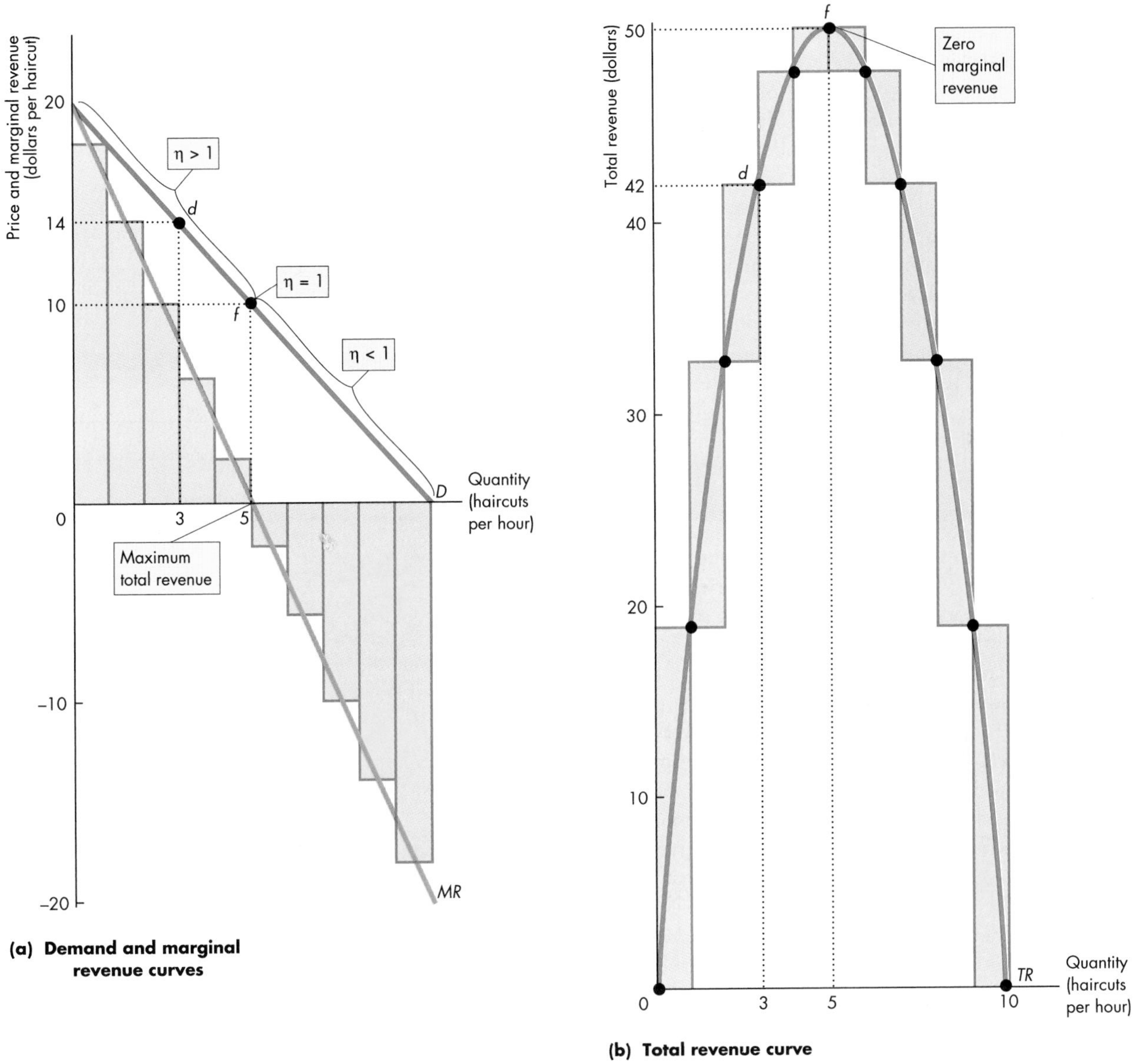

Bobbie's demand curve *(D)* and marginal revenue curve *(MR)*, shown in part (a), and total revenue curve *(TR)*, shown in part (b), are based on the numbers in Table 13.1. For example, at a price of $14, Bobbie sells 3 haircuts an hour (point *d* in part a) for a total revenue of $42 (point *d* in part b). Over the range 0 to 5 haircuts an hour, total revenue is increasing and marginal revenue is positive, as shown by the blue bars. Over the range 5 to 10 haircuts an hour, total revenue declines—marginal revenue is negative, as shown by the red bars. Over the output range for which marginal revenue is positive, the elasticity of demand is greater than 1—demand is elastic. Over the output range for which marginal revenue is negative, the elasticity of demand is less than 1—demand is inelastic. At the output at which marginal revenue is zero, total revenue is at a maximum and the elasticity of demand equals 1—point *f*.

We've seen what happens to marginal revenue and total revenue when the elasticity of demand is greater than 1 and when it is less than 1. If the elasticity of demand is exactly 1, the percentage decrease in price equals the percentage increase in the quantity demanded. In this case, a price change results in no change in total revenue. Marginal revenue is zero. Thus when the elasticity of demand is 1, total revenue is at its maximum and marginal revenue is zero.

The relationship that you have just discovered has an interesting implication: A profit-maximizing monopoly will never produce an output in the inelastic range of its demand curve. If it does so, marginal revenue will be negative—each additional unit sold will lower total revenue. In such a situation, it will always pay to charge a higher price and sell a smaller quantity. But exactly what price and quantity does a profit-maximizing monopoly firm choose?

Price and Output Decision

Profit is the difference between total revenue and total cost. To determine the output level and price that maximize a monopoly's profit, we need to study the behavior of both revenue and costs as output varies.

A monopoly faces the same types of technology and cost constraints as a competitive firm. The monopoly has a production function that is subject to diminishing returns. The monopoly buys its inputs in competition with other firms, at prices that it cannot influence. The sole difference between the monopoly that we'll study here and a perfectly competitive firm lies in the market constraint for the output that each firm faces. The competitive firm is a price taker, whereas the monopoly supplies the entire market. Because the monopoly supplies the entire market, its output decision affects the price at which that output is sold. It is this fact that gives rise to the difference between the decisions faced by these two types of firm.

We have already looked at Bobbie's revenue in Table 13.1 and Figs. 13.1 and 13.2. The revenue information contained in Fig. 13.3 is extracted from Table 13.1. The figure also contains information on Bobbie's costs and profit.

Total cost *(TC)* rises as output rises and so does total revenue (*TR*). Profit equals total revenue minus total cost. As you can see in the table, the maximum profit ($12) occurs when Bobbie sells 3 haircuts for $14 each. If she sells 2 haircuts for $16 each or 4 haircuts for $12 each, her profit will be only $8.

Figure 13.3 A Single-Price Monopoly's Profit-Maximizing Output and Price

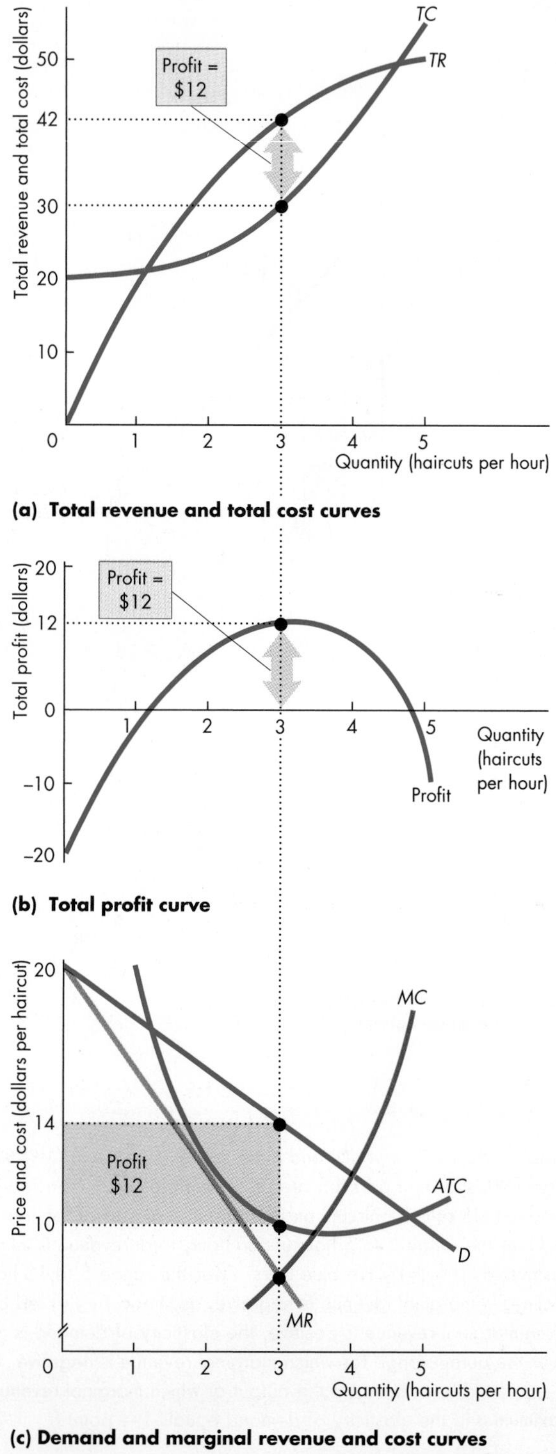

Figure 13.3 A Single-Price Monopoly's Profit-Maximizing Output and Price

Price P (dollars per haircut)	Quantity demanded Q (haircuts per hour)	Total revenue $TR = P \times Q$ (dollars)	Marginal revenue $MR = \Delta TR/\Delta Q$ (dollars per haircut)	Total cost TC (dollars)	Marginal cost $MC = \Delta TC/\Delta Q$ (dollars per haircut)	Profit $TR - TC$ (dollars)
20	0	0		20		−20
			18		1	
18	1	18		21		−3
			14		3	
16	2	32		24		+8
			10		6	
14	3	42		30		+12
			6		10	
12	4	48		40		+8
			2		15	
10	5	50		55		−5

The table adds information about total cost *(TC)*, marginal cost *(MC)*, and profit *(TR − TC)* to the information on demand and revenue in Table 13.1. For example, at a price of $16, 2 haircuts will be sold for a total revenue of $32. The total cost of producing 2 haircuts is $24, so profit equals $8 ($32 − $24). Profit is at a maximum in the row highlighted in red.

The numbers in the table are graphed in the three parts of the figure. The total cost and total revenue curves appear in part (a). The vertical distance between total revenue *(TR)* and total cost *(TC)* equals total profit. Maximum profit occurs at 3 haircuts an hour. Part (b) shows the total profit curve. This curve reaches a maximum at 3 haircuts an hour. The total profit curve is at a maximum (part b) when the vertical distance between the total revenue and total cost curves is also at a maximum (part a). Where total revenue equals total cost (in part a), the total profit curve cuts the horizontal axis (in part b). Part (c) shows that at the profit-maximizing output of 3 haircuts, marginal cost *(MC)* equals marginal revenue *(MR)*. The monopoly sells the output for the maximum possible price as determined by its demand curve. In this case, that price is $14. The monopoly's profit is illustrated in part (c) by the blue rectangle. That profit is $12—the profit per haircut ($4) multiplied by 3 haircuts.

You can see why 3 haircuts is the profit-maximizing output by looking at the marginal revenue and marginal cost columns. When Bobbie raises output from 2 to 3 haircuts, marginal revenue is $10 and marginal cost is $6. Profit increases by the difference—$4. If Bobbie increases output yet further, from 3 to 4 haircuts, she generates a marginal revenue of $6 and a marginal cost of $10. In this case, marginal cost exceeds marginal revenue by $4, so profit falls by $4. It always pays to produce more if marginal revenue exceeds marginal cost and to produce less if marginal cost exceeds marginal revenue. It pays to produce neither more nor less when marginal cost and marginal revenue are equal to each other. Thus the profit-maximizing output occurs when marginal revenue equals marginal cost.

The information set out in the table is shown graphically in Fig. 13.3. Part (a) shows Bobbie's total revenue curve *(TR)* and total cost curve *(TC)*. Profit is the vertical distance between *TR* and *TC*. Bobbie maximizes her profit at 3 haircuts an hour—profit is $42 minus $30, or $12. Part (b) shows how Bobbie's profit varies with the number of haircuts sold.

Figure 13.3(c) shows the demand curve *(D)* and the marginal revenue curve *(MR)* along with the marginal cost curve *(MC)* and average total cost curve *(ATC)*. The profit-maximizing output is 3 haircuts, where marginal cost equals marginal revenue. The price charged is found by reading from the demand curve the price at which 3 haircuts can be sold. That price is $14. When Bobbie produces 3 haircuts, average total cost is $10 (read from the *ATC* curve).

Figure 13.4 Short-run Profit, Costs, and Demand

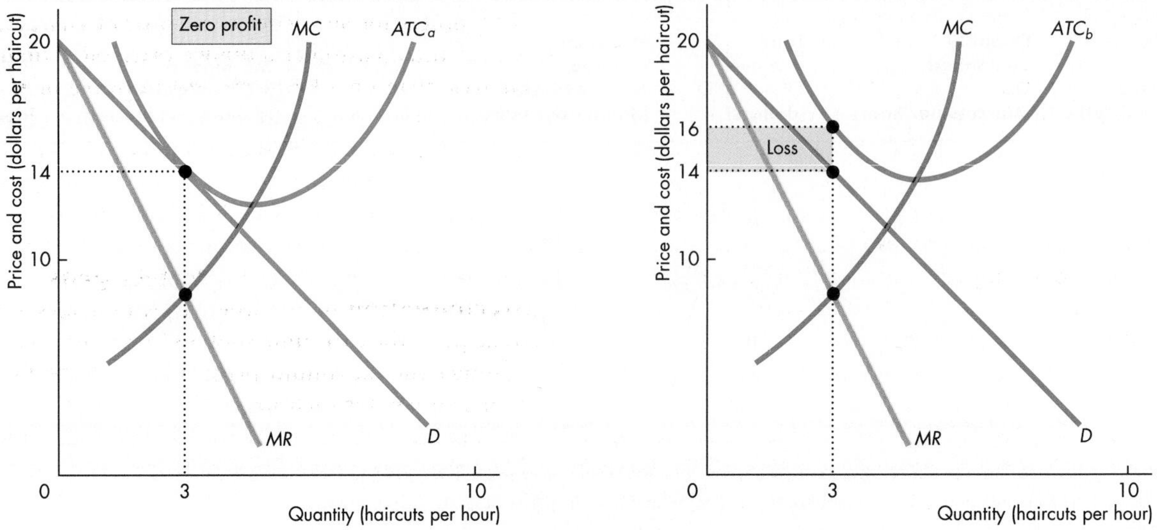

(a) Zero profit

(b) Loss

In the short run, a monopoly can make zero profit or even a loss. Part (a) shows a monopoly making zero profit. At the profit-maximizing output—3 haircuts an hour—average total cost and price are each $14. Part (b) shows a monopoly making a short-run loss. In this case, at the profit-maximizing output (again 3 haircuts an hour) average total cost is $16 and price is $14, so the firm incurs a loss of $6. The loss is represented by the red rectangle.

Her profit per haircut is $4 ($14 minus $10). Bobbie's total profit is indicated by the blue rectangle, which equals the profit per haircut ($4) multiplied by the number of haircuts (3), for a total profit of $12. Since price always *exceeds* marginal revenue and at the profit-maximizing output marginal revenue equals marginal cost, price always exceeds marginal cost.

Bobbie makes a positive profit. But there is nothing to guarantee that a monopoly will be able to make a profit. A monopoly can make a zero profit or even, in the short run, a loss. Figure 13.4 shows the conditions under which these other two outcomes will occur.

If Bobbie's average total cost is ATC_a, as shown in Fig. 13.4(a), then the profit-maximizing output, where marginal revenue equals marginal cost, will be 3 haircuts. At this output, average cost just equals price, so both the profit per haircut and total profit are zero. If Bobbie's average total cost curve is ATC_b, as shown in Fig. 13.4(b), then marginal cost equals marginal revenue at 3 haircuts and average total cost is $16. But 3 haircuts can only be sold for $14 each, so Bobbie makes a loss of $2 a haircut. That loss, however, is the minimum possible loss, so Bobbie is still maximizing profit. A monopoly that makes a loss will only do so in the short run. If the situation shown in Fig. 13.3(b) were permanent, Bobbie would go out of business.

When we studied a competitive firm, we checked to see whether price was higher or lower than average variable cost. With a price below average variable cost, it pays a firm to shut down temporarily and produce nothing. It makes a loss equal to total fixed cost. Like a competitive firm, Bobbie also needs to check her average variable cost to see whether it pays to shut down temporarily. There is no point in any firm, competitor or monopoly, making a loss that exceeds total fixed cost.

If firms in a perfectly competitive industry are making a positive economic profit, new firms enter. That does not happen in a monopoly industry. Barriers to entry prevent new firms from entering. So a firm can make a positive economic profit and continue to do so indefinitely in a monopoly industry. Sometimes that profit is large, as in the cable TV industry (see Reading Between the Lines, pp. 324–325.)

No Monopoly Supply Curve Unlike a perfectly competitive firm, a monopoly does not have a supply curve. Recall that a supply curve shows the quantity supplied at each different price. A change in demand in a competitive industry results in the industry moving along its supply curve and each firm moving along its marginal cost curve. A change in demand in a monopoly also produces a change in price and quantity, but the monopoly does not slide along a supply curve. Instead, given the new demand conditions, the monopoly picks the combination of output and price that maximizes profit, given its cost curves. As in competitive conditions, the monopoly chooses to sell a quantity such that marginal revenue equals marginal cost. But the relationship between price and marginal revenue, and between price and marginal cost, depends on the shape of the demand curve. For a given profit-maximizing quantity, the steeper the demand curve, the higher is the price at which that quantity is sold. It is for this reason that there is no unique relationship between the monopoly's profit-maximizing quantity and price, and therefore no such thing as a monopoly's supply curve.

R E V I E W

A single-price monopoly maximizes profit by producing an output at which marginal cost equals marginal revenue. At that output, the monopoly charges the highest price that consumers are willing to pay. Since a monopoly's price exceeds its marginal revenue, its price also exceeds its marginal cost. But there is no guarantee that a monopoly will make a profit in the short run. Depending on its cost curves and the demand for its output, the monopoly might make a positive economic profit, or a zero profit, or incur a loss. But a monopoly can make a positive economic profit even in the long run since there are barriers to the entry of new firms. There is no unique relationship between the quantity that a monopoly produces and its price—there is no monopoly supply curve. ■

Price Discrimination

Price discrimination is the practice of charging some customers a higher price than others for an identical good or of charging an individual customer a higher price on a small purchase than on a large one. An example of price discrimination is the practice of charging children or students a lower price than adults to see a movie. Another example is the common practice of barbers and hairdressers giving discounts to senior citizens and students. Price discrimination can be practiced in varying degrees. **Perfect price discrimination** occurs when a firm charges a different price for each unit sold and charges each consumer the maximum price that he or she is willing to pay for each unit. Though perfect price discrimination does not happen in the real world, it shows the limit to which price discrimination can be taken.

Not all price *differences* imply price *discrimination.* In many situations, goods that are similar but not identical have different costs and sell for different prices *because* they have different costs. For example, we saw in Chapter 12 that the marginal cost of producing electricity depends on the time of day. If an electric power company charges a higher price for consumption between 7:00 and 9:00 in the morning and between 4:00 and 7:00 in the evening than it does at other times of the day, this practice is not called price discrimination. Price discrimination charges varying prices to consumers, not because of differences in the cost of producing the good, but because different consumers have different demands for the good.

At first sight, it appears that price discrimination contradicts the assumption of profit maximization. Why would a movie operator allow children to see movies at half price? Why would a hairdresser or barber charge students and senior citizens less? Aren't these producers losing profit by being nice guys?

Deeper investigation shows that far from losing profit, price discriminators actually make a bigger profit than they would otherwise. Thus a monopoly has an incentive to try to find ways of discriminating among groups of consumers and charging each group the highest possible price. Some people may pay less with price discrimination, but others pay more. Let's see how price discrimination brings in more total revenue.

Local Monopoly in Cable TV

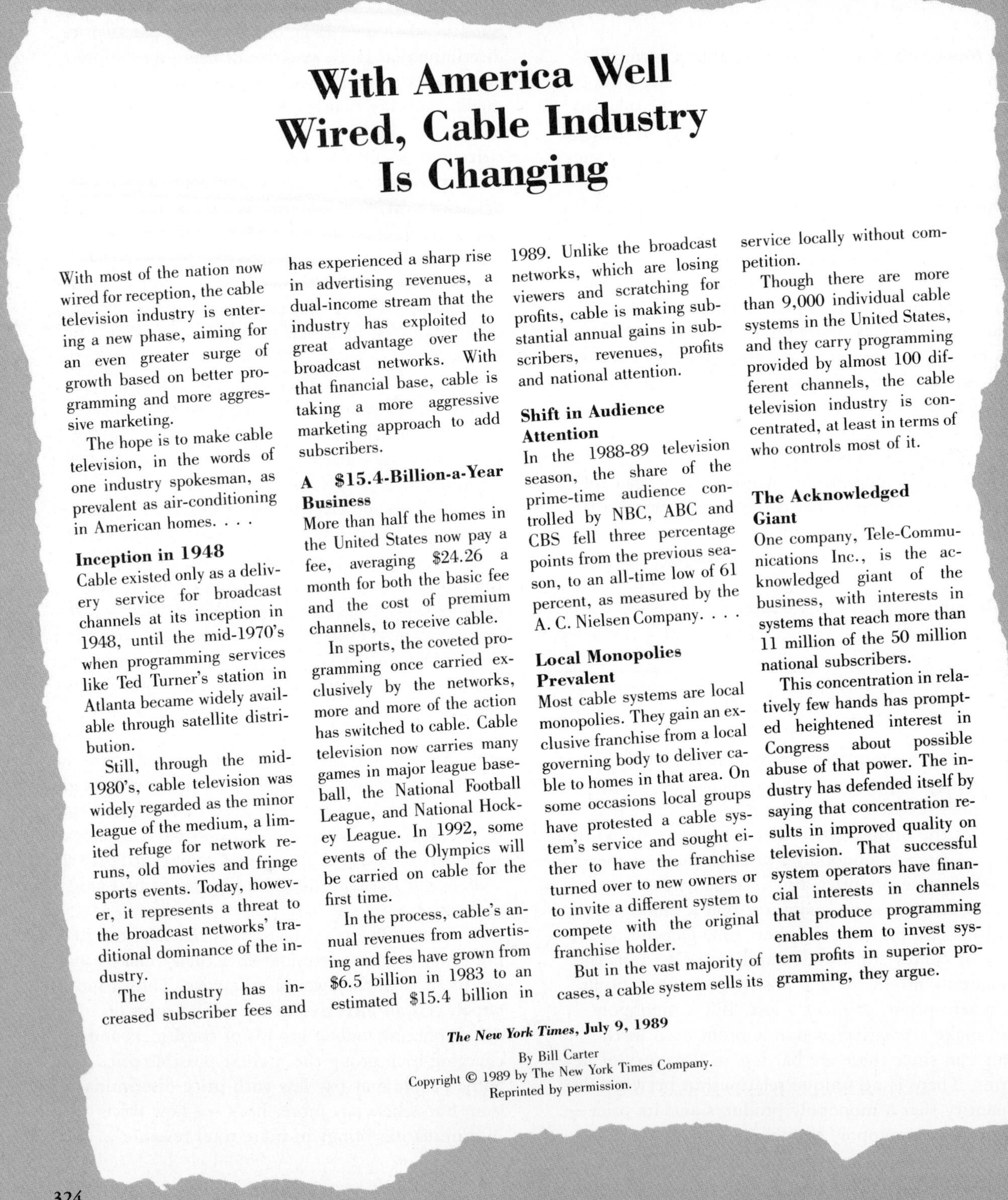

With America Well Wired, Cable Industry Is Changing

With most of the nation now wired for reception, the cable television industry is entering a new phase, aiming for an even greater surge of growth based on better programming and more aggressive marketing.

The hope is to make cable television, in the words of one industry spokesman, as prevalent as air-conditioning in American homes. . . .

Inception in 1948

Cable existed only as a delivery service for broadcast channels at its inception in 1948, until the mid-1970's when programming services like Ted Turner's station in Atlanta became widely available through satellite distribution.

Still, through the mid-1980's, cable television was widely regarded as the minor league of the medium, a limited refuge for network reruns, old movies and fringe sports events. Today, however, it represents a threat to the broadcast networks' traditional dominance of the industry.

The industry has increased subscriber fees and has experienced a sharp rise in advertising revenues, a dual-income stream that the industry has exploited to great advantage over the broadcast networks. With that financial base, cable is taking a more aggressive marketing approach to add subscribers.

A $15.4-Billion-a-Year Business

More than half the homes in the United States now pay a fee, averaging $24.26 a month for both the basic fee and the cost of premium channels, to receive cable.

In sports, the coveted programming once carried exclusively by the networks, more and more of the action has switched to cable. Cable television now carries many games in major league baseball, the National Football League, and National Hockey League. In 1992, some events of the Olympics will be carried on cable for the first time.

In the process, cable's annual revenues from advertising and fees have grown from $6.5 billion in 1983 to an estimated $15.4 billion in 1989. Unlike the broadcast networks, which are losing viewers and scratching for profits, cable is making substantial annual gains in subscribers, revenues, profits and national attention.

Shift in Audience Attention

In the 1988-89 television season, the share of the prime-time audience controlled by NBC, ABC and CBS fell three percentage points from the previous season, to an all-time low of 61 percent, as measured by the A. C. Nielsen Company. . . .

Local Monopolies Prevalent

Most cable systems are local monopolies. They gain an exclusive franchise from a local governing body to deliver cable to homes in that area. On some occasions local groups have protested a cable system's service and sought either to have the franchise turned over to new owners or to invite a different system to compete with the original franchise holder.

But in the vast majority of cases, a cable system sells its service locally without competition.

Though there are more than 9,000 individual cable systems in the United States, and they carry programming provided by almost 100 different channels, the cable television industry is concentrated, at least in terms of who controls most of it.

The Acknowledged Giant

One company, Tele-Communications Inc., is the acknowledged giant of the business, with interests in systems that reach more than 11 million of the 50 million national subscribers.

This concentration in relatively few hands has prompted heightened interest in Congress about possible abuse of that power. The industry has defended itself by saying that concentration results in improved quality on television. That successful system operators have financial interests in channels that produce programming enables them to invest system profits in superior programming, they argue.

The New York Times, July 9, 1989

By Bill Carter

The Essence of the Story

- Cable television service began in 1948 as a method of delivering broadcast television channels.
- In the mid-1970s, the Turner Broadcasting System in Atlanta started supplying television programming services distributed via satellite to local cable companies.
- At first, most programming offered by cable companies was limited to network reruns, old movies, and special interest sporting events. But by 1989, cable programming companies were offering top sporting attractions, and material similar to that on the broadcast networks.
- Cable fees have increased to an average of $24.26 a month; advertising revenue has grown from $6.5 billion in 1983 to an estimated $15.4 billion in 1989; and cable companies' profits are substantial.
- The prime time audience is switching from NBC, ABC, and CBS to the cable channels, and cable television is now in more than 50 million homes.
- Cable television services are operated by local monopolies that gain exclusive franchises from a local government body.
- There are 9000 individual cable systems carrying almost 100 different channels, but some very big companies service a significant proportion of the market and make much of the programming.
- The industry defends monopoly and large-scale producers, saying that large profits are used to make better programs, thereby improving the quality of television.

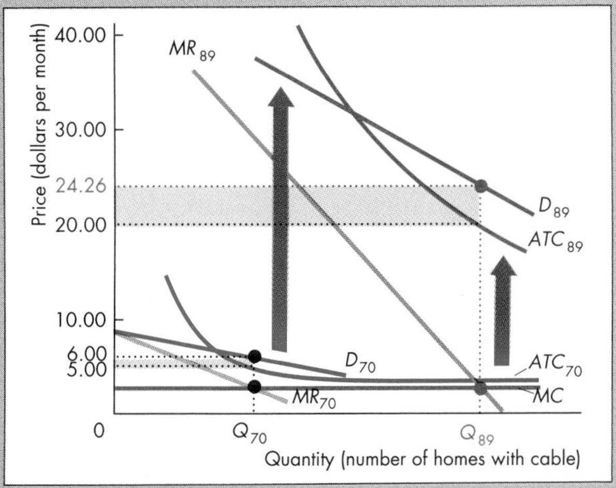

Background and Analysis

- Until the mid-1970s, all television programming could be received (in major population centers) by either broadcast or cable. Hence cable was a close substitute for broadcasting, and the demand for cable services was low, as shown in the figure by demand curve D_{70}. The marginal revenue curve was MR_{70}.
- The marginal cost of adding homes to cable service is low (shown as MC in the figure) and in the mid-1970s average total cost was ATC_{70}.
- In the 1970s, profit was maximized by providing cable service to Q_{70} homes at a price of $6.00 a month. Profits were modest, as shown by the smaller blue-shaded rectangle in the figure.
- The development of satellite technology made it possible for cable programmers to sell via cable services that were not available by broadcast. As a result, the cable companies created improved-quality television services, available exclusively on cable. Consequently, the demand for cable service increased, and the demand curve shifted to D_{89}. The marginal revenue curve shifted to MR_{89}.
- The increased cost of providing the improved cable services shifted the average total cost curve to ATC_{89}, but the marginal cost of adding homes to cable service (probably) did not change, so the marginal cost curve remained at MC.
- The profit-maximizing situation in 1989 was for cable service to be sold to Q_{89} homes—the quantity that makes marginal cost and marginal revenue equal—at a price of $24.26 a month. Profits were high (large blue rectangle).
- Cable programming companies do not "invest their profits in superior programming," as they are reported to argue. To maximize profit, they operate on two margins—the number of homes serviced and the quality of programming. Superior programs cost more but increase demand and bring in more revenue. To maximize profit, cable programmers make the marginal cost of superior programs equal to the marginal revenue they generate.

Figure 13.5 Total Revenue and Price Discrimination

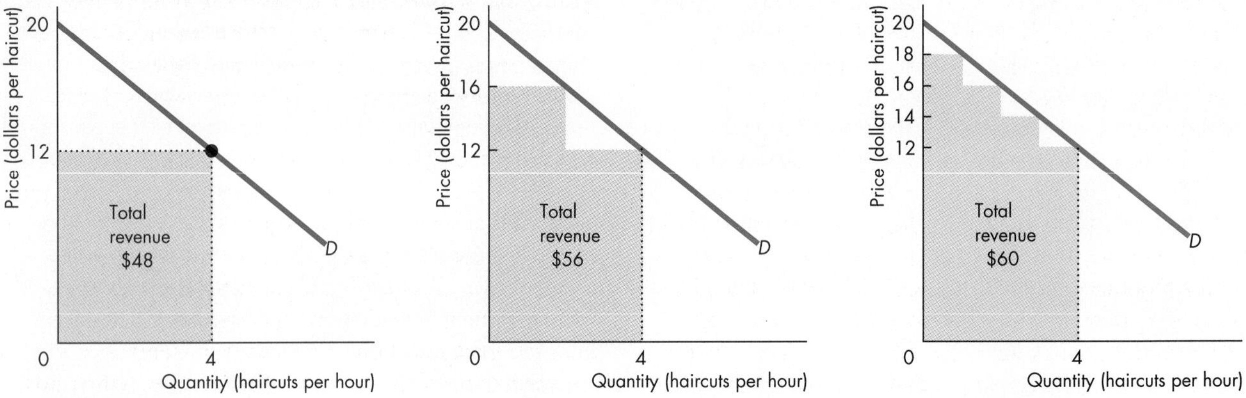

(a) One price **(b) Two prices** **(c) Many prices**

If Bobbie sells 4 haircuts for the same price—$12 each—her total revenue is $48, as shown by the blue rectangle in part (a). If she charges two prices—$16 each for the first 2 haircuts and $12 each for the next 2—her total revenue will be $56, as shown by the blue area in part (b). If Bobbie charges four different prices—$18 for the first haircut, $16 for the second haircut, $14 for the third haircut, and $12 for the fourth haircut—her total revenue will be $60, as shown by the blue area in part (c). The more finely a monopoly can discriminate, the larger the total revenue from a given level of sales.

Price Discrimination and Total Revenue

The total revenue received by a single-price monopoly equals the quantity sold multiplied by the single price charged. That revenue is illustrated in Fig. 13.5(a). Suppose that Bobbie sells 4 haircuts for a single price of $12 each. Bobbie's total revenue, $48, is the area of the blue rectangle—the quantity sold, 4 haircuts, multiplied by the price, $12.

Now suppose that Bobbie can sell some haircuts for one price and some for another, higher price. Figure 13.5(b) illustrates this case. The first 2 haircuts are sold for $16 each and then two more are sold for the original price, $12. In this case, Bobbie has greater total revenue than when she charges a single price. The extra revenue earned on the first 2 haircuts sold has to be added to the original revenue. Total revenue, the blue area shown in part (b), is $56 (2 at $12 plus 2 at $16).

What will happen if Bobbie can perfectly price discriminate? The answer is shown in Fig. 13.5(c). Each haircut is sold for the maximum possible price. The first haircut sells for $18, the next for $16, the third for $14, and the fourth for $12. Total revenue, the blue area in part (c), is $60.

Price Discrimination and Consumer Surplus

Demand curves slope down because the value that an individual places on a good falls as the quantity consumed of that good rises. When all the units consumed can be bought for a single price, consumers make a surplus—*consumer surplus.* (If you need to refresh your understanding of consumer surplus, flip back to Chapter 7, p. 167.) Price discrimination can be seen as an attempt by a monopoly to capture the consumer surplus (or as much of the surplus as possible) for itself.

Discriminating among Units of a Good One form of price discrimination charges each single buyer a different price on each unit of a good bought. An example of this type of discrimination is a discount for bulk buying. The larger the order, the larger is the discount—and the lower is the price. This type of price discrimination works because each individual's demand curve slopes downward. For example, suppose that Lisa is willing to pay $7 to see one movie a month, $6 to see two, and $5 to see three. If movies cost $5, she sees three and pays $5 for each. But the value to her of the first movie is $7—$2 more than she pays for it. And the value to her of the second movie is $6—$1 more than she pays for it. Lisa's consumer surplus is $3.

Now imagine that a movie theater offers the following monthly subscription. For $7, you can see one movie a month; for $13, you can see two a month; for $18, you can see three movies a month. If Lisa opts for the three-movie package, the movie theater extracts from Lisa her entire consumer surplus. But to extract every dollar of consumer surplus from every buyer, the monopolist would have to offer each individual customer a separate contract based on that customer's own demand curve. Clearly such price discrimination cannot be carried out in practice, because a firm does not have sufficient information about each individual consumer's demand curve to be able to do the necessary calculations. But by making arrangements of the type just described that extract most of the consumer surplus of a typical customer, firms can move somewhere toward perfect price discrimination.

Discriminating among Individuals Even when it is not possible to charge each individual a different price for each unit bought, it may still be possible to discriminate among individuals. This possibility arises from the fact that some people place a higher value on consuming one more unit of a good than do other individuals. By charging such an individual a higher price, the producer can obtain some of the consumer surplus that would otherwise accrue to their customers.

Let's look a bit more closely at the price and output decisions of a monopoly that practices price discrimination.

Price and Output Decisions with Price Discrimination

Price discrimination often takes the form of discriminating between different groups of consumers on the basis of age, employment status, or other easily distinguished characteristics. Price discrimination works only if each group has a different price elasticity of demand for the product. If one group has a high elasticity and the other a low elasticity, then a firm can increase profit by charging a lower price to the group with the high elasticity and a higher price to the group with a low elasticity.

Let's stick with the example of haircuts. Bobbie suspects that the students and the elderly of Cairo have a higher elasticity of demand for haircuts than do other people—they do not seem to care as much about getting a bit shaggy as the business people and homemakers. Let's see how Bobbie exploits these differences in demand and raises her profit by price discriminating. Until now, Bobby has sold 3 haircuts an hour at $14 a haircut, for a total revenue of $42. With a total cost of $30 an hour, Bobbie makes an hourly profit of $12. Bobbie's costs, revenues, and profit were shown in the table in Fig. 13.3.

Bobbie has noticed that students and elderly customers come in less frequently than other clients. In fact, of the 3 haircuts she does each hour, 2 are for business people or homemakers and only 1 for an elderly customer or a student. Bobbie also suspects that the business people and homemakers will still turn up for haircuts at the rate of 2 an hour, even if she charges them a higher price. She knows that to get more students and seniors, she has to lower the price she charges them. Bobbie decides to try price discriminating between the two groups. But she has to figure out what price to charge each group to maximize her profit. Table 13.2 sets out the calculations that Bobbie performs. It shows Bobbie's estimates of the demand schedules for her two groups of customers. It also shows the total revenue and marginal revenue calculations for the two separate groups. Bobbie's marginal costs are the same for both groups—hair is hair, whether it belongs to a student or a homemaker. But marginal revenue differs between the two groups of customers. For example, when the price falls from $18 to $16, the marginal revenue from students and the elderly is zero, while for others, it is $14. When the price falls from $16 to $14, the marginal revenue from students and the elderly is $14, while that from others is *minus* $4.

Bobbie maximizes her profit by lowering the price and increasing output when marginal revenue exceeds marginal cost and by raising the price and

Table 13.2 Profiting from Price Discrimination

Price *P* (dollars per haircut)	Students and the elderly: Quantity demanded *Q* (haircuts per hour)	Total revenue *TR* (dollars)	Marginal revenue *MR* (dollars per haircut)	Others: Quantity demanded *Q* (haircuts per hour)	Total revenue *TR* (dollars)	Marginal revenue *MR* (dollars per haircut)
20	0	0		0	0	
			0			18
18	0	0		1	18	
			0			14
16	0	0		2	32	
			14			−4
14	1	14		2	28	
			10			−4
12	2	24		2	24	
			6			−4
10	3	30		2	20	

Profit Calculation

Profit = $TR - TC$

= (\$12 × 2) + (\$16 × 2) − \$40

= \$16

As a single-price monopoly, Bobbie sells 3 haircuts an hour for \$14 each and makes a maximum profit of \$12, as was shown in Fig. 13.3. By discriminating between two groups of customers—the first group consisting of students and the elderly and the second group consisting of all other customers—Bobbie is able to make a bigger profit. She raises the price of regular haircuts to \$16 and lowers the price for students and the elderly to \$12. Her sales rise to 4 haircuts an hour and her profit rises to \$16.

decreasing output when marginal cost exceeds marginal revenue. In this example, Bobbie calculates her profit-maximizing prices and output in the following way. She knows that the marginal cost of the third haircut that she is producing, without price discrimination, is \$6. (To see this, look back at the table for Fig. 13.3.) If her output increases, with price discrimination, the marginal cost of the fourth haircut is \$10. She looks at her marginal revenues and compares them with this \$10 marginal cost. She notices that by charging her business and homemaking customers \$16, this group buys 2 haircuts an hour for a marginal revenue of \$14. If she charges her students and elderly customers \$12, that group buys 2 haircuts an hour and brings in a marginal revenue of \$10. Thus when she sells a total of 4 haircuts (2 to students and elderly and 2 to other customers) the marginal revenue from the students and elderly, \$10, just equals the marginal cost of the fourth haircut.

But she can see that if she lowers the price to either group, marginal revenue will fall short of marginal cost. Marginal cost will climb to \$15 for a fifth haircut and marginal revenue will fall to \$6 if an extra haircut is sold to students and the elderly. Other customers have an inelastic demand curve and will not buy any more than 2 haircuts, so that marginal revenue from lowering the price to that group is negative. Thus Bobbie can make no more profit than that arising from charging students and the elderly \$12 and other customers \$16 and producing 4 haircuts an hour. The profit from such price discrimination is \$16. (The calculation is set out at the foot of Table 13.2.)

Figure 13.6 Output and Profit with Perfect Price Discrimination

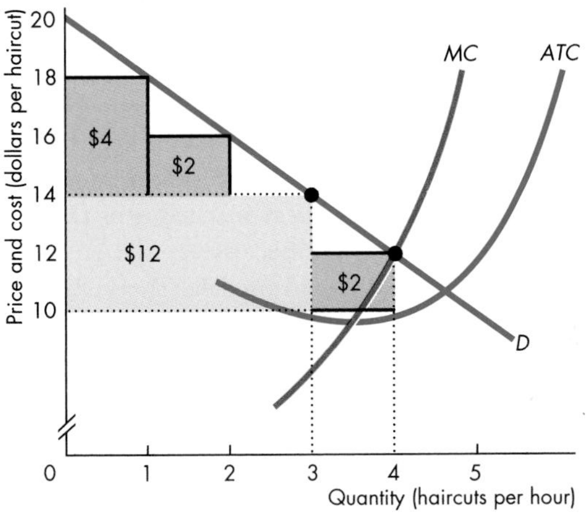

Bobbie's profit as a single-price monopoly, shown by the the light blue area, is $12. With perfect price discrimination, Bobbie charges $18 for the first haircut, $16 for the second, $14 for the third, and $12 for the fourth. Marginal revenue equals price in each case because, with perfect price discrimination, the marginal revenue curve is the same as the demand curve. Profit is maximized when the demand curve intersects the marginal cost curve. It does not pay Bobbie to sell a fifth haircut because its marginal revenue (price) is less that its marginal cost. Bobbie's additional profit as a perfect price discriminator, shown by the dark blue areas, is $8. Her maximum total profit with perfect price discrimination is $20.

Maximum profit with single price:			$12	Quantity: 3 haircuts
add	extra profit from 1st haircut		+4	
add	extra profit from 2nd haircut		+2	
add	extra revenue from 4th haircut	$12		
less	marginal cost of 4th haircut	−10		
add	extra profit from 4th haircut		+2	
equals	maximum profit with price discrimination		$20	Quantity: 4 haircuts

Perfect Price Discrimination

Suppose that Bobbie is able to devise a means of being a perfect price discriminator. How much profit can she make in this case? Bobbie's demand and cost curves are shown in Fig. 13.6. As a single-price monopoly, she produces 3 haircuts, sells them for $14 each, and makes a profit of $12—the light blue rectangle. (Refresh your memory if necessary by referring back to Fig. 13.3c.) If Bobbie can get each of her customers to pay the maximum price that each is willing to pay for a haircut, then she can sell the first haircut for $18. She makes an extra profit of $4 ($18 minus $14) from that first haircut sold. She can sell the second haircut for $16, $2 more than before. She will still sell the third for $14, since that is the maximum price that the third customer is willing to pay for a haircut. If Bobbie continues to produce 3 haircuts, her profit rises to $18, an increase of $6.

But Bobbie will not stop at 3 haircuts an hour. To see why, consider the marginal revenue from selling a fourth haircut and the marginal cost of producing it. The fourth haircut can be sold for $12. The marginal cost of the fourth haircut, from the table in Fig. 13.3, is only $10. So by producing a fourth haircut and selling it for $12, Bobbie makes a further $2 profit. The maximum profit with price discrimination occurs when Bobbie sells 4 haircuts, each for the maximum price that the consumers are willing to pay. That profit is illustrated in the figure as the sum of the light blue and the dark blue rectangles. The table in the figure summarizes the calulation.

When a firm practices perfect price discrimination, its output exceeds that of a single-price monopoly. It produces up to the point at which the marginal cost curve cuts the demand curve. The less perfect the price discrimination, the smaller is the additional output produced.

REVIEW

Price discrimination increases a monopoly's profit by increasing its total revenue. By charging the highest price for each unit of the good that each person is willing to pay, a monopoly perfectly price discriminates and captures all of the consumer surplus. Much price discrimination takes the form of discriminating among different groups of customers, charging a higher price to some and a lower price to others. Such price discrimination increases total revenue and profit, but it is possible only if the two groups have different elasticities of demand. A price-discriminating monopoly produces a larger output than a single-price monopoly. ■

Discrimination among Groups

You can now see why it pays to price discriminate. The sign in Bobbie's window—"Haircuts $16: Special for students and seniors, only $12"—is no generous gesture. It is profit-maximizing behavior. The model of price discrimination that you have just studied explains a wide variety of familiar pricing practices, even by firms that are not pure monopolies. For example, airlines offer lower fares for advance-purchase tickets than for last-minute travel. Last-minute travelers usually have a low elasticity of demand, while vacation travelers who can plan ahead have a higher elasticity of demand. Retail stores of all kinds hold seasonal "sales" when they reduce their prices, often by substantial amounts. These "sales" are a form of price discrimination. Each season, the newest fashions carry a high price tag but retailers do not expect to sell all their stock at such high prices. At the end of the season, they sell off what is left at a discount. Thus such stores discriminate between buyers who have an inelastic demand (for example, those who want to be instantly fashionable) and buyers who have an elastic demand (for example, those who pay less attention to up-to-the-minute fashion and more attention to price).

Limits to Price Discrimination

Since price discrimination is profitable, why don't more firms do it? Why don't we see senior citizen discounts on speeding tickets? What are the limits to price discrimination?

Profitable price discrimination can take place only under certain conditions. First, it is possible to price discriminate only if the good cannot be resold. If a good can be resold, then customers who get the good for the low price can resell it to someone willing to pay a higher price. Price discrimination breaks down. It is for this reason that price discrimination usually occurs in markets for services rather than in markets for storable goods. One major exception, price discrimination in the sale of fashion clothes, works because at the end of the season when the clothes go on sale, the fashion plates are looking for next season's fashions. People buying on sale have no one to whom they can resell the clothes at a higher price.

Second, a price discriminating monopoly must be able to identify groups with different elasticities of demand. The characteristics used for discrimination must also be within the law. These requirements usually limit price discrimination to cases based on either age or employment status, or on the timing of the purchase.

Despite these limitations, there are some ingenious criteria used for discriminating. For example, TWA discriminates between five different passenger groups on many of its international flights. The economy class alternatives between New York and London at one point in 1989 were:

- $1730—no restrictions
- $821—14-day advance purchase
- $771—14-day advance purchase mid-week only
- $658—30-day advance purchase
- $608—30-day advance purchase mid-week only

These different prices discriminate between different groups of customers with different elasticities of demand.

Comparing Monopoly and Competition

We have now studied a variety of ways in which firms and households interact in markets for goods and services. In Chapter 12, we saw how perfectly competitive firms behave and discovered the price and output at which they operate. In this chapter, we have studied the price and output of a single-price monopoly and a monopoly that price discriminates. How do

"Yoo-hoo! My husband gets the senior-citizen discount! Yoo-hoo, Officer, yoo-hoo!"

the quantities produced, prices, and profits of these different types of firms compare with each other?

To answer this question, let's imagine an industry made up of a large number of identical competitive firms. We will work out what the price charged and quantity traded will be in that industry. Then we will imagine that a single firm buys out all the individual firms and creates a monopoly. We will then work out the price charged and quantity produced by the monopoly, first when it charges a single price, and second when it price discriminates.

Price and Output

We will conduct the analysis by using Fig. 13.7. The industry demand curve is *D* and the industry supply curve is *S*. In perfect competition, the market equilibrium occurs where the supply curve and the demand curve intersect. The quantity produced by the industry is *C* and the price is P_C.

Each firm takes the price P_C and maximizes its profit by producing the output at which its own marginal cost equals the price. Since each firm is a small part of the total industry, there is no incentive for any firm to try to manipulate the price by varying its output.

Now suppose that this industry is taken over by a single firm. No changes in production techniques occur, so the new combined firm has identical costs to the original separate firms. The new single firm recognizes that by varying output it can influence price. It also recognizes that its marginal revenue curve is *MR*. To maximize profit, the firm chooses an output at which marginal revenue equals marginal cost. But what is the monopoly's marginal cost curve? To answer this question, you need to recall the relationship between the marginal cost curve and the supply curve of a competitive firm. The supply curve of an individual competitive firm is its marginal cost curve. The supply curve of a competitive industry is derived from the supply curves of each individual firm. The industry supply curve tells us how the sum of the quantities supplied by each firm varies as the price varies. Thus the industry supply curve is also the industry's marginal cost curve. (The supply curve has also been labeled *MC* to remind you of this fact.) Therefore, when the industry is taken over by a single firm, that firm's marginal cost curve is the

Figure 13.7 Monopoly and Competition Compared

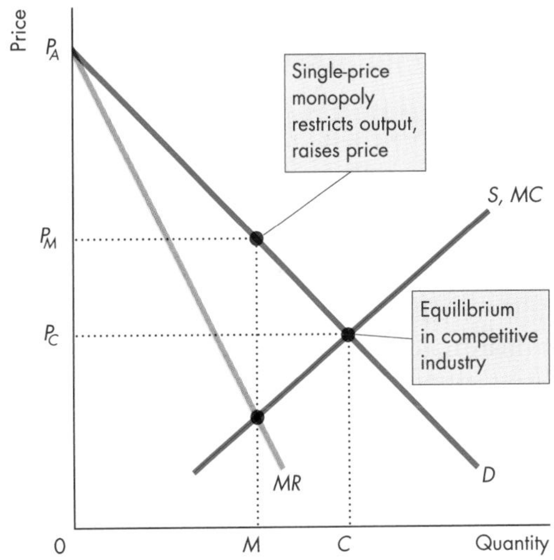

A competitive industry has a demand curve *D* and a supply curve *S*. Equilibrium occurs where the quantity demanded equals the quantity supplied at quantity *C* and price P_C. If all the firms in the industry are taken over by a single producer who sells the profit-maximizing output for a single price, marginal revenue is *MR* and the supply curve of the competitive industry, *S*, becomes the monopoly's marginal cost curve, *MC*. The monopoly produces the output at which marginal revenue equals marginal cost. A single-price monopoly produces *M* and sells that output for the price P_M. A perfectly price-discriminating monopoly produces *C* and charges a different price for each unit sold. The prices charged range from P_A to P_C. Monopoly restricts output and raises the price. But the more perfectly a monopoly can price discriminate, the closer its output gets to the competitive output.

same as what used to be the competitive industry's supply curve.

A competitive industry operates at the point of intersection of its supply and demand curves—in Fig. 13.7, at a price of P_C and quantity *C*. The single-price monopoly maximizes profit by restricting output to *M*, where marginal revenue equals marginal cost. Since the marginal revenue curve is below the demand curve, output *M* will always be smaller than output *C*. The monopoly charges the highest price for which output *M* can be sold, and that price is P_M.

If the monopoly can perfectly price discriminate, it will charge a different price on each unit sold and increase output to *C*. The highest price charged is P_A and the lowest price charged is P_C, the price in a competitive market. The price P_A is the highest that is charged because at yet higher prices nothing can be sold. The price P_C is the lowest charged because when a monopoly perfectly price discriminates, its marginal revenue curve is the same as the demand curve and at prices below P_C marginal cost exceeds marginal revenue.

The key price and output differences between competition and monopoly are the following:

- Monopoly price exceeds the competitive price.
- Monopoly output is less than competitive output.
- The more perfectly the monopoly can price discriminate, the closer its output gets to the competitive output.

Allocative Efficiency

Monopoly is less efficient than competition. It prevents some of the gains from trade from being achieved. To see why, look at Fig. 13.8. The maximum price that consumers are willing to pay for each unit is shown by the demand curve. The difference between the maximum price that they are willing to pay for each unit bought and the price they do pay is *consumer surplus*. Under perfect competition (part a), consumers have to pay only P_C for each unit bought and obtain a consumer surplus represented by the green triangle.

A single-price monopoly (part b) restricts output to *M* and sells that output for P_M. Consumer surplus is reduced to the smaller green triangle. Consumers lose partly by having to pay more for what is available and partly by getting less of the good. But is the consumers' loss equal to the monopoly's gain? Is there simply a redistribution of the gains from trade? A closer look at Fig. 13.8(b) will convince you that there is a reduction in the gains from trade. It is true that some of the loss in consumer surplus does accrue to the monopoly—the monopoly gets the difference between the higher price (P_M) and P_C on the quantity sold *(M)*. So the monopoly has taken the blue rectangle part of the consumer surplus.

What though has become of the rest of the consumer surplus? The answer is that because output has been restricted, it is lost. But more than that has been lost. The total loss resulting from the lower monopoly output *(M)* is the area of the gray triangle in Fig. 13.8(b). The part of the gray triangle above P_C is the loss of consumer surplus and that part of the triangle below P_C is a loss to the producer—a loss of producer surplus. **Producer surplus** is the difference between a producer's revenue and the opportunity cost of production. It is calculated as the sum of the differences between price and the marginal cost of producing each unit of output. Under competitive conditions, the producer sells the output between *M* and *C* for a price of P_C. The marginal cost of producing each extra unit of output through that range is shown by the supply curve. Thus the vertical distance between the marginal cost curve and price represents a producer surplus. Part of the producer surplus is lost when a monopoly restricts output below its competitive level.

The gray triangle, which measures the total loss of both consumer and producer surplus, is called the deadweight loss. **Deadweight loss** measures allocative inefficiency as the reduction in consumer and producer surplus resulting from a restriction of output below its efficient level. A monopoly's reduced output and higher price results in the monopoly capturing some of the consumer surplus. It also results in the elimination of the producer surplus and consumer surplus on that output that a competitive industry would have produced but which the monopoly does not.

We have seen that a single-price monopoly creates a deadweight loss by restricting output. What is the deadweight loss if the monopoly practices perfect price discrimination? The answer is zero. A perfect price discriminator produces the same output as the competitive industry. The last item sold costs P_C, the same as its marginal cost. Thus from the point of view of allocative efficiency, a perfect price-discriminating monopoly achieves the same result as perfect competition.

Figure 13.8 The Allocative Inefficiency of Monopoly

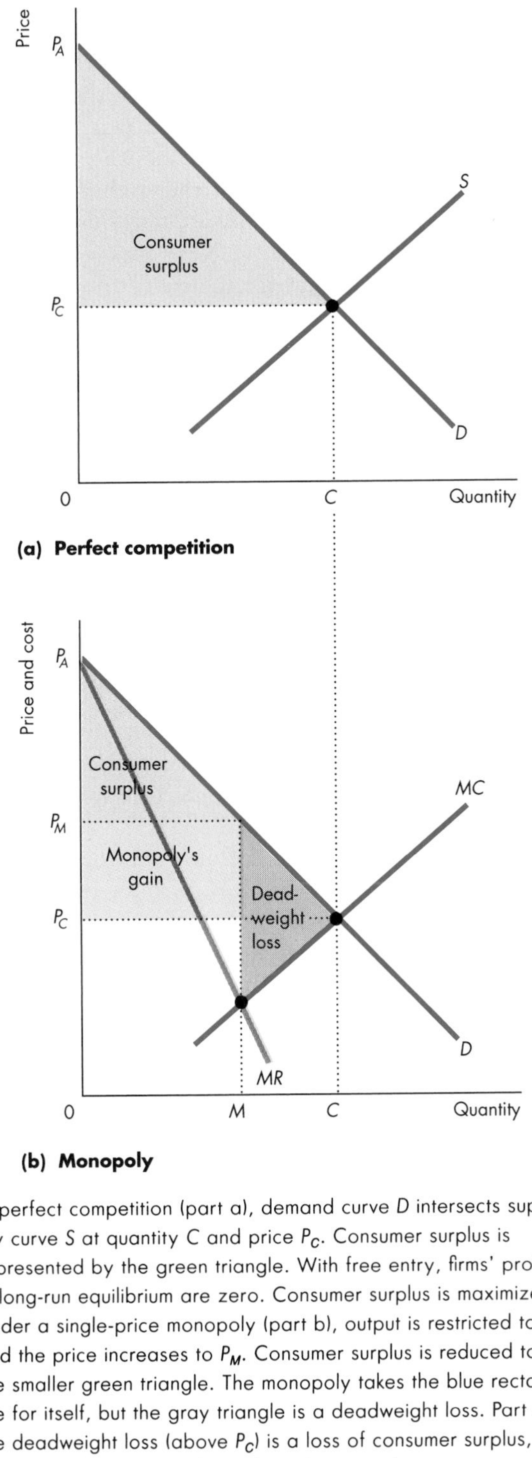

In perfect competition (part a), demand curve *D* intersects supply curve *S* at quantity *C* and price P_C. Consumer surplus is represented by the green triangle. With free entry, firms' profits in long-run equilibrium are zero. Consumer surplus is maximized. Under a single-price monopoly (part b), output is restricted to *M* and the price increases to P_M. Consumer surplus is reduced to the smaller green triangle. The monopoly takes the blue rectangle for itself, but the gray triangle is a deadweight loss. Part of the deadweight loss (above P_C) is a loss of consumer surplus, and part (below P_C) is a loss of producer surplus.

Redistribution

Under perfect competition, the consumer surplus is the green triangle in Fig. 13.8(a). With free entry, the long-run equilibrium economic profit of each perfectly competitive firm is zero. We've just seen that the creation of monopoly reduces consumer surplus. Further, in the case of a single-price monopoly, a deadweight loss arises. But what happens to the distribution of surpluses between producers and consumers? The answer is that the monopoly always wins. In the case of a single-price monopoly (Fig. 13.8b), the monopoly gains the blue rectangle at the expense of the consumer. It has to offset against that gain its loss of producer surplus—its share of the deadweight loss. But there is always a net positive gain for the monopoly and a net loss for the consumer. We also know that because there is a deadweight loss, the consumer loses more than the monopoly gains.

In the case of a perfect price-discriminating monopoly, there is no deadweight loss but there is an even larger redistribution away from consumers to the monopoly. In this case, the monopoly captures the entire consumer surplus, the green triangle in Fig. 13.8(a).

R E V I E W

The creation of a monopoly results in a redistribution of economic gains away from consumers and to the monopoly producer. If the monopoly can perfectly price discriminate, it captures the entire consumer surplus. If the monopoly cannot perfectly price discriminate, a deadweight loss results from restricting output below its perfectly competitive level. The monopoly gains and the consumer loses, but the loss of the consumer exceeds the gain of the monopoly. ■

Rent Seeking

Operating a monopoly is more profitable than operating a firm in a perfectly competitive industry. Economic profit can be made in a competitive industry in the short run but not in the long run. Freedom of entry brings new firms into a profitable industry and results in economic profit being competed away. Barriers to entry prevent this process in a monopoly industry, so a monopoly can enjoy economic profit even in the long run. Because monopoly is more profitable than perfect competition, there is an incentive to attempt to create monopoly. The activity of creating monopoly is called **rent seeking.** The name rent seeking arises from the fact that another name for consumer surplus and producer surplus is rent. We've just seen that a monopoly makes its profit by diverting part of the consumer surplus to itself. Thus pursuing maximum monopoly profit is the same thing as diverting consumer surplus, or rent seeking.

Rent seeking is not a costless activity. To obtain a monopoly right, resources have to be used. Furthermore, everyone has an incentive to seek monopoly power, so there will be competition for monopoly rights. There are two ways in which people compete for monopoly rights—they buy an existing right or they create a new one. But existing monopoly rights had to be created at some time, so ultimately, competition for monopoly rights is a process that uses productive resources in order to establish a monopoly right. What is the value of the resources that a person will use to obtain a monopoly right? The answer is any amount up to the monopoly's profit. If the value of resources spent trying to acquire a monopoly exceeds the monopoly's profit, the net result is an economic loss. But as long as the value of the resources used to acquire a monopoly falls short of the monopoly's profit, there is a profit to be earned. If there is no barrier to entry, the value of the resources used up in rent seeking will, in equilibrium, equal the monopoly's profit.

Because of rent seeking, monopoly imposes costs that exceed the deadweight loss that we calculated earlier. To calculate that cost, we must add to the deadweight loss the value of resources used in rent seeking. That amount equals the entire monopoly profit since that is the value of the resources that it pays to use in rent seeking. Thus the cost of monopoly is the deadweight loss plus monopoly profit.

What exactly are the resources used in rent seeking? What do rent seekers do? One form of rent seeking is the searching out of existing monopoly rights that can be bought for a lower price than the monopoly's economic profit—that is, seeking to acquire existing monopoly rights. This form of rent seeking results in a market price for monopoly rights that is close to the economic profit. There are many real world examples of this type of rent-seeking activity. One that is well known is the purchase of taxicab licenses. In most cities, taxicabs are regulated. The city restricts both the fares and the number of taxis that are permitted to operate. Operating a taxi is profitable—resulting in economic profit or rent being earned by the operator. A person who wants to operate a taxi has to buy the right to do so from someone who already has that right. Competition for that right leads to a price sufficiently high to eliminate long-run economic profit. For example, in New York City, the price that has to be paid for the right to operate a taxi is close to $100,000.[1]

Another example occurred in the airline industry. In 1986, United Airlines bought the rights to all the international air routes across the Pacific Ocean that had previously been owned and operated by Pan American Airlines. United paid Pan Am $500 million for the exclusive rights to these routes. Pan Am had originated these Pacific routes, and other U.S. airlines were prohibited from competing on them by an international air transportation agreement entered into by the United States and other governments. To acquire these routes, United had to pay Pan Am a price that provided as much profit as Pan Am hanging onto the rights and operating the routes themselves would have made. Competition among airlines to buy these rights resulted in them being bought by the most efficient potential operator, because that operator was willing to offer the highest price for them.

Although a great deal of rent-seeking activity involves searching out existing monopoly rights that can be profitably bought, much of it is devoted to the creation of monopoly. This type of rent-seeking activity takes the form of lobbying and seeking to influence the political process. Such influence is sometimes sought by making campaign contributions in exchange for legislative support or in the form of indirectly seeking to influence political outcomes through publicity in the media or more direct contacts with politicians and bureaucrats. (This type of rent seeking is discussed and explained more fully in Chapters 20 and 21.)

---

[1]Taxis do not earn $100,000 in a single year; if they did, there would be fewer economics professors and far more cabbies. Since profits on a taxi will be earned over several future years, the $100,000 price tag on the right to operate a taxi is the *present value* of the expected future profits—see Chapter 9.

R E V I E W

When rent seeking is taken into account, there are no guaranteed long-run profits, even from monopoly. Competition for monopoly rights results in the use of resources to acquire those rights equal in value to the potential monopoly profit. As a consequence, monopoly imposes costs equal to the deadweight loss plus the monopoly's economic profit. ■

Gains from Monopoly

In our comparison of monopoly and competition, monopoly comes out in a pretty bad light. If monopoly is so bad, why do we put up with it? Why don't we have laws that crack down on monopoly so hard that it never rears its head? As we'll see in Chapter 21, we do indeed have laws that limit monopoly power. We also have laws that regulate those monopolies that exist. But monopoly is not all bad. Let's look at its potential advantages and some of the reasons for its existence.

The main reasons for the existence of monopoly are:

- Economies of scale and economies of scope
- Incentive to innovate

Economies of Scale and Scope You met economies of scale in Chapters 9 and 10. There, we defined *economies of scale* as decreases in average total cost resulting from increasing a firm's scale. The scale of a firm increases when it increases all its inputs—capital, labor, and materials—in the same proportions. For example, if all inputs double, total cost also doubles. If output more than doubles, average total cost declines or, equivalently, the firm has economies of scale.

Economies of scope are decreases in average total cost made possible by increasing the number of different goods produced. For example, McDonald's can produce both hamburgers and French fries at an average total cost that is lower than what it would cost two separate firms to produce the same goods. Economies of scope are important when highly skilled (and expensive) technical inputs can be shared by different goods. For example, computer programmers and designers and marketing experts can apply their skills to producing a variety of goods, thereby spreading their costs and lowering the cost of production of each of the goods.

Large-scale firms that have control over supply and can influence price—and that therefore behave like the monopoly firm that we've been studying in this chapter—can reap these economies of scale and scope. Small, competitive firms cannot. As a consequence, there are situations in which the comparison of monopoly and competition that we made earlier in this chapter is not a valid one. Recall that we imagined the takeover of a large number of competitive firms by a single monopoly firm. But we also assumed that the monopoly would use exactly the same technology as the small firms and have the same costs. But if one large firm can reap economies of scale and scope, its marginal cost curve will lie below the supply curve of a competitive industry made up of thousands of small firms. It is possible for such economies of scale and scope to be so large as to result in a higher output and lower price under monopoly than a competitive industry would achieve.

Figure 13.9 illustrates such a situation. Here, the demand curve and the marginal revenue curve are the same regardless of whether the industry is a competitive one or a monopoly. With a competitive industry, the supply curve is *S*, the quantity produced is *C*, and the price is P_C. With a monopoly that can exploit economies of scale and scope, the marginal cost curve is MC_M. The monopoly maximizes profit by producing the output *(M)* at which marginal revenue equals marginal cost. The price that maximizes profit is P_M. By exploiting a superior technology not available to each of the large number of small firms, the monopoly is able to achieve a higher output and lower price than the competitive industry.

There are many examples of industries in which economies of scale are so important that they lead to an outcome similar to that shown in Fig. 13.9. Public utilities such as gas, electric power, water, local telephone service, and garbage collection are all such cases. There are also many examples where a combination of economies of scale and economies of scope are important. Examples are the brewing of beer, the manufacture of refrigerators and other household appliances, pharmaceuticals, and the refining of petroleum.

Figure 13.9 When Economies of Scale and Scope Make Monopoly More Efficient

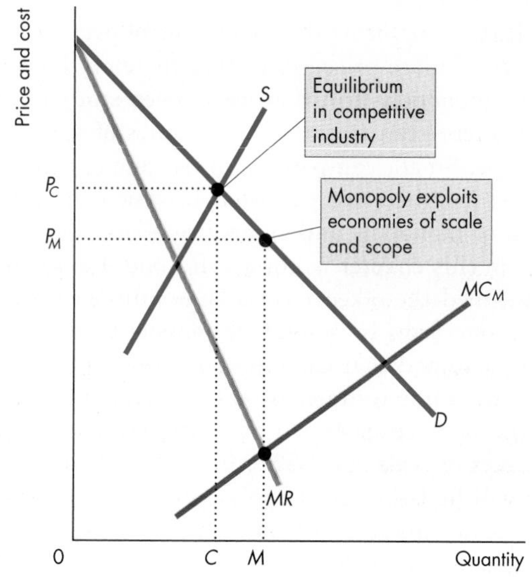

In some industries, economies of scale and economies of scope result in the monopoly's marginal cost curve (MC_M) lying below the competitive industry supply curve (S). In such a case, it is possible that the single-price monopoly output (M) exceeds the competitive output (C) and that the monopoly price (P_M) is below the competitive price (P_C).

Innovation Innovation is the first-time application of new knowledge in the production process. Innovation may take the form of developing a new product or a lower-cost way of making an existing product. Controversy has raged among economists over whether large firms with monopoly power or small competitive firms lacking such monopoly power are the most innovative. It is clear that some monopoly power (temporary monopoly power) arises from innovation. A firm that develops a new product or process and patents it obtains exclusive right to that product or process for the term of the patent. But does the granting of a monopoly, even a temporary one, to an innovator increase the pace of innovation? One line of reasoning suggests that it does. With no protection, an innovator is not able to enjoy the profits from innovation for very long. Thus the incentive to innovate is weakened. A contrary argument is that monopolies can afford to be lazy while competitive firms cannot. Competitive firms must strive to innovate and cut costs even though they know that they cannot hang on to the benefits of their innovation for long. But that knowledge spurs them on to greater and faster innovation.

A matter such as this one cannot be resolved by listing arguments and counterarguments. It requires a careful empirical investigation. Many such investigations have been conducted. But the evidence that they bring to bear on this question is mixed. They show that large firms do much more research and development than do small firms. They also show that large firms are significantly more prominent at the development end of the research and development process. But measuring research and development is measuring the volume of inputs into the process of innovation. What matters is not input but output. Two measures of the output of research and development are the number of patents and the rate of productivity growth. On these measures, there is no clear evidence that big is best. But there is a clear pattern in the process of diffusion of technological knowledge. After innovation, a new process or product spreads gradually through the industry. Whether an innovator is a small firm or a large firm, large firms jump on the bandwagon more quickly than do the remaining small firms. Thus large firms are important in speeding the process of diffusion of technological advances.

In determining public policy toward monopoly (matters discussed in Chapter 21), laws and regulations are designed that balance these positive aspects of monopoly against the deadweight loss and redistribution that they also generate.

■ We've now studied two models of market structure—perfect competition and monopoly. We've discovered the conditions under which perfect competition achieves allocative efficiency and we've compared the efficiency of competition with that of monopoly. We've also used these two models to make predictions about the effects on prices and quantities of changing cost and demand conditions.

Although there are examples of markets in the U.S. economy that are highly competitive or highly monopolistic, the markets for most goods and services lie somewhere between these two extremes. In the next chapter, we're going to study this middle ground between monopoly and competition. We're going to discover that many of the lessons that we learned from these two extreme models are still relevant and useful in understanding behavior in real world markets.

SUMMARY

How Monopoly Arises

Monopoly arises because of barriers to entry that prevent competition. Barriers to the entry of new firms may be legal or natural. Legal barriers take the form of public franchises, government licenses, or patents. Natural barriers exist when a single firm possesses total control of a mineral or natural resource or when economies of scale are so large that a single firm can supply an entire market at a lower average total cost than can several firms. (pp. 316–317)

Single-Price Monopoly

A monopoly is an industry in which there is a single supplier of a good, service, or resource. A single-price monopoly is a firm that charges the same price for each unit of output. The monopoly's demand curve is the market demand curve for the good. For a single-price monopoly, marginal revenue is less than price. Total revenue rises at first, but above some output level it begins to decline. When total revenue is rising, marginal revenue is positive. When total revenue is falling, marginal revenue is negative. When marginal revenue is positive (total revenue rising), the elasticity of demand is greater than 1. The elasticity of demand equals 1 when total revenue is at a maximum.

A monopoly's technology and costs behave in a way similar to those of any other type of firm. The monopoly maximizes profit by producing the output that makes marginal revenue equal to marginal cost, and by charging the maximum price that consumers are willing to pay for that output. The price charged always exceeds marginal cost. There is no supply curve in a monopoly. (pp. 317–323)

Price Discrimination

Price discrimination is the practice of charging some consumers a higher price than others for an identical item or charging an individual customer a higher price on a small purchase than on a large one. Price discrimination is an attempt by the monopoly to convert consumer surplus into profit. Perfect price discrimination extracts all the consumer surplus. Such a monopoly charges a different price for each unit sold and obtains the maximum price that each consumer is willing to pay for each unit bought. With perfect price discrimination, the monopoly's marginal revenue curve is the same as its demand curve and the monopoly produces the same output as would a perfectly competitive industry.

A monopoly can discriminate between different groups of customers on the basis of age, employment status, or other distinguishable characteristics. Such price discrimination increases the monopoly's profit if each group has a different elasticity of demand for the product. To maximize profit with price discrimination, the monopoly produces an output such that marginal cost equals marginal revenue, but then charges each group the maximum price that it is willing to pay.

Price discrimination can be practiced only when it is impossible for a buyer to resell the good and when consumers with different elasticities can be identified. (pp. 323–330)

Comparing Monopoly and Competition

If a monopoly takes over all the firms in a perfectly competitive industry and if the technology and input prices in the industry remain unchanged, the monopoly charges a higher price and produces a lower quantity than would prevail in a perfectly competitive industry. If the monopoly can perfectly price discriminate, it produces the competitive quantity and sells the last unit for the competitive price.

Monopoly is less efficient than competition because it prevents some of the gains from trade from being achieved. A monopoly captures some part of the consumer surplus, but to do so it has to restrict output so that when it maximizes profit it creates a deadweight loss. The more a monopoly is able to price discriminate, the smaller the deadweight loss but the larger the monopoly profit and the smaller the consumer surplus.

Monopoly redistributes away from consumers toward the producer. The more perfectly a monopoly can price discriminate, the smaller the deadweight loss but the larger the reallocation of surpluses from consumers to the producer.

Monopoly imposes costs that equal its deadweight loss plus the cost of the resources devoted to rent seeking—searching out profitable monopoly opportunities. It pays to use resources equal in value to the entire monopoly profit that might be attained. As a result, the cost of monopoly equals its deadweight loss plus the entire monopoly profit.

There are some industries in which a monopoly is more efficient than a large number of perfectly competitive firms. Such industries are those in which economies of scale and scope are so large that the monopoly's output is higher and price lower than those that would arise if the industry had a large number of firms. There are also situations in which monopoly may be more innovative than competition, resulting in a faster pace of technological change. (pp. 330–336)

KEY CONCEPTS

Key Figures

REVIEW QUESTIONS

1 What is a monopoly? What are some examples of monopoly in your state?

2 How does monopoly arise?

3 Distinguish between a legal monopoly and a natural monopoly. Give examples of each type.

4 Explain why marginal revenue is always less than average revenue for a single-price monopoly.

5 Why does a monopoly's profit increase as output rises initially but eventually decrease when output gets too big?

6 Explain how a monopoly chooses its output and price.

7 Does a monopoly operate on the inelastic part of its demand curve? Explain why it does or does not.

8 Explain why a monopoly produces a smaller output than an equivalent competitive industry.

9 Is monopoly as efficient as competition?

10 What is deadweight loss?

11 Can any monopoly price discriminate? If yes, why? If no, why not?

12 Show graphically the deadweight loss under perfect price discrimination.

13 As far as allocative efficiency is concerned, is single-price monopoly better or worse than perfect price discrimination? Why?

14 Explain why people indulge in rent-seeking activities.

15 When taking account of the cost of rent seeking, what is the social cost of monopoly?

16 What are economies of scale and economies of scope? What effects, if any, do they have on allocative efficiency of monopoly?

17 Monopoly redistributes consumer surplus. Explain why the consumer loses more under perfect price discrimination than under single-price monopoly.

PROBLEMS

1 Minnie's Mineral Springs, a single-price monopoly, faces the following demand schedule for bottled mineral water:

Price (dollars per bottle)	Quantity demanded (bottles)
5	0
4	1
3	2
2	3
1	4
0	5

a) Calculate Minnie's total revenue schedule.

b) Calculate its marginal revenue schedule.

c) At what price is the elasticity of demand equal to one?

2 Minnie's has the following total cost:

Quantity produced (bottles)	Total cost (dollars)
0	1
1	2
2	4
3	7
4	11
5	16

Calculate the profit-maximizing levels of

a) Output

b) Price

c) Marginal cost

d) Marginal revenue

e) Profit

3 Suppose that Minnie's can perfectly price discriminate. What is its profit-maximizing

a) Output

b) Total revenue

c) Profit

4 How much would someone be willing to pay Minnie's for a license to operate its mineral spring?

5 Two demand schedules for round-trip flights between New York and Los Angeles are set out below. The schedule for weekday travelers is for those making round-trips on weekdays and returning within the same week. The schedule for weekend travelers is for those who stay through the weekend. (The former tend to be business travelers and the latter vacation and pleasure travelers.)

Weekday travelers		Weekend travelers	
Price (dollars per round trip)	*Quantity demanded (thousands of round trips)*	*Price (dollars per round trip)*	*Quantity demanded (thousands of round trips)*
1500	0	500	0
1000	10	250	10
500	20	125	10
250	25	0	20
125	27.5		
0	30		

The marginal cost of a round trip is $125. If a single-price monopoly airline controls the New York–Los Angeles route, use a graph to find out the following:

a) What price is charged?

b) How many passengers travel?

c) What is the consumer surplus?

6 If the airline in problem 5 discriminates between round-trips within a week and round-trips through the weekend:

a) What is the price for the round-trip within the week?

b) What is the price of the airline ticket with a weekend stay?

c) What is the consumer surplus?

7 Barbara runs a truck stop on the prairies, miles from anywhere. She has a monopoly and faces the following demand for meals:

Price (dollars per meal)	Quantity demanded (meals per week)
1.00	160
1.50	140
2.00	120
2.50	100
3.00	80
3.50	60
4.00	40
4.50	35
5.00	30
5.50	25

Barbara's marginal cost and average total cost are a constant $1 per meal.

a) If Barbara charges all customers the same price for a meal, what price is it?

b) What is the consumer surplus of all the customers who buy a meal from Barbara?

c) What is the producer surplus?

d) What is the deadweight loss?

8 Barbara discovers that some of the people stopping for meals are truck drivers and some are tourists. She estimates that the demand schedules for the two groups are:

Price (dollars per meal)	Quantity demanded (meals per week)	
	Truck drivers	*Tourists*
1.00	70	90
1.50	65	75
2.00	60	60
2.50	55	45
3.00	50	30
3.50	45	15
4.00	40	0
4.50	35	0
5.00	30	0
5.50	25	0

If Barbara price discriminates between the two,

a) What price does she charge truck drivers?

b) What price does she charge tourists?

c) What is her output per week, and is it higher, lower, or the same as when she did not price discriminate?

d) What is her weekly profit, and is it higher, lower, or the same as when she did not price discriminate?

Chapter 14

Monopolistic Competition and Oligopoly

After studying this chapter, you will be able to:

- Describe and distinguish among market structures that lie between perfect competition and monopoly
- Define monopolistic competition
- Explain how price and output are determined in a monopolistically competitive industry
- Define oligopoly and duopoly
- Explain what game theory is
- Explain the prisoner's dilemma game
- Explain duopoly and oligopoly as games that firms play
- Predict the price and output behavior of duopolists
- Make predictions about price wars and competition among small numbers of firms

Fliers and War Games

Every week, we receive a newspaper stuffed with supermarket fliers describing this week's "specials," providing coupons and other enticements, all designed to grab our attention and persuade us that A & P, Kroger, Safeway, Alpha Beta, Winn Dixie, Stop & Shop, Shop 'n' Save, and H.E.B.'s have the best deals in town. Supermarkets are not the only businesses that cut prices in order to attract customers. Every few months, clothing and furniture stores hold sales designed partly to clear space for the new season's inventory, but also partly to attract new customers. ■ Firms do not only compete with each other on price. They also compete on product quality. Millions of dollars are spent on TV and magazine advertising, all designed to enable us to pick the best brand and, having picked it, to keep buying it again and again, even if its price is slightly higher than that of some competing brands. ■ How do firms that are locked in fierce competition with other firms set their prices, pick their product, and choose the quantities to produce? How are the profits of such firms affected by the actions of other firms? ■ Suddenly in 1973, the prices that people paid for gasoline, heating oil, and other petroleum products depended on the whims of the Organization of Petroleum Exporting Countries (OPEC). In that year, OPEC acted like a monopoly, restricting the production of oil and raising prices. For almost a decade, the price of oil kept rising until, in 1982, it stood at 11 times the price of a decade before. Horrified consumers speculated about the day when it would cost $50, $60, $70 a barrel. ■ Equally suddenly, and to the surprise of millions of people, OPEC fell apart. Oil prices faltered for a bit, and then, in a matter of months, they fell by more than half. Headlines in early 1986 screamed, "The Price War Is Here," and "Frenzied Gas Wars Push Down Pump Prices." ■ Why did OPEC's stranglehold on oil prices, which had brought its members enormous riches, suddenly disappear? Not only did OPEC stop raising prices, it saw them fall dramatically. Why did prices suddenly break? Will OPEC ever control oil prices again? ■ Price-fixing arrangements such as those practiced by OPEC are illegal in the United States. This means that any conspiracies by firms to fix prices have to be undertaken in secrecy. As a result we get to know about such agreements only after they have been cracked by the Justice Department. One famous price-fixing arrangement, involving almost 30 firms, has been called "the incredible electrical conspiracy."[1] For most of the 1950s, 30 producers of electrical equipment, including such giants as General Electric and Westinghouse, fixed prices "on items ranging from $2 insulators to huge turbine generators costing several million dollars."[2] Though the electrical equipment pricing conspiracy operated throughout the 1950s, the individual firms conspiring often changed. In particular, General Electric sometimes participated in the price-fixing agreement and sometimes dropped out, undercutting the agreed price and dragging down the industry price and profit. ■ Why do firms start price wars and drag down the industry's profit? Do competitors always follow suit? When do price wars end?

■ The theories of monopoly and perfect competition, which we studied in Chapters 12 and 13, do not predict the kind of behavior that we've just described. There are no fliers and coupons or price wars in perfect competition because each firm is a price taker. There are none in monopoly either because each monopoly firm has the entire market to itself and so never needs to fear the actions of a competitor. To understand fliers, coupons, discounts, sales, price-fixing agreements, and price wars, we need richer models of the behavior of firms in markets than those of perfect competition and monopoly. This chapter presents such models. The industries that we're going to study lie between the two extremes of perfect competition and monopoly. We'll study two cases: One in which there are many firms but each produces a slightly different product from the others so that, although the firms are in competition with each other, each has a small element of monopoly power arising from the uniqueness of its own product. This model will enable us to understand markets such as those for food and clothing, soft drinks and plastics, printing and book publishing. The second model applies to industries that contain only a few firms. These few firms are locked in an unusual game. Each one has to keep a wary eye on how its competitors are acting. And in choosing its own actions, each firm must work out what its competitors' response will be and what its own best response is to its competitors' actions. Our model of the competition that arises in this type of situation will enable us to understand industries like oil and electrical equipment supply. ■ But first, before turning to these two additional models, we are going to describe the characteristics of different types of markets so that we can identify those to which each model applies.

[1]Richard A. Smith, "The Incredible Electrical Conspiracy," Part I and Part II, *Fortune* (April 1961): 132 and (May 1961): 161.

[2]James V. Koch, *Industrial Organization and Prices,* 2nd ed. (Englewood Cliffs, N.J.: Prentice-Hall, 1980): 423.

Varieties of Market Structure

We have studied two types of market structure—perfect competition and monopoly. In perfect competition, a large number of firms produce identical goods and there are no barriers to the entry of new firms into the industry. In this situation, each firm is a price taker and, in the long run, there is no economic profit. The opposite extreme, monopoly, is an industry in which there is one firm. That firm is protected by barriers preventing the entry of new firms. The firm sets its price to maximize profit and the firm enjoys economic profit even in the long run.

Although there are some industries in the real world that have the characteristics of a perfectly competitive or a monopoly industry, most do not. Most industries lie somewhere between these two extreme cases. There are many situations in which firms are in fierce competition with a large number of other firms but they do have some power to set prices. There are other cases in which the industry consists of very few firms and each firm has considerable power in price determination. In order to tell how close to the competitive or monopolisitic extreme an industry comes, economists have developed a measure of industrial concentration. This measure is designed to indicate

Table 14.1 Concentration Ratio Calculations (hypothetical)

Tiremakers Firm	Sales (millions of dollars)	**Printers** Firm	Sales (millions of dollars)
Top, Inc.	200	Fran's	2.5
ABC, Inc.	250	Ned's	2.0
Big, Inc.	150	Tom's	1.8
XYZ, Inc.	100	Jill's	1.7
Top 4 sales	700	Top 4 sales	8.0
Other 10 firms	175	Other 1000 firms	1592.0
Industry sales	875	Industry sales	1600.0

Four-firm concentration ratios:

Tiremakers:	700/875	=	80%
Printers:	8/1600	=	0.5%

the degree of control that a small number of firms have over a market. The most commonly used measure of concentration is called the four-firm concentration ratio. The **four-firm concentration ratio** is the percentage of the value of sales accounted for by the largest four firms in an industry. (Concentration ratios are also defined and measured for the largest eight, 20, and 50 firms in an industry.) Table 14.1 sets out two hypothetical concentration ratio calculations, one for tires and one for printing. In this example, there are 14 firms in the tire industry. The biggest four have 80 percent of the sales of the industry, so the four-firm concentration ratio for that industry is 80 percent. In the printing industry, with 1004 firms, the top four firms account for only 0.5 percent of total industry sales. In that case, the four-firm concentration ratio is 0.5 percent.

Using data on each firm's sales, the Department of Commerce calculates concentration ratios for a large number of industry groups. Some industries, such as commercial printing, plastic products, and soft drinks have low concentration ratios. These industries are highly competitive. At the other extreme are industries with a high concentration ratio—such as electric light bulbs, motor vehicles, and household refrigerators. These are examples of industries in which there is competition but among a small number of firms, each of which has considerable control over its price. Medium concentration ratios exist in the newspaper, pharmaceutical preparation, and meat packing industries.

The idea behind calculating concentration ratios is to provide information about the degree of competitiveness of a market: A low concentration ratio indicates a high degree of competition and a high concentration ratio indicates an absence of competition. In the extreme case of monopoly, the concentration ratio is 100—the largest (and only) firm makes the entire industry sales. But there are problems with concentration ratios as measures of competitiveness and, although the ratios themselves are useful, they have to be supplemented by other information. There are three key problems:

1. Geographical Scope of Market Concentration ratio data are based on a national view of the market.

Many goods are indeed sold on a national market but some are sold on a regional market and some on a global one. The newspaper industry is a good example of one in which the local market is more important than the national market. Thus although the concentration ratio for newspapers is not high, there is nevertheless a high degree of concentration in the newspaper industry in most cities. The automobile industry is an example of one for which there is a global market. Thus although the biggest four U.S. car producers account for 92 percent of all cars sold by U.S. producers, they account for a much smaller percentage of the total U.S. car market (including imports) and an even smaller percentage of the global market for cars.

2. Barriers to Entry and Turnover Measures of concentration do not tell us how severe are the barriers to entry in an industry. Some industries, for example, are highly concentrated but have virtually free entry and experience an enormous amount of turnover of firms. A good example is the market in local restaurants. Many small towns have few restaurants. But there are no restrictions on entering the restaurant industry and indeed firms do enter and exit with great regularity.

3. Market and Industry The classifications used to calculate concentration ratios allocate every firm in the U.S. economy to a particular industry. Markets for particular goods do not always correspond exactly to particular industries. For example, Westinghouse is classified by the Department of Commerce as being in the electrical goods and equipment industry. That is indeed the main product line of Westinghouse. But Westinghouse also produces, among other things, gas-fired incinerators and plywood. Thus this one firm operates in three quite separate markets. Furthermore, the market or markets in which a firm operates depend on the profit opportunities that exist. There are many spectacular examples of firms that have built their initial organization on one product but then diversified into a wide variety of others.

Nevertheless, concentration ratios, combined with information about the geographical scope of the market, barriers to entry, and the extent to which large, multiproduct firms straddle a variety of markets, do provide the basis for classifying industries. The less concentrated an industry and the lower its barriers to entry, the more closely it approximates the perfect competition case. The more concentrated an industry and the higher the barriers to entry, the more it approximates the monopoly case.

But there is a great deal of space between perfect competition and monopoly. That space is occupied by two other market types that we'll now identify. The first of these is monopolistic competition. **Monopolistic competition** is a market type in which a large number of firms compete with each other by making similar but slightly different products. Making a product slightly different from the product of a competing firm is called **product differentiation.** Because of product differentiation, a monopolistically competitive firm has an element of monopoly power. The firm is the sole producer of the particular version of the good in question.

For example, in the market for microwave popcorn, only Nabisco makes Planters Premium Select, only General Mills makes Pop Secret, and only American Popcorn makes Jolly Time. Each of these firms has a monopoly on a particular brand of microwave popcorn. Differentiated products are not necessarily different in an objective sense. For example, the different brands of microwave popcorn may actually be only different ways of packaging an identical commodity. What matters is that consumers perceive products to be differentiated. In fact, there are claims that the different brands of microwave popcorn are different in ways other than their packaging—for example, in popability.

Oligopoly is a market type in which a small number of producers compete with each other. There are hundreds of examples of oligopolistic industries. Oil and gasoline production, the manufacture of electrical equipment, and international air transportation are but a few. In some oligopolistic industries, each firm produces an almost identical product while in others products are differentiated. For example, oil and gasoline are essentially the same whether they are made by Texaco or Exxon. But Chrysler's Plymouth Reliant is a differentiated commodity from Chevrolet's Celebrity and Ford's Mercury Topaz.

Table 14.2 summarizes the characteristics of the two market types that we're going to study in this chapter, monopolistic competition and oligopoly, along with those of perfect competition and monopoly.

Table 14.2 Market Structure

Characteristic	Perfect competition	Monopolistic competition	Oligopoly	Monopoly
Number of firms in industry	Many	Many	Few	One
Product	Identical	Differentiated	Either identical or differentiated	No close substitutes
Barriers to entry	None	Some	Scale and scope economy barriers	Scale and scope economics or legal barriers
Firm's control over price	None	Some	Considerable	Considerable or regulated
Concentration ratio (0 to 100)	0	Low	High	100
Examples	Wheat, corn	Food, clothing	Automobiles, cereals	Local phone service, electric and gas utilities

Monopolistic Competition

Three conditions define a monopolistically competitive industry:

- Each firm faces a downward-sloping demand curve.
- There is free entry.
- There are a large number of firms in the industry.

Because each firm faces a downward-sloping demand curve, it has to choose its price as well as its output. Also a firm's marginal revenue curve is different from its demand curve. These features of monopolistic competition are also present in monopoly. The important difference between monopoly and monopolistic competition lies in free entry.

In monopoly, there is no entry. In monopolistic competition, there is free entry and, as a consequence, though monopolistic competition enables economic profits to occur in the short run, they cannot persist forever. When profits are available, new firms will enter the industry. Such entry will result in lower prices and lower profits. When losses are being incurred, firms will leave the industry. Such exit will increase prices and increase profits. In long-run equilibrium, firms will neither enter nor leave the industry, and firms will be making a zero economic profit.

Because the industry consists of a large number of firms, no one firm can effectively influence what other firms will do. That is, if one firm changes its price, that firm is such a small part of the total industry that it will have no effect on the actions of the other firms in the industry.

Price and Output in Monopolistic Competition

To see how price and output are determined by a firm in a monopolistically competitive industry, let's look at Fig. 14.1. Part (a) deals with the short run and part (b) the long run. To keep things simple, we will suppose that the industry consists of a large number of firms with a differentiated product and that all firms in the industry have identical demand and cost curves. Let's concentrate initially on the short run. The demand curve *D* is the demand curve for the firm's own variety of the product. For example, it is the demand for Bayer aspirin rather than for aspirin in general; or for McDonald's hamburgers rather than for hamburgers in general. The curve *MR* is the marginal revenue curve associated with the

Figure 14.1 Monopolistic Competition

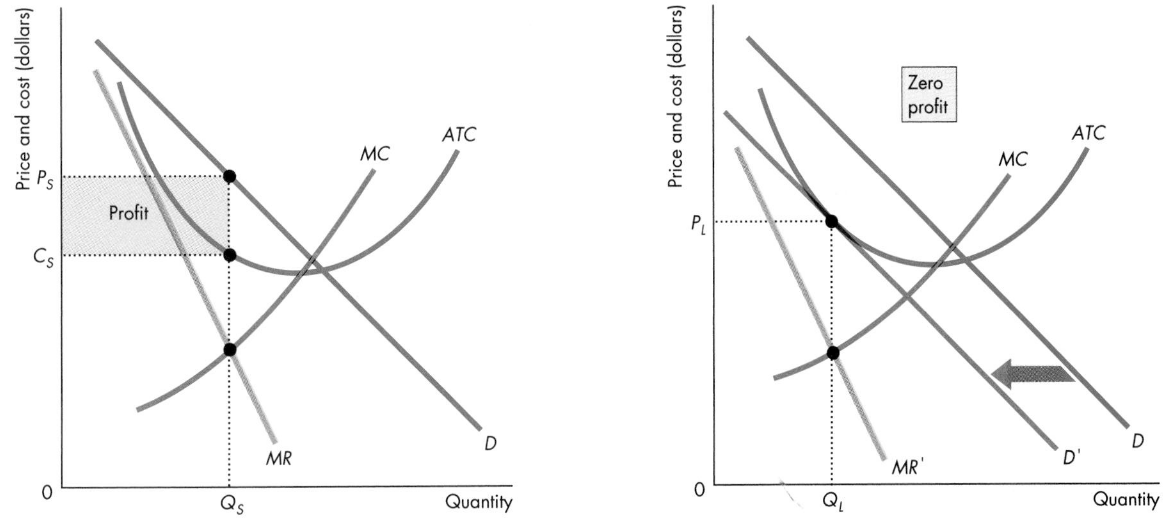

(a) Short run **(b) Long run**

Under monopolistic competition, a firm faces a downward-sloping demand curve and so has to choose its price and the quantity to produce. Profit is maximized where marginal revenue equals marginal cost. Part (a) of the figure shows a short-run profit-maximizing situation. The quantity produced is Q_S, the price is P_S, average total cost is C_S, and profit is represented by the blue rectangle.

Profit encourages new entrants, and so the firm's demand curve begins to shift to the left, as shown in part (b). As the demand curve shifts to the left, so too does the firm's marginal revenue curve. When the demand curve has shifted all the way from D to D', the marginal revenue curve is MR', and the firm is in a long-run equilibrium. The output that maximizes profit is Q_L and the price is P_L. Profit, in long-run equilibrium, is zero. There is no further entry into the industry.

demand curve. The firm's average total cost *(ATC)* and marginal cost *(MC)* are also shown in the figure. A firm maximizes profit in the short run by producing output Q_S, where marginal revenue equals marginal cost, and charging the price P_S. The firm's average total cost is C_S and the firm makes a short-run profit, as measured by the blue rectangle.

So far, the monopolistically competitive firm looks just like a monopoly. It produces the quantity at which marginal revenue equals marginal cost and then charges the highest possible price for that quantity. The key difference between monopoly and monopolistic competition lies in what happens next. There is no restriction on entry so, with economic profit being earned, new firms will enter the industry. As new firms enter the industry, they take some of the market away from the existing firms. As they do so, the firm's demand curve starts to shift to the left. The marginal revenue curve also starts to shift to the left. At each point in time, the firm will seek to maximize its short-run profit. That is, output will be chosen so that marginal revenue equals marginal cost and the highest possible price will be charged for the good. But as the demand curve shifts to the left, the profit-maximizing quantity and price fall. In the long run, shown in part (b), the firm produces Q_L and sells it at a price of P_L. In this situation, the firm is making a zero economic profit. Average total cost exactly equals price.

Excess Capacity Notice that in the long run the firm in monopolistic competition always has excess capacity in that it produces a lower output than that which minimizes average total cost. This result arises from the fact that the firm faces a downward-sloping demand curve. Only if the demand curve facing the firm is perfectly elastic will the long-run equilibrium be at the point of minimum average total cost. The demand curve slopes down because of product differentiation. If each firm produces an identical product, each firm's output will be a perfect substitute for the outputs of all other firms and so the demand curve will be perfectly elastic. Thus it is product differentiation that produces excess capacity.

Efficiency of Monopolistic Competition

When we studied a perfectly competitive industry, we discovered that in some circumstances, such an industry achieves allocative efficiency. A key feature of allocative efficiency is that price equals marginal cost. Recall that price measures the value placed on the last unit bought by the consumer and marginal cost measures the opportunity cost of producing the last unit. We also discovered that monopoly is allocatively inefficient because it restricts output below the level at which price equals marginal cost. As we have just discovered, monopolistic competition shares this feature with monopoly. Even though there is zero profit in long-run equilibrium, the monopolistically competitive industry produces an output at which price equals average total cost and exceeds marginal cost.

Does this feature of monopolistic competition mean that this market structure, like monopoly, is allocatively inefficient? It does not. It is true that if the firms in a monopolistically competitive industry each produce an identical product, so that they are perfect substitutes, then each firm will face a perfectly elastic demand curve and will produce, in the long run, at the point of minimum average total cost and charge a price equal to marginal cost. But achieving that outcome will itself have a cost. The cost is the absence of product differentiation. Variety is valued by consumers but variety is only achievable if firms make differentiated products. The loss in allocative efficiency occurring in monopolistic competition has to be offset against the gain of greater product variety.

Product Innovation

Another source of gain from monopolistically competitive industries is product innovation. Monopolistically competitive firms are constantly seeking out new products that will provide them with a competitive edge, even if only temporarily. A firm that manages to introduce a new and differentiated variety will temporarily face a steeper demand curve than before and will be able to temporarily increase its price. Entry of new firms will, eventually, compete away the profit arising from this initial advantage.

Advertising

Monopolistically competitive firms seek to differentiate their products partly by designing and introducing products that actually are different from those of the other firms in the industry. But they also attempt to differentiate the consumer's perception of the product. Advertising is the principal means whereby firms seek to achieve this end. But advertising increases the monopolistically competitive firm's costs above those of a competitive firm or a monopoly that does not advertise.

To the extent that advertising provides consumers with information about the precise nature of the differentiation of products, it serves a valuable purpose to the consumer, enabling a better product choice to be made. But the opportunity cost of the additional information through advertising has to be offset against the gain to the consumer from making a better choice.

The bottom line on the question of allocative efficiency of monopolistic competition is ambiguous. In some cases, the gains from extra product variety unquestionably offset the costs in the form of advertising and excess capacity. The tremendous varieties of books and magazines, of clothing, food, and drink are examples of such gains. It is less easy to see the gains from being able to buy brand name drugs that have an identical chemical composition to a generic alternative. But some people do willingly pay more for the brand name alternative.

R E V I E W

A firm in a monopolistically competitive industry faces a downward-sloping demand curve and so has to choose its price as well as the quantity to produce. Such firms also compete on product variety and by advertising. A lack of barriers to entry into such industry ensures that economic profit is competed away. In long-run equilibrium, firms make zero economic profit, charging a price equal to average total cost. But price exceeds marginal cost and the quantity produced is below that which minimizes average total cost. The cost of monopolistic competition is excess capacity and high advertising expenditure; the gain is a wide product variety. ■

We can use the model of monopolistic competition to interpret and analyze many real world industries. One such industry is that for microwave popcorn (see Reading Between the Lines, pp. 350–352). Although this industry has a small number of producers that dominate the market (it has a high concentration ratio), it does have differentiated products and there are no obvious restrictions on the entry of new firms. Thus it is an industry in which entry may result in economic profit being competed away in the long run. There are some industries, however, in which barriers to entry prevent such an outcome. In such industries, competition is restricted to a small number of firms, each of whose actions affect not only its own profits but those of the other firms in the industry. This is the case of oligopoly, to which we now turn.

Oligopoly

We have defined oligopoly as a market in which a small number of producers compete with each other. In such a market, each producer is interdependent. The sales of any one producer depends upon that producer's price and the prices charged by the other producers. If one firm lowers its price, its own sales increase but the sales of the other firms in the industry decrease. In such a situation, the other firms will, most likely, lower their prices, too. Then the price cuts of the other firms will lower the profits of the first firm. So, before deciding to cut its prices, the first firm tries to predict how other firms will react and attempts to calculate the effects of those reactions on its own profit.

The situation faced by firms in an oligopolistic industry is not unlike that faced by military planners. For example, in deciding whether to build additional weapons or to dismantle existing ones, U.S. military planners have to take into account the effects of U.S. actions on the behavior of the Soviet Union. Similarly, in making its plans, the Soviet Union has to take into account the reactions of the United States. Neither side can assume that its rival's behavior will be independent of its own actions.

Whether we're studying price wars or star wars, we need a method of analyzing choices that takes into account the interactions between agents. Such a method has been developed and is called game theory.

Game Theory

Game theory is a method of analyzing strategic interaction. **Strategic interaction** is acting in a way that takes into account the expected behavior of others and the mutual recognition of interdependence. Game theory was invented by John von Neumann in 1937 and further extended by von Neumann and Oskar Morgenstern in 1944 (see Our Advancing Knowledge, pp. 354–355). It is the topic of a massive amount of current research.

Game theory seeks to understand oligopoly as well as political and social rivalries by using a method of analysis specifically designed to understand games of all types, including the familiar games of everyday life. We will begin our study of game theory, and its application to the behavior of firms, by considering those familiar games.

Familiar Games: What They Have in Common

What is a game? At first thought, the question seems silly. After all, there are many different games. There are ball games and parlor games, games of chance and games of skill. What do games of such diversity and variety have in common? In answering this question, we will focus on those features of games that are relevant and important for game theory and for analyzing oligopoly as a game. All games have three things in common:

- Rules
- Strategies
- Payoffs

Let's see how these common features of ordinary games apply to oligopoly.

Monopolistic Competition in Action

Microwave Key to Popcorn War

Poor Orville Redenbacher. The executives of General Mills, Pillsbury and Nabisco Brands are out to get the king of popcorn.

Their passion for popcorn—or to be more precise, microwave popcorn—is easy to understand. In the last four years, the nation has developed a seemingly insatiable appetite for microwave popcorn, making it the fastest-growing segment of the popcorn business.

Five years ago, microwave popcorn did not exist. In 1983, the first full year that microwave popcorn was available nationally, it generated retail sales of $53 million, according to Packaged Facts, a New York-based consumer research concern. Last year, consumers popped an estimated $250 million worth of the stuff, according to the Popcorn Institute, a Chicago-based trade group.

One pattern in the highly competitive packaged-snack-food industry is that, where there is demand, an abundance of supply will surely follow. Indeed, there are now five major brands slugging it out: Pillsbury's Microwave Popcorn, General Mills' Pop Secret, American Pop Corn's Jolly Time, Nabisco's Planters Premium Select and, of course Beatrice's Orville Redenbacher's Microwave Popping Corn. Several smaller companies, including the food concern of the actor Paul Newman, have also jumped into the fray.

Calling the market "keenly competitive," Donald L. Knutzen, the general manager of the General Mills snack food division said: "This is easily the hottest microwave product General Mills has ever introduced."

Two consumer trends are responsible for microwave popcorn's rise: the health craze and the growing popularity of microwave ovens.

Since popcorn (at least in its unadulterated form) is low in calories and sodium and high in fiber, Americans are now annually gobbling up 675 million pounds of all types, or an average of 46 quarts a person—twice the amount consumed in 1970.

65% of Homes Have Microwaves

With microwave ovens now in about 65 percent of households in the United States, popcorn that can be prepared in those ovens is increasingly the kind of popcorn that Americans are eating. Total popcorn retail sales (popped and unpopped) are expected to double to $2 billion by 1990. And the microwave variety, which now accounts for 44 percent of unpopped popcorn sold, will probably become the dominant form in its category, with retail sales of $430 million by 1990, said Dennis P. Mitchell, managing editor of Snack Food Magazine.

Given these projections, it is easy to understand why some of the biggest guns of the packaged-foods industry have entered the business.

Consumers are willing to pay an average of $2 for a package of microwave popcorn—substantially more than the 89 cents that a much larger generic bag of regular popcorn typically costs. Even with their high technology and marketing costs, microwave-popcorn manufacturers have margins of 10 to 20 percent or more, according to several makers.

Pillsbury introduced the first popcorn geared for microwaves in 1982, when it came out with a frozen microwave popcorn. But Orville Redenbacher, the dominant power in the traditional unpopped-popcorn market, burst onto the microwave scene in 1983. By 1985, Redenbacher, a Beatrice Companies unit, had taken the lead in the microwave segment.

Since then, General Mills' Betty Crocker Pop Secret has caught up with Redenbacher. Each company now holds about 26 percent of the market, measured in retail dollars.

General Mills promoted Pop Secret as the first popcorn appropriate for all microwave ovens—no matter what the wattage. More of Pop Secret's kernels will pop than the competition's, General Mills says.

Some of General Mills' competitors disagree—and for understandable reasons. Because packaging is pretty much the same, "popability" is a big deal.

Redenbacher asserts that virtually every single one of its kernels pops. Nabisco Brands U.S.A. makes the same claim for its Planters Premium Select Popcorn.

One With Butter
For its part, the American Pop Corn Company is trying to distinguish its fourth-ranked Jolly Time Microwave Popcorn from the pack by noting that Jolly Time is the only microwave popcorn to contain butter. Meanwhile, all the big contenders have introduced salt-free versions for health-conscious consumers.

Despite the growing popularity of microwave popcorn, many in the industry are already predicting a shakeout. "Like wine coolers, two or three winners will entrench in the microwave market, which will become a big, mainstream staple," said Faith B. Popcorn, chairman of Brainreserve, a marketing consulting firm in New York. "All the others will fall into the ocean."

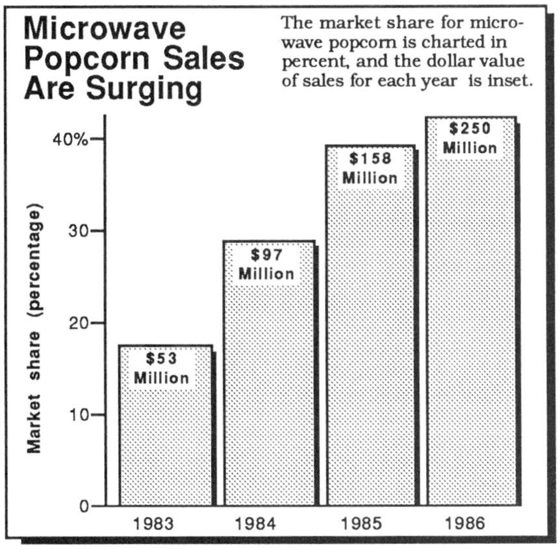

The New York Times, June 22, 1987

The Essence of the Story

- Popcorn that pops in a microwave oven became available in 1982.
- Between 1983 and 1986, sales of microwave popcorn grew from \$53 million (18 percent of popcorn market) to \$250 million (44 percent of popcorn market).
- Growth in demand has been generated by increased awareness of health value of popcorn, and the spread of microwave ovens (to 65 percent of homes by 1986).
- Projected microwave popcorn sales by 1990 are \$430 million.
- Price of a package of microwave popcorn is \$2, more than twice the price of regular popcorn.
- Manufacturers' profit is at least 10 percent and perhaps more than 20 percent of total cost.
- In 1982, there was only one producer of microwave popcorn—Pillsbury. In 1983, Orville Redenbacher entered the market and by 1985 had become the biggest producer.
- There were five major producers of microwave popcorn by 1986 (see table below).
- The producers attempt to distinguish their products from each other on the basis of "popability" and additives (or their absence).
- Some industry observers are predicting that despite further growth in demand, the number of major producers will settle down to two or three.

(Continued on next page.)

Producer	Brand name	Sales in 1986 (if known)
Pillsbury	Microwave Popcorn	—
Orville Redenbacher	Microwave Popping Corn	\$ 65 million*
Betty Crocker (General Mills)	Pop Secret	\$ 65 million*
American Pop Corn	Jolly Time	—
Nabisco	Planters Premium	—
		\$250 million

*About 26 percent of market according to the article.

Background and Analysis

(Continued)

- The microwave popcorn industry may be studied using the model of monopolistic competition: While a small number of firms dominate the market, there is product differentiation and free entry.

- In 1983, there were two major producers, Pillsbury and Orville Redenbacher. A typical firm sold 13.25 million packages of popcorn at $2 a package and had a total revenue of $26.5 million.

- The revenue, cost, and profit of a typical producer in 1983 are shown in the first figure below.

  —The demand curve is *D*
  —The marginal revenue curve is *MR*
  —The average total cost curve is *ATC*
  —The marginal cost curve is *MC*
  —The producer maximizes profit by producing 13.25 million packages of microwave popcorn (the quantity that makes marginal revenue equal marginal cost)
  —Price is $2 a package
  —Profit, the blue area, is 20 percent of total cost.

- After 1983, demand continued to grow; existing firms expanded their plant; new firms entered the industry.

- By 1986, the biggest firms were producing 32.5 million packages of popcorn a year and making profits in excess of 20 percent.

- A typical producer in 1986 had cost and revenue curves similar to those shown in the figure but at larger scales of production than those shown there.

- While profit opportunities are available, existing firms will expand and/or new firms will enter the industry.

- The prediction reported in the article is that there will be no new entry but that existing firms will expand. Furthermore, two or three of the existing firms will expand so successfully that the others will be unable to survive.

- The second figure illustrates a possible situation after the predicted "shake-out." Three firms produce 72 million packages each. Their average total cost curve (*ATC*) just touches their demand curve (*D*) at that quantity. Maximum profit is being earned but that profit is zero. In such a situation, there is no further incentive to expand or for new firms to try to enter the industry. The industry has excess capacity as a consequence of product differentiation. Each firm is selling 72 million packages at $2 a package for a total revenue of $144 million and industry revenue is three times that amount, the $430 million predicted by Dennis P. Mitchell in the article.

- In both figures, the cost curves and demand curves have been *assumed* to change so that the price stays constant at $2 a package. Nothing in the article predicts a constant price. The diagrams have been drawn to generate a constant price so that the analysis is neutral in that regard. It is possible that the price will rise or fall depending on exactly how the demand and cost curves shift over time.

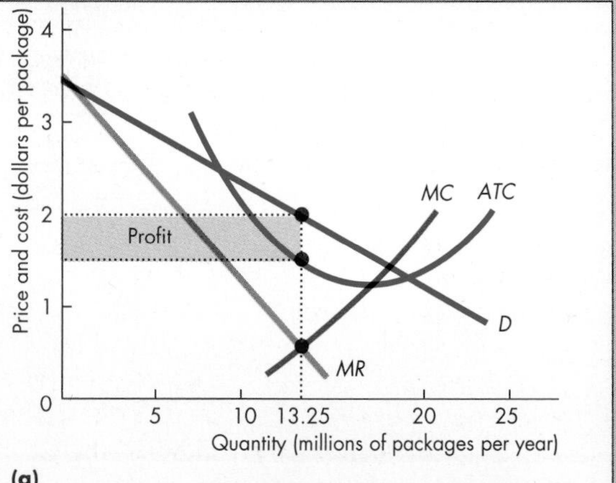

(a)

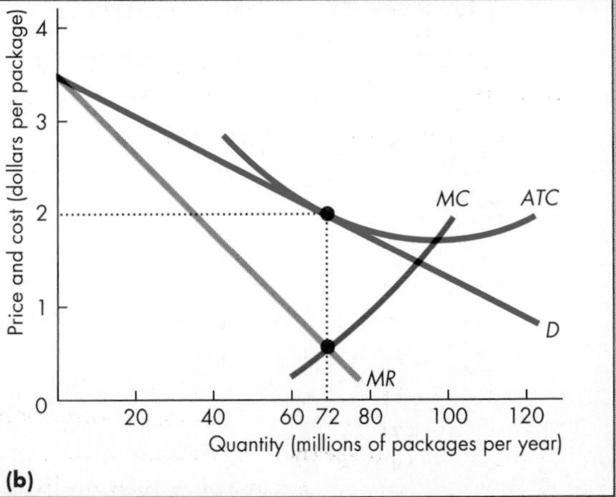

(b)

Rules of the Oligopoly Game

The rules of the oligopoly game have not been written down by the "National Oligopoly League." They arise from the economic, social, and political environment in which the oligopolists operate.

One rule of the oligopoly game is the number of players—the number of firms in the market. Another rule is the method of calculating the score. This rule states that the score of each player is the player's economic profit or loss. The goal of each player of the oligopoly game is to make the largest possible profit. The remaining rules of the oligopoly game are determined by the framework of laws within which the oligopolists are operating. Oligopolists' actions are restricted only by the legal code.

Strategies in the Oligopoly Game

In game theory as in ordinary games, **strategies** are all the possible actions of each player. A comprehensive list of strategies in the oligopoly game would be very long, but it would include, for each player, such actions as:

- Raise price, lower price, hold price constant.
- Raise output, lower output, hold output constant.
- Increase advertising, cut advertising, hold advertising constant.
- Enhance features of product, simplify product, leave product unchanged.

Payoffs in the Oligopoly Game

In game theory, the score of each player is called the **payoff.** In the oligopoly game, the payoffs are the profits and losses of the players. These payoffs are determined by the oligopolists' strategies and by the constraints that they face. Constraints come from customers who determine the demand curve for the product of the oligopoly industry, from the technology available, and from the prices of the resources used by the oligopolists.

To understand how an oligopoly game works, it is revealing to study a special case of oligopoly called duopoly. **Duopoly** is a market structure in which there are two producers of a commodity competing with each other. There are few cases of duopoly on a national and international scale but many cases of local duopolies. For example, in some communities, there are two suppliers of milk, two local newspapers, two taxi companies, two car rental firms. But the main reason for studying duopoly is not its "realism" but the fact that it captures all the essential features of oligopoly and yet is more manageable to analyze and understand. Furthermore, there is a well-known game called "the prisoner's dilemma" that captures some of the essential features of duopoly and that provides a good illustration of how game theory works and how it leads to predictions about the behavior of the players. Let's now turn our attention to studying a duopoly game, beginning with the prisoner's dilemma.

The Prisoner's Dilemma

Alf and Bob have been caught red-handed stealing a car. Facing airtight cases, they will receive a sentence of two years each for their crime. During his interviews with the two prisoners, the district attorney begins to suspect that he has stumbled on the two people who were responsible for a multimillion-dollar bank robbery some months earlier. The district attorney also knows, however, that this is just a suspicion. He has no evidence on which he can convict them of the greater crime unless he can get each of them to confess. The district attorney comes up with the following idea.

He places the prisoners in separate rooms so that they cannot communicate with each other. Each prisoner is told that he is suspected of having carried out the bank robbery and that if he and his accomplice both confess to that crime, each will receive sentences of three years. Each is also told that if he alone confesses and his accomplice does not, he will receive an even shorter sentence of one year while his accomplice will receive a ten-year sentence. The prisoners know that if neither of them confesses, then they will only be tried for and convicted of the lesser offense of car theft, which carries a two-year prison term. How do the prisoners respond to the district attorney?

Models of Oligopoly

Economists have studied oligopoly and duopoly since the time of Cournot (see Our Advancing Knowledge, p. 84). The earliest models were based on assumptions about the beliefs of each firm concerning the reactions of another firm (or firms) to its own actions. A particularly influential model was proposed in the 1930s by Paul M. Sweezy, editor of the *Monthly Review* for the past 40 years.

Sweezy's concern was to explain why prices did not fall more quickly during the years of the Great Depression. He proposed a theory based on the following propositions about the beliefs held by firms:

- If we increase our price, we will be on our own—others will not follow us.
- If we decrease our price, so will everyone else.

If these beliefs are correct, a firm faces a demand curve for its product that has a kink occurring at the current price, *P* (see figure). At prices above *P* the demand curve is relatively flat, reflecting the belief that if the firm increases its price, it will be out of line with all of the other firms and so will experience a large fall in the quantity demanded. At prices below *P*, the demand curve is relatively steep, reflecting the belief that since all other firms are matching the price cut, the increase in the quantity demanded will not be as large as the decrease in the quantity demanded resulting from a price rise.

The kink in demand curve *D* results in a break in the marginal revenue curve (*MR*). The profit-maximizing output (*Q*) is where the marginal cost curve passes through the discontinuity in the marginal revenue curve—the gap *ab*. If marginal cost fluctuates between *a* and *b*, an example of which is shown in the figure with the marginal cost curves, MC_0 and MC_1, the firm will change neither its price nor its quantity of output. Only if marginal cost fluctuates outside the range *ab* will the firm change its price and quantity produced.

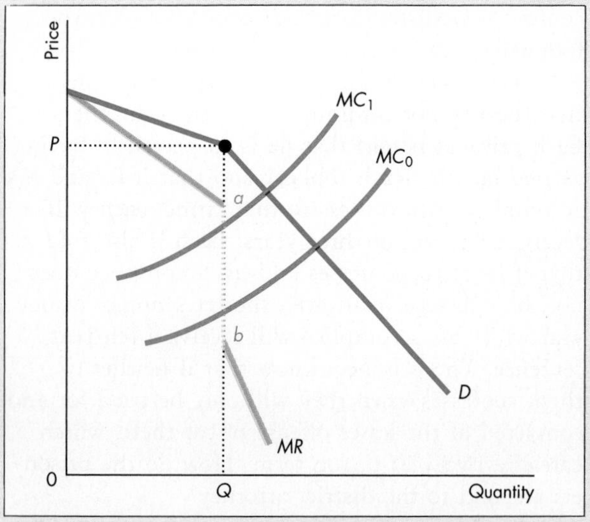

There are two problems with Sweezy's model:

- It does not tell us how the price, *P*, is determined
- It does not tell us what happens if firms discover that their belief about the demand curve is incorrect.

Suppose, for example, that marginal cost increased by enough to cause the firm to increase its price and that all firms experience the marginal cost increase. In such a case, all firms increase their prices together and the belief that other firms will not match the price increase is incorrect. The firm's beliefs are inconsistent with reality and the demand and marginal revenue curves, which summarize those beliefs, are not the correct ones for the purpose of calculating the new profit-maximizing price and output. A widespread dissatisfaction with the state of the theory of oligopoly was a primary impetus to the development of game theory.

Game theory was invented in 1928 by John von Neumann, a brilliant mathematician, physicist, and pioneer in mathematical economics. He established the logical basis for the computer and built the first modern computing machine. He also worked on the "Manhattan Project," which developed the atomic bomb in Los Alamos, New Mexico. Born in Budapest, Hungary, in 1903, von Neumann studied in Budapest and Zurich, and from 1931 worked at the Institute for Advanced Study at Princeton University.

John von Neumann

Von Neumann's mathematical brilliance was recognized at an early age and his first mathematical publication which grew out of lessons with his tutor appeared when he was only 18. But it was at the age of 25, in 1928, that von Neumann published an article that started a flood of research in game theory. In that article, von Neumann studied a game with two players in which the sum of the payoffs is zero—what one player gains the other player loses. Bargaining for shares of a fixed pie is an example. Such a game is called a zero-sum game, a phrase which has entered common usage in English. He proved that there existed, in a zero-sum game, a best strategy for each player. In 1944, von Neumann and his collaborator Oskar Morgenstern published *Theory of Games and Economic Behavior*, a book in which they extended von Neumann's earlier results to games involving any number of players and to cases where the payoffs added up to more than zero.

Von Neumann strongly believed that the social sciences would progress by applying mathematical tools, but he also believed that they required completely different mathematical tools from the physical sciences.

The next major step in the development of game theory was taken in 1951 by John F. Nash, Jr., a mathematician at MIT, who developed the equilibrium concept that now bears his name and that you have learned about in this chapter.

Today there is an enormous volume of research being done on game theory, and a large number of brilliant economists and mathematicians are at work on the subject. Among these is John Harsanyi who teaches decision science—the mathematical analysis of economic decisions—at the University of California at Berkeley. Harsanyi has studied games in which the players are not fully informed and each knows some things that the others do not know. Another interesting contribution is by Eric Maskin of Harvard and Jean Tirole of MIT, who have recently shown that even the kinked demand curve theory of Sweezy can be viewed as the outcome of a game. The particular game is one in which firms take turns at determining the market price and all other firms accept the price that has been set. The model proposed by Maskin and Tirole overcomes all the problems of the original Sweezy theory: Firms' beliefs, on the average, are correct, and the model even predicts where the kink in the demand curve will occur—at the monopoly profit-maximizing price and quantity point.

Game theory has now firmly established itself as one of the main tools of analysis in mathematical economics.

First, notice that the prisoner's dilemma is a game with two players. Each player has two strategies: To confess to the multimillion-dollar bank robbery or to deny the charge. Because there are two players, each with two strategies, there are four possible outcomes.

1 Neither player confesses.
2 Both players confess.
3 Alf confesses but Bob does not.
4 Bob confesses but Alf does not.

Each prisoner can work out exactly what will happen to him—his payoff—in each of these four situations. We can tabulate the four possible payoffs for each of the prisoners in what is called a payoff matrix for the game.

The Payoff Matrix

A **payoff matrix** is a table that shows the payoffs for every possible action by each player for every possible action by each other player.

Table 14.3 shows a payoff matrix for Alf and Bob. The squares show the payoffs for each prisoner—*A* for Alf and *B* for Bob. If both prisoners confess (top left), they each get a prison term of 3 years. If Bob confesses but Alf denies (top right), Alf gets a 10-year sentence and Bob gets a 1-year sentence. If Alf confesses and Bob denies (bottom left), Alf gets a 1-year sentence and Bob gets a 10-year sentence. Finally, if both of them deny (bottom right), neither can be convicted of the bank robbery charge but both are sentenced for the car theft—a 2-year sentence.

Table 14.3 Prisoner's Dilemma Payoff Matrix

Bob's strategies		Alf's strategies: Confess	Alf's strategies: Deny
	Confess	*A* 3 years *B* 3 years	*A* 10 years *B* 1 year
	Deny	*A* 1 year *B* 10 years	*A* 2 years *B* 2 years

Each square shows the payoffs for the two players, *A* for Alf and *B* for Bob, for each possible pair of actions. For example, if both confess, the payoffs are in the top left square. Alf reasons as follows: If Bob confesses, it pays me to confess because then I get 3 years rather than 10. If Bob denies, it pays me to confess because then I get 1 year rather than 2. Regardless of what Bob does, it pays me to confess. Alf's dominant strategy is to confess. Bob reasons similarly: If Alf confesses, it pays me to confess and get 3 years rather than 10. If Alf denies, it pays me to confess and get 1 year rather than 2. Bob's dominant strategy is to confess. Since each player's dominant strategy is to confess, the equilibrium of the game is for both players to confess and to each get 3 years.

The Dilemma The dilemma is seen by considering the consequences of confessing and not confessing. Each prisoner knows that if he and his accomplice remain silent about the bank robbery, they will only be sentenced to 2 years for stealing the car. Neither prisoner, however, has any way of knowing that his accomplice will remain silent and refuse to confess. Each knows that if the other confesses and he denies, the other will receive only a 1-year sentence while the one denying will receive a 10-year sentence. Each poses the following questions: Should I deny and rely on my accomplice to deny so that we may both get only 2 years? Or should I confess in the hope of getting just 1 year (providing my accomplice denies), but knowing that if my accomplice does confess we will both get 3 years in prison? Resolving the dilemma involves finding the equilibrium for the game.

Equilibrium

The equilibrium of a game is called a Nash equilibrium: It is so named because it was first proposed by John Nash (see Our Advancing Knowledge, pp. 354–355). A **Nash equilibrium** occurs when *A* takes the best possible action given the action of *B* and *B* takes the best possible action given the action of *A*. In the case of the prisoner's dilemma, the equilibrium occurs when Alf makes his best choice given Bob's choice and when Bob makes his best choice given Alf's choice.

The prisoner's dilemma is a game that has a special kind of Nash equilibrium. Its equilibrium is called a dominant strategy equilibrium. A **domi-**

nant strategy is a strategy that is the same regardless of the action taken by the other player. In other words, there is a unique best action regardless of what the other player does. A **dominant strategy equilibrium** occurs when there is a dominant strategy for each player. The equilibrium in the prisoner's dilemma is an example of a dominant strategy equilibrium. In the prisoner's dilemma, no matter what Bob does, Alf's best strategy is to confess, and no matter what Alf does Bob's best strategy is to confess. Thus each player confessing is the equilibrium of the prisoner's dilemma.

If each prisoner plays the prisoner's dilemma game in his own individual best interest, the outcome of the game will be that each confesses. To see why each player confesses, let's consider again their strategies and the payoffs from the alternative courses of action.

Strategies and Payoffs

Look at the situation from Alf's point of view. Alf realizes that his outcome depends on the action Bob takes. If Bob confesses, it pays Alf to confess also, for in that case, he will be sentenced to 3 years rather than 10 years. But if Bob does not confess, it still pays Alf to confess (in that case he will receive 1 year rather than 2 years). Alf reasons that regardless of Bob's action, his own best action is to confess.

The dilemma from Bob's point of view is identical to Alf's. Bob knows that if Alf confesses, he will receive 10 years if he does not confess or 3 years if he does. Therefore if Alf confesses, it pays Bob to confess. Similarly, if Alf does not confess, Bob will receive 2 years for not confessing and 1 year if he confesses. Again, it pays Bob to confess. Bob's best action, regardless of Alf's action, is to confess.

Each prisoner sees that regardless of what the other prisoner does, his own best action is to confess. Since each player's best action is to confess, each will confess, each will get a 3-year prison term, and the district attorney has solved the bank robbery. This is the equilibrium of the game.

A Bad Outcome

The equilibrium of the game, where each player confesses, is not for the prisoners the best outcome. A better outcome would be for neither of them to confess, because they would each get only 2 years for the lesser crime. Isn't there some way in which this better outcome can be achieved? It seems that there is not, because the players cannot communicate with each other. Each player can put himself in the other player's place and, as a result, each player can figure out that there is a dominant strategy for each of them. The prisoners are indeed in a dilemma. Each prisoner knows that he can serve 2 years only if he can trust the other not to confess. Each prisoner also knows, however, that it is not in the best interest of the other to not confess. Thus each prisoner knows that he has to confess, thereby delivering a bad outcome for both.

Let us now see how we can use the ideas that we have just developed to understand price fixing, price wars, and the behavior of duopolists.

A Duopoly Game

To study a duopoly game, we're going to build a model of a duopoly industry. The model is inspired by "the incredible electrical conspiracy." But don't lose sight of the fact that what follows is a model. It is not a description of a real historical episode.

Suppose that only two firms make a particular kind of electric switchgear. We will call the firms Trick and Gear. Our goal is to make predictions about the prices charged and the outputs produced by each of the two firms. We are going to pursue that goal by constructing a duopoly game that the two firms will play. To set out the game, we need to specify the strategies of the players and the payoff matrix.

We will suppose that the two firms enter into a collusive agreement. A **collusive agreement** is an agreement between two (or more) producers to restrict output in order to raise prices and profits. Such an agreement is illegal and is undertaken in secret. A group of firms that has entered into a collusive agreement to restrict output and increase prices and profits is called a **cartel.** The strategies that firms in a cartel can pursue are to:

- Comply
- Cheat

Complying simply means sticking to the agreement. Cheating means breaking the agreement in a manner designed to benefit the cheating firm and harm the other firm.

Since each firm has two strategies, there are four possible combinations of actions for the two firms:

- Both firms comply.
- Both firms cheat.
- Trick complies and Gear cheats.
- Gear complies and Trick cheats.

We need to work out the payoffs to each firm from each of these four possible sets of actions. To do that we need to explore the cost and demand conditions in the industry.

Cost and Demand Conditions

The cost of producing switchgears is the same for both Trick and Gear. The average total cost curve *(ATC)* and the marginal cost curve *(MC)* for each firm are shown in Fig. 14.2(a). The market demand curve for switchgears *(D)* is shown in Fig. 14.2(b). Each firm produces an identical switchgear product, so one firm's switchgear is a perfect substitute for the other's. The market price of each firm's product, therefore, is identical. The quantity demanded depends on that price—the higher the price, the lower is the quantity demanded.

Notice that in this industry, there is room for only two firms. For each firm the *minimum efficient scale* of production is 3000 switchgear units a week. When the price equals the average total cost of production at the minimum efficient scale, total industry demand is 6000 switchgear units a week. Thus there is no room for three firms in this industry. If there were only one firm in the industry, it would make an enormous profit and invite competition. If there were three firms, at least one of them would make a loss. The number of firms that an industry can sustain depends on the relationship between cost and the industry's demand conditions. In the model industry that we're study-

Figure 14.2 Costs and Demand

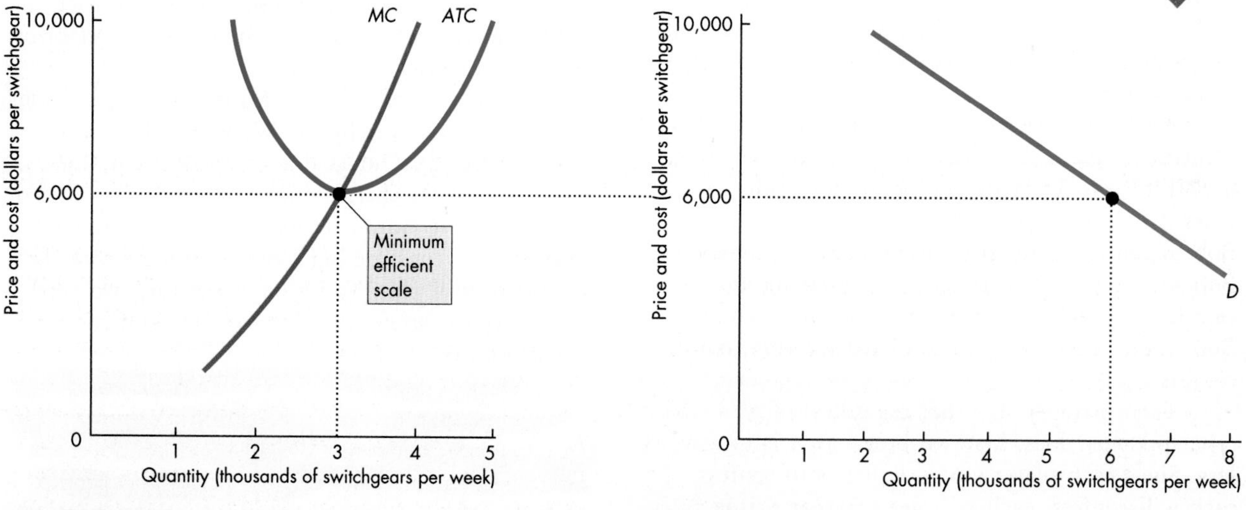

(a) Individual firm **(b) Industry**

Part (a) shows the costs facing Trick and Gear, two duopolists who make switchgears. Each firm faces identical costs. The average total cost curve for each firm is *ATC* and the marginal cost curve is *MC*. For each firm, the minimum efficient scale of prduction is 3000 units per week and the average total cost of producing that output is $6000 a unit. Part (b) shows the industry demand curve. At a price of $6000 a unit, the quantity demanded is 6000 units per week. There is room for only two firms in this industry.

Figure 14.3 Colluding to Make Monopoly Profits

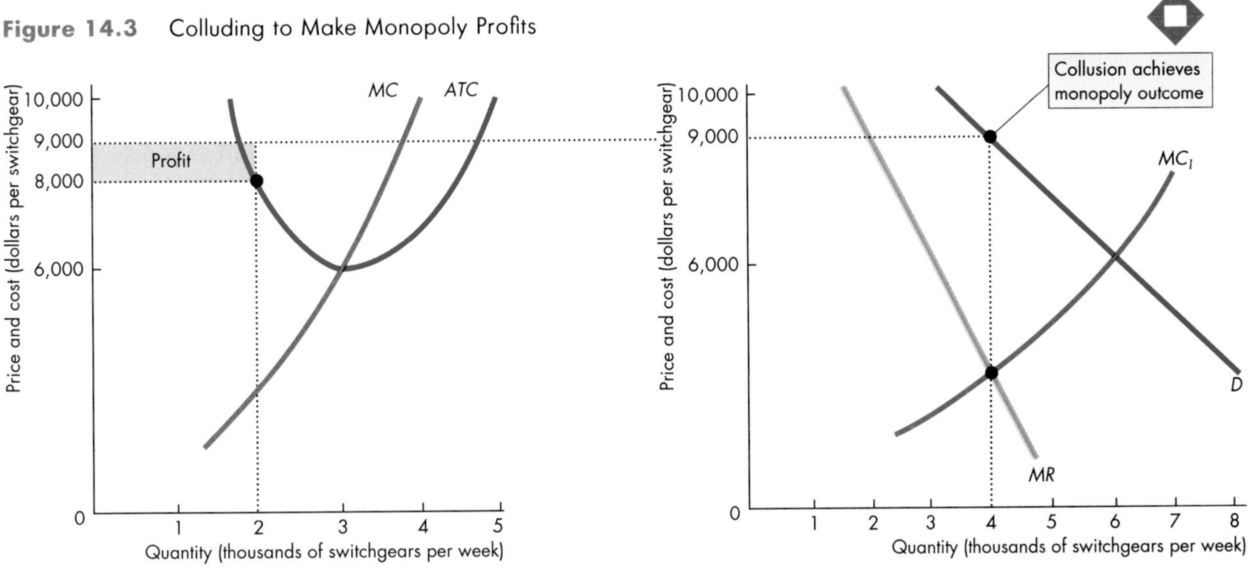

(a) Individual firm **(b) Industry**

If Trick and Gear come to a collusive agreement, they can act as a single monopolist and maximize profit. Part (a) shows the consequences of reaching such an agreement for each firm and part (b) shows the situation in the industry as a whole.

To maximize profit, the firms first calculate the industry marginal cost curve (MC_I) shown in part (b)—the horizontal sum of the two firms' marginal cost curves (MC) in part (a). Next they calculate the industry marginal revenue, MR in part (b). They then choose the output rate that makes marginal revenue equal to marginal cost (4000 units per week). They agree to sell that output for a price of $9000, the price at which 4000 switchgear units are demanded.

The costs and profit of each firm are seen in part (a). Each firm produces half the total output—2000 units per week. Average total cost is $8000 per unit, so each firm makes a profit of $2 million (blue rectangle)—2000 units multiplied by $1000 profit per unit.

ing here, the particular cost and demand conditions assumed are designed to generate an industry in which two firms can survive in the long run. In real world oligopoly and duopoly, barriers to entry may arise from economies of scale of the type featured in our model industry but there are other possible barriers as well (as discussed in Chapter 13, pp. 316–317).

Colluding to Maximize Profits

Let's begin by working out the payoffs to the two firms if they collude to make the maximum industry profit—the profit that would be made by a single monopoly. The calculations that the two firms will perform are exactly the same calculations that a monopoly performs. (You have already studied such calculations in the previous chapter, pp. 320–321.) The only additional thing that the duopolists have to do is to agree on how much of the total output each of them will produce.

The price and quantity that maximizes industry profit for the duopolists is shown in Fig. 14.3. Part (a) shows the situation for each firm and part (b) for the industry as a whole. The curve labeled MR is the industry marginal revenue curve. The curve labeled MC_I is the industry marginal cost curve if each firm produces the same level of output. That curve is constructed by adding together the outputs of the two firms at each level of marginal cost. That is, at each level of marginal cost, industry output is twice as much as the output of each individual firm. Thus the curve MC_I in part

(b) is twice as far to the right as the curve *MC* in part (a).

To maximize industry profit, the duopolists agree to restrict output to the rate that makes the industry marginal cost and marginal revenue equal. That output rate, as shown in part (b), is 4000 switchgear units a week. The highest price for which the 4000 units can be sold is $9000 each. Let's suppose that Trick and Gear agree to split the market equally so that each firm produces 2000 switchgear units a week. The average total cost (*ATC*) of producing 2000 units a week is $8000, so the profit per unit is $1000 and the total profit is $2 million (2000 units × $1000 per unit). The profit of each firm is represented by the blue rectangle in Fig. 14.3(a).

We have just described one possible outcome for the duopoly game: The two firms collude to produce the monopoly profit-maximizing output and divide that output equally between themselves. From the industry point of view, this solution is identical to a monopoly. A duopoly that operates in this way is indistinguishable from a monopoly. The profit that is made by a monopoly is the maximum profit that can be made by colluding duopolists.

Cheating on a Collusive Agreement

Under a collusive agreement, the colluding firms restrict output to make their joint marginal revenue equal to their joint marginal cost. They set the highest price for which the quantity produced can be sold—a price higher than marginal cost. In such a situation, each firm recognizes that if it cheats on the agreement and raises its output, even though the price will fall below that agreed to, more will be added to revenue than to cost, so its profit will increase. Since each firm recognizes this fact, there is a temptation for each firm to cheat. There are two possible cheating situations: One in which one firm cheats and one in which both firms cheats. What happens if one of the firms cheats on the agreement?

One Firm Cheats What is the effect of one firm cheating on a collusive agreement? How much extra profit does the cheating firm make? What happens to the profit of the firm that sticks to the agreement in the face of cheating by the other firm? Let's work out the answers to these questions.

There are many different ways for a firm to cheat. We will work out just one possibility. Suppose that Trick convinces Gear that there has been a fall in industry demand and that it cannot sell its share of the output at the agreed price. It tells Gear that it plans to cut its price in order to sell the agreed 2000 switchgear units each week. Since the two firms produce a virtually identical product, Gear has no alternative but to match the price cut of Trick.

In fact, there has been no fall in demand and the lower price has been calculated by Trick to be exactly the price needed to sell the additional output that it plans to produce. Gear, though lowering its price in line with that of Trick, restricts its output to the previously agreed level.

Figure 14.4 illustrates the consequences of Trick cheating in this way: Part (a) shows what happens to Gear (the complier); part (b) shows what happens to Trick (the cheat); and part (c) shows what is happening in the industry as a whole.

Suppose that Trick decides to raise output from 2000 to 3000 units a week. It recognizes that if Gear sticks to the agreement to produce only 2000 units a week, total output will be 5000 a week and, given demand in part (c), the price will have to be cut to $7500 a unit.

Gear continues to produce 2000 units a week at a cost of $8000 a unit, and so incurs a loss of $500 a unit or $1 million. This loss is represented by the red rectangle in part (a). Trick produces 3000 units a week at an average total cost of $6000 each. With a price of $7500, Trick makes a profit of $1500 a unit and therefore a total profit of $4.5 million. This profit is the blue rectangle in part (b).

We have now described a second possible outcome for the duopoly game—one of the firms cheats on the collusive agreement. In this case, the industry output is larger than the monopoly output and the industry price is lower than the monopoly price. The total profit made by the industry is also smaller than the monopoly's profit. Trick (the cheat) makes a profit of $4.5 million and Gear (the complier) incurs a loss of $1 million, and the industry makes a profit of $3.5 million. Thus the industry profit is $0.5 million less than the maximum profit would be with a monopoly outcome. But that profit is distributed unevenly. Trick makes an even bigger profit than it would under the collusive agreement, while Gear makes a loss.

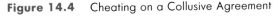

Figure 14.4 Cheating on a Collusive Agreement

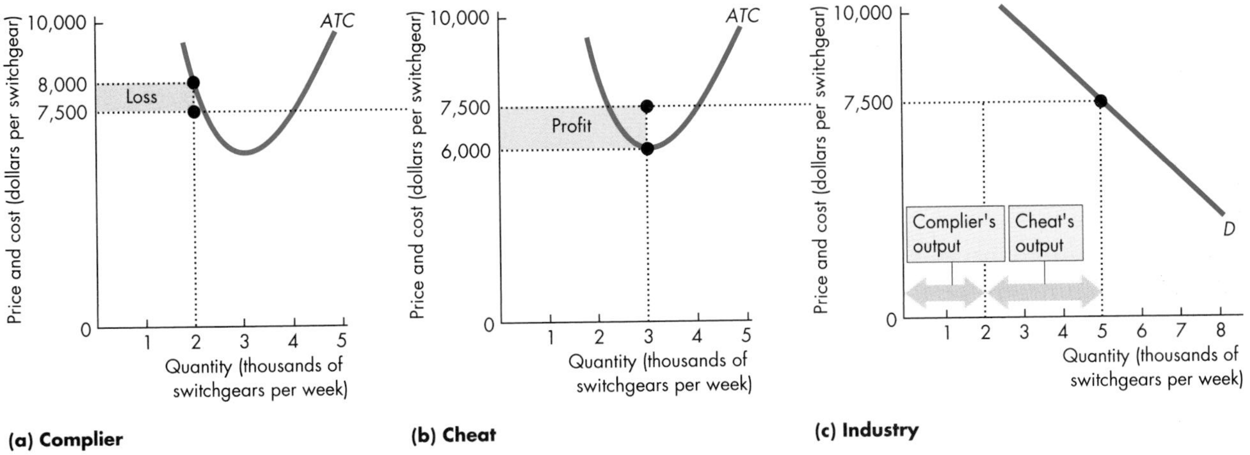

In part (a), one firm complies with the agreement. In part (b), the other firm cheats by raising output above the agreed limit to 3000 switchgears per week. Either firm can be the complier and the other the cheat. In part (c), the effect on the industry price of the actions of the cheat are shown. As a result of cheating, industry output rises to 5000 units a week and the market price falls to $7500—the price at which 5000 switchgear units can be sold.

Part (a) describes the complier's situation. Output remains at 2000 units and average total cost remains at $8000 per unit. The firm loses $500 per switchgear and makes a total loss of $1 million (red rectangle). Part (b) describes the cheat's situation. Average total cost is $6000 per unit and profit per switchgear is $1500, so the cheat's total profit is $4.5 million (blue rectangle).

We have just worked out what happens if Trick cheats and Gear complies with the collusive agreement. There is another similar outcome that would arise if Gear cheated and Trick complied with the agreement. The industry profit and price would be the same but in this case Gear (the cheat) would make a profit of $4.5 million and Trick (the complier) a loss of $1 million.

There is yet another possible outcome: Both firms cheat on the agreement.

Both Firms Cheat Suppose that instead of just one firm cheating on the collusive agreement, both firms cheat. In particular, suppose that each firm behaves in exactly the same way as the cheating firm that we have just analyzed. Each firm tells the other that it is unable to sell its output at the going price and that it plans to cut its price. But since both firms are cheating, each will propose a successively lower price. They will only stop proposing lower prices when the price has reached $6000. That is the price that equals minimum average cost. At a price of less than $6000, each firm will make a loss. At a price of $6000, each firm will cover all its costs and make zero economic profit. Also, at a price of $6000, each firm will want to produce 3000 units a week, so that the industry weekly output will be 6000 units. Given the demand conditions, 6000 units can be sold at a price of $6000 each.

The situation just described is illustrated in Fig. 14.5. Each firm, shown in part (a) of the figure, is producing 3000 units a week, and this output level occurs at the point of minimum average total cost ($6000 per unit). The market as a whole, shown in part (b), operates at the point at which the demand curve *(D)* intersects the industry marginal cost curve. This marginal cost curve is constructed as the horizontal sum of the marginal cost curves of the two firms. Each firm has lowered its price and increased its output in order to try to gain an advantage over the other firm, and they have each pushed this process as far as they can without incurring losses.

Figure 14.5 Both Firms Cheat

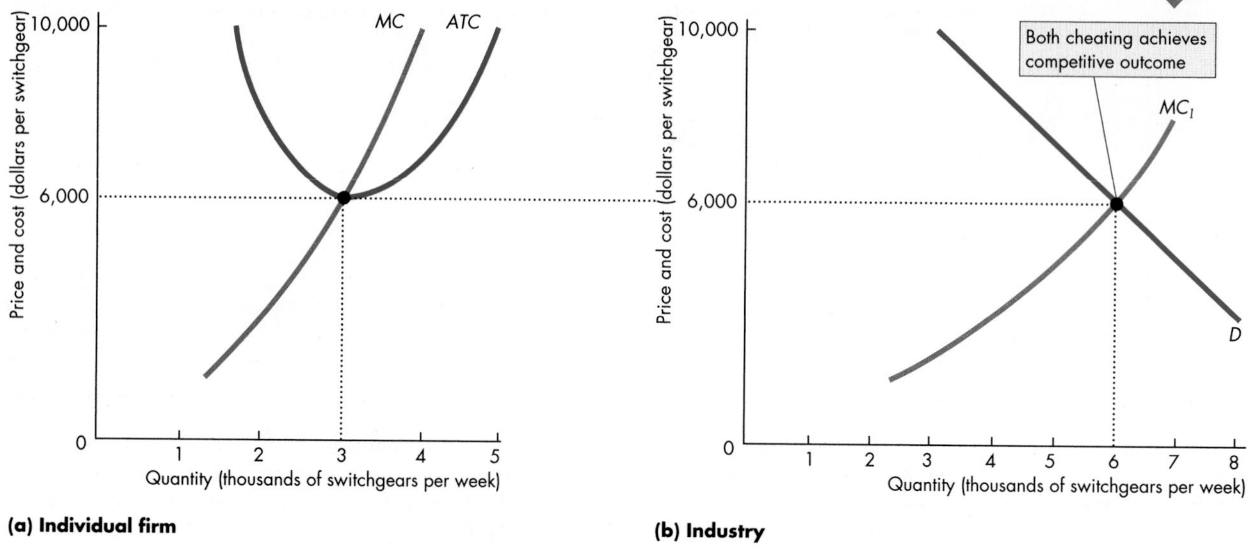

If both firms cheat by raising their output and lowering the price, the collusive agreement completely breaks down. The limit to the breakdown of the agreement is the competitive equilibrium. Neither firm will want to cut the price below $6000 (minimum average total cost), for to do so will result in losses.

Part (a) shows the situation facing each firm. At a price of $6000, the firm's profit-maximizing output is 3000 units. At that output rate, price equals marginal cost, and it also equals average total cost. Economic profit is zero. Part (b) describes the situation in the industry as a whole. The industry marginal cost curve (MC_I)—the horizontal sum of the individual firms' marginal cost curves (MC)—intersects the demand curve at 6000 switchgear units per week and at a price of $6000. This output and price is the one that would prevail in a competitive industry.

We have now described a third possible outcome of this duopoly game—both firms cheat. If both firms cheat on the collusive agreement, the output of each firm is 3000 units a week and the price is $6000. Each firm makes zero profit.

The Payoff Matrix and Equilibrium

Now that we have described the strategies and payoffs in the duopoly game, let's summarize the strategies and the payoffs in the form of the game's payoff matrix and then calculate the equilibrium.

Each firm has two possible actions—cheat or comply. Since each firm has two possible actions and there are two firms, there are four possible outcomes:

- Both firms cheat.
- Both firms comply.
- Gear complies and Trick cheats.
- Trick complies and Gear cheats.

What are the payoffs from these alternative actions? Table 14.4 sets out the payoff matrix for this game. It is constructed in exactly the same way as the payoff matrix for the prisoner's dilemma in Table 14.3. The squares show the payoffs for the two firms—Gear and Trick. In this case, the payoffs are profits. (In the case of the prisoner's dilemma, the payoffs were losses.)

The table shows that if both firms cheat (top left), they achieve the perfectly competitive outcome—each firm makes zero economic profit. If both firms comply (bottom right), the industry makes the monopoly profit and each firm earns a profit of $2 million. The top-right and bottom-left squares show what happens if one firm cheats while the other complies. The firm that cheats collects a profit of $4.5 million and the one that complies makes a loss of $1 million.

This duopoly game is, in fact, the same as the prisoner's dilemma that we examined earlier in this chapter; it is a duopolist's dilemma. You will see this once you have determined what the equilibrium of this game is.

To find the equilibrium, let's look at things from the point of view of Gear. Gear reasons as follows: Suppose that Trick cheats. If we comply with the agreement, we make a loss of $1 million. If we also cheat, we make a zero profit. Zero profit is better than a $1 million loss, so it will pay us to cheat. But suppose Trick complies with the agreement. If we cheat, we will make a profit of $4.5 million, and if we comply, we will make a profit of $2 million. A $4.5 million profit is better than a $2 million profit so it would again pay us to cheat. Thus regardless of whether Trick cheats or complies, it pays us to cheat. Gear's dominant strategy is to cheat.

Trick comes to the same conclusion as Gear. Therefore both firms will cheat. The equilibrium of this game then is that both firms cheat on the agreement. Although there are only two firms in the industry, the price and quantity is the same as in a competitive industry.

Although we have done this analysis for only two firms, it would not make any difference (other than to increase the amount of arithmetic) if we were to play the game with three, four, or more firms. In other words, though we have analyzed duopoly, the game theory approach can also be used to analyze oligopoly. The analysis of oligopoly is much harder, but the essential ideas that we have learned apply to oligopoly.

Table 14.4 Duopoly Payoff Matrix

		Gear's strategies: Cheat	Gear's strategies: Comply
Trick's strategies	Cheat	Gear $0 Trick $0	Gear −$1.0m Trick +$4.5m
	Comply	Gear +$4.5m Trick −$1.0m	Gear +$2.0m Trick +$2.0m

Each square shows the payoffs from a pair of actions. For example, if both firms comply with the collusive agreement, the payoffs are recorded in the square at the bottom right corner of the table. Gear reasons as follows: If Trick cheats, it pays me to cheat and make a zero economic profit rather than a $1 million loss. If Trick complies, it pays me to cheat and make a $4.5 million profit rather than a $2 million profit. Cheating is Gear's dominant strategy. Trick reasons similarly: If Gear cheats it pays me to cheat and make a zero profit rather than a $1 million loss. If Gear complies, it pays me to cheat and make a $4.5 million profit rather than a $2 million profit. The equilibrium is a Nash equilibrium in which both firms cheat.

Repeated Games

The first game that we studied, the prisoner's dilemma, was played just once. The prisoners did not have an opportunity to observe the outcome of the game and then play it again. The duopolist game that we have just studied was also played just once. But unlike the duopolists that we have just studied, real world duopolists do get an opportunity to play repeatedly against each other. This fact suggests that real world duopolists might find some way of learning to cooperate so that their efforts to collude are more effective. If Gear cheats this week, won't Trick cheat next week? Shouldn't Gear take account of the possibility of Trick cheating next week before it decides to cheat this week?

If a game is played repeatedly, one player always has the opportunity to penalize the other player for previous "bad" behavior. If Trick refuses to cooperate this week, then Gear can refuse to cooperate next week (and vice versa).

What is the equilibrium of this more complicated prisoner's dilemma game when it is repeated indefinitely? Actually there is more than one possibility. One is the Nash equilibrium that we have just analyzed. Both players cheat with each making zero profit forever. In such a situation, it will never pay one of the players to start complying unilaterally, for to do so would result in a loss for that

Table 14.5 Repeated Duopoly Game

Period of play	Collude: Trick (Profit in millions of dollars)	Collude: Gear	Cheat with tit-for-tat strategy: Trick (Profit in millions of dollars)	Cheat with tit-for-tat strategy: Gear
1	2	2	2.0	2.0
2	2	2	4.5	−1.0
3	2	2	−1.0	4.5
4	2	2	2.0	2.0
.	.	.	.	.
.	.	.	.	.
.	.	.	.	.

If duopolists repeatedly play the "cooperate" strategy, they each make $2 million in each period. If one player cheats in one period, the other player cheats in the following period—tit-for-tat. The profit from cheating can be made only for a single period. In the following period, the other player cheats and the first player must cooperate if the cooperative agreement is to be restored in period 4. The profit from cheating, calculated over 4 periods of play, is lower than that from colluding. Under collusion, each player makes $8 million; with a single cheat responded to with a tit-for-tat, each makes a profit of $7.5 million. It pays each player to cooperate, so cooperation is an equilibrium.

player and a profit for the other. The price and quantity will remain at the competitive levels forever.

But another equilibrium is possible in which the players make and share the monopoly profit. How might this equilibrium come about? Why wouldn't it always pay each firm to try to get away with cheating? The key to answering this question is the fact that when a prisoner's dilemma game is played repeatedly, the players have an increased array of strategies. Each player can punish the other player for previous actions. There are two extremes of punishment. The smallest penalty that one player can impose on the other is what is called "tit-for-tat". A **tit-for-tat strategy** is one in which a player cooperates in the current period if the other player cooperated in the previous period but cheats in the current period if the other player cheated in the previous period. The most severe form of punishment that one player can impose on the other arises in what is called a trigger strategy. A **trigger strategy** is one in which a player cooperates if the other player cooperates but plays the Nash equilibrium strategy forever thereafter if the other player cheats. Since a tit-for-tat strategy and a trigger strategy are the extremes of punishment—the most mild and most severe—there are evidently other intermediate degrees of punishment. For example, if one player cheats on the agreement, the other player could punish by refusing to cooperate for a certain number of periods. In the duopoly game between Gear and Trick, it turns out that a tit-for-tat strategy keeps both players cooperating and earning monopoly profits. Let's see why.

Table 14.5 sets out the profits that each firm will make in each period of play under two sets of conditions: First, if they cooperate and second, if cheating is responded to with a tit-for-tat strategy. As you can see, as long as both firms stick to the collusive agreement, they make the monopoly profit ($2 million per period each). Suppose that Trick contemplates cheating in period 2. The cheating produces a quick $4.5 million profit and inflicts a $1 million loss on Gear. The next period Gear will hit Trick with its tit-for-tat response and cheat. If Trick reverts to cooperating (to induce Gear to cooperate in period 4), Gear now makes a profit of $4.5 million and Trick makes a loss of $1 million. Adding up the profits over two periods of play, Trick comes out ahead by cheating ($6.5 million compared with $4 million). But if we run the game forward for four periods, Trick would be better off having cooperated. In that case, it would have made $8 million in profit compared with $7.5 million from cheating and generating Gear's tit-for-tat response.[3]

Though we have just worked out what happens if Trick cheats, we can turn the tables and perform the same thought experiment for Gear cheating. We will come up with the same conclusion—it pays Gear to collude. Since it pays both firms to stick with the collusive agreement, both firms will do so and the monopoly price, quantity, and profit will prevail in the industry. This equilibrium is called a **cooperative equilibrium**—an equilibrium resulting from each player responding rationally to the credible threat of the other player to inflict heavy damage if the agreement is broken. But in order for this strategy to work, the threat must be credible: That is, each player must recognize that it is in the interest of the other player to respond with a tit-for-tat. The tit-for-tat and the trigger strategies are credible because if one player cheats, it clearly does not pay the other player to continue complying. So the threat of cheating in response to cheating is credible and sufficient to support the monopoly equilibrium outcome.

[3]In calculating Trick's profits from colluding compared with cheating, we've ignored the fact that future profits have a smaller *present value* than current profits (see pp. 214–216). However, provided that the interest rate at which future profits are discounted is not too high, it will still pay Trick to cooperate rather than cheat.

Uncertainty

In reality, there are random fluctuations in demand and in costs that make it impossible for one firm to detect whether the other firm is cheating. For example, a fall in demand can also lower the industry price. One firm increasing its output can also lower the industry price. If a firm observes only that the industry price has fallen, it cannot tell which of these forces caused it. If it knew that the price resulted from a fall in demand, its profit-maximizing action would be to continue cooperating with the other firm to maintain the monopoly agreement. But if the price fall resulted from the other firm cheating and increasing its output, the profit-maximizing response will be to hit the other firm with a tit-for-tat in the next period. But, by only observing the price fall, neither firm can tell whether the other firm has cheated. What can the firms do in a situation such as this one?

If they each always *assume* that whenever the price falls it is because the other firm has cheated, the monopoly agreement will repeatedly break down and the firms will fail to realize the potentially available monopoly profits. If, on the other hand, one firm assumes that the other firm is always cooperating and that any price falls have resulted from market forces beyond the control of either firm, then that other firm will have an incentive to cheat. (Recall that with one firm cheating and the other cooperating, the cheat makes even bigger profits than when they both cooperate.) To remove that incentive to cheat, each firm will assume that the other is cooperating, provided the price does not fall by more than a certain amount. If the price does fall below that predetermined amount, each firm will react as if the other firm had cheated. When market forces take the price back up above the critical level, the firms will cooperate again.

Other Oligopoly Models

The oligopoly model that we have studied in this section, based on the prisoner's dilemma game, is only one of several models that have been suggested for understanding this important type of market. But it is the approach that dominates current research in the area. Earlier attempts to understand oligopoly are briefly explained and reviewed in Our Advancing Knowledge, pp. 354–355.

Games and Price Wars

Let's see whether the theory of price and output determination under duopoly can help us understand real world behavior and, in particular, price wars. Suppose that two (or more) producers reach a collusive agreement and set their prices at the monopoly profit-maximizing level and that the agreement is enforced by each firm pursuing a strategy that involves cooperating in the agreement unless the price falls below a certain critical level, as described above. Fluctuations in demand will lead to fluctuations in the industry price and output. Most of the time, these fluctuations will be small ones and the price, although it will rise and fall, will not normally fall far enough to make either firm depart from the agreement. Occasionally, however, a large decrease in demand will bring about a large decrease in price. When the price falls by a large enough amount, each firm will respond by abandoning the agreement. The events that take place in such a situation will look exactly like a price war. For it is extremely unlikely that each firm would abandon the agreement, lowering its price, at exactly the same moment. It will appear as if one firm abandoned the agreement and then the other abandoned it in retaliation. But what is actually happening is that each firm is reacting to the large price fall in a manner that maintains a credible threat to the other firm that preserves the monopoly cooperative equilibrium in normal demand conditions. When demand increases again and market forces increase the price, the firms revert to their cooperative behavior reaping the monopoly profit.

Thus there will be cycles of price wars and the restoration of collusive agreements. The behavior of prices and outputs in the oil industry (see Reading Between the Lines, pp. 368–369) can be explained by the type of game that you have just studied.

Preserving Secrecy

Because collusion is illegal, one special problem that colluding firms face is hiding the fact of their collusion and preserving secrecy. The real world 1950s case of "the incredible electrical conspiracy" provides a fascinating view of one way in which this problem has been solved. The particular device used in this conspiracy was called the "phases of the moon" pricing formula.

> [These pricing formulas were listed on] sheets of paper, each containing a half dozen columns of figures. . . . One group of columns established the bidding order of the seven switchgear manufacturers—a different company, each with its own code number, phasing into the priority position every two weeks (hence "phases of the moon"). A second group of columns, keyed into the company code numbers, established how much each company was to knock off the agreed-upon book price. For example, if it were No 1's (G.E.'s) turn to be low bidder at a certain number of dollars off book, then all Westinghouse (No 2), or Allis-Chalmers (No 3) had to do was look for their code number in the second group of columns to find how many dollars they were to bid *above* No 1. These bids would then be fuzzed up by having a little added to them or taken away by companies 2, 3, etc. Thus, there was not even a hint that the winning bid had been collusively arrived at.[4]

Before stumbling on the "phases of the moon" papers, the Justice Department was having a very hard time proving conspiracy but, with the formula in hand, they were able to put the conspiracy under the spotlight and end it.

Other Strategic Variables

We have focused here on firms that play a simple game and consider only two possible strategies—complying and cheating—concerning two variables—price and quantity produced. However, the approach that we have used can be extended to deal with a much wider range of choices facing firms. For example, a firm has to decide whether to enter or leave an industry; whether to mount an expensive advertising campaign; whether to modify its product; how reliable to make its product (the more reliable a product, usually, the more expensive it is to produce);

---

[4]Richard A. Smith, "The Incredible Electrical Conspiracy," Part II, *Fortune* (May 1961): 210.

whether to price discriminate and if so among which groups of customers and to what degree; whether to undertake a large research and development (R&D) effort aimed at lowering production costs. All of these choices that firms make can be analyzed by using game theory. The basic method of analysis that you have studied can be applied to these problems by working out the payoff for each of the alternative strategies and then finding the equilibrium of the game. Let's look at an example—based on an important, real world case—of an R&D game.

An R&D Game in the Disposable Diaper Industry

Disposable diapers were first marketed in 1966. The two market leaders from the start of this industry have been Procter & Gamble (makers of Pampers) and Kimberly-Clark (makers of Huggies). Procter & Gamble has 60 to 70 percent of the total market while Kimberly-Clark has 25 percent. The disposable diaper industry is fiercely competitive. When the product was first introduced in 1966, it had to be cost-effective in competition against reusable, laundered diapers. A massive research and development effort resulted in the development of machines that could make disposable diapers at a low enough cost to achieve that initial competitive edge. But, as the industry has matured, a large number of firms have tried to get into the business and take market share away from the two industry leaders and the industry leaders themselves have battled against each other to maintain or increase their own market share.

The disposable diaper industry is one in which technological advances that result in small decreases in the average total cost of production can provide an individual firm with an enormous competitive advantage. The current machines can produce disposable diapers at a rate of 3000 an hour—a rate that represents a tenfold increase on the output rate just a decade earlier. The firm that develops and uses the least-cost technology gains a competitive edge, undercutting the rest of the market, increasing its market share, and increasing its profit. But the research and development effort that has to be undertaken to achieve even small cost reductions is itself very costly. This cost of research and development has to be deducted from the profit resulting from the increased market share

Table 14.6 Pampers versus Huggies: An R&D Game

		Procter & Gamble's strategies	
		R&D	No R&D
Kimberly-Clark's strategies	R&D	K-C $ 5m P&G $45m	K-C $85m P&G −$10
	No R&D	K-C −$10m P&G $85m	K-C $30m P&G $70m

If both firms undertake R&D, their payoffs are those shown in the top left square. If neither firm undertakes R&D, their payoffs are in the bottom right square. When one firm undertakes R&D and the other one does not, their payoffs are in the top right and bottom left squares. The dominant strategy equilibrium for this game is for both firms to undertake R&D. The structure of this game is the same as that of the prisoner's dilemma.

that lower costs achieve. If no firm does R&D, every firm can be better off, but if one firm initiates the R&D activity, all must.

Each firm is in a research and development dilemma situation. Table 14.6 illustrates the dilemma (with hypothetical numbers) for the R&D game that Kimberly-Clark and Procter & Gamble are playing. Each firm has two strategies: to spend $25 million a year on R&D, or to spend nothing on R&D. If neither firm spends on R&D, they make a joint profit of $100 million, $30 million for Kimberly-Clark and $70 million for Procter & Gamble (bottom right square in payoff matrix). If each firm conducts R&D, market shares are maintained but each firm's profit is lower, by the amount spent on R&D (top left square of payoff matrix). If Kimberly-Clark pays for R&D but Procter & Gamble does not, Kimberly-Clark gains a large part of Procter & Gamble's market. Kimberly-Clark profits and Procter & Gamble loses (top right square of payoff matrix). Finally, if Procter & Gamble invests in R&D, and Kimberly-Clark does not, Procter & Gamble gains market share from Kimberly-Clark, increasing its profit while Kimberly-Clark makes a loss.

Oligopoly in Action

The Price War Is Here

Saudi Arabia's Oil-production Binge May Cost Its Competitors Dearly

When petroleum prices were doubling and redoubling during the 1970s, oil buyers wondered whether the increases would ever hit a ceiling. Last week the problem was reversed: as global prices continued to plummet, traders despaired about the lack of a firm floor. "The market is in a careening tailspin," said one Manhattan oil-futures analyst. Warned another: "Put on your hard hat. The sky is falling." The price for next month's delivery of West Texas Intermediate, a major U.S. crude, plunged $3.39 on Monday and Tuesday to $15.44 per bbl., its lowest point since 1979 and a nearly 50% decline from just three months ago. Only toward the end of the week did the markets calm down a bit, and the price recovered part of its losses, to finish at $17.68.

The steep slide early in the week occurred when members of the Organization of Petroleum Exporting Countries confirmed that the group has in effect abandoned any effort to curb its production, thus ensuring a worsening global glut. Meeting in Vienna under dark snow clouds, a committee of oil ministers from five OPEC nations—Venezuela, Indonesia, Iraq, Kuwait and the United Arab Emirates—declined to propose any new output limit for the 13-member group. Their decision goes along with the strategy being pursued by Saudi Arabia, Kuwait and other wealthy oil producers, who are flooding the market with excess petroleum. . . .

How did OPEC go from a strategy of one-for-all to a free-for-all? The cartel's disintegration began in 1981, when prices started sliding because of worldwide overproduction, partly caused by consumption cutbacks in many oil-dependent nations. To sop up the surplus, OPEC imposed output limits on its members. But that only provided a chance for such new producers as Mexico and Britain to steal business from OPEC countries, whose market share consequently dropped from 63% in 1979 to 38% currently.

Saudi Arabia tried for years to set an example of self-restraint in OPEC. The country slashed its production from a peak 10.3 million bbl. a day in 1981 to a low of 2 million bbl. a day last June. But gradually the Saudis began to feel that they were being played for a sucker by other OPEC members like Colonel Muammar Gaddafi's Libya, which has exceeded its quotas, and by some non-OPEC countries, which were producing at peak capacity. Finally fed up, the Saudis quietly began opening their spigots last autumn, when a seasonal increase in demand temporarily camouflaged the additional supply. By now the kingdom has more than doubled its output, to nearly 4.5 million bbl. a day.

***Time*, February 17, 1986**

By Stephen Koepp. Reported by Robert Ball/Vienna and Raji Samghabadi/New York, with other bureaus

The Essence of the Story

- In the 1970s, oil prices rose sharply.
- In 1986, OPEC abandoned its efforts to curtail production and oil prices fell quickly.
- OPEC's cartel came under pressure in 1981, but Saudi Arabia kept total production limited and maintained high prices by cutting its own output from 10.3 million barrels a day in 1981 to 2 million barrels a day in 1985.
- Other OPEC members produced more than their agreed output, and by 1985 Saudi Arabia decided to abandon its efforts to single-handedly restrain OPEC production.

Background and Analysis

- OPEC is made up of 13 countries (Algeria, Ecuador, Gabon, Indonesia, Iran, Iraq, Kuwait, Libya, Nigeria, Qatar, Saudi Arabia, United Arab Emirates, and Venezuela) and seeks to achieve the best available returns for its members' exports of crude oil and petroleum products.
- The world oil industry is an oligopoly.
- In 1973, the OPEC producers controlled two thirds of the world's oil supply. In that year, they entered into a collusive agreement to restrict world oil production and raise its price.
- The OPEC producers stuck to their agreement from the early 1970s until 1982.
- Faced with a fall in demand and lower profits, individual OPEC members began to abandon the collusive agreement. By 1985, all members except Saudi Arabia were cheating. In 1985, Saudi Arabia also abandoned the agreement.
- The events just summarized can be understood in terms of the game that we have analyzed in this chapter. The OPEC members are playing an oligopoly game similar to the duopoly game that we have studied.
- They began by colluding and stuck to the agreement for a remarkable length of time. Eventually, responding to falling profits, the smaller producers abandoned the agreement. Ultimately the big producer, Saudi Arabia, abandoned its production limits in order to punish its partners who had previously abandoned their own part of the agreement.
- Although at this writing it has not happened, OPEC has a strong incentive to try to restore its collusive agreement and again restrict output and raise the world price of oil.

The two firms, confronted with the payoff matrix in Table 14.6, calculate their best strategies. Kimberly-Clark reasons as follows: If Procter & Gamble does not undertake R&D, we make $85 million if we do and $30 million if we do not; therefore it pays to conduct R&D. If Procter & Gamble conducts R&D, we lose $10 million if we don't and make $5 million if we do. Again, R&D pays off. Thus conducting R&D is a dominant strategy for Kimberly-Clark. It pays Kimberly-Clark to do R&D regardless of Procter & Gamble's decision. Procter & Gamble reasons similarly: If Kimberly-Clark does not undertake R&D, we make $70 million if we follow suit and $85 million if we conduct R&D. It therefore pays to conduct R&D. If Kimberly-Clark does undertake R&D, we make $45 million by doing the same and lose $10 million by not doing R&D. Again, it pays to conduct R&D. So, for Procter & Gamble, R&D is also a dominant strategy. Since R&D is a dominant strategy for both players, it is the Nash equilibrium. The outcome of this game is that both firms conduct R&D. They make lower profits than they would if they could collude to achieve the cooperative outcome of no R&D.

In this real world situation, there are actually more players than Kimberly-Clark and Procter & Gamble. There are a large number of other firms sharing a small portion of the market all of them ready to eat into the share of Procter & Gamble and Kimberly-Clark. So, the R&D effort by these two firms not only serves the purpose of maintaining shares in their own battle, but helps to keep barriers to the entry of other firms high enough to preserve their joint market share.

■ We have now studied the four main market types—perfect competition, monopolistic competition, oligopoly, and monopoly—and discovered how prices and outputs, revenue, cost, and profit are determined in these industries. We have used the various models to make predictions about behavior and to assess the efficiency of alternative market structures. A key element in our analysis of the markets for goods and services is the behavior of costs. Costs are determined partly by technology and partly by the prices of factors of production. We have treated those factor prices as given. It is now time to turn our attention to an examination of the way in which factor prices are themselves determined. Factor prices interact with the goods market that we have just studied in two ways. First, they determine the firm's production costs. Second, they determine household incomes and therefore influence the demand for goods and services. Factor prices also have an important effect upon the distribution of income. The firms that we've been studying in the past five chapters decide *how* to produce; the interactions of households and firms in the markets for goods and services decide *what* will be produced. But the factor prices determined in the markets for factors of production determine *for whom* the various goods and services are produced.

S U M M A R Y

Varieties of Market Structure

Most industries in the real world lie between the extremes of perfect competition and monopoly. The degree of competition is sometimes measured by the concentration ratio. The four-firm concentration ratio measures the percentage of the value of the sales of an industry accounted for by its four largest firms. High concentration ratios indicate a relatively low degree of competition and vice versa, with some important qualifications. There are three key problems related to concentration ratios: (1) concentration ratios refer to the national market, but some industries are local while others are international; (2) concentration ratios do not tell us about the degree of turnover of firms and the ease of entry; and (3) some firms classified in one particular industry operate in several others.

There are two models of industries that lie between monopoly and perfect competition: monopolistic competition and oligopoly. Monopolistic competition is a market type where a large number of firms compete, each making a slightly differentiated product from the others by competing on price, quality, and advertising. Oligopoly is a market type in which a small number of firms compete with each other and in which the actions of any one firm have an important impact on the profit of the others. (pp. 343–346)

Monopolistic Competition

Monopolistic competition occurs when a large number of firms compete with each other by making slightly different products. Under monopolistic competition, each firm faces a downward-sloping demand curve and so has to choose its price as well as its output level. Because there is free entry, in long-run equilibrium zero economic profit is earned. When profit is maximized, with marginal cost equal to marginal revenue, average cost also equals price in the long run. But average cost is not at its minimum point. That is, in monopolistic competition firms operate with excess capacity. (pp. 346–349)

Oligopoly

Oligopoly is a situation in which a small number of producers compete with each other. The key feature of oligopoly is that the firms strategically interact. Each firm has to take into account the effects of its own actions on the behavior of other firms and the effects of the actions of other firms on its own profit.

Game theory is a method of analyzing strategic interaction. Game theory focuses on three aspects of a game:

- Rules
- Strategies
- Payoffs

The rules of the oligopoly game specify the permissible actions by the players. These actions are limited only by the legal code and involve such things as raising or lowering prices; raising or lowering output; raising or lowering advertising effort; enhancing or not enhancing the product. The strategies in the oligopoly game are all the possible actions that each player can take given the action of the other player. The payoff of the oligopoly game is the player's profit or loss. It depends on the actions of both the players and on the constraints imposed by the market, technology, and input costs. (pp. 349–353)

The Prisoner's Dilemma

Duopoly is a market structure in which there are two producers of a good competing against each other. Duopoly is a special case of oligopoly. The duopoly game is similar to the prisoner's dilemma game. Two prisoners are faced with the problem of deciding whether or not to confess to a crime. If neither confesses, they are tried for a lesser crime and receive a light penalty. If both confess, they receive a higher penalty. If one confesses and the other does not confess, the one confessing receives the lightest of all penalties and the one not confessing receives a very heavy penalty.

The prisoner's dilemma has a dominant strategy Nash equilibrium. That is, regardless of the action of the other player there is a unique best action for each player—to confess. (pp. 353–357)

A Duopoly Game

A duopoly game can be constructed in which two firms contemplate the consequences of colluding to achieve a monopoly profit or of cheating on the collusive agreement to make a bigger profit at the expense of the other firm. Such a game is identical to the prisoner's dilemma. The equilibrium of the game will be one in which both firms cheat on the agreement. The industry output will be the same in this case as it would be if the industry was perfectly competitive. The industry price will also be the competitive price and firms will make zero economic profit. If the firms are able to enforce the collusive agreement, the industry will look exactly like a monopoly industry. Price, output, and profit will be the same as in a monopoly.

If a game is repeated indefinitely, there is an opportunity for one player to punish another player for previous "bad" behavior. In such a situation, a tit-for-tat strategy can produce an equilibrium in which both firms stick to the agreement. A tit-for-tat strategy is one in which the players begin by colluding. If one player cheats, the other player responds at the next play by also cheating. Since each knows that it pays the other to respond in this manner, no one cheats. This equilibrium is a cooperative equilibrium—one in which each player cooperates because such behavior is a rational response to the credible threat of the other to inflict damage if the agreement is broken. Uncertainty makes it possible for such an equilibrium to break down from time to time. (p. 357–365)

Games and Price Wars

Price wars can be interpreted as the outcome of a repeated duopoly game. The competing firms comply with the agreement unless market forces bring about a sufficiently large fall in price. A large fall in price is responded to as if it had resulted from the other firm cheating. Only by responding in this manner can each firm maintain the credible threat that it will punish a cheat and thereby ensure that the ever-present temptation to cheat is held in check and the monopoly agreement maintained. When market conditions bring about an increase in price, the firms revert to their cooperative behavior. Industries will go through cycles, starting with a monopoly price and output and occasionally, when demand falls by enough, temporarily pursuing non-cooperative actions. At these times, the industry price and output will be the competitive ones. (p. 366)

Other Strategic Variables

Firms in oligopolistic industries have to make a large range of decisions: Whether to enter or leave an industry; how much to spend on advertising; whether to modify its product; whether to price discriminate; whether to undertake research and development. All these choices result in payoffs for the firm and the other firms in the industry and a game can be constructed to predict the outcome of such choices.

An interesting real world example is the research and development game played between producers of disposable diapers. The equilibrium of that game results in a large amount of research and development being undertaken and lower profits than would emerge if the firms could collude somehow to keep out new entrants and undertake less research and development. Thus that game is similar to the prisoner's dilemma. (pp. 366–370)

KEY CONCEPTS

Cartel, 357
Collusive agreement, 357
Cooperative equilibrium, 365
Dominant strategy, 357
Dominant strategy equilibrium, 357
Duopoly, 353
Four-firm concentration ratio, 344
Game theory, 349
Monopolistic competition, 345
Nash equilibrium, 356
Oligopoly, 345
Payoff, 353
Payoff matrix, 356
Product differentiation, 345
Strategic interaction, 349
Strategies, 353
Tit-for-tat strategy, 364
Trigger strategy, 364

Key Figures and Tables

REVIEW QUESTIONS

1 What are the main varieties of market structure? What are the main characteristics of each of those market structures?

2 What is a four-firm concentration ratio? If the four-firm concentration ratio is 90 percent, what does that mean?

3 Give some examples of U.S. industries that have a high concentration ratio and of U.S. industries that have a low concentration ratio.

4 What are barriers to entry? Give some examples of barriers to entry that exist in the U.S. economy?

5 Explain how a firm can differentiate its product.

6 What is the difference between monopolistic competition and perfect competition?

7 Is monopolistic competition more efficient or less efficient than perfect competition?

8 What is the difference between duopoly and oligopoly?

9 What is the essential feature of both duopoly and oligopoly?

10 List the key features that all games have in common with each other.

11 What are the features of duopoly that make it reasonable to treat duopoly as a game between two firms?

12 What is the prisoner's dilemma?

13 What is a dominant strategy equilibrium?

14 What is meant by a repeated game?

15 Explain what a tit-for-tat strategy is.

16 What is a price war? What is the effect of a price war on the profit of the firms in the industry and on the profitability of the industry itself?

PROBLEMS

1 A monopolistically competitive industry is in long-run equilibrium as illustrated in Fig. 14.1(b). An increase in demand for the industry's product shifts the demand curves of each firm to the right. Using diagrams similar to those in Fig. 14.1, analyze the short-run and long-run effects on price, output, and profit of this change in demand.

2 Another monopolistically competitive industry is in long-run equilibrium, as illustrated in Fig. 14.1(b), when it experiences a large increase in wages which raises the costs of all the firms. Using diagrams similar to those in Fig. 14.1, analyze the short-run and long-run effects on price, output, and profit of this change in costs.

3 Describe the game known as the prisoner's dilemma. In describing the game:

a) Make up a story that motivates the game.

b) Work out a payoff matrix.

c) Describe how the equilibrium of the game is arrived at.

4 Consider the following game. There are two players and they are each asked a question. They can answer the question honestly or they can lie. If they both answer honestly, they each receive a payoff of \$100. If one answers honestly and the other lies, the liar gains at the expense of the honest player. In that event, the liar receives a profit of \$500 and the honest player gets nothing. If they both lie, then they each receive a payoff of \$50.

a) Describe this game in terms of its players, strategies, and payoffs.

b) Construct the payoff matrix.

c) What is the equilibrium for this game?

5 Explain the behavior of oil prices by using a repeated prisoner's dilemma game.

Part 6

Markets for Factors of Production

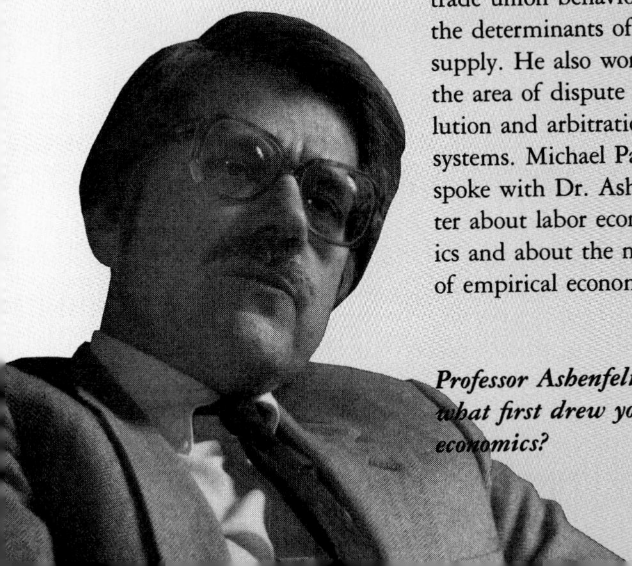

Talking with Orley Ashenfelter

Orley Ashenfelter is a professor of economics at Princeton University and director of the Industrial Relations Section of the Woodrow Wilson School. He has held visiting appointments in the U.S. Department of Labor. His work has covered various aspects of the labor market, including the relationship between racial discrimination and trade union behavior and the determinants of labor supply. He also works in the area of dispute resolution and arbitration systems. Michael Parkin spoke with Dr. Ashenfelter about labor economics and about the nature of empirical economics.

Professor Ashenfelter, what first drew you to economics?

I enjoyed economics from the very first course I took. I found it easy, if you can believe that. I went to graduate school on the recommendation of the professor who taught me labor economics, who claimed that academia was the only place you could do economics where there was a demand for—and payment for—honest opinions. I've always valued that.

Why do you think economics seemed easy to you?

Beginning students are often troubled by the powerful hypothesis that people act in their own self-interest, but that assumption always seemed perfectly natural to me. The practical conse-

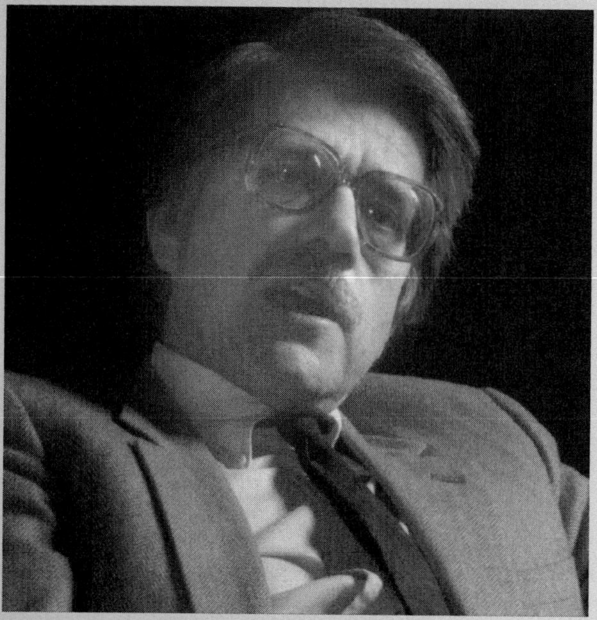

"Academia was the only place you could do economics where there was a demand for honest opinions."

quences of rational self-interest didn't seem harmful. Sometimes students get this economic assumption confused with the moral judgments people make in other contexts about whether it's wrong to act in your own self-interest. But if you find it a hospitable assumption in the context of economic analysis, then you'll find that the questions your professors ask you on exams will also seem completely natural.

How did you become interested in labor economics in particular?

I think my family background contributed. My father belonged to a trade union most of his life. I worked in a factory in the summers during college. At that time, in the late 1950s, there was substantial unemployment in my part of California. When a human resource—a person—is underutilized—out of work or in the wrong job—it has always seemed to me to be more of a waste, in human terms, than when a machine is down. Labor problems have always seemed to be a more important set of concerns than most others.

One of the most controversial issues in the labor market deals with discrimination of all kinds. Against blacks, or women, or young people, for example. Are economic tools useful in studying the extent and effects of discrimination?

The study of discrimination originated as a study of an anomaly in the labor market. As an economist, if you look at equally qualified workers, you expect to find that their wage rates would be unrelated to race, sex, or any such personal characteristic. But the data have shown many times that there *has* historically been a correlation between pay and race or sex. If you think that employers are acting in their self-interest, then any difference in wage rates between equally qualified groups of workers ought to lead rational employers to hire only the workers who are discriminated *against*. Once they have hired the workers that had been earning less, the difference in pay between the two groups should disappear. In other words, most economic theories imply that there isn't actually discrimination in the long run. But that doesn't explain the facts.

How do you, as an economist, explain the facts?

The economic model doesn't work that well here, probably because employers abide by cultural constraints. I'll give you an example. Jim Heckman, at Yale, has studied the employ-

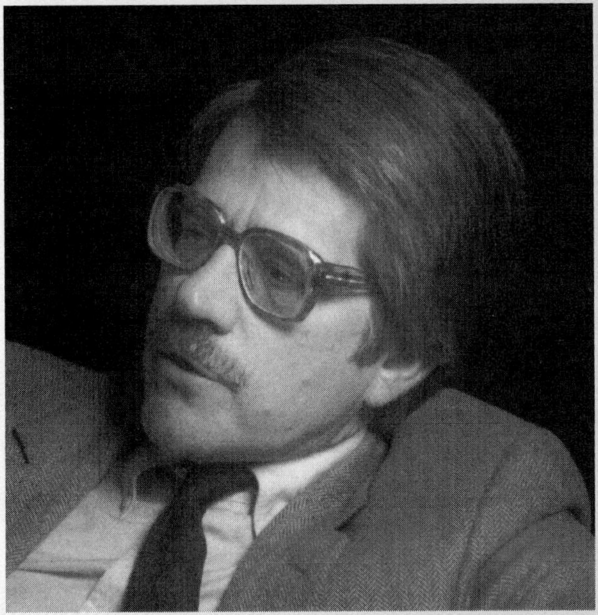

ment of black workers in the South Carolina textile industry. Apparently, employers used the 1964 Civil Rights Act to break down racial discrimination, which was a cultural institution that forced them to act against their own self-interest. Until 1965, there were no black workers to speak of in that industry, even though there had been a terrific labor shortage of white workers since 1954. Naturally, the wage rates of the white workers were increasing dramatically. Many employers would have liked to hire black workers, and ease the labor shortage, but they didn't. Not until 1965, when the employers announced that the government was forcing them to hire black workers—which was in their interest also. All of a sudden, there was an enormous increase in the hiring of black workers in the textile industry. Wages began to level off. The labor shortage disappeared. The only way you can account for these events is by looking at the cultural factors.

What about the role of labor unions?

I have studied in great detail the occurrence of discrimination against blacks in the labor unions themselves. My experience in looking at these issues reveals how important I think empirical economics is. In the 1960s, I began to wonder whether black workers would be as likely as white workers to belong to trade unions. I couldn't get any data, no numbers, on that question. There wasn't much progress on this question until the late 1960s when the Office of Economic Opportunity sponsored a government survey. That information suggested that black workers are better off with trade unions, or at least not worse off.

The union movement has been in decline in recent years. Why is that?

No one really knows. To understand unions, you have to realize that unions act as agents for workers. Everyone would like to have the kinds of agents that movie stars have, but they're expensive. A union is a cost-effective way of providing agents for workers. Of course, agents have drawbacks. The interests of the agent may not be precisely the same as the interests of the people they represent. It may be that workers today in new industries and occupations don't see the value of unions acting as their agents. My personal belief is that the union movement will grow again if it can find a way of providing cost-effective services as agents for the new kinds of jobs in service, high-tech, and government sectors.

"Economic theories imply that there isn't discrimination in the long run. But that doesn't explain the facts."

> "Ninety percent of an economist's job is doing the work, not getting the answers."

What are some of the ways to do empirical economics and get solid answers?

Experiments in the field—where you actually take an idea and test it with real people in a real economy—have much higher credibility than any other kind of work in empirical economics. Of course, they're very hard to carry out. Recently, one remarkable field experiment, the Illinois Unemployment Insurance Bonus, looked at ways to lower unemployment insurance payments and simultaneously help unemployed workers. Some economists have wondered whether people look hard enough for a

new job when they're collecting unemployment insurance. So in this experiment, half the people in certain unemployment offices were offered the following: If you get a job within 10 weeks of collecting your unemployment benefits and keep it for six months, you'll get your insurance *and* a $500 bonus. There was a dramatic drop in unemployment among the people that were offered the bonus.

What principles have been most important to you and your work?

I've always tried to understand the fundamental tension between any

simple economic model and the real world. To recognize the limitations of any model by measuring variations in the real world. Understanding those variations deepens and expands your original model. It allows you to quantify your predictions as a probability. And if you predict right more often than not, then you're improving economic policy.

What advice would you give to a student

interested in studying economics?

I'd say that you should study economics because you love it, not because of any vocational reason. Ninety percent of an economist's job is doing the work, not getting the answers. If you care about the problems that economics tries to deal with and if you like doing the work itself, then you'll do really interesting research. Of course, then it's hard to keep your strong feelings from influencing your work. I'll pass on the advice that my former teacher, Richard Musgrave, shared with me—let your interests and passions guide you in choosing the questions you ask, but keep those passions out of the answers you form.

Chapter 15

Pricing and Allocating Factors of Production

After studying this chapter, you will be able to:

- Explain how firms choose the quantities of labor, capital, and land to employ in their production activities
- Explain how households choose the quantities of labor, capital, and land to supply
- Explain how wages, interest, and rent are determined in competitive factor markets
- Explain the concept of economic rent
- Distinguish between economic rent and transfer earnings

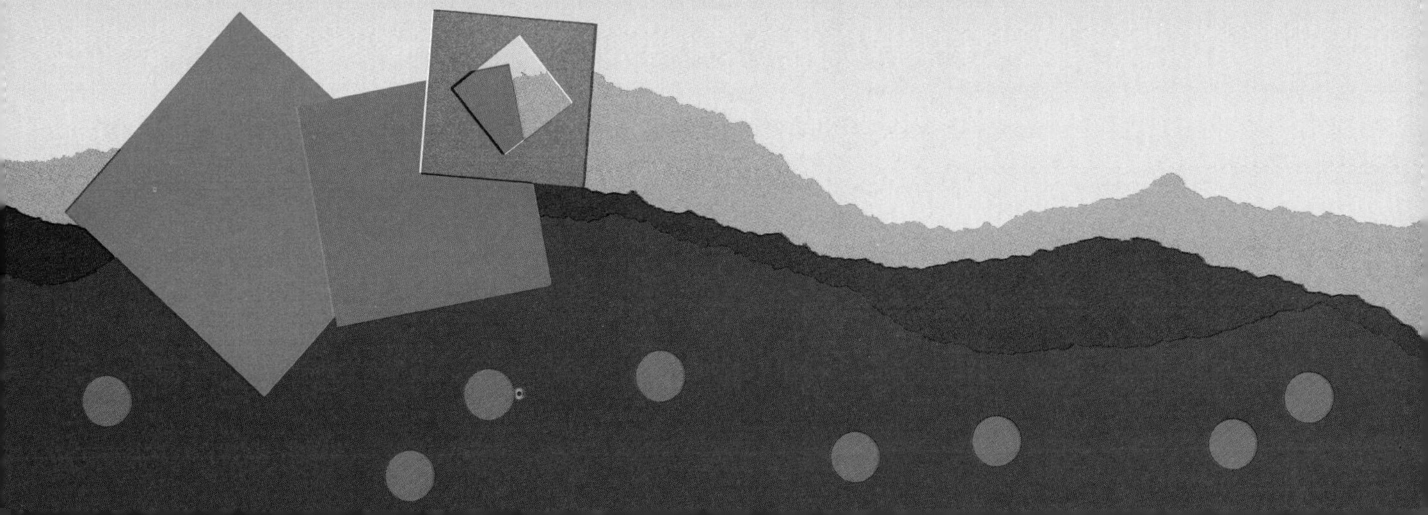

Many Happy Returns

It may not be your birthday and, even if it is, chances are that you are spending most of the day working. But at the end of the week, or month (or, if you're devoting all your time to college, when you graduate), you will receive the *returns* from your labor. ■ Of course, those returns vary a lot from one person to another and from one kind of job to another. An average person in full-time employment in 1987 earned $21,000—about $12 an hour. Most of us are clustered around that average. Such a person is Pedro Lopez. Pedro spends his day in a small container, suspended by cables attached to the top of Chicago's John Hancock Tower. With the wind whipping off Lake Michigan, and with chilly toes, fingers and ears, Pedro cleans the several acres of glass that form the windows of that skyscraper. Pedro works hard for his $12 an hour, but when those happy returns come in at the end of the week, it all seems worthwhile. ■ For some workers, the returns are very happy indeed. Dan Rather is one such worker. Dan collects a cool $3.6 million a year for that 30-minute news show he puts on each weekday evening. And he's not alone on those dizzy heights of happy paychecks. Barbara Walters, Tom Brokaw, Bryant Gumbel, and Diane Sawyer are all up there with him in the million-dollar plus annual pay range. ■ At the other extreme are those working for the minimum wage and, in some cases, for even less than the minimum wage. Student help at McDonald's and farm workers in the fields of southern California labor away for just a few dollars an hour. But even for those workers, the returns are worthwhile. Sure they'd like more, but they prefer working for low wages than not working at all and having no income. ■ What determines the wages that we are paid? What determines the kinds of jobs we do? How does our economy allocate its labor resources to the many thousands of different tasks that must be performed?

■ Most of us have little trouble spending our pay. But most of us manage to save some of what we earn. Some of our savings we put on deposit in the bank or at the savings and loan. With some we buy bonds and stocks. The returns that we get on our savings depend on which of these various things we do with them. If we put the money in the bank or in a savings and loan, we earn interest on it. If we buy bonds and stocks, we're paid a dividend and enjoy stock price increases—or suffer decreases. The size of our return on a stock depends on the company whose stock we've bought. We may be lucky and get a huge return or unlucky and get little or nothing at all. For example, the people who invested in Service Merchandise, a Nashville-based retail company, made a staggering 400 percent return in 1988; those investing in Borman's, Inc., the Detroit-based supermarket chain, doubled their money; and those investing in Murray Ohio, a bicycle maker, almost doubled theirs. But the people buying Texas American Bancshares, a troubled Texas bank, and Berkey, Inc., a photographic processing concern in White Plains, New York, gave their money away. The value of those investments fell by 90 percent. ■ What determines the amount of saving that people do and the returns they make on that saving? How do the returns on saving influence the allocation of savings across the many industries and activities that use our capital resources? ■ Savings can also be used to buy land. That use of a person's savings generates a return in the form of rent. The amount of rent earned varies enormously with the location and quality of land. For example, if you buy an acre of farmland in Iowa, you will be able to rent it out for something approaching $1000 a year. If you buy a block on Chicago's "Magnificent Mile," you'd collect several million dollars a year in rent income. ■ What determines the rent that people are willing to pay for different blocks of land? Why are rents so enormously high in big cities and so relatively low in the great farming regions of the nation? ■ It is not only land rents that are much higher in cities than in other parts of the country. Many of the things we buy are more expensive in a city than in a small town. For example, a cup of coffee that costs a quarter in your university cafeteria costs 50¢ in a central city snack bar, $1.25 in New York City, and $2 in Tokyo. Why? Obvious, you answer. High rent leads to high cost, so coffee shops in high rent areas have to charge high prices for their coffee. But wait! Is it high rents that lead to high prices of coffee in big cities, or is it that a high demand for coffee leads to high prices which in turn lead to high rents?

■ In this and the following three chapters, we deal with the kinds of questions that have just been posed. We study markets for factors of production—for labor, capital, and land—and learn how the prices of these factors of production are determined. This first chapter provides an overview of all three types of factor markets and also introduces you to the important concept of economic rent. It begins by introducing you to the terminology of factor markets and setting out the link between factor prices and incomes.

Factor Prices and Incomes

Factors of production are divided into three broad categories: *labor, capital,* and *land.* (We defined these factors of production in Chapter 1, p. 14.) The owners of factors of production receive an income from the firms that use those factors as inputs into their production activities. These incomes are *wages* paid for labor, *interest* paid for capital, and *rent* paid for land. Wages include all labor income including salaries, commissions, and any other supplementary forms of income paid in compensation for labor. Interest includes all forms of capital income including dividends paid by firms. Rent is the income paid for the use of land and natural resources. Apartment rents include an element of rent and also an element of interest—a payment for the use of capital.

Labor is by far the most important factor of production and generates about 70 percent of all income, and that percentage has been steadily increasing over the years.

In the rest of this chapter, we're going to build a model of a factor market. We'll use that model to determine factor prices, the quantities of factors traded, and the incomes that factors of production earn.

An Overview

Factor prices are determined in factor markets, and we can understand those prices by using the model of demand and supply. The quantity of a factor of production demanded depends upon the factor's price. That is, the quantity of labor demanded

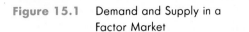

Figure 15.1 Demand and Supply in a Factor Market

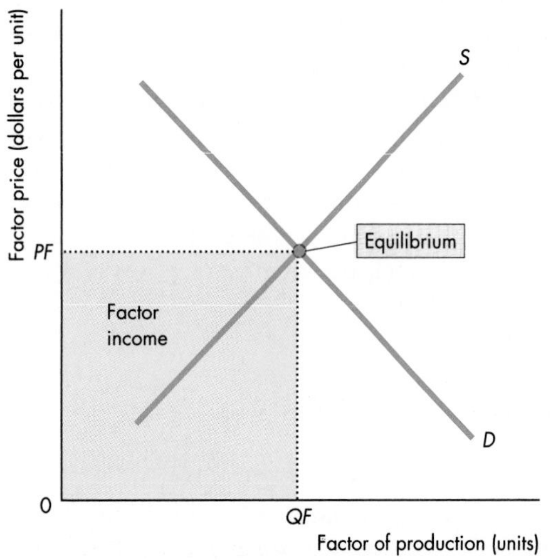

The demand curve for a factor of production (*D*) slopes downward and the supply curve (*S*) slopes upward. Where the demand and supply curves intersect, the factor price (*PF*) and the quantity of a factor traded (*QF*) are determined. The factor income is the product of the factor price and the quantity, as represented by the blue rectangle of the factor.

depends on the wage rate, the quantity of capital demanded depends on the interest rate, and the quantity of land demanded depends on the rent. The law of demand applies to factors of production just as it applies to all other economic entities. Thus as the price of a factor of production decreases, the quantity of the factor demanded increases. The demand curve for a factor of production is shown in Fig. 15.1 as the curve labeled *D*.

The quantity supplied of a factor of production depends on its price. With some exceptions that we'll identify later in this chapter, the law of supply applies to factors of production, so that as the price of a factor of production increases, the quantity of the factor supplied increases. The supply of a factor of production is shown in Fig. 15.1 as the curve labeled *S*.

The equilibrium factor price is determined at the point of intersection of the factor demand and factor supply curves. Figure 15.1 shows such an equilibrium—*QF* is the quantity of the factor of production traded and *PF* is the factor price.

The income earned by a factor of production is its price multiplied by the quantity traded. In this case, the price is measured by the distance from the origin to *PF* in Fig. 15.1, and the quantity traded is measured by the distance from the origin to *QF*. The factor income is the product of these two distances and it is equivalent to the blue shaded area in the figure.

All the influences on the quantity of a factor bought other than its price result in a shift in the factor demand curve. We'll study what those influences are in the next section. For now, let's simply work out the effects of a change in the demand for a factor of production. An increase in demand for a factor of production, as illustrated in Fig. 15.2(a), shifts the demand curve to the right, leading to an increase in the quantity of the factor traded and an increase in its price. Thus when the demand curve shifts from D_0 to D_1, the quantity traded increases from QF_0 to QF_1 and the price increases from PF_0 to PF_1. An increase in the demand for a factor of production increases that factor's income. The dark blue area in Fig. 15.2(a) illustrates the increase in income.

When the demand for a factor of production decreases, its demand curve shifts to the left. Figure 15.2(b) illustrates the effects of a decrease in demand: the demand curve shifts to the left from D_0 to D_2; the quantity traded decreases from QF_0 to QF_2; and the price decreases from PF_0 to PF_2. When the demand for a factor of production decreases, the income of that factor also decreases. The light blue area in Fig. 15.2(b) illustrates the decrease in income.

The extent to which a change in the demand for a factor of production changes the factor price and the quantity traded depends on the elasticity of supply. If the supply curve is very flat (supply is elastic), the change in the quantity traded is large and the change in price is small. If the supply curve is very steep (supply is inelastic), the change in the price is large and the change in the quantity traded is small.

A change in the supply of a factor of production also changes the price and quantity traded as well as the income earned by those supplying the factor. An increase in supply results in an increase in the quantity traded and a decrease in the factor price. A decrease in supply results in a decrease in the quantity traded and an increase in the factor price. But whether a change in supply increases or decreases income depends on the elasticity of demand for the factor.

Figure 15.2 Changes in Demand

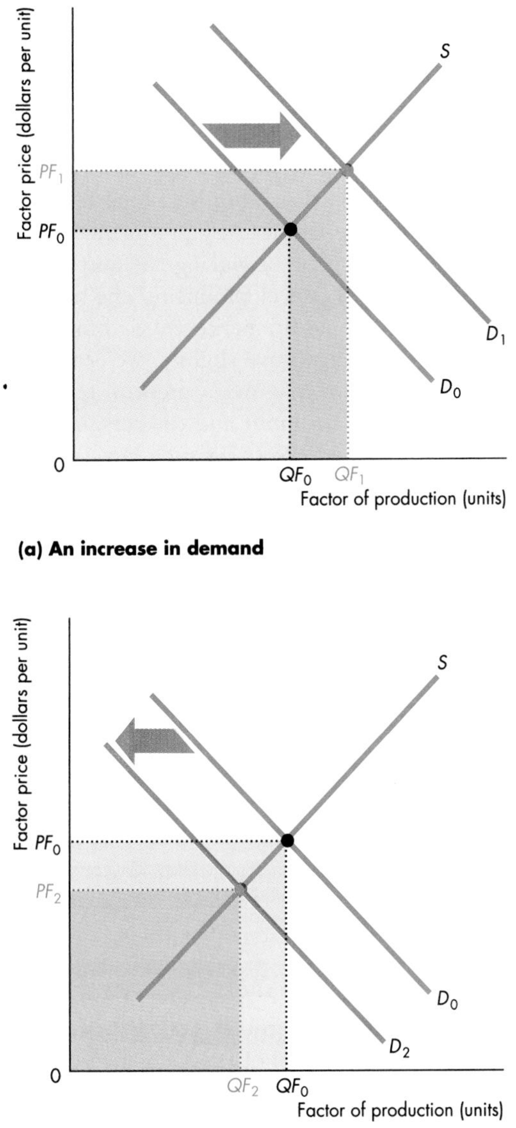

(a) An increase in demand

(b) A decrease in demand

An increase in the demand for a factor of production (part a) shifts its demand curve to the right—from D_0 to D_1. The quantity traded increases from QF_0 to QF_1 and the price increases from PF_0 to PF_1. The factor income increases, and that income increase is shown by the dark blue area. A decrease in the demand for a factor of production, from D_0 to D_2, results in a decrease in the quantity traded, from QF_0 to QF_2, and a decrease in the factor price, from PF_0 to PF_2. The decrease in demand results in a decrease in the factor income. That decrease in income is illustrated by the light blue area.

Figure 15.3 Factor Income and Demand Elasticity

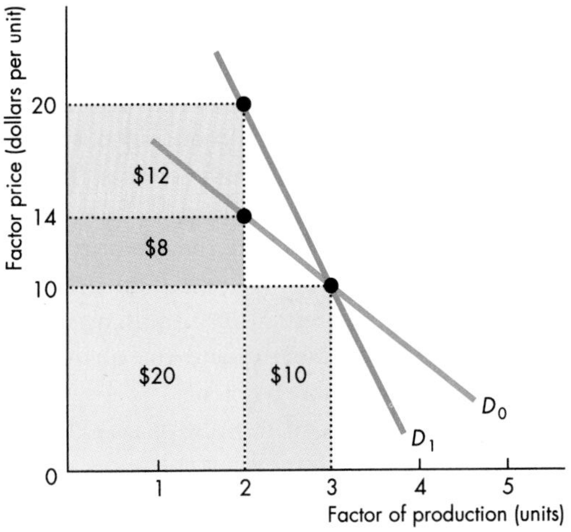

A decrease in the quantity traded of a factor of production may result in a decrease or an increase in the factor's income. If the demand curve is D_0 (an elastic demand curve over the relevant range), a decrease in the quantity traded, from 3 to 2, results in a decrease in the factor income, from $30 to $28. If the demand curve is D_1 (an inelastic demand curve over the relevant range), a decrease in the quantity traded, from 3 to 2, results in an increase in the factor's income, from $30 to $40.

Suppose that the quantity traded of the factor of production illustrated in Fig. 15.3 decreases from 3 units to 2 units. Initially, the price is $10 a unit. If the demand curve is D_0, the decrease in supply results in an increase in the price of the factor but a decrease in the income of those supplying this factor of production. You can see that income decreases by multiplying the factor price by the quantity traded. Initially, when 3 units are traded at a price of $10 each, the income earned by the suppliers of this factor of production is $30 (the $20 light blue area plus the $10 red area). When the quantity traded decreases to 2 units and the price increases to $14, income decreases (by the $10 red area) but increases (by the $8 dark blue area), for a net decrease to $28. Over the range of the price change that we've just considered, the demand curve D_0 is elastic—its elasticity is greater than 1.

Conversely, suppose that the demand curve is D_1. In this case, when the quantity traded decreases to 2 units, the price increases to $20 a unit. Income increases to $40. The smaller quantity traded lowers income by $10 (red area), but the higher factor price increases income by $20 (dark blue plus green areas). Over the range of the price change that we've just considered, the demand curve D_1 is inelastic—its elasticity is less than 1.

The markets for factors of production determine factor prices in much the same way as goods markets determine the prices of goods and services. These markets also determine factor incomes. Factor income is the factor price multiplied by the quantity of the factor traded. Thus to work out the influences on incomes we have to pay attention simultaneously to the determination of the prices and the quantities traded of the factors of production.

We're going to spend the rest of this chapter exploring more closely the influences on the demand for and supply of factors of production. We're also going to discover what determines the elasticities of supply and demand for factors. These elasticities are important because of their effects on factor prices and the incomes earned. Let's begin by studying the demand for inputs.

Demand for Factors

The demand for any factor of production is a derived demand. A **derived demand** is a demand for an input not for its own sake but in order to use it in the production of goods and services. A firm's derived demand for inputs depends on the constraints the firm faces—its technology constraint and its market constraint. It also depends on the firm's objective. The objective of the model firms that we have studied is to maximize profit. We'll continue to study the behavior of such firms.

A firm's demand for factors stems from its profit-maximization decision. *What* to produce and *how* to produce it are the questions that the firm must answer in order to make maximum profit. Those choices have implications for the firm's demand for inputs, which we'll now investigate.

Profit Maximization

A firm's inputs fall into two categories: fixed and variable. In most industries, the fixed inputs are capital (i.e., plant, machinery, and buildings) and land; and the variable inputs are labor and raw materials. A firm meets permanent changes in output by changing the scale of its inputs of capital and land. It meets short-run variations in output by varying its labor and raw material inputs.

Profit-maximizing firms produce the output at which marginal cost equals marginal revenue. This principle holds true whether the firm is in a perfectly competitive industry, in monopolistic competition, in oligopoly, or a monopoly. If one more unit of output adds less to total cost than it adds to total revenue, the firm can increase its profit by producing more. A firm maximizes profit by producing the output at which the additional cost of producing one more unit of output equals the additional revenue from selling it. If we shift our perspective slightly, we can also state the condition for maximum profit in terms of the marginal cost of an input and the marginal revenue that input generates. Let's see how.

Marginal Revenue Product and Factor Price

The change in total revenue resulting from employing one more unit of any factor is called the factor's **marginal revenue product.** The concept of marginal revenue product sounds a bit like the concept of marginal revenue that you have met before. These concepts are indeed related but there is an important distinction between the two. *Marginal revenue product* is the extra revenue generated as a result of employing one extra unit of a factor; *marginal revenue* is the extra revenue generated as a result of selling one additional unit of output.

A profit-maximizing firm hires the quantity of a factor that makes the marginal revenue product of the factor equal to the marginal cost of the factor. For a firm that buys its factors of production in competitive factor markets, the marginal cost of a factor is the factor's price. That is, in a competitive factor market, each firm is such a small demander of the factor that it has no influence on its price. The firm simply has to pay the going factor price—market wage rate for labor, interest rate for capital, and rent for land. We have defined the additional revenue resulting from employing one more unit of a factor as the factor's marginal revenue product. We have seen that in competitive factor markets, the marginal cost of a factor equals its price. Therefore a profit-maximizing firm—a firm that makes the marginal revenue product equal to the marginal cost of each input—hires each factor up to the point at which its

Table 15.1 Marginal Revenue Product and Average Revenue Product at Max's Wash 'n' Wax

	Quantity of labor *L* (workers)	Output Q (cars washed per hour)	Marginal product of labor *MP* = Δ*Q*/Δ*L* (washes per worker)	Total revenue TR = P × Q (dollars)	Marginal revenue product *MRP* = Δ*TR*/Δ*L* (dollars per worker)	Average revenue product *ARP* = *TR*/*L* (dollars per worker)
a	0	0		0		
			5		20	
b	1	5		20		20
			4		16	
c	2	9		36		18
			3		12	
d	3	12		48		16
			2		8	
e	4	14		56		14
			1		4	
f	5	15		60		12

The marginal revenue product of labor is the change in total revenue that results from a one-unit increase in labor input. To calculate marginal revenue product, first work out total revenue. If Max hires 1 worker (row *b*), output is 5 washes an hour, and total revenue, at $4 a wash, is $20. If he hires 2 workers (row *c*), output is 9 washes an hour, and total revenue is $36. By hiring the second worker, total revenue rises by $16—the marginal revenue product of labor is $16. The average revenue product of labor is total revenue per unit of labor employed. For example, when Max employs 2 workers, total revenue is $36, and average revenue product is $18 ($36 divided by 2).

marginal revenue product equals the factor's price. As the price of a factor varies, the quantity demanded of it also varies. The lower the price of a factor, the larger is the quantity demanded of that factor. Let's illustrate this proposition by working through an example—that of labor.

The Firm's Demand for Labor

Labor is a variable input. A firm can change the quantity of labor it employs in both the short run and the long run. Let's focus first on a firm's short-run demand for labor.

A firm's short-run technology constraint is described by its *short-run production function.* Table 15.1 sets out the production function for a car wash operated by Max's Wash 'n' Wax. (This production function is similar to the one that we studied in Chapter 10, Fig. 10.1.) The numbers in the first two columns of the table tell us how the maximum number of car washes each hour varies as the amount of labor employed varies. The third column shows the *marginal product of labor*—the change in output resulting from a one-unit increase in labor input. (Since marginal product refers to a *change* in the quantity of labor employed, these numbers appear midway between the two levels of employment from which they are calculated.) Max's market constraint is the demand curve for his product. If in the goods market a firm is a monopoly or engaged in monopolistic competition or oligopoly, it faces a downward-sloping demand curve for its product. If a firm is perfectly competitive, it faces a fixed price for its product regardless of its output level and therefore faces a horizontal demand curve for its product. We will assume that Max operates his car wash in a perfectly competitive market and can sell as many washes as he chooses at a constant price of $4 a wash. Given this information, we can calculate Max's total revenue (fourth column) by multiplying the number of cars washed per hour by $4. For example, if 9 cars are washed each hour (row *c*), total revenue is $36.

Table 15.2 A Compact Glossary of Factor Market Terms

Factors of production	Labor, capital, and land (including raw materials)
Factor prices	Wages—price of labor; interest—price of capital; rent—price of land
Marginal product	Output produced by last unit of input hired; e.g., the marginal product of labor is additional output produced by employing one more person
Average product	Output per unit of input; e.g., average product of labor is output divided by labor input
Marginal revenue	Revenue resulting from selling one additional unit of output
Marginal revenue product	Revenue resulting from hiring one additional unit of a factor of production; e.g., the marginal revenue product of labor is the additional revenue resulting from selling the output produced by employing one more person.
Average revenue product	Total revenue per unit of input; calculated as total revenue divided by labor input

The fifth column shows the calculation of marginal revenue product of labor—the change in total revenue per unit change in labor input. For example, if Max hires a second worker (row *c*), total revenue increases from \$20 to \$36, so marginal revenue product is \$16. There is an alternative way of calculating the marginal revenue product of labor—multiply marginal product by marginal revenue. To see that this method gives the same answer, multiply the marginal product of hiring a second worker—4 cars an hour—by marginal revenue—\$4 a car—and notice that we get the same \$16 as before.

Total revenue divided by the quantity of the factor hired is called the **average revenue product** of the factor. Thus average revenue product is the average contribution of each unit of an input to the firm's total revenue. The last column of Table 15.1 shows the average revenue product of labor. For example, when Max employs 3 workers (row *d*), total revenue is \$48. Thus the average revenue product of labor is \$48 divided by 3 workers, which is \$16 per worker.

Notice that as the quantity of labor rises, the marginal revenue product of labor falls. When Max hires the first worker, the marginal revenue product of labor is \$20. If Max hires a second worker, the marginal revenue product of labor is \$16. Marginal revenue product of labor continues to decline as Max hires more workers.

Marginal revenue product diminishes as Max hires more workers because of the principle of diminishing returns that we first studied in Chapter 10. With each additional worker hired, the marginal product of labor falls and so brings in a smaller marginal revenue product. Because Max's Wash 'n' Wax is a perfectly competitive firm, the price of each additional car wash is the same and brings in the same marginal revenue. If instead Max had a monopoly, he would have to lower his price to sell more washes. In such a case, the marginal revenue product of labor diminishes even more quickly than in perfectly competitive conditions. Marginal revenue product diminishes because of diminishing marginal product of labor and also because of diminishing marginal revenue. Table 15.2 provides a compact glossary of factor market terms.

We can illustrate the marginal revenue product and average revenue product of labor as curves. The **average revenue product curve** shows the average revenue product of a factor at each quantity of the factor hired. The **marginal revenue product curve** shows the marginal revenue product of a factor at each quantity of the factor hired. Figure 15.4(a) shows the marginal revenue product and average revenue product curves for workers employed by Max. Let's study this figure.

The horizontal axis measures the number of workers that Max hires and the vertical axis measures the marginal and average revenue product of labor. The curve labeled *ARP* is the average revenue product curve and is based on the numbers in Table 15.1. For example, point *d* on the *ARP* curve represents

Figure 15.4 Marginal Revenue Product and the Demand for Labor at Max's Wash 'n' Wax

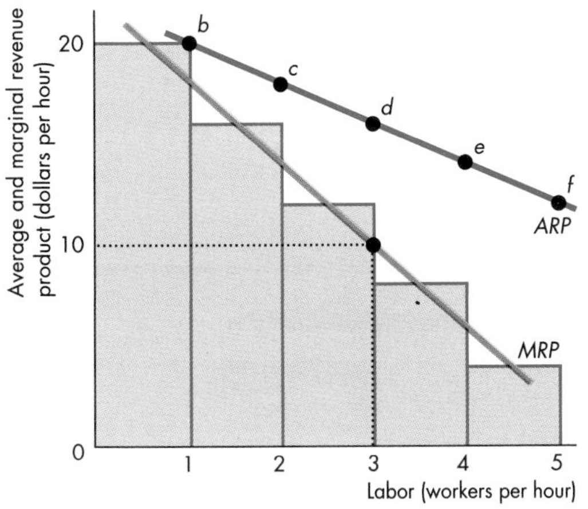

(a) Average and marginal revenue product

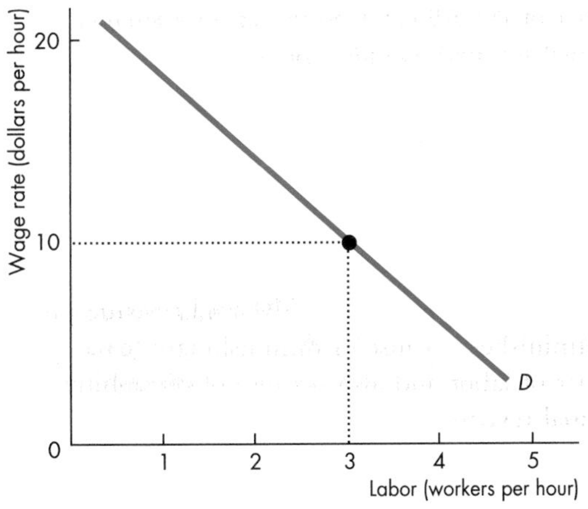

(b) Demand for labor

Part (a) shows the average and marginal revenue product curves for Max's Wash 'n' Wax. Points *b* through *f* on the average revenue product curve correspond to the rows of Table 15.1. The blue bars representing marginal revenue product are also based on the numbers in that table. (Each point is plotted midway between the labor inputs used in its calculation.) Average revenue product and marginal revenue product decline and the marginal revenue product curve is always below the average revenue product curve. Part (b) shows Max's demand for labor curve. It is identical to his marginal revenue product curve. Max demands labor up to the point at which the wage rate (the worker's marginal cost) equals marginal revenue product.

row *d* in the table. Max employs 3 workers and the average revenue product of labor is $16 a worker. The blue bars show the marginal revenue product of labor as Max employs more workers. These bars correspond to the numbers in Table 15.1. The curve *MRP* is the marginal revenue product curve.

The firm's demand for labor curve is based on its marginal revenue product curve. You can see Max's demand for labor curve (*D*) in Fig. 15.4(b). The horizontal axis measures the number of workers hired—the same as part (a). The vertical axis measures the wage rate in dollars per hour. The demand for labor curve is exactly the same as the firm's marginal revenue product curve. For example, when Max employs 3 workers an hour, his marginal revenue product is $10 an hour, as in Fig. 15.4(a); and at a wage rate of $10 an hour, Max hires 3 workers an hour, as in Fig. 15.4(b).

But why is the demand for labor curve identical to the marginal revenue product curve? Because the firm hires the profit-maximizing quantity of labor. If the cost of hiring one more worker—the wage rate—is less than the additional revenue that worker will bring in—the marginal revenue product of labor—then it pays the firm to employ one more worker. Conversely, if the cost of hiring one more worker is greater than the additional revenue that worker will bring in—the wage rate exceeds the marginal revenue product—then it does not pay the firm to employ one more worker. When the cost of the last worker hired equals the revenue brought in by that worker, the firm is making the maximum possible profit. Such a situation occurs when the wage rate equals the marginal revenue product. Thus the quantity of labor demanded by the firm is such that the wage rate equals the marginal revenue product of labor.

R E V I E W

A firm chooses the quantity of labor to hire so that its profit is maximized. The additional total revenue generated by hiring one additional worker is called the marginal revenue product of labor. It is the change in total revenue generated by a one-unit change in labor input. In a competitive industry, the marginal cost of labor is the wage rate. Profit is maximized when the marginal revenue product of labor equals the wage rate. The marginal revenue product of labor curve is the firm's demand for labor curve. The lower the wage rate, the higher is the quantity of labor demanded. ■

Two Conditions for Profit Maximization When we studied firms' output decisions, we discovered that a condition for maximum profit is that marginal revenue equals marginal cost. We've now discovered another condition for maximum profit—that marginal revenue product equals the factor price. How can there be two conditions for a maximum profit? There are two conditions for a maximum profit because they are equivalent to each other. That marginal revenue equals marginal cost is the condition that tells us the quantity of goods a firm produces; and that marginal revenue product equals the factor price is the condition that tells us the quantity of a factor that a firm hires to produce its profit-maximizing output. The equivalence of the two conditions is set out in Table 15.3.

Table 15.3 Two Conditions for Maximum Profit

Symbols

Marginal revenue	*MR*
Marginal cost	*MC*
Marginal revenue product	*MRP*
Factor price	*PF*

Two conditions for maximum profit

1. $MR = MC$
2. $MRP = PF$

Equivalence of conditions

1.	$MRP / MP = \mathbf{MR}$	=	$\mathbf{MC} = PF / MP$
	Multiply by *MP* to give		Multiply by *MP* to give
2.	$MR \times MP = \mathbf{MRP}$	=	$\mathbf{PF} = MC \times MP$

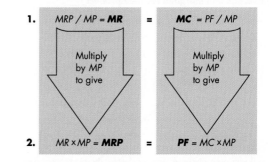

Marginal revenue (*MR*) equals marginal cost (*MC*) , and marginal revenue product (*MRP*) equals the price of the factor (*PF*). The two conditions for maximum profit are equivalent because marginal revenue product (*MRP*) equals marginal revenue (*MR*) multiplied by marginal product (*MP*), and the factor price (*PF*) equals marginal cost (*MC*) multiplied by marginal product (*MP*).

We have just derived the law of demand as it applies to the labor market. Let's now study the influences that result in a change in the demand for labor and, therefore, in a shift in the demand for labor curve.

Shifts in the Firm's Demand for Labor Curve The position of the demand for labor curve depends on three factors:

- The price of the firm's output
- The prices of other inputs
- Technology

The higher the price of a firm's output, the greater is the quantity of labor demanded by the firm, other things being equal. The price of output affects the demand for labor through its influence on marginal revenue product. A higher price for the firm's output increases marginal revenue which, in turn, increases the marginal revenue product of labor. A change in the price of a firm's output leads to a shift in the firm's demand for labor curve. If the output price increases, the demand for labor increases.

The other two influences on the demand for labor have their main effects not in the short run but in the long run. The **short-run demand for labor** is the relationship between the wage rate and the quantity of labor demanded when the firm's capital is fixed and labor is the only variable input. The **long-run demand for labor** is the relationship between the wage rate and the quantity of labor demanded when all inputs can be varied. A change in the relative price of inputs—such as the relative price of labor and capital—leads to a substitution away from the input whose relative price has increased and toward the input whose relative price has decreased. Thus if the price of using capital decreases relative to that of using labor, the firm substitutes capital for labor, increasing the quantity of capital demanded and decreasing its demand for labor.

Finally, a technological change that influences the marginal product of labor also affects the demand for labor. Again, this effect is felt in the long run when the firm takes the opportunity to adjust all its inputs and incorporate the new technology into its production process. A technological change that decreases the marginal product of labor results in a decrease in the demand for labor, and one that increases the marginal product of labor results in an increase in the demand for labor. Table 15.4 summarizes the influences on a firm's demand for labor.

As we saw earlier, Fig. 15.2 illustrates the effects of a change in the demand for a factor. If that factor is labor, then Fig. 15.2 shows the effects of a change in the demand for labor on the wage rate and the quantity of labor hired. But we can now say why the demand for labor curve shifts. For example, an increase in the price of the firm's output, an increase in the price of capital, or a technological change that increases the marginal product of labor shifts the demand for labor curve from D_0 to D_1 in Fig. 15.2(a). Conversely, a decrease in the price of the firm's output, a decrease in the price of capital, or a technological change that lowers the marginal product of labor shifts the demand curve for labor from D_0 to D_2 in Fig. 15.2(b).

Table 15.4 A Firm's Demand for Labor

The law of demand

The quantity of labor demanded by a firm

Decreases if:	Increases if:
• The wage rate increases	• The wage rate decreases

Changes in demand

A firm's demand for labor

Decreases if:	Increases if:
• The firm's output price decreases	• The firm's output price increases
• The prices of other inputs decrease	• The prices of other inputs increase
• A technological change decreases the marginal product of labor	• A technological change increases the marginal product of labor

Market Demand

So far, we've studied only the demand for labor by an individual firm. Let's now look at the market demand. The market demand for a factor of production is the total demand for that factor by all firms. The market demand curve for a given factor is obtained by adding up the quantities demanded of that factor by each firm at each given factor price. Thus the concept of the market demand for labor curve is exactly like the concept of the market demand curve for a good or service. In the case of a good or service, the market demand curve is obtained by adding together the quantities demanded of that good by all households at each price. In the case of labor, the market demand curve is obtained by adding together the quantities of labor demanded by all firms at each wage rate.

Elasticity of Demand for Labor

The elasticity of demand for labor measures the responsiveness of the quantity of labor demanded to the wage rate. We calculate this elasticity in the same way that we calculate a price elasticity: the elasticity of demand for labor equals the percentage change in the quantity of labor demanded divided by the percentage change in the wage rate. The elasticity of demand for labor depends on the elasticity of demand for the good that the firm is producing and on the properties of the firm's production function. However, there is a slight difference in the things that affect the elasticity of demand for labor in the short run and the long run.

Short-run Elasticity The term **short-run elasticity of demand for labor** is the percentage change in the quantity of labor demanded divided by the percentage change in the wage rate when labor is the only variable input. Since the quantity of labor demanded always falls when the wage rate rises, there is no need to attach a negative sign. The elasticity of demand for labor, in positive numbers, tells us the responsiveness of a quantity *fall* to a wage rate *rise*. A higher elasticity means a more responsive demand. The short-run elasticity of demand for labor depends on three things:

1 *The short-run elasticity of demand for the product.* If the demand for the good that labor produces is elastic, then a small change in the price of the good creates a large change in the quantity demanded of the good. One thing that can change the price of the good is a change in costs, and costs change in the short-run if the wage rate changes. For a given wage rate change, the price changes, and the larger the elasticity of demand for the good, the larger is the change in the quantity of the good demanded and, therefore, the larger is the change in the labor input used to produce that good. Other things being equal, the higher the elasticity of demand for the product, the higher is the elasticity of demand for labor.

2 *Labor intensity.* The proportion of labor in the production of a good—the labor intensity of the production process—also affects the elasticity of demand for labor. Suppose that the cost of labor is 90 percent of the total cost of producing a good. In such a situation, a 10 percent change in the cost of labor generates a 9 percent change in total cost. Conversely, if the cost of labor is only 10 percent of the total cost, then a 10 percent change in the cost of labor produces only a 1 percent change in total cost. The larger the percentage change in total cost, the larger is the percentage change in price and, for a given elasticity of demand for the product, the larger is the percentage change in output. The larger the change in output, the larger is the change in labor input. So, the larger the proportion of total cost coming from labor (labor intensity), the more elastic is the demand for labor, other things being equal.

3 *The slope of the marginal product of labor curve.* The slope of the marginal product of labor curve depends on the production technology. In some processes, marginal product diminishes quickly; in others, it remains fairly constant as a firm hires more workers. The steeper the slope of the marginal product curve, the more responsive is the marginal revenue product to a change in labor input. When the revenue brought in by an extra worker diminishes quickly, a firm will not hire many new workers to produce more of its product. Therefore, the steeper the marginal product curve, the less elastic is the firm's demand for labor.

Long-run Elasticity The **long-run elasticity of demand for labor** is the percentage change in the quantity of labor demanded divided by the percentage change in the wage rate when all inputs are varied. Long-run elasticity, like short-run elasticity, depends on the elasticity of demand for the product in the long run rather than in the short run, and on *labor intensity.* In addition, the long-run elasticity depends on the *substitutability of capital for labor.* The more easily capital can be substituted for labor in production, the larger is the long-run elasticity of demand for labor. For example, it is fairly easy to substitute robots for assembly line workers in car factories and automatic picking machines for labor in vineyards and orchards. At the other extreme, it is difficult (though not impossible) to substitute robots for newspaper reporters, bank loan officers, and stockbrokers. The more readily can capital be substituted for labor, the more elastic is the firm's demand for labor.

R E V I E W

The short-run elasticity of demand for labor depends on three factors:

- The short-run elasticity of demand for the product
- Labor intensity
- The slope of the marginal product of labor curve

The long-run elasticity of demand for labor also depends on three factors:

- Long-run elasticity of demand for the product
- Labor intensity
- Substitutability of capital for labor ■

Supply of Factors

The supply of factors is determined by the decisions of households. Households allocate the factors of production that they own to their most rewarding uses. The quantity supplied of any factor of production depends on its price. Usually, the higher the price of a factor of production, the larger is the quantity supplied. There is an important possible exception to this general law of supply concerning the supply of labor. It arises from the fact that labor is the single most important factor of production and the source of the largest portion of household income.

Let's examine household factor supply decisions, beginning with the supply of labor.

Supply of Labor

A household chooses how much labor to supply as part of its time allocation decision. Time is allocated between two broad activities:

- Market activity
- Nonmarket activity

Market activity is the same thing as supplying labor. **Nonmarket activity** consists of leisure and nonmarket production activities including education and training. The household obtains an immediate return from market activities in the form of an income. Nonmarket activities generate a return in the form of goods and services produced in the home, in the form of a higher future income, or in the form of leisure, which is valued for its own sake and which is classified as a good.

In deciding how to allocate its time between market activity and nonmarket activity, a household weighs the returns that it can get from the different activities. We are interested in the effects of the wage rate on the household's allocation of its time and on how much labor it supplies.

Wages and Quantity of Labor Supplied To induce a household to supply labor, it must be offered a high enough wage rate. Nonmarket activities are valued by households either because the time is used in some productive activity or because of the value they attach to leisure. In order for it to be worthwhile to supply labor, a household has to be offered a wage rate that is at least equal to the value it places on the last hour it spends in nonmarket activities. This wage rate—the lowest one for which a household will supply labor to the market—is called its **reservation wage.** At wage rates below the reservation wage, the household supplies no labor. Once the wage rate reaches the reservation wage, the household begins to supply labor. As the wage rate rises above the reservation wage, the household varies the quantity of labor that it supplies. But a higher wage rate has two offsetting effects on the quantity of labor supplied—a *substitution effect* and an *income effect.*

1. Substitution Effect Other things being equal, the higher the wage rate, the more will people economize on their nonmarket activities and increase the time they spend working. As the wage rate rises, the household will discontinue any nonmarket activity that yields a return that is less than the wage rate; instead, the household will switch to market activity. For example, a household might use some of its time to cook meals and do laundry—nonmarket activities—that can, alternatively, be bought for $10 an hour. If the wage rate available to the household is less than $10 an hour, the household will cook and wash for itself. If the household's wage rate rises above $10 an hour, it will be worthwhile for the household to work more hours and use part of its income ($10) to buy laundry services and to eat out. The higher wage rate induces a switch of time from nonmarket activities to market activities.

2. Income Effect The higher the household's wage rate, the higher is its income. A higher income, other things being equal, induces a rise in demand for most goods. Leisure, a component of nonmarket activity, is one of those goods. Since an increase in income creates an increase in the demand for leisure, it also creates a decrease in the amount of time allocated to market activities and, therefore, to a fall in the quantity of labor supplied.

Backward-bending Household Supply of Labor Curve The substitution effect and the income effect work in opposite directions. The higher the wage rate, the higher is the quantity of labor supplied via the substitution effect, but the lower is the quantity of labor supplied via the income effect. At low wage rates, the substitution effect is larger than the in-

Figure 15.5 The Supply of Labor

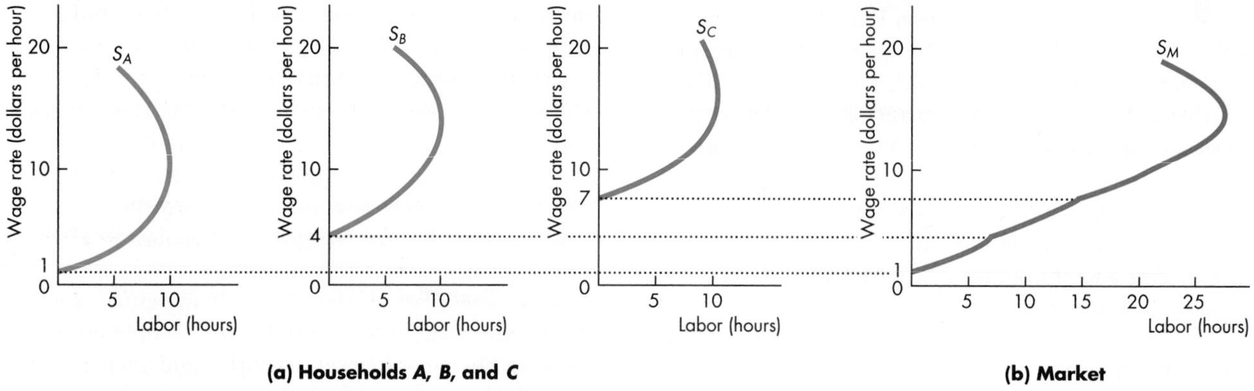

Part (a) shows the labor supply curves of three households (S_A, S_B, and S_C). Each household has a reservation wage below which it will supply no labor. As the wage rises above the reservation wage, the quantity of labor supplied rises to a maximum. If the wage continues to rise, the quantity of labor supplied begins to decline. Each household's supply curve eventually bends backward. When the quantity of labor supplied increases as the wage increases, the substitution effect dominates the income effect. When the quantity of labor supplied begins to fall as the wage rate increases, the income effect (which leads people to demand more leisure) dominates the substitution effect.

Part (b) shows how, by adding together the quantities of labor supplied by the individual households at each wage rate, we derive the market supply curve of labor (S_M). The market supply curve also eventually bends backward, but in the real world at a higher wage rate than that currently experienced. The upward-sloping part of the labor supply curve before it bends backward is the part along which the market operates.

come effect. As the wage rate rises, the household supplies more labor. But as the wage rate continues to rise, there comes a point at which the substitution effect and the income effect just offset each other. At that point, a change in the wage rate has no effect on the quantity of labor supplied. If the wage rate continues to rise, the income effect begins to dominate the substitution effect and the quantity of labor supplied declines. The household's supply of labor curve does not slope upward throughout its entire length but begins to bend back on itself. This curve is called a backward-bending supply curve.

Three individual household labor supply curves are shown in Fig. 15.5(a). Each household has a different reservation wage. Household *A* has a reservation wage of $1 an hour, household *B* of $4 an hour, and household *C* of $7 an hour. Each household's labor supply curve is backward-bending.

Market Supply The quantity of labor supplied to the entire market is the total quantity supplied by all households. The market supply of labor curve is the sum of the supply curves of all the individual households. Figure 15.5(b) shows the market supply curve (S_M) derived from the supply curves of the three households (S_A, S_B, S_C) in Fig. 15.5(a). At wage rates of less than $1 an hour, the three households do laundry and cook, but they do not supply any market labor. The household most eager to supply market labor has a reservation wage of $1 an hour. As the wage rate rises to $4 an hour, household *A* increases the quantity of labor that it supplies to the market. The reservation wage of household *B* is $4 an hour, so as the wage rate rises above $4 an hour, the quantity of labor supplied in the market is the sum of the labor supplied by households *A* and *B*. When the wage rate reaches $7 an hour, household *C* begins to supply some labor to the market. At wage rates above $7 an hour, the quantity supplied in the market is equal to the sum of the quantities supplied by the three households.

Notice that the market supply curve S_M, like the individual household supply curves, eventually bends backward. But the market supply curve has a long upward-sloping section. The reason why the market supply curve slopes up for such a long stretch is that the reservation wages of individual households are not equal and at higher wage rates additional households are confronted with their reservation wage and so begin to supply labor.

Though the market supply curve eventually bends backward, no real world economy has reached a wage rate so high that it operates on the backward-bending portion of its labor supply curve. Many individual households are on the backward-bending portion of their own labor supply curve. Thus as wage rates rise, some people work fewer hours. But higher wage rates induce those workers who are on the upward-sloping part of their labor supply curve to supply more hours and induce additional workers to enter the work force. The response of these workers to higher wage rates dominates that of those whose work hours decline as wage rates rise. Therefore, for the economy as a whole, the labor supply curve slopes upward. For this reason, we will restrict our attention to the upward-sloping part of the labor supply curve in Fig. 15.5(b).

Supply to Individual Firms We've studied the labor supply decisions of individual households and seen how those decisions add up to the total market supply. But how is the supply of labor to each individual firm determined? The answer to this question depends on the degree of competitiveness in the labor market.

In a perfectly competitive labor market, each firm faces a perfectly elastic supply of labor curve. This situation arises because the individual firm is such a small part of the total labor market that it has no influence on the wage rate.

Some labor markets are noncompetitive in the sense that firms can and do influence the price of the labor that they hire. In these cases, firms face an upward-sloping supply of labor curve. The more labor they wish to employ, the higher is the wage rate they have to offer. We examine how this type of labor market operates in Chapter 16. Here, we deal only with the case of perfectly competitive input markets.

R E V I E W

A household chooses the quantity of labor to supply as part of its time allocation decision. If the wage rate is below the household's reservation wage, the household supplies no labor to the market and uses all its time for nonmarket activities. At wage rates above the household's reservation wage, the household supplies some labor to the market. A rising wage has two opposite effects on the quantity of labor that the household supplies: a substitution effect and an income effect. Other things being equal, the higher wage rate induces the household to economize on leisure and other nonmarket time and to work more hours—the substitution effect. The higher wage rate also raises the household's income, which increases its demand for most goods including leisure. More time taken for leisure means less labor is supplied. That is, other things being equal, the higher wage rate induces the household to spend more time on leisure and work fewer hours—the income effect.

The market supply of labor is the total quantity of labor supplied by all households. The market supply curve, like a household's supply curve, bends backward above a certain wage rate. Actual economies operate on the upward-sloping part of the market supply of labor curve. The supply of labor curve faced by each individual firm depends on the degree of competitiveness of the labor market. In a perfectly competitive labor market, each firm faces a perfectly elastic supply curve. ■

Next, let's examine the supply of capital.

Supply of Capital

Households supply capital to firms by consuming less than their income—they save. Thus the scale on which a household supplies capital depends on how much of its income it saves.

The most important factors determining a household's savings are:

- Its current income in relation to its expected future income
- The interest rate

Current and Future Income A household with a current income that is low compared with its expected future income saves little and might even

Figure 15.6 Short-run and Long-run Supply of Capital

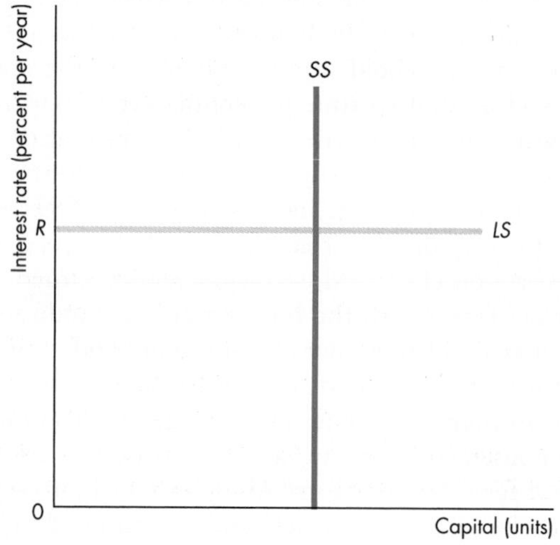

The long-run supply of capital *(LS)* is highly elastic (perfectly elastic in this figure). If the interest rate is above *R*, households increase their saving and increase the total amount of capital supplied. If the interest rate is below *R*, households decrease their saving and reduce the amount of capital supplied. The short-run supply of capital *(SS)* is highly inelastic (perfectly inelastic in the figure). For the economy as a whole and for individual firms in the short run, once capital is put in place, it is difficult to vary its quantity easily and quickly. Thus, no matter what the interest rate, at a given point in time there is a given amount of capital supplied.

have negative saving. A household with a current income that is high compared with its expected future income saves a great deal in the present in order to be able to consume more in the future. The stage in the household's life cycle is the main factor influencing whether current income is high or low compared with expected future income. Young households typically have a low current income compared with their expected future income, while older households have a high current income relative to their expected future income. The consequence of this pattern in income over the life cycle is that young people have negative saving and older people have positive saving. Thus the young incur debts (such as mortgages and consumer credit) to acquire durable goods and to consume more than their income, while older people save and accumulate assets (often in the form of pension and life insurance arrangements) to provide for their later retirement years.

Interest Rate and Capital Supply Curve A household's supply of capital is the stock of capital that it has accumulated as a result of its past saving. The household's supply curve of capital shows the relationship between the quantity of capital supplied and the interest rate. Other things being equal, a higher interest rate encourages people to economize on current consumption in order to take advantage of the higher return available from saving. Thus the higher the interest rate, the greater is the quantity of capital supplied.

Market Supply The market, or aggregate, quantity of capital supplied is the sum of the supplies of all the individual households. The market supply curve of capital shows how the aggregate quantity of capital supplied varies as the interest rate varies. The market supply curve of capital is likely to be highly elastic and might even be perfectly elastic. Such a market supply curve is shown in Fig. 15.6 as that labeled *LS*. At interest rates above *R*, enough households are willing to save so that the total stock of capital supplied increases. At interest rates below *R*, a sufficient number of households plan to consume more than their income, and the total quantity of saving supplied decreases.

Supply to Individual Firm When studying the supply of capital to an individual firm, it is important to distinguish between the short-run and long-run supply of capital. Recall the distinction between the short run and the long run. The short run is a period during which a firm can vary its labor input but not its capital input. Thus in the short run, the firm's capital input is fixed. The long run is a period during which a firm can vary all its inputs. Thus in the long run, the firm can vary its capital as well as its labor inputs. In the long run, a firm operating in a competitive capital market can obtain any amount of capital at the going market interest rate. Thus it faces a perfectly elastic supply curve of capital. In the short run, the firm has acquired a specific set of assets. For example, an auto producer has acquired a production assembly line; a laundromat operator has

Figure 15.7 The Supply of Land

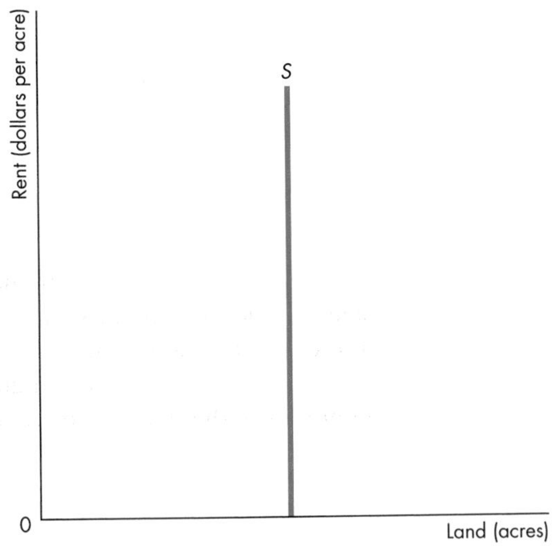

The supply curve of a given piece of land is perfectly inelastic. No matter what the rent, no more land than exists can be supplied.

acquired a number of washing machines and dryers; the campus print shop has acquired a number of photocopying and other printing machines. In the short run, the supply of capital facing an individual firm can be highly inelastic. Specific pieces of machinery and equipment have been bought and have been bolted in place. They cannot be quickly disposed of or added to. In the extreme case, the short-run supply of capital is perfectly inelastic. Such a case is illustrated as the vertical line (*SS*) in Fig. 15.6.

The inelastic short-run supply and the elastic long-run supply of capital have important implications for the returns obtained from different types of capital. We'll explore those implications later in this chapter when we study equilibrium in the capital market. But before that, let's complete our analysis of the supply of factors of production by examining the supply of land.

Supply of Land

Land is the stock of natural resources and its aggregate quantity supplied cannot be changed by any individual decisions. Individual households can vary the amount of land they own, but whatever land is acquired by one household is sold by another so that the aggregate quantity of land supplied of any particular type and in any particular location is fixed regardless of the decisions of any individual household. This fact means that the supply of each particular piece of land is perfectly inelastic. Figure 15.7 illustrates such a supply. Regardless of the rent available, the quantity of land supplied on Chicago's Magnificent Mile is a fixed number of square feet.

Expensive land can be, and is, used more intensively than inexpensive land. For example, high rise buildings enable land to be used more intensively. However, to use land more intensively, it has to be combined with another factor of production—capital. Increasing the amount of capital per block of land does nothing to change the supply of land itself.

Although the supply of each type of land is fixed and its supply is inelastic, each individual firm, operating in competitive land markets, faces an elastic supply of land. That is, each firm can acquire the land that it demands at the going rent, as determined in the marketplace. Thus provided land markets are highly competitive, firms are price takers in these markets, just as they are in the markets for other factors of production.

R E V I E W

The supply of capital is determined by households' saving decisions. Other things being equal, the higher the interest rate, the greater is the amount of capital supplied. The supply of capital to individual firms is highly inelastic in the short run but elastic in the long run.

Individual households can vary the amount of land that they supply but the aggregate supply of land is determined by the fact that there is a given, fixed quantity of it available. Thus the supply of each particular piece of land is perfectly inelastic. In a competitive land market, each firm faces an elastic supply of land at the going rent. ■

Let's now see how factor prices and quantities are determined.

Figure 15.8 Labor Market Equilibrium

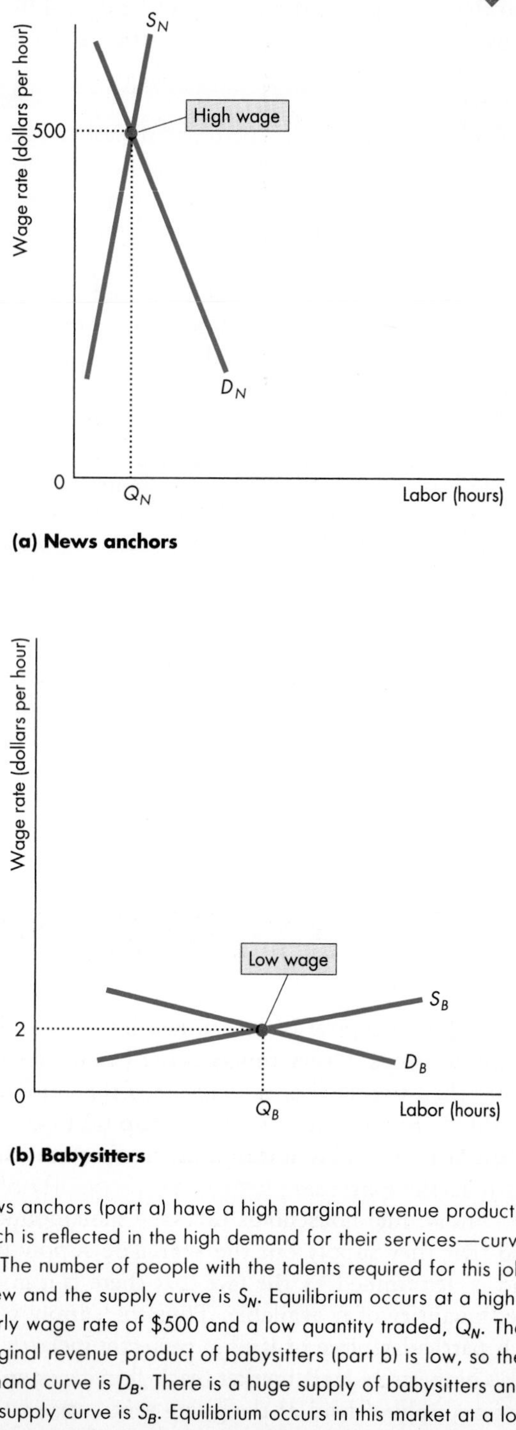

News anchors (part a) have a high marginal revenue product, which is reflected in the high demand for their services—curve D_N. The number of people with the talents required for this job is few and the supply curve is S_N. Equilibrium occurs at a high hourly wage rate of $500 and a low quantity traded, Q_N. The marginal revenue product of babysitters (part b) is low, so the demand curve is D_B. There is a huge supply of babysitters and the supply curve is S_B. Equilibrium occurs in this market at a low wage rate of $2 an hour and a high quantity traded, Q_B.

Competitive Equilibrium

The price of a factor of production and the quantity of it traded are determined by the interaction of the demand for the factor and its supply. We'll illustrate competitive equilibrium by looking at the markets for labor, capital, and land and by looking at two examples of each.

Labor Market Equilibrium

Figure 15.8 shows two labor markets. That in part (a) is the labor market for national news anchors. Such people have a very high marginal revenue product and this is reflected in the demand curve for their services, curve D_N. The supply of individuals with the required talents for this kind of job is low, and this fact is reflected in supply curve S_N. Equilibrium occurs at a high hourly wage rate ($500 in this example) and a low quantity traded, Q_N.

Figure 15.8(b) shows another market, that for babysitters. Although people value the output of babysitters, the marginal revenue product of these services is low, a fact reflected in demand curve D_B. There are many households, typically those with high school students, willing to supply these services and the supply curve is S_B. This market achieves an equilibrium at a low wage rate ($2 an hour in this example) and at a relatively high quantity traded, Q_B.

If there is an increase in the demand for news anchors, the demand curve D_N in Fig. 15.8(a) shifts to the right, increasing their wage and increasing the quantity traded. The higher wage rate will induce more households to offer their services in this activity. If there is an increase in demand for babysitters, the demand curve D_B in Fig. 15.8(b) shifts to the right, increasing their wage rate and increasing the quantity traded. Again, a higher wage rate will induce an increase in the quantity supplied. Movements in wage rates occur to achieve a balance between the quantities demanded and supplied in each individual labor market. Changes in demand result in changes in the wage rate that achieve a reallocation of the labor force.

Capital Market Equilibrium

Figure 15.9 shows capital market equilibrium. In Fig. 15.9(a), we illustrate that part of the capital

Figure 15.9 Capital Market Equilibrium

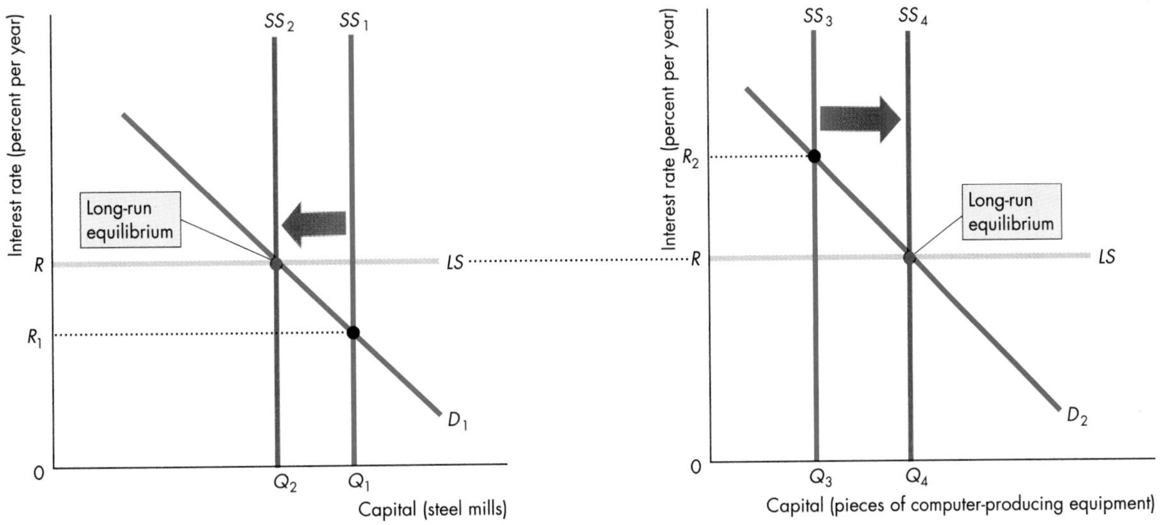

(a) Steel industry **(b) Computer industry**

The long-run supply curve of capital (*LS*) in the steel industry (part a) and the computer industry (part b) is perfectly elastic. The number of steel mills in place is fixed at Q_1, so the short-run supply curve in the steel industry is SS_1. The demand curve for steel mills is D_1. The interest rate on capital invested in steel is R_1. The amount of computer-producing equipment in place is fixed at Q_3, so the short-run supply curve in the computer industry is SS_3. The demand curve for computer-producing equipment is D_2. The interest rate in the computer industry is R_2. With a higher interest rate in the computer industry, capital leaves the steel industry and goes into the computer industry. The short-run supply curves shift. In the steel industry, the short-run supply curve shifts to the left, to SS_2, and the interest rate rises. In the computer industry, the short-run supply curve shifts to the right, to SS_4, and the interest rate falls. In long-run equilibrium, interest rates are the same in both industries.

market in the steel industry—the market for steel mills. The long-run supply of capital to the steel industry is shown as the perfectly elastic supply curve *LS*. But the actual quantity of steel mills in place is Q_1, and the short-run supply curve is SS_1. The demand curve for steel mills, determined by their marginal revenue product, is D_1. The interest rate earned by the owners of steel mills—the stockholders in U.S. Steel and similar firms—is R_1.

Figure 15.9(b) shows that part of the capital market in the computer industry. Again, the long-run supply curve is *LS*, the same curve as in the steel industry. That is, in the long run, capital is supplied to each of these industries at an interest rate *R*. But the amount of computer-producing capital in place is Q_3, and the short-run supply curve is SS_3 in part (b). The interest rate earned by the owners of computer production equipment—the stockholders of IBM and similar firms—is R_2.

You can see that the interest rate paid to owners of capital in the steel industry is lower than that in the computer industry. This inequality of interest rates on capital sets up an interesting dynamic adjustment process that gradually lowers the stock of capital in the steel industry and increases the stock of capital in the computer industry. With a low interest rate on capital in the steel industry and a high interest rate on capital in the computer industry, it pays people to take their investments out of the steel industry and to put them into the computer industry. But physical plant and equipment have been built in the steel industry and

Figure 15.10 Land Market Equilibrium

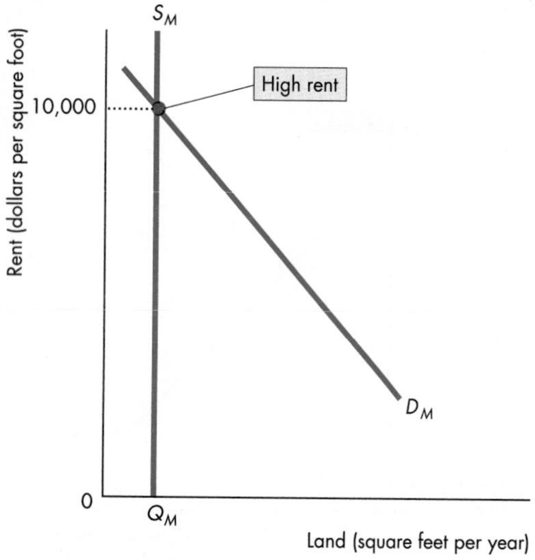

(a) Magnificent Mile

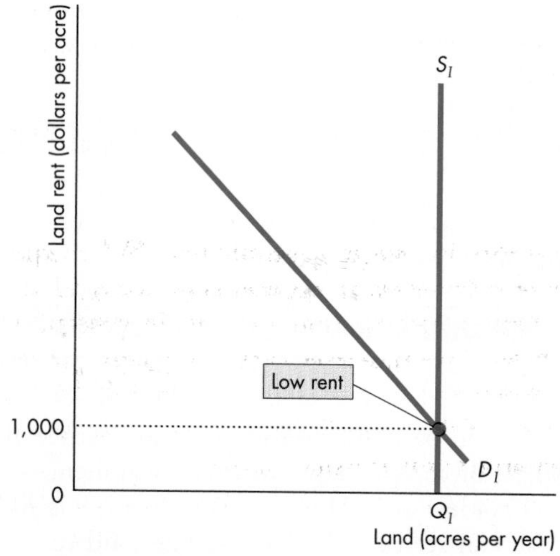

(b) Iowa farmland

The marginal revenue product of land on Chicago's Magnificent Mile gives rise to the demand curve D_M (part a). The quantity of land on the Magnificent Mile is fixed at Q_M, so the supply curve is S_M. Equilibrium occurs at an annual rent of \$10,000 a square foot. The marginal revenue product of farmland in Iowa (part b) gives rise to a demand curve D_I. The quantity of farmland in Iowa is fixed at Q_I and the supply curve is S_I. Equilibrium occurs at an annual rent of \$1000 an acre.

cannot be readily transformed into computer-making equipment. Its owners must wait until their investment has worn out. But as capital equipment depreciates in the steel industry, it is not replaced and so the capital stock declines. The short-run supply curve shifts to the left, to SS_2. Conversely, as capital is freed up and additional saving is made, it is directed toward the computer industry, so that its short-run supply curve shifts to the right, to SS_4. The interest rates adjust in the two industries during this process. The interest rate increases in the steel industry and decreases in the computer industry. Eventually, in long-run equilibrium, the interest rate on capital in the two industries will have equalized at R.

Land Market Equilibrium

Equilibrium in the land market occurs at rents that allocate the fixed amounts of land available to their highest value uses. Figure 15.10 illustrates two land markets. Part (a) shows the market for land on Chicago's Magnificent Mile. Its marginal revenue product gives rise to the demand curve D_M. There are a fixed number of square feet of land (Q_M), so the supply is inelastic, as shown by the curve S_M. Equilibrium occurs at a rent of \$10,000 a square foot a year.

Figure 15.10(b) illustrates the market for farmland in Iowa. Here, the marginal revenue product produces the demand curve D_I. There is a vast amount of land available but again, only a fixed quantity—in this case, Q_I. Thus the supply curve lies a long way to the right but is vertical—perfectly inelastic—at S_I. Here the equilibrium rent occurs at \$1000 an acre a year.

We've now studied the markets for the three factors of production and seen how wages, interest, and rent are determined. We now turn to our final task in this chapter—defining and distinguishing between economic rent and transfer earnings.

Economic Rent and Transfer Earnings

The total income of a factor of production is made up of its economic rent and its transfer earnings. **Economic rent** is an income received by the owner of a factor over and above the amount required to induce that owner to offer the factor for use. The income required to induce the supply of a factor of production is called **transfer earnings.**

These concepts of economic rent and transfer earnings are illustrated in Fig. 15.11. The figure shows the market for a factor of production. It could be *any* factor of production—labor, capital, or land. The demand curve for the factor of production is D and its supply curve is S. The factor price is PF and the quantity traded QF. The income of the factor is the sum of the yellow and green areas. The yellow area below the supply curve measures transfer earnings and the green area below the factor price but above the supply curve measures economic rent.

To see why the area above the supply curve measures economic rent, recall that a supply curve can be interpreted in two different ways. The standard intepretation is that a supply curve indicates the quantity supplied at a given price. But the alternative interpretation of a supply curve is that it shows the minimum price at which a given quantity is willingly supplied. If suppliers receive only the minimum amount required to induce them to supply each unit of the factor of production, they will be paid a different price for each unit and the prices will trace the supply curve and the income received is entirely transfer earnings—the yellow area in Fig. 15.11.

The concept of economic rent is similar to the concept of consumer surplus that you met in Chapter 7, pp. 167–168. Consumer surplus, recall, is the difference between the price the household pays for a good and the maximum price it would be willing to pay, as indicated by the demand curve. In a parallel sense, economic rent is the difference between the factor price a household actually receives and the minimum factor price at which it would be willing to supply a given amount of a factor of production.

It is important to distinguish between *economic rent* and *rent.* Rent is the price paid to the factor of production, land. Economic rent is a component of the income received by every factor of production.

The portion of the income of a factor of production that consists of economic rent depends on the elasticity of the supply of the factor of production. When the supply of a factor of production is inelastic, its entire income is economic rent. When the supply of a factor of production is perfectly elastic, none of its income is economic rent. In general, when the supply curve is neither perfectly elastic nor perfectly inelastic (like that illustrated in Fig. 15.11), some part of the factor income is economic rent and and the other part transfer earnings.

Figure 15.11 Economic Rent and Transfer Earnings

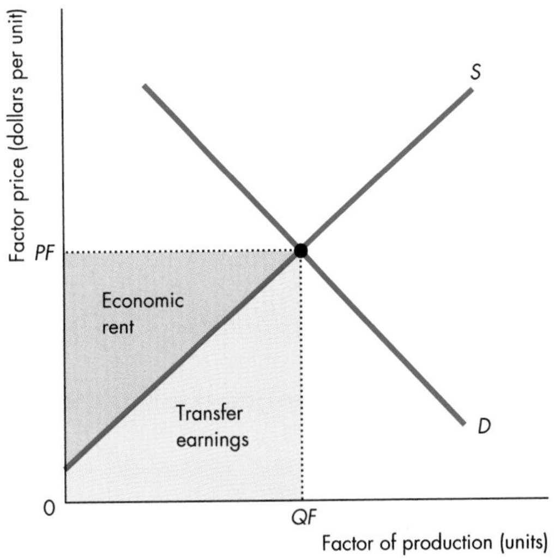

The total income of a factor of production is made up of its economic rent and its transfer earnings. Transfer earnings are measured by the yellow area under the supply curve and economic rent, by the green area above the supply curve and below the factor price.

Figure 15.12 illustrates the three possibilities. Part (a) of the figure shows the market for a particular parcel of land in New York City. The land is fixed in size at L square yards. Therefore the supply curve of the land is vertical—perfectly inelastic. No matter what the rent on the land is, there is no way of increasing the quantity that can be supplied.

The demand for that block of land is determined by its marginal revenue product. The marginal revenue product in turn depends on the uses to which the land can be put. In a central business district such as Manhattan, the marginal revenue

Figure 15.12 Economic Rent and Supply Elasticity

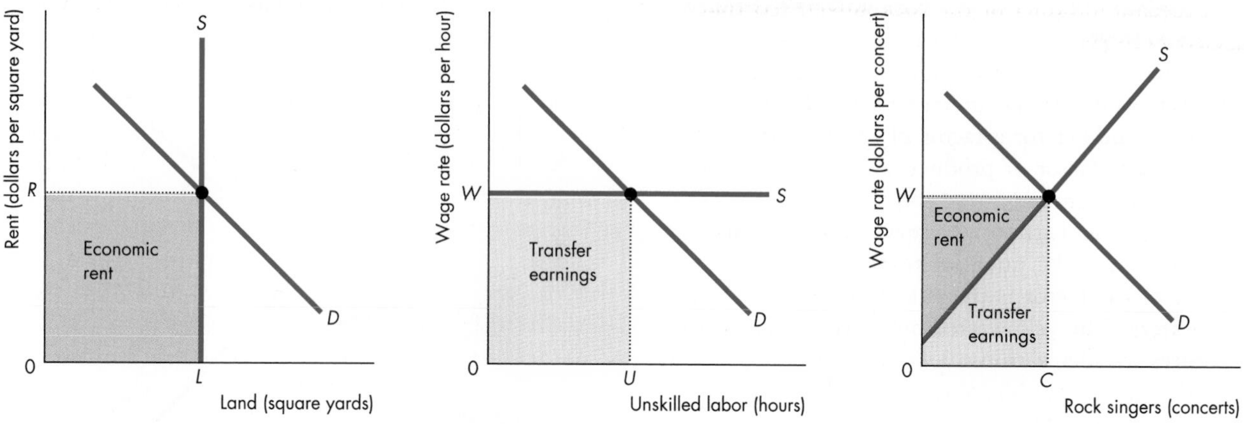

(a) All economic rent **(b) All transfer earnings** **(c) Intermediate case**

When the elasticity of supply is zero (the supply curve is vertical) as in part (a), the entire factor income is economic rent. When the supply of the factor of production is perfectly elastic, as in part (b), the factor's entire income is transfer earnings. When a factor supply curve slopes upward, as in part (c), part of the factor income is economic rent and part is transfer earnings. Land is the example shown in part (a); unskilled labor in poor countries such as India and China in part (b); and rock singers in part (c).

product is high because a large number of people are concentrated in that area, making it a prime place for conducting valuable business. Suppose that the marginal revenue product of this block of land is shown by the demand curve in Fig. 15.12(a). Then it commands a rent of *R*. The entire income accruing to the owner of the land is the green area in the figure. This income is *economic rent.* The rent charged for this piece of land depends entirely on its marginal revenue product—on the demand curve. If the demand curve shifts to the right, the rent rises. If the demand curve shifts to the left, the rent falls. The quantity of land supplied remains constant at *L*.

The conclusion that we have just reached concerning the determination of the rent of a block of land in Manhattan answers one of the questions posed at the beginning of this chapter: Is coffee expensive in New York City because rents are high or are rents high because people are willing to pay a high price for coffee in New York City? We've seen that the rent of a New York City block is determined entirely by the demand for it and that the demand, in turn, is determined by marginal revenue product. Land has a high marginal revenue product only if people are willing to pay a high price to use the land. Of course, from the point of view of McDonald's, they feel that they have to charge a high price for their coffee at their 57th Street restaurant because of the high rent they pay there. But the rent wouldn't be high if McDonald's (and other potential users) did not have a high marginal revenue product "attached" to that land, making them willing to pay those high rents.

Figure 15.12(b) shows the market for a factor of production that is in perfectly elastic supply. An example of such a market might be that for unskilled labor in a poor country such as India or China. In those countries, large amounts of labor flock to the cities and are available for work at the going wage rate (in this case, *W*). Thus, in these situations, the supply of labor is almost perfectly elastic. The entire income earned by this labor is transfer earnings. They receive no economic rent.

Figure 15.12(c) shows the market for rock singers. To induce a rock singer to sing at a larger number of concerts, a higher income has to be offered—the rock singer's supply curve is upward-sloping. The demand curve—measuring the marginal revenue product of the rock singer—is that labeled D in the figure. Equilibrium occurs where the rock singer receives a wage of W and sings in C concerts. The green area above the rock singer's supply curve is economic rent and the yellow area below the supply curve is the rock singer's transfer earnings. If the rock singer is not offered at least the amount of the transfer earnings, then the singer will withdraw from the rock concert market and perform some alternative activity.

■ We've now studied the market for the three factors of production—labor, capital, and land—and we've seen how the returns to these factors of production—wages, interest, and rent—are determined. We've seen the crucial role played in determining the demand for a factor of production by the factor's marginal revenue product. We've seen how the interaction of demand and supply determines factor prices and factor incomes. We've also seen how changes in these prices and incomes come about from changes in demand and supply. Finally, we've distinguished between economic rent and transfer earnings.

In the next chapter, we're going to examine some detailed features of the labor market more closely, explaining differences in wage rates among the skilled and the unskilled, males and females, and racial and ethnic minorities.

SUMMARY

Factor Prices and Incomes

The factors of production—labor, capital, and land—earn a return—wages, interest, and rent. Labor is the most important source of income. Factor prices are determined by the demand for and supply of factors of production. Incomes are determined by the prices of factors of production and the quantities traded. An increase in the demand for a factor of production increases the factor's price and income; a decrease in the demand for a factor of production decreases its price and income. An increase in supply increases the quantity traded of a factor of production but decreases its price. A decrease in supply decreases the quantity traded and increases the factor's price. Whether an increase in supply leads to an increase or decrease in the income of a factor of production depends on the elasticity of demand of the factor. When elasticity of demand is greater than 1, an increase in supply leads to an increase in the factor's income. When the elasticity of demand for a factor is less than 1, an increase in supply leads to a decrease in the factor's income. (pp. 381–384)

Demand for Factors

A firm's demand for a factor stems from its desire to maximize profit. The extra revenue generated by hiring one more unit of a factor is called the marginal revenue product of the factor. A firm's demand curve for a factor is derived from that factor's marginal revenue product curve. A firm demands an input up to the point at which the marginal revenue product of the factor equals the factor's price.

A firm's labor input is variable in both the short run and the long run. The firm's capital input may be varied only in the long run. The elasticity of the demand for labor in the short run depends on the short-run elasticity of demand for the firm's product, on the labor intensity of the production process, and on the slope of the marginal product of labor curve. The long-run elasticity of a firm's demand for labor depends on the long-run elasticity of demand for the product, on labor intensity, and on the ease with which capital can be substituted for labor.

The market demand for labor is the sum of the demands by each individual firm. (pp. 384–390)

Supply of Factors

The supply of factors is determined by households' decisions on the allocation of their time and the division of their income between consumption and saving. In choosing how much time to allocate to market activities, each household compares the wage rate that can be earned with the value of its time in other nonmarket activities. The household will supply no market labor at wage rates below its reservation wage. At wage rates above the household's reservation wage, the quantity of labor supplied rises as long as the substitution effect of the higher wage rate is larger than the income effect. As the wage rate continues to rise, the income effect, which leads to more time taken for leisure, becomes larger than the substitution effect, and the quantity of labor supplied by the household falls.

The market supply curve of labor is the sum of the supply curves of all households. Like the household's labor supply curve, the market supply of labor curve eventually bends backward. However, the response to higher wage rates of those on the upward-sloping part of the labor supply curve dominates the response of those on the backward-bending part, and the market supply curve slopes upward over the range of wage rates that we experience.

Households supply capital by saving. Saving increases as the interest rate increases. The supply of capital to an individual firm is highly inelastic in the short run but highly elastic in the long run.

The supply of land is fixed and independent of its rent. (pp. 391–395)

Competitive Equilibrium

In a competitive factor market, the factor price and quantity traded are determined at the point of intersection of the demand and supply curves. High factor prices occur for factors of production that have a high marginal revenue product and a low supply. Low factor prices occur for factors of production with a low marginal revenue product and a high supply. (pp. 396–398)

Economic Rent and Transfer Earnings

Economic rent is that part of the income received by a factor owner over and above the amount needed to induce the owner to supply the factor of production for use. The rest of a factor's income is transfer earnings. When The supply of a factor is perfectly inelastic, its entire income is made up of economic rent. Factors that have a perfectly elastic supply receive only transfer earnings. In general, the supply curve of a factor of production is upward-sloping, and part of the income received is transfer earnings (below the supply curve) and part is ceonomic rent (above the supply curve but below the factor price). (pp. 398–401)

KEY CONCEPTS

Average revenue product, 386
Average revenue product curve, 386
Derived demand, 384
Economic rent, 398
Long-run demand for labor, 388
Long-run elasticity of demand for labor, 390
Marginal revenue product, 384
Marginal revenue product curve, 386
Market activity, 391
Nonmarket activity, 391
Reservation wage, 391
Short-run demand for labor, 388
Short-run elasticity of demand for labor, 389
Transfer earnings, 399

Key Figures and Tables

REVIEW QUESTIONS

1 Explain what happens to the price of a factor of production and its income if the following occurs:

a) There is an increase in demand for the factor.

b) There is an increase in the supply of a factor.

c) There is a decrease in demand for the factor.

d) There is a decrease in supply of the factor.

2 Explain why the effect of a change in supply of a factor on a factor's income depends on the elasticity of demand for the factor.

3 Define marginal revenue product and distinguish between marginal revenue product and marginal revenue.

4 Why does marginal revenue product decline as the quantity of a factor employed increases?

5 What is the relationship between the demand curve for a factor of production and its marginal revenue product curve? Why?

6 Show that the condition for maximum profit in the product market—marginal cost equals marginal revenue—is equivalent to the condition for maximum profit in the factor market—marginal revenue product equals marginal cost of factor (equals factor price in a competitive factor market).

7 Review the main influences on the demand for a factor of production—the influences that shift the demand curve for a factor.

8 What determines the short-run and the long-run elasticity of demand for labor?

9 What determines the supply of labor?

10 Why might the supply of labor curve bend backward at a high enough wage rate?

11 What determines the supply of capital?

12 Define economic rent and transfer earnings and distinguish between these two components of income.

13 Suppose that a factor of production is in perfectly inelastic supply. If the marginal revenue product of the factor decreases, what happens to its price, quantity traded, income, transfer earnings, and rent?

PROBLEMS

1 Wendy owns an apple orchard. She employs students to pick the apples. Students can pick the following amounts of apples in an hour:

Number of students	Quantity of apples (pounds)
1	20
2	50
3	90
4	120
5	145
6	165
7	180
8	190

a) Draw the average and marginal product curves of these students.

b) If Wendy can sell her apples for 50 cents a pound, draw the average and marginal revenue product curves.

c) Draw Wendy's demand for labor curve.

d) If all apple growers in Wendy's neighborhood pay their pickers $7.50 an hour, how many students will Wendy hire?

2 The price of apples falls to 33.33¢ a pound, and apple pickers' wages remain at $7.50 an hour.

a) What happens to Wendy's average and marginal product curves?

b) What happens to her average and marginal revenue product curves?

c) What happens to her demand for labor curve?

d) What happens to the number of students that she hires?

3 Apple pickers' wages increase to \$10 an hour but the price of apples remains at 50¢ a pound.

a) What happens to the average and marginal revenue product curves?

b) What happens to Wendy's demand curve?

c) How many pickers does Wendy hire?

4 Using the information provided in problem 1, calculate Wendy's marginal revenue and marginal cost, marginal revenue product, and marginal cost of labor. Show that when Wendy is making maximum profit, marginal cost equals marginal revenue and marginal revenue product equals the marginal cost of labor.

5 You are given the following information about the labor market in an isolated town in the Rocky Mountains. Everyone works for logging companies, but there are many logging companies in the town. The market for logging workers is perfectly competitive. The town's labor supply is given as follows:

Wage rate (dollars per hour)	Quantity of labor supplied (hours)
2	120
3	160
4	200
5	240
6	280
7	320
8	360

The market demand for labor from all the logging firms in the town is as follows:

Wage rate (dollars per hour)	Quantity of labor demanded (hours)
2	400
3	360
4	320
5	280
6	240
7	200
8	160

a) What is the competitive equilibrium wage rate and the quantity of labor employed?

b) What is total labor income?

c) How much of that labor income is economic rent and how much is transfer earnings? (You may find it easier to answer this question by drawing graphs of the demand and supply curves and then finding the economic rent and transfer earnings as areas on the graph in a manner similar to what was done in Fig. 15.11.)

Chapter 16

Labor Markets

After studying this chapter, you will be able to:

- Explain why college graduates earn more, on the average, than high school graduates
- Explain why skilled workers earn more, on the average, than unskilled workers
- Explain why union workers earn higher wages than nonunion workers
- Explain why, on the average, men earn more than women and whites earn more than minorities
- Predict the effects of a comparable worth program
- Explain why some people are paid by the hour and others by formulas based on performance
- Explain how performance-related compensation rules induce greater effort and higher profit

The Sweat of Our Brows

As you well know, college is not just a ball. Those exams, quizzes, tests, and problem-sets require a lot of hard work. Are they worth all the effort that goes into them? What is the payoff? Part of the payoff is a higher income. At age 22, college graduates earn 30 percent more, on the average, than high-school graduates, and when they reach middle age their earnings are more than 50 percent higher than high school graduates and three times the level of those who attended elementary school only. But have you ever wondered why? After all, an accountant or a lawyer or even an economist doesn't sweat as hard as a person who works as a laborer. Why do they earn more? ■ Suppose that you do earn more after college. Ignoring the many cultural and social benefits of college, and focusing only on money, let's ask a simple question: How much more income will you have to earn after graduation to make up for four years of tuition, room and board, and lost wages? (You could, after all, be washing dishes now instead of slogging through this economics course.) ■ Many workers, both blue collar and white collar, belong to labor unions. Usually, union workers earn a higher wage than nonunion workers in comparable jobs. Why? How are unions able to get higher wages for their members than the wages that nonunion workers are paid? ■ Among the most visible and persistent differences in earnings are those between men and women and between whites and minorities. White men, on the average, earn incomes that are one third higher than the incomes earned by black men. Black men earn more, in descending order, than Hispanic men, white women, black women, and Hispanic women, who earn only 56 cents for each dollar earned by the average white man. Certainly a lot of individuals defy the averages. But why do minorities and women so consistently earn less than white men? Is it because of discrimination and exploitation? Or could it be because of economic factors? Or is it a combination of the two? ■ Equal pay legislation has resulted in comparable-worth programs, which try to ensure that jobs of equivalent value receive the same pay regardless of the pay set by the market. Can comparable-worth programs bring economic help to women and minorities? ■ Most people work for an hourly wage rate. The total amount earned depends on the total hours worked. But not everyone is paid in this way. For example, some doctors get paid by the number of X-rays or appendectomies they perform. Garment workers receive an income based on the number of shirts they make. Sales people receive a percentage of the value of their sales. Senior managers often get to share in their company's profits. Tennis players and boxers are compensated by prize money. Managers and production workers sometimes receive bonuses for achieving target profits or output levels. Why is there such variety in the ways in which people are compensated for their work? Why don't we all get an hourly wage rate?

■ In this chapter, we study the way labor markets work and answer questions such as these. We begin by using the model of a competitive labor market, such as that developed in Chapter 15, to analyze the effects on wages of differences in education and training. We then extend the model to explain differences in union and nonunion wages, in pay among men, women, and minorities, and to analyze the effects of comparable-worth laws. Finally, we study compensation arrangements based not on hours of work but on performance. We explain how such schemes lead to greater effort and higher profits. We'll even discover that chief executives and tennis stars get paid in a similar way.

Skill Differentials

Differences in earnings between workers with varying levels of education and training can be explained using a model of competitive labor markets. In the real world, there are many different levels and varieties of education and training. To keep our analysis as clear as possible, we'll study a model economy in which there are just two different levels that result in two types of labor, what we will call skilled labor and unskilled labor. We'll study the demand for and supply of these two types of labor and see why there is a difference in their wages and what determines that difference. Let's begin by looking at the demand for the two types of labor.

The Demand for Skilled and Unskilled Labor

Skilled workers can perform a wide variety of tasks that unskilled workers would perform badly or perhaps could not even perform at all. Imagine an untrained, inexperienced person performing surgery or piloting an airplane. Because skilled workers perform complex tasks, they have a higher marginal revenue product than unskilled labor. As we learned in Chapter 15, the demand for labor curve is derived from the marginal revenue product curve. The higher the marginal revenue product of labor, the higher is the demand for labor.

Figure 16.1(a) shows the demand curves for skilled and unskilled labor. At any given level of employment, firms are willing to pay a higher wage to a skilled worker than to an unskilled worker. The gap between the two wages is the difference between the marginal revenue products of a given number of skilled and unskilled workers. This difference is the marginal revenue product of skill. For example, at an employment level of 2000 hours, firms are willing to pay $12.50 for a skilled worker and only $5 for an unskilled worker. The difference in the marginal revenue product of the two workers is $7.50 an hour. Thus the marginal revenue product of skill is $7.50 an hour.

The Supply of Skilled and Unskilled Labor

Skills are costly to acquire. Furthermore, a worker pays the cost of acquiring a skill before benefiting from a higher wage. For example, attending college usually leads to a higher income, but the higher income is not earned until after graduation. These facts make the acquisition of skills similar to investment. To emphasize the investment nature of acquiring a skill, we call that activity an investment in human capital. **Human capital**, as we defined it in Chapter 3, is the accumulated skill and knowledge of human beings. The value of a person's human capital is the *present value* of the extra earnings *received* as a result of acquiring skill and knowledge. (The concept

Figure 16.1 Skill Differentials

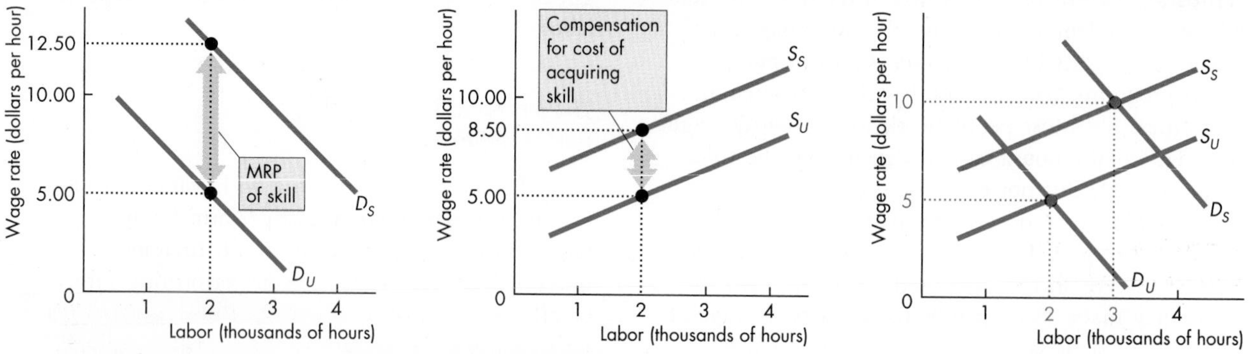

(a) Demand for skilled and unskilled labor

(b) Supply of skilled and unskilled labor

(c) Markets for skilled and unskilled labor

Part (a) illustrates the marginal revenue product of skill. Unskilled workers have a marginal revenue product that gives rise to the demand curve marked D_U. Skilled workers have a higher marginal revenue product than unskilled workers. Therefore the demand curve for skilled workers (D_S) thus lies to the right of D_U. The vertical distance between these two curves is the marginal revenue product of skill.

Part (b) shows the effects of the cost of acquiring skills on the supply curves of labor. The supply curve for unskilled workers is S_U. Skilled workers have to incur costs in order to acquire their skills. Therefore they will only supply labor services at a wage rate that exceeds that of unskilled labor. The supply curve for skilled workers is S_S. The vertical distance between these two curves is the required compensation for the cost of acquiring a skill.

Part (c) shows the determination of the equilibrium levels of employment and the skilled and unskilled wage differential. Unskilled workers earn the wage rate $5 an hour where the quantities demanded and supplied of unskilled workers are equal. The employment level of unskllled workers is 2000 hours. Skilled workers earn the wage rate $10 an hour where the quantities demanded and supplied of skilled workers are equal. The employment level of skilled workers is 3000 hours. Wages for skilled workers are always greater than those for unskilled workers.

of present value is explained in Chapter 9.) It is equivalent to a sum of money which, if invested today at the average interest rate, will yield a stream of income equivalent to the extra earnings resulting from a person's acquired knowledge and skills.

The cost of acquiring a skill includes actual expenditures on such things as tuition and room and board, and also costs in the form of lost or reduced earnings while the skill is being acquired. When a person goes to school full time, that cost is the total earnings foregone. However, some people acquire skills on the job. Such skill acquisition is called on-the-job training. Usually a worker undergoing on-the-job training is paid a lower wage than one doing a comparable job but not undergoing training. In such a case, the cost of acquiring the skill is the difference between the wage paid to a person not being trained and that paid to a person being trained.

Supply Curves of Skilled and Unskilled Labor

The position of the supply curve of skilled workers reflects the cost of acquiring the skill. Figure 16.1(b) shows two supply curves, one for skilled workers and the other for unskilled workers. The supply curve for skilled workers is S_S and for unskilled workers S_U.

The skilled worker's supply curve lies above the unskilled worker's supply curve. The vertical distance between the two supply curves is the compensation for the cost of acquiring the skill. (The difference is the amount that has a present value equal to the cost of acquiring the skill.) For example, suppose that the quantity of unskilled labor supplied is 2000 hours at a wage rate of $5 an hour. This wage rate compensates the unskilled workers purely for their time on the job. Consider next the supply of skilled workers. To induce 2000 hours of skilled labor to be supplied, firms have to pay a wage rate of $8.50 an hour. This wage rate for skilled labor is higher than that for unskilled labor since skilled labor must be compensated not only for the time on the job but also for the time and other costs of acquiring the skill.

Wage Rates of Skilled and Unskilled Labor

To work out the wage rates of skilled and unskilled labor, all we have to do is bring together the effects of skill on the demand and supply of labor. Figure 16.1(c) shows the demand curves and the supply curves for skilled and unskilled labor. These curves are exactly the same as those plotted in parts (a) and (b). Equilibrium occurs in the market for unskilled labor where the supply and demand curves for unskilled labor intersect. The equilibrium wage rate is $5 an hour and the quantity of unskilled labor employed is 2000 hours. Equilibrium in the market for skilled workers occurs where the supply and demand curves for skilled workers intersect. The equilibrium wage rate is $10 an hour and the quantity of skilled labor employed is 3000 hours.

As you can see in part (c), the equilibrium wage rate of skilled labor is higher than that of unskilled labor. There are two reasons why this occurs: First, skilled labor has a higher marginal revenue product than unskilled labor; second, skills are costly to acquire. The wage differential (in this case $5 an hour) depends on both the marginal revenue product of the skill and the cost of acquiring it. The higher the marginal revenue product of the skill, the larger is the vertical distance between the demand curves for skilled and unskilled labor. The more costly it is to acquire a skill, the larger is the vertical distance between the supplies of skilled and unskilled labor. The higher the marginal revenue product of the skill and the more costly it is to acquire, the larger is the wage differential between skilled and unskilled workers.

Do Education and Training Pay?

There are large and persistent differences in earnings based on the degree of education and training. An indication of those differences can be seen in Fig. 16.2. This figure highlights two important sources of earnings differences. The first is the degree of education itself. The higher the level of education, other things being equal, the higher are a person's earnings. The second source of earnings differences apparent in Fig. 16.2 is age. Age is strongly correlated with experience and the degree of on-the-job training a person has had. Thus as a person gets older, up to middle age, earnings increase.

We can see, from Fig. 16.2, that going through high school, college, and postgraduate education leads to higher incomes. But do they pay in the sense of yielding a higher income that compensates for the cost of education and for the delay in the start of earnings? For most people, college does indeed pay. Rates of return have been calculated suggesting that a

Figure 16.2 Education and Earnings

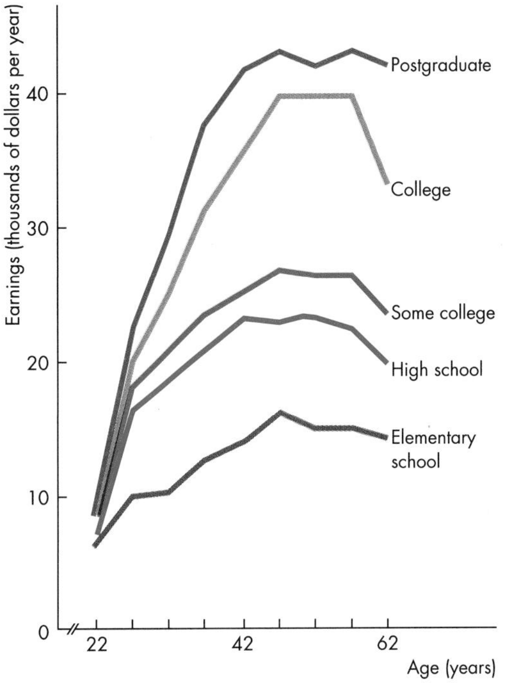

Earnings of male employees at various ages and with varying school levels are shown. Earnings increase with length of education and also with age, but only up to the mid-forties. Beyond that age, earnings decrease. These differences show the importance of experience and education in influencing skill differentials.

college degree is a better investment than almost any other that a person can undertake. Rates of return as high as 15 percent, after allowing for inflation, are not uncommon.

Differences in education and training are an important source of differences in earnings. But they are not the only source. Another is the activities of labor unions. Let's see how unions affect wages and why, on the average, union wages exceed nonunion wages.

Union-Nonunion Wage Differentials

A **labor union** is an organized group of workers whose purpose it is to increase wages and influence other job conditions. A labor union acts in the labor market like a monopolist in the product market. The union seeks to restrict competition and, as a result, raises the price at which labor is traded. A compact glossary on unions can be found in Table 16.1.

There are two main types of union: craft unions and industrial unions. A **craft union** is a group of workers who have a similar range of skills but work for many different firms in many different industries and regions. An example of a craft union is the carpenters' union. An **industrial union** is a group of workers who have a variety of skills and job types but work for the same firm or industry. The United Auto Workers (UAW) is an example of an industrial union.

Most unions are members of the AFL-CIO. The AFL-CIO was created in 1955 when two labor organizations combined: the American Federation of Labor (AFL), which was founded in 1886 to organize craft unions, and the Congress of Industrial Organizations (CIO), founded in 1938 to organize industrial unions. The AFL-CIO acts as the national voice of organized labor in the media and in politics. Unions vary enormously in size. Craft unions are the smallest and industrial unions the biggest.

Union strength peaked in the 1950s when 35 percent of the work force belonged to unions. That percentage has declined steadily since 1955 and is now less than 20 percent. Changes in union membership, however, have been uneven. Some unions have declined dramatically while others, especially those in government, have increased in strength.

Table 16.1 A Compact Glossary on Unions

Labor union	An organized group of workers that attempts to increase wages and improve other conditions of employment
AFL-CIO	A federation of unions formed in 1955 by a merger of the American Federation of Labor (AFL) and the Congress of Industrial Organizations (CIO); acts as the voice of organized labor in media and political arenas
Craft union	A union in which workers have a similar range of skills but work for many firms and in many different industries
Industrial union	A union in which workers have a variety of skills and job types but work in same industry
Local	A sub-unit of a union that organizes individual workers. In craft unions, the local is geographical; in industrial unions, the local is based on a plant or a company
Open shop	A place of work that has no union restriction on who can work in the shop; here, the union bargains for its members but not for nonmembers
Closed shop	A place of work where only union members may be employed; illegal since 1947, when Congress passed the Labor-Management Relations Act (the Taft-Hartley Act)
Union shop	A place of work that may hire nonunion workers but only if they join the union within a specified period; illegal in 20 states where "right-to-work" legislation has been passed
Right-to-work law	A law that protects the right of an individual to work without joining a union
Collective bargaining	Negotiations between representatives of employers and unions on wages and other employment conditions
Strike	A group decision to refuse to work under prevailing conditions
Lockout	A firm's refusal to allow its labor force to work
Binding arbitration	Determination of wages and other employment conditions by a third party (an arbitrator) acceptable to both parties

Union organization is based on a subdivision known as the local. The **local** is a sub-unit of a union that organizes the individual workers. In craft unions, the local is based on a geographical area, while in industrial unions the local is based on a plant or an individual firm.

There are three possible forms of organization for a local: an open shop, a closed shop, or a union shop. An **open shop** is an arrangement in which workers have a right to be employed without joining the union—there is no union restriction on who can work in the "shop." A **closed shop** is an arrangement in which only union members may be employed by a firm. Closed shops have been illegal since the passage of the Taft-Hartley Act in 1947. A **union shop** is an arrangement in which a firm may hire nonunion workers, but in order for such workers to remain employed they must join the union within a brief period specified by the union. Union shops are illegal in the 20 states that have passed "right-to-work" laws. A **right-to-work law** allows an individual to work at any firm without joining a union.

Unions negotiate with employers or their representatives in a process called **collective bargaining.** The main weapons available to the union and the employer in collective bargaining are the strike and the lockout. A **strike** is a group decision to refuse to work under prevailing conditions. A **lockout** is a firm's refusal to operate its plant and employ its workers. Each party uses the threat of a strike or a lockout to try to get an agreement in its own favor. Sometimes when the two parties in the collective bargaining process cannot agree on wages and other conditions of employment, they agree to put their disagreement to binding arbitration. **Binding arbitration** is a process in which a third party—an arbitrator—determines wages and other employment conditions on behalf of the negotiating parties.

Though not labor unions in a legal sense, professional associations act, in many ways, like labor unions. A **professional association** is an organized group of professional workers such as lawyers, dentists, or doctors that seeks to influence the compensation and other labor market conditions affecting its members. An example of a professional association is the American Medical Association (AMA).

Unions' Objectives and Constraints

Unions have three broad objectives:

- Improving compensation
- Improving working conditions
- Improving employment prospects

Each of these objectives contains a series of more detailed goals. For example, in seeking to improve its members' compensation unions operate on a variety of fronts: wages, fringe benefits, retirement pay, and such things as vacation allowances. In seeking to improve working conditions, unions are concerned with occupational health and safety as well as the environmental quality of the workplace. In seeking to improve employment prospects, unions try to obtain greater job security for existing union members and to expand their job opportunities.

A union's ability to pursue its objectives is restricted by two sets of constraints—one on the supply side and the other on the demand side of the labor market. On the supply side, the union's activities are limited by how well it can restrict nonunion workers from offering their labor. The larger the fraction of the work force controlled by the union, the more effective the union can be. For example, unions find it difficult to be effective in markets for unskilled farm labor in southern California because of their inability to control the flow of nonunion, often illegal, labor from Mexico. At the other extreme, unions in the construction industry can better pursue their goals because they can influence the number of people obtaining skills as electricians, plasterers, and carpenters. Those best able to restrict supply are the professional associations for such groups as lawyers, dentists, and doctors. These groups control the number of qualified workers by controlling the examinations that new entrants must pass.

The constraint facing a union on the demand side of the labor market arises because the union cannot force firms to hire more labor than they demand. Anything that raises wages or other employment costs will lower the quantity of labor demanded. Unless the union can take actions that shift the demand curve for the labor that it represents, it will have to accept the fact that the higher wage can be obtained only at the price of lower employment. Recognizing the importance of the demand for labor curve, unions try to make the demand for their labor inelastic and to increase the demand for labor. Here are some of the methods that they employ:

- Encouraging import restrictions
- Supporting minimum wage laws
- Supporting immigration restrictions
- Increasing product demand
- Increasing the marginal product of union members

Figure 16.3 A Union in a Competitive Labor Market

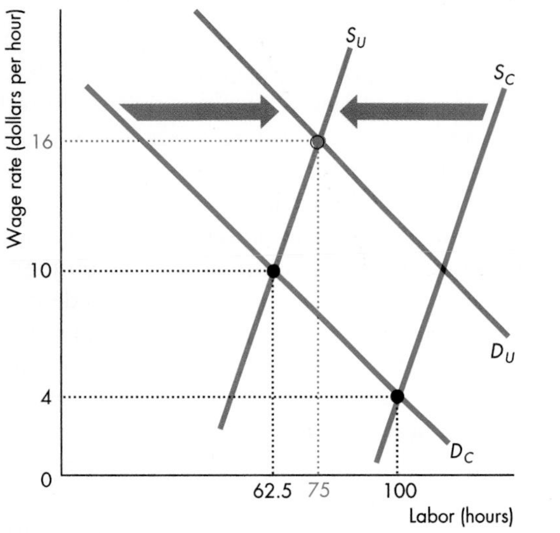

In a competitive labor market, the demand curve is D_C and the supply curve S_C. Competitive equilibrium occurs at a wage rate of \$4 an hour with 100 hours employed. By restricting employment below its competitive level, the union shifts the supply of labor to S_U. If the union can do no more than that, the wage rate will rise to \$10 an hour, but employment will fall to 62.5 hours. If the union can increase the demand for labor (by increasing the demand for the good produced by the union members or by raising the price of substitute labor) and shift the demand curve to D_U, then it can raise the wage rate still higher to \$16 an hour and achieve employment of 75 hours.

One of the best examples of import restrictions is the support by the United Auto Workers union for import restrictions on foreign cars. Unions support minimum wage laws in order to increase the cost of unskilled labor, a substitute for skilled union labor. Supporting restrictive immigration laws leads indirectly to an increase in the wages of unskilled workers and again increases the cost of labor that might otherwise be substituted for the higher cost union labor. Increasing product demand indirectly increases the demand for labor. The best examples of attempts by unions in this activity are in the textile and auto industries. Garment workers are encouraged to buy union-made clothes and auto workers to buy only U.S.-produced cars. Increasing the marginal product of union members directly shifts the demand curve for their services. Unions use apprenticeship, training, and professional certification to increase the marginal product of their members.

Unions in a Competitive Labor Market

When a union operates in an otherwise competitive labor market, it seeks to raise wages and other compensation and to limit employment reductions by increasing demand for the labor of its members.

Figure 16.3 illustrates a labor market. The demand curve is D_C and the supply curve is S_C. If the market is a competitive one with no union, the wage rate is \$4 an hour and 100 hours of labor will be employed. Suppose that a union is formed to organize the workers in this market and that the union has sufficient control over the supply of labor to be able to artificially restrict that supply below its competitive level—to S_U. If that is all the union does, employment will fall to 62.5 hours of labor and the wage rate will rise to \$10 an hour. If the union can also take steps that increase the demand for labor to D_U, it can achieve an even bigger rise in the wage rate with a smaller fall in employment. By maintaining the restricted labor supply at S_U, the union raises the wage rate to \$16 an hour and achieves an employment level of 75 hours of labor.

An example of a union operating in an industry with a competitive output market is that of coal mining. Some recent developments in that industry are analyzed in Reading Between the Lines on pp. 414–416.

We next turn our attention to the case in which employers have considerable influence in the labor market.

Monopsony

A **monopsony** is a market structure in which there is just a single buyer. With the growth of large-scale production over the last century, large manufacturing plants such as coal mines, steel and textile mills, and car manufacturers became the major employer of labor in some regions, and in some places a single firm employed almost all the labor. Such a firm is a monopsonist in the labor market.

A monopsonist can make a bigger profit than a group of firms that have to compete with each other for their labor. Figure 16.4 illustrates how a monopsonist operates. The monopsonist's marginal revenue product curve is *MRP*. This curve tells us the extra revenue from selling the output produced by the last hour of labor hired. The curve labeled *S* is the supply curve of labor. This curve tells us how many hours are supplied at each wage rate. It also tells us the minimum wage that is acceptable at each level of labor supplied.

In deciding how much labor to hire, the monopsonist recognizes that to hire more labor it must pay a higher wage or, equivalently, by hiring less labor the monopsonist can get away with paying a lower wage. The monopsonist takes account of this fact when calculating its marginal cost of labor. The marginal cost of labor is shown by the curve *MCL*. The relationship between the marginal cost of labor curve and the supply curve is similar to the relationship between the marginal cost and average total cost curves that you studied in Chapter 10. The supply curve is like the average total cost of labor curve. For example, in Fig. 16.4 the firm can hire 50 hours of labor at $5 an hour, so its average total cost is $5 an hour. The total cost of labor is $5 an hour multiplied by 50 hours, which equals $250 an hour. But suppose that the firm hires slightly less than 50 hours of labor, say 49 hours. The wage rate at which 49 hours of labor can be hired is $4.90 an hour. The firm's total labor cost is 49 multiplied by $4.90, which equals $240.10. Hiring the fiftieth hour of labor raises the total cost of labor from $240.10 to $250, which is almost $10. The curve *MCL* shows the $10 marginal cost of hiring the fiftieth hour of labor.

To calculate the profit-maximizing quantity of labor to hire, the firm sets the marginal cost of labor equal to the marginal revenue product of labor. That is, the firm wants the cost of the last worker hired to equal the extra revenue brought in. In Fig. 16.4, this outcome occurs when the monopsony employs 50 hours of labor. To hire 50 hours of labor, the firm has to pay $5 an hour. The marginal revenue product of labor, however, is $10 an hour, which means that the firm makes an economic profit of $5 on the last hour of labor that it hires. Each worker gets paid $5, and marginal revenue product is $10. So the firm gets an extra $5 economic profit out of the last hour of labor hired.

The ability of a monopsonist to make an economic profit depends on the elasticity of labor supply. The more elastic the supply of labor, the less opportunity a monopsonist has to make an economic profit.

Figure 16.4 A Monopsony Labor Market

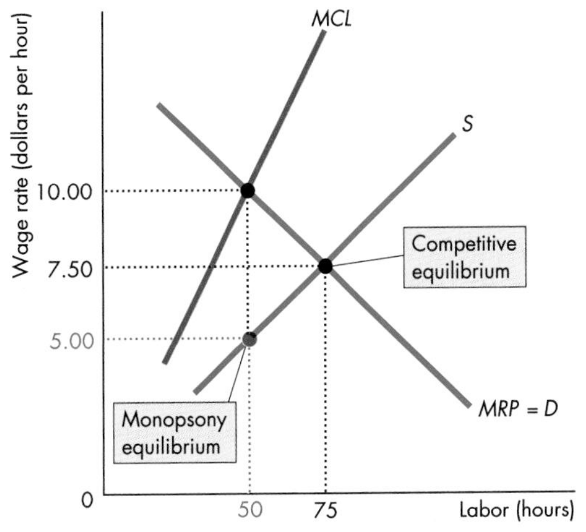

A monopsony is a market structure in which there is a single buyer. A monopsonist whose marginal revenue product curve is *MRP* faces a labor supply curve *S* and has a marginal cost of labor curve *MCL*. Profit is maximized by making the marginal cost of labor equal to marginal revenue product. The monopsonist hires 50 hours of labor and pays the lowest wage for which that labor will work—$5 an hour.

If this labor market were competitive, the wage rate would be $7.50 and the level of employment would be 75 hours. Compared with a competitive labor market, employment and the wage rate are lower under monopsony.

Monopsony Tendencies With today's low costs of transportation, it is unlikely that many pure monopsonists remain. Workers can easily commute long distances to a job, and so for most people there is not just one potential employer. Nevertheless, many firms still face an upward-sloping supply of labor curve. Though they are not monopsonists, there is a monopsony tendency in their market in the sense that to attract more workers they have to offer higher wages. A firm's monopsony element may come from its location, if it is more conveniently reached by some workers than others. Firms compete with each other for labor by offering wages that not only compensate their workers for time on the job but also for commuting time. The more workers a firm hires, the longer the commute for the marginal worker and,

A Labor Union Faces a Fall in Demand

Weaker UMW's Hard Task

The master labor contract, which covers the workers who produce roughly half of the nation's coal supply, will expire next Jan. 31 [1988], an event for which the industry is already preparing. Although formal negotiations have yet to begin, at least 10 of the 30 or so coal producers in the Bituminous Coal Operators Association, the industry bargaining group, have already dropped out, thinking they can cut a better deal with the union on their own. These companies are meeting with union representatives on their own timetable, and some have even signed preliminary agreements.

Dwindling Membership

The defections will almost certainly weaken a union that has been steadily losing ground, industry and labor experts say. The U.M.W.'s dues-paying membership has dwindled to about 73,000 from 144,000 in 1980 according to Leo Troy, a Rutgers University expert on unions. And in a decade when demand for coal has been weakened by the wide availability and low price of oil, the union, like its counterpart in the automobile industry, will have to make job security a top priority in upcoming talks. At the same time, it plans not to give up any of its wage gains, although it hasn't articulated its pay demands as yet.

"Trumka's [U.M.W. president] got a tough assignment," said Bud Ogden, head of the Island Creek Coal Company, the coal subsidiary of the Occidental Petroleum Corporation.

Island Creek, which broke away from the B.C.O.A. in 1984, has decided to go it alone again this year. By negotiating on his own, Mr. Ogden is hoping to customize the industry contract to address the particular needs of some of Island Creek's operations. "Working through the association leaves us once removed at best," he said.

As it has in the steel industry, the deterioration of industrywide bargaining has caused concern among union leaders and labor experts. Charles R. Perry, an associate professor at the University of Pennsylvania's Wharton School who has written extensively on coal mining, said the trend toward fragmentation could stretch the union's resources. "It makes their life more complicated because now they have to deal with a more fragmented bargaining structure."

Thomas A. Grames, a miner in Price, Utah, who serves part-time as president of his union local, agreed. "We have limited numbers of people capable of doing the negotiation, and if the companies are playing hardball and making you negotiate each one of them, it makes it hard," he said.

Threats Foreign and Domestic

Such a scenario would have been unthinkable in the Lewis era.* Back then, nearly all the nation's coal was produced by U.M.W. mines, and the industry considered a master contract in its best interests. It was expedient, and it assured all producers of the same labor costs.

Coal Miners' Pay Exceeds Some Other Workers'...

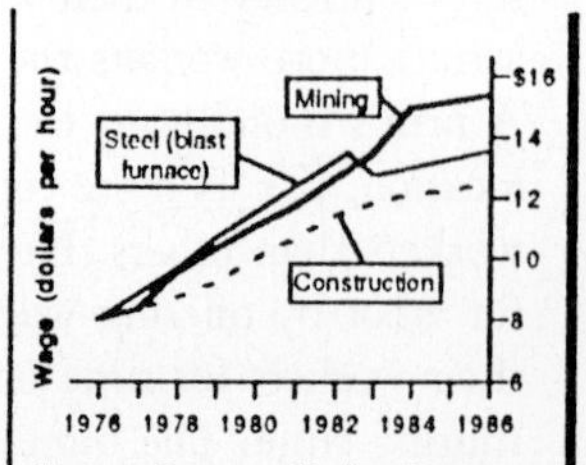

Source: Bureau of Labor Statistics

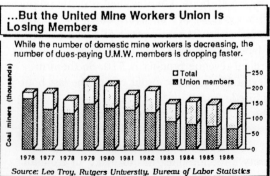

...But the United Mine Workers Union Is Losing Members

While the number of domestic mine workers is decreasing, the number of dues-paying U.M.W. members is dropping faster.

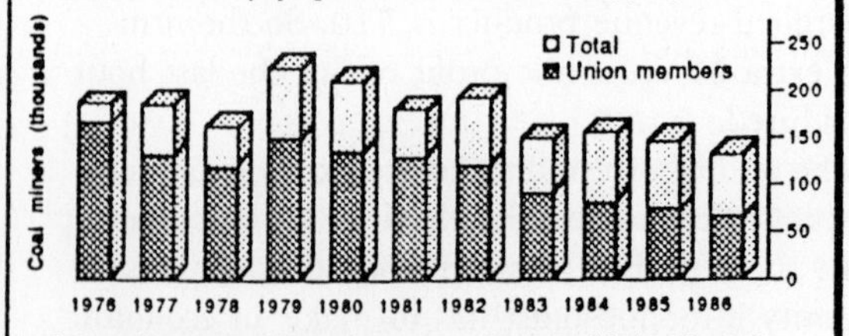

Source: Leo Troy, Rutgers University, Bureau of Labor Statistics

That level playing field no longer suffices because the B.C.O.A. companies are not the only coal producers. Foreign coal not represented by the B.C.O.A. has made inroads, but the bigger threat is homegrown. Nonunion mines can produce coal for $2 to $5 a ton less than similar union operations. A ton typically costs about $20, but the price can range from as little as $3 in some of the newer Western surface mines to $35 in some of the older Eastern mines. The result: Union coal now accounts for only 60 percent of all bituminous, or soft, coal mined in the United States, according to the U.M.W., and independent estimates are closer to 40 percent.

Making the U.M.W.'s task all the more daunting is the coal industry's failing health. Producers are still reeling from a decade of overexpansion, fueled by an anticipated growth in demand that was expected to accompany soaring oil prices. That surge in demand never materialized. "People back in the 1970's believed some of their own press releases," said Richard M. Holsten, the president of the Pittsburg and Midway Coal Mining Company, based in Denver, which has never been in the B.C.O.A.

Lower oil prices and a slump in the steel industry, the second-largest user of coal after utilities, have caused prices to fall 33 percent since 1982 and led to layoffs. "The industry is definitely in a lot of trouble and in a period of stagnation," said Forrest Hill, a consultant based in Annapolis, Md.

At the same time, productivity has soared, although management and labor disagree about who deserves the credit. Island Creek officials, for instance, said new mining methods had helped to raise production at its Virginia Pocahontas No. 6 mine near Rowe, Va.

Five years ago, using continuous mining machines to scoop out the coal, the mine produced 12 tons of coal per worker per eight-hour shift. It now averages 19.8 tons, relying primarily on $10 million long-wall mining machines that can extract the coal from a 600-foot panel in about 20 minutes by remote control. "Just like your microwave," said George King, the mine's superintendent, demonstrating the push-button device.

And as long as productivity continues to outpace sluggish demand, mine workers will keep losing their jobs. . . .

---

*John L. Lewis was the founder of the U.M.W. and its leader for 40 years.

The New York Times, August 10, 1987

By Alison Leigh Cowan

The Essence of the Story

- The Bituminous Coal Operators Association (B.C.O.A.), an association of mine employers, traditionally has negotiated a "master labor contract," governing all its members, with the United Mine Workers Union (U.M.W.).

- In mid-1987, as the existing contract approached its expiration date (January 31, 1988), 10 of the 30 members of B.C.O.A. decided to bargain separately with the U.M.W.

- The U.M.W. is in a weak bargaining position because of several reasons:

  —Its membership is declining, down from 144,000 in 1980 to 73,000 in 1987.
  —The demand for coal has fallen as a result of a lower price of oil and a slump in the steel industry.
  —Competition from foreign and nonunion domestic producers has reduced domestic union-produced coal to 60 percent of the market.
  —Costs in nonunion mines are $2 to $5 a ton less than costs in union mines.
  —New but expensive machines have raised output per worker from 12 tons a shift in 1982 to 19.8 tons a shift in 1987.
  —Productivity growth is faster than the growth in demand and the number of jobs available is declining.

- Job security is the U.M.W.'s top priority, though it also wants to maintain the wage gains that it has achieved in the past (see illustration in the news article comparing wages in mining with steel and construction).

(Continued on next page)

Background and Analysis

(Continued from previous page)

- The ability of the U.M.W. to maintain wage and employment levels depends on the demand for coal miners, which in turn is determined by the marginal revenue product of coal miners.

- The marginal revenue product of coal miners depends on:

  —The marginal revenue of coal producers
  —The marginal product of coal miners

- Coal mining is a competitive industry and no single mine can exert a significant influence on the price of coal. As a consequence, a coal producer's marginal revenue is equal to the price of coal.

- The price of coal is determined by supply and demand in the market for coal. The demand for coal has been falling because of two factors:

  —The price of oil, a substitute for coal, has been falling.
  —The price of steel, a major user of coal, has been falling.

- The price of coal has fallen by 33 percent since 1982.

- The marginal product of coal miners depends on the technology used for coal production. The installation of long-wall mining machines has increased average productivity by 65 percent in the past five years.

- The figure illustrates what has been happening to the demand for coal miners in the past few years. In 1982, the marginal revenue product (and demand) was the curve labeled MRP_{82}. The industry operated at the point marked 1982 on that demand curve, employing 200,000 workers at a wage rate of $13 an hour.

- If there had been no technical advances in coal mining, the fall in the price of coal (33 percent) between 1982 and 1986 would have lowered the marginal revenue product of coal miners, and the demand for coal, to the line labeled MRP_0.

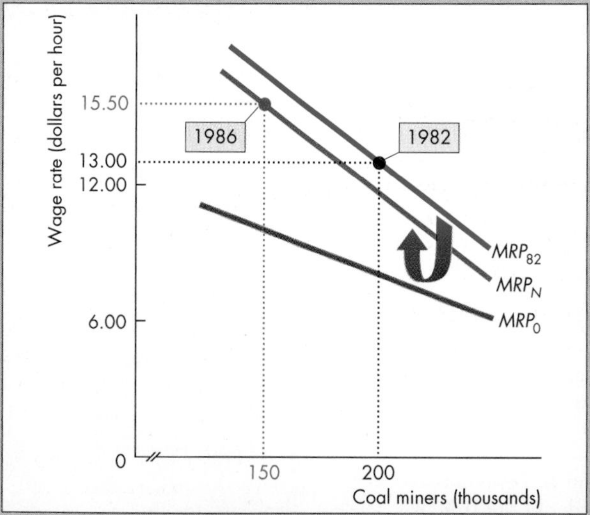

- Between 1982 and 1986, technological changes in coal mining resulted in massive productivity gains. The introduction of long-wall machines raised the marginal revenue product of miners. As a consequence, the marginal revenue product curve and, equivalently, the demand curve shifted to that labeled MRP_N. The average wage rate rose to $15.50 an hour and 150,000 coal miners were employed (the point marked 1986).

- The combination of the two factors—the fall in the price of coal and the rise in the productivity of coal miners resulting from the use of long-wall machines—only slightly lowered the demand for coal miners.

- The U.M.W. pushed up coal miners' wages in the period since 1982 and accepted a cut in employment. To have maintained employment at 200,000 miners, it would have been necessary to accept a pay cut. If wages had been held constant at $13 an hour, employment would have fallen but by less than the fall that oc-curred with higher wages.

therefore, the higher the wage that the firm has to pay to attract that worker. How strong such a monopsony tendency is depends on the size and density of the urban area in which the labor market is situated. Next, let's see the effects of minimum wage laws and unions in a monopsonistic labor market.

Monopsony, Minimum Wage, and Unions

In Chapter 6, we saw how a minimum wage usually decreases employment. However, in a situation where a firm is a monopsonist, minimum wage regulations can actually raise both the wage rate and employment. A union can also raise the wage rate and employment. Let's see how.

Minimum Wages and Monopsony Suppose that the labor market is that shown in Fig. 16.5 and that the wage rate is $5 an hour with 50 hours of labor being employed. The government now passes a minimum wage law that prohibits anyone from hiring labor for less than $7.50 an hour. Firms can hire labor for $7.50 an hour or more but not for less than that wage. The monopsonist in Fig. 16.5 now faces a perfectly elastic supply of labor at $7.50 an hour up to 75 hours. Above 75 hours, a higher wage than $7.50 an hour has to be paid to hire additional hours of labor. Since the wage rate is a fixed $7.50 an hour up to 75 hours, the marginal cost of labor is also constant at $7.50 up to 75 hours. Beyond 75 hours, the marginal cost of labor rises above $7.50 an hour. To maximize profit, the monopsonist sets the marginal cost of labor equal to its marginal revenue product. That is, the monopsonist hires 75 hours of labor at $7.50 an hour. The minimum wage law has made the supply of labor perfectly elastic and made the marginal cost of labor the same as the wage rate up to 75 hours. The law has not affected the supply of labor curve or the marginal cost of labor at employment levels above 75 hours. The minimum wage law has succeeded in raising wages by $2.50 an hour and raising the amount of labor employed by 25 hours.

Monopsony and Unions When we studied monopoly in Chapter 13, we discovered that a single seller in a market is able to determine the price in that market. We have just studied monopsony—a market with a single buyer—and discovered that in such a market the buyer is able to determine the price. Suppose that a union starts to operate in a

Figure 16.5 Minimum Wage in Monopsony

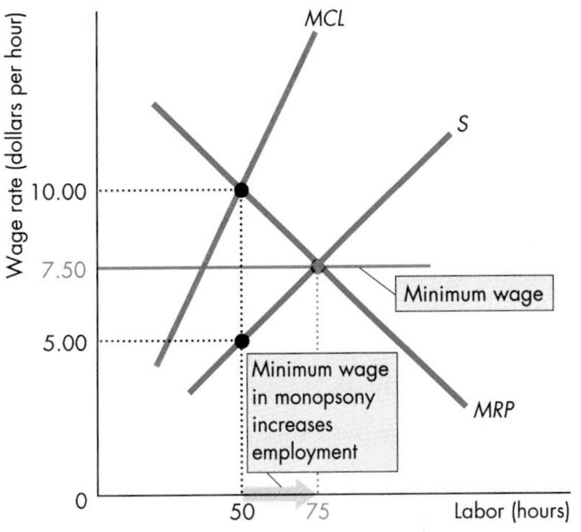

In a monopsony labor market, the wage rate is $5 an hour. If a minimum wage law raises the wage rate to $7.50 an hour, employment rises to 75 hours. Equivalently, if a union enters the market, it will attempt to increase the wage rate to above $5 an hour. If the union is all-powerful, the highest wage rate it can achieve is $10 an hour. If the union and the firm are equally powerful, they will bargain and agree to a wage rate of $7.50 an hour—the wage rate that splits the difference between marginal revenue product and the lowest wage for which labor will work equally.

monopsony labor market. A union is like a monopoly. It controls the supply of labor and acts like a single seller of labor. If the union (monopoly seller) faces a monopsony buyer, the situation is one of **bilateral monopoly.** In bilateral monopoly, the wage rate is determined by bargaining between the two traders. Let's study the bargaining process.

We saw that if the monopsony in Fig. 16.4 is free to determine the wage rate and the level of employment, it hires 50 hours of labor for a wage rate of $5 an hour. If a union that represents the workers can maintain employment at 50 hours but charge the highest wage rate acceptable to the employer, the wage rate will be $10 an hour. That is, the wage rate will equal the marginal revenue product of labor. If the monopsonist and the union bargain over the wage rate, the result will be a wage rate between $10 an hour (the maximum that the union can achieve) and $5 an hour (the minimum that the firm can achieve).

The actual outcome of the bargaining depends on the costs that each party can inflict on the other as a result of a failure to agree on the wage rate. The firm can shut down the plant and lock out its workers and the workers can shut down the plant by striking. Each party knows the strength of the other and knows what it has to lose if it does not agree to the demands of the other. If the two parties are equally strong, and they realize it, they will split the difference and agree to a wage rate of $7.50 an hour. If one party is stronger than the other—and both parties know that—the agreed wage will favor the stronger party. Usually, an agreement is reached without a strike or a lockout. The threat—the knowledge that such an event can occur—is usually enough to bring the bargaining parties to an agreement. When strikes or lockouts do occur, it is because one party has misjudged the situation.

The Scale of Union-Nonunion Wage Differentials

We have seen that unions can influence the wages of their members partly by restricting the supply of labor and partly by manipulating the demand for labor. How much of a difference to wage rates do unions make in practice?

In 1985, union wage rates were, on the average, 33 percent higher than nonunion wage rates. In mining and financial services, union and nonunion wages are similar, and in services, manufacturing, and transportation the differential is between 11 and 19 percent. But in the wholesale and retail trades the differential is 42 percent and in construction it is 77 percent.

These union-nonunion wage differentials do not give a true measure of the effects of unions on wages, however. In some industries, union wages are higher than nonunion wages because union members do jobs that involve greater skill. Even without a union, those who perform such tasks receive a higher wage. To calculate the effects of unions, we have to examine the wages of unionized and nonunionized workers who do nearly identical work. The evidence suggests that after allowing for the effects of skill differentials, the union-nonunion wage differential lies between 10 percent and 25 percent. For example, airline pilots who belong to the Airline Pilots' Union earn about 25 percent more than nonunion pilots with the same level of skill.

Wage Differentials between Sexes and Races

There are persistent earnings differences between the sexes and the races. Figure 16.6 provides a snapshot of these differences in 1984. The wages of each race and sex group are expressed as a percentage of the wages of white men. By definition, then, the wages of white men are 100. As you can see, the wages of each group fall progressively from 81 percent for other men down to 64 percent for women of Hispanic origin.

Why do the differentials shown in Fig. 16.6 exist, and why do they persist? Do they arise because there is discrimination against women and members of minority races, or is there some other explanation? These controversial questions generate an enormous amount of passion. It is not my intention to make you angry, but that may happen as an unintended consequence of this discussion. The objective of this section is to show you how to use economic analysis to address controversial and emotionally charged issues.

We are going to examine three possible explanations for these earnings differences:

- Discrimination
- Differences in human capital
- Differences in degree of specialization

Discrimination

To see how discrimination can affect earnings, let's look at an example—the market for investment advisors. Suppose that there are two groups of investment advisors who are identical in terms of picking good investments. One group consists of black females and the other of white males. The supply curve of black females (S_{BF}) is shown in Fig. 16.7(a). The supply curve of white males (S_{WM}) is shown in Fig. 16.7(b). These supply curves are identical. The marginal revenue product of investment advisors, whether they are black female or white male is also identical and is shown by the two curves labeled *MRP* in parts (a) and (b). (Their revenues are the fees their customers pay for investment advice.)

Suppose that everyone in this society is free of prejudice about color and sex. The market for black female investment advisors determines a wage rate of $40,000 a year and there are 2000 black female investment advisors. The white male investment ad-

Figure 16.6 Sex and Race Differentials

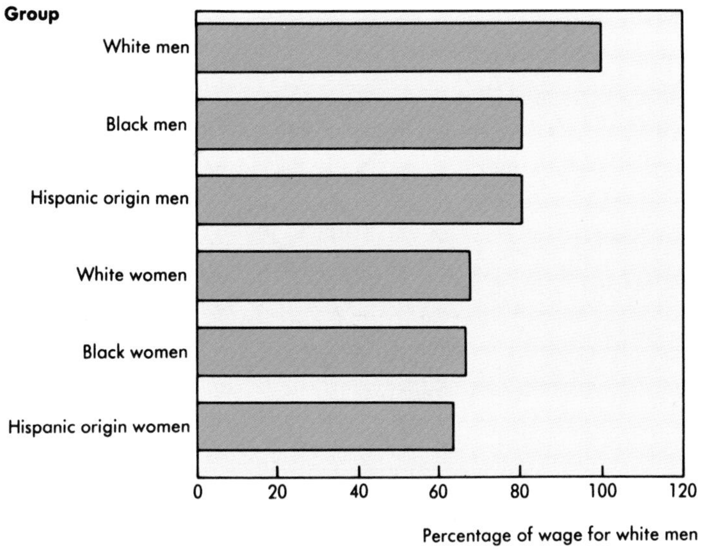

Median hourly wages are shown as percentages of white male income. These differentials have persisted over many years.

Source: Statistical Abstract of the United States: 1987, 107th ed., p. 404.

visor market also clears at a wage rate of $40,000 a year, and there are 2000 white male investment advisors.

In contrast to the previous situation, suppose that the customers of investment houses are prejudiced against women and against members of racial minorities. The two types are equally able, as before, but the degree of prejudice is so strong that the customers are not willing to pay as much for investment advice given by a black female as they will pay for advice from a white male. Because of the differences in the amounts that people are willing to pay, based purely on their prejudices, the marginal revenue products of the two groups are different. The ability of the two groups is the same but the value that prejudiced consumers place on their outputs is not the same. Suppose that the marginal revenue product of the black females, when discriminated against, is the line labeled MRP_{DA}—DA standing for discriminated against. Suppose that the marginal revenue product for white males, the group discriminated in favor of, is MRP_{DF}—DF standing for discriminated in favor of. Given these marginal revenue product curves, the markets for the two groups of investment advisors will now determine very different wages and employment levels. Black females will earn $20,000 a year and only 1000 will work as investment advisors. White males will earn $60,000 a year and 3000 of them will work as investment advisors. Thus, purely on the basis of the prejudice of the demanders of investment advice, black women will earn one third the wages of white men, and three quarters of all investment advisors will be white men and only one quarter will be black women.

The case that we have just examined is a hypothetical example of how prejudice can produce differences in earnings. But economists disagree about whether or not prejudice actually causes wage differentials for a simple but difficult reason: You can recognize prejudice when you see it, but you cannot easily measure it. Our model shows that sex and race differentials may come from prejudice. But without a way of measuring prejudice in the real world, we cannot easily test that model to see if it is true.

We need to make another point as well. Our model of prejudice, like all economic models, is in an equilibrium, albeit an unhappy one. But simply because a model is in equilibrium does not mean that such a real situation is either desirable or inevitable. Economic theory makes predictions about the way things will be, not moral statements about the way things ought to be. Policies designed to bring equal wages and employment prospects to women and minorities can be devised. But to be successful, such

Figure 16.7 Discrimination

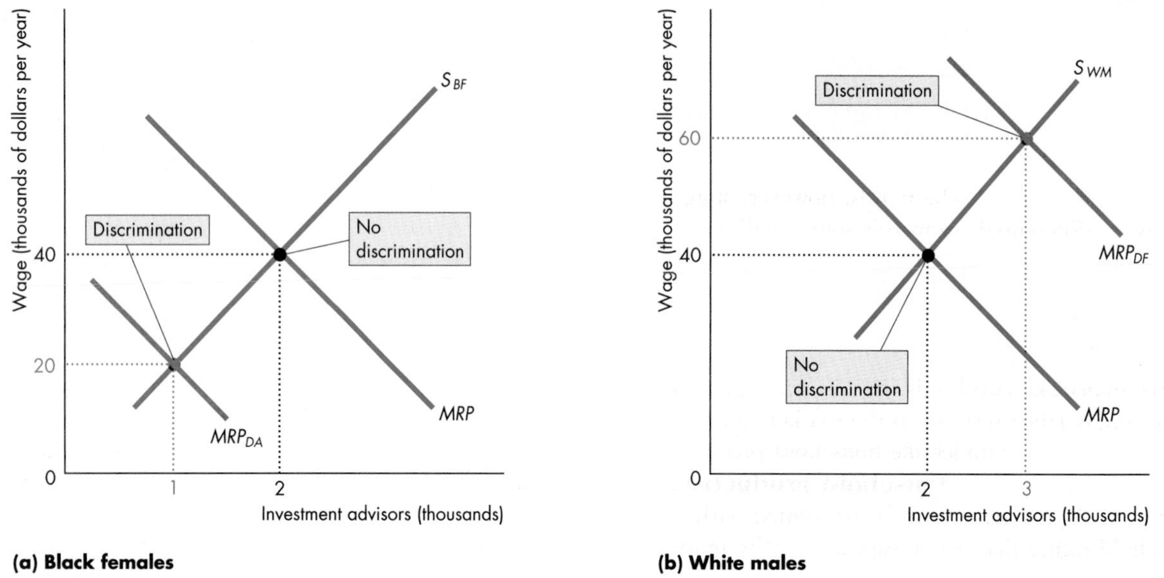

The supply curve for black female investment advisors is S_{BF} in part (a) and the supply curve for white male investment advisors is S_{WM} in part (b). If the marginal revenue product of both groups of investment advisors is *MRP* (the same curve in each part), then the equilibrium wage rate for each group is \$40,000 a year and 2000 of each type of advisor are employed. If there is discrimination against blacks and women, the marginal revenue product curve is to the left of the original curve. It is the curve labeled MRP_{DA}—*DA* standing for discriminated against. There is discrimination in favor of white males, so their marginal revenue product curve is MRP_{DF}—*DF* standing for discriminated in favor of. The wage rate for black women falls to \$20,000 a year and only 1000 are employed. The wage rate for white males rises to \$60,000 a year and 3000 are employed.

policies must be based on careful economic analysis. Good intentions are not enough to bring about equality.

Human Capital Differences

As we saw above (pp. 407–410), wages are compensation, in part for time spent on the job and in part for the cost incurred in acquiring skill—in acquiring human capital. The more human capital a person supplies, the higher is that person's earnings, other things being equal. Measuring human capital with any precision is difficult. But there are some rough indicators. One such indicator is the number of years of schooling that a person has had. A second indicator is the number of years of work experience. The most recent figures indicate that the median years in school for all races and both sexes are almost equal at about 12½ years. But this equality in median years of schooling is recent. In 1960, whites, on the average, spent about 11 years in school while blacks, on the average, had about 8 years of schooling. By 1970, that differential had been cut to two years and today it has virtually disappeared.

A third possible indicator of human capital is the number of job interruptions. Interruptions to a career disrupt and reduce the effectiveness of job experience and slow down the accumulation of human capital. Also, during a job interruption, it is possible that human capital depreciates through lack of use. Traditionally, women's careers have been interrupted more frequently than men's, usually for bearing and rearing children. This factor is a possible source of lower wages, on the average, for women.

Just as education differences are virtually disappearing, so career interruptions for women are becoming less severe. Maternity leave and day-care facilities are providing an increasing number of women with uninterrupted employment that makes their human capital accumulation indistinguishable from that of men.

Thus it seems that human capital differences possibly can account for earnings differentials among races and sexes in the past and some of the differentials that still remain. The trends, however, suggest that wage differentials from this source will eventually disappear.

Degrees of Specialization

People undertake two kinds of production activities: They supply labor services to the market (market activities) and they undertake household production (nonmarket activities). **Household production** creates goods and services to be consumed within the household rather than to be supplied to the market. Such activities include cooking, cleaning, minor repair work, education, and various organizational services such as arranging vacations and other leisure activities. Bearing and rearing children is another important nonmarket activity.

In Chapter 3, we discovered that people can gain from specializing in particular activities and trading their output with each other. Specialization and the gains from trade do not operate exclusively in the marketplace. They also operate within the household and among its members. It is not uncommon for one member of a household to specialize in shopping, another in cleaning, another in laundry, and so on. Specialization in bearing children is a biological necessity, although rearing them is not.

Consider, for example, a household that has two members—Bob and Sue. Bob and Sue have to decide how they will allocate their time between various nonmarket household production activities and market activity. One solution is for Bob to specialize in market activity and Sue to specialize in nonmarket activity. Another solution is to reverse the roles and have Sue specialize in market activity and Bob in nonmarket activity. Alternatively, one or both of them can become diversified doing some market and some nonmarket activity. A completely egalitarian allocation will have them each share the nonmarket tasks equally and each devote the same amount of time and energy to market activity. But unequal allocations of time are also possible with one of the household members specializing in market activity and the other being diversified.

In deciding which of the many alternative time allocations to choose, Bob and Sue will take into consideration their future plans for having children. The particular allocation chosen by Bob and Sue will depend on their preferences and on the market earning potential of each of them. An increasing number of households are choosing the egalitarian allocation with each person diversified between nonmarket household production and market activity. Most households, however, still choose an allocation that would have Bob almost fully specialized in market activity and Sue covering a greater diversity of tasks both in the job market and the household. What are the effects of this more common assignment of market and nonmarket tasks? Though there will always be exceptions, on the average, it seems likely that if Bob specializes in market production and Sue diversifies between market and nonmarket production, Bob will have higher earning potential in the marketplace than Sue. If Sue is devoting a great deal of productive effort to ensuring Bob's mental and physical well-being, the quality of Bob's market labor will be higher than if he were undertaking his household production tasks on his own. If the roles were reversed, Sue would be able to supply market labor capable of earning more than Bob.

Economists have attempted to test whether the degree of specialization can account for earnings differentials between the sexes by examining the wages of men and women where, as far as possible, the degree of specialization is held constant. For example, if the degree of specialization is an important factor influencing a person's wage, then men and women of identical ages and educational backgrounds in identical occupations will be paid different wages depending on whether they are single, married to a spouse who specializes in household production, or married to a spouse who works. Single men and women who live alone and who are equally specialized in household and market production and who have the same amounts of human capital and who do similar jobs will be paid the same wage. To make nonmarket factors as similar as possible, two groups have been chosen for analysis. They are "never married" men and women. The available evidence suggests that, on the average, when they have the same amount of human capital—measured by years of schooling, work experience, and career interruptions—the wages of these two groups are not identical but they are much closer than the difference between average wages for men and women. As we saw in Fig. 16.6(b), women are paid on the average about 66 percent of the wages of men. When allowance is made for degree of specialization and human capital, this wage differential comes down to between 5 and 10 percent, by some estimates. Some economists suspect the remaining discrepancy stems from discrimination against women, although the difficulty of measuring such discrimination makes this hypothesis hard to test.

Most of the difference in men's and women's wages arises from the fact that men and women do different jobs and, for the most part, men's jobs are better paid than women's jobs. There are, however, an increasing number of women entering areas that were traditionally the preserve of men. This trend is particularly clear in professions such as architecture, medicine, economics, law, accounting, and pharmacology where the percentage of total enrollments in university courses in these subjects for women has increased from less than 20 percent in 1970 to approaching, and in some cases exceeding, 50 percent today.

Comparable-Worth Laws

In 1963, Congress passed the Equal Pay Act and in 1964 the Civil Rights Act. These acts require equal pay for equal work. They are attempts to remove the most blatant forms of discrimination between men and women and whites and minorities. But many people believe that these acts do not go far enough. In their view, getting paid the *same* wage for doing the *same* job is just the first tiny step that has to be taken. What's important is that *comparable* jobs receive the *same* wages regardless of whether they are done by men or women, or by blacks or whites. Paying the same wage for different jobs that are judged to be comparable is called **comparable worth.**

Advocates of comparable-worth laws argue that wages should be determined by analyzing the characteristics of jobs and determining their worth on objective grounds. However, such a method of determining wage rates does not achieve the objectives sought by supporters of wage equality. Let's see why.

Figure 16.8 shows two markets: that for oil rig operators in part (a) and that for nurses in part (b). The marginal revenue product curves (MRP_R and MRP_N) and the supply curves (S_R and S_N) are shown for each type of labor. Competitive equilibrium generates a wage rate W_R for oil rig operators and W_N for nurses.

Suppose that the knowledge and skills required in those two occupations—the mental and physical demands, the responsibilities and the working conditions—result in a judgment that these two jobs are of comparable worth. Suppose that the wage rate that is judged to apply to each of them is W_C. Suppose that a court enforces that wage rate as part of a comparable-worth ruling. What will happen? First, there will be a shortage of oil rig operators. Oil rig companies will be able to hire only S_r workers at the wage rate W_C. They will have to cut back their production or build more expensive labor-saving oil rigs. There will also be a fall in nursing employment. But this fall occurs because hospitals will demand fewer nurses. At the higher wage W_C, hospitals will demand only D_n nurses. The quantity of nurses supplied will be S_n and the difference between S_n and D_n will be the number of unemployed nurses looking for jobs.

Thus legislated comparable wages for comparable work may have serious and costly unintended consequences.

R E V I E W

Differences in earnings based on skill or education level arise because skilled labor has a higher marginal revenue product than unskilled labor and because skills are costly to acquire. Union workers have higher wages than nonunion workers because unions are able to control the supply of labor and, indirectly, influence the marginal revenue product of their members. Wage differences between the sexes and the races are harder to explain. They may arise from discrimination and from differences in human capital. Sex differentials may also in part arise from differences in the degree of specialization. Comparable worth law cannot, on its own, eliminate wage differentials. Differentials will be reduced only if differences in marginal revenue product are reduced. The process of equalization of human capital and of the degree of specialization will lead to lower differentials and possibly will eliminate them. ■

Figure 16.8 The Problem with Comparable Worth

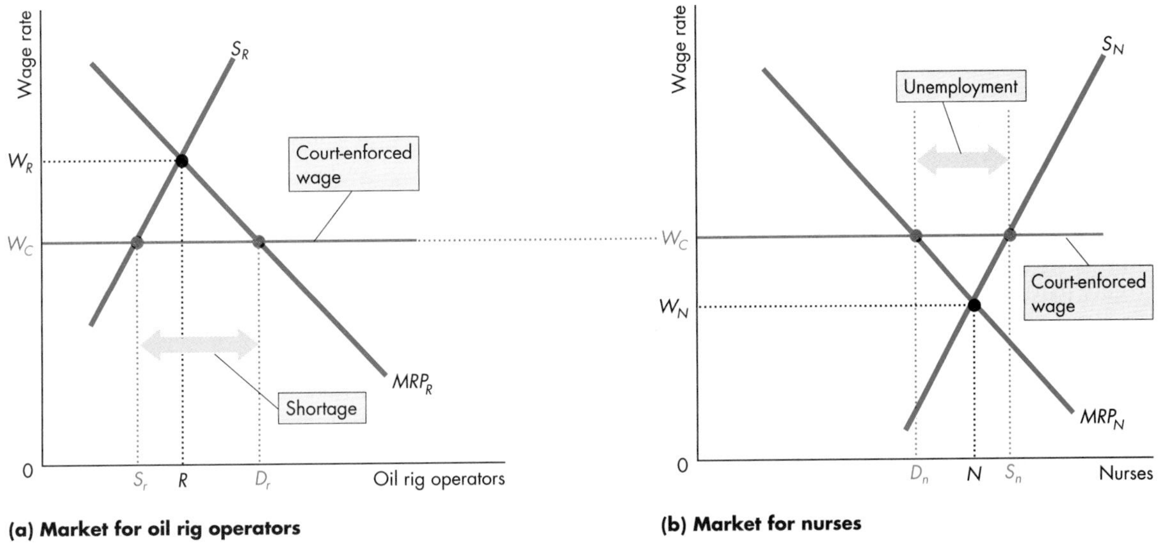

The demand for and supply of oil rig operators (MRP_R and S_R) are shown in part (a) and for nurses (MRP_N and S_N) in part (b). The competitive equilibrium wage rate for oil rig operators is W_R and for nurses it is W_N. If an evaluation of the two jobs finds that they have comparable worth and it is ruled that the wage rate W_C be paid to both types of workers, there will be an excess demand for oil rig operators and an excess supply of nurses. There will be $S_n - D_n$ nurses unemployed and a shortage of $D_r - S_r$ oil rig operators. Oil producers will have to find other ways of producing oil (that are more expensive) and nurses will have to find other jobs (that are less desirable to them and less well paid).

Our next task is to study alternative compensation arrangements—those based on workhours and those based on performance.

Alternative Compensation Rules

A **compensation rule** is a formula for calculating a person's income. There are four commonly used compensation rules:

- Time-related payments
- Performance-related payments
- Payments based on the performance of a team or group
- Payments based on the performance of one person compared with that of another

Non-standard compensation arrangements have become increasingly common in recent years (see Reading Between the Lines, pp. 428–429). Let's look at the four basic alternatives.

Time-related Compensation Rules

Time-related compensation rules are called time rates. **Time rates** are compensation rules based on the number of hours an individual works; they are expressed in dollars per hour. Many occupations are compensated on a time basis and almost all production line jobs are rewarded in this way.

Performance-related Compensation Rules

There are three measures of performance that are commonly used as the basis for performance-related compensation rules. They are:

- Physical production (piece rates)
- Value of sales (commissions and royalties)
- Profit (profit-sharing)

Piece Rates A compensation rule based on the amount of output a worker produces is called a **piece rate.** Workers are paid a dollar amount for each piece they produce. The piece may be a very simple item such as a shirt sleeve, or a more complicated service such as performing an appendectomy or writing a will. In all of these cases, the worker gets paid for the number of units of output produced, not for the number of hours worked.

Commissions and Royalties **Commissions and royalties** are a form of compensation based on the value of sales. This method of compensation is common among salespersons, realtors, stockbrokers, pop singers, and authors. In all these cases, the person buying the output does not observe the amount of time that the individual works and the amount of effort exerted.

Profit-Sharing **Profit-sharing** is a compensation rule that allocates a certain fraction of a firm's profit to its employees. Such compensation schemes are not as common as the others that we have just considered, and they are usually reserved for senior executives of corporations. Each year, newspapers and magazines publish lists of the top money-making executives of the year. Usually most of their multimillion dollar income is not from salary but from profit-sharing.

Team Performance

In some production situations with teams of workers, the output of the entire team decides the compensation of each of the members of the team. This method of compensation is used in some team sports, for example, where a win results in higher pay for each member of the team. It is also used in team production where a bonus is paid if the team achieves particular target output levels.

Besides bonuses, there are also penalties for failure. For example, a price is sometimes agreed to provided delivery takes place by a certain time. Failure to meet the agreed deadline results in a penalty being paid by the supplier. Such penalty clauses are not common in labor contracts but they are common in transactions between firms.

Comparative Performance

Compensation rules based on comparative performance are a major form of compensation in professional sports. The winner of a tennis tournament typically is paid twice as much as the runner-up, who in turn receives twice as much as the defeated semifinalists. They in turn earn twice as much as the defeated quarterfinalists, and so on. As we'll see below, compensation of senior executives in firms can also be interpreted as having a "prize element" for winning.

Our goal is to work out why firms use compensation schemes based on performance. To achieve that understanding, we study what is known as the principal-agent model.

Principals and Agents

A **principal** is an individual who sets a compensation rule to motivate an agent to choose activities advantageous to the principal. An **agent** is a person who works for a principal and performs various activities, some of which are not observable by the principal. A principal may hire just one or many agents.

The compensation rule chosen by the principal will contain appropriate incentives. An **incentive** is an inducement to an agent to behave in a particular way. The word incentive is derived from Latin and means "setting the tune." Thus an incentive can be thought of as a "tune" that induces an agent to "sing the appropriate song."

The observation of an agent's actions by a principal is called **monitoring.** A principal cannot monitor an agent without incurring costs. Such costs are called **monitoring costs.** In some situations, monitoring costs are modest; in others they are high. There are even situations in which no matter how much is spent on monitoring, the relevant actions of an agent cannot be observed. An example of low monitoring costs occurs in quality control work. A quality control worker's effort can be checked by observing how many defective items are missed. An example of expensive monitoring costs (which we don't observe in reality) would occur on a car assembly line. If an auto manufacturer hires a second worker to monitor every assembly line worker, it will probably go broke. An example of a situation in which monitoring is impossible is in the work of designers, film makers, and other creative artists.

Where monitoring is impossible, a principal has no choice but to use a compensation rule based on those parts of the agent's actions that can be observed. Where monitoring is possible but costly, the principal may be able to avoid monitoring costs by using a compensation rule based on only those aspects of an agent's behavior that can be observed at low cost. Let's look more closely at the monitoring of an agent's actions.

There are many situations where getting a job done presents problems of monitoring either the output of the worker or the effort that the worker is exerting. Often it is fairly easy to observe output but virtually impossible to measure effort.

Observing Output

Some of the best examples where we can observe output but not effort are those of professional services. Doctors, dentists, lawyers, and accountants provide services that in many cases are easily observed and evaluated by their clients. Performing an appendectomy, crowning a tooth, drawing up a will, or preparing an income tax return are all reasonably well defined activities that can be monitored and observed by the client. The client cannot observe how much effort the doctor, dentist, lawyer, or accountant exerts to produce the service. These are all cases where the quantity and quality of the product is known to the buyer, but the time and effort needed to produce the product is known only to the supplier—the worker.

Other examples concern the effort of people who work in a different geographical location from their employer, such as salespersons. These people are hired to sell as much as they can. Their output, measured in sales, can be readily observed by their employers, but not the time and energy they put into their job. It would be easy for a salesperson to take off a day or two, or to mix pleasure with business to the point where no business was being done. Provided the salesperson's output, measured in terms of sales, was large, the employer would never discover the low volume of effort.

There are other cases in which it is possible to observe effort but hard or impossible to observe output.

Observing Effort

It is often easy to observe effort but impossible to observe an individual's output when people work together as a team. The team effort produces the output. No one individual can produce the output alone and the contribution of any one individual to the final output cannot be determined.

Individual effort can be observed, however, when there are precise standards by which to judge it. These standards are present when the output is controlled by some objective circumstance, such as the speed at which a production line is running. In such a case, an individual worker has no choice but to put in the effort required to keep up with the production line. Examples of jobs in which effort can be observed are car assembly lines and steel rolling mills.

In some cases, neither the output nor the effort of an individual can be observed. Let's now consider these.

Observing neither Output nor Effort

The best examples of cases in which it is difficult or impossible to observe either the effort being exerted or the output achieved by a single individual is in the area of sports. The effort exerted by a tennis player, a boxer, a football player, and so on is known only to the individual player. The output is a sports event the quality of which depends on the joint efforts and interactions of all the players. Each individual player's contribution to the output is virtually impossible to assess. And it is also not possible to calculate each player's contribution to the commercial successes of the event, the revenue from selling tickets and broadcast rights.

Although sporting examples are the most obvious ones, there are many other cases in which neither individual effort nor output can be easily monitored. The effort exerted in the board rooms and executive suites of large corporations by chief executives is virtually impossible for their employers, the shareholders of the company, to monitor. The value of the executive's output, the extent to which his or her effort increases the profitability of the corporation, cannot be calculated directly.

If we cannot observe effort and output, how can we compensate people so that they do nevertheless supply the right amount of effort and a high quality output? In a nutshell, how can a principal devise a compensation rule that spurs an agent to take an action that is not observed but brings maximum attainable benefit to the principal?

Efficient Compensation Rules

Efficient compensation rules have two characteristics. The first characteristic is that the compensation rule delivers a maximum expected profit for the principal. A compensation rule that does not maximize the principal's expected profit (net of monitoring costs) can be improved upon. Profit-maximizing principals will constantly seek out an efficient compensation rule in each situation. A second characteristic of an efficient compensation rule is that it is acceptable to the agent. That is, whatever rule the principal proposes, it delivers a compensation package that the agent is willing to accept. In a competitive environment, an agent will have alternative job possibilities. An efficient compensation rule makes the agent at least as well off as in the best available alternative job. Let's consider an example.

Jenny has invented a revolutionary new vacuum cleaner—the Dustbeater—and she is going to hire a salesperson to go on the road and sell her product. She knows that a salesperson can put in a great deal of effort or take a lot of leisure on the job. The salesperson who takes leisure on the job is not going to encounter many potential customers and sales will be low. The salesperson who works hard might have bad luck and do no better than the lazy salesperson but might also have good luck and find a lot of customers with filthy rugs and worn out vacuum cleaners. But Jenny does not have the time to follow the salesperson around checking on the amount of effort being expended. How is she to tell the difference between a hardworking salesperson who has bad luck and a lazy one?

She structures the compensation package for the salesperson in such a way as to induce him to exert an effort that maximizes her expected income. In figuring out the appropriate contract, she begins by working out the effects of the effort of the salesperson on her income.

Income, Effort, and Luck

Suppose that the total income of Jenny and the salesperson depends on two things: the effort of the salesperson and luck; let's also suppose that there are two levels of effort—"work" and "shirk"—and that there are two levels of luck—"good" and "bad." Income depends on the combination of effort and luck. The incomes arising from each of these considerations are set out in Table 16.2. Income is \$60 if the agent shirks, regardless of whether there is good or bad luck. If the agent works, income is \$140 if there is good luck and \$60 if there is bad luck. The probability (or chance) of good luck occurring is 50 percent, or one half.

Jenny, the principal, can figure out the four possible outcomes shown in Table 16.2, but she cannot observe the effort of the agent nor tell whether the agent had good or bad luck. The agent—the salesperson—knows whether or not he is shirking but has no incentive to tell Jenny.

Jenny's problem is to figure out how to compensate the salesperson given the possible outcomes shown in the table. Her next step is to figure out what the salesperson's next best alternative employment prospect is.

Agent's Preferences and Alternatives The agent has alternative employment prospects (selling encyclopedias or brushes) and also has preferences that Jenny has to take into account when designing the compensation rule. Let's suppose that the agent places a \$20 value on shirking. That is, he prefers shirking to working but a day of working compensated with \$20, or a day of shirking, are equally acceptable to him.

The agent does not have to sell vacuum cleaners. Let's suppose that selling encyclopedias will yield him an income of \$70 a day but that \$20 worth of work has to be expended to earn to \$70, so the net gain to the agent is \$50 a day. To attract the agent, the principal has to offer compensation worth at least \$50. Jenny compares two compensation rules: Rule 1 is a daily wage and Rule 2 is a commission.

Table 16.2 Compensation Schemes for Dustbeater Salespersons

Incomes, effort, and luck

Luck	Effort: Work	Effort: Shirk
Good	$140	$60
Bad	$ 60	$60

There is an equal (50 percent) chance of good luck or bad luck.

Agent's preferences and alternative employment

Value of time spent working is $20 per day.

Income from alternative employment is $70 per day.

Value of work is $70 minus $20, which is $50 per day.

Compensation rules and outcomes

Rule 1: Principal pays $50.

	Value to agent
If the agent works:	$50 − $20 = $30
If the agent shirks:	$50 − $ 0 = $50

Outcome:
Agent's choice is to shirk.

Total income	=	Principal's income	+	Agent's income
$60	=	$10	+	$50

Rule 2: Principal pays agent $20 plus 51 percent of value of output.

Value to agent

If the agent works: $\$20 + 0.51\left(\frac{\$140}{2} + \frac{\$60}{2}\right) - \$20 = \$51.00$

If the agent shirks: $\$20 + 0.51(\$60) - \$\ 0 = \$50.60$

Outcome:
Agent's choice is to work.

Total income	=	Principal's income	+	Agent's income
$100	=	$29	+	$71

Under Rule 1, Jenny pays the agent $50 a day. The agent calculates the value of working and shirking. If the agent works, that value is $30—the $50 paid by Jenny minus $20 worth of work effort. If the agent shirks, that value is $50. Nothing has to be subtracted from the wage for work effort. In this situation, the agent chooses to shirk. Table 16.2 shows the outcome. Total income generated is $60. That income is divided between Jenny and the salesperson in accordance with the compensation rule. Jenny gets $10 and the salesperson $50. Tough luck for Jenny.

Under Rule 2, Jenny pays the salesperson $20 a day plus 51 percent of the total income generated. Let's look at the salesperson's choices under this scheme. If the agent shirks, regardless of his luck, he generates a total income for Jenny and himself of $60. He is paid 51 percent of that income—$30.60—plus the fixed payment of $20. Thus his income from shirking is $50.60. If the agent works, his income depends on whether he has good or bad luck. So he calculates his expected or average income. With good luck, total income is $140 but with bad luck, it is $60. Since there is an equal chance of good luck and bad luck, total income on the average is $100. The agent gets 51 percent of this amount or, $51. Over and above this amount, Jenny pays $20 a day but this payment is offset by the value of the effort expended by the agent in working. Thus the expected net value of work under this compensation scheme is $51.

The agent compares the outcome from working, $71, with that from shirking, $50.60, and concludes that work yields a sufficiently higher income than shirking to induce him to work. Since expected total income is $100, and the salesperson is paid an average income of $71, Jenny has an average income of $29.

Let's compare Rule 1 with Rule 2 from the point of view of both Jenny and the salesperson. Under Rule 1, the salesperson has an income of $50. Under Rule 2, the salesperson has an income of $71 on the average, but because he has to work, its value is only $51. Still, even when accounting for the distaste of having to work, the salesperson has $1 more under Rule 2 than under Rule 1. Jenny has an average income under Rule 1 of $10 and under Rule 2 of $29. She is better off under Rule 2 by $19. Since both the salesperson and

Bonus Schemes in Action

Bonuses Replace Wage Rises and Workers Are the Losers

Seeking to hold down labor costs, thousands of companies are changing the way they increase workers' pay. Instead of the traditional annual increase, millions of workers in industries as diverse as supermarkets and aerospace are receiving cash bonuses—and this new form makes a big difference.

While many corporate executives are promoting the bonus programs as a tool to share the wealth and increase productivity, the plans clearly mean less money for most workers.

The bonuses take many forms and names. . . . But virtually all of them have two things in common: They can vary with a company's fortunes, disappearing in hard times, and they are not permanent. . . .

In a recent survey, 1,120 of the 1,600 companies that responded had one or more of these bonus plans, and 69 percent of those companies had instituted the plans in the last five years, according to the American Productivity Center, a research organization. . . .

"The new bonus raise is contributing to a flattening of wages nationally," said Robert Reich, a Harvard economist. "We don't know how important the contribution is yet, but it is a factor." Total compensation—pay plus benefits, adjusted for inflation—grew by a scant three-tenths of 1 percent for all American workers in the year ended March 31 and only 1.8 percent in the previous year, the Labor Department reported.

The vast change developing in pay practices should, on the face of it, have labor unions up in arms. But unions, more concerned about losing jobs to nonunion companies and foreign countries with lower labor costs, are reluctant to fight the trend. . . .

Stephen P. Yokich, a United Automobile Workers vice president, insists that standard wage increases must be restored to the Ford and General Motors agreements in the contract negotiations that start July 22. Such increases have been absent since 1982, replaced by profit-sharing formulas that produced an average bonus of $2,100 a worker at Ford for 1986, but not a penny for G.M. workers.

The U.A.W. gave in on wage increases in 1982 because of the trauma of thousands of layoffs in the auto industry, and job security is still the main concern. "Wages don't mean a hill of beans if you don't have a job," Mr. Yokich said. "Wages are not the most important thing anymore; job security is." . . .

***The New York Times*, June 26, 1987**

By Louis Uchitelle

The Essence of the Story

- A 1987 survey revealed that 70 percent of companies (1,120 out of 1,600) had profit-sharing bonus schemes and 69 percent of them had started such schemes between 1982 and 1987.
- Real wages increased very slowly during this period, and the more widespread use of bonus schemes was partly responsible for the slow wage growth.
- All the schemes have two things in common. Bonuses:

  —vary with company profits
  —are not built into base pay.
- Unions did not oppose the trend to greater use of profit-sharing bonuses, believing them to contribute to job security.

Background and Analysis

- Profit sharing is used when team effort is important and when the principal cannot observe the effort of each individual agent.
- It is unlikely that changes in the importance of team effort and in the cost of monitoring individual workers can explain the scale of the increase in profit sharing in the years since 1982.
- Also, it is unlikely that profit sharing has much effect on average wage rates (as claimed in the article). For a principal must reward an agent with the market average wage rate; otherwise the agent will quit and seek work with another principal.
- Slow growth in real wages between 1982 and 1987 can be explained by the forces of demand and supply. During those years, both demand and supply increased, increasing employment but keeping real wages steady.
- Profit sharing enables wages to adjust quickly when demand changes, and its spread in the 1980s may have arisen because demand changes have been large.
- With no bonus (top figure), the wage rate consists entirely of base pay. With a demand curve LD_0 and a supply curve LS, the wage rate is W_0 and employment is L_0. If demand decreases to LD_1, and if the wage rate does not fall, employment falls to L_1. To restore equilibrium, the base pay rate eventually falls.
- In the bottom figure, the same equilibrium wage rate, W_0, is made up of base pay and a bonus.
- In this case, if demand decreases to LD_1, the bonus shrinks, the wage rate falls to W_1, and employment falls to L_2, a smaller decrease than if wages failed to fall.
- Bonuses that make wage rates adjust quickly reduce the effects of demand fluctuations on employment.

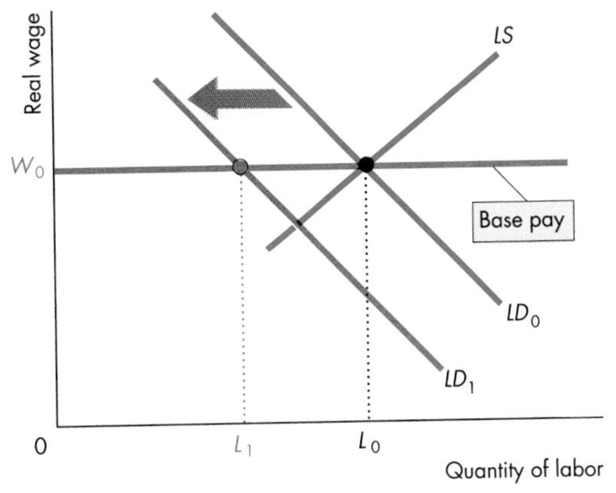

(a)

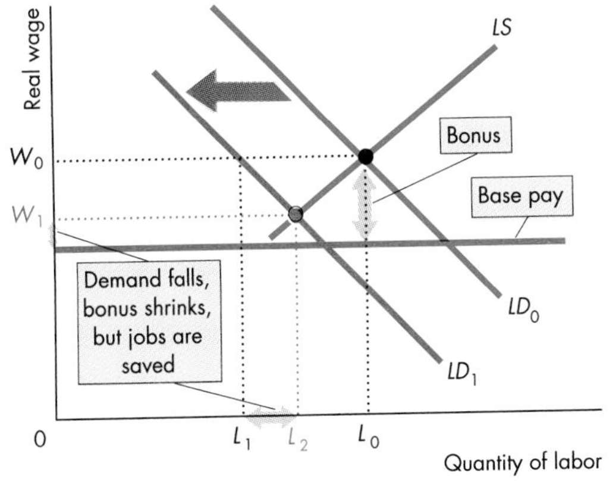

(b)

Jenny gain by using Rule 2, that is the compensation rule Jenny offers. This example illustrates why most salespersons are compensated for their work by a commission rather than a fixed daily wage rate. It also explains why piece rates are used to compensate textile workers and why royalties compensate authors. All of these cases are examples in which output—the value of the final product—can be measured but the effort of the individual worker in producing that output cannot.

Compensation Rules and Teams The compensation scheme that we have just considered arises in a situation in which effort cannot be observed but an agent's output can. There are some situations in which neither individual effort nor individual output can be directly observed. These situations occur when the production process involves a team whose combined efforts determine how much is produced and at what cost. In these cases, performance-related compensation rules can be employed, but they have to be based on the total output of the team rather than on the effort of any one individual. The most comprehensive team compensation rule is profit-sharing.

Profit-Sharing The objective of any firm is to maximize profit. Since that is the objective, why isn't *everyone* paid by a profit share? Profit sharing is, in fact, becoming more common (see Reading Between the Lines, p. 428), but there are many situations in which there is only a loose connection between profit and an *individual* agent's output where profit sharing is not used. Profit is the consequence of the joint output of all the firm's inputs. But profit gives a good indication of the effectiveness of senior management. It is their job to coordinate the other inputs to achieve maximum profit. That is why profit-sharing arrangements are usually seen in compensation rules for senior managers.

Compensation Rules Based on Rank

Compensation rules that are based on rank deliver a payment related not to the *absolute* output performance of an agent but on the performance of one agent *relative* to another. This type of compensation rule is also common in sports, and because of this, such a rule is usually referred to as a rank-tournament compensation rule. A **rank-tournament compensation rule** is one in which the payment to the agent depends on the agent's rank in the tournament.

Let's see how rank-tournament compensation rules work. Table 16.3 contains an example that we'll use in our exploration of such rules. Suppose that there are ten agents, each of whom generates a value of output based on effort and luck in the same way as the agent in Table 16.2. Each agent has the same preferences as before and has the opportunity, from alternative employment, to generate a net return of $50. Compensation Rule 1 simply has the principal paying each agent $50. The agents accept this compensation rule but shirk. Total income is $600 (10 × $60); the principal pays the agents $500 and makes $100 of income.

Now consider Rule 2. The principal pays a prize of $260 to the agent with the highest output —the agent that comes first in rank—and pays $50 each to all the other agents. If two or more agents tie in producing the highest output, the prize is shared. How does the agent respond to this compensation rule? The answer is worked out in the final part of Table 16.3.

Each agent figures that by working there is a one in ten chance of winning the prize and nine in ten chances of not winning the prize. Therefore, the agent who works will expect an income of $71 (1/10 of $260 plus 9/10 of $50). The cost of working as opposed to shirking is $20, so subtracting that from the expected income leaves the working agent with an expected dollar value of work effort of $51. If the agent shirks, there is no chance of winning the prize, so income is $50. In this situation, each agent will choose to work. Since they all work, they will in fact all share the prize, so they will each receive an income of $71. This income is made up of $50, the income for coming in second, plus 1/10 of $210, the excess of the prize income over the normal income.

The total value of the work done by the agents, and therefore the principal's income, depends on whether good or bad luck occurs. On the average, the value of the output of a single agent is $100 (the average of $140 and $60). The total income generated by the 10 agents is, on the average, $1000 ($100 multiplied by 10). The agents receive $710 and the principal $290.

Comparing the outcome of Rule 1 with that of Rule 2, it is clear that both the principal and

Table 16.3 Rank-Tournament Compensation Scheme

Value of output of each agent

	Effort	
Luck	Work	Shirk
Good	$140	$60
Bad	$ 60	$60

There is an equal (50 percent) chance of good or bad luck.
There are 10 agents and the output of each agent is observable.

Compensation rules and outcomes

Rule 1: Principal pays each agent $50.

Outcome:
Each agent's choice is to shirk.

Total income	=	Principal's income	+	Agent's income
$600	=	$100	+	$500

Rule 2: Principal pays a prize of $260 to the agent with highest output and $50 to each other agent (a tie results in sharing the prize).

Value to each agent

If the agent works: $\frac{1}{10}(\$260) + \frac{9}{10}(\$50) - \$20 = \$51$

If the agent shirks: $= \$50$

Outcome:
Each agent's choice is to work.

Total income	=	Principal's income	+	Agent's income
$1000	=	$290	+	$710

the agents gain by operating under Rule 2 rather than Rule 1.

Though rank tournaments in practice usually involve somebody winning outright rather than agents tying, rank tournaments work for exactly the same reason that this example works. By giving the agent the incentive to try for the prize, the agent finds it advantageous to work, thereby raising the income of the principal as well as that of the agent.

Professional tennis illustrates this type of compensation rule very well. If Martina Navratilova and Steffi Graff were paid by the hour, it would be in their interest to play a match where the game length was such that the cost to each of them of the last hour played equaled the hourly wage rate. If the wage rate was fairly high, they would play a long and boring game. If the wage rate was low, the game would be short (and probably equally boring). It wouldn't matter to either of them who won—they could even agree on the winner before the game began. Compensating such people with a prize for the best player induces each to try to be the best and produces a greater total output. In this case, it produces a greater total output by generating a higher quality and more exciting game of tennis that people are willing to pay more to watch.

Similar situations can be found in network newsrooms. Newscasters such as Tom Brokaw, Peter Jennings, and Dan Rather receive compensation packages well in excess of $1 million a year. They are talented broadcasters. But there are dozens of other talented broadcasters, working with them in their newsrooms and news-gathering organizations around the world. It is hard to monitor the activities of reporters, but the quality of the job that they do influences such things as total audience size and total revenue that can be generated from advertising during the newscasts. In such a situation, the news-gathering and reporting business can be treated like a tennis match. Though the rules are less precise and the rules for scoring are more complicated, those who perform best win the prize of being promoted to the most prestigious position in the news organization. The top prize, anchor on the nightly news, has to be worth enough to keep the people below that position working hard and competing for it.

The same considerations apply to the executive suites and boardrooms of large corporations. By having large differences in compensation between the chief executive officer and the people on the next rung below that level and so on down the executive ladder, a competitive environment similar to that of tennis or other sports tournaments is created. The result is an average level of effort that, though not observed and monitored by anyone, is higher than it otherwise would be. Paying the chief executive twice as much as everybody else makes everybody work harder!

Many individuals are compensated by a combination of the schemes we have just reviewed. For example, some senior executives are rewarded partly with a prize for winning a tournament, partly with profit-sharing, and partly on an hourly basis.

We have now seen how simple compensation rules based on observable characteristics of performance can spur agents to work hard for the principal, even when much of their effort cannot be observed. Where it is impossible to observe the agent's actions, the principal has no choice but to use such compensation rules. But in some situations, the principal can monitor the agent, at a cost, and make sure that the agent behaves in the principal's interest. An implication of the compensation rules that we have just examined is that sometimes, with appropriate compensation rules, principals can avoid monitoring costs.

Avoiding Monitoring Costs

To see why a principal can avoid monitoring costs, let's go back to the example of Jenny's vacuum cleaner summarized in Table 16.2. Suppose that by spending \$1, Jenny can monitor the salesperson's effort. If a principal can monitor an agent's effort, then it is possible to base the agent's compensation on that effort. Suppose that Jenny incurs the cost of \$1 to monitor the salesperson and offers the following compensation rule: If you work, I will pay you \$71. If you shirk, I will pay you \$50. The salesperson knows that Jenny can monitor his actions and therefore computes the value of working and shirking in the following way:

- If I work, I receive an income of \$71 but incur a cost of working of \$20; so the net value of my effort is \$51.
- If I shirk, I receive an income of \$50 but avoid the cost of working; so the net value I receive is \$50.
- It pays me to work.

The salesperson works and receives an income of \$71. Jenny receives an average income of \$28. This income is arrived at in the following way. The average income generated by the agent that works is \$100 (the average of \$140 for good luck and \$60 for bad luck). Jenny pays \$71 to the salesperson and incurs a \$1 monitoring cost. Subtracting these costs from the average total income of \$100 leaves her with an average of \$28.

Now compare the results in the case that we have just worked through with the example in Table 16.2 if Rule 2 is employed. Recall that under Rule 2 Jenny pays the salesperson \$20 plus 51 percent of the value of the output. The salesperson works and receives an income, on the average, of \$71. Jenny receives an average income of \$29. The only difference between monitoring and not monitoring is Jenny's income. Her income falls by the cost of monitoring. The salesperson earns the same income in both situations. This example shows that a compensation rule can encourage an agent to work hard for a principal without the principal having to incur the cost of monitoring the agent's efforts.

Labor Market Equilibrium

You may be wondering, in light of this discussion of performance-related compensation, what has become of the idea that wages and employment are determined by equilibrium in the labor market. We have simply added a more detailed account of the labor market and one that requires a more detailed notion of labor market equilibrium.

Workers supply their time and effort in whatever way makes them best off. They have a variety of choices concerning not only the type of job to take and the number of hours to work but also the type of compensation scheme to accept. On the demand side of the market, firms decide not only how much of each type of labor to hire but also what to choose among the available compensation schemes for paying those workers. An equilibrium in the labor market consists of wage rates for different types of jobs, employment quantities in different jobs and industries, and a list of compensation rules that are actually used in each different type of employment. In labor market equilibrium, no individual worker (agent) can switch from one job to another or from one compensation rule to another and become better off. Moreover, no firm (principal) can offer a different compensation rule that will raise profit.

This description of equilibrium does not mean that clever principals cannot devise new, previously unthought of compensation rules that work better than existing compensation rules. There is technical progress in devising compensation rules just as there is technical progress in devising ways of getting cows to produce milk or tomato plants to produce fruit. But at any given point in time, given the alternative rules that have been invented, the best available compensation rule for each situation is being used. That is the compensation rule that provides the agent with at least as good a deal as the next best alternative employment and which maximizes the principal's profit.

■ In this chapter, we have extended and applied the factor markets model to understand a wide variety of phenomena in labor markets such as wage differentials and alternative compensation schemes. In the next chapter, we apply and extend the factor markets model to deal with markets for capital and for natural resources.

SUMMARY

Skill Differentials

Skill differentials arise partly because skilled labor has a higher marginal product than unskilled labor and partly because skills are costly to acquire. The higher marginal product of skilled workers results in a higher marginal revenue product. Since the demand for labor curve is derived from the marginal revenue product curve, the higher the marginal revenue product of skilled labor, the greater is the demand for skilled labor.

Skills are costly to acquire because households have to invest in human capital to become skilled. Investment sometimes means direct payments such as tuition and other training fees and sometimes means working for a lower wage during on-the-job training. Because skills are costly to acquire, households supply skilled labor on terms that compensate them for both the time spent on the job and the costs of acquiring the skills. Thus the supply curve of skilled labor lies above the supply curve of unskilled labor.

Wage rates of skilled and unskilled labor are determined by demand and supply in the two labor markets. The equilibrium wage rate for skilled labor exceeds that for unskilled labor. The difference in wages reflects the higher marginal product of skill and the cost to acquire skill. (pp. 407–410)

Union-Nonunion Wage Differentials

Labor unions influence wages by controlling the supply of labor. In competitive labor markets, unions obtain higher wages only at the expense of lower employment. Even so, unions can increase the total wage bill by forcing firms to hire at the point on their marginal revenue product curve where the demand for labor is less elastic. Unions in competitive industries also influence the marginal revenue product of their members by restricting imports, raising minimum wages, supporting immigration restrictions, increasing demand for their product, and increasing the marginal product of their members.

In a monopsony—a market in which there is a single buyer—unions increase wages without sacrificing employment. Bilateral monopoly occurs when the union is a monopoly seller of labor, the firm is a monopsony buyer of labor, and the wage rate is determined by bargaining between the two parties.

In practice, union workers earn an estimated 10 to 25 percent more than comparable nonunion workers. (pp. 410–418)

Wage Differentials between Sexes and Races

There are persistent differentials in earnings between men and women and whites and minorities. Three possible explanations for these differentials are discrimination, differences in human capital, and differences in degree of specialization.

Discrimination results in lower wages and lower employment for those discriminated against and higher wages and higher employment levels for those discriminated in favor of. Human capital differences result from differences in schooling and work experience. Differentials based on schooling have been falling and have almost been eliminated. Differentials based on work experience have kept women's pay below that for men because women's careers have traditionally been interrupted more frequently than those of men, resulting on the average in a smaller accumulation of human capital. This difference is less important today than in the past. Differentials arising from different degrees of specialization are probably important and may persist. Men have traditionally been more specialized in market activity, on the average, than women. Women have traditionally undertaken both nonmarket, household production activities, as well as market activities. Attempts to test for the importance of the degree of specialization suggest that it is an important source of the difference between the earnings of men and women. (pp. 418–422)

Comparable-Worth Laws

Comparable-worth laws determine wages by assessing the value of different types of jobs on objective characteristics rather than on what the market will pay. Determining wages through comparable worth will result in a cut in the number of people employed in those jobs where the market places a lower value, and shortages of those workers that the market values more highly. Thus the attempt to achieve comparable wages for comparable work has costly, unintended consequences. (pp. 422–423)

Alternative Compensation Rules

There are four commonly used compensation rules:

- Time-related payments
- Performance-related payments
- Payments based on the performance of a team or group
- Rank-related payments (pp. 423–424)

Principals and Agents

Compensation rules are studied by using a principal-agent model. A principal is a person who specifies the compensation rule and the agent is a person who works for a principal and receives an income determined by the compensation rule. The principal's goal is to devise a compensation rule that will spur the agent to maximize the principal's profit.

There are many production situations in which observing or monitoring a person's effort or output is either expensive or impossible. In some situations, output is easily observed but effort is not. In other situations, effort is easily observed but output is not. In some cases, neither output nor effort is readily observable. For situations in which either effort or output or both are unobservable, principals have to devise compensation rules that induce agents to work in a profit-maximizing way. (pp. 424–426)

Efficient Compensation Rules

Compensation rules have two characteristics: acceptability to the agent and profit maximization for the principal. When an individual agent's effort can be easily monitored but output is harder to observe, principals commonly use time rates of pay. When effort is not easily measured but output is, a compensation rule based on the agent's output can result in maximum profit for the principal. By paying an agent an amount that varies with output, or some fraction of the value of the agent's output, the principal can induce the agent to work harder and produce more.

Even when the principal can at some expense monitor the agent, it may still be possible to use a compensation rule that enables the principal to make maximum profit while avoiding the monitoring costs.

In labor market equilibrium, no individual worker or firm can become better off by adopting a different compensation rule. On the supply side, workers determine how much time and effort to supply, but they also decide which compensation scheme to accept. On the demand side, firms decide not only how much labor to hire but also what compensation schemes to offer. Labor market equilibrium consists of wage rates for different types of labor, the amount of employment in different jobs and industries, and a list of compensation rules for each different type of job. (pp. 426–433)

KEY CONCEPTS

Agent, 424
Bilateral monopoly, 417
Binding arbitration, 411
Closed shop, 411
Collective bargaining, 411
Commissions and royalties, 424
Comparable worth, 422
Compensation rule, 423
Craft union, 410
Human capital, 407
Household production, 421
Incentive, 424
Industrial union, 410
Labor union, 410
Local, 410
Lockout, 411
Monitoring, 424
Monitoring costs, 424
Monopsony, 412
Open shop, 411
Piece rate, 424
Principal, 424
Professional association, 411
Profit-sharing, 424
Rank-tournament compensation rule, 430
Right-to-work law, 411
Strike, 411
Time rates, 423
Union shop, 411

Key Figures and Tables

REVIEW QUESTIONS

1 Explain why skilled workers are paid more than unskilled workers.

2 What are the main types of labor union?

3 How does a labor union try to influence wages?

4 What can a union do in a competitive labor market?

5 How might a union increase the demand for its members' labor?

6 Under what circumstances would a minimum wage increase employment?

7 How big are the union-nonunion wage differentials in the United States today?

8 What are the three main reasons why sex and race differentials in earnings exist?

9 How do comparable-worth laws work and what are their predicted effects?

10 What are the main alternative compensation schemes?

11 Define and distinguish between a principal and an agent.

12 What are monitoring costs?

13 Why are student helpers at McDonald's paid by the hour rather than by the number of hamburgers they sell?

14 Why does Dan Rather make a higher wage than the news cameraman filming the war-torn streets of Beirut for the evening news?

PROBLEMS

1 Wendy owns an apple orchard. She employs students to pick the apples. They can pick the following amounts of apples in an hour:

Number of students	Quantity of apples (pounds)
1	20
2	50
3	90
4	120
5	145
6	165
7	180
8	190

a) Draw the average and marginal product curves of these students.

b) If Wendy can sell her apples for 50 cents a pound, draw Wendy's average and marginal revenue product curves.

c) Draw Wendy's demand for labor curve.

d) If all apple growers in Wendy's neighborhood pay their pickers $7.50 an hour, how many students will Wendy hire?

2 Assume that fruit pickers become unionized and student pickers are outlawed. If the union gets the wage increased to $10 an hour, how many unionized pickers will Wendy hire?

3 In a small isolated town in the Rocky Mountains the only firm hiring workers is a logging company. The firm's demand for labor and the town's supply of labor are given by:

Wage rate (dollars per hour)	Quantity demanded (hours)	Quantity supplied (hours)
2	400	120
3	360	160
4	320	200
5	280	240
6	240	280
7	200	320
8	160	360

a) What is the wage rate and how much labor does the firm hire?

b) If the townspeople form a union that is more powerful than the logging company in the labor market, what is the wage rate and how much labor does the firm hire?

4 The value of the output of labor in a particular production is as follows:

Marginal revenue products

	Work hard	*Average effort*	*Shirk*
Lots of bugs	$100	$ 70	$ 70
Average bugs	140	100	70
No bugs	180	140	100

An agent might work hard, give average effort, or shirk and the production process may have lots of bugs, average bugs, or no bugs. Depending on which combination of these situations prevail, the marginal revenue product of a worker will be one of the numbers set out in the table.

From the worker's point of view, shirking has no cost. Supplying average effort has a cost of $10, and working hard has a cost of $20. The worker has to be offered a compensation arrangement that is worth at least $50. Devise a compensation scheme that will make the maximum possible profit for the principal.

5 Suppose that there are three national football leagues: the Time League, the Goal Difference League, and the Bonus for Win League. The difference between the three leagues is in the way the players are paid. In the first league, the players are paid by the hour for time spent practicing and time spent playing. In the second league, the players are paid an amount that depends on the number of points that the team scores minus the number of points scored against it. In the third league, the players are paid one wage for a loss, a higher wage for a draw, and the highest wage of all for a win.

Provide a brief description of the predicted differences in the quality of the game in each of these three football leagues. Which league will be the most attractive and generate the biggest profits?

Chapter 17

Capital and Natural Resource Markets

After studying this chapter, you will be able to:

- Define and distinguish among financial and real assets, capital, and investment
- Define and distinguish between saving and portfolio choice
- Describe the structure of capital markets in the United States today
- Explain how interest rates and stock prices are determined and why the stock market fluctuates
- Define natural resources and explain how their prices are determined
- Explain how markets regulate the pace at which we use exhaustible resources such as oil

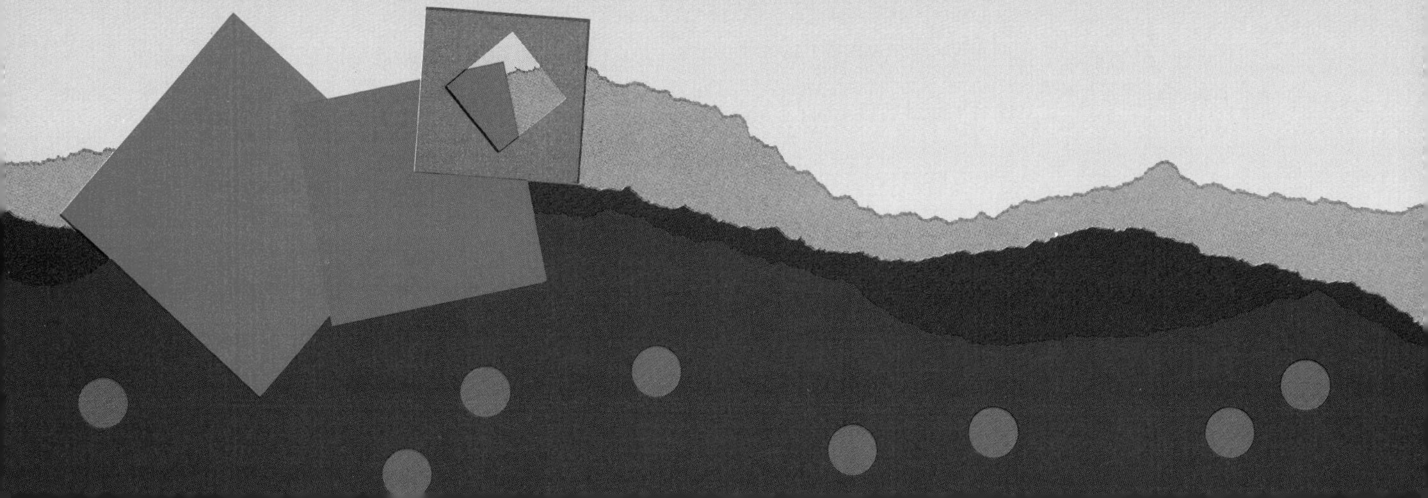

Boom and Bust

An air of panic filled the cavernous New York Stock Exchange on Monday, October 19, 1987. It had taken five years, from August 1982, for the average price of a common stock to climb 200 percent. But on that single day, stock prices fell an unheard of 22 percent—knocking billions of dollars off the value of people's investments. The crash touched off other stock market plunges from Tokyo to London. Why did the stock market boom for five years and then crash so suddenly and so spectacularly? ■ If you had bought $1000 worth of the stock of Circuit City Stores in August 1982, five years later your $1000 would have grown in value to an impressive $3,337,300. In contrast, if in 1982 you had bought $1000 worth of the stock of Brock Hotel Corporation, you would, by August 1987, have had only $17 left. Why do some companies' stocks boom and others slump? What determines the prices of individual companies' stocks? ■ The New York Stock Exchange, large as it is, is only a part of the enormous capital market of the United States. And the capital market of the United States is just a part of an even more enormous worldwide capital market. Every year, billions of dollars are saved and flow into the nation's and the world's capital markets. Savings flow by various channels—through banks, insurance companies, and stock exchanges—and end up financing the purchases of machinery, factory and office buildings, cars, homes, and a host of other capital goods. How does a dollar saved and placed on deposit in a bank help a firm to finance the purchase of a shiny new machine? How does your purchase of life insurance result in your savings enabling Pepsi-Cola to open a new bottling plant? ■ Giant firms, such as Shell Oil, and household names, such as Revlon and E. F. Hutton, have been taken over by other companies in recent years. Other firms, such as Sperry and

Burroughs, two computer makers, have merged to pool their strength. Takeovers and mergers affect the jobs of hundreds of thousands of people and change the competitive balance in entire industries. Why do firms merge or get taken over? ■ Many of our natural resources are exhaustible and yet we are using up these resources at an alarming rate. Every year we burn billions of cubic feet of natural gas and petroleum. We burn millions of tons of coal, we extract bauxite to make aluminium, and iron ore and other minerals to make steel. Aren't we one day going to run out of natural gas, oil, coal, bauxite, iron ore, and other natural resources? How do markets allocate these exhaustible resources? How are their prices determined? And do their prices adjust to encourage us to conserve such resources, or does the market need help to ensure that we do not pillage the exhaustible endowments of nature?

■ In this chapter, we're going to study capital and natural resource markets. We'll find out why people save as much or as little as they do, and why firms buy the amount of new capital equipment that they do. We will find out how interest rates and stock values are determined. In our study of natural resource markets, we'll discover that these markets obey some of the same economic laws as capital markets. We'll pay special attention to markets for exhaustible resources and discover how market forces act to encourage conservation.

Capital, Investment, and Saving

Let's begin with some capital market vocabulary and define three key terms:

- Asset
- Liability
- Balance sheet

An **asset** is anything of value that a household, firm, or government *owns.* A **liability** is a debt—something that a household, firm, or government *owes.* A **balance sheet** is a list of assets and liabilities.

Table 17.1 shows an example of a balance sheet—that for Rocky's Mountain Bikes. It lists three assets—cash in the bank, an inventory of bikes, and fixtures and fittings—that add up to $243,000. The balance sheet contains two liabilities—a bank loan of $120,000 and Rocky's equity of $123,000. Rocky's equity is the amount that the company owes to Rocky.

Financial Assets and Real Assets

Assets fall into two broad classes: financial and real. **Financial assets** are sophisticated IOUs—pieces of paper that represent a claim against another household, firm, or government. When you hold an IOU, it means that somebody else owes you money. Similarly, if you own a financial asset, someone else has a financial liability—owes you money. For example, the savings deposit that you own (your asset) is a liability of your bank. The difference between financial assets and financial liabilities is called **net financial assets.** Net financial assets are the net value of the paper claims that one household, firm, or government has against everyone else.

Real assets are physical things such as buildings, plant and equipment, inventories, and consumer durable goods. Real assets are also called capital. **Capital** is the real assets owned by a household, firm, or government.

Table 17.2 illustrates the distinction between financial assets and real assets by again presenting the information contained in the balance sheet of Rocky's Mountain Bikes. But this time the information is sorted into financial and real items. The financial items in the balance sheet are the cash in bank (an asset) and the bank loan and Rocky's equity (liabilities). To calculate net financial assets, we have to subtract financial liabilities from financial assets, so the bank loan and Rocky's equity appear with negative signs. The net financial assets of Rocky's Mountain Bikes are −$225,000. The real assets are the inventory of bikes and the fixtures and fittings—the firm's capital—which add up to $225,000.

Capital and Investment

All the assets and liabilities recorded in a balance sheet are stocks. A **stock** is a quantity measured at a point in time. An example of a stock is the amount of water in Lake Powell at a given moment. Capital is a stock because it is the quantity of buildings, plant, and machinery in existence at a given point in time.

Table 17.1 Balance Sheet of Rocky's Mountain Bikes

Assets		Liabilities	
Cash in bank	$ 18,000	Bank loan	$120,000
Inventory of bikes	15,000	Rocky's equity	123,000
Fixtures and fittings	210,000	Total liabilities	$243,000
Total assets	$243,000		

A related concept to the stock of capital is the flow of investment. A **flow** measures a quantity per unit of time. An example of a flow is the number of gallons of water per hour passing from the San Juan and Colorado Rivers into Lake Powell. It is a flow that adds to the stock of water in the lake. **Investment** is the amount of new capital equipment purchased in a given time period. It is a flow that adds to the stock of capital.

There is another flow that reduces the stock of capital—like the water flowing out of Lake Powell into the Colorado River. That flow is called depreciation. **Depreciation** is the fall in the value of capital resulting from its use and from the passage of time. Investment adds to the capital stock; depreciation lowers the capital stock. The net change in the capital stock is the difference between investment and depreciation. To emphasize this fact, we distinguish between **gross investment,** the value of all the new capital purchased in a given time period and **net investment,** which equals gross investment minus depreciation.

Table 17.2 Financial Assets and Real Assets of Rocky's Mountain Bikes

Financial assets	
Cash in bank	$ 18,000
Bank loan	− 120,000
Rocky's equity	− 123,000
Net financial assets	−$225,000
Real assets	
Inventory of bikes	$ 15,000
Fixtures and fittings	210,000
Capital	$225,000

Saving and Portfolio Choice

The quantity of capital supplied results from people's saving decisions. Saving is the opposite of consuming. **Saving** is income minus consumption. The sum of a household's past saving, together with any inheritances it has received, is the household's **wealth.** Wealth is allocated across a variety of financial and real assets in a manner described by the household's balance sheet. A household's choice regarding how much to hold in various assets and how much to owe in various liabilities is called a **portfolio choice.** For example, if a household decides to borrow $100,000 from a bank and to use that $100,000 to buy stocks in a corporation, the household is making a portfolio choice. It is choosing the amount of an asset (the equity in a corporation) and the amount of a liability (the bank loan).

In everyday language, we often refer to the purchase of stocks and bonds as investment. That everyday use of the word investment can cause confusion in economic analysis. It is to avoid that confusion that we use the term *portfolio choice* to refer to the choices that households make in allocating their wealth across the various assets available to them. We reserve the word *investment* to refer to the purchases of new real assets by firms and households.

We can illustrate the concepts of saving, wealth, and portfolio choice by looking at Rocky's *personal*

Table 17.3 Rocky's Income, Consumption, Saving, and Wealth

	Income	Consumption	Savings	Wealth
Initial net worth				$150,000
Year 1	$58,000	$50,000	$8000	158,000

situation—at Rocky's household balance sheet. Rocky has an initial wealth of $150,000 (see Table 17.3). During year 1, Rocky earns an income of $58,000, consumes $50,000, and saves $8000. His wealth rises to $158,000.

How has Rocky allocated his wealth among the various assets and liabilities? Table 17.4 separates out Rocky's financial assets and liabilities from his real assets. His financial assets include, first of all, his equity in Rocky's Mountain Bikes. Second, Rocky has some cash in the bank. This is his own personal bank account and is completely separate from the cash in the bike business. Third, Rocky has a mortgage on his home of $140,000 and a bank loan of $10,000 secured by the value of his car. Rocky's personal net financial assets are −$17,000. Note the minus sign. It tells us that Rocky *owes* $17,000 more than he owns—his net financial assets are negative.

Rocky's real assets are his house (valued at $160,000), and his car (valued at $15,000), so his capital stock is $175,000. Rocky's wealth is the sum of his capital stock and his net financial assets. Since Rocky's net financial assets are negative (he owes more than he owns), his wealth is his capital stock minus what he owes—$158,000.

With exactly the same savings, investment, and wealth, Rocky could have chosen a different portfolio allocation. For example, he could have used his bank deposit to pay off part of his bank loan or part of his mortgage. Alternatively, he could have taken a bigger mortgage and a smaller bank loan. Savings and investment decisions determine how much wealth a person has. Portfolio decisions determine how that wealth is held and financed.

Table 17.4 Rocky's Financial Assets and Real Assets at End of Year 1

Financial assets	
Equity in Rocky's Mountain Bikes	$123,000
Cash in bank	10,000
Mortgage	− 140,000
Car loan	− 10,000
Net financial assets	−$ 17,000
Real assets	
House	$160,000
Car	15,000
Capital	$175,000
Wealth	$158,000

R E V I E W

There are two kinds of assets: financial and real. Financial assets are the paper claims that lenders have on borrowers. One person's financial asset is another person's financial liability. Real assets are buildings, plant and equipment, and inventories. Physical capital is the stock of real assets in existence at a point in time. Additions to the stock of capital are called investment. Capital wears out over time. This process is called depreciation. The quantity of capital supplied results from people's saving decisions. Saving is income minus consumption. The accumulated sum of past saving is wealth. The allocation of wealth among different assets and liabilities is called a portfolio choice. ■

Capital Markets in the United States Today

Capital markets are the channel whereby savings are translated into investment—into the accumulation of capital. There are three broad ways in which investment takes place:

- Households buy capital.
- Firms buy capital and finance it by selling stocks and bonds to households.
- Firms buy capital and finance it by loans from financial intermediaries who in turn take in households' savings.

Figure 17.1 illustrates the structure of capital markets and the financing of investment. The green arrows in the figure show that households can employ their savings (allocate their portfolio of wealth) in the three ways just listed.

- They can directly own firms (proprietorships and partnerships).
- They can buy stocks or bonds issued by firms.
- They can place deposits with financial intermediaries.

Financial intermediaries are firms whose principal business is taking deposits, making loans, and buying securities. The best known type of financial intermediary is a commercial bank. A **commercial bank** is a financial intermediary that takes deposits and makes loans. There is another important type of bank called an investment bank. An **investment bank** is a bank that trades in firms' equities and bonds. (The distinction between a commercial bank and an investment bank is a legal one made by the Glass-Steagall Act passed in 1932.)

Other important types of financial intermediaries are insurance companies and savings and loan associations. Insurance companies take in the savings of households and provide life insurance and pen-

Figure 17.1 Capital Market Flows

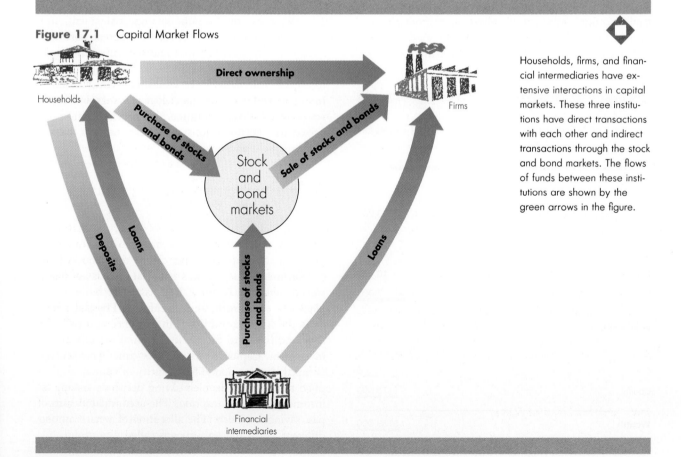

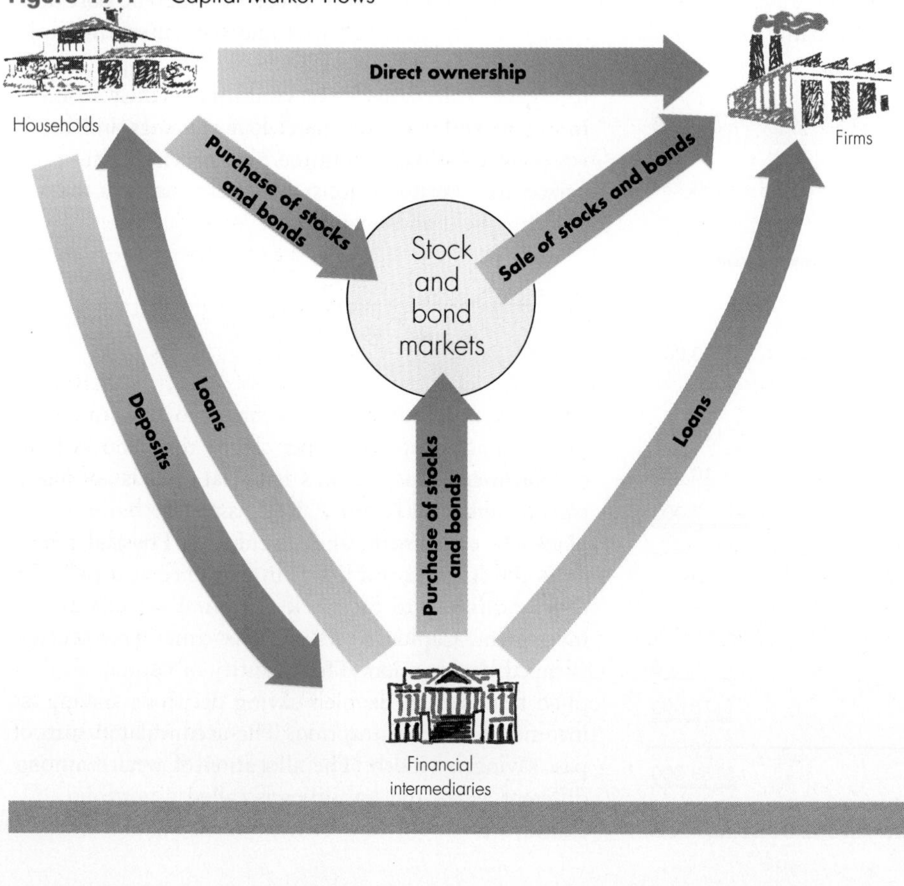

Households, firms, and financial intermediaries have extensive interactions in capital markets. These three institutions have direct transactions with each other and indirect transactions through the stock and bond markets. The flows of funds between these institutions are shown by the green arrows in the figure.

sions. They lend the money received from households to firms by buying equity or bonds. Savings and loan associations take in savings from households and make loans, mainly back to households in the form of mortgages.

Coordinating the actions of households, firms, and financial intermediaries are the markets for stocks and bonds. The **stock market** is the market in which the equities of firms are traded. The **bond market** is the market in which the bonds issued by firms and governments are traded. (Governments are not shown in the figure but are important participants in the bond market.) The distinction between equity and bonds was made in Chapter 9 (pp. 211–216). Firms sell stocks and bonds in exchange for money to finance their investment. Governments also sell bonds to finance their budget deficits. Households and financial intermediaries buy new stocks and bonds and also buy and sell existing stocks and bonds.

The direct ownership of capital by a household is the riskiest portfolio choice. It is placing all one's eggs in a single basket. For instance, if Rocky's bike firm fails, his household loses its wealth. If the bike firm succeeds, Rocky can earn an enormous return. Buying stocks such as shares in IBM or bonds in General Electric, is the second most risky way of allocating one's wealth. By holding a diverse collection of stocks, a household can spread its risk and avoid the extremes that can occur from lending to a single firm or a single project. Even so, there is still some risk because stock prices fluctuate. When stock prices fall, a household loses some of its wealth. Nevertheless, buying stocks is a much safer portfolio choice than putting everything into a single firm or project.

Bonds are less risky than stocks but their prices also fluctuate, so they are not a completely safe group of assets to hold.

The safest place to put one's wealth is depositing it into a financial intermediary. The risk associated with this portfolio choice is that a financial intermediary may make bad loans and be unable to repay its depositors. Although financial intermediaries fail on occasion, such failures are rare. Furthermore, deposit insurance provides guarantees in the event of a failure.

The Nation's Balance Sheet

How large are the U.S. capital markets? How big a role do the various elements play? The borrowing and lending pictured in Fig. 17.1 can be measured in the nation's balance sheet. This balance sheet lists the assets and liabilities of each of the major groups of agents in the economy—households, financial intermediaries, firms and governments. Figure 17.2 provides a picture of those balance sheets. The data, in trillions of dollars, are from December 31, 1984, and are the most recent available. Assets are shown in blue and liabilities in red. The green arrows show the direction of the flow of funds.

First look at the households. They have financial assets in the form of deposits with financial intermediaries, savings in life insurance and pension funds, and holdings of equity and bonds. The total of these items is \$6.2 trillion. Households have financial liabilities in the form of mortgages and consumer credit totalling \$1.7 trillion. Total financial assets of households exceed their liabilities by \$4.5 trillion, that is \$6.2 trillion less \$1.7 trillion. Households own real assets in the form of houses and consumer durable goods valued at a total of \$4.2 trillion (\$3.0 trillion in houses plus \$1.2 trillion in consumer durables). Total household wealth is the sum of net financial assets and real assets and is \$8.7 trillion.

Next look at the financial intermediaries. Their liabilities are the deposits and life insurance and pension funds, which we have just seen as the assets of households. They are liabilities of financial intermediaries because the financial intermediaries "owe" them to households. The assets of financial intermediaries represent loans by these institutions to households, firms, and governments. Financial intermediaries make loans to households in the form of mortgages and consumer credit. The financial intermediaries make loans to firms and governments as a result of purchasing bonds issued by these institutions. Financial intermediaries also make mortgage loans to firms. These bond purchases and mortgages provide firms and governments with funds to buy real assets. The financial assets and liabilities of financial intermediaries are each \$4.2 trillion.

The financial liabilities of firms—bonds (\$1.3 trillion), mortgages (\$0.4 trillion), and equity (\$1.5 trillion)—totaling \$3.2 trillion—are matched by their capital (real assets)—plant and equipment (\$1.5 trillion) and buildings (\$1.7 trillion).

Government financial liabilities (bonds) generate funds to finance the purchase of plant and equipment and buildings. The value of the government sector's real assets exceeds the value of its liabilities, and the difference is the wealth of the government sector.

Figure 17.2 The Nation's Balance Sheet

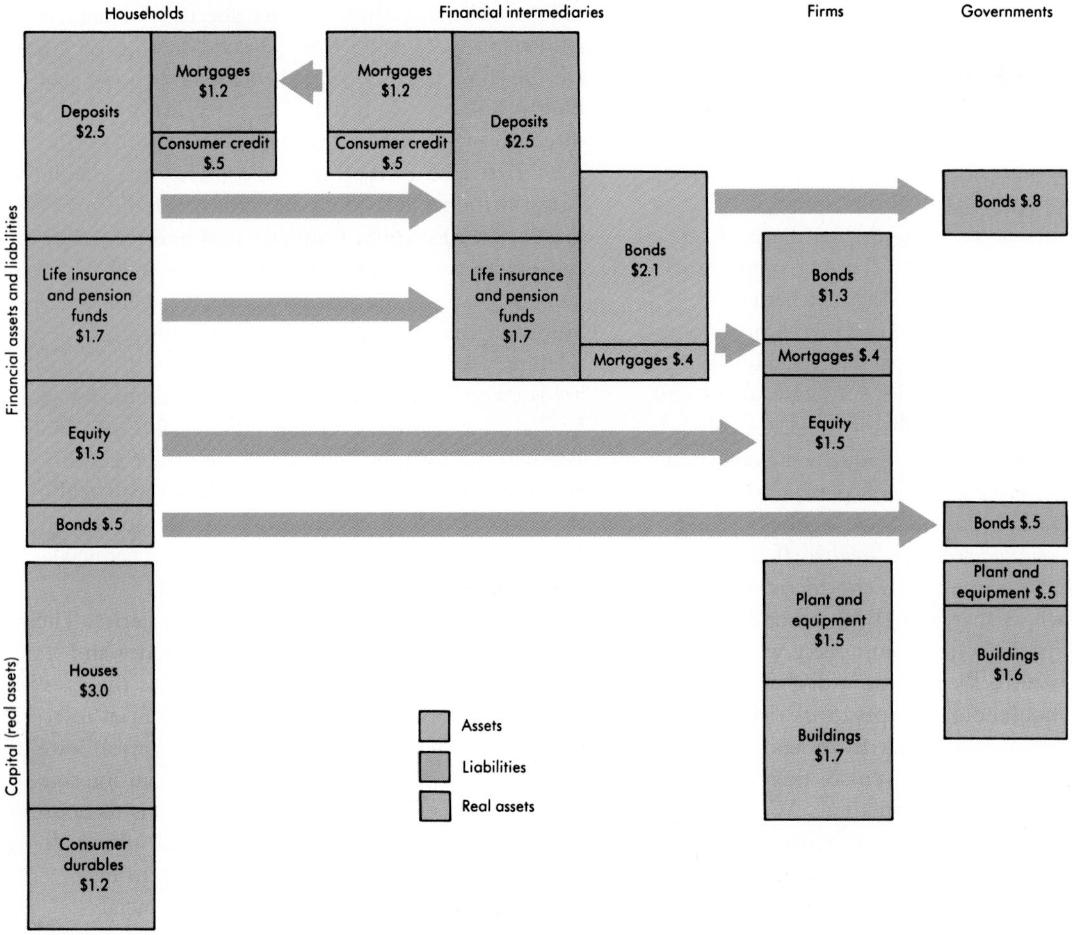

The nation's balance sheet records the indebtedness between the sectors of the economy—households, financial intermediaries, firms, and governments. The financial assets (blue) and liabilities (red) are shown in the top part of the figure, and real assets or capital (orange) appear in the bottom part. All numbers are trillions of dollars.

Households' financial assets are deposits with financial intermediaries, life insurance and pension funds, equity, and bonds. These assets are the liabilities of financial intermediaries, firms, and governments. Financial intermediaries take deposits and life insurance and pension fund contributions from households. Then they lend some of these funds back to households as mortgages and consumer credit; the remainder is lent to firms and governments in the form of bonds and mortgages. Both firms and governments borrow from financial intermediaries and households.

Capital (real assets) consists of houses and consumer durables owned by households and of plant and equipment and buildings owned by firms and governments.

Source: Statistical Abstract of the United States: 1986, 106th ed. p. 488.

The numbers in Fig. 17.2 give you an idea of the scale of the operations of the various elements in the capital markets. But they do not provide a flavor of the huge volume of transactions that take place—the flow of activity each day—nor of the dynamic change over time in the scale of capital market transactions. The daily turnover in the ownership of stocks and bonds is enormous. On an average day in 1987, more than 200 million individual stocks changed hands on the New York Stock Exchange. On what has come to be called Black Monday—October 19, 1987—a record 605 million shares were traded.

Demand for Capital

The demand for capital, like the demand for any other input, stems from firms' profit-maximization choices. As a firm increases the quantity of capital employed, other things being equal, the marginal revenue product of capital diminishes. To maximize profit, a firm uses additional amounts of capital until the marginal revenue product of capital equals the opportunity cost of a unit of capital. That is, the firm increases its capital stock until the additional total revenue generated by one extra unit of capital equals the opportunity cost of one unit of capital. When a firm rents capital equipment, its calculations are identical to those made to choose its labor input. The firm faces an hourly rate for renting a machine and it simply calculates the marginal revenue product of the machine per hour and compares that number with the hourly rental rate. Many machines are rented—for example, earth-moving equipment, cars, and airplanes—so these calculations are relevant in such cases.

But most capital is not rented. Firms *buy* buildings, plant, and equipment and operate them for several years. To decide how much capital equipment to buy, the firm must compare the price of the equipment to be paid, here and now, with the returns—the marginal revenue products—that the equipment will generate over its entire life. To see how a firm decides how much capital to buy, we need to convert the future stream of marginal revenue products into its present value so that it can be directly compared with the price of buying a new piece of capital equipment. You have already met the concept of present value in Chapter 9 (pp. 212–213) and you may like to flip back to it to refresh your memory before moving on.

Net Present Value of Investment

Let's calculate the present value of the marginal revenue product of a capital input and see how we can use the result to make an investment decision. Table 17.5 summarizes the data that we'll use.

Tina runs a firm called Taxfile, Inc. The firm sells advice to taxpayers designed to minimize the taxes that they have to pay. Tina is considering buying a new computer that will cost $10,000. The computer has a life of two years, after which it will be worthless. Although Tina works hard all year

Table 17.5 Net Present Value of an Investment—Taxfile, Inc.

(a) Data

Price of computer	$10,000
Life of computer	2 years
Marginal revenue product	$5900 at end of each year
Interest rate	4% a year

(b) Present value of the flow of marginal revenue product

$$PV = \frac{MRP}{1+r} + \frac{MRP}{(1+r)^2}$$

$$= \frac{\$5900}{1.04} + \frac{\$5900}{(1.04)^2}$$

$$= \$5673 + \$5455$$

$$= \$11{,}128$$

(c) Net present value of investment

$$NPV = PV \text{ of Marginal revenue product} - \text{Cost of computer}$$

$$= \$11{,}128 - \$10{,}000$$

$$= \$1128$$

studying tax law and writing sophisticated computer programs that will enable her to corner a good share of the market, she generates an income only once each year—at tax filing time. If she buys the computer that she is now evaluating, Tina expects to be able to sell tax advice in each of the next two years that will bring in $5900 at the end of each year. The interest rate that she has to pay is 4 percent a year.

We can calculate the present value of the marginal revenue product of Taxfile's computer by using a formula similar to the one that you met on p. 213. The formula is set out in Table 17.5(b). The present value *(PV)* of $5900 one year in the future is $5900 divided by 1.04 (one plus the interest rate expressed as a proportion—4 percent as a proportion is 0.04). The present value of $5900 two years in the future is $5900 divided by $(1.04)^2$. Working out those two present values and then adding them gives the present value of the flow of marginal revenue product from the machine as $11,128.

To decide whether or not to buy the computer, Tina compares the present value of its stream of marginal revenue product with its price. She makes this comparison by calculating the net present value *(NPV)* of the investment. The **net present value of an investment** is the present value of the stream of marginal revenue product generated by the investment minus the cost of the investment. If the net present value of an investment is positive, it pays to buy the item. If the net present value is negative, it does not pay to buy this item. Only investments that have a positive net present value increase a firm's net worth. Part (c) of Table 17.5 shows this calculation. The net present value of Tina's investment in a computer is $1128. Therefore the investment is worth undertaking and Tina buys the computer.

Whenever the net present value of an investment is positive, a firm will increase its net worth by making the investment. Like all other inputs, capital is subject to diminishing marginal returns. The more capital is added, the lower is its marginal product and the lower is its marginal revenue product. We have seen in the above example that it pays the firm to buy one machine because that investment yields a positive net present value. Should Tina invest in two computers or three? To answer this question, she must do more calculations similar to those summarized in Table 17.5.

Suppose, in particular, that Taxfile's investment opportunities are as set out in Table 17.6. Tina can buy any number of computers. They each cost $10,000 and have a life of two years. The marginal revenue product generated by each computer depends on how many Taxfile operates. If it operates just one computer, it has a marginal revenue product of $5900 a year (the case just reviewed). If Taxfile uses a second computer, marginal revenue product falls to $5600 a year, and in the case of a third computer to $5300 a year. Part (b) calculates the present value of the marginal revenue product of each of these three levels of investment in computers.

We have seen that with an interest rate of 4 percent it pays to invest in the first computer—the net present value of that computer is positive. It also pays to invest in a second computer. The present value of the marginal revenue product resulting from using two computers, $10,562, exceeds the cost of

Table 17.6 Taxfile's Investment Decision

(a) Data

Price of computer	$10,000
Life of computer	2 years
Marginal revenue product:	
Using 1 computer	$5900 a year
Using 2 computers	$5600 a year
Using 3 computers	$5300 a year

(b) Present value of the stream of marginal revenue product

If r = 0.04 (4% a year):

Using 1 computer:	$PV = \frac{5900}{1.04} + \frac{5900}{(1.04)^2} = \$11,128$
Using 2 computers:	$PV = \frac{5600}{1.04} + \frac{5600}{(1.04)^2} = \$10,562$
Using 3 computers:	$PV = \frac{5300}{1.04} + \frac{5300}{(1.04)^2} = \$\ 9996$

If r = 0.08 (8% a year):

Using 1 computer:	$PV = \frac{5900}{1.08} + \frac{5900}{(1.08)^2} = \$10,521$
Using 2 computers:	$PV = \frac{5600}{1.08} + \frac{5600}{(1.08)^2} = \$\ 9986$

If r = 0.12 (12% a year):

Using 1 computer:	$PV = \frac{5900}{1.12} + \frac{5900}{(1.12)^2} = \$\ 9971$

the second machine by $562. You can also see that it does *not* pay to invest in a third computer. The present value of the marginal revenue product resulting from using three computers is $9996. But the computer costs $10,000, so the net present value of the third computer is −$4. Tina buys a second computer but does not buy a third one. If she does, the net worth of Taxfile will fall by $4.

We have just discovered that at an interest rate of 4 percent a year it pays Tina to buy two computers but not three. Suppose that the interest rate is higher than 4 percent a year—say, 8 percent a year. In this case, the present value of one machine (see calculations in Table 17.6b) is $10,521. Therefore it still pays to buy the first machine. But its net present value is smaller when the interest rate is 8 percent than at the lower 4 percent interest rate. At an 8 percent interest rate, the net present value resulting from using two machines is negative. The present value of the marginal revenue product, $9986, is less than the $10,000 that the second computer costs. Therefore at an interest rate of 8 percent it pays Tina to buy one computer but not two.

Suppose that the interest rate is even higher, say, 12 percent a year. In this case, the present value of the marginal revenue product of one computer is $9971 (see Table 17.6b). At this interest rate, it does not pay to buy even one computer.

The calculations that you have just reviewed trace out Taxfile's demand schedule for capital. The demand schedule for capital shows the number of computers demanded by Taxfile at each rate of interest. As the interest rate falls, the quantity of capital demanded increases. At an interest rate of 12 percent a year, the firm demands no computers. At an interest rate of 8 percent a year, one computer is demanded; at 4 percent a year, the quantity demanded is two; and at an interest rate below 4 percent a year, the quantity demanded is three. (Although we have stopped our calculations at three computers, at lower interest rates Tina would buy yet more machines.)

Figure 17.3 A Firm's Demand for Capital

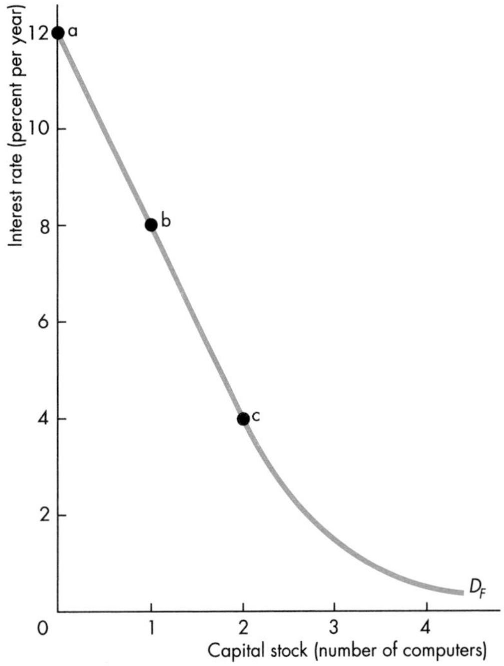

Taxfile demands capital (computers) until the present value of the stream of marginal revenue product of computers equals the price of a computer. The present value depends on the interest rate. The lower the interest rate, the higher the number of computers demanded. At an interest rate of 12 percent a year, Taxfile demands no computers (point *a*). At an interest rate of 8 percent, the firm demands 1 computer (point *b*). At an interest rate of 4 percent, the firm demands 2 computers (point *c*). If computers of different types (fractions of a $10,000 computer) can be bought, a demand curve that passes through points *a*, *b*, and *c* is generated.

Demand Curve for Capital

A firm's demand curve for capital relates the quantity of capital demanded to the interest rate. Figure 17.3 illustrates the demand for computers (D_F) by Tina's firm. The horizontal axis measures the number of computers that Taxfile owns and the vertical axis measures the interest rate. Points *a, b,* and *c* correspond to the example that we have just worked through. At an interest rate of 12 percent a year, it does not pay Tina to buy any computers—point *a*. At an interest rate of 8 percent, it pays to buy 1 computer—point *b*. At an interest rate of 4 percent, it pays to buy 2 computers—point *c*.

In our example, we've only considered one type of computer—that which costs exactly $10,000. In practice, Tina could consider buying a different type of computer the power of which could be expressed as a multiple or fraction of one of the $10,000 computers that we've been considering here. For example, there may be a $5000 computer that has half

Figure 17.4 The Market Demand for Capital

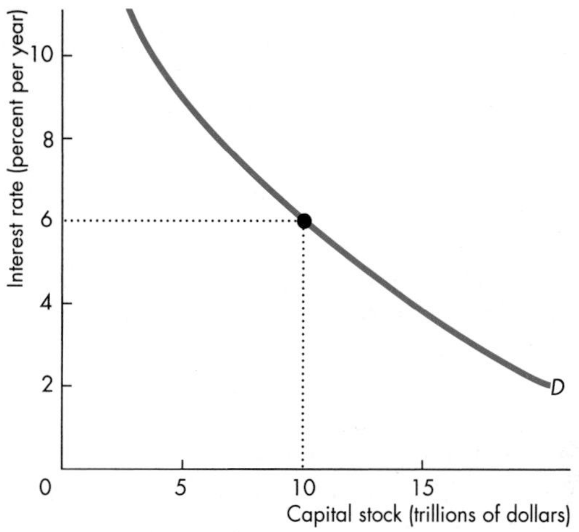

The market demand curve for capital is obtained by adding together the demand curve for capital of all the firms in the economy. An example of a market demand curve is *D*. On this demand curve, the quantity of capital demanded is $10 trillion when the interest rate is 6 percent a year, and the quantity of capital demanded falls as the interest rate rises, other things being equal.

the power of a $10,000 machine. Or a bigger machine costing $12,500 that has one and a quarter times the power of a $10,000 machine. If we consider all the different types of computers that Tina can buy, we will generate not just the three points *a, b,* and *c* but an entire demand curve like that shown in the figure.

The market demand curve for capital is obtained by adding all the individual firm's demand curves. Since different firms demand different types of machines (and since even the same firm demands different types of machines), we have to use common units of measurement to calculate the market demand curve for capital. The dollar value is a convenient unit. The market demand curve is shown in Fig. 17.4. It measures the total quantity of capital demanded (in trillions of dollars) on the horizontal axis and the interest rate on the vertical axis. On that curve, at an interest rate of 6 percent per year the quantity of capital demanded is $10 trillion. Like the firm's demand curve, the market demand curve slopes down.

Changes in the Demand for Capital

The demand for capital is constantly changing and the demand curve for capital is constantly shifting. Also, the composition of the demand for capital is constantly changing, the demand for some types of capital increases while the demand for other types decreases. Technological change is the main force generating these changes in the demand for capital. For example, the development of diesel engines for railroad transportation resulted in a decrease in demand for steam engines, an increase in demand for diesel engines, and not much change in the overall demand for capital in the railroad industry. In contrast, the development of desktop computers has led to a large increase in demand for office and research computing equipment.

The general trend resulting from the development of new technology and its exploitation through innovation is for the demand for capital to steadily increase over time with a steady rightward shift of the demand curve for capital.

R E V I E W

The demand for capital is determined by firms' profit-maximizing choices. The marginal product of capital declines as the amount of capital used rises. As a consequence, the marginal revenue product of capital declines as more capital is used. Capital is demanded up to the point where the present value of its stream of marginal revenue products equals its price. The interest rate is an important factor in the present value calculation. The higher the interest rate, the lower is the present value of the stream of marginal revenue products.

The demand curve for capital is the relationship between the quantity of capital demanded and the interest rate. The higher the interest rate, the lower is the present value of the stream of marginal products and the smaller is the quantity of capital demanded by a firm. The demand curve for capital slopes downward. The demand for capital changes as a result of technological change. There is a general tendency for the demand for capital to increase over time with the demand curve for capital shifting to the right. ■

The Supply of Capital

The quantity of capital supplied results from the saving decisions of households. The most important factors determining a household's savings are:

- The household's current income in relation to its expected future income
- The interest rate

The stage in the household's life cycle is the major factor influencing whether current income is high or low compared with expected future income. Households typically smooth their consumption over the life cycle. Consumption smoothing is one of the main influences on the savings of a household. As we saw in Chapter 15 some young households typically have low current income compared with their expected future income, and older households have high income relative to expected future income; young people incur debts, older people save and accumulate assets. A household's savings depends on how much it smoothes its consumption over the life cycle.

Interest Rate

There are two distinct effects of interest rates on the level of savings:

- Substitution effect
- Income effect

Substitution Effect A higher interest rate increases the future payoff from today's saving. It therefore increases the opportunity cost of current consumption. Thus a higher interest rate encourages people to economize on current consumption and take advantage of the higher interest rate available on savings. As the interest rate rises, people substitute higher future consumption for current consumption, and savings increase.

Income Effect A change in the interest rate changes people's incomes. Other things being equal, the higher a person's income, the higher is the level of current consumption and the higher are the levels of future consumption and of saving.

The effect of a change in the interest rate on income depends on whether a person is a borrower or a lender. For a lender—a person with positive net financial assets—an increase in interest rates increases income, so the income effect is positive. The income effect reinforces the substitution effect and a higher interest rate results in higher savings.

For a borrower—a person with negative net financial assets—an increase in interest rates decreases the income available for consumption. In this case, the income effect is negative—higher interest rates lower consumption and savings. The income effect works in a direction opposite to that of the substitution effect and savings may decrease.

Supply Curve of Capital

The supply of capital is the total stock of accumulated savings by a household. The supply curve of capital shows the relationship between the quantity of capital supplied and the interest rate. We've seen that this relationship depends on the relative strengths of the income effect and the substitution effect, and for an individual household may be either positive or negative. For the economy as a whole, however, the substitution effect is stronger than the income effect, so a higher interest rate encourages saving and the supply curve of capital is upward-sloping. Figure 17.5 illustrates the supply curve of capital. On that

Figure 17.5 The Supply of Capital

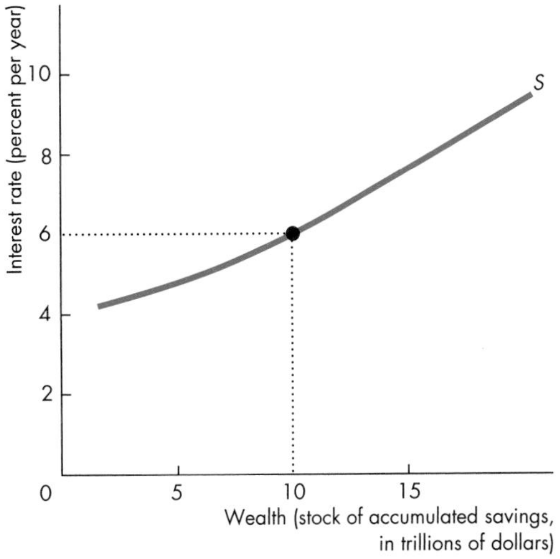

The higher the interest rate, the more capital households supply—the supply curve of capital slopes upward. At an interest rate of 6 percent a year, the quantity of capital supplied is $10 trillion.

curve, at an interest rate of 6 percent per year, the quantity of capital supplied is $10 trillion.

Changes in the Supply of Capital

The supply of capital changes constantly. The main influences on the supply of capital are demographic. As the population changes and as its age distribution changes, so does the supply of capital. A population with a larger proportion of young people has a smaller supply of capital than a population with a larger proportion of middle-aged people. The age distribution of the population affects the supply of capital as a result of the life-cycle consumption smoothing described above.

Another influence on the supply of capital is the average income level. The higher the level of income, the larger is the supply of capital. A growing population and steadily rising income result in the supply of capital curve gradually shifting to the right over time.

Portfolio Choices

Households have to choose not only how much to save (the total quantity of capital to supply) but also how to allocate their savings across various financial assets—which financial assets to hold.

In making portfolio choices, households take account of two primary factors:

- Relative interest rates
- Relative degrees of risk

Relative Interest Rates Other things being equal, the higher the interest rate on a particular asset, the more of that asset and the less of other assets will households choose to hold. For example, if the interest rate on bonds is 10 percent a year and on equities 5 percent a year, households will want to switch their portfolios away from holding equities and into holding bonds. If the gap widens even further so that bonds are yielding 12 percent a year and equities 3 percent a year, households will want to switch out of equities and hold even more bonds.

If the interest rates on equities and bonds are identical and if all other things are equal, then households will be indifferent between putting their wealth into bonds or equities.

Relative Degrees of Riskiness In general, when comparing two securities, there are more things to take into account than their interest rates. The certainty with which those interest rates are available is also an important consideration. To make this clear, suppose that you have the following two choices:

1. Put your money in the bank for a guaranteed interest rate of 5 percent a year.
2. Lend your money to a friend who has an exciting business idea. If his business succeeds, he will pay you back with interest at a rate of 150 percent. If his business fails, not only will he pay you no interest, he will not even give you your original money back.

The first option has no risk. For every dollar you put in the bank you will have $1.05 one year from now for sure. The second option has a great deal of risk. To compare this second risky project with the first safe project, you need to calculate the expected interest rate that you would make and also to make some assessment of the degree of risk. Suppose that your friend has been involved in several other business ventures and you know from experience that half of them succeeded and the other half failed. Let's suppose also that you have no reason to expect this project to be any different from the others. If you were to put your savings into a large number of your friend's projects, half of the time you'd lose your savings and the other half of the time you'd receive $2.50 on every dollar put into these projects. On the average, you would receive $1.25 on each dollar. You will expect an interest rate of 25 percent on your financial stake in your friend's projects. Whether an interest rate of 25 percent with a lot of risk is better or worse than an interest rate of 5 percent with no risk is something that only you can decide. It depends on your attitude toward risk. Some people feel that the risk is worth taking. Others would rather sleep well at night. In general, the wealthier the person and the larger the number of projects they can put their savings into, the more willing they are to take risks on any individual project. But one thing is clear: The higher the degree of risk, the higher is the interest rate required to make a project worthwhile.

REVIEW

The quantity of capital supplied is determined by households' saving decisions. Savings depend on the amount of consumption smoothing the household undertakes over its life cycle and the interest rate. The more the household smoothes its consumption and the higher the interest rate, the larger the amount people save. The supply curve of capital is the relationship between the interest rate and the quantity of capital supplied. It slopes upward—the higher the interest rate, the larger the quantity of capital supplied, other things being equal. The supply of capital changes as a result of changes in the population and its age composition, and the level of income. Increasing population and increasing income result in a steady increase in the supply of capital—with the supply curve shifting steadily to the right.

People allocate their savings to different types of assets depending on relative interest rates and relative degrees of risk. Other things being equal, the higher the interest rate and the lower the riskiness of a particular asset, the larger the amount of savings people will allocate to that asset. ■

Now that we have studied the demand for and supply of capital, we can bring these two sides of the capital market together and study the determination of interest rates and asset prices. We'll then be able to answer some of the questions posed at the beginning of this chapter about the stock market and understand the forces that produce stock market booms and crashes.

Interest Rates and Asset Prices

Households' saving plans and firms' investment plans are coordinated through capital markets. Asset prices and interest rates adjust to make these plans compatible. We are now going to study the way in which these market forces work. And we are going to discover what determines the stock market value of a firm.

Two Sides of the Same Coin

Interest rates and asset prices can be viewed as two sides of the same coin. We'll look first at interest rates, then at asset prices, and finally at the connection between them. Some assets, such as bank deposits, earn a guaranteed interest rate. Other assets, such as bonds and shares in the stocks of firms, do not. The interest rates on these assets are usually called bond yields and stock yields. A **bond yield** is the interest on a bond, expressed as a percentage of the price of the bond. A **stock yield** is the income from a share in the stock of a firm, expressed as a percentage of the price of the share—the stock market price. A bond earns a guaranteed dollar income, but its market price fluctuates and hence its yield also fluctuates. A share in the stock of a firm earns a dividend based on the profitability of the firm. Also the stock market value of the share fluctuates. Thus a stock yield fluctuates for two reasons—fluctuations in the dividend and fluctuations in its stock market price.

Let's now look at the two sides of the same coin—the price of an asset and its yield or interest rate. To calculate a bond yield or stock yield, we divide the earnings of the asset by the price paid for it. For example, if Taxfile, Inc., pays a dividend of $5 a share and if a share can be bought for $50, the stock yield will be 10 percent ($5 divided by $50, expressed as a percent). It follows from this calculation that for a given amount of earnings, the higher the price of an asset, the lower its yield. For example, if the price of a share in Taxfile increases to $100 but its dividend remains constant at $5, its yield falls to 5 percent. This connection between the price of an asset and its yield or interest rate means that we can study the market forces in capital markets as simultaneously determining asset yields (interest rates) and asset prices. We will first look at capital market equilibrium in terms of interest rate (or yield) determination and then in terms of the stock market value of a particular firm.

Equilibrium Interest Rate

Figure 17.6 brings together the relevant parts of the previous analysis of the demand for and supply of capital. The diagram shows the entire capital market. The horizontal axis measures the total quantity of capital. Notice that the axis is labeled "Capital stock

Figure 17.6 Capital Market Equilibrium

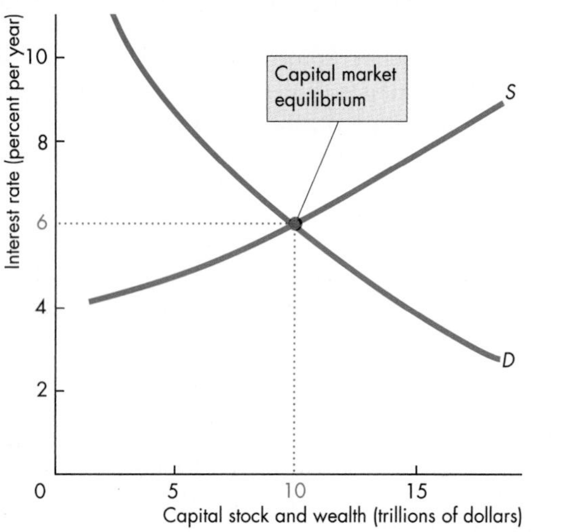

Capital market equilibrium occurs when the interest rate is such that the quantity of capital demanded equals the quantity of capital supplied. The demand curve is *D* and the supply curve is *S*. These curves intersect at an interest rate of 6 percent a year and a capital stock of $10 trillion.

and wealth." This label emphasizes the fact that the value of the capital stock and of wealth are equivalent. The vertical axis measures the interest rate. The demand curve *(D)* is the market demand for capital that you met in Fig. 17.4. The supply curve *(S)* is the market supply of capital shown in Fig. 17.5.

Capital market equilibrium occurs where the quantity of capital supplied equals the quantity of capital demanded. In Fig. 17.6, this equilibrium occurs at an interest rate of 6 percent a year where $10 trillion of capital is supplied and demanded. The market forces that bring about the equilibrium are exactly the same as those that we have discussed in the context of the markets for goods and services. In the case of the capital market, there are organized institutions, banks, insurance companies, and specialized dealers that constantly trade, thus maintaining equality between the quantity of capital demanded and quantity supplied.

The interest rate determined in Fig. 17.6 is the *average* interest rate. Interest rates on individual assets will be distributed around that average, based on the relative degree of riskiness of individual assets. An asset with a high degree of risk will earn an interest rate that exceeds the average and a very safe asset will earn an interest rate that is below the average. For example, if the average interest rate is 6 percent a year as shown in Fig. 17.6, the interest rate on a bank deposit might be 4 percent a year (a safer asset) and that on equities 8 percent a year (riskier assets).

We've now seen how asset yields or interest rates are determined. Let's look at the other side of the coin—asset prices. To determine asset prices, we will change our focus and look not at the capital market in aggregate but at the stock market value of an individual firm.

Stock Market Value of a Firm

We've seen that there is a connection between an asset's yield (or interest rate) and that asset's price. The yield is the earnings on the asset divided by its price (expressed as a percent). Let's use this fact to work out the stock market value of a firm. Suppose that a firm finances its purchases of capital by selling shares of its stock. What determines the price of a share? What determines the total value of all the shares sold?

The value of a share depends on the total value of the firm and on the number of shares sold. The value of one share is equal to the value of a firm divided by the number of shares sold, or, equivalently, the value of the firm is equal to the value of one share multiplied by the number of shares sold. So for a firm with a given number of shares, asking what determines the price of a share is the same as asking what determines the value of the firm?

When a person buys a share in the stock of a firm, that person becomes entitled to receive a profit each year. The price of a share depends on the expected future profit to be paid out by the firm. As we discovered in Chapter 9 (pp. 215–216) when we looked at the value of a share in Wisconsin Toy, the price of a share is the present value of its expected future profit. If a firm is expected to pay out no profits at all in the future, its shares will be worthless. If it is expected to pay out $10 a year on a share and if the interest rate is 10 percent a year, its shares will be worth $100 each. If it is expected to pay out $20 a year on a share and the interest rate is 10 percent, its shares will be worth $200 each.

The price of a share is determined by current expectations of the future profitability of the firm. Stockholders must therefore form expectations about future profit. How do they go about that task?

Rational Expectations

We defined a rational expectation in Chapter 6 (pp. 139) as the best forecast that can be made on the basis of all the available and relevant information. To make a rational expectation about future profit, it is necessary to make a forecast of the future profitability of the firm.

Stockholders calculate the profitability of a firm by making forecasts of conditions in the firm's output markets, input markets, and the technological developments that will influence the firm. For example, forecasts are made of the demand for the firm's product, the degree of competition that it faces, new cost-saving technologies that might become available to it, and the prices of the inputs that it employs to produce a good. Armed with forecasts of all these things, stockholders can forecast the future profit of the firm. By discounting the forecasted future profit, stockholders can calculate the price that it is worth paying today for a share of the stock of the firm.

Price-Earnings Ratio

A commonly used measure to describe the performance of a firm's stock is its price-earnings ratio. A *price-earnings ratio* is the current price of a share in a firm's stock divided by the most recent year's profit per share. In 1982, the average price-earnings ratio of the stocks that formed the Dow-Jones Industrial Average was 8.1. By 1987, the price-earnings ratio had risen to 20.5, but that was a peak year. The ratio then fell off and, at the beginning of 1989, stood at about 12.

What determines a price-earnings ratio? Why, at the beginning of 1989, was Ford's price-earnings ratio only 5 while Sony's was 33?

We have seen that the price of a share of stock is determined by the present value of the expected future profit of the firm. The higher the *expected future* profit, the higher is *today's* price. The price-earnings ratio of a firm depends on its current profit in relation to its expected future profit. When expected future profit is high relative to current profit, the price-earnings ratio is high. When expected future profit is low relative to current profit, the price-earnings ratio is low. Fluctuations in the price-earnings ratio arise from fluctuations in expected future profit relative to current profit.

Stock Market Volume and Prices

Sometimes the prices quoted on the stock market rise or fall with little trading taking place. At other times, stock market prices rise or fall with an enormous volume of trading. On yet other occasions, there is little change in the stock prices but there is an enormous volume of trading. Why do stock prices rise or fall and what determines the volume of trading on the stock market?

Stock prices rise and fall because of changes in expectations of future profit. Consider the firm whose profit per share is $1. Suppose that the interest rate on assets that are as risky as a share of this firm's stock is 8 percent a year. Further suppose that the firm's profit in each future year is expected to be exactly the same as this year's. The price of the firm's stock will adjust until a share can be bought for the price that makes the stock yield equal to 8 percent a year. That price is $12.50. People will buy shares in this company for $12.50 and expect, on the average, to make $1 a share each year, or a stock yield of 8 percent ($1 is 8 percent of $12.50). The price-earnings ratio will be 12.5—today's price ($12.50) divided by last year's profit ($1 per share).

Suppose that market conditions change and people now expect the firm's profit to double to $2 per share starting next year. With an expected profit of $2 a share, the stock market price jumps to $25. It's true that at $25 a share this year's profit ($1 per share) represents only a 4 percent stock yield ($1 is 4 percent of $25), but with profit expected to be $2 per share next year and every year thereafter, the expected yield is 8 percent a year—the interest rate available on other assets of similar risk. This price jump to $25 occurs with no change in the current year's profitability of the firm. It occurs entirely because people observe some event today that leads them to expect higher profit in the future.

Suppose that the change in market conditions leading to expected higher future profit is so obvious that everyone can see it and everyone agrees that this firm's earnings are indeed going to double next year. In such a situation, the market value of the firm's shares rises to $25 but no one buys or sells shares. Stockholders are happy with the shares that they already hold. If the price does not rise to $25, everyone will want to buy some shares. If the price rises to more than $25, everyone will want to sell some shares. If the price rises to exactly $25, everyone will be indifferent between hanging on to those shares or buying some other shares that are currently yielding 8 percent a year.

On the other hand, suppose that the event that changed expectations about this firm's profitability is difficult to interpret. Some people think the event will lead to a rise in the firm's profit and others think it will not have any effect on profit. Let's call the first group optimists and the second group pessimists. The optimists will want to buy the stock and will be willing to do so as long as its price is less than $25. The pessimists will sell the stock as long as its price is above $12.50. In such a situation, the pessimists will sell out and the optimists will buy in. The price will not necessarily change, but there will be a large volume of trading activity. What causes the trading activity is the disagreement, not the event that triggered the change in expected profitability. High volume of trading on the stock market implies a large amount of disagreement. Large price changes with low volume of trading imply a great deal of agreement that something fundamental has changed. A large volume of trading with hardly any price change means that the underlying changes are difficult to interpret: Some people predict that things will move in one direction while others predict the opposite.

Reading Between the Lines (pp. 456–458) looks at the long upswing in the stock market that occurred between 1982 and 1987 and illustrates some of the principles that you've just studied.

Takeovers and Mergers

The theory of capital markets that you've now studied can be used to explain why takeovers and mergers occur. A **takeover** is the purchase of the stock of one firm by another firm. A takeover occurs when the stock market value of a firm is lower than the present value of the expected future profit from operating the firm. For example, suppose that Taxfile Inc., has a stock market value of $120,000. But suppose also that the present value of the future profit of the firm is $150,000. It will pay for someone to try to take over the firm. Takeover activity affects the price of a firm and often the threat of a takeover drives the price to the point at which the takeover is no longer profitable.

There are other takeover situations in which the expected future profit of a firm depends on the firm taking it over. A recent example illustrates this point very well. The Atari Computer Company was having difficulty in breaking into the retail computer market on the scale that it desired. To overcome its problems, Atari searched out, surprisingly, a retail chain that was losing money. The present value of a firm that is making a loss is less than the value of its plant and equipment. So, Atari was able to buy retail outlets for a lower price from its current owners than it could have done by starting afresh. Atari believed that by buying the firm and using its retail stores to sell Atari computers, Atari could convert that firm's loss into a profit.

A **merger** is the combining of the assets of two firms to form a single, new firm. Mergers take place when two firms perceive that by combining their assets, they can increase their combined stock market values. For example, the merger of Piedmont and U.S. Air enabled the resulting firm to increase its profit by integrating their routes and schedules.

REVIEW

Saving plans and investment plans are coordinated through capital markets. Adjustments in asset prices and interest rates make the saving plans and investment plans compatible. Interest rates and asset prices are two sides of the same coin. The interest rate on an asset is the income on the asset divided by its price. The average interest rate makes the quantity of capital demanded equal to the quantity of savings supplied.

The value of a share of a firm's stock is determined by the firm's current and expected future profit. Expected future profit is based on rational expectations of future prices, costs, and technologies that the firm will face. The stock market value of a firm is often expressed as a ratio of the firm's current profit per share—the price-earnings ratio. The price-earnings ratio depends on expected profit growth.

Stock market prices sometimes move dramatically and the volume of trading on the stock market is sometimes high and sometimes low. Prices change quickly when there are changes in expectations of future profitability. The volume of stock market trading rises when people disagree strongly about the future.

Mergers and takeovers occur when the stock market value of a firm is lower than the present value of the future profit stream that another firm believes it could generate with the first firm's assets. ■

The lessons that we've just learned about capital markets have wider application than explaining fluctuations in the stock market. They also enable us to understand how natural resource markets operate. These lessons are particularly important and interesting in the cases of exhaustible natural resources—resources that we are using up and will eventually use up completely. Let's now turn to this important range of issues.

Natural Resource Markets

Natural resources are the nonproduced factors of production with which we are endowed. Natural resources fall into two categories: exhaustible and nonexhaustible. **Exhaustible natural resources** are natural resources that can be used only once and that cannot be replaced once used. Examples of exhaustible natural resources are coal, natural gas, and oil—the so-called hydrocarbon fuels. **Nonexhaustible natural resources** are natural resources that can be used repeatedly without depleting what's available for future use. Examples of nonexhaustible natural resources are land, sea, rivers and lakes, rain and sunshine. Plants and animals are also examples of nonexhaustible natural resources. By careful cultivation and husbandry, more of these natural resources can be produced to replace those used up in production and consumption activities.

Natural resources have two important economic dimensions—a stock dimension and a flow dimension. There is a stock of each natural resource determined by nature and by the previous rate of use of the resource. The flow of a natural resource is the rate at which it is being used. This flow is determined by human choices and those choices determine whether a given stock of natural resources is used up quickly, slowly, or not at all. In studying the operation of natural resource markets, we'll begin by considering the stock dimension of a natural resource.

Supply and Demand in a Natural Resource Market

The stock of a natural resource supplied is the amount of the resource in existence. For an exhaustible natural resource, that amount is not influenced by the price of the resource. In such a case, the supply of the stock of the natural resource is perfectly inelastic. Its position depends on the amount of the resource available initially, and on the rate at which it has been used up in the past. The smaller the initial stock and the faster the rate of use, the smaller is the stock of a resource available.

The demand for a stock of a natural resource is one aspect of portfolio choice. People own stocks of natural resources as an alternative to owning equities in corporations, other financial assets such as bonds, or other real assets such as plant, equipment, and buildings.

The demand for a stock of a natural resource is determined in the same way as the demand for any other asset—by the income that it is expected to earn, expressed as an interest rate or yield. If the expected yield—or interest rate—on a stock of a natural resource exceeds that on other assets (with comparable risk), people will allocate more of their net worth to owning the natural resource and less to other assets. Conversely, if the expected interest rate on a natural resource falls short of that on other assets (with comparable risk), portfolios will be reallocated by selling the stock of a natural resource and buying other assets. When the yield, or interest rate, from owning a stock of a natural resource equals the yield on other comparably risky assets, there will be no tendency for people to either buy or sell stocks of natural resources or other assets. People will be satisfied with their existing portfolio allocation and with the quantity of the stock of the natural resource that they are holding.

Equilibrium occurs in the market for a stock of a natural resource when the price of the resource is *expected* to rise over time, at a rate equal to the interest rate. This proposition is known as the **Hotelling Principle.**[1] Why is the price of a

[1] The Hotelling Principle, discovered by Harold Hotelling, first appeared in "Economics of Exhaustible Resources," *Journal of Political Economy* 39 (April 1931): 137–75.

A Stock Market Boom

How Much Power Is Left in the Bull?

Conventional wisdom on Wall Street says the bull market began in August 1982. But not everyone agrees.

One respected market analyst dates the move from December 1974. Another professional views the five-year advance as part of a supercycle that began in 1932. Still another takes his cues from the stars and the moon, rather than rates and the economy; he sees the market's movements as a series of celestial-based cycles lasting three to eight weeks. . . .

Several experts say the market may go through a wrenching correction in the next few months, giving investors a rough ride. They differ on exactly when and where the market will top out, and they're more ready to say how high it will go than when it's going to get there. In many cases, their thoughts on when the bull market will end are linked to when they believe it began. Here's a sample of when some of them think that was, and what they see for the future.

1932: The current bull market is really the final phase of a big stock market move that began 55 years ago, says Mr. Prechter, author of an investment newsletter based on the Elliott wave theory, the mathematical application of crowd psychology to market behavior.

Yardsticks for the Rally

	CHG FROM 8/12/82	P/E 8/7/87
DJIA	+233.6%	20.5
S&P 500	+215.4	19.8
NYSE Composite	+207.6	18.9
Wilshire 5000	+202.4	19.6
Amex	+204.3	24.1
Nasdaq Composite	+171.3	23.5

Source: Wilshire Associates

He says large stock market moves occur in a series of five waves. If the trend is up, there are five sub-waves: up, down, up, down, up. . . .

The first wave was from 1932 to 1937, an advance that carried the stock market out of the Great Depression. From 1937 to 1942, the Dow Jones Industrial Average declined more than 50%. In the next 24 years, ending in 1966, stocks enjoyed a prolonged bull market. Mr. Prechter sees the 1966 to 1982 experience as "a sideways market." The fifth wave began in August 1982. Mr. Prechter . . . believes the Dow Jones Industrial Average can eventually reach 3600 to 3700 before the 1932 supercycle ends. But, the rally could be interrupted by a substantial correction, he warns. . . .

1974: Robert Farrell, chief technical analyst at Merrill Lynch Capital Markets, sees the bull market as a series of "theme stages.". . .

The first theme stage began in late 1974 and lasted through 1980. It was led by companies that benefited from accelerating inflation and the energy crisis, but that didn't make this stage "any less of a bull market," Mr. Farrell contends.

. . . The second stage [starting] in late 1981 [and] lasting through 1986 was the era of disinflation and lower interest rates and leaps in stock values. Low inflation made investors willing to pay more for companies' future profits. The market is now beginning a third stage, where earnings growth is the key, he says.

1982: The first sign this bull market started five years ago, says Philip Erlanger, a technical analyst with Advest Inc. in Hartford, Conn., was that the Dow Jones Transportation Average finally broke through a level it had been bumping against for 15 years.

Mr. Erlanger reasons that transportation companies foreshadow major positive shifts in the economy. The fortunes of railroads, truckers and airlines begin to brighten as they start to haul the raw materials that manufacturers need. Later on, they transport the finished goods.

His charts showed the action in the transportation stocks was similar to the start of what he calls the 1949–1966 bull market. So he estimated this advance could be as strong and long-lived.

Archibald Crawford, an investment newsletter writer in New York City, believes the heavens dictated the start of the bull market in 1982. And now he's expecting some momentous happenings in the galaxy to signal an eventful close in the weeks ahead. Among the powerful events in the sky, Mr. Crawford says, there will be a solar eclipse on the fall equinox and five planets will be lined up in a tight conjunction for six days. "We'll be in for a decline," he declares.

Whatever the causes of great market moves, the stars may be as good as any other guide for charting their beginnings and ends. On Aug. 13, 1982—Friday the 13th—the Dow Jones Industrial Average closed at 788.05, up 11.13. It was the first daily gain in a week, but on that day, most seers saw gloom, not hope. Many were forecasting a renewed decline to as low as 700. Hardly a one would have believed, much less foretold, that a run to 2600 or beyond had just begun.

***Wall Street Journal*, August 10, 1987**

By Beatrice E. Garcia

Bull's Run

Stock prices have soared more than 200% in the past five years, but national output has increased barely 40% before inflation—and only 20% if inflation is taken into account.

The stock market "strikes me as being all by itself," says Charles P. Kindleberger, emeritus professor of economics at Massachusetts Institute of Technology. "There is no real industrial investment boom behind it. It's a puzzle."

Stock Market's Advance...

	8/12/82	8/7/87	PCT CHG
DJIA	776.92	2592.00	+233.6%

...vs. Economy's Gains

	3rd QTR 1982	2nd QTR 1987	PCT CHG
Real GNP[1]	$3.15	$3.80	+20.3%
Consumer spending[1]	2.05	2.49	+21.3
After-tax income[1]	2.26	2.65	+17.2

	AUG. '82	LATEST	PCT CHG
Industrial production index ('77=100)	102.0	128.2	+25.7%
Employment[2] (in millions)	101.2	114.4	+13.0
Jobless rate[2]	9.7%	5.9%	−39.2

[1] Seasonally adjusted annual rate, in trillions of 1982 dollars

[2] Based on total employment

***Wall Street Journal*, August 10, 1987**

By Tim Metz

The Essence of the Stories

- The U.S. stock market rose by more than 200 percent in the five years from August 1982 to August 1987.

- In the same five year period, national output grew by 20 percent, industrial production by 25 percent, employment by 13 percent, consumer spending by 21 percent, and after tax income by 17 percent.

- Some economists, such as Professor Kindleberger, are puzzled by the fact that the stock market has advanced on a scale 10 times greater than most indicators of underlying real economic performance.

- Stock market analysts differ in their explanations for the rise and their predictions about the stock market's future course:

  —Wave theorist Prechter sees the advance as the last upward sub-wave of a 55-year trend and predicts a further 40 percent rise before the peak is reached.

  —Technical analyst Farrell identifies a series of "theme stages"—rising inflation and the energy crisis in the 1970s and falling inflation in the 1980s as the source of movements and predicts that earnings growth is now the key to the future performance of the stock market.

  —Technical analyst Erlanger emphasizes the performance of transportation stocks.

  —Celestial-based cycle theorist Crawford looks to solar eclipses and planetary conjunctions.

- For all their differences, virtually no one predicted on August 13, 1982 that day 1 of a sustained five-year upward movement in the stock market had begun.

(continued on next page)

Background and Analysis

What Are All Those Indexes of Stock Market Performance?

- Here is a brief description of all the different indexes in the table "Yardsticks for the Rally."

  —DJIA: the Dow Jones Industrial Average, an index made up from the value of 30 industrial stocks including such household names as American Express, Coca-Cola, IBM, and McDonald's
  —S&P 500: Standard and Poor's index of 500 securities
  —NYSE Composite: an index compiled by the New York Stock Exchange covering a broad range of stocks
  —Wilshire 5000: an index constructed by Wilshire Associates
  —Amex: an index of prices on the American stock exchange
  —Nasdaq Composite: an index compiled by the National Association of Security Dealers Automated Quotations, for stock not traded on any particular stock exchange

- Each index gives a slightly different measure of the change in the stock market, but they all agree that the percent change in the five years ending August 1982 was around 200 percent.

What Is a Bull Market?

- A bull market is simply a rising market. The opposite of a bull market is a bear market. A bear market is a falling market.

Why Was There Such a Strong Bull Market between 1982 and 1987?

- In 1982, the U.S. economy was in a depressed state, there had been no economic growth for a fourth successive year, and income per head was declining. People were pessimistic about the future and were predicting poor earnings performance for U.S. industry.

- Starting in the final quarter of 1982, the U.S. economy made a spectacular recovery. Real income grew by 7 percent during the next seven quarters.

- Bit by bit, industry by industry, it became clear that the pessimistic expectations that had prevailed in 1982 were inappropriate. Optimism replaced pessimism.

- People's assessments of the present value of expected future earnings increased, so they placed higher values on corporate equity.

- There is no mystery or puzzle about the strong rise in the stock market substantially outpacing the underlying change in the economy. The economic theory of the value of an asset predicts a relationship between the price of a stock and the expected future growth rate in its earnings. A change in expectations about growth rates has a large effect on the value of a stock. Replacing an expected decline of 4 percent by an expected rise of 1 percent, combined with a moderate fall in interest rates, is enough to produce a 200 percent rise in the value of stocks.

Where Is the Stock Market Heading?

- No one forecasted the current 1980s upsurge in the stock market.

- The analysis that we have just performed is a rationalization of what happened but could not have been used to make a prediction ahead of time.

- As a matter of fact, it is an implication of the economic theory of the value of stocks that it is impossible to forecast future changes.

- The current price is based on forecasts about future earnings. There are no better forecasts available than the ones that people have made.

- Therefore we cannot use economic theory to predict that the stock market is going to rise further or that it is going to crash.

- But we can use the theory to calculate the implications of different assumptions about earnings and interest rates. For example, historically the interest rate in the United States has been 5 percent a year and earnings have grown at about 2 percent a year. If these conditions emerged in the United States economy, the price-earnings ratio would be 34. With a price-earnings ratio of 34 and with earnings at their current level, the Dow Jones Industrial Average would be 4300.

- This last statement is not a prediction. But it does serve to show that the bull market was not really extraordinary.

natural resource expected to grow at a rate equal to the interest rate? It is to make the expected yield on the natural resource equal to the yield available on other comparably risky assets. But the yield (or interest rate) on a stock of a natural resource is the rate of change in the price of the resource. If you buy a stock of a natural resource, you buy it at today's price. If you sell your natural resource stock a year later, you sell it at the price prevailing at that time. The percentage change in the price of the resource over the year is your yield or interest rate. Thus the more rapid the increase in the price of a natural resource, other things being equal, the larger is the yield on that natural resource.

But there is only one yield that is consistent with an equilibrium portfolio allocation. That yield is the same as the interest rate or yield on other comparably risky assets. Thus the equilibrium yield on a stock of a natural resource occurs when the price of the natural resource rises at a rate equal to the interest rate. Of course, when making a portfolio allocation decision, future prices are not known and decisions are based on expectations. Thus when the price of a natural resource is expected to rise at a rate equal to the interest rate, the portfolio allocation is in equilibrium.

The supply of and demand for the stock of a natural resource determines the yield or interest rate from owning that stock. That yield is determined by the expected rate of increase in the price of the natural resource. But the supply of and demand for the stock of the resource does not determine the current *level* of the price—only its future expected rate of change. To determine the level of the price of a natural resource, we have to consider not only the supply of and demand for the stock of the resource but also the demand for its flow—the rate at which the resource is used up.

The Price of a Natural Resource

To determine the price of a natural resource, we first consider the influences on the demand for the flow of the natural resource and then we study the equilibrium that emerges from the interaction of the demand for the flow with the available stock.

Demand for a Flow The demand for a flow of a natural resource is determined in the same way as the demand for any other input. It arises from firms' profit-maximization decisions. A firm maximizes profit when the marginal revenue product of an input equals the marginal cost of the input. In a perfectly competitive market, the marginal cost of an input equals the factor price. The quantity demanded of a flow of a natural resource is the amount that makes the marginal revenue product of that flow equal to the price of the resource. As in the case of all other inputs, the marginal revenue product of a natural resource diminishes as the quantity of the resource used increases. Thus the lower the price of a resource, the greater is the quantity demanded of the flow of the natural resource—as illustrated in Fig. 17.7.

There is one special feature of the demand for a flow of a natural resource. For any resource, there is a high price at which it does not pay anyone to use the resource. The price at which it no longer pays to use a natural resource is called the **choke price.** Figure 17.7 shows a choke price of P_C. Everything has substitutes and at a high enough price, a substitute is used. For example, we do not have to use aluminum to make cans for soft drinks; we can use plastic

Figure 17.7 Demand for a Flow of a Natural Resource

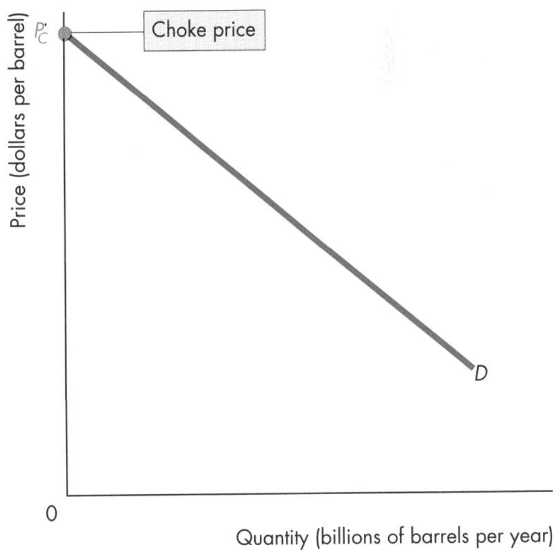

Natural resources have substitutes. If the price of a natural resource is too high, then a substitute will be used. At P_C, none of this resource is demanded and a substitute will be used. At a price below P_C, the quantity demanded is positive and the lower the price, the larger is the quantity demanded. The price P_C is called the choke price.

Figure 17.8 An Exhaustible Natural Resource Market

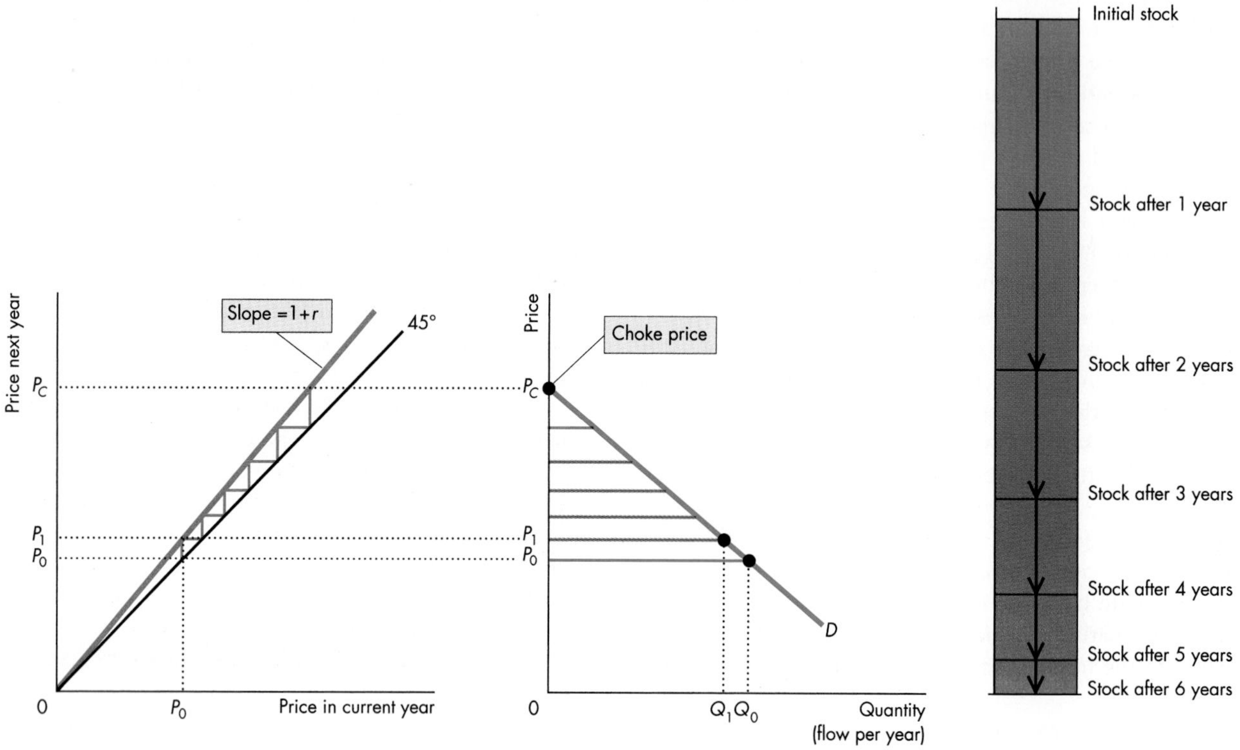

(a) Expected price path **(b) Rate of use** **(c) Remaining stock**

The expected rate of increase in the price of a natural resource equals the interest rate. Starting at P_0 in part (a), the price increases at first to P_1 and eventually to P_C. The price path follows the steps shown, with each step bigger than the previous one. Part (b) shows the rate at which the resource is used up. Its demand curve *(D)* determines the quantity demanded for use (a flow) at each price. Initially, when the price is P_0, that flow is Q_0. As the price increases, the flow decreases. When the price reaches P_C, the choke price, the flow is zero. Part (c) illustrates the remaining stock after each year. The initial stock is used up in decreasing amounts until, after six years, the stock is exhausted. The price P_0 is the equilibrium price because it achieves equality between the sum of the flows in each year and the initial stock.

instead. We do not have to use oil as the fuel for cars; we can use alcohol or electric cars instead. We do not have to use gas and electric power to heat our homes; we can use solar energy instead. The natural resources that we *do* use are the least expensive resources available. They cost us less than the next best alternative would.

Equilibrium Stock and Flow The price and the flow of a natural resource depend on three things:

- The interest rate
- The demand for the flow
- The stock of the resource remaining

Figure 17.8 shows how these three factors combine to determine the price of a natural resource, the expected path of that price, the rate at which the resource is used up, and the stock of the resource remaining. Let's take in the figure one part at a time.

In part (a), you can see the expected price path of the natural resource. That path is determined by the interest rate *r*. The line with a slope of $1 + r$ shows the relationship between the price in the current year and the price next year if the price rises at a rate equal to the interest rate. Suppose that initially the price is P_0. Next year, the price will rise to P_1, the price that is r percent higher than P_0. You can see the rise in price by following the "steps" between the 45° line and the line with a slope of $1 + r$. Each step represents a price increase. The steps become larger but the height of each step is a constant percentage of the previous year's price. Since the price keeps rising, eventually it reaches the choke price, identified as P_C in the figure.

Next, consider Fig. 17.8(b), which shows the rate at which the resource is used up. The demand for the flow, based on the marginal revenue product of the natural resource, is illustrated by the curve D. In the initial year, at a price of P_0 the quantity Q_0 is used. In the following year, we know from part (a) that the price increases to P_1. At this price, the quantity used up is Q_1. As the price increases each year, the quantity used each year decreases. When the price reaches P_C, the choke price, the quantity used is zero.

Figure 17.8(c) shows the remaining stock. The initial stock is identified in the figure and the stock remaining after each year is also identified. For example, the stock after one year is the initial stock minus Q_0, the amount used up in the first year. In this example, after six years, there is no stock left. The price has increased from P_0 to the choke price P_C and the quantity used in each year has declined until, in the final year, it has become zero—the quantity of the flow of natural resources demanded at the choke price.

How do we know that P_0 is the current price? It is because it is the price that achieves an equilibrium between the remaining stock and the current year's flow and the future years' expected flows. That is, it is the only current price that leads to a sequence of future prices (growing at the interest rate) that generate a sequence of flows such that the stock is exhausted in the same year that the choke price is reached. If the current price is higher than P_0 and if the future prices are expected to rise at the interest rate, the choke price will be reached before the stock is exhausted. If the current price is below P_0 and, again, if the future prices are expected to rise at the interest rate, the stock will be exhausted before the choke price is reached.

We can now see how the current price is determined by the three factors that we identified above. First, the higher the interest rate, the lower is the current price of a natural resource. The higher interest rate means that the price is going to increase more quickly. Thus starting from the same initial price, the choke price will be reached sooner. But if the choke price is reached sooner, the stock available will not be used up at that point in time. Thus the initial price has to be lower when the interest rate is higher to ensure that by the time the price does reach the choke price, the total stock available has been used.

Second, the higher the marginal revenue product of the natural resource—the higher the demand for the flow of the natural resource—the higher is the current price of the resource. You can see why this relationship exists by looking again at Fig. 17.8(b). If the demand for the flow of the resource were higher than that shown in this figure, the demand curve would lie to the right of the demand curve shown. In this case, the current price would be higher than P_0.

Third, the larger the initial stock of the natural resource, the lower the current price. You can also see why this relationship holds by considering Fig. 17.8(c). If the initial stock is larger than that shown in the figure, P_0 cannot be the equilibrium price for it leads to a sequence of prices that generate a sequence of quantities demanded that do not exhaust the stock by the time the choke price is reached. Thus the initial price would have to be below P_0 to ensure that the larger stock is exhausted by the time that the choke price is reached.

Equilibrium in the market for a natural resource determines the current price of the natural resource and the expected path of future prices. But the price path actually followed is rarely the same as its expected path. For example, in 1984 expectations about the future price of oil were that it would rise at a rate equal to the interest rate. Opinions differed about the long-term average interest rate, so projections ranged from a low growth rate of 1.8 percent a year to a high growth rate of 7.1 percent a year. But, as events have turned out, the price of oil fell after 1984 (see Fig. 17.9).

Why do natural resource prices change unexpectedly, sometimes even falling rather than following their expected path?

Unexpected Price Changes

The price of a natural resource depends on expectations about future events. It depends on expectations about the interest rate, the future demand for the flow of the resource, and the size of the remaining stock. Natural resource markets are constantly being

Figure 17.9 Unfulfilled Expectations

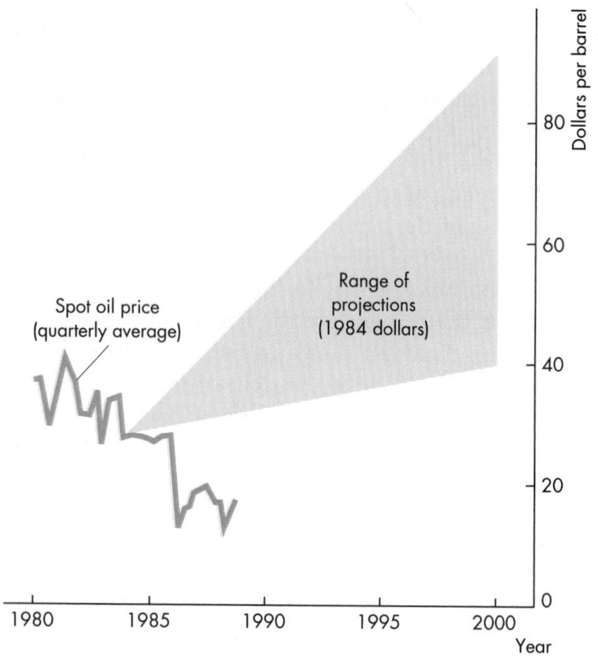

In 1984, the price of oil was expected to increase at a rate equal to the interest rate. There were different views of the future interest rate, so there was a range of expected price increases. The events of the 1980s unfolded in a way that was different from what had been expected in 1984. Higher interest rates, the discovery of increased reserves, and new energy-saving technologies all contributed to a falling price of oil. The breakup of the OPEC cartel also contributed significantly to falling oil prices.

Source: "Future Imperfect," *The Economist:* Feb. 4, 1989, p. 67. © 1989 The Economist Newspaper Limited. Reprinted with permission.

bombarded by new information that leads to new expectations. For example, new information about the stock of a resource or the technologies available for its use can lead to sudden and perhaps quite large changes in the price of a natural resource.

All of these forces have been at work in many of the markets for exhaustible natural resources in recent years. The market for oil illustrates these effects very well. Increased interest rates and the discovery of new supply sources have taken place in recent years, and at the same time the price of oil, far from rising at a rate equal to the interest rate, has actually fallen. Changes in the marginal revenue product of an input are harder to document but, for example, the development of energy-efficient automobile and airplane engines represents a technological change that increases the marginal revenue product of capital—engines—and decreases the marginal revenue product of the exhaustible resource—the oil that those engines burn.

An additional force leading to price changes in natural resource markets in general and in the oil market in particular is the degree of competitiveness in the markets. The model market that we have been studying is a perfectly competitive one. But the real world market for oil has oligopolistic elements (some of which we analyzed in Chapter 14, pp. 349–366). Oligopolistic influences on price can produce price fluctuations over and above the fluctuations arising from the forces at work in a competitive market. Furthermore, in forecasting the future price of a natural resource, it is necessary to forecast future changes in market structure. Adding this complication to an already complex forecasting problem makes it clear that the fluctuations in prices of natural resources such as oil are, for the most part, unforecastable.

Conservation and Doomsday

The analysis that you have just reviewed concerning the price of a natural resource and its expected change over time has important implications for the popular debate concerning natural resources and their use. Many people fear that we are using the earth's exhaustible natural resources at such a rapid pace that we shall eventually (and perhaps in the not very distant future) run out of important sources of energy and of other crucial raw materials. Such people urge a slowing down in the rate of use of exhaustible natural resources so that the limited stocks available will last longer.

This topic is an emotional one and generates passionate debate. It is also a matter that involves economic issues that can be understood using the economic model of a depletable natural resource that you have just studied.

The economic analysis of an exhaustible natural resource market predicts that doomsday—the using up of the entire stock of a natural resource—will eventually arise if our use of natural resources is organized in competitive markets. The economic model also implies that a competitive market will provide an automatic conservation program arising from a steadily rising price. As a natural resource gets closer and closer to being depleted, its price gets closer to the choke price—the price at which no one wants to use the resource any more. Each year, as the price rises, the quantity demanded of the flow declines.

But what if the resource gets completely used up? Don't we have a real problem then? We have the problem of scarcity but in no more acute a form than we had it before. The resource that is no longer available was used because to use it was more efficient than to use some alternative. Once that resource is completely used up, then and only then does it pay to turn to using a more expensive substitute. So, the market economy handles the depleting stocks of natural resources by persistently forcing up their prices. Higher prices cause us to ration our use and eventually drive the quantity demanded of the flow to zero when the supply of the stock disappears.

There is an important economic issue as to whether or not a competitive market leads us to use our scarce exhaustible natural resources at an efficient rate. Recall that we have studied the allocative efficiency of a perfectly competitive market in Chapter 12 (pp. 307–309). There we discovered that perfectly competitive markets achieve allocative efficiency if there are no external costs and benefits. The same conclusion applies to markets for natural resources. If there are no external costs or benefits impinging upon these markets, then the rate of use determined in a perfectly competitive exhaustible natural resource market is the allocatively efficient rate of use. But if there are external costs associated with the use of the natural resource, allocative efficiency will result from a slowdown in the rate of use of the resource compared with that arising in the competitive market. For example, if burning hydrocarbon fuels increases the carbon dioxide in the atmosphere and a warming of the earth's atmosphere results—the so-called greenhouse effect—the costs associated with this atmospheric change have to be added to the costs of using oil and coal as fuels. When these costs are taken into account, the allocatively efficient rate of use of these fuels is lower than that resulting from a perfectly competitive market. We examine ways in which government intervention can achieve allocative efficiency in such a situation in Chapter 19.

■ We have now studied the way in which factor markets allocate scarce productive resources—labor, capital, and land—and the determination of factor prices and factor incomes. The outcome of the operation of the factor markets is the determination of the distribution of income among individuals and families—the determination of *for whom* goods and services are produced. We are now going to examine that distribution and discover the main features and sources of income and wealth inequality in our economy.

SUMMARY

Capital, Investment, and Saving

There are two kinds of assets: financial and real. Financial assets are all the paper claims of one economic agent against another. Real assets, or capital, are the stock of all the productive assets owned by households and firms. Investment is the flow of additions to the stock of capital. Depreciation is the flow reduction in the stock of capital through use or the passage of time.

The quantity of capital supplied results from people's saving decisions. Saving equals income minus consumption. People allocate their savings to a variety of alternative financial and real assets. (pp. 439–441)

Capital Markets in the United States Today

Capital markets provide the link between the savings decisions of households and the investment decisions of firms and governments. Households finance firms' investment by buying equity and bonds or by making deposits in financial intermediaries who in turn make loans to firms. Households also make loans to governments by buying bonds and indirectly through deposits with financial intermediaries. (pp. 442–445)

Demand for Capital

The demand for capital is determined—like the demand for factors—by firms' profit-maximization choices. The quantity of capital demanded by a firm is such that the marginal revenue product of capital equals its opportunity cost. A firm can make the comparison between marginal revenue product and cost by calculating the present value of marginal revenue product and comparing that present value with the price of a new piece of capital.

The quantity of capital demanded by a firm depends on the interest rate. The higher the interest rate, the lower is the present value of the future stream of marginal revenue products, and the smaller is the quantity of capital equipment a firm buys. The lower the interest rate, the greater is the quantity of capital demanded—the demand curve for capital is downward sloping. The demand curve for capital shifts steadily to the right as a result of technological change and the general tendency to exploit innovations over time. (pp. 445–448)

The Supply of Capital

The quantity of capital supplied results from the saving decisions of households. Savings depend on how much households smooth their consumption over the life cycle and on the interest rate. The particular assets into which people will put their savings depend on the relative rates of return. Relative rates of return, in turn, reflect differing degrees of riskiness. The supply curve for capital is upward sloping—as interest rates rise, the quantity of capital supplied increases. The supply curve of capital shifts over time as a result of changes in the population, and its age composition, and the level of income. (pp. 449–451)

Interest Rates and Asset Prices

Interest rates and asset prices can be viewed as two sides of the same coin. Interest rates and asset prices adjust to achieve equality between the quantity of capital demanded and the quantity supplied. Interest rates on particular assets are distributed around the average rate according to the degree of riskiness of different types of assets.

The stock market value of a firm depends on the firm's current profit and expectations of its future profit. The higher the expected growth rate of a firm's profit, the higher is the price of a share of its stock. The price-earnings ratio is the ratio of the current price of a share in a firm's stock to its current profit per share. That ratio depends on the expected growth rate of profit.

The volume of trading on the stock market is determined by the extent of the divergence of expectations of the future. When everyone agrees about the future, volume of trading is low. When there is widespread disagreement, volume of trading is high. There can be large changes in prices with low or high volume of trading. Price changes occur when there is a change in expectations about profit growth.

Mergers and takeovers occur as part of the process of maximizing profit. If a firm's stock market value is lower than the value of its assets when used by another firm, it will pay that other firm to take over the first firm. Mergers occur when there is a mutually agreed benefit from combining the assets of two (or more) firms. (pp. 451–455)

Natural Resource Markets

Natural resources are the nonproduced factors of production with which we are endowed. The price of a natural resource is determined by the interest rate, its marginal revenue product (which determines the demand for its flow), and the stock of the natural resource (which determines the supply of its stock). The price of a natural resource is such that its future price is expected to rise at a rate equal to the interest rate and to reach the choke price at the time at which the resource is exhausted. The actual price is constantly changing to take into account new information. Even though the future price is expected to increase, the actual price often decreases as a result of new information leading to an increase in the estimate of the remaining stock or to a decrease in the demand for the flow of the resource. (pp. 455–463)

KEY CONCEPTS

Asset, 439
Balance sheet, 439
Bond market, 443
Bond yield, 451
Capital, 439
Choke price, 459

Key Figures and Tables

REVIEW QUESTIONS

1 Why does the quantity of capital demanded by a firm rise as the interest rate falls?

2 Set out the key reasons for differences in interest rates on different types of assets.

3 What is the relationship between interest rates and asset prices?

4 Explain how the stock market value of a firm is determined.

5 Define the price-earnings ratio and explain how it is determined.

6 Why are there some occasions on which stock market prices change a lot but with little trading and other times when prices are stable but trading volumes are high?

7 Why do mergers and takeovers occur?

8 Distinguish between the stock and the flow of an exhaustible natural resource.

9 Explain why the price of an exhaustible natural resource is expected to rise at a rate equal to the interest rate.

10 What determines the price of a natural resource?

11 Why are most of the fluctuations in the price of a natural resource unforecastable?

PROBLEMS

1 At the end of 1989, a firm had a production plant worth $1 million. The plant depreciated during 1990 by 10 percent. During the same year, the firm also bought new capital equipment for $250,000. What is the value of the firm's stock of capital at the end of 1990? What was the firm's gross investment during 1990? What was the firm's net investment during 1990?

2 You earn $10,000 per year for three years and you spend $8000 each year. How much do you save each year? What happens to your wealth during this three-year period?

3 What are the different ways in which a holder of wealth can channel capital into firms?

4 How can a holder of wealth lower the risk of supplying capital to firms?

5 Why is a deposit in a financial intermediary less risky than buying equity or bonds?

6 A firm is considering buying a new machine. It is estimated that the marginal revenue product of the machine will be $1000 a year for five years. The machine will have a scrap value at the end of five years of $1000. The interest rate is 10 percent a year.

a) What is the maximum price that the firm will pay for the machine?

b) If the machine costs $4000, will the firm buy the machine at an interest rate of 10 percent? What is the highest interest rate at which the firm will buy the machine?

Chapter 18

The Distribution of Income and Wealth

After studying this chapter, you will be able to:

- Describe the distribution of income and wealth in the United States today
- Explain why the data on wealth distribution show greater inequality than the data on income distribution
- Explain how the distribution of income arises from the prices of productive resources and the distribution of endowments
- Explain how the distribution of income and wealth is affected by individual choices
- Explain the different views about fairness in the distribution of income and wealth
- Explain the effects of redistribution policies on the distribution of income and wealth

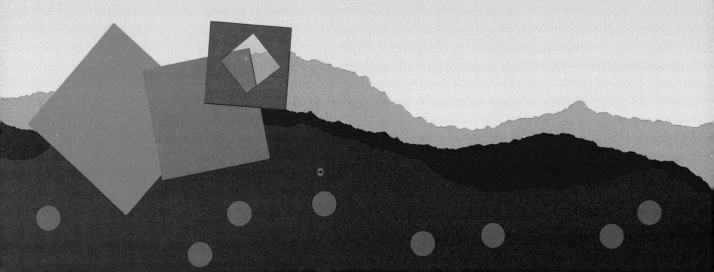

Riches and Rags

Fifty-three stories above Manhattan there is for sale a 3363 square foot penthouse with unobstructed views of Central Park, the Hudson River, and the city skyline: The price? $4 million. "Now, you can be one of the enviable few to fly Around the World by Supersonic Concorde. Less than 400 Americans have done it before. Space very limited. $26,800 per person," trumpets an advertisement in the *New Yorker.* What kind of people can afford homes and vacations as costly as these? Obviously only the very richest. And there are some very rich people in the United States today. It has been estimated that the richest 1 percent of families own more than 40 percent of the nation's wealth and the richest 20 percent earn over 40 percent of the nation's income. ■ At the other end of the scale there is abject poverty. Not quite within view of the $4 million penthouse, but not far from it, is Fort Washington Armory in Upper Manhattan. What was opened as a temporary shelter in 1981 now permanently houses 850 men sleeping in one huge room. "As the men at Fort Washington stretch out on cots on the coarse wooden drill floor in a room the size of a football field, there is pervasive fear—fear of AIDS and tuberculosis, fear for physical survival. And there is widespread despair over the future. . . . There, side by side, are predators and their prey, the mentally ill, alcoholics, men with limbs thinned by disease and malnutrition, others with muscles trained through exercise in prison."[1] ■ Though Fort Washington is an extreme example of poverty and despair, many thousands of families, often with a single (and usually female) parent, struggle to obtain even such basics as adequate food, clothing, and shelter. It is estimated that the poorest 50 percent of the families in the United States own a mere 1 percent of the nation's net assets. The

[1]*New York Times* (February 18, 1988): 1, 42.

poorest 20 percent of families earn only 5 percent of the nation's income. ■ What determines the distributions of wealth and income? Why are some people exceedingly rich while others earn very little and own almost nothing? Are there any trends in the distribution of income? Is the distribution becoming more equal or more unequal? Is it fair that some people should be so incredibly rich while others live in miserable poverty? And what do we mean by fairness?

■ In this chapter, we study the sources of income and wealth inequality. We'll see how factor prices and the quantities of factors hired, as determined in factor markets, result in unequal incomes. We'll study the connection between income and wealth and discover why the distribution of wealth is much more uneven than that of income. We'll also see how inequality results in part from the choices that people make. ■ Most of the chapter deals with positive issues—with trying to understand the world as it is—and not normative matters—commenting on or making judgments about what is desirable. Nevertheless, in the final section of the chapter we do review some of the key contributions to the perennial search for a widely acceptable concept of fairness. ■ Let's begin by looking at some facts about the distributions of income and wealth.

Distributions of Income and Wealth in the United States Today

The incomes earned by the factors of production are the wages (including salaries and other forms of compensation) paid to labor, the interest (and dividend) income paid to the owners of capital, and the rental incomes received by the owners of land and minerals. Labor earns the largest share of total income and that share has increased slightly over the years.

The distribution of income among individuals and families depends on the amount of labor, capital, and natural resources that they supply and on the wage rates, interest and dividend rates, and rental rates they receive. The resource that everyone has in identical amounts is time. But the price at which a person can sell his or her time, the wage rate, depends on the individual's marginal product. That marginal product in turn depends partly on natural ability, partly on luck or chance, and partly on the amount of human capital that the individual has built up. The income from working is a mixture of a return on human capital as well as a compensation for forgoing leisure.

There is a great deal of inequality in the distribution of ownership of all other factors of production. We will more closely examine that inequality shortly. For now, let's just note that the total income of a family depends on its labor income (including its returns on human capital) as well as its income from other assets.

In 1987, the median U.S. household income was $30,853. The median household is located in the middle of the income distribution—50 percent of households have higher incomes and 50 percent have lower incomes than the median income. Twenty-three percent of all households had incomes of $50,000 or more.[2] One fifth of all households had incomes of less than $15,000.

Figure 18.1 illustrates the distribution of income. It shows the percentage of total income received by each of five equal-sized groups from the poorest 20 percent to the richest 20 percent of families. The 20 percent of families with the lowest incomes receive just 5 percent of total income. The second lowest 20 percent received 11 percent of total income. You can continue reading across the figure to see the percentages of income received by families that are increasingly better off. The 20 percent of families with the highest incomes received 43 percent of total income.

Although the data on the distribution of income display considerable inequality, a picture of even greater inequality emerges from the data on the distribution of wealth. Wealth and income are linked in a way that we will examine shortly, but it's important to remember the distinction: Income is what you earn, wealth is what you own. Data on the wealth distribution measure the value of individual and family holdings of real estate and financial assets. These data are expensive to collect and are updated only infrequently. The most comprehensive data available measure the wealth of families in 1973. In that year, the average family owned net assets of $37,657. The range about that average was enormous. The poorest 40 percent of families owned only

[2]The most recent year for which complete data on income distribution are available is 1987.

Figure 18.1 Family Income Shares

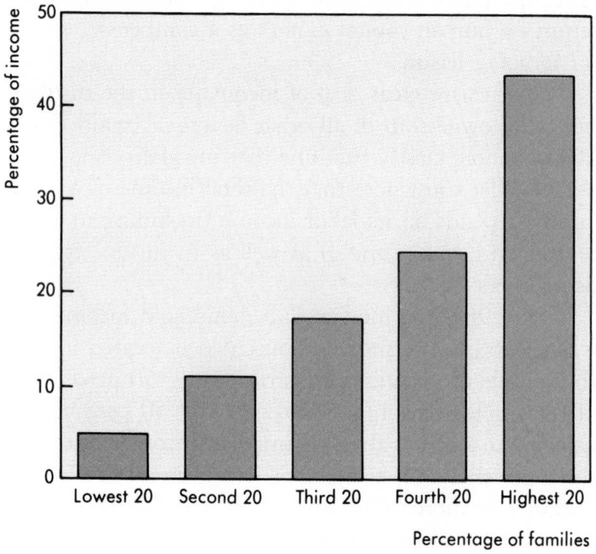

One way of measuring income inequality is to calculate the percentage of total income earned by a given percentage of families, starting with the poorest. The figure shows us that the poorest 20 percent of families earn only 5 percent of the income while the richest 20 percent earn 43 percent of the income. The richest 20 percent are almost nine times as well off, on the average, as the poorest 20 percent.

Source: U.S. Bureau of the Census, *Current Population Reports*, Series P-60.

0.1 percent of the total wealth. The richest 10 percent owned almost 70 percent of total wealth.

Figure 18.2 provides a picture of the distribution of wealth in the United States in 1973. The figure is arranged in a way that enables you to compare the distribution of wealth with the distribution of income.

As in the case of the distribution of income, there is considerable inequality in the distribution of wealth. But there is even more inequality in the case of wealth than of income. For example, the poorest 80 percent of families own 15.4 percent of the wealth but earn 57 percent of total income. The highest 20 percent own 84.6 percent of the wealth and earn 43 percent of total income.

The amount of inequality in the distribution of wealth is even greater if we break down the richest group. Within that group, the richest 1 percent of all families own 33 percent of total wealth. The next 1 percent own 10 percent of the wealth, and the next 3 percent own 15 percent of the wealth.

Lorenz Curves for Income and Wealth

Another way of describing the distributions of income and wealth is presented in Fig. 18.3. The table records the cumulative percentages of income and wealth of various cumulative percentages of families. For example, row *a* of the table shows the percentages of income and wealth of the lowest 20 percent of families; row *b* shows the data for the lowest 40 percent of families, and so on. These data can be illustrated graphically in what is called a Lorenz curve. A **Lorenz curve** shows the cumula-

Figure 18.2 Income and Wealth Distributions

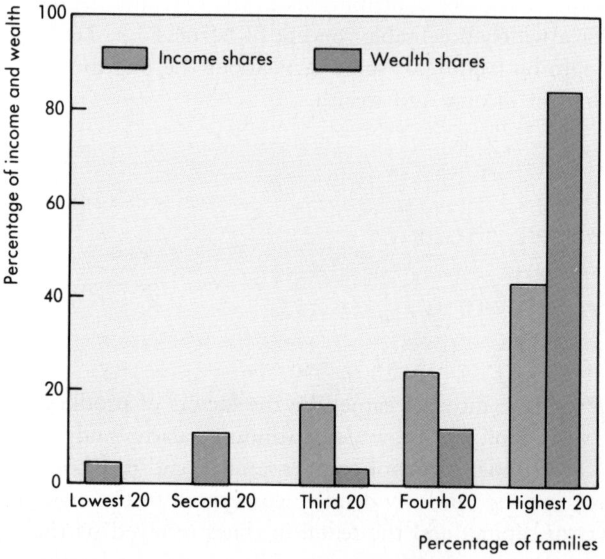

Wealth is distributed even more unequally than income. The poorest 40 percent of the population owns only 0.1 percent of the wealth in the economy. The richest 20 percent owns more than 80 percent of total wealth. Even the middle 20 percent of the population owns only 3.5 percent of total wealth.

Sources: Wealth: Lars Osberg, *Economic Inequality in the United States* (Armonk, N.Y.: M.E. Sharpe, 1983) 44. Income: *Statistical Abstract of the United States: 1987*, 107th ed., p. 437

Figure 18.3 Lorenz Curves for Income and Wealth

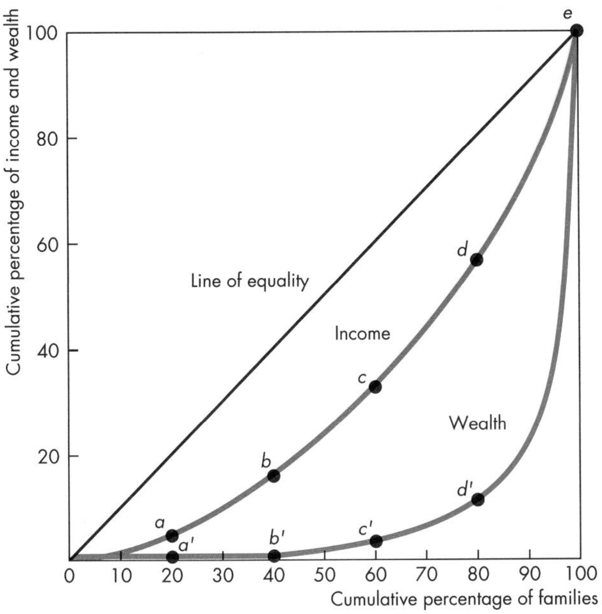

The cumulative percentages of income and wealth are graphed against the cumulative percentage of families. If income and wealth were distributed equally, each 20 percent of families would have 20 percent of the income and wealth—the line of equality. Points *a* through *e* on the Lorenz curve for income correspond to the rows of the table showing family income and points *a'* through *e* on the Lorenz curve for wealth correspond to the rows of the table showing family wealth. Wealth is distributed more unequally than income.

	Cumulative percentage of families	Cumulative percentage of income	Cumulative percentage of wealth	
a	Lowest: 20	5	0	*a'*
b	40	16	0	*b'*
c	60	33	4	*c'*
d	80	57	15	*d'*
e	100	100	100	*e'*

Sources: Income: *Statistical Abstract of the United States: 1987*, 107th ed., p. 437. The data are for 1985. Wealth: Lars Osberg, *Economic Inequality in the United States* (Armonk, N.Y.: M.E. Sharpe, 1983) 44. The data are for 1973.

tive percentage of income or wealth of any given cumulative percentage of families. The Lorenz curve derives its name from its founder, Konrad Lorenz, who devised this type of figure in 1905.

The horizontal axis of the figure measures the cumulative percentages of families ranked from the poorest to the richest. For example, the point marked 40 on the horizontal axis represents the 40 percent of families with the lowest income and wealth. The vertical axis measures the cumulative percentages of income and wealth. For example, the point marked 40 indicates 40 percent of total income or total wealth.

If each family had the same amount of income and wealth, the cumulative percentages of income received and wealth owned by the cumulative percentages of families would fall along the straight line labeled "Line of equality." The actual distributions of income and wealth are shown by the two curves labeled "Income" and "Wealth." The points on the income distribution curve labeled *a* through *e* correspond to the family income shares shown in the table. The points on the wealth distribution curve labeled *a′* through *e* correspond to family wealth shares shown in the table.

The advantage of using Lorenz curves to describe the distribution of income and wealth is that they provide a graphic illustration of the degree of inequality. The closer the Lorenz curve is to the line of equality, the more equal the distribution. As you can see from the two Lorenz curves in Fig. 18.3, the distribution of wealth is much more unequal than the distribution of income. That is, the Lorenz curve for the wealth distribution is much farther away from the line of equality.

The numbers in the table tell the same story. For example, the poorest 60 percent of all families own only 4 percent of the total wealth but earn 33 percent of total income. The poorest 80 percent of all families own only 15 percent of the wealth but earn 57 percent of the income.

Table 18.1 A Comparison of the Distribution of Income in 1955 and 1985

Cumulative percentage of families	Cumulative percentage of income 1955	1985
Lowest: 20	5	5
40	16	16
60	32	33
80	55	57
100	100	100

The distributions of income in 1955 and 1985 are remarkably similar. At the low end, they are identical. The 1985 distribution has a slightly lower degree of inequality than the 1955 distribution. The richest 20 percent of families had 45 percent of the income in 1955 but only 43 percent by 1985.

Source: The 1955 figures are from Historical Statistics of the United States, Colonial Times to 1957, p. 166; the 1985 figures are from Statistical Abstract of the United States, 107th ed., p. 437.

Lorenz curves, and the data from which they are drawn, are useful not only for comparing two different distributions, such as that of income and of wealth, but also for comparing distributions at different points in time. Such comparisons reveal whether the distribution of income has become more or less equal over time.

Inequality over Time

Let's take a look at the distribution in the United States 30 years earlier than the numbers that we have just been studying. Table 18.1 provides a comparison. It shows the cumulative percentage of income shares in 1955 and compares those numbers with the same income shares in 1985 (the figures in Fig. 18.3). As you can see from Table 18.1, there was remarkably little change in the distribution of income in the 30 years between 1955 and 1985.

We have seen that there is a great deal of inequality in income and wealth. But *who* are the rich and *who* are the poor? What are the key characteristics of rich and poor families? Let's now turn our attention to these questions.

Who Are the Rich and the Poor?

The poorest person in the United States today is most likely to be a black woman living on her own, probably widowed, who is over 65 years of age, has had less than eight years of elementary school, and lives in the South. The highest income family in the United States today is likely to be a married couple, between ages 45 and 54, with two children. The adult household members in this family have had four years or more of college education, are white, and live in California. These snapshot profiles are the extremes in Fig. 18.4. That figure illustrates the importance of education, marital status, size of household, age of householder, race, and region of residence in influencing the size of a family's income.

Education is the single most important factor. On the average, those with less than eight years of elementary school earn around $10,000 a year while those with four years or more of college earn nearly $40,000 a year. Marital status is also important. Widowed females or those living without a husband, on the average, have incomes of less than $10,000 a year while married couples earn an average income of more than $30,000 a year. Household size has an obvious effect on household income but the house-

Figure 18.4 The Distribution of Income of Families by Selected Family Characteristics in 1985

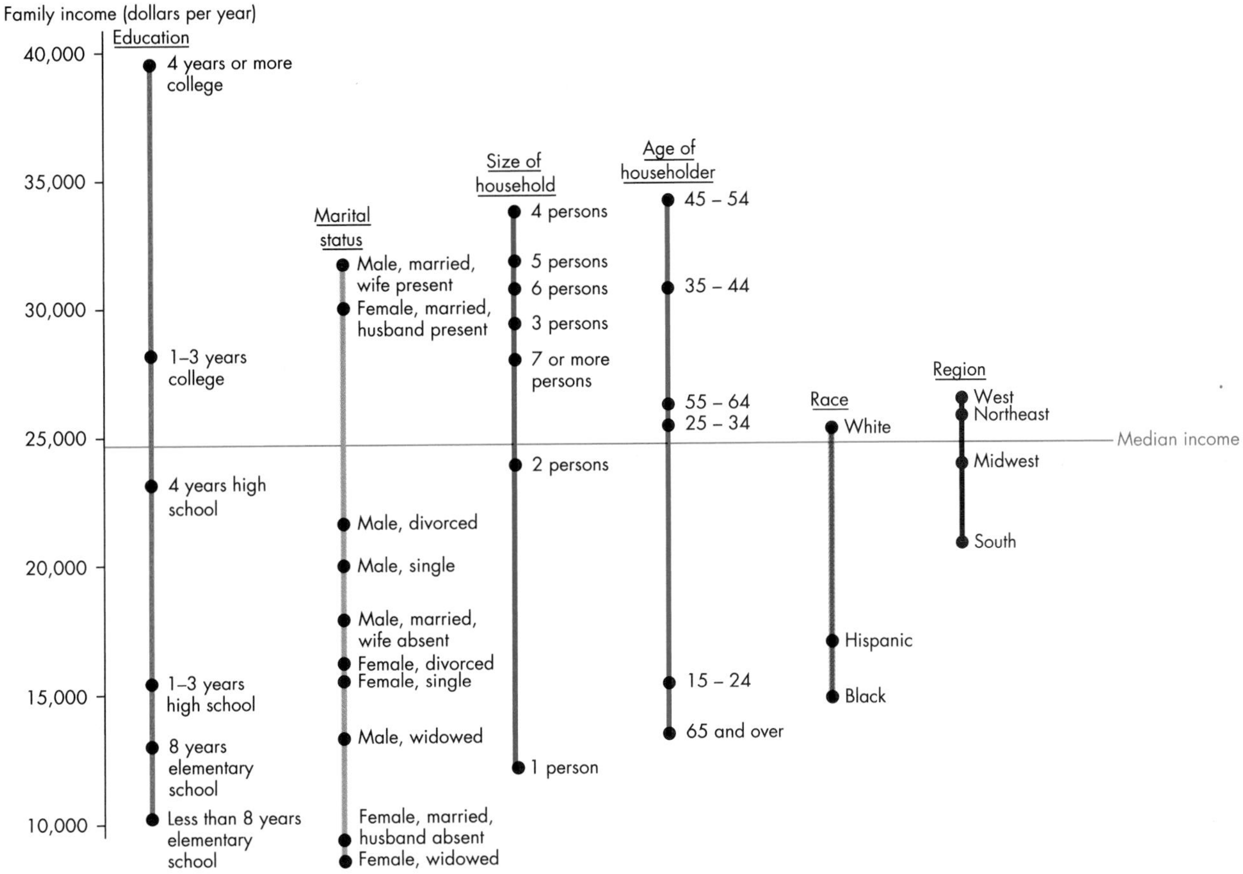

Education is the single biggest factor affecting family income distribution, but marital status, size of household, and age of householder are also very important. Race and region of residence also play a role.

Source: Statistical Abstract of the United States: 1988.

hold size at which income is highest is four persons. Age also is important, with the oldest and youngest households having the lowest incomes and middle-aged households the highest. Race and region of residence also influence the income distribution but on a smaller scale than the other characteristics that we have just examined. Black families have an average income of $15,000 while white families have an average income of $25,000. Incomes are lowest in the South and highest in the West, with those in the Northeast fairly close to those in the West and incomes in the Midwest lying midway between these two.

Poverty Families at the bottom end of the income distribution are so poor that they are considered to be living in poverty. **Poverty** is an income level measured by a poverty index first calulated by the Social Security Administration in 1964. The index is based on Department of Agriculture assessments of the minimum consumption requirements of families based on their size and composition. In 1987, the poverty level for a two-person family was $7397. For a four-person family, it was $11,611. The distribution of poverty is very unequal by race, with 11 percent of white families and 31 percent of black families being below the poverty level. Poverty is also heavily influenced by family status. More than a third of families where the householder is a female and no husband is present is below the poverty level, while less than 10 percent of other families are.

Extreme wealth We've seen that there are a large number of very poor families—families living in poverty. Are there a similarly large number of extremely rich families? The answer is no. Extremely rich families are rare compared with extremely poor families. For example, in 1985 there were only 32,000 families in the United States whose wealth exceeded $5 million, and those families had an average wealth of $10 million each. There were, in that same year, only 375,000 families with wealth of more than $1 million but less than $5 million. These families had average wealth of almost $2 million each.

Income Redistribution

Because poverty is so dreadful for those experiencing it and so fearful for everyone else, there is almost universal agreement that the government can play the role of a kind of giant insurance company (a sort of institutionalized Robin Hood, taking from the rich and giving to the poor). There are two main ways in which governments redistribute income in the United States today:

- Income taxes
- Welfare programs

Income Taxes The amount and nature of the redistribution achieved through income taxes depend on the form that the income taxes take. Income taxes may be progressive, regressive, or proportional. A **progressive income tax** is one that taxes income at a marginal rate that rises with the level of income. The term "marginal," applied to income tax rates, refers to the fraction of the last dollar earned that is paid in taxes. A **regressive income tax** is one that taxes income at a marginal rate that falls with the level of income. A **proportional income tax** is one that taxes income at a constant rate regardless of the level of income.

The income tax rates that apply in the United States are composed of two parts: federal and state taxes. There is a good deal of variety in the detailed tax arrangements in the individual states but the tax system, at both the federal and state levels, is progressive. However, tax reforms introduced in 1986 have reduced the amount of progressiveness. Under the 1986 tax law, there are just two federal income tax rates, one of 15 percent for low income households and 28 percent for all others.

Welfare Programs A second way governments redistribute income is by making direct payments to those at the low end of the income distribution. The detailed arrangements vary from state to state. Using California as an example (with data from 1982), Table 18.2 provides the details of the monthly value of Aid to Families with Dependent Children (AFDC) payments and food stamp programs that were available to families with zero or very low earnings. Although the figures in the table refer to just one state in one year, the key point that this table makes is not affected by either the state or year chosen. The situation is similar in all the states.

Notice two key things about the numbers in this table. First, the poor receive benefits from the government on a scale that ensures that no family has an income that falls below a certain level. In California in 1982, that level was $669 a month or $8028 a year. Second, the poor face astonishingly high "taxes" on anything that they might earn. It is true that the poor don't actually pay taxes to the government. Instead, the government withdraws benefits as the earnings of the poor increase. But the effect is the same as paying taxes. Imagine giving every family $669 a month, regardless of their earned income, and then imposing a tax on them as their income rises successively by the amounts shown in the first column of Table 18.2. Looked at in this way, we can calculate the marginal tax rates faced by the poor.

The change in earnings (fourth column) is simply the rise in monthly earnings given in the first column. The change in total income is the rise in the total income given in the third column. When earnings rise from nothing to $200 a month, total income rises by less than that amount—it rises by $78 a month. The reason why income only goes up by $78 a month while earnings go up by $200 a month is that the value of the AFDC and food stamp benefits fall by $122 a month. If income rises by another $200 a month, from $200 to $400 a month, an even larger reduction in AFDC and food stamps occurs. This time total income rises by only $17 a month, with a reduction of AFDC and food stamps of $183 a month. A similar thing happens as

Table 18.2 Welfare Payments and Earnings in California in 1982

Monthly earnings	AFDC and food stamps	Total income	Change in earnings	Change in total income	Marginal tax rate (percent)
0	$669	$669	—	—	—
$200	547	747	$200	$78	61
400	364	764	200	17	92
600	201	801	200	37	82

Welfare payments can be thought of as negative taxes (taxes that the government pays to a household). When household earnings rise, welfare benefits fall. The change in benefits divided by the change in income is similar to the marginal tax rate (negative tax rate). Marginal tax rates for welfare recipients are among the highest—even exceeding 90 percent in some cases.

Source: Lars Osberg, *Economic Inequality in the United States* (Armonk, N.Y.: M. E. Sharpe, 1983), 244.

income rises from $400 to $600. In this event, AFDC and food stamp benefits fall by $163 a month, leaving the family with an extra $37 a month.

We can consider the initial $669 of AFDC and food stamps as a kind of negative tax paid *to* families rather than paid *by* families. We can consider the reduction of benefits as a positive tax paid by families as their incomes rise. We can calculate the marginal tax rate paid by these poor families in the final column in the table. The rise in monthly earnings from nothing to $200 results in benefits falling by $122; this fall is similar to paying a 61 percent tax. The rise in monthly earnings from $200 to $400 results in a drop in benefits of $183, which is similar to paying a tax of almost 92 percent. The rise in monthly earnings from $400 to $600 results in a drop in benefits of $163, which is similar to paying a tax of almost 82 percent.

Marginal income tax rates as high as those shown in Table 18.2 substantially exceed the marginal income tax rates faced by the earners of the highest incomes. Such tax rates act as a considerable disincentive for the poor to seek employment. As a consequence of tax rates of this magnitude, some economists have advocated introducing an explicit *negative income tax.* Such a scheme would pay every family a bare minimum income of, say, $669 a month. Any earnings that the family makes over and above that would be taxed at a constant, flat rate, regardless of the magnitude of those earnings. A tax rate of perhaps 25 or 30 percent might be applied. Such a scheme would lower the disincentives faced by the poor and encourage them to seek additional employment.

Other Policies that Redistribute In addition to income taxes and welfare programs, governments undertake other measures not primarily aimed at redistributing income but having that effect. The most important of these measures is the provision of public education and subsidized health care. Because of such programs, the poor are better educated and healthier and so have more human capital and are able to increase their earnings.

The Scale of Income Redistribution The distribution of income that would prevail in the absence of government policies is called the **market distribution.** The income distribution that takes account of government policies is called the **distribution after taxes and transfers.** Calculating the effects of all the many tax and transfer arrangements in place is a

Figure 18.5 The Effect of Taxes and Transfers on the Distribution of Income

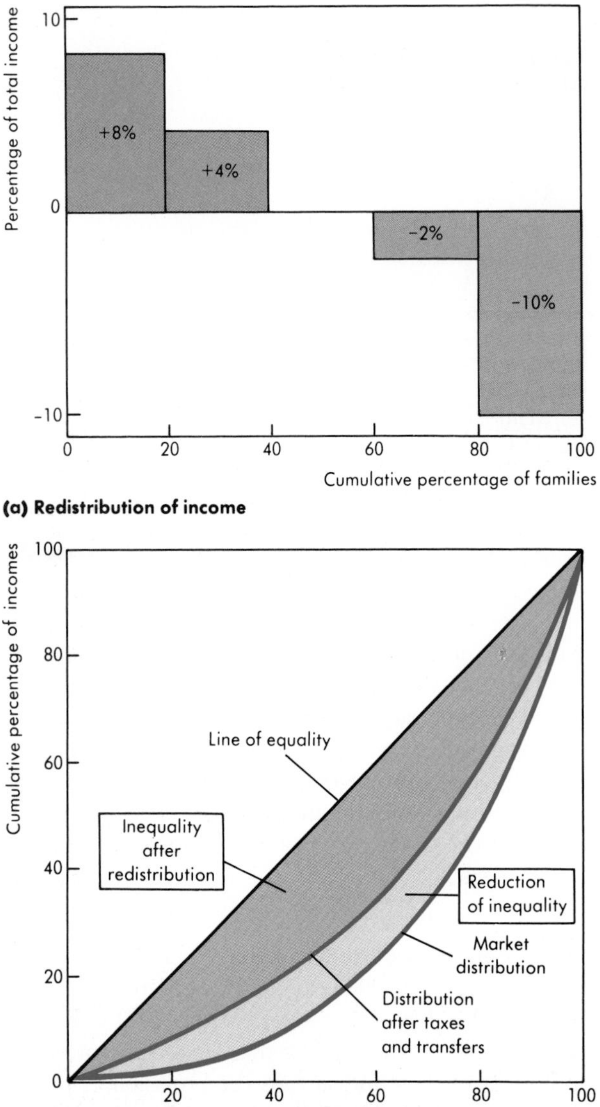

Taxes and transfers reduce the degree of inequality that the market generates. Part (a) shows that 10 percent of income is taken from the richest fifth of the population and 2 percent from the second-richest fifth and redistributed to the poorest two fifths. The poorest fifth receives 8 percent and the second-poorest fifth, 4 percent. The middle income group breaks even. Part (b) shows the effects of this redistribution on the Lorenz curve for income.

complicated matter and the most recent year for which we have a thorough analysis is 1976. Figure 18.5 (a) illustrates the scale of redistribution. The amount of redistribution that takes place between the five groups is 12 percent of total income. Of this, 10 percent is taken from the richest group and 2 percent from the second-richest group. The poorest group receives 8 percent and the second-poorest group receives 4 percent. The middle group just about breaks even. The effects of redistribution policies may also be seen by comparing the Lorenz curves for the market distribution of income and the distribution after taxes and transfers. Figure 18.5 (b) shows these Lorenz curves. As you can see, there is a considerable amount of redistribution undertaken, especially to boost the incomes of the very poor, but a great deal of inequality remains after redistribution.

Another measure of the scale of redistribution is provided by an examination of the sources of income of families at different points on the income distribution scale. The poorest families receive almost two thirds of their income in the form of payments from the government—called transfer income. Even the second 20 percent of families receives a third of its income in government transfers. In contrast, the richest 20 percent receive hardly anything from the government but receive a third of their income from capital—interest and dividends from financial assets. The fraction of income from that source for the other 80 percent of families is remarkably constant at about 8 percent.

We have now examined the distributions of income and wealth in the United States and have seen that a considerable amount of inequality exists. We've seen that the distribution of wealth is much more unequal than that of income. We've also looked at some of the characteristics of rich and poor families and, finally, we have examined the role of redistribution. We've also looked at some of the characteristics of rich and poor families and, finally, we have examined the role played by government in redistributing income.

But what is the reason for the enormous inequality that exists? And why is the distribution of wealth so much more unequal than that of income? Which of these two distributions paints the more accurate picture concerning the degree of inequality? In the next section, we examine the reasons for the *differences* in the degree of inequality as measured by wealth and income. After that we study some of the reasons for inequality itself.

Comparing Like with Like

In order to determine just how much inequality there is, it is necessary to make the correct comparisons. But what are the correct comparisons? Should we be looking at income or should we be looking at wealth? And should we, as we have been doing, look at annual income or should we look at income over some other time period—for example, over a family's lifetime?

Wealth versus Income

The main reason wealth is distributed much more unequally than income is that the data on wealth and income measure different things. The wealth data refer only to nonhuman capital—tangible assets that are traded on capital markets (such as those items analyzed in Chapter 17). The data on income distribution refer to income from all sources, not only from nonhuman capital but also from human capital. Let's explore the sources of these differences a bit more closely by looking at an example. We will begin however by refreshing our memory on the distinction between *income* and *wealth.*

Income and Wealth: Flow and Stock Income and wealth can be considered different ways of looking at precisely the same thing. *Wealth* is the *stock* of assets owned by an individual. *Income* is the *flow* of earnings received by an individual. *Income* is the *flow of earnings* that results from the *stock of wealth.* It is easiest to see the relationship between income and wealth by considering an example. Suppose that Lee owns assets worth $1 million. Thus Lee's wealth is $1 million. If the rate of return on assets is 5 percent a year, then Lee will receive an income of $50,000 a year from his assets of $1 million. We can describe Lee's economic condition by saying that he has either wealth of $1 million or an income of $50,000. If the rate of return is 5 percent, these two statements are equivalent to each other.

In order to talk about the distribution of income and wealth, let's consider two individuals: Lee, who has wealth of $1 million and income of $50,000, and Peter, who has assets of $500,000. Peter and Lee have the same investment opportunities and they invest their assets at the same rate of return—5 percent a year. Peter has an income of $25,000 (5 percent of $500,000). We can now talk about the distribution of wealth and income between Peter and Lee. Lee has wealth of $1 million compared with Peter's wealth of $500,000. Thus Lee has twice as much wealth as Peter. Lee has an income of $50,000 and Peter has an income of $25,000. Again, Lee's income is twice as much as Peter's. Regardless of whether we compare Peter and Lee on the basis of their wealth or their income, we reach the same conclusion: Lee is twice as rich as Peter, both in terms of wealth and income.

Human Capital

So far, we have discussed only the earnings that Peter and Lee receive from their nonhuman wealth. We sometimes refer to physical and financial assets as *tangible assets* or, to contrast them with human capital, as *nonhuman capital.* What about their work effort? The earnings received from work are partly a compensation for giving up leisure time and partly a return on *human capital.* Although human capital represents intangible things like skills, we can put a value on it. We value human capital by looking at the earnings that a person can make from working over and above what would be earned by someone who has had no education or training. The extra earnings are the income from human capital. The value of human capital is the amount of money that a person would have to be given today so that, if invested, it would generate an interest income equal to the income from that individual's human capital.

Consider Peter and Lee again. Suppose now that each of them has no assets other than their productive skills. Lee earns $50,000 a year and if the interest rate is 5 percent a year, then Lee has $1 million of human capital. A million dollars invested at an interest rate of 5 percent a year will earn $50,000 a year. Peter earns $25,000 a year and, again, if the interest rate is 5 percent a year, Peter has human capital of $500,000. Lee earns twice as much income as does Peter and Lee has twice as much human capital.

Human and Nonhuman Capital

We have now considered the distributions of income and wealth in two extreme cases. In the first case, Lee and Peter owned no human capital so their entire income was generated by their financial and real assets. In the second case, Lee and Peter had only human capital—their productive skills. Most people have both nonhuman and human capital. Wealth, correctly measured, includes both of these types of capital.

No matter what the source of income—whether human capital or nonhuman capital—the distribution of wealth and income is the same when we count both the human and nonhuman capital. In both cases that we have just examined, Lee has twice the wealth and twice the income of Peter. So the distribution of wealth between Lee and Peter is identical to the distribution of income between them.

Let's finally examine the case in which Peter and Lee have both human capital and nonhuman capital. For a reason that will become apparent shortly, however, let's suppose that Peter has much more human capital than does Lee and that Lee has more nonhuman capital than does Peter. Table 18.3 sets out some hypothetical numbers to illustrate this case. As before, Lee has twice the total wealth and twice the total income of Peter. Lee's human capital is only \$200,000, so Lee's labor income is just \$10,000. But Lee has nonhuman capital of \$800,000, which generates an income of \$40,000. In contrast, Peter's wealth is almost exclusively human capital. Peter earns \$24,950 of income from \$499,000 worth of human capital. Peter has only \$1000 worth of tangible assets (nonhuman capital), which generates an annual income of \$50.

Suppose that a national wealth and income surveyor is examining this economy comprised of Peter and Lee and observes their incomes of \$25,000 and \$50,000 respectively. The surveyor concludes that on the basis of income, Lee is twice as rich as Peter. The surveyor then measures their assets. The only assets that are measured are tangible assets. The surveyor observes that Lee owns \$800,000 worth of such assets and Peter has \$1000 worth. The assets are listed in a distribution of wealth table and the national surveyor concludes that, in terms of assets, Lee is 800 times as wealthy as Peter. The national survey concludes that wealth is much more unevenly distributed than income.

You can see that the national survey techniques measure the distribution of wealth in a way that does not include human capital. The distribution of income takes into account human capital and is the correct measure of the distribution of economic resources. Measured wealth distributions that ignore the distribution of human capital overstate the inequality among individuals.

Annual or Lifetime Income and Wealth?

The income distributions that we have examined earlier in this chapter are based on annual incomes. And the wealth distributions are based on measuring family wealth in a given year. There are many sources of inequality in annual income and in wealth in a given year, but these do not imply inequality over a family's entire lifetime. For example, young people earn less, on the average, than middle-aged people. Thus in a given year, a young family has a lower income

Table 18.3 Capital, Wealth, and Income

	Lee		Peter	
	Wealth	Income	Wealth	Income
Human capital	\$ 200,000	\$10,000	\$499,000	\$24,950
Nonhuman capital	800,000	40,000	1,000	50
Total	\$1,000,000	\$50,000	\$500,000	\$25,000

When wealth is measured to include the value of human capital as well as nonhuman capital, the distribution of income and the distribution of wealth display the same degree of inequality.

than a middle-aged family. But when the young family becomes middle-aged itself, its income will be no different, on the average, from the current middle-aged family. This is an example of an inequality in annual income that does not reflect an inequality across families over their entire lifetimes. The case of wealth is more extreme. Most young families have few assets and often have debts that exceed those assets. Families with people between middle age and retirement age are at a stage in life when they're building up their assets to provide for a retirement income. Again, the older family looks wealthier than the younger family but, by the time the younger family reaches that same later stage in the life cycle, it will have accumulated assets similar in scale to those of the existing older family.

In order to compare the income and wealth situation of one family with another, it is important that we take into account the family's stage in the life cycle and not be misled by differences arising purely from that factor. To illustrate the importance of this source of inequality, we'll work through an example.

Figure 18.6 shows a family's income, consumption, and wealth over its entire life cycle. The horizontal axis of each part measures age. The vertical axis measures thousands of dollars of income and consumption in part (a) and of wealth in part (b).

Part (a) shows the pattern of income and consumption. This family consumes at a steady rate of \$20,000 a year throughout its life. The family's income from employment starts out at \$18,000 a year. It gradually rises until, just before retirement, the family is earning \$30,000 a year. After retirement, the family's income from work is zero but it continues to receive an income in the form of interest on the capital that it has accumulated in the years before retirement. (Some of the transactions of this hypothetical family are being ignored—for example, the purchase of a house, an automobile, and other consumer durable goods. For the purpose of this example, let's imagine that when the family bought these items, it financed their purchase by borrowing. Thus any real assets owned by the family had offsetting financial liabilities and therefore did not change the family's wealth).

Part (b) shows the family's nonhuman wealth. At first, the family has to borrow to sustain its consumption level. As it does so, it incurs debt and also has to pay interest on the debt. The family is at its deepest point of debt at age 35. After that age,

Figure 18.6 Life-Cycle Income, Consumption, and Wealth

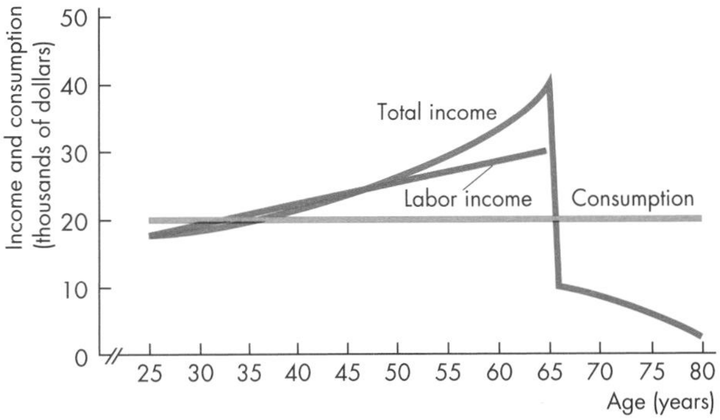

(a) Income and consumption

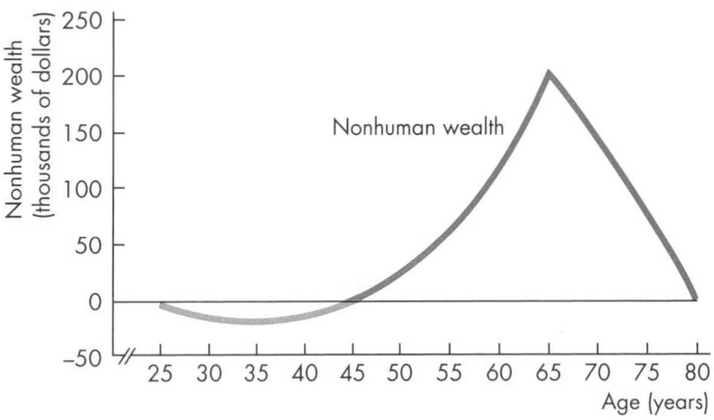

(b) Nonhuman wealth

Part (a) of the figure shows the consumption and income of a household. Consumption is constant at \$20,000 a year throughout the lifetime. Labor income starts at \$18,000 and gradually increases to \$30,000 at retirement. After retirement, the household has no labor income. Total income is labor income plus interest on capital (on nonhuman wealth). Part (b) shows the household's nonhuman wealth. In its early years, the household is consuming more than its income and going into debt. At age 35, the household is at its maximum debt. After that time, the household gradually gets out of debt and begins to accumulate nonhuman wealth up to retirement age. After retirement, the household spends its nonhuman wealth throughout the rest of its life. An economy populated by households like this one but with each household at a different stage in its life cycle will have highly unequal distributions of annual income and wealth. The small fraction of the population close to (both before and after) retirement will own almost all the economy's nonhuman wealth.

Figure 18.7 Lorenz Curves for Imaginary and Actual Economies

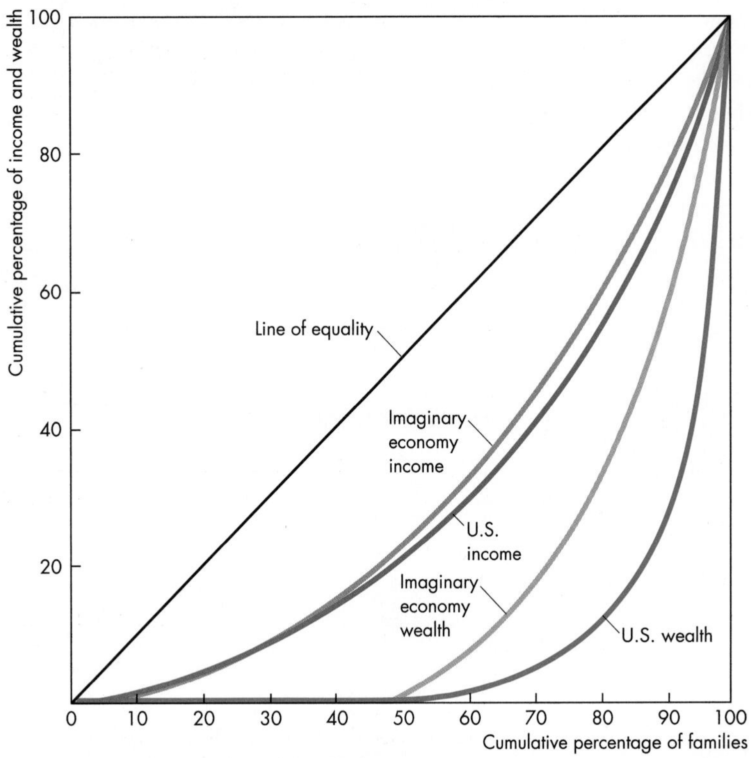

The Lorenz curves for income and wealth in the U.S. economy are shown alongside those for an imaginary economy in which everyone has the same lifetime income and consumption. The degree of lifetime inequality is exaggerated by looking only at the distribution of annual income and the distribution of nonhuman wealth.

the family gradually gets out of debt and through its sixties starts accumulating a great deal of nonhuman wealth. After retirement, that nonhuman wealth is spent on postretirement consumption.

Now suppose that there are two families identical to the one that we've looked at here but at different stages of the life cycle. One of these families is 25 years old and the other is 66. If all we look at is income, we will conclude that the 25-year-old family is almost twice as well off as the 66-year-old family. If all we look at is nonhuman wealth, we will conclude that the 66-year-old family, which has accumulated assets worth $200,000, is much better off than the 25-year-old family. Yet from the point of view of consumption, these two families are identical.

If the entire population of this imaginary economy is made up of families that are identical except for their stage of the life cycle, and if there are an equal number of people at each age, we discover some startling facts about the distributions of wealth and annual income. First, let's look at the distribution of nonhuman wealth in this imaginary economy. That distribution is illustrated in Fig. 18.7. For comparison, the wealth distribution in the United States is also shown. As you can see, the Lorenz curve for the imaginary economy's wealth distribution lies inside that for the actual U.S. economy, so wealth in the United States is more unequally distributed than wealth in the imaginary economy. This means that although inequality in wealth arising from measuring different families at different points in the life cycle accounts for some of the inequality in the real world, it does not account for it all.

Second, let's consider the distribution of annual income. The Lorenz curve for the imaginary economy is plotted against that for the U.S. economy, again in Fig. 18.7. As you can see, there is more inequality in the United States than in the imaginary economy, but the difference is smaller than it appears when we do not take account of the differences in the stage of the life cycle.

The example through which we have just worked shows that some of the measured inequality in income and wealth arises purely from the fact that different families are at different stages in the life cycle. It also shows, however, that there are important remaining inequalities in income and wealth in the United States today. In the next two sections, we're going to explore the sources of those inequalities.

Factor Prices and Endowments

Each individual owns factors of production and sells the services of those factors to provide an income. A person's income is the price paid for the use of each factor multiplied by the quantity supplied. Factor prices are determined by the forces that we analyzed in Chapters 15 through 17. The amount of each factor service that an individual supplies depends partly on the endowment of the factor owned by the individual and partly on the choices that individual makes. Let's now examine the extent to which differences in income arise from differences in factor prices and from differences in the quantity of factors that people supply.

Labor Market and Wages

We've seen that the biggest single source of income is labor. To what extent do variations in wage rates account for the unequal distribution of income? Table 18.4 helps answer this question. It sets out the average hourly earnings of private sector employees in seven industry groups in the United States in 1985. Average hourly earnings for all industries are $8.57. As a group, those working in construction earn $12.31, substantially more than the average, and those working in the retail trades earn $5.94, substantially less than the average. Within the seven groups, there is a large variation in individual wage rates. For example, in the mining group the highest paid work is in coal mining ($15.25 an hour) and the lowest paid work is in nonmetallic minerals ($10.19 an hour). In the lowest paid industry, retail trades, the highest-paid work is in food stores ($7.35 an hour), while the lowest-paid work is in eating and drinking places ($4.33 an hour).

Table 18.4 Average Hourly Earnings in 1985

Industry	Average hourly earnings (dollars)	
Mining		**11.98**
Coal mining	15.25	
Non-metallic minerals	10.19	
Manufacturing		**9.53**
Primary, nonferrous metals	13.75	
Children's outerwear	5.07	
Construction		**12.31**
Transportation		**11.40**
Pipeline transport	15.26	
Local transit	7.69	
Retail trade		**5.94**
Food stores	7.35	
Eating and drinking places	4.33	
Finance, insurance, and real estate		**7.94**
Services		**7.89**
Motion pictures	12.08	
Hotels and lodging places	5.83	
Average, all industries (private sector)		**8.57**

There is considerable inequality in average hourly earnings across different occupations. But the range of inequality is much lower than inequality of income. For example, the highest paid group, pipeline transportation workers, earns only 3½ times the income of the lowest-paid group, those who work in eating and drinking places.

Source: Statistical Abstract of the United States: 1987, 107th ed., pp. 396–398.

We can measure the spread between the highest- and lowest-paid workers in these employment categories. Take the highest-paid group of workers, those in pipeline transport who earn $15.26 an hour on the average, and divide that wage by the wage of the lowest-paid group, those working in eating and

Figure 18.8 A Normal Distribution

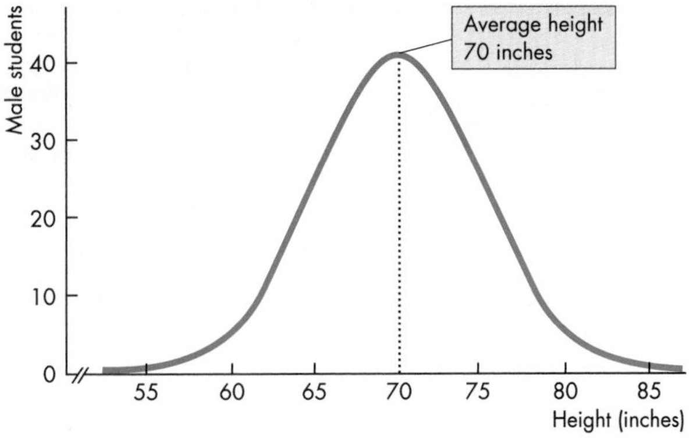

A normal distribution is shaped like a bell and is symmetric around the average. The distribution shown here is the height of a group of male students. The average height is 70 inches. For every person with a height above 70 inches, there is a mirror-image person with a height an equal distance below 70 inches. A symmetric, bell-shaped distribution describes a large number of human characteristics.

drinking places who earn $4.33 an hour. That calculation, which we call a wage differential, is 15.26 divided by 4.33, which is (approximately) 3.5. This differential says that the highest-paid group of workers earns 3.5 times as much as the lowest-paid group.

One of the things that a wage differential undoubtedly includes is the difference in skills, or human capital. For example, the most highly paid people in manufacturing work in nonferrous metals (copper, brass, and aluminum), while the least-paid workers make children's outerwear. The wage differential between those two categories probably reflects, to some degree, differences in training and skill. Similarly, in transportation, operating highly sophisticated pipeline-transport networks requires more skill than driving a local train or bus. Again, this difference in human capital is reflected in the wage differential. You can see other examples in the table.

The distribution of income is generated not only by differences in wage rates but also by differences in the endowments or abilities of individuals. Let's now consider this source of difference.

Distribution of Endowments

Ability Although we are all endowed with equal amounts of time, we are not endowed with equal abilities. Physical and mental differences (some inherited, some learned) are such an obvious feature of human life that they hardly need mentioning. But these differences produce differences in earnings and, therefore, differences in income and wealth.

It is impossible to know for sure how such an intangible thing as "earnings potential based on ability" is distributed among the population. There are, however, many measurable characteristics of people that probably influence their earnings. For example, physical attributes such as height, weight, strength, and endurance can all be measured objectively. All of these measurable attributes appear to have what is called a normal distribution in the population. For example, Fig. 18.8 shows the distribution of heights of male students. The horizontal axis measures those heights in inches. The average height is 70 inches (5′10″). The vertical axis measures the number of students at each height. The curve in the figure traces the percentage of students at each height. The distribution is symmetric. That is, for each person above the average height there is another person who is below the average by the same amount so that the two are like a mirror image of each other. There are more people at the average and clustered around the average than there are at the two extremes.

Figure 18.9 The Distribution of Income

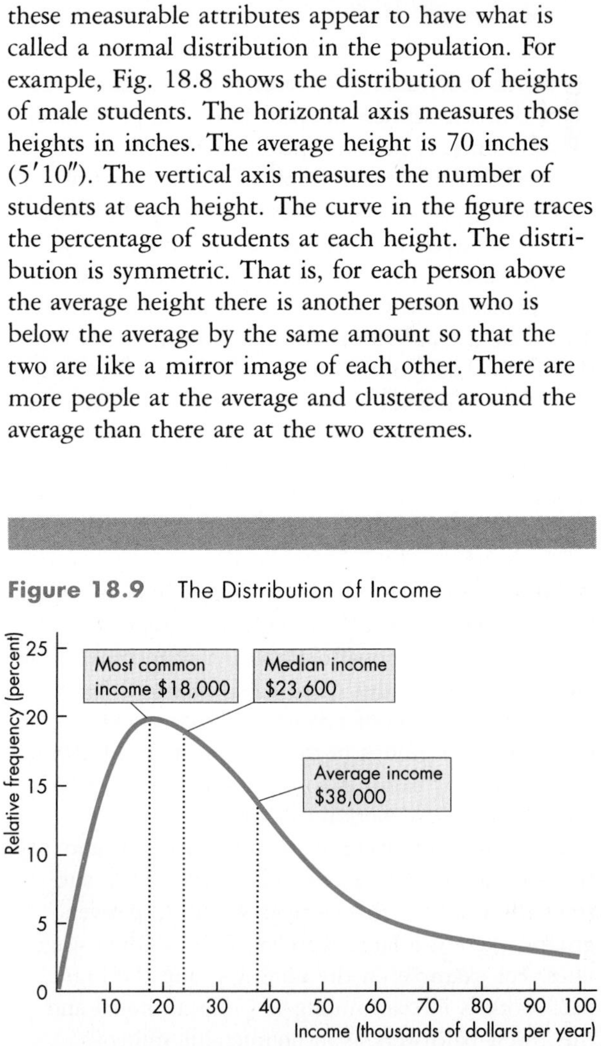

The distribution of income is unequal and is not symmetric around the average. There are many more people below the average than above the average. Also, the distribution has a long thin upper tail representing the small number of people earning very large incomes.

The range of individual ability is a major source of differences in income and wealth. But it is not the only source. If it were, the distributions of income and wealth would look like the bell-shaped curve that describes the distribution of heights in Fig. 18.8. In fact, the distribution of income looks like Fig. 18.9. Figure 18.9 shows different levels of income on the horizontal axis and the percentage of the population on the vertical axis. The median income is shown as $23,600. There are many more people below the average than above it and a relatively small number of people receive extremely high incomes. Because of this, the most common income is below the median—at $18,000—and the average income is above the median—at $38,000. The asymmetric shape of the distribution of income and wealth has to be explained by something more than the distribution of individual abilities.

Choices and the Distribution of Income and Wealth

A person's income and wealth depend in part on the choices that he or she makes. Households get paid for supplying factors of production—labor services, capital, and natural resources. The income received depends partly on the price of those factors of production and partly on the quantities that the household chooses to supply. In most cases, people can't influence the prices of the factors of production. They can't go to a bank and demand that it pay a higher interest rate, or to the New York Stock Exchange and demand that stocks improve their performance. People can't demand higher wages than the equilibrium wage rate for their babysitting, truck driving, car washing, or taxation advice work. An investment banker earns more than a parking lot attendant because of differences in human capital, but the market still determines the wages at which labor is traded.

In contrast, people can and do choose how much of each factor to supply. They also choose whether to baby-sit or to work in a bank, whether to put their savings in the bank or in stocks. Each individual chooses how much of each factor to supply. So the distribution of income depends not only on factor prices but also on people's choices about supplying factors.

We are going to discover that the choices that people make exaggerate the differences among individuals. Their choices make the distribution of income more unequal than the distribution of abilities and also make the distribution of income skewed. A skewed distribution is one in which there are a larger number of people on one side of the average than on the other. In the case of income distribution, there are more people below the average than above the average.

Let's now go on to see why people's choices lead to an unequal and skewed income distribution.

Wages and the Supply of Labor

A family's supply curve of labor shows the relationship between the quantity of labor the household supplies and the wage rate. Suppose that a family has a labor supply curve like the one shown in Fig. 18.10. At a wage rate at or below $1 an hour, the household supplies no labor. As the wage rate in-

Figure 18.10 The Supply of Labor

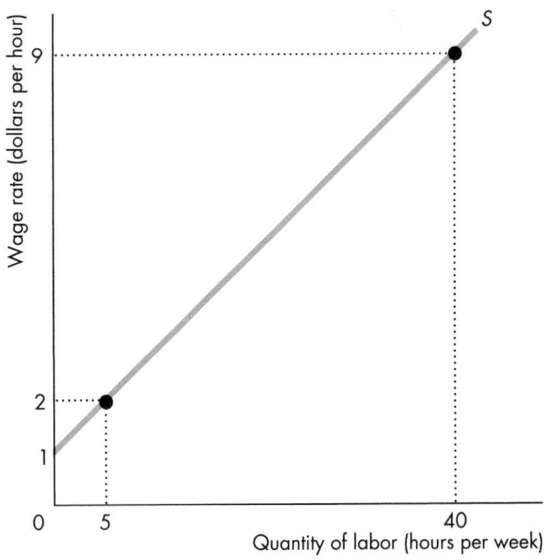

As the wage rate increases so does the quantity of labor supplied. A person facing a wage rate of $2 an hour works for 5 hours and so earns $10 a week. A person facing a wage rate of $9 an hour works for 40 hours and earns $360 a week. The wage rate of the second person is 4.5 times that of the first, but the second person's income is 36 times larger.

creases, the quantity of labor supplied increases, and at a wage rate of $9 an hour, 40 hours a week of labor are supplied. The fact that the quantity of labor supplied increases as the wage rate increases results in the distribution of income being more unequal than the distribution of hourly wages. It also results in the distribution of income being skewed even if the distribution of wages is symmetric. To see why these features of the income distribution occur, let's imagine a population of 1000 people, each one of whom has a labor supply curve like the one shown in Fig. 18.10.

Although everyone has the same labor supply curve, suppose that they each have a different marginal revenue product of labor and so are paid a different wage rate (see pp. 407–410). Figure 18.11 describes this artificial economy. Part (a) shows the distribution of marginal revenue products—and hourly wage rates—for the 1000 people. This distribution is a normal curve—bell-shaped, like the distribution of students' heights. The average wage rate is $5 an hour and the wage ranges from $1 an hour to $9 an hour.

Figure 18.11(b) shows the distribution of weekly income. Since people who earn a higher hourly wage work longer hours, their weekly income is disproportionately larger than that of people with low hourly wages who work shorter hours. As you can see from Fig. 18.11(b), the most common income is $100 a week, but the average income is $128 a week. Those who earn $2 an hour only work 5 hours a week for a weekly wage of $10. Those who earn $9 an hour work 40 hours a week for a wage of $360. Thus the range of income from the highest to the lowest is 36 to 1. In contrast, the wage rate of the highest paid is only 4.5 times that of the lowest paid.

Choices also make the distribution of income skewed. You can see this by looking again at Fig. 18.11(b). A larger proportion of the population has an income below the average than above the average.

The example through which we have just worked is, of course, artificial. But the point that it illustrates applies in the real world. Other things being equal, the higher the wage rate, the more labor will a person supply; therefore the distribution of income is more unequal than the underlying distribution of abilities. Even if the distribution of abilities is symmetric, the distribution of income will be skewed. More people will have incomes below the average than above the average.

How important is this source of income inequality? It is impossible to give a firm and precise answer to this question, but we can get some idea of its importance by comparing the distribution of hours of work with the distribution of income. The poorest 20 percent of the population has 5 percent of the income but does only 2 percent of the hours of work. The richest 20 percent receives 43 percent of the income but does only 35 percent of the work. It is the middle groups who do a larger percentage of the work than the percentage of income that they receive. There is a direct relationship between the percentage of the work performed and the percentage of income received by each of the five groups. But the poorest and the richest groups each obtain a bigger fraction of the income than the fraction of the work that they perform, while the middle groups perform a bigger fraction of the work than the fraction of the income that they receive. This feature of the distribution of income and work reflects the fact that the poorest families receive a large amount of their income directly from the government while the richest receive a large amount of their income in the form of dividends and interest.

Another choice that makes for unequal distributions in income and wealth is savings and bequests. Let's now look at this source of inequality.

Savings and Bequests

A **bequest** is a gift from one generation to the next. The wealthier the family, the more that family tends to save and bequeath to later generations. By making a bequest, a family can spread good and bad luck across the generations.

Savings and bequests are not inevitably a source of increased inequality. Savings that merely redistribute uneven income over the life cycle to enable consumption to be constant are an example of savings having no effect on inequality. A generation that is lucky might make a bequest to a generation that is unlucky, in which case the bequest would be a source of equality not inequality. But there are two important features of bequests that do make intergenerational transfers of wealth a source of increased inequality:

- Debts cannot be bequeathed
- Mating is assortative

Bequeathing debts Though a person may die with debts in excess of assets, those debts cannot be forced onto the remaining members of the family of the deceased debtor. Also, as a rule, it is difficult to incur

Figure 18.11 The Distribution of Wages, Hours, and Income

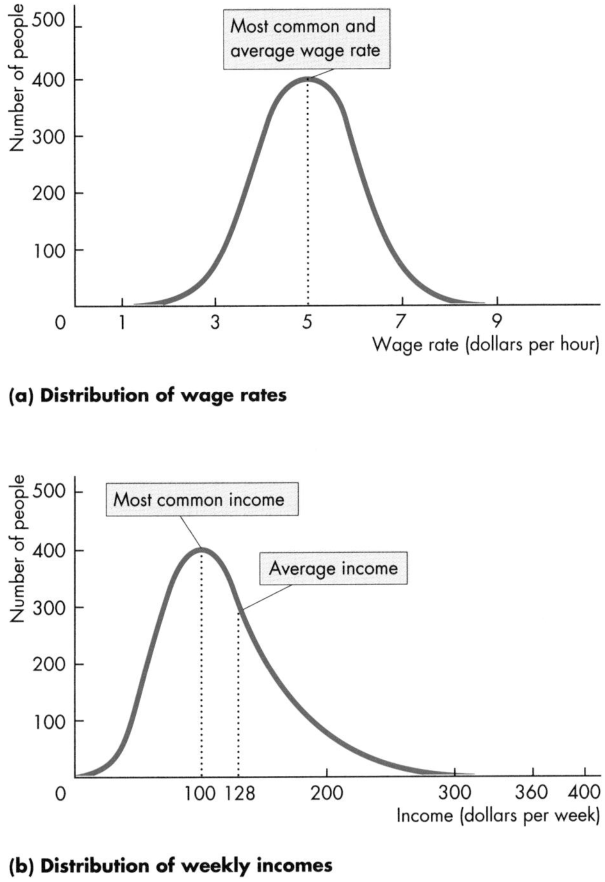

Economic choices create a skewed income distribution. Part (a) graphs the distribution of wages. It is symmetric around the average wage rate of \$5 an hour. Part (b) graphs the distribution of weekly income. A majority of the people earn less than the average income. The higher the wage rate, the more labor will a person supply; therefore the distribution of income is more unequal and not symmetric around the average. The range of inequality in wage rates—\$1 to \$9—is accentuated in the inequality of weekly income—\$0 to \$360.

debts in excess of assets. It is hard to find anyone willing to lend if there is not some kind of security either in the form of assets that could be seized and sold or in the form of a future earnings potential.

Because a zero inheritance is the smallest inheritance that anyone can receive, savings and bequests can only add to future generations' wealth and income potential. The vast majority of people inherit nothing or a very small amount from the previous generation. A tiny number of people inherit enormous fortunes. As a result of bequests, the distribution of income and wealth is not only more unequal than the distribution of ability and job skills but also more persistent. A family that is poor in one generation is more likely to be poor in the next. A family that is enormously wealthy in one generation is more likely to be enormously wealthy in the next. But there is a tendency for income and wealth to converge, across the generations, to the average. Though there can be long runs of good luck or bad luck, or good judgment or bad judgment, across the generations, such long runs are uncommon. However, one additional feature of human behavior slows down convergence to the average and makes wealth and income inequalities persist—assortative mating.

Assortative Mating **Assortative mating** means that people tend to marry within their own socioeconomic class. In the vernacular, "like attracts like." Although there is a good deal of folklore that "opposites attract," perhaps such Cinderella tales appeal to us because they are so rare in reality. Marriage partners tend to have similar socioeconomic characteristics. Wealthy individuals seek wealthy partners. The consequence of assortative mating is that inherited wealth becomes more unequally distributed.

We've now completed our positive analysis of inequality in the distribution of income and wealth. We've described the extent of inequality and have identified some of the reasons that it exists. But we have not attempted to make any assessment about fairness or justice in the distribution of income and wealth. Is it fair that some people can be so incredibly rich and others so abjectly poor? In the final section of this chapter, we examine the way in which economists and philosophers have tried to wrestle with this type of question.

Ideas about Fairness

We all have views about fairness and what constitutes a "fair" distribution of income and wealth. These views are diverse, and they are a source of political and philosophical debate. Throughout the ages, moral philosophers have tried to find a satisfactory theory of distributive justice. A **theory of distributive justice** is a set of principles against which we can test whether a particular distribution of economic well-being is fair. There are two broad classes of theories of distributive justice: end-state theories and process theories.

An **end-state theory of distributive justice** focuses on the justice or fairness of the outcomes or ends of economic activity. A **process theory of distributive justice** focuses on the justice or fairness of the *mechanisms* or *means* whereby the ends are achieved. For example, the belief that everyone should have exactly the same income and wealth is an end-state theory. The belief that everyone should have the same *opportunity* to earn and accumulate wealth is a process theory. Equality of income and wealth requires an equality of outcomes or ends. That is, when the process is over, everyone has to have the same income and wealth. Requiring that people have equal opportunity does not imply that they will have equal income and wealth because people will use their opportunities in different ways. Depending on how they use their opportunities and on a variety of chance events (good and bad luck), unequal income and wealth will emerge.

End-State Theories

The two leading end-state theories of distributive justice are the utilitarian and Rawlsian theories.

The **utilitarian theory** is that the fairest outcome is the one that makes the sum of the utilities of all the individuals in a society as large as possible. If Rob gets less utility than does Ian from the last dollar spent, then fairness requires that a dollar be taken from Rob and given to Ian. The reduction in Rob's utility is less than the gain in Ian's utility, so society is better off. Redistribution should take place until the marginal utility of the last dollar spent by each individual is the same. Utilitarian theories of fairness were developed in the eighteenth and nineteenth centuries by such economists as David Hume, Adam Smith, Jeremy Bentham, and John Stuart Mill.

The **Rawlsian theory of fairness** is that the fairest distribution is that which gives the least well-off member of society the biggest income possible. In the Rawlsian view, if the poorest person can be made better off by taking income from any other person, justice requires that such redistribution take place. The Rawlsian theory of fairness was developed in the 1960s by John Rawls, a contemporary philosopher at Harvard University, and published in his classic work, *A Theory of Justice,* in 1971.[3]

As you can see, the two end-state theories of justice differ in what they regard as the desirable end-state or desirable outcome: For the utilitarian, it is the average or sum of all the individuals that counts; for Rawls, it is the least well-off individual or individuals that count.

How Much Inequality Is Consistent with End-State Theories?

It used to be thought that an end-state theory of justice implied that complete equality in the distribution of income was the best outcome. This conclusion was reached by reasoning along the following lines. First, people are pretty much alike in their capacity for enjoyment. (In the technical language of economics, they have the same marginal utility of income schedule.) Second, marginal utility declines with income. Therefore by taking a dollar from a rich person and giving it to a poorer person, the marginal utility lost by the rich person is less than the marginal utility gained by the poorer person. Thus, taking from the rich and giving to the poor increases total utility. Maximum utility occurs when each individual has the same marginal utility, a point that is reached, only when incomes—after redistribution—are equal. When incomes have been equalized, total utility of the society has been maximized and "fair shares" have been achieved.

The Big Tradeoff

Although it used to be thought that justice implied complete equality, it is now recognized that there exists what has been called a "big tradeoff" between fairness and economic efficiency. The term comes from the title of a book[4] by Arthur Okun, chairman of the Council of Economic Advisors to President Lyndon Johnson.

The big tradeoff is based on the following idea. Greater equality can be achieved only by taxing productive activities. Taxing people's income from their

---

[3]John Rawls, *A Theory of Justice* (Cambridge: Harvard University Press, 1971).

[4]Arthur Okun, *Equality and Efficiency: The Big Tradeoff* (Washington, D.C.: Brookings Institution, 1975).

work and savings lowers the after-tax income they receive. This lower income makes them work and save less. In economic terms, lower after-tax factor prices result in reduced factor supplies. Lower factor supplies result in smaller output and the smaller output results in less consumption not only for the rich but also, possibly, for the poor. According to this line of reasoning, the correct amount of redistribution to undertake depends on the balance between greater equality and lower average level of consumption.

It also must be recognized that taking resources from the rich to give to the poor cannot be achieved without using resources to administer the redistribution. Tax-collecting agencies such as the Internal Revenue Service as well as all the tax accountants, auditors, and lawyers together with the welfare-administering agencies use massive quantities of skilled labor and capital equipment, such as computers, to do their work. A dollar collected from a rich person does not translate into a dollar received by a poor person. The bigger the scale of redistribution, the greater are the costs of administering the process.

When these aspects of redistribution are taken into account, it is not obvious that taking a dollar from a rich person to give to a poor person increases the welfare of the poor person. The wealth available for redistribution could be reduced to the point where everyone is worse off. Taking account of the disincentive effects of redistribution and the resource costs of administering the redistribution is what produces the "big tradeoff." A more equally shared pie results in a smaller pie.

The Process View of Justice

The process view of distributive justice was given its most recent statement by Harvard philosopher Robert Nozick in his book *Anarchy, State, and Utopia.*[5] Nozick argues that no end-state theory of justice can be valid and that a theory of justice must be based on the justice of the mechanisms through which the distribution of income and wealth arises. Nozick argues for the justice of a system based on private property rights, where private property can be acquired and transferred only through voluntary exchange. His argument can be illustrated with the following story.

We start out with a distribution that you personally regard as the best possible. Now suppose that your favorite rock singer enters into a contract with a recording company and a rock concert organizer. The deal is that she will get 5 cents on every record sold and 50 cents for every ticket sold to her rock concerts. In a given year, she sells 5 million records and 500,000 people attend her concerts. Her total income is half a million dollars. This income is much larger than the average and much larger than she had under the original "ideal" distribution.

Is she entitled to this income? Is the new distribution unfair? The original distribution was fair. You and five million other fans contributed 5-cent and 50-cent pieces to the income of this successful singer. Was there something illegitimate about you buying a record and attending a rock concert? Nozick believes that she is entitled to the income and that there is nothing illegitimate about you and your friends buying records and attending rock concerts. According to Nozick's definition of fairness, the new distribution is also fair.

The philosophical debate continues and will perhaps never be settled. This state of affairs is no deterrent to those in the practical world of politics. While moral philosophers continue their disagreement about fairness, politicians are creating and implementing policies designed to chop off the extremes of the distribution of income and achieve a greater measure of equality.

■ We have examined the distributions of income and wealth in the United States and seen that there is a large amount of inequality across families and individuals. Some of that inequality arises from comparing families at different stages in the life cycle. But even taking a lifetime view, there remains a great deal of inequality. Some of that inequality arises from differences in rates of pay. But economic choices accentuate those differences. Also, savings and bequests result in the growth of huge wealth concentrations over the generations.

The topic that we have examined in this chapter is highly political and, as we've seen, governments attempt to redistribute income to alleviate the worst aspects of poverty. In the next three chapters, we're going to undertake a systematic study of a broad range of political economic issues and of the economic behavior of government. We'll return to questions concerning the distribution of income and wealth as part of that broader study.

[5] Robert Nozick, *Anarchy, State, and Utopia* (New York: Basic Books, 1974).

SUMMARY

Distribution of Income and Wealth in the United States Today

Labor's share in income is the largest and it has grown slightly over the years. It is approximately three quarters of total income. The distribution of wealth and income among individuals is uneven. The richest 1 percent of Americans own almost one third of the total wealth in the country. The poorest 50 percent own only 1 percent of the total wealth. Income is distributed less unevenly than wealth. The income distribution has changed only slightly over time and in the direction of a lower degree of inequality. The poorest people in the United States are most likely to be older, single, black women, with less than eight years of schooling, living in the South. The richest are most likely to live on the West Coast and to be college-educated, middle-aged, white families with husband and wife living together. Income tax and social welfare programs result in a redistribution of income, taking more from the rich than the poor and, to some degree, alleviating poverty. (pp. 469–476)

Comparing Like with Like

In order to judge the extent of inequality, it is important that we make valid comparisons. The measured distribution of wealth exaggerates the degree of inequality because it fails to take into account the distribution of human capital. The distributions of annual income and wealth exaggerate the degree of lifetime inequality because they do not take into account the stage in a family's life cycle. (pp. 477–481)

Factor Prices and Endowments

Differences in income and wealth arise partly from differences in individual endowments and partly from differences in factor prices. Wage rates vary considerably, depending on skill and other factors. But these differences, on their own, are not enough to account for differences in the distribution of income and wealth. Those differences get exaggerated by the economic choices that people make. (pp. 481–483)

Choices and the Distribution of Income and Wealth

The economic choices that people make have an important influence on income and wealth. Attitudes toward work result in some people taking a larger amount of leisure, earning a smaller income than others, and consuming a smaller amount of goods. Also, savings and bequests affect wealth across the generations. Because of assortative mating—the tendency for wealthy individuals to seek wealthy marriage partners—bequests accentuate inequality. (pp. 483–485)

Ideas about Fairness

People disagree on what constitutes a fair distribution of income. Moral philosophers have tried to resolve the issue by finding principles on which we can all agree, but agreement still has not been reached. Two broad groups of theories have been developed: end-state theories and process theories. End-state theories of fairness assert that it is the outcome that matters. Process theories assert that it is equality of opportunity that matters. (pp. 485–487)

KEY CONCEPTS

Assortative mating, 485
Bequest, 484
Distribution after taxes and transfers, 476
End-state theory of distributive justice, 486
Lorenz curve, 470
Market distribution, 475

Key Figures

REVIEW QUESTIONS

1 Which of the following describe the distributions of personal income and wealth in the United States today?
   a) The distributions of income and wealth are best represented by normal or bell-shaped curves.
   b) The richest people are more than 800 times as wealthy as the poorest people, but there is the same percentage of people at each different level of wealth.
   c) More than 50 percent of the population is wealthier than the average.
   d) More than 50 percent of the population is poorer than the average.

2 Which is more unequally distributed, income or wealth? In answering this question, pay careful attention both to the way in which income and wealth are measured by official statistics and to the fundamental concepts of income and wealth.

3 What is wrong with the way in which the official statistics measure the distribution of wealth?

4 Explain why the work/leisure choices made by individuals can result in a distribution of income and consumption that is more unequal than the distribution of ability. If ability is distributed normally (bell-shaped), will the resulting distribution of income also be bell-shaped?

5 Explain how the distribution of income and wealth is influenced by bequests and assortative mating.

6 What is a Lorenz curve? How does a Lorenz curve illustrate inequality? Explain how the Lorenz curves for the distributions of income and wealth in the United States economy differ from each other?

PROBLEMS

1 Imagine an economy in which there are five people who are identical in all respects. They each live for 70 years. For the first fourteen of those years, they earn no income. For the next 35 years, they work and earn $30,000 a year from their work. For their remaining years, they are retired and have no income from labor. To make the arithmetic easy, let's suppose that the interest rate in this economy is zero; the individuals consume all their income during their lifetime and at a constant annual rate. What are the distributions of income and wealth in this economy if the individuals have the following ages:
   a) All are 45
   b) 25, 35, 45, 55, 65

   Is case (a) one of greater inequality than case (b)?

2 You are given the following information about income and wealth shares:

	Income shares (percent)	Wealth shares (percent)
Lowest 20%	5	0
Second 20%	11	1
Third 20%	17	3
Fourth 20%	24	11
Highest 20%	43	85

Draw the Lorenz curves for income and wealth for this economy. Explain which of the two variables—income or wealth—is more unequally distributed.

3 An economy consists of 10 people, each of whom has the following labor supply schedule:

Hourly wage rate (dollars per hour)	1	2	3	4	5
Hours worked per day	0	1	2	3	4

The people differ in ability and earn different wage rates. The distribution of *wage rates* is as follows:

Wage rate (dollars per hour)	1	2	3	4	5
Number of people	1	2	4	2	1

a) Calculate the average wage rate.
b) Calculate the ratio of the highest to the lowest wage rate.
c) Calculate the average daily income.
d) Calculate the ratio of the highest to the lowest daily income.
e) Sketch the distribution of hourly wage rates.
f) Sketch the distribution of daily incomes.
g) What important lesson is illustrated by this problem?

Part 7

Markets and Government

Talking with Alfred Kahn

During his career, Alfred E. Kahn has been the chairman of the New York Public Service Commission and has received presidential appointments as chairman of the Civil Aeronautics Board, chairman of the Council on Wage and Price Stability, and Advisor on Inflation. Dr. Kahn is a professor of political economy at Cornell University. Michael Parkin spoke with him about his experience in public service and about his views on regulation and deregulation.

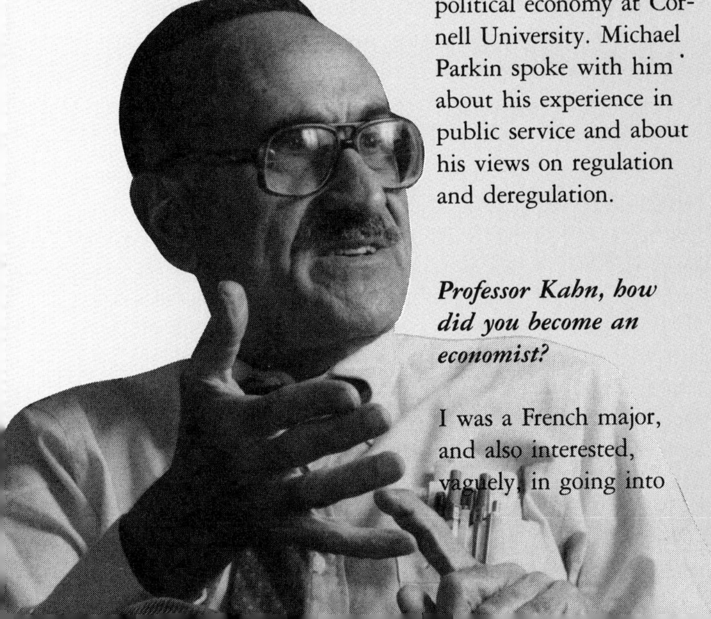

Professor Kahn, how did you become an economist?

I was a French major, and also interested, vaguely, in going into the theater. I also loved mathematics, but decided, foolishly, that it had no practical usefulness. Then I took a course in economics and found it terribly interesting. I went to school during the Depression, when the world's worst problems seemed to be economic; and I wanted to make a difference in the world. I always thought—even 12 years after my Ph.D.—that I would go to law school, so as to be able to participate actively in public policy.

Just at that time, however, I was invited to be a member of the Attorney General's National Committee to Study the Antitrust Laws, since my second book was in that field, and shortly after that to the senior staff of the Council of Economic Advisers; and

I realized that I could be involved in making policy in the real world and be an academic economist as well.

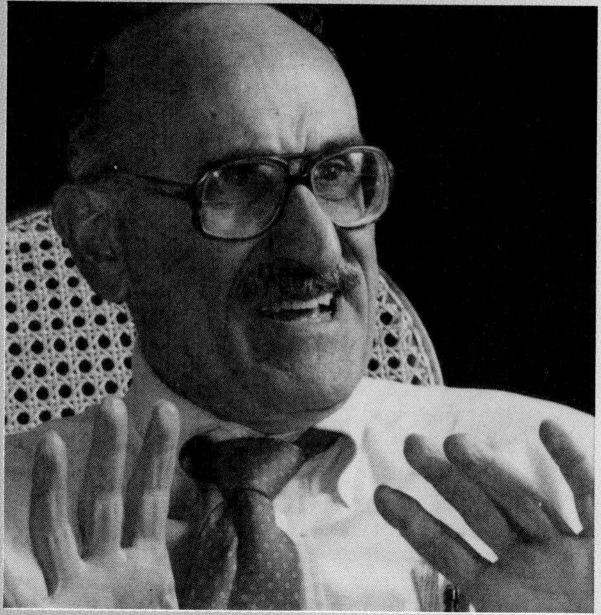

In 1978, as chairman of the Civil Aeronautics Board, you helped bring about the deregulation of the airline industry. How does airline deregulation look to you today?

Although there have been surprises and disappointments, it has done most of the things I expected it would do. The principal purpose by far was to unleash competition. Regulation had thoroughly cartelized the industry; the result was monstrous inefficiency, and a failure to give travelers the benefits of price competition.

"Prohibit involuntary bumping, and require airlines to solicit volunteers. How? Offer bribes."

And this has been accomplished?

The industry is unquestionably far more competitive than it was under regulation, even with the disappearance of low-cost carriers like People Express. The release of the existing airlines to invade one another's markets, and the removal of restraints on pricing has produced savings to travelers amounting to $10 to $15 billion a year. And under the pressures of price competition, some of the worst inefficiencies encouraged by regulation have been eliminated—overscheduling, half-empty planes, inefficient route structures and work practices—while accident rates are down 35 to 45 percent.

But there have been problems?

Of course. There has been enormous turmoil and confusion. That was no surprise; competition is much messier and more turbulent than regulation, but that's because it is also much more creative.

While the explosion of competitive entry was beyond my wildest hopes, the rapid departure of most of the new airlines has left us with a handful of carriers with significant monopoly power. Travelers in and out of hubs that are dominated by a single carrier, especially travelers whose demand is inelastic, are probably being exploited; discretionary travelers, who can stay over a weekend, can still get real bargains.

Of course, we all now sit around in airports much longer. Is this a consequence of deregulation?

Yes, but in large part it is a measure of its success. It is the result of the fantastic response of travelers to the bargain fares that are now available. But we have not had a corresponding response on the supply side. We rely on government agencies for the supply of safety inspectors and air traffic controllers and for the availability of air channels and airport space; and those agencies have been grossly delinquent in expanding capacity.

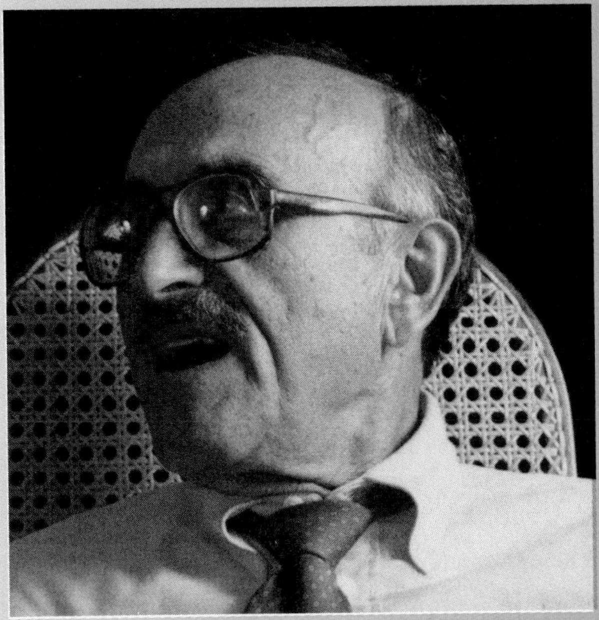

Had you anticipated these problems when you set out to deregulate the industry?

Yes, indeed. Back in 1977 and 1978 I warned the Federal Aviation Administration that with more people and new airlines flying, they were going to need bigger budgets to fulfill their responsibilities for air safety. I also warned them about airport congestion. If you see airplanes waiting for an hour on a runway for the chance to take off, elementary economics will tell you that it reflects one of two failures—a failure to expand supply efficiently or a failure to price correctly.

Was a background in economics good training for a new chairman of the Civil Aeronautics Board?

I think it was indispensable. I'll give you an example. In one of my early cases, transatlantic cargo carriers wanted to charge lower rates per pound for flights, as I recall, from east to west than from west to east, because they had a lot of empty space on their planes going that way. The CAB lawyers opposed such differences as discriminatory. But elementary economics tell us that price differences are not discriminatory if the marginal costs differ; and the marginal cost of space in a plane that would otherwise be partially empty could be as low as zero. The CAB's requirement of uniform charges prevented the carriers from filling their planes on the back hauls.

Were there other opportunities to apply elementary economics?

Yes, consider the rules we established for bumping passengers on overbooked flights. The board had been trying for years to set equitable bumping priorities. But there are no acceptable principles.

I pointed out that allocating the scarce seats was a problem of economic efficiency, with a simple market solution. All we needed to do was prohibit involuntary bumping, and require the airlines instead to solicit volunteers. How? By offering bribes. The elegant result is that nobody to whom the value of staying on the plane, or the cost of getting off, exceeds the bribe, need give up the seat. And nobody takes the bribe unless its value to him or her exceeds that cost.

Has the climate for deregulation changed? Are there new industries that are candidates for deregulation, or are we done with it?

"If competition is to work, government has a vital role to play."

"Regulation had thoroughly cartelized the airline industry. The result was monstrous inefficiency."

The process of liberalization, once begun, tends to become cumulative: I think we will see continued infusion of competition and deregulation, for example, in telecommunications and in the electric and gas utilities.

On the other hand, in some ways we may be coming to the end of the era, partly because the failure of governments to do their job has resulted in severe dissatisfactions. In the case of the airlines, the major derelictions have been in strenuous enforcement of the antitrust laws and expanding air traffic capacity. In case of the

savings and loan institutions, it has been a failure to close down recklessly run or insolvent banks, or to force their owners to put up more capital, leaving them free to continue to attract depositors: why should depositors worry, so long as their dollars are federally insured?

The failure to recognize that in many ways deregulation can mean increased responsibilities of government has been discrediting deregulation itself.

What guiding principles of economics do you apply to your work?

First, the importance of economic efficiency, which calls for prices equated to marginal cost. That carries you a tremendous distance. But, second, it doesn't answer the question of what institutional mechanisms are best adapted to give you the efficient result, including the incentive constantly to improve efficiency. The answer is competition, wherever it is remotely feasible.

Third, if competition is to work, government has a vital role to play—for example, in enforcing the antitrust laws, protecting consumers from deception, protecting the environment, and in hundreds of other ways.

Finally, we must never forget that economics is only a means to an end; the end is a good society and a good life for its people. We are never going to make good policy if we ignore the requirements of economic efficiency; but we are never going to make it either unless we keep clearly in mind the social goals and ultimate values we are trying to serve.

What advice would you give to young people today who are interested in pursuing careers in the public sector?

I don't see how anybody can participate intelligently in the making of public policy without an understanding of economics. But do not study only economics; study also politics, history, and literature. Like every other discipline, economics is limited by its own implicit assumptions and goals. We all look for keys lost in the dark under the street lamp familiar to us, because that's the only place we have any hope of finding them; but they may not be under that lamp at all. The particular principles and hypotheses that most economists employ are one kind of street lamp. It sheds a great deal of light; but we should always be open to the challenge of looking under other people's street lamps as well.

Chapter 19

Market Failure

After studying this chapter, you will be able to:

- Describe the range of economic actions governments undertake
- Outline the structure of the government sector of the United States economy
- Distinguish between a normative and a positive analysis of government economic behavior
- Define market failure and explain how it might be overcome by government action
- Distinguish between private goods and public goods
- Explain the free-rider problem
- Explain how government provision of public goods avoids the free-rider problem
- Explain how property rights and taxes and subsidies may be used to achieve a more efficient allocation of resources when externalities are present

Government—the Solution or the Problem?

Government is big business—one of the biggest. In 1989, the U.S. federal government employed more than 5 million people and spent more than $1 trillion. State and local governments employed a further 14 million people, spending $0.7 trillion between them. Independent government agencies employed yet another million people. What do all these people and all these dollars do for us? Is the government sector of our economy doing more than it should? Is it simply too big? Is government, as President Ronald Reagan often suggested, "the problem"? Or, despite its enormous size, is government doing less than it should? Is government too small? Is more government activity and intervention the solution to many outstanding problems? ■ Governments provide an enormous array of goods and services. Some are intangibles like laws and their enforcement; others are tangibles like schools and highways. Why does government supply some goods and not others? You've probably seen a Wells Fargo security truck delivering cash to your local bank. Why does Wells Fargo, a private company, supply security services to banks while the local police department provides similar services to residential neighborhoods, streets, and highways? What is so special about roads and highways, nuclear weapons, and judicial services that results in such services always being provided by government and never by private firms? ■ We've been hearing a lot recently about our endangered planet. The massive quantities in which we burn fossil fuels—coal, natural gas, and oil—have some obvious and immediate effects on the atmosphere that result in acid rain. And there are harder to measure but potentially more serious effects on the chemical balance of the earth's atmosphere, increasing the proportion of carbon dioxide and reducing the proportion of other elements. It is predicted that the continuation of this process will result in a gradual warming up of the planet—the so-called greenhouse effect. It is also predicted that the persistent and large-scale use of chlorofluorocarbons (CFCs) will cause irreparable damage to the earth's ozone layer, thereby exposing us to an increased amount of radiation. These environmental issues are simultaneously everybody's problem and nobody's problem. Everyone is put at risk by the continued damage to our atmosphere and yet no one individual can take the necessary action to protect the environment. What, if anything, might government do to protect our environment? How can the government help us to take account of the damage that we cause others every time we turn on our heating or air conditioning systems?

■ We have spent a great deal of time studying the economic choices of households and firms. We have seen how households make choices governing the allocation of the factors of production that they own and how those choices determine their incomes. We've also seen how they choose their spending and saving. We've seen how firms choose the quantities of goods and services to produce and the techniques with which to produce them. We've seen how households and firms interact in markets for goods and services and for factors of production. ■ We've also seen that households and firms do not make their choices in a political vacuum. Their choices are influenced by actions taken by government. For example, rent controls and minimum wage laws influence the way competitive markets operate. We've also seen that many markets are not competitive. They have monopoly elements, and those elements often arise from legal restrictions on competition. ■ In this chapter and the next two, we turn our attention to the economic choices that governments make and to the effects of those choices on the economy. In this chapter, our main concern is to describe the government sector and explain how the market economy, in the absence of a government, would fail to achieve an efficient allocation of resources. We also provide a brief sketch of the economic theory of government behavior that serves as an outline that will be elaborated and applied in the subsequent two chapters on this broad and important topic.

■ We begin by describing the main components of the government sector of the economy and by looking at the size of government and the way in which it has grown over the past 50 years.

The Government Sector

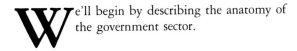

We'll begin by describing the anatomy of the government sector.

The Structure and Scale of Government

The government sector of the U.S. economy consists of more than 80,000 separate organizations, some tiny like the Yuma, Arizona, School District, and some enormous like the U.S. federal government. The total government sector of the U.S. economy accounts for 35 percent of spending on goods and services and 36 percent of total employment.

There are three levels of government in the United States: federal, state, and local. The federal government spends more than the state and local governments do—about $1 trillion a year—but local government has the highest number of employees—close to 10 million. Each level of government is organized into branches and departments. The branches of government are the legislature, judiciary, and executive, and the departments are the bureaucracies that take care of the day-to-day business of government. The bulk of government economic activity takes place in the Departments of Defense, Health, and Treasury. Including military personnel, the Defense Department employs almost two thirds of total government-sector employees and spends almost one third of the budget. The Department of Health and Human Services, which administers welfare programs (including social security), spends more than one third of the total budget. Even the Treasury Department spends close to one fifth of the budget (mainly on debt interest and tax collection).

The Scale and Growth of Government

The scale of government has changed dramatically over the years. In 1940, for example, government-sector expenditure accounted for less than 20 percent of the economy's total expenditure, while in 1990 it had reached 35 percent. But the growth of government expenditure over the past 50 years probably understates the growth of the importance of government in economic life. That importance stems partly from the government's expenditure and partly from the extent of the laws and regulations passed by government that affect the economic actions of individual households and firms. We look at this aspect of government in Chapter 21 where we study regulation and antitrust.

Our main task in this chapter is not to describe the anatomy of government and the pace at which it has grown but to analyze the failure of markets to achieve *allocative efficiency* and to explore the role of government in coping with market failure. Before we embark on that main task, we're going to take an overview of the alternative approaches that economists use to study the economic behavior of government.

The Economic Theory of Government

We all have opinions on political matters and some of those opinions are strongly held. As students of economics, our task is to understand, explain, and predict the economic choices that the government sector makes. Although we cannot suppress our political views, it is important, if we are to make progress in studying political behavior, to continually remind ourselves of the important distinction between positive and normative analysis. We first reviewed that distinction in Chapter 1 (pp. 17–18). But because the distinction is so important for the economic study of political behavior, let's remind ourselves of what that distinction is.

Positive and Normative Analysis An economic analysis of government choices may be either *positive* or *normative.* The positive analysis of government seeks to explain the reasons for and effects of government economic choices. A normative analysis seeks to evaluate the desirability of a government action and argues for or against some particular proposal. Positive analysis seeks to understand what is; normative analysis seeks to reach conclusions on what *ought* to be. The economic analysis used in both of these activities is similar. But the use to which the analysis is put differs. Here we undertake a positive study of government action; that is, we seek to understand the reasons for and the effects of the actions that we see being undertaken by governments in the United States today. We do not seek to establish the desirability of any particular course of action or to argue for or against any particular policy.

All government economic action stems from two aspects of economic life:

- Market failure
- Redistribution

Market Failure One explanation for government intervention in the economy is market failure. **Market failure** is the inability of an unregulated market to achieve, in all circumstances, allocative efficiency. There are three types of situations in which market failure arises:

- The provision of goods and services that we consume in common with everyone else
- The production of goods and services where *external costs* or *external benefits* are present
- The restriction of output by monopolies and cartels

In all three cases, the unregulated market produces waste in the sense that a different allocation would result in producing more of some goods without producing less of others and could make someone better off without making anyone worse off. It is important not to take this last statement as being normative. The presence or absence of waste is a positive matter. It is a statement about what *is.* A prediction that government action will (or will not) occur to eliminate such waste is also a positive statement. The proposition that government *ought* (or ought not) to intervene to eliminate waste is normative. In dealing with market failure, it is the positive aspects that will be our concern.

Redistribution Another explanation for government intervention in the economy is to redistribute income and wealth. Such redistribution is usually justified on the basis of some notion of equity or distributive justice, which we discussed in Chapter 18. But not all redistribution is explained in this way. The creation of monopoly and government protection of cartels also results in the redistribution of income and wealth. And the *rent-seeking* activities that we described in Chapter 13 have an important political dimension.

Again, it is important to keep the distinction between positive and normative aspects of the redistributive role of government clear. The proposition that most people believe that the market distributions of income and wealth are unfair is positive. The proposition that government intervention can redistribute income from the rich to the poor is also positive. The statement that the government *ought* to redistribute income and wealth is normative. We have described the scale of income redistribution in Chapter 18 and we will study it further in Chapter 20. When we do so, our focus will be entirely on its positive aspects.

Public Interest and Public Choice There are two broad classes of economic theories of government behavior:

- Public interest theories
- Public choice theories

A **public interest theory** of government behavior predicts that government action will take place to eliminate waste and achieve an efficient allocation of resources. A **public choice theory** predicts that the behavior of the government sector of the economy is the outcome of individual choices made by voters, politicians, and bureaucrats interacting with each other in a political marketplace. According to the public interest theory of government, whenever there is market failure, government action can be designed to eliminate the consequences of that failure and to achieve allocative efficiency. According to the public choice theory, matters are not that simple. Not only is there the possibility of market failure (arising in the situations that we have outlined above), but there is also the possibility of "government failure." That is, it is possible that when voters, politicians, and bureaucrats each pursue their own best interests and interact in the political "marketplace," the resulting "public choice" no more achieves the elimination of waste and the attainment of allocative efficiency than does an unregulated market. Understanding why not is the main topic of Chapter 20.

In the next section, we're going to explain more fully the economic role of the government arising from two of the sources of market failure—the provision of goods and services that we consume in common with everyone else, and the production of goods and services where external costs or external benefits are present. The other source of market failure, arising from monopoly and cartels, and the government regulation of such industries, is dealt with in Chapter 21.

Public Goods

Why does the government provide certain goods and services such as a legal system, a system of national defense, schools and highways, and public health services? Why don't we simply leave the provision of these goods and services in the hands of private firms that sell their output in markets? How much national defense would we have if a private firm, Star Wars, Inc., had to compete for our dollars in the marketplace in the same way that McDonald's and Coca-Cola do?

Most of the answers to these questions lie in the distinction between private goods and public goods.

Private Goods and Public Goods

A **private good** is a good or service each unit of which is consumed by only one individual. An example of a private good is a can of soda. There are two important features of a private good. The first feature is called *rivalry.* Rivalry emphasizes the idea that one person's consumption can take place only at the expense of another person's. If you increase your consumption of soda by one can, other things being equal, someone else has to consume one can less. The second feature of a private good is called *excludability.* Once you have bought a can of soda, the soda is yours to do with as you choose. You can exclude others from using it.

A **pure public good** is a good or service each unit of which is consumed by everyone and from which no one can be excluded. An example of a pure public good is the national defense system. There are two important features of a pure public good that parallel the two features that we identified concerning a private good. The first feature is called *nonrivalry.* One person's consumption of a pure public good does not reduce the amount available for someone else. For example, your consumption of the security provided by a national defense system does not decrease the security of anyone else. The second feature is called *nonexcludability.* No one can be excluded from the additional security that every citizen enjoys from the national defense system.

Many goods lie between a pure public good and a private good. Such goods are called **mixed goods.** An example of a mixed good is a highway. A highway is like a pure public good until it becomes congested. One more car or truck on a highway with plenty of space on it does not reduce the consumption of highway services of anyone else. But once the highway is congested, the addition of one more user lowers the quality of the service available for everyone else—it becomes like a private good.

Pure public goods and mixed goods with a large public element—all referred to as public goods —give rise to what is called the free-rider problem.

Free Riding

A **free rider** is someone who consumes a good without paying for it. The **free-rider problem** is the tendency for the scale of provision of a public good to be too small if it is produced and sold privately. The free-rider problem arises because there is no incentive for a person to pay for a good if the payment makes no difference to the quantity of the good that the person is able to consume. Public goods are such goods. To see why, let's look at an example.

Imagine that an effective, antimissile laser weapon has been developed. One of these new weapons can attack and destroy 400 intercontinental ballistic missiles within seconds of their being launched. The larger the number of antimissile laser weapons deployed, the larger is the number of missiles destroyed. Potential enemies have 1500 missile launchers and four of the new weapons can eliminate all of them. Three can do a pretty good job and even two can severely limit the amount of damage that will be inflicted by missiles that get through the laser defense.

But the new weapons system is very expensive. To build it, resources have to be diverted from peaceful space programs and from the development of other productive uses of lasers in medicine. As a result, the larger the number of weapons installed, the greater is their marginal cost.

Our task is to work out the scale on which to install this new defense system to achieve allocative efficiency. We'll then examine whether private provision can achieve allocative efficiency and we'll discover that it cannot—that there is a free-rider problem.

Benefits and Costs

The benefits provided by a weapons system are based on the preferences and beliefs of the consumers of the services of that system. The costs are based on technology and the prices of the factors of production used to produce the system. When studying private goods, we observed that the value of a good to an individual is the maximum amount that the person is willing to pay for one more unit of the good. We worked out this value from the individual's demand curve. That is, the demand curve tells us the quantity demanded at a given price, or for a given quantity, the maximum price that is willingly paid for the last unit bought. We can work out the value a person places on a public good in a similar manner. That is, the value that a person places on a public good is the maximum amount willingly paid for one additional unit of the good.

To calculate the maximum amount that a person is willing to pay for one more unit of a public good, we first need to establish that person's total benefit schedule. **Total benefit** is the total dollar value that a person places on a given level of provision of a public good. The greater the scale of provision, the larger is the total benefit. The table in Fig. 19.1 sets out an example of the total benefits to Lisa and Max of different scales of provision of the proposed antimissile lasers. Lisa and Max believe that the weapons system reduces the chance of a nuclear war occurring and, if it does occur, increases the chance of preventing nuclear warheads from reaching their targets. The more lasers there are in place, the greater is the degree of security, but up to a maximum level. Each additional laser is believed to provide less additional security than the previous one. The increase in total benefit resulting from a unit increase in the scale of provision of a public good is called its **marginal benefit.** The marginal benefits to Lisa and Max are calculated in the table in Fig. 19.1 As you can see, the greater the scale of provision, the smaller is the marginal benefit. By the time 4 lasers are deployed, Lisa perceives no additional benefits, and Max perceives only $10 worth. Lisa's and Max's marginal benefits are graphed as MB_L and MB_M, respectively, in parts (a) and (b) of the figure.

The marginal benefit of a public good is the maximum amount that a person is willing to pay for one more unit of the good. This maximum amount varies with the quantity of the good consumed. The greater the quantity, the smaller is the maximum amount that will be paid for one more unit.

Part (c) of the figure shows the economy's marginal benefit curve, *MB* (where the economy has only two people, Lisa and Max). The marginal benefit curve of a public good for an individual is similar to the demand curve for a private good. But there is an important difference between the economy's marginal benefit curve for a public good and the market demand curve for a private good. To obtain the market demand curve for a private good, we add up the quantities demanded by each individual at each price. In other words, we sum the individual demand curves horizontally (see Fig. 7.1, p. 157). In contrast,

Figure 19.1 Benefits of a Public Good

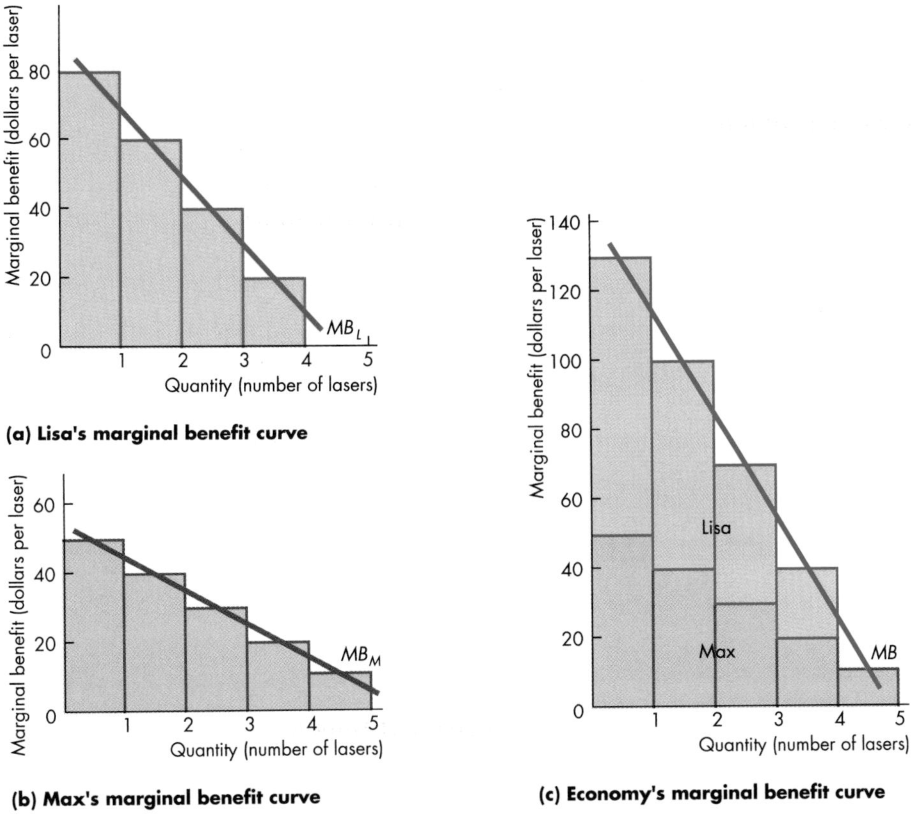

The table shows various scales of provision of an antimissile laser defense system. It also lists the total benefits accruing to Lisa, Max, and the economy (comprised of only Lisa and Max) of different scales of provision. The table also calculates the marginal benefit—the change in total benefit resulting from a unit increase in the scale of provision—to Lisa, Max, and the economy. The marginal benefits are graphed in the figure, for Lisa in part (a) and for Max in part (b). The marginal benefit to the economy at each level of provision is the sum of the marginal benefits to each individual and is shown in part (c). The marginal benefit curves are MB_L for Lisa, MB_M for Max, and MB for the economy.

Quantity (number of antimissile lasers)	**Lisa** Total benefit (dollars)	**Lisa** Marginal benefit (dollars per laser)	**Max** Total benefit (dollars)	**Max** Marginal benefit (dollars per laser)	**Economy** Total benefit (dollars)	**Economy** Marginal benefit (dollars per laser)
0	0		0		0	
		80		50		130
1	80		50		130	
		60		40		100
2	140		90		230	
		40		30		 70
3	180		120		300	
		20		20		 40
4	200		140		340	
		 0		10		 10
5	200		150		350	

to find the economy's marginal benefit curve of a public good, we sum the marginal benefits to each individual at each quantity of provision. That is, we sum the individual marginal benefit curves vertically. The resulting marginal benefit for the economy comprised of just Lisa and Max is calculated in the table,

Figure 19.2 The Efficient Scale of Provision of a Public Good

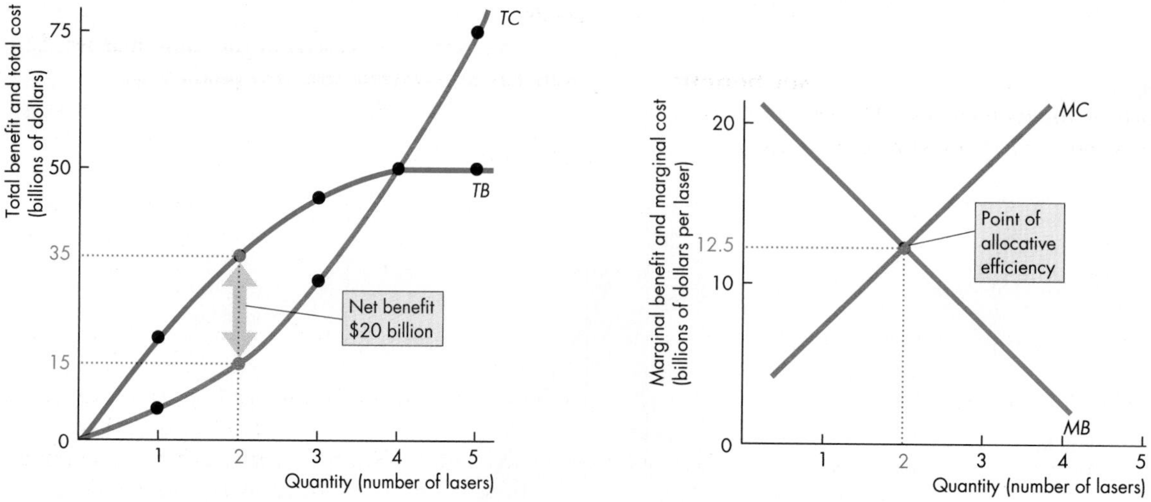

(a) Total benefit and total cost curves

(b) Marginal benefit and marginal cost curves

Quantity (number of antimissile lasers)	Total benefit (billions of dollars)	Marginal benefit (billions of dollars)	Total cost (billions of dollars)	Marginal cost (billions of dollars)	Net benefit (billions of dollars)
0	0		0		0
		20		5	
1	20		5		15
		15		10	
2	35		15		20
		10		15	
3	45		30		15
		5		20	
4	50		50		0
		0		25	
5	50		75		−25

The table shows the total benefit and marginal benefit to the entire economy of various scales of provision of a laser weapons system. It also shows the total cost and marginal cost of the various scales of provision. Total benefit and total cost are graphed in part (a) as the total benefit curve, *TB*, and the total cost curve, *TC*. Net benefit is visible as the vertical distance between these two curves and is maximized when 2 lasers are installed. Part (b) shows the marginal benefit curve, *MB*, and marginal cost curve, *MC*. Where marginal cost equals marginal benefit, net benefit is maximized and allocative efficiency is achieved.

and the economy's marginal benefit curve is graphed in part (c)—the curve labeled *MB*.

An economy with just two people would certainly not buy any antimissile lasers—their total benefits fall far short of their cost. But an economy with 250 million people might. To determine the efficient scale of provision, consider the example set out in Fig. 19.2. The first two columns of the table show the hypothetical total and marginal benefits to the entire economy (consisting of 250 million people).

The next two columns show the total and marginal cost of producing antimissile lasers. These costs are opportunity costs and are derived in exactly the same way as the costs associated with the production of sweaters that we studied in Chapter 10. The final column of the table shows net benefit. **Net benefit** is total benefit minus total cost. The efficient scale of provision is the one that maximizes net benefit.

Total benefit and total cost are graphed as the total benefit curve, *TB*, and total cost curve, *TC*, in part (a). Net benefit is also visible in that part of the figure as the vertical distance between the two curves. Net benefit is maximized when that distance is at its largest, a situation that occurs at a scale of provision of 2 lasers. This is the efficient scale of provision.

Another way of describing the efficient scale of provision is in terms of marginal benefit and marginal cost. The marginal benefit and marginal cost of lasers are graphed as the marginal benefit curve, *MB*, and marginal cost curve, *MC*, in part (b). When marginal benefit exceeds marginal cost, net benefit increases if the quantity produced increases. When marginal cost exceeds marginal benefit, net benefit increases if the quantity produced decreases. When marginal benefit equals marginal cost, net benefit cannot be increased—it is at its maximum possible level. Thus when marginal benefit equals marginal cost, allocative efficiency has been achieved.

Now that we have worked out the efficient scale of provision of a public good, let's go on to see how much of such a good would be provided by a private producer.

Private Provision

We have now worked out the scale of provision of a national defense system that maximizes net benefit. Would a private firm—Star Wars, Inc.—deliver that scale of provision? It would not. To do so, it would have to collect $15 billion to cover its costs—or $60 from each of the 250 million people in the economy. But no one would have any incentive to buy his or her "share" of the laser weapon system. Each person would reason as follows: The number of antimissile lasers provided by Star Wars, Inc., is not going to be affected by my $60. But my own private consumption is going to be affected by whether or not I pay. If I do not pay, I will enjoy the same level of security from the laser weapons and more of other goods. Therefore it pays me to keep my $60 and spend it on other goods, my consumption of which is affected by my spending on them. In other words, it pays me to free ride on the public good and buy private goods.

Since everyone reasons in the same manner, Star Wars has zero revenue and zero production.

Public Provision

Suppose that the people in this economy have instituted a government that makes the following proposition: The government will collect $60 from each person and will spend the resulting $15 billion to provide 2 antimissile lasers. Will the people vote for this proposition? Clearly they will. If there is no antimissile system (the output of Star Wars, Inc.), the marginal benefit of installing one laser greatly exceeds its marginal cost. By proposing to provide 2 antimissile lasers, the government is offering each voter a level of security that maximizes net benefit. The voters obtain a benefit of $35 billion—$140 each—for a total cost of $15 billion—$60 each. Since the voters recognize this as an improvement over the zero provision by Star Wars, Inc., they will vote for it.

Whether or not actual governments produce public goods on a scale that maximizes net benefit is something that we examine in Chapter 20. But we have established a key proposition: A government is able to provide any public good on a scale larger than that provided by a private producer.

R E V I E W

If people make their own decisions about the provision of public goods and buy those goods in private markets, there is a free-rider problem. It is in everyone's individual interest to free ride, with the result that the scale of provision of the goods is smaller than that required for allocative efficiency. A government that balances marginal cost and marginal benefit provides the public good on a scale that achieves allocative efficiency. ■

Let's now turn to the second source of market failure, externalities.

Externalities

An **externality** is a cost or a benefit arising from an economic transaction that falls on a third party and that is not taken into account by those who undertake the transaction. For example, when a chemical factory dumps its waste products into a river and kills the fish, it imposes an externality—in this case, an external cost—on the fisherman who lives downstream. Since these costs are not borne by the chemical factory, they are not taken into account in deciding whether to dump waste into the river, and if so, how much. When a person in Los Angeles drives a car that burns leaded gasoline and does not have a catalytic converter, an externality—again, an external cost—is imposed on everyone who tries to breathe the unbreathable air. When a homeowner fills her garden with beautiful spring bulbs, she generates an externality—in this case an external benefit—for all the joggers and walkers who pass by. In deciding how much to spend on this lavish display, she takes into account only the benefits accruing to herself.

Two particularly dramatic externalities have received a lot of attention in recent years. The first arises from the use of chlorofluorocarbons (CFCs). These man-made chemicals are used in a wide variety of products—from coolants in refrigerators and air conditioners, to plastic phones, to cleaning solvents for computer circuits. Though the precise chemistry of the process is not understood, and even the subject of dispute, many atmospheric physicists believe that the consumption of CFCs damages the atmosphere's protective ozone layer. Discoveries of depleted ozone over Antarctica in 1983 have heightened fears of extended ozone depletion. The National Academy of Sciences has estimated that a 1 percent drop in ozone levels might cause a 2 percent rise in the incidence of skin cancer. Diminished ozone is also believed to be a possible cause of cataracts.

The second externality arises from burning fossil fuels that add carbon dioxide and other gases to the atmosphere, which prevents infrared radiation from escaping, resulting in what has been called the "greenhouse effect." If the greenhouse scenario turns out to be correct, it is predicted that much of the Midwest will become a dustbowl and many eastern and Gulf Coast regions will disappear under an expanded Atlantic Ocean (see Reading Between the Lines, pp. 506–508.)

When you take a cold drink from the refrigerator or switch on the air conditioner on a steamy August evening, you do not take into account the consequences of your actions on global atmospheric matters. You compare the private benefits to yourself of drinking the cold can of soda or having a comfortable night's sleep with the cost that *you* have to incur. You do not count the costs of an increase in the incidence of skin cancer as part of the price that has to be paid for the cold soda.

Externalities are not always negative—they are not always external costs. In fact, many activities bring external benefits. Education is a good example. Not only do more highly educated people derive benefits for themselves in the form of higher incomes and the enjoyment of a wider range of artistic and cultural activities, but they also bring benefits to others through social interaction. But in deciding how much schooling to undertake, we make our calculations on the basis of the costs borne by us and the benefits accruing to us as individuals. We do not take into account the extra benefits that we're creating for others.

Health services also create external benefits. The pursuit of good health and personal hygiene reduces the risk that people with whom we come into contact will be infected by transmitted diseases. Again, in making economic choices about the scale of resources to devote to health and hygiene, we take account of the costs borne by ourselves and the benefits accruing to ourselves and not the greater benefit that our actions bring to others.

The existence of externalities—both costs and benefits—is another source of market failure. There are two possible types of action that governments can take to achieve a more efficient allocation of resources in the face of externalities:

- Establish and enforce private property rights.
- Tax those activities producing external costs and subsidize those that bring external benefits.

First, let's briefly consider the use of private property rights for dealing with externalities.

Private Property Rights and Externalities

There are some cases in which externalities arise because of an absence of private property rights. A **private property right** is a legally established title to the sole ownership of a scarce resource. A private property right is enforceable in the courts.

The creation of externalities in the absence of private property rights is illustrated well by the example of the chemical factory and a private fishing club. Members of a private fishing club use a particular stretch of a stream that is well stocked with excellent fish. A chemical factory opens upstream from the fishing club. It has to make a decision about how it will dispose of some of its waste products.

Consider two different legal situations. In the first, no one owns the stream. If the chemical factory dumps its waste products in the stream, its cost of waste disposal is zero. But the waste kills the fish and the fishing club goes out of business.

In the second situation, there are property rights established in the stream. The fishing club owns its stretch of the stream and the fish that swim in it. The chemical factory might still dump its waste into the stream but if it does so, and if it kills the fish, the fishing club will successfully bring a lawsuit against the chemical plant for damages. The damages paid to the fishing club are the cost to the chemical company of disposing of the chemical waste by dumping it in the river. If some other method of waste disposal is available that has a lower cost than killing the fish, the chemical factory will choose that alternative.

Whenever externalities arise from the nonexistence of property rights that can easily be established and enforced, this method of dealing with externalities is a natural one for governments to contemplate. But there are many situations in which private property rights simply cannot be established and enforced. In these cases, governments resort to the alternative method of coping with externalities—using taxes and subsidies. Let's see how these government tools work.

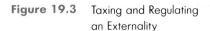

Figure 19.3 Taxing and Regulating an Externality

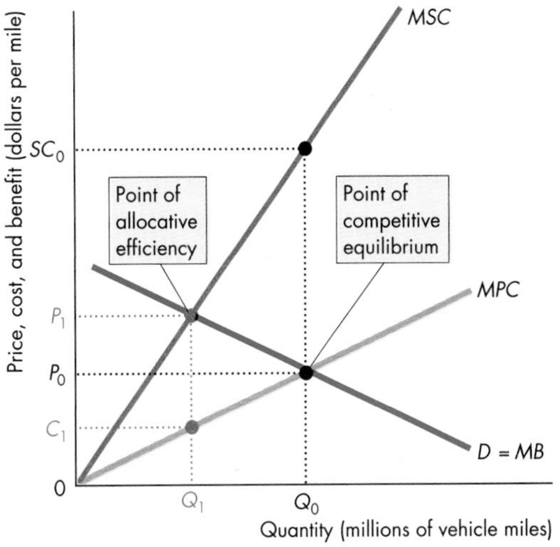

The demand curve for transportation services is also the marginal benefit curve (D = MB). The marginal private cost curve is MPC. Because of congestion and environmental pollution, the marginal cost of providing transportation services exceeds the marginal private cost. Marginal social cost is shown by curve MSC. If the market is competitive, output is Q_0 and the price is P_0. Marginal social cost is SC_0. If a tax is imposed to confront producers of transportation services with their full marginal social cost, the MSC curve becomes the relevant marginal cost curve for suppliers' decisions. The price increases to P_1 and the quantity decreases to Q_1. Allocative efficiency is achieved.

Taxes and External Costs

As we've just noted, every time you burn fossil fuel you release CO_2 into the atmosphere. These CO_2 emissions impose unintended costs on others. Let's see how the government might modify your choices and encourage you to take account of the potential costs that you're imposing on others.

One activity that creates CO_2 is driving a gasoline-fuelled vehicle. To study the demand for this activity, we'll examine the market for transportation services. Fig. 19.3 illustrates this market. The demand curve is also the marginal benefit curve, the curve $D=MB$. It tells us how much consumers value each different level of output. Curve MPC measures the marginal private cost of producing transportation services. **Marginal private cost** is the marginal cost directly incurred by the producer of a good. Thus the MPC curve shows the marginal cost directly incurred by the producers of transportation services. But there are externalities in transportation. The fact that fossil fuels are burned creates atmospheric pollution and contributes to the greenhouse effect. It also causes other, more immediate health problems. Furthermore, one person's decision to use a highway imposes congestion costs on others. These costs also are external costs. When all the external costs are added to the private costs, we obtain the marginal social cost of transportation services. **Marginal social cost** is the marginal cost incurred by the pro-

The Greenhouse Effect

Feeling the Heat

For more than a decade, many scientists have warned that cars and factories are spewing enough gases into the atmosphere to heat up the earth in a greenhouse effect that could eventually produce disastrous climatic changes. But until recently, the prophets of global warming garnered about as much attention as the religious zealots who insist that Armageddon is near.

Unfortunately, scientists cannot agree on how much global warming has occurred, how much more is on the way and what the climatic consequences will be, giving policymakers an excuse for delay. But no one disputes the fact that the amount of CO_2 in the atmosphere has risen and continues to increase rapidly. The possible consequences are so scary that it is only prudent for governments to slow the buildup of CO_2 through preventive measures, from encouraging energy conservation to developing alternatives to fossil fuels.

Recent research has confirmed that [the CO_2 buildup] is more than just theory. By drilling deep into Antarctic and Arctic ice, scientists have been able to measure the amount of CO_2 in air bubbles trapped in ancient layers of snow. They have also looked at fossilized plant tissues for clues as to how warm the air was during the same period. The conclusion: CO_2 levels and global temperatures have risen and fallen together, over tens of thousands of years. And there is evidence from space: Mars, which has little CO_2 in its atmosphere, has a surface temperature that reaches −24° F at best, while Venus, with lots of CO_2, is a hellish 850° F.

Carbon dioxide is released in large quantities when wood and such fossil fuels as coal, oil and natural gas are burned. As society industrialized, coal-burning factories began releasing CO_2 faster than plants and oceans, which absorb the gas, could handle it. In the early 1900s, people began burning oil and gas at prodigious rates. And increasing population led to the widespread cutting of trees in less developed countries. These trees are no longer available to soak up excess CO_2, and whether they are burned or left to rot, they instead release the gas. By the late 1800s atmospheric CO_2 had risen to between 280 and 290 parts per million. Today it stands at 350 p.p.m., and by 2050 it could reach 500 to 700 p.p.m., higher than it has been in millions of years.

By far the most efficient and effective way to spur conservation is to raise the cost of fossil fuels. Current prices fail to reflect the very real environmental costs of pumping carbon dioxide into the air. The answer is a tax on CO_2 emissions—or a CO_2 user fee, if that is a more palatable term. The fee need not raise a country's overall tax burden; it could be offset by reductions in income taxes or other levies.

Imposing a CO_2 fee would not be as difficult as it sounds. It is easy to quantify how much CO_2 comes from burning a gallon of gasoline, a ton of coal or a cubic yard of natural gas. Most countries already have gasoline taxes; similar fees, set according to the amount of CO_2 produced, could be put on all fossil-fuel sources. At the same time, companies could be given credits against their CO_2 taxes if they planted trees to take some of the CO_2 out of the air.

A user fee would have benefits beyond forcing a cutback in CO_2 emissions. The fuels that generate carbon dioxide also generate other pollutants, like soot, along with nitrogen oxides and sulfur dioxide, the primary causes of acid rain. The CO_2 tax would be a powerful incentive for consumers to switch from high-CO_2 fuels, such as coal and oil, to power sources that produce less CO_2, notably natural gas.

Ultimately, though, the world must move away from fossil fuels for most of its energy needs. Said Berrien Moore, director of the Institute for the Study of the Earth, Oceans and Space at the University of New Hampshire: "Even if you cut emissions of CO_2 in half, the atmospheric concentration will keep going up. You're still adding CO_2 faster than you're withdrawing it, so the balance keeps rising."

Of all the known nonfossil energy sources, only two are far enough along in their development to be counted on: solar and nuclear, neither of which generates any greenhouse gases at all. Solar power is especially attractive. It produces no waste, and it is inexhaustible. Not all solar power comes directly from the sun: both wind and hydroelectric power are solar, since wind is created by the sun's uneven warming of the atmosphere and since the water that collects behind dams was originally rain, which in turn was water vapor evaporated by solar heating.

But wind and hydroelectric power can be generated at only a relatively few sites, and so governments should redouble financing for research to develop efficient, low-cost photovoltaic power. Photovoltaic cells, which produce electric current when bathed in sunlight, were briefly in vogue during the energy crises of the 1970s, and while public attention and Government funding have waned, research into the technology has continued. "The capital costs have come down from about $50 a peak watt to $5," said [Gus] Speth [of the World Resources Institute]. If they drop to $1, solar power will become competitive. That could happen without significant Government research support—but it will happen sooner with it.

***Time*, January 2, 1989**

By Michael D. Lemonick

The Essence of the Story

- The amount of carbon dioxide (CO_2) in the earth's atmosphere has been increasing and continues to do so.

- In the late 1800s, atmospheric CO_2 was between 280 and 290 p.p.m.; in the late 1900s, it has been 350 p.p.m.; by 2050, it could reach 500 to 700 p.p.m.

- Although there is disagreement among scientists, many predict that these increasing concentrations of CO_2 are leading, and will continue to lead, to an increase in the earth's average temperature.

- The relationship between CO_2 and temperature is suggested by evidence from CO_2 air bubbles in ancient snow layers and fossilized plant tissue. Evidence is also provided by the relationship between CO_2 content and surface temperature on the neighboring planets of Mars and Venus.

- There are two ways government can intervene to control the greenhouse effect:

  —Imposing a tax on CO_2 emission
  —Subsidizing the development of solar energy

Background and Analysis

- The marginal private cost of generating electricity by using fossil fuels is the curve *MPC* (in each figure). The marginal cost of generating electricity using solar power is the curve *MC*.

- The power generated by solar energy has no externalities.

- The power generated by fossil fuel creates a carbon dioxide buildup with a possible greenhouse effect.

- The greenhouse effect imposes potentially large social costs: By changing weather patterns and land use patterns, it will increase the cost of food production; by melting the polar ice caps, it will raise the ocean levels, reducing the amount of usable land.

- The marginal social cost of generating electricity by using fossil fuels, including the external costs of the greenhouse effect, is the curve *MSC*.

- The market demand curve for electricity is *D*.

- With no intervention (Fig. a), the market supply curve is *S*; this curve is made from the *MPC* curve for fossil fuels and the *MC* curve for solar power.

- Equilibrium occurs at price P_0 and quantity Q_0; only fossil fuels are used; the marginal social cost is MSC_0, which exceeds the price; there is an allocative inefficiency—too much electricity is generated.

(Continued on next page.)

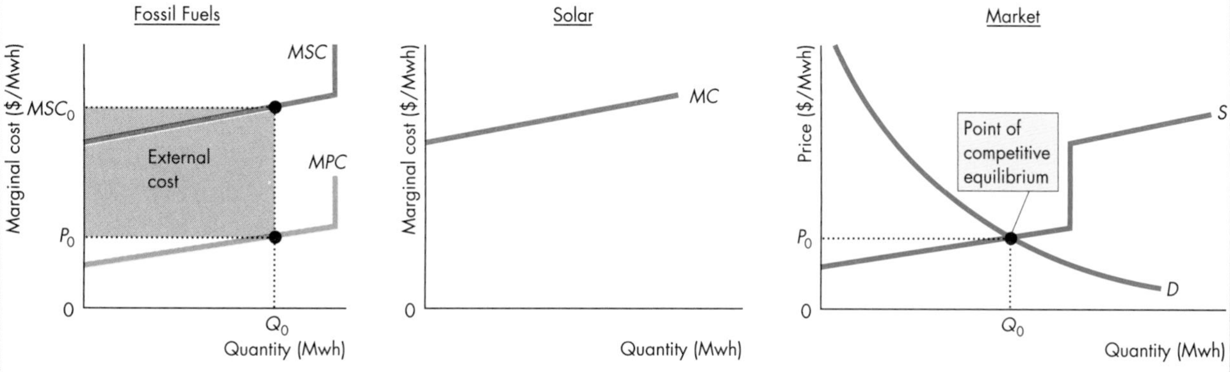

(a) No intervention

Background and Analysis (cont.)

- If a CO_2 tax is imposed (Fig. b) equal to the external costs, fossil fuel producers of electricity face costs shown by the curve "*MPC* + *tax* = *MSC*."
- The market supply curve becomes curve "*S* +*tax*."
- Equilibrium occurs at price P_1 and quantity Q_1; Q_{1F} is produced by fossil fuels and Q_{1S} by solar energy; marginal social cost is MSC_1, which equals the price P_1; allocative efficiency is achieved.
- If the development of solar energy is subsidized and fossil fuels are not taxed, (Fig. c), fossil fuel producers of electricity face the marginal cost curve *MPC* and solar producers face the marginal cost curve "*MC* − *subsidy*."
- The market supply curve is "*S* − *subsidy*."
- Equilibrium occurs at price P_2 and quantity Q_2; Q_{2F} is produced using fossil fuels and Q_{2S} using solar energy.
- Marginal social cost is MSC_2, which exceeds price P_2 and an allocative inefficiency remains; too much electric power is generated.
- A similar parallel analysis can be applied to CFCs and other atmospheric pollutants.

Conclusion

- To achieve allocative efficiency in the face of an externality, the externality has to be identified and its magnitude assessed.
- If a tax is imposed equal to the external marginal cost, allocative efficiency is achieved.
- Subsidizing a substitute activity that does not have external costs is not equivalent to taxing an activity that does have an external cost and does not achieve allocative efficiency.

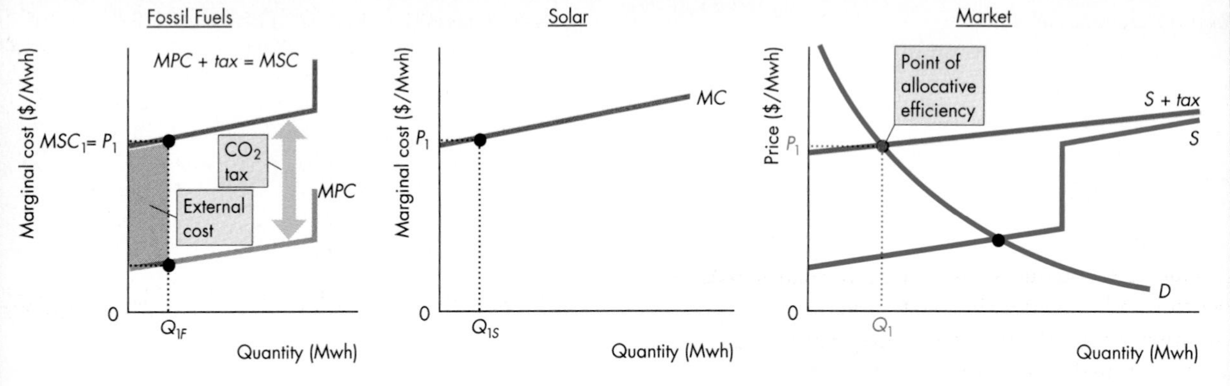

(b) CO_2 tax

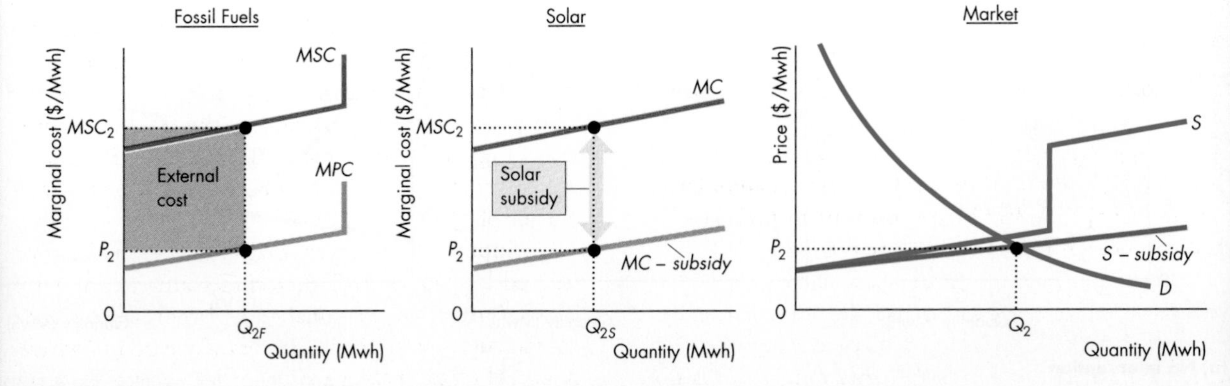

(c) Solar subsidy

ducer of a good together with the marginal cost imposed as an externality on others. Marginal social cost is illustrated by the curve *MSC* in the figure.

Suppose that the transportation market is competitive and unregulated. People will balance the marginal private cost against the marginal benefit and travel Q_0 million miles at a price of P_0 per mile. At this scale of travel, a large amount of external costs will be borne. The marginal social cost is SC_0. The difference between P_0 and SC_0 represents the marginal cost imposed on others—the external marginal cost.

Suppose that the government taxes transportation and that it sets the tax equal to the external marginal cost. By imposing such a tax, the government raises the marginal private cost—the original marginal private cost *plus* the tax—to equal the marginal social cost. The *MSC* curve is now the relevant marginal cost curve for each person's decision since each person now faces a marginal cost of transportation equal to its marginal social cost. The market supply curve shifts upward to become the *MSC* curve. The price rises to P_1 and the amount of travel falls to Q_1. The marginal cost of the resources used in producing Q_1 million miles of travel is C_1 but the marginal external cost generated is P_1 minus C_1. That external marginal cost is paid by the consumer through the tax.

The situation depicted at the price P_1 and the quantity Q_1 is allocatively efficient. At an output rate above Q_1, social marginal cost exceeds the marginal benefit; at an output below Q_1, social marginal cost is less than the marginal benefit. In the first situation, producing less reduces costs by more than it reduces benefits and increases the net benefit. In the second situation, by producing more, marginal benefit exceeds marginal cost and net benefit increases.

Figure 19.4 Subsidizing an External Benefit

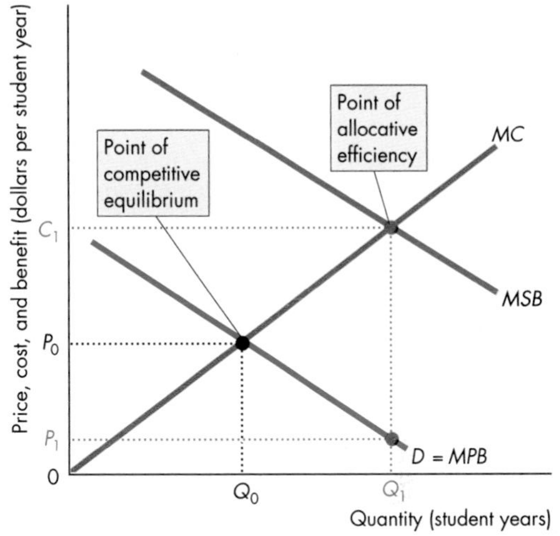

The demand curve for education also measures the marginal private benefit to education ($D = MPB$). The marginal cost of education is shown by curve *MC*. If education is provided in a competitive market with no government intervention, the price of education is P_0 and the quantity bought Q_0. But education produces a social benefit and the marginal social benefit is shown by the curve *MSB*. Allocative efficiency is achieved if the government provides education services on a scale such that marginal social cost equals marginal social benefit. This scale of provision is Q_1, which is achieved if the government subsidizes education, making it available for a price of P_1. The quantity demanded at a price of P_1 is Q_1, and at that quantity marginal cost equals marginal social benefit at a level of C_1.

Subsidies and External Benefits

Some goods bring external benefits—benefits to people who do not directly consume the good. In some cases, the government induces additional consumption of such goods by subsidizing them. A **subsidy** is a payment made by the government to producers that depends on the level of output. Figure 19.4 shows how subsidized education can increase the amount of education and achieve allocative efficiency. Suppose that the marginal cost of producing education is shown by the curve *MC* (assuming there is no difference between marginal private cost and marginal social cost). The demand curve for education tells us the quantity of education demanded at each price when people are free to choose the amount of education that they undertake and have to pay for it themselves. It also measures the marginal private benefit—the benefit perceived by the individual undertaking education. That curve is $D = MPB$. A private competitive education market will produce an output of Q_0 at a price of P_0.

Suppose that the external benefit—the benefit derived by people other than those undertaking education—results in marginal social benefits described by the curve *MSB*. Allocative efficiency occurs where marginal cost equals marginal social benefit, at output Q_1. By providing the quantity of education Q_1 and by making it available at a price P_1, the government can achieve allocative efficiency in the education sector. In this case, by providing education at a low price, the government is able to encourage people to undertake the amount of education that makes its marginal social benefit equal to its marginal cost, rather than making the marginal private benefit equal to marginal cost.

We've now looked at two examples of the way in which government action can achieve an economic outcome different from that of a private unregulated market, by helping market participants take account of the external costs and benefits deriving from their actions. We've also illustrated government interventions that achieve allocative efficiency where the unregulated market fails to do so—where there is market failure. Because we can design a level of government intervention that achieves allocative efficiency in an economic model, it does not automatically mean that actual governments are able to achieve this outcome. Just as in the case of public goods, it is possible that the political equilibrium resulting from the interactions of voters, politicians, and bureaucrats leads to an outcome other than one of allocative efficiency. We'll explore this possibility in the next chapter.

REVIEW

When externalities are present, the market allocation is not efficient. Sometimes an efficient allocation can be achieved by establishing private property rights. But in many cases, private property rights simply cannot be established and enforced. In such cases, if the government confronts people with taxes equivalent to the external marginal costs, or subsidies equivalent to external marginal benefits, it induces people to produce goods on a scale that achieves allocative efficiency, even in the face of externalities. ■

■ We've seen that markets do not always achieve allocative efficiency. When the market fails, we can describe an allocation that is efficient. But showing an efficient allocation is not the same thing a designing institutions to achieve one. Do governments in fact achieve allocative efficiency? Or are there economic problems arising from the functioning of a political system leading to "government failure" and preventing the attainment of an efficient allocation of resources? These questions are dealt with in the next chapter.

SUMMARY

The Government Sector

The government sector of the U.S. economy accounts for 35 percent of all expenditure on goods and services and 36 percent of total employment. The biggest departments of government deal with the provision of defense and health services. The Treasury Department is also a large one. The government share of the economy has grown over the years, increasing from less than 20 percent in 1940 to more than 35 percent in 1990.

But when economists study political behavior, they are careful to maintain the distinction between positive and normative analysis. Their main focus is on positive matters—on what *is* and on how the political system works rather than on what *ought* to be and how the political system *ought* to function.

All government economic actions stem from either market failure or the redistribution of income and wealth. Market failure arises from the provision of public goods and services, from externalities, and from monopolies and cartels. The redistribution of income and wealth arises partly from notions of equity and justice and partly from rent-seeking activities.

There are two broad approaches to the economic analysis of government—public interest theories and public choice theories. Public interest theories emphasize the idea of government as an eliminator of waste and an achiever of allocative efficiency. Public choice theories emphasize the idea that government operates in a political marketplace in which politicians, bureaucrats, and voters interact with each other. According to the public choice view, government failure to achieve allocative efficiency is as real as the possible failure of the market. (pp. 497–499)

Public Goods

Pure public goods have two features: nonrivalry and nonexcludability. One person's consumption does not reduce the amount available for someone else (nonrivalry) and no one can be kept from sharing the consumption of such a good (nonexcludability). An example of a pure public good is the national defense system.

The existence of public goods gives rise to the free-rider problem. This problem is the tendency for the scale of provision of a public good to be too small if it is produced and sold privately. The free-rider problem arises because there is insufficient incentive for a person to pay for a good if that payment has no effect on the quantity of the good the person consumes. It thus pays everyone to free ride, so with private provision no revenue can be raised from the sale of a public good. In such a situation, no public goods will be produced. In contrast, the government can produce a public good, paying for it out of taxation. People will vote for taxes and a public good provided that the net benefits are positive. The government is able to provide any public good on a scale larger than that provided by a private producer, but it does not necessarily produce an allocatively efficient amount of a public good. (pp. 499–503)

Externalities

An externality is a cost or a benefit arising from an economic transaction that falls on a third party and that is not taken into account by those undertaking the transaction. When external costs are present, allocative efficiency requires a reduction in the scale of output below what the market will produce. When external benefits are present, allocative efficiency requires an increase in output. There are two ways in which government can deal with externalities: Establishing and enforcing private property rights or using taxes and subsidies. If the government uses taxes and subsidies, it imposes taxes where there are external costs and gives subsidies where there are external benefits. (pp. 504–510)

KEY CONCEPTS

Externality, 504
Free rider, 500
Free-rider problem, 500
Marginal benefit, 500
Marginal private cost, 505
Marginal social cost, 505
Market failure, 498
Mixed good, 499
Net benefit, 503
Private good, 499
Private property right, 504
Public choice theory, 499
Public interest theory, 499
Pure public good, 499
Subsidy, 509
Total benefit, 500

Key Figures

REVIEW QUESTIONS

1 How big is the government sector of the U.S. economy today?

2 Set out the main economic functions of government.

3 Provide an example of each function.

4 What is a pure public good?

5 Name examples of three goods: a pure public good, a private good, and a mixed good.

6 What is the free-rider problem and how does government help overcome it?

7 What is an externality?

8 Give three examples of externalities.

PROBLEMS

1 You are given the following information about a sewage disposal system that a city of 1 million people is considering installing:

Capacity (thousands of gallons a day)	Marginal private benefit to one person (dollars)	Total cost (millions of dollars)
0		0
	50	
1		5
	40	
2		15
	30	
3		30
	20	
4		50
	10	
5		75

a) What is the capacity that achieves maximum net benefit?

b) How much will each person have to pay in taxes in order to pay for the efficient capacity level?

c) What are the total and net benefits?

2 A chemical factory dumps waste in a river. Damage is done to the local fish stock and membership fees at a nearby fishing club are lowered by the following amounts:

Output of chemical plant (gallons per hour)	Lost fees to fishing club
0	0
100	10
200	30
300	70
400	210

a) The local government plans to tax the chemical factory. Devise a tax that will achieve allocative efficiency.

b) How might private property rights be used in this situation?

3 Explain why your state government should operate a university system and permit students to attend for a tuition fee below the full cost of the education provided.

Chapter 20

Public Choice

After studying this chapter, you will be able to:

- Describe the components of the political marketplace
- Define a political equilibrium
- Explain how the main political parties choose an economic policy platform
- Explain how government bureaucracy interacts with politicians to determine the scale of provision of public goods and services
- Explain why we vote for redistributions of income and wealth
- Explain why we tax some goods at much higher rates than others
- Predict the effects of taxes on prices, quantities produced, and profits
- Explain why we subsidize the producers of some goods
- Predict the effects of subsidies on prices, quantities produced, and profits

Rhetoric and Reality

Franklin Delano Roosevelt was elected president in 1932, at the depths of the greatest depression in history. During the election campaign, Roosevelt set forth a program for economic recovery and reform that came to be called the New Deal. Roosevelt promised to provide aid for farmers and millions of other Americans and to strengthen the forces of competition. He promised that the increase in government spending would not increase the government deficit. Rather, his New Deal would result in an economic recovery that would bring in extra taxes and a balance in the government's budget. ■ Ronald Reagan was elected president in 1980, at a time of severe and stubborn inflation. Reagan's main economic theme was smaller government and lower taxes. Reagan argued that lower tax rates would not lead to a bigger government deficit. Instead, he predicted that with lower revenue, the spending plans of Congress would be kept under firmer discipline. Furthermore, he believed that lower tax rates would stimulate such a large upsurge in economic activity that sufficient additional revenue would flow into the government to balance its budget. ■ Despite dramatic differences in the economic environment of 1932 and 1980, and despite differences in the details of the political rhetoric, political reality resulted in outcomes different from those promised and foreseen. In the 1930s, the promised recovery was slow to arrive and the government's budget remained in deficit through most of that decade. In the 1980s, government spending was not curtailed—in fact it increased—and, although there was an unprecedented expansion of economic activity, tax revenue did not catch up with spending and the budget deficit persisted. ■ One important difference between the 1980s and the 1930s is in the scale of government. In the 1930s, the government undertook less than one fifth of all economic activity. In the 1980s, the government's budget represented two fifths of the nation's total expenditure. What determines the scale of government? What are the forces that generate the level of provision of public goods and services and why has government grown over the years to command an increasing fraction of the economy's resources? ■ Government pervades many aspects of our lives. It is present at our birth, supporting the hospitals in which we are born and training the doctors and nurses who deliver us. It is present throughout our education, supporting schools and colleges and training our teachers. It is present throughout our working lives, taxing our incomes, regulating our work environment, and paying us benefits when we are unemployed. It is present throughout our retirement, paying us a small income, and when we die, taxing our bequests. But the government does not make all our economic choices. We decide for ourselves what work to do, how much to save, and what to spend our income on. Why does the government intervene in some aspects of our lives but not others? Why doesn't the government provide more of our health services? Why doesn't it provide less of our education services? ■ There are many situations in which it is obvious why the government intervenes. Attempting to stem the flow of dangerous drugs is an example. But there are other areas in which the government does not intervene and yet many people believe it should. One such area is the protection of the quality of our air. Why doesn't the government do more to protect air quality? ■ Republicans and Democrats battle to dominate politics. Yet many people complain that there aren't really all that many differences in their policies. Why do two opposing political parties take similar positions on most topics? ■ Almost everyone grumbles about government bureaucracy. The poor single mother complains about the treatment that she receives from bureaucrats that administer the social welfare programs that she uses; the wealthy taxpayer complains about her treatment by the bureaucrats at the Internal Revenue Service; and even presidents, senators, and representatives complain that the bureaucracy is too big, too slow, and inefficient. Why is the bureaucracy so unpopular and the target of so much scorn? How do government bureaus operate to deliver the many public services for which they are responsible? ■ Government taxes almost all the goods and services that we buy. Some of these taxes are very high—for example, those on gasoline, alcohol, and tobacco products. A few items that we buy are not taxed and their producers are even subsidized by the government. Examples are milk and wheat. Why does government impose heavy taxes on some goods and subsidies on others? What are the effects of taxes on prices, on the quantities bought and sold, and on the amount of revenue raised by the government?

■ In this chapter, we study the economic interactions of voters, politicians, and bureaucrats and discover how the scale and variety of government economic activity are determined. Our focus here is on the provision of public goods and services, the taxation needed to pay for those services, the control of externalities, and the redistribution of income. In Chapter 21, we'll apply the same basic theory of government economic behavior to the regulation and control of monopolies and cartels.

The Political Marketplace

Government is not a huge computer that grinds out solutions to resource allocation problems plagued with free riders and externalities. It does not simply calculate and balance marginal social costs and benefits, automatically achieving allocative efficiency. Rather, it is a complex organization made up of thousands of individuals. These individuals have their *own* economic objectives, and government policy choices are the outcome of the choices made by these individuals. To analyze these choices, economists have developed a theory of the political marketplace that parallels theories of ordinary markets—*public choice theory.*

There are three types of actors in the economic model of the marketplace:

- Voters
- Politicians
- Bureaucrats

Voters are the consumers of the outcome of the political process. In ordinary markets for goods and services, people express their demands by their willingness to pay. In the political marketplace, voters express their demands in three principal ways. First, they express them by a willingness to vote, either in an election or on a referendum issue. Second, and less formally, they express their demands through campaign contributions. Third, they express their demands by lobbying. **Lobbying** is the activity of bringing pressure to bear on government agencies or institutions through a variety of informal mechanisms. The pro-life and pro-choice lobbies are two of the most prominent examples of such organizations in the United States today.

Politicians are the elected officials in federal, state, and local government—from chief executives (the president, state governor, or mayor) to members of the legislatures (state and federal senators and representatives, city councilors). Politicians are chosen by voters.

Bureaucrats are the appointed officials who work at various levels in the many government departments, again at the federal, state, and local levels. The most senior bureaucrats are appointed by politicians. Junior bureaucrats are appointed by senior ones.

Voters, politicians, and bureaucrats make their economic choices in a way that best furthers their own objectives, but they each face two types of constraints. First, each group is constrained by the preferences of the others. Bureaucrats are constrained by the preferences of politicians; politicians are constrained by the preferences of bureaucrats and voters; and voters are constrained by the preferences of bureaucrats and politicians. Second, voters, bureaucrats, and politicians cannot ignore technological constraints. They can only do things that are technologically feasible. We are going to examine the objectives of voters, politicians, and bureaucrats and the constraints they face when making their choices. We're also going to study the interactions among the three types of actors. In so doing, we are going to discover how the political system actually works.

The predictions of an economic model of voter, politician, and bureaucrat behavior are the equilibrium of the political process—the political equilibrium. A **political equilibrium** is a situation in which the choices of voters, politicians, and bureaucrats are all compatible and in which no one group of agents will be better off by making a different choice. Thus a political equilibrium has the same characteristics as an equilibrium in the markets for goods and services and factors of production.

The theory of public choice that we are about to study is a relatively new branch of economics that has grown rapidly in the past 30 years. It was recently recognized by the awarding of the Nobel Prize for economics to one of its principal architects, James Buchanan (see Our Advancing Knowledge, pp. 518-519).

Let's begin our study of public choice theory by looking at the behavior of politicians.

The Behavior of Politicians and Voters

All kinds of people go into politics. Some have noble ideals and want to make a lasting contribution to improving the conditions of their fellow citizens. Others are single-minded in pursuit of their own self-interest and profit. Most politicians, no doubt, blend these two extremes. Economic models of public choice are based on the assumption that in a democratic political system their central objective is to get enough votes to be elected and to keep enough support to remain in office. Votes, to a politician, are similar to dollars to a private firm. In order to obtain enough votes, politicians form coalitions with each other; we call these coalitions political parties. A political party is simply a collection of politicians who have banded together for the purpose of achieving and maintaining office. A political party attempts to develop policies that appeal to a majority of the voters.

Public choice theory assumes that voters support policies that they believe make them better off and oppose policies that they believe make them worse off. They neither oppose nor support—they are indifferent among—policies that they believe have no effect on them. Voters' *perceptions* rather than reality are what guide their choices.

To obtain the support of voters, a politician (or political party) must offer a package of policies that voters believe will make them better off than the policies proposed by the opposing political parties. There are two ways in which a political program can seek to make a voter better off. One way is to implement policies that make *everyone* better off. Providing national defense or protecting the environment are examples of such policies. Another way is to implement policies that make some voters worse off but that make at least 50 percent of the voters better off. Redistributing income in such a way that at least one half of the electorate reaps net benefits is one example. Supporting or opposing abortion is another and supporting or opposing gun control yet another.

Political programs that make everyone better off feature in the platforms of all parties. Policies that favor one group against another differ from party to party and depend on which segment of the population or particular interest group a political party wants to appeal to. Let's see how politicians and voters interact and how the policy platforms of political parties emerge by examining how the political process handles the provision of public goods and external costs and benefits.

Public Goods In Chapter 19, we compared the scale of provision of public goods that achieves allocative efficiency with the scale that would be provided through the private marketplace. Now we want to work out the scale of provision of public goods that a political system will actually deliver.

For the moment, let's ignore differences among individual voters and suppose that people have identical views about the benefits of public goods and externalities. We'll consider what happens when people disagree and have different preferences shortly. To be concrete, let's stick with the example of national defense that we studied in Chapter 19.

Suppose that the total costs and total benefits of producing antimissile lasers are the ones shown in Fig. 20.1. (These are the same costs and benefits that we used in Chapter 19, p. 504.) Suppose also that there are two political parties. Let's call one the Hawks and the other the Doves. Suppose that the Hawks and the Doves propose exactly the same policy platform in all respects except for national defense. The Hawks offer a high level of national defense. They propose to provide 4 antimissile lasers at a cost of $50 billion, with benefits of $50 billion and a net benefit of zero. The Doves propose to provide just 1 laser at a cost of $5 billion, with a benefit of $20 billion and a net benefit of $15 billion ($20 billion total benefit minus $5 billion total cost).

In an election in which voters are presented with the two platforms just described, the Doves will win. Recall that we assumed that both parties are offering identical programs in every respect except for defense. The defense program of the Doves provides the voters with a net benefit of $15 billion over and above the taxes that they are asked to pay, while the Hawks are offering no net benefit, so the Doves will get all the votes.

Now suppose that the Hawks, contemplating the election outcome that we have just described, realize that their party is offering too high a level of defense—that it is too hawkish—to get elected. It figures that it has to offer net benefits in excess of $15 billion if it is to beat the Doves. It therefore scales back its plans and proposes to build 2 antimissile lasers. At this level of provision, the total cost is $15 billion and total benefit is $35 billion, so net benefit is $20 billion. The Hawks are now offering a package that the voters prefer to the one offered by the Doves. Now in an election, the Hawks will win.

The Doves, contemplating this outcome, realize that the best they can do is to match the Hawks. They too propose to provide 2 lasers on exactly the same terms as the Hawks. The voters are now indifferent between the proposals of the two parties and are indifferent about which one they vote for.

Figure 20.1 Provision of a Pulbic Good in a Political System

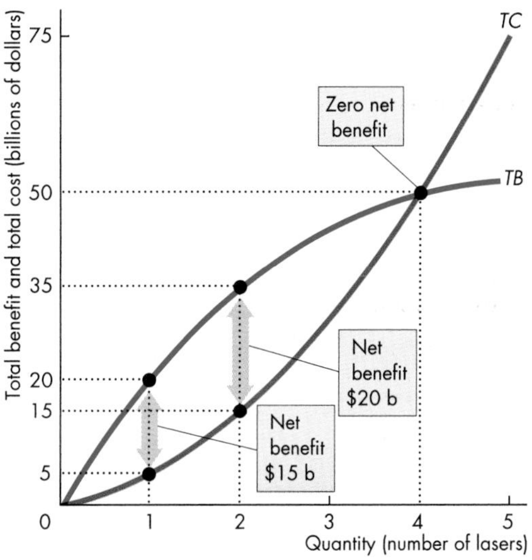

The total benefit curve for an antimissile laser weapon is *TB*, and the total cost curve is *TC*. Net benefit is maximized if 2 antimissile lasers are installed, with a total benefit of $35 billion and a total cost of $15 billion. There are two political parties offering platforms on this defense systems: the Doves and the Hawks. Their platforms are identical on all matters except defense. The Doves propose to install 1 antimissile laser and the Hawks 4. In an election, the Doves will win since their proposal generates a larger net benefit than the Hawks' proposal. But if the Hawks propose to install 2 lasers, they will beat the Doves since the net benefit resulting from 2 lasers exceeds that from 1. To get even, the Doves will have to match the Hawks. If voters are well informed and in general agreement about the value of a public good, competition between political parties for their votes can achieve an efficient scale of provision.

Public Choice

The past 30 years have seen an enormous growth in work on the economic choices of government and on the interactions of politicians, bureaucrats, and voters. The result of this work is a well-recognized discipline within economics called *public choice theory*.

The father of modern public choice is Duncan Black. Born in Motherwell, Scotland, in 1908, Black studied first mathematics and physics and then economics and politics at the University of Glasgow (where, 150 years earlier, Adam Smith had worked). Black's work is monumental. His vision was to develop a science of politics—having the same rigor as economics—based on a theory of committees. In Black's model, consumers' preferences are replaced by the preferences of committee members; goods and services are replaced by motions or propositions before a committee. Black's work of the 1940s and 1950s was summarized in his book *The Theory of Committees and Elections* (Cambridge University Press, 1958).

Cycles in Voting

	Possible income distribution		
	1	2	3
Ann	150	50	100
Ben	100	150	50
Con	50	100	150

An example of one of Black's discoveries is the possibility of *cyclical voting*. Such a possibility is illustrated in the accompanying table. There are three people and three possible income distributions. If the distribution is 1, then Ben and Con vote for distribution 2. Ann opposes distribution 2, but in a majority vote she loses. If the distribution is 2, Ann and Con vote for distribution 3. Ben votes against that distribution but, again, if the majority decides the day, Ben loses. But if the distribution is 3, Ann and Ben vote for distribution 1 while Con opposes that distribution. Again, majority vote results in distribution 1 winning. But we are now back where we started. Ben and Con can now vote that distribution down and so the whole cycle begins again.

The possibility of voting cycles is just one potential flaw in democracy. Another was suggested by Kenneth Arrow. Arrow, a Nobel Prize winner in economic science in 1972, was born in New York City in 1921 and studied at Columbia and the University of Chicago. He has taught at Harvard and at Stanford, where he currently holds two positions—professor of economics and of operations research. Arrow's contributions to economics span an amazing range (as his dual professorship signifies), but in the public choice area his book *Social Choice and Individual Values* (John Wiley & Sons, 1951) has been of substantial influence. In that book, Arrow demonstrates what has come to be called the "Arrow impossibility theorem." In simplified terms, the theorem states that it is not, in general, possible

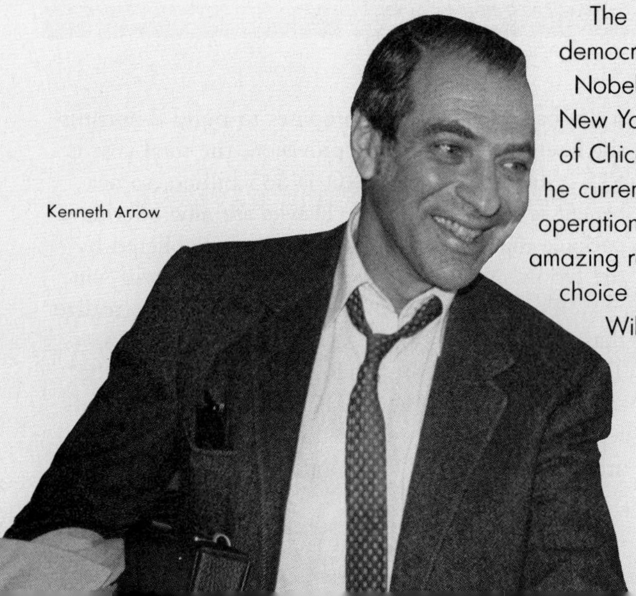

Kenneth Arrow

James Buchanan

to aggregate the preferences of individuals to arrive at social preferences that can be used to guide government choice.

One of the major contributors to modern public choice theory is James Buchanan, whose work was recognized by his being awarded the Nobel Prize in economic science in 1986. Born in Murfreesboro, Tennessee, in 1919, Buchanan received his Ph.D. at the University of Chicago in 1948. Buchanan has devoted his lifetime to understanding political decision-making by using the same tools of analysis that economists use to understand all economic choices. Buchanan's ideas are given their most extensive development in *The Calculus of Consent: Logical Foundation of Constitutional Democracy* (University of Michigan Press, 1962) which he wrote with his colleague, Gordon Tullock. In this book, Buchanan and Tullock analyze the effects of different voting systems: for example, simple majority versus qualified majority—qualified majority being two-thirds majority or unanimity—and the effects of having two legislative chambers—a congress and a senate. The authors also examine the economics and ethics of pressure groups, special interests, and the constitution.

Two other Americans have made important contributions that we are studying in this chapter. They are Anthony Downs and William Niskanen.

Downs, born in Evanston, Illinois, in 1930, received his Ph.D. at Stanford in 1956. His doctoral thesis turned into what has become a great classic: *An Economic Theory of Democracy* (Harper and Row, 1957). In that book, Downs first set out the "median voter theorem." He also pointed out what has come to be called the "paradox of voting." The paradox centers on a question: Why do we bother to vote? From a purely economic point of view, voting seems silly. If the political parties offer the policies that best benefit the median voter, no one individual's vote is going to make any difference to the outcome of an election. Since it takes time and effort to vote, the individually rational thing to do is to stay home and give the election a miss. The fact that most of us do vote implies either that the economic theory of voting is overlooking an important aspect of economic behavior or that voting is not to be understood purely and narrowly in economic terms.

William Niskanen, born in Bend, Oregon, in 1933, received his Ph.D. at the University of Chicago in 1962. Niskanen has had an interesting and highly varied career: He has worked as an economist in the Department of Defense and in the armed forces and has been a professor at the University of California at Berkeley and Los Angeles. He also served as head of the economic division of the Ford Motor Company and as a member of the Council of Economic Advisors to President Reagan. With this rich variety of experience, Niskanen has made significant advances in the theory of bureaucracy. His classic book *Bureaucracy and Representative Government* (Aldine-Atherton) was published in 1971. It is in this work that Niskanen proposes the theory of budget maximization that we have studied in this chapter.

Competition for votes among political parties, even when there are only two of them, produces a political platform that maximizes the perceived net benefit accruing to the voters. For this outcome to occur, it is necessary that the voters be able to evaluate the alternatives. We'll see below that this condition is not necessarily going to be satisfied.

Externalities

The example that we have just worked through deals with a situation in which the voters are in agreement about and can calculate the benefits arising from different proposals. The same line of reasoning applies to policies concerning the control of externalities. Provided the voters are in agreement about the benefits and can evaluate them, the political party that offers the level of control of externalities that maximizes net benefits will be the one that wins an election. The political party that proposes a total ban on the production of CFCs or sulfur dioxide emission will lose an election to a party that proposes more limited controls. A party that proposes a free-for-all on CFCs and sulfur dioxide emissions will lose an election to a party that proposes restraint in the production of goods that generate these external costs. Competition for votes will force each party to find the degree of control that maximizes net benefit.

In the examples of public goods and externalities that we have just worked out, we have ignored differences of opinion among the voters. We'll now go on to consider cases in which the preferences of voters differ and in which these differences are crucial in determining the outcome of the political process.

Interest Groups and Redistribution

Most matters decided in the political arena are ones on which people have different opinions. Some people favor a large national defense program while others urge disarmament; some favor a large scale of income redistribution while others urge tax cuts; some want massive government intervention to protect the environment while others want more limited environmental controls. Faced with this diversity of opinion, no political party can propose a platform that pleases everyone. But to attain office, a party must put together a package that attracts a majority of the votes. To do so, each party has to deliver a package that makes a majority of the voters better off (as the voters perceive it) than under the policies proposed by the opposing party (or parties). This search for a majority results in each political party offering policies that are very close to the policies of the others. This tendency toward similar policies is known as the principle of minimum differentiation.

Figure 20.2 The Principle of Minimum Differentiation

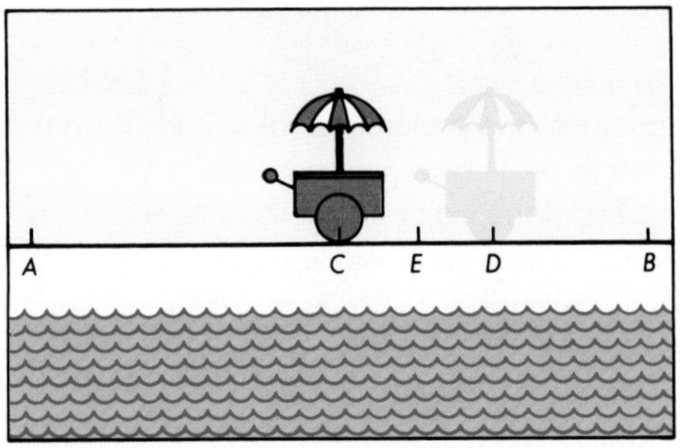

A beach stretches from *A* to *B*. Sunbathers are distributed at even intervals along the whole beach. An ice cream seller sets up a stand at point *C*. The distance that people have to walk for ice cream is the same no matter on which side of the ice cream stand they are located. If a second ice cream seller sets up a stand, it will pay to place it exactly next to *C* in the middle of the beach. If the second stand is placed at *D*, only the customers on the beach between *E* and *B* will buy ice cream from *D*. Those between *A* and *E* will go to *C*. By moving as close to *C* as possible, the second ice cream vendor picks up half of the ice cream customers.

The Principle of Minimum Differentiation The **principle of minimum differentiation** is the tendency for competitors to make themselves almost identical in order to appeal to the maximum number of clients or voters. Let's study the principle of minimum differentiation by looking at a problem that is more familiar and concrete than that faced by political parties.

There are two ice cream vendors on a beach. The beach is one mile long and is illustrated in Fig. 20.2 as the distance from *A* to *B*. Sunbathers lounge at equal intervals over the entire beach. One of the ice cream vendors comes along and sets up a stand. Where will she locate? The answer is at position *C*—exactly halfway between *A* and *B*. By locating in this position, the farthest that anyone has to walk to buy an ice cream is a mile (half a mile to the ice cream stand and half a mile back to the beach towel).

Now suppose that a second ice cream vendor comes along. Where will he place his ice cream stand? The answer is right next to the original one at point *C*. To understand why, imagine that the second vendor locates his stand at point *D*—halfway between *C* and *B*. How many customers will he attract and how many will go to the stand at *C*? The stand at *D* will pick up all the customers on the beach between *B* and *D*, because this stand is closer for them. It will also pick up all the customers between *D* and *E* (the point halfway between *C* and *D*), because they too will have a shorter trip for an ice cream by going to *D* than by going to *C*. All the people between *A* and *C* and all those between *C* and *E* will go to stand *C*. So the ice cream stand located at *C* will pick up all the people on the beach between *A* and *E* and the stand located at *D* will pick up all the people located between *E* and *B*.

Now suppose that the vendor with a stand at *D* moves to *C*. There are now two stands at *C*. Half the customers will go to the first vendor and the other half to the second vendor. Only by each locating bang in the center of the beach can each pick up half the customers. If either of them moves slightly away from the center, then that vendor picks up less than half the customers and the one remaining at the center picks up a majority of the customers.

This example illustrates the principle of minimum differentiation. By having no differentiation in location, both ice cream vendors do as well as they can and share the market evenly.

The principle of minimum differentation has been applied to explain a wide variety of choices—how supermarkets choose their locations; how the makers of automobiles and microwave popcorn design their products; and how political parties choose their platforms.

The principle of minimum differentiation predicts that political parties will be similar to each other. But it does not tell us which policies they will favor, only that they will favor similar ones. In the case of the ice cream vendor, the location is determined by technological considerations—minimizing the distance that the bathers have to walk. But what determines a political party's choice of platform? Let's now address this question.

The Median Voter Theorem An interesting proposition about a political party's choice of platform is provided by the median voter theorem. The **median voter theorem** states that political parties will pursue policies that maximize the net benefit of the median voter. (The median of a distribution of, say, student heights is the height of the student in the middle. One half of the students are taller and one half of the students are shorter than the median.) Let's see how the median voter theorem applies to the question of how large a tax to impose on sulfur dioxide emissions that cause acid rain.

Imagine arranging all the voters along a line running from *A* to *B*, as shown in Fig. 20.3. The voter wanting the highest tax is at *A* and the one wanting no tax is at *B*, and all the other voters are arranged along the line based on the level of the tax that they favor. The curve in the figure shows the tax

Figure 20.3 The Median Voter Theorem

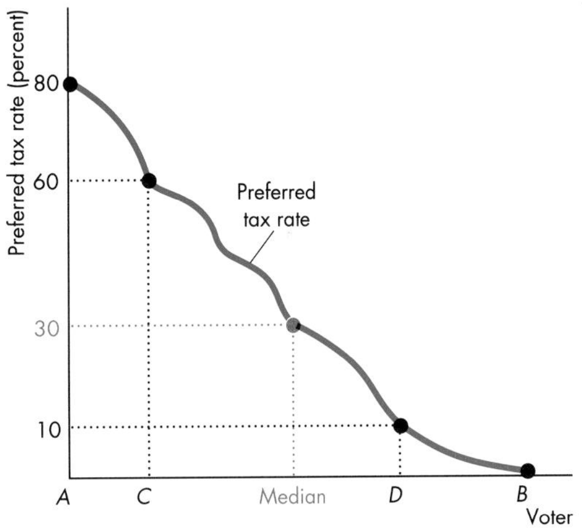

A political party can win an election by proposing policies that appeal to the median voter and to all the other voters on one side of the median. If the median mildly favors a policy, that policy will be proposed. In the figure, voters have different preferences concerning the rate at which to tax an externality. They are ranked from *A* to *B* in descending order of their preferred tax. There are two political parties. If one proposes a 61 percent tax and the other a 59 percent tax, the lower tax party will win the election—voters between *A* and *C* will vote for the high tax and those between *C* and *B* for the low tax. If both parties propose low taxes—11 percent and 9 percent—the party proposing the higher tax will win. It will pick up the votes between *A* and *D*, leaving only the votes between *D* and *B* for the lower tax party. Each party will have an incentive to move toward the tax rate preferred by the median voter. At that point, each party picks up a half of the votes and neither can improve its share.

rate favored by each voter between *A* and *B*. As shown in the graph, the median voter favors a tax rate of 30 percent.

Suppose that two political parties propose similar but not quite identical taxes on emissions of sulfur dioxide. One party proposes a tax of 61 percent and the other of 59 percent. All the voters lying between *A* and *C* prefer the higher tax and will vote for it. All the voters lying between *C* and *B* prefer the lower tax and will vote for it. The lower tax party will win the election.

Alternatively, suppose that the two political parties offer a low tax rate—and again, slightly different rates. One party offers a rate of 11 percent and the other of 9 percent. The voters between *A* and *D* will vote for the higher tax rate and those between *D* and *B* for the lower rate. This time, the higher tax party will win.

But each party, in either of these situations, will see that it can win the election by moving closer to the tax rate preferred by the median voter. Once the two parties are offering that tax rate, however, neither will be able to increase its share of the vote by changing its proposal. One party will get the votes between *A* and the median and the other the votes between the median and *B*. All the voters except the median will be dissatisfied—for those between *A* and the median the tax rate is too low and for those between *B* and the median the tax is too high. But no political party can propose a tax other than 30 percent and expect to win the election. Of course, if the two parties proposed exactly 30 percent, the voters will be indifferent and will either not bother to vote or will flip a coin to decide which party to vote for.

The principle of minimum differentiation and the median voter theorem seem to imply that all political parties will be identical in all respects. If that is so, it is too bad for the principle and the theorem. The world that we live in has political parties that certainly do differ. Many of us are heated in our support for and opposition to particular parties and policy proposals. It is in the area of the redistribution of income and wealth that one of the major differences in political parties arises. Let's use the principle of minimum differentiation and the median voter theorem to see if we can understand why all political parties favor some redistribution but why, also, there are differences in the parties in this respect.

Voting for Income Redistribution

The first model of redistribution that we'll consider is one that results in voting cycles. Imagine a society with 100 voters. These voters are divided into four different income groups, as set out in Table 20.1. Twenty-five of the voters earn $10,000 a year, another 25 earn $20,000 a year, another 25 earn $40,000 a year, and the richest 25 earn $90,000 a year. The average income in this community is $40,000 a year.

Suppose that a political party proposes to tax the richest 25 people $5000 and the second richest

Table 20.1 Voting for Income Redistribution: A Tie

Number of voters	Income before redistribution (thousands of dollars)	Income after redistribution (thousands of dollars)	Gain (+)/loss (−) (thousands of dollars)
25	10	15	+5
25	20	23	+3
25	40	37	−3
25	90	85	−5
Total 100	Averages: 40	40	0

Table 20.2 Voting for Income Redistribution: The Rich Lose

Number of voters	Income before redistribution (thousands of dollars)	Income after redistribution (thousands of dollars)	Gain (+)/loss (−) (thousands of dollars)
25	10	15	+5
25	20	23	+3
25	40	40	0
25	90	82	−8
Total 100	Averages: 40	40	0

$3000. It proposes to make transfers of $5000 to the poorest 25 people and $3000 to the next poorest 25. The incomes resulting from the tax and transfers in this proposal are set out in the third column of Table 20.1. The average income is still $40,000. The final column of the table shows the gains and losses to each income group. The poorest gain and the richest lose.

Suppose that there is a second political party in this society that opposes the redistribution scheme just described. Which party will win the election? The answer is that it will be a tie. The party proposing the redistribution scheme will pick up 50 percent of the votes—those of the poorer half of the electorate. The party opposing the redistribution scheme will pick up the other half of the votes (those at the wealthier end of the income distribution).

Now suppose that one of the parties offers the modified scheme set out in Table 20.2. The proposal is to tax the richest quarter of the people not $5000 but $8000, and not to tax the second richest quarter at all. Under this scheme, the two poorest groups of people will receive benefits of $5000 and $3000 respectively. One party supports these measures and the other opposes them and proposes no redistribution at all. Which party will win? The answer is the party supporting redistribution. All the people with original incomes of $10,000 and $20,000 will vote for the scheme. Those with incomes of $30,000 will be indifferent between the two parties so we may suppose that half will vote for one party and half the other. The party opposing the redistribution scheme will collect the votes of the richest quarter of the people plus half of those in the second richest group.

This example shows one particular redistribution proposal that could gain the support of the majority of voters. But there will be many other proposals that could also gain majority support (but with different people making up the majority in each case). There is no end to the different proposals that could win a majority. As these different schemes are proposed, there are cycles in the voting similar to those described in Our Advancing Knowledge, pp. 518–519.

Why do we not observe voting cycles in reality? Why do we see a tendency for redistribution policies to remain in place for very long periods of time? The answer is suggested by a second model of redistribution—a median voter model. A key feature of this model is what has been called the "big tradeoff" (see Chapter 18, pp. 486–487). The greater the amount of income that is redistributed, the smaller is the incentive to work and the lower is the average level of income. As a consequence, redistributive taxes have two effects on the median voter: They raise the median voter's income by taking from those above the median and redistributing to those at and below the median; they also lower the median voter's income by reducing the incentive to work, which lowers average income. Which of these two opposing effects is stronger depends on the scale of redistribution. At low tax rates, the disincentive effects are small, so an increase in taxes makes the median voter better off. The higher income resulting from transfers from the rich is more than enough to offset the lower income resulting from disincentive effects. If tax rates are set too high, a cut in taxes will make the median voter better off. In this case, the lower income resulting from smaller transfers from the rich is more than made up for by the higher average income resulting from improved incentives. But there is a level of taxes and an amount of redistribution that is exactly right from the point of view of the median voter. This scale of redistribution is the one that balances these two considerations and maximizes the median voter's income. This amount of redistribution is a possible political equilibrium.

Model and Reality

We've now looked at two models of equilibrium redistribution—a voting cycles model and a median voter model. In the voting cycles model, there is a never-ending sequence of different majorities for different directions of redistribution. In the median voter model, there is a unique equilibrium that maximizes the net benefit to the median voter.

Which of these models best fits the facts about income redistribution? The median voter model comes closest. Its strengths lie in its predictions that the political parties will differ in their rhetoric but be very close to each other in the actual redistribution measures for which they vote. This prediction accords well with reality and especially well with what occurred in 1986, the most recent occasion on which a major change in redistributive taxes took place. (See Reading Between the Lines, pp. 526–527). In contrast, the voting-cycles model predicts a sequence of different majorities for different directions of redistribution that we do not observe in reality.

R E V I E W

Politicians seek to obtain enough votes to achieve and maintain power. They do this by appealing to slightly more than half of the electorate. The key voter is the median voter. To appeal to the median voter, political parties offer programs that favor a majority of the electorate. Each party tries to outdo the other by appealing to the median voter. In part, that appeal results from the political parties proposing income-increasing policies. It also, in part, results from the redistribution of income to the point where no one can invent a way of raising the income of the median voter. ■

We have analyzed the behavior of politicians but not that of the bureaucrats who translate the choices of the politicians into programs. Let's now turn to an examination of the economic choices of bureaucrats.

The Behavior of Bureaucrats

An interesting model of the behavior of bureaucrats has been suggested by William Niskanen (see Our Advancing Knowledge, pp. 518–519). In that model, bureaucrats aim to maximize the budget of the agency in which they work. The bigger the budget of the agency, the greater is the prestige of the agency chief and the larger is the opportunity for promotion for people further down the bureaucratic ladder. Thus all the members of an agency have an interest in maximizing the agency's budget. In seeking to obtain the largest budget it can, each government agency and department marshals its best arguments for why it should have more funds to spend. Since each agency does its best to obtain more funds, the net result is upward pressure for expenditure on all publicly provided goods and services.

The constraints on maximizing the budget of a government department or agency are the taxes that the politician has to levy and the implications of those taxes for the politician's own ability to win votes. But government departments and agencies recognize and appreciate the interplay between their own objectives and those of the politician and so do their best to help the politician appreciate the vote-winning consequences of spending more on their own particular department or agency. Thus budget maximization, to some degree, translates itself into political campaigns designed to explain to voters why they need more defense, more health services, and so on.

Let's examine the consequences of bureaucratic budget maximization for the provision of public goods and their cost by looking again at the example of national defense. We've studied this example twice before. The first time (in Chapter 19, p. 504) our concern was to establish that a government could overcome the free-rider problem and produce a larger quantity of a public good than would be produced by the private market. In this chapter, (on pp. 517–520), we examined the way in which political parties competing for votes determine the scale of provision of a public good in a situation in which the voters are in agreement about the benefits of the public good and in which they are able to assess the costs and benefits of different scales of provision. In that example, no bureaucrats intervene in the process.

But the creation and operation of weapons and defense systems require the establishment of a large and complex government bureaucracy. How does the defense bureaucracy influence the scale and cost of the defense program? Let's answer this question by returning to the example of the installation of an antimissile laser defense system.

Take a look at Fig. 20.4. You will recognize it as being similar to Fig. 20.1. The horizontal axis shows the number of antimissile lasers and the vertical axis their total benefit and total cost. The curve labeled *TB* shows the total benefit as perceived by all the individuals in the economy and the curve labeled *TC* shows the total cost.

We saw earlier that the level of provision that maximizes net benefit is 2 lasers. This level of defense costs $15 billion, and it yields a total benefit of $35 billion and a net benefit of $20 billion. A political party that proposes installing 2 lasers will win an election because there is no higher net benefit possible. But will the Pentagon press Congress to vote for 2 lasers? According to Niskanen's model of bureaucracy, it will not. The Pentagon will push to expand the scale of provision and budget for national defense to the largest possible level. If it is able to increase the number of antimissile lasers to 4, for example, it can increase the budget to $50 billion. In this situation, total benefit equals total cost and net benefit is zero. If the Pentagon is able to increase defense to an even higher level, its budget increases yet further and net benefit becomes negative.

But how would it be possible for the Pentagon to get away with pressing the politicians for a scale of defense spending in excess of that which maximizes net benefit? Won't it always pay the politicians to take control of the Pentagon and cut back on the scale of military spending?

We've already seen that when there are two political parties competing for votes, the party that gets closest to maximizing net benefit is the one that picks up the most votes. Don't these forces of competition for votes dominate the wishes of the bureaucrats and ensure that the maximum budget allowed to them is that which maximizes net benefit?

Figure 20.4 Bureaucratic Overprovision

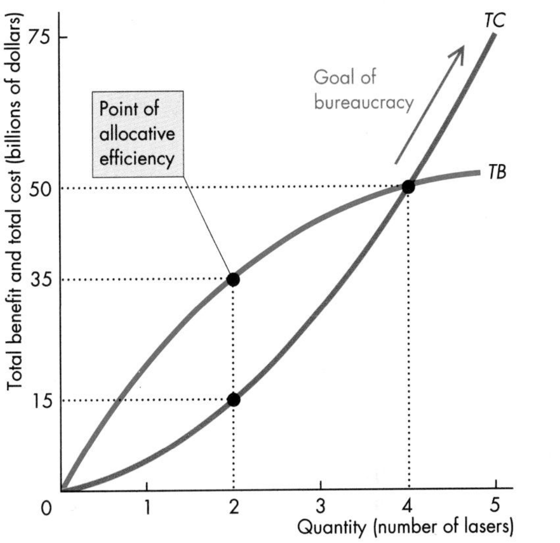

A bureau that maximizes its budget will seek to expand output and expenditure as far as possible. For example, the Pentagon prefers 4 antimissile lasers at a cost of $50 billion to the allocatively efficient number—2 at a cost of $15 billion. The goal of the bureau is to move as far up the total cost curve as possible. If voters are well informed, politicans will not be able to deliver the taxes that enable the bureau to get beyond the point of allocative efficiency. But if some voters are rationally ignorant while others are well informed, it is possible that the bureau will be able to increase its budget above the allocatively efficient level. In general, the bureau will produce a higher quantity than the one that maximizes net benefit.

If voters are well informed and if their perception of their self-interest is correct, the political party that wins the election is the one that holds the Pentagon budget to the level that provides the efficient level of defense. But there is another possible equilibrium. It is one based on the principle of voter ignorance and well-informed interest groups.

Voter Ignorance and Well-Informed Interest Groups

One of the major propositions of public choice theory is that it does not pay voters to be well-informed

The Political Economy of Tax Reform

The Making of a Miracle

They said it couldn't be done . . . couldn't be done . . . couldn't be done. Scrap the gargantuan federal tax code and write a simpler, fairer one? How naive! Drastically reduce top tax rates to their lowest levels in 58 years by throwing out the special breaks and deductions that have accrued over the past four decades? . . . Get real! Such a drastic overhaul would amount to putting the public interest ahead of special interests—in this case nearly every interest with enough clout to hire a lobbyist. And everybody knows the political process does not work that way.

Except that once in a great while the process *does* work that way. Thus it was with tax reform, a political miracle that was brought to the verge of fruition by an amazingly varied group of conservatives and liberals, Republicans and Democrats. . . .

The Tax Reform Act of 1986 is one of the few pieces of legislation that can truly be called historic. It reverses the whole direction that federal taxation has been following for decades: instead of adding exceptions and deductions, it wipes them out by the hundreds; instead of shifting the tax burden from business to individuals, it switches that load the other way. . . .

The bill by 1988 would erase the complex schedule of 15 tax rates on individual incomes, ranging from 11% to 50%, and replace them with just two: 15% and 28%.

To get these benefits, individuals will have to give up some cherished tax breaks. The bill preserves the most popular: deductions for state and local income taxes and for mortgage interest on first and second homes. But there will be no more deductions for interest on loans to buy cars, boats, clothes and furniture. Nor will there be any for sales taxes. The special deduction for families in which both husband and wife work will be eliminated, along with credits for child-care expenses. Charitable contributions will be deductible only for those who choose to send in itemized returns (at present they can be written off by users of the short form). Profits on the sale of stocks, bonds, houses and other assets, which have been subject to low capital-gains rates, will be taxed at the same rate as ordinary income: 28% tops.

One of the bill's greatest benefits will be psychological rather than monetary. It will foster a public perception that the tax laws have become fairer by levying approximately the same amount on people with similar incomes. Most significantly, it will wipe out those complex schemes that allow wealthy individuals with wily accountants to claim large paper losses through small cash investments in real estate syndicates and other tax shelters.

At the bottom of the scale, some 6 million people with incomes at or below the poverty line will be freed from paying any income tax at all, doing away with a pernicious unintended consequence of the current law: for the past several years the poor have been sending a growing share of their meager pay to Washington. About 80% of taxpayers will owe less; though many of the reductions will be small, they add up to big money. Collectively, individuals over the next five years will keep in their wallets $121.7 billion that they would have to hand over to the Internal Revenue Service under present law.

Business taxes will rise by $120 billion. (One of the principles that tax reformers settled on early was "revenue neutrality," on the theory that a radical rewrite of the tax code would be difficult enough without getting it tangled up in the debate over whether the Government should raise its total tax take in order to reduce deficits.) Although the top tax rate on business profits will drop from 46% to 34%, it will apply to far more corporate income. Scores of special breaks that benefited such industries as banking and real estate will be wiped out.

Time, August 25, 1986

The Essence of the Story

- In the summer of 1986, few believed that the federal income tax code could be reformed.
- But a coalition of conservatives and liberals, Republicans and Democrats passed the Tax Reform Act of 1986.
- That act is "revenue neutral," cutting personal taxes and increasing corporate taxes—each by about $120 million.
- The act cuts the top tax rates but eliminates many deductions, including interest on loans to buy cars and boats, state sales taxes, and child care expenses.
- Capital gains, previously taxed at a lower rate, are taxed at the same rate as other income.
- Six million low-income families no longer have to pay income taxes.
- 80 percent of taxpayers pay less under the reformed plan.
- The rate of tax on corporations declines, but the amount of profit subject to tax increases.
- Special tax breaks for banks and real estate companies are eliminated.

Background and Analysis

- Taxes influence both allocative efficiency and the distribution of income.
- The Tax Reform Act of 1986 was "revenue neutral"—a reform that left the total amount of taxes paid constant.
- Tax *rates* were lowered, but because many previously allowed deductions from income were eliminated, the tax *base* was increased.
- Lower tax *rates* on a larger tax *base* may result in greater economic efficiency and potential gains for all—serving the public interest.
- But tax reform is driven by its effects on the distribution of income—by special interests.
- According to the estimates in the article, 80 percent of taxpayers pay less tax under the new plan, and 20 percent of taxpayers pay more. (The table summarizes the main winners and losers.)
- A tax reform that benefits 80 percent of the population and harms 20 percent does not seem as miraculous as the article claims.
- It is true that each loser has more at stake in the reform than each winner and therefore will lobby harder.
- But gainers lobby, too, and members of Congress, valuing votes, pay attention to both gainers and losers.
- Further, this tax reform was a highly publicized event, and one that directly and significantly affected each voter.
- Also, the voting record of each legislator was highly publicized.
- The increase in corporate taxes to some degree obscures the redistribution of the tax burden brought about by the reform.
- Higher corporate taxes mean less income for the *owners* of corporations—for the people who invest in them.
- The reform, therefore, lowered taxes on labor income but increased taxes on income from capital.
- Thus, the winners are those whose income is primarily from labor; the losers are those whose income is primarily from capital.
- As the labor force participation rate has been increasing steadily, over the years, an increasing number of taxpayers (voters) stood to gain from such a reform.
- If this explanation for the 1986 reform is correct, it implies that, as the population ages and more people become dependent on income from capital (retirement income), the tax burden will shift from capital income toward labor income—personal income taxes will rise, and corporate income taxes will decline.

Winners and Losers from Tax Reform

Winners	Losers
(a) Direct	
80 percent of taxpayers	20 percent of taxpayers
Low-income families	High-income families using tax shelters
Families with high labor income, low capital income, and few deductions	Families with high capital income and capital gains and low labor income
One-income families	Two-income families with child care expenses
(b) Indirect	
Potentially everyone, from greater allocative efficiency resulting from lower tax rates	Tax accountants
	Charities and foundations
	Makers of cars, boats, and durable goods
	Investors in banks and real estate companies
	Providers of day care services

about the issues on which they are voting unless those issues have an immediate and direct consequence for their own income. In other words, it pays voters to be rationally ignorant. **Rational ignorance** is the decision *not* to acquire information, because the cost of acquiring the information is greater than the benefit derived from having it. For example, each voter knows that he or she can make virtually no difference to the actual defense policy pursued by the U.S. government. Each voter also knows that it would take an enormous amount of time and effort to become even moderately well-informed about alternative defense technologies and the most effective ways of achieving different levels of defense. As a result, voters see it as being in their best interests to remain relatively uninformed about the technicalities of national defense issues. (Though we are using national defense as an example, the same applies to all aspects of government economic activity).

All voters are consumers of national defense. But not all voters produce it. Only a small number are in this latter category. Those voters who produce national defense, whether they be members of the military or firms and households that work in producing defense equipment, have a direct personal interest in defense because it affects their incomes. Unlike other voters, therefore, it pays these voters to become well informed about national defense issues and to operate a political lobby aimed at furthering their own interests. These voters, in collaboration with the bureaucracies that deliver national defense, will exert a larger influence through the voting process than the relatively uninformed general voters who only consume this public good.

If the rationality of the uninformed voter and the rationality of the informed special interest group are taken into account, a political equilibrium emerges in which the scale of provision of public goods exceeds the one that maximizes net benefit.

R E V I E W

Politicians implement their policies through departments and agencies that are staffed by bureaucrats. In the economic model of bureaucracy, bureaucrats pursue the objective of budget maximization. Each agency tries to persuade politicians that its own budget should be increased. The politician has to balance the need for a bigger bureau budget against the cost of losing votes through higher taxes. If voters are well-informed about the costs and benefits of the activities of a bureau, the maximum budget permitted to the bureau will be that which maximizes net benefit. If voters are rationally ignorant, the best-informed voters will be those who both produce and consume a public good. Voters who only consume a public good will be relatively uninformed. The well-informed voters, in collaboration with the bureaucracies that produce public goods, will exert a larger influence than the uninformed voters who only consume the public goods, and so the scale of provision of public goods will exceed the one that maximizes net benefit. ■

We've now seen how voters, politicians, and bureaucrats interact to determine the scale of provision of public goods and services and the scale of redistribution, and how they deal with external costs and benefits. But public goods and services have to be paid for with taxes. How does the political marketplace determine the scale and variety of taxes that we pay? And why is it that some goods not only are untaxed but are actually subsidized by the government? We've seen one partial answer to some of these questions already—taxes and subsidies might be used as a part of the government's attempt to deal with externalities. But that is not the entire story, as we'll now see.

Taxes and Subsidies

The bulk of the government's revenue arises from income taxes. The highest tax rates are levied on such commodities as gasoline, alcoholic beverages, tobacco products, and some imported goods. Taxes on these types of items account for more than one fifth of the revenue of federal, state, and local governments. Why are some goods taxed very highly and others hardly at all? Why are some goods even subsidized? And what are the effects of taxes and subsidies on prices and on the quantities of the goods bought and sold? And who winds up paying the tax? Does the consumer pay, does the producer pay, or do they somehow share the tax between them?

Excise Taxes

An **excise tax** is a tax on the sale of a particular commodity. The tax may be set as a fixed dollar amount per unit of the commodity, in which case it is called a *specific tax*. Alternatively, the tax may be set as a fixed percentage of the value of the commodity, in which case it is called an *ad valorem tax*. The taxes on gasoline, alcoholic beverages, and tobacco products are all examples of excise taxes.

Let's study the effects of an excise tax by considering the tax on gasoline. We'll assume that the market for gasoline is competitive. The presence of monopolistic elements does affect the answer to the question that we're now examining and we'll consider what that effect is when we've worked through the competitive case.

Figure 20.5 illustrates the market for gasoline. The quantity of gasoline, measured in millions of gallons a day, is shown on the horizontal axis and the price of gasoline (measured in cents per gallon) is on the vertical axis. The demand curve for gasoline is *D* and the supply curve is *S*. If there is no tax on gasoline, its price is 60¢ a gallon and 400 million gallons of gasoline a day are bought and sold.

Let's suppose that a tax is imposed on gasoline at the rate of 60¢ a gallon. If producers are willing to supply 400 million gallons a day for 60¢ when there is no tax, then they will be willing to supply that same quantity in the face of a 60¢ tax only if the price increases to $1.20 a gallon. That is, they will want to get the 60¢ a gallon they received before, plus the additional 60¢ that they now have to hand over to the government in the form of a gasoline tax. As a result of the tax, the supply curve shifts upward by the amount of the tax and becomes the red curve labeled "*S* + *tax*." The new supply curve intersects the demand curve at a quantity of 300 million gallons a day and at a price of $1.10 a gallon. This situation is the new equilibrium after the imposition of the tax. Why doesn't the equilibrium occur at $1.20—the original price plus the tax? Let's find out.

Who Pays the Tax? When a tax of 60¢ a gallon is imposed on gasoline, Fig. 20.5 illustrates that the price of gasoline increases, but only by 50¢, to $1.10. Thus the price paid by gasoline consumers increases by less than the tax. The government collects 60¢ a gallon in tax, but the consumer pays only an extra 50¢ a gallon for gasoline. Who pays the

Figure 20.5 An Excise Tax

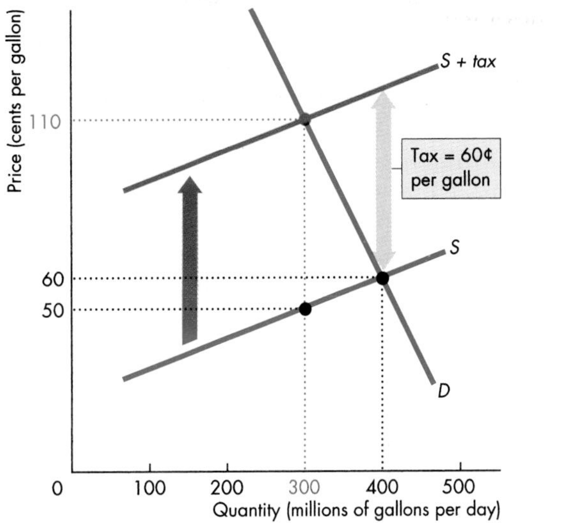

The demand curve for gasoline is *D* and the supply curve is *S*. In the absence of any taxes, gasoline will sell for 60¢ a gallon and 400 million gallons a day will be bought and sold. When a tax of 60¢ a gallon is imposed, the supply curve shifts upward to "*S* + *tax*." The new equilibrium price is $1.10 a gallon and 300 million gallons a day are traded. The tax is shared between the consumer, who pays 50¢, and the producer, who pays 10¢.

other 10¢? The answer must be the producer. You can see that the producer does in fact pay the missing 10¢ because the receipts of the producer fall from 60¢ a gallon to 50¢ a gallon when the quantity traded falls to 300 million gallons a day.

The way the tax payment is divided between an increase in price paid by the consumer and the fall in the price received by the producer depends on the elasticity of demand and supply. If supply is perfectly elastic—a horizontal supply curve—the rise in price will be equal to the tax. If supply is perfectly inelastic—a vertical supply curve—there will be no change in either the price or the quantity traded and the producer will pay the entire amount of the tax.

If demand is perfectly elastic, the tax will leave the price unchanged. The entire burden of the tax will fall on the producers. The producers will decrease the quantity supplied until marginal cost is below the price by the amount of the tax. The more inelastic the demand, the larger is the rise in price and the smaller is the fall in the quantity traded that results from the imposition of a tax. Furthermore, the more inelastic the demand, the larger is the fraction of the tax paid by the consumer and the smaller is the fraction borne by the producers.

Although we have just examined the effects of an excise tax on gasoline, the same basic analysis has widespread application. Taxes on alcohol and tobacco, sales taxes, and even taxes imposed in the labor market—for example, personal income taxes and social security taxes—can be analyzed in the same manner. The imposition of a tax shifts the supply curve upward by the amount of the tax. The new equilibrium is determined at a higher price and a lower quantity traded. The division of the burden of the tax between a rise in the price of the good being traded and a fall in the receipts of its producer depends on the elasticities of demand and supply.

Monopoly Markets A monopoly industry has a higher price and smaller quantity traded than the same industry would have in competitive conditions. The monopoly determines its profit-maximizing price by making marginal revenue and marginal cost equal. The imposition of a sales tax or excise tax on a monopoly works in a manner similar to the way it works in a competitive industry. The tax represents an increase in the monopoly's marginal cost. Its marginal cost curve shifts upward by the amount of the tax. Monopoly profit is maximized by producing the output at which marginal cost plus tax equals marginal revenue. Thus the imposition of a sales tax or an excise tax on a monopoly industry has the effect of raising the price and lowering output in the same way that it does in a competitive industry.

Why Do Tax Rates Vary?

Why is the structure of taxes the way it is? Why do we tax alcohol, tobacco, and gasoline at a very high rate and some goods not at all? There are two main reasons why some commodities are taxed very highly and others hardly at all. First, the consumption of some goods, as we saw in Chapter 19, imposes external costs. By placing taxes on the purchase and consumption of such goods, people can be made to take into account the external costs they are imposing on others when they make their own consumption choices. Second, taxes create *deadweight losses*, and by levying taxes at different rates on different commodities, the deadweight loss arising from raising a given amount of revenue can be minimized. Let's look at these two explanations for variable tax rates a bit more closely.

External Costs External costs are associated with many goods that are taxed at a high rate. For example, the high tax on gasoline in part enables road users to be confronted with the marginal social cost of the congestion that they impose on others. The high taxes on alcohol and tobacco products in part serve to confront drinkers and smokers with the external costs that their consumption habits impose on others. The impairment of long-term health that results from using these products, and the subsequent health-care costs, as well, perhaps, as a decline in their efficiency as workers, may lead to costs that are borne by others. These costs are not taken into account when a person is deciding whether or not to drink or smoke.

Some goods that have high external costs associated with their consumption are not taxed. Instead, they are made illegal. Marijuana and cocaine are important examples of such goods. Large amounts of these goods are consumed every day in the United States and the illegal markets in which they are traded generate large external costs. An alternative way of organizing these markets would be to make these drugs legal but to impose heavy taxes on them. Sufficiently high taxes would leave the quantities consumed similar to (and perhaps even smaller than) what they currently are, and would confront the users of these drugs with the marginal social cost of their actions. Such taxes would also result in a source of revenue (perhaps a large one) for the government. (Of course, matters relating to drugs have dimensions that go beyond a narrow economic calculation. Some people believe that the consumption of these drugs is so immoral that it would be equally immoral for the government, or anyone else, to legally profit from their production and consumption. These considerations, important though they are, go beyond the scope of economics.)

Let's now look at the deadweight loss that arises from taxes and the way in which this loss can be minimized.

Minimizing the Deadweight Loss of Taxes It's easy to see that taxes create deadweight loss by returning to the example of the gasoline tax that you studied in Fig. 20.5. The deadweight loss associated with the gasoline tax is illustrated in Fig. 20.6. Without a tax, 400 million gallons of gasoline a day are consumed at a price of 60¢ a gallon. With a 60¢ tax, the price paid by the consumer rises to $1.10 a gallon and the quantity consumed declines to 300 million gallons a day. There is a loss of consumer surplus arising from this price increase and quantity decrease. There is also a loss of producer surplus. Producers now receive 50¢ a gallon for 300 million gallons compared with 60¢ a gallon for 400 million gallons in the absence of taxes. The deadweight loss —the sum of the loss of consumer surplus and producer surplus—is indicated by the gray triangle in Fig. 20.6. The dollar value of that triangle is 30 million dollars a day.[1] But how much revenue is raised by this tax? Since 300 million gallons of gasoline are sold each day and since the tax is 60¢ a gallon, total revenue from the gasoline tax is $180 million a day (300 million gallons multiplied by 60¢ a gallon). Thus to raise tax revenue of $180 million a day using the gasoline tax, a deadweight loss of $30 million a day—one sixth of the tax revenue—is incurred.

One of the main influences on the deadweight loss arising from a tax is the elasticity of demand for the product. The demand for gasoline is fairly inelastic. As a consequence, when a tax is imposed the quantity demanded falls by a smaller percentage than the percentage rise in price. In the example that we've just studied, the quantity demanded falls by 25 percent but the price increases by 83.33 percent. To see the importance of the elasticity of demand, let's consider a different commodity—orange juice. So that we can make a quick and direct comparison, let's assume that the orange juice market is exactly as big as the market for gasoline. Figure 20.7 illustrates this market. The demand curve for orange juice is *D* and the supply curve is *S*. Orange juice is not taxed, and so the price of orange juice is 60¢ a gallon—where the supply curve and the demand curve intersect—and the quantity of orange juice traded is 400 million gallons a day.

Figure 20.6 The Deadweight Loss from an Excise Tax

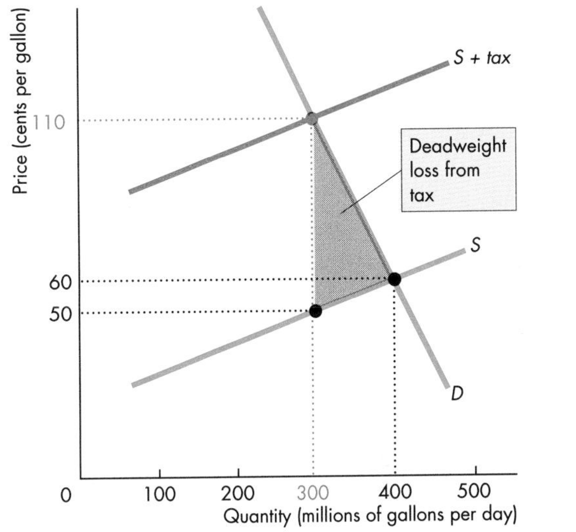

An excise tax creates a deadweight loss represented by the gray triangle. The tax revenue collected is 60¢ a gallon on 300 million gallons, or $180 million a day. The deadweight loss from the tax is $30 million a day. That is, to raise a tax revenue of $180 million a day, a deadweight loss of $30 million a day is incurred.

Now suppose that the government contemplates abolishing the gasoline tax and taxing orange juice instead. The demand for orange juice is more elastic than the demand for gasoline. It has many more good substitutes in the form of other fruit juices. The government wants to raise $180 million a day so that its total revenue is not affected by this tax change. The government's economists, armed with their statistical estimates of the demand and supply curves for orange juice that appear in Fig. 20.7, work out that a tax of 90¢ a gallon will do the job. With such a tax, the supply curve shifts upward to the curve labeled "*S* + *tax*." This new supply curve intersects the demand curve at a price of $1.30 a gallon and at a quantity of 200 million gallons a day. The price at which suppliers are willing to produce 200 million gallons a day is 40¢ a gallon. The government collects a tax of 90¢ a gallon on 200 million gallons a day, so it collects a total revenue of $180 million dollars a day—exactly the amount that it requires.

But what is the deadweight loss in this case? The answer can be seen by looking at the gray

[1] You can calculate the area of that triangle by using the following formula:

$$\frac{\text{Base} \times \text{height}}{2}$$

Turn the triangle on its side so that its base is 60¢, the size of the tax. Its height then becomes the reduction in the quantity sold—100 million gallons a day. Multiplying 60¢ by 100 million gallons and dividing by 2 gives $30 million a day.

Figure 20.7 Why We Don't Tax Orange Juice

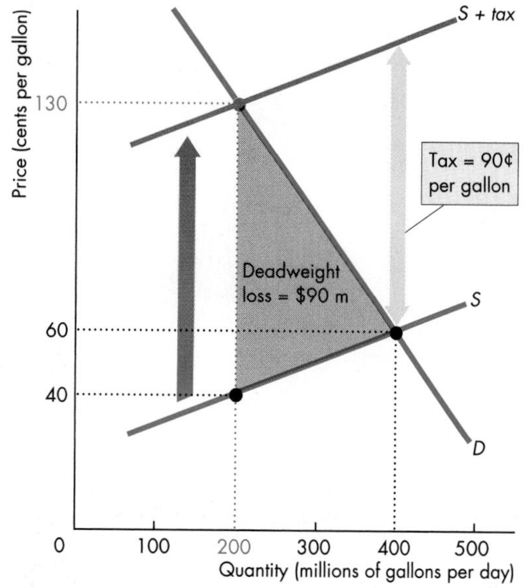

The demand curve for orange juice is *D* and the supply curve is *S*. The equilibrium price is 60¢ a gallon and 400 million gallons of juice a day are traded. To raise $180 million of tax revenue, a tax of 90¢ a gallon will have to be imposed. The introduction of this tax shifts the supply curve to "*S + tax*." The price rises to $1.30 a gallon and the quantity traded falls to 200 million gallons a day. The deadweight loss is represented by the gray triangle and equals $90 million a day. The deadweight loss from taxing orange juice is much larger than that from taxing gasoline (Fig. 20.6) because the demand for orange juice is more elastic than the demand for gasoline. Items that are taxed more heavily than items that have a low elasticity of demand have a high elasticity of of demand.

triangle in Fig. 20.7. The magnitude of that deadweight loss is $90 million.[2] Notice how much bigger the deadweight loss is from taxing orange juice than that from taxing gasoline. In the case of orange juice, the deadweight loss is one half the revenue raised, while in the case of gasoline it is only one sixth. The difference between these two markets is the elasticity of demand. The supply curves are identical in each case and the examples were also set up to ensure that the initial no-tax prices and quantities were identical. The difference between the two cases is the elasticity of demand: In the case of gasoline, the quantity demanded falls by only 25 percent when the price almost doubles. In the case of orange juice, the quantity demanded falls by 50 percent when the price only slightly more than doubles.

You can see why taxing orange juice is not on the political agenda of any of the major parties. Vote-seeking politicians seek out taxes that benefit the median voter. Other things being equal, this means that they try to minimize the deadweight loss of raising a given amount of revenue. Equivalently, they tax items with an inelastic demand more heavily than items with an elastic demand.

Let's now turn to an examination of subsidies.

Subsidies

In the aggregate, subsidies do not constitute a large fraction of government expenditure either at the federal, state, or local levels. Nevertheless, there is one industry in which subsidies constitute an important component of income— agriculture. More than 10 percent of the total receipts of grain producers, for example, are in the form of government subsidies. Let's study subsidies by examining the market for wheat.

Suppose that the wheat market is as illustrated in Fig. 20.8. The demand curve is *D* and the supply curve is *S*. Two billion bushels a year are produced at a price of $3.50 a bushel. Now suppose that the government offers wheat growers a subsidy of $1 a bushel. If suppliers are willing to supply 2 billion bushels a year for $3.50 without a subsidy, then they will be willing to supply that same quantity for $2.50 with a $1 subsidy. The supply curve for wheat, therefore, shifts downward by the amount of the subsidy. The new supply curve becomes that labeled "*S* − *subsidy*." The new supply curve intersects the demand curve at a price of $3 a bushel and at a quantity of 3 billion bushels a year. This price and quantity is the new equilibrium. The price of wheat falls by 50¢ a bushel. Consumers pay 50¢ a bushel less and producers' costs rise by 50¢ a bushel. The 50¢ cost increase and the 50¢ price cut are made up by the one-dollar subsidy to the producer.

---

[2]This deadweight loss is calculated in exactly the same way as our previous calculation of the deadweight loss from the gasoline tax. Turning the deadweight loss triangle on its side, the base is 90¢ and the height is 200 million gallons. Using the formula for the area of the triangle—base multiplied by height divided by 2—we calculate the deadweight loss as 90¢ multiplied by 200 million divided by 2, which equals $90 million a day.

Figure 20.8 Subsidies

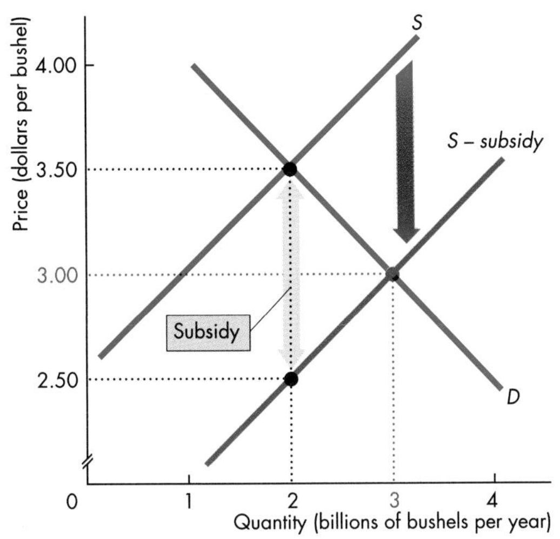

The demand curve for wheat is *D* and the supply curve is *S*. A competitive market with no taxes or subsidies produces 2 billion bushels of wheat a year at a price of $3.50 a bushel. If the government subsidizes wheat production by $1 a bushel, the supply curve shifts downward to "*S*−*subsidy*." The price of wheat falls to $3 a bushel and the quantity produced increases to 3 billion bushels a year. Wheat growers receive just enough revenue from the market, along with the subsidy, to cover their costs.

Subsidies with Quotas

In the United States, in addition to subsidies on production in the farm sector, there are also quotas. A **quota** is a limit on the quantity that a firm is permitted to produce. When a group of producers can enforce quotas, it is possible to restrict output and thereby obtain monopoly profit. We can see the effects of quotas and subsidies in Fig. 20.9. Suppose that the government establishes and enforces quotas for each producer that result in total output being 2 billion bushels a year (shown by the vertical line marked "*Quota*" in the figure). At this output level, consumers are willing to pay $3.50 a bushel for the wheat, and so that will be its market price. Producers also get a subsidy of a dollar a bushel on everything they produce so the supply curve becomes "*S* − *subsidy*." With the subsidy and a market price of $3.50, producers would like to supply 4 billion bushels a year—the quantity read off from the new red supply curve at a price of $3.50. But they're prevented from doing so by the quota.

With output restricted to 2 billion bushels of wheat, producers' costs are $3.50 a bushel. They are also selling their wheat for $3.50 a bushel. In addition, they are receiving $1 a bushel in subsidies from the government. The subsidy is like a monopoly profit.

It is interesting to contrast this situation with the one in which there is a subsidy but no quota. Without a quota, output is 3 billion bushels and marginal cost is $4 a bushel. The market price is $3 a bushel so the subsidy of $1 a bushel makes up the difference between the market price and marginal cost. Without a quota, the price plus the subsidy just cover marginal cost. With a quota, price covers mar-

Figure 20.9 Subsidies with Quotas

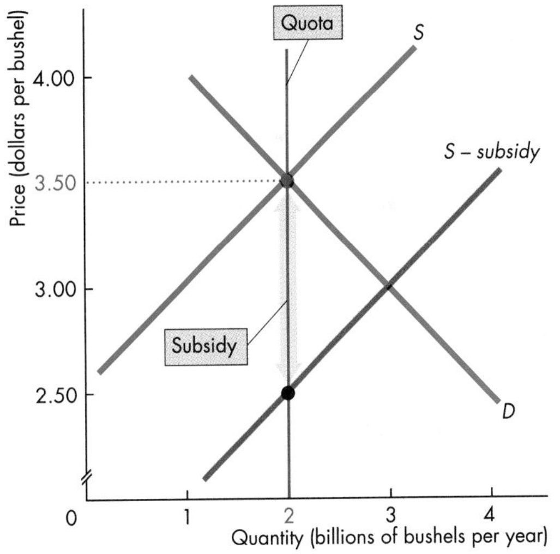

A competitive wheat market with no taxes or subsidies produces 2 billion bushels a year at a price of $3.50 a bushel—the point of intersection of the curves *D* and *S*. A subsidy of $1 a bushel shifts the supply curve to "*S*−*subsidy*." But if a quota is introduced at the same time as the subsidy, the output of each producer is restricted so that total output stays at 2 billion bushels a year, and the price remains $3.50 a bushel. With the quota, producers receive $3.50 from the market plus $1 from the government. Producers gain from the quota. The revenue from the market covers costs, so the subsidy is like a monopoly's profit.

ginal cost and the subsidy is a surplus for the producer—an excess revenue over cost.

Subsidies with quotas are clearly a good thing from the point of view of producers. But they are a bad thing from the point of view of consumers. To pay a subsidy the government has to raise taxes that create deadweight loss. So why do we have subsidies with quotas?

Why Subsidies and Quotas? The existence of quotas and subsidies is explained by the fact that those who stand to gain from a system of quotas and subsidies are relatively well defined and easily organized into a political force. Those who stand to lose are highly diffuse and much more difficult and costly to organize. As a result, the political equilibrium that prevails is one in which a relatively small number of people gain a significant per person amount while a relatively large number of people each lose an almost unnoticeable amount.

■ We have now reviewed the structure of the government sector, market failure, and the theory of public choice that explains how politicians, bureaucrats, and voters interact to determine the scale of provision of public goods, the extent to which taxes and subsidies are used to cope with externalities, the amount of income redistribution, and the levels of taxes and subsidies.

We have seen that a political equilibrium emerges in which no individual can improve his or her own situation by proposing or implementing a different policy. Each political party devises a program that appeals as closely as possible to half of the electorate. The parties differ in their rhetoric because of differences in the particular half of the electorate to which they appeal, but their actions are similar to each other. Bureaus grow to a size such that politicians perceive the benefit from increasing the bureaus' budgets still further is matched by the perceived cost of higher taxes and their consequences for lost votes. Voters are as well informed as it pays them to be—they are rationally ignorant.

In the next chapter, we're going to study a further range of government actions—their interventions in markets for goods and services in which there are monopoly and cartel elements.

SUMMARY

The Political Marketplace

There are three types of actors in the political marketplace: voters, politicians, and bureaucrats. Voters are the consumers of the outcome of the political process. They express their demands through their votes, campaign contributions, and lobbying. Public choices are made by politicians and implemented by bureaucrats. The objective of politicians is to win enough votes to be elected and then to remain in office. They do so by offering policies that are likely to appeal to a majority of voters. To appeal to a majority of voters, politicians have to appeal to the median voter. Since politicians aim for the vote of the median voter, their policies will resemble each other—they will be minimally differentiated. For example, in designing income redistribution policies, politicians transfer from the rich not only to the poor but to all those with incomes at or below the median. Redistribution will be aimed at making the median voter as rich as possible.

Bureaucrats, in pursuing their own objectives, seek to maximize the budget of their own bureau. If voters are well informed, politicians will not be able to collect taxes to enable bureaucrats to achieve budgets in excess of those that maximize net benefit. But if voters are rationally ignorant, producer interests may result in voting to support taxes that in turn support a level of provision of public goods in excess of that which maximizes net benefit. (pp. 515–528)

Taxes and Subsidies

The imposition of a tax on a good shifts the supply curve upward, raises the price of the good, and lowers the quantity traded. A tax is shared between the consumer and the producer and creates a deadweight loss. The size of the deadweight loss depends on the elasticity of demand. By taxing goods that have a low elasticity of demand, deadweight loss of raising a given amount of tax revenue is minimized. The highest tax rates are applied to goods with a low elasticity of demand.

Subsidizing a good shifts the supply curve downward, lowers the price of the good and increases the quantity traded. Subsidies combined with quotas generate additional income for producers at the expense of consumers. (pp. 528–534)

KEY CONCEPTS

Bureaucrats, 516
Excise tax, 529
Lobbying, 516
Median voter theorem, 521
Political equilibrium, 516
Politicians, 516
Principle of minimum differentiation, 520
Quota, 533
Rational ignorance, 528
Voters, 515

Key Figures

REVIEW QUESTIONS

1 What are the three types of actors in the political marketplace?

2 Describe the economic functions of voters and explain how they make their economic choices.

3 Describe the economic functions of politicians and explain how they make their economic choices.

4 What is meant by "political equilibrium"?

5 What is the principle of minimum differentiation?

6 How does the principle of minimum differentiation explain political parties' policy platforms?

7 What is the median voter theorem?

8 What features of political choices does the median voter theorem explain?

9 What are the economic functions of bureaucrats and how do they make their economic choices?

10 Describe the ways in which government redistributes income.

11 Why is it rational for voters to be ignorant?

12 Explain why it is likely that the scale of provision of public goods will exceed the allocatively efficient scale.

PROBLEMS

1 Your local city council is contemplating upgrading its system for controlling traffic signals. By installing a sophisticated computer with sensing mechanisms at all the major intersections, the council believes that it can better adjust the timing of the changes in signals and improve the speed of the traffic flow. The bigger the computer it buys, the better job it can do; the more sensors

it installs, the more intersections it can monitor and the faster the overall traffic flow that will result. The mayor and the other elected officials who are working on the proposal want to determine the scale and sophistication of the system that will win them the most votes. The city bureaucrats in the traffic department want to maximize the budget. Suppose that you are an economist who is observing this public choice. Your job is to calculate the scale of provision of this public good that maximizes net benefit—that achieves allocative efficiency.

a) What data would you need in order to reach your own conclusions?

b) What does the public choice theory predict will be the scale of provision chosen?

c) How could you, as an informed voter, attempt to influence the choice?

2 Three people—Joe, Jim, and Jon—have incomes of \$1000, \$500, and \$250. Set up a proposed redistribution of income between these three people that will achieve majority support. Once you've determined the new distribution (after implementing your proposal), set up another scheme that will also command a majority support. Show that you can find a voting cycle.

3 A community of 9 people, identified by letters *A* through *I*, have strong views about a local factory that is polluting the atmosphere. Some of them work at the factory and don't want the government to take any action against it while others want to see the imposition of a huge tax based on the scale of pollution. The preferences of each person concerning the scale of the tax that should be imposed are as follows:

A	*B*	*C*	*D*	*E*	*F*	*G*	*H*	*I*
100	90	80	70	60	0	0	0	0

Suppose that there are two political parties competing for office in this community. What tax rate will the parties propose?

4 You are given the following information about a perfectly competitive market for cookies.

Price (dollars per pound)	Quantity demanded (pounds per month)	Quantity supplied (pounds per month)
10	0	12
8	1	10
6	2	8
4	3	6
2	4	4
0	5	0

a) What are the competitive equilibrium price and quantity traded?

b) Suppose that a 10 percent tax is imposed on cookies.

(i) What is the new price of cookies?

(ii) What is the new quantity traded?

(iii) What is the total amount of tax revenue raised by the government?

(iv) What is the deadweight loss?

c) Now suppose that cookies are not taxed but are instead subsidized by 10 percent.

(i) What happens to the price of cookies?

(ii) What happens to the quantity traded?

(iii) How much is the subsidy paid out by the government?

(iv) Suppose that along with the subsidy, a quota is imposed on cookie producers. What is the scale of the quota that will maximize profit for the producer?

Chapter 21

Regulation and Antitrust Law

After studying this chapter, you will be able to:

- Define regulation
- State which parts of the economy are subject to regulation
- Describe the main trends in regulation and deregulation
- Describe the main elements of antitrust law
- Explain how antitrust law has been applied in a number of landmark cases
- Distinguish between the "public interest" and "capture" theories of regulation
- Explain how regulation of natural monopolies affects prices, outputs, profits, and the distribution of the gains from trade between consumers and producers
- Explain how the regulation of cartels affects prices, outputs, profits, and the distribution of the gains from trade between consumers and producers

Public Interest or Special Interests?

Some of the most important things that you consume are bought from regulated natural monopolies. Water, electric power, gas, cable TV, and subway services are all examples of such goods. Why are the industries that produce goods and services regulated? How are they regulated? And do the regulations work in the interests of consumers—the public interest—or do they serve the interests of the producer—special interests? ■ Regulation extends beyond natural monopoly, to cartels. For example, until 1978, the price of air transportation in the United States, and the routes that airlines could fly, were regulated by the Civil Aeronautics Board (CAB). But in 1978, domestic air travel was deregulated, and the CAB was disbanded. The government still regulates the airline industry to ensure adequate safety standards, but airlines are now free to choose their routes and decide their own fares. The initial result was that more airlines sprang up, prices fell, and the number of airline passengers increased dramatically. Subsequently, however, prices began to edge upward and competition lessened. ■ Regulation and deregulation are not confined to the airline industry. Interstate trucking, and the financial sector—banking and insurance and other financial services—were regulated in the past but in recent years were deregulated. Why do we sometimes regulate an industry and at other times deregulate that same industry? Whose interest is served by regulation and deregulation—the consumer or the producer? ■ Regulation and deregulation represent just one aspect of the actions governments can take to influence the market economy. They also pass laws—antitrust laws—that block mergers between large competing companies and that result in other companies being broken up. For example, until a few years ago, if you made a long-distance phone call, you had no choice but to use the American Telephone and Telegraph Company (AT&T). Our antitrust laws were used to break up AT&T and to create a number of independent producers of long-distance telephone service. Today, after the breakup of AT&T, and also following deregulation in the phone business, you can choose your long-distance carrier, and such alternatives as MCI and U.S. Sprint compete with AT&T. The price of a long-distance phone call has gone down considerably. ■ What are the antitrust laws? How have they evolved over the years? How are they used today? Do antitrust laws serve consumer interests—the public interest—or the special interests of producer groups?

■ This chapter studies the actions taken by government to regulate, control, and influence trading in markets for goods and services. It begins by describing the various ways in which government intervenes in monopolistic and oligopolistic markets. The chapter draws on your earlier study of how competitive, monopolistic, and oligopolistic markets work, and on your knowledge of the gains from trade—of consumer and producer surplus. It shows how consumers and producers might redistribute those gains, and identifies who stands to gain and who stands to lose from various types of government intervention. And since such intervention is supplied by politicians and bureaucrats, the chapter also looks at the economic behavior of these groups, expanding on what you learned in the previous chapter about public choice and the political "marketplace."

Market Intervention

There are two main ways in which the government intervenes in monopolistic and oligopolistic markets to influence *what, how,* and *for whom* various goods and services are produced:

- Regulation
- Antitrust law

Regulation

Regulation consists of rules administered by a government agency to restrict economic activity by determining prices, product standards and types, and the conditions under which new firms may enter an industry. In order to implement its regulations, the government establishes agencies to oversee the regulations and ensure their enforcement. The first such agency to be set up in the United States was the Interstate Commerce Commission (ICC), established in 1887. Over the years since then and up to the late 1970s, regulation of the economy grew until, at its peak, almost a quarter of the nation's output was produced by regulated industries. Regulation applied to banking and financial services, telecommunications, gas and electric utilities, railroads, trucking, airlines and buses, and many agricultural products. Since the late 1970s, there has been a tendency to deregulate the U.S. economy.

Deregulation is the process of removing restrictions on prices, product standards and types, and entry conditions. In recent years, deregulation has occurred in domestic air transportation, telephone service, interstate trucking, and banking and financial services.

Antitrust Law

An **antitrust law** is a law that regulates and prohibits certain kinds of market behavior, such as monopoly and monopolistic practices. Antitrust law is enacted by Congress and enforced through the judicial system. Lawsuits under the antitrust laws may be initiated either by government agencies or by privately injured parties.

The main thrust of the antitrust law is the prohibition of monopoly practices and of restricting output in order to achieve higher prices and profits. The first antitrust law was enacted in 1890—the Sherman Act. Successive acts and amendments have strengthened and refined the body of antitrust law. Antitrust law (like all law) depends as much on decisions of the courts and of the Supreme Court as on the statutes passed by Congress. Over the 100 years since the passage of the Sherman Act, there have been some interesting turns of direction in the interpretation of the law by the courts and the vigor with which the law has been enforced. We'll study these later in this chapter.

To understand why the government intervenes in the market economy and to work out the effects of its interventions, we need to identify the gains and losses that government actions can create. These gains and losses are the consumer surplus and producer surplus associated with different output levels and prices. You've already met these concepts in Chapters 7 (pp. 167–168) and 13 (p. 332). All we need to do here, therefore, is refresh our understanding of these concepts and of the way in which their magnitudes are affected by the price at which a good is sold and the quantity traded.

Surpluses and Their Distribution

Consumer surplus is the difference between the maximum amount that consumers are willing to pay and the amount that they actually do pay for a given quantity of a good. Consumer surplus is the gain from trade accruing to consumers. *Producer surplus* is the difference between the producer's revenue and the opportunity cost of production. Producer surplus is the gain from trade accruing to producers. **Total surplus** is the sum of consumer surplus and producer surplus.

The lower the price and the larger the quantity traded, the larger is consumer surplus. The closer are the price and quantity traded to the monopoly profit-maximzing levels, the larger is producer surplus.Total surplus is maximized (in the absence of external costs and benefits) when marginal cost equals price. In this situation, allocative efficiency is achieved.

There is a conflict between maximizing producer surplus and maximizing total surplus. Monopoly firms have an incentive to restrict output below the competitive level, increasing producer surplus but reducing consumer surplus and creating deadweight loss. Thus there is a tension between the public interest of maximization of total surplus and the producer's interest of maximizing monopoly profit and producer surplus. This tension is of central importance in the economic theory of regulation. Let's now examine that theory.

The Economic Theory of Regulation

The economic theory of regulation is part of the broader theory of public choice. You have already met that theory in Chapter 20 and seen the main components of a public choice model. We're going to reexamine the main features of such a model but with an emphasis on the regulatory aspects of government behavior. We'll examine the demand for government actions, the supply of those actions, and the political equilibrium—the balancing of demands and supplies.

The Demand for Regulation

The demand for regulation is expressed through political institutions. Both consumers and producers vote, lobby, and campaign for regulations that best further their own interests. None of these activities are costless. Voters incur costs in order to acquire information on the basis of which to decide their vote. Lobbying and campaigning cost time, effort, and contributions to the campaign funds of political parties. Individual consumers and producers demand political action only if the benefit that they individually receive from such action exceeds the costs incurred by them in obtaining the action. There are four main factors that affect the demand for regulation:

- Consumer surplus per buyer
- Number of buyers
- Producer surplus per firm
- Number of firms

The larger the consumer surplus per buyer resulting from regulation, the greater is the demand for regulation by buyers. Also, as the number of buyers increases, so does the demand for regulation. But numbers alone do not necessarily translate into an effective political force. The larger the number of buyers, the greater is the cost of organizing them, so the demand for regulation does not increase proportionately with the number of buyers.

The larger the producer surplus per firm arising from a particular regulation, the larger is the demand for that regulation by firms. Also, as the number of firms that might benefit from some regulation increases, so does the demand for that regulation. But again, as in the case of consumers, large numbers do not necessarily mean an effective political force. The larger the number of firms, the greater is the cost of organizing them.

For a given surplus, consumer or producer, the smaller the number of households or firms who share that surplus, the larger is the demand for the regulation that creates it.

The Supply of Regulation

Regulation is supplied by politicians and bureaucrats. As we saw in the previous chapter, politicians choose policies that appeal to a majority of voters, thereby enabling themselves to achieve and maintain office, and bureaucrats support policies that maximize their budgets. Given these objectives of politicians and bureaucrats, the supply of regulation depends on the following factors:

- Consumer surplus per buyer
- Producer surplus per firm
- The number of persons affected

The larger the consumer surplus per buyer or producer surplus per firm generated, and the larger the number of persons affected by a regulation, the greater is the tendency for politicians to supply that regulation. If regulation benefits a large number of people significantly enough for it to be noticed and if the recipients know who is the source of the benefits, that regulation appeals to politicians and it is supplied. If regulation affects markets that benefit a large number of people but by a small amount per person, and if such benefits do not attract notice, that regulation does not appeal to politicians and it is not supplied. Regulation that bestows clear and large benefits on a small number of people may be attractive to politicians provided some of those benefits flow back and thus enable the politicians to fight more effective election campaigns.

Equilibrium

In equilibrium, the regulation that exists is such that no interest group feels it is worthwhile to use additional resources to press for changes, and no group of politicians feels it is worthwhile to offer different regulations. Being in a political equilibrium is not the same thing as everyone being in agreement. Lobby groups will devote resources to trying to change regulations that are already in place. And others will devote resources to maintaining the existing regulations. But no one will feel it is worthwhile to *increase* the resources they are devoting to such activities. Also, political parties will not agree with each other. Some support the existing regulations and others propose different regulations. In equilibrium, no one wants to change the proposals that they are making.

What will a political equilibrium look like? There are two theories of political equilibrium: one is called the public interest theory and the other the capture theory. Let's look at these two theories.

Public Interest Theory The **public interest theory of regulation** states that regulations are supplied to satisfy the demand of consumers and producers for the maximization of total surplus—or the attainment of allocative efficiency. Public interest theory predicts that the political process will relentlessly seek out deadweight loss and introduce regulations that eliminate it. For example, where monopoly or monopolistic practices by collusive oligopoly exist, the political process will introduce price regulation to ensure that output and price are close to their competitive levels.

Capture Theory The **capture theory of regulation** states that the regulations that exist are those that maximize producer surplus. The key idea of capture theory is that the cost of regulation is high and that only those regulations that increase the surplus of small, easily identified groups who have low organization costs will be supplied by the political process. Such regulations will be supplied even where they impose costs on others, provided those costs are spread thinly and widely enough so that they do not have negative effects on votes.

The predictions of the capture theory of regulation are less precise than the predictions of the public interest theory. According to the capture theory, regulations benefit cohesive interest groups by large and visible amounts and impose costs on everyone else that are so small, in per capita terms, that no one feels it is worthwhile to incur the cost of organizing an interest group to avoid these costs. To make these predictions concrete enough to be useful, the capture theory needs a model of the costs of political organization.

Whichever theory of regulation is correct, the political system delivers an amount and type of regulation that best furthers the electoral success of politicians. Since we have seen that producer-oriented and consumer-oriented regulation are in direct conflict with each other, it is clear that the political process cannot satisfy both groups in any particular industry. Only one group can win. This makes the regulatory actions of government a bit like a unique product—for example, a painting by Rembrandt. There is only one original and it will be sold to just one buyer. Normally, a unique commodity is sold through an auction; the highest bidder takes the prize. Equilibrium in the regulatory process can be thought of in much the same way: The suppliers of regulation will satisfy the demands of the higher bidder. If the producer demand offers a bigger return to the politicians, either directly through votes or indirectly through campaign contributions, then the producers' interests will be served. If the consumer demand translates into a larger number of votes, then the consumers' interests will be served by regulation.

We have now completed our study of the theory of regulation in the marketplace. Let's turn our attention to an examination of the regulations that exist in our economy today.

Regulation and Deregulation

The past 20 years have seen dramatic changes in the way in which the U.S. economy is regulated by government. We're going to examine some of the more important of those changes. To begin, we'll look at what is regulated and also at the scope of regulation. Then we'll turn to the regulatory process itself and examine how regulators control prices and other aspects of market behavior. Finally, we'll tackle the more difficult and controversial questions: Why do we regulate some things but not others? Who benefits from the regulation that we have?

The Scope of Regulation

The first federal regulatory agency, the Interstate Commerce Commission (ICC), was set up in 1887 to control prices, routes, and the quality of service of interstate transportation companies—railroads, trucking lines, bus lines, water carriers, and, in more recent years, oil pipelines. Following the establishment of the ICC, the regulatory environment remained static until the years of the Great Depression. Then, in the 1930s, more agencies were established —the Federal Power Commission, the Federal Communications Commission, the Federal Maritime

Table 21.1 Federal Regulatory Agencies Controlling Prices, Entry, and Services in 1978

Organization	Year established	Controls and regulates
Interstate Commerce Commission	1887	Prices, routes, and services of railroads, trucks, bus lines, oil pipelines, and domestic water carriers
Federal Power Commission	1930	Wellhead gas prices and wholesale prices of natural gas and electricity sold for resale in interstate commerce
Federal Communications Commission	1934	Prices for telephone and telegraph service; entry into telecommunications and broadcasting
Federal Maritime Commission	1936	Fares and schedules of transoceanic freight shipments
Civil Aeronautics Board	1938	Airline passenger fares; entry of airlines into city-to-city air routes
Postal Rate Commission	1970	Classes of mail and rates for those classes; sets fees for other services
Federal Energy Regulatory Commission	1974	Wellhead crude-oil prices and refinery, wholesale, and retail prices of petroleum products; allocation levels for wholesalers and retailers of crude oil, residual fuel oil, and most refined petroleum products produced in or imported into the United States during a period of energy emergency
Copyright Royalty Tribunal	1976	Fees and charges on copyright materials

Source: Paul W. MacAvoy, *The Regulated Industries and the Economy* (New York: W.W. Norton, 1979), 146–147.

Commission, and, in the late 1930s, the Civil Aeronautics Board. There was a further lull until the establishment in the 1970s of the Postal Rate Commission and the Energy Regulatory Administration and finally, the Copyright Royalty Tribunal. Table 21.1 provides a summary of the federal regulatory agencies and their functions.

In the mid-1970s, almost one quarter of the economy was subject to some form of regulation, as seen in Table 21.2 (a). The most heavily regulated industries—those subject both to price regulation and to regulation of entry of new firms—were electricity, natural gas, telephones, airlines, highway freight services, and railroads (see Table 21.2b). It has been estimated that in 1975 regulation was costing the U.S. economy $100 billion a year—more than 6¢ on every dollar earned.

Regulation reached its peak in 1977. Since then, there has been a gradual and important deregulation process in place. Deregulation has had the most significant impact in the telecommunication, banking and finance, railroad, bus, trucking, and airline industries.

What exactly do regulatory agencies do? How do they regulate?

The Regulatory Process

Though regulatory agencies vary in size and scope and in the detailed aspects of economic life that they control, there are certain features common to all agencies.

First, the senior bureaucrats who are the key decision makers in a regulatory agency are appointed by the administration or Congress. In addition, all agencies have a permanent bureaucracy made up of experts in the industry being regulated and often recruited from the regulated firms. Agencies have financial resources, voted by Congress, to cover the costs of their operations.

Second, each agency adopts a set of practices or operating rules for controlling prices and other aspects of economic performance based on well-defined physical and financial accounting procedures that are relatively easy to administer and to monitor.

In a regulated industry, individual firms are free to determine the technology that they will use in production. But they are not free to determine the prices at which they will sell their output, the quantities that they will sell, or the markets that they will serve. The regulatory agency grants certification to a company to serve a particular market and with a particular line of products, and it determines the level and structure of prices that will be charged. In some cases, the agency also determines the scale of output permitted.

To analyze the way in which regulation works, it is convenient to distinguish between the regulation

Table 21.2 How Much Regulation?

(a) Regulation as a percentage of total output

	Year 1965	1975
Price regulation	5.5	8.8
Financial regulation	2.7	3.0
Health and safety regulation	—	11.9
Total	8.2	23.7

(b) Industries subject to price and entry regulation

Industry	Jurisdiction and extent of regulation
Electricity	Federal Energy Regulatory Commission and 49 state agencies certify service.
Natural gas	Federal Energy Regulatory Commission controls interstate transportation and 49 state agencies set rates for distribution.
Telephones	Federal Communications Commission and 50 state agencies set rates, entry, and service conditions.
Airlines	Civil Aeronautics Board regulations set fares and entry conditions before the Airline Deregulation Act of 1978; 21 state agencies set fare and entry conditions interstate.
Highway freight	Interstate Commerce Commission and 47 state agencies regulate rates; the ICC and 45 state agencies control entry into common-carrier services.
Railroads	Interstate Commerce Commission and 44 state agencies set freight rates; the ICC and 26 state agencies certify entry into the provision of rail services.

Source: Paul W. MacAvoy, *The Regulated Industries and the Economy* (New York: W.W. Norton, 1979), 18, 25.

Figure 21.1 Natural Monopoly: Marginal Cost Pricing

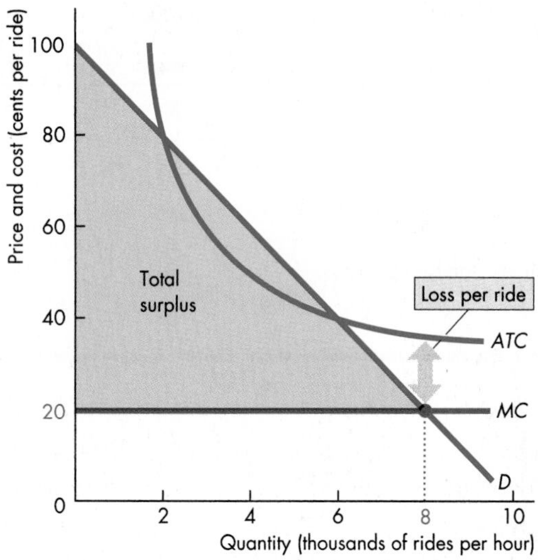

A natural monopoly is an industry in which average total cost is falling even when the entire market demand is satisfied. A natural monopoly for subway rides has a demand curve *D*. Marginal costs are constant at 20¢ a ride, as shown by the curve *MC*. Fixed costs are heavy and the average total cost curve, which includes average fixed cost, is shown as *ATC*. A marginal cost pricing rule that maximizes total surplus sets the price of a ride at 20¢, with 8000 rides an hour being taken. The resulting consumer surplus is shown as the green area. The producer makes a loss on each ride indicated by the red arrow. In order to remain in business, the producer must either price discriminate or receive a subsidy.

of natural monopoly and the regulation of cartels. Let's begin with natural monopoly.

Natural Monopoly

Natural monopoly was defined in Chapter 13 (pp. 316–317) as an industry in which one firm can supply the entire market at a lower price than two or more firms can. As a consequence, a natural monopoly experiences economies of scale, no matter how high an output rate it produces. Examples of natural monopolies include gas and electric utilities and subway services. It is much more expensive to have two or more competing sets of pipes, wires, and train lines serving every neighborhood than it is to have a single set.

Let's consider the example of a subway train service. The demand for the subway service and the subway's cost curves are illustrated in Fig. 21.1. The demand curve is *D*. The marginal cost curve is *MC*. Notice that the marginal cost curve is horizontal at 20¢ a ride—that is, the cost of each additional ride is a constant 20¢. The subway company has a heavy investment in track, trains, and control equipment and so has high fixed costs. These fixed costs feature in the company's average total cost curve, shown as *ATC*. The average total cost curve slopes downward because as the number of rides increases the fixed cost is spread over a larger number of rides. (If you need to refresh your memory on how the average total cost curve is calculated, take a quick look back at pp. 237–241.)

Regulation in the Public Interest How will this industry be regulated according to the public interest theory? Recall that the public interest theory states that regulation maximizes total surplus—achieves allocative efficiency. Allocative efficiency occurs when marginal cost equals price. Equivalently, it occurs when total surplus (the green area) is maximized—when the area above the marginal cost curve and below the demand curve has reached a maximum. As you can see in the example shown in Fig. 21.1, that outcome occurs if the price is regulated at 20¢ a ride and if 8000 rides an hour are produced. Such a regulation is called a marginal cost pricing rule. A **marginal cost pricing rule** sets price equal to marginal cost. It maximizes total surplus in the regulated industry.

A natural monopoly that is regulated to set price equal to marginal cost makes an economic loss. Because its average total cost curve is falling, marginal cost is below average total cost. Because price equals marginal cost, price is below average total cost. The difference between price and average total cost is the loss per unit produced, a shown by the red arrow in Fig. 21.1. It's pretty obvious that a private subway company that is required to use a marginal cost pricing rule will not stay in business for long. How can a company cover its costs and, at the same time, obey a marginal cost pricing rule?

One possibility is price discrimination. Some natural monopolies can fairly easily price discriminate. For example, local phone companies can charge consumers a monthly fee for being connected to the telephone system and then charge a low price (perhaps even zero) for each local call. A subway company can price discriminate by offering discounts on weekly or monthly season tickets.

But a natual monopoly cannot always price discriminate. When a natural monopoly cannot price discriminate, it can only cover its total cost and follow a marginal cost pricing rule if it receives a subsidy from the government. In such a case, the government would have to raise the revenue for the subsidy by taxing some other activity. But as we saw in Chapter 20, taxes themselves generate deadweight loss. Thus the deadweight loss resulting from additional taxes has to be offset against the allocative efficiency gained by forcing the natural monopoly to adopt a marginal cost pricing rule. It is possible that deadweight loss will be minimized by permitting the natural monopoly to charge a higher price than marginal cost rather than by taxing some other sector of the economy in order to subsidize the natural monopoly. Such a pricing arrangement is called an average cost pricing rule. An **average cost pricing rule** sets price equal to average total cost. The average cost pricing solution is shown in Fig. 21.2. The subway company charges 40¢ for each ride and sells 6000 rides an hour. Consumer surplus (the green area) falls below its maximum possible amount, and deadweight loss arises, represented by the gray triangle in the figure.

Even though there is a deadweight loss, this situation may well be allocatively efficient. Recall that the subway company goes out of business if it doesn't cover its costs. If a subsidy is required to cover costs and if the subsidy requires a tax that has a deadweight loss larger than the one shown in the figure, then the average cost pricing rule is the best available.

Capturing the Regulator What does the capture theory predict about the regulation of this industry? Recall that according to the capture theory, regulation serves the interests of the producer. The interests of the producer, in this case, are best satisified by maximizing profit. To work out the price that achieves this goal, we need to look at the relationship between marginal revenue and marginal cost. As you know, a monopoly maximizes profit by producing the output at which marginal revenue equals marginal cost. The monopoly's marginal revenue curve in Fig. 21.3 is the orange curve *MR*. Marginal revenue equals marginal cost when output is 4000 rides an hour. The subway company sells three rides at a price of 60¢ a ride (as determined by the demand curve). The subway company's average total cost is 50¢ a ride, its profit is 10¢ a ride, and its total profit is shown by the blue triangle. Consumer surplus shrinks (green triangle), and deadweight loss expands (gray triangle).

Figure 21.2 Natural Monopoly: Average Cost Pricing

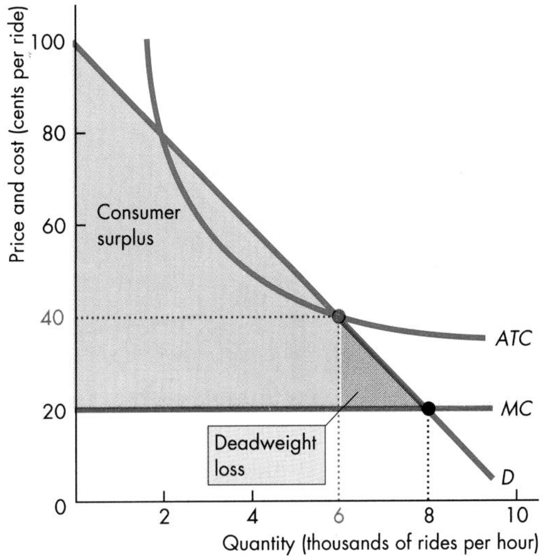

Average cost pricing sets price equal to average total cost. The Subway Company charges 40¢ a ride and sells 6000 rides an hour. In this situation the Subway Company will break even—average total cost equals price. Deadweight loss, shown by the gray triangle, is generated. Consumer surplus is reduced to the green area.

We have discovered that a regulation that best serves the interest of the producer will set the price at 60¢ a ride. But how can a producer go about obtaining regulation that results in this monopoly profit-maximizing outcome? To answer this question, we need to look at the way in which agencies determine the level at which to set a regulated price. The key method used is called rate of return regulation.

Rate of Return Regulation **Rate of return regulation** determines a regulated price by setting the price at a level that enables the regulated firm to earn a specified target percent return on its capital. The target rate of return is determined with reference to what is normal in competitive industries. This rate of

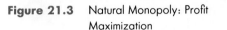

Figure 21.3 Natural Monopoly: Profit Maximization

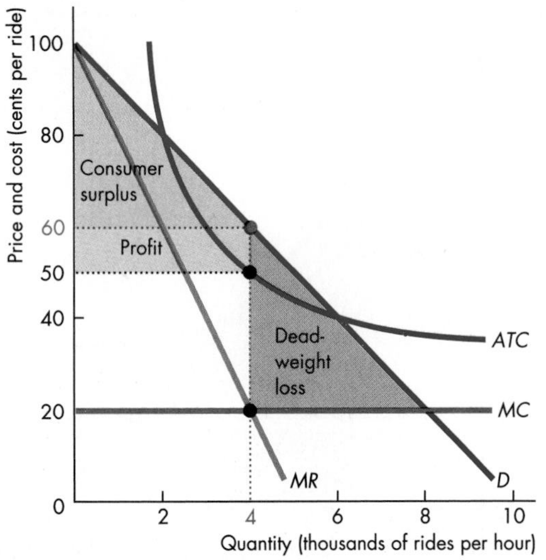

The subway company would like to maximize profit. To do so, marginal revenue (*MR*) is made equal to marginal cost (*MC*). At a price of 60¢ a ride, 4000 rides an hour are sold. Consumer surplus is reduced to the green triangle. The deadweight loss increases to the gray triangle. Monopoly makes the profit shown by the blue rectangle. If the producer can capture the regulator, the outcome will be the situation shown here.

return is part of the opportunity cost of the natural monopolist and is included in the firm's average total cost. By examining the firm's total cost, including the normal rate of return on capital, the regulator attempts to determine the price at which average total cost is covered. Thus rate of return regulation is equivalent to average cost pricing.

In the example that we have just been examining (Fig. 21.2), average cost pricing results at a regulated price of 40¢ a ride with 6000 rides an hour being sold. Thus rate of return regulation, based on a correct assessment of the producer's average total cost curve, results in a price and quantity that favors the consumer and does not enable the producer to maximize monopoly profit. The special interest group will have failed to capture the regulator and the outcome will be closer to that predicted by the public interest theory of regulation.

But there is an important feature of many real world situations that the above analysis does not take into account—the ability of the monopoly firm to mislead the regulator about its true costs.

Inflating Costs The senior managers of a firm might be able to inflate the firm's costs by spending part of the firm's revenue on inputs that are not strictly required for the production of the good. By this device, the firm's apparent cost curves exceed the true cost curves. On-the-job luxury in the form of sumptuous office suites, limousines, free baseball tickets (disguised as public relations expenses), company jets, lavish international travel, and entertainment are all ways in which managers can inflate costs.

If the subway company manages to inflate its costs and persuade the regulatory agency that its true cost curve is that shown as *ATC*(inflated) in Fig. 21.4, then the regulator, applying the normal rate of return principle, will regulate the price at 60¢ a ride. In this example, the price and quantity will be the same as those under unregulated monopoly. Though it might be impossible for firms to inflate their costs by as much as that shown in the figure, to the extent

Figure 21.4 Natural Monopoly: Inflating Costs

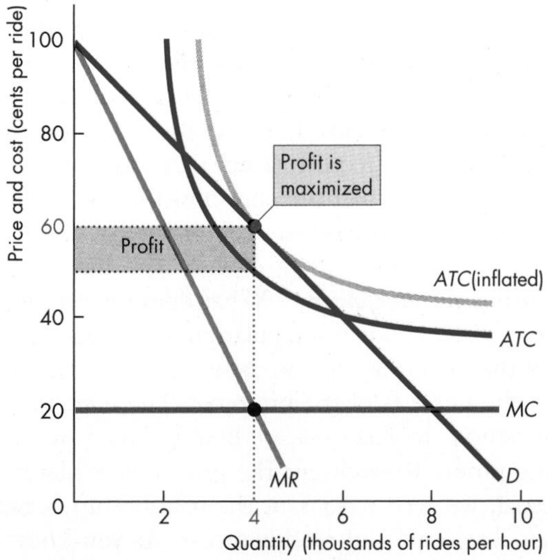

If the subway company is able to inflate its costs to *ATC*(inflated) and persuade the regulator that these are genuine minimum costs of production, rate of return regulation will result in a price of 60¢ a ride—the profit-maximizing price. To the extent that the producer can inflate costs above average total cost, the price will rise, output will fall, and deadweight loss will increase.

that costs can be inflated, the apparent average total cost curve lies somewhere between the true *ATC* curve and *ATC*(inflated). The greater the ability of the firm to pad its costs in this way, the closer its profit (measured in economic terms) approaches the maximum possible. The shareholders of this firm don't receive this economic profit. It gets used up by the managers of the firm on the self-serving activities that they have used to inflate the company's costs.

Public Interest or Capture?

It is not clear whether actual regulation produces prices and quantities that more closely correspond with the predictions of capture theory or with public interest theory. One thing is clear, however. Price regulation does not require natural monopolies to use the marginal cost pricing rule. If it did, most natural monopolies would make losses and receive hefty government subsidies to enable them to remain in business. But there are even exceptions to this conclusion. For example, many local telephone companies do appear to use marginal cost pricing for local phone calls. They cover their total cost by charging a flat fee each month for being connected to their telephone system but then permitting each call to be made at its marginal cost—zero or something very close to it.

A test of whether natural monopoly regulation is in the public interest or the interest of the producer is to examine the rates of return earned by regulated natural monopolies. If those rates of return are significantly higher than those in the rest of the economy, then, to some degree, the regulator may have been captured by the producer. If the rates of return in the regulated monopoly industries are similar to those in the rest of the economy, then we cannot tell, for sure, whether the regulator has been captured or not for we cannot know the extent to which costs have been inflated by the managers of the regulated firms.

Table 21.3 shows the rates of return in regulated natural monopolies as well as the economy's average rate of return. In the 1960s, rates of return in regulated natural monopolies were somewhat below the economy average; in the 1970s, those returns exceeded the economy average. Overall, the rates of return achieved by regulated natural monopolies are not very different from those in the rest of the economy.

We can conclude from these data either that natural monopoly regulation does, to some degree,

Table 21.3 Rates of Return in Regulated Natural Monopolies

	Years	
	1962–69	1970–77
Electricity	3.2	6.1
Gas	3.3	8.2
Railroad	5.1	7.2
Average of above	3.9	7.2
Economy average	6.6	5.1

Source: Paul W. MacAvoy, The Regulated Industries and the Economy (New York: W.W. Norton, 1979), 49–60.

serve the public interest, or that natural monopoly managers inflate their costs by amounts sufficiently large to disguise the fact that they have captured the regulator and that the public interest is not being served.

We've now examined the regulation of natural monopoly. Let's next turn to regulation in oligopolistic industries—to the regulation of cartels.

Cartel Regulation

A *cartel* is a collusive agreement among a number of firms designed to restrict output and achieve a higher profit for the members of the cartel. Cartels arise in oligopolistic industries. An oligopoly is an industry in which a small number of firms compete with each other. We studied oligopoly (and duopoly—two firms competing for a market) in Chapter 14. There we saw that if firms manage to collude and behave like a monopoly, they can set the same price and sell the same total quantity as a monopoly firm would. But we also discovered that in such a situation, each firm will be tempted to "cheat," increasing its own output and profit at the expense of the other firms. The result of such "cheating" on the collusive agreement is the unraveling of the monopoly equilibrium and the emergence of a competitive outcome with zero profit for producers. Such an outcome benefits consumers at the expense of producers.

Figure 21.5 Collusive Oligopoly

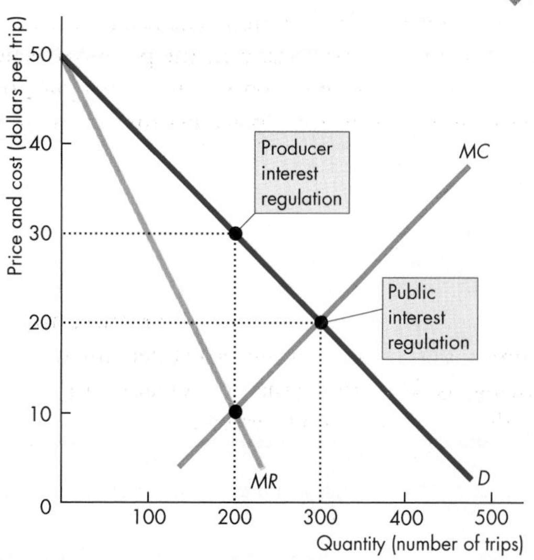

Ten trucking firms transport tomatoes from the San Joaquin valley to Los Angeles. The demand curve is *D* and the industry marginal cost curve is *MC*. Under competition, the *MC* curve is the industry supply curve. If the industry is competitive, the price of a trip will be $20 and 300 trips will be made each week. Producers will demand regulation that restricts entry and restricts the output of producers to 200 trips a week. This regulation will raise the price to $30 a trip and result in each producer making maximum profit —as if it is a monopoly. The industry marginal revenue will be equal to industry marginal cost.

How is oligopoly regulated? Does regulation prevent monopoly practices or does it encourage those practices?

According to the public interest theory, oligopoly is regulated to ensure a competitive outcome. Consider, for example, the market for trucking tomatoes from the San Joaquin valley to Los Angeles, illustrated in Fig. 21.5. The demand curve for trips is *D*. The industry marginal cost curve—and the competitive supply curve is *MC*. Public interest regulation will regulate the price of a trip at $20 and there will be 300 trips a week.

How would this industry be regulated according to the capture theory? Regulation that is in the producer interest will set the price at $30 a trip and, to ensure that that price is maintained, will restrict the number of trips to 200 a week. Each producer will make a maximum profit, and the industry marginal revenue will be equal to the industry marginal cost. If there are 10 trucking companies, this outcome can be achieved by issuing a production quota to each trucking company restricting it to 20 trips a week so that the total number of trips in a week is 200. Penalities can be imposed to ensure that no single producer violates its quota.

What does regulation of oligopoly do in practice? Though there is disagreement about the matter, the consensus view is that regulation tends to favor the producer. Trucking (regulated by the Interstate Commerce Commission), taxicabs (regulated by cities), and airlines (regulated by the Civil Aeronautics Board) are all specific examples in which it has been calculated that increased profits have accrued to producers as a result of regulation. In some cases—and trucking is one of these—the work force, through unionization, also manages to take a large part of the total surplus.

Some further evidence in support of the conclusion that regulation sometimes increases profit is presented in Table 21.4. If regulation ensures a competitive outcome, rates of return in a regulated oligopoly will be no higher than those in the economy as a whole. As the numbers in Table 21.4 show, rates of return in airlines and trucking exceeded twice the economy average rate of return in the 1960s. In the 1970s, the rate of return in trucking remained higher than the economy average (although by a smaller margin than had prevailed in the 1960s). Airline rates of return in the 1970s fell to below the economy average. The overall picture that emerges from examining data on rates of return is mixed. The regulation of oligopoly does not always result in higher profit but there are many situations in which it does.

Further evidence on cartel and oligopoly regulation can be obtained from the performance of prices and profit following deregulation. If, following deregulation, prices and profit fall, then, to some degree, the regulation must have been serving the interest of the producer. In contrast, if, following deregulation, prices and profit remain constant, or increase, then the regulation may be presumed to have been serving the public interest. Since there has been a substantial amount of deregulation in recent years, we may use this test of oligopoly regulation to see which of the two theories better fits the facts. The evidence is mixed, but there are many cases in which deregulation has been accompanied by falling prices. Airlines, trucking, railroads, long-distance telephones, and banking and financial services are all industries in

Table 21.4 Rates of Return in Regulated Oligopolies

	Years	
	1962–69	1970–77
Airlines	12.8	3.0
Trucking	13.6	8.1
Economy average	6.6	5.1

Source: Paul W. MacAvoy, The Regulated Industries and the Economy (New York: W.W. Norton, 1979), 49–60.

which deregulation was, initially at least, associated with more competition, lower prices, and a large increase in the volume of transactions.

Interpreting the deregulation evidence, however, is made difficult by the possibility that firms in oligopoly industries will find other ways of restricting competition in a deregulated environment. There is evidence, for example, that the airlines managed to do this in the 1980s (see Reading Between the Lines, pp. 550–551.)

Making Predictions

Most industries have a few producers and many consumers. In these cases, public choice theory predicts that regulation will protect producer interests because a small number of people stand to gain a large amount and they would be fairly easy to organize as a cohesive lobby. Under such circumstances, politicians will be rewarded with campaign contributions rather than votes. But there are situations where the consumer interest is sufficiently strong and well organized and thus able to prevail. There are also cases in which the balance switches from producer to consumer, as seen in the deregulation process that began in the late 1970s.

Deregulation raises one of the hardest questions for economists seeking to understand and make predictions about regulation. Why has the transportation sector been deregulated? If the producers gained from regulation, and if the producer lobby was strong enough to achieve regulation, what happened in the late 1970s to change the equilibrium to one in which the consumer interest prevailed? We do not have a good and convincing answer to this question at the present time. One possibility—though it is an after-the-fact rationalization—is that regulation had become so costly to consumers, and the potential benefits to them from deregulation so great, that the cost of organizing the consumer voice became a cost worth paying. Furthermore, as communication technology improves, and the cost of communication falls, it is probable that the cost of organizing larger groups of individuals will also fall. If this line of reasoning is correct, we should expect to see more consumer-oriented regulation in the future. In practice, more consumer-oriented regulation means deregulation—removing the regulations that are already in place to serve the interests of producer groups.

There is another puzzling feature of the deregulation movement. Although the movement was begun by a Democratic administration (see "Talking with Alfred Kahn," which opens Part 7 on pp. 491–494), its major impetus in the 1980s has come not from the Ralph Nader consumer movement but from the Republican party and the business interests that it is perceived to support. If the regulator really has been captured and serves the interests of producers, why are producers the ones pressing hardest for deregulation? This is another question to which we don't know the answer.

Let's now leave regulation and turn to the other main method of intervention in markets—antitrust law.

Antitrust Law

Antitrust law provides an alternative way in which the government may influence the marketplace. As in the case of regulation, antitrust law can be formulated in the public interest, to maximize total surplus, or in private interests, to maximize the surpluses of particular special interest groups such as producers.

Landmark Antitrust Cases

The antitrust laws themselves are brief and easily summarized. The first antitrust law, the Sherman Act, was passed in 1890 in an atmosphere of outrage and disgust at the actions and practices of the "rob-

Airline Deregulation

Why Flying Is Unpleasant

Why are airline fares skyrocketing? Why is airline service going to the dogs? Why can't some pilots find the right runway or even the right airport? Why are some planes flying into the flight paths of others? The fashion is to blame deregulation and to search for a solution in some form of re-regulation.

This reflects both ignorance of history and an analytical failure to distinguish a disease from its symptoms. The problem lies not in deregulation but in the Reagan Administration's failure to enforce antitrust laws and build up safety regulation and oversight—all of which are needed for fair and constructive competition.

The initial results of the 1978 deregulation of routes, rates and entry were impressive: the number of scheduled carriers nearly tripled. Fares (in inflation-adjusted terms) fell 13 percent on average. The proportion of travelers flying on low-cost discount fares rose from 48 percent to 80 percent by 1982.

Productivity in the industry improved by an estimated 80 percent, with cumulative cost savings of possibly as much as $10 billion in the first several years. And air travel expanded at significantly higher annual rates, as larger numbers of people found it increasingly affordable.

Why, then, the current disenchantment? It is rooted in a profound misunderstanding of deregulation. Deregulation is not synonymous with rambunctious, laissez-faire anarchy. If regulations barring entry to the industry are dropped and price regulation is abandoned, then they must be replaced with another regulatory mechanism—competition. And this requires that Government enforce antitrust laws so that competition is not subverted by unrestrained mergers and oligopolistic collusion.

Yet, the Reagan Administration has abandoned this responsibility. It has tolerated the most widespread merger and acquisition movement in the industry's history. In all, the Administration has countenanced 38 airline mergers and acquisitions, which have created a highly concentrated, noncompetitive industry. Once the USAir-Piedmont consolidation is completed, just eight carriers will collectively control 94 percent of the nation's airline business.

In regional markets, the impact of the absence of competition is clear. Before 1978, St. Louis was served by five airlines. While nine more carriers entered the St. Louis market after decontrol, their numbers quickly dwindled. Today, T.W.A. controls 82 percent of the city's air passenger traffic. The problem is replicated across the country. At 15 of the nation's largest airports (including Denver, Detroit, Houston, Minneapolis and Pittsburgh), either half of the business is now controlled by a single carrier or two carriers share more than 70 percent of the traffic.

The problems posed by the lack of competition have been exacerbated by a proliferation of anticompetitive practices among the airlines.

Computerized reservation systems—which are widely used by travel agents to book flights and are crucial to the ability of all carriers to compete—are dominated by two of the nation's biggest air carriers.

United's Apollo system and American Airlines' Sabre system together account for 70 percent of passenger revenues booked by travel agents nationwide. Control of these computerized systems has enabled the airlines to stifle competition in a number of ways: biasing screen displays by listing competitors' flights last, using information gained through the systems to unfair advantage and charging exorbitant rates for access to these key systems by other carriers.

Monopolization of airport terminal gates has further eroded competition. The airline oligopoly blocks potential competitors by tying up gates through exclusive long-term leases and by obstructing expansion plans by local airport authorities. In some cities, gates go unused because established carriers either refuse to lease them or demand astronomical rents.

(Walter Adams is Professor of Economics at Michigan State University, and James W. Brock is Associate Professor of Economics at Miami University of Ohio.)

The New York Times, **August 6, 1987**

By Walter Adams and James W. Brock

The Essence of the Story

- Domestic air travel was deregulated in 1978.
- In the past year or so, air fares have been rising and service quality falling.
- Deregulation is blamed for the recent developments in the airline industry.
- Deregulation is not the problem.
- Since 1978, the number of air carriers has tripled, fares have fallen, the proportion of discount fare travelers has risen, and larger numbers of people can afford air travel.
- The airline industry's problems arise from mergers and acquisitions that lower competition.
- Fifteen of the largest airports are served by one or two dominant carriers.
- There has been a proliferation of anticompetitive practices, including computerized reservation systems that manage information on flight schedules and availability and the monopolization of terminal facilities by long-term leases.

Background and Analysis

- The figure analyzes the market for air transportation out of one of the nation's 15 largest airports.
- If the airline industry were perfectly competitive, the price would be P_C and quantity Q_C, where the competitive supply curve (*S*) cuts the demand curve (*D*).
- If the industry were monopolized, the price would be P_M and the quantity traded Q_M. This quantity makes marginal revenue equal to marginal cost (the marginal cost curve is the supply curve, so *MR* equals *S*) and the price is the maximum price at which Q_M can be sold.
- When the airline industry was regulated, the price was above the competitive price, P_C. The airline industry regulation process had been "captured" by the producers and operated more in their favor than in the interests of the consumers.
- Deregulation injected competition into the industry and brought the price down toward its competitive level.
- More recently the industry has become increasingly monopolized. This monopoly movement has resulted partly from mergers and acquisitions reducing the number of competitors, and partly from the use of practices that restrict entry of new competition.

Conclusion

The conclusion is provided by the authors of the article:

" . . .Deregulation without competition does not serve the public interest. The competitive market is neither a self-perpetuating nor an immutable artifact of nature. If it is to perform its role as economic regulator, it must be protected from subversion, and that is the inescapable responsibility of government. It calls for strict antitrust enforcement, especially against oligopolistic mergers and market concentration . . ."

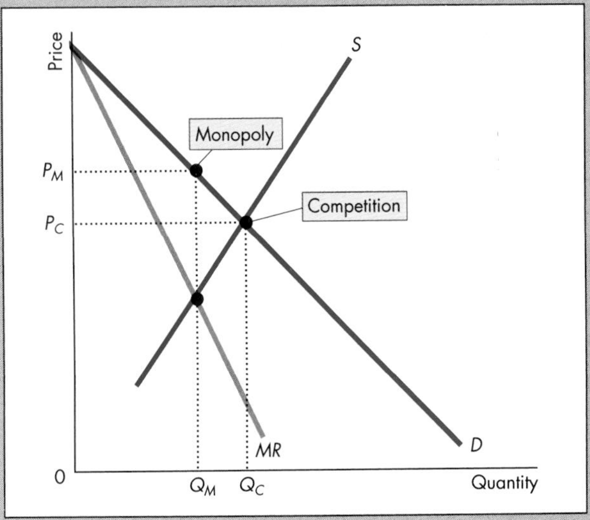

Table 21.5 Antitrust Laws

Name of law	Year passed	What the law prohibits
Sherman Act	1890	• Combination, trust, or conspiracy to restrict interstate or international trade • Monopolization, or attempt to monopolize interstate or international trade
Clayton Act	1914	• Price discrimination where effect is to substantially lessen competition or create monopoly and where such discrimination is not justified by cost differences • Contracts that force other goods to be bought from same firm • Acquisition of competitors' shares or assets if effect is to reduce competition • Interlocking directorships among competing firms
Robinson-Patman Amendment	1936	
Cellar-Kefauver Amendment	1950	
Federal Trade Commission Act	1914	• Unfair methods of competition and unfair or deceptive business practices

ber barons."[1] The most lurid stories of the actions of the robber barons are not of their monopolization and exploitation of consumers but of their sharp practices against each other. Nevertheless, monopolies did emerge—for example, the spectacular control of the oil industry by John D. Rockefeller. But once the Sherman Act was passed it had little effect until the early part of this century. Table 21.5 gives a summary of the main antitrust laws.

The real force of any law arises from its interpretation. Interpretation of the antitrust laws has ebbed and flowed. At times, it has appeared to favor producers and at other times consumers. Lets see how.

Table 21.6 summarizes the landmark antitrust cases. The first important cases were those of the American Tobacco Company and Standard Oil Company, decided in 1911. These two companies were found guilty of violations under the Sherman Act and ordered to divest themselves of large holdings in other companies. The breakup of John D. Rockefeller's Standard Oil Company resulted in the creation of many oil companies that today are household names—such as Exxon.

In finding these companies to be in violation of the provisions of the Sherman Act, the Supreme Court enunciated the "rule of reason." The rule of reason states that monopoly arising from mergers and agreements among firms is not necessarily illegal. Only if there is an unreasonable restraint of trade does the arrangement violate the provisions of the Sherman Act. The rule of reason was widely regarded as removing the force of the Sherman Act itself. This view was reinforced in 1920 when U.S. Steel was acquitted of violations under the act even though it had a very large (more than 50 percent) share of the U.S. steel market. Applying the "rule of reason," the court declared that "size alone is not an offense."

Matters remained much as they were in 1920 until 1940 when the *Socony-Vacuum Oil Company* case resulted in the first chink in the armor of the "rule of reason." The court found Socony-Vacuum Oil Company guilty because a combination had been formed for the purpose of price fixing. The court ruled that no consideration of reasonableness should be applied to such a case. Where the purpose of the agreement was price fixing, the automatic interpretation was to be that the agreement was unreasonable.

The "rule of reason" received its death blow in the *ALCOA* case, decided in 1945. ALCOA was judged to be in violation of the law because it was too big. It had too large a share of the aluminum market. A relatively tough interpretation of the law continued through the late 1960s. In 1961, General Electric, Westinghouse, and other electrical component manufacturers were found guilty of a price-fixing conspiracy. This case was the first one in which the executives (as opposed to the company itself) were fined and also jailed.

Tough antimerger decisions were taken in 1962 against Brown Shoe and in 1965 against Von's Grocery. In the first of these cases, Brown Shoe was required to divest itself of ownership of Kinney's—a shoe retail chain. This case is an example of the court ruling that a vertically integrated firm is capable of restraining competition. **Vertical integration** is the merger of two or more firms operating at different stages in a production process of a single good or

[1]Business practices of this era are discussed by Matthew Josephson, *The Robber Barons: The Great American Capitalists, 1861–1901* (New York: Harcourt Brace Jovanovich, 1934).

Table 21.6 Landmark Antitrust Cases

Case	Year	Verdict and consequence
American Tobacco Company	1911	*Guilty:* Ordered to divest themselves of large holdings in other companies; "rule of reason" enunciated—only *unreasonable* combinations guilty under Sherman Act.
Standard Oil Company	1911	
U.S. Steel Company	1920	*Not guilty:* Although U.S. Steel had a very large market share (near monopoly), mere "size alone is not an offense"; application of the "rule of reason."
Socony-Vacuum Oil Company	1940	*Guilty:* Combination was formed for purpose of price fixing; no consideration of "reasonableness" applied.
ALCOA	1945	*Guilty:* Too big—had too large a share of the market; end of "rule of reason."
General Electric, Westinghouse, and others	1961	*Guilty:* Price-fixing conspiracy; first time executives fined and jailed.
Brown Shoe	1962	*Guilty:* Ownership of Kinney, a retail chain, reduced competition; ordered to sell Kinney (Brown supplied 8% of Kinney's shoes and Kinney sold 2% of nation's shoes).
Von's Grocery	1965	*Guilty:* Merger of two supermarkets in Los Angeles would restrain competition (the merged firm would have had 7½% of the L.A. market).
IBM	1982	*Case dismissed* as being "without merit"; back to the "rule of reason"?
AT&T	1983	*Agreement* between AT&T and government that company would divest itself of all local telephone operating companies—80% of its assets.

service. For example, the merger of a firm that produces raw materials, a firm that converts those raw materials into a manufactured good, and a firm that retails the finished product will be a vertically integrated firm. The vertically integrated Brown Shoe and Kinney retail chain was ordered to be broken up even though Brown supplied only 8 percent of Kinney's shoes and Kinney sold only 2 percent of the nation's shoes.

Von's Grocery is an example of a horizontally integrated firm. **Horizontal integration** is a merger of two or more firms providing essentially the same product or service. In the *Von's Grocery* case, the court ruled that the combination of two supermarkets in Los Angeles would restrict competition even though the combined sales of the two firms would have been only 7.5 percent of total supermarket sales in the Los Angeles area.

The two most visible recent antitrust cases, and two cases that were settled in interesting ways, are those involving AT&T and IBM. Though important and highly visible cases, neither of the two was decided by the courts. The *AT&T* case was resolved by an agreement between AT&T and the Department of Justice, and the *IBM* case, after 13 years of litigation, was dismissed by the government as being "without merit."

The present attitude toward monopoly is pragmatic. AT&T's monopoly on telephone services has gone. IBM's position in the computer industry is much less secure and looks much less like a monopoly today than it did in 1967 when the Justice Department began its proceedings against that firm. Also, increased international competition has reduced the monopoly power of any particular firm or group of firms.

Regulating Long Distance Phone Rates

FCC Hopes New Regulations Will Cut Phone Rates—But Others Aren't So Sure

Since the breakup of the Bell System 3½ years ago, federal regulators have forced American Telephone & Telegraph Co. to cut long-distance rates a whopping 33.5%. But whether phone bills will go even lower under newly proposed regulation is a matter of heated debate.

Earlier this week, the Federal Communications Commission proposed removing its limit on AT&T's profits and replacing it with a price cap. FCC Chairman Dennis Patrick and AT&T executives contend that the company would have more incentive to cut costs, passing part of the savings to consumers, with the rest fattening AT&T's bottom line. Moreover, says Larry Garfinkel, an AT&T vice president, the company would be more inclined to put new technology in its network, which would generate new services.

But consumer groups are skeptical. "Based on what we know, rates go down more under profit regulation," says Fred Goldberg, the Washington counsel to the National Association of State Utility Consumer Advocates.

Monitoring Costs

Currently, AT&T's interstate rates are set by limiting how much it can earn on its $9.1 billion investment in interstate plant and equipment. The allowed rate of return is now 12.2%. Under price regulation, the FCC would instead set a ceiling on what AT&T can charge. The ceiling would rise or fall depending on inflation, taxes, the industry's productivity, and AT&T's costs to connect to local phone companies.

The debate over which system is best centers in large part on how good the FCC is at monitoring AT&T's costs. Under profit regulation, prices should drop as technological advances reduce the company's costs. But if AT&T can keep its costs artificially high—and many people think it has—prices won't drop as fast as they could. One analyst estimates that AT&T could easily cut $2 billion of costs without affecting service.

AT&T denies it pads its costs, but acknowledges it doesn't have any incentive to cut them under profit regulation. "With price-cap regulation instead of rate-of-return, prices will go down more because we'll have the incentive to really try to be more efficient. We would pass some of that (savings) on to customers," says Wendell Lind, administrator of rates and trariffs for AT&T. But Mr. Goldberg says that even if AT&T does pad its costs, the current regulatory system still does a better job of ensuring that the industry's declining costs are reflected in lower rates than a price-cap approach would. FCC studies say phone rates overall have only doubled since 1935 while overall prices have risen eightfold. With price-caps tied to an inflation index, Mr. Goldberg fears the caps will effectively become price floors for future increases.

Price Cuts Since the Breakup

Percentage reductions in basic long-distance service costs since the AT&T breakup in January 1984:

May 1984	6.4
June 1985	5.6
June 1986	11.8
January 1987	11.4
July 1987	4.8

Wall Street Journal, **August 6, 1987**

By Janet Guyon, staff reporter

The Essence of the Story

- The Bell System long-distance phone monopoly was broken in January 1984.
- Prices of long-distance phone calls fell steadily between January 1984 and August 1987.
- The long-distance phone industry is regulated by the Federal Communications Commission (FCC).
- Long-distance phone rates are regulated by allowing a maximum rate of return of 12.2 percent on capital (rate of return regulation).
- The FCC is proposing to replace rate of return regulation with a price cap—a maximum price that may be charged.
- The proposed change is controversial: Some argue that prices will be more effectively controlled by rate of return regulation than by a price cap.

Background and Analysis

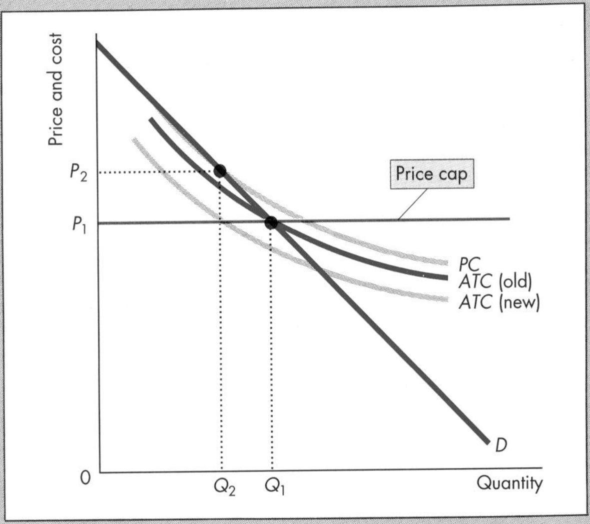

Costs and Demand

- The figure analyzes AT&T's costs and demand under different regulations.
- *D* is the demand curve that AT&T faces.
- Average total cost, using existing technologies, is shown by the curve *ATC* (old). That curve is AT&T's average total cost curve including an allowed rate of return of 12.2 percent.

Rate of Return Regulation

- At the point where the average total cost curve *ATC* (old) cuts the demand curve at price P_1 and quantity Q_1, AT&T just makes its allowed rate of return. (Recall that the rate of return is included in the cost curve).
- Suppose that AT&T pads its costs so that they rise to the curve labeled *PC* for padded costs. (The padded curve is not a cost curve because a cost curve shows the minimum possible cost. Padding takes the firm off its cost curve.) With rate of return regulation, there will be nothing to stop AT&T from raising the price to P_2 and cutting output to Q_2. Thus rate of return regulation does not provide an incentive for the producer to be economically efficient.
- Suppose that a new technology becomes available and results in costs falling to the curve labeled *ATC* (new). There is no incentive for AT&T to adopt the new technology because it can make its maximum permissible 12.2 percent return by using the existing technology, selling Q_1 phone calls for a price of P_1.

Price Cap

- Suppose that rate of return regulation is replaced by a price cap, with P_1 being the cap price. This regulation means that AT&T cannot charge a price higher than P_1.
- Under the price cap regulation, if AT&T produces Q_1 calls with the cost curve *ATC* (old), it will make exactly the same rate of return as under rate of return regulation.
- But there is now no incentive for AT&T to pad costs, for to do so will simply cause it to make losses.

(Continued on next page.)

Background and Analysis (*cont.*)

- If a new technology becomes available, it pays AT&T to adopt it. If it can continue to charge P_1 and produce Q_1, it makes a higher profit—the difference between average total cost with the new technology and the cap price.

- The theory is clear in its predictions: Rate of return regulation provides no incentive to minimize cost, while a price cap encourages cost minimization, though not necessarily ensuring that lower costs result in lower prices for consumers.

Empirical Issues

- Though the theory makes clear predictions, experience has generated controversy.

- In Maryland, AT&T has not been subject to rate of return regulation since mid-1986. The company made a profit of 125 percent in Maryland in the year ended March 31, 1987.*

- After Maryland dropped rate of return regulation in mid-1986, "the cost of a 5-minute day time phone call within 100 miles dropped 27 percent."**

*John M. Glynn, Maryland Peoples' Council, *Wall Street Journal* (August 21, 1987).

***Wall Street Journal* (August 21, 1987).

Conclusion

- As the *Wall Street Journal* reminds us, "It's always good to keep in mind that the folks who run consumerist organizations have a conflict with the very people they say they represent. If deregulation continues to grow in popularity with consumers, simple market competition will substitute for regulatory hearings. And when those hearing rooms are closed, consumerists will have to find other work. No wonder they are not happy with the FCC's latest proposal."†

†*Wall Street Journal* (August 21, 1987).

Public or Special Interest?

It is clear from the historical contexts in which antitrust law has evolved that its intent has been to protect and pursue the public interest and restrain the profit-seeking and anticompetitive actions of producers. But it is also clear from the above brief history of antitrust legislation and cases that from time to time the interest of the producer has had an influence on the way in which the law has been interpreted and applied. Nevertheless, the overall thrust of antitrust law appears to have been directed toward achieving allocative efficiency and, therefore, to serving the public interest.

It is interesting to note that there is an important difference between the way in which antitrust law and regulation are administered. Regulation is produced by a bureaucracy. Antitrust law is interpreted and enforced by the legal process—the courts. Economists are now beginning to extend theories of public choice to include an economic analysis of the law and the way the courts interpret the law. It is interesting to speculate that the legal institutions that administer antitrust law are more sensitive to the public interest than the political and bureaucratic institutions that deal with regulation.

The breakup of the AT&T monopoly is a strikingly good example of the consumer and public interest emerging and dominating that of the producer. The effects of the breakup and deregulation of long-distance telecommunications, while controversial, appear to have brought some visible benefits to consumers (see Reading Between the Lines, pp. 554–556.)

■ In this chapter, we've seen how the government intervenes in markets to affect prices, quantities, the gains from trade, and the division of those gains between consumers and producers when there is monopoly or oligopoly. We've seen that there is a conflict between the pursuit of the public interest—achieving allocative efficiency—and the pursuit of the special interests of producers—maximizing monopoly profit. The political and legal arenas are the places in which these conflicts are resolved. We've reviewed the two theories—public interest and capture—concerning the type and scope of government intervention.

SUMMARY

Market Intervention

There are two ways in which the government intervenes to regulate monopolistic and oligopolistic markets: regulation and antitrust law. In the United States, both of these methods are widely used. In studying regulation, we seek to understand the reasons for and the effects of regulation.

Government action can influence consumer surplus, producer surplus, and total surplus. Consumer surplus is the difference between what consumers are willing to pay for a given consumption level and what they actually pay. Producer surplus is the difference between a producer's revenue from sales and the opportunity cost of production. Total surplus is the sum of consumer surplus and producer surplus. Total surplus is maximized under competition. Under monopoly, producer surplus is increased and consumer surplus decreased, and a deadweight loss is created. (pp. 539–540)

The Economic Theory of Regulation

Consumers and producers express their demand for the regulation that influences their surpluses by voting, lobbying, and making campaign contributions. The larger the surplus that can be generated by a particular regulation and the smaller the number of people affected, the larger is the demand for that regulation. A smaller number of people are easier to organize into an effective political lobby. Regulation is supplied by politicians who pursue their own best interest. The larger the surplus per head generated and the larger the number of persons affected by it, the larger is the supply of regulation.

In equilibrium, the regulation that exists is such that no interest group feels it is worthwhile to employ scarce resources to press for further changes. There are two theories of political equilibrium: public interest theory and capture theory. Public interest theory predicts that total surplus will be maximized, thereby achieving allocative efficiency; capture theory predicts that producer surplus will be maximized. (pp. 540–542)

Regulation and Deregulation

Regulation began with the establishment of the Interstate Commerce Commission in 1887. A further expansion of regulation occurred in the 1930s. There was further steady growth of regulatory activity to the mid-1970s. Since 1978, the transportation, telecommunication, and financial sectors have been deregulated.

Regulation is conducted by regulatory agencies controlled by politically appointed bureaucrats and staffed by a permanent bureaucracy of experts. Regulated firms are required to comply with rules about price, product quality, and output levels. Two types of industries are regulated: natural monopolies and cartels. In both cases, regulation has enabled firms in the regulated industries to achieve profit levels equal to or greater than those attained on the average in the rest of the economy. This outcome is closer to the predictions of the capture theory of regulation than to the predictions of the public interest theory. (pp. 542–549)

Antitrust Law

Antitrust law provides an alternative way in which the government can control monopoly and monopolistic practices. The law itself is brief and its interpretation has fluctuated between favoring the consumer and favoring the producer.

But the overall thrust of the law has been directed toward serving the public interest. In recent years, increased international competition has reduced monopoly power. (pp. 549–557)

KEY CONCEPTS

Antitrust law, 539
Average cost pricing rule, 545
Capture theory of regulation, 541
Deregulation, 539
Horizontal integration, 553
Marginal cost pricing rule, 544
Public interest theory of regulation, 541
Rate of return regulation, 545
Regulation, 539
Total surplus, 540
Vertical integration, 552

Key Figures and Tables

REVIEW QUESTIONS

1 What are the two main ways in which the government can intervene in the marketplace?

2 What is consumer surplus? How is it calculated and how is it represented in a diagram?

3 What is producer surplus? How is it calculated and how is it represented in a diagram?

4 What is total surplus? How is it calculated and how is it represented in a diagram?

5 Why do consumers demand regulation? In what kinds of industries are their demands for regulation greatest?

6 Why do producers demand regulation? In what kinds of industries are their demands for regulation greatest?

7 Explain the public interest and capture theories of the supply of regulation. What does each theory imply about the behavior of politicians?

8 How is oligopoly regulated in the United States? In whose interest is it regulated?

9 What are the main antitrust laws in force in the United States today?

10 What is the "rule of reason"? When was this rule formulated? How has it been applied? When was it abandoned?

PROBLEMS

1 Cascade Springs, Inc., is a natural monopoly that bottles water from a natural spring high in the Grand Tetons. The total fixed cost incurred by Cascade Springs is $80,000 and its marginal cost is 10¢ a bottle. The demand for bottled water from Cascade Springs is as follows:

Price (cents per bottle)	Quantity demanded (thousands of bottles per year)
100	0
90	100
80	200
70	300
60	400
50	500
40	600
30	700
20	800
10	900
0	1000

What is the price of a bottle of water and how many bottles does Cascade Springs sell?

2 Does Cascade Springs maximize total surplus or producer surplus?

3 If the government regulates Cascade Springs by imposing a marginal cost pricing rule, what is the price of a bottle of water and how many bottles will Cascade Springs sell?

4 Is the regulation in problem 3 in the public interest or in the private interest?

5 If the government regulates Cascade Springs by imposing an average cost pricing rule, what is the price of a bottle of water and how many bottles does Cascade Springs sell?

6 Is the regulation in problem 5 in the public interest or in the private interest?

7 Compare consumer surplus in problem 3 with that in problem 5. Which situatin has the larger consumer surplus?

Part 11

International Trade and Comparative Systems

Talking with Anne Krueger

Anne Krueger pioneered the study of the effects of international trade protection on economic growth and development. Currently professor of economics at Duke University, she served for five years as vice president for economics and research at the World Bank. Michael Parkin talked with Professor Krueger about her experiences and insights into the role of trade policy.

Professor Krueger, what led you into economics?

I started out in political science and found that most of the things I wanted to understand were economics. I got waylaid into economics and never got back.

There are two broad views about trade and development. One is that free trade permits resources to go to their highest value use, enhancing and accelerating development. The other is that people or countries "learn by doing," and need protection until they're mature. What's your view?

As you're asking it, the choice is either doing nothing or else inhibiting trade. I think the whole insight of the past 30 years has been that trade restriction actually inhibits the learning by doing. There probably is lots of learning—by governments on how to operate effectively, and by individuals on how to do their business. If you impose trade restrictions,

"Every protectionist says 'I am for free trade . . . But this is special.'"

what people learn is how to try and circumvent the trade restrictions. They learn how to do other things that do not contribute to higher productivity or standards of living.

Can you then give us a thumbnail sketch of what we have learned about the contribution of good trade policy toward the development process?

The evidence is fairly overwhelming that the economic costs of a highly protectionist policy are substantial. If you have high levels of protection for domestic industries, you will find yourself with a wasteful regime and very slow growth. The evidence that there are very high costs for import substitution is strong. My view is that the incentive side of the story is terribly important. And by incentive I do mean competition, not simply the reward. I mean the knowledge that if you just sit around and your firm takes losses, it may go under. This is perhaps the most powerful incentive there is. In short, the intellectual case for free trade is so overwhelming that every protectionist starts by saying "I am for free trade . . . But this is special and here's why."

We're holding this conversation the day after a general election in Canada, in which the people of Canada endorsed the free trade agreement between the United States and Canada. How important is that agreement?

It's potentially more important in the long run than the short run. It's not obvious that all the trade restrictions are going to be removed. Some of them will gradually be relaxed and some will not be intensified. I think there's still a big question about what's going to come out of the multilateral negotiations that started in 1986 under the auspices of the General Agreement on Tariffs and Trade. That will make a huge difference to how important the U.S.–Canadian trade pact will be. A great deal still depends on Europe 1992, on how the European Economic Community works out. And what happens to the bilateral U.S.–Canadian pact if the U.S. signs a U.S.–Australia or a U.S.–Japan pact. I think the world trading system is in a state of flux. The U.S.–Canada agreement represents a recognition that trade is too important not to be given its due. But there's a lot else going on.

Suppose the United States did enter into bilateral pacts with Japan and Australia. How would that affect the U.S.–Canada deal?

If the Canadians, for example, relax their protection of a domestic industry in order to have better access to the U.S. market for wheat, and the United States turns around and offers the better access to the U.S. market to Australia, then the Canadians have lost part of what they bargained for. And then, too, you'll have a U.S.–Canada bilateral commission and presumably also a U.S.–Australia bilateral commission. What happens when their rulings are inconsistent?

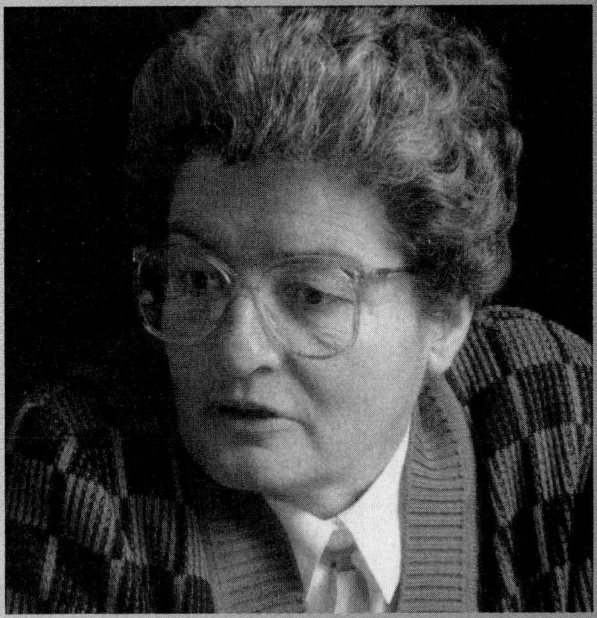

How serious is the debt problem for developing countries? Was there an international crisis?

Debt is an assessor of everything you've done in the past. If you borrowed and used the loan to finance productive activities that generate earnings streams, there's no problem unless you hit an unpleasant surprise. If, on the other hand, you borrow because you're spending beyond your income, when you have to pay the loan back, sometime in the future, you're going to have to cut your expenditures relative to your income. In the late 1970s, many developing countries were spending perhaps more than they should have and had great difficulties, when the worldwide recession hit in the early 1980s because many of them had excessive domestic programs, or programs that had low rates of return on investment. Then when the cost of borrowing went up, simultaneously, their export earnings fell and they couldn't cut their imports fast enough, their debt almost doubled. Mexico was the first very big debtor and, of course, had lots of oil revenue. The only trouble was that Mexico knew how to spend it faster than it could discover new oil fields.

Not all countries borrowed so much. India and Pakistan, whatever else they did, did not borrow a great deal and did not have great difficulties with debt repayments. Other countries, like Korea, Taiwan, Singapore, and Colombia, borrowed but put the loans to productive use.

At the World Bank, we were looking at the debt problem from the developing countries' viewpoints. The commercial banks that made the loans thought about their bottom lines. But the idea that all the countries would default at the same time and bring about an international financial crisis I really think is close to inconceivable.

"Debt is an assessor of everything you've done in the past."

You were a pioneer in the development of "rent seeking," the concept not the practice! How did you hit on this important idea?

I was studying trade regimes in India and Turkey, and I discovered everywhere that the local people were using resources that could have been used productively

in order to try to get their share of something the government had placed under restriction. For example, the government of India used to assign all importers who applied for licenses to import, say, copper to produce utensils, a certain ceiling on how much copper they could import, according to their capacity. The government couldn't figure out why these producers kept expanding their factories. Now the bigger their capacity, the more copper they could import, right? So it paid to expand, just to get hold of more copper, even though they'd never use their bigger factories. That's rent seeking.

"It took my friend about 10 hours to turn my $10 into $200."

You've done some interesting direct observations on rent seeking, haven't you?

Indeed. I was once staying in a hotel in India and encountered a bellboy who studied economics at night. He was very entrepreneurial in his spare time. He wanted to borrow $10 in U.S. currency. I said I would lend him the money if I could come along with him to see how he made money out of the $10 during the day by rent seeking. He said, "You'll have to ride on the back of my motor scooter, O.K?" I said, "Fine, if you'll buy my lunch."

What sort of things did he do?

We engaged in about 40 transactions. Mostly small stuff, but with a little money in U.S. currency you could buy this and sell that and buy some more stuff and so on and so forth. If you rode a motor scooter, nobody noticed you, so you could do things that you couldn't otherwise. For example, there were prohibitions on selling liquor on certain days of the week in certain states. So the bellboys would go into another state to pick up beer and then sell it in the local hotels for quite a profit. There were other things. Sulfur was not allowed across state lines and price differentials were very large. It took my friend about 10 hours to turn my $10 into $200. And we had a nice lunch.

What advice do you give a student interested in working in international or development issues?

The obvious part is to get your union card by going to graduate school. I guess I'd argue for a couple of years of applied experience in between college and graduate school. Or the Peace Corps. I've seen lots of people go off into the Peace Corps and come back transformed. One of the hardest things in the generally wealthy United States or Canada is to teach young people that economics is called the dismal science because it recognizes that resources are not unlimited. And the hardest thing in the world is to convince people that in this magnificent economic phenomenon, our magnificent living standards haven't come for free and you can't take them for granted. Any economist who really understands that is already halfway there.

Chapter 35

Trading with the World

After studying this chapter, you will be able to:

- Describe the trends and patterns in international trade
- Explain comparative advantage
- Explain why all countries can gain from international trade
- Explain how prices adjust to bring about balanced trade
- Explain how economies of scale and diversity of taste lead to gains from international trade
- Explain why trade restrictions lower the volume of imports and exports, and lower our consumption possibilities
- Explain why we have trade restrictions even though they lower our consumption possibilities

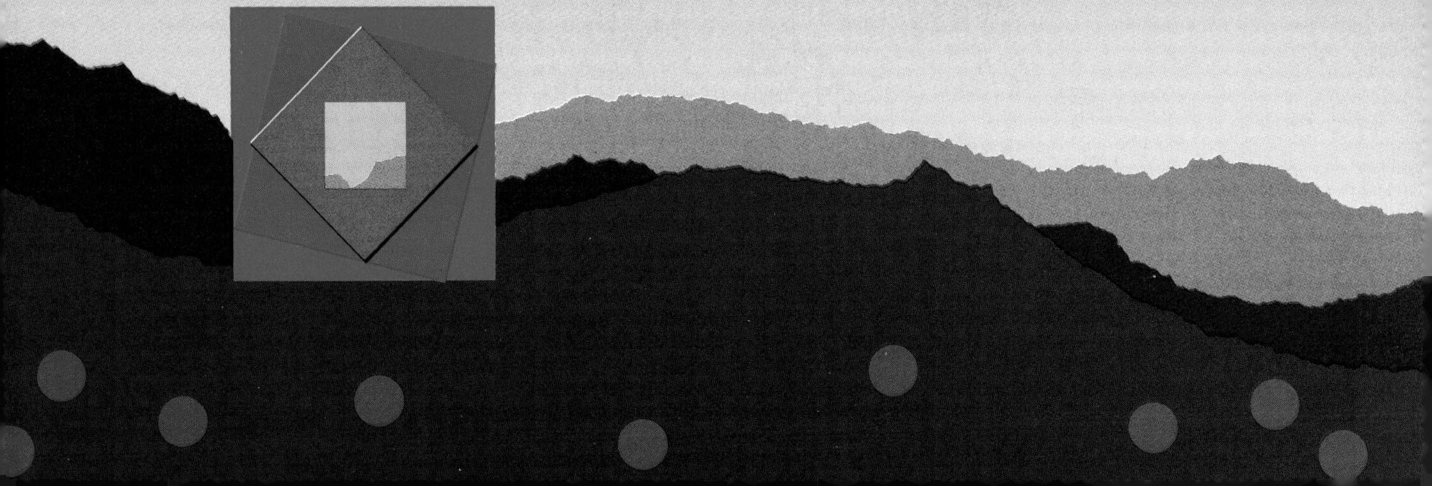

Silk Routes and Rust Belts

Since ancient times, people have strived to expand their trading as far as technology allowed. The maritime nations of southern Europe, the Middle East and North Africa had flourishing trades in the Mediterranean 5000 years ago. Roman coins have been found in the ruins of ancient Indian cities. Marco Polo opened up the silk route between Europe and China in the thirteenth century. Merchants of Venice imported goods from the entire known world in the fifteenth century. Adventurers such as Christopher Columbus paved the way for the beginnings of trade between Europe and the Americas. Today, container ships laden with cars and machines and Boeing 747s stuffed with fresh fruit, fresh New Zealand lamb, and French cheeses ply the sea and air routes, carrying billions of dollars worth of goods and services. Why do people go to such great lengths to trade with those in other nations? What does the pattern of international trade look like today? And what have been the recent trends in international trade? ■ International trade obviously brings enormous benefits. It enables us to consume fresh tropical fruit that doesn't grow here; to use raw materials such as chromium that are not found here; to buy low cost electrical energy generated by Canadian water power; to buy a wide range of manufactured goods such as cars, VCRs, TVs, and textiles that are available at lower prices from other countries. It also enables producers—workers and the firms that employ them—in export industries to earn more by expanding the markets for their products. ■ But international trade also has its costs. In recent years, a massive increase in the penetration of the foreign car industry into the United States has brought about a severe contraction of our own car-producing sector. Jobs in Detroit and other car-producing cities have disappeared, creating what has come to be called the Rust Belt. Do the benefits of international trade make up for the cost of jobs displaced by foreign competition? Could we, as politicians often claim, improve our economy by restricting imports? ■ The rich countries of the European Communities, Japan, and the United States import vast quantities of raw materials from Third World countries and from resource-rich developed countries such as Australia and Canada. To pay for these raw material imports, the rich countries sell manufactured goods to these countries. Do resource suppliers become poorer when they sell their bauxite, coal, and copper to the rich countries and buy farm combines and commercial jets in return? ■ The wages earned by the workers in the textile and electronics factories of Singapore, Taiwan, and Hong Kong are incredibly low compared with wages in the United States. Obviously, these countries can make manufactured goods much more cheaply than we can. How can we possibly compete with countries that pay their workers a fraction of U.S. wages? Are there any industries, besides perhaps the Hollywood movie industry, where we have an advantage? ■ The United States is a major actor in international economic affairs and, on many occasions, has taken initiatives that have had an enormous impact on world prosperity—sometimes for good but sometimes for ill. Perhaps its darkest hour was in 1930 when Congress passed the Smoot-Hawley Act, an act that increased taxes on imports to 60 percent, provoking widespread retaliation from the world's major trading countries. As a consequence, within two years, international trade almost dried up. In contrast, its finest hour came after World War II, when a process of trade liberalization brought about the creation of the General Agreement on Tariffs and Trade (GATT). The result this time was one of rapid world recovery from the devastation of war and an unprecedented expansion of world trade. What are the effects of trade restrictions? Why don't we have completely unrestricted international trade?

■ In this chapter, we're going to learn about international trade. We'll begin by looking at some facts about international trade, examining the patterns of imports and exports and trends in the main items that the United States buys from and sells to other countries. Then we will discover how *all* nations can gain by specializing in producing the goods and services at which they have an advantage compared with other countries and by exchanging some of their output with each other. We'll discover that all countries can compete, no matter how high their wages. We will also explain why, despite the fact that international trade brings benefits to all, countries restrict trade. We'll discover who suffers and who benefits when international trade is restricted.

Patterns and Trends in International Trade

The goods and services that we buy from people in other countries are called **imports.** The goods and services that we sell to people in other countries are called **exports.** What are the most important things that we import and export? Most people would probably guess that a rich nation such as the United States imports raw materials and exports manufactured goods. While that is one feature of U.S. international trade, it is not its most important feature. The vast bulk of our exports *and* imports is manufactures. We sell earth-moving equipment, airplanes, supercomputers, and scientific equipment and we buy TVs, VCRs, blue jeans, and T-shirts. Also, we are a major exporter of agricultural products and raw materials. We also import and export a huge volume of services. Let's look at the international trade of the United States in a recent year.

U.S. International Trade

Table 35.1 classifies U.S. international trade in four major categories of goods—agricultural products, industrial supplies and materials, manufactures, and miscellaneous goods—and services. The first column gives the value of U.S. exports and the second column U.S. imports. The third column tells us the balance of trade in the various categories. The **balance of trade** is the value of exports minus the value of imports. If the balance is positive, then the value of exports exceeds the value of imports and the United States is a **net exporter.** But if the balance is negative, the value of imports exceeds the value of exports and the United States is a **net importer.**

Trade in Goods Two thirds of U.S. international trade is trade in goods. One third is trade in services. Of the categories of goods traded, by far the most important is manufactures. But the total value of exports of manufactures is less than imports—the

Table 35.1 U.S. Exports and Imports in 1988

Category	Exports	Imports	Balance
	(billions of dollars)		
Agricultural products	38.1	24.9	13.2
Industrial supplies and materials (excluding agricultural)	83.7	122.4	−38.7
Manufactures	169.1	286.1	−117.0
Miscellaneous goods	28.4	13.1	15.3
Services	210.5	195.2	−15.3
Total	529.8	641.7	−111.9

Source: Survey of Current Business (June 1989), vol. 69, pp. 50, 72, 74.

Table 35.2 U.S. Exports and Imports of Goods in 1988: Some Large Individual Items

Item	Exports	Imports	Balance
	(billions of dollars)		
Grains	15.4	0	15.4
Chemicals	26.0	12.4	13.6
Aircraft	20.6	7.5	13.1
Machinery	89.9	93.4	−3.5
Automobiles	32.5	87.9	−55.4
Fuels	9.5	43.4	−33.9
Manufactured consumer goods	24.2	96.4	−72.2

Source: Survey of Current Business (June 1989), vol. 69, pp. 72, 74.

United States is a net importer of manufactured goods. The United States is a net exporter of agricultural products and miscellaneous goods. In all other categories, it is a net importer.

Table 35.2 highlights some of the major items of imports and exports of goods. As you can see, the United States exports large quantities of machinery and cars. These are both larger than the exports of grains. However, the United States also imports large quantities of machinery, cars, and car parts. The United States is a small net importer of machinery, but it is a large net importer of cars and manufactured consumer goods. The country's biggest single net export is grains.

Trade in Services One third of U.S. international trade is not of goods but of services. You may be wondering how a country can "export" and "import" services. Let's look at some examples.

Suppose that you decide to vacation in France, traveling there on an Air France flight from New York. What you buy from Air France is not a good, but a transportation service. Although the concept may sound odd at first, in economic terms you are importing that service from France. Since you pay U.S. money to a French company in exchange for a service, it doesn't matter that most of your flight time is over the Atlantic Ocean. For that matter, the money you spend in France on hotel bills, restaurant meals, and other things are also classified as the import of services. Similarly, the vacation taken by a French student in the United States counts as an export of services to France.

When we import TV sets from South Korea, the owner of the ship that carries those TV sets might be Greek and the company that insures the cargo might be British. The payments that we make for the transportation and insurance to the Greek and British companies are also payments for the import of services. Similarly, when an American shipping company transports Californian wine to Tokyo, the transportation cost is an export of a service to Japan.

Whenever you look at a photograph or see a movie that features a major city such as Hong Kong, Tokyo, or London, although you're looking at a foreign country, you see many familiar names: American Express, Citicorp, McDonald's, to mention just a few. These American corporations are producing goods and services in foreign countries for the citizens of those countries. Such corporations are exporting the services of U.S. capital to the rest of the world. The income that they receive for these services are payments made by foreigners for the services imported from the United States. Similarly, many foreign corporations establish plants in the United States or buy established firms. For example, Toyota has established car-making facilities in the United States. Robert Campeau, a Canadian financier, has bought retail interests in the United States, including Bloomingdale's. The income that we pay to these foreign corporations on their investments in the United States are part of our imports of services from foreigners.

The importance of the various components of trade in services is set out in Table 35.3. As you can see, the income from assets (that is, income we receive from our foreign operations and that we pay to foreigners for their economic activity here) is the biggest component of services traded. But transportation and travel are also very important.

Geographical Patterns The United States has important trading links with almost every part of the world except for Eastern Europe—which includes the Soviet giant—where trade is almost nonexistent. As you can see from Table 35.4, the bulk of our international trade is with Canada, Japan, the countries of the European Communities (notably West Germany and Britain), Latin America, and the newly industrializing countries of Asia such as Singapore, South Korea, and Taiwan.

Trends in Trade

International trade.has become an increasingly important part of our economic life. In 1950, we exported less than 5 percent of total output and imported only 4 percent of the goods and services that we consumed ourselves. Over the years since then, that percentage has steadily increased and today it is more than double its level of 1950.

On the export side, all the major commodity categories have shared in the increased volume of international trade. Machinery, food, and raw materials have remained the most important components of exports and have roughly maintained their share in total exports.

But there have been dramatic changes in the composition of imports. Food and raw material imports have declined steadily. Imports of fuel increased dramatically in the 1970s but declined in the 1980s. Imports of machinery of all kinds, after being a fairly stable percentage of total imports until the middle 1980s, now approaches 50 percent of total imports.

There have been important trends in the overall balance in U.S. international trade in recent years. That overall *balance of trade* (of goods and services) is shown in Fig. 35.1. As you can see, the balance fluctuates around zero, but in the years since 1982 there has been a large excess of imports over exports (a negative balance of trade). The country with which we have the largest trade deficit is Japan.

Table 35.3 U.S. Trade in Services in 1988

	Exports	Imports (billions of dollars)	Balance
Travel and transportation	57.0	59.6	−2.6
Other services	35.2	15.4	19.8
Income from assets	107.8	105.5	2.3
Military services	10.6	14.7	−4.1
Total	210.6	195.2	15.4

Source: *Survey of Current Business* (June 1989), vol. 69, pp. 62, 63.

Table 35.4 U.S. Exports and Imports in 1988: Geographical Patterns

	Exports	Imports (billions of dollars)	Balance
Canada	73.6	84.4	−10.8
Japan	37.1	89.8	−52.7
European Communities	74.5	85.6	−11.1
Latin America	43.6	51.4	−7.8
Other Western Europe	12.0	16.6	−4.6
Eastern Europe	3.8	2.2	1.6
Other Asia and Africa	67.9	113.0	−45.1
Australia, New Zealand, South America	6.8	3.5	3.3
Total	319.3	446.5	−127.2

Source: *Survey of Current Business* (June 1989), vol. 69, pp. 68–70.

Balance of Trade and International Borrowing When people buy more than they sell, they have to finance the difference by borrowing. When they sell

Figure 35.1 The U.S. Balance of Trade

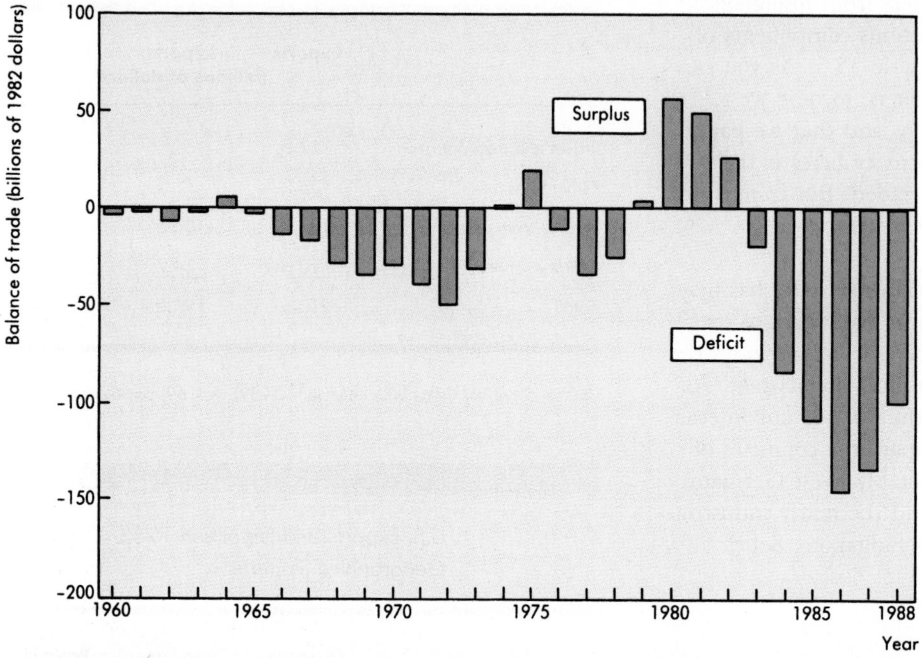

The balance of trade has fluctuated around zero, but since 1982 imports have grown more quickly than exports and a huge deficit has emerged.

Source: Economic Report of the President (1989), p. 311.

more than they buy, they can use the surplus to make loans to others. This simple principle that governs the income and expenditure and borrowing and lending of individuals and firms is also a feature of our balance of trade. If we import more than we export, we have to finance the difference by borrowing from foreigners. When we export more than we import, we make loans to foreigners to enable them to buy goods in excess of the value of the goods they have sold to us.

This chapter does not cover the factors that determine the balance of trade and the scale of international borrowing and lending that finance that balance. It is concerned with understanding the volume, pattern, and directions of international trade rather than its balance. So that we can keep our focus on these topics, we'll build a model in which there is no international borrowing and lending—just international trade in goods and services. We'll find that we are able to understand what determines the volume, pattern, and direction of international trade and also establish its benefits and the costs of trade restrictions within this framework. This model can be expanded to include international borrowing and lending, but such an extension does not change the conclusions that we'll reach here about the factors that determine the volume, pattern, and directions of international trade. Let's now begin to study those factors.

Opportunity Cost and Comparative Advantage

Let's apply the lessons that we learned in Chapter 3 about the gains from trade between Jane and Joe, to the trade between nations. We'll begin by recalling how we can use the production possibility frontier to measure opportunity cost.

Opportunity Cost in Pioneerland

Pioneerland (a fictitious country) can produce grain and cars at any point inside or along the production possibility frontier shown in Fig. 35.2. (We're holding constant the output of all the other goods that Pioneerland produces.) The Pioneers (the people of

Pioneerland) are consuming all the grain and cars that they produce and they are operating at point *a* in the figure. That is, Pioneerland is producing and consuming 15 billion bushels of grain and 8 million cars each year. What is the opportunity cost of a car in Pioneerland?

We can answer that question by calculating the slope of the production possibility frontier at point *a*. For, as we discovered in Chapter 3 (pp. 53–55), the slope of the frontier measures the opportunity cost of one good in terms of the other. To measure the slope of the frontier at point *a*, place a straight line tangential to the frontier at point *a* and calculate the slope of that straight line. Recall that the formula for the slope of a line is the change in *y* divided by the change in *x* as we move along the line. Here, *y* is billions of bushels of grain and *x* is millions of cars. So the slope (opportunity cost) is the change in the number of bushels of grain divided by the change in the number of cars. As you can see from the red triangle in the figure, at point *a*, if the number of cars produced increases by 2 million, grain production decreases by 18 billion bushels. Therefore, the slope is 18 billion divided by 2 million, which equals 9000. To get one more car, the people of Pioneerland must give up 9000 bushels of grain. Thus the opportunity cost of 1 car is 9000 bushels of grain. Equivalently, 9000 bushels of grain cost 1 car.

Figure 35.2 Opportunity Cost in Pioneerland

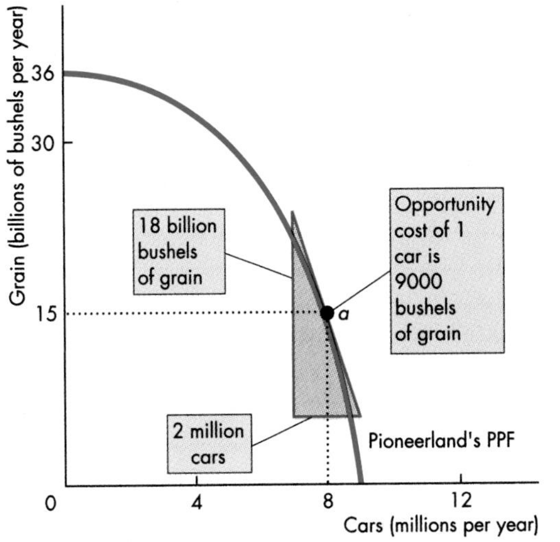

Pioneerland produces and consumes 15 billion bushels of grain and 8 million cars a year. That is, it produces and consumes at point *a* on its production possibility frontier. Opportunity cost is measured as the slope of the production possibility frontier. At point *a*, 2 million cars cost 18 billion bushels of grain. Equivalently, 1 car costs 9000 bushels of grain or 9000 bushels cost 1 car.

Opportunity Cost in Magic Empire

Now consider the production possibility frontier in Magic Empire (another fictitious country and the only other country in our model world). Figure 35.3 illustrates its production possibility frontier. Like the Pioneers, the Magicians (the people in Magic Empire) consume all the grain and cars that they produce. Magic Empire consumes 18 billion bushels of grain a year and 4 million cars, at point *a′*.

We can do the same kind of calculation of opportunity cost for Magic Empire that we have just done for Pioneerland. At point *a′*, 1 car costs 1000 bushels of grain, or, equivalently, 1000 bushels of grain costs 1 car.

Figure 35.3 Opportunity Cost in Magic Empire

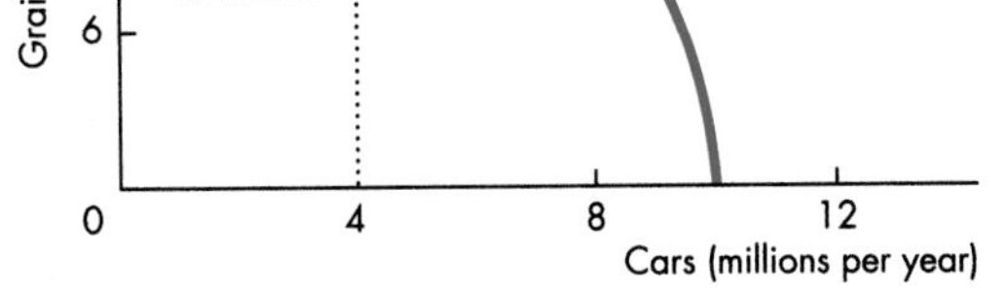

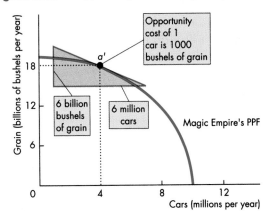

Magic Empire produces and consumes 18 billion bushels of grain and 4 million cars a year. That is, it produces and consumes at point *a′* on its production possibility frontier. Opportunity cost is measured as the slope of the production possibility frontier. At point *a′*, 6 million cars cost 6 billion bushels of grain. Equivalently, 1 car costs 1000 bushels of grain or 1000 bushels cost 1 car.

Comparative Advantage

Cars are cheaper in Magic Empire than in Pioneerland. One car costs 9000 bushels of grain in Pioneerland but only 1000 bushels of grain in Magic Empire. But grain is cheaper in Pioneerland than in

Magic Empire—9000 bushels of grain costs only 1 car in Pioneerland while that same amount of grain costs 9 cars in Magic Empire.

Magic Empire has a comparative advantage in car production. Pioneerland has a comparative advantage in grain production. A country has a **comparative advantage** in producing a good if it can produce that good at a lower opportunity cost than any other country. Let's see how opportunity cost differences and comparative advantage generate gains from international trade.

The Gains from Trade

The Basic Idea

If Magic Empire bought grain for what it costs Pioneerland to produce it, then Magic Empire could buy 9000 bushels of grain for 1 car. That is much lower than the cost of growing grain in Magic Empire, for there it costs 9 cars to produce 9000 bushels of grain. If the Magicians buy at the low Pioneerland price, they will reap some gains.

If the Pioneers buy cars for what it costs Magic Empire to produce them, they will be able to obtain a car for 1000 bushels of grain. Since it costs 9000 bushels of grain to produce a car in Pioneerland, the Pioneers would gain from such an activity.

In this situation, it makes sense for Magicians to buy their grain from Pioneers and for Pioneers to buy their cars from Magicians. Let's see how such profitable international trade comes about.

Reaping the Gains from Trade

We've seen that the Pioneers would like to buy their cars from the Magicians and that the Magicians would like to buy their grain from the Pioneers. Let's see how the two groups do business with each other, concentrating attention on the international market for cars.

Figure 35.4 illustrates such a market. The quantity of cars traded internationally is measured on the horizontal axis. On the vertical axis we measure the price of a car but it is expressed as its opportunity cost—the number of bushels of grain that a car costs. If no international trade takes place, that price in Pioneerland is 9000 bushels of grain, indicated by point *a* in the figure. Again, if no trade takes place, that price is 1000 bushels of grain in Magic Empire, indicated by point *a′* in the figure. The points *a* and *a′* in Fig. 35.4 correspond to the points identified by those same letters in Figs. 35.2 and 35.3.

The lower the price of a car (in terms of bushels of grain), the greater is the quantity of cars that Pioneers import from Magicians. This fact is illustrated in the downward-sloping curve that shows Pioneerland's import demand for cars.

The Magicians respond in the opposite direction. The higher the price of cars (in terms of bushels of grain), the greater is the quantity of cars that Magicians export to Pioneers. This fact is reflected in Magic Empire's export supply of cars—the upward-sloping line in the figure.

Figure 35.4 International Trade in Cars

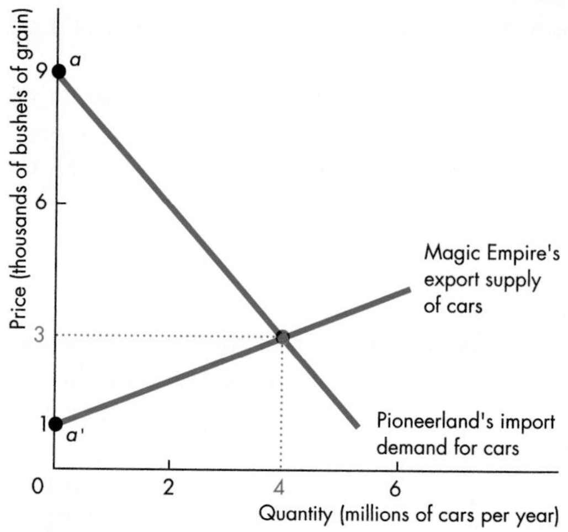

As the price of a car decreases, the quantity of imports demanded by Pioneerland increases—Pioneerland's import demand curve for cars is downward-sloping. As the price of a car increases, the quantity of cars supplied by Magic Empire for export increases—Magic Empire's export supply curve of cars is upward-sloping. Without international trade, the price of a car is 9000 bushels of grain in Pioneerland (point *a*) and 1000 bushels of grain in Magic Empire (point *a′*). With free international trade, the price of a car is determined where the export supply curve intersects the import demand curve—at a price of 3000 bushels of grain. At that price, 4 million cars a year are imported by Pioneerland and exported by Magic Empire. The value of grain exported by Pioneerland and imported by Magic Empire is 12 billion bushels a year, the quantity required to pay for the cars imported.

The international market in cars determines the equilibrium price and quantity traded. This equilibrium occurs where the import demand curve intersects the export supply curve. In this case, the equilibrium price of a car is 3000 bushels of grain. Four million cars a year are exported by Magic Empire and imported by Pioneerland. Notice that the price at which cars are traded is lower than the initial price in Pioneerland but higher than the initial price in Magic Empire.

Balanced Trade

Notice that the number of cars exported by Magic Empire—4 million a year—is exactly equal to the number of cars imported by Pioneerland. How does Pioneerland pay for its cars? By exporting grain. How much grain does Pioneerland export? You can find the answer by noticing that for 1 car Pioneerland has to pay 3000 bushels of grain. Hence, for 4 million cars they have to pay 12 billion bushels of grain. Thus Pioneerland's exports of grain are 12 billion bushels a year. Magic Empire imports this same quantity of grain.

Magic Empire is exchanging 4 million cars for 12 billion bushels of grain each year and Pioneerland is doing the opposite, exchanging 12 billion bushels of grain for 4 million cars. Trade is balanced between these two countries. The value received from exports equals the value paid out for imports.

Changes in Production and Consumption

We've seen that international trade makes it possible for Pioneers to buy cars at a lower price than they can produce them for themselves. It also enables Magicians to sell their cars for a higher price, which is equivalent to saying that Magicians can buy grain for a lower price. Thus everybody seems to gain. Magicians buy grain at a lower price and Pioneers buy cars at a lower price. How is it possible for everyone to gain? What are the changes in production and consumption that accompany these gains?

An economy that does not trade with other economies has identical production and consumption possibilities. Without trade, the economy can only consume what it produces. But with international trade an economy can consume different quantities of goods from those that it produces. The production possibility frontier describes the limit of what a country can produce but it does not describe the limits to what it can consume. Figure 35.5 will help you to see the distinction between production possibilities and consumption possibilities when a country trades with other countries.

First of all, notice that the figure has two parts, part (a) for Pioneerland and part (b) for Magic Empire. The production possibility frontiers that you saw in Figs. 35.2 and 35.3 are reproduced here. The slopes of the two black lines in the figure represent the opportunity costs in the two countries when there is no international trade. Pioneerland produces and consumes at point *a* and Magic Empire produces and consumes at *a'*. Cars cost 9000 bushels of grain in Pioneerland and 1000 bushels of grain in Magic Empire.

With international trade, Magic Empire can sell cars to Pioneerland for 3000 bushels of grain each. Pioneerland can buy cars from Magic Empire for that same price. Thus both countries can exchange cars for grain or grain for cars at a price of 3000 bushels of grain per car.

With international trade, the producers of cars in Magic Empire can now get a higher price for their output. As a result, they increase the quantity of car production. At the same time, grain producers in Magic Empire are now getting a lower price for their grain and so they reduce production. Producers in Magic Empire adjust their output until the opportunity cost in Magic Empire equals the opportunity cost in the world market. This situation arises when Magic Empire is producing at point *b'* in Fig. 35.5(b).

But the Magicians do not consume at point *b'*. That is, they do not increase their consumption of cars and decrease their consumption of grain. They sell some of their car production to Pioneerland in exchange for some of Pioneerland's grain. But to see how that works out, we first need to check in with Pioneerland to see what's happening there.

In Pioneerland, cars are now less expensive and grain more expensive than before. As a consequence, producers in Pioneerland decrease car production and increase grain production. They do so until the opportunity cost of a car in terms of grain equals the cost on the world market. They move to point *b*, in part (a). But the Pioneers do not consume at point *b*. They exchange some of their additional grain production for the now cheaper cars from Magic Empire.

The figure shows us the quantities consumed in the two countries. We saw in Fig. 35.4 that Magic

Figure 35.5 Expanding Consumption Possibilities

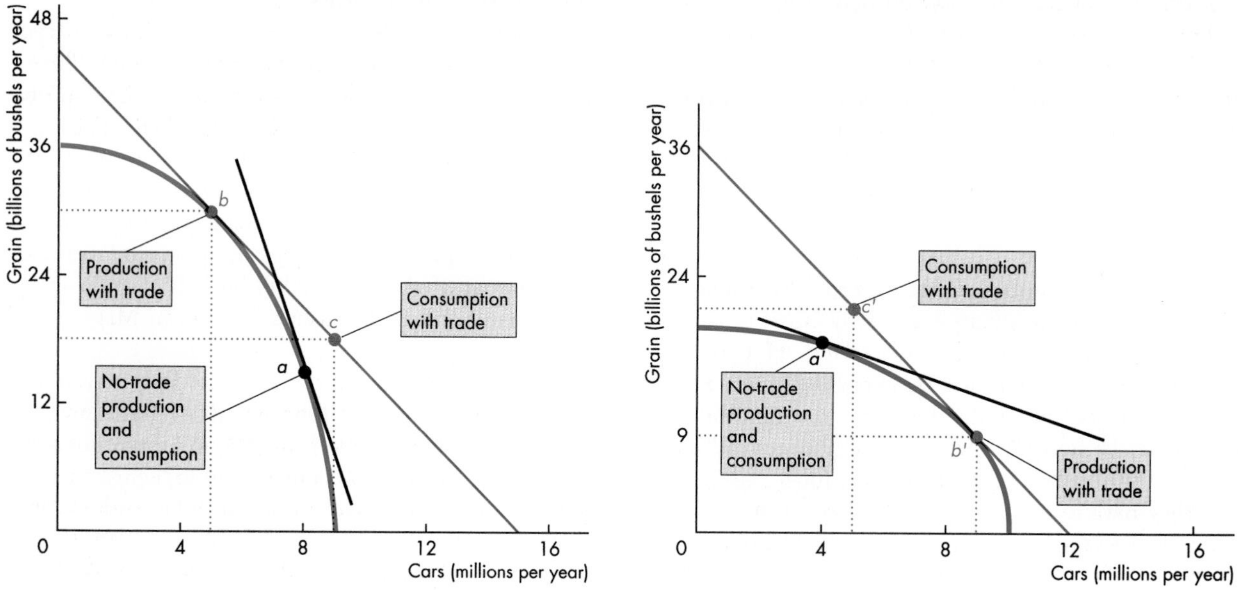

(a) Pioneerland **(b) Magic Empire**

With no international trade, the Pioneers produce and consume at point *a* and the opportunity cost of a car is 9000 bushels of grain (the slope of the black line in part a). Also, with no international trade, the Magicians produce and consume at point *a′* and the opportunity cost of 1000 bushels of grain is 1 car (the slope of the black line in part b).

Goods can be exchanged internationally at a price of 3000 bushels of grain for 1 car along the red line. In part (a), Pioneerland decreases its production of cars and increases its production of grain, moving from *a* to *b*. It exports grain and imports cars, and it consumes at point *c*. The Pioneers have more of both cars and grain than they would if they produced all their own consumption goods—at point *a*. In part (b), Magic Empire increases car production and decreases grain production, moving from *a′* to *b′*. Magic Empire exports cars and imports grain, and it consumes at point *c′*. The Magicians have more of both cars and grain than they would if they produced all their own consumption goods—at point *a′*.

Empire exports 4 million cars a year and Pioneerland imports those cars. We also saw that Pioneerland exports 12 billion bushels of grain a year and Magic Empire imports that grain. Thus Pioneerland's consumption of grain is 12 billion bushels a year less than it produces and its consumption of cars is 4 million a year more than it produces. Pioneerland consumes at point *c* in Fig. 35.5(a).

Similarly, we know that Magic Empire consumes 12 billion bushels of grain more than it produces and 4 million cars fewer than it produces. Thus Magic Empire consumes at *c′* in Fig. 35.5(b).

Calculating the Gains from Trade

You can now literally "see" the gains from trade in Fig. 35.5. Without trade, Pioneers produce and consume at *a* (part a)—a point on Pioneerland's production possibility frontier. With international trade, Pioneers consume at point *c* (in part a)—a point *outside* the production possibility frontier. At point *c*, Pioneers are consuming 3 billion bushels of grain a year and 1 million cars a year more than before. These increases in consumption of cars and grain, beyond the limits of the production possibility frontier, are the gains from international trade.

But Magicians also gain. Without trade, they consume at point a' (part b)—a point on Magic Empire's production possibility frontier. With international trade, they consume at point c'—a point outside the production possibility frontier. With international trade, Magic Empire consumes 3 billion bushels of grain a year and 1 million cars a year more than without trade. These are the gains from international trade for Magic Empire.

Gains for All

When Pioneers and Magicians trade with each other, potentially everyone can gain. Domestic sellers add the net demand of foreigners to their domestic demand, and so their market expands. Buyers are faced with domestic supply plus net foreign supply and so have a larger total supply available to them. As you know, prices increase when there is an increase in demand and they decrease when there is an increase in supply. Thus the increased demand (from foreigners) for exports increases their price and the increased supply (from foreigners) of imports decreases their price. Gains in one country do not bring losses in another. Everyone, in this example, gains from international trade.

Absolute Advantage

Suppose that in Magic Empire, fewer workers are needed to produce any given output of either grain or cars than in Pioneerland. In this situation, Magic Empire has an absolute advantage over Pioneerland. A country has an **absolute advantage** if its output per unit of inputs of all goods is higher than that of another country. With an absolute advantage, isn't it the case that Magic Empire can outsell Pioneerland in all markets? Why, if Magic Empire can produce all goods using fewer factors of production than Pioneerland, does it pay Magic Empire to buy *anything* from Pioneerland?

The answer is that the cost of production in terms of the factors of production employed is irrelevant for determining the gains from trade. It does not matter how much labor, land, and capital are required to produce 1000 bushels of grain or a car. What matters is how many cars must be given up to produce more grain or how much grain must be given up to produce more cars. That is, what matters is the opportunity cost of one good in terms of the other good. Magic Empire may have an absolute advantage in the production of all things, but it cannot have a comparative advantage in the production of all goods. The statement that the opportunity cost of cars in Magic Empire is lower than in Pioneerland is identical to the statement that the opportunity cost of grain is higher in Magic Empire than in Pioneerland. Thus *whenever opportunity costs diverge, everyone has a comparative advantage in something.* All countries can potentially gain from international trade.

R E V I E W

When countries have divergent opportunity costs, they can gain from international trade. Each country can buy goods and services from another country at a lower opportunity cost than it can produce them for itself. Gains arise when each country increases its production of those goods and services in which it has a comparative advantage (of goods and services that it can produce at an opportunity cost that is lower than that of other countries) and exchanges some of its production for that of other countries.

All countries gain from international trade. Everyone has a comparative advantage at something. ■

Gains from Trade in Reality

The gains from trade that we have just studied between Pioneerland and Magic Empire in grain and cars are taking place in a model economy—in an economy that we have imagined. But these same phenomena are occurring every minute of every day in real-world economies. We buy cars made in Japan and American producers of grain and lumber sell large parts of their output to Japanese households and firms. We buy cars and machinery from European producers and sell airplanes and computers to Europeans in return. We buy shirts and fashion goods from the people of Hong Kong and sell them machinery in return. We buy TV sets and VCRs from South Korea and Taiwan and sell them financial and other services as well as manufactured goods in return.

Thus much of the international trade that we see in the real world takes precisely the form of the trade that we have studied in our model of the world economy. But as we discovered earlier in this chapter, a great deal of world trade is heavily concentrated among industrial countries and primarily involves the international exchange of manufactured goods. Thus the type of trade that we have just analyzed—exchanging cars for grain—although an important and clearly profitable type of trade, is not the most prominent type. Why do countries exchange manufactured goods with each other? Can our model of international trade explain such exchange?

A Puzzle

At first thought, it seems puzzling that countries would trade manufactured goods. Consider, for example, America's trade in cars and auto parts. Why does it make sense for the United States to produce cars for export and at the same time to import large quantities of cars from Canada, Japan, Korea, and Western Europe? Wouldn't it make more sense to produce all the cars that we buy here in the United States? After all, we have access to the best technology available for producing cars. Auto workers in the United States are surely as productive as their fellow workers in Canada, Western Europe, and the Pacific countries. Capital equipment, production lines, robots, and the like used in the manufacture of cars are as available to American car producers as they are to any others. This line of reasoning leaves a puzzle concerning the sources of international exchange of similar commodities produced by similar people using similar equipment. Why does it happen?

Diversity of Taste The first part of the answer to the puzzle is that people have a tremendous diversity of taste. Let's stick with the example of cars. Some people prefer a sports car, some prefer a limousine, some prefer a regular full-size car, and some prefer a compact. In addition to size and type of car, there are many other dimensions in which cars vary. Some have low fuel consumption, some have high performance, some are spacious and comfortable, some have a large trunk, some have four-wheel drive, some have front-wheel drive, some have manual transmission, some have automatic transmission, some are durable, some are flashy, some have a radiator grille that looks like a Greek temple, others look like a wedge. People's preferences across these many dimensions vary.

The tremendous diversity in tastes for cars means that people would be dissatisfied if they were forced to consume from a limited range of standardized cars. People value variety and are willing to pay for it in the marketplace.

Economies of Scale The second part of the answer to the puzzle is economies of scale. *Economies of scale* are the tendency, present in many production processes, for the average cost of production to be lower, the larger the scale of production. In such situations, larger and larger production runs lead to ever lower average production costs. Many manufactured goods, including cars, experience economies of scale. For example, if a car producer makes only a few hundred (or perhaps a few thousand) cars of a particular type and design, they have to use production techniques that are much more labor-intensive and much less automated than those actually employed to make hundreds of thousands of cars in a particular model. With low production runs and labor-intensive production techniques, costs are high. With very large production runs and automated assembly lines, production costs are much lower. But to obtain lower costs, the automated assembly lines have to produce a large number of cars.

It is the combination of diversity of taste and economies of scale that produces such a large amount of international trade in similar commodities. Diversity of taste and the willingness to pay for variety does not guarantee that variety will be available. It could simply be too expensive to provide a highly diversified range of different types of cars, for example. If every car bought in the United States today was made in the United States and if the present range of diversity and variety was available, production runs would be remarkably short. Car producers would not be able to reap economies of scale. Although the current variety of cars could be made available, it would be at a very high price, and perhaps at a price that no one would be willing to pay.

But with international trade, each manufacturer of cars has the whole world market to serve. Each producer specializes in a limited range of products and then sells its output to the entire world market. This arrangement enables large production runs on the most popular cars and feasible production runs even on the most customized cars demanded by only a handful of people.

The situation in the market for cars is also present in many other industries, especially those producing specialized machinery and specialized machine tools. Thus international exchange of similar but slightly differentiated manufactured products is a highly profitable activity.

This type of trade can be understood with exactly the same model of international trade that we studied earlier. Although we normally think of cars as a single commodity, we simply have to think of sports cars and sedans and so on as different goods. Different countries, by specializing in a few of these "goods" are able to enjoy economies of scale and, therefore, a comparative advantage in their production.

You can see that comparative advantage and international trade bring gains regardless of the goods being traded. When the rich countries of the European Communities, Japan, and the United States import raw materials from the Third World and from Australia and Canada, the rich importing countries gain and so do the exporting countries. When we buy cheap TV sets, VCRs, shirts, and other goods from low wage countries, both we and the exporters gain from the exchange. It's true that if we increase our imports of cars and produce fewer cars ourselves, jobs in our car-producing sector disappear. But jobs in other sectors, sectors in which we have a comparative advantage and supply to other nations, expand. *After the adjustment is completed,* those whose jobs have been lost find employment in the expanding sectors and usually at higher wages than they had previously. They buy goods produced in other countries at even lower prices than those at which they were available before. The gains from international trade are not gains for some at the expense of losses for others.

But changes in comparative advantage that lead to changes in international trade patterns can take a long time to adjust to. For example, the increase in automobile imports and the corresponding relative decline in domestic car production has not immediately brought increased wealth for displaced auto workers. Better jobs take time to find and often people go through a period of prolonged search putting up with inferior jobs and lower wages than they had before. Thus only in the long run does everyone potentially gain from international specialization and exchange. Short-run adjustment costs, that can be large and relatively prolonged, may be borne by groups that have lost their comparative advantage.

Partly because of the costs of adjustment to changing international trade patterns, but partly also for other reasons, governments intervene in international trade restricting its volume. Let's examine what happens when governments restrict international trade. We'll contrast restricted trade with free trade. We'll see that free trade brings the greatest possible benefits. We'll also see why, in spite of the benefits of free trade, governments sometimes restrict trade.

Trade Restrictions

Governments restrict international trade in order to protect domestic industries from foreign competition. The restriction of international trade is called **protectionism.** There are two main protectionist methods employed by governments:

- Tariffs
- Nontariff barriers

A **tariff** is a tax that is imposed by the importing country when a good crosses an international boundary. A **nontariff barrier** is any action other than a tariff that restricts international trade. Examples of nontariff barriers are quantitative restrictions and licensing regulations limiting imports. We'll consider nontariff barriers in more detail below. First, let's look at tariffs.

The History of Tariffs

Average tariff levels in the United States today are quite modest compared with their historical levels. As you can see from Fig. 35.6, tariff levels have averaged around 40 percent through most of U.S. history. During certain periods, such as the 1830s and, with the passage of the Smoot-Hawley Act in the Great Depression years of the 1930s, they reached 60 percent.

Today, average tariffs represent only 4 percent of total imports and only 6 percent of that part of imports that are subject to a tariff. But some sectors have high tariffs. The sector with the highest tariffs is textiles and footwear. Ninety-two percent of all our imports of textiles and footwear are protected at an average rate of more than 10 percent. For example, when you buy a pair of blue jeans for $20, you are paying about $5 more than you would have to if there were no trade restrictions on textiles. If you buy a $20,000 automobile, you are paying close to $5000 more than the free trade price would be. Other

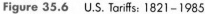

Figure 35.6 U.S. Tariffs: 1821–1985

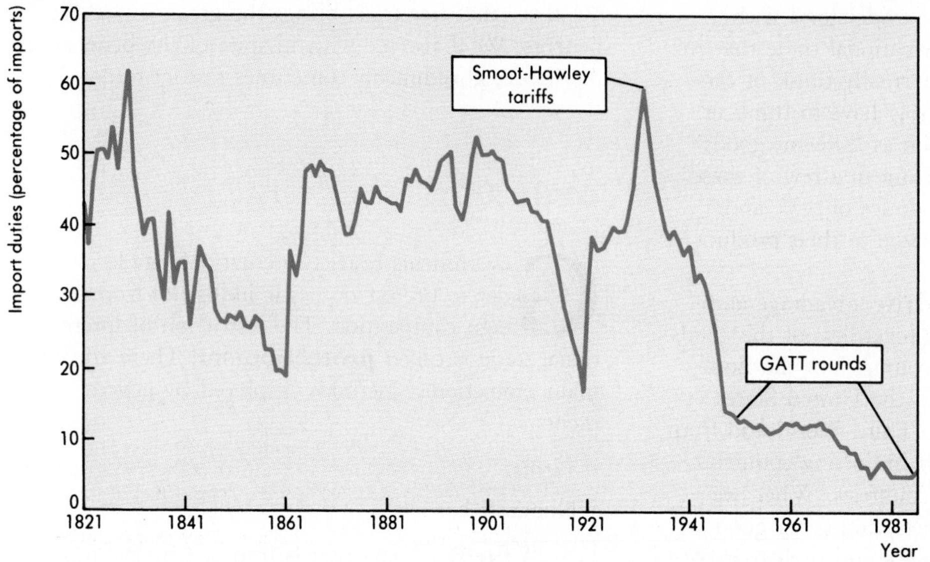

Tariffs in the United States have for most of its history, averaged around 40 percent. On occasion, they have increased to 60 percent. Since World War II, tariffs have steadily declined and are now at the lowest levels they have ever been.

***Source: Historical Statistics of the United States*, Series no. U-20.**

sectors protected by tariffs are agricultural products, energy and chemicals, minerals and metals. Almost all the meat and cheese that you consume costs significantly more because of protection than it would with free international trade.

The temptation, on governments, to impose tariffs is a strong one. First, tariffs provide revenue to the government. Second, they enable the government to satisfy special interest groups in import-competing industries. But, as we've seen, free international trade brings enormous benefits. Because free trade brings benefits and because the temptation to restrict trade is so great, countries have attempted to enter into a multilateral agreement whose goal is the enhancement of free international trade—the General Agreement on Tariffs and Trade (GATT). The **General Agreement on Tariffs and Trade** is an international agreement designed to limit government intervention to restrict international trade. It was negotiated immediately following World War II and was signed in October 1947. Its goal is to liberalize trading activity and to provide an organization to administer more liberal trading arrangements. GATT itself is a small organization that is located in Geneva, Switzerland.

Since the formation of GATT, several rounds of negotiations have resulted in general tariff reductions (see Table 35.5). One of these, the Kennedy Round that began in the early 1960s, resulted in large tariff cuts. Yet further tariff cuts resulted from the Tokyo Round that took place between 1973 and 1979. The Uruguay Round, currently in progress, is attempting to achieve less restricted international trade in services and agricultural products, two large and important areas excluded from all previous GATT negotiations.

In addition to the multilateral agreements under GATT, the United States is a party to several important bilateral trade agreements. One of these is the Canada–United States free trade agreement that became effective on January 1, 1989 (see Reading Between the Lines, pp. 580–581). Under this agreement, barriers to international trade between Canada and the United States will be virtually eliminated after a 10-year phasing-in period. Less ambitious, but important, is the United States–Mexico Framework, a consultative mechanism to review trade and investment issues and to negotiate the removal of trade barriers. Within Western Europe, trade barriers among the member countries of the European Communities will have been completely eliminated by 1992, creating the largest unified tariff-free market in the world.

How Tariffs Work

To analyze how tariffs work, let's return to the example of trade between Pioneerland and Magic Empire. Suppose that these two countries are trading cars and grain in exactly the same way that we analyzed before. Magic Empire exports cars and Pioneerland exports grain. The volume of car imports into Pioneerland is 4 million a year and cars are selling on the world market for 3000 bushels of grain. Let's suppose that grain costs a dollar a bushel so, equivalently, cars are selling for $3000. Figure 35.7 illustrates this situation. The volume of trade in cars and their price are determined at the point of intersection of Magic Empire's export supply curve of cars and Pioneerland's import demand curve for cars.

Now suppose that the government of Pioneerland, perhaps under pressure from car producers, decides to impose a tariff on imported cars. In particular, suppose that a tariff of $4000 per car is imposed. (This is a huge tariff, but the car producers of Pioneerland are pretty fed up with competition from Magic Empire.) What happens?

The first part of the answer is obtained by studying the effects on the supply of cars in Pioneerland. Cars are no longer going to be available at the Magic Empire export supply price. The tariff of $4000 must be added to that price—the amount paid to the government of Pioneerland on each car

Table 35.5 Summary of U.S. Tariffs

		Percentage tariff rate on U.S. imports: Dutiable imports	Total imports
1930	Smoot-Hawley—"high point" of retaliatory protection during the Depression	53	18
1947	Setting up of GATT		
1947–1956	GATT negotiating rounds: Geneva in 1947, Annecy in 1949, Torquay in 1951, Geneva in 1956—agreements on tariff rates and modest tariff cuts	25	9
1961	Dillon Round of tariff negotiations—further modest tariff cuts		
1967	Kennedy Round of tariff negotiations—significant tariff cuts	12	7
1979	Tokyo Round of negotiations—further tariff cuts	6	4
1988	Uruguay Round of negotiations—in progress		

Source: Based on John Whalley, *Trade Liberalization among Major World Trading Areas* (Cambridge, Mass.: MIT Press, 1985), Table 1.3, p. 16.

Figure 35.7 The Effects of a Tariff

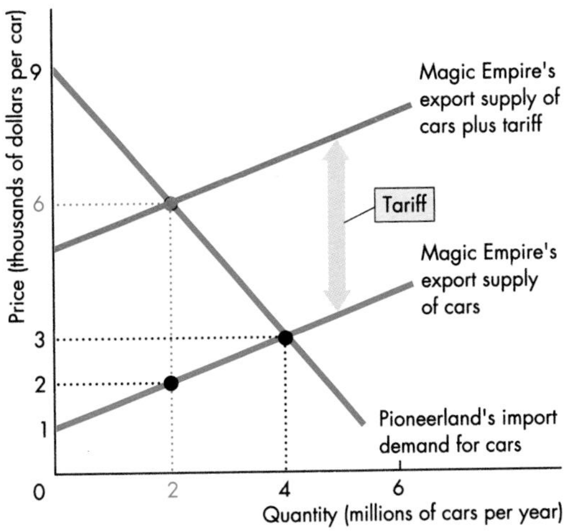

Pioneerland imposes a tariff on car imports from Magic Empire. The tariff increases the price that Pioneers have to pay for cars. It shifts the supply curve of cars in Pioneerland upward. The distance between the original supply curve and the new one is the amount of the tariff. The price of cars in Pioneerland increases and the quantity of cars imported decreases. The government of Pioneerland collects a tariff revenue of $4000 per car—a total of $8 billion on the 2 million cars imported. Pioneerland's exports of grain decrease since Magic Empire now has a lower income from its exports of cars.

Winners and Losers

North Americans Ponder How They Will Fare after Free Trade Becomes a Reality

Norm Dyck, 47, sours a little as he contemplates the prospects of greater free trade between the U.S. and Canada, which could become a reality by the end of the year. A slim, bespectacled wheat farmer, Dyck owns a 1,000-acre homestead near Debolt, Alta., a farming community about 560 miles north of the Canadian–U.S. border. In his view, free trade will soon lead to a flood of cheap U.S. wheat pouring into Canada's domestic market. Says Dyck: "This is not time to expand production." This spring, he plans to plant 800 of his acres in grass and clover rather than wheat, in anticipation of falling wheat prices.

On the other side of Canada, executives at Hydro-Québec, the province's government-owned electrical utility, can barely hide their delight at the prospects contained in the version of the free-trade pact signed by President Ronald Reagan and Prime Minister Brian Mulroney in January. As a supplier of 16.4 billion kilowatt-hours of electricity to Northeastern U.S. markets —$351.8 million worth in 1987—Hydro-Québec has been worrying that Washington will restrict the firm's access to U.S. customers. Clauses in the Canada–U.S. free-trade agreement would explicitly ban any such barriers to the export of Canadian energy supplies. Says Jacques Guevremont, Hydro-Québec vice president for external sales: "We were already operating in a pretty free market. Now we'll be operating in one that's completely open."

South of the 49th parallel, in Peoria, Ill., salesmen for giant Caterpillar, Inc., are also anticipating a future bonanza from the trade treaty. Under the agreement, a 10% Canadian tariff on earth-moving equipment would be phased out over the next eight years, offering new sales opportunities for the U.S. firm. Says William Lane, a Caterpillar spokesman: "It will definitely make our products more competitive in Canada."

Out in Montana, Cattle Rancher Jimme Wilson, 56, has mixed feelings. On his 1,200-acre ranch in a mountainous section of Sanders County, Wilson keeps 400 Herefords, some of which he would like to sell in Canada. Currently he cannot, because Canadian agricultural regulations restrict the importation of live animals from the U.S., in part through costly quarantine rules. Only some of the regulations would be loosened under the free-trade accord. Most of the rules are "just an excuse" to keep out U.S. livestock, says Wilson.

With equal parts of consternation and anticipation, U.S. and Canadian businessmen are beginning to realize that the prospective free-trade accord could bring about dramatic changes in the economic lives of the two countries. The promise of the treaty is of a "win-win" future for both. Under the pact, most remaining tariffs and duties would be removed on almost $150 billion worth of mutual trade, a move that in turn should expand what is already the world's largest two-way trading relationship. U.S. exports to Canada reached $61.5 billion last year, or 26% of the U.S. worldwide total, while Canadian exports to the U.S. came to $73.7 billion, or 78% of Canada's shipments abroad.

***Time*, March 14, 1988**

by Edward Desmond, reported by Beth Austin and Peter Stoler

The Essence of the Story

- U.S. exports to Canada in 1987 were $61.5 billion—26 percent of U.S. total exports.
- Canadian exports to the United States in 1987 were $73.7 billion—78 percent of Canada's total exports.
- A free-trade agreement between the United States and Canada will remove the remaining tariffs and expand what is already the world's largest two-way trading relationship.
- Many predictions were being made in 1988 about the consequences of the Free Trade Agreement:

—Wheat prices will fall, cutting Canadian wheat production.
—A completely free market in electricity will be created in the United States and Canada.
—Exports of earth-moving equipment will increase as the 10 percent Canadian tariff is phased out.
—Nontariff barriers such as quarantine rules for cattle will limit the extent of free trade in livestock.
—Large changes in economic life in both countries will produce gains for all.

Background and Analysis

- With tariffs, international trade is restricted.
- International trade in earth-moving equipment is an example (see figure)
- Under free trade, the quantity of earth movers exported by the United States and imported by Canada is Q_2. The price at which this trade takes place is P_2.
- Canada imposes a 10 percent tariff on earth-moving equipment imports.
- The supply curve facing Canada is the U.S. export supply curve plus the 10 percent tariff.
- The quantity of Canadian imports of earth-moving equipment is Q_1 and the price paid by Canadian buyers is P_1.
- American producers sell such equipment for a price of C.
- The difference between P_1 and C is the tariff collected by the Canadian government on each earth mover.
- The removal of tariffs results in an increased volume of trade—from Q_1 to Q_2—a lower price for importers—from P_1 to P_2—and a higher price for exporters, from C to P_2.

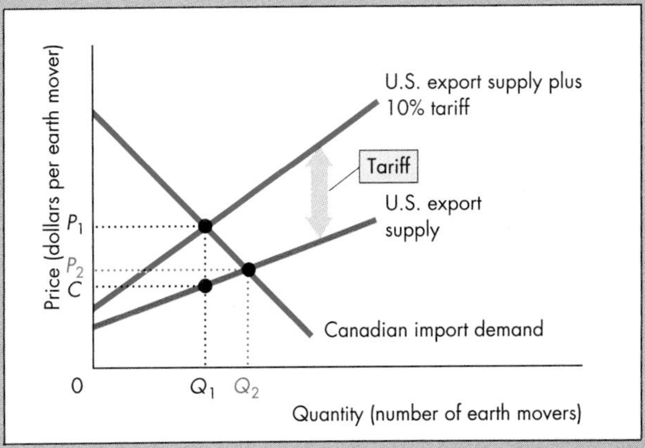

- The removal of the tariff shifts the supply curve faced by Canada downward—to the red curve.
- The situation shown in the figure is identical for exporters of all goods, whether U.S. or Canadian.
- The introduction of free trade brings an expansion in export industries and a contraction in import competing industries—making large changes in economic life as foreseen by U.S. and Canadian businesses.
- The removal of tariffs does not bring complete free trade. Nontariff barriers remain. An example is the quarantine rules on moving live animals across the U.S.–Canadian border. Such rules restrict international trade even though that is not their initial or main intent.
- To reap the gains from trade, exporting industries must expand. This expansion can occur only if importing industries contract.
- At the time of the change to free trade, exporters are happy but importers complain.
- Eventually, those moving from import industries will find jobs in the expanding export sector and share in the gains from freer international trade.

imported. As a consequence, the supply curve in Pioneerland shifts in the manner shown in Fig. 35.7. The new supply curve becomes that labeled "Magic Empire's export supply of cars plus tariff." The vertical distance between Magic Empire's export supply curve and the new supply curve is the tariff imposed by the government of Pioneerland.

The next part of the answer is found by determining the new equilibrium. Imposing a tariff has no effect on the demand for cars in Pioneerland and so has no effect on Pioneerland's import demand for cars. The new equilibrium occurs where the new supply curve intersects Pioneerland's import demand curve for cars. That equilibrium is at a price of $6000 a car and with 2 million cars a year being imported. Imports fall from 4 million to 2 million cars a year. At the higher price of $6000 a car, domestic car producers increase their production. Domestic grain production decreases to free up the resources for the expanded car industry.

The total expenditure on imported cars by the Pioneers is $6000 a car multiplied by the 2 million cars imported ($12 billion). But not all of that money goes to the Magicians. They receive $2000 a car or $4 billion for the 2 million cars. The difference—$4000 a car or a total of $8 billion for the 2 million cars—is collected by the government of Pioneerland as tariff revenue.

Obviously, the government of Pioneerland is happy with this situation. It is now collecting $8 billion that it didn't have before. But what about the Pioneers? How do they view the new situation? The demand curve tells us the maximum price that a buyer is willing to pay for one more unit of a good. As you can see from Pioneerland's import demand curve for cars, if one more car could be imported, someone would be willing to pay almost $6000 for it. Magic Empire's export supply curve of cars tells us the minimum price at which additional cars are available. As you can see, one additional car would be supplied by Magic Empire for a price only slightly more than $2000. Thus since someone is willing to pay almost $6000 for a car and someone is willing to supply one for little more than $2000, there is obviously a gain to be had from trading an extra car. In fact, there are gains to be had—willingness to pay exceeds the minimum supply price—all the way up to 4 million cars a year. Only when 4 million cars are being traded is the maximum price that a Pioneer is willing to pay equal to the minimum price that is acceptable to a Magician. Thus restricting international trade reduces the gains from international trade.

It is easy to see that the tariff has lowered Pioneerland's total import bill. With free trade, Pioneerland was paying $3000 a car and buying 4 million cars a year from Magic Empire. Thus the total import bill was $12 billion a year. With a tariff, imports have been cut to 2 million cars a year and the price paid to the foreign country has also been cut to only $2000 a car. Thus the import bill has been cut to $4 billion a year, a "saving" of $8 billion a year. Doesn't this fact mean that Pioneerland's balance of trade has changed? Is Pioneerland now importing less than it is exporting?

To answer that question, we need to figure out what's happening in Magic Empire. We've just seen that the price that Magic Empire receives for cars has fallen from $3000 to $2000 a car. Thus the price of cars in Magic Empire has fallen. But if the price of cars has fallen, the price of grain has increased. With free trade, the Magicians could buy 3000 bushels of grain for one car. Now they can buy only 2000 bushels for a car. With a higher price of grain, the quantity demanded by the Magicians decreases. As a result, Magic Empire's import of grain declines. But so does Pioneerland's export of grain. In fact, Pioneerland's grain industry suffers from two sources. First, there is a decrease in the quantity of grain sold to Magic Empire. Second, there is increased competition for inputs from the now expanded car industry. Thus the tariff leads to a contraction in the scale of the grain industry in Pioneerland.

It seems paradoxical at first that a country imposing a tariff on cars would hurt its own export industry, lowering its exports of grain. It may help to think of it this way: Foreigners buy grain with the money they make from exporting cars. If they export fewer cars, they cannot afford to buy as much grain. In fact, in the absence of any international borrowing and lending, Magic Empire has to cut its imports of grain by exactly the same amount as the loss in revenue from its export of cars. Grain imports into Magic Empire will be cut back to a value of $4 billion, the amount that can be paid for by the new lower revenue from Magic Empire's car exports. Thus trade is still balanced in this post-tariff situation. Although the tariff has cut imports, it has also cut exports, and the cut in the value of exports is exactly equal to the cut in the value of imports. The tariff, therefore, has no effect on the balance of trade—it reduces the volume of trade.

The result that we have just derived is perhaps one of the most misunderstood aspects of international economics. On countless occasions, politicians and others have called for tariffs in order to remove a balance of trade deficit or have argued that lowering tariffs would produce a balance of trade deficit. They reach this conclusion by failing to work out all the implications of a tariff. Because a tariff raises the price of imports and cuts imports, the easy conclusion is that the tariff strengthens the balance of trade. But the tariff also changes the *volume* of exports as well. The equilibrium effects of a tariff are to reduce the volume of trade in both directions and by the same value on each side of the equation. The balance of trade itself is left unaffected.

Learning the Hard Way Although the analysis that we have just worked through leads to the clear conclusion that tariffs cut both imports and exports and make everyone worse off, we have not found that conclusion easy to accept. Time and again in our history we have imposed high tariff barriers on international trade (as Fig. 35.6 illustrates). Whenever tariff barriers are increased, trade collapses. The most vivid historical example of this interaction of tariffs and trade occurred during the Great Depression years of the early 1930s when in the wake of the Smoot-Hawley tariff increases and the retaliatory tariff changes that other countries introduced as a consequence, world trade almost dried up.

Let's now turn our attention to the other range of protectionist weapons—nontariff barriers.

Nontariff Barriers

There are two important forms of nontariff barriers:

- Quotas
- Voluntary export restraints

A **quota** is a quantitative restriction on the import of a particular good. It specifies the maximum amount of the good that may be imported in a given period of time. A **voluntary export restraint** is an agreement between two governments in which the government of the exporting country agrees to restrain the volume of its own exports. Voluntary export restraints are often called VERs.

Nontariff barriers have become important features of international trading arrangements in the period since World War II and there is now general agreement that nontariff barriers are a more severe impediment to international trade than tariffs.

It is difficult to quantify the effects of nontariff barriers in a way that makes them easy to compare with tariffs, but some studies have attempted to do just that. Such studies attempt to assess the tariff rate that would restrict trade by the same amount as the nontariff barriers do. With such calculations, nontariff barriers and tariffs can be added together to assess the total amount of protection. When we add nontariff barriers to tariffs for the United States, the overall amount of protection increases more than threefold. Even so, the United States is the least protectionist country in the world. Total protection in the European Communities is higher, and higher still in other developed countries and Japan. The less developed countries and the so-called newly industrializing countries have the highest protection rates of all.

Quotas are especially important in the textile industries, where there exists an international agreement called the Multifibre Arrangement, which establishes quotas on a wide range of textile products. Agriculture is also subject to extensive quotas. Voluntary export restraints are particularly important in regulating the international trade in cars between Japan and the United States.

How Quotas and VERs Work

To understand how nontariff barriers affect international trade, let's return to the example of trade between Pioneerland and Magic Empire. Suppose that Pioneerland imposes a quota on car imports. Specifically, suppose that the quota restricts imports to not more than 2 million cars a year. What are the effects of this action?

The answer is found in Fig. 35.8. The quota is shown by the vertical red line at 2 million cars a year. Since it is illegal to import more than that number of cars, car importers buy only that quantity from Magic Empire producers. They pay $2000 a car to the Magic Empire producer. But what do they sell their cars for? The answer is $6000 each. Since the import supply of cars is restricted to 2 million cars a year, people with cars for sale will be able to get $6000 each for them. The quantity of cars imported equals the quantity determined by the quota.

Importing cars is now obviously a profi[illegible] business. An importer gets $6000 for an [illegible] costs only $2000. Thus there is severe

Figure 35.8 The Effects of a Quota

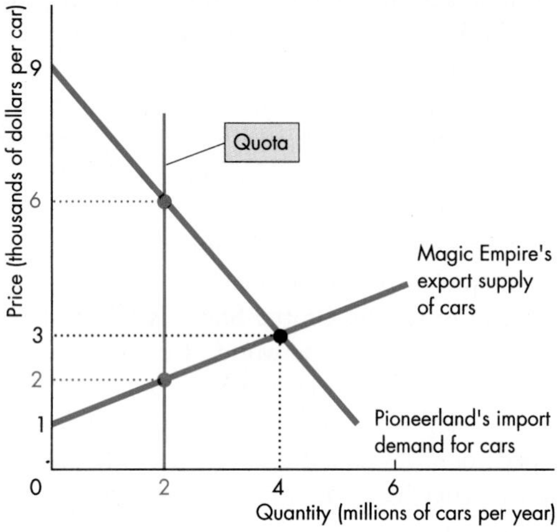

Pioneerland imposes a quota of 2 million cars a year on car imports from Magic Empire. That quantity appears as the vertical red line marked "Quota." Since the quantity of cars supplied by Magic Empire is restricted to 2 million, the price at which those cars will be traded increases to $6000. Importing cars is profitable since Magic Empire is willing to supply cars at $2000 each. There is competition for import quotas—rent seeking.

among car importers for the available quotas. It is the pursuit of the profits from quotas that Anne Krueger calls "rent seeking" (see "Talking with Anne Krueger," pp. 561–564).

The value of imports—the amount paid to Magic Empire—declines to $4 billion, exactly the same as in the case of the tariff. Thus with lower incomes from car exports and with a higher price of grain, the Magicians cut back on their imports of grain in exactly the same way they did under a tariff.

The key difference between a quota and a tariff lies in who gets the profit represented by the difference between the import supply price and the domestic selling price. In the case of a tariff, that difference goes to the government. In the case of a quota, that difference goes to the person who has the right to import under the import-quota regulations.

A voluntary export restraint is like a quota arrangement where quotas are allocated to each exporting country. The effects of voluntary export restraints are imilar to those of quotas but differ from them in that e gap between the domestic price and the export price is captured not by domestic importers but by the foreign exporter. The government of the exporting country has to establish procedures for allocating the restricted volume of exports among its producers.

Paying with Your Shirt! Two of the most heavily protected industries in the United States today are apparel and textiles. It has been estimated that the total protection on these industries, most of which takes the form of quotas, costs the average American family between $200 and $400 a year. Despite this fact, the House of Representatives passed a new act (the Textile and Apparel Trade Act) in 1975 which, if it had become law, would have increased protection in those industries even further, adding $300 to $400 a year in additional costs for the average household.[1] Taking all protection together, it has been estimated that the cost per year to an individual U.S. family is more than $1000.[2]

Another way of looking at the cost of protection is to calculate the cost per job saved. It has been estimated, for example, that to protect one job in the textile industry costs $46,000 a year; one job in the footwear industry costs close to $80,000 a year, and one job in the carbon, steel, and auto industries costs more than $80,000 a year. In all these cases, it costs many times more to save a job through international trade barriers than the wages of the workers involved.[3]

R E V I E W

When a country opens itself up to international trade and trades freely at world market prices, it expands its consumption possibilities. When trade is restricted, some of the gains from trade are lost. A country may be better off with restricted trade than with no trade but not as well off as it could be if it engaged in free trade. A tariff reduces the volume of imports,

[1]For more on this topic, see "Expanding Trade and Avoiding Protectionism," *Economic Report of the President* (1988), pp. 127–162.

[2]Murray Weidenbaum and N. Munger, "Protection at Any Price?" *Regulation* (July/August 1983), pp. 14–18.

[3]Keith E. Maskus, "Rising Protectionism and U.S. International Trade Policy," *Economic Review* (July/August 1984), Federal Reserve Bank of Kansas City, pp. 3–17.

but it also reduces the volume of exports. Under both free trade and restricted trade (and without international borrowing and lending), the value of imports equals the value of exports. With restricted trade, both the total value of exports and the total value of imports are lower than under free trade, but trade is still balanced. ■

Why Quotas and VERs Might Be Preferred to Tariffs

At first sight, it seems puzzling that countries would ever want to use quotas and even more puzzling that they would want to use voluntary export restraints. We have seen that the same domestic price and the same quantity of imports can be achieved by using any of the three devices for restricting trade. However, a tariff provides the government with a source of revenue; a quota provides domestic importers with a profit; and a voluntary export restraint provides the foreigner with a profit. Why, then, would a country use a quota or a voluntary export restraint rather than a tariff?

There are three possible reasons. First, a government can use quotas to reward its political supporters. Under a quota, licenses to import become tremendously profitable. So the government bestows riches on the people to whom it gives licenses to import. Second, quotas are more precise instruments for holding down imports. As demand fluctuates, the domestic price of the good fluctuates but not the quantity of imports. You can see this implication of a quota by going back to Fig. 35.8. Suppose that the demand for imports fluctuates. With a quota, these demand fluctuations simply produce fluctuations in the domestic price of the import but no change in the volume of imports. With a tariff, fluctuations in demand lead to no change in the domestic price but to large changes in the volume of imports. Thus if for some reason the government wants to control the quantity of imports and does not care about fluctuations in the domestic price, it will use a quota. Third, different branches of government have jurisdiction over different aspects of international trade restriction. Congress has the power to impose tariffs. The administration has the power to impose nontariff barriers. Thus changing tariffs is a slow and cumbersome matter requiring the passage of an act of Congress. In contrast, nontariff barriers can be changed quickly provided the administration is persuaded of the need for the change.

Why would a government use voluntary export restraints rather than a tariff or quota? The government may want to avoid a tariff or quota war with another country. If one country imposes a tariff or a quota, that might encourage another country to impose a similar tariff or quota on the exports of the first country. Such a tariff and quota war would result in a much smaller volume of trade and a much worse outcome for both countries. A voluntary export restraint can be viewed as a way of achieving trade restrictions to protect domestic industries but with some kind of compensation to encourage the foreign country to accept that situation and not retaliate with its own restrictions. Finally, VERs are often the only form of trade restriction that can be legally entered into under the terms of the General Agreement on Tariffs and Trade.

Dumping and Countervailing Duties

Dumping is the selling of a good in a foreign market for a lower price than in the domestic market or for a lower price than its cost of production. Such a practice can arise from discriminating monopoly seeking to maximize profit. An example of alleged dumping has occurred with Japanese sales of steel to the United States. Under current U.S. law and under GATT, dumping is illegal and antidumping duties may be imposed on foreign producers if U.S. producers can show that they have been injured by dumping.

Countervailing duties are tariffs that are imposed to enable domestic producers to compete with subsidized foreign producers. Often, foreign governments subsidize some of their domestic industries. Two examples are the Canadian pork and lumber industries. Under current U.S. law, if American producers can show that a foreign subsidy has damaged their market, a countervailing duty may be imposed.

Why Is International Trade Restricted?

There are many reasons why international trade is restricted. We've just seen two reasons—to offset the effects of dumping and of foreign subsidies. Even in these cases, it does not obviously benefit a country to protect itself from cheap foreign imports. However, more generally, we've seen that international trade benefits a country by raising its consumption possibilities. Why do we restrict international trade when such restrictions lower our consumption possibilities?

The key reason is that consumption possibilities increase *on the average* but not everyone shares in the gain and some people even lose. Free trade brings benefits to some and costs to others, with total benefits exceeding total costs. It is the uneven distribution of costs and benefits that is the principal source of impediment to achieving more liberal international trade.

Returning to our example of international trade in cars and grain between Pioneerland and Magic Empire, the benefits from free trade accrue to all the producers of grain and those producers of cars who would not have to bear the costs of adjusting to a smaller car industry. The costs of free trade are borne by those car producers and their employees who have to move and become grain producers. The number of people who gain will, in general, be enormous compared with the number who lose. The gain per person will, therefore, be rather small. The loss per person to those who bear the loss will be large. Since the loss that falls on those who bear it is large, it will pay those people to incur considerable expense in order to lobby against free trade. On the other hand, it will not pay those who gain to organize to achieve free trade. The gain from trade for any one individual is too small for that individual to spend much time or money on a political organization to achieve free trade. The loss from free trade will be seen as being so great by those bearing that loss that they *will* find it profitable to join a political organization to prevent free trade. Each group is optimizing—weighing benefits against costs and choosing the best action for themselves. The anti–free trade group will, however, undertake a larger quantity of political lobbying than the pro–free trade group.

Compensating Losers

If, in total, the gains from free international trade exceed the losses, why don't those who gain compensate those who lose so that everyone is in favor of free trade? To some degree, such compensation does take place. It also takes place indirectly as a consequence of unemployment compensation arrangements. But, as a rule, only limited attempts are made to compensate those who lose from free international trade. The main reason why full compensation is not attempted is that the costs of identifying the losers would be enormous. Also, it would never be clear whether or not a person who has fallen on hard times is suffering because of free trade or for other reasons, and perhaps reasons largely under the control of the individual. Furthermore, some people who look like losers at one point in time may, in fact, wind up gaining. The young auto worker who loses his job in Michigan and becomes a computer assembly worker in Minneapolis resents the loss of work and the need to move. But a year or two later, looking back on events, he counts himself fortunate. He's made a move that has increased his income and given him greater job security.

It is because we do not, in general, compensate the losers from free international trade that protectionism is such a popular and permanent feature of our national economic and political life.

Political Outcome

The political outcome that emerges from this activity is one in which a modest amount of restriction on international trade occurs and is maintained. Politicians react to constituencies pressing for protection and find it necessary, in order to get re-elected, to support legislative programs that protect those constituencies. The producers of protected goods are far more vocal and much more sensitive swing-voters than the consumers of those goods. The political outcome, therefore, leans in the direction of maintaining protection.

The politics of trade can be seen easily today. The United States restricts imports of sugar by quota. Who profits from the quotas? Not the foreign exporters. Whereas voluntary export restraints give exporters like Toyota and Honda big profits, quotas do not help foreign producers. In this case, the quotas have brought real economic and political suffering to Central American and Caribbean countries which produce sugar. The U.S. sugar growers, on the other hand, benefit from the quotas.

Do sugar growers participate in politics? They certainly do, as surfaced in a debate among Democratic candidates during the presidential primaries in 1988. Missouri congressman Richard Gephardt was campaigning for the Democratic nomination for president on a platform of trade restrictions. One of his opponents, Massachusetts governor Michael Dukakis, questioned Mr. Gephardt on contributions to his campaign from the sugar industry.

Mr. Gephardt defended his willingness to take money from corporate and labor groups, arguing that those who contributed to him did not always agree with him.

"Don't give us this establishment stuff," Mr. Dukakis retorted, "when you're out there taking their money."

Mr. Gephardt in turn challenged the Governor for accepting money from companies that did business with Massachusetts.

"These two guys have eliminated themselves," Mr. Jackson cut in. "I am the choice."

The Reverend Jesse Jackson went on to demonstrate his understanding of the economics of politics, observing that "lobbyists would lose their jobs if they gave their money continuously against the interests they were working for."[4]

■ You've now seen how free international trade enables everyone to gain from increased specialization and exchange. By producing goods at which we have a comparative advantage and exchanging some of our own production for that of others, we expand our consumption possibilities. Placing impediments on that exchange when it crosses national borders restricts the extent to which we can gain from specialization and exchange. By opening our country up to free international trade, the market for the things that we sell expands and the price rises. The market for the things that we buy also expands and the price falls.

Although all countries can gain from international trade, virtually no country engages in completely free trade. Some countries even restrict the trade that may take place *within* their borders. We are going to study and compare such countries in the next chapter. One of these, Japan, has attained a position among the world's richest and most powerful trading nations. Another, the Soviet Union, undertakes very little international trade, and uses an economic system that is very different from the one that we employ in the United States.

[4]*New York Times* (March 1, 1988), p. B7.

SUMMARY

Patterns and Trends in International Trade

Large flows of trade take place between rich and poor countries. Resource-rich countries exchange natural resources for manufactures, and resource-poor countries import their resources in exchange for their own manufactures. However, by far the biggest volume of trade is in manufactures exchanged among the rich industrialized countries. The biggest single U.S. export item is machinery. However, its biggest single net export is grain. Trade in services has grown in recent years. Total trade has also grown over the years. The U.S. balance of trade fluctuates around zero, but since 1982 the United States has had a balance of trade deficit. (pp. 567–570).

Opportunity Cost and Comparative Advantage

When opportunity costs differ between countries, the country with the lowest opportunity cost of producing a good is said to have a comparative advantage in that good. Comparative advantage is the source of the gains from international trade. A country can have an absolute advantage, but not a comparative advantage, in the production of all goods. Every country has a comparative advantage in something. (pp. 570–572)

The Gains from Trade

Countries can gain from trade if their opportunity costs differ. Through trade, each country can obtain goods at a lower opportunity cost than it could if it produced all goods at home. Trading allows consumption to exceed production. By specializing in producing the good in which it has a comparative advantage and then trading some of that good for imports, a country can consume at points outside its production possibility frontier. Each country can consume at such a point.

In the absence of international borrowing and lending, trade is balanced as prices adjust to reflect the international supply and demand for goods. The world price is established at the level that balances the production and consumption plans of the trading parties. At the equilibrium price, trade is balanced and domestic consumption plans exactly match a combination of domestic production and international trade.

Comparative advantage explains the enormous volume and diversity of international trade that takes place in the world. But much trade takes the form of exchanging similar goods for each other—one type of car for another. Such trade arises because of economies of scale in the face of diversified tastes. By specializing in producing a few goods, having long production runs, and then trading those goods internationally, consumers in all countries can enjoy greater diversity of products at lower prices. (pp. 572–577)

Trade Restrictions

A country can restrict international trade by imposing tariffs or nontariff barriers—quotas and voluntary export restraints. All trade restrictions raise the domestic price of imported goods, lower the volume of imports, and reduce the total value of imports. They also reduce the total value of exports by the same amount as the reduction in the value of imports.

All trade restrictions create a gap between the domestic price and the foreign supply price of an import. In the case of a tariff, that gap is the tariff revenue collected by the government. But the government raises no revenue from a quota. Instead, domestic importers who have a license to import increase their profit. A voluntary export restraint resembles a quota except that a higher price is received by the foreign exporter.

Governments restrict trade because restrictions help the producers of the protected commodity and the workers employed by those producers. Because their gain is sufficiently large and the loss per consumer sufficiently small, the political equilibrium favors restricted trade. Politicians pay more attention to the vocal and active concerns of the few who stand to lose than to the quieter and less strongly expressed views of the many who stand to gain. (pp. 577–587)

KEY CONCEPTS

Absolute advantage, 575
Balance of trade, 567
Comparative advantage, 572
Countervailing duty, 585
Dumping, 585
Exports, 567
General Agreement on Tariffs and Trade, 578
Imports, 567
Net exporter, 567
Net importer, 567
Nontariff barrier, 577
Protectionism, 577
Quota, 583
Tariff, 577
Voluntary export restraint, 583

Key Figures

REVIEW QUESTIONS

1 What are the main exports and imports of the United States?

2 How does the United States trade services internationally?

3 Which items of international trade have been growing the most quickly in recent years?

4 What is comparative advantage? Why does it lead to gains from international trade?

5 Explain why international trade brings gains to all countries.

6 Distinguish between comparative advantage and absolute advantage.

7 Explain why all countries have a comparative advantage in something.

8 Explain why we import and export such large quantities of certain similar goods—such as cars, for example.

9 What are the main ways in which we restrict international trade?

10 What are the effects of a tariff?

11 What are the effects of a quota?

12 What are the effects of a voluntary export restraint?

13 Describe the main trends in tariffs and nontariff barriers.

14 Which countries have the largest restrictions on their international trade?

15 Why do countries restrict international trade?

PROBLEMS

1 a) Using Fig. 35.2, calculate the opportunity cost of cars in Pioneerland at the point on the production possibility frontier at which 4 million cars are produced.

b) Using Fig. 35.3, calculate the opportunity cost of a car in Magic Empire when it produces 8 million cars.

c) With no trade, Pioneerland produces 4 million cars and Magic Empire produces 8 million cars. Which country has a comparative advantage in the production of cars?

d) If there is no trade between Pioneerland and Magic Empire, how much grain is consumed and how many cars are bought in each country?

2 Suppose that the two countries in problem 1 trade freely.

a) Which country exports grain?

b) What adjustments will be made to the amount of each good produced by each country?

c) What adjustment will be made to the amount of each good consumed by each country?

d) What can you say about the price of a car under free trade?

3 Compare the total production of each good produced in problems 1 and 2.

4 Compare the situation in problems 1 and 2 with that analyzed in this chapter (pp. 570–574). Why does Magic Empire export cars in the chapter but import them in problem 2?

5 The following figure depicts the international market for soybeans.

a) What is the world price of soybeans if there is free trade between these countries?

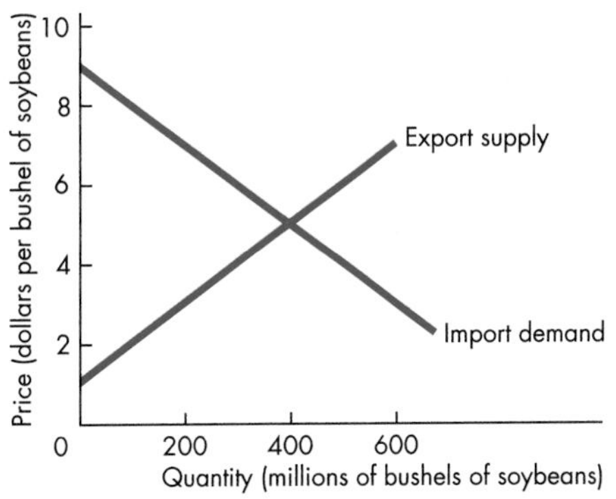

b) If the country that imports soybeans imposes a tariff of \$2 per bushel, what is the world price of soybeans and what quantity of soybeans gets traded internationally? What is the price of soybeans in the importing country? Calculate the tariff revenue.

6 If the importing country in problem 5a imposes a quota of 300 million bushels, what is the price of soybeans in the importing country? What is the revenue from the quota and who gets this revenue?

7 If the exporting country in problem 5a imposes a VER of 300 million bushels of soybeans, what is the world price of soybeans? What is the revenue of soybean growers in the exporting country? Which country gains from the VER?

8 Suppose that the exporting country in problem 5(a) subsidizes production by paying its farmers \$1 a bushel for soybeans harvested.

a) What is the price of soybeans in the importing country?

b) What action might soybean growers in the importing country take? Why?

Chapter 38

Comparing Economic Systems

After studying this chapter, you will be able to:

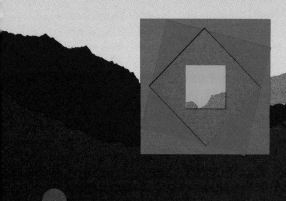

- Explain why the economic problem of scarcity is common to all economic and political systems
- Describe the various political systems that have been proposed to deal with the economic problem
- Explain the difference between capitalism and socialism
- Describe the varieties of capitalism in the United States, Japan, and Western Europe
- Describe the main features of the economy of the Soviet Union
- Explain the economic restructuring—or *perestroika*—being undertaken in the Soviet Union
- Describe the economic reforms being undertaken in China
- Assess the efficiency of alternative economic systems

From Moscow and Beijing to Washington, London, and Tokyo, dramatic changes are taking place in the way governments manage their nations' economies. ■ In Moscow, it is called *perestroika*—restructuring. At the June 1987 meeting of the Central Committee of the Communist party, Mikhail Gorbachev presented his model for the "radical restructuring of economic management" in the Soviet Union. He preached his message in meetings with ordinary Russians, and proclaimed the virtues of "working an extra bit harder" with an almost religious intensity. In his book, *Perestroika,* which became a best seller even in the United States, he described the origins and the first steps being taken to implement his "*perestroika* revolution." ■ In Beijing,

Perestroika

widespread reforms in the Chinese economic system are being encouraged and implemented. In that country, the goal declared by the architect of the modern Chinese economy, Deng Xiaoping, is to build "a socialist nation with Chinese characteristics" that will embody "one country and two systems." The two systems are the socialist system of China and the Soviet Union, and the capitalist system of the United States, Western Europe, and Japan. ■ Changes in government economic management are less dramatic in Washington, London, and Tokyo than those in the Soviet Union and China. But change, nevertheless, is in the air. In the United States, that change has taken the form of a steady process of deregulation, a process begun during the years when Jimmy Carter was president and given greater momentum during the Reagan years. In Great Britain, and many other Western European countries, deregulation has been accompanied by the selling off of state-operated businesses such as railroads, telecommunications, and public utilities to private enterprise. In Japan, change is taking place that results in a greater liberalization of the Japanese economy and of its international trading and financial relations. ■ What are the main differences in the economic systems of the Soviet Union and China, and of the United States, Western Europe, and Japan? What exactly are capitalism and socialism? Why are the socialist countries undergoing such massive changes in their methods of economic management? Why are countries in Western Europe and Japan privatizing large parts of their economies? How do the alternative economic systems of capitalism and socialism perform? Can a single country successfully combine the two different economic systems?

■ In this chapter, we're going to describe some of the key differences in the economic systems of the world's major countries. We will learn how capitalist and socialist economies operate. We'll examine some of the diversity among the capitalist economies—the United States, Japan, and Western Europe. We'll study the economic system of the Soviet Union and see why *perestroika* is taking place. We'll examine the reforms in China and describe its economic goals. Finally, we'll compare the performances of the alternative economic systems.

The Fundamental Economic Problem

The first thing that we learn when we begin to study economics is that the source of all economic problems is the universal fact of *scarcity.* In embarking on a study of comparative economic systems, it will be worthwhile to review and reinforce our understanding of the implications of scarcity.

Scarcity

Scarcity arises because we all want to consume more goods and services than the available resources make possible. The *production possibility frontier* describes the limits of what we can produce—it separates the attainable from the unattainable (see Chapter 3, pp. 51–53). Our consumption possibilities are maximized if we arrange our economic affairs in such a way that we produce at a point on our production possibility frontier. The first aspect of solving the economic problem, therefore, involves getting onto the frontier itself.

Getting onto the Production Possibility Frontier

If we operate at a point on the production possibility frontier rather than at some point inside it, we produce more of all goods. We cannot take it for granted, however, that we will automatically operate on the frontier. We might waste resources. Resources are wasted, for example, if we produce more of some perishable commodity at a given moment than can be quickly consumed. Some of the commodity rots and may as well not have been produced. Therefore the resources used to produce that commodity are wasted.

Another more subtle form of waste arises if productive resources are combined in a way that makes the cost of production higher than it needs to be. For example, electricity can be generated by using either coal, oil, or nuclear power as the energy source. If the cost of producing a megawatt of electricity is lowest using nuclear power, but instead coal and oil are used, then productive resources are wasted. Don't lose sight, however, that in economics the word "cost" includes all costs. In the case of power production, the costs include environmental costs such as pollution, the hazard of nuclear accident and contamination, and many other costs not borne by the producer of electricity.

Different economic systems use different methods to get the economy to a point on its production possibility frontier. We will look at those methods in the next section. Once the economy is on its production possibility frontier, no more of any one good can be produced without producing less of some other good. It is this fact that gives rise to the concept of *opportunity cost.* The opportunity cost of producing one more unit of any particular good is the amount of some other good or goods forgone. Because it is only possible to produce more of one good by producing less of another good, a second aspect of solving the economic problem involves getting to the right point on the frontier.

Producing the Right Quantities of Goods and Services

Determining how much of each of the various goods and services to produce requires that people's preferences of the alternatives be taken into account. For example, if people place a high value on clean air and a low value on quick and convenient transportation, we would produce fewer cars and highways and have more stringent methods of controlling exhaust emission. If people value vacations on the moon highly and place little or no value at all on any of the other things that we currently produce and consume, then we would use an enormous amount of our resources to build lunar transportation systems and holiday resorts! If we all become addicted to fruit and ice cream and refuse to eat meat, Burger King and McDonald's fast-food outlets would either go out of business or radically change their mix of products. Baskin Robbins would be booming.

The way in which individual preferences influence the quantities of goods and services produced varies from one economic system to another. As we'll see shortly, our own economic system takes individual consumers' preferences as the dominant force determining what is produced. But there are other systems in which individual preferences play a limited role and those of the government's planning agency play the dominant role.

Getting onto the production possibility frontier and choosing the right point on it are two aspects of solving the economic problem. There is a third aspect —determining the distribution of economic well-being.

The Distribution of Economic Well-Being

An economy could be at a point on the production possibility frontier and further, that point could be one that exactly reflects consumers' preferences concerning the values of the various goods. At that point, production of more of any one good and less of any other good would make somebody worse off. There are, however, many such points possible, each of which is associated with a different distribution of economic well-being. One such point would be where everyone is equally well off. Another is where 90 percent of the population is almost starving and the other 10 percent are living in enormous luxury. Economic systems, in effect, make decisions about who gets what. Some economic systems favor, in principle at least, considerable equality in the distribution of economic well-being. Other systems favor equality of opportunity but pay little attention to the distribution that results from equal opportunities.

R E V I E W

The best we can do in the face of scarcity is to get ourselves onto the production possibility frontier. The point on the frontier that we go to depends on whose preferences determine which goods and services the economy produces and on how the economic system distributes well-being. No economic system can abolish the economic problem. Each system, at best, can only help people cope with scarcity. ■

Let's see how different economic systems cope with the fundamental economic problem.

Alternative Economic Systems

Economic systems vary in two dimensions:

- Who owns capital and land
- Who allocates of resources

Figure 38.1 summarizes the possibilities. Capital and land may be owned entirely by individuals, entirely by the state, or by a mixture of the two. Resources may be allocated entirely by markets, entirely by government economic planners, or by a mixture of the two. The two highlighted corners of the figure represent two idealized extreme cases: capitalism and socialism.

Capitalism is an economic system based on the private ownership of capital and land and on market allocation of resources. **Socialism** is an economic system based on state ownership of capital and land and on a centrally planned allocation of resources. **Central planning** is a method of allocating resources by command. It involves plans being made by a central planning authority and then communicated to the various production and distribution organizations in the country. The plans are monitored by a large team of bureaucrats. Hardly any country has ever used an economic system that precisely corresponds to one of these extreme types, but the United States and Japan come close to being capitalist economies and the Soviet Union and China to being socialist economies.

Figure 38.1 Alternative Economic Systems

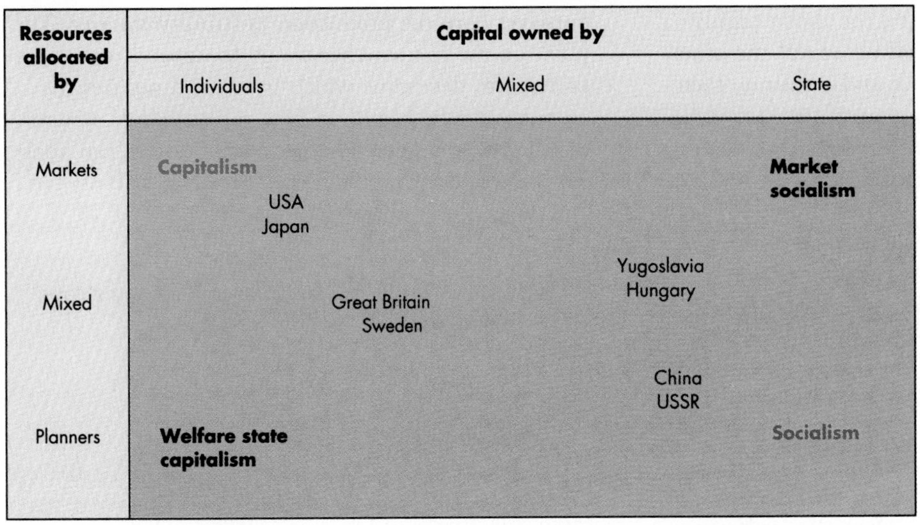

Under capitalism, individuals own capital—farms and factories, plant and equipment—and resources are allocated by markets. Under socialism, the state owns capital and resources are allocated by a planning and command system. Market socialism combines state ownership of capital with a market allocation of resources. Welfare state capitalism combines private capital ownership with a high degree of state intervention in the allocation of resources.

Some countries combine private and state ownership and market allocation and planning in unusual ways. **Market socialism** (also called **decentralized planning**) is an economic system that combines socialism's state ownership of capital and land with capitalism's market allocation of resources. Yugoslavia and Hungary are examples of market socialist economies. In such economies, the planners communicate a set of prices to the various production and distribution organizations and then leave those organizations free to produce whatever quantities they choose at those prices. Another combination is welfare state capitalism. **Welfare state capitalism** combines capitalism's private ownership of capital and land with a heavy degree of state intervention in the allocation of resources. Sweden, the United Kingdom, and other Western European countries provide examples of such economies.

Since all the economic systems in Fig. 38.1 are made up of a combination of capitalism and socialism, let's examine these two extreme types a bit more closely.

Capitalism

Let's describe a country that has a pure (hypothetical) form of capitalism. Such a country is one in which a concern for individual liberty is paramount. Its foundation is the establishment and enforcement of individual property rights. Each individual owns what he or she has produced or legitimately acquired. Resources are legitimately acquired as a result of buying them from a willing seller or receiving them as a gift. These are the only ways in which resources can be transferred between individuals. Any other method of transferring resources is illegal. Preventing illegal transfers is the only proper role of the state. No other economic action by any individual or group of individuals may be blocked by the force of the state. All individuals are free to form coalitions or groups to buy and sell whatever goods and services they choose and in whatever quantities they choose.

Governments may be viewed as coalitions among individuals that provide certain types of goods and services. Furthermore, if a government can offer better terms than any other coalition so that people choose to trade with it rather than with some other group, then a government may legitimately undertake economic actions. A government may not, however, coerce individuals in any way other than to prevent them from attempting to violate other people's property rights.

In capitalist economies, the allocation of resources is determined by individual choices expressed through markets. *What* is produced is determined by consumers' preferences; *how* goods are produced is determined by profit-maximizing firms; *for whom* goods are produced is determined by individual decisions on the supply of factors of production and by the market-determined prices at which those factors of production trade.

Socialism

Socialism is an economic system based on the political philosophy that the private ownership of capital and land enables the rich (owners of capital and land) to exploit the poor (workers who have no capital and land). To avoid such exploitation, capital and land are owned by the state. Individuals are permitted to own only their *human capital* and capital equipment used for consumption purposes such as consumer durable goods. All other capital is owned by the state. Thus the state owns all factories and farms and the plant and equipment to operate them. All labor works for the state and all consumption goods and services are produced by and bought from the state.

Under socialism, some people are wealthier than others (and have higher incomes than others), but gross inequalities of wealth arising from the ownership of massive industrial and commercial complexes are not permitted. The principles governing the distribution of income are "from each according to his ability, to each according to his contribution." That is, the state pays each individual a wage that reflects the state's own opinion of the value of the output of the individual.

A variant of socialism is communism. **Communism** is an economic system based on the state ownership of capital and land, on central planning, and on distributing income in accordance with the rule "from each according to his ability, to each according to his need." The word communism is commonly used to describe Eastern European and Soviet-style socialism. In ordinary speech, the words communism and socialism are virtually interchangeable. It is worthwhile keeping the two words distinct, however, when thinking about economic systems.

In socialist (and communist) economies, resources are allocated not by markets but by central planners and it is their preferences and priorities that determine *what, how,* and *for whom* the various goods and services are produced.

The Pros and Cons of Capitalism

Advantages of Capitalism The major advantages of capitalism arise because each individual's judgment about his or her own well-being is paramount in determining what economic actions take place. Each individual decides how much work to do and for whom to work, how to spend time away from work, and how to dispose of the income made from selling his or her resources. Individual incentives are strong. Adam Smith wrote:

> As every individual . . . endeavors as much as he can both to employ his capital in the support of domestic industry and so to direct that industry that its produce be of the greatest value; every individual necessarily labors to render the annual revenue of society as great as he can. . . . He intends only his own gain, and he is in this, as in many other cases, led by an invisible hand to promote an end which was no part of his intention.[1]

Adam Smith went on to reject any detailed state intervention in economic life:

> The statesman, who should attempt to direct private people in what manner they ought to employ their capitals, would not only load himself with a most unnecessary attention, but assume an authority which could safely be trusted, not only to no single person, but to no counsel or senate whatever, and which would nowhere be so dangerous as in the hands of a man who had the folly and presumption enough to fancy himself fit to exercise it.

Disadvantages of Capitalism A major disadvantage of capitalism is seen, even by those who support this economic system, as arising from the fact that

---

[1]Adam Smith, *The Wealth of Nations* (New York: Random House, 1937) 423.

the historical distribution of endowments is arbitrary and indeed is the result of massive illegitimate transfers. For example, the European colonizers of North America took land from the native people of this continent. Because there have in the past been illegitimate transfers—violations of private property rights—the current distribution of wealth has no legitimacy. If there were no large inequality in the distribution of wealth, its historical origins would not be a matter of much concern. But the fact that wealth is distributed very unequally leads most people to the conclusion that there is a role for state intervention to redistribute income and wealth.

A further disadvantage of capitalism arises from the belief that some people do not, in fact, know what is good for them and will, if left to their own devices, make the wrong choices. We all agree that children should not be permitted to exercise complete freedom of choice. Most people would also extend some restrictions to the mentally ill, the senile, and to those who are addicted (or even potentially addicted) to dangerous drugs. Some advocates of socialism go further, arguing that socialist planners are able to make better choices than people would make for themselves.

We have reviewed some arguments against capitalism that might be used to persuade people that such a system is not desirable. But there is a more fundamental problem with capitalism: It has an internal contradiction.

The Contradiction Private property rights can be enforced only if the state has a monopoly on coercion. If the state were simply competing with others to enforce property rights, then every time a disagreement arose between two parties each would hire its own enforcers to settle the dispute. Battles would ensue. Only when a single supplier of coercive power has emerged victorious can private property rights be successfully enforced without indulging in a process of open physical violence and conflict. The state is the monopolist in the provision of coercion for enforcing property rights. But once the state has achieved that monopoly position, there is no way of preventing it from expanding its range of coercive activities further. There is no check on those individuals who hold offices of state and who exercise the state's powers. Furthermore, there is no way of preventing private individuals and coalitions of private individuals from attempting to persuade the state to use its powers in a broader manner.

Whether it is because of the persuasiveness of the arguments against capitalism or because of the fundamental internal contradiction in the system, capitalism is a hypothetical rather than an actual economic system. No country ever has or ever will experience that pure form of economic organization. It is a philosophical ideal or reference point against which to compare actual systems. If we could have such a system and if we could remedy the historical violations of property rights, then many people would agree that we would have done the best we could to solve the economic problem. But such a solution is simply not available to us. It is for this reason that most capitalist economies include some element of state ownership and control of economic activity.

The Varieties of Capitalism

There is no unique model of capitalism. Most of this book illustrates and elaborates the principles of economics, using examples drawn from the largest and most important capitalist economy—the United States. But not all capitalist economies follow the U.S. model. In this section, we take a quick look at some of the key differences among the capitalist economies and some of the trends that are emerging in those countries.

Japan

Japan's economic performance since World War II is known as the "Japanese economic miracle." Emerging from war with per capita incomes less than one fifth of those in the United States, Japan has transformed itself into an economic giant whose per capita income now approaches that of our own. The most spectacular growth period occurred in the 25 years from 1945 to 1970, when per capita income increased eightfold. Today, the Japanese have a dominant position in world markets for cars and computers, audio and video equipment and a whole range of "high-tech" commodities. The camera-laden Japanese tourist is now as common a sight in London, Paris, and Rome as the North American tourist. And there are many more Japanese visitors to North America than Americans visiting Japan. What has led to this transformation of Japan into one of the world's most powerful and richest economies?

There are four features of the Japanese economy that appear to be responsible for its dramatic success:

- Reliance on free-market, capitalist methods
- Self-disciplined, hardworking, loyal, and cooperative people
- Small scale of government
- Pro-business government intervention

The economic system in Japan is like that in the United States. People are free to pursue their ideas, to own firms, to hire labor and other inputs, and to sell their outputs in relatively free markets.

The Japanese people have a long tradition of loyalty and a strong work ethic. As a consequence, Japanese workers are loyal to their employers and firms are loyal to their workers. This cooperative atmosphere is one that results in hard work and high productivity.

The Japanese government is the smallest in the capitalist world. The total scale of government is less than one fifth of the economy. That is, average taxes and government spending account for slightly less than one fifth of GNP. This contrasts with close to 30 percent in the United States and more than 40 percent in some Western European capitalist countries. Small scale of government means that taxes are low and therefore, do not constitute a major discouragement to work and to saving and accumulating capital. To the extent that the Japanese government does intervene in the economy, that intervention is pro-business.

The main vehicle of government intervention is the **Ministry of International Trade and Industry** (MITI)—a government agency responsible for stimulating Japanese industrial development and international trade. In the years immediately following World War II, MITI encouraged the development of basic industries such as coal, electric power, shipbuilding, and steel. It used tariffs and quotas to protect these industries in their early stages of development, subsidized them, and ensured that capital resources were abundantly available for them. MITI is almost entrepreneurial in its activities. During the 1960s, with the basic industries in place, MITI turned its attention to helping the chemical and lighter manufacturing industries. In the 1980s, it helped Japanese industry dominate the world computer market.

MITI not only is active in fostering the growth and development of certain industries, but it also helps speed the decline of those industries that are not contributing to rapid income growth. For example, in the mid-1970s when the price of oil increased dramatically, the smelting of bauxite to create aluminium became inefficient in Japan. Within two years, Japan's bauxite-smelting industry had been closed down, and Japan was importing all its aluminium from Australia. By identifying industries for profitable growth and those for profitable decline, MITI helps speed the adjustment process in reallocating resources to take maximum advantage of technological change and trends in prices.

The result of Japan's economic system and government economic intervention has been a high rate of capital accumulation. There has also been a high rate of accumulation of human capital, especially in the applied sciences. Going along with a high rate of capital accumulation—both physical and human—has been a high rate of technological advance and with no inhibitions about using the best technologies available, wherever in the world they might have been developed.

Welfare State Capitalism

Capitalism in Western Europe is more heavily tinged with socialism than in either the United States or Japan. It is welfare state capitalism. The countries of Western Europe, many of which now belong to the European Communities, are basically capitalist market economies in the sense that most productive resources are owned by private individuals and most resources are allocated by individuals trading freely in markets for both goods and services and factors of production. But the scale of government, and the degree and direction of government intervention, is much larger in these countries than in the United States and Japan.

Government expenditure and taxes range between 40 and 50 percent of GNP in European countries. Tax rates this high create disincentives that result in less effort and lower saving rates than in countries with lower taxes. The European countries also have a large, nationalized industry sector. A **nationalized industry** is an industry owned and operated by a publicly owned authority that is directly responsible to the government. Railways, airlines, gas, electricity, telephones, radio and television broadcasting, coal, steel, banking and finance, and even automobiles are among the list of industries that are either wholly or partly publicly owned in some

European countries. Nationalized industries are often managed on a command rather than market principle and usually are less efficient than privately owned, competitive firms.

Increasingly in recent years, European governments have been selling state-owned enterprises. The process of selling state-owned enterprises is called **privatization.** There has also been a retreat, in some countries, from very high tax rates. European countries have noticed the economic success of Japan and the United States and, right or wrong, have drawn the conclusion that the greater reliance on capitalism in those economies is, in part, responsible for their economic success. That conclusion is reinforced by a widespread belief that the socialist methods employed by the Soviet Union and China are no longer serving those countries well. Let's take a closer look at socialism—first in the Soviet Union and then in China.

The Soviet Union

The Soviet Union, or the Union of Soviet Socialist Republics, was founded in 1917 following the Bolshevik revolution led by Vladimir Ilyich Lenin. The Soviet Union is a vast, resource-rich, and diverse nation. Its land area is three times that of the United States; its population is approaching 300 million; it has vast reserves of coal, oil, iron ore, natural gas, timber, and almost every other mineral resource; it is a nation of enormous ethnic diversity, with Russians making up only 50 percent of the population. The remaining population includes many European, Asian, and Arabic ethnic groups.

Table 38.1 A Compact Summary of Key Periods in the Economic History of the Soviet Union

Period	Main economic events/characteristics
1917–1921 (Lenin)	• Bolshevik revolution • Nationalization of banking, industry, and transportation • Forced requisitioning of agricultural output
1921–1924 (Lenin)	• New Economic Policy (NEP), 1921 • Market allocation of most resources
1928–1953 (Stalin)	• Abolition of market • Introduction of command planning and five-year plans • Collectivization of farms • Emphasis on capital goods and economic growth • Harsh conditions
1953–1970 (Khrushchev to Brezhnev)	• Steady growth • Increased emphasis on consumer goods
1970–1985 (Brezhnev to Chernenko)	• Deteriorating productivity in agriculture and industry • Slowdown in growth
1985– (Gorbachev)	• *Perestroika*—reforms based on increased accountability

History

A compact economic history of the Soviet Union appears in Table 38.1. Although the nation was founded in 1917, its modern economic management system was not put in place until the 1930s. The architect of this system was Joseph Stalin. The financial, manufacturing, and transportation sectors of the economy had been taken into state ownership and control by Lenin. Stalin added the farms to this list. He abolished the market and introduced a command planning mechanism, initiating a series of five-year plans that placed their major emphasis on setting and attaining goals for the production of capital goods. The production of consumer goods was given a secondary place and personal economic conditions were harsh. With emphasis on the production of capital goods, the Soviet economy grew quickly.

By the 1950s, after Stalin's death, steady economic growth continued but the emphasis in economic planning gradually shifted away from capital goods toward consumer goods production. In the 1960s, the growth rate began to sag and by the 1970s and early 1980s, the Soviet economy was running into serious problems. Productivity was actually declining, especially in agriculture but also in industry. Growth stopped and, on some estimates, per capita income in the Soviet Union began to fall.

It was in this situation that Mikhail Gorbachev came to power with plans to restructure the Soviet economy, based on the idea of increased individual accountability and rewards based on performance.

Although the Soviet economy is now undergoing a major restructuring process, its essential organization is that established in the 1930s by Stalin. Let's see what that organization is.

Planning and Command System

There are two parallel organizations in the Soviet Union: the state and the Communist party. Power resides in the Communist party. The most important policy-making body in the Soviet Union is the Politburo, a small group of party officials appointed by the Central Committee of the Communist party, in turn appointed by the Party Congress, as shown in Fig. 38.2. The Party Congress, made up of delegates from all levels of the party and all regions of the country, exercises only nominal control over the Central Committee and the Politburo.

These organs of the Communist party parallel the state institutions. The Soviet parliament is the Supreme Soviet. This body meets infrequently and appoints a Presidium to conduct work between sessions. The Council of Ministers is the government bureaucracy. This bureaucracy controls 60 ministries responsible for detailed aspects of production. The figure provides a sample of the names and responsibilities of some of the 60 ministries. Twenty committees report to the Council of Ministers and of these, two play a central role in economic planning

Figure 38.2 Organization Chart of the Soviet Union

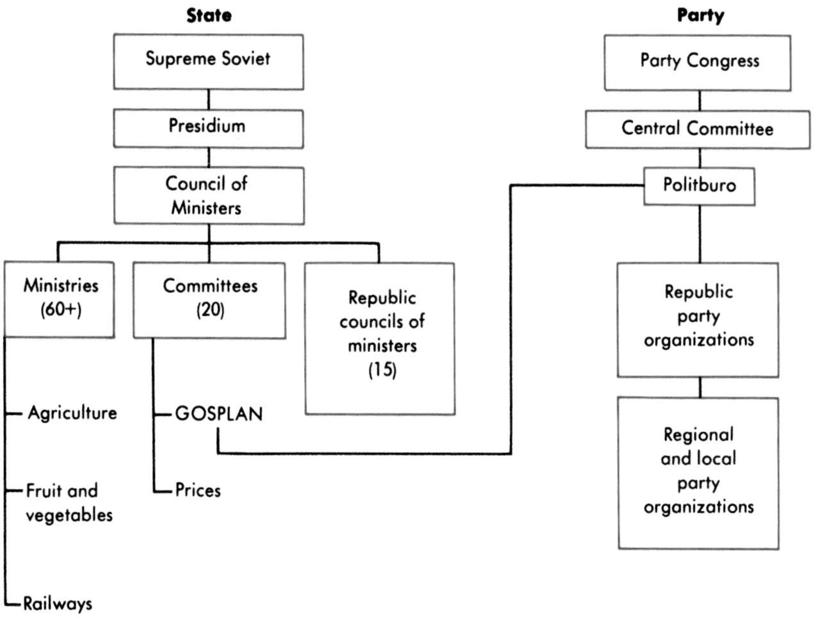

Two parallel organizations—the state and the party—manage the Soviet economy. Although the two organizations are parallel, the party is the dominant partner. GOSPLAN—the State Committee for Economic Planning—has direct links to the Politburo, the chief organ of party power. Economic plans are administered by ministries that deal with each sector of the economy. Plans are also monitored by regional and local party organizations. This chart shows only the tip of a bureaucratic iceberg. Each of the 15 republics of the Soviet Union has an organization similar to that shown here and each local region within each republic has yet another similar organization.

and control. The first of these is the State Committee for Economic Planning, whose acronym, in Russian, is GOSPLAN. **GOSPLAN** is the committee responsible for drawing up and implementing the state's economic plans. The second important economic committee is one that determines prices. Also reporting to the Council of Ministers are the Councils of Ministers of the 15 republics of the Soviet Union.

The organization chart shown in Fig. 38.2 is just the tip of a bureaucratic iceberg, for each of the 15 republics of the Soviet Union has a set of institutions that almost exactly parallels the institutions of the central government just described. This organizational form is also replicated at the regional level and then, yet again, at the local level. Thus there are ministries and party organizations whose influence stretches deep into the most detailed aspects of economic life in the Soviet Union.

The Communist party of the Soviet Union exercises control over the state by three main methods:

- GOSPLAN reports to the Politburo
- Party approves all major projects
- Party controls appointments

The detailed plans for economic activity, drawn up by GOSPLAN (and described below), are reported to and approved by the Politburo. The party exercises detailed day-to-day control over all major projects and production activities through its regional and local organizations. The Communist party's most powerful tool for influencing the Soviet economy is its control over all major appointments in the state bureaucracy, in industry, and in the military.

State Enterprises The **state enterprise** is the basic production unit in the Soviet economy. An enterprise is run by a state-appointed director who is in charge of all the enterprise's operations but is required to follow the instructions imposed by the state's economic plans. State enterprises operate in both the industrial and agricultural sectors of the economy and the enterprise manager plays a key role in the fulfillment of plans. Soviet managers are rewarded through a complex system of performance-related payments.

Planning at GOSPLAN Every five years, GOSPLAN draws up a five-year plan. The **five-year plan** is a broad outline of the general targets and directions set for a period of five years. Each year, GOSPLAN draws up an annual plan. The **annual plan** is a month-by-month set of targets for output, prices, inputs, investment, and money and credit flows. The plans are approved by the Politburo and the Council of Ministers and then communicated to the individual enterprises—farms and factories—that produce the goods and services. Enterprises are overseen both by the ministries that are responsible for the various industries and by local party organizations.

The annual plan is organized around five basic balances:

1 Consumer goods
2 Labor
3 Credit
4 Capital goods
5 Materials

1. Consumer Goods Balance Consumer goods balance is the achievement of a balance between the quantities supplied and demanded for each individual category of consumer goods and services. Soviet planners have three ways of achieving consumer goods balance: changing output, changing incomes, changing prices. Figure 38.3 illustrates these three possibilities. The demand for some good (say, shoes) is D_0; the quantity of shoes that the planners intend to produce is Q_0; the supply curve is S_0; and the cost of producing shoes is C. If the price of shoes is set by the planners at C, there will be an excess of the quantity demanded over the quantity supplied—equal to Q_1 minus Q_0. The planners will not have achieved consumer goods balance in the market for shoes. They can achieve a balance by increasing production to Q_1, in which case the supply curve will shift to the right to S_1 (part a). They can also achieve a balance by imposing higher income taxes, thereby reducing after-tax income and lowering the demand for shoes (part b). They will have to increase taxes by enough to shift the demand curve to the left from D_0 to D_1. At a price of C, the quantity of shoes demanded equals the quantity supplied (Q_0).

In practice, although these two methods of achieving consumer goods balance are available to the Soviet planners, they are not the main methods used. The easiest way of achieving consumer goods balance, and the one most frequently used, is to adjust the price. Soviet planners adjust prices by imposing turnover taxes. The **turnover tax** in the Soviet Union is a tax on a consumer good designed to make its market price high enough to achieve a balance be-

Figure 38.3 Consumer Goods Balance

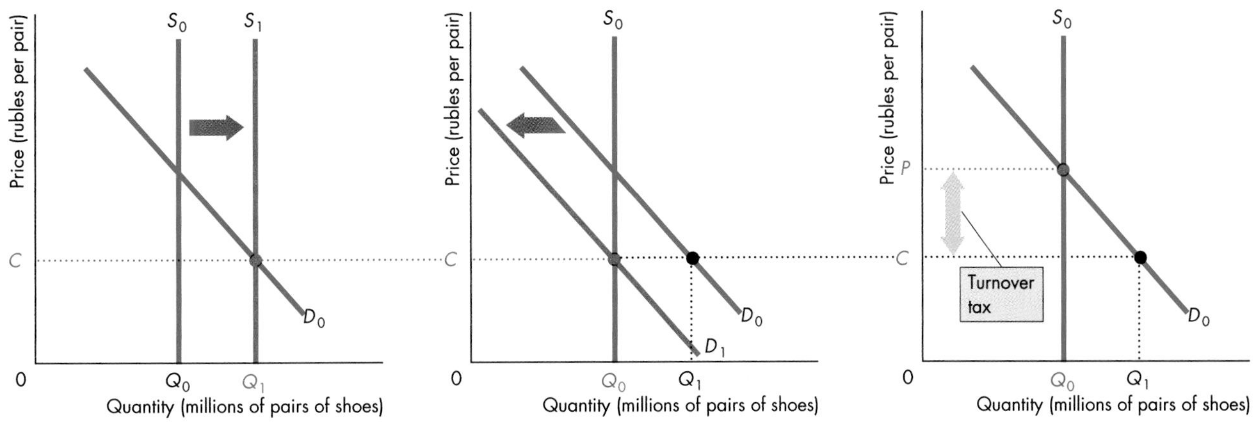

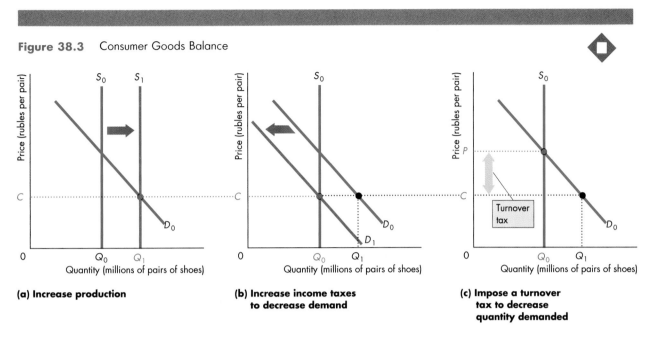

(a) Increase production

(b) Increase income taxes to decrease demand

(c) Impose a turnover tax to decrease quantity demanded

The cost of producing a consumer good (say, shoes) is C. The demand for shoes is D_0, and the quantity produced is Q_0. Three ways of achieving consumer goods balance are available. In part (a), the decision to increase output results in a shift in the supply curve to S_1. When the price is C and the quantity of shoes produced and consumed is Q_1, consumption goods balance is achieved. In part (b), income taxes are increased, reducing after-tax income. The demand for shoes decreases and the demand curve shifts to the left to D_1. The price is C and the quantity of shoes produced and consumed is Q_0. In part (c), the planners impose a turnover tax on shoes. A tax equal to the difference between P and C is imposed, raising the price of shoes to P. The quantity demanded decreases to Q_0 and consumer goods balance is achieved. The Soviet planner uses the turnover tax more frequently than the other two methods for achieving consumer goods balance.

tween the quantity demanded and quantity supplied. In this example (Fig. 38.3c), a turnover tax sufficient to increase the price to *P* ensures consumer goods balance in the market for shoes.

2. Labor Balance Labor balance is the achievement of a balance between the quantities supplied and demanded for each individual category of labor services. It is achieved, in the short run, by adjusting wage rates. Large differentials in wages—larger than those common in the United States—are necessary to achieve labor balance. In the long run, labor balance is also influenced by the planners' ability to direct resources allocated to education and training, favoring the acquisition of skills in short supply.

3. Credit Balance Credit balance is the achievement of a balance between the quantities of credit supplied and demanded. The banking system in the Soviet Union is owned and controlled by the state. Credit balance is achieved by the state banking system making available the credit that the planners have decided is required.

4. Capital Goods Balance Capital goods balance is the achievement of a balance between the quantities supplied and demanded of each type of capital good. The central planners decide how to allocate the scarce capital goods available and, through their control of credit, influence the demand for capital goods by individual production enterprises.

5. Materials Balance Materials balance is the achievement of a balance between the quantities demanded and supplied for each and every raw material and intermediate good used in the production of final

Table 38.2 Materials Balance

	Quantity Supplied			Quantity demanded				
				Intermediate goods			Final goods	
Material	Production	Inventories	Imports	Coal	Electric power	Nylon	Domestic	Foreign
Coal (tons)	490	10	0	50	300	50	75	25
Electric power (kilowatt-hours)	10,000	0	0	2,000	1,000	1,500	5,500	0
Nylon (yards)	20,000	200	2,000	0	0	0	22,200	0

Materials can be supplied from production, inventories, or imports. They are demanded as an input in the production of intermediate goods, for final domestic consumption, or export. Plans are drawn up to ensure that the quantity supplied equals the quantity demanded. To achieve materials balance, Soviet planners can increase production, decrease inventories, increase imports, decrease the quantity demanded as an intermediate good, decrease final demand, or decrease exports. Reductions in final domestic demand are the main method employed for achieving materials balance.

consumer goods and capital goods. This balancing exercise is the most complex aspect of Soviet planning. There are literally billions of raw materials and intermediate goods and the detailed plans for the material balances fill 70 volumes, or 12,000 pages, each year.

An example of a simplified materials balance schedule is set out in Table 38.2. There are just three materials. (The actual Soviet plans consider more than 30,000 separate materials at the central planning level, and a further 50,000 at the regional and local levels.) There are three sources of any material used in the production process: production, inventories, and imports. There are three broad categories of uses of any raw material or produced input: an intermediate input into the production of other goods, final domestic use either for consumption or investment purposes, and exports. For each material, a detailed plan showing the balance between the quantity supplied and quantity demanded is drawn up. For example, the first row of the table shows that 490 tons of coal are produced and 10 tons are taken from inventory. The quantity supplied is 500 tons of coal. The quantity demanded is made up of 50 tons as inputs in the coal industry itself, 300 tons to produce electric power, 50 tons to extract chemicals that are converted into nylon, 75 tons for domestic heating, and the 25 tons exported. The total quantity demanded is 500 tons. The plan for coal balances. The second row of the table shows the plan for electric power and the third row that for nylon.

Table 38.2 shows a balance between the quantity demanded and the quantity supplied of each material. Suppose that there is an excess of the quantity demanded over the quantity supplied of electric power. What can the Soviet planners do in such a situation? They can plan to produce more electric power or they can plan to produce less coal and less nylon, thereby reducing the amount of electric power demanded, or they can reduce the quantity of electric power for final domestic use. The Soviet planners usually choose the last of these options. If they were to increase the output of electric power, there would then be an increase in the quantity of coal demanded in the electric power industry. The increase in the quantity demanded of coal would result in a shortage in the coal sector that would require further adjustments in that sector. To balance the quantity supplied and quantity demanded of electric power by reducing the amount going to some other industry would result in that industry failing to achieve its targets.

The Market Sector Although the economy of the Soviet Union is a planned one, a substantial amount of economic activity takes place outside the planning and command economy. The most important component of the market sector is in agriculture. It is estimated that there are 35 million private plots worked by rural households. These private plots constitute less than 3 percent of the agricultural land of the Soviet Union but produce close to 25 percent of total agricultural output and a third of all the meat and milk produced. Some estimates suggest that the productivity on private plots is 40 times that of state enterprise farms and collective farms.

There are other economic activities undertaken by Soviet citizens outside the planning systems. Many of these are legal but some are not. Often they involve the illegal buying and selling of goods brought in illegally from abroad.

Perestroika At the June 1987 meeting of the Central Committee of the Communist party, Mikhail Gorbachev announced the first step in his reform plan, now universally known as *perestroika.* The key elements in this plan are:

- Increased independence for state enterprises
- Reform of accounting methods to calculate enterprises' full cost, revenue, and profit
- Requirement that each enterprise achieve the "highest end results" (maximum profits)
- The establishment of a direct link of income to performance
- Reduction in the power of central planners, relieving them of "interference in day-to-day activities"
- Reform of planning and pricing
- Decreased reliance on command system of management and increased role for individual incentives

Gorbachev spoke of the need to "create a powerful system of motives and stimuli [to] encourage workers to reveal their capability, work fruitfully [and] use productive resources most effectively." Remarkably, he declared that "there is only one criterion of justice [in the distribution of income]: whether or not it is earned."[2] Gorbachev even talked of abolishing job security and of closing down unprofitable state enterprises.

By the standards that have prevailed in the Soviet Union since 1928, Gorbachev's plans are revolutionary. They call for a redistribution of economic power and as such they are likely to meet a great deal of resistance. But to the extent that they contain the basis for improved economic performance, they also have a large number of supporters. How quickly and how far the Soviet Union will be able to travel along the road charted by Mikhail Gorbachev, we cannot yet say. But the direction that the Soviet economy is now taking is exciting and at least holds out the promise of a more efficient, productive, and prosperous Soviet Union.

We'll assess the performance of the Soviet economy and compare its performance with that of capitalist economies later in this chapter. But first, let's look at the other socialist giant, China.

China

China is the world's largest nation, with a population of more than a billion people. Chinese civilization is ancient and has a splendid history, but the modern nation—the People's Republic of China—dates only from 1949. A compact summary of key periods in the economic history of the People's Republic is presented in Table 38.3.

Modern China began when a revolutionary Communist movement, led by Mao Zedong, captured control of China, forcing the country's previous leader, Chiang Kai-shek (Jiang Jie-shi) onto the island of Formosa—now Taiwan. Like the Soviet Union, China is a socialist country. But unlike the Soviet Union, China is largely nonindustrialized—it is a developing country.

During the early years of the People's Republic, the country followed the Soviet model of economic planning and command. Urban manufacturing industry was taken over and operated by the state and the farms were collectivized. Also, following the Stalin model of the 1930s, primary emphasis was placed on the production of capital equipment.

The Great Leap Forward

In 1958, Mao Zedong set the Chinese economy on a sharply divergent path from that which the Soviet Union had followed. Mao called his new path the Great Leap Forward. The **Great Leap Forward**

[2] Mikhail Gorbachev, *Perestroika: New Thinking for Our Country and the World* (New York: Harper & Row, 1987).

Table 38.3 A Compact Summary of Key Periods in the Economic History of the People's Republic of China

Period	Main economic events/characteristics
1949	• People's Republic established under Mao Zedong
1949–1952	• Economy centralized under new communist government • Emphasis on heavy industry and "socialist transformation"
1952–1957	• First five-year plan
1958–1960	• The Great Leap Forward: an economic reform plan based on labor-intensive production methods; • Massive economic failure
1966	• Cultural Revolution: revolutionary zealots
1976	• Death of Mao Zedong
1978	• Deng's reforms: under leadership of Deng Xiaoping, liberalization of agriculture and introduction of individual incentives • Growth rates accelerated
1989	• Democracy movement; government crackdown

was an economic plan based on small-scale, labor-intensive production. The Great Leap Forward paid little or no attention to linking individual pay to individual effort. Instead, a revolutionary commitment to the success of collective plans was relied upon. The Great Leap Forward was an economic failure. Productivity increased, but so slowly that living standards hardly changed. In the agricultural sector, massive injections of modern, high-yield seeds, improved irrigation, and chemical fertilizers were insufficient to enable China to feed its population. The country became the largest importer of grains, edible vegetable oils, and even raw cotton.

The popular explanation within China for poor performance, especially in agriculture, was that the country had reached the limits of its arable land and that its population explosion was so enormous that agriculture was being forced to use substandard areas for farming. The key problem was that the revolutionary and ideological motivation for the Great Leap Forward degenerated into what came to be called the Cultural Revolution. Revolutionary zealots denounced productive managers, engineers, scientists, and scholars, and banished them to the life of the peasant. Schools and universities were closed and the accumulation of human capital was severely disrupted.

1978 Reforms

By 1978, two years after the death of Mao Zedong, the new Chinese leader, Deng Xiaoping, proclaimed major economic reforms. Collectivized agriculture was abolished. Agricultural land was distributed among households on long-term leases. In exchange for a lease, a household agreed to pay a fixed tax and contracted to sell part of its output to the state. But the household made its own decisions on cropping patterns, the quantity and types of fertilizers and other inputs to use, and also hired its own workers. Private farm markets were liberalized and farmers received a higher price for their produce. Also, the state increased the price that it paid to farmers, especially for cotton and other nongrain crops.

The results of the reforms of Deng Xiaoping have been astounding. Annual growth rates of output of cotton and oil-bearing crops increased a staggering fourteenfold. Soybean production, which had been declining at an annual rate of 1 percent between 1957 and 1978, now started to grow at 4 percent a year. Growth rates of yields per acre also increased dramatically. By 1984, a country that six years earlier had been the world's largest importer of agricultural products became a food exporter!

The reforms not only produced massive expansion in the agricultural sector. Increased rural incomes brought an expanding rural industrial sector that, by the middle 1980s, was employing a fifth of the rural population.

Reform of the manufacturing sector has provided stronger incentives for enterprise managers and a greater degree of independence for making production decisions. These reforms, similar to those now being proposed by Gorbachev in the Soviet Union, have resulted in rapid growth in industrial output. China has gone even further and is encouraging foreign investment and joint ventures. In addition, China is experimenting with formal capital markets and now has a stock market.

Motivated partly by political considerations, China is proclaiming the virtues of what it calls the "one country, two systems" approach to economic management. The political source of this movement is the existence of two capitalist enclaves in which China has a close interest—Taiwan and Hong Kong. China claims sovereignty over Taiwan. As such, it wants to create an atmosphere in which it becomes possible for China to be "reunified" at some future date. Hong Kong, a British crown colony, is currently leased by Britain from China and that lease terminates in 1997. When the lease expires, Hong Kong will become part of China. Anxious not to damage the economic prosperity of Hong Kong, China is proposing to continue operating Hong Kong as a capitalist economy. With Hong Kong and Taiwan as part of the People's Republic of China, the stage will be set for the creation of other capitalist "islands" in such dynamic cities as Shanghai.

Whether China has invented a new economic system—one country, two systems—is too early to say. And the violent suppression of the democracy movement in Tiananmen Square in the summer of 1989 further clouds our view of where China is heading. But the experiment in comparative economic systems currently going on in China is one of the most exciting that the world has seen. Economists of all political shades of opinion will closely watch its outcome, and its lessons will be of enormous value for future generations—whatever those lessons turn out to be.

Comparing Capitalism and Socialism

We have now defined capitalist and socialist economic systems and have described the economic organization of some of the leading examples of the alternative types. In this final section, we'll use some of the economic models that we have studied to analyze the workings of capitalist and socialist economic systems. We'll also compare the performances of the two systems in practice.

To make our comparison of the working of a capitalist and socialist economy as clear as possible, we're going to study a model economy. The model economy, under capitalism, will have perfect competition and no external economies or diseconomies. We'll study the same economy under socialism.

Capitalism

Under capitalism, individual households choose the quantities of productive resources to supply and the quantities of goods and services to demand. Each firm seeks to make the biggest possible profit and to produce at the lowest possible cost. The demand for a good or service is summarized by its market demand curve. The market demand curve also shows the value placed on each extra unit of the good. The supply of the good is summarized by the market supply curve. The supply curve also shows the marginal cost of producing each unit of the good. The equilibrium price and quantity are determined where the supply and demand curves intersect.

Figure 38.4 illustrates a market in a perfectly competitive capitalist economy—the market for shoes. The demand curve for shoes (D) and the supply curve of shoes (S) intersect at quantity Q_C and price P_C. At this price and quantity, the perfectly competitive capitalist economy achieves *allocative* efficiency. The value placed on the last pair of shoes

Figure 38.4 Prices and Quantities Under Capitalism

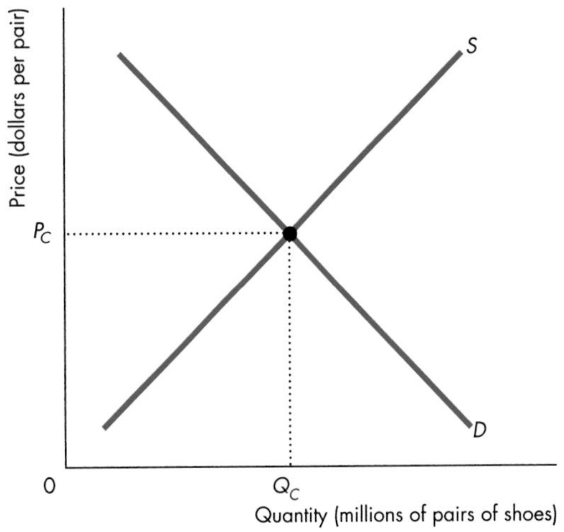

The preferences and choices of households determine the demand for shoes (curve D). The profit-maximization decisions of firms determine the supply of shoes (curve S). With a perfectly competitive shoe market, capitalism produces quantity Q_C at price P_C. If there are no external costs and benefits, this outcome achieves allocative efficiency.

produced (P_C) is the same as the marginal cost of producing them.

What happens under socialism?

Socialism

Now imagine that the economy whose market for shoes is depicted in Fig. 38.4 is taken over by a socialist government. Instead of operating under a capitalist system, it is now operated under centralized socialist planning. Let's see how the shoe market will perform under this new system of economic control. Figure 38.5 illustrates the shoe market in a socialist economy.

Consumers still have their views about the value they place on goods and services, so the demand for shoes is represented by the same demand curve. There is a difference, however, on the supply side.

Figure 38.5 Prices and Quantities under Socialism

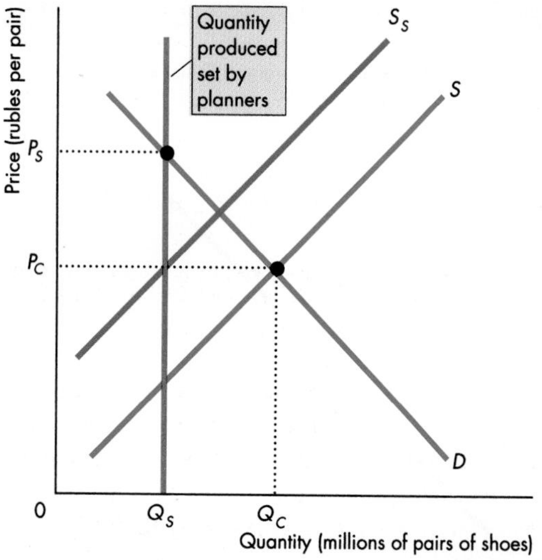

Consumers determine the demand for shoes (curve D). Socialist managers determine the supply of shoes (curve S_S). Socialist managers have less incentive than capitalist entrepreneurs to supply goods at least cost, so the supply curve S_S lies to the left of the capitalism supply curve S. The central planning process sets a target output of shoes for the economy of Q_S. To achieve a balance of the quantity demanded and the quantity supplied, a tax is imposed on shoes to raise the price to P_S. Socialism delivers a lower quantity of shoes traded and a higher price of shoes than does capitalism.

Under socialism, firms do not own the means of production, and so the individual manager of a plant has no incentive to maximize profit and minimize cost. The manager's income is determined by the central planner and the manager receives a bonus if the firm achieves its target output, but there is no incentive for output to be produced in the most efficient possible way. On the contrary, the manager has an incentive to produce inefficiently. To see this, we need to consider how production targets are determined under socialism.

The central planner sets targets for total output and allocates those targets to the different production plants. The target output rate for any individual plant depends on what that plant has historically been able to produce. Therefore it always pays for a manager of a plant to pretend that his plant can produce less than what in fact it can. Therefore the supply curve under socialism is, in general, to the left of the supply curve under capitalism. The line labeled S_S in Fig. 38.5 is a possible supply curve for shoes under socialism, given the supply curve S under capitalism.

The gap between the socialist and capitalist supply curves is waste or inefficiency. The gap arises because the manager of the socialist factory has little incentive to produce the target output at minimum cost, and a high incentive to hide the true potential of his plant so that he will be assigned an easier production target.

The next big difference between capitalism and socialism concerns the way in which prices and quantities are determined. The quantity supplied is determined partly by the plans of the central planners and partly by the actions of the individual enterprises and the incentives that they face. Suppose that the outcome of the planning process is a quantity of shoes produced of Q_S. To achieve a balance between the quantity demanded and quantity supplied, the socialist planners will have to introduce a tax on shoes, raising their price to P_S. At this price, there is a balance between the quantity demanded and quantity supplied.

Central planning with state ownership produces a smaller quantity of shoes, Q_S compared with Q_C, at a higher price, P_S compared with P_C, than the perfectly competitive capitalist economy. This inferior performance has arisen from two sources: inefficient production resulting in higher average cost and production of the wrong quantity. Part of this problem is addressed by market socialism, but part is not. Let's see the difference that market socialism makes.

Market Socialism

Again, in order to compare the different systems, we will continue to look at the same economy and its shoe market. The demand for shoes remains as before and is shown again in Fig. 38.6. Again, the socialist manager has less incentive than the capitalist manager to maximize profit and produce at least cost, so his supply curve is S_S rather than the capitalist supply curve S. But the price is now determined in a decentralized manner in the market for shoes. The supply curve S_S and the demand curve D intersect at price P_{MS} and at quantity Q_{MS}. This price is higher than the competitive capitalist price and the quantity is smaller, but more shoes are produced and sold at a lower price under market socialism than under centrally planned socialism, as depicted in Fig. 38.5.

To get the economy to produce the capitalist quantity of shoes at the capitalist price, incentives have to be put in place at the individual firm level to encourage socialist factory managers to produce at least cost and be as efficient as capitalist managers.

Figure 38.6 Prices and Quantities under Market Socialism

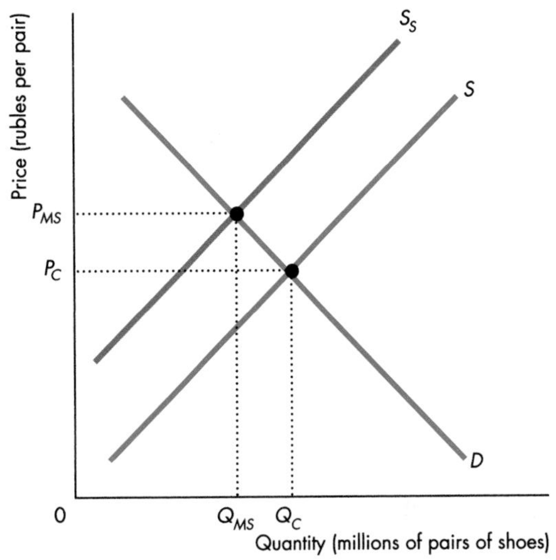

The market socialist demand and supply curves are the same as they are under socialism. The price of shoes is set in a decentralized way, so that the quantity demanded and the quantity supplied are equal. If the price is set too low, the central planner will gradually increase it. If the price is set too high, the central planner will gradually decrease it. On the average, the price is P_{MS} and the quantity traded is Q_{MS}. A smaller quantity of shoes is traded and at a higher price than in a perfectly competitive capitalist economy. But more shoes are traded and at a lower price than under socialism.

Perestroika in the Model Economy

You can interpret *perestroika* in this model economy. Under the central planning methods of Stalin, the Soviet economy is producing too few shoes at too high a price. It is the situation depicted in Fig. 38.5. By moving to the decentralized planning that countries such as Hungary and Yugoslavia employ, the socialist economy can do better, lowering the price and increasing the quantity produced, as shown in Fig. 38.6. Such a move is one part of *perestroika*. But the socialist economy can do even better still, provided it can place strong enough incentives at the factory level to achieve maximum profits and produce efficiently. If that does prove to be possible, the socialist economy will be able to lower the price and increase the quantity produced to equal the competitive capitalist levels.

Inefficiencies in Capitalism

In the previous model economies, elements of inefficiency in capitalism have been ignored. That does not mean that they are not present in the real world. Capitalist economies do not function like the perfectly competitive ideal. There are external costs and benefits, monopoly elements, taxes and subsidies, all of which move the economy away from the competitive ideal. But these problems are present in socialist economies as well. They do not directly enter into an evaluation of the two systems. Thus we cannot compare the performance of capitalist and socialist economies merely by looking at an idealized, perfectly competitive model.

The ultimate test of capitalism and socialism comes not in a comparison of models, but of actual performance. How have socialist economies performed and how does that performance compare with that of capitalist economies?

Economic Growth and Average Living Standards

One way of comparing the success of alternative economic systems is to look at their capacity to deliver

Table 38.4 Annual Growth Rates in the United States, Japan, and the Soviet Union

Years	Annual growth rate (percentage)		
	United States	Japan	Soviet Union
1840–1885	4.4		
1885–1905	3.7	5.7	3.3 (1885–1913)
1905–1929	3.4	7.4	
1929–1950	2.8		5.4 (1928–1937)
1950–1960	3.2	11.5	6.0 (1940–1960)
1960–1970	4.0		5.1
1970–1979	3.1		4.0
1980–1986	3.1		4.0

Source: Paul R. Gregory and Robert C. Stuart, *Soviet Economic Structure and Performance*, 2nd ed. (New York: Harper & Row, 1981).

economic growth and high standards of living. Table 38.4 tells us what has happened in the United States, Japan, and the Soviet Union over 140 years of history. As you can see, throughout this period, the United States has experienced steady and sustained economic growth rates of between 3 and 4 percent a year. This growth rate has produced a living standard for Americans that is the highest in the world. Impressive though the American growth performance has been, Japan, another capitalist economy, has done better. By growing in excess of 10 percent a year in many of the postwar years, it has transformed itself from a war-devastated country in 1945 to one of the richest industrial giants in the world today.

Compare these performances with that of the Soviet Union. The Soviet Union was a capitalist country until the revolution in 1917. It was, however, a very poor country and most people worked in the agricultural sector. Eleven years after the Revolution, in 1928, the Soviet Union instituted central planning and established its first five-year plan. Since that date, Soviet economic growth has been impressive. The growth rates are set out in Table 38.4. As you can see, Soviet growth rates are larger than those of the United States. They are not as high, however, as those of Japan. Nevertheless, they have resulted in the Soviet Union having, by 1978, a per capita gross national product that approached one half that of the United States.

The Soviet Union achieved its rapid growth primarily by squeezing consumption and focusing on capital accumulation and investment. In the United States, consumption and investment have grown at roughly the same rate over the long term. In the Soviet Union, consumption has grown at a pace that is approximately one half that of the growth rate of investment. During the first two five-year plans (the period from 1928 to 1937), consumption grew by only 0.7 percent a year while GNP grew by 5.4 percent a year and investment grew by 14.5 percent a year. Not until the late 1960s did consumption and investment in the Soviet Union grow at a similar pace. Thus although the Soviet Union has grown quickly, it has done so at enormous cost—Soviet planners have squeezed consumption to a point that capitalist countries would not have tolerated.

The growth performance of China also provides interesting evidence on the performance of a socialist economy. Figure 38.7 illustrates the rise in per capita income since 1965. During the Cultural Revolution of the 1960s, per capita income actually fell. The growth rate increased quickly in the late 1960s, but it then became modest until Deng's reforms of the late 1970s. Following those reforms, per capita income began to grow at a rate that, if maintained, will double the standard of living every ten years. Thus when China has relied most heavily on socialist methods, its growth rate has been negative or slow, and when it has relied on capitalist methods, its growth rate has increased.

Productivity How productive are the socialist economies? We have noted that there is less incentive for managers under socialism to use the least-cost method of production and be efficient than there is under capitalism. Calculations by Soviet experts suggest that national income per unit of productive resources used in the Soviet Union is slightly less than 50 percent of what it is in the U.S. economy and only 65 percent of the productivity of France, West Germany, and the United Kingdom.[3]

[3]Paul R. Gregory and Robert C. Stuart, *Soviet Economic Structure and Performance*, 2nd ed. (New York: Harper & Row, 1981).

Figure 38.7 Economic Growth in China

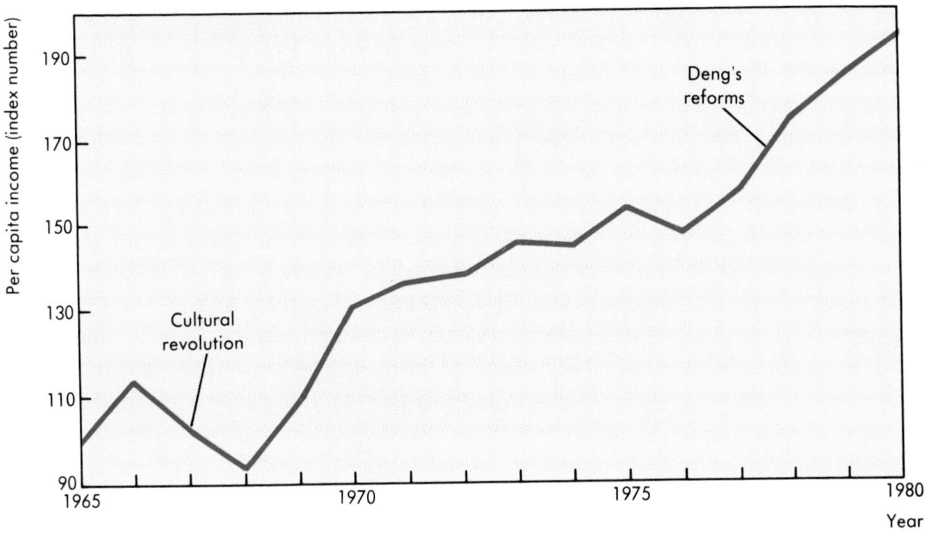

The growth of per capita income in China is strongly influenced by the economic system. During the Cultural Revolution, per capita income fell. Under a central planning and command mechanism in the early 1970s, per capita income grew at a moderate pace. Under capitalist methods of production in agriculture following the 1978 reforms, per capita income growth increased dramatically.

Source: **International Monetary Fund, *International Financial Statistics* (1988).**

From the available evidence, it appears as if socialism is substantially less successful than capitalism at producing high living standards. Does it, however, produce greater equality in the distribution of income?

Income Inequality under the Two Systems

There is considerable inequality of income and wealth in our own economy. Is the same true of the socialist economies of Eastern Europe and the Soviet Union? The answer appears to be yes. The Soviet Union has not published much data on the distribution of income among individuals and families. But from the evidence that is available it appears that the distribution of wage income in the Soviet Union is about the same as that in the capitalist economies of Western Europe and North America. But the overall distribution of income also depends on the distribution of income from the ownership of capital. Comparing this overall distribution of income is possible only in approximate terms, as Fig. 38.8 shows. The broad conclusion that emerges from the studies that have been done is that the overall distribution of after-tax income in the Soviet Union is about as equal as the distribution in the welfare state economies of Western Europe, such as the United Kingdom, and more equal than other capitalist economies, such as the United States.

Ceteris Paribus Making comparisons between countries is a bit like trying to compare apples and oranges. They differ in so many respects that it is hardly clear that we have been able to isolate the factors responsible for differences in their performances. One important difference between nations is their cultural history and the customs and habits of their people. Ideally, we'd like to be able to compare the performances of countries in which these historical and cultural factors are similar. That is, we'd like to be able to hold all these other things constant.

A few comparisons between socialist and capitalist economies are available that do almost satisfy this *ceteris paribus* condition. Examples are East Germany and West Germany, and North Korea and South Korea. East Germany and West Germany are historically and culturally similar and, at the end of World War II, were in per capita terms almost the same. West Germany became a capitalist economy

Figure 38.8 Socialist and Capitalist Lorenz Curves

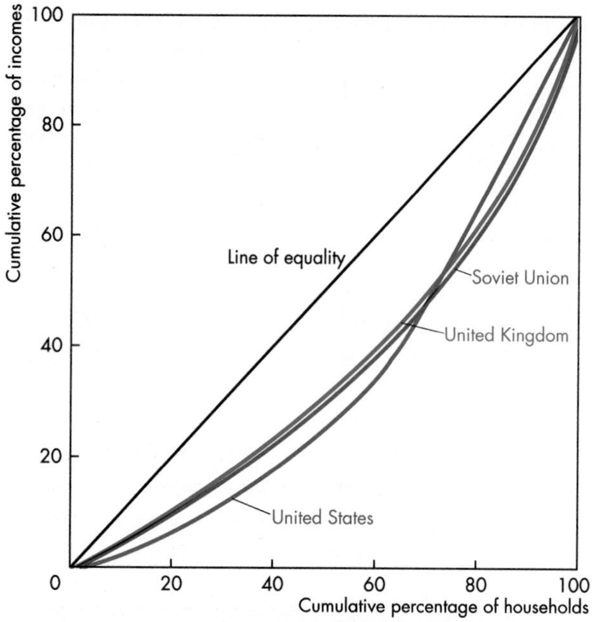

The degree of income inequality is illustrated by the Lorenz curve. If a given percentage of households have that same given percentage of income, incomes are distributed equally. The further the Lorenz curve is from the line of equality, the greater the degree of inequality. The Lorenz curves for the Soviet Union and the United Kingdom show that those two countries have an almost identical distribution of income and one that is more equal than that in the United States.

and East Germany a socialist one. Today, per capita income in West Germany exceeds that in East Germany by a sizable margin. At the end of the Korean War, in 1953, North Korea and South Korea embarked upon opposite roads. North Korea adopted the socialist model and South Korea the capitalist one. South Korea had fewer resources than North Korea, but today South Korea, a capitalist country, dominates socialist North Korea in per capita income and wealth.

We've seen that socialist economies can achieve rapid growth rates by choosing a resource allocation that favors the production of capital equipment and holds the growth of consumer goods production in check. We've also seen, however, that prolonged and sustained growth can be achieved by capitalist economies. Also, capitalist economies appear to achieve a greater measure of economic and allocative efficiency. The degree of inequality is less pronounced in the Soviet Union than in the United States but similar to the welfare state capitalist economies of Western Europe.

■ This comparison of the economic performance of socialist and capitalist economies seems to favor capitalism. A practical consequence of this comparison is the universal movement that is now taking place toward greater reliance on private enterprise and market mechanisms and less emphasis on government intervention, regulation, and control. For the moment, right or wrong, the view is increasingly widely held that capitalism works and socialism does not. The evidence generated by the variety of experiments conducted since World War II appears to support that conclusion. But it is the hallmark of a good scientist to maintain an open and skeptical mind even in the face of strong evidence. A great deal of work is required and no doubt more will be done before the final verdict on the superiority of one economic system over another is delivered.

SUMMARY

The Fundamental Economic Problem

No economic system can abolish the fundamental economic problem of scarcity. Each system attempts to get the economy onto its production possibility frontier, choose a point on the frontier, and distribute the gains from economic activity. (pp. 592–593)

Alternative Economic Systems

Economic systems vary in two dimensions—who owns capital and land and who allocates resources. Under capitalism, capital and land are privately owned and resources are allocated by markets. Under socialism, capital and land are owned by the state and resources are allocated by a command planning system.

Capitalism is based on the political philosophy that individual liberty is paramount. Individual preferences guide the production of goods and services. Socialism is an economic system based on the political philosophy that the private ownership of capital and land enables the wealthy to exploit the poor. The goods and services produced under socialism reflect the preferences not of individual consumers but of central planners.

Welfare state capitalism combines private ownership of capital and land with a large degree of state intervention. Market socialism combines state ownership of capital with market-determined prices.

All countries employ economic systems that contain some elements of capitalism and socialism. The United States and Japan come closest to being capitalist economies and the Soviet Union and China are examples of socialist economies. The countries of Western Europe employ welfare state capitalism, while Eastern European countries such as Hungary and Yugoslavia employ market socialism. (pp. 593–596)

The Varieties of Capitalism

The capitalist economy whose performance has been most spectacular is Japan. Its performance has been based on a strong reliance on the free market and capitalist methods of production, a small scale of government and low taxes, and pro-business government intervention. Japan's Ministry of International Trade and Industry (MITI) has taken an active and entrepreneurial role in protecting and subsidizing industries identified as priority growth areas and fostering the decline of inefficient industries.

Capitalism in Western Europe has larger elements of socialism than capitalism in Japan or the United States. Government expenditure and taxes are higher and many industries are publicly owned or nationalized. In recent years, European welfare states have been retreating from state ownership and high taxes. (pp. 596–598)

The Soviet Union

The Soviet Union is a vast, resource-rich nation that uses a socialist economic system with a central planning and command mechanism. Soviet planning is managed by GOSPLAN and is based on a series of detailed plans for consumer goods, labor, credit, capital goods, and materials. Targets are specified for production enterprises and enterprises are encouraged to achieve their targets by a complex system of incentives. They are also monitored by local officials of the Communist party and of state ministries. Since 1987, the Soviet Union has embarked upon a process of economic restructuring called *perestroika*. This restructuring involves a move away from central planning and command toward decentralized incentives and market prices. (pp. 598–603)

China

Since the foundation of the People's Republic of China, economic management has been through turbulent changes. At first, China used the Soviet system of central planning. It then introduced the Great Leap Forward, which in turn degenerated into the Cultural Revolution. China at first grew quickly with heavy reliance on state planning and capital accumulation, but growth slowed and, at times, per capita income actually fell. In 1978, China revolutionized its economic management, placing greater emphasis on private incentives and markets. As a consequence, productivity grew at a rapid rate and per capita income increased.

When Hong Kong becomes part of China at the end of this century, and if Taiwan is reunified with China, as the Chinese wish, these two islands will be permitted to remain capitalist. Furthermore, China is establishing what are, in effect, capitalist zones within China. Recent political events cast a serious shadow across the Chinese economy and raise doubts about its future course. But if the Chinese experiment continues, it will become an exciting real-world laboratory test of alternative economic systems. (pp. 603–605)

Comparing Capitalism and Socialism

The historical record of capitalism and socialism shows that socialism is capable of achieving high growth rates of per capita income. But it does so at the cost of squeezing consumption to levels below those that would be tolerated in capitalist economies. The most spectacular growth performance has been achieved by capitalist economies or by socialist economies when they have relaxed their central planning and command mechanisms and relied on decentralized incentives and markets. Productivity is higher in capitalist economies than in socialist economies. The distribution of income is more equal in socialist economies than in some capitalist economies but it is similar to that in welfare state capitalist countries. (pp. 605–610)

KEY CONCEPTS

Key Figures and Tables

REVIEW QUESTIONS

1 What are the three aspects of the economic problem that any economic system has to tackle?

2 What are the main economic systems? Set out the key features of each.

3 How does capitalism solve the economic problem? What determines how much of each good to produce?

4 How does socialism solve the economic problem? What determines how much of each good to produce?

5 How does market socialism determine the price and quantity of each good?

6 Give examples of countries that are capitalist, socialist, market socialist, and welfare state capitalist. (Do not cite those countries that appeared in Fig. 38.1).

7 Describe the capitalist economy of Japan. What are the sources of its dramatic success?

8 Describe the role of the Ministry of International Trade and Industry (MITI) in Japan. Compare and contrast capitalism in Western Europe with that in the United States and Japan. Describe the planning and command system in the Soviet Union.

9 How does GOSPLAN achieve consumer goods balance?

10 How does GOSPLAN achieve materials balance?

11 What are the main components of *perestroika?*

12 Review the main episodes in China's economic management since 1949.

13 Compare the economic growth performance of the United States, the Soviet Union, and Japan. What do we learn from this comparison?

14 Compare the degree of income inequality in socialist and capitalist economies. Why is the distribution of income more unequal in the United States than in the Soviet Union?

15 What might we learn from the current "one-country, two-systems" experiment that is going on in China?

Glossary

Absolute advantage A person has an absolute advantage in production if that person can produce more of all goods than anyone else. A country has an absolute advantage if its output per unit of inputs of all goods is higher than that of another country.

Agent A person who works for a principal and performs various activities, some of which are not observable by the principal. *See also* Principal.

Allocative efficiency The situation that occurs when no resources are wasted—when no one can be made better off without someone else's being made worse off.

Annual plan A plan of the Soviet government specifying month-by-month targets for output, prices, inputs, investment, and money and credit flows.

Antitrust law A law prohibiting certain kinds of market activity, such as monopoly and monopolistic practices.

Asset Anything of value that a household, firm, or government owns.

Assortative mating Marrying within one's own socioeconomic group.

Assumptions The foundation on which a model is built.

Average cost pricing rule A rule that sets the price equal to average total cost.

Average fixed cost Total fixed cost per unit of output—total fixed cost divided by output.

Average product Total product per unit of variable input.

Average revenue Total revenue divided by the quantity sold. Average revenue also equals price.

Average revenue product Total revenue divided by the quantity of the factor hired.

Average revenue product curve A curve that shows the average revenue product of a factor at each quantity of the factor hired.

Average total cost Total cost per unit of output—total cost divided by output.

Average variable cost Total variable cost per unit of output—total variable cost divided by output.

Axes The scale lines on a graph.

Balance of trade The value of exports minus the value of imports.

Balance sheet A list of assets and liabilities.

Barriers to entry Restrictions on the entry of new firms into an industry.

Barter The direct exchange of goods for goods.

Bequest A gift from one generation to the next.

Bilateral monopoly A market structure in which a single buyer and a single seller confront each other.

Binding arbitration A process in which a third party—an arbitrator—determines wages and other employment conditions.

Black market An illegal trading arrangement in which buyers and sellers do business at a price higher than the legally imposed price ceiling.

Bond A legally enforceable obligation to pay specified sums of money at specified future dates.

Bond market The market in which the bonds issued by firms and governments are traded.

Bond yield The interest on a bond, expressed as a percentage of the price of the bond.

Break-even point An output rate at which total revenue equals total cost (and at which profit is zero).

Budget equation An equation that states the maximum possible consumption of one good, given income, prices, and consumption of other goods.

Budget line The limits to a household's consumption choices.

Bureaucrats Appointed officials who work at various levels in government departments.

Capacity The output rate at which a plant's average total cost is at a minimum.

Capacity output The output at which the firm's cost per unit produced is minimized.

Capital The real assets—equipment, buildings, tools, and other manufactured goods used in production—owned by a household, firm, or government.

Capital accumulation The growth of capital resources.

Capital goods Goods that are added to capital resources.

Capital-intensive technique A method of production that uses a relatively large amount of capital and a relatively small amount of labor to produce a given quantity of output.

Capitalism An economic system based on the private ownership of capital and land used in production and on market allocation of resources.

Capital resources Goods that have been produced and can now be used in the production of other goods and services.

Capital stock The stock of plant, equipment, and buildings (including residential housing).

Capture theory of regulation A theory of regulation that states that the regulations that exist are those that maximize producer surplus.

Cartel A group of producers who enter into a collusive agreement to restrict output in order to raise prices and profits.

Central planning A method of allocating resources by command.

Ceteris paribus Other things being equal, or other things remaining constant.

Change in demand A shift of the entire demand curve that occurs when some influence on buyers' plans, other than the price of the good, changes.

Change in quantity demanded A movement along a demand curve that results from a change in the price of the good.

Change in quantity supplied A movement along the supply curve that results from a change in the price of the good.

Change in supply A shift in the entire supply curve that occurs when some influence on producers' plans, other than the price of the good, changes.

Choke price The price at which it no longer pays to use a natural resource.

Closed economy An economy that has no links with any other economy.

Closed shop An arrangement (illegal since the passage of the Taft-Hartley Act in 1947) in which only union members may be hired.

Collective bargaining A process of negotiation between representatives of employers and unions.

Collusive agreement An agreement between two (or more) producers to restrict output in order to raise prices and profits.

Command mechanism A method of determining *what*, *how*, and *for whom* goods and services are produced, based on the authority of a ruler or ruling body.

Commercial bank A financial intermediary that takes deposits and makes loans.

Commissions and royalties A compensation rule based on the value of sales.

Common stock Stock that entitles its holder to vote at stockholders' meetings but gives a claim to dividends only if the directors vote to pay one. Such a dividend is paid at a variable rate, determined by the directors and varying according to the firm's profits.

Communism An economic system based on state ownership of capital and land, on central planning, and on distributing income in accordance with the rule "from each according to ability, to each according to need."

Comparable worth The payment of equal wages for different jobs that are judged to be comparable.

Comparative advantage A person has a comparative advantage in producing a good if he or she can produce that good at a lower opportunity cost than anyone else. A country has a comparative advantage in producing a good if it can produce that good at a lower opportunity cost than any other country.

Compensation rule A formula for calculating a person's income.

Competition A contest for command over scarce resources.

Complement A good that is used in conjunction with another good.

Constant returns to scale Technological conditions under which the percentage increase in a firm's output is equal to the percentage increase in its inputs.

Consumer equilibrium A situation in which a consumer has allocated his or her income in a manner that maximizes utility.

Consumer surplus The difference between the value of a good and its price.

Consumption The process of using up goods and services.

Consumption goods Goods that are used up as soon as they are produced.

Convertible stock Stock that entitles its holder to receive a fixed coupon payment, as a bondholder does, and to convert the stock into a fixed number of shares of common stock.

Cooperation People working with others to achieve a common end.

Cooperative equilibrium An equilibrium resulting from each player responding rationally to the credible threat of the other player to inflict heavy damage if the agreement is broken.

Coordinates Lines running from a point on a graph perpendicularly to the axes.

Coordination mechanism A mechanism that makes the choices of one individual compatible with the choices of others.

Corporation A firm owned by one or more limited liability stockholders.

Cost Total payment made by a firm for the services of factors of production.

Countervailing duty A tariff that is imposed to enable domestic producers to compete with subsidized foreign producers.

Coupon payment The amount paid each year to the holder of a bond.

Craft union A group of workers have a similar range of skills but work for different firms and industries.

Cross elasticity of demand The percentage change in the quantity demanded of a good divided by the percentage change in the price of a substitute or complement.

Curve Any relationship between two variables plotted on a graph, even a linear relationship.

Deadweight loss A measure of allocative inefficiency as the reduction in consumer and producer surplus resulting from restricting output below its efficient level.

Decentralized planning *See* Market socialism.

Decision maker Any person or organized group of persons who make economic choices.

Decreasing returns to scale Technological conditions under which the percentage change in a firm's output is less than the percentage change in the scale of inputs; sometimes called diseconomies of scale.

Demand The entire relationship between the quantity demanded of a good and its price.

Demand curve A graph showing the relationship between the quantity demanded of a good and its price, holding everything else constant.

Demand schedule A list of the quantities demanded at different prices, holding everything else constant.

Depreciation The fall in the value of capital or the value of a durable input resulting from its use and from the passage of time.

Deregulation The removal of rules restricting prices, product standards and types, and entry conditions.

Derived demand Demand for an input not for its own sake but in order to use it in the production of goods and services.

Diminishing marginal rate of substitution The general tendency for the marginal rate of substitution to diminish as the consumer moves along an indifference curve, increasing the consumption of good x and decreasing the consumption of good y.

Diminishing marginal return A situation in which the marginal product of the last worker hired falls short of the marginal product of the second last worker hired.

Diminishing marginal utility The decline in marginal utility that occurs as more and more of a good is consumed.

Discounting The conversion of a future sum of money to its present value.

Distribution after taxes and transfers The income distribution that takes account of taxes levied and transfers made by the government.

Dominant strategy A strategy in a game that is the unique best action regardless of the action taken by the other player.

Dominant strategy equilibrium A Nash equilibrium in which there is a dominant strategy for each player in a game. *See also* Nash equilibrium.

Double coincidence of wants A situation that occurs when person A wants to buy what person B is selling and person B wants to buy what person A is selling.

Dumping The sale of a good in a foreign market for a lower price than in the domestic market or for a lower price than its cost of production.

Duopoly A market structure in which two producers of a commodity compete with each other.

Durable input A factor of production that is not entirely used up in a single production period.

Economic activity What people do to cope with scarcity.

Economic depreciation The change in the market price of a durable input over a given period. Economic depreciation over a year is calculated as the market price of the input at the beginning of the year minus its market price at the end of the year.

Economic efficiency A state in which the cost of producing a given output is as low as possible.

Economic growth The persistent expansion of our production possibilities.

Economic rent An income received by the owner of a factor over and above the amount required to induce that owner to offer the factor for use.

Economics The study of how people use their limited resources to try to satisfy unlimited wants.

Economic theory A generalization that enables us to understand and predict economic choices.

Economies of scale *See* Increasing returns to scale.

Economies of scope Decreases in average total cost made possible by increasing the number of different goods produced.

Economizing Making the best use of scarce resources.

Economy A mechanism that allocates scarce resources among competing uses.

Efficient market A market in which the actual price embodies all currently available relevant information.

Elastic demand Elasticity is greater than 1; the quantity demanded of a good drops by a larger percentage than its price rises.

Elasticity of demand *See* Price elasticity of demand.

Elasticity of supply The percentage change in the quantity supplied of a good divided by the percentage change in its price.

Endowment The resources that people have.

End-state theory of distributive justice A theory of distributive justice that examines the fairness of the outcome of economic activity.

Entry The act of setting up a new firm in an industry.

Equilibrium A situation in which everyone has economized—that is, all individuals have made the best possible choices in the light of their own preferences and given their endowments, technologies, and information—and in which all choices have been coordinated and made compatible with all other choices. Equilibrium is the solution or outcome of an economic model.

Equilibrium price The price at which the quantity demanded equals the quantity supplied. At this price, opposing forces exactly balance each other.

Equity or equity capital The owner's stake in a business.

Excess capacity A state in which output is below that at which average total cost is at a minimum.

Excise tax A tax on the sale of a particular commodity. The tax may be set as a fixed dollar amount per unit of the commodity, in which case it is called a *specific tax.* Alternatively, the tax may be set as a fixed percentage of the value of the commodity, in which case it is called an *ad valorem tax.*

Exhaustible natural resources Natural resources that can be used only once and that cannot be replaced once used.

Exit The act of closing down a firm and leaving an industry.

Expenditure The amount spent for the purchase of a good. It equals the price of the good multiplied by the quantity bought.

Exports The goods and services that one country sells to people in other countries.

External benefits Those benefits accruing to people other than the buyer of a good.

External costs Those costs borne not by the producer but by other members of society.

External diseconomies Factors outside the control of a firm that raise its costs as industry output rises.

External economies Factors beyond the control of a firm that lower its costs as industry output rises.

Externality A cost or benefit arising from an economic transaction that falls on a third party and that is not taken into account by those who undertake the transaction.

Factor market A market in which the factors of production are bought and sold.

Factors of production The economy's productive resources—land, labor, and capital.

Fair Labor Standards Act An act making it illegal to hire an adult worker for less than $3.35 an hour.

Financial assets Paper claims of the holder against another household or firm.

Financial intermediary A firm whose principal business is taking deposits, making loans, and buying securities.

Firm An institution that buys or hires factors of production and organizes them to produce and sell goods and services.

Five-year plan A plan of the Soviet government specifying in broad outline general targets and directions for a period of five years.

Fixed cost A cost that is independent of the output level.

Fixed inputs Those inputs whose quantity used cannot be varied in the short run.

Flow A quantity measured over a period of time.

Four-firm concentration ratio The percentage of the value of sales accounted for by the largest four firms in an industry.

Free rider Someone who consumes a good without paying for it.

Free-rider problem The tendency for the scale of provision of a public good to be too small—to be allocatively inefficient—if it is privately provided.

Game theory A method of analyzing strategic behavior.

General Agreement on Tariffs and Trade (GATT) An agreement that limits government taxes and restrictions on international trade.

Goods and services All the valuable things that people produce. Goods are tangible, and services are intangible.

Goods market A market in which goods and services are bought and sold.

GOSPLAN The Soviet planning committee responsible for drawing up and implementing the state's economic plans.

Government An organization that provides goods and services to households and firms, and redistributes income and wealth.

Government firm A firm that is owned and operated by a government.

Government license A license that controls entry into particular occupations, professions, or industries.

Great Leap Forward An economic plan for postrevolutionary China based on small-scale, labor-intensive production motivated by revolutionary zeal.

Gross investment The value of new capital equipment purchased in a given time period.

Historical cost Cost that values resources at the prices actually paid for them.

Horizontal integration The merger of two or more firms providing essentially the same product or service.

Hotelling principle The proposition that the market for a stock of a natural resource is in equilibrium when the price of the resource is expected to rise at a rate equal to the interest rate.

Household Any group of people living together as a decision-making unit.

Household production The production of goods and services for consumption within the household.

Human capital The accumulated skill and knowledge of human beings.

Human resources The muscle power and brain power of human beings.

Implications The outcome of a model that follows logically from its assumptions.

Implicit rental rate The rent that a firm implicitly pays to itself for the use of the durable inputs that it owns.

Imports The goods and services that we buy from people in other countries.

Imputed cost An opportunity cost that does not involve an actual expenditure of cash.

Incentive An inducement to an agent to behave in a particular way.

Income The amount received by households in payment for the services of factors of production.

Income effect The effect of a change in income on the quantity consumed.

Income elasticity of demand The percentage change in the quantity demanded divided by the percentage change in income.

Increasing marginal returns A situation in which the marginal product of the last worker hired exceeds the marginal product of the second last worker hired.

Increasing returns to scale Technological conditions under which the percentage increase in a firm's output exceeds the percentage increase in its inputs. Under these conditions, reductions in the cost of producing a unit of a good occur as the scale of output increases.

Indifference curve A line showing all possible combinations of two goods among which the consumer is indifferent.

Individual demand The relationship between the quantity demanded by a single individual and the price of a good.

Industrial union A group of workers with a variety of skills and job types but who work for the same firm or industry.

Inelastic demand Elasticity is between 0 and 1; the quantity demanded of a good drops by a smaller percentage than its price rises.

Inferior good A good the demand for which decreases when income increases.

Intellectual property The intangible product of creative effort, protected by copyrights and patents. This type of property includes books, music, computer programs, and inventions of all kinds.

Inventories Stocks of raw materials, semifinished goods, and finished goods held by firms.

Investment The amount of new capital equipment purchased in a given time period.

Investment bank A bank that trades in firms' equities and bonds.

Isocost equation An equation that states the relationship between the quantities of inputs that can be hired for a given total cost.

Isocost line A line that shows all the combinations of capital and labor that can be bought for a given total cost.

Isocost map A map that shows a series of isocost lines, each for a different total cost.

Isoquant A curve that shows the different combinations of labor and capital required to produce a fixed quantity of output.

Isoquant map A map that shows a series of isoquants, each for a different output.

Joint unlimited liability The liability of each and every partner for the full debts of a partnership.

Labor *See* Human resources.

Labor-intensive technique A method of production that uses a relatively large amount of labor and a relatively small amount of capital to produce a given quantity of output.

Labor union An organized group of workers whose purpose is to increase wages and influence other job conditions.

Land Natural resources of all kinds.

Law of diminishing marginal rate of substitution A law stating that the marginal rate of substitution of capital for labor falls as the amount of capital decreases and the amount of labor increases.

Law of diminishing returns The general tendency for marginal product to eventually diminish as more of the variable input is employed, holding the quantity of fixed inputs constant.

Least-cost technique The combination of inputs that minimizes total cost of producing a given output.

Legal monopoly A monopoly that occurs when a law, license, or patent restricts competition by preventing entry.

Liability A debt—something that a household, firm, or government owes.

Limited liability The limitation of liability of the firm's owners for debts only up to the value of the initial investment.

Linear relationship The relationship between two variables depicted by a straight line on a graph.

Lobbying The activity of bringing pressure to bear on government agencies or institutions through a variety of informal mechanisms.

Local A subunit of a union that organizes individual workers.

Lockout The refusal by a firm to operate its plant and employ its workers.

Long run A period of time in which the quantities of all inputs can be varied.

Long-run average cost curve A curve that traces the relationship between the lowest attainable average total cost and output when all inputs can be varied.

Long-run cost The cost of production when a firm uses the economically efficient plant size.

Long-run demand curve The demand curve that describes the response of buyers to a change in price after all possible adjustments have been made.

Long-run demand for labor The relationship between the wage rate and the quantity of labor demanded when all inputs can be varied.

Long-run elasticity of demand for labor The percentage change in the quantity of labor demanded divided by the percentage change in the wage rate when all inputs are varied.

Long-run supply curve The supply curve that describes the response of the quantity supplied to a change in price after all technologically possible adjustments to supply have been made.

Lorenz curve A curve that shows the cumulative percentage of income or wealth against the cumulative percentage of population.

Loss The difference between a firm's revenue and cost when cost exceeds revenue.

Macroeconomics The branch of economics that studies the economy as a whole. Macroeconomics is concerned with aggregates and averages of behavior rather than with detailed individual choices.

Marginal benefit The increase in total benefit resulting from a one)unit increase in the scale of provision of a public good.

Marginal cost The increase in total cost resulting from a unit increase in output.

Marginal cost pricing rule The rule that sets price equal to marginal cost. It maximizes total surplus in the regulated industry.

Marginal private cost The marginal cost directly incurred by the producer of a good.

Marginal product The change in total product resulting from a one-unit increase in a variable input.

Marginal product of capital The change in total product resulting from a one-unit increase in the quantity of capital employed, holding the quantity of labor constant.

Marginal product of labor The change in total product resulting from a one-unit increase in the quantity of labor employed, holding the quantity of capital constant.

Marginal rate of substitution The rate at which a person will give up one good in order to get more of another good and at the same time remain indifferent.

Marginal rate of substitution of capital for labor The decrease in capital per unit increase in labor that keeps output constant.

Marginal revenue The change in total revenue resulting from a one-unit increase in the quantity sold.

Marginal revenue product The change in total revenue resulting from employing one more unit of a factor.

Marginal revenue product curve A curve that shows the marginal revenue product of a factor at each quantity of the factor hired.

Marginal social benefit The dollar value of the benefit from one additional unit of consumption, including the benefit to the buyer and any indirect benefits accruing to any other member of society.

Marginal social cost The cost of producing one additional unit of output, including the costs borne by the producer and any other costs indirectly incurred by any other member of society; the marginal cost incurred by the producer of a good, together with the marginal cost imposed as an externality on others.

Marginal utility The additional utility or change in utility resulting from the last unit of a good consumed.

Marginal utility per dollar spent The marginal utility obtained from the last unit of a good consumed divided by the price of the good.

Market Any arrangement that facilitates buying and selling (trading) of a good, service, factor of production, or future commitment.

Market activity The supplying of labor through the market. *See also* Nonmarket activity.

Market constraints The conditions under which a firm can buy its inputs and sell its output.

Market demand The relationship between the total quantity of a good demanded and its price.

Market distribution The distribution of income that would prevail in the absence of government policies.

Market failure The inability of an unregulated market to achieve, in all circumstances, allocative efficiency.

Market mechanism A method of determining *what*, *how*, and *for whom* goods and services are produced, based on individual choices coordinated through markets.

Market socialism An economic system that combines socialism's state ownership of capital and land with capitalism's market allocation of resources.

Maturity structure The distribution of future dates on which bonds are to be redeemed.

Median voter theorem The proposition that political parties will pursue policies that maximize the net benefit of the median voter.

Medium of exchange Anything that is generally acceptable in exchange for goods and services.

Merger Combining the assets of two firms to form a single new firm.

Microeconomics The branch of economics that studies the decisions of individual households and firms and the way in which individual markets work. Microeconomics also studies the way in which taxes and government regulation affect economic choices.

Minimum wage law A regulation that makes it illegal to trade labor below a specified wage.

Ministry of International Trade and Industry (MITI) A Japanese government agency responsible for stimulating Japanese industrial development and international trade.

Mixed economy An economy that relies partly on a command mechanism and partly on a market mechanism to coordinate economic activity.

Mixed good A good that lies between a private good and a pure public good.

Momentary supply curve The supply curve that describes the immediate response of the quantity supplied to a change in price.

Monetary exchange A system in which some commodity or token serves as the medium of exchange.

Money A medium of exchange.

Monitoring The observation of the actions of an agent by a principal.

Monitoring costs The costs of observing the actions of an agent.

Monopolistic competition A market type in which a large number of firms compete with one another by making similar but slightly different products.
Monopoly The sole supplier of a good, service, or resource that has no close substitutes. Monopoly arises from the existence of a barrier preventing the entry of new firms.
Monopsony A market structure in which there is only a single buyer.
Nash equilibrium The outcome of a game in which the strategy chosen by player A is the best possible response to the strategy of player B and in which player B's strategy is the best possible response to the strategy of player A.
Nationalized industry An industry owned and operated by a publicly owned authority directly responsible to a government.
Natural monopoly A monopoly that occurs when there is a unique source of supply for a raw material or when one firm can supply the entire market at a lower price than two or more firms can.
Natural resources The nonproduced factors of production with which we are endowed—all the gifts of nature, including land, water, air, and all the minerals they contain.
Negative relationship A relationship between two variables that move in opposite directions.
Net benefit Total benefit minus total cost.
Net borrower A country that is borrowing more from the rest of the world than it is lending to it.
Net exporter A country whose value of exports exceeds its value of imports.
Net financial assets Financial assets minus financial liabilities.
Net importer A country whose value of imports exceeds its value of exports.
Net investment Gross investment minus depreciation.
Net lender A country that is lending more to the rest of the world than it is borrowing from it.
Net present value The sum of the present values of payments spread over several years.
Net present value of an investment The present value of a stream of marginal revenue product generated by the investment minus the cost of the investment.
Nonexhaustible natural resources Natural resources that can be used repeatedly without depleting what is available for future use.
Nonmarket activity Leisure and nonmarket production activities, including education and training.
Nontariff barriers Any action, other than a tariff, that restricts international trade.
Normal good A good the demand for which increases when income increases.
Normative statement A statement about what *ought* to be. An expression of an opinion that cannot be verified by observation.
Not-for-profit firm An organization that chooses or is required to have equal costs and revenue.
Oligopoly A market type in which a small number of producers compete with one another.
Open economy An economy that has economic links with other economies.
Open shop An arrangement in which no requirement is placed on an individual worker to join a union.
Opportunity cost The best alternative forgone.
Optimizing Balancing benefits against costs to do the best within the limits of what is possible.
Origin The zero point that is common to both axes on a graph.
Overutilized capacity When a plant produces more than the output at which average total cost is at a minimum.
Partnership A firm with two or more owners who have unlimited liability.
Patent An exclusive right granted by the government to the inventor of a product or service.
Payoff The score of each player in a game.
Payoff matrix A table that shows the payoffs resulting from every possible action by each player for every possible action by each other player.
Perfect competition A state that occurs in markets in which a large number of firms sell an identical product; there are many buyers; there are no restrictions on entry; firms have no advantage over potential new entrants; and all firms and buyers are fully informed about the prices of each and every firm.
Perfectly competitive firm's supply curve A curve that shows how a perfectly competitive firm's output varies as the market price varies.
Perfectly elastic demand Elasticity is infinity; the quantity demanded becomes zero if the price rises by the smallest amount, and the quantity demanded becomes infinite if the price falls by the smallest amount.
Perfectly inelastic demand Elasticity is zero; the quantity demanded does not change as the price rises.
Perfect price discrimination The practice of charging each consumer the maximum price that he or she is willing to pay for each unit bought.
Physical limits The maximum output that a plant can produce.
Piece rate A compensation rule based on the output of a worker.
Political equilibrium A situation in which the choices of voters, politicians, and bureaucrats are all compatible and in which no one group of agents will be better off by making a different choice.
Politicians Elected officials in federal and state government—from chief executives (the president, state governor, or mayor) to members of the legislatures (state and federal senators and representatives).

Portfolio choice A choice concerning which assets and liabilities to hold.

Positive relationship A relationship between two variables that move in the same direction.

Positive statement A statement about what *is.* Something that can be verified by careful observation.

Poverty An income level measured by a poverty index first calculated by the Social Security Administration in 1964.

Preferences A ranking of likes and dislikes and the intensity of those likes and dislikes.

Preferred stock Stock that conveys no voting rights but gives a prior claim on dividends at a fixed rate, regardless of the profit level.

Present value The value in the present of a future sum of money; equal to the amount which, if invested today, will grow as large as that future sum, taking into account the interest it will earn.

Price discrimination The practice of charging some customers a higher price than others for an identical good or of charging an individual customer a higher price on a small purchase than on a large one.

Price-earnings ratio The current price of a share divided by the current profit per share.

Price effect The effect of a change in the price on the quantity of a good consumed.

Price elasticity of demand The percentage change in the quantity demanded of a good divided by the percentage change in its price.

Price taker A firm that cannot influence the price of its product.

Principal An individual who sets a compensation rule to motivate an agent to choose activities advantageous to the principal.

Principle of minimum differentiation The tendency for competitors to make themselves almost identical in order to appeal to the maximum number of clients or voters.

Private enterprise An economic system that permits individuals to decide on their own economic activities.

Private good A good or service each unit of which is consumed by only one individual.

Private property right A legally established title to sole ownership of a scarce resource.

Privatization The process of selling state-owned enterprises to private individuals and firms.

Process theory of distributive justice A theory of distributive justice that examines the fairness of the *mechanism* or *process* that results in a given distribution.

Producer surplus The difference between a producer's revenue and the opportunity cost of production.

Product differentiation Making a product slightly different from that of a competing firm.

Production The conversion of natural, human, and capital resources into goods and services.

Production function The relationship between the maximum output attainable and the quantities of inputs used.

Production possibility frontier The boundary between attainable and unattainable levels of production.

Professional association An organized group of professional workers, such as lawyers, dentists, or doctors, that seeks to influence the compensation and other labor market conditions affecting its members.

Profit The difference between a firm's revenue and cost when revenue exceeds cost.

Profit maximization Making the largest possible profit.

Profit sharing A compensation rule that allocates a certain fraction of a firm's profit to its employees.

Progressive income tax An income tax at a marginal rate which rises with the level of income.

Property Anything of value that is owned.

Property rights Social arrangements that govern the ownership, use, and disposal of economic resources.

Proportional income tax An income tax that is at a constant rate regardless of the level of income.

Proprietorship A firm with a single owner who has unlimited liability.

Protectionism The restriction of international trade.

Public choice theory A theory predicting the behavior of the government sector of the economy as the outcome of the individual choices made by voters, politicians, and bureaucrats interacting in a political marketplace.

Public franchise An exclusive right granted to a firm to supply a good or service.

Public interest theory A theory predicting that government action will take place to eliminate waste and achieve an efficient allocation of resources.

Public interest theory of regulation A theory of regulation that states that regulations are supplied to satisfy the demand of consumers and producers for the maximization of total surplus—or the attainment of allocative efficiency.

Pure public good A good each unit of which is consumed by everyone and from which no one can be excluded.

Quantity demanded The amount of a good or service that consumers plan to buy in a given period of time.

Quantity supplied The amount of a good or service that producers plan to sell in a given period of time.

Quantity traded The quantity actually bought and sold.

Quota A restriction on the quantity of a good that a firm is permitted to produce or that a country is permitted to import.

Rank-tournament compensation rule A compensation rule under which the payment to an agent depends on the agent's rank in a tournament.

Rate of return regulation A regulation that sets the

price at a level that enables the regulated firm to earn a specified target percentage return on its capital.

Rational choice The best possible course of action from the point of view of the individual making the choice.

Rational expectation The best forecast that can be made on the basis of all the available and relevant information.

Rational ignorance The decision not to acquire information, because the cost of acquiring the information is greater than the benefit derived from having it.

Rawlsian theory of fairness A theory of distributive justice that gives the biggest income possible to the least well off.

Real assets Land, buildings, plant and equipment, inventories, and consumer durable goods.

Real income Income expressed in units of goods. Real income in terms of a particular good is income divided by the price of that good.

Redemption date The date on which the final payment on a bond is made.

Redemption value The amount paid to a bondholder on the redemption date of a bond.

Regressive income tax An income tax at a marginal rate which falls with the level of income.

Regulation Rules enforced by a government agency to restrict economic activity by determining prices, product standards and types, and the conditions under which new firms may enter an industry.

Relative price The price of one good divided by the price of another good.

Rent ceiling A regulation making it illegal to charge a rent higher than a specified level.

Rent seeking The activity of attempting to create a monopoly.

Reservation wage The lowest wage rate for which a household will supply labor to the market.

Residual claimant An agent who receives the firm's profits and is responsible for its losses.

Returns to scale Increases in output that result from increasing all the inputs by the same percentage.

Revenue The amount received from the sale of a good. Revenue equals the price of the good multiplied by the quantity sold.

Right-to-work law A law allowing an individual to work at any firm without joining a union.

Saving Income minus consumption.

Scarcity The universal state in which wants exceed resources.

Scatter diagram A diagram that plots the value of one economic variable associated with the value of another.

Search activity The time and effort spent in searching for someone with whom to do business.

Self-sufficiency A state that occurs when people produce only enough for their own consumption.

Share A fraction of the stock of a corporation.

Short run A period of time in which the quantities of some inputs are fixed and others can be varied.

Short-run demand curve The demand curve that describes the initial response of buyers to a change in the price of a good.

Short-run demand for labor The relationship between the wage rate and the quantity of labor demanded when the firm's capital input is fixed and labor is the only variable input.

Short-run elasticity of demand for labor The percentage change in the quantity of labor demanded divided by the percentage change in the wage rate when labor is the only variable input.

Short-run industry supply curve A curve that shows how the total quantity supplied in the short run by all firms in an industry varies as the market price varies.

Short-run production function A function that describes how the maximum attainable output varies as the quantity of labor employed in a given production plant varies.

Short-run supply curve The supply curve that describes the response of the quantity supplied to a change in price when only *some* of the technologically possible adjustments have been made.

Shutdown point The point at which a firm's maximum profit is the same regardless of whether the firm produces a positive amount of output or produces nothing—temporarily shuts down.

Single-price monopoly A monopoly that charges the same price for each unit of output.

Slope The change in the value of y divided by the change in the value of x (where y is measured on the vertical axis and x is measured on the horizontal axis of a graph).

Socialism An economic system based on state ownership of capital and land and on a centrally planned allocation of resources.

Specialization The production of only one good or a few goods.

State enterprise The basic production unit of the Soviet economy.

Stock A quantity measured at a point in time.

Stock exchange An organized market for trading in stock.

Stock market The market in which the equities of firms are traded.

Stock yield The income from a share in the stock of a firm, expressed as a percentage of the price of the share.

Strategic interaction Acting in a way that takes into account the expected behavior of others and the mutual recognition of interdependence.

Strategies All the possible actions of each player.

Strike The refusal of a group of workers to work under the prevailing conditions.

Substitute A good that may be used in place of another good.

Substitution effect The effect of a change in price on the quantities consumed when the consumer remains indifferent between the original and the new combinations of goods consumed.

Sunk costs The historical cost of buying plant and machinery that have no current resale value.

Supply The entire relationship between the quantity supplied of a good and its price.

Supply curve A graph showing the relationship between the quantity supplied and the price of a good, holding everything else constant.

Supply schedule A list of quantities supplied at different prices, holding everything else constant.

Takeover The purchase of the stock of one firm by another firm.

Tariff A tax on an import by the government of the importing country.

Tastes A person's attitudes or preferences toward different goods and services.

Tax base The activity on which a tax is levied.

Tax rate The percentage rate at which a tax is levied on a particular activity.

Tax revenue The product of the tax rate and the tax base.

Team production A production process in which each individual in a group specializes in mutually supportive tasks.

Technique Any feasible way of converting inputs into output.

Technological efficiency A state in which it is not possible to increase output without increasing inputs.

Technological progress The development of new and better ways of producing goods and services.

Technology A method for converting resources into goods and services.

Theory of distributive justice A set of principles against which we can test whether a particular distribution of economic well-being is fair.

Time rates A compensation rule based on the number of hours an individual works.

Time-series graph A graph showing the value of a variable on the y-axis plotted against time on the x-axis.

Tit-for-tat strategy A strategy in which a player cooperates in the current period if the other player cooperated in the previous period but cheats if the other player cheated in the previous period.

Total benefit The total dollar value that people place on a given level of provision of a public good.

Total cost The sum of the costs of all the inputs used in production.

Total fixed cost The cost of all fixed inputs.

Total product The total quantity produced by a firm in a given period of time.

Total product curve A graph showing the maximum output attainable with a given amount of capital as the amount of labor employed is varied.

Total surplus The sum of consumer surplus and producer surplus.

Total variable cost The cost of variable inputs used in production.

Transactions costs The costs arising from finding a trading partner, negotiating an agreement about the price and other aspects of the exchange, and ensuring that the terms of the agreement are fulfilled.

Transfer earnings The income required to induce the supply of a factor of production.

Trend A general tendency for a variable to rise or fall.

Trigger strategy A strategy in which a player cooperates if the other player cooperates but plays the Nash equilibrium strategy forever thereafter if the other player cheats.

Turnover tax A Soviet tax on a consumer good designed to make its market price high enough to achieve a balance between the quantity demanded and the quantity supplied.

Union shop An arrangement in which a firm may hire nonunion workers, but in order for such workers to remain employed, they must join the union within a brief time period specified by the union.

Unit elastic demand An elasticity of 1; the quantity demanded of a good and its price change in equal proportions.

Unlimited liability The legal responsibility for all debts incurred by a firm up to an amount equal to the entire wealth of its owner.

Utilitarian theory The theory that the fairest outcome is the one that maximizes the sum of all individual utilities in society.

Utility The benefit or satisfaction that a person obtains from the consumption of a good or service.

Utility maximization The attainment of the greatest possible utility.

Value The maximum amount that a person is willing to pay for a good.

Variable cost A cost that varies with the output level.

Variable inputs Those inputs whose quantity used can be varied in the short run.

Vertical integration The merger of two or more firms operating at different stages in the production process of a single good or service.

Voluntary export restraint A self-imposed restriction by an exporting country on the volume of its exports of a particular good; often called VER.

Voters The consumers of the outcome of the political process.

Wants People's unlimited desires or wishes for goods and services.

Wealth Total assets of a household, firm, or government minus its total liabilities.

Welfare state capitalism An economic system combining capitalism's private ownership of capital and land with a heavy degree of state intervention in the allocation of resources.

***x*-axis** The horizontal scale on a graph.

***x*-coordinate** A line running horizontally from a point on a graph to the *y*-axis; called the *x*-coordinate because its length is the same as the value marked off on the *x*-axis.

***y*-axis** The vertical scale on a graph.

***y*-coordinate** A line running vertically from a point on a graph to the *x*-axis; called the *y*-coordinate because its length is the same as the value marked off on the *y*-axis.

Index

Key concepts and pages where they are defined appear in boldface.

Additional Credits (continued from p. iv)

Assar Lindbeck (pp. 1–4): Robin Bade. ***Adam Smith*** (p. 22): Archiv fur Kunst und Geschichte, Berlin. ***Antoine-Augustin Cournot*** (p. 84): Historical Pictures Service, Chicago. ***Alfred Marshall*** (p. 85): Historical Pictures Service, Chicago. ***Jeremy Bentham*** (p. 194): Mary Evans Picture Library. ***General Cinema Corporation advertisement*** (p. 212): Courtesy of General Cinema Corporation. ***Wisconsin Toy Company, Inc., advertisement*** (p. 215): The reproduction of this advertisement and the tradename and logo of Wisconsin Toy Company, Inc., is reproduced in this textbook with the express authorization of Wisconsin Toy Company, Inc., for this limited purpose. ***Jacob Viner*** (p. 250): Seeley G. Mudd Library, Special Collections, Princeton University. ***John von Neuman*** (p. 354): Historical Pictures Service, Chicago. ***Kenneth Arrow*** (p. 518): UPI/Bettman Newsphotos. ***James Buchanan*** (p. 519): George Mason University, Center for Public Choice.